ATLAS OF THE

UNITED STATES

AND THE WORLD

CRESCENT BOOKS
New York

Edited by
Bill Willett, Cartographic Editor,
David Gaylard, Assistant Cartographic Editor,
and Geoffrey Atkinson, Lilla Prince-Smith, Raymond Smith
and Joan Williamson

Maps prepared under the direction of Alan Poynter,
Director of Cartography

The maps of the United States are based on material appearing in
the National Atlas of the United States. The material was supplied
by the National Cartographic Information Center, U.S. Geological
Survey, Reston, Va.

Printed in Hong Kong

1986 edition published by Crescent Books, distributed by Crown Publishers Inc.

ISBN O-517-61036-1

h g f e d c b a

PREFACE

This atlas is purposefully entitled an atlas of the United States and the World for nearly half of the pages are devoted to maps covering the United States and the other half to the rest of the World. The dimensions of the atlas make it easily handleable. It is not too large to be cumbersome nor too small for the maps to have no value as a reference atlas. The scale of 1:2.5 million (40 miles to the inch) has been used as far as possible for the State maps. The more densely populated and really smaller states in the east are shown at twice this basic scale, namely 1:1.25 million (20 miles to the inch) and the geographically larger Alaska, Montana, and Texas are shown at smaller scales. Each state is shown on a separate page and is arranged in the atlas alphabetically except where the shape of two or more states taken together fit more comfortably on to the page, Vermont and New Hampshire being examples. In these cases one or two states are out of alphabetical sequence and these exceptions are clearly indicated.

Each of the State maps shows the boundaries of the State, naturally, and also the county boundaries together with the county seat. Recreation areas and reservations, roads, rails, and airports are shown. The land surface is depicted with contours and hill shading. The symbols and type for the cities and towns are graded according to their population at the 1980 Census.

This atlas contains a lot of information and to answer a specific query the reader can find the particular map or place that he requires via the contents list and the index. In the contents list which follow this preface there are lists of states and map titles and also outline maps of the United States and the Continents showing the extent of individual map pages. The index gives the page number of the map which holds the place name required. The reader is then directed to a point on that page by way of the geographical co-ordinates.

The forms of place names on the map and in the index are those that are used locally in the country concerned. The normally-used name form in English, if it differs from the local form, often appears on the map in brackets and in the index it is cross-referenced to the locally spelled form (Vienna = Wien, for example). In countries that do not use a Roman script the place names have been transcribed using a system which is accepted by the U.S. and British authorities on geographic names. In China the Pinyin system is used. This is the system which the Chinese themselves prefer and which is being increasingly used outside China.

The reader is reminded that a map is a scaled down representation of the Earth. The General Reference at the beginning of the map section shows the symbols that are used on the maps and the introduction to the index explains how to use it in conjunction with the maps.

B. M. WILLETT

CONTENTS I

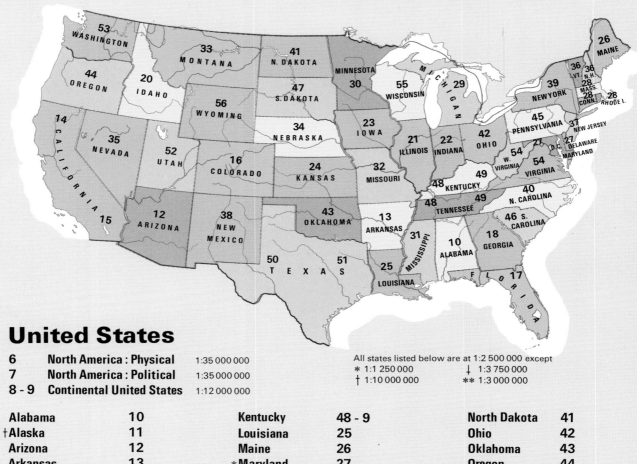

CONTENTS II

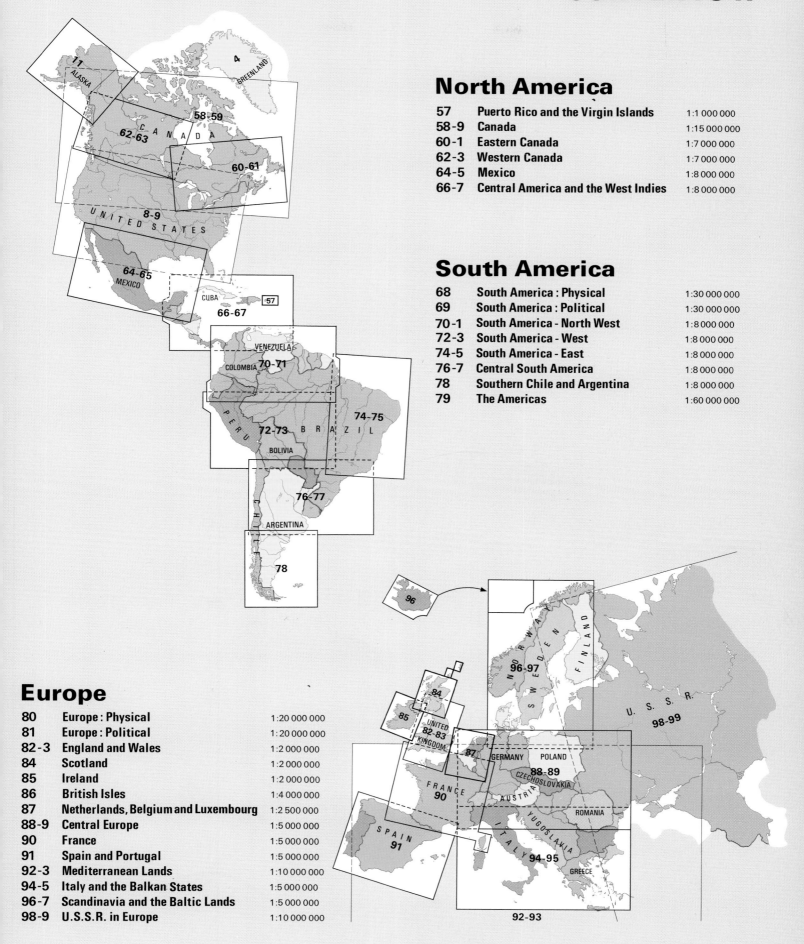

North America

South America

Europe

CONTENTS III

Asia

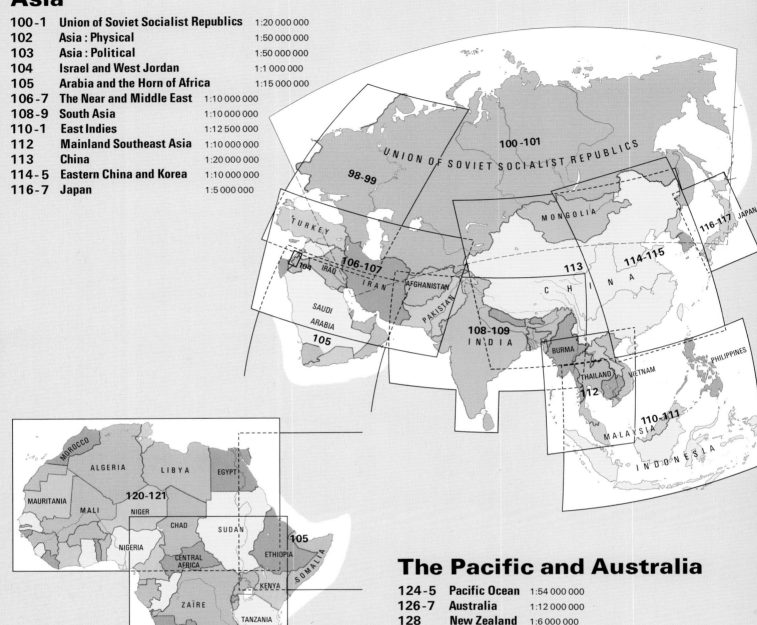

Africa

The Pacific and Australia

Index

PRINCIPAL COUNTRIES OF THE WORLD

Country	Area in thousands of square km.	Population in thousands	Density of population per sq. km.	Capital Population in thousands
Afghanistan	647	17 222	27	Kabul (1 036)
Albania	29	2 841	98	Tiranë (202)
Algeria	2 382	20 500	9	Algiers (1 740)
Angola	1 247	8 339	7	Luanda (700)
Argentina	2 767	29 627	11	Buenos Aires (9 927)
Australia	7 687	15 369	2	Canberra (251)
Austria	84	7 549	90	Vienna (1 516)
Bangladesh	144	94 651	657	Dhaka (3 459)
Belgium	31	9 856	318	Brussels (989)
Belize	23	156	5	Belmopan (3)
Benin	113	3 720	33	Porto-Novo (132)
Bhutan	47	1 360	29	Thimphu (60)
Bolivia	1 099	6 082	5	Sucre (63) La Paz (881)
Botswana	600	1 007	2	Gaborone (60)
Brazil	8 512	129 662	15	Brasilia (1 306)
Brunei	6	209	35	Bandar Seri Begawan (58)
Bulgaria	111	8 946	81	Sofia (1 064)
Burkina Faso	274	6 607	24	Ouagadougou (286)
Burma	677	36 750	54	Rangoon (2 276)
Burundi	28	4 540	162	Bujumbura (157)
Cambodia (Kampuchea)	181	6 981	39	Phnom Penh (400)
Cameroon	475	9 165	19	Yaoundé (485)
Canada	9 976	24 907	2	Ottawa (738)
Central African Rep.	623	2 450	4	Bangui (302)
Chad	1 284	4 789	4	Ndjamena (303)
Chile	757	11 682	15	Santiago (4 132)
China	9 597	1 039 677	108	Peking (9 231)
Colombia	1 139	27 190	24	Bogota (4 056)
Congo	342	1 651	5	Brazzaville (422)
Costa Rica	51	2 379	47	San José (272)
Cuba	115	9 884	86	Havana (1 951)
Cyprus	9	655	73	Nicosia (161)
Czechoslovakia	128	15 415	120	Prague (1 186)
Denmark	43	5 118	119	Copenhagen (1 382)
Djibouti	22	332	15	Djibouti (150)
Dominican Republic	49	5 962	121	Santo Domingo (1 313)
Ecuador	284	9 251	32	Quito (881)
Egypt	1 001	45 915	46	Cairo (5 074)
El Salvador	21	5 232	249	San Salvador (429)
Equatorial Guinea	28	381	14	Rey Malabo (37)
Ethiopia	1 222	33680	28	Addis Abeba (1 478)
Fiji	18	670	37	Suva (68)
Finland	337	4 863	14	Helsinki (922)
France	547	54 652	99	Paris (8 510)
French Guiana	91	78	1	Cavenne (39)
Gabon	268	1 127	4	Libréville (252)
Gambia	11	696	63	Banjul (109)
Germany, East	108	16 864	156	East Berlin (1 173)
Germany, West	249	61 638	248	Bonn (294)
Ghana	239	12 700	53	Accra (738)
Greece	132	9 848	75	Athens (3 027)
Greenland	2 176	52	0.02	Godthåb (10)
Guatemala	109	7 699	71	Guatemala (793)
Guinea	246	5 704	23	Conakry (763)
Guinea-Bissau	36	836	23	Bissau (109)
Guyana	215	922	4	Georgetown (188)
Haiti	28	5 201	186	Port-au-Prince (888)
Honduras	112	4 092	37	Tegucigalpa (485)
Hong Kong	1	5 313	5 313	Hong Kong (1 184)
Hungary	93	10 702	115	Budapest (2 067)
Iceland	103	236	2	Reykjavik (84)
India	3 288	732 256	223	Delhi (5 729)
Indonesia	2 027	156 442	77	Jakarta (6 503)
Iran	1 648	42 070	26	Tehran (4 496)
Iraq	435	14 654	34	Baghdad (2 969)
Irish Republic	70	3 508	50	Dublin (525)
Israel	21	4 097	195	Jerusalem (424)
Italy	301	56 836	189	Rome (2 831)
Ivory Coast	322	9 300	29	Abidjan (850)
Jamaica	11	2 260	205	Kingston (671)
Japan	372	119 259	320	Tokyo (8 139)
Jordan	98	3 489	36	Ammän (681)
Kenya	583	18 784	32	Nairobi (1 048)
Korea, North	121	19 185	158	Pyŏngyang (1 500)
Korea, South	98	39 951	408	Seoul (8 367)
Kuwait	18	1 672	93	Kuwait (775)
Laos	237	4 209	18	Vientiane (90)
Lebanon	10	2 739	274	Beirut (702)
Lesotho	30	1 444	48	Maseru (45)
Liberia	111	2 113	19	Monrovia (306)
Libya	1 760	3 356	2	Tripoli (980)
Luxembourg	3	365	121	Luxembourg (79)
Madagascar	587	9 400	16	Antananarivo (400)
Malawi	118	6 429	54	Lilongwe (103)
Malaysia	330	14 860	45	Kuala Lumpur (938)
Mali	1 240	7 528	6	Bamako (419)
Malta	0.3	377	1 256	Valletta (14)
Mauritania	1 031	1 779	2	Nouakchott (135)
Mauritius	2	993	496	Port Louis (149)
Mexico	1 973	75 103	38	Mexico (14 750)
Mongolia	1 565	1 803	1	Ulan Bator (419)
Morocco	447	22 110	49	Rabat (842)
Mozambique	783	13 311	17	Maputo (384)
Namibia	824	1 040	1	Windhoek (61)
Nepal	141	15 738	112	Katmandu (210)
Netherlands	41	14 362	350	Amsterdam (936)
New Zealand	269	3 203	12	Wellington (343)
Nicaragua	130	3 058	23	Managua (820)
Niger	1 267	6 040	5	Niamey (225)
Nigeria	924	89 022	96	Lagos (1 477)
Norway	324	4 129	13	Oslo (624)
Oman	212	1 131	5	Muscat (25)
Pakistan	804	89 729	112	Islamabad (201)
Panama	76	2 089	27	Panama (655)
Papua New Guinea	462	3 190	7	Port Moresby (123)
Paraguay	407	3 472	8	Asunción (602)
Peru	1 285	18 790	15	Lima (4 601)
Philippines	300	52 055	173	Manila (1 630)
Poland	313	36 571	117	Warsaw (1 641)
Portugal	92	10 056	109	Lisbon (818)
Puerto Rico	9	3 350	372	San Juan (1 086)
Romania	238	22 638	95	Bucharest (1 979)
Rwanda	26	5 700	219	Kigali (116)
Saudi Arabia	2 150	10 421	5	Riyadh (667)
Senegal	196	6 316	32	Dakar (799)
Sierra Leone	72	3 672	51	Freetown (214)
Singapore	0.6	2 502	4 170	Singapore (2 517)
Somali Republic	638	5 269	8	Mogadishu (400)
South Africa	1 221	31 008	25	Pretoria (739) Cape Town (2 517)
Spain	505	38 228	76	Madrid (3 159)
Sri Lanka	66	15 416	234	Colombo (1 412)
Sudan	2 506	20 362	8	Khartoum (561)
Surinam	163	407	2	Paramaribo (151)
Swaziland	17	605	36	Mbabane (23)
Sweden	450	8 331	19	Stockholm (1 409)
Switzerland	41	6 482	158	Bern (289)
Syria	185	9 660	52	Damascus (1 251)
Taiwan	36	18 700	519	Taipei (2 271)
Tanzania	945	20 378	22	Dar-es-Salaam (757)
Thailand	514	49 459	96	Bangkok (5 468)
Togo	56	2 756	49	Lomé (247)
Trinidad and Tobago	5	1 202	240	Port of Spain (66)
Tunisia	164	6 886	42	Tunis (597)
Turkey	781	47 279	61	Ankara (2 239)
Uganda	236	14 625	62	Kampala (332)
United Arab Emirates	84	1 206	14	Abu Dhabi (449)
U.S.S.R.	22 402	272 500	12	Moscow (8 396)
United Kingdom	245	56 377	230	London (6 755)
United States	9 363	234 496	25	Washington (3 061)
Uruguay	178	2 968	17	Montevideo (1 173)
Venezuela	912	16 394	18	Caracas (2 944)
Vietnam	330	57 181	173	Hanoi (2 571)
Western Samoa	3	159	53	Apia (36)
Yemen, North	195	6 232	32	Sana' (448)
Yemen, South	288	2 158	7	Aden (285)
Yugoslavia	256	22 800	89	Belgrade (1 407)
Zaïre	2 345	31 151	13	Kinshasa (2 242)
Zambia	753	6 242	8	Lusaka (641)
Zimbabwe	391	7 740	20	Harare (656)

PRINCIPAL CITIES OF THE WORLD

The population figures used are from censuses or more recent estimates and are given in thousands for towns and cities over 500,000 (over 750,000 in China, India, the U.S.S.R. and the U.S.A.) Where possible the population of the metropolitan area is given e.g. Greater London, Greater New York, etc.

AFRICA

ALGERIA (1977)
- Alger — 1 740
- Oran — 543

ANGOLA (1982)
- Luanda — 700

CAMEROON (1983)
- Douala — 708

EGYPT (1976)
- El Qâhira — 5 074
- El Iskandarîya — 2 318
- El Giza — 1 230

ETHIOPIA (1983)
- Addis Abeba — 1 478

GHANA (1970)
- Accra — 738

GUINEA (1980)
- Conakry — 763

IVORY COAST (1976)
- Abidjan — 850

KENYA (1983)
- Nairobi — 1 048

MOROCCO (1981)
- Casablanca — 2 409
- Rabat-Salé — 842
- Fès — 562
- Marrakech — 549

NIGERIA (1975)
- Lagos — 1 477
- Ibadan — 847

SENEGAL (1976)
- Dakar — 779

SOUTH AFRICA (1980)
- Johannesburg — 1 726
- Cape Town — 1 491
- Durban — 961
- Pretoria — 739
- Port Elizabeth — 585

SUDAN (1980)
- El Khartûm, — 561

TANZANIA (1978)
- Dar-es-Salaam — 757

TUNISIA (1984)
- Tunis — 597

ZAIRE (1975)
- Kinshasa — 2 242

ZAMBIA (1980)
- Lusaka — 641

ZIMBABWE (1983)
- Harare — 681

ASIA

AFGHANISTAN (1979)
- Kābul — 1 036

BANGLADESH (1982)
- Dhaka — 3 459
- Chittagong — 1 388
- Khulna — 623

BURMA (1977)
- Rangoon — 2 276

CHINA (1970)
- Shanghai — 11 860
- Beijing — 9 231
- Tianjin — 7 764
- Shenyang — 2 800
- Wuhan — 2 560
- Guangzhou — 2 500
- Chongqing — 2 400
- Nanjing — 1 750
- Harbin — 1 670
- Dalian — 1 650
- Xi'an — 1 600
- Lanzhou — 1 450
- Taiyuan — 1 350
- Qingdao — 1 300
- Chengdu — 1 250
- Changchun — 1 200
- Kunming — 1 100
- Jinan — 1 100
- Fushun — 1 080
- Anshan — 1 050
- Zhengzhou — 1 050
- Hangzhou — 960
- Tangshan — 950
- Baotou — 920
- Zibo — 850
- Changsha — 825
- Shijiazhuang — 800
- Qiqihar — 760

HONG KONG (1981)
- Kowloon — 2 450
- Hong Kong — 1 184
- Tsuen Wan — 599

INDIA (1981)
- Calcutta — 9 194
- Bombay — 8 243
- Delhi — 5 729
- Madras — 4 289
- Bangalore — 2 922
- Ahmedabad — 2 548
- Hyderabad — 2 546
- Pune — 1 686
- Kanpur — 1 639
- Nagpur — 1 302
- Jaipur — 1 015
- Lucknow — 1 008
- Coimbatore — 920
- Patna — 919
- Surat — 914
- Madurai — 908
- Indore — 829
- Varanasi — 797
- Jabalpur — 757

INDONESIA (1980)
- Jakarta — 6 503
- Surabaya — 2 028
- Bandung — 1 462
- Medan — 1 379
- Semarang — 1 026
- Palembang — 787
- Ujung Pandang — 709
- Malang — 512

IRAN (1976)
- Tehrān — 4 496
- Esfahān — 672
- Mashhad — 670
- Tabrīz — 599

IRAQ (1970)
- Baghdād — 2 969

JAPAN (1982)
- Tōkyō — 11 676
- Yokohama — 2 848
- Ōsaka — 2 623
- Nagoya — 2 093
- Kyōto — 1 480
- Sapporo — 1 465
- Kobe — 1 383
- Fukuoka — 1 121
- Kitakyūshū — 1 065
- Kawasaki — 1 055
- Hiroshima — 898
- Sakai — 809
- Chiba — 756
- Sendai — 662
- Okayama — 551
- Kumamoto — 522
- Kagoshima — 514
- Amagasaki — 510
- Higashiōsaka — 501

JORDAN (1981)
- 'Ammān — 681

KOREA, NORTH (1972)
- Pyŏngyang — 1 500

KOREA, SOUTH (1980)
- Sŏul — 8 367
- Pusan — 3 160
- Taegu — 1 607
- Inchŏn — 1 085
- Kwangju — 728
- Taejon — 652

KUWAIT (1975)
- Al-Kuwayt — 775

LEBANON (1980)
- Bayrūt — 702

MALAYSIA (1980)
- Kuala Lumpur — 938

PAKISTAN (1981)
- Karachi — 5 103
- Lahore — 2 922
- Faisalabad — 1 092
- Rawalpindi — 806
- Hyderabad — 795
- Multan — 730
- Gujranwala — 597
- Peshawar — 555

PHILIPPINES (1981)
- Manila — 1 630
- Quezon City — 1 166
- Davao — 610

SAUDI ARABIA (1974)
- Ar Riyād — 667
- Jiddah — 561

SINGAPORE (1983)
- Singapore — 2 517

SRI LANKA (1981)
- Colombo — 1 412

SYRIA (1982)
- Dimashq — 1 112
- Ḥalab — 985

TAIWAN (1981)
- Taipei — 2 271
- Kaohsiung — 1 227
- Taichung — 607
- Tainan — 595

THAILAND (1982)
- Bangkok — 5 468

TURKEY (1982)
- İstanbul — 2 949
- Ankara — 2 276
- İzmir — 1 083
- Adana — 864
- Konya — 691
- Bursa — 658
- Gaziantep — 526

VIETNAM (1973-79)
- Phanh Bho Ho Chi Minh — 3 420
- Hanoi — 2 571
- Haiphong — 1 279

AUSTRALIA AND NEW ZEALAND

AUSTRALIA (1982)
- Sydney — 3 310
- Melbourne — 2 837
- Brisbane — 1 124
- Adelaide — 960
- Perth — 948

NEW ZEALAND (1982)
- Auckland — 839

EUROPE

AUSTRIA (1981)
- Wien — 1 516

BELGIUM (1983)
- Brussel — 989

BULGARIA (1982)
- Sofiya — 1 064

CZECHOSLOVAKIA (1983)
- Praha — 1 186

DENMARK (1981)
- København — 1 382

FINLAND (1982)
- Helsinki — 922

FRANCE (1982)
- Paris — 8 510
- Lyon — 1 170
- Marseille — 1 080
- Lille — 935
- Bordeaux — 628
- Toulouse — 523

GERMANY, EAST (1982)
- East Berlin — 1 173
- Leipzig — 557
- Dresden — 521

GERMANY, WEST (1980)
- West Berlin — 1 896
- Hamburg — 1 645
- München — 1 299
- Köln — 977
- Essen — 648
- Frankfurt am Main — 629
- Dortmund — 608
- Düsseldorf — 590
- Stuttgart — 581
- Duisburg — 558
- Bremen — 555
- Hannover — 535

GREECE (1981)
- Athínai — 3 027
- Thessaloníki — 706

HUNGARY (1983)
- Budapest — 2 067

IRISH REPUBLIC (1981)
- Dublin — 525

ITALY (1981)
- Roma — 2 831
- Milano — 1 635
- Napoli — 1 211
- Torino — 1 104
- Genova — 760
- Palermo — 700

NETHERLANDS (1983)
- Rotterdam — 1 025
- Amsterdam — 936
- 's-Gravenhage — 674

NORWAY (1980)
- Oslo — 624

POLAND (1983)
- Warszawa — 1 641
- Lodz — 848
- Kraków — 735
- Wrocław — 631
- Poznań — 571

PORTUGAL (1981)
- Lisboa — 818

ROMANIA (1982)
- București — 1 979

SPAIN (1981)
- Madrid — 3 159
- Barcelona — 1 753
- Valencia — 745
- Sevilla — 646
- Zaragoza — 572
- Málaga — 502

SWEDEN (1983)
- Stockholm — 1 409

SWITZERLAND (1982)
- Zürich — 705

U.S.S.R. (1983)
- Moskva — 8 396
- Leningrad — 4 779
- Kiyev — 2 355
- Tashkent — 1 944
- Baku — 1 638
- Kharkov — 1 519
- Minsk — 1 405
- Gorkiy — 1 382
- Novosibirsk — 1 370
- Sverdlovsk — 1 269
- Kuybyshev — 1 242
- Dnepropetrovsk — 1 128
- Tbilisi — 1 125
- Odessa — 1 097
- Yerevan — 1 095
- Omsk — 1 080
- Chelyabinsk — 1 077
- Donetsk — 1 055
- Perm — 1 037
- Ufa — 1 034
- Kazan — 1 031
- Alma-Ata — 1 023
- Rostov — 977
- Volgograd — 962
- Saratov — 887
- Riga — 867
- Krasnoyarsk — 845
- Zaporozhye — 835
- Voronezh — 831

UNITED KINGDOM (1983)
- London — 6 754
- Birmingham — 1 013
- Glasgow — 751
- Leeds — 714
- Sheffield — 543
- Liverpool — 502

YUGOSLAVIA (1981)
- Beograd — 1 407
- Zagreb — 1 175
- Skopje — 507

SOUTH AMERICA

ARGENTINA (1980)
- Buenos Aires — 9 927
- Córdoba — 982
- Rosario — 955
- Mendoza — 597
- La Plata — 560

BOLIVIA (1982)
- La Paz — 881

BRAZIL (1980)
- São Paulo — 8 732
- Rio de Janeiro — 5 539
- Belo Horizonte — 1 937
- Salvador — 1 502
- Recife — 1 433
- Fortaleza — 1 307
- Brasília — 1 306
- Pôrto Alegre — 1 221
- Nova Iguaçu — 1 184
- Curitiba — 943
- Belém — 934
- Goiánia — 680
- Duque de Caxias — 666
- São Gonçalo — 660
- Santo André — 634
- Campinas — 587

CHILE (1983)
- Santiago — 4 132

COLOMBIA (1978)
- Bogotá — 4 056
- Medellin — 1 507
- Cali — 1 316
- Barranquilla — 855

ECUADOR (1982)
- Guayaquil — 1 279
- Quito — 881

PARAGUAY (1978)
- Asunción — 602

PERU (1981)
- Lima — 4 601

URUGUAY (1981)
- Montevideo — 1 173

VENEZUELA (1980)
- Caracas — 2 944
- Maracaibo — 901
- Valencia — 506

NORTH AMERICA

CANADA (1983)
- Toronto — 3 067
- Montréal — 2 862
- Vancouver — 1 311
- Ottawa — 738
- Edmonton — 699
- Calgary — 634
- Winnipeg — 601
- Québec — 580
- Hamilton — 548

CUBA (1981)
- La Habana — 1 925

DOMINICAN REP. (1981)
- Santo Domingo — 1 313

GUATEMALA (1979)
- Guatemala — 793

HAITI (1982)
- Port-au-Prince — 888

JAMAICA (1980)
- Kingston — 671

MEXICO (1979)
- Mexico — 14 750
- Guadalajara — 2 468
- Netzahualcóyotl — 2 331
- Monterrey — 2 019
- Puebla de Zaragoza — 711
- Ciudad Juárez — 625
- León de los Aldamas — 625
- Tijuana — 566

NICARAGUA (1981)
- Managua — 820

PANAMA (1981)
- Panama — 655

PUERTO RICO (1980)
- San Juan — 1 086

UNITED STATES (1980)
- New York — 16 121
- Los Angeles — 11 498
- Chicago — 7 870
- Philadelphia — 5 548
- San Francisco — 5 180
- Detroit — 4 618
- Boston — 3 448
- Houston — 3 101
- Washington — 3 061
- Dallas — 2 975
- Cleveland — 2 834
- Miami — 2 644
- St. Louis — 2 356
- Pittsburgh — 2 264
- Baltimore — 2 174
- Minneapolis-St. Paul — 2 114
- Seattle — 2 093
- Atlanta — 2 030
- San Diego — 1 817
- Cincinnati — 1 660
- Denver — 1 621
- Milwaukee — 1 570
- Tampa — 1 569
- Phoenix — 1 509
- Kansas City — 1 327
- Indianapolis — 1 306
- Portland — 1 243
- Buffalo — 1 243
- New Orleans — 1 187
- Providence — 1 096
- Columbus — 1 093
- San Antonio — 1 072
- Sacramento — 1 014
- Dayton — 1 014
- Rochester — 971
- Salt Lake City — 936
- Memphis — 913
- Louisville — 906
- Nashville — 851
- Birmingham — 847
- Oklahoma — 834
- Greensboro — 827
- Norfolk — 807
- Albany — 795
- Toledo — 792
- Honolulu — 763

The World Today

The planet earth

THE earth was formed approximately four-and-a-half billion years ago, although some of the materials that form its surface today may have been laid in place, by the action of rivers for example, only yesterday. By contrast to the age of the planet, the history of man on earth dates back only one million years, and the period of man's occupance of which we have any direct knowledge represents only a minute fraction of this shorter span of time.

During this short period of time, nevertheless, human beings have developed a remarkable variety of races, languages and cultures. Since the earth is a sphere, natural conditions of temperature, landscape and fertility range widely between polar and tropical, and some of the variety of mankind's development is clearly due to this variety in nature. Man has adapted to living in both hot and cold climates, and not only his lifestyle but some of his institutions, such as religion, reflect this adaptation. Yet there is a much greater variety in human life-forms and customs than can be accounted for by environment alone. For one thing, members of the same race, or language group, may be bitterly opposed to one another on political or religious grounds. For another, a sense of belonging draws people together in national or tribal groupings, which develop their own particular means of cultural expression.

Basic resources

Man's primary need is his own life support. Alone among the planets, as far as we know, the earth provides the conditions necessary to sustain life. These conditions we know as resources. Fundamental to the resource structure of the earth is the energy of the sun: it is the power plant that drives all other systems. At a secondary level are the mineral deposits, soils and water on the earth; and thirdly, there are the plants that support animal life, and those animals which exist by preying, species upon species. All these can be classed as the earth's natural resources.

At the highest level, where man exists in total isolation from the natural world, there is a further resource component: what is normally referred to as human resources. These are represented by the ability of man to think, work, invent and find uses for natural materials; to apply skill or power to these materials and transform them. Many animals can build them-

selves a home in ways that display great engineering skill. Most creatures, however, can only build one kind of structure. Man can build a whole range of structures and design new forms to suit his needs as he anticipates them.

Unequal distribution

The distribution of natural resources over the earth's surface is far from even. The whereabouts of mineral deposits depend on random events in a remote geological past; patches of fertile soil depend on events more recent but, to man, equally capricious — the flow of rivers or the movement of ice. When it comes to agriculture, the activity that has been basic to the survival of man and his increase in numbers, we find that, in round figures, 20 per cent of the earth's surface is barred to him by ice or perennially frozen soil; 20 per cent is composed of highlands too cold, rugged or barren for the cultivation of crops; 20 per cent is arid or desert, and between five and 10 per cent of the remainder has no soil, either because it has been scraped by ice or because it is permanently wet or flooded. This leaves only 30-35 per cent of the land surface where food production is possible, together with the oceans and whatever resources may be obtained from that source.

We can think of these natural resources as forming a cover, or coating, of varying thickness over the earth's surface: in some places it is deep and rich; in others it is for all practical purposes non-existent. In the same way, observation shows that human resources vary in quality from place to place. What, in fact, we are observing are different levels of technical ability and equipment among different peoples. Whereas, however, we can accept that natural resource distribution is either random or climatically determined, and therefore unchangeable, the explanation for different development levels of human resources is a much more complex matter.

Why have some nations or groups advanced more rapidly than others in technology? Why have some lost the lead they once had? A number of explanations have been offered in order to answer these questions. One of these is climatic — that some environments are more stimulating to effort and inventiveness than others. Some are racial — and may, in due course, become racist — arguing that one race is more gifted than another. Yet others

▲The earth in space *was an unfamiliar view we obtained when* man first ventured beyond his *natural environment: a small, rocky*

Pluto: diameter approx. 3,000km; 5,900 million km from sun

Neptune: diameter 49,500km; 4,496.6 million km from sun

focus on the structure of society, and the opportunities it affords for the use of individual talents and the freedom to innovate.

The key to exploitation

Each of these theories in isolation can be disproved, simply by pointing out the exceptions to it. Whatever the explanation, however, the fact is clear: that the ability to make use of what nature has provided in the way of resources varies critically from society to society, and that a high level of human resource input can provide a good living for people in areas, such as Scandinavia, where the natural endowment is meagre, while people may live on top of a veritable treasure chest of natural riches, as, it would appear, the Brazilians do, without necessarily obtaining the benefit of

them. It is, after all, only a few years since the oil states of the Middle East were among the world's poorest nations. If we think of the earth as a storehouse of natural wealth, then it is human ingenuity — the human resources represented by technical skills — which provides the key to open it.

Fortunately, no nation today possesses a monopoly of these skills, or is, for that matter, debarred from acquiring them. It is a slow process to do so, but one that can be speeded up if those societies which are relatively advanced will help those that are only at the beginning. Human resources have transformed parts of this planet once judged to be too cold, or too dry, or too poor to support the dense populations, either on the land or in the great cities, that now occupy them.

planet with much surface water
and a dense atmosphere.

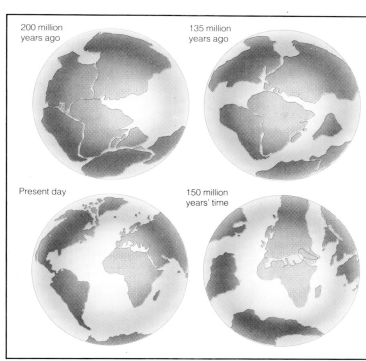

200 million
years ago

135 million
years ago

Present day

150 million
years' time

Plate Tectonics

The migration of the continents is a
feature unique to Planet Earth. The
complementary, almost jigsaw-puzzle fit
of the coastlines on each side of the
Atlantic Ocean inspired Alfred
Wegener's theory of continental drift at
the beginning of the twentieth century.
The theory suggested that an ancient
supercontinent, which Wegener named
Pangaea, incorporated all of the earth's
land masses and gradually split up to
form the continents we see today. The
modern theory of plate tectonics
attributes continental drift to movements
in crustal plates underlying the oceans
as well as the continents. These
movements are caused by the slow but
continuous welling-up of material from
deep within the earth along a series of
mid-ocean ridges. Geological evidence
that the continents once formed a single
land mass is provided by distinctive rock
formations that can be assembled into
continuous belts when Africa and South
America are lined up next to each other.
Distribution of some plants and animals
in the past, as well as ancient climatic
zones, can only be explained by the
theory of plate tectonics.

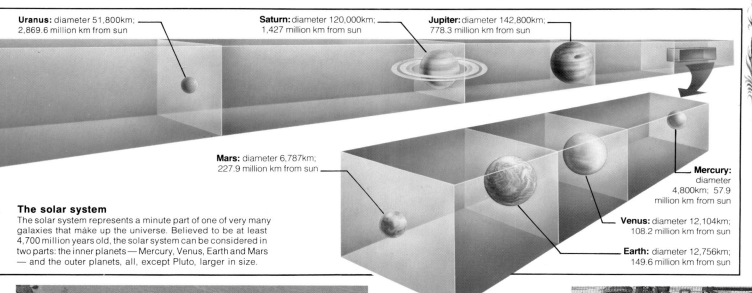

Uranus: diameter 51,800km;
2,869.6 million km from sun

Saturn: diameter 120,000km;
1,427 million km from sun

Jupiter: diameter 142,800km;
778.3 million km from sun

Mars: diameter 6,787km;
227.9 million km from sun

Mercury:
diameter
4,800km; 57.9
million km from sun

Venus: diameter 12,104km;
108.2 million km from sun

Earth: diameter 12,756km;
149.6 million km from sun

The solar system

The solar system represents a minute part of one of very many
galaxies that make up the universe. Believed to be at least
4,700 million years old, the solar system can be considered in
two parts: the inner planets — Mercury, Venus, Earth and Mars
— and the outer planets, all, except Pluto, larger in size.

▶ **The evolution of man** as a
unique social and cultural animal
has produced a variety of races,
languages, religious and social
systems. A political rally in China
illustrates one aspect of culture.

◀ **The Amazon basin** is one of the
few remaining wildernesses on
earth. Such vast areas of forest play
a vital role in global ecology — by
helping to maintain the balance of
oxygen in the atmosphere.

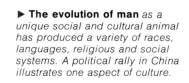

▶ **Throughout history** man has
found various ways of expressing
his beliefs in supernatural powers.
Here, monks follow the teachings of
the Dalai Lama in a temple in Tibet
— one facet of religion today.

A crowded planet

FROM man's earliest ancestors on the planet earth, more than one million years ago, until the beginnings of settled agriculture some 10,000 years ago, the number of human beings alive at any one time did not exceed five million. By 1800 the world was home to one billion people. The second billion was reached by 1930, the third by 1960 and the fourth billion by 1970. The likelihood is that the fifth billion will be reached by 1987 and that a sixth billion will be added by the end of the century, when United Nations demographers estimate that the earth will "carry" 6,250,000,000 human beings.

The key to population growth

What happens after that depends on the speed at which the rate of population growth slows down over the coming decade. The annual growth rate is believed to have peaked at about two per cent in 1970, declining to between 1.7 and 1.8 per cent today. This deceptively small statistic is adding some 80 million people to the world's population each year and, because the world's total population includes such a high proportion of young people who have yet to grow up and have children, it is going to take a long time for the population to stabilize at somewhere between eight and 15 billion, some time in the twenty-first century.

The cause of this extraordinary explosion in human numbers over the past 200 years lies essentially in declining death rates rather than in increasing birth rates. Medical advances and improved conditions of life first cut death rates in Europe. The subsequent explosion in the numbers surviving was partly masked by the massive exodus to new countries, with some 60 million migrants travelling to the Americas and elsewhere before World War II. An even greater and faster increase in numbers began in the developing countries of Asia, Africa and Latin America before World War II as a much more rapid drop in death rates followed the spread of scientific technology to prevent and control disease and improvements in the availability of food.

As death rates declined in Europe birth rates also slowly came down, and today population growth in all modern industrialized countries is low or non-existent. In a few cases, such as West Germany and Austria, the population has even begun to decrease. But less than one-third of the world's population lives in these developed regions, and it is among the two-thirds in the developing countries that population is growing fast. Although the rates of growth have begun to fall in many countries, the proportion of the world's population in the developing countries of Asia, Africa and Latin America will continue to rise until the year 2000.

The distribution of people

At the moment Europe remains the most densely populated area of the globe, with an average of 90 people per square kilometre. The vast territories of southern and eastern Asia are, however, not far behind, and within the next 100 years they are likely to have three times the density of present-day Europe, according to United Nations estimates. In Asia as a whole, population is likely to increase from 2.5 billion to 3.6 billion in the next 20 years. Africa, by contrast, is relatively lightly populated at present, though individual countries such as Egypt, Rwanda and Lesotho have high populations in relation to productive land. The African continent is likely to add another 400 million people to its 1979 population of 455 million by the turn of the century, while Latin America's population will grow from 360 million to some 600 million in the same period.

Of more concern to many governments than overall density of population is the distribution within national boundaries. The growth of cities is one of the most striking features of our time. At the beginning of this century there were only 250 million city dwellers in the world. Today 1,500 million people live in urban areas and by the year 2000, it is believed, more than half the world's population, or some 3,000 million people, will be living in towns and cities.

The call of the city

The growth of cities is partly the result of natural increase, but more significantly the result of migration from the countryside, where population growth often coincides with rural stagnation and a shortage of work. Unlike the situation in the nineteenth century, there are few unused fertile areas left in the world. And the only job opportunities are those which appear to beckon from the growing cities. Already one-third of the urban inhabitants in less-developed countries are squatters living on the fringes of cities such as Djakarta, Bombay, Calcutta, Rio de Janeiro, Manila and Mexico City. These are among the fastest grow-

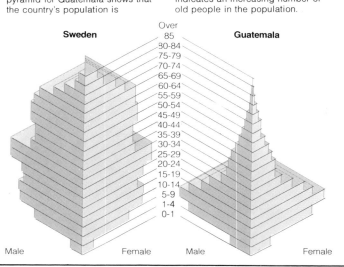

▲ **Most of the world's poor** *live in appalling conditions. Having migrated to the cities in the hope of greater opportunities, many people find themselves in even worse surroundings. Shanty towns, such as this one in Sao Paulo, are home to a large proportion of the inhabitants of the world's fastest-growing cities.*

Age/sex structure

Age pyramids illustrate the differences in population structure between developed and developing countries. The broad base of the pyramid for Guatemala shows that the country's population is increasing rapidly. In general, as birth and death rates decline, such a diagram loses its pyramid shape and becomes barrel-shaped. This indicates an increasing number of old people in the population.

Sweden | Guatemala

Over 85
80-84
75-79
70-74
65-69
60-64
55-59
50-54
45-49
40-44
35-39
30-34
25-29
20-24
15-19
10-14
5-9
1-4
0-1

Male | Female | Male | Female

ing settlements in the world today.

Taking both rural and urban areas of the developing world together, more than 40 per cent of the population is either unemployed or underemployed, two billion are continually undernourished and some 1,400 million are illiterate. The causes of such problems are complex, but rapid population growth makes all of them more difficult to solve. As a result, four-fifths of the developing world's population now live in countries which have adopted policies aimed at slowing down the rate of population growth.

Since the world conference on population in Bucharest in 1974, governments have increasingly come to realize that such policies stand the best chance of success if they involve social and development policies which create a wish for smaller families, as well as access to family planning information and services. The motivation for small families involves the reduction of infant and child mortal-

ity, the expansion of basic education, especially for girls, an increase in the income of the rural poor, a more equal distribution of wealth and — of particular importance — the improvement of the status of women in society. Where such measures have been taken along with the provision of family planning services, including access to early abortion and a range of fertility control methods, rapid declines in fertility have taken place. The most spectacular example in recent years has been China.

Millions of people in the developing world, however, have no access to modern birth control methods and, indeed, some governments, on religious grounds or for strategic reasons, actively discourage family planning programmes. With greater pressures being put upon the earth's limited resources, from agricultural land to mineral wealth, and the ever-increasing impact of man's activities on the environment, the prospect of further population growth poses many and varied problems.

▲ **India,** with the second-largest population in the world, has introduced many birth control methods. At this sterilization clinic many vasectomies are carried out at one session.

▶ **The status of women** in a society affects attitudes to population control. In China women are considered to be an essential part of the work force and birth control is encouraged.

▲ **Birth rates remain high** in many of the less-developed countries. Large numbers of children are very often encouraged by the societies, for religious, economic and political reasons.

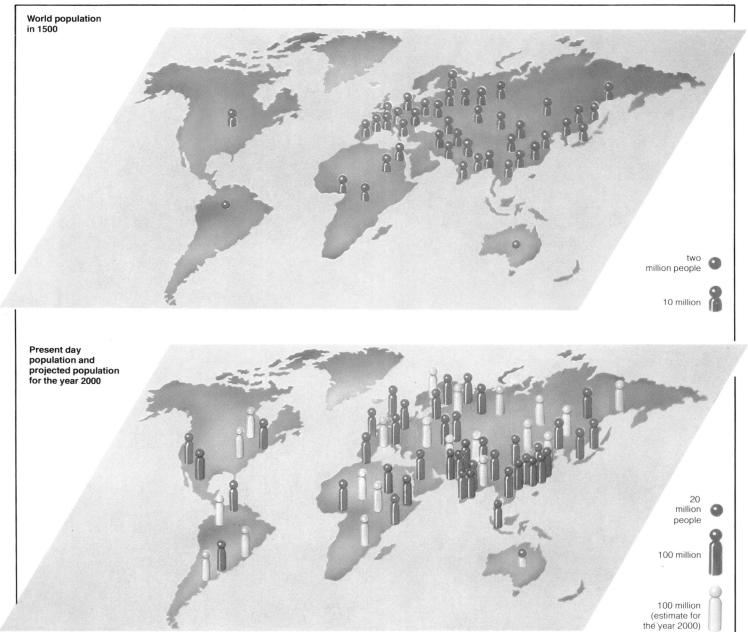

World population in 1500

two million people

10 million

Present day population and projected population for the year 2000

20 million people

100 million

100 million (estimate for the year 2000)

By about 8000 BC there were approximately five million people on earth. From then on, numbers increased by between 0.04 and 0.06 per cent a year until about 1650. The "doubling time" of human numbers had been reduced from 1,500 to 200 years by 1800, by which time world population had reached one billion.

Environment in danger

ALL life on our planet is confined to a thin skin of earth, air and water that is no more than 10 kilometres thick. It depends for its healthy existence on green vegetation which turns sunlight into chemical energy and maintains the balance of oxygen and carbon dioxide in the atmosphere. On this process are based the complex food chains made up of many thousands of plant and animal species, all of which are vulnerable to the activities of man.

The mounting impact of man on the environment is partly the result of his increased numbers. It is also due to the enormous increase in industrial activity and consumption of the earth's resources, particularly in the countries of the northern hemisphere. A two per cent annual increase in population since the middle of this century has been accompanied by a four per cent annual increase in consumption, a rate of growth which, if maintained for a century, will increase consumption 50 times and create an even greater impact on the biological environment.

The impact of man

The oceans, grasslands, croplands and forests have all felt the impact of man's rapidly increasing exploitation of these resources for food, fuel and living space. Forests play a vital role in maintaining the ecological status quo, preserving watersheds, preventing soil erosion and the silting of dams, moderating climate and providing fuel, building materials and paper. But the destruction of trees for farmland and firewood has a long history, and by the middle of this century between one-third and one-half of the earth's original forest cover had gone.

Forest management in western Europe, the Soviet Union and North America now shows an awareness of the need to conserve existing woodland, while China is striving to undo the destruction of past generations. Almost everywhere in the developing world, however, the remaining tree cover is under pressure as the growing population increases the demand for firewood supplies and farmland. Serious deforestation is occurring in the Himalayas, causing erosion and flooding in the plains below, and similar problems are reported from eastern India, Pakistan, Thailand, the Philippines, Malaysia, Tanzania and elsewhere. The tropical forests of southeast Asia, central and west Africa and Amazonia are also severely threatened, and with them the earth's richest store of rare plants and animals.

The loss of farmland

Arable land, which makes up one-tenth of the earth's land surface, is also under great pressure. The area of cropland is being reduced by serious erosion and conversion to non-agricultural use at a faster rate than new land is brought under the plough. Japan, for example, lost six per cent of cropland in the 1960s.

The oceans, too, have recently been exploited more intensively than ever before: the fish catch trebled from 21 to 72 million tonnes between 1950 and 1980. As a result, many areas have been overfished, particularly in the North Atlantic, where there have been sudden declines in catches of cod, haddock, sole and herring. The Peruvian anchovy has been grossly overfished and several species of whale have been hunted almost to the point of extinction.

The oceans are suffering also from another consequence of man's escalating consumption: the generation of excessive and dangerous wastes. The seas, which cover two-thirds of the earth's surface, have become a dustbin for oil, chemicals, radioactive materials, sewage, junk metal, pesticides and detergents, among many other products. Approximately one million tonnes of oil seep into the sea from ships and drilling rigs each year, and many inland seas and estuaries are now so heavily polluted that fish, if they survive at all, are not safe to eat. Pollution is also having its effect on human health through the air we breathe and the food and water we consume. Some 600,000 different chemicals are in daily use and every year several thousand new ones enter into significant use. Among the illnesses they have produced are parasitic infections, emphysema, heart disease and some cancers. With polluted rivers running across national frontiers and acid rain falling over a wide area of Europe, pollution can now be considered an international problem.

A growing concern

The long-term effects of some of man's activities are uncertain. There is considerable concern about the fluorocarbons contained

Environmental pollution

The possibility that the earth's climate may be changing has been a subject much discussed in recent years. Untypical, "freak" weather during the 1970s may well be the result of natural trends of cooling and warming that the earth has experienced throughout its history, but there are suggestions that the activities of man may fundamentally alter the world's climatic patterns. A manifestation of this is what is known as the "greenhouse effect". Carbon dioxide in the atmosphere is transparent to the shortwave infra-red heat radiation from the sun, but opaque to longwave infra-red radiation emitted from warm objects on earth. What this means, in effect, is that heat can get in but it cannot get out as easily. Measurements show that the level of carbon dioxide in the air has increased significantly during this century, possibly by as much as 15 per cent. The combustion of fossil fuels produces carbon dioxide and is the chief culprit, but ploughing land also releases large amounts of soil-held gas into the atmosphere.

Industrial effluent and untreated sewage are the most common pollutants of water, but the increasing use of fertilizers in food production means that larger amounts of nitrates and phosphates are leached into river systems. The over-abundance of chemicals such as phosphates in lakes and coastal waters produces an increase in algae on the surface, which blots out the light necessary for plant life. This, in turn, reduces the oxygen content and, ultimately, marine life. More and more water systems are "dying" as a result.

in aerosol cans. Half a million tonnes of these chemicals are released into the atmosphere each year, and it is thought they may be destroying the ozone layer which filters out the harmful ultraviolet radiation from the sun. The result of this could be an increase in the incidence of skin cancer, damage to crops and even a change in climate. The ozone layer may be threatened also by the release of nitrous oxides from nitrogen fertilizers, on which man depends for greater crop yields.

Of more immediate concern is the environmental stress caused by rapid urbanization. By the end of the century more than half the world's six billion people will be city dwellers if present trends continue. The lack of basic services in many cities and the crowding and stress suffered by the majority of urban dwellers in the less-developed countries pose a great environmental problem, albeit local in effect.

There is a rapidly increasing awareness of the environmental impact of man's activities. It is, however, often difficult to put a price on the conservation of nature and the protection of our vulnerable environment.

▲ **The world is in danger** of losing some of its rarest fauna as a result of man's activities. Such animals are either hunted into extinction or their habitats are ruined by human encroachment.

▼ **Road vehicles** consume vast amounts of oil and other raw materials, pollute the air and eat up land space for roads and car parks.

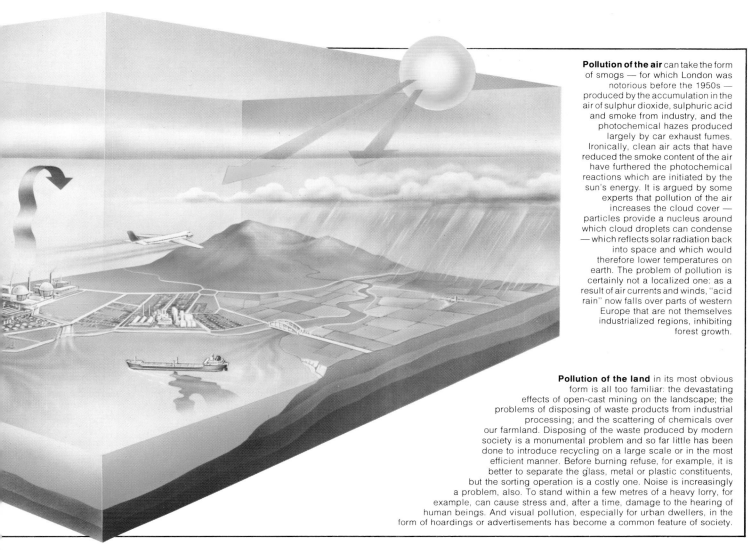

Pollution of the air can take the form of smogs — for which London was notorious before the 1950s — produced by the accumulation in the air of sulphur dioxide, sulphuric acid and smoke from industry, and the photochemical hazes produced largely by car exhaust fumes. Ironically, clean air acts that have reduced the smoke content of the air have furthered the photochemical reactions which are initiated by the sun's energy. It is argued by some experts that pollution of the air increases the cloud cover — particles provide a nucleus around which cloud droplets can condense — which reflects solar radiation back into space and which would therefore lower temperatures on earth. The problem of pollution is certainly not a localized one: as a result of air currents and winds, "acid rain" now falls over parts of western Europe that are not themselves industrialized regions, inhibiting forest growth.

Pollution of the land in its most obvious form is all too familiar: the devastating effects of open-cast mining on the landscape; the problems of disposing of waste products from industrial processing; and the scattering of chemicals over our farmland. Disposing of the waste produced by modern society is a monumental problem and so far little has been done to introduce recycling on a large scale or in the most efficient manner. Before burning refuse, for example, it is better to separate the glass, metal or plastic constituents, but the sorting operation is a costly one. Noise is increasingly a problem, also. To stand within a few metres of a heavy lorry, for example, can cause stress and, after a time, damage to the hearing of human beings. And visual pollution, especially for urban dwellers, in the form of hoardings or advertisements has become a common feature of society.

▶ **Pollution of the air** can be manifested in what is known as a photochemical haze, seen here lingering over a Californian beach. Car exhausts provide many of the raw materials needed for the atmospheric reactions: nitrogen dioxide, hydrocarbons and other organic compounds. Reactions are initiated by the sun's energy.

▼ **The destruction of tree cover,** overgrazing and overcropping contribute to the spread of deserts. The Sahara has crept both north and south – as in the Sahel region shown here – at a rate of almost 100 kilometres in the last 17 years, with the recent loss of 650,000 sq kilometres of productive land.

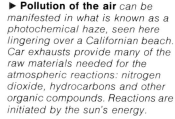

▲ **The air is still clear** and the land unscarred in regions of the earth that are apparently remote from the industrialized world. Studies of tissues from certain animals in the far northern and southern latitudes, however, shows evidence of pollution in the form of insecticides and other man-made chemicals that are carried to all parts of the globe by the earth's wind and water systems.

Feeding the world

WORLD food supplies have been increasing steadily and, in spite of predictions of impending disaster, have not yet been outstripped by population growth. Although current methods for determining accurately either world population or global food production figures are woefully inadequate, official United Nations statistics estimate that the earth's population has been increasing at less than two per cent annually while food production is growing at 2.9 per cent. While these figures are encouraging they do mask a high level of malnutrition, which is thought to affect between 60 and 400 million people. The cause of this problem is poverty created by an unequal distribution of land, wealth and opportunity rather than actual food shortages.

Nutritional requirements

Over the past two decades, as the young science of nutrition gathered more information, our understanding of nutritional requirements has become more exact. Figures on how many people were inadequately fed were previously based on the assumption that each person needed at least 3,000 kilocalories, including 90 grams of protein, a day. More recent findings have had the effect of revising these figures downwards to 1,990 kilocalories a day for developing countries and 2,320 kilocalories a day for developed countries. These figures are still only an average. Individual nutritional requirements vary, depending on age, sex, level of physical activity and even the climate of the region in which one lives. For example, the range extends from 820 kilocalories for a female child of less than one year to 3,100 kilocalories for a teenage boy.

The new recommended kilocalorie requirements mean that, on average, every individual needs the equivalent of 250 kilograms of grain a year. If the marketed supplies of food could have been equally distributed, then during the early 1970s, when concern about the amount of food available was so high, every person could have had 2,240 kilocalories a day, which is more than enough to engage in a healthy and active life. By the end of the 1970s approximately 1,300 million tonnes of food were reaching the market each year. That would have been enough to feed almost 5,200 million people, more than 1,000 million more than are on earth at the present time.

How much land is available?

During the same period in which nutritional requirements have been revised, our knowledge of how much food can be produced has also improved. Findings based on detailed studies of soil conditions, water availability, climate and crop characteristics indicate that there is the physical capability to produce enough food for even the highest estimate of population in the next 100 years. Studies show that a great deal more land is suitable for agricultural use than was previously believed. In southeast Asia, for example, only about 75 per cent of land which could be put under production is presently farmed.

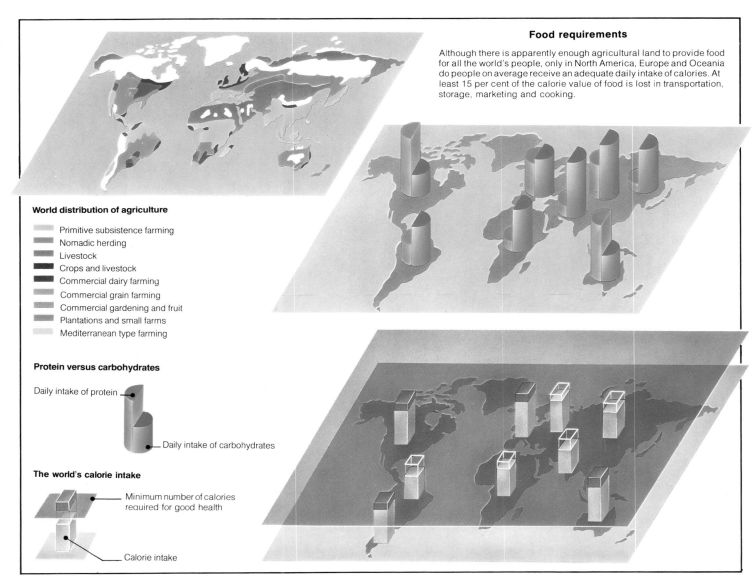

Food requirements

Although there is apparently enough agricultural land to provide food for all the world's people, only in North America, Europe and Oceania do people on average receive an adequate daily intake of calories. At least 15 per cent of the calorie value of food is lost in transportation, storage, marketing and cooking.

World distribution of agriculture

- Primitive subsistence farming
- Nomadic herding
- Livestock
- Crops and livestock
- Commercial dairy farming
- Commercial grain farming
- Commercial gardening and fruit
- Plantations and small farms
- Mediterranean type farming

Protein versus carbohydrates

- Daily intake of protein
- Daily intake of carbohydrates

The world's calorie intake

- Minimum number of calories required for good health
- Calorie intake

From the use of United Nations soil maps and studies of crops by the International Biological Programme it is estimated that there are 3,714 million hectares of land suitable for farming. Of these, 1,900 million have the potential for irrigation, a technique which can improve crop yields dramatically. Of course, competing uses for this land and the inability, for social and economic reasons, to gain access to "best-practice" techniques will mean that not all of this area is used to the fullest of its potential. If, however, only 1,208 million hectares were to be irrigated and crop yields were to reach 65 per cent of their potential, then 32,390 million tonnes of grain could be produced each year. That would be enough to feed 30 times the number of people on earth today.

Animal and plant resources

In addition to availability and productivity of land, food production depends on effective utilization of animals and plants. Plant-eating mammals and birds are all potentially edible. There are also numerous other animals, fish, insects and crustaceans which are eaten in some parts of the world but not in others. Many of these are in serious danger of elimination if industrial development takes place without consideration for the environmental requirements of these creatures. We need a world inventory of edible species so that these food sources are not lost by accident and not reduced without replacement.

Many of the hoofed animals thrive better in their home countries than imported sheep and cattle. They can be managed as wild herds by culling a calculated proportion each year for food. A further development would be domestication, as was performed on the original wild cattle of Europe. With modern knowledge of genetics animal breeding programmes could achieve targets in shorter periods than were necessary for the familiar breeds, and such animals as the eland and saiga antelope could be improved to meet the desired characteristics of meat, milk and hides that have been developed successfully in familiar domestic breeds.

More plants to eat

Just as the animal resources of most of the world are hardly yet developed, so too are indigenous plants in many regions where it is urgent that more food is produced locally. The International Biological Programme of 1963-74 identified several hundreds of plants which can fix nitrogen and, therefore, do not need nitrogen fertilizers. Many of these plants produce edible parts and could be improved by selection to become crops. Social anthropological studies show that people eat a much wider variety of plants and parts of plants than is generally supposed. An inventory of these would indicate which have the widest degree of acceptance and these could then be the subject of deliberate programmes of improvement to increase production.

The third factor in food production is technology, and its suitability to the societies that adopt it. So far, wherever a new technology has been introduced into a society where land and other resources are unequally distributed, the effect has been to increase the gap between rich and poor. Even when more food has been produced, poor people seldom get more of it, and there are many documented instances when they have got less.

The future of food production raises many issues, but the overriding aim should be to increase the food supplies available to the millions of people who still go hungry. The problem is to try to ensure that technical advance will for the present keep pace with population growth, and will in the long run overtake it so that those millions can have an adequate diet in the future. The question is what kind of food production is most suitable.

▲ **Nomadic pastoralism** *is practised on marginal lands where extremes of temperature or lack of water make cultivation virtually impossible. Subsistence farming makes no impact on world food markets, but half the world's population lives off the land and produces little or no surplus.*

▲ **The rolling plains** *of the North American continent have made the United States the granary of the world, on which millions of hungry mouths depend. (The USSR is actually the largest grain producer, but also the greatest consumer.) A series of bad harvests in the 1970s reduced world grain reserves to a few days' supply.*

▶ **The dire conditions** *of most of the world's poor — here typified by a mother and her children in the slums of an Indian city — do not offer much opportunity for an adequate diet.*

▼ **It is claimed** *that half the food bought in the United States ends up in the waste bin. We are constantly encouraged to buy more even though obesity is an extensive problem in the western world.*

▲ **Commercial livestock ranching** *is big business, especially in North America. It is often argued that we do not need as much meat as we eat and that cattle consume too much grain.*

What kind of food production?

WITH the world's population increasing by 70 or 80 million each year, and with many of the present population living off a totally inadequate diet, there can be little doubt about the urgency of increasing available food supplies. Nor is there any question about the two principal ways of doing so. They are to increase the area at present cultivated or grazed by farmers, and to obtain higher production per unit area from the existing farmlands.

In certain respects, these two objectives overlap. The effective area of cultivation will be doubled, for example, if a single, annual crop can be replaced by double-cropping. To obtain two crops in place of one, however, will probably require either a new breed of plant, which will mature faster, or an addition to the water supply, probably by irrigation, to provide enough water for double-cropping.

Extending the farming frontier
The principal methods by which the cultivated or pastured area can be extended are by clearance of forest, by irrigation, by drainage, by breeding hardier stocks and by removing the barriers presented by disease. The first three date back to antiquity. Irrigation was the basis of the Egyptian, Mesopotamian and some Central American civilizations, while in Europe, where nearly 90 per cent of the potentially arable land is cultivated, forest clearance has historically been the main method of extending the farming frontier, just as it has been for the past three centuries in eastern North America. Forest clearance assumes that the need for, or value of, land under agriculture is greater than the value of land under trees, an assumption that could realistically be made in medieval Europe, but that has ceased to hold good, for example, along the Canadian margins of agriculture. It is probable, in fact, that worldwide at present the forest is advancing on the farmland rather than the reverse. The potential for extra cropland, however, does exist in many areas of the world.

Irrigation and drainage both involve re-directing natural water supplies, and together they have already transformed great areas of Asia (the continent with by far the largest irrigated area, and where the Chinese have been using valley and delta drainage for millennia), the Middle East and North America. The Mississippi Valley and the Central Valley of California are today two of the world's most productive farming regions, yet a century ago one was a tangle of swamps and trees, and the other an area of desert and salt pans. Irrigation and drainage hold out good prospects for further increasing the area of farmland, but the capital costs are enormous, and the more irregular the water supply, the higher those costs become.

The breeding of hardy and quick-maturing plants has already served to push back frontiers by permitting the use of land formerly unsuitable for cultivation because of low temperatures or a short growing season. It is by this means that the great cereal areas of the Canadian prairies and the Soviet steppes have been enlarged still further.

The removal of barriers raised by disease would open up other great areas to the food producer. Africa, one of the most seriously food-deficient regions of the world, would be the principal target in this respect: only 22 per cent of its potentially arable land is cultivated, and much of it is unproductive because of diseases such as sleeping sickness.

A green revolution
The other main method of producing more food is by increasing yields per hectare. If yields worldwide were at the level of those in northwest Europe or the American Midwest, then every hectare of the world's farmland could support between 15 and 20 people on average, instead of the present global figure of between 2.8 and 3.0. The problems are not those of technology, but of supply, economics and education.

On the technical side, the major contribution so far has been made by the plant breeders. The heart of the so-called green revolution of the past four decades has been the scientific creation of high-yielding strains of corn, wheat, rice and other crops, together with improved breeds of livestock. A series of international institutes, most of them located in less-developed countries, now provide a focus for this work. Sometimes the development concerns the period necessary for the plant to mature: a rice that matures in 120 days instead of 160 may permit two crops to be grown each year instead of one. Sometimes it is a case of altering the density of planting: it is possible by scientific breeding to double the number of plants per square metre without overcrowding or loss of growth. Alternatively, the actual structure of the plant may be involved: it must have a shorter stem, for instance, in order to be able to support a heavier head.

Other areas of technical innovation are in the use of chemical fertilizers and pesticides, and in educating the farmer in a wider range of expertise, thus encouraging him to make more innovations. There is, however, the limitation imposed on adopting the new farming techniques by economics. Not only are supplies of seed for the new "wonder crops" limited at present, but the additional fertilizer input and the equipment to harvest and store larger crops have to be paid for. And this cost is not purely financial. Chemical fertilizer production involves far greater energy inputs than the additional food energy yielded by their use. It is necessary, therefore, to possess the raw materials, whose price has been soaring, and to consume other resources, before the farmer can produce more food. It is small wonder that many farmers cling to traditional methods.

Certainly, improvements in food supply can be made: by cutting down losses due to pests and disease; by mariculture, or farming the sea for food; by organizing the marketing of products through co-operatives and re-organizing the tenure of land; and in the future, perhaps, by the development of synthetic food stuffs. Most of these, however, are long-term projects and, like the cross-breeding of plants, cannot be hurried.

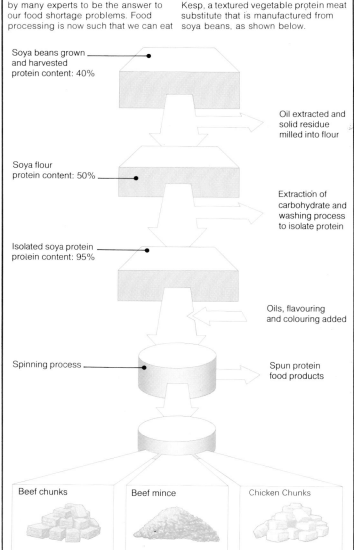

Textured vegetable protein

Textured vegetable protein is thought by many experts to be the answer to our food shortage problems. Food processing is now such that we can eat what appears to be meat but is in fact Kesp, a textured vegetable protein meat substitute that is manufactured from soya beans, as shown below.

Soya beans grown and harvested protein content: 40%

Oil extracted and solid residue milled into flour

Soya flour protein content: 50%

Extraction of carbohydrate and washing process to isolate protein

Isolated soya protein protein content: 95%

Oils, flavouring and colouring added

Spinning process

Spun protein food products

Beef chunks

Beef mince

Chicken Chunks

▲ **Deserts** *are not necessarily infertile regions and, once water is supplied, they can be transformed into highly productive areas, as in the Algerian Sahara. Water can be pumped from underground reservoirs, or basins can be dug so that the root systems of crops can reach groundwater supplies. Fences protect crops from sand.*

▼ **The world fish catch** *reached more than 60 million tonnes a year in the 1970s as a result of greater efficiency and better technology. Some species have been seriously overfished. Attention is now being paid to aquaculture — the artificial culturing of fish — and fish farming, which increases natural stocks in the open sea or seawater tanks.*

▲ **Terracing** *is the traditional method of cultivation on the densely populated island of Bali in Indonesia and is being usefully employed in other regions where land is in short supply. In contrast to the terraces shown here, however, modern schemes often involve mechanized excavations and produce non-irrigated crops.*

▶ **Sorghum** *could be grown as an energy crop as well as for food. It has a high concentration of carbon dioxide around its green pigment and can convert solar energy 10 times as efficiently as other crops.*

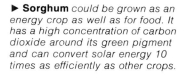

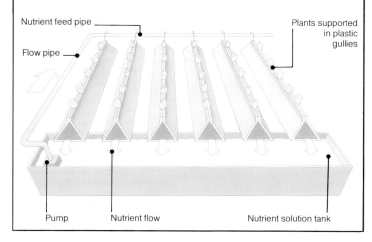

Nutrient film technique

Technology has come to play an increasingly important role in modern agriculture and one new method — the nutrient film technique — means that the farmer can actually grow crops without any soil. This is done with the aid of the device shown here, whereby crops are planted, either outdoors or in greenhouses, in plastic trays. A solution containing all the vital nutrients the plant needs is constantly circulated through the trays. This method — first developed by the Glasshouse Crops Research Institute in England — has proved highly successful and is used in many parts of the world.

Nutrient feed pipe

Flow pipe

Plants supported in plastic gullies

Pump

Nutrient flow

Nutrient solution tank

Man's quest for energy

SINCE the Industrial Revolution there has been a close relationship between economic activity and world energy use. For many years a one per cent increase in economic growth has been matched by a similar increase in energy demands. Because of this close, historic relationship, and given fears of impending resource scarcity, energy is very much at the centre of the debate about man's future. Energy underlies everyday life: it heats and lights homes, offices and factories, drives machinery and raises steam for industrial processes, fuels trans-port systems, and is a key require-ment for food production — directly for tractors and food processing and indirectly for the production of fertilizers and pesticides.

Since man learnt to utilize fire, the quest for energy has been a key feature of every civilization. Humans, animals, wood, wind and water were harnessed and the availability of such sources of energy set the limits to economic activity within societies.

First use of fossil fuels
Since the process of industrializa-tion and urbanization began, man has increasingly supplemented the use of renewable sources of energy by exploiting the depletable fossil fuels. At first coal was mined at or near the surface, but as demand grew and technology improved, underground mining complexes were developed. Coal was used in boilers, steam engines and locomo-tives and in open fires to heat homes; converted to coke it fuelled a breakthrough in iron and steel production, and as gas it supplied street lighting and domestic heat-ing; some was used to make chemi-cals, dyes and explosives.

Coal dominated world energy supplies until the 1950s, although oil and natural gas were by then widely used in the United States. In 1900, coal accounted for 94 per cent of the world's use of commer-cial fuels, oil four per cent and natural gas one per cent, and wood and hydroelectric power for the remainder. By 1950, these percen-tages had changed to 62, 25 and nine respectively, and in 1974, the year after the oil crisis, to 32, 45 and 21. Today oil and natural gas account for more than two-thirds of world fossil fuel supplies.

The other dramatic development since the beginning of this century has been a change in the scale of demand for energy. World con-sumption of fossil fuels increased ten-fold between 1900 and 1980 from 760 million tons of coal equi-valent (tce) to 8,500 million tce. The western industrialized economies, mainly North America, Western Europe and Japan, consumed 60 per cent of the total, the USSR and Eastern Europe 23 per cent, and the poorer, less-developed countries (including those with large popula-tions such as India and China) only 17 per cent of the total.

World energy supplies
Coal production reached 3,740 mil-lion tonnes in 1980 and is forecast by the World Energy Conference to double by the year 2000. The main producers are the USSR, USA,

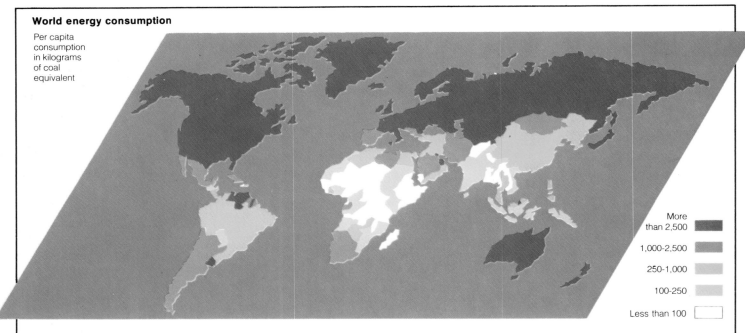

World energy consumption

Per capita consumption in kilograms of coal equivalent

More than 2,500

1,000-2,500

250-1,000

100-250

Less than 100

A continuation of current trends of energy consumption for 75 years would lead to an annual world consumption of about 80,000 million tce in the year 2050: today's poor countries, with 75 per cent of the world's people, would still account for only one-third of total energy consumption.

▶ **Large pipelines** — *used here to carry oil across the desert in Qatar — have higher capital costs but lower running costs than other forms of transport. They also raise international political issues.*

◀ **Modern, industrialized society** — *epitomized by the New York skyline — is dependent upon vast supplies of energy. In 1981 the total amount of energy produced commercially was the equivalent of 2.1 tonnes of coal per person.*

China, Poland, the UK and West Germany. Amongst developing countries, India is the major producer. Ultimately recoverable resources are vast — more than one million, million tonnes.

Oil production rose to 4,330 million tce in 1980, the major producers being the USSR, USA, Saudi Arabia, Iran, Venezuela and Iraq. A major recent development has been the exploitation of offshore oil resources. Ultimate crude oil reserves are estimated at between 250 and 300 thousand million tonnes, with a similar quantity in unconventional forms such as oil shales, tar sands and synthetic oils, exploitable at higher costs. Natural gas has become a major world fuel only relatively recently. Proved reserves are estimated at between 70 and 90 thousand million tce, but this is thought to be conservative.

Nuclear power is based on the fission (or splitting) of uranium atoms in a range of reactor types, the dominant categories being water-cooled (mainly in the USA, France, West Germany and Japan) and gas-cooled (mainly in the UK). Future reactor types include fast breeders based on a mixture of uranium and plutonium fuel and the high temperature reactor. Nuclear power at present provides about four per cent of world electricity requirements but a substantial increase is planned by 2000. The extent of uranium reserves is subject to considerable uncertainty and this also applies to thorium, which may prove a suitable alternative fuel, although no commerical thorium reactors have been put into operation yet.

Only about 14 per cent of world hydroelectric potential is exploited at present, mainly at sites in industrialized countries. The capital costs of major hydro schemes are often beyond the reach of developing countries unless aided by massive financial assistance.

Industry is the largest consumer of energy in the developed world, accounting for 35-40 per cent of total demand. Those industries concerned with processing of materials — iron and steel, chemicals, aluminium, bricks — account for two-thirds of this total. Technical changes in industrial processes have led to improved energy efficiency and recent fuel price increases will encourage this further. Increased recycling of materials will also reduce the energy demand per unit of output. Public and private services account for 10-15 per cent of energy demands in the developed countries, mainly for heating and lighting.

Energy use in the home
Domestic use accounts for 20-25 per cent of energy demand. Of this about 60 per cent is used for space heating and air conditioning; 20-25 per cent for water heating; 10 per cent for cooking and between five and 10 per cent (almost entirely as electricity) for appliances such as washing machines, televisions and so on. Many appliances, for example hi-fi, use little electricity, but others such as tumble driers and dishwashers may be key future growth areas. Improved insulation of buildings could reduce domestic energy demands.

Transport accounts for 25 per cent of energy demand in the USA and 20 per cent in Western Europe. The largest proportion is used by road transport, especially the private car. A range of new technologies might reduce fuel consumption per mile by 20-40 per cent in the coming decades and there is scope for improving the efficiency of public transport systems.

Over the next 20-30 years, the world will experience a transition from a dependence on oil and gas towards greater use of coal, nuclear power and renewable energy sources. Major technical changes will be necessary and will require a considerable developmental period before widespread application is possible.

How one nuclear reactor works

Certain atoms of uranium break into fragments when a neutron is added to the nucleus. If this occurs, the uranium atom is split into two and energy is released in the form of heat. At the same time neutrons are given off and they continue the process by splitting other nuclei. This is called a chain reaction and it forms the basis of the generation of nuclear power. In a nuclear reactor the chain reaction is kept going at a steady rate and the heat is used to produce steam to drive electricity generators. In order to maintain a steady rate the number of neutrons that continue the reaction has to be controlled. This is done by absorbing excess neutrons in control rods made of boron. If neutrons produced by the reaction are slowed down they can split the nuclei more easily. The slowing down is achieved by surrounding the fuel with a moderator — so-called because it moderates the speed of the neutrons. The reactor is protected by a concrete shield to prevent the escape of dangerous radiation. In a gas-cooled reactor, such as the one shown here, the heat produced by the reaction is removed by circulating carbon dioxide gas. Alternatively, the heat can be removed by circulating water through the system. The heat is used to convert water to steam.

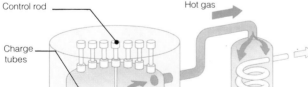

Reactor   **Heat exchanger**

- Control rod
- Charge tubes
- Graphite moderator
- Fuel element
- Hot gas
- Steam
- Water
- Gas blower
- Cold gas
- Concrete shield

▲ **Natural gas** was once considered to be a useless by-product of drilling for oil and was burnt off. Today, however, technical developments, such as liquefied natural gas tankers and large pipeline networks, have enabled a rapid growth in its use. Deposits are found in association with oil or on their own, as in this Iranian field.

▶ **Millions of people** in the less-developed countries are dependent for energy on what nature supplies, mainly firewood and dung. Non-commercial consumption of energy is difficult to assess accurately, but is probably in the region of 1,500 tce. Such energy sources are steadily being replaced by fossil fuels, however.

▶ **Recoverable coal reserves** are vast enough to last for almost 3,000 years at current rates of consumption. Greater concern for the environment may affect production techniques, however. Open-cast mining — seen here in West Virginia — is one of the most economical mining methods but it usually has a devastating effect on the landscape.

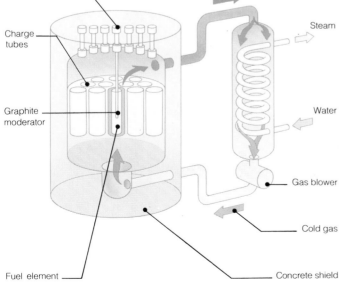

Energy alternatives

AT PRESENT the world depends almost entirely on non-renewable sources for its energy. More than 90 per cent of our energy is derived from the major non-renewable fossil fuels: coal, oil and natural gas. A high proportion of the rest, especially in countries of the Third World, comes from wood which, although renewable in principle, is being rapidly depleted. We are never likely to run out of any of these resources completely, but we are already experiencing large increases in the cost of obtaining each unit of fossil fuel. This trend will continue and will impose an ever-increasing strain on the world's systems of production and the societies built on them.

We are at the moment ill-equipped to deal with this eventuality: none of the possible renewable sources of energy are anywhere near ready to start replacing fossil fuels. Moreover, the processes of developing and commercializing major new technologies are extremely difficult and lengthy. Nuclear power, for instance, has been under intensive and massively funded development for more than 30 years, and yet it is still far from being a mature technology and supplies only one per cent of the world's energy demand. Renewable energy, by which we mean direct solar, geothermal, hydroelectric, wind, wave and tidal power, biomass fuels and nuclear breeding and fusion, will require a similar, if not greater, volume and intensity of effort if it is to make a substantial impact on world energy supplies in 50 years' time.

Renewable energy and lifestyles

Renewable energy sources (with the exception of nuclear) are often called "alternative" energy. Alternative energy tends to be linked with the idea of alternative culture — implying a radical change in lifestyle both at an individual level and in the political, economic and social spheres. It is perhaps unfortunate that practitioners of 'alternative culture' in the West are rarely good advertisements for the advantages of their lifestyle but it is certainly true that at their existing (mainly rudimentary) stage of development, most renewable energy sources are most compatible with a low energy-using, rural society with limited industrialization. This is because the majority of renewables provide only diffuse, low-grade energy, which is subject to considerable variability in supply.

Much of the development effort in renewable energy must, therefore, be concentrated on making it as compatible as possible with urban, industrial society. The difficulties of achieving this (through effective storage and the up-grading of low-grade heat, for instance) are what makes the development of renewable energy sources so expensive. In the long term, therefore, widespread reliance on renewable energy will probably not require major and fundamental changes to existing lifestyles. Renewable nuclear sources (breeders and fusion), on the other hand, are specifically designed to fit existing industrial societies and their development in the future may well be compatible only with even more centralized and interdependent societies than exist at present.

Sources of renewable energy

Direct solar energy is the most obviously attractive source because of its abundance. The major problems in its development (common to a number of renewables) concern its low efficiency and its variability, which requires the development of storage technologies. High yields of useful energy from the sun are therefore likely to need heavy capital investment. Domestic space heating technology is reasonably well developed and electricity production from direct solar sources has been demonstrated, but enormous problems remain to be solved.

Hydroelectricity is the only renewable source in significant commercial use, and it provides more than one-fifth of the world's electricity. Its main problems are that it is not a genuinely renewable source in the long term (because of reservoir silting) and that most sites suitable for large-scale development have already been used in

▲ **Wind power** was used traditionally for pumping water or grinding corn and modern wind power generators have been built in some areas, such as the Orkneys. Wind is an attractive energy source since its use produces no extra heat load on the environment.

◄ **The world's largest solar furnace,** at Odeillo in the French Pyrenees, uses a large concave mirror to focus the sun's rays. In regions where there is strong sunshine during the day, solar energy can be used for space heating or to supply hot water to homes or larger buildings that have a low requirement for hot water.

many industrialized countries. Geothermal sources make use of the earth's internal heat to supply either heat or electricity. Limited commercial development has already taken place. Diffuseness is again a major developmental problem.

Wind power has improved significantly since the heyday of traditional windmills. It may well prove extremely suitable for rural use (pumping and electricity) where climatic conditions are suitable. Wave power could in principle supply large amounts of electricity, but has not yet been substantially demonstrated, and its development faces major technical and economic problems. Tidal power has already been demonstrated on a fairly large scale, but there are few suitable sites in the world.

Biological sources of energy (wood, dung, wastes and crops) are already of vital importance to the Third World, though there are major problems of depletion. The main long-term problem for biomass fuels is competition with food production for the use of land.

The future of nuclear power

Fast breeder nuclear reactors — which "breed" their own fuel in the form of plutonium — and fusion reactors — in which common light elements fuse and release energy — can be considered as renewable sources. Breeders are being built on a commercial scale, but technical, safety and environmental problems remain to be solved. They are, nevertheless, a long-term possibility for electricity production and have massive government backing in both capitalist and communist countries as the main "technical fix" for fossil fuel scarcities. Nuclear fusion is an attempt to reproduce on earth the fusion reaction of the sun, and it would mean an end to the world's energy problems. Fusion occurs, however, at temperatures of about 100 million degrees and the problems of holding the resulting "plasma" stable and then safely extracting energy are currently well beyond our technical capabilities.

The obvious and enormous difficulties that still need to be overcome before renewable energy can by widely used, together with the ever-rising costs of non-renewable sources, lead to two main conclusions: that there is a critical need to promote energy conservation as a way of reducing demand and buying time; and that we will almost certainly need to rely on a combination of a large number of renewable energy sources.

▲ **A considerable number** of sites suitable for hydroelectric power schemes remain unexploited in less-developed countries, but constructing a dam such as the Kariba poses enormous financial, technical and political problems for the developing nations.

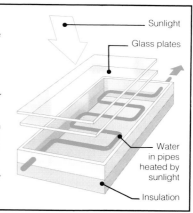

Solar power

Solar collectors operate in much the same way as a greenhouse. Air inside a metal-backed box with a transparent lid of either glass or plastic is heated by the sun. The glass traps the infra-red radiation and so the box becomes a collector for the heat. Another version has copper pipes in which water is heated instead of air. A solar system can only be effective if the heat can be stored for release when the house needs warming. This is done by means of the heating of a rock store, usually placed beneath the house, or by heating water in a storage tank.

Sunlight

Glass plates

Water in pipes heated by sunlight

Insulation

▲ **Power from geothermal sources** makes use of heat stored in the earth in volcanic regions or deep sedimentary basins. Electricity can be generated from turbines driven by the pressure of underground streams of hot water and steam. Geothermal power is produced commercially in Iceland, the USA, Italy and New Zealand.

Power from the sea

One wave power converter consists of a "duck" that rocks backwards and forwards on a spindle and can extract up to 90 per cent of the energy contained in a wave that it intercepts. No commercial wave power station has yet been built, but to produce power in quantity a long series of ducks in concrete rafts would be needed. They would drive a generator within the axle linking them. It is agreed that, for greatest efficiency, wave power stations should be designed to extract energy not from the biggest waves that occur only a few times a year but from the average-sized waves that flow all the time. The stations will still have to withstand powerful storm waves, however. The average Atlantic wave can produce a power equivalent of about 70 kilowatts per metre. That is enough to heat seven medium-sized houses in a temperate climate for an hour. In a tidal power scheme a basin reservoir is created by constructing a barrage across a tidal estuary. Seawater enters and leaves the basin through ducts containing turbines that power generators. Such schemes are restricted to estuaries whose tidal range between high and low water is extremely large, such as the Rance estuary in northwestern France. The Severn estuary in England is a possible site for the future development of tidal power.

Tidal power

Wave power

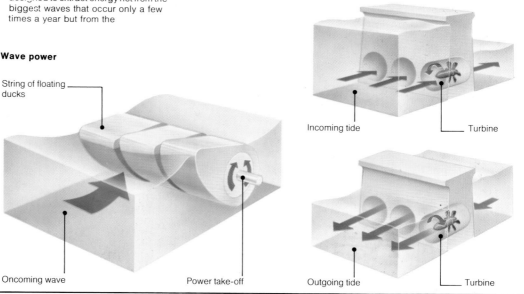

String of floating ducks

Incoming tide

Turbine

Oncoming wave

Power take-off

Outgoing tide

Turbine

The earth's mineral wealth

MODERN industrial society is dependent upon an assured supply of a wide variety of mineral commodities besides those that are used as a source of energy. Very few countries are totally devoid of all non-fuel minerals but, conversely, even the few exceptionally mineral-rich nations, such as Australia, Canada and South Africa, usually need to import at least one critically important commodity.

Bulk minerals used for construction purposes, for example crushed stone, sand, gravel, cement and clay, are widely distributed geographically and are therefore unimportant in terms of international trade. Moreover, although they are consumed in large quantities, they have a low intrinsic value and can rarely be transported economically for any great distance even within their countries of origin.

Of other important mineral commodities, some, such as iron ore and bauxite (the raw material of the aluminium industry), are mined and consumed in vast quantities, but because of an unequal global distribution of resources, the considerable cost of transportation has to be borne by the many consumer nations. At the other extreme, minerals such as the various precious metals, diamonds, cobalt, chromium and many others have a high intrinsic value, are not consumed in vast tonnages and, in their case, transportation costs have relatively little significance.

Three categories

When considered in terms of their end-use, the minerals entering international trade fall broadly into three categories. Minerals required as raw materials for the iron and steel industry include, in addition to the iron ore itself, the ores of the alloying metals such as tungsten, nickel, manganese and chromium and sometimes special grades of limestone for smelting purposes.

Non-ferrous metals used in their own right and not mainly as an adjunct to the iron and steel industry form a distinct category of their own. These include the base metals such as copper, lead, tin and zinc and also the precious metals.

A third category includes those substances that are loosely termed industrial minerals, and embraces those which are not utilized as a source of metal. Some, like phosphate rock, fluorspar and potash, are essential raw materials in the large-scale manufacture of important chemicals. Others, like ceramic and refractory clays, asbestos, talc and mica, are sought because of certain distinctive physical and chemical properties.

The growth and survival of the world's mineral industry demands considerable expertise at all levels of exploitation, including prospecting, mining, processing and utilization. The widespread search for minerals on and beyond continental limits requires much investment in geological, geophysical and geochemical exploration methods, and reflects the reality that mineral resources are far from being randomly or equally distributed.

A geological revolution

An intellectual revolution in the earth sciences in the last two decades has led to a better understanding of how continental segments or "plates" have evolved and moved relative to each other through more than three billion years of planetary history. In turn, this wider understanding of geological processes has encouraged a broader insight into the mechanism of formation and the reasons for the distribution of many key mineral commodities. For example, the presence of many large copper-bearing ore bodies of the so-called porphyry type along the geologically active western margins of both North and South America can be related to the present-day seismic and volcanic activity in those regions. This kind of correlation provides guidelines for the location of analogous ore bodies in much more ancient terrains.

Other major mineral resources, well exemplified by the major iron ore deposits of Australia, Brazil and South Africa and bauxite in several tropical countries, have a distribution related not so much to deep-seated crustal processes as to climatic or other physical conditions that were prevalent at specific periods in the earth's history. The recognition of the role that such palaeo-environmental factors have had on the formation of these ores serves to focus the search for further mineral deposits.

Exploration for new mineral deposits is also assisted by increasingly refined methods of detection. Discovery of such deposits is now rarely dependent upon the recognition of visible traces of ore but instead requires detection of the subtle physical and chemical effects which may be the only tangible manifestation of important ore bodies concealed beneath considerable thicknesses of barren rock. Such improvement in prospecting techniques owes much to modern methods of rapid chemical analysis, complex electronic circuitry in geophysical instruments, automatic data processing and remote sensing, using both aircraft and satellite-borne detection devices.

A success story so far

In the fields of mining, handling and milling of ore, economies resulting from the increasingly larger scale of operation have enabled the mining industry to keep pace with ever increasing demand for most commodities. The development of large and highly mechanized open-cast mining operations at the expense of labour-intensive underground methods has resulted in a significant reduction of the economic ore cut-off grade. Further developments in the processing of low-grade ores, for example by chemical and bacterial leaching, suggest that the process of technical improvement may continue. Mining of sub-sea mineral resources can also be expected to commence in the near future, although there the barriers are of a political nature.

Despite the continuing success of the mining industry, demand for most commodities continues to rise. Investigation of the potential resources that, it is hoped, will provide the necessary margin of reserves ahead of production must therefore be pursued vigorously. Although this search has so far proved successful, some alarm has been expressed that shortages may soon appear in the supply of some key mineral commodities.

Where economic minerals occur

The distribution and concentration of minerals of economic significance is controlled by the major geological processes of magmatism (the melting, movement and solidification of volcanic and other igneous rocks), metamorphism (chemical and physical changes to rocks brought about by heat and pressure below the zone of weathering) and sedimentation (the transport and deposition of material derived from the weathering of other rocks)

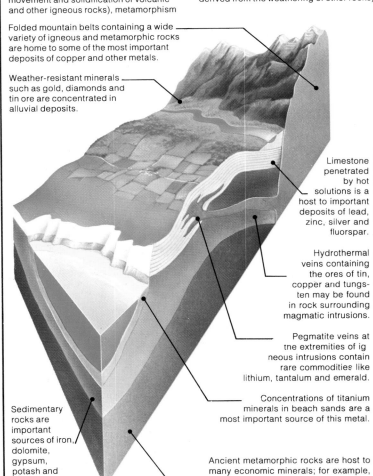

Folded mountain belts containing a wide variety of igneous and metamorphic rocks are home to some of the most important deposits of copper and other metals.

Weather-resistant minerals such as gold, diamonds and tin ore are concentrated in alluvial deposits.

Limestone penetrated by hot solutions is a host to important deposits of lead, zinc, silver and fluorspar.

Hydrothermal veins containing the ores of tin, copper and tungsten may be found in rock surrounding magmatic intrusions.

Pegmatite veins at the extremities of igneous intrusions contain rare commodities like lithium, tantalum and emerald.

Concentrations of titanium minerals in beach sands are a most important source of this metal.

Sedimentary rocks are important sources of iron, dolomite, gypsum, potash and others.

Ancient metamorphic rocks are host to many economic minerals; for example, gold, nickel, iron, asbestos.

▲ **Satellite surveying** *includes taking photographs that emphasize certain bands of the light spectrum and reveal many large-scale geological features that would be*

unrecognizable from the ground. Satellite-borne detection devices have reduced the time and increased the efficiency of mineral prospecting on the ground.

▲ **More than two-thirds** *of the world's metallic mineral output is produced by open-cast methods which are cheaper and easier now that technology is available to remove thick overburden.*

▶ **The precious metals,** *long valued as a store of wealth, are of increasing importance to industries such as electronics, dentistry, photography and aerospace.*

Major mineral deposits

Relatively few mineral deposits are of economic value, and of those the metals are the most important. Iron, the fourth most abundant element in the earth's crust, occurs widely and 500 million tonnes are produced annually. Aluminium is the most common metal, but only 18 million tonnes are produced a year. Tin deposits are restricted to a few areas which makes it an expensive metal (production: 210,000 tonnes). Other major metals include copper (7.7 million tonnes), gold (less than 1,500 tonnes), silver (about 10,000 tonnes), uranium (38,000 tonnes) and lead and zinc, which usually occur together (4.4 and 6 million tonnes respectively). The distribution of major deposits of the world's most valuable minerals is shown on the map below.

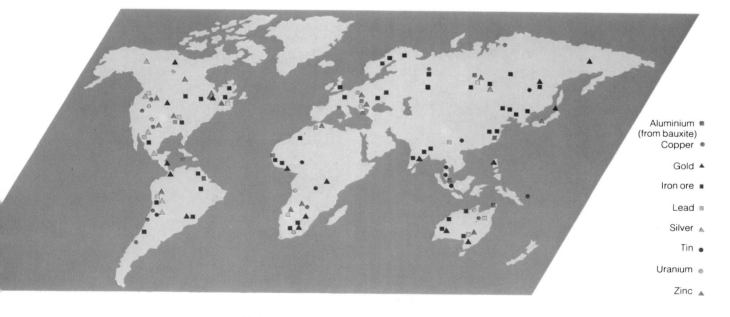

Aluminium ▪
(from bauxite)
Copper ●

Gold ▲

Iron ore ▪

Lead ▫

Silver ▲

Tin ●

Uranium ●

Zinc ▲

Asbestos (chrysotile)

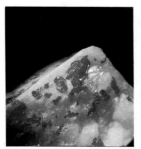

Mercury (cinnabar)

Uranium (autunite)

Iron (haematite)

Copper (bornite)

A conserving future

IN THE context of an ever-increasing world population and the consequent rise in demand for living space, food and raw materials, it has been predicted by some economic forecasters that a crisis in the supply of our most important mineral resources is imminent. Although the mining industry has been successful in continuing to discover new resources ahead of demand, it is suggested that the number of new discoveries of ore yet to be made must be finite and that sooner or later mankind will be faced with an absolute shortage of many key commodities which are essential to an industrial society.

The question of conservation
At the simplest level of argument, conservation of minerals is proposed as a desirable object of international co-operation simply to delay for as long as possible the point at which society can no longer rely on supplies. A diametrically opposed view is, however, often supported, not least by the mining industry itself. This argues that the efficient utilization of all resources that are available and can be extracted economically at the present time, far from being discouraged, should be vigorously pursued. Only this will give an innovative society the economic encouragement that it needs to discover

technical solutions to the problems of raw material shortages that may occur in the near future.

Expressed in this way, arguments for and against mineral conservation appear to be somewhat academic. However, recent history has shown that for two reasons, political and environmental, conservation or, more accurately, the efficient utilization of mineral resources is a desirable end. In the political sphere, the growth of producer cartels such as OPEC (petroleum), CIPEC (copper) and the IBA (bauxite) may well have the effect of encouraging countries which are net importers of the commodities concerned to examine more closely the efficiency with which those commodities are utilized.

The growing pressure of mining on the environment is partly the result of increased demand requiring bigger mines, but it can also be attributed to the exhaustion of high-grade ore deposits, resulting in a shift of emphasis towards large-scale extractive operations that are able to work vast low-grade deposits at a profit.

Political and environmental pressures, although fundamental in encouraging the efficient use of non-renewable resources,• can often act indirectly. For example, the increases imposed for political reasons upon the price of crude

petroleum not only encourage less wasteful use of the refinery products themselves but also, at second hand, the efficient use of, say, metals produced in smelters dependent upon oil-based energy.

How to improve efficiency
The efficient use and therefore, ultimately, the conservation of mineral resources involves a critical examination of the way in which they are utilized at all stages from their removal from the ground, through processing, fabrication, usage and recovery as scrap.

At the point at which minerals are mined there is often scope for improvement in recovery ratios. Open-cast mining often permits the recovery of almost 100 per cent of the ore available, but such favourable recoveries are rarely attainable with underground mining. And it must be admitted that in some cases the installation of mechanization to improve the economic performance of underground mining results in a concomitant reduction in the attainable reserves available. Mechanical cutters on longwall faces, for example, can only work on seams that are more than a minimum thickness.

The processing and fabrication stages in the conversion of raw material to finished product offer the opportunity for resource conservation in the way in which energy is used and also in terms of the way in which the final products are designed. Nevertheless, scrutiny of the energy input of manufacturing processes demands a sophisticated degree of analysis. For example, the use of the light metals aluminium and magnesium in automobile components can only be justified if the amount of fuel

saved during the lifetime of the vehicle more than offsets the higher energy cost of smelting these substitute metals.

Substitution of many important commodities to meet specific shortages can be envisaged. A good example is aluminium which can substitute for copper as an electrical conductor or for steel in the construction industry. But the physical properties of substitutes are never identical, and in some cases substitution does not appear to be a realistic possibility. Silver, for example, is probably irreplaceable for photographic purposes.

Recycling
It is probable that in the short term recycling of scrap and waste will create more impact than substitution on resource conservation. Once again, however, the trade-offs have to be considered. While little energy input is involved in collecting high-quality process scrap from the floor of a machine shop, the same is not necessarily true if useful materials have to be separated at great expense from general industrial waste. There also tend to be restrictions on the uses to which recovered material can be put. Scrap aluminium usually contains some silicon and can therefore be used for making castings but not for many fabrication purposes. The total efficiency of scrap recovery is closely related to the purpose to which the material is put.

The technical aspects of mineral conservation appear to be fairly well understood. Encouragement for their implementation requires social and political initiative although the operation of the simple law of supply and demand will be effective in time.

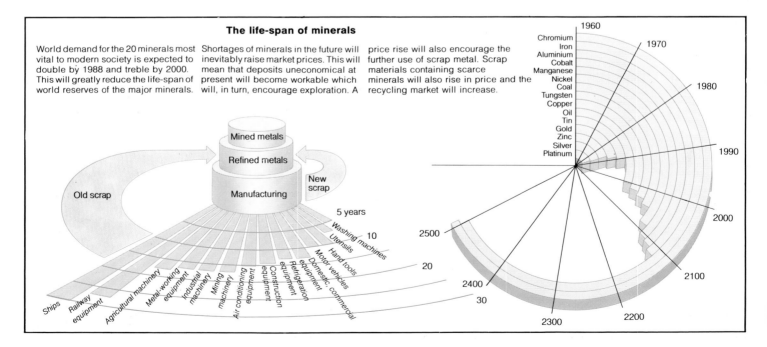

The life-span of minerals
World demand for the 20 minerals most vital to modern society is expected to double by 1988 and treble by 2000. This will greatly reduce the life-span of world reserves of the major minerals.

Shortages of minerals in the future will inevitably raise market prices. This will mean that deposits uneconomical at present will become workable which will, in turn, encourage exploration. A

price rise will also encourage the further use of scrap metal. Scrap materials containing scarce minerals will also rise in price and the recycling market will increase.

▲ **Iron,** and its principal alloy, steel, are the most important and widely used metals. Iron and steel mills, consuming vast quantities of energy and water as well as raw materials, and the steel-consuming industries such as ship-building represent more than anything else the road to industrialization for the less-developed world.

▶ **More and more** food and drink is sold in non-returnable containers, especially bottles and cans, which create mountains of litter. Aluminium cans, for instance, are no good for composting, they do not degrade and therefore have to be removed. They can be recycled but separation is a costly process.

▲ **Millions of cars** are dumped each year when they could be recycled. Since they contain plastic, rubber and other metals as well as steel the end-product from crushing has to be refined before it can be re-used.

▲ **If more motor vehicles** could be produced economically from substitute materials such as glass reinforced plastic, a significant saving of metals would be made.

◀ **Bridges** constructed from reinforced concrete as opposed to metal are another step towards the conservation of minerals.

▼ **Manganese nodules,** found beyond depths of about three kilometres below the surface of the oceans, may be commercially dredged in the future. The origin of these nodules is uncertain, but they may prove an invaluable source of heavy metals as land deposits become increasingly depleted.

Marine mineral deposits

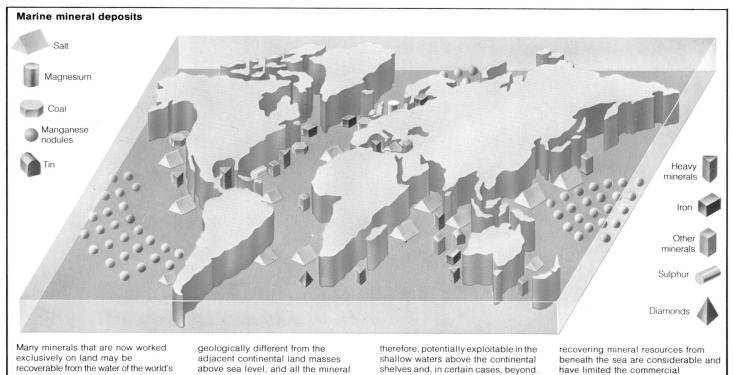

- Salt
- Magnesium
- Coal
- Manganese nodules
- Tin
- Heavy minerals
- Iron
- Other minerals
- Sulphur
- Diamonds

Many minerals that are now worked exclusively on land may be recoverable from the water of the world's oceans. Continental shelves are not geologically different from the adjacent continental land masses above sea level, and all the mineral resources available on land are, therefore, potentially exploitable in the shallow waters above the continental shelves and, in certain cases, beyond. However, the costs involved in recovering mineral resources from beneath the sea are considerable and have limited the commercial development of marine deposits so far.

19

Economic trends

THE object and function of international trade is to make the world as a whole richer in the supply of material goods, whether they be raw materials (including food) or manufactured products. Two countries will engage in trade only if each of them gains by it, except in circumstances which allow one country to exercise compulsion over the other.

Growth of world trade

In the last 20 years the value of world trade has increased about twenty-fold (although inflation magnifies the real extent of this expansion). In 1948 the value of imports stood at US $62,700 million and exports were valued at $57,000 million. In 1980 the corresponding totals (in millions) were $2,045,800 and $2,001,700. Nevertheless, the continuing growth of international trade has done little to bring about a more equal distribution of wealth among the nations of the world. With a few exceptions, such as Australia, New Zealand and Denmark, those countries that have concentrated in the last 100 years or more on developing their manufactures have come to appropriate a disproportionate share of the world's wealth.

In the nineteenth century, the influential German economist Friedrich List argued strongly that only when a country had developed its own national industries could it share in the profits that were the reward of the international division of labour. He went even further and gave his opinion that only a country that exported manufactured products and imported food could rise in the international wealth tables. His influence is still felt today. Most leaders of Third World countries are engaged in an effort to industrialize their economies. Yet it may well be that many of them would profit more from international trade if they ceased to identify prosperity and national pride with steel mills and oil refineries.

A Third World

About 140 countries comprise what has come to be called the Third World. These countries are variously described as "less-developed", "under-developed" or "developing", names that assume Western patterns of development and industrial growth as norms, and desirable norms at that. The people of the Third World, comprising some two-thirds of the world's population, live, for the most part, in dire poverty. National per capita income figures

for the seven major regions of the globe show how marked is the divide between the standard of living enjoyed by those living in developed countries and that of the rest of the world. In 1978 annual per capita income was £4,187 in North America, £3,149 in Europe, £2,834 in Oceania. In stark contrast were the figures for the Middle East (£1,013), Latin America (£684), Africa (£276) and Asia excluding Japan (£138). In the 1970s the national income of some oil-producing countries of the Third World has risen dramatically, but there is no guarantee that their present prosperity will survive the depletion of their oil resources.

It is rare for more than 10 per cent of the gross national product of a Third World country to consist of manufactures. Most developing economies lack the required capital and trained skills for large-scale industry. Their chief preoccupation is with providing enough food for their people. As a result they contribute only a small part of the total volume of world trade. Again, 1980 import/export figures (in millions of US dollars) reveal large discrepancies between North America (319,359/238,879) or Europe (1,014,128/895,062) and, for instance, Africa (85,513/95,875) or Central and South America (113,824/105,099). The same point is made by comparing the figures for Australia and New Zealand (27,864/27,308) with those for less-developed Oceania (3,539/2,439).

Patterns of trade

A breakdown of world trade figures reveals a number of trends that have become apparent in recent years. Although the developed market economies of the West retain the lion's share of world trade, the volume of their international trade has been growing at a slower rate than that of the Third World and the centrally planned economies (the Soviet bloc members of COMECON and China). Between 1970 and 1976 the volume of world trade rose by 21.2 per cent. The rate of growth in the developed market economies was only 16.7% in the second half of the decade but increased to 22.9% in 1978–9. The comparative figures for the Third World countries were 18.5% and 39.1%.

This dramatic shift in trading patterns reflects, of course, the oil boom enjoyed by those members of OPEC, whose exports rose by 48.2 per cent between 1973 and 1976. That rise is almost entirely explained by exports of oil and was

GNP and world trade

Gross national product and patterns of export trade reveal much about the world economy. The nations with the largest GNPs are those which dominate international trade, and have done so for at least a century. The most apparent feature of patterns of international trade is the fact that approximately 75 per cent of it flows between developed, capitalist countries. Since the distribution of resources is uneven across the globe, the production of goods varies from one region to another and gives some a "comparative advantage". Such differences in the cost of production of goods leads, through the development of trade, to specialized areas of production. Some experts argue, however, that this is the result of relationships between developed and under-developed economies. Wealth is extracted from less-developed countries and accumulated in the economic capitals of the developed world. This reflects the free trade philosophy of the nineteenth century when what we now know as the Third World supplied primary products for industrial centres in the Western world. Resource-rich countries, however, have come to command rather more respect in trading agreements today.

Exports ——————

Gross national product ——————

not shared by the rest of the Third World. It does not, therefore, represent a permanent shift in the patterns of international trade.

More important, in the long run, may be the perceptible rise in the Third World's share of the trade in manufactured goods. World exports of machinery and transport equipment, for example, rose by 19.3 per cent between 1970 and 1979. The developing economies increased their exports of these goods by 35.2 per cent in the same period. Their exports of primary materials and food, on the other hand, moved at exactly the same rate as those of the world as a whole — increasing by about 16 per cent. In time, if this trend continues, the relative wealth of the industrialized West and its partners may decline.

The cry for a new international economic order is an attempt by developing countries to strengthen and realize the potential of their resources and at the same time mitigate the relations of dependency that have characterized their integration into the international economic order. Moves have already been made to stabilize export earnings, increase the flow of aid and technology from the developed to the developing world, and gain favourable trading privileges. But such developments have yet to make a truly significant mark on patterns of international trade and the overwhelming dominance of the Western world in the global economic system.

▲ **The London stock exchange** epitomizes the sophistication and the dominance of developed countries in the world of finance and trade. Bidding and counter-bidding in stock and commodity markets reflect the economic climate of the world.

▼ **In many parts** of the developing world, goods are traded in relatively primitive market conditions, such as here in Morocco. For most people economic activity does not extend beyond the local market place.

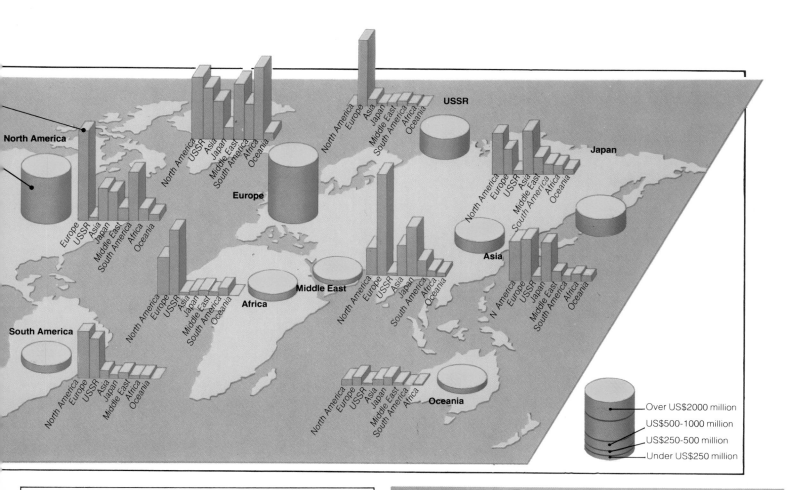

North America

Europe
USSR
Asia
Japan
Middle East
South America
Oceania

USSR

Europe

North America
USSR
Asia
Japan
Middle East
South America
Oceania

Japan

North America
Europe
USSR
Asia
Middle East
South America
Africa
Oceania

Middle East

Africa

North America
Europe
USSR
Asia
Japan
Middle East
South America
Oceania

Asia

N America
Europe
USSR
Japan
Middle East
South America
Africa
Oceania

South America

North America
Europe
USSR
Asia
Japan
Middle East
Africa
Oceania

North America
Europe
USSR
Asia
Japan
Middle East
South America
Africa

Oceania

Over US$2000 million
US$500-1000 million
US$250-500 million
Under US$250 million

The multinationals

The emergence of vast multinational companies is of more than economic and industrial significance. The activities of such organizations affect governmental policy and the relationships between nations. The operations of multinationals span the earth and represent a startling example of international co-operation. Many have annual sales exceeding the gross national product of a small nation.

total sales

profit as proportion of sales (% below)

| Exxon 5.5% | Royal Dutch Shell 6.7% | Mobil Oil 5.5% | General Motors 1.3% loss | Texaco 5.2% |

| British Petroleum 6.9% | Standard Oil (Chevron) 5.9% | Ford 4.2% loss | Gulf Oil 5.3% | IBM 13.6% |

| General Electric 6.1% | Unilever 2.8% | Renault 0.9% | ITT 4.8% | Philips 0.9% |

▲ **The export of luxury goods** *such as motor cars is obviously important for a healthy balance of payments. Another characteristic of developed economies is the export of what is known as "capital" goods — equipment and machinery used in the production of other items, such as farm implements.*

▶ **Regional trading groups** are *formed to stimulate production and trade, but can produce economic anomalies. Certain products can be over-priced because prices are maintained by government subsidies. This leads to wastage. Here French farmers protest against Common Market policies.*

The politics of possession

WHEN the various resource categories — people, land, minerals and energy — are examined in relation to one another, we discover their full political significance. The resources possessed by a nation combine to form the resource structure on which economic and military strength are based. Agriculture, for instance, is essential for a healthy and productive labour force, while substantial energy inputs are required to exploit and develop mineral resources and increase agricultural production.

Resources and power

The power base that is formed by the multifarious links between resources defies the temptation to make a direct correlation between the possession of a single resource and political power. In the case of population, for example, what are regarded as the three most powerful countries in the world — the USA, the USSR and the People's Republic of China — are among the four most populous countries in the world. When one looks to India and Bangladesh, however, with the second- and eighth-largest populations respectively, any direct correlation between power and the size of population breaks down. Quite clearly, the population in these latter countries is out of all proportion to the possession and development of other resources. The access that a population has to other resources, including capital and knowledge, will determine how much it will add to or detract from the political power of the state.

In isolation one can observe the political importance assigned to the categories of resources as links in the power base of a state. In a pariah state such as Israel, self-sufficiency in agriculture is of strategic importance, enabling the country to resist external pressures.

Energy is an increasingly important component of the resource structure, driving countries such as the United Kingdom, France, Brazil and India to develop politically unpopular nuclear power programmes. Industrialized countries such as the United States hold strategic stockpiles of the most important minerals to mitigate any interruption in supply that could arise during political conflicts.

It is bordering on a truism to state that an optimal mix of resources enhances the power of a state while the greater the sum total of that mix, the stronger will be the base from which a state exercises power. The USA and the USSR, as superpowers, derive much of their power from the possession of large amounts of all categories of resources. Saudi Arabia, a country with a sparse population and few agricultural and mineral resources, stands as an

▲ **International conventions,** whether they be conferences on population or desertification, or political gatherings such as this International Socialist Convention, are a feature of the modern world.

◄ **Rockets on display** in Moscow's Red Square during May Day celebrations in fact, through the media, show off the Soviet Union's military might to the world.

The Arab-Israeli conflict is a serious threat to world peace. This picture was taken when Israeli-occupied territory extended to the Suez canal.

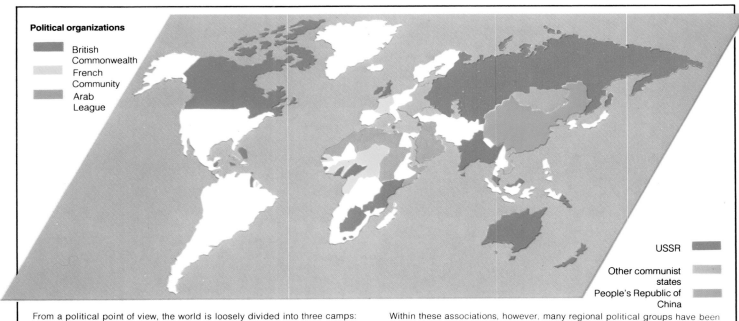

Political organizations

- British Commonwealth
- French Community
- Arab League

USSR
Other communist states
People's Republic of China

From a political point of view, the world is loosely divided into three camps: the capitalist, Western bloc, the socialist states and the so-called "Group of 77". Within these associations, however, many regional political groups have been formed since World War II.

aberration to this pattern. As the world's largest exporter of oil, Saudi Arabia is able to exercise power in world politics far beyond the capability of other single resource states — a power that belies the country's scarcity of resources.

Dependency and power

An abundance or lack of resources is also critical to the dependency structure. A country that is deficient in certain resources often becomes reliant upon external sources. This dependence on external sources for resources is reinforced when a country depends on foreign exchange to finance development and when that foreign exchange is earned primarily by the export of a few commodities. Such nations are forced to look to external sources for aid in financing development and in turn become politically vulnerable as aid is tied to exports

from the donor country or preconditions set by lending institutions.

It is contended by some observers that today's world is one of interdependence, where even the most self-reliant countries such as the USSR and China depend on imports of wheat and high technology from the West, while the West's own power is diminished because of its dependence on developing countries for raw materials.

The lessons of World War II altered the utility of war as a political tool by which a state could seize resources. Total war had become exceptionally costly in terms of the drain on resources and the destruction wrought by modern warfare. What emerged from the War was a bipolar political world characterized by two distinct blocs, with two resource-rich superpowers, the USA and the USSR, serving as respective leaders of each bloc.

The West sought to reduce competition over resources and institutions such as the General Agreement on Tariffs and Trade (GATT) and the International Monetary Fund (IMF) were founded to encourage free trade and stable monetary relations at an international level. The socialist bloc sought a system in which states were to be as self-reliant as possible, with centrally planned economies.

Recent political trends

Two apparent trends have led some to believe that the rift between East and West is diminishing. The first is the disintegration of both political blocs. In 1971 the USA ceased to exchange gold for dollars, marking an end to the post-war monetary system and America's unchallenged leadership of the West. And the socialist bloc has developed rifts within itself. The second trend

is that of convergence between East and West. Western countries such as the UK and Denmark often include a high degree of central planning in their economies, while socialist countries rely on trade with the West to obtain many products.

The rise of a new political bloc of developing countries, otherwise known as the Group of 77, has recently given prominence to a new confrontation over the allocation of resources — the "North-South dialogue". In the mid-1970s the United Nations General Assembly adopted resolutions calling for the transfer of real resources from developed (both capitalist and socialist) to developing countries.

The preoccupation of all countries with political self-interest where ownership and control of resources is concerned shows that resources remain inseparable from the achievement of political ends.

▲ **The education gap** *between developed and less-developed countries is of great significance in a world where an educated population is considered to be a vital resource. Practical training rather than theoretical learning is perhaps the most crucial element of education in the Third World.*

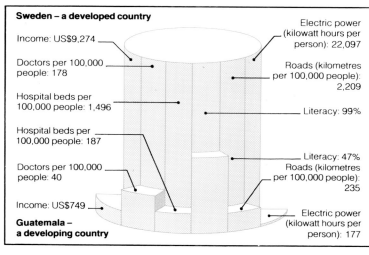

Sweden – a developed country

Income: US$9,274

Doctors per 100,000 people: 178

Hospital beds per 100,000 people: 1,496

Hospital beds per 100,000 people: 187

Doctors per 100,000 people: 40

Income: US$749

Guatemala – a developing country

Electric power (kilowatt hours per person): 22,097

Roads (kilometres per 100,000 people): 2,209

Literacy: 99%

Literacy: 47%
Roads (kilometres per 100,000 people): 235

Electric power (kilowatt hours per person): 177

The North/South dialogue

The "haves" versus "have-nots" debate concerning the differences in standards of living or opportunities between the developed and Third worlds has become polarized in what is known as the "North-South dialogue". This is what amounts to a confrontation over the allocation of resources and is an attempt on the part of developing countries to take full advantage of the resources they possess and, at the same time, do away with their dependence on the developed countries which has been a feature of their integration into the international economic system so far. Their goal can only be reached when they have true economic as well as political independence.

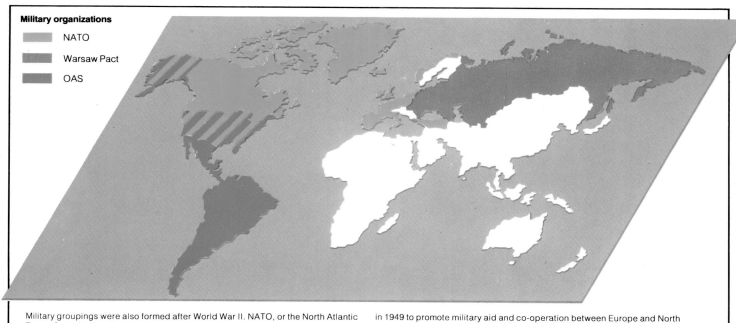

Military organizations

NATO

Warsaw Pact

OAS

Military groupings were also formed after World War II. NATO, or the North Atlantic Treaty Organization, for example, is a Western defensive alliance that was formed in 1949 to promote military aid and co-operation between Europe and North America during peacetime.

Transport and communication

TWO hundred years ago there began a revolution in the speed, availability and cost of transport. For centuries prior to the end of the eighteenth century, speeds had been limited to those of the horse on land and the sailing vessel at sea, while the carriage of heavy goods was prohibitively expensive and restricted in practice to movement by water. The period since then, however, has seen one transforming event after another — road improvement, canal building, railway construction, the steamship, pipeline, aeroplane and hovercraft. Men who sailed before the mast on the old clipper ship have lived to travel by supersonic jet. Modes of transport have superseded one another rapidly. Since World War II an extensive network of motorways has been built in Britain and much traffic that used to be carried by rail now goes by road, despite the fact that road transport uses energy less efficiently.

The transport revolution
The revolution in transport, in turn, made other changes possible. The Industrial Revolution of the nineteenth century involved, among other things, the assembly of huge quantities of raw materials, such as coal or iron ore. It involved also the transfer of other materials, such as cotton or rubber, from distant parts of the world to the new industrial areas, and the new industry necessitated the concentration of workers near to mines or factories in regions that may previously have had only a sparse population. Basic to all these changes was a transport system that could ensure rapid, predictable flows of traffic to keep industry supplied.

Transport was a key factor also in the "urban revolution" of the same period, as population drained away from the countryside and into the new industrial towns. These new townsmen no longer produced their own food: they had to be supplied from farms elsewhere, and supplied as cheaply as possible. As the nineteenth century drew to a close, the cheapest sources of food were found, on the whole, in countries thousands of miles away from the city markets — in the Americas and Australasia.

Such rapid changes in transport technology have inevitably meant that its development has seen a good deal of waste: waste of capital invested in quickly-outmoded facilities, and waste in the construction of competing routes. Scarcely had the canals in Britain been built when they were superseded by the railways and, in regions such as Britain and North America, not only by one railway but by two or three. Every day, hundreds of empty seats cross the Atlantic in aircraft which fly not so much because there are enough passengers to fill them as for reasons of prestige or competitive pressure. New types of plane, car or train are outdated almost before they can complete the transfer from drawing board to assembly line. A rational transport policy, whereby everybody and everything travelled by the most economical transport mode available, would represent a huge saving in world resources of capital and energy. At present, however, no such policy for transport is in sight.

On land the railway dominated the nineteenth century as road transport has dominated the twentieth. Railways are still being built here and there, but almost exclusively either to tap a particular mineral deposit or for strategic purposes. Some regions have never seen the railway and probably never will. By contrast, every year sees the extension of road networks to accommodate some 350 million motor vehicles that now use them.

This last figure indicates another aspect of the transport revolution. There was a time when travel was the privilege of a few: most people never had the opportunity to travel for pleasure. It is estimated today, however, that there are 300 million tourists worldwide each year: that is, one in 14 of the world's population makes a journey purely for pleasure. Travel has truly been democratized.

Economy of scale
Technical changes in transportation continue, and economies are being made in what has been, in the past, a wasteful industry. The most dramatic of these economies is represented by the rise of the supertanker, the bulk carrier and the jumbo jet — the economies of scale in using a large vehicle. Economies have been made also in loading and unloading techniques as a result of the "container revolution", which has placed small cargoes in easily-handled modules of standard size, and produced the roll-on, roll-off vessel that cuts out trans-

▲ **"Containerization"** has been the major development in the transport of goods in the last two decades. Containers are all of an internationally agreed size and can be quickly loaded into purpose-built vessels.

◀ **Road transport** has benefited in the last half-century by the investment by governments in motorway systems. It is, however, not as efficient as rail transport in terms of energy consumption, and threatens the environment.

shipment of cargo altogether. These changes have been necessary if only because of the great increase in international waterborne commerce — from some 900 million tonnes in 1955 to 3.8 billion tonnes in 1979, the bulk of this increase accounted for by the movement of oil.

Communications
If the past two decades have seen revolutionary changes in transport, there have been equally striking developments in communications. These began in 1843 with the transmission of messages by key and code down electric wires: they continued with the telephone, the radio (or wire-less), television and the satellite, and have reached their present degree of sophistication with the involvement of computers, data storage and instant electronic recall of information.

It seems clear that the impact of these changes has still to be fully felt. Already, however, we can see how business structures and, indeed, whole industries, can be transformed by electronics. Branch offices, for example, have immedi-

ate access to central records; executives can "sit in on" conferences at which they are not physically present; and machines are built by other machines rather than by human hand.

The contribution of satellites to the development of communications systems has been particularly dramatic. A number of tasks which previously involved the presence on the ground of a human agent — for example, to map land use or military installations — can now be done much faster and just as effectively from the sky. Satellite pictures help weather forecasters and mineral prospectors, and people across the world can watch an event on television as it happens, instead of the next day or even the following week.

All these developments — whether in transportation or communications systems — are a far cry from the relatively recent days when news was conveyed by runners, goods were moved by barge and empires were administered by issue of orders which could take years to be received and even longer to be implemented.

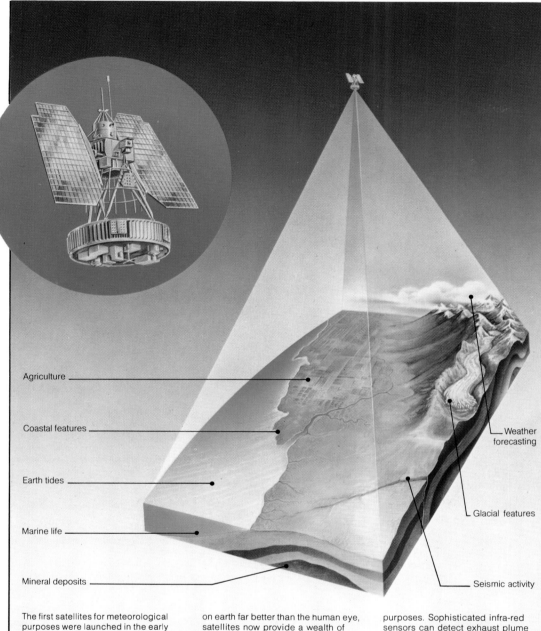

Agriculture

Coastal features

Earth tides

Marine life

Mineral deposits

Weather forecasting

Glacial features

Seismic activity

The first satellites for meteorological purposes were launched in the early 1960s. By means of multi-band cameras and infra-red and microwave sensors that can discriminate conditions on earth far better than the human eye, satellites now provide a wealth of information from their constant surveillance of much of the globe. Satellites can also be used for defence purposes. Sophisticated infra-red sensors can detect exhaust plume emissions from missiles as they are launched and thus give an early warning of possible attack.

▲ **Supertankers** *can be loaded and unloaded quickly with the aid of specialized port facilities and they require few crew members.*

▼ **Transport by air,** *especially of passengers, has increased enormously in the last 30 years, particularly over long distances.*

▲ **Traffic flow** *through the city centre can be monitored from the traffic control room by means of close circuit television cameras mounted in strategic places throughout the city. Details are then relayed to the traffic police in the streets. Highly sophisticated communications systems have revolutionized many industries.*

The shrinking world

As with other aspects of man's activities, from consumption of the earth's resources to the increase in human numbers, the development of transport systems has shown an exponential growth in the speed of the various modes of travel since the take-off point in the nineteenth century. But what of the future of transport? Since social and commercial life depends upon an efficient transport system and as concern for increasingly depleted resources and a threatened environment grows, governments are playing an ever greater role in decision-making within the transport sector. Support for public transport systems, for instance, could see the future development of extensive and rapid mass-transit systems at the expense of private transport which is being made to carry an ever heavier burden of taxation.

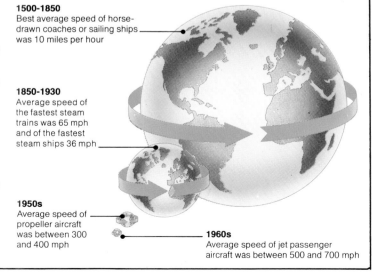

1500-1850
Best average speed of horse-drawn coaches or sailing ships was 10 miles per hour

1850-1930
Average speed of the fastest steam trains was 65 mph and of the fastest steam ships 36 mph

1950s
Average speed of propeller aircraft was between 300 and 400 mph

1960s
Average speed of jet passenger aircraft was between 500 and 700 mph

Industry and technology

WITHIN the last 30 years there have been a number of changes in the overall pattern of world industry or, at least, of industrial science and technology, which are the mainsprings of industrial advance. Before World War II most industrial research was carried out in university laboratories, supported by meagre funds. The technological fruits of that research were, in turn, developed by private companies with their own capital. In both fields — scientific research and technological development — the countries of Western Europe maintained the lead which they had established in the nineteenth century. In the 1950s and 1960s, however, three major changes took place.

Significant developments
In the first place there was an explosive growth in the amount of scientific and technological knowledge and output. Second, there was a massive assumption by government departments and agencies of responsibility for supporting industrial research and development. Third, the United States became the pre-eminent centre of world industry, both in its role as the discoverer of new technologies and in the command which it has come to exercise over worldwide industrial empires. By 1970 the United States was spending 3.5 per cent of its gross national product — about $30 billion, or more than twice the total investment of the rest of the western world — on industrial research and development. This massive capital investment by the

government has given the USA its present dominance of industries such as electronics and aerospace.

There have also been changes of direction in other areas. In industries such as chemicals, transport, steel and paper production, there has been a shift away from the simple search for "bigger and better" products. Industry has begun to direct its attention to finding safer chemical products, quieter industrial plants and goods which are both destructible and made from synthetic materials. In such ways . industry is beginning to respond to the need for a reduction in the consumption of the earth's natural resources and to the concern of the public that the environment should be protected.

Several trends have manifested themselves in the organization of industry. There has been a move away from adapting organization to technological requirements and towards adapting technology to human and organizational needs. There has been a shift away from plants of maximum size to medium-sized and small units which are more responsive both to market changes and to technological changes in production methods. This change has been especially noticeable in the chemicals and electronics industries and in mechanical engineering works.

In the last 20 years it has been the low-income countries (annual per capita income of less than US $250) and the middle-income countries (more than US $250) that have shown an increase in manufacturing as a percentage of gross

domestic product. For all countries, however, the rate of industrial growth has slowed down during the 1970s. A growth rate of 6.7 per cent in low-income countries between 1960 and 1970 fell to 4.5 between 1970 and 1976. In industrial states for the same periods the growth rate fell from 5.7 to 3.2 per cent.

Energy and industrial growth
Undoubtedly, the major cause of this trend has been the increasing cost of energy. Industry will not take strides forward again until alternatives to non-renewable sources of energy (chiefly oil and natural gas) are developed. The high cost of energy in the 1970s is only partly the result of the decision of the oil-exporting countries to raise their prices. It is in the very nature of a non-renewable commodity that the more it is used, the more expensive it becomes. As the most easily exploitable oil fields become exhausted, the cost of developing less accessible and smaller resource deposits automatically rises. This cost is passed on to the major consumer items: housing (fuel and electricity), clothing (synthetic materials based on petroleum) and food (fertilizers and pesticides made from petroleum and natural gas).

This steady and irreversible rise in the price of non-renewable energy sources leads necessarily to industrial stagnation. It produces inflation, a shortage of capital and an unwillingness to invest in high-risk manufacturing enterprises (because the basic cost of energy is so unstable). The future of industry depends upon the current search to find marketable ways of exploiting alternative sources of energy, and the making of plans today for using alternative energy tomorrow.

Technological breakthrough
Two developments, pioneered in the United States, represent a startling technological advance. One is the manufacture of integrated cir-

cuits — postage stamp sized chips containing electric currents sufficiently elaborate to operate complex computer systems. Production began in the early 1960s and the results have been successful enough for the product to enter the mass market in the form of digital watches and pocket calculators.

A more recent and equally important development is the photovoltaic cell. This is a thin, chemically-treated slice of silicon, mounted on a metal base. When light hits it, an electric current is generated. This development could eventually provide the answer to a substantial proportion of our electricity demands. The difficulty is to create a market large enough to reduce costs to the point where the cells could be made in large quantities.

Creating a demand
A vicious circle is in operation: because the demand for photovoltaic cells is at present too low to support an efficient scale of production, the cost of the cells remains too high for them to compete on the energy market. The demand has therefore to be created and only governments have the resources to create such a demand. It was huge orders from the American defence department, placed deliberately in order to stimulate production, that made integrated circuits competitive. If any new commodity is to have the same degree of success, a similar stimulation from governments — on a scale that private industry cannot meet — will have to be provided.

This final point helps to explain why, when one looks globally at industrial and technological development, and despite intense efforts in recent decades to transform many Third World countries from subsistence-level, agricultural economies to industrialized, manufacturing economies, the world remains divided into a relatively rich, industrial north and a relatively poor, agricultural south.

▲ **The North American farmer** has tended to become a small link in a vast agricultural production line that has earned itself the title of agribusiness. Investment in the farm is massive and trends in food production are dictated by the large food corporations.

The labour shift

The growth of service industries has been the most significant development within the economic structure of developed countries since World War II. More than 60 per cent of all workers in the United States are employed in the service sector. A service industry is distinguished from other industries in that it supplies the needs of industry or the consumer in the form of such things as banking and insurance, entertainment, education, transport and communications, legal or financial advice, medical and social services, government and the distribution and sale of goods by wholesalers and retailers. The increase in services reflects greater per capita income levels. As people earn more than is required to meet their basic needs they desire and can afford more services. The growth of services does not necessarily reflect a proportional increase in demand. Service industries are labour-intensive and output per worker is not as great as in other sectors. Service industries (personal servants excepted) are of much less significance in developing countries where most growth has been in the retail trade.

▲ **Assembly line work,** *such as this Ford production line in Detroit, represents for many workers a sophisticated form of drudgery. Wages are high to compensate for the repetitiveness of the work.*

◄ **Textiles** *have played a pioneer role in the economic development of Third World countries. Mechanization exacerbates already high levels of under-employment.*

► **Since the advent** *of the transistor radio, electronic devices have become more diverse and increasingly sophisticated. The range of their application today extends from telecommunications to data processing and automatic control. The latter raises serious questions about possibly greater unemployment in the future.*

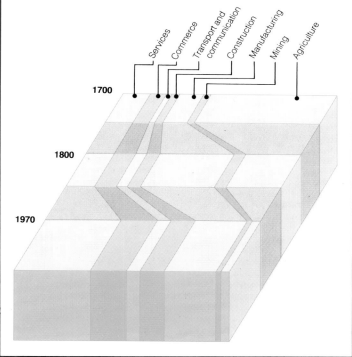

Services · Commerce · Transport and communication · Construction · Manufacturing · Mining · Agriculture

1700

1800

1970

Industrial relations

Good industrial relations have become an increasingly important ingredient for the economic well-being of a nation. The purpose of trade unions is to represent the interests of workers and unions now exist in most countries of the world. The level of organization, however, varies enormously from one country to another. It depends, for instance, on social attitudes, political policies and the economic framework of the country. Disputes and strikes are an inevitable part of a democratic system of industrial relations. Britain does not fare too badly within a league of developed countries, but strikes in Britain differ from many other countries in one important respect: a large proportion of them are unofficial, that is, they are in breach of union rules.

Japan .13 hrs

France .576 hrs

United Kingdom 3.63 hrs

Switzerland .015 hrs

Time lost as a result of industrial disputes (working man ... per year)

Working population

Sweden 8.39 hrs

West Germany .037 hrs

Australia 4.37 hrs

Canada 6.38 hrs

United States 2.54 hrs

10 20 50 100 million

The quality of life

THAT people should wish for an improvement in the quality of life for themselves and their children seems to most of those people who live in the world's developed countries both reasonable and "normal". For them change is constant and advance is taken for granted. It is important to realize, however, that this state of affairs is relatively recent in the history even of the developed world, and it does not apply, even today, to millions of inhabitants of the developing countries.

The element of choice
What underlies an improvement in the quality of life is the idea of choice: the freedom of human beings, either individually or as communities, to choose among several possibilities the one that best serves their own interests, whether it be type of work, location and kind of dwelling, or use of leisure time. In a society where the dawn to dusk efforts of every single member of the community are required merely to keep starvation at bay, there are no such choices. Everybody must live wherever the work is, in whatever kind of shelter is available, and there is little opportunity for leisure activities.

Sometimes, of course, the absence of choice is imposed not by economic necessity but by political and social restraint. In the feudal society of medieval Europe, for example, most of the population were tied to the soil: they had no right to move from their birthplace, or to withhold their labour when it was required by their overlord. For many centuries, in fact, the only changes that occurred were almost always disastrous — the passage of marauding armies, or the withdrawal of common rights by the landlord. In any totalitarian society, choice is the privilege of those who rule that society.

Industrialization and choice
In the developed world, freedom of choice broadened gradually with the breakdown of feudalism and serfdom, with a growing diversity of work opportunities (especially after the onset of industrialization), with an increasing margin in the economy above the level of mere survival, and with the coming of cheap and rapid movement by public transport. Even so, change was no friend to the first generation

or so of the new, freer society. Craftsmen were rendered unemployed by factory-based machines, and small farmers were dispossessed. Thousands of country people found themselves in the new slums of the industrial cities, their only "choice" being to starve on the land or work 12- or 16-hour days in the factories. It has taken time for choice to percolate down through society so that today even the most poorly paid worker has some choice about where he lives or how he spends his leisure hours.

Improvement of the quality of life is a goal also in the centrally planned economies of the Communist world no less than in Western Europe or North America, although the emphasis is on improvement for the community as a whole, rather than for its individual members. Even in these countries, however, it is impossible in practice to eliminate the idea of personal incentive and achievement: in sport, in recreation, in striving for a better job, or in the rewards that come with higher output per worker.

What of the less-developed world, however? There is no reason to suppose that, given the opportunity, millions of inhabitants in developing countries would not welcome the same range of choice that is enjoyed by others. At the moment, most of these people are tied to particular patches of earth which afford their only means of subsistence, and if and when they have the opportunity and the courage to break away, they are as likely as not to find themselves in the shanty towns that have grown up on the outskirts of many large cities in less-developed countries. There they live in appalling conditions and experience great deprivation.

A standard of living
The term normally used to identify differences in the quality of life is standard of living, although the two concepts are subtly different in character. Standard of living is generally expressed by the level of income per person. If we compare nation with nation in this respect, the differences in standards are enormous: $14,044 per person in Switzerland (1979 figures) compared with $192 in India, $218 in Sri Lanka, or $200 per person in Rwanda. Within these countries, needless to say, the range variation about the average figure is

▲ **The clamour** for extensive, unpolluted open spaces in which to spend our leisure time has meant that millions of hectares in the form of national parks or game reserves have been put aside for just that purpose. Areas of outstanding natural beauty are now protected by law from human encroachment that could damage the environment.

great. In many Latin American countries, for example, the idea of an "average" standard of living is meaningless.

Nevertheless, it is the policy of more or less every government, whatever its political complexion, to raise the standard of living of its people. Standards may rise, however, without a corresponding improvement in the quality of life. In general we can say that advance in either will be accompanied by certain signs of change within the society or economy that reflect the improvement of living standards.

Indications of change
As the standard of living rises, it will probably be marked by a decrease in the proportion of the population engaged in primary production — in working on the land, or in forestry, fishing or mining — which implies a broadening variety of other forms of occupation — in manufacturing, transport, education and other service industries. In other words, the society requires fewer people to supply its basic needs. In the United States today only three workers out of ten actually produce anything at all, by farming the land or manufacturing goods.

Another indicator is an increase in the volume of circulation, whether of goods or of people, within society. This implies a greater and wider range of demand for commodities beyond those produced locally, and a greater freedom, financial and personal, to come and go at will. Finally, an improvement in the quality of life will be marked by the increased allocation of resources, especially of land, to leisure pursuits, from golf courses and waterfronts to national parks, in some cases the size of a small country. This involves setting aside some part of land resources from ordinary productive use, and expresses a growing concern for the facilities available to the population when they are not working in offices or factories.

There is an increasing awareness now, however, that the path to industrialization and a higher standard of living in the past will not lead to an improvement in the quality of life in the future. That improvement may well necessitate a fourth indication of change within society — the conservation of the earth's limited resources and the protection of the natural and our man-made environment.

Labour migration

The migration of people has been a recurrent theme throughout history, but a high degree of individual mobility is a characteristic of recent times. Migration has been an essential part of the processes of urbanization and industrialization. To a large extent this has reflected the greater job opportunities and higher income levels in urban centres. For similar reasons, rural-urban migration has been on the increase in less-developed countries. Migration represents one way by which people can improve their standard of living. On the other hand, the post-war prosperity of Europe, for example, has been increased by a vast pool of immigrant labour. The economic recession of recent years, however, has meant that many countries have closed their doors to unlimited foreign labour and only let migrant workers in according to the needs of the country. To some extent, therefore, a migrant workforce may shield the native workforce from the effects of a recessionary period as a contraction in employment will result in fewer migrant workers being admitted or allowed to stay in the host country. In times of growth, on the other hand, immigrant workers will help support economic expansion.

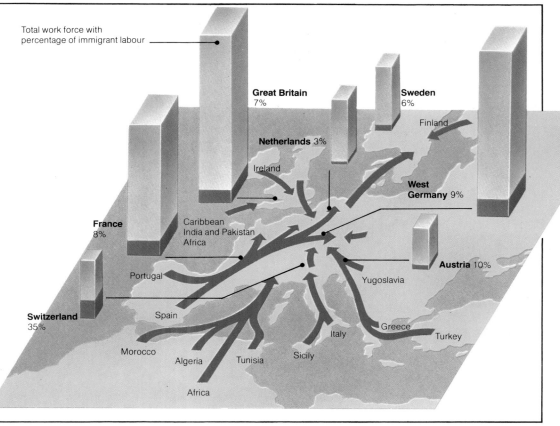

Total work force with percentage of immigrant labour

Great Britain 7%
Sweden 6%
Finland
Netherlands 3%
Ireland
West Germany 9%
France 8%
Caribbean India and Pakistan Africa
Austria 10%
Portugal
Yugoslavia
Switzerland 35%
Spain
Greece
Turkey
Italy
Morocco
Algeria
Tunisia
Sicily
Africa

► **The greater opportunities** *for migrant workers in post-war Europe has meant an escape from poverty for, for example, millions of Turkish factory workers in West Germany.*

▼ **In the West** *we tend to take social improvement for granted, but for the underprivileged in New York's Bowery, life in the developed world offers little opportunity.*

▼ **An ever-shorter** *working week and more leisure time leads to increasing demands for leisure facilities. Many sports, such as American baseball, are now big business ventures.*

Life expectancy

Not only do we expect better opportunities in life and an ever-higher standard of living, we also expect a healthier and longer life than did our forebears. With the advances of medical science, the length of life the average new-born baby in the developed world can expect has more than doubled in the last two centuries to about 70 years today. Although death rates in many Asian and South American countries have been dramatically reduced, death rates in parts of the African continent have only just begun to decline and remain very high.

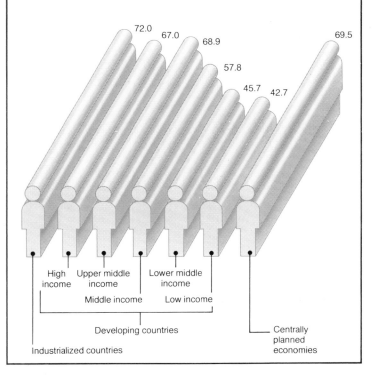

72.0   67.0   68.9   57.8   45.7   42.7   69.5

High income
Upper middle income
Lower middle income
Middle income
Low income
Developing countries
Centrally planned economies
Industrialized countries

One earth

WITH people everywhere, both in less-developed and developed countries, clamouring for an improved standard of living, it is necessary to appreciate what this implies on an earth whose resources are finite. One way of defining standard of living is as the total amount of resources consumed in a year by the average person in a nation or community. At present, people in countries with a high standard of living are consuming huge and varied quantities of materials derived, in one way or another, from the earth — not only more food per person than their bodies actually require,

but steel and petrol for their cars and a whole range of goods, in fact, that are part of everyday life. Such a community leaves behind it mountains of waste. By contrast, the total resource consumption in a poor community may be represented by small amounts of food and clothing.

Between these levels of consumption there is manifestly no comparison. Yet if we are to visualize that, in the course of time, all living standards will rise and converge upon the highest level we now know, then that implies a colossal drain on the earth's resources. To envisage all of mankind living as North Americans or

Western Europeans currently do, in the present state of our knowledge and technology, is an extremely daunting prospect.

Resources and technology

In past eras, inequalities in living standards were confronted very simply: groups preyed on one another, and the strong grew rich while the poor starved. Not only is this unacceptable by present-day standards, but a new factor has been introduced into the competition for resources — the technical ability to use them. A community with a high level of technology can, in practice, reach out and tap the resources of others: by contrast, a country richly endowed with natural resources may not have the technical expertise to exploit them, and so may have to bring in outsiders and share its wealth with them in return for their assistance. All this means,

however, is that, without resorting to force, the rich grow richer, often at the expense of the poor.

There are several possible remedies for this situation. One is to set up a world organization with sufficient power to introduce some form of international rationing. However, not only would it be exceedingly difficult to decide what constituted "fair shares" for nations with entirely different needs and lifestyles, but such an arrangement could, in practice, only be introduced with the consent and help of the most wealthy nations, and they would naturally be the losers by it.

A question of distribution

The second possibility is that the largest consumers of resources should limit their usage and leave more for the rest of mankind. It has even been agreed that the living standards of the rich would not

▲ **The rehabilitation** of land spoiled by man's activities has become an exact science. Here in Wales colliery spoil is spread over toxic metal waste and planted with a special strain of grass whose short root system does not reach the toxic soil beneath the top layer.

The United Nations

The United Nations was established in 1948 by 50 nations. It now has three times as many members and stands as a symbol of world unity. The political sector of the UN is the General Assembly and the Security Council. The Economic and Social Council, under the supervision of the General Assembly, co-ordinates the economic and social work of the UN

and 14 specialized agencies. The Trusteeship Council was set up to supervise the affairs of 11 territories all of which except one, the Pacific Islands, are now independent. The International Court of Justice is the principal judicial body and the Secretariat services all other departments and is responsible for implementing their policies.

General Assembly   1

Security Council   Secretariat   Economic and Social Council   Trusteeship Council   International Court of Justice

2   3   4   5   6   7   8   9

IMF International Monetary Fund	IDA International Development Association	ITU International Telecommunications Union
WHO World Health Organization	IBRD International Bank for Reconstruction and Development	WMO World Meteorological Organization
FAO Food and Agriculture Organization	IFC International Finance Corporation	GATT General Agreement on Tariffs and Trade
ILO International Labour Organization	Universal Postal Union	IMCO Inter-Governmental Maritime Consultative Organization
UNESCO Educational, Scientific and Cultural Organization	ICAO International Civil Aviation Organization	

1 UNCTAD Conference on Trade and Development
2 UNIDO Industrial Development Organization
3 UNITAR Institute for Training and Research
4 UNHCR High Commission for Refugees
5 UN Capital Development Fund
6 UNDP Development Programme
7 Trade and Development Board
8 UNICEF Children's Fund
9 UN-FAO World Food Programme

IAEA International Atomic Energy Authority
Peace keeping forces/Military observers
Disarmament Commission

necessarily fall. Their present consumption patterns are so wasteful of resources that any loss in supply could be recouped by the proper use of the resources they still possessed. By eliminating waste, improving efficiency and recycling materials, the developed countries could live on a lot less.

All this is true, and there is no doubt that the average consumer in the developed world today has a far more tender conscience, and a far greater awareness of the needs of others, than was the case a few decades ago, thanks in part to the development of communications and the immediate coverage of famine, catastrophe and living conditions worldwide. Reduced consumption by the well-to-do will not, however, solve the problem of transferring the resources saved by one country in order to supply the needs of another. If the United

States were to reduce its consumption of petroleum, this would not necessarily make it cheaper or easier for a poor and oil-less state such as Bangladesh to obtain petroleum. The connection between supply and demand is not that simple. While there is, therefore, an obvious argument that there should be fairness for all, the machinery for achieving this has yet to be created, at least on an international level.

The provision of aid
The only workable alternative to these two ideas, and one which has received a lot of attention in the years since World War II, is that of giving technical aid. Since it is the difference in technical standards and capacities which chiefly distinguish the rich nation from the poor one, a levelling up of those standards ought to lead directly towards an equalization of living

standards. Furthermore, it should be possible to do this with a minimum of disturbance to ordinary trade relations, and without the need to move large quantities of food and materials from one place to another. By upgrading the poor nation's ability to make use of its own resources, the poor may gain much and the rich will lose little, at least in the short term. Over a longer period, however, the technically-advanced nation is creating competitors for its own producers. But it is reasonable to expect that, by the time that happens, the advanced economy will have moved on again to different levels of technology.

Experience has shown, however, that aid from the developed countries to the developing has been double-edged. Much of the aid has been in the form of loans, on which interest has to be paid, or there are strings attached, such as the

demand that purchases of equipment for the developing economy shall be made only from the aid-granting country. Sometimes technical aid to agriculture benefits only the large farmers and makes life more difficult for the small operator, and industries are established which are not only controlled but also staffed largely by technicians from abroad, so that their presence makes little impact on unemployment in the area.

What this means is not that aid should be stopped, but that it should take carefully chosen forms, and that the basic objective of every aid programme should be to give the maximum assistance to those most in need. In the world today, it is not by the condition of the average man, and certainly not by the wealth of the richest, but by the circumstances of the most needy that future generations will judge us.

▲ **The most constructive form** of aid to less-developed countries is education and the introduction of a technology that is best suited to their requirements.

◄ **Massive foreign aid** is granted to developing countries each year. Aid at times of catastrophe is widely publicized — less well known is the work of the United Nations and other international organizations in assisting economic development in the less developed world.

▶ **Proponents of an alternative society** advocate a return to a pre-industrial way of life in which men live more simply and without generating the problems of modern times. The Amish of Pennsylvania, however, have never succumbed to the pressures of American society and have lived in relative seclusion for the past two centuries.

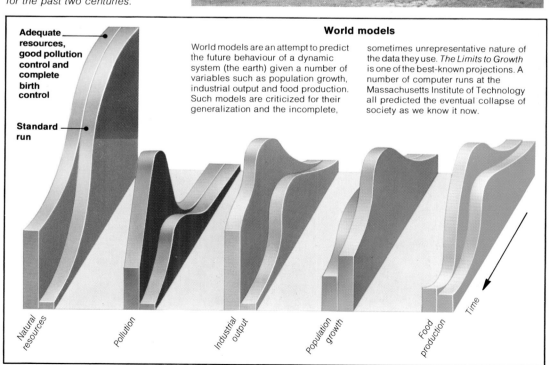

World models

World models are an attempt to predict the future behaviour of a dynamic system (the earth) given a number of variables such as population growth, industrial output and food production. Such models are criticized for their generalization and the incomplete, sometimes unrepresentative nature of the data they use. *The Limits to Growth* is one of the best-known projections. A number of computer runs at the Massachusetts Institute of Technology all predicted the eventual collapse of society as we know it now.

Adequate resources, good pollution control and complete birth control

Standard run

Natural resources

Pollution

Industrial output

Population growth

Food production

Time

Earth data

The earth's dimensions

Superficial area	510,000,000km²
Land surface	149,000,000km²
Land surface as % of total area	29.2%
Water surface	361,000,000km²
Water surface as % of total area	70.8%
Equatorial circumference	40,077km
Meridional circumference	40,009km
Equatorial diameter	12,757km
Polar diameter	12,714km
Volume	1,083,230×10⁶km³
Mass	5.9×10²¹ tonnes

The earth's surface

Highest point (Mount Everest, Tibet-Nepal border)	8,848m
Lowest point (Dead Sea, Israel-Jordan)	395m below sea level
Greatest ocean depth (Challenger Deep, Mariana Trench)	11,022m
Average height of land	840m
Average depth of sea	3,808m

The largest oceans and seas

Pacific Ocean	165,721,000km²
Atlantic Ocean	81,660,000km²
Indian Ocean	73,442,000km²
Arctic Ocean	14,351,000km²
Mediterranean Sea	2,966,000km²
Bering Sea	2,274,000km²
Caribbean Sea	1,942,000km²
Mexico, Gulf of	1,813,000km²
Okhotsk, Sea of	1,528,000km²
East China Sea	1,248,000km²

The longest rivers

	LENGTH	LOCATION
Nile	6,669km	Africa
Amazon	6,516km	South America
Mississippi-Missouri	6,050km	North America
Yangtze-Kiang	5,989km	Asia
Ob-Irtysh	5,149km	Asia
Amur	4,666km	Asia
Zaire	4,373km	Africa
Hwang Ho (Yellow River)	4,344km	Asia
Lena	4,256km	Asia
Mackénzie	4,240km	North America

The largest lakes and inland seas

	AREA	LOCATION
Caspian Sea	393,896km²	Asia
Lake Superior	82,413km²	North America
Lake Victoria	69,484km²	Africa
Aral Sea	68,681km²	Asia
Lake Huron	59,596km²	North America
Lake Michigan	58,015km²	North America
Lake Tanganyika	32,893km²	Africa
Great Bear Lake	31,792km²	North America
Lake Baykal	30,510km²	Asia
Lake Nyasa	29,604km²	Africa

The highest mountains

	HEIGHT	LOCATION
Everest	8,848m	Tibet-Nepal
K2 (Godwin Austen)	8,616m	Kashmir
Kanchenjunga	8,591m	Nepal-Sikkim
Makalu	8,481m	Tibet-Nepal
Dhaulagiri	8,177m	Nepal
Nanga Parbat	8,131m	Kashmir
Annapurna	8,078m	Nepal
Gasherbrum	8,073m	Kashmir
Gosainthan	8,019m	Tibet
Nanda Devi	7,822m	India

The largest islands

	AREA	LOCATION
Greenland	2,175,000km²	Atlantic
New Guinea	885,780km²	Pacific
Borneo	743,330km²	Pacific
Madagascar	587,045km²	Indian
Baffin	476,070km²	Arctic
Sumatra	473,600km²	Indian
Honshu	230,540km²	Pacific
Great Britain	218,050km²	Atlantic
Ellesmere	212,690km²	Arctic
Victoria	212,200km²	Arctic

The continents

	AREA
Asia	44,250,000km²
Africa	30,264,000km²
North America	24,398,000km²
South America	17,807,800km²
Antarctica	13,209,000km²
Europe	9,906,000km²
Australia and New Zealand	8,842,400km²

The greatest waterfalls

	HEIGHT	LOCATION
Angel	980m	Venezuela
Tugela	853m	South Africa
Mongefossen	774m	Norway
Yosemite	738m	California
Mardalsfossen	655m	Norway
Cuquenan	610m	Venezuela
Sutherland	579m	New Zealand
Reichenbach	548m	Switzerland
Wollomombi	518m	Australia
Ribbon	491m	California

Notable volcanoes

	HEIGHT	LOCATION
Etna	3,340m	Sicily
Fuji	3,778m	Japan
Mauna Loa	4,160m	Hawaii
Ngaurone	2,290m	New Zealand
Njamiagira	3,059m	Zaire
Nyiragongo	3,472m	Zaire
Pacaya	2,546m	Guatemala
Popocatepetl	5,456m	Mexico
Saint Helens	2,744m	USA
Stromboli	927m	Italy
Tristan da Cunha	2,026m	Atlantic Ocean
Vesuvius	1,278m	Italy

SETTLEMENTS

U.S.A.

Settlement symbols in order of size

BALTIMORE   ■ **NEWARK**   ▣ **Allentown**   ◉ **Trenton**   ◎ **Norristown**   ⊚ Bridgeton   ⊙ Quakertown   ○ Parkesburg   ○ Avondale

ADMINISTRATION

County seat towns have red infill   **RICHMOND** State Capital   **WASHINGTON** National Capital

——— County Boundary
(census area in Alaska)

OHIO / INDIANA — State Boundary   ADDISON Counties   National Parks, Recreation Areas, Monuments, Seashores, Lakeshores

Indian Reservations   MARK TWAIN NATIONAL FOREST National Forests

COMMUNICATIONS

Interstates and Major Turnpikes   ——— Railroads   ········ Transportation Canals   ✈ Major Airfields
Other Highways   →--← Railroad Tunnels   ········ Other Canals   + Other Airfields
          ≍ Passes

PHYSICAL FEATURES

Perennial Streams   Perennial Lakes   Dry Lakes   ▲ 733 Elevation in meters
Intermittent Streams   Swamps, Marshes   Glaciers, Icefields   ▼ 329 Sea Depth in meters
Waterfalls   Intermittent Lakes   Dams with Reservoirs   174 Height of Lake Surface Above Sea Level in meters

SETTLEMENTS

WORLD

Settlement symbols in order of size

⬡ **LONDON**   ■ **Stuttgart**   ◉ **Sevilla**   ◎ **Bergen**   ⊙ **Bath**   ○ Biarritz   ○ Srikolayatji

Settlement symbols and type styles vary according to the scale of each map and indicate the importance of towns on map rather than specific population figures

ADMINISTRATION

——— International Boundaries   ········ Internal Boundaries
--- --- International Boundaries (Undemarcated or undefined)   National and Provincial Parks

International boundaries show the *de facto* situation where there are rival claims to territory

COMMUNICATIONS

Principal Roads   Principal Railroads   ········ Principal Canals   Trails and Seasonal Roads
Other Roads   Other Railroads   Principal Oil Pipelines   ✿ Airfields
≍ Passes   --·--·-- Railroads (under construction)   __3386__ Principal Shipping Routes

PHYSICAL FEATURES

Perennial Streams   Perennial Lakes   Permanent Ice   ▲▼ 8848 Elevation, Sea Depth in meters
Intermittent Streams   Swamps, Marshes   Wells in Desert   Height of Lake Surface
          Intermittent Lakes   1134 Above Sea Level in meters

Height of Land Above Sea Level in meters / in feet

| 6060 | 4000 | 3000 | 2000 | 1500 | 1000 | 400 | 200 | 0 |
| 18 000 | 12 000 | 9000 | 6000 | 4500 | 3000 | 1200 | 600 |

Land Below Sea Level

| 6000 | 12 000 | 15'000 | 18 000 | 24 000 | in feet |
| 200 | 2000 | 4000 | 5000 | 6000 | 8000 |

Depth of Sea in meters

Some of the maps have different contours to highlight and clarify the principal relief features

Abbreviations of measures used   mm Millimeters   m. Meters   km. Kilometers

Projection: *Hammer Equal Area*

1 : 80 000 000

3

ARCTIC OCEAN

Zemlya Frantsa Iosifa
Novaya Zemlya
Barents Sea
Nord Kapp
Murmansk
Arkhangelsk

Severnaya Zemlya
Laptev Sea
New Siberian Is.
East Siberian Sea

Tiksi
Verkhoyansk
Nizhne-Kolymsk
Arctic Circle
Anadyr

Salekhard
Ob

Yenisey

Vilyuysk
Lena
Yakutsk

Okhotsk

Bering Sea

Kamchatka
Petropavlovsk-Kamchatskiy
C. Lopatka

SWEDEN
FINLAND
Helsinki
Stockholm
EST. LITH.
WHITE
LATVIA
POLAND Warszawa
RUSSIA
Berlin
Wien
CZECH. HUNG.
Praha
Milano
Budapest
ROMANIA
Beograd
YUGOSLAVIA Bucuresti
Sofiya BULGARIA
Napoli GREECE
Sardinia
Sicily Athinai
MALTA Crete
CYPRUS
Mediterranean Sea
Tarābulus
TUNISIA

UNION OF SOVIET SOCIALIST REPUBLICS
RUSSIAN SOVIET FEDERATIVE SOCIALIST REPUBLIC

Leningrad
Yaroslavl
Moskva
Kuybyshev
Perm Sverdlovsk
Kazan
Ufa
Chelyabinsk Omsk
Novosibirsk
Tomsk Krasnoyarsk
Barnaul Novokuznetsk
Irtysh
Ulan Ude
L. Baykal
Irkutsk

Minsk
Kiyev UKRAINE
Lvov Kharkov
Volga
Odessa Rostov Volgograd
Black Sea
Groznyy Astrakhan
Istanbul Ankara Tbilisi Yerevan
TURKEY Baku
Izmir
Halab Bayrūt SYRIA Dimashq Baghdad
Tel Aviv-Yafo ISR. Tabriz
El Iskandariya JORDAN IRAQ
El Qâhira Bûr Saîd Al Riyād

KAZAKHSTAN
Karaganda
Aral Sea L. Balkhash
UZBEKISTAN Alma Ata
Samarkand Tashkent KIRGIZIA
TURKMENISTAN Dushanbe
Ashkhabad AFGHANISTAN
Mashhad Kabul
Tehrān Rawalpindi
IRAN (PERSIA) Eşfahān
Ābādān Shiraz
KUWAIT The Gulf
BAHRAIN QATAR
Srinagar
Lahore
U.A.E.
OMAN

MONGOLIA
Ulaanbaatar

CHINA
Lanzhou
Xi'an
Chengdu
Chongqing
Kunming

Harbin
Changchun
Shenyang
Beijing
Tianjin
Taiyuan Dalian
Jinan
Huang He
Nanjing
Wuhan
Chang Jiang
Changsha

Vladivostok
N. KOREA
Pyŏngyang
Sŏul S. KOREA
Pusan
Qingdao
Shanghai
East China Sea
Fuzhou
Taibei
TAIWAN (FORMOSA)
Guangzhou
Hong Kong

Komsomolsk
Khabarovsk
Amur
Kuril Is.
Sakhalin
Sapporo
Hakodate
JAPAN
Tōkyō
Kyoto Yokohama
Kōbe Nagoya
Ōsaka
Kitakyūshū
Ryukyu Is.

PACIFIC

Tropic of Cancer
Wake I. (U.S.)
Northern Marianas (U.S.)

OCEAN

LIBYA
EGYPT
Aswân
Red Sea
SAUDI ARABIA
Makkah
NIGER CHAD
SUDAN
L. Chad
Ndjamena
El Khartûm Omdurman
Blue Nile
Asmera YEMEN
DJIBOUTI SOUTH YEMEN
Aden
Gulf of Aden
Socotra (S. Yemen)
CENTRAL AFRICAN REPUBLIC
ETHIOPIA
Addis Abeba
SOMALI REP.
Muqdisho
KENYA
Nairobi
UGANDA Kampala
Kisangani
ZAÏRE (CONGO)
Kinshasa
Kananga
CONGO Kasai
ANGOLA
Benguela
Lubumbashi
ZAMBIA
Lusaka
Zambezi
ZIMBABWE
Bulawayo Harare
BOTSWANA
NAMIBIA
Windhoek
Gaborone
Pretoria
Johannesburg
SOUTH AFRICA
Cape Town
C. of Good Hope
Port Elizabeth
Durban

OMAN
Karachi
PAKISTAN
Ahmadabad
Bombay Pune
Hyderabad
Bangalore Madras
Colombo
SRI LANKA (CEYLON)
Dôndra Hd
MALDIVES

Delhi
Agra
Kanpur Lucknow
INDIA
Ganga
Calcutta
Nagpur
Arabian Sea
Bay of Bengal
Lakshadweep Is.
Andaman Is. (India)
Nicobar Is. (India)

NEPAL Katmandu
Kathmandu
XIZANG (TIBET)
Lhasa
BANGLA DESH Dhaka
BURMA
Mandalay
Rangoon
THAILAND
Bangkok
Hainan
Hanoi
VIET-NAM
South China Sea
Phnom Penh
CAMBODIA
Phanh Bho Ho Chi Minh

PHILIPPINES
Manila
Cebu

Guam (U.S.)
Yap
Belau
TRUST TERRITORY OF THE PACIFIC ISLANDS (U.S.)
Caroline Is.
Truk
Ponape
Marshall Is.

KIRIBATI
NAURU

INDIAN
SEYCHELLES
Amirante Is.
Chagos Arch. (Br.)
Diego Garcia (Br.)
OCEAN
Cocos (Keeling Is.) (Australia)
Christmas I. (Australia)

Equator
Medan
Kuala Lumpur
PEN. MALAYSIA
SINGAPORE
Palembang
MALAYSIA
BRUNEI SABAH
Kuching SARAWAK
Borneo
Banjarmasin
Jakarta Surabaya
Bandung Jawa
Ujung Pandang
Sulawesi
INDONESIA
Sumatra
Sunda Islands
Maluku
Irian Jaya
Timor
Timor Sea
Darwin

Comores
COMORO IS.
Mombasa
Zanzibar
Dar es Salaam
TANZANIA
L. Tanganyika
Aldabra
MALAWI
Zomba
MOZAMBIQUE
MADAGASCAR
Antananarivo
Réunion (Fr.)
MAURITIUS
Rodriguez

PAPUA NEW GUINEA
Rabaul
Port Moresby
C. York
New Ireland
New Britain
SOLOMON IS.
Louisade Arch.
Santa Cruz Is.
VANUATU
Vanua Levu
FIJI Viti Levu Suva
New Caledonia (Fr.)

Tropic of Capricorn
North West C.
Amsterdam (Fr.)
St. Paul (Fr.)

WESTERN AUSTRALIA
Perth
Fremantle
C. Leeuwin
Kalgoorlie-Boulder
SOUTH AUSTRALIA
Alice Springs
NORTHERN TERRITORY
Townsville
Cairns
QUEENSLAND
Rockhampton
Brisbane
AUSTRALIA
Great Australian Bight
Adelaide
VICTORIA
Canberra
Melbourne
NEW SOUTH WALES
Darling
Newcastle
Sydney
Lord Howe (Australia)
Norfolk I. (Australia)
Tasman Sea
Auckland
North I.
NEW ZEALAND
Wellington
North C.
TUVALU

Pr. Edward Is. (South Africa)
Crozet Is. (Fr.)
Kerguelen (Fr.)
McDonald I. (Australia)
Heard I. (Australia)

TASMANIA
Hobart
Stewart I.
Bounty Is.
Antipodes Is. (N.Z.)
Auckland I. (N.Z.)
Macquarie I. (Australia)
Campbell I. (N.Z.)
South I.
Christchurch
C. Farewell
Dunedin

SOUTHERN OCEAN

Antarctic Circle
Enderby Land
Wilkes Land
AUSTRALIAN DEPENDENCY
S. Magnetic Pole 1980
TERRE ADÉLIE
Balleny Is.
Ross Sea

From Greenwich

COPYRIGHT. GEORGE PHILIP & SON. LTD.

ARCTIC REGIONS

Arctic Explorers
——— Cook 1778
– – – Franklin 1826–47
·–·–· McClure 1850–53
–··–··– Nordenskiöld ("Vega") 1878–79
······· De Long 1881
–·–·– Nansen ("Fram") 1893–96
+++++ Abruzzi & Cagni 1899–1900
■■■■ Sverdrup 1902
········ Peary 1892–1906
–·–·– Amundsen 1903–6 & 1926
·–·–·– Peary 1908–9
◊◊◊◊ Knud Rasmussen 1912
·•·•· Koch 1913
○○○○ Stefánsson 1914–15
+·+·+ Byrd 1926 (by air)
×·×·× Wilkins 1928 (by air)
–·–·– Lindsay 1934
.... Papanin (Drift of Soviet
          Expedition) 1937–38
–––– "Sedov" 1937–40
–×–×– Knuth (Danish Pearyland
          Expedition) 1948–49

Projection: Zenithal Equidistant

Seas open all ye[...]
Extreme limits [...]
drift-ice
Seas covered by[...]
pack-ice in Spri[...]
Seas permanent[...]
covered by pac[...]
Ice-caps and
permanent ice[...]

Progress of Exploration
Coasts explored before   1800
    „   „   between 1800 & 1[...]
    „   „   between 1850 & 1[...]
    „   „   since 1900
+ Byrd   Highest latitudes reached by explore[...]
1926   with [...]

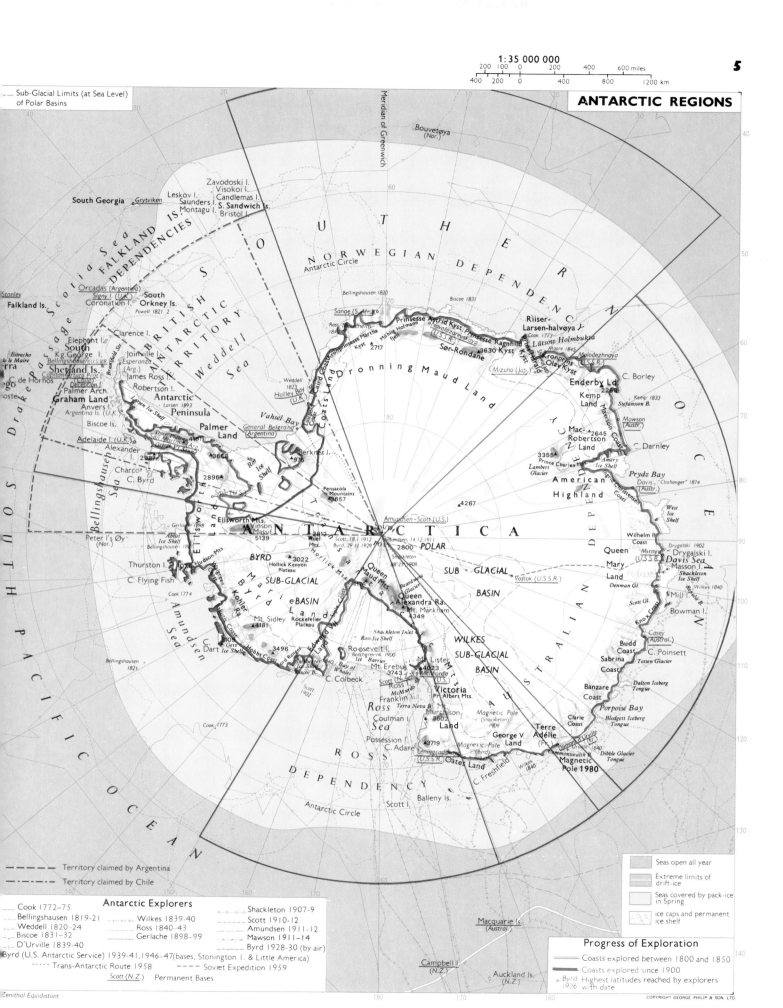

1 : 35 000 000

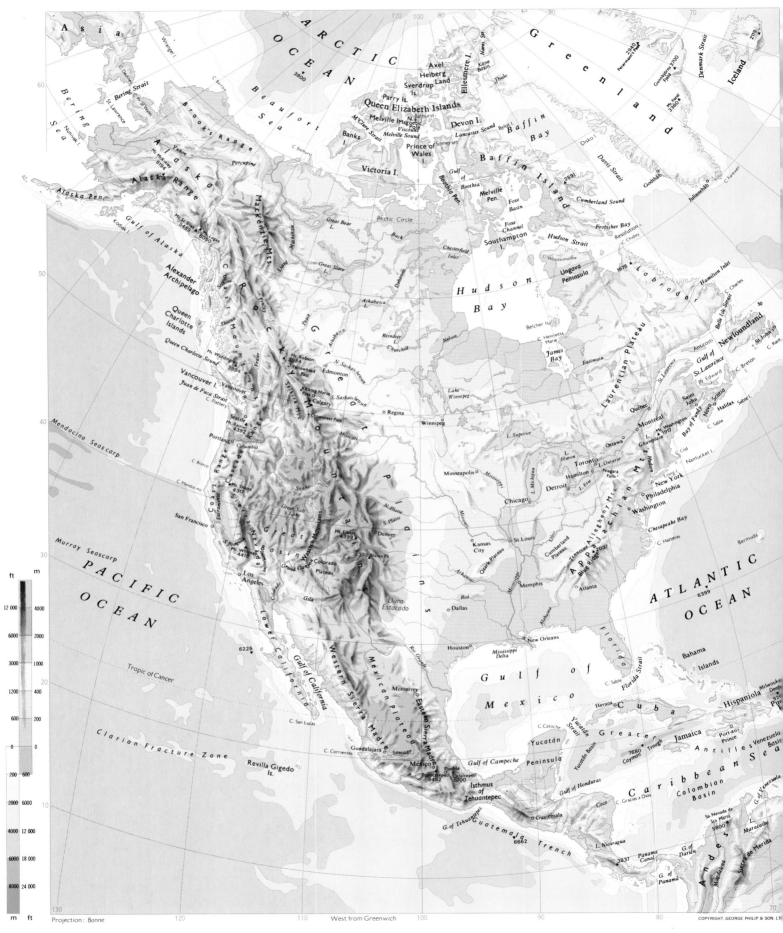

ft   m

PACIFIC

OCEAN

Projection: Bonne   West from Greenwich   COPYRIGHT. GEORGE PHILIP & SON, LT

1 : 35 000 000

200   0   200   400   600   800 miles
400   0   400   800   1200 km

ARCTIC OCEAN

U.S.S.R.

Bering Strait

Bering Sea

Beaufort Sea

Queen Elizabeth Is.

Ellesmere I.

GREENLAND (Denmark)

Denmark Strait

Reykjavik   ICELAND

ALASKA

Arctic Circle

Yukon

Fairbanks

Anchorage

Juneau

Gulf of Alaska

Porcupine

YUKON TERRITORY

INUVIK

Victoria I.

KITIKMEOT

NORTHWEST TERRITORIES

BAFFIN

Baffin Bay

Davis Strait

Godthåb

Baffin I.

FORT SMITH

Great Bear L.

Mackenzie

Liard

Great Slave L.

Back

Dubawnt

KEEWATIN

Hudson Strait

Farvel

NEWFOUNDLAND

BRITISH COLUMBIA

Skeena

Finlay

Peace

Fraser

Athabasca

Athabasca

CANADA

ALBERTA

Edmonton

N. Saskatchewan

SASKATCHEWAN

Churchill

Nelson

MANITOBA

Eastmain

Hudson Bay

QUÉBEC

Labrador

Calgary

Victoria

Vancouver

S. Saskatchewan

Regina

L. Winnipeg

ONTARIO

Winnipeg

St. Lawrence

Québec

NEW BRUNSWICK

SCOTIA

Fredericton

NOVA

Halifax

PR. EDWARD I.

Charlottetown

St. John's

SPM

Ottawa

Montréal

MAINE

Montpelier

VER. N.H. Concord

L. Ontario

Toronto

Buffalo

Augusta

WASHINGTON

Seattle

Olympia

Portland

Salem

Columbia

OREGON

IDAHO

Boise

Snake

MONTANA

Helena

Missouri

NORTH DAKOTA

Bismarck

SOUTH DAKOTA

Pierre

MINNESOTA

St. Paul

Minneapolis

WISCONSIN

Madison

Milwaukee

L. Superior

L. Michigan

L. Huron

MICHIGAN

Lansing

Detroit

Toledo

Cleveland

Chicago

Pittsburgh

PENNSYLVANIA

Harrisburg

Columbus

OHIO

Cincinnati

Frankfort

Indianapolis

INDIANA

ILLINOIS

Springfield

Jefferson City

St. Louis

KENTUCKY

Nashville

TENNESSEE

Memphis

NEW YORK

Albany

MASS.

Boston

Hartford

C. R.I. Providence

N.Y.

Trenton

Philadelphia

Baltimore

Annapolis

M. D. Dover

WEST VIRGINIA

Charleston

Washington

VIRGINIA

Richmond

Raleigh

NORTH CAROLINA

Columbia

SOUTH CAROLINA

WYOMING

Cheyenne

N. Platte

NEBRASKA

Lincoln

IOWA

Des Moines

UNITED STATES

Salt Lake City

Carson City

NEVADA

UTAH

COLORADO

Denver

Arkansas

KANSAS

Topeka

Kansas City

MISSOURI

Sacramento

San Francisco

San Jose

CALIFORNIA

Las Vegas

LOS ANGELES

San Diego

Colorado

ARIZONA

Phoenix

Gila

Tucson

Santa Fe

Albuquerque

NEW MEXICO

El Paso

Oklahoma City

OKLAHOMA

ARKANSAS

Little Rock

Red River

Fort Worth

Dallas

TEXAS

Austin

Birmingham

MISSISSIPPI

Jackson

ALABAMA

Montgomery

GEORGIA

Atlanta

Tennessee

Alabama

LOUISIANA

Baton Rouge

New Orleans

Tallahassee

Jacksonville

FLORIDA

Tampa

Miami

C. Sable

Str. of Florida

Bermuda

ATLANTIC OCEAN

PACIFIC OCEAN

Houston

Monterrey

Golfo de California

Tropic of Cancer

MEXICO

Baja California

Rio Grande

Revillagigedo Is.

Guadalajara

MEXICO

Gulf of Mexico

Havana

CUBA

BAHAMAS

Nassau

JAMAICA

HAITI

Port-au-Prince

Kingston

DOMINICAN REP.

Santo Domingo

San Juan

PUERTO RICO

Caribbean Sea

Belmopan

BELIZE

GUATEMALA

HONDURAS

Guatemala

San Salvador

EL SALVADOR

Tegucigalpa

NICARAGUA

Managua

L. de Nicaragua

COSTA RICA

San José

PANAMA

Panamá

Maracaibo

Barranquilla

VENEZUELA

Medellín

COLOMBIA

Bogotá

SOUTH AMERICA

Montgomery : State capital ⊙

C.	CONNECTICUT
D.	DELAWARE
D.C.	DISTRICT OF COLUMBIA
M.	MARYLAND
MASS.	MASSACHUSETTS

N.H.	NEW HAMPSHIRE
N.J.	NEW JERSEY
R.I.	RHODE ISLAND
VER.	VERMONT
SPM	ST. PIERRE ET MIQUELON

Projection : Bonne

West from Greenwich

COPYRIGHT. GEORGE PHILIP & SON. LTD.

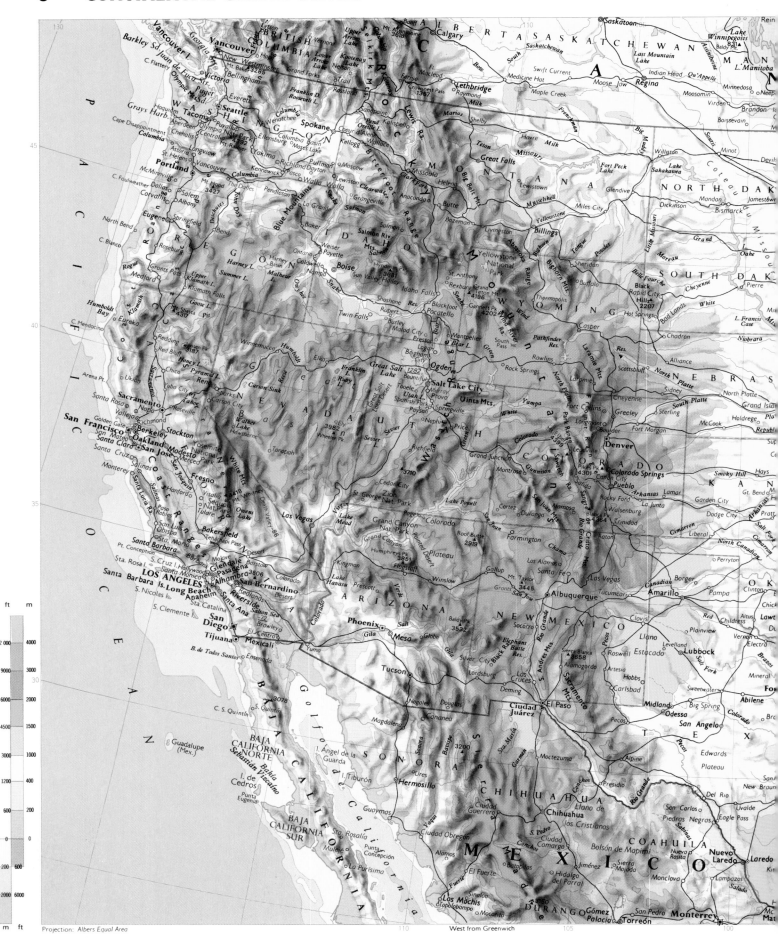

1:12 000 000

50 0   50 100   150   200   250   300 miles
50 0 50 100 150 200 250 300 350 400 450 km

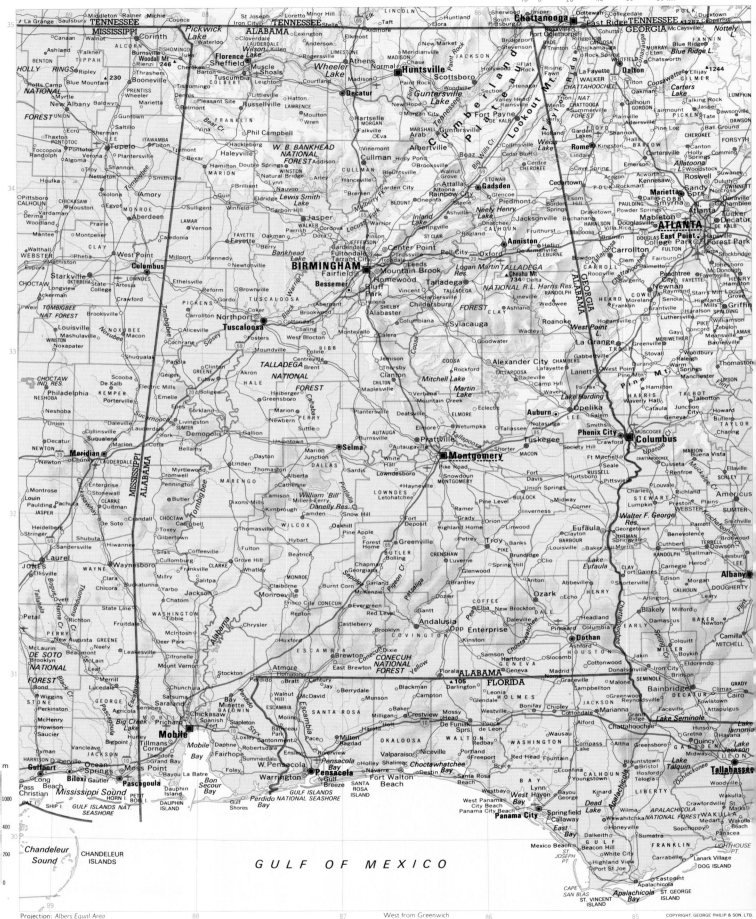

1:2 500 000

Projection: Albers Equal Area   West from Greenwich   COPYRIGHT. GEORGE PHILIP & SON. LTD.

1:10 000 000

50 0 50 100 150 200 250 miles
50 0 50 100 150 200 250 300 350 400 km

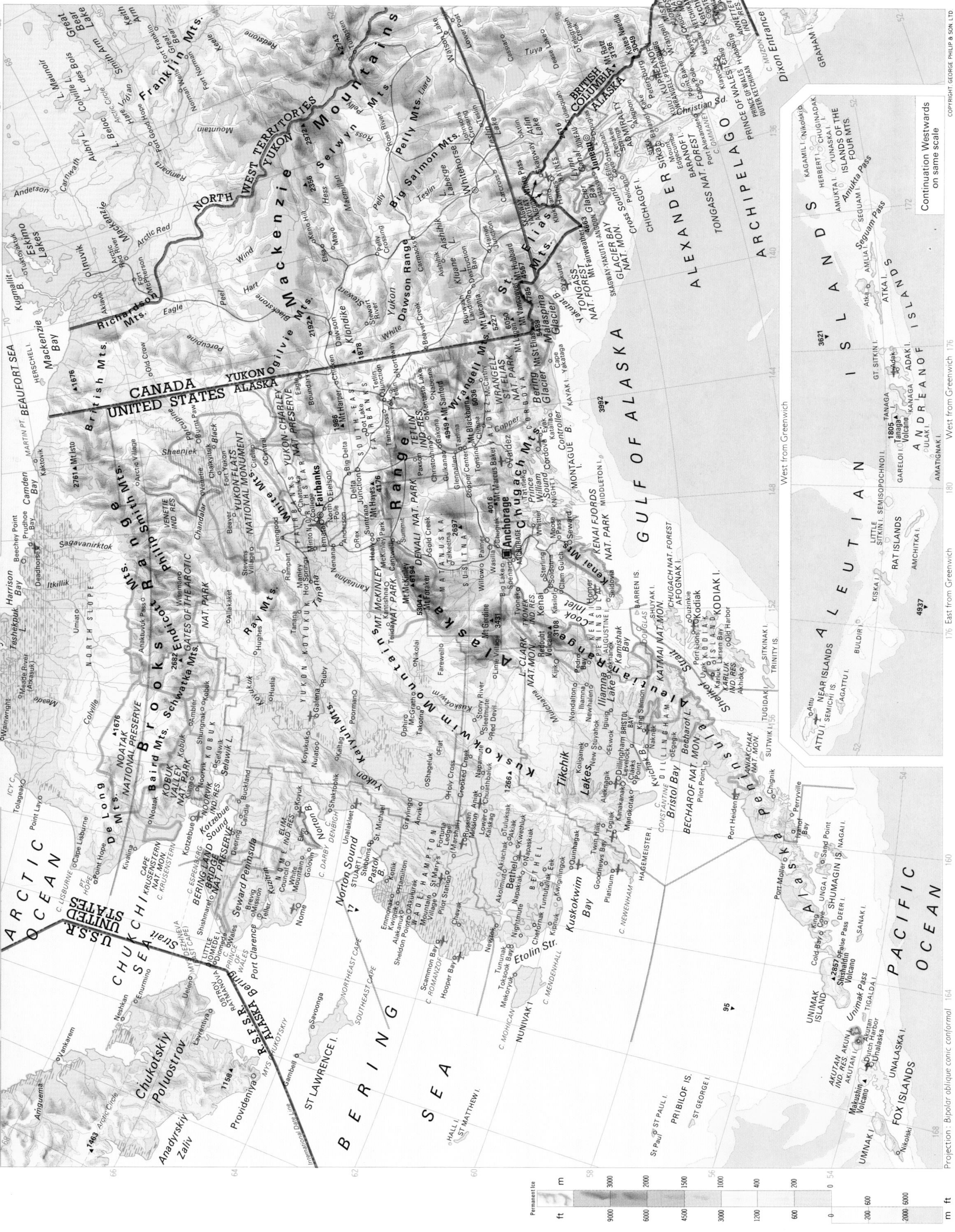

Continuation Westwards
on same scale

ARCTIC OCEAN

BEAUFORT SEA

Franklin Mts.

WEST TERRITORIES

NORTH

YUKON

Selwyn Mts.

Mackenzie Mountains

Pelly Mts.

Big Salmon Mts.

Richardson Mts.

British Mts.

Ogilvie Mts.

Dawson Range

St. Elias Mts.

BRITISH COLUMBIA

ALASKA

Juneau

TONGASS NAT. FOREST

ALEXANDER ARCHIPELAGO

PRINCE OF WALES

Dixon Entrance

GRAHAM I.

CANADA
UNITED STATES

YUKON
ALASKA

Brooks Range

Philip Smith Mts.

Schwatka Mts.

Baird Mts.

Endicott Mts.

GATES OF THE ARCTIC NAT. PARK

NOATAK NATIONAL PRESERVE

KOBUK VALLEY NAT. PARK

Ray Mts.

White Mts.

YUKON-CHARLEY NAT. PRESERVE

YUKON FLATS NATIONAL MONUMENT

Fairbanks

DENALI NAT. PARK

MT McKINLEY
5304 MT McKINLEY

Mt Hayes 4216

WRANGELL MTS.

WRANGELL ST. ELIAS NAT. PARK

Mt Sanford 4949

Mt Blackburn 5036

Chugach Mts.

Anchorage

MATANUSKA

SUSITNA

KENAI FJORDS NAT. PARK

Kenai Mts.

Kuskokwim Mountains

L. CLARK NAT. PARK

LAKE CLARK NAT. PARK

Alaska Range

Cook Inlet

GULF OF ALASKA

Kodiak I.

KODIAK I.

AFOGNAK I.

KATMAI NAT. MON.

Bristol Bay

Kuskokwim Bay

Norton Sound

Seward Peninsula

BERING LAND BRIDGE NAT. PRESERVE

NOME

BERING SEA

ST LAWRENCE I.

NUNIVAK I.

ST MATTHEW I.

HALL I.

PRIBILOF IS.
ST PAUL
ST GEORGE I.

Alaska Peninsula

BECHAROF NAT. MON.

Aleutian Range

FOX ISLANDS

UNIMAK ISLAND

Dutch Harbor

Unalaska

ALEUTIAN ISLANDS

Islands of the Four Mts.

ANDREANOF ISLANDS

RAT ISLANDS

NEAR ISLANDS

Attu

CHUKCHI SEA

USSR
UNITED STATES

R.S.F.S.R.
ALASKA

Chukotskiy Poluostrov

Anadyrskiy Zaliv

International Date Line

PACIFIC OCEAN

Projection: Bipolar oblique conic conformal

West from Greenwich

East from Greenwich

Permanent ice

ft   m
9000   3000
6000   2000
4500   1500
3000   1000
1200   400
600   200
0   0
       200   600
       2000   6000
m   ft

1:2 500 000

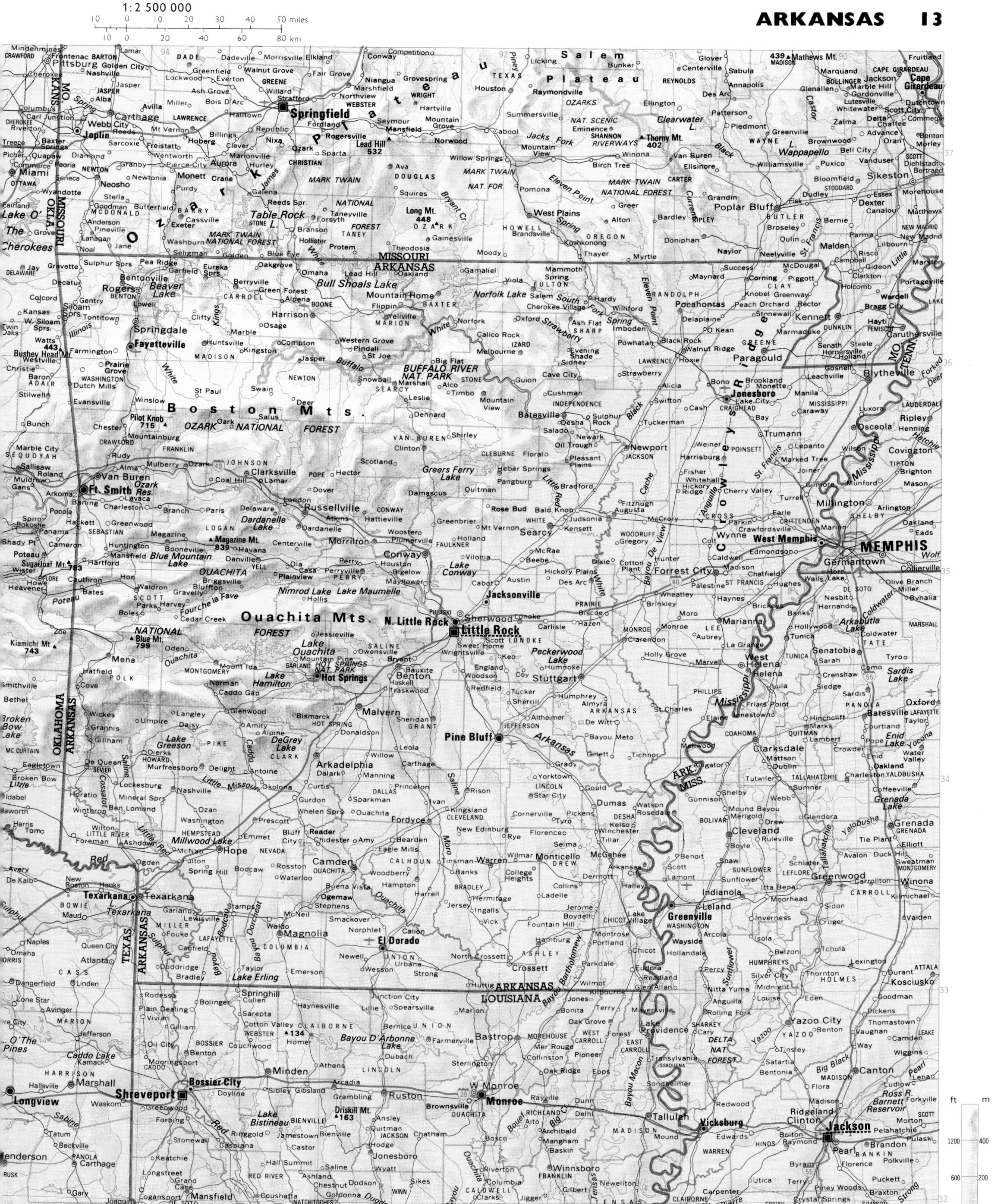

10 0 10 20 30 40 50 miles
20   0   20   40   60   80 km

ARKANSAS

MISSOURI

OKLAHOMA

TEXAS

LOUISIANA

MISSISSIPPI

TENN.

Ozark Plateau

Salem Plateau

Boston Mts.

Ouachita Mts.

OZARK NATIONAL FOREST

OUACHITA NATIONAL FOREST

MARK TWAIN NATIONAL FOREST

BUFFALO RIVER NAT. PARK

Springfield

Joplin

Fayetteville

Springdale

Rogers

Bentonville

Harrison

Mountain Home

Ft. Smith

Van Buren

Russellville

Conway

Little Rock

N. Little Rock

Jacksonville

Hot Springs

Benton

Malvern

Pine Bluff

Camden

El Dorado

Texarkana

Hope

Magnolia

Jonesboro

Paragould

Blytheville

West Memphis

MEMPHIS

Forrest City

Helena

West Helena

Greenville

Vicksburg

Jackson

Clinton

Monroe

W Monroe

Bossier City

Shreveport

Longview

CAPE GIRARDEAU

Poplar Bluff

Sikeston

Bull Shoals Lake

Norfolk Lake

Table Rock

Lake Ouachita

Lake Hamilton

Greers Ferry Lake

Lake Conway

DeGray Lake

Millwood Lake

Nimrod Lake

Lake Maumelle

Blue Mountain Lake

Dardanelle Lake

Beaver Lake

Magazine Mt. 839

Driskill Mt. 163

Kiamichi Mt. 743

Blue Mt. 799

Pilot Knob 715

Mathews Mt. 439

Thorny Mt. 402

Long Mt. 448

Lead Hill 532

Arkansas

White

Red

Buffalo

Ouachita

Little Missouri

Cossatot

Mississippi

St. Francis

Black

Current

Spring

L'Anguille

Cache

Bayou Bartholomew

Bayou Macon

ft   m
1200   400
600   200
0   0

1:2 500 000

PACIFIC OCEAN

OREGON
CALIFORNIA

NEVADA
CALIFORNIA

San Francisco
Oakland
Berkeley
Sacramento
Stockton
Modesto
San Jose
Salinas
Monterey
Santa Cruz
Fresno

Eureka
Redding
Chico
Reno
Carson City
Lake Tahoe

Projection : Albers Equal Area   West from Greenwich

COPYRIGHT. GEORGE PHILIP & SON. LTD.

1 : 2 500 000

10   0   10   20   30   40   50 miles
10   0   20   40   60   80 km

NEBRASKA
COLORADO

KANSAS
COLORADO

WYOMING
COLORADO

UTAH
COLORADO

COLORADO
NEW MEXICO

COLORADO
OKLAHOMA

DENVER
Colorado Springs
Pueblo
Fort Collins
Greeley
Boulder
Aurora
Lakewood
Arvada
Cheyenne

PAWNEE NAT. GRASSLAND
COMANCHE NAT. GRASSLAND
ROOSEVELT NATIONAL FOREST
ROUTT NATIONAL FOREST
WHITE RIVER NATIONAL FOREST
PIKE NATIONAL FOREST
GUNNISON NATIONAL FOREST
SAN ISABEL NATIONAL FOREST
RIO GRANDE NATIONAL FOREST
SAN JUAN NATIONAL FOREST
UNCOMPAHGRE NATIONAL FOREST

Rocky Mountains
Front Range
Sawatch Range
Sangre de Cristo Mountains
Park Range
Elk Mountains
San Juan Mountains
Grand Mesa
Danforth Hills
Roan Plateau
Book Cliffs
Uncompahgre Plateau
San Luis Valley

Mt. Elbert 4399
Pikes Peak 4300
Mt. Evans 4349

m   4000 3000 2000 1500 1000
ft   12000 9000 6000 4500 3000

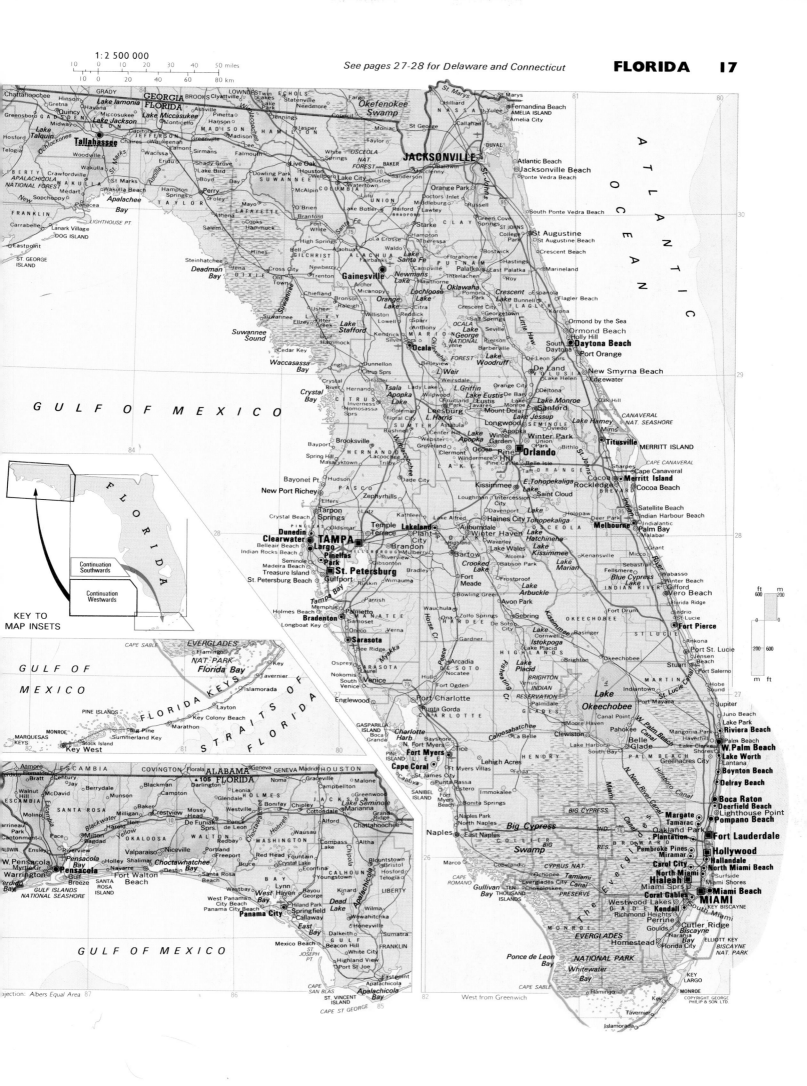

1:2 500 000

1:2 500 000

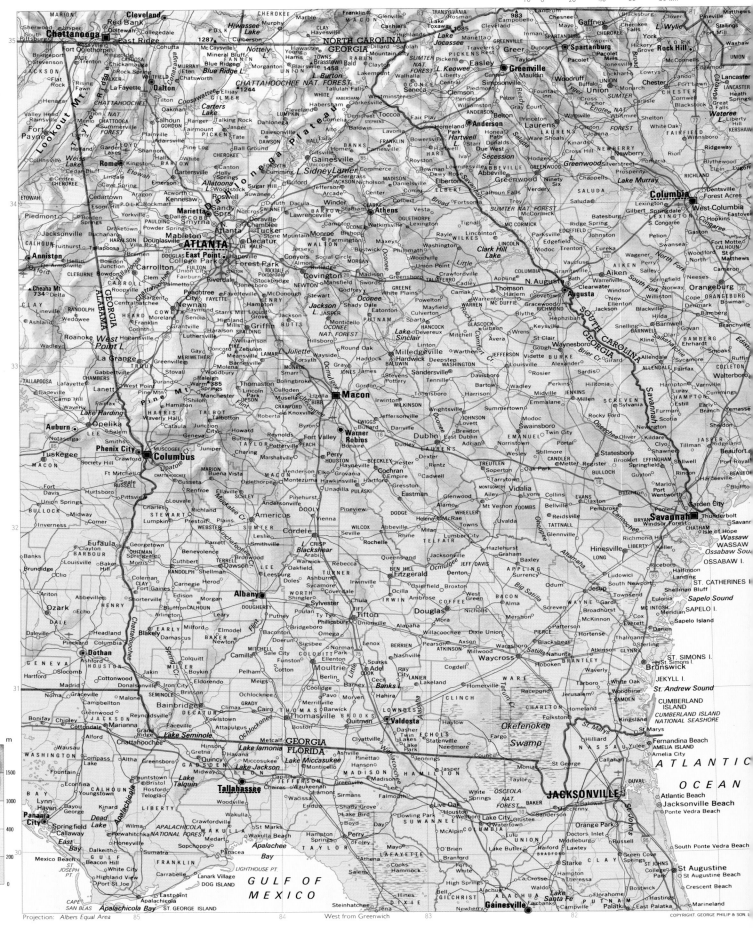

1 : 2 500 000

10 0   10 20 30   40   50 miles
10 0   20   40   60   80 km

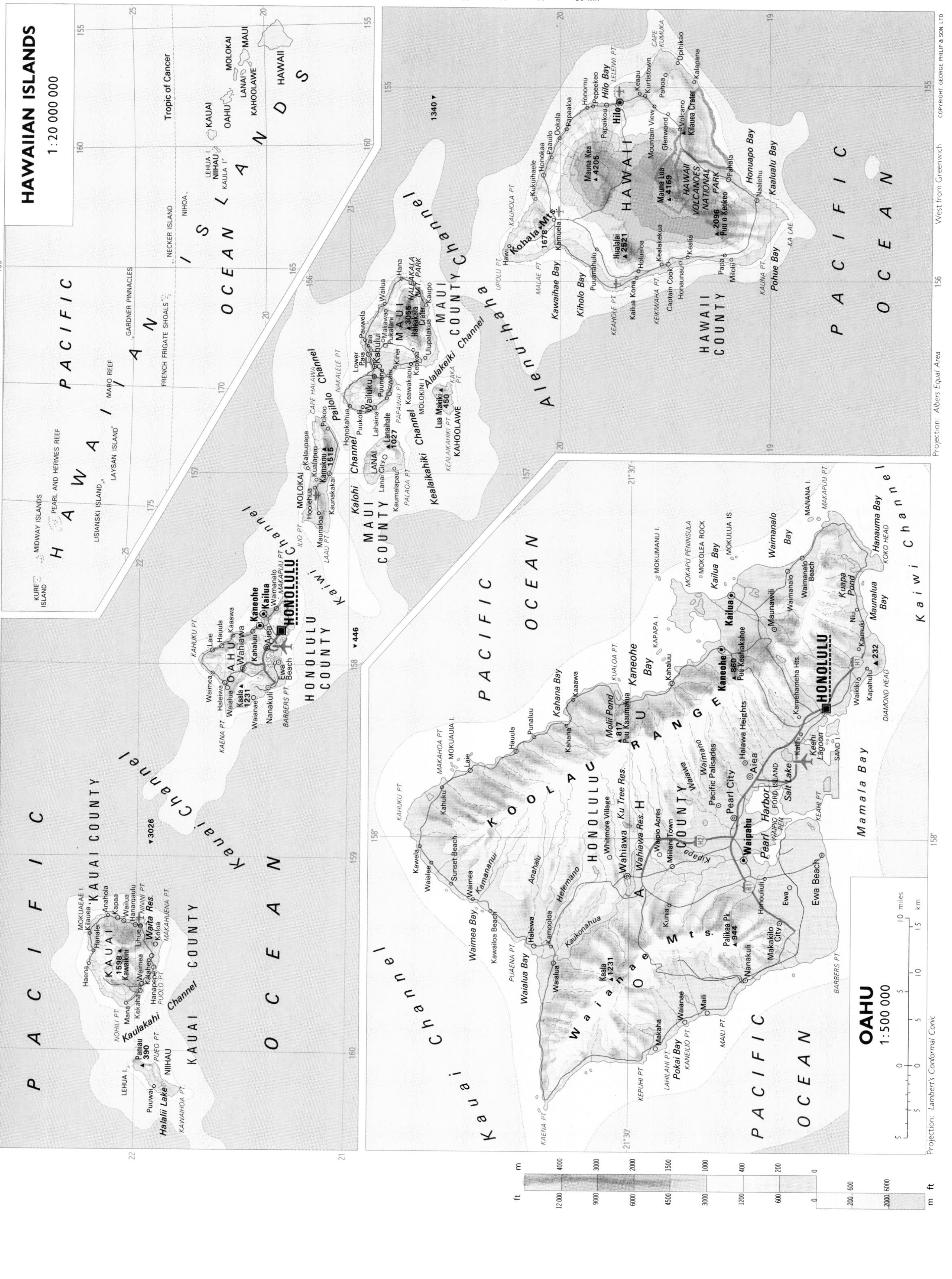

HAWAIIAN ISLANDS
1 : 20 000 000

Tropic of Cancer

KAUAI
OAHU
MOLOKAI
MAUI
LANAI
KAHOOLAWE
HAWAII

LEHUA I. NIIHAU
KAULA I.

NIHOA

NECKER ISLAND

GARDNER PINNACLES

FRENCH FRIGATE SHOALS

MARO REEF

LAYSAN ISLAND

LISIANSKI ISLAND

PEARL AND HERMES REEF

MIDWAY ISLANDS

KURE ISLAND

H A W A I I A N   I S L A N D S

L E E W A R D   I S L A N D S

PACIFIC   OCEAN

West from Greenwich

COPYRIGHT GEORGE PHILIP & SON LTD

Projection: Albers Equal Area

HAWAII

Kohala Mts. 1678
Mauna Kea ▲4205
Mauna Loa ▲4169
Hualalai ▲2521
▲2096 Puu o Keokeo
Kilauea Crater
HAWAII VOLCANOES NATIONAL PARK

Hilo
Hilo Bay
CAPE KUMUKA
Opihikao
Kalapana
Pahoa
Volcano
Glenwood
Mountain View
Keaau
Kurtistown
Pepeekeo
Honomu
Papaikou
Rapaokala
Ookala
Paauilo
Honokaa
Kukuihaele
Kukaiau
Kamuela
Waimea
Honaunau
Captain Cook
Keauhou
Kealakekua
Kealia
Kailua Kona
Keahole
KEAHOLE PT.
KEKAHA PT.
Kiholo Bay
Kawaihae Bay
Puuanahulu
Holualoa
Pahala
Naalehu
Waiohinu
KA LAE
Pohue Bay
Kaalualu Bay
Honuapo Bay
UPOLU PT.
KAUHOLA PT.
MALAE PT.
Hawi
Kapaau

HAWAII COUNTY

1340 ▼

Alenuihaha   Channel

PACIFIC   OCEAN

MAUI
MAUI COUNTY

Haleakala ▲3055
HALEAKALA NAT. PARK
Puu Kukui ▲

Wailuku
Kahului
Paia
Lower Paia
Pauwela
Huelo
Keanae
Nahiku
Hana
Kipahulu
Kaupo
Ulupalakua
Makena
Kihei
Keokea
Puunene
Olowalu
Lahaina
Kaanapali
Napili
Kapalua

MAUI COUNTY CHANNEL

MOLOKAI
1515
Kaunakakai
Kamalo
Halawa
Kalaupapa
Kualapuu
Hoolehua
Maunaloa
Kaluakoi

LANAI
1027
Lanai City
Palaoa PT.

KAHOOLAWE
450
Lua Makika ▲

Iialakeiki Channel
Kealaikahiki Channel
Kalohi Channel
Pailolo Channel
Kaiwi Channel
Auau Channel
Papawai PT.
Laau PT.
Ilio PT.
NAKALELE PT.
CAPE HALAWA
Kalaupapa
Nakalele PT.

OAHU (inset, Hawaiian Islands map)
HONOLULU
Kaneohe
Kailua
Waimanalo
Ewa
Wahiawa
Haleiwa
Kahuku
Laie
Hauula
Kaaawa
Kaneohe
Waianae
Nanakuli
Kahaluu
Kaala 1231
KAENA PT.
BARBERS PT.
MAKAPUU PT.
446 ▼
HONOLULU COUNTY
Kaiwi Channel
Kauai Channel

KAUAI
KAUAI COUNTY
Kawaikini 1598
MOKUAEAE I.
Kilauea
Anahola
Kapaa
Wailua
Lihue
Nawiliwili
Koloa
Waita Res.
Hanapepe
Waimea
Kekaha
Mana
Haena
Hanalei
Kalaheo
NOHILI PT.
PUOLO PT.
MAKAHUENA PT.
HANAPEPE PT.
KIPUNI PT.
TUNINI PT.
Kalihiwai

NIIHAU
Puuwai 390
Paniau 390
Halalii Lake
LEHUA I.
KAWAIHOA PT.
3026 ▼

Kauai Channel

P A C I F I C   O C E A N

OAHU
1 : 500 000

Projection: Lambert's Conformal Conic

HONOLULU
Waikiki
DIAMOND HEAD
Kapahulu
▲232
Kaimuki
Kamehameha Hts.
Keehi Lagoon
SAND I.
Salt Lake
Aiea
Halawa Heights
Pearl City
Pacific Palisades
Pearl Harbor
Waimalu
Waipahu
Waiau
FORD ISLAND
KAIPIO PEN.
Ewa
Ewa Beach
BARBERS PT.
Nanakuli
Makakilo City
Honouliuli
Kunia
Wahiawa
Whitmore Village
Wahiawa Res.
Ku Tree Res.
Miliani Town
Wahiawa
Waipio Acres
Kipapa
Mililani
Pearl Harbor
Puu Kaaumakua 817
Pacific City
Aiea
Kaneohe
Kailua
Waimanalo
Waimanalo Beach
Puu Keahiakahoe 860
Maunawili
Niu
Maunalua Bay
Kuapa Pond
Hanauma Bay
KOKO HEAD
MAKAPUU PT.
MANANA I.
MOKUMANU I.
MOKAPU PENINSULA
MOKULEA ROCK
MOKOLEA IS.
KAPAPA I.
Kaneohe Bay
Kailua Bay
Kahaluu
KUALOA PT.
Kahana
Kaaawa
Punaluu
Hauula
Laie
Kahuku
KAHUKU PT.
Kawela
Waialee
Sunset Beach
Waimea
Waialua
Haleiwa
Kamananui
Waialua Bay
Waimea Bay
PUAENA PT.
KAENA PT.
KAHUKU PT.
Mokuleia
Kaukonahua
Makua
Kaena
Kamaile
Makaha
Waianae
Maili
Nanakuli
Lualualei
Kaala ▲1231
KOOLAU RANGE
WAIANAE MTS.
Palikea Pk. 944
Molii Pond
Anahulu
Helemano
HONOLULU   COUNTY
Mamala Bay
Kaiwi Channel
Kauai Channel
LAHILAHI PT.
POKAI BAY
KANEILIO PT.
MAILI PT.
KEPUHI PT.
H₂
H₁

P A C I F I C   O C E A N

10 miles
5   10   15 km
km
0   5   10   15
5   0

ft
12000
9000
6000
4500
3000
2000
1500
600
200
m
4000
3000
2000
1500
1000
400
200
0
200 600
2000 6000
m   ft

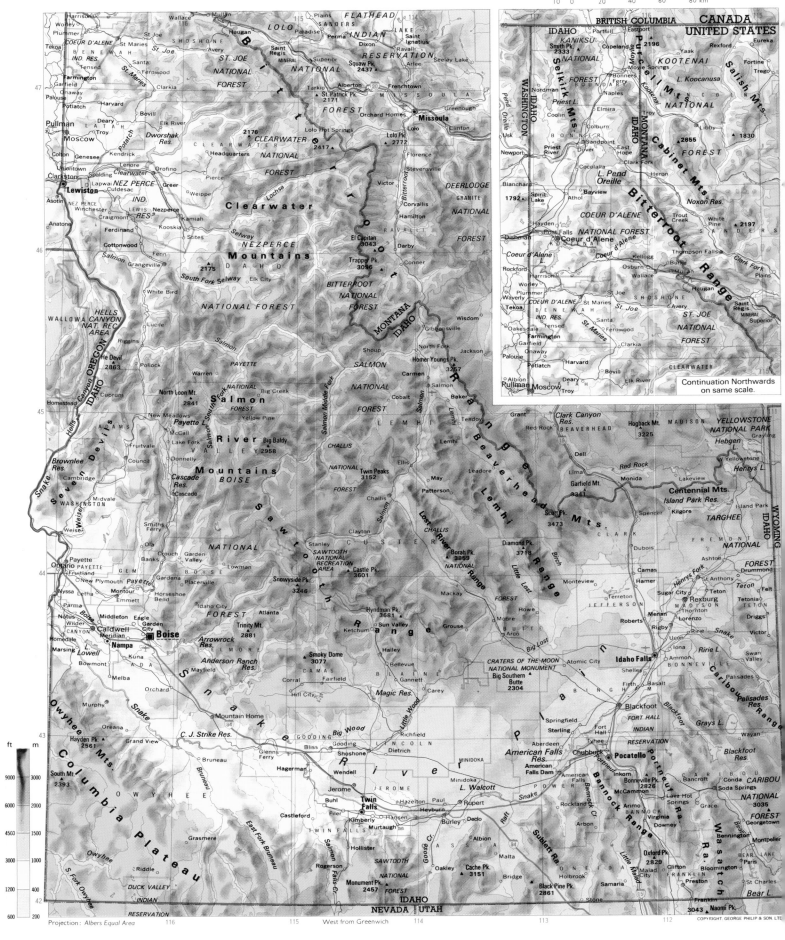

1 : 2 500 000

Continuation Northwards on same scale.

Projection : Albers Equal Area

West from Greenwich

COPYRIGHT GEORGE PHILIP & SON, LTD.

1:2 500 000

10 0 10 20 30 40 50 miles
10 0 20 40 60 80 km

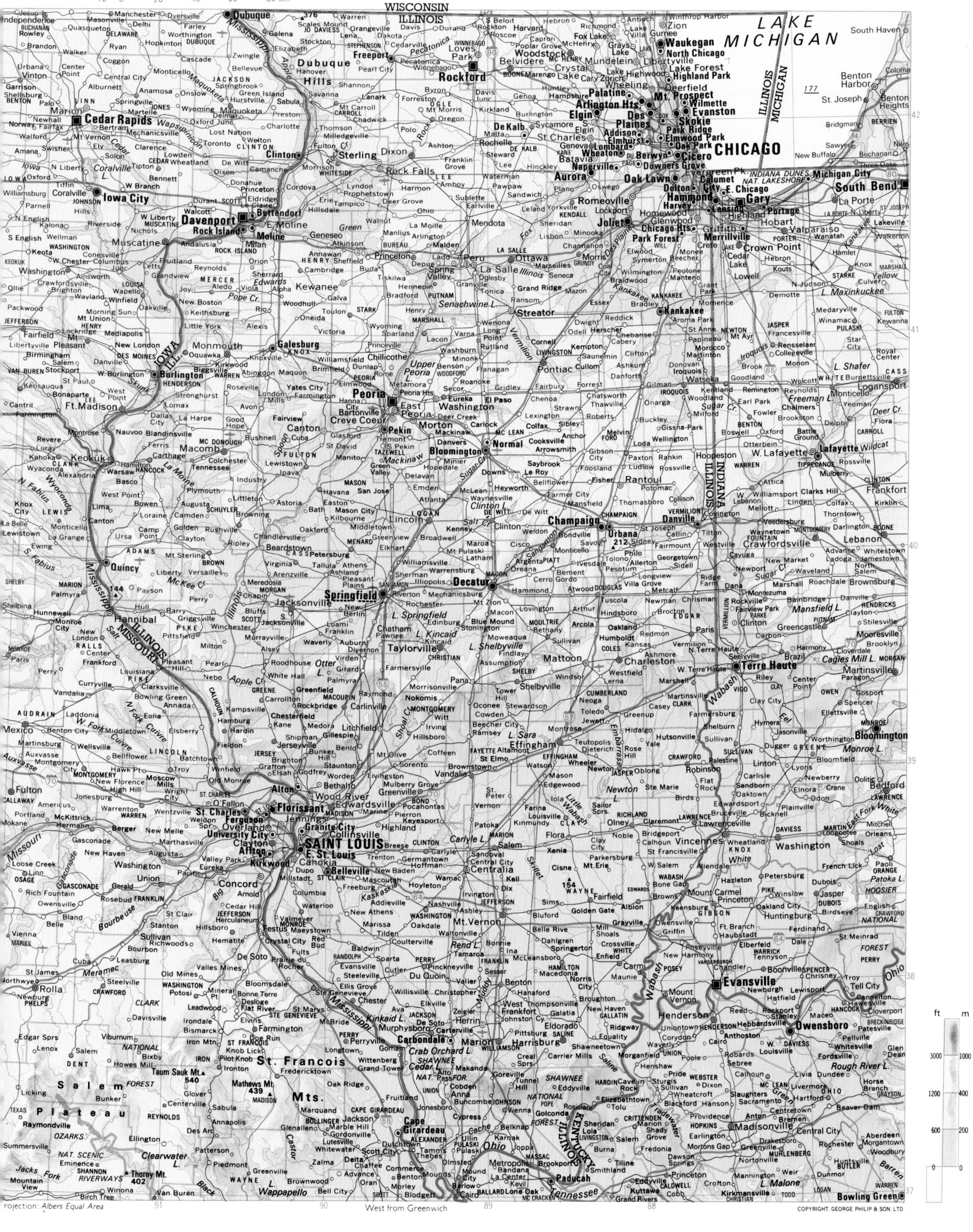

WISCONSIN
ILLINOIS

LAKE MICHIGAN

Projection: Albers Equal Area

West from Greenwich

COPYRIGHT GEORGE PHILIP & SON LTD.

ft m
3000 1000
1200 400
600 200

1:2 500 000

10   0   10   20   30   40   50 miles

10   0   20   40   60   80 km

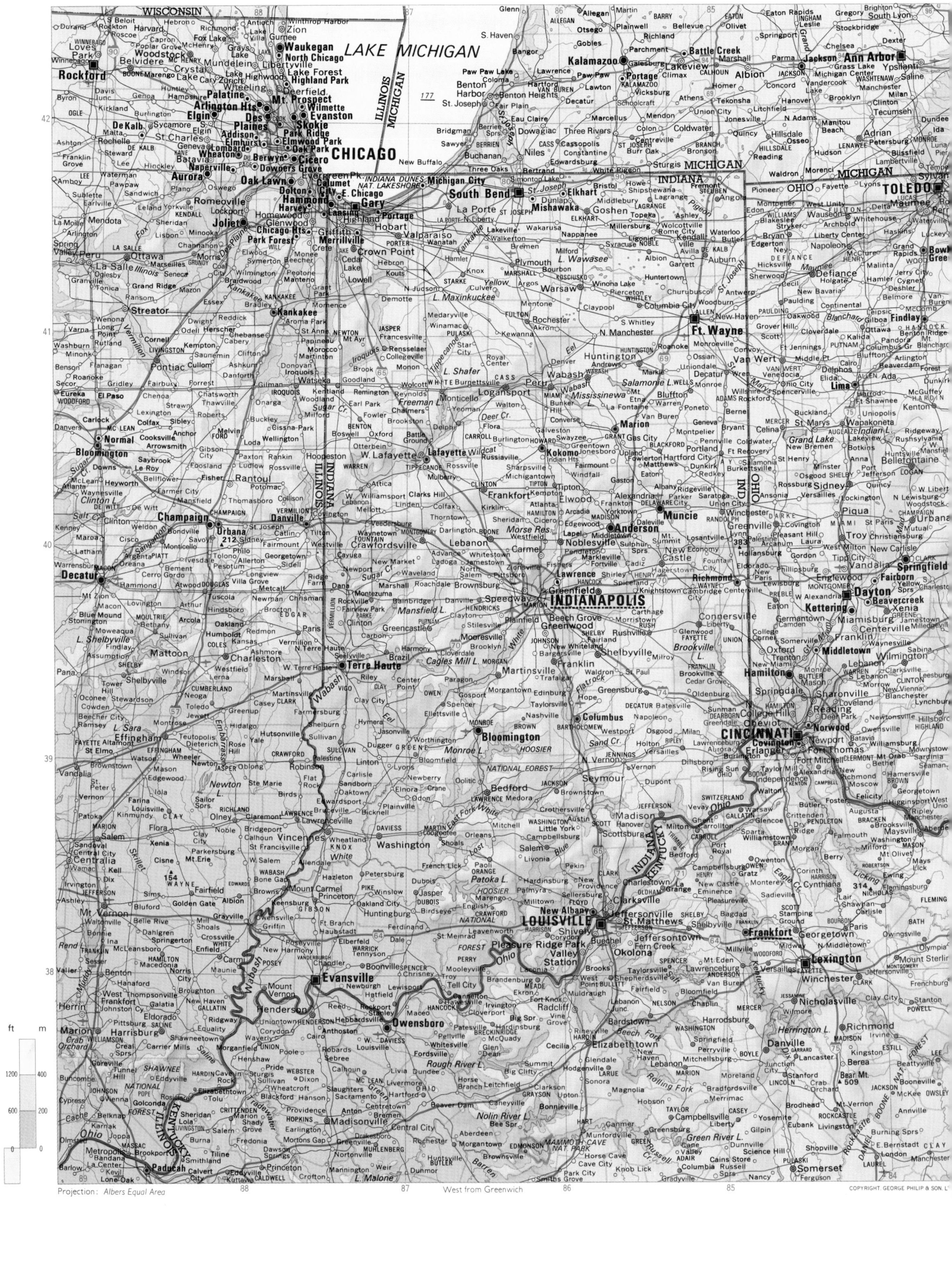

LAKE MICHIGAN

CHICAGO

INDIANAPOLIS

Projection: Albers Equal Area   West from Greenwich   COPYRIGHT GEORGE PHILIP & SON. L

1 : 2 500 000

10 0 10 20 30 40 50 miles
10 0 20 40 60 80 km

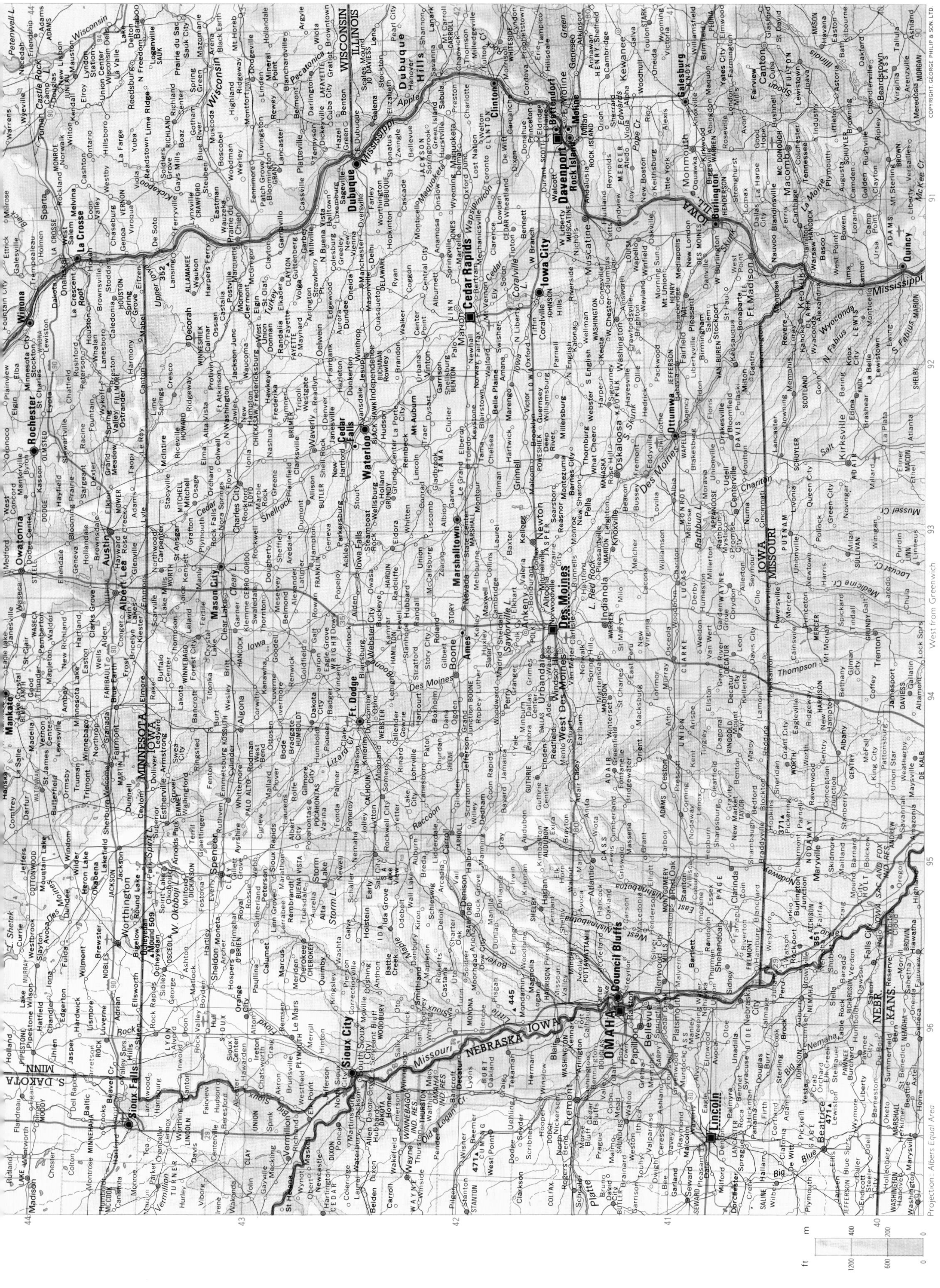

WISCONSIN

ILLINOIS

MINNESOTA

IOWA

MISSOURI

NEBRASKA

KANS.

S. DAKOTA

MINN.

Sioux City

Council Bluffs

OMAHA

Lincoln

Des Moines

Ames

Cedar Rapids

Iowa City

Davenport

Rock Island

Moline

Waterloo

Cedar Falls

Mason City

Fort Dodge

Ottumwa

Marshalltown

Dubuque

Clinton

Burlington

La Crosse

Winona

Rochester

Owatonna

Austin

Albert Lea

Mankato

West Des Moines

Ankeny

Urbandale

Bellevue

Boone

Nevada

Quincy

Galesburg

Mississippi

Missouri

Des Moines

Iowa

Cedar

West from Greenwich

Projection : Albers Equal Area

COPYRIGHT GEORGE PHILIP & SON LTD

ft   m
1200 400
600 200
0 0

1 : 2 500 000

10   0   10   20   30   40   50 miles
10   0   20   40   60   80 km

1:2 500 000

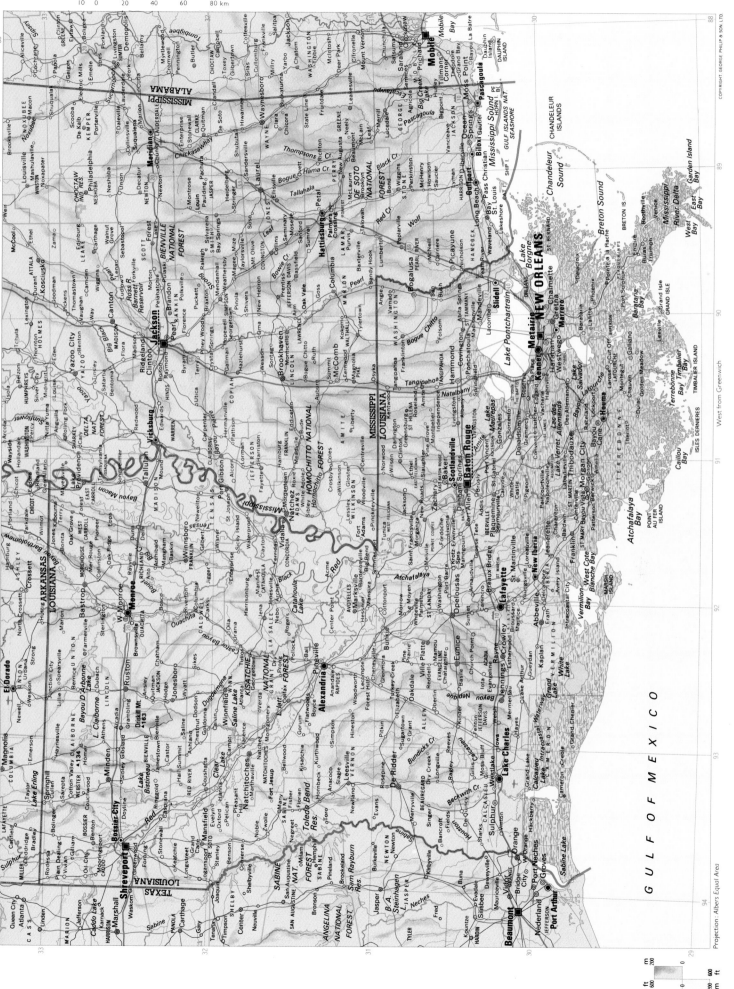

GULF OF MEXICO

West from Greenwich

Projection: Albers Equal Area

COPYRIGHT GEORGE PHILIP & SON LTD

1:2 500 000

10 0 10 20 30 40 50 miles
10 0 20 40 60 80 km

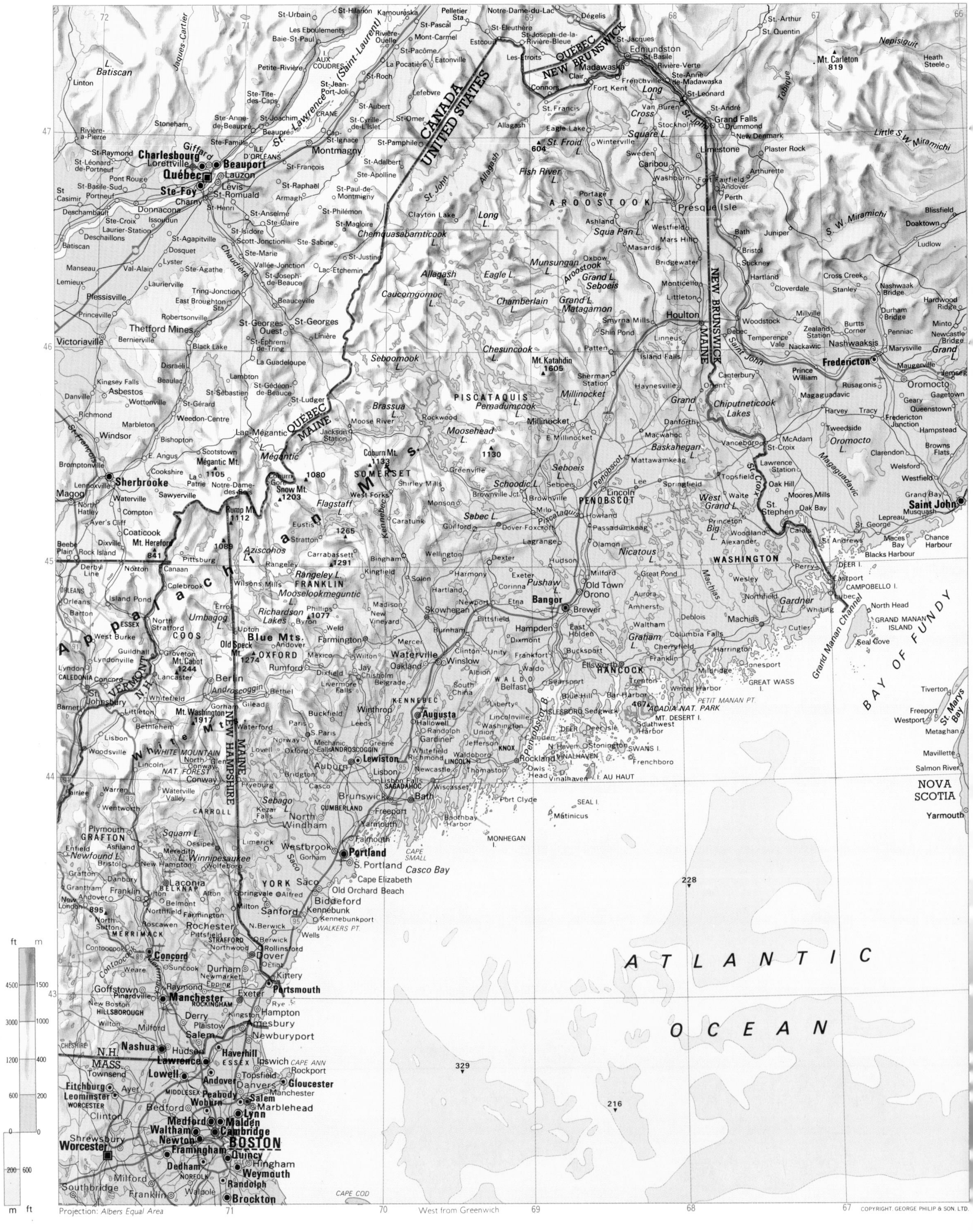

CANADA
UNITED STATES
QUEBEC
NEW BRUNSWICK
MAINE
NEW HAMPSHIRE
VERMONT
MASS.
N.H.

AROOSTOOK
PISCATAQUIS
SOMERSET
FRANKLIN
OXFORD
KENNEBEC
PENOBSCOT
WASHINGTON
HANCOCK
WALDO
KNOX
LINCOLN
SAGADAHOC
ANDROSCOGGIN
CUMBERLAND
YORK
COOS
GRAFTON
CARROLL
BELKNAP
STRAFFORD
ROCKINGHAM
HILLSBOROUGH
MERRIMACK
CHESHIRE
WORCESTER
MIDDLESEX
ESSEX
NORFOLK

Québec
Charlesbourg
Beauport
Lauzon
Ste-Foy
Lévis
Sherbrooke
Fredericton
Saint John
Bangor
Brewer
Augusta
Lewiston
Auburn
Portland
S. Portland
Biddeford
Saco
Brunswick
Bath
Rockland
Waterville
Skowhegan
Houlton
Presque Isle
Caribou
Fort Kent
Madawaska
Van Buren
Edmundston
Grand Falls
Mt. Carleton 819
Mt. Katahdin 1605
Moosehead L.
Flagstaff L.
Chesuncook L.
Chamberlain L.
Eagle L.
Allagash
Sebago L.
L. Winnipesaukee
Concord
Manchester
Nashua
Lowell
Lawrence
Haverhill
Worcester
BOSTON
Cambridge
Newton
Waltham
Quincy
Brockton
Gloucester
Salem
Lynn
Medford
Malden
Portsmouth
Dover
Rochester
Sanford
Kennebunk
Kittery

ATLANTIC OCEAN
BAY OF FUNDY
NOVA SCOTIA
Yarmouth
Casco Bay
CAPE SMALL
CAPE COD
CAPE ANN
Grand Manan Channel
GRAND MANAN ISLAND
ACADIA NAT. PARK
MT. DESERT I.
Bar Harbor

APPALACHIAN
WHITE MOUNTAIN NAT. FOREST
Mt. Washington 1917
Mt. Cabot 1244
Old Speck Mt. 1274
Snow Mt. 1203
Pump Mt. 1112
Coburn Mt. 1133
1130
1080
1105
1089
841
1291
1077
1265
604
228
329
216
467

Projection: Albers Equal Area
West from Greenwich
COPYRIGHT GEORGE PHILIP & SON LTD.

ft m
4500 1500
3000 1000
1200 400
600 200
0 0
200 600
m ft

1:1 250 000

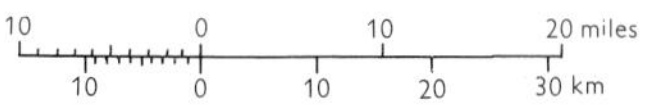

10   0   10   20 miles
10   0   10   20   30 km

NEW JERSEY

DELAWARE

MARYLAND

PENNSYLVANIA

VIRGINIA

WEST VIRGINIA

Delaware Bay

Chincoteague Bay

ATLANTIC OCEAN

Chesapeake Bay

Tangier Sound

Eastern Shore

Delmarva Peninsula

Tidewater

Appalachian Mountains

South Mountain

Catoctin Mt.

Potomac

Susquehanna

BALTIMORE
WASHINGTON D.C.
Annapolis
Dover
Wilmington
Salisbury
Cumberland

West from Greenwich

Continuation Westwards on same scale

Projection: Lambert's Conformal Conic

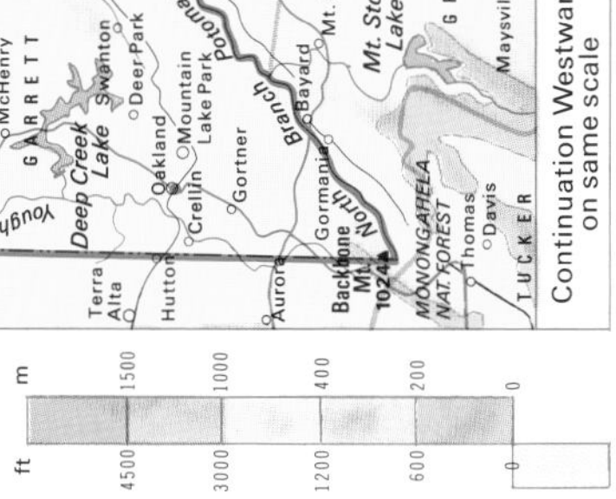

m 1500 1000 400 200 0
ft 4500 3000 1200 600 0

Mt. Davis ▲979
High Rock ▲912
Backbone Mt. ▲1024

MONONGAHELA NAT FOREST
SHENANDOAH NATIONAL PARK
WASHINGTON NATIONAL FOREST

1:1 250 000

10   0   10   20 miles
10   0   10   20   30 km

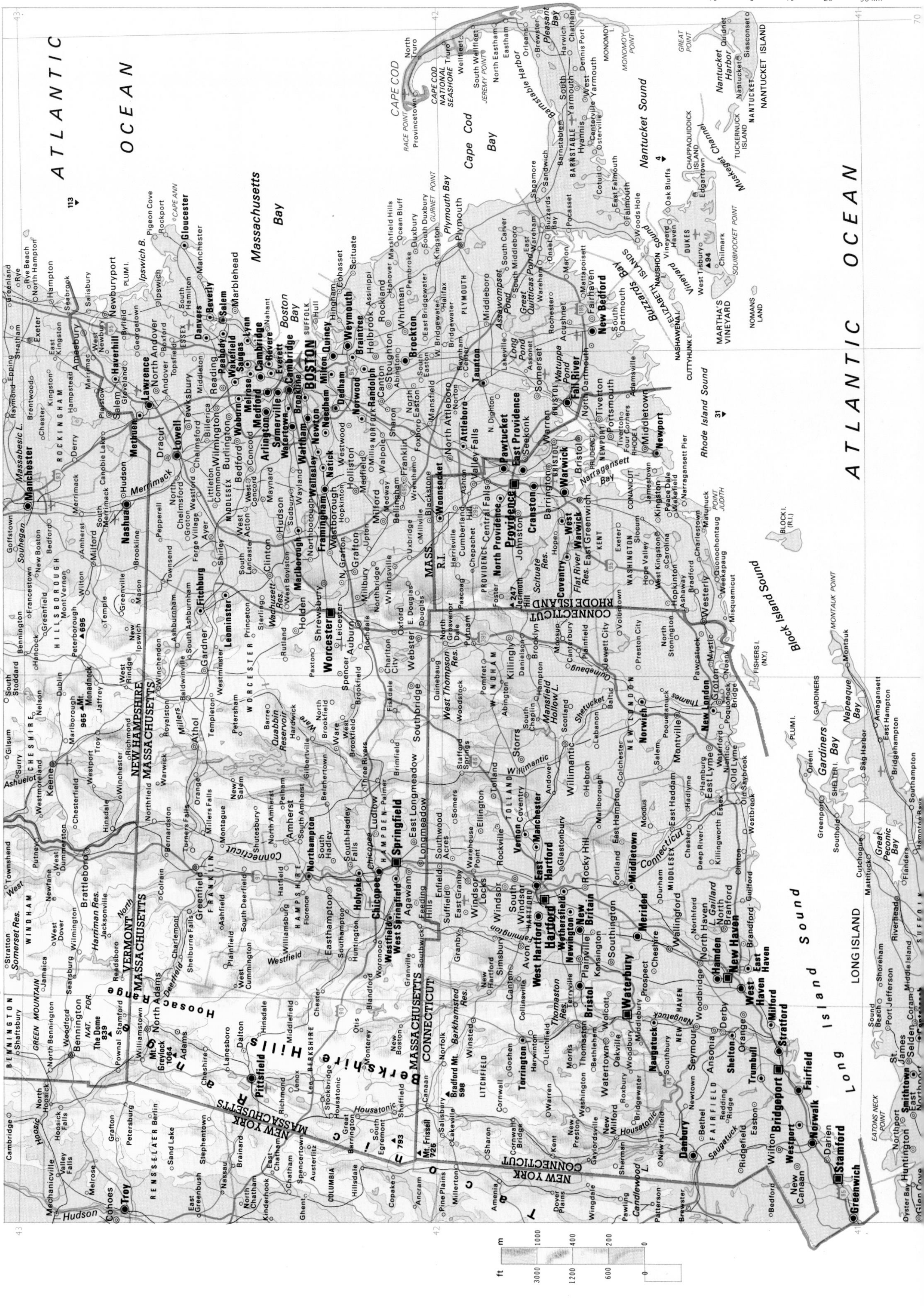

ATLANTIC OCEAN

ATLANTIC OCEAN

CAPE COD

Cape Cod Bay

Massachusetts Bay

Nantucket Sound

NANTUCKET ISLAND

MARTHA'S VINEYARD

NOMANS LAND

Rhode Island Sound

Narragansett Bay

Buzzards Bay

Block Island Sound

Long Island Sound

LONG ISLAND

NEW HAMPSHIRE

VERMONT

MASSACHUSETTS

CONNECTICUT

RHODE ISLAND

NEW YORK

BOSTON

Worcester

Springfield

Providence

Hartford

New Haven

Bridgeport

Stamford

Manchester

Nashua

Lowell

Lawrence

Cambridge

Quincy

Brockton

Fall River

New Bedford

Newport

Pawtucket

Cranston

Warwick

Woonsocket

Pittsfield

Keene

Fitchburg

Leominster

Gloucester

Salem

Lynn

Quabbin Reservoir

Connecticut

Housatonic

Berkshire Hills

Green Mountains

Hoosac

ft   m
3000 1000   400   200
1200 600   0

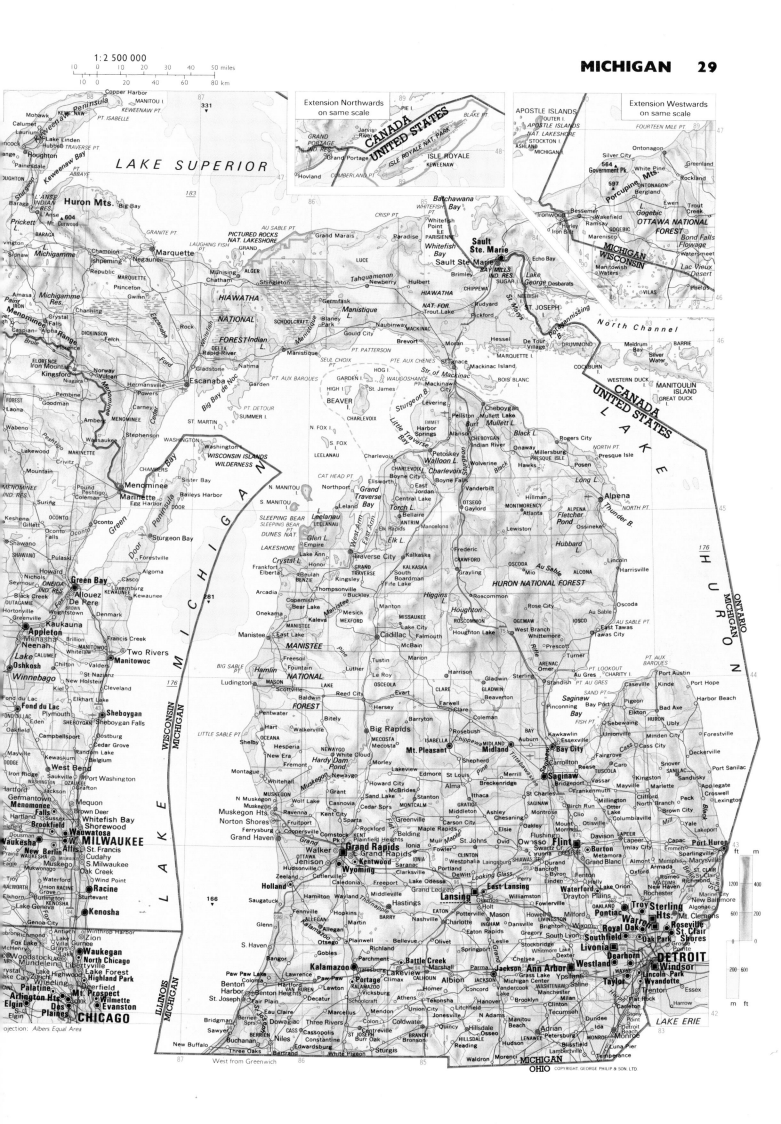

1:2 500 000

Projection : Albers Equal Area

West from Greenwich

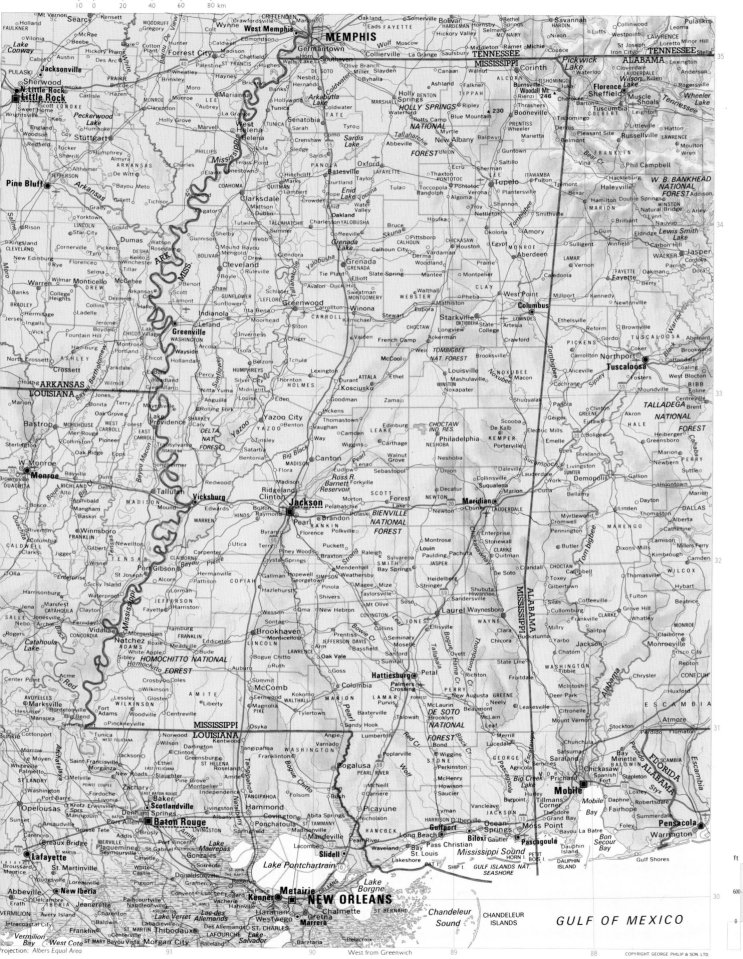

1 : 2 500 000

10 0   10   20   30   40   50 miles
10 0   20   40   60   80 km

Projection: Albers Equal Area

West from Greenwich

COPYRIGHT GEORGE PHILIP & SON. LTD.

GULF OF MEXICO

1:2 500 000

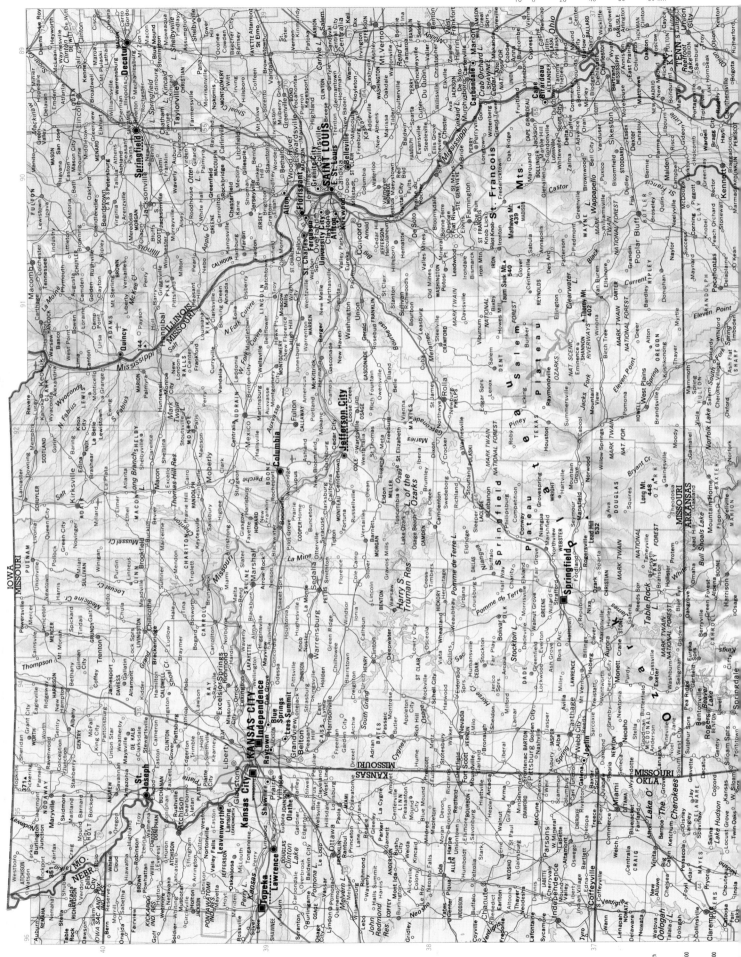

1:3 750 000

MONTANA

NORTH DAKOTA
MONTANA

CANADA
UNITED STATES

SASKATCHEWAN
MONTANA

ALBERTA
MONTANA

MONTANA
WYOMING

IDAHO
MONTANA

Billings

Great Falls

Helena

Butte

Bozeman

Missoula

Kalispell

Lethbridge

Medicine Hat

ROCKY   MOUNTAINS

Bighorn Mts.

Beartooth Range

Bitterroot Range

Salmon River Mountains

YELLOWSTONE NATIONAL PARK

Projection: Albers' Equal Area

COPYRIGHT GEORGE PHILIP & SON LTD.

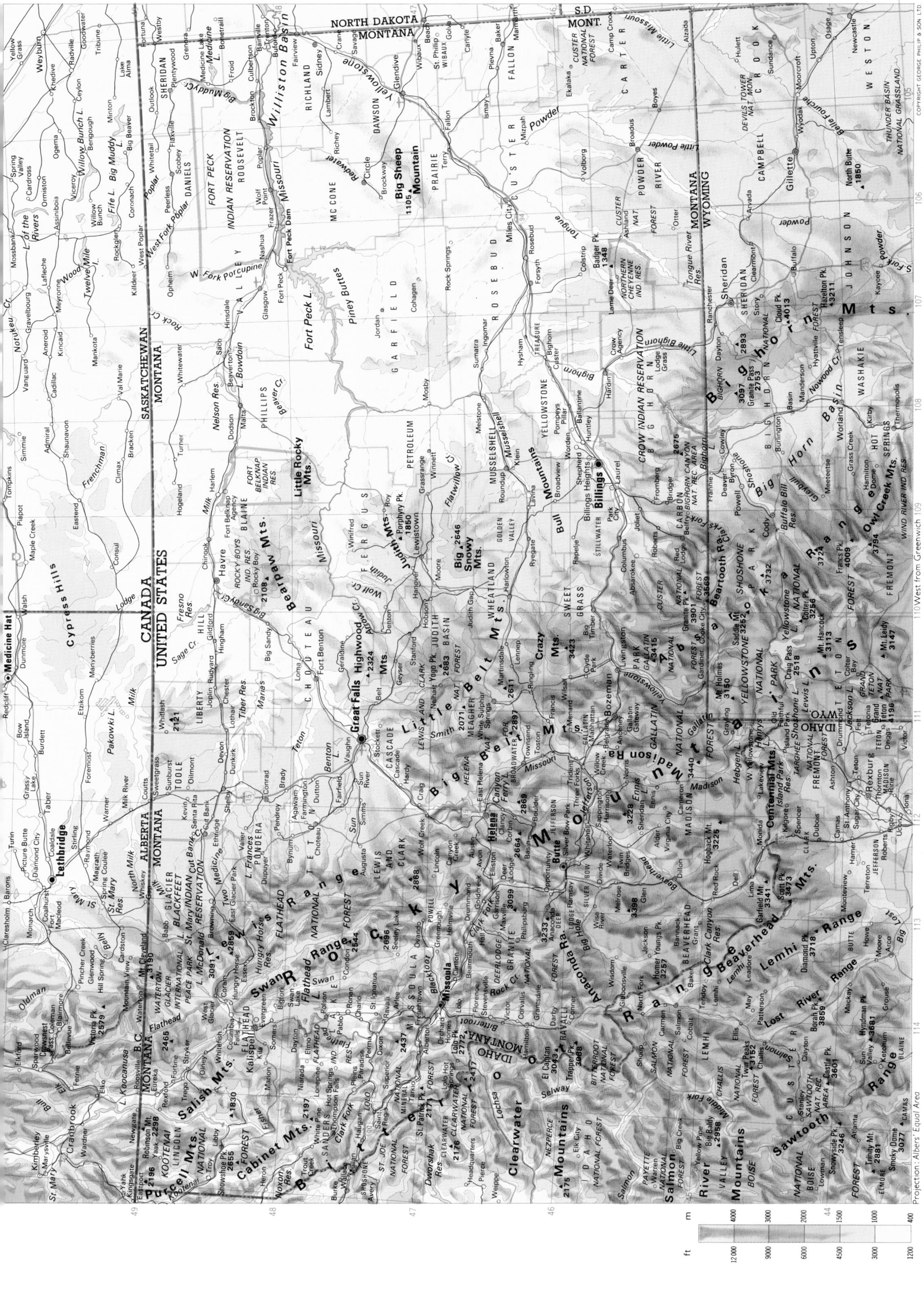

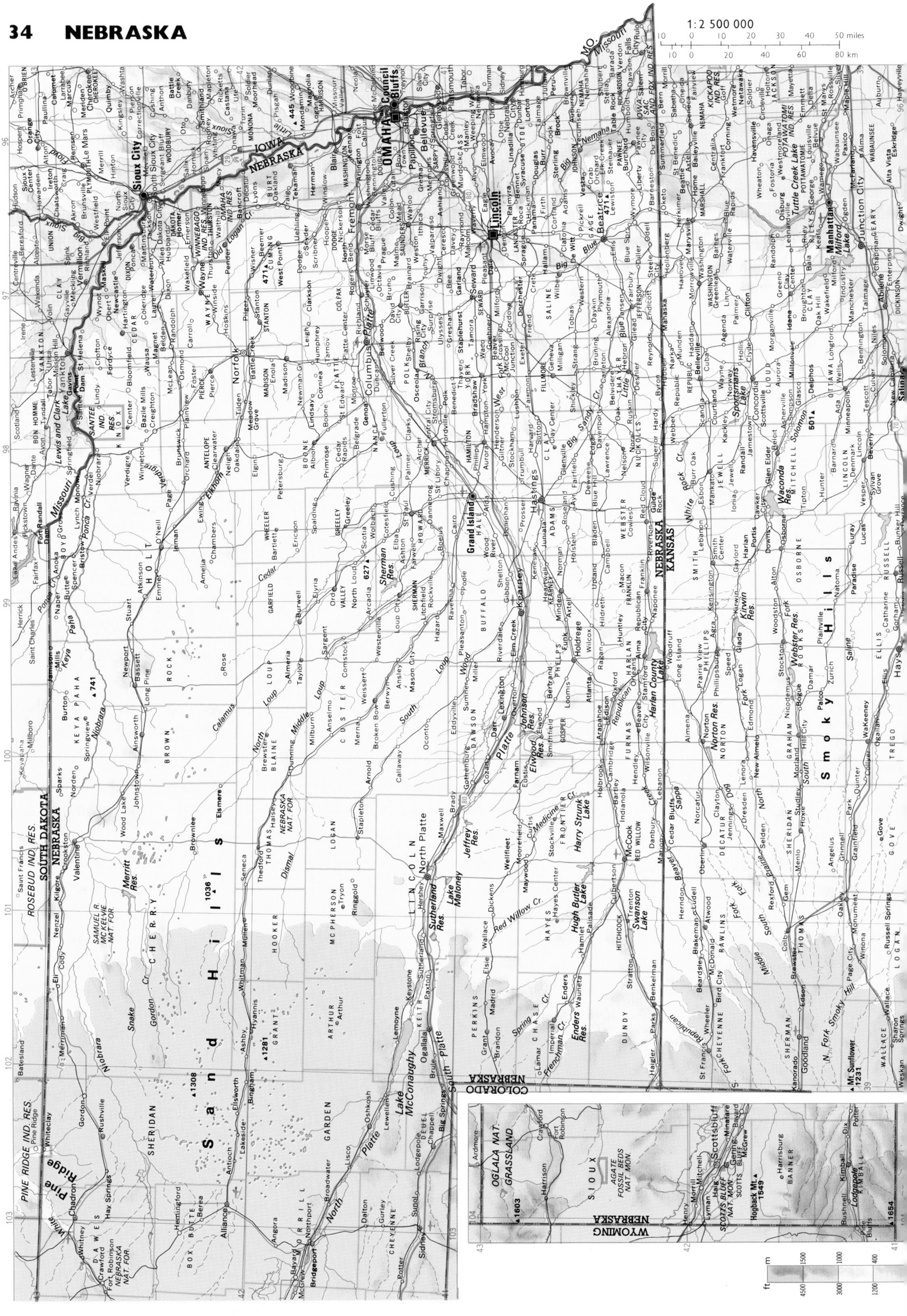

1:2 500 000

10   0   10   20   30   40   50 miles
10   0   20   40   60   80 km

States and major labels

IOWA

NEBRASKA

OMAHA

Council Bluffs

Lincoln

Sioux City

MISSOURI

SOUTH DAKOTA

NEBRASKA

KANSAS

COLORADO

WYOMING

Sand Hills

Smoky Hills

ROSEBUD IND. RES.

PINE RIDGE IND. RES.

Pine Ridge

SAMUEL R. McKELVIE NAT. FOR.

NEBRASKA NAT. FOR.

Grand Island

Norfolk

Columbus

Fremont

Hastings

Beatrice

Manhattan

Salina

Lake McConaughy

Missouri

Niobrara

Platte

North Platte

South Platte

Loup

Middle Loup

North Loup

South Loup

Elkhorn

Republican

Lewis and Clark Lake

Fort Randall Dam

Gavins Point Dam

Merritt Res.

Sherman Res.

Lake Maloney

Sutherland Res.

Harlan County Lake

Swanson Lake

Enders Res.

Medicine Creek Res.

Harry Strunk Lake

Hugh Butler Lake

Jeffrey Res.

Red Willow Cr.

Frenchman Cr.

Keya Paha

Snake

Dismal

Calamus

Tuttle Creek Lake

Milford Lake

Waconda Res.

Webster Res.

Kirwin Res.

Norton Res.

▲741   ▲1281   ▲1308   ▲1036   ▲627   ▲501   ▲471

Inset (Western Nebraska panhandle)

WYOMING

NEBRASKA

COLORADO

SIOUX

OGLALA NAT. GRASSLAND

AGATE FOSSIL BEDS NAT. MON.

SCOTTS BLUFF NAT. MON.

Scottsbluff

Fort Robinson

Hogback Mt. ▲1549

Mt. Sunflower ▲1231

▲1603   ▲1654

m 1500 1000 400
ft 4500 3000 1200

1:2 500 000

10 0 10 20 30 40 50 miles
10 0 20 40 60 80 km

IDAHO
NEVADA

Great Basin

Benio
Trident Peak 2558
Continental Lake
McDermitt
FORT MC DERMITT IND. RES.
DUCK VALLEY IND. RES.
Owyhee
S. Fork Owyhee
Owyhee
Mountain City
Jackpot
San Jacinto 2485
Contact

Alkali Lake
Massacre Lake
Vya
HUMBOLDT
Santa Rosa Range
HUMBOLDT NATIONAL FOREST
Wild Horse Res.
Matterhorn 3304
N. Fork Humboldt
Saqnon Falls

SUMMIT LAKE IND. RES.
Summit Lake
2864
Bull Creek Mts.
NAT. 2966 FOREST
Granite Peak
Quinn
Desert Ranch Res.
Tuscarora Mts.
Independence Mts. 3182
Bishop Creek Res.
Montello

High Rock Lake 2593
Black Rock Desert
Quinn
HUMBOLDT
Little Humboldt
Paradise Valley
Willow Creek Res.
Tuscarora
N. Fork Humboldt
Bruneau
Deeth
Wells
Cobre
Oasis
3265

Granite Range
Jackson Mts. 2720
Desert Valley
2645
Rock Cr.
Carlin
Humboldt
Elko
ELKO
Snow Water Lake
Pequop Mts.
Goshute Valley
Toana Ra.

WASHOE
Smoke Creek Desert
Gerlach
Empire
GREAT
Humboldt
Winnemucca
Golconda
Battle Mountain
Beowawe
SOUTH FORK IND. RES.
Ruby Dome 3471
Halleck 3437
3128
3050

PYRAMID LAKE IND.
Pyramid Lake
Sutcliffe
Seven Troughs Range
Rye Patch Res.
2997
PERSHING
Mill City
Valmy
2950
Cortez Mts.
Sulphur Springs Ra.
Ruby Valley Franklin Lake
Currie
Goshute Lake
3188
Antelope Ra.
Goshute Mts.

Virginia Mts. 2550
Black Springs
Wadsworth
Fernley
Hazen
Trinity Range
Humboldt Ra.
2236
Oreana
Unionville
2979
2566
Tobin Ra.
Reese
SHOSHONE Ra.
2793
Pine Cr.
Ruby Lake
3275
Alkali Flats
Cherry Creek
WHITE PINE
NATIONAL

Reno
Sparks
STOREY
Silver Springs
Carson Sink
Humboldt Sink
Humboldt Salt Marsh
Stillwater Range
2713
Austin
LANDER
Simpson Park Mts.
3089
EUREKA
Newark Lake
3235
Diamond Mts.
North Schell Peak 3622
McGill

Washoe
Virginia City
FALLON IND. RES.
Stillwater
Fallon
Carson Lake
2679
Clan Alpine Mts.
3040
Desatoya Mts.
Bunker Hill 3497
Reese
3189
Eureka
3189
3080
Ruth
Ely
East Ely
Schell Creek Range
NATIONAL
Mt. Moriah 3673

Carson City
Wabuska
WALKER
DOUGLAS
Weed Heights
Gardnerville
LYON
Smith
Wellington
Topaz Lake
Lahontan Reservoir
Walker
BASIN
3143
Toiyabe Range
TOIYABE
3593
Arc Dome
Mt. Jefferson 3599
3309
Toquima Range
Monitor Range
3123
Hot Creek Range
Duckwater
Lund
Preston 3509
White Pine Range
Railroad Valley
Grant Range
3351
3383
EGAN RANGE
Snake Range
Wheeler Peak 3982
Spring Valley

Artesia Lake
Walker Lake
Gillis Ra.
Gabbs Valley Ra.
2548
MINERAL
Gabbs
NATIONAL FOREST
Round Mountain
Warm Springs
Troy Peak 3444
Adams-McGill Res.
Coal Valley
Seaman Ra.
Pahroc Ra.
Pioche
Ursine
Caselton

3426
Mt. Grant
Babbitt
Hawthorne
Luning
Mina
TOIYABE NAT. FOR.
Excelsior Mts.
Columbus Salt Marsh
Tonopah
N Y E
2866
Kawich Ra.
Cactus Flat
Warm Springs
3123
Panaca
Caliente
3351
Hiko 2664
Templute
LINCOLN

Mono Lake 3610 3794
Brawley Peaks 2913
TOIYABE NAT.
Mount Montgomery
Boundary Peak 4007
ESMERALDA
Mud Lake
Cactus Ra.
Belted Ra.
2566
Groom Lake
Alamo
Elgin
Pahranagat Ra.

Sierra Nevada
Lee Vining 3031 3975
Mt. Ritter 4010
Mammoth Lakes
Benton
Dyer
Goldfield
Lida
Gold Point
Pahute Mesa
Sarcobatus Flat
Frenchman L.
Indian Springs
Spotted Ra.
Pintwater Ra.
Desert Ra.
Mormon Mts.
2259

YOSEMITE NAT. PARK
MARIPOSA MADERA
INYO NAT. FOR.
Lake Crowley
Waucoba Mt. 3390
Tin Mt. 2729
2151
Yucca L.
Beatty
Amargosa
Lathrop Wells
Hayford Peak 3021
Sheep Range
Mesquite
Bunkerville

DEATH VALLEY NAT. MON.
Saline Valley
Cottonwood Mts.
Panamint Ra.
Amargosa Ra.
Amargosa Desert
Amargosa Valley
CLARK
Moapa
Logandale
Overton
ARIZONA NEVADA

Lone Pine
Owens L.
INYO
Cartago
Pahrump
Charleston Peak 3633
North Las Vegas
Spring Mts.
LAKE MEAD NAT. REC. AREA
Muddy Mts. 1635
Las Vegas
Sunrise Manor
East Las Vegas
Henderson
Lake Mead
1757
Winchester
Paradise
Virgin

Inset (lower left):

NEVADA
CALIFORNIA
Spring Mts.
Winchester
Paradise
Henderson
Las Vegas
East Las Vegas
Lake Mead
Blue Diamond
Goodsprings
Jean
Roach L.
Mesquite L.
Clark Mt. 2417
Nipton
1442
Cima
SAN BERNARDINO
Baker
CLARK
McCullough Mts.
2142
LAKE MEAD NAT. REC. AREA
Colorado
Boulder City
Searchlight
Davis Dam
ARIZONA
Providence Mts.

Continuation outwards on same scale
Projection : Albers Equal Area
West from Greenwich
COPYRIGHT GEORGE PHILIP & SON LTD.

0 200 400 1000 1500 2000 3000 4000 m
0 600 1200 3000 4500 6000 9000 12,000 ft

1:1 250 000

10   0   10   20 miles
10   0   10   20   30 km

Delson • St-Luc • Ste-Brigide-d'Iberville • Ange-Gardien • Bromont • Waterloo • Deauville • **Sherbrooke** • Lennoxville • La Patrie • Notre-Dame-des-Bois

St-Jean • Iberville • St-Alexandre • Farnham • East-Farnham • Adamsville • Eastman • L. Magog • Sawyerville • Salmon Mt. 1025 • Rump Mt. 1112

Napierville • Henryville • Pike River • Stanbridge-East • Dunham • Sutton • Brome • Lac-Brome • Magog • Waterville • Compton • Second L. • Kennebago L.

Barrington • Lacolle • Bedford • Sutton 972 • Mansonville • Ayer's Cliff • L. Massawippi • Coaticook • Mt. Hereford 841 • Pittsburg • First Connecticut • Aziscohos L. • Oquossoc • FRANKLIN

Hemmingford • Philipsburg • Abercorn • **QUEBEC** • **CANADA** • Stewartstown • Francis • Rangeley

Houses Point • Missisquoi B. • SUTTON MTS. • North Troy • Derby Line • **UNITED STATES** • Beecher Falls • West Stewartstown • Wilsons Mills • Mooselookmeguntic L.

45 • Champlain • Alburg • Highgate Center • Richford • East Berkshire • Jay Peak 1177 • Newport • Derby • Morgan • Gore Mt. 1015 • Colebrook • Dixville Notch • Upper Richardson L. • Elephant Mt. 1150

Mooers • Swanton • Sheldon • Enosburg Falls • Montgomery Center • Troy • ORLEANS • East Charleston • Island Pond • Lemington • Errol • Lower Richardson L.

West Chazy • Chazy • Isle La Motte • St. Albans • East Fairfield • Bakersfield • Lowell • Belvidere Mt. 1024 • Irasburg • Orleans • Barton • L. Willoughby • ESSEX • North Stratford • COOS • OXFORD • Andover

North Hero • Grand Isle • Georgia Center • FRANKLIN • Waterville • Albany • Glover • Westmore • Nulhegan • Stratford • Umbagog L. • Rumford

CLINTON • GRAND ISLE • Fairfax • Eden • Belvidere Mt. • Greensboro • Sutton • West Burke • Groveton • West Milan • Blue Mt. 1135 • Milan • Hanover

Morrisonville • South Hero • Milton • Jeffersonville • Johnson • LAMOILLE • Hardwick • Lyndonville • Passumpsic • Guildhall • Berlin • Mt. Success 1094 • Bethel

Plattsburg • Lake Champlain • Cambridge • Mt. Mansfield 1339 • Morrisville • Hyde Park • Lamoille • CALEDONIA • Stone Mt. 839 • Mt. Cabot 1244 • Gorham • Old Speck Mt. 1274 • Gilead

Port Kent • Keeseville • Winooski • Essex Jct. • Underhill Flats • Stowe • Cabot • St. Johnsbury • Concord • Lunenburg • Lancaster • Whitefield • Meadows • WHITE MOUNTAIN NAT. FOR. • North Waterford

Clintonville • **Burlington** • Williston • CHITTENDEN • Waterbury Center 1083 • WORCESTER MTS. • Marshfield • Danville • Barnet • Moore Res. • Littleton • Bethlehem • Twin Mountain • Mt. Washington 1917 • Mt. Carrigain 1476 • **NEW HAMPSHIRE** • MAINE

South Burlington • Shelburne • Richmond • Waterbury • WASHINGTON • Plainfield • Groton • Ammonoosuc • Franconia • Mt. Lafayette 1600 • WHITE MOUNTAIN • WHITE Mountains

Lewis • Essex • Hinesburg • Huntington • Camels Hump 1244 • **Montpelier** • Barre • Lisbon • Woodsville • Benton • GRAFTON • Lincoln • NATIONAL FOREST • North Conway • Jackson • Glen • Lovell

Winooski • NEW YORK • VERMONT • Mad • Waitsfield • Northfield • Wells • West Topsham • Mt. Moosilauke 1466 • Mt. Tecumseh 1220 • Bartlett • Intervale • Bridgton

Westport • Ferrisburg • Warren • Roxbury • Brookfield • East Corinth • Haverhill • East Haverhill • Glencliff • Woodstock • Waterville Valley 1059 • Conway • North Waterford

Addison • Bristol • Vergennes • GREEN MOUNTAIN • Granville • Randolph Center • Chelsea • Bradford • Warren • West Thornton • Passaconaway • Denmark

ADDISON • Middlebury • East Middleburg • NATIONAL FOREST • Randolph • East Randolph • West Fairlee • Fairlee • Carr Mt. 1058 • Stinson Lake • Sandwich Mt. 1217 • Wonalancet • CARROLL • CUMBERLAND

Crown Point • Bridport • Cornwall • Salisbury • Hancock • Rochester • ORANGE • Bradford • Wentworth • West Campton • Sandwich • West Ossipee • East Sebago • Sebago

44 • Shoreham • Leicester • Forest Dale • Bethel • South Royalton • South Strafford • Lyme • Rumney • Center Sandwich • Tamworth • Kezar Falls

Chilson • Whiting • VERMONT • NEW HAMPSHIRE • White • Sharon • West Plymouth • Squam L. • Ossipee L. • Effingham Falls

Ticonderoga • Brandon • Stockbridge • Pittsfield • Barnard • Norwich • Smarts Mt. 988 • Dorchester • Plymouth • Holderness • Moultonboro • Center Ossipee

Hague • Hubbardton • Pittsford • Chittenden • Sherburne • Woodstock • South Pomfret • Quechee • Wilder • Hanover • West Canaan • Hebron • Ashland • Center Harbor • Melvin Village • Ossipee

WARREN • L. George • Benson • Proctor • Mendon • Bridgewater • White River Junc. • Canaan • Mt. Cardigan 951 • Meredith • Lake Winnipesaukee • Tuftonboro • West Newfield

Huletts Landing • L. Bomoseen • Castleton • Rutland 1293 • WINDSOR • Hartland • Lebanon • Enfield • Alexandria • Newfound L. • New Hampton • YORK

Whitehall • Fair Haven • West Rutland • Plymouth • South Woodstock • Meriden • Enfield Center • Grafton • Bristol • Winnipesaukee • Wolfeboro • North Shapleigh

Poultney • RUTLAND • Clarendon • Tyson • Plainfield 848 • Danbury • Laconia • Alton Bay • Sanbornville • Shapleigh • Waterboro

Fort Ann • Middletown Springs • Wallingford • East Wallingford • Healdville • Amsden • Grantham • Andover • BELKNAP • Wakefield

Kingsbury • Tinmouth • Wells • Ludlow 1028 • Ascutney • Sugar • SULLIVAN • Croydon Flat • Sunapee • New London • Northfield • Franklin • Tilton • Belmont • Gilmanton • Milton • Alfred

South Hartford • Pawlet • Danby • Proctorsville • Windsor • Claremont • Mt. Kearsarge 895 • Salisbury Heights • Lower Gilmanton • Farmington • Sanford

Hartford • West Pawlet • East Rupert 1160 • North Springfield • Newport • Mt. Sunapee • North Sutton • Salisbury • Center Barnstead • Strafford • Rochester • North Berwick

WASHINGTON • Rupert • Dorset • East Dorset • Peru • Weston • Chester • North Charlestown • Newbury • MERRIMACK • Warner • Boscawen • Pittsfield • Loudon • Center Strafford • Somersworth • Ogunquit

West Hebron • Salem • Manchester • GREEN • Londonderry • Grafton • South Charlestown • Washington • Penacook • North Chichester • Gossville • Northwood • East Barrington • Dover

Equinox Mt. 1164 • Rawsonville • Cambridgeport • Bellows Falls • Lempster • East Lempster • Henniker • Hopkinton • **Concord** • Northwood • Durham • Great B. • Portsmouth • Newmarket

MOUNTAIN • GREEN • Jamaica • Walpole • Marlow • Hillsboro • Upper Village • Bow • Suncook • Nottingham • Epping • Greenland • Kittery

Middle Falls • Greenwich • Stratton 1176 • Somerset Res. • Townshend • Westminster • Gilsum • South Stoddard • Hillsboro • Dunbarton • Hooksett • South Deerfield • Raymond • Stratham • Rye Beach

Cambridge • BENNINGTON • Shaftsbury • WEST • WINDHAM • Surry • CHESHIRE • Nelson • Hancock • Bennington • Goffstown • **Manchester** • Massabesic L. • Brentwood • North Hampton

Hoosick • North Hoosick • NATIONAL • Jamaica • West Dover • Newfane • West Dummerston • Keene • Dublin • Greenfield • New Boston • Chester • Exeter • Hampton

Hoosick Falls • North Bennington • Woodford • Wilmington • Marlborough • West Swanzey • Troy • HILLSBOROUGH • Mont Vernon • Amherst • Bedford • Derry • Kingston • Seabrook

RENSSELAER • **Bennington** • The Dome 839 • Harriman Res. • Jacksonville • Chesterfield • Westport • Mt. Monadnock 965 • Jaffrey • Milford • Merrimack • South Merrimack • Canobie Lake • Plaistow • West Newbury • Newburyport

FOREST • Readsboro • West Westport • Winchester • Hinsdale • West Rindge • New Ipswich • Temple • Wilton • Salem • Haverhill • ATLANTIC OCEAN

VERMONT • **MASSACHUSETTS** • Northfield • **NEW HAMPSHIRE** • **MASSACHUSETTS** • Richmond • Winchester • Greenville • Mason • Brookline • **Nashua** • Hudson • **Methuen** • **Lawrence** • Ipswich B.

Williamstown • North Adams • Mt. Greylock 1064 • Adams • Colrain • Bernardston • Warwick • Royalston • Millers • Ashburnham • Townsend • Groton • North Chelmsford • **Lowell** • Dracut • North Andover • Boxford • **Gloucester**

43

Lake Champlain • Richelieu • ESSEX • Otter Cr. • GREEN MOUNTAIN RANGE • TACONIC RANGE • HOOSAC RANGE • BATTEN KILL • Connecticut R. • OMPOMPANOOSUC • Wells R. • Williams R. • Black R. • West R. • Deerfield R. • North R. • Ashuelot R. • Contoocook R. • Souhegan R. • Merrimack R. • Salmon Falls R. • Saco R. • Androscoggin R. • Pemigewasset R.

ft   m
4500 1500
3000 1000
1200 400
600   200
0

1:1 250 000

10   0   10   20 miles
10   0   10   20   30 km

ATLANTIC

OCEAN

LONG ISLAND

Long Island Sound

NEW YORK

PENNSYLVANIA

NEW JERSEY

CONNECTICUT

DELAWARE

MARYLAND

Delaware Bay

Kittatinny Mts.

Pocono Mts.

PHILADELPHIA

NEWARK

NEW YORK

Projection: Lambert's Conformal Conic

West from Greenwich

COPYRIGHT. GEORGE PHILIP & SON. LTD.

ft   m
4500 1500
3000 1000
1200 400
600   200
0

1:2 600 000

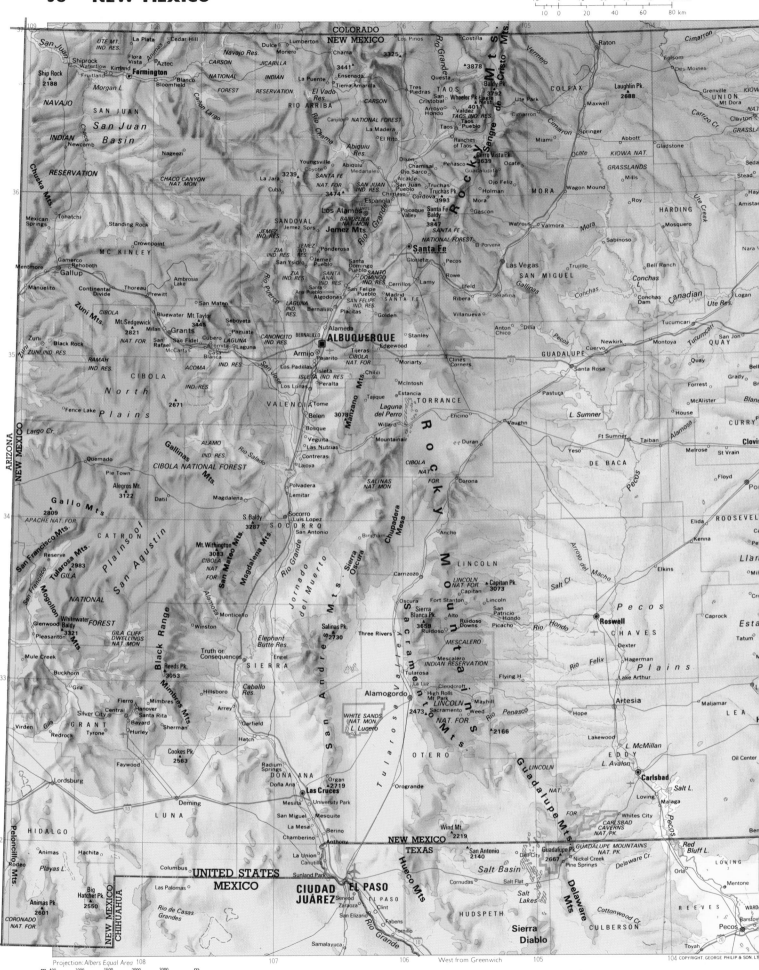

Projection: Albers Equal Area

West from Greenwich

COPYRIGHT. GEORGE PHILIP & SON. LT

1:2 500 000

10 0 10 20 30 40 50 miles
10 0 20 40 60 80 km

ATLANTIC OCEAN

NEW YORK CITY
1:1 250 000

CANADA
UNITED STATES

LAKE ONTARIO

LAKE ERIE

TORONTO
MISSISSAUGA

St. Catharines

Projection: Albers Equal Area

West from Greenwich

COPYRIGHT GEORGE PHILIP & SON, LTD

1:2 500 000

10   0   10   20   30   40   50 miles
10   0   20   40   60   80 km

ATLANTIC OCEAN

VIRGINIA

NORTH CAROLINA

SOUTH CAROLINA

GEORGIA

TENNESSEE

W. VA.

KENTUCKY

Chesapeake Bay

Virginia Beach
Chesapeake
Norfolk
Portsmouth
Newport News
Hampton
Suffolk

Richmond
Lakeside
Bon Air
Petersburg
Hopewell
Colonial Heights

Lynchburg
Roanoke
Salem
Vinton
Blacksburg

Elizabeth City
Edenton
Washington
Greenville
Kinston
New Bern

Rocky Mount
Wilson
Goldsboro

Raleigh
Durham
Chapel Hill
Cary

Henderson
Oxford

Greensboro
Burlington
High Point
Winston-Salem

Danville
Eden
Reidsville

Fayetteville
Jacksonville
Wilmington

Charlotte
Gastonia
Kannapolis
Concord
Albemarle
Salisbury
Statesville
Hickory
Lenoir

Rock Hill
Gaffney
Spartanburg
Greer

Boone

Myrtle Beach
North Myrtle Beach

Georgetown

Cape Hatteras
Hatteras Island
Ocracoke I.
Cape Lookout
Pamlico Sound
Albemarle Sound
Roanoke I.
Kill Devil Hills
Nags Head
Currituck Sound

Smith I.
Cape Fear

Continuation Westward on same scale

TENNESSEE   **NORTH CAROLINA**   **GEORGIA**

Knoxville
Asheville
Hendersonville
Waynesville
Spartanburg
Greenville

Great Smoky Mts. Nat. Park
Nantahala Nat. Forest
Cherokee
Pisgah Nat. Forest

Mt. Mitchell 2037

m 1500 1000 400 200 0
ft 4500 3000 1200 600 0 200 600 6000

1:2 500 000

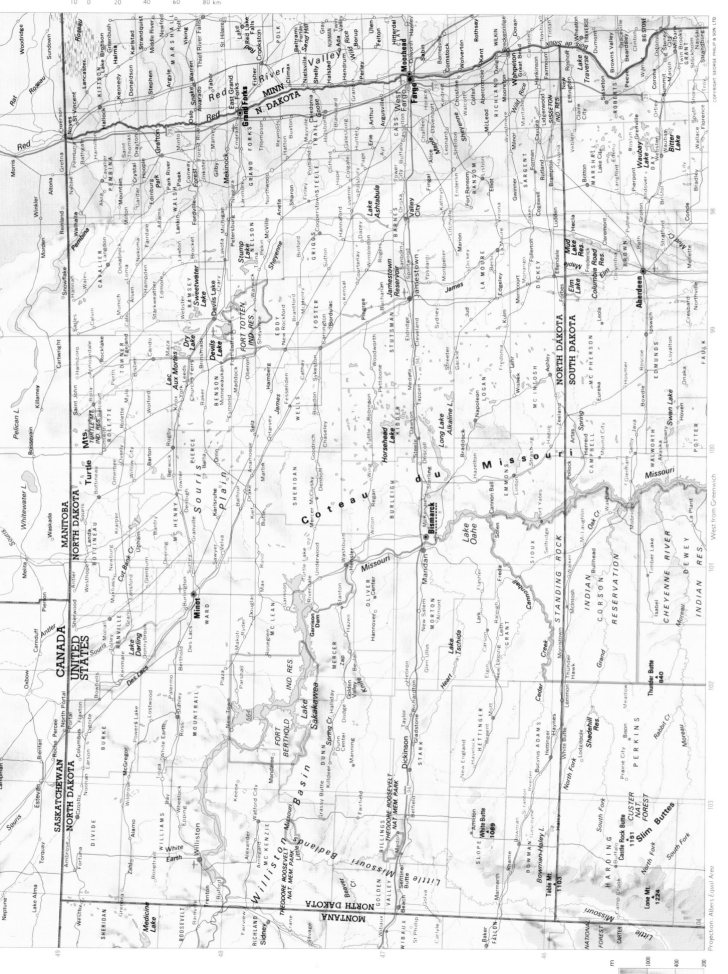

1 : 2 500 000

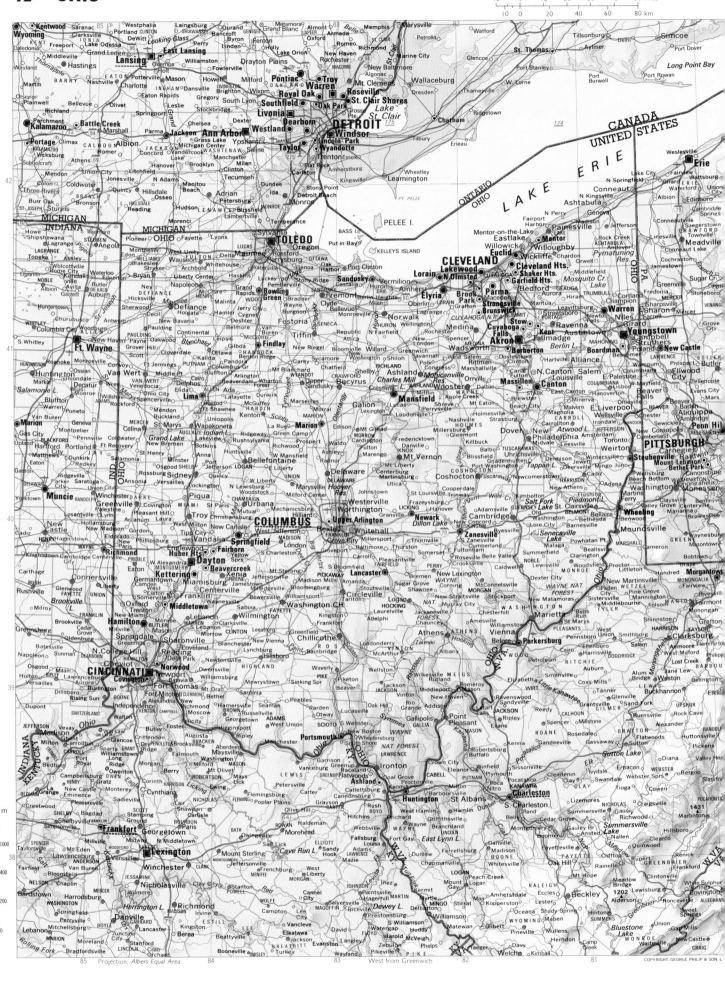

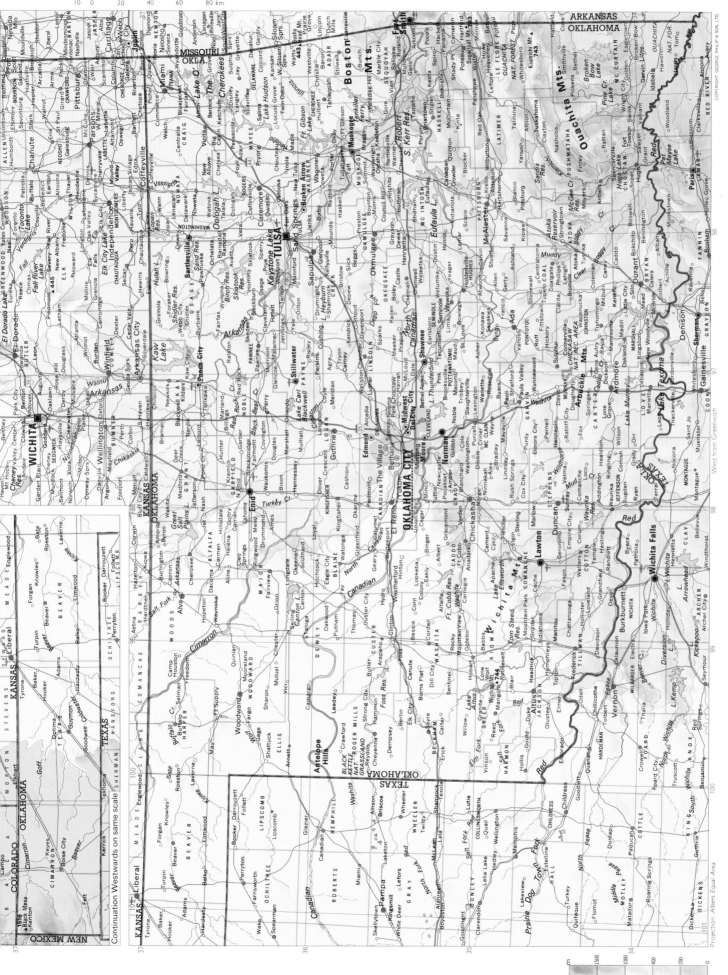

1 : 2 500 000

10 0 10 20 30 40 50 miles
10 0 20 40 60 80 km

COPYRIGHT GEORGE PHILIP & SON LTD.

Continuation Westwards on same scale

Projection: Albers Equal Area

1:2 500 000

Projection: Albers Equal Area

1 : 2 500 000

10   0   10   20   30   40   50 miles

10   0   20   40   60   80 km

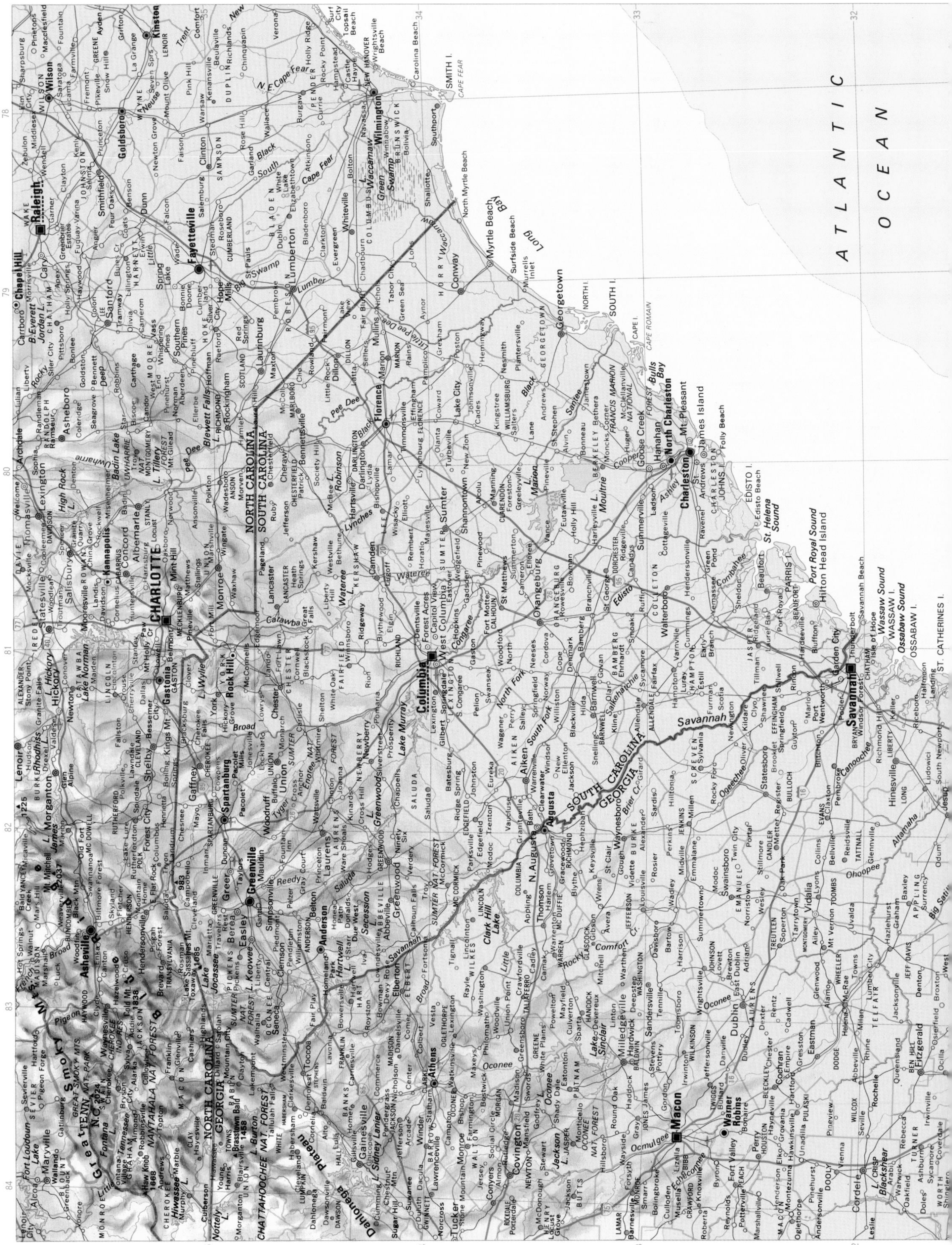

ATLANTIC OCEAN

m 1500 1000 400 200 0

ft 4500 3000 1200 600 0 -200 -600

1 : 2 500 000

10 0 10 20 30 40 50 miles
10 0 20 40 60 80 km

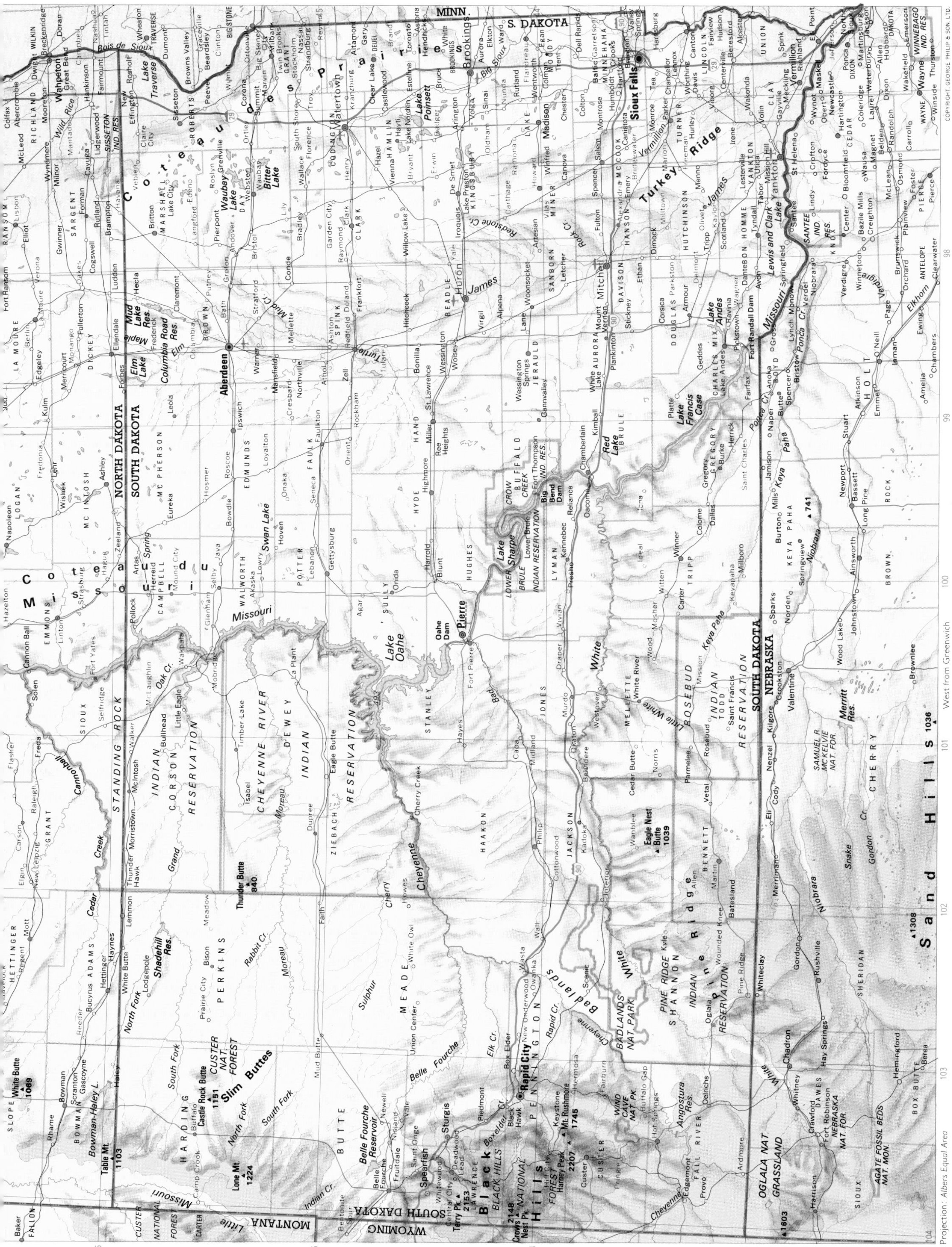

MINN.

S. DAKOTA

NORTH DAKOTA
SOUTH DAKOTA

MONTANA
WYOMING | SOUTH DAKOTA

SOUTH DAKOTA
NEBRASKA

Sioux Falls
Brookings
Watertown
Aberdeen
Huron
Pierre
Mitchell
Yankton
Rapid City
Sturgis

Missouri
Lake Oahe
Oahe Dam
Lake Sharpe
Big Bend Dam
Lake Francis Case
Fort Randall Dam
Lewis and Clark Lake

Cheyenne River
White River
Bad River
Belle Fourche
Grand
Moreau

STANDING ROCK INDIAN RESERVATION
CHEYENNE RIVER INDIAN RESERVATION
LOWER BRULE INDIAN RESERVATION
CROW CREEK IND. RES.
PINE RIDGE INDIAN RESERVATION
ROSEBUD INDIAN RESERVATION
SISSETON IND. RES.
SANTEE IND. RES.
WINNEBAGO IND. RES.

Black Hills
BLACK HILLS NATIONAL FOREST
CUSTER NAT. FOREST
BADLANDS NAT. PARK
WIND CAVE NAT. PK
Mt. Rushmore 1745
Harney Peak 2207
Crows Nest Pk. 2148
Terry Pk. 2153

OGLALA NAT. GRASSLAND
AGATE FOSSIL BEDS NAT. MON.

Thunder Butte 840
Eagle Nest Butte 1039
White Butte 1069
Castle Rock Butte 1151
Table Mt. 1103
Lone Mt. 1224
1308
1603
1036
741

Turkey Ridge
Coteau des Prairies
Coteau du Missouri
Sand Hills
Pine Ridge
Keya Paha

Lake Traverse
Big Stone Lake
Lake Poinsett
Bitter Lake
Waubay Lake
Mud Lake Res.
Elm Lake
Swan Lake
Shadehill Res.
Angostura Res.
Belle Fourche Reservoir
Merritt Res.

Niobrara
Little White
Missouri

Projection: Albers Equal Area
West from Greenwich
COPYRIGHT GEORGE PHILIP & SON LTD

ft m
6000 2000
4500 1500
3000 1000
1200 400
600 200

Projection: Albers Equal Area

1:2 500 000

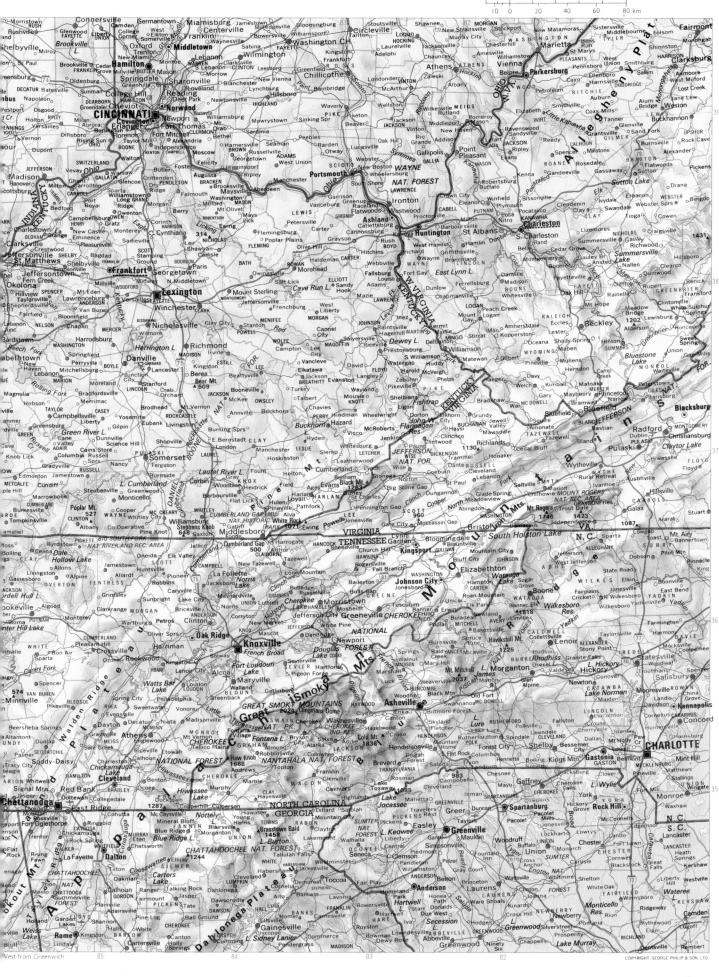

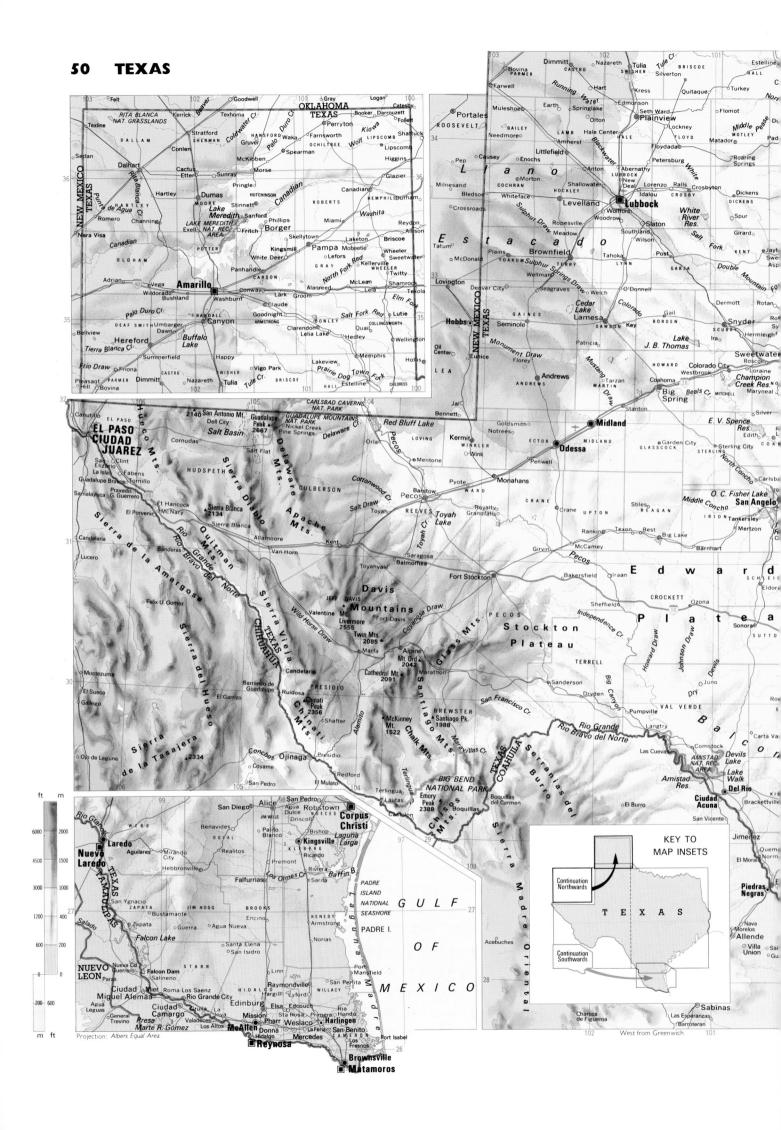

Map Insets and Labels

Top Left Inset (Oklahoma/Texas Panhandle)

OKLAHOMA
TEXAS

Felt, Goodwell, Gray, Logan, Catesby
RITA BLANCA NAT. GRASSLANDS, Kerrick, Texhoma Cr., Beaver, Booker, Darrouzett, Follett
Texline, Stratford, Farnsworth, Perryton, Kiowa, Lipscomb, Shattuck
DALLAM, SHERMAN, Gruver, Waka, OCHILTREE, Wolf, LIPSCOMB
Sedan, Dalhart, Conlen, McKibben, Spearman, HEMPHILL, Durham, Higgins
Rio Blanca Cr., Dumas, Hartley, MOORE, Stinnett, Canadian, ROBERTS, Canadian, WASHITA
punta de Agua, HARTLEY, Channing, Lake Meredith, Sanford, Miami, Reydon, Allison
Romero, LAKE MEREDITH NAT. REC. AREA, Exell, Fritch, Phillips, Borger, Skellytown, Briscoe
Nara Visa, Nara Visa, Pringle, Morse, Kingsmill, Mobeetie, Laketon, Wheeler, Sweetwater
OLDHAM, Adrian, POTTER, White Deer, Pampa, Lefors, WHEELER, Twitty
Vega, Wildorado, Bushland, Washburn, Conway, Lark, Groom, McLean, Shamrock, Lela, Texola
Amarillo, CARSON, GRAY, North Fork Red, Elm Fork
Canyon, RANDALL, ARMSTRONG, Claude, DONLEY, Clarendon, COLLINGSWORTH
Bellview, DEAF SMITH, Umbarger, Dawn, Goodnight, Lelia Lake, Hedley, Wellington
Hereford, Buffalo Lake, Happy, Quail, CHILDRESS
Frio Draw, Tierra Blanca Cr., Friona, Summerfield, SWISHER, Lakeview, Memphis, Hollis
Pleasant Hill, PARMER, Dimmitt, CASTRO, Nazareth, Tulia, Vigo Park, BRISCOE, Prairie Dog Town Fork, HALL
Bovina, Tule Cr., Estelline, CHILDRESS

Top Right Inset (Llano Estacado)

Dimmitt, Nazareth, Tulia, Tule Cr., BRISCOE, Estelline
Bovina, PARMER, Silverton, HALL
Farwell, Running Water, Hart, Kress, Quitaque, Turkey, Nort
Portales, Muleshoe, Earth, Springlake, Olton, Edmonson, Flomot, Pease
ROOSEVELT, BAILEY, Needmore, Amherst, Springlake, Plainview, Lockney, Floydada, Roaring Springs, MOTLEY, Pad
Pep, Causey, Enochs, Littlefield, Anton, Abernathy, Petersburg, FLOYD, Matador
Milnesand, COCHRAN, Morton, HOCKLEY, Shallowater, New Deal, Lorenzo, Rails, Crosbyton, DICKENS, Dickens
LAMB, HALE, Hale Center, Blackwater, White, Spur
Whiteface, Levelland, Lubbock, Wolfforth, Woodrow, Slaton, CROSBY, White River Res., Girard
Tatum, McDonald, Plains, Meadow, Southland, Wilson, Post, KENT, Jayt, Swe
Lovington, Denver City, YOAKUM, Brownfield, Tahoka, LYNN, GARZA, Double Mountain
Hobbs, Seagraves, O'Donnell, Patricia, Welch, DAWSON, Key, Lake J. B. Thomas, Dermott, Rotan
NEW MEXICO, Oil Center, Eunice, Florey, Tarzan, HOWARD, Colorado City, Westbrook, SCURRY, Snyder, Hermleigh
LEA, Jal, Bennett, ANDREWS, Andrews, Martin, Coahoma, Big Spring, Beals Cr., MITCHELL, Champion Creek Res., Maryneal, Sweetwate, Roscoe

Main Map (Central/South Texas and Rio Grande)

Canutillo, EL PASO, San Antonio Mt. 2140, Guadalupe Peak 2667, GUADALUPE MOUNTAINS NAT. PARK, CARLSBAD CAVERNS NAT. PARK
EL PASO, CIUDAD JUAREZ, Hueco Mts., Dell City, Nickel Creek, Pine Springs, Delaware, Red Bluff Lake
San Elizario, Clint, Salt Basin, Sierra Diablo Mts., Delaware Mts., Orla, Goldsmith, Notrees, Kermit, E. V. Spence Res.
Elizario, Fabens, Cornudas, Salt Flat, LOVING, WINKLER, Wink, ECTOR, Midland, MIDLAND, Garden City, GLASSCOCK, Sterling City, COKE
Guadalupe Bravos, Tornillo, Salt Flat, HUDSPETH, Apache Mts., Mentone, Pyote, Penwell, Odessa, STERLING
Samalayuca, G. Guerrero, Praxedis, Ft Hancock, Sierra Blanca 2134, CULBERSON, Cottonwood Cr., Barstow, Monahans, WARD, Crane, UPTON, Stiles, REAGAN, O. C. Fisher Lake, Middle Concho, San Angelo
El Porvenir, McNary, Sierra Blanca, Salt Draw, Toyah, Pecos, CRANE, Rankin, Texon, Big Lake, IRION, Tankersley, Mertzon
Candelaria, Sierra de la Amargosa, Quitman Mts., Allamoore, Kent, REEVES, Toyah Lake, Royalty, Grandfalls, Girvin, McCamey, Barnhart, SCHLE, Eldor
Lucero, Rio Grande, Van Horn, Toyahvale, Saragosa, Balmorhea, Pecos, Bakersfield, Iraan, EDWARD, PLATEA
Sierra Vieja, Banderas, Sierra del Hueso, Toyahvale, Fort Stockton, CROCKETT, Ozona, Sonora, SUTTO
Felix U. Gomez, Rio Bravo del Norte, JEFF DAVIS, Davis Mountains, Mt. Livermore 2555, Fort Davis, Coyangosa Draw, PECOS, Stockton Plateau, Sheffield, Independence Cr., Balcon
Moctezuma, TEXAS CHIHUAHUA, Valentine, Twin Mts. 2085, Marfa, Alpine, Mt. Ord 2042, Glass Mts., Howard Draw, Johnson Draw, TERRELL, Devils, Juno
El Sueco, Candelaria, Cathedral Mt. 2091, Marathon, Sanderson, Dryden, DRY, VAL VERDE, Langtry
Gallego, Wild Horse Draw, PRESIDIO, Ruidosa, Chinati Peak 2356, McKinney Mt. 1522, Santiago Pk. 1988, BREWSTER, San Francisco Cr., Pumpville, Comstock, Las Cuevas, Carta Val
Barranco de Guadalupe, El Garrizo, Shafter, Chalk Mts., Santiago Mts., Maravillas Cr., Rio Grande, Rio Bravo del Norte, AMISTAD NAT. REC. AREA, Devils Lake
Sierra de la Tasajera 2334, Concho, Ojinaga, Alamito, Terlingua, TEXAS COAHUILA, Serranias del Burro, Amistad Res., Lake Walk, Del Rio
Ojo de Legune, Coyame, Presidio, Redford, BIG BEND NATIONAL PARK, Lajitas, Boquillas del Carmen, Las Cuevas, El Burro, Ciudad Acuña
El Mulato, Terlingua, Emory Peak 2388, Chisos Mts., Boquillas, Sierra Madre Oriental, San Vicente, Brackettville

Bottom Left Inset (South Texas/Rio Grande Valley)

Rio Grande, San Diego, Alice, San Pedro, Robstown, NUECES, Corpus Christi
Laredo, WEBB, Benavides, JIM WELLS, Agua Dulce, Driscoll, Bishop
Nuevo Laredo, Aguilares, Mirando City, DUVAL, Palito Blanco, Kingsville, Laguna Larga
TEXAS TAMAULIPAS, Hebbronville, Realitos, Premont, Riviera, KLEBERG, Ricardo, Baffin B
San Ygnacio, ZAPATA, Falfurrias, BROOKS, Sarita, PADRE ISLAND NATIONAL SEASHORE
Salado, Bustamante, JIM HOGG, Encino, KENEDY, Armstrong, PADRE I.
Zapata, Guerra, Agua Nueva, Norias, GULF OF MEXICO
Falcon Lake, Santa Elena, San Isidro, Laguna Madre
NUEVO LEON, Nueva Cd. Guerrero, Falcon Dam, STARR, Linn, San Manuel, Port Mansfield
Paras, Ciudad Mier, Roma-Los Saenz, Rio Grande City, Raymondville, San Perlita
Miguel Aleman, Salineno, HIDALGO, Edinburg, Elsa, Lyford, WILLACY
Agua Leguas, Ciudad Camargo, Gruila, Mission, Pharr, Weslaco, Rio Hondo, CAMERON
General Trevino, Presa Marte R. Gomez, Valadeces, Los Altos, McAllen, Donna, La Feria, San Benito, Harlingen
Reynosa, Hidalgo, Mercedes, Los Fresnos, Port Isabel
Brownsville, Matamoros

Scale bar (left):
ft / m
6000 / 2000
4500 / 1500
3000 / 1000
1200 / 400
600 / 200
0 / 0
200 / 600
m / ft

Projection: Albers Equal Area

Key to Map Insets (bottom right):

KEY TO MAP INSETS
Continuation Northwards
TEXAS
Continuation Southwards

West from Greenwich
Jimenez, Piedras Negras, El Moral, Quema, Norm, Nava, Morelos, Allende, Villa Union, Sabinas, Las Esperanzas, Barroteran, Charcos de Figueroa, Acebuches

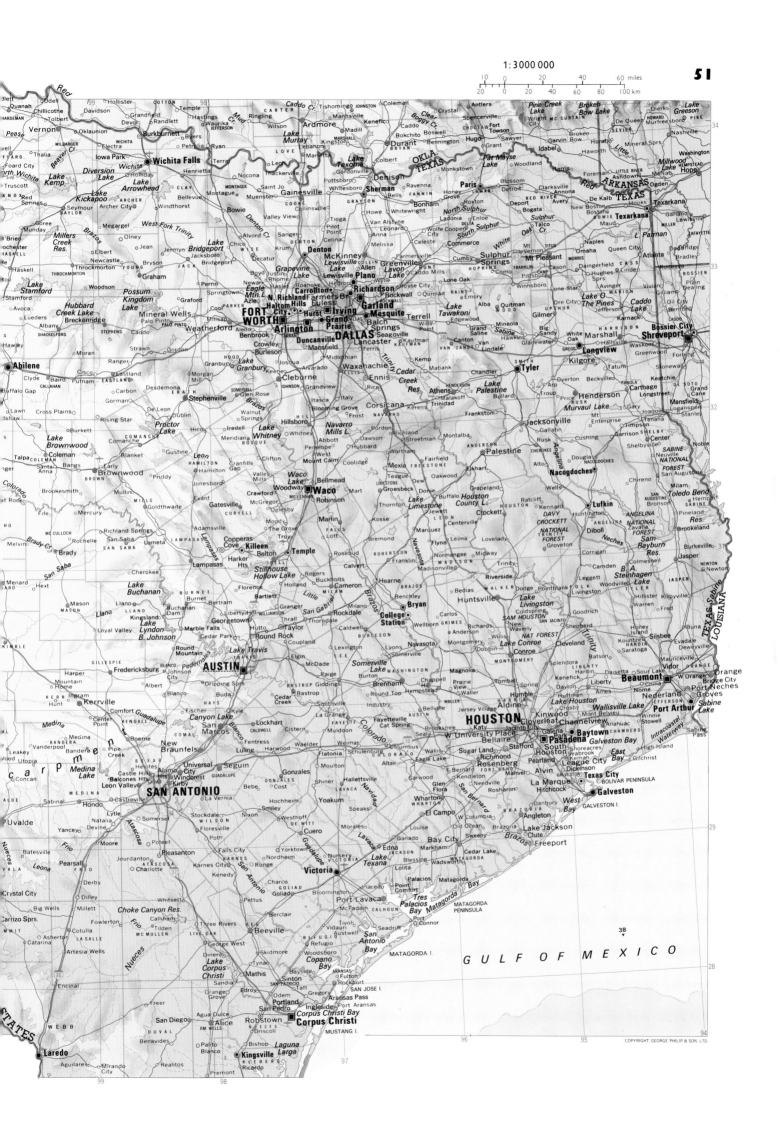

1 : 3 000 000

51

GULF OF MEXICO

1 : 2 500 000

10   0   10   20   30   40   50 miles

10   0   20   40   60   80 km

ft   m

12 000   4000

9000   3000

6000   2000

4500   1500

3000   1000

1200   400

Projection: Albers Equal Area

West from Greenwich

COPYRIGHT GEORGE PHILIP & SON Lᵗᵈ

Projection: Albers Equal Area

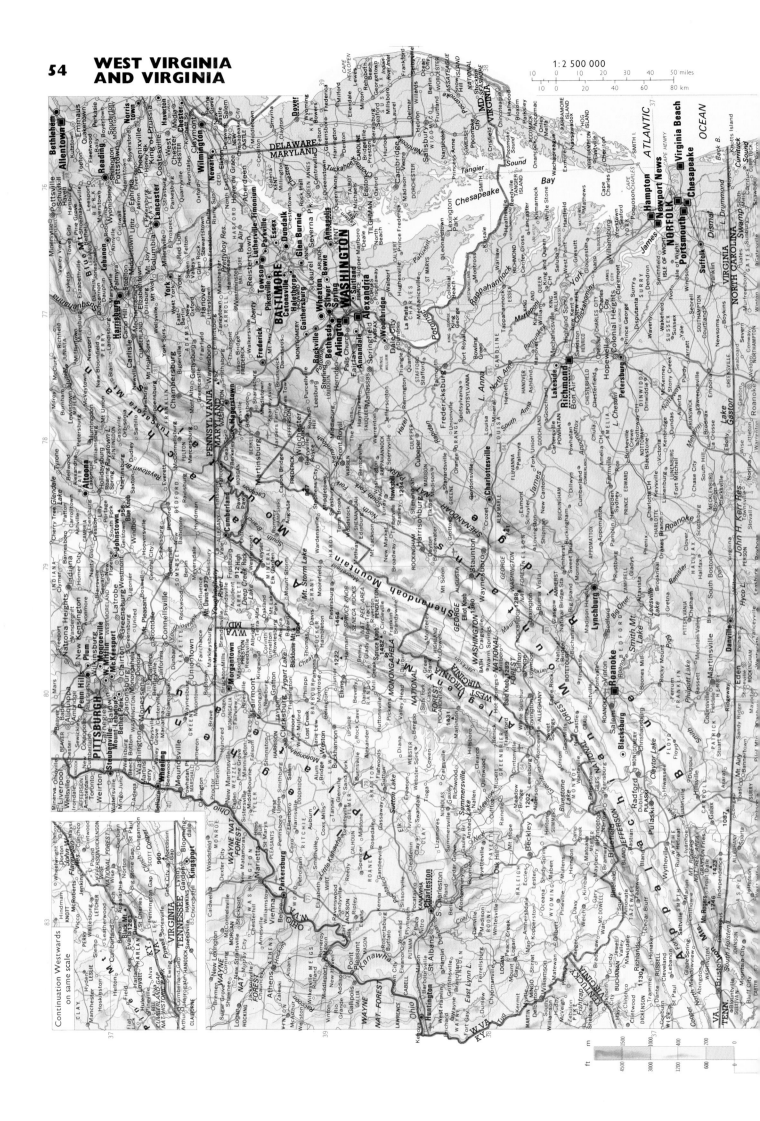

1:2 500 000

1:2 500 000

Projection: Albers Equal Area

West from Greenwich

COPYRIGHT GEORGE PHILIP & SON. LTD.

1 : 2 500 000

10   0   10   20   30   40   50 miles
10   0   20   40   60   80 km

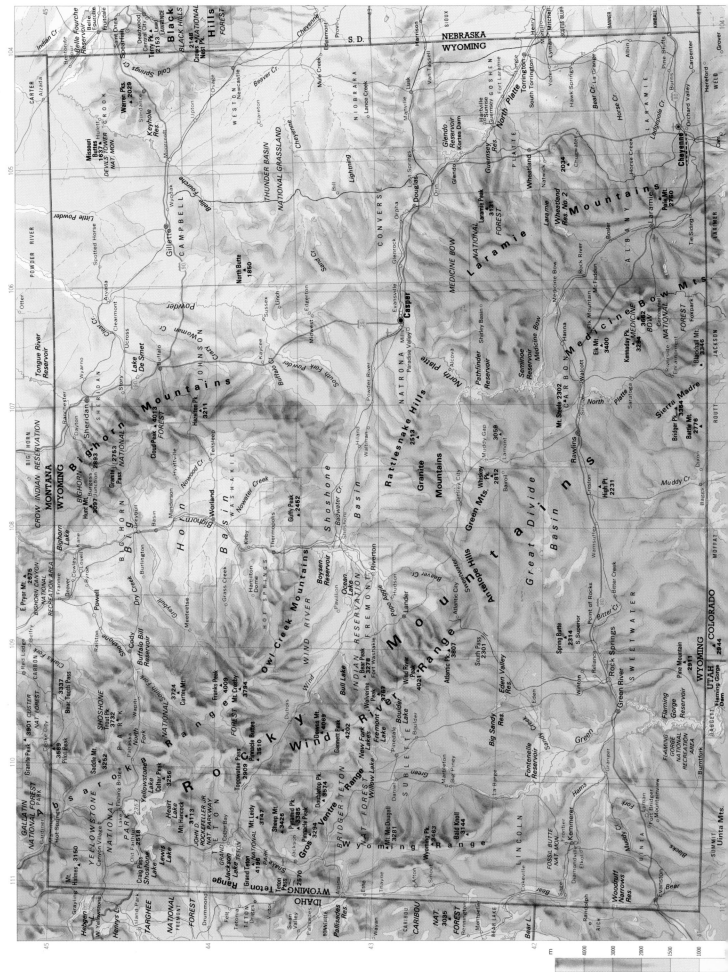

MONTANA
WYOMING

NEBRASKA
WYOMING

S.D.

UTAH   COLORADO
WYOMING

CARTER

Indian Cr.

Belle Fourche
Reservoir

Belle
Fourche

Fruitdale

Berinote   Aladdin

Spearfish

Deadwood
Central City   Lead   2153
Terry Pk.

Alzada

Cold Springs Cr.

Beulah

Warren Pks. ▲2029

**Black
Hills**   **FOREST**

Missouri
Buttes   DEVILS TOWER
1317   NAT. MON.
Hulett   2148   Crow
Nest Pk.
Keyhole
Res.

BLACK HILLS

CROOK   LAWRENCE

Sundance

Cheyenne

Osage   Upton

W E S T O N

Newcastle

Clareton

Mule Creek

Lance Creek

N I O B R A R A

SIOUX

Henry   Lyman   SCOTTS BLUFF
Mitchell   BANNER
KIMBALL

Harrison

Van Tassell
Lusk   Node

Manville

Hartville
Hat Creek   Sunrise
Guernsey
Glendo
Reservoir
Kortes Dam

Fort Laramie

North Platte

G O S H E N

Torrington
South Torrington

Yoder   Lingle
Veteran
Fort Laramie
La Grange

Hawk Springs

Burns

Hereford

L A R A M I E

Bear Cr.

Horse Cr.

Lodgepole Cr.

Orchard Valley

Pine Bluffs
Carpenter

2034
Chugwater

Wheatland
Res. No. 2

Cheyenne

Pole Mt. 2760

LARIMER

Grover

THUNDER BASIN

NATIONAL GRASSLAND

Lightning

Bill

C A M P B E L L

Gillette

90

P O W D E R   R I V E R

Little Powder

Otter

Spotted Horse

Wyodak

Arvada
Clearmont

Leiter

Sussex

Linch

Edgerton
Midwest

North Butte
1850

C O N V E R S E

Glenrock
Orpha
Douglas

Evansville
Casper
Mills

Paradise Valley
Alcova

Glendo

Shawnee

N A T I O N A L   **F O R E S T**
Laramie Peak
3131

M E D I C I N E   B O W

Laramie   **Mountains**

Boser

Rock River

McFadden

A L B A N Y

Laramie

Tie Siding

Sierra Madre

Bridger Pk. 3354

Battle Mt. 2176

ROUTT

MOFFAT

Boxelder Cr.

Powder

Clear Cr.

S H E R I D A N

Dayton   Ranchester
Sheridan
Parkman

Big Horn
Story
Banner

Buffalo

Kaycee

J O H N S O N

Ucross

Clearmont

Buffalo Cr.
South Fork Powder

Crazy Woman Cr.

Powder River

Hiland
Waltman

N A T R O N A

North Platte

Pathfinder
Reservoir

Seminoe
Reservoir
Medicine Bow

Shirley Basin

Muddy Gap

Lamont

Bairoil

Whiskey 2812
Peak

Baroil

Walcott
Sinclair
Rawlins

Creston

C A R B O N

Medicine Bow
Elk Mt.
3400

Hanna

Mt. Steele 2302

3059

Kennaday Pk. 3682
3294
Centennial

Riverside
Encampment

Savery

Dixon

Blackhall Mt.
3346

High Pt.
2231

Muddy Cr.

Bapts

G r e a t   D i v i d e   B a s i n

Wamsutter

Bitter Creek

Point of Rocks

S W E E T W A T E R

Bitter Cr.

Rock Springs
Reliance

Winton
S. Superior

Superior

Spring Butte
2314

Rattlesnake Hills
2513

**Granite
Mountains**

Jeffrey City

Green Mts.
3807

A n t e l o p e   H i l l s

Sweetwater

Atlantic City

South Pass
2301

Lander
Hudson

F R E M O N T

Riverton

Arapahoe
Hudson
Pavillion

Boysen
Reservoir

Ocean
Lake

WIND RIVER INDIAN RESERVATION

Fort Washakie

Bull Lake

Wind River

Dubois

Bear Peak
3278

Wolverine
Peak 3787

Fremont Pk.
4202

New Fork Lakes

Boulder Lake

Pinedale

Boulder

Big Sandy
Res.

Eden Valley
Res.

Farson

Eden

Reliance

Green River

Granger

Hams Fork

Fontenelle
Reservoir

La Barge

Big Piney

Marbleton

Daniel

S U B L E T T E

L I N C O L N

Pine Mountain
2911

Flaming Gorge
Reservoir

FLAMING
GORGE
NATIONAL
RECREATION
AREA

Burntfork

Mountainview

Fort Bridger

Lyman

Blacks

Fork

U I N T A

Granger

Carter

Green
River

SUMMIT

Uinta Mts.

BRIDGER

2644

SHOSHONE   **P A R K**

NATIONAL   **F O R E S T**

Granite Peak ▲3901
Pilot Peak
3669

CUSTER   NAT. FOREST

Red Lodge

CARBON

Bear Tooth Pass

3337

Saddle Mt.
3252

Trout Pk.
3732

Pahaska

North Fork

Wapiti
Cody

Ralston
Powell

Garland

Byron   Cowley
Lovell

Frannie

Deaver

Emblem

Burlington
Otto

Basin

Greybull

Manderson

Worland

Ten Sleep

W A S H A K I E

Nowater Creek

Gooseberry Cr.

Kirby
Thermopolis

H O T   S P R I N G S

Grass Creek

Hamilton
Dome

Meeteetse

Owl Creek Mountains

Shoshone

Basin

Guffey Peak ▲2452

Badwater Cr.

Shoshoni

Hazelton Pk.
3211

Cloud Peak ▲4013
NATIONAL   Granite ▲2753
Hunt Mt.   Pass
Burgess   Junction
2893

Hyattville

B I G   H O R N

BIG HORN

Bighorn
Lake

Frannie

BIGHORN CANYON
NATIONAL
RECREATION AREA

E. Pryor Mt. ▲2575

CROW INDIAN RESERVATION

B I G   H O R N

Bighorn

Lake

Kane

Cowley

Lovell

Garland

Dry Creek

Bighorn   **Mountains**

FOREST

B i g h o r n

B a s i n

Bighorn

Horn

Franks Peak
3724

Carter Mt.
3426

McCrosby
3794

Pinnacle Buttes ▲3510

Dunoir

Wind River

B R I D G E R - T E T O N

NATIONAL

FOREST

Wind   River   Range

Gannett Peak ▲4202

Dinwoody Pk. 4069

R o c k y   M o u n t a i n s

Union Peak 3463

Wyoming Pk. ▲3463

Bald Knoll
3144

Wyoming   Range

Afton

Alpine

Etna

Thayne

Grover

Smoot

Cokeville

Kemmerer
Diamondville
Elkol
Oakley

FOSSIL BUTTE
NAT. MON.

Sage

Frontier

Granger

Cumberland

Opal

Mountainview

Bear

L I N C O L N

Cokeville

Muddy Cr.

Randolph

Woodruff
Narrows
Res.

Evanston

R I C H

Bear L.

GALLATIN
NATIONAL FOREST

Mt. Holmes ▲3150

Gardiner

Gallatin
River

Grayling

Y E L L O W S T O N E

NATIONAL   **PARK**

Old Faithful

Lewis
Lake

Shoshone
Lake

Yellowstone
Lake

West Yellowstone

Henrys L.

Madison

Hebgen L.

TARGHEE

NATIONAL

FOREST

Drummond

Felt
Tetonia
Driggs

Victor

T E T O N
NAT.
PARK

Craig Pass
2518

Heart
Lake

Mt. Hancock

JOHN D.
ROCKEFELLER JR.
MEMORIAL PARKWAY

Mt. Leidy
3147

Sheep Mt.
3426

Pyramid Pk. ▲3385

Mt. McDougall
3281

Bondurant

G r o s   V e n t r e   R a n g e

Jackson
Lake
GRAND
TETON
PARK

Grand Teton
4196

Teton Pass
2570

T E T O N
Range

Wyoming   Range

Jackson

Hoback

IDAHO
WYOMING

Swan
Valley

Wayan

Palisades
Res.

CARIBOU

NAT.
FOREST

3035

Alton

Freedom

Thayne

Auburn

Bedford

Turnerville

45

104

105

106

107

108

109

110

111

104

45

44

43

42

41

m   4000   3000   2000   1500   1000

ft   12000   9000   6000   4500   3000

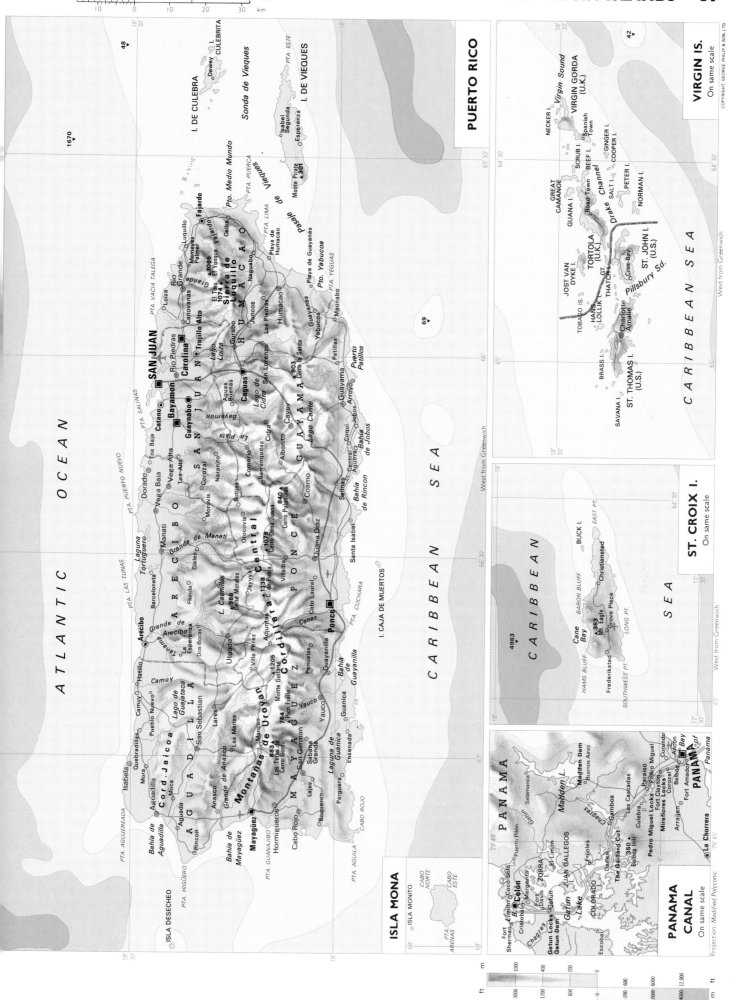

1:1 000 000

PUERTO RICO

ATLANTIC OCEAN

I. DE CULEBRA
Dewey I.
CULEBRITA
PTA. ESTE
Sonda de Vieques
Esperanza
Isabel Segunda
I. DE VIEQUES
Monte Pirate ▲301
PTA. PUERCA
PTA. LIMA
Pasaje de Vieques

1670 ▼
48 ▼

PTA. VACIA TALEGA
Fajardo
Luquillo
Mameyes
Palmer
Ceiba
Rio Grande
El Toro ▲1065
Sierra de Luquillo
El Yunque 1074 ▲
Loíza
Canóvanas
Playa de Humacao
Gurabo
Juncos
Las Piedras
Humacao
SAN JUAN
Rio Piedras
Carolina
Trujillo Alto
Lago Loíza
Aguas Buenas
Caguas
San Lorenzo
Cerro la Santa ▲903
Yabucoa
Pto. Yabucoa
Bayamón
Cataño
Guaynabo
Lago de Cidra
Cidra
Cayey
Guayama
Arroyo
Puerto Patillas
Patillas
Maunabo

PTA. SALINAS
Toa Baja
Dorado
Vega Alta
Toa Alta
Naranjito
Comerío
Aibonito
Cerro Doña Juana ▲1079
Coamo
Juana Díaz
Santa Isabel
Salinas
Coquí
Central Aguirre
Bahía de Jobos
Jobos
Guayanilla

PTA. PUERTO NUEVO
Vega Baja
Corozal
Morovis
Barranquitas
Orocovis
Ciales
Barceloneta
Manatí
Grande de Manatí
Florida
Cerro Morales ▲840
Cerro Punta ▲1338
Villalba
Canas
Coto Laurel
Ponce
Peñuelas
Bahía de Guayanilla
Yauco
Guánica
Ensenada
Laguna de Guánica
Laguna Tortuguero
PTA. LAS TUNAS
Arecibo
Grande de Arecibo
Utuado
Villa Pérez
▲1205
Monte Guilarte
Adjuntas
Pico Fraile ▲
Cordillera
Maricao
Las Tetas de Cerro Gordo ▲831
Montañas de Uroyán
Mayagüez
Hormigueros
San Germán
Sabana Grande
Lajas
Boquerón

ISLA MONA
CABO NORTE
CABO ESTE
PTA. ARENAS
ISLA MONITO

CARIBBEAN SEA

CABO ROJO
PTA. AGUILA
Laguna de Guánica
Parguera

Bahía de Mayagüez
PTA. GUANAJIBO
Añasco
Grande de Añasco
Rincón
Aguada
Aguadilla
Bahía de Aguadilla
PTA. HIGÜERO
ISLA DESECHEO
AGUADILLA
Quebradillas
Isabela
Camuy
Moca
Mora
Pueblo Nuevo
Hatillo
Camuy
Lares
Las Marías
San Sebastián
Lago de Guajataca
ARECIBO
Dos Bocas
La Esperanza
Jayuya
L. Caonillas ▲998
MAYAGÜEZ
▲764
Pico Fraile

CABO ROJO
PTA. AGUEREADA

18°30'
18°
67°
66°30'
66°
65°30'

West from Greenwich

ISLA MONA

VIRGIN IS.
On same scale

18°30'
42 ▼
NECKER I.
Virgin Sound
VIRGIN GORDA (U.K.)
Spanish Town
GINGER I.
COOPER I.
SALT I.
PETER I.
NORMAN I.
GREAT CAMANOE
SCRUB I.
BEEF I.
GUANA I.
Road Town
TORTOLA (U.K.)
Drake Channel
JOST VAN DYKE I.
TOBAGO IS.
HANS LOLLIK I.
THATCH
ST. JOHN I. (U.S.)
Cruz Bay
Pillsbury Sd.
BRASS I.
Charlotte Amalie
ST. THOMAS I. (U.S.)
SAVANA I.

CARIBBEAN SEA

65°
64°30'
18°30'

West from Greenwich

COPYRIGHT. GEORGE PHILIP & SON LTD

ST. CROIX I.
On same scale

CARIBBEAN
4983 ▼
HAMS BLUFF
BARON BLUFF
Cane Bay
Mt. Eagle ▲353
Grove Place
Frederiksted
SOUTHWEST PT.
BUCK I.
EAST PT.
Christiansted
LONG PT.

SEA

17°30'
65°
64°30'

West from Greenwich

PANAMA CANAL
On same scale

PANAMA
Fort Sherman
Cristobal
Colón
Coco-Solo
Margarita
Fort Davis
Gatún Locks
Gatún Dam
Gatún
Chagres
Limón Bay
ZORRA I.
JUAN GALLEGOS I.
COLORADO I.
Escobal
Frijoles
Gamboa
The Gaillard Cut
Culebra
Las Cascadas
Paraiso
Pedro Miguel Locks
Fort Clayton
Miraflores Locks
Arraiján
Balboa
La Chorrera
Gatún Lake
Madden L.
Madden Dam
Buenos Aires
Salamanca
Puerto Pilón
El Limón
Darién
Fort Amador
Corozal
Curundú
Ancón
Balboa Hill ▲350
PANAMA
Bay of Panama
PANAMA

79°45'

m
ft
1000
400
200
0
3000
1200
600
0
-200
-600
2000
6000
4000
12,000
m
ft

Projection: Modified Polyconic

1:15 000 000

100 50 0   100   200   300   400 miles

100   0   100   200   300   400   500   600 km

GREENLAND

A T L A N T I C

Baffin Bay

Angmagssalik

Svartenhuk Halvø

2136

Lancaster Sound

Arctic Bay

Bylot I.

Pond Inlet

Milne Inlet

Pond Inlet

Scott I.

C. Hewett

Clyde

Home B.

Broughton Island

2591

Cumberland Peninsula

Pangnirtung

C. Dyer

Cape Dyer

Disko (Qeqertarsuaq)

Disko B.

Christianshåb (Qasigiannguit)

Søndre Strømfjord

Holsteinsborg (Sisimiut)

2850

Sukkertoppen (Manitsoq)

Gotthåb (Nuuk)

Fiskenæsset

Frederikshåb (Paamiut)

Ivigtut

Julianehåb (Qaqortoq)

Narssarssuaq (Narsaq)

Nanortalik

Kap Farvel

Kong Frederik VIs Kyst

Prince Charles I.

Melville Peninsula

Hall Lake

Foxe Basin

C. Mercy

Nettilling L.

Hoare B.

Cumberland Sd.

Fury & Hecla Str.

Igloolik Island

Repulse B.

Boothia Isthmus

C. Dorchester

Foxe Channel

Southampton I.

Coral Harbour

Bell Pen.

Frobisher Bay

Resolution I.

C. Chidley

Amadjuak

Amadjuak L.

Frobisher Bay

Foxe Penin.

Cape Dorset

Lake Harbour

Hudson Strait

Ross Welcome Sd.

Coats I.

Digges Is.

Mansel I.

Ivujivik

Saglouc (Sugluk)

Maricourt (Wakeham)

Koartac Notre Dame de Koartac

Akpatok I.

Ungava Bay

Arnaud (Bellin) (Payne Bay)

3809

Ottawa Isd.

Portland Promontory

Inoucdjouac (Port Harrison)

Payne L.

Feuilles

1676

Port Nouveau-Québec (George R.)

Hebron

Nutak

Nain

NEWFOUNDLAND

Bay

257

Sleeper Is.

King George Is.

Baker's Dozen Is.

King George Is.

Belcher Is.

La L'Eau Claire

Lac Bienville

Scheffersville

Petitsikapau

Lobstick L.

COAST OF LABRADOR

Smallwood Reservoir

North West Falls

Churchill

Churchill Falls

Hopedale

Rigolet

Makkovik

C. Harrison

Indian Harbour

Goose Bay

Battle Harb.

Belle Isle

Cartwright

Str. of Belle Isle

C. Henrietta Maria

Pte. Louis-XIV

Winisk

Grand Baleine Poste-de-la-Baleine Great Whale River

Kanaaupscow

Ft. George

La Grande

Ashuanipi

Kaniapiskau L.

Moisie

Natashquan

St. Augustin

Saguenay

Notre-Dame B.

Twillingate

Lewisporte

Gander

Bonavista

Trinity B.

Carbonear

St. John's

C. Race

Trepassey

Placentia

QUEBEC

1128

Gagnon

Moisie

Mingan

Î. d'Anticosti

Sept-Îles

Port-Cartier

C. Ray

Channel Port aux Basques

Grand Falls

Harbour Grace

James Bay

Attawapiskat

Akimiski I.

Nouveau Comptoir (Paint Hills)

Eastmain

Eastmain

Fort Rupert (Rupert House)

Mistassini

L. Albanel

Péribonca

L. Mistassini

Rupert

Nottaway

Baie-Comeau

Bétsiamites

Matane

Pén. de Gaspé

Gaspé

Percé

Chaleur

Îs. de la Madeleine

Gulf of St. Lawrence

Cape Breton I.

Glace Bay

Sydney

Port Hawkesbury

Mulgrave

Sable I. (Nova Scotia)

6309

ST-PIERRE et MIQUELON (Fr.)

Ft. Albany

Albany

Charlton

Moosonee

Chibougamau

Rés. de Gouin

Mattagami

Dolbeau

St-Jean

Roberval

Lac St-Jean

Jonquière

Chicoutimi

Rimouski

Rivière-du-Loup

Dalhousie

Bathurst

Newcastle

Chatham

Northumberland Str.

P.R. EDWARD I.

Summerside

Charlottetown

NOVA SCOTIA

New Glasgow

Pictou

Truro

Windsor

Dartmouth

Halifax

Bridgewater

Liverpool

Shelburne

C. Sable

Yarmouth

Nakina

Longlac

Cochrane

L. Abitibi

Taschereau

Senneterre

Val d'Or

La Tuque

Shawinigan

Trois-Rivières

Sorel

St-Hyacinthe

Granby

Joliette

Sherbrooke

Thetford Mines

Edmundston

St-Léonard

Woodstock

Fredericton

NEW BRUNSWICK

Moncton

Amherst

Springhill

Saint John

Digby

B. of Fundy

MAINE

Bangor

Augusta

Kentville

Heron Bay

Michipicoten

Hearst

Timmins

Noranda

Rouyn

Kirkland Lake

Haileybury

Cobalt

Rés. de Cabonga

L. Témiscamingue

Ft. Coulonge

Pembroke

Arnprior

Ottawa

Hull

1190

Lévis

QUÉBEC

MONTRÉAL

Lachine

L. Champlain

VERMONT

1917

Concord

NEW HAMPSHIRE

Manchester

Lewiston

Portland

Franz

Nder Bay

Kenogami

Heron Bay

Superior

Michipicoten

Batchawana

Sault Ste. Marie

Sault Ste. Marie

Copper Cliff

Sudbury

North Bay

Parry Sound

Georgian Bay

Kingston

Belleville

Cobourg

Cornwall

Massena

Watertown

Plattsburg

Burlington

MASS.

Boston

Worcester

CONN.

Providence

C. Cod

Columet

Keweenaw Bay

Marquette

M.

S.

Manistique

Escanaba

Menominee

Green Bay

Appleton

Oshkosh

Manitowoc

Cheboygan

Petosky

Traverse City

Cadillac

Ludington

Muskegon

Lake Huron

Owen Sound

Orillia

Georgian Bay

Oshawa

Toronto

Guelph

Kitchener

Stratford

L. Ontario

Hamilton

St. Catharines

Niagara Falls

Buffalo

Rochester

Syracuse

Utica

Albany

Springfield

Hartford

New Haven

Bridgeport

Milwaukee

Racine

Kenosha

Evanston

GO

GARY

INDIANA

South Bend

Toledo

DETROIT

Windsor

Chatham

Lake Erie

London

Brantford

Woodstock

Saginaw

Flint

Jamestown

Williamsport

Scranton

Allentown

Reading

Trenton

Binghamton

Elmira

NEW YORK

PENNSYLVANIA

OHIO

Cleveland

Akron

Youngstown

Erie

Newark

NEW YORK

Jersey City

NEW JERSEY

West from Greenwich

60   COPYRIGHT. GEORGE PHILIP & SON. LTD

N . W   T E R R I T O R I E S

MANITOBA

H U D S O N

B A Y

Belcher
Islands

Baker's
Dozen Is.

Nastapoka Is.

L. Minto

L. Guillaume-
Delisle

L. à
l'Eau Claire

J A M E S

B A Y

Akimiski
I.

Grand Baleine

Eastmain

Q

ONTARIO

LAKE SUPERIOR

Thunder
Bay

Duluth
Superior

Timmins

Kirkland
Lake

OTTAWA

North
Bay

Sudbury

Sault Ste. Marie

WISCONSIN

MILWAUKEE

CHICAGO

ILLINOIS

INDIANA

O H I O

P E N N S Y L V A N I A

CLEVELAND

DETROIT

BUFFALO

TORONTO

HAMILTON

Rochester

LAKE   ONTARIO

LAKE   ERIE

LAKE   HURON

LAKE   MICHIGAN

Green Bay

Grand Rapids

Madison

Rockford

Kalamazoo

London

Windsor

Toledo

Lambert's Equivalent Azimuthal

ft   m

4500   1500

3000   1000

1200   400

600   200

0   0

200   600

2000   6000

4000   12 000

m   ft

1 : 7 000 000

50   0   50   100   150   200 miles
50   0   50   100   150   200   250   300 km

South Aulatsivik I.
High I.
N E W
C O A S T   O F
L A B R A D O R
Z   E

Erlandson   Whale   Fraser   Paul I.   60
L.   George
Fort
McKenzie
Nachicapau
L.
Chakonipau L.   Kogaluk
Otelnuk L.   Voiseys B.
Wheeler   Tunungayualok I.
Champdoré   Davis Inlet
Mistastin   Nunaksaluk I.
L.   Hopedale
610   L. Tudor   Big Bay
Whitegull   L.
L.   Kanairiktok   Makkovik
Harp L.   Nakaupi   Aillik   C. Harrison
Seal L.   Adlavik I.
Nipishish   Rigolet   Holton
Smallwood   Grand   Indian Harbour
Reservoir   North-West River   L. Melville   Groswater
Lac Verneuil   L.   Hamilton   B.
Lac Petitsikapau   Lobstick L.   Goose   Happy Valley-   Separation   Cartwright   Island of Ponds
Clairambault   Churchill Falls   Goose Bay   Point   Sandwich B.
Lac Delorme   Ossokmanuan   Churchill   Square Islands
Kaniapiskau   L.   Alexis   Paradise
L. Bermen   Winokapau L.   St. Lewis   Battle Harbour
Shabogamo   Minipi   Mary's   Hamilton Inlet
Opiscoteo   L.   L.   Harbour   Red   Bay
Opiskotish   Burnt   Little Mecatina   Bay   Belle I.
Naococane   L. Joseph   L.   St. Paul   Str. of Belle Isle
Labrador City   Alikonak   Anse au Loup   Griquet
Woolish   L.   Fortean   St. Anthony
1128   Ashuanipi   Bradore Bay   Lourdes   Cook's Harbour
Mouchalagane   L.   Petit Lac   St. Augustin   Blanc-Sablon   Great   Conche
L.   Manicouagan   Natashquan   Harbour   Bell I.
Plétipi   Monts   St-Augustin   Deep   Englee
West Main   Saguenay   Outer I.   White B.   Groais I.
Petit   I. du   Port   Horse Is.
Gagnon   Romaine   Olomane   Petit-Mécatina   Saunders
Rés.   Aguanus   Harrington Harbour   Daniel's
Manicouagan   1048   Natashquan   Harbour   Baie   La Scie
Ste-Marguerite   Nipissi   Musquaro   Verte   Notre Dame   Fogo I.
Manouane   St-Jean   Etamamu   Seal Cove   Mts.   Twillingate
Quiardes   Lac   Springdale   Lewisporte   Fogoville
Allardville   GROS MORNE   South   Gander   C. Freels
Rés.   Manitou   NAT. PARK   Brook   Norwood   Glenwood
Péribonca   Sheldrake   Trout River   Deer   Howley   Grand Falls   Gambo   Westerville
Pipmuacan   Havre-St-Pierre   Bay of Islands   Lake   Bishop's Falls   Dark Cove   Bonavista
Clarke   Mingan   Cove   Red Indian   Windsor   Gloverton   C. Bonavista
City   Moisie   Det. de Jacques-Cartier   Corner Brook   814   L.   Trinity B.   Bonavista
Betsiamites   Port-Cartier   I. d'Anticosti   Long P.   NEWFOUNDLAND   Catalina
Forestville   Sept-Îles   Jupiter   Long   Grey   Port Blandford
Godbout   Rivière-Pentecôte   Heath Pt.   Port au Port   Range   Res.   Bonavista   Bay de Verde
Baie-   Det.   Victoria   Salmon   381   Content
Comeau   Baie-Trinité   Sud Ouest   Mts.   Res.   Clarenville   Torbay
Pte. des Monts   d'Honguedo   St. George's B.   Terrenceville   Harbour   Spaniard's
Baie-   Cap-Chat   Grande-Vallée   Pte. Sud   572   St. David's   White   Conception B.
St-Paul   Mont-   Ste-Anne   PARC PROV.   Mt. Jacques-   South Branch   Bear   Grace   St. John's
Joli   des   Monts   1310   Cartier   GULF OF   St. Andrew's   Res.   Harbour   Ferryland
Forestville   DE LA   St. Lawrence   C. Ray   Belloram   Marystown   Avalon
Chicoutimi   Mts. Chic-Chocs   C. de Gaspé   ST. LAWRENCE   François   Placentia   Peninsula
Bergeronnes   Pén. de Gaspé   Gaspé   Rose   Grand   Argentia   C. St. Mary's
Tadoussac   Amqui   Bonnerive   Douglastown   Blanche   Bank   Placentia   C.
Alfred   Rimouski   Percé   Channel-Port   Burgeo   Buria   St. Mary's B.   Spassey
St-Siméon   Bic   Anne   Grande-Rivière   aux Basques   Romea   B.
La Malbaie   Causapscal   Chandler   Î. Brion   Langlade
PROV.   Trois-Pistoles   Matapédia   Paspébiac   Grande-Entrée   Miquelon
ENTIDES   Rivière-du-Loup   Chaleur Bay   Miscou I.   Îs. de la   St-Pierre
1190   Dalhousie   Lamèque   Madeleine   Cap-aux-Meules   SAINT-PIERRE
Cabano   Belledune   Shippegan   (Quebec)   ET MIQUELON
St-Pascal   Campbellton   Tracadie   Havre-Aubert   (Fr.)
Edmundston   Redgwick   Straits   Bathurst   North Pt.   St. Paul
St-Jean-Port-Joli   St. Arthur   Heath Steele   Tignish   C. North
Pacôme   Clabano   Heath   Neguac   Alberton   Cabot   Ingonish   Cap Breton
Ft. Kent   St. Leonard   819   Miramichi B.   Strait   CAPE BRETON
Montmagny   Grand Falls   Plaster   Newcastle   Summerside   NAT. PARK
Lauzon   Plaster   Chatham   Richibucto   Kensington   Chéticamp   532   Sydney Mines
Lévis   Van Buren   Rock   Blackville   PRINCE EDWARD   East Pt.   New Waterford
Beaugeville   Caribou   Nashwaak   Doaktown   Borden   ISLAND   Souris   N. Sydney   Glace Bay
St-Georges   Ashland   Blissfield   Montague   Charlottetown   Inverness   Sydney
Thetford Mines   Presqu'isle   Chipman   Dame   Northumberland   Peters   Murray Hr.   Georgetown   Baddeck   Cape Breton
Eagle L.   Houlton   Str.   Tormentine   Pictou   Bras d'Or   Island
Lac-   Woodstock   Stanley   Minto   Havelock   Pleasant Bay   St. Peters   Louisbourg
Mégantic   Chesuncook   Hartland   Grand   Petitcodiac   Shediac   New Glasgow   Fourchu
brooke   Patten   Island Falls   Gagetown   Amherst   Stellarton   Antigonish
M A I N E   1606   Fredericton   Sussex   Moncton   Springhill   Pictou   Mulgrave   I. Madame
ticook   Moosehead   Millinocket   Jct.   Elgin   Sussex   Chedabucto B.
Mooselook-   Lincoln   Gage   Truro   Sherbrooke   Canso
megantic   Grand   town   Chignecto B.   N O V A   S C O T I A
Bingham   Oakfield   Fredericton   Sackville   Stewiacke   Upper
Waterville   Skowhegan   Jct.   Minas   Musquodoboit
Berlin   Mattawamkeag   St. John   St. Martins   Basin   Upper Musquodoboit
Guilford   Old Town   Chipman   Windsor   Sheet Hr.
Bangor   Brewer   Gage   Rothesay   Middleton   Dartmouth
Rumford   Dover-Foxcroft   Ellsworth   Saint   Bay of Fundy   Kentville   Musquodoboit Hr.   A T L A N T I C
Augusta   Machias   John   Blacks   Bridgetown   Halifax
Belfast   Bar Harbor   Calais   Harbour   Annapolis   Windsor
Auburn   Camden   Mt. Desert I.   Eastport   Royal   Mahone Bay
Lewiston   Rockland   Jonesport   Grand   Digby   Lunenburg   Sable I.
Bethel   Manan I.   St. Mary's B.   Weymouth   Bridgewater   (Nova Scotia)
Sebago   Bath   St. Stephen   Freeport   Liverpool
Brunswick   Yarmouth   Rossignol   Port   O C E A N
Sanford   Portland   Wedgeport   Res.   Mouton
Saco   Clark's Harbour   Shelburne
Biddeford   C. Sable   Lockeport
Con-   Dover
Cord   Portsmouth
Manchester
Nashua   Haverhill
Lawrence
Gloucester
BOSTON   Lynn   C. Ann
Brockton

70   West from Greenwich   65   60   COPYRIGHT GEORGE PHILIP & SON, LTD

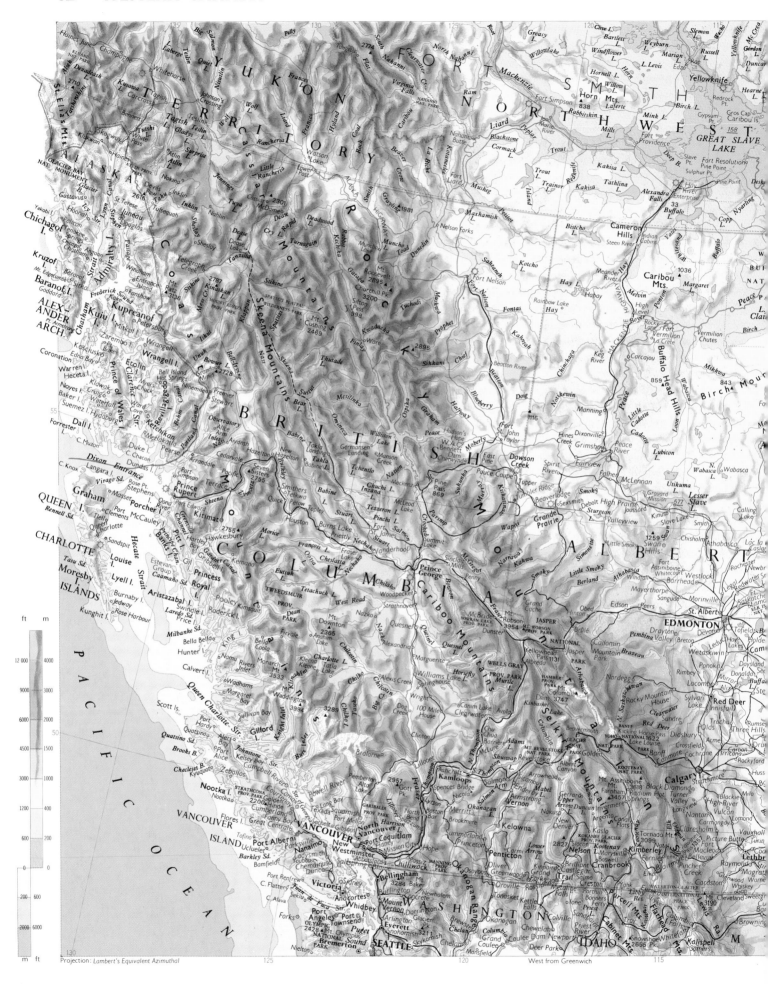

Projection: Lambert's Equivalent Azimuthal   West from Greenwich

50 0 50 100 150 200 miles
50 0 50 100 150 200 250 300 km

HUDSON

BAY

KEEWATIN

REGION

TERRITORIES

SASKATCHEWAN

MANITOBA

ONTARIO

Athabasca

Cree L.

Reindeer L.

Southern Indian L.

LAKE WINNIPEG

Lake Winnipegosis

Lake Manitoba

Prince Albert

North Battleford

Saskatoon

Regina

Moose Jaw

Swift Current

WINNIPEG

Brandon

Portage la Prairie

Selkirk

Dauphin

Yorkton

Weyburn

Estevan

Kenora

Lake of the Woods

NORTH DAKOTA

MINNESOTA

MONTANA

Fort Peck Res.

Williston

Minot

Devils Lake

Grand Forks

Duluth

Bemidji

International Falls

Thief River Falls

COPYRIGHT GEORGE PHILIP & SON. LTD.

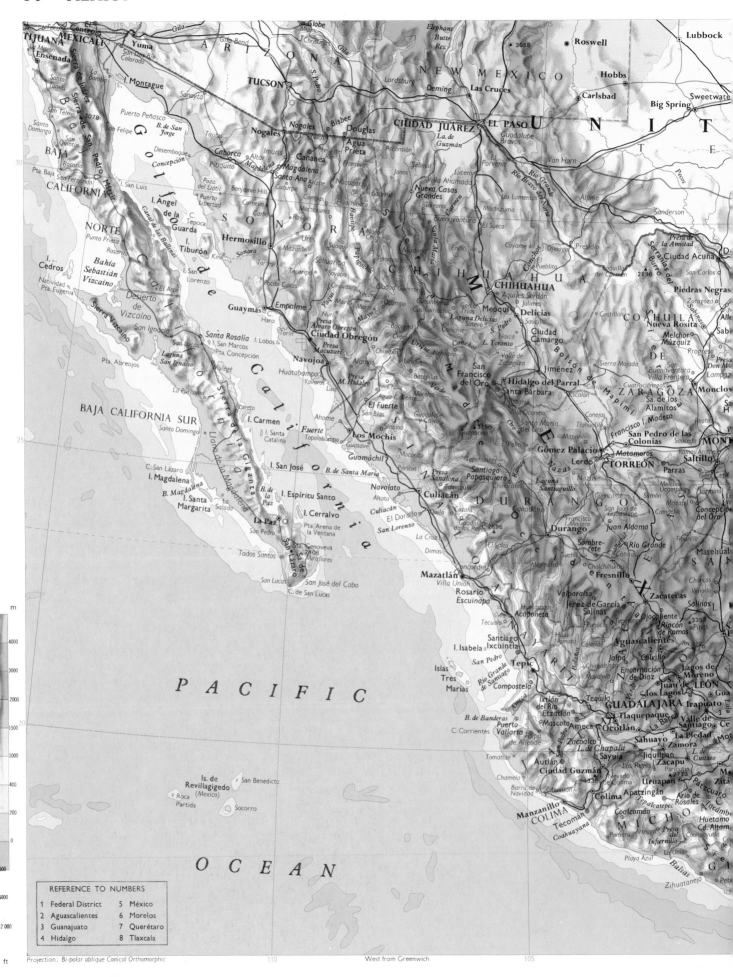

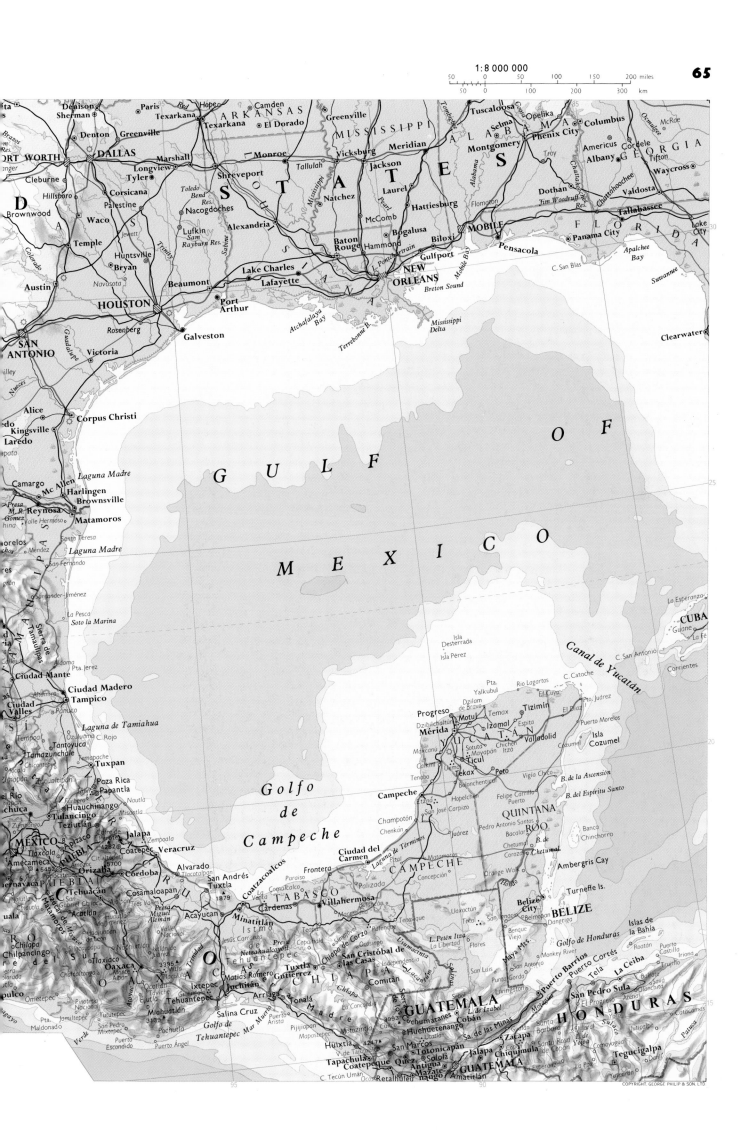

1 : 8 000 000

50   0   50   100   150   200 miles
50   0   100   200   300 km

A T L A N T I C

O C E A N

Tropic of Cancer

S

ht

San Salvador
(Watling I., Guanahani)
Inception I.

ng I.
Rum Cay

lorence
Town
Crooked I. Passage

Crooked I.
Richmond
Albert
Town
Plana Cays
Snug
Corner
Mira por vos Cay
Mayaguana I.
Acklins I.
Hogsty Reef
Little Inagua I.
Lake Rose
Great
Inagua I.
Matthew
Town

Caicos
Islands
(Br.)
Caicos Passage
Turks I. Passage
Turks Islands
(Br.)

Mod

Baracoa
Pta. de
Maisi
Pta de Vientos
Paso de los Vientos
(Windward) Passage
Jean-Rabel
Cap-à-Foux

Î. de la
Tortue
Port-de-Paix
Cap-Haïtien
Fort-Liberté
Monte Cristi
La Isabela
C. Frances Viejo
Puerto Plata

namo
Golfe de la
Gonâve
St.-Marc
Santiago de
los Caballeros
La Vega
San Francisco de Macoris
Nagua
Sánchez

Jérémie
Î. de la Gonâve
Dame
Marie
carcasse
Massif de la Hotte
Les Cayes
Aquin
Jacmel
PORT-
AU-PRINCE
Pédernales
San Juan
2280 Enriquillo
Pointe-à-Gravois
L. de
Enriquillo
Î.a-Vache
Î. Beata
C. Beata

HAITI
Cord.
Central
3175
Hinche
DOMINICAN
REP.
San Pedro
de Macoris
Higüey
Hato Mayor
C. Engaño
Azua de
Compostela
Bani
Barahona
San Cristóbal
SANTO DOMINGO
La Romana
B. de
Yuma
I. Saona
Sabana de La Mar

Sánchez
Aguadilla
Arecibo
Bayamón
SAN JUAN
Fajardo
1338
Mayagüez
Isla
Mona
(U.S.A.)
Ponce
Caguas
Guayama
PUERTO
RICO
(U.S.A.)

Virgin Gorda
Tortola
Virgin Is.
(Br.)
Anegada
Anguilla Passage
Sombrero (Anguilla)
Road Town
St. Thomas
Virgin Is.
(U.S.A.)
St. Croix
Frederiksted
Christiansted
Charlotte Amalie
Anguilla (Br.)
St.-Martin (Guad.)
St.-Barthélemy (Fr.)
St. Maarten
(Neth.)
Saba (Neth.)
St. Eustatius
(Neth.)
Basseterre
Nevis
ST.
CHRISTOPHER-
NEVIS
St. Johns
Redonda
Montserrat

Barbuda
ANTIGUA
& BARBUDA
Antigua

HISPANIOLA
ANTILLES
LESSER
GREATER

Guadeloupe Passage
Ste-Rose
Moule
Désirade
(Fr.)
GUADELOUPE
Basse-Terre
Pointe-a-Pitre
Marie-Galante (Fr.)
Grand-Bourge
Î. des Saintes
(Guad.)
I. de Aves (Bird I.)
(Venezuela)
Dominica Passage
Portsmouth
Roseau
DOMINICA

LEEWARD ISLANDS

B E A N   S E A

Martinique Passage
Ste-Marie
Mt. Pelée
1397
Fort-de-France
François
Rivière-Pilot
MARTINIQUE
(Fr.)
St. Lucia Channel
Castries
Soufrière
ST. LUCIA

St. Vincent Passage
Soufrière 1234
Kingstown
ST. VINCENT
Speightstown
Bridgetown
& THE
BARBADOS
Hillsborough
The Grenadines
GRENADINES
St. George's
GRENADA

WINDWARD ISLANDS

LESSER ANTILLES

Aruba
(Neth.)
Curaçao
(Neth.)
Bonaire (Neth.)
Willemstad
Neth.
Antilles
I. Blanquilla (Ven.)
J. Los Hermanos
(Ven.)

Pta. Gallinas
C. San Román
Pen. de
Paraguaná
Pta.
Espada
Pen. de la
Guajira
Is. de Aves
(Ven.)
Is. Los Roques
(Ven.)
J. Orchila
(Ven.)
Is. Los Testigos
(Ven.)
Tobago
Scarborough

Ríohacha
Uribia
San Juan
de Guia
GUAJIRA
Punto Fijo
Punta
Cardón
Puerto
Cumarebo
Coro
La Vela de Coro
I. Margarita
La Asunción
NUEVA
ESPARTA
Porlamar
Galera
Pt.
Pen. de Paria
Güiria
Port
of
Spain
Arima
Trinidad
Dragon's Mouth
Pta. Mejillones

Santa
Marta
Ciénaga
Soledad
Sabanalarga
Fundación
Calamar
MAGDALENA
Plato
Zambrano
Magangué
Mompós
El Banco
NORTE
DE
Majagual
El Callao

Nevada
de
Santa Marta
5800
MARACAIBO
La
Concepción
Santa Rita
Cabimas
Ciudad
Ojeda
Lago de
Maracaibo
Machiques
ZULIA
La Ceiba
TRUJILLO
San Carlos
del Zulia
Catatumbo
Encontrados
San
Agustín
Codazzi
CÉSAR
Valledupar
Villa del
Rosario
Agustín
Codazzi
Cúcuta
SANTANDER
NORTE
Ocaña
BOLÍVAR
Simiti
Cucasia
cual

San
Rafael
Altagracia
Mene de Mauroa
FALCÓN
Baragua
San Felipe
Carora
Mene
Grande
BARQUISIMETO
LARA
El Tocuyo
Acarigua
Valera
MÉRIDA
Mérida
Cord. de Mérida
Tovar
TÁCHIRA
San Cristóbal
Santa Bárbara
Ciudad
Bolivia
La Fria
Barinas
BARINAS
Libertad
San
Fernando de
Apure
Bruzual
Achaguas
V E N E Z U E L A
Apure

Tucuyo
Yaritagua de
los Morros
Valencia
Maracay
Villa
de Cura
S. Juan de
los Morros
San Carlos
COJEDES
GUÁRICO
Calabozo
El Baúl
Guanare
PORTUGUESA
Portuguesa
Río de Nutrias
Maquetía
La Guaira
CARACAS
DISTRITO
FEDERAL
Puerto
Cabello
MIRANDA
Los Teques
Ocumare del Tuy
Río Chico
Higuerote
El Sombrero
Aragua de
Barcelona
Valle de la
Pascua
Santa María
de Ipire
Uname
I. La Tortuga
(Ven.)
C. Codera

Cumaná
Carúpano
Río
Caribe
SUCRE
Caripito
Barcelona
Puerto La Cruz
Caicara
Anaco
MONAGAS
Maturín
El Tigre
Camaura
Pariaguan
El Pao
ANZOÁTEGUI
Soledad
Ciudad Guayana
Upata
AMACUR
Tucupita
DELTA-
San Fernando
Golfo de Paria
Serpent's Mouth
Caripe
Río Claro
TRINIDAD
& TOBAGO
Sierra Imataca
Ciudad
Bolívar
El Pao
Orinoco
Mapire
Emb de Guri
Caroní
Guasipati
Tumeremo
Caicara
Guárico
Manapire
Aragua de
Barcelona

75   West from Greenwich   70   65   COPYRIGHT. GEORGE PHILIP & SON. LTD.

ft   m
12.000 4000
9000   3000
6000   2000
4500   1500
3000   1000
1200   400
600   200
0   0
200   600
2000   6000
4000   12 000
6000   18 000
8000   24 000
m   ft

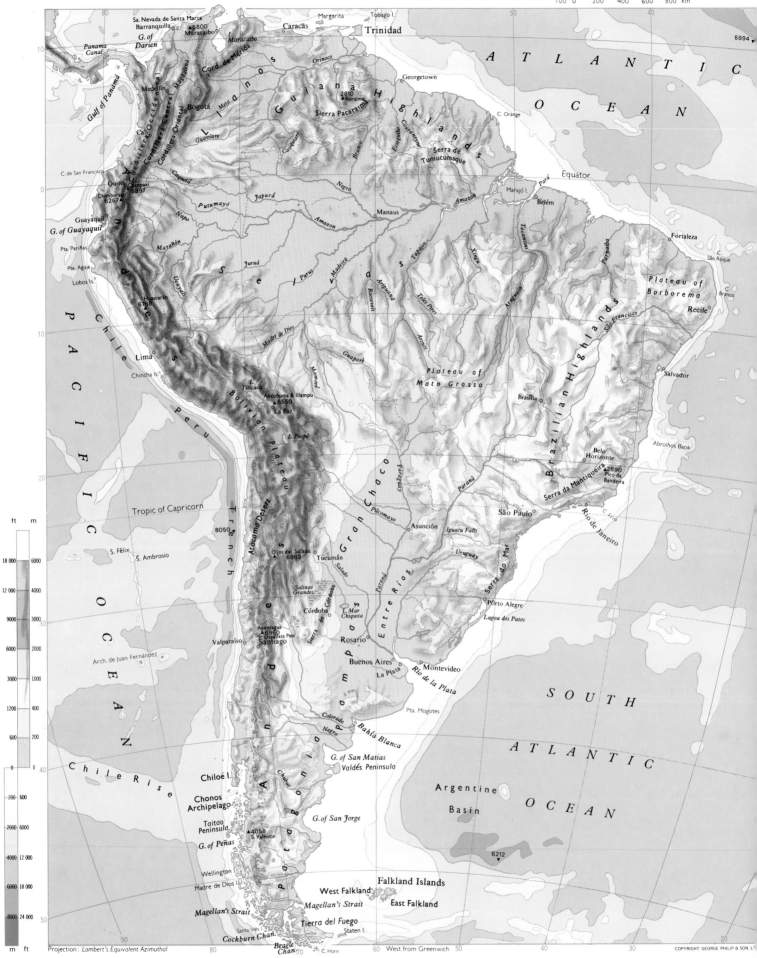

1:30 000 000

100   0   100 200 300   400   500 miles
100   0   200   400   600   800 km

ft   m

18 000   6000
12 000   4000
9000   3000
6000   2000
3000   1000
1200   400
600   200
0   0

200   600
2000   6000
4000   12 000
6000   18 000
8000   24 000

m   ft

Projection: *Lambert's Equivalent Azimuthal*

ATLANTIC OCEAN

5994▾

Sa. Nevada de Santa Marta
Barranquilla ▲5800
Maracaibo
L. Maracaibo
Caracas
Margarita
Tobago I.
Trinidad

Panama Canal
G. of Darien
Cord. de Mérida
Orinoco
Georgetown
C. Orange

Medellín
Bogotá
Llanos
Guiana Highlands
Sierra Pacaraima
▲2810 Roraima
Serra de Tumucumaque

Cali
Guaviare
Casiquiare
Branco
Essequibo
Courantyne

C. de San Francisco
Quito
Cotopaxi 5897
Chimborazo 6267
Caquetá
Negro
Equator

Putumayo
Japurá
Amazon
Marajó I.
Pará
Belém

Guayaquil
G. of Guayaquil
Napo
Manaus

Pta. Pariñas
Marañón
Juruá
Purus
Madeira
Amazon
Tapajós
Xingu
Tocantins
Parnaíba
Fortaleza

Pta. Agua
Lobos Is.
Ucayali
Selvas
Roosevelt
Aripuanã
Teles Pires
Araguaia
São Roque
C. Branco

Huascarán 6768
Madre de Dios
Arinos
Plateau of Borborema
Recife

Lima
Chincha Is.
Guaporé
Mamoré
Plateau of Mato Grosso
São Francisco

Bolivian Plateau
L. Titicaca
Ancohuma & Illampu ▲6550
La Paz
L. Poopó
Brasília
Salvador
Abrolhos Bank

Belo Horizonte
▲2890 Pico da Bandeira
Serra da Mantiqueira
Brazilian Highlands

Tropic of Capricorn
8050
Atacama Desert
Gran Chaco
Paraná
São Paulo
Iguaçu Falls
Rio de Janeiro
C. Frio

S. Félix
S. Ambrosio
Ojos del Salado ▲6863
Tucumán
Salado
Asunción
Uruguay
Serra do Mar

PACIFIC OCEAN
Chile Rise
Arch. de Juan Fernández
Salinas Grandes
Córdoba
Sierra de Córdoba
L. Mar Chiquita
Rosario
Paraná
Entre Rios
Pôrto Alegre
Lagoa dos Patos

Aconcagua ▲6960
Uspallata Pass
Santiago
Valparaíso
Buenos Aires
La Plata
Montevideo
Río de la Plata

SOUTH ATLANTIC OCEAN
Pta. Mogotes
Pampas
Colorado
Negro
Bahía Blanca
Argentine Basin

Chiloé I.
Chonos Archipelago
Taitao Peninsula
G. of Peñas
Patagonia
G. of San Matías
Valdés Peninsula
G. of San Jorge

Wellington
Madre de Dios I.
▲4058 S. Valentín
6212▾

West Falkland
Falkland Islands
East Falkland

Magellan's Strait
Tierra del Fuego
Santa Inés I.
Cockburn Chan.
Beagle Chan.
C. Horn
Staten I.

West from Greenwich

COPYRIGHT. GEORGE PHILIP & SON. L

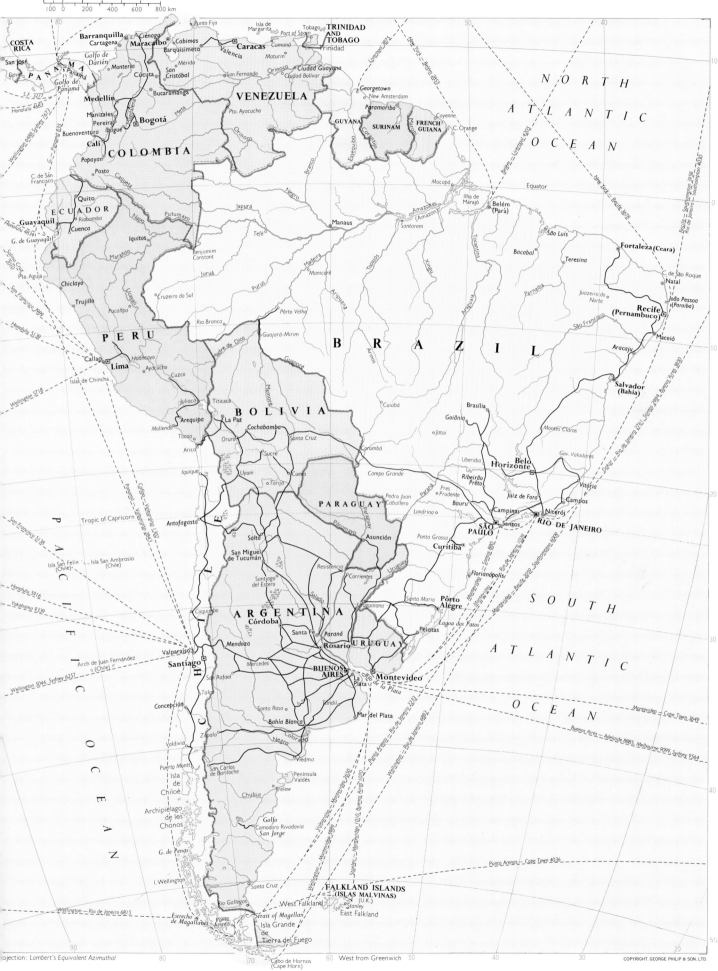

1:30 000 000

100   0   100   200   300   400   500 miles
100   0   200   400   600   800 km

COSTA
RICA

San José

PANAMA
Panamá

S.F. 3277
Golfo de
Panamá

Honolulu 4683

Barranquilla
Cartagena
Maracaibo
Cabimas
Golfo de
Darién
Monteria
Medellin
Cúcuta
San
Cristóbal
Manizales
Pereira
Ibagué
Buenaventura
Bogotá
Cali
COLOMBIA
Popayan
Pasto

C. de San
Francisco

Quito
ECUADOR
Guayaquil
Riobamba
Cuenca
G. de Guayaquil
Pta. Aguja

Honolulu 4341

San Cruz
2010

Chiclayo
Trujillo

San Francisco 7699

PERU

Honolulu 5139

Callao
Lima
Wellington 5718

Islas de Chincha

Ciénaga
Punta Fijo
Valencia
Barquisimeto
Caracas
Maturin
Cumaná
VENEZUELA
Mérida
San Fernando
Orinoco
Pto. Ayacucho
Orinoco

Port of Spain
Tobago
TRINIDAD
AND
TOBAGO
Trinidad

Isla de
Margarita

Ciudad Guayana
Ciudad Bolívar

Georgetown
New Amsterdam
GUYANA
Paramaribo
SURINAM
FRENCH
GUIANA
Cayenne

Napo

Iquitos

Putumayo

Japurá

Marañon

Benjamim
Constant

Juruá

Cruzeiro do Sul

Pucallpa

Purus

Rio Branca

Madre de Dios

Guajará-Mirim

Pôrto Velho

Huancayo
Ayacucho
Cuzco

Juliaca
Titicaca

Arequipa
Mollendo
Tacna
Arica
Iquique

La Paz
BOLIVIA
Oruro
Sucre
Cochabamba
Santa Cruz
Corumbá

Uyuni
Cueva
Tarija

Antofagasta

Isla San Felix
(Chile)
Isla San Ambrosio
(Chile)

Honolulu 5916

Yokohama 9339

Arch de Juan Fernández
(Chile)

Wellington 5044, Sydney 6257

Tropic of Capricorn

Collao – Valparaiso 1302
Panama – Valparaiso 2947

Salta
San Miguel
de Tucumán
Santiago
del Estero

CHILE

Coquimbo

Valparaíso
Santiago

San Rafael
Mendoza

ARGENTINA
Córdoba
Santa Fe
Paraná
Rosario
Mercedes

Resistencia

Corrientes

Salado

Salado

Buenos
Aires
La
Plata

Talca

Concepción

Valdivia

Zapala

Puerto Montt

Isla
de
Chiloé

San Carlos
de Bariloche

Archipiélago
de los
Chonos

Chubut

Colorado

Viedma

Peninsula
Valdés
Trelew

Golfo
Comodoro Rivadavia
San Jorge

G. de Penas

I. Wellington

Santa Cruz

Rio Gallegos

Estrecho
de Magallanes
Punta
Arenas
Strait of Magellan

Isla Grande
de
Tierra del Fuego

Cabo de Hornos
(Cape Horn)

FALKLAND ISLANDS
(ISLAS MALVINAS)
(U.K.)
West Falkland
Stanley
East Falkland

Negro

Tefé

Manaus

Santarem

Amazonas
(Amazon)

Ilha de
Marajó

Belém
(Pará)

Macapá

Equator

São Luis

Bacabal

Teresina

C. Orange

Fortaleza (Ceara)

C. de São Roque
Natal
João Pessoa
(Paraiba)
Recife
(Pernambuco)
Maceió

Manicoré

Aripuaná

Tapajós

Xingu

Araguaia

Tocantins

Parnaiba

Juazeiro do
Norte

São Francisco

Aracaju

B R A Z I L

Cuiabá

Goiânia

Brasília

Jataí

Montes Claros

Gov. Valadares

Aracaju

Salvador
(Bahía)

Campo Grande

PARAGUAY

Pedra Juan
Caballero

Asunción

Pilcomayo

Paraguay

Paraná

Uberaba
Ribeirão
Prêto
Uberaba
Belo
Horizonte

Pres
Prudente
Bauru
Londrina

Campinas

Juiz de Fora
Vitória
Campos
Niterój
RIO DE JANEIRO
SÃO
PAULO
Santos
Curitiba
Ponta Grossa

Florianópolis

Santa Maria
Pôrto
Alegre

Uruguaiana

Uruguay

URUGUAY
Montevideo

Pelotas

Lagoa dos Patos

Rio de la Plata

Tandil

Mar del Plata

Bahía Blanca

Santa Rosa

NORTH
ATLANTIC
OCEAN

SOUTH
ATLANTIC
OCEAN

PACIFIC
OCEAN

Montevideo – Cape Town 3649

Buenos Aires – Adelaide 8885, Melbourne 9099, Sydney 9564

Punta Arenas – Cape Town 4036

Projection: Lambert's Equivalent Azimuthal

West from Greenwich

COPYRIGHT. GEORGE. PHILIP & SON. LTD.

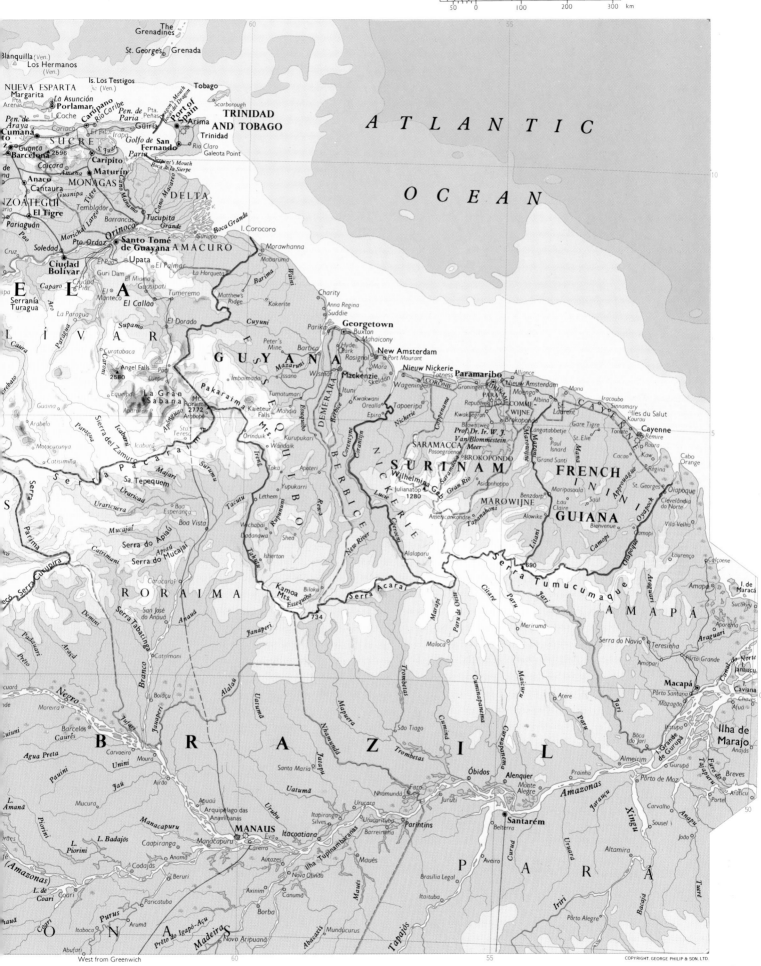

1:8 000 000

50 0 50 100 150 200 miles
50 0 100 200 300 km

ATLANTIC

OCEAN

TRINIDAD
AND TOBAGO

NUEVA ESPARTA

SUCRE

MONAGAS

DELTA

AMACURO

VENEZUELA

BOLÍVAR

GUYANA

SURINAM

FRENCH
GUIANA

RORAIMA

BRAZIL

PARÁ

AMAPÁ

Georgetown

Paramaribo

Cayenne

MANAUS

Santarém

Macapá

Ilha de
Marajó

West from Greenwich

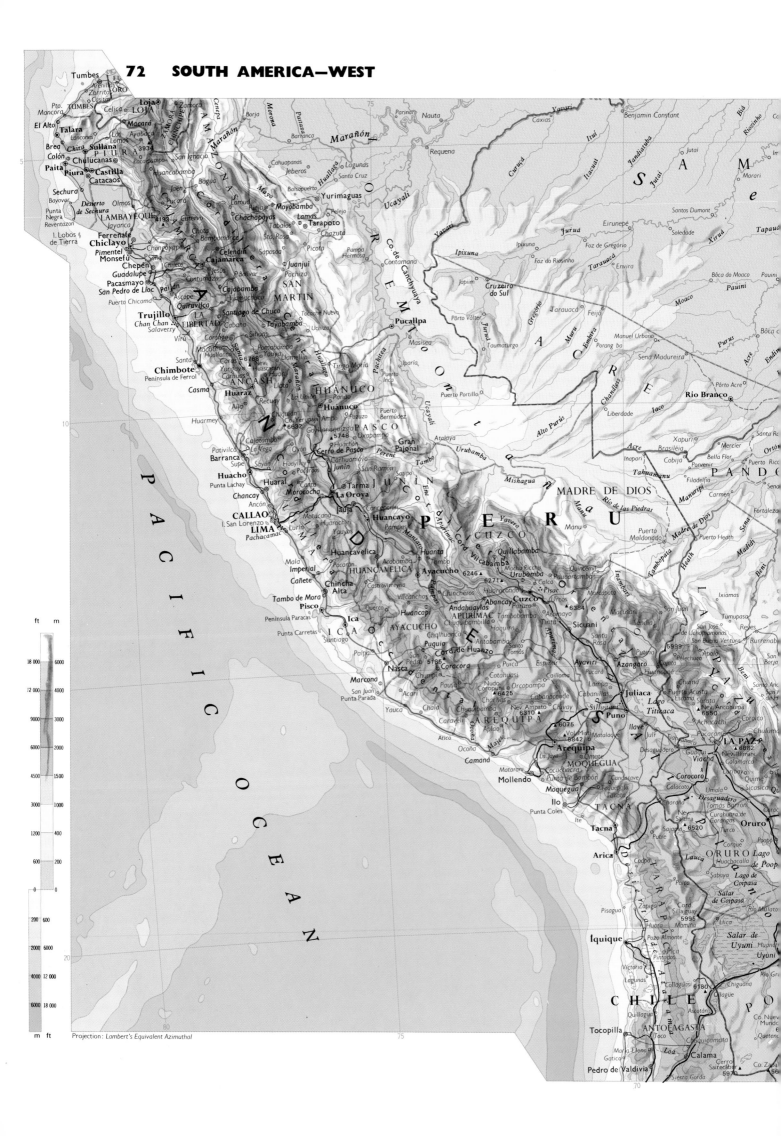

Projection: Lambert's Equivalent Azimuthal

1:8 000 000

50   0   50   100   150   200 miles
50   0   50   100   200   300 km

BRAZIL

AMAZONAS

PARÁ

L. de Coari · Coari
Itanhauā · Coari
Purus · Itaboca · Arumā · Paricatuba · Axinim · Canumā
Itatuba · Tapauá · Manicoré · Novo Aripuanã · Capoeira · Borba · Maués · Itaituba · Pôrto Alegre · Bacajá
Canutama · Santa Maria dos Marmeles · Itapinima · Miriti · Sai-Cinza · Tucunaré · Entre Rios · São Félix · Nazaré · Riosinho
Axioma · Três Casas · Canudos · Crepori · Cachimba · Alto Iriri · São Benedito · Irirí Novo
Lábrea · Majuriã · Mucium · Humaitá · Prainha · Samaúma · Recreio · Barracão do Barreto · Peixoto de Azevedo
Calama · Jamari · Tabajara · Aripuanã · S. Benedito · Pôrto Cajueiro · Campo de Diauarum
Pôrto Velho · Jaciparaná · Caritianas · Nova Vida · Diamantino · Cuiabá · Suiá Missu · Liberdade

RONDÔNIA
Guajará-Mirim · Guayaramerin · Ariquemes · Jaru · Rondônia · Presidente Hermes · Nortelândia · Arenápolis · Pouso Alegre
Sa. dos Pacaás Novos · Pimenta Bueno · Barão de Melgaço · Vilhena · 663 · Nhambiquara · Juruena · Utiariti
Principe da Beira · Versalles · Pedras Negras · 669 · Arinos · Alto Paraguai · Serra Azul
Matequa · Magdalena · Puerto Villazón · Serrania de Huanchaca · Mato Grosso · Tapirapuã · Barra do Bugres · Rosário Oeste · Chavantina · 915

MATO GROSSO
Planalto do Mato Grosso

BOLIVIA
San Javier · Trinidad · Perseverancia · 1995 · Guaporé · Acorizal · Chapada dos Guimarães · Mortes · Aruanã · Araguaial
de Mojos · Loreto · Concepción · San Ignacio · Mato Grosso · Varzea Grande · **Cuiabá** · Coronel Ponce · Barro do Garças · Araguaiana
San Francisco · San Javier · Santa Ana · San Miguel · Pôrto Esperidião · Cáceres · Santo Antônio do Leverger · Poxoréu · Jaciara · Tesouro · Aragarças
San Carlos · Santa Rosa del Palmar · Aguapei · San Matías · Poconé · Barão de Melgaço · Guiratinga · Ponte Branca · Iporá · Ivolândia
Portachuelo · Montero · Warnes · El Cerro · Laguna Concepción · Cuiabá · São Lourenço · Rondonópolis · Baliza · Caiapônia · Sa. das Divisões

SANTA CRUZ
Santa Cruz · Pompa Grande · Cotoca · San José · Santo Corazón · Lagoa Uberaba · Itiquira · Alto Garças · Santa Rita do Araguaia · Rio Verde
Samaipata · El Palmar · Llanos de Chiquitos · La Cal · Pôrto Jofre · Itiquira · Correntes · Taquari · Jataí
Villegrande · Abapó · Bañados de Izozog · 1425 · Robore · Serr. de Santiago · Pantanal do São Lourenço · Alto Araguaia · Baús · Mineiros · Serra do

MATO GROSSO DO SUL
Santa Ana · Puerto Suárez · **Corumbá** · Ladário · Lagoa Mandioré · Taquari · Pantanal do Rio Negro · Rio Verde de Mato Grosso · Itrumã · Cachoeira Alta · Caçu
Charagua · Fortín General Pando · Albuquerque · Nhecolândia · Coxim · Paraíso · Cassilândia · Apore
Fortín Ingavi · Coimbra · Pôrto Esperança · Negro · Corguinho · Alto Sucuriú · Paranaíba
Camiri · **OLIMPO** · Bahía Negra · Miranda · Rochedo · Aquidauana · Jaraguari · Aparecida do Taboado · Bubinha

CHUQUISACA
Carandaiti · Fortín Coronel Eugenio Garay · Fuerte Olimpo · Terenos · Ribas do Rio Pardo · Pereira Barreto
TARIJA · Fortín Madrejón · Puerto Guaraní · **Campo Grande** · Água Clara · Três Lagoas · **Andradina**
PARAGUAY · **BOQUERÓN** · Fortín Garrapatal · Pôrto Murtinho · Bonito · Nioaque · Sidrolândia · Maracaju · Xavantina · Mirandópolis · Aguapei
Tarija · Villa Montes · Yacuiba · Chaco Boreal · Jardim · Guia Lopes da Laguna · Panorama
SALTA · Tartagal · La Esmeralda

Pôrto Velho 404
5603

1:8 000 000

50　0　50　100　150　200 miles
50　0　100　200　300 km

ATLANTIC OCEAN

SALVADOR (Bahia)
ESPÍRITO SANTO
Tropic of Capricorn

Feira de Santana
Vitória da Conquista
Teófilo Otoni
Gov. Valadares
Caratinga
Montes Claros
Diamantina
BELO HORIZONTE
Vitória
Vila Velha
CAMPOS
RIO DE JANEIRO
NITERÓI
Juiz de Fora
BRASÍLIA
DISTRITO FEDERAL
GOIÂNIA
Anápolis
Uberlândia
Uberaba
Araguari
SÃO PAULO
SANTO ANDRÉ
SANTOS
São Vicente
CAMPINAS
Sorocaba
Jundiaí
Bauru
Marília
Presidente Prudente
Londrina
Maringá
CURITIBA
Ponta Grossa
Guarapuava
Paranaguá

M I N A S   G E R A I S
S Ã O   P A U L O
P A R A N Á
G O I Á S
B A H I A

West from Greenwich

Projection: Lambert's Equivalent Azimuthal
COPYRIGHT GEORGE PHILIP & SON LTD

m　ft
6000
4500
3000
1200
600
0
200
600
6000
12 000

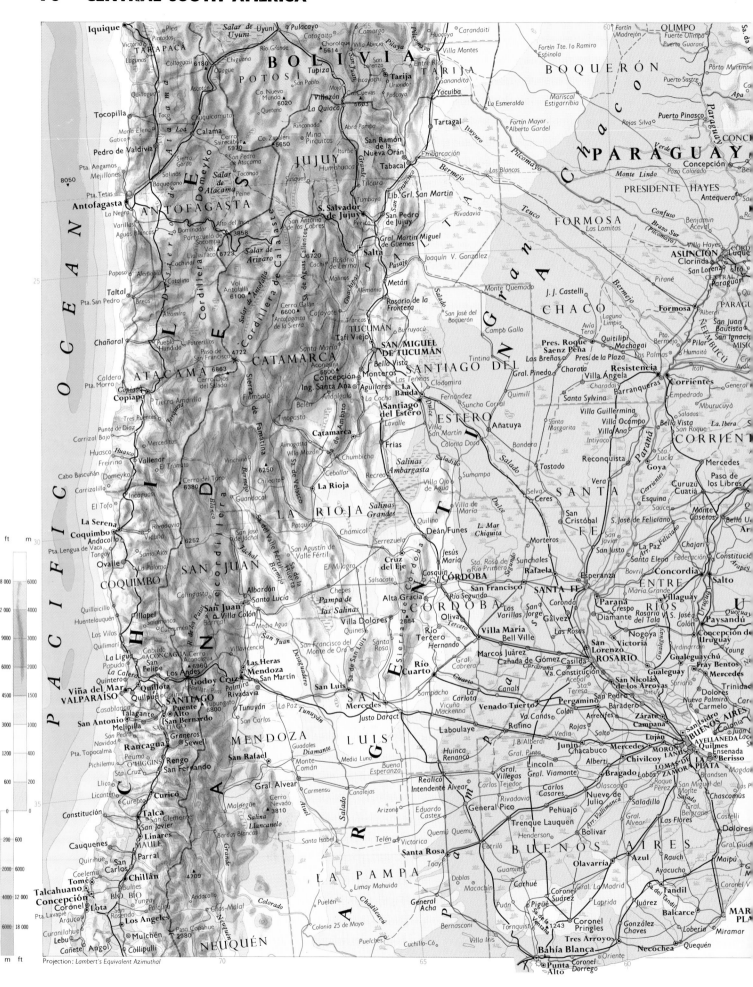

1:8 000 000

50   0   50   100   150 miles

50 0 50 100 150 200 km

BELO
HORIZONTE

GROSSO
SUL

Anhanguera
Macaúba
Três Lagoas
Xavantina
Mirandópolis
Andradina
Mirassol
Olímpia
S. José
do Rio Prêto
Passos
N. Lima
Itabirito
Congonhas
Cons.
Lafaiete
Ouro
Prêto
Ponte Nova
Vitória
Itaquari
Vila
Velha
Guarapari

Dourados
Rio Brilhante
Panorama
Araçatuba
Catanduva
Bebedouro
Ribeirão
Prêto
Batatais
Oliveira
Represa de
Furnas
Campo Belo
Carangola
Pico da
Bandeira
2890
Castelo
Cachoeiro
de Itapemirim

Pora
ro Juan Caballero
Pardo
Pres.
Epitácio
Adamantina
Tupã
SÃO
Jaboticabal
PAULO
Guaxupé
São João
da Boa Vista
Casa
Branca
São João
del Rei
Ubá
Muriaé
Alegre
Itaperuna
Guarus

Pôrto São José
Santo Anastácio
Presidente
Prudente
Martinópolis
Marília
Bauru
Araraquara
São
Carlos
Pinhal
Poços de
Caldas
Pouso
Alegre
Lavras
Barbacena
Cataguases
Leopoldina
Cambuci
CAMPOS

Paranavaí
Nova
Esperança
Assis
Santa Cruz
do Rio Pardo
Piracicaba
Limeira
Americana
Mogi-Mirim
Serra Cruzeiro
Bragança
Paulista
Três
Corações
Juiz de Fora
Três
Rios
Além Paraíba
RIO DE JANEIRO
Nova Friburgo
Macaé

PARANÁ
BRAZIL
Londrina
Rolândia
Maringá
Apucarana
CAMPINAS
Jundiaí
Itu
Sorocaba
S. J. dos Campos
Jacareí
Taubaté
Volta
Redonda
Barra do Pirai
Petrópolis
DUQUE DE CAXIAS
SÃO GONÇALO
Cabo Frio

Ponta Grossa
CURITIBA
SÃO PAULO
SANTO ANDRÉ
Angra dos Reis
NITERÓI
RIO DE JANEIRO
Tropic of Capricorn

SANTOS
São Vicente
Guarujá
Ilha de São Sebastião

Guaíra
Cascavel
Foz do Iguaçu
Iguaçu
Falls
Guarapuava
Irati
Palmeira
Antonina
Paranaguá
Guaratuba

MISIONES
Obera
Uruguai
Santa Rosa
Erechim
SANTA CATARINA
São Francisco do Sul
Joinvile
Itajaí
Blumenau
Brusque

Carazinho
Passo Fundo
Lajes
Ilha de Santa Catarina
Florianópolis

Cruz Alta
Vacaria
Tubarão
Laguna
Cabo Santa Marta Grande

RIO GRANDE
Caxias do Sul
Criciúma
Ararangua

Santa Maria
Santa Cruz
do Sul
Nôvo Hamburgo
Taquara

DO SUL
São Gabriel
PÔRTO ALEGRE
Osorio

Dom Pedrito
Camaquã
Lagoa dos Patos

Bagé
Pelotas
Mostardas

AY
Melo
Rio Grande

Jaguarão
Lagoa
Mirim

Treinta y Tres
Lagoa Mangueira

Santa Vitória do Palmar

Aigua
Castillos

Minas
Rocha

San Carlos
Maldonado

VIDEO

A T L A N T I C

O C E A N

5304

55   West from Greenwich   50   45   40   COPYRIGHT. GEORGE PHILIP & SON, LTD

1:8 000 000

50   0   50   100   150 miles
50   0   100   200 km

LA PAMPA

Colonia 25 de Mayo   Bernasconi   Tornquist 1243   Coronel Pringles   Juárez   Balcarce
Villa Iris   González Chaves   Loberia
Arauco   Mulchén   Paso Copahue   Collipulli 2880   Loncopué   **BUENOS AIRES**   Quequén
Cañete   Angol   Victoria   Colorado   Bahía Blanca   Punta Alta   Necochea
Capitán Pastene   Curacautín   Las Lajas   Barda del Medio   Médanos   B. Blanca   Coronel Dorrego
I. Mocha   Traiguén   Paso de los Indios   Neuquén   Fortín Uno   Mayor Buratovich
Temuco   Lautaro 3124   Paso Pino Hachado   Cipolletti   Oriente
Puerto Saavedra   Freire   Cherquenco 1824   Zapala   Cutral-Có   Neuquén   Allen   Gral. Roca   Río Colorado   I. Trinidad
Nueva Imperial   Pitrufquén   **NEUQUÉN**   Chelforó   Negro   Choele Choel   Colorado
ARAUCANIA   Tolten   Loncoche   Villarrica   Picún Leufú   Lamarque
Paso Mamuil Malal   **RÍO NEGRO**   Salina Gualicho   B. Anegada
Valdivia   Los Lagos   Las Coloradas   Junín de los Andes   Piedra del Águila   Gral. Conesa
Corral   L. Panguipulli 1253   3776   El Cuy   Stroeder
Pta. Galera   San Martín de los Andes   La Esperanza 1314   Sa. Colorada   Valcheta   Negro   Carmen de Patagones
La Unión   L. Ranco   Futrono   Paso Flores   Comallo   Los Menucos   Aguada Cecilio   San Antonio Oeste   Viedma
Osorno   Río Bueno   Lago Ranco   Pta. Rasa
Río Negro   Puyehue   L. Nahuel Huapi   Maquinchao   **Golfo San Matías**
LOS LAGOS   Vol. Osorno 2660   3554   San Carlos de Bariloche   Ingeniero Jacobacci   El Caín   Sierra Grande   G. José   Pta. Norte
L. Llanquihue   La Ensenada   Mte. Tronador   Quetrequile   Cona Niyeu   Verde   Puerto Lobos
Puerto Varas   Maullín   **Puerto Montt**   2185   El Bolsón   Norquinco   G. San José   Puerto Pirámides   **Pen. Valdés**
G. de los Coronados   El Maitén   G. Nuevo   Punta Delgada
Pta. Huechucuicui   G. de Ancud   Leleque   Gastre   Telsen   Puerto Madryn
Ancud 820   Achao   Gan Gan   Gaimán
Isla de Chiloé   **Castro**   Menéndez 2470   Gualjaina   **CHUBUT**   Rawson   Trelew
C. Quilán   Chaitén   Esquel   Chubut   Perdido   Chubut
Puerto Quellón   2440   Tecka   Pampa de Agnia   Las Plumas   Meseta de Montemayor
Boca del Guafo   2300   Yelcho   El Corcovado 2075   Paso de Indios   C. Raso
I. Guafo   Golfo Corcovado   Palena   José de San Martín   Chico
Islas Guaitecas   L. Gral. Vintter 1245   Gran Laguna Salada
Río Pico   Camarones   B. Camarones
Archipiélago   I. Magdalena   La Plata 2020   Genoa   C. Dos Bahías
I. Guamblin   **de los**   L. Fontana   L. Musters   B. Bustamante
I. Moraleda   Alto Río Senguer   L. Colhué Huapi   **Golfo**
Chonos   Coihaique   Facundo   Sarmiento   **San Jorge**
C. Taitao 1372   Puerto Aisén   Mayo   Río Mayo   Holdich   **Comodoro Rivadavia**
Balmaceda   Los Monos   Caleta Olivia
Península de Taitao   Mte. San Valentín 4058   L. Buenos Aires   Colonia Las Heras
Chile Chico   Perito Moreno   Pico Truncado
C. Tres Montes   I. Javier   Co. Arenales   L. Gral. Carrera   Los Antiguos   Fitz Roy   Mazaredo   C. Tres Puntas
Golfo de   3437   Cochrane   L. Pueyrredón 2726   1335   Jaramillo   C. Blanco
Penas   San Lorenzo 3700   Lago Posadas   Deseado   Puerto Deseado
Archipiélago   Las Horquetas   Pta. Medanosa
Guayaneco   Canal Baker   2280   Mt. Inés 1120   **SANTA CRUZ**   Bahía Laura
I. Campana   Mellizo Sur 3050   Gob. Gregores
I. Patricio Lynch   San Martín   L. Cardiel   **Altiplanicie Central**   San Julián
I. Esmeralda   Mte. Fitzroy 3375   Chico
G. Ladrillero   Co. Murallón 3600   L. Viedma   Tres Lagos   Cmte. Luis Piedrabuena
I. Mornington   Lago Argentino   Shehuen   Santa Cruz
G. Trinidad   **Bahía Grande**
I. Madre de Dios   Calafate   Puerto Coig
I. Duque de York   Chatham   **FALKLAND ISLANDS (ISLAS MALVINAS)**
C. Santiago   Esperanza   Coig   Jason Is.   Pebble I.   C. Dolphin
B. Salvación   I. Hanover   **Puerto Natales**   El Turbio   **Río Gallegos**   King George B.   Mt. Adam 700   Mt. Usborne 705
C. Jorge   Estrecho Nelson   Gallegos   Monte Dinero   Queen Charlotte B.   Port Darwin   Stanley
Arch. Reina Adelaida   G. Almirante Montt   C. Virgenes   Weddell I.   **West Falkland**   C. Meredith   **East Falkland**
C. Deseado   Pen. Muñoz   Seno Skyring   **Strait of Magellan**   Beauchêne I.
I. Riesco   Seno de Otway   Cerro Sombrero
I. Desolación   Gamero   Porvenir   **Isla**
Punta Arenas   Pen. Brunswick   San Sebastián   **Grande**
Santa Inés   B. Inútil   **de Tierra**
I. Otway   Dawson   Río Grande   **del**
Clarence   Capt. Aracena   Whiteside   **TIERRA**   **Fuego**
Pen. Brecknock 2469   Misión Fagnano   **DEL**   C. San Diego
Canal Cockburn   Mte. Darwin   L. Fagnano   **FUEGO**   I. de los Estados (Staten I.)
I. Stewart   Ushuaia   Est. de Le Maire
I. Londonderry   Gordon   Canal Beagle   I. Picton   I. Nueva
B. Cook   I. Hoste   I. Navarino   I. Lennox
Pen. Hardy   B. Nassau
Islas Wollaston
Is. Hermite   Cabo de Hornos (Cape Horn)
Islas Diego Ramírez

PACIFIC OCEAN

SOUTH ATLANTIC OCEAN

Projection: Lambert's Equivalent Azimuthal

West from Greenwich

COPYRIGHT, GEORGE PHILIP & SON, L

ft	m
	50
9000	3000
6000	2000
4500	1500
3000	1000
1200	400
600	200
0	0
200	600
2000	6000
4000	12 000

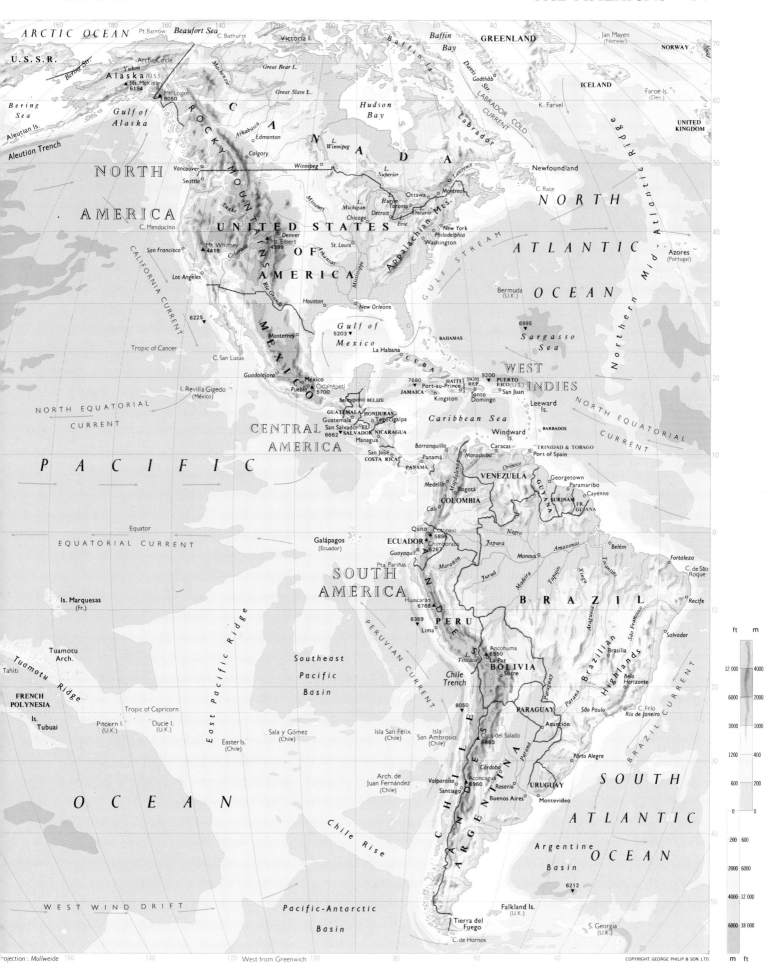

ARCTIC OCEAN   Pt.Barrow   *Beaufort Sea*   C. Bathurst   Victoria I.   Baffin Is.   *Baffin Bay*   **GREENLAND**   Jan Mayen (Norway)   **NORWAY**

U.S.S.R.   Arctic Circle   *Yukon*   **Alaska** (U.S.)   ▲Mt.McKinley 6194   Mackenzie   Great Bear L.   Great Slave L.   Godthåb   Str.   ICELAND   K. Farvel   Faroe Is. (Den.)

Bering Sea   Gulf of Alaska   ▲Mt Logan 6050   C A N A D A   Athabasca   Edmonton   Hudson Bay   LABRADOR COLD CURRENT   Labrador   **UNITED KINGDOM**

Aleutian Is.   Calgary   L. Winnipeg   Newfoundland   **NORTH**

Aleutian Trench   NORTH   Vancouver   ROCKY MOUNTAINS   Winnipeg   L. Superior   Ottawa   Montreal   C. Race   **ATLANTIC**

Seattle   Snake   L. Huron   Toronto   St. Lawrence Mts.

AMERICA   C. Mendocino   UNITED STATES   Missouri   Michigan   Detroit   Erie   Ontario   New York   Northern Mid-Atlantic Ridge   **OCEAN**

San Francisco   ▲Mt. Whitney 4418   Denver   Mt. Elbert 4399   Chicago   Philadelphia   Washington   Azores (Portugal)

CALIFORNIA CURRENT   Colorado   OF   St. Louis   Arkansas   Appalachian Mts.   GULF STREAM

Los Angeles   Rio Grande   AMERICA   Houston   Bermuda (U.K.)

6225 ▼   M E X I C O   New Orleans

Tropic of Cancer   C. San Lucas   5203 ▼   Gulf of Mexico   BAHAMAS   6995 ▼   *Sargasso Sea*

Monterrey   La Habana   CUBA   WEST

NORTH EQUATORIAL   Guadalajara   México ▲Citlaltépetl 5700   Puebla   9200 ▼   HAITI   DOM. REP.   PUERTO RICO (U.S.)   **INDIES**   NORTH EQUATORIAL

I. Revilla Gigedo (México)   7680 ▼   Port-au-Prince   Santo Domingo   San Juan

CURRENT   Belmopan BELIZE   JAMAICA   Kingston   Leeward Is.   CURRENT

GUATEMALA HONDURAS   *Caribbean Sea*   BARBADOS

CENTRAL   Guatemala   Tegucigalpa   Windward Is.   TRINIDAD & TOBAGO

San Salvador EL 6662 ▲   SALVADOR NICARAGUA   Port of Spain

P A C I F I C   AMERICA   Managua   Barranquilla   Caracas

San José   PANAMA   Maracaibo   Orinoco

COSTA RICA   Panamá   **VENEZUELA**   Georgetown   Paramaribo

Medellín   Magdalena   Bogotá   **GUYANA** SURINAM   Cayenne   FR. GUIANA

COLOMBIA   Cali

Equator   Galápagos (Ecuador)   Quito   Cotopaxi   Negro

EQUATORIAL CURRENT   **ECUADOR**   5896   Chimborazo 6267   Japurá   Amazonas   Belém

Guayaquil   Marañón   Manaus   C. de São Roque

Pta. Pariñas   Juruá   Madeira   Tapajós   Xingu   Fortaleza

Is. Marquesas (Fr.)   **SOUTH**   Huascarán 6768   **B R A Z I L**   Recife

Tahiti   **AMERICA**   PERUVIAN CURRENT   6369 ▼   **PERU**   Tocantins

East Pacific Ridge   Lima   São Francisco   Salvador   ft   m

FRENCH POLYNESIA   Tuamotu Arch.   *Southeast Pacific Basin*   Ancohuma 6550   **BOLIVIA**   Brazilian Highlands   Brasília   12 000 4000

Tuamotu Ridge   L. Titicaca   La Paz   Belo Horizonte

Is. Tubuai   *Chile Trench*   Sucre   6000 2000

Tropic of Capricorn   8050 ▼   PARAGUAY   São Paulo   C. Frío   3000 1000

Pitcairn I. (U.K.)   Ducie I. (U.K.)   Asunción   Río de Janeiro   1200 400

Easter Is. (Chile)   Sala y Gómez (Chile)   Isla San Félix (Chile)   Isla San Ambrosio (Chile)   Ojos del Salado 6863   Paraguay   Paraná   Pôrto Alegre   600 200

Arch. de Juan Fernández (Chile)   Córdoba   Aconcagua 6960   Rosario   **URUGUAY**   **SOUTH**   0 0

O C E A N   Valparaíso   Santiago   Buenos Aires   Montevideo   **ATLANTIC**   200 600

CHILE   ARGENTINA   *Argentine Basin*   2000 6000

WEST WIND DRIFT   *Pacific-Antarctic Basin*   6212 ▼   4000 12 000

Chile Rise   Falkland Is. (U.K.)   **OCEAN**   6000 18 000

Tierra del Fuego   S. Georgia (U.K.)

C. de Hornos

1:20 000 000

100   0   100   200   300   400   500 miles
100   0   200   400   600   800 km

CASPIAN SEA
-28

Ural Mountains
Ob
Pechora
Kama
1617
1894
Obshchiye
Volga Uplands
Volga
Mezen
N. Dvina
Onega
Kanin Peninsula
Kola Peninsula
White Sea
Tundra
Lapland
Finland
Scandinavia
Nordkinn
North Cape
Vesterålen
Lofoten
2123 Tromsø
Snøhetta
Umeå
Indals
Muonio
Inari

Central Russian Uplands
Don
Tsimlyansk Res.
Manych
Kuban
Terek
5633 Caucasus
Rion
Kura
Araks
5165
Ararat
Armenia
Kurdistan
Euphrates
Tigris
Anatolia
Taurus

Don
Rybinsk Res.
Volga
Oka
Ukraine
Dnepr (Dnieper)
Bug
Sea of Azov
Str. of Kerch
Crimea
Danube
BLACK SEA
2211
Bosporus
Ida 1766
5121
Aegean Sea

Russian Plain
Pripyat (Pripet) Marshes
Dnestr (Dniester)
Prut
Carpathians
Transylvanian Alps
2655 Tatra
Wallachia
Danube
Mures
Tisza
Plain of Hungary
Balkans
Balkan Peninsula
Pindus
Morea
Ionian Is.
Ionian Sea

L. Ladoga
Neva
Chudskoye
L. Onega
L. Ladoga
Gulf of Finland
Gulf of Riga
Gotland
Niemen
Wisła (Vistula)
Odra (Oder)
Elbe
Sudetes
Er. Geb.
Bohemian For.
Morava
Drava
Sava
Danube
Dinaric Alps
ADRIATIC SEA
Str. of Otranto
Calabria
3263 Etna
Sicily

Väner
Vätter
Mälaren
BALTIC SEA
North Sea
Harz 1142
Thür. For.
Weser
Weser
Elbe
Taunus
Erz. Geb.
Black For.
Rhine
2655
Alps
4807
Apennines
Vesuvius 1237
2914 Gr. Sasso
Tiber
Tyrrhenian Sea

Skagerrak
Kattegat
Jutland
Lindesnes
Heligoland
Netherlands
Weser
Ardennes
Eifel
Vosges
Jura
Rhône
Ligurian Sea
Corsica
Str. of Bonifacio
Sardinia

3734
NORWEGIAN SEA
Shetland Is.
Orkney Is.
Faroe Is.
Fisher Bank
Dogger Bank
NORTH SEA
Great Britain
Ireland
Irish Sea
Thames
English Channel
Brittany
Seine
Loire
Gironde
Garonne
Central Massif
1886
Cévennes
Gulf of Lions

Arctic Circle
Iceland
1491
Vatna Jökull 2119
ATLANTIC
Rockall
Hebrides
1343
1085
British Isles
Land's End
Valentia
C. Clear
Bay of Biscay
4861
Cantabrian Mts.
Old Castile
New Castile
Iberian Peninsula
Pico de Aneto 3404
Pyrenees
Sa. de Guadarrama
Douro
Duero
Sa. da Estrela
C. Finisterre
C. Roca
C. St. Vincent
C. Trafalgar
C. Spartel
Str. of Gibraltar
Sierra Morena
Guadalquivir
Andalusia
Sierra Nevada 3478
Maritime Atlas
Plateau of the Shotts
MEDITERRANEAN SEA
Balearic Is.
C. Bon
C. Blanco
Sr. of Messina
Ionian Sea

OCEAN

m
4000
2000
1000
500
200
0
ft
12 000
6000
3000
1200
600
0
200
2000
4000
6000
12 000

1:20 000 000

100   0   100   200   300   400   500 miles
100   0   200   400   600   800 km

ICELAND

ATLANTIC OCEAN

UNITED KINGDOM
SCOTLAND
IRELAND
WALES
ENGLAND
LONDON

NORWAY
SWEDEN
FINLAND
DENMARK
NETHER-LANDS
BELGIUM
GERMANY
West · East
POLAND
CZECHOSLOVAKIA
AUSTRIA
HUNGARY
FRANCE
SWITZERLAND
ITALY
SPAIN
PORTUGAL
MOROCCO
ALGERIA
TUNISIA

UNION OF SOVIET SOCIALIST REPUBLICS
RUSSIAN S.F.S.R.
ESTONIAN S.S.R.
LATVIAN S.S.R.
LITHUANIAN S.S.R.
BYELORUSSIAN S.S.R.
UKRAINIAN S.S.R.
MOLDAVIAN
GEORGIAN S.S.R.
ARMENIAN S.S.R.
AZERBAIJAN S.S.R.
KAZAKH S.S.R.

ROMANIA
BULGARIA
YUGOSLAVIA
ALBANIA
GREECE
TURKEY
CYPRUS
SYRIA
IRAQ
IRAN (PERSIA)

BLACK SEA
CASPIAN SEA
MEDITERRANEAN SEA
ADRIATIC SEA
NORTH SEA
BAY OF BISCAY

Arctic Circle

Projection: Bonne   West from Greenwich   East from Greenwich

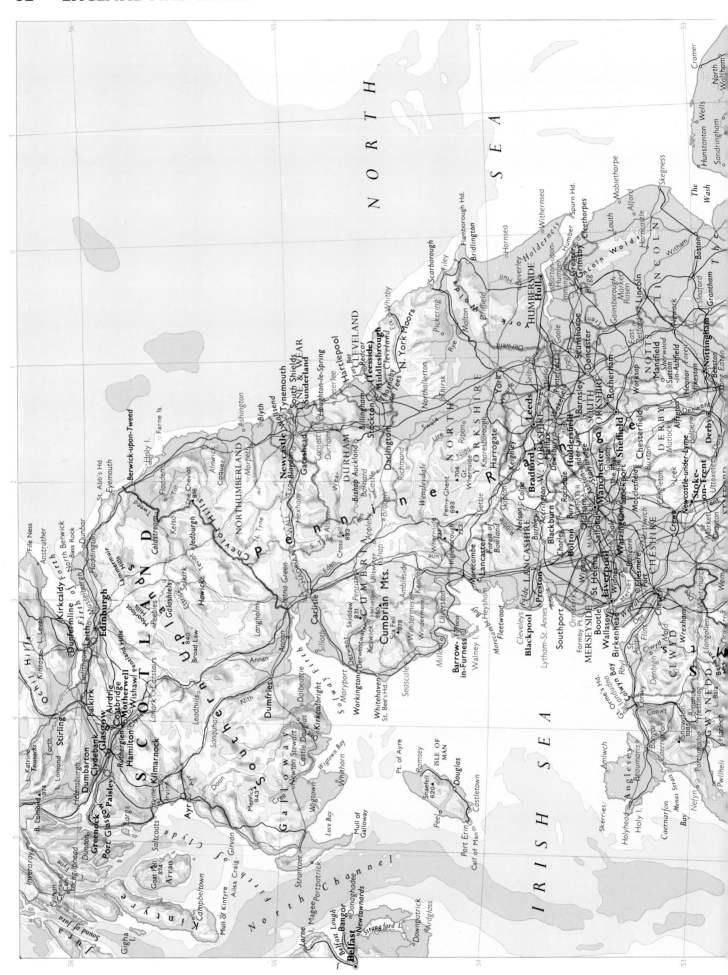

N O R T H   S E A

NORTH SEA

I R I S H   S E A

S C O T L A N D

Southern Uplands

Galloway

Cheviot Hills

NORTHUMBERLAND

P e n n i n e s

CUMBRIA

Cumbrian Mts.

LANCASHIRE

N. York Moors

York Wolds

CHESHIRE

DURHAM

YORKSHIRE

NORTH YORKSHIRE

WEST YORKSHIRE

SOUTH YORKSHIRE

DERBY

NOTTS

LINCOLN

Lincoln Wolds

HUMBERSIDE

Holderness

MERSEYSIDE

CLWYD

GWYNEDD

North Channel

Kintyre

Firth of Clyde

Sound of Jura

ISLE OF MAN

Anglesey

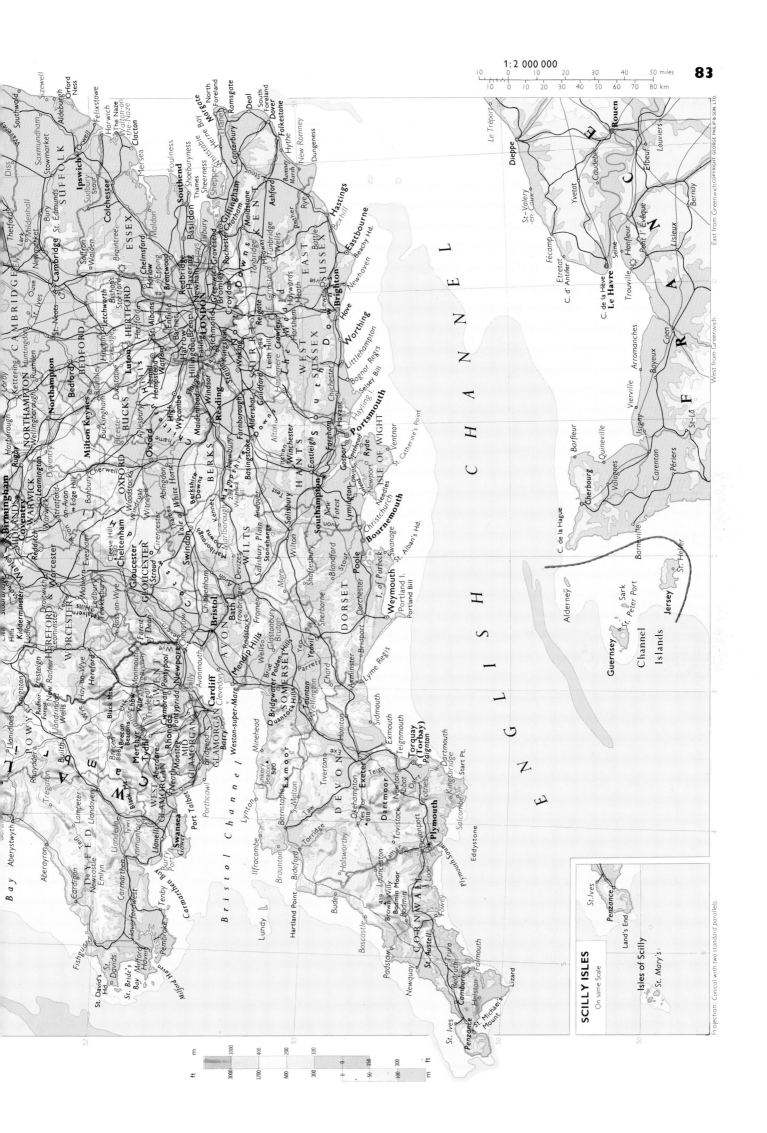

1 : 2 000 000

Projection: Conical with two standard parallels.

East from Greenwich COPYRIGHT GEORGE PHILIP & SON LTD.

West from Greenwich

SCILLY ISLES
On same Scale

Isles of Scilly

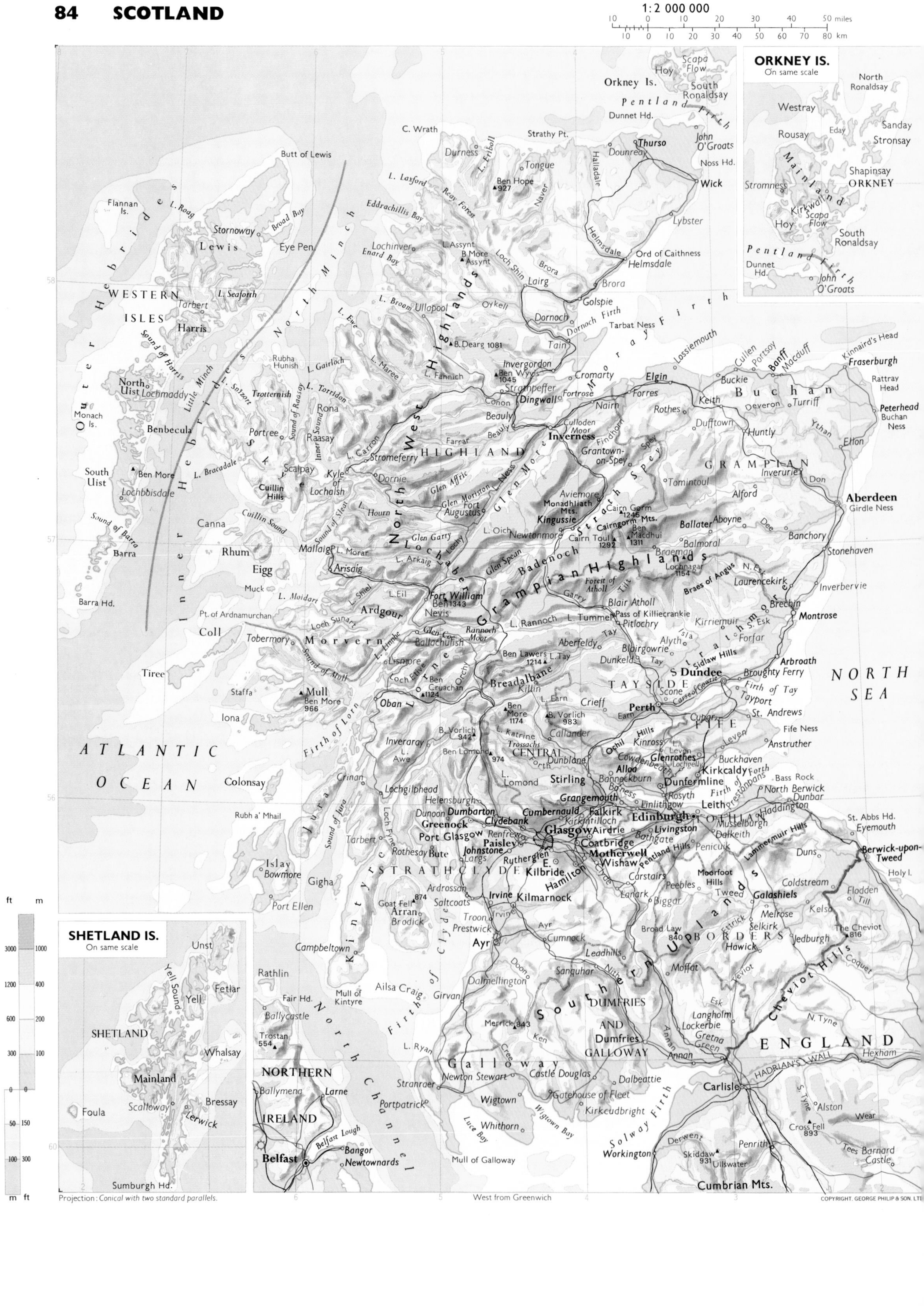

1 : 2 000 000

10 0 10 20 30 40 50 miles
10 0 10 20 30 40 50 60 70 80 km

ORKNEY IS.
On same scale

North Ronaldsay
Westray
Rousay   Eday   Sanday
Stronsay
Mainland   Shapinsay
Stromness   ORKNEY
Kirkwall
Hoy   Scapa Flow
South Ronaldsay
Pentland Firth
Dunnet Hd.
John O'Groats

Hoy   Scapa Flow
Orkney Is.   South Ronaldsay
Pentland Firth
Dunnet Hd.
John O'Groats   Noss Hd.
Wick
Thurso   Lybster
Dounreay
Strathy Pt.
C. Wrath   Halladale
Durness   L. Friboll
Tongue   Naver
Ben Hope 927
L. Laxford   Reay Forest
Eddrachillis Bay   Ord of Caithness
Lochinver   L. Shin   Helmsdale
Enard Bay   B. More Assynt   Lairg   Brora
L. Assynt   Golspie
Ullapool   Oykell   Dornoch
L. Broom   Dornoch Firth
B. Dearg 1081   Tain   Tarbat Ness
L. Fannich   Moray Firth
Butt of Lewis   Invergordon   Cullen   Portsoy
Ben Wyvis 1045   Lossiemouth   Banff   Macduff   Kinnaird's Head
Strathpeffer   Cromarty   Elgin   Buckie   Fraserburgh
Flannan Is.   L. Roag   Conon   Dingwall   Nairn   Forres   Keith   BUCHAN   Rattray Head
Stornoway   Broad Bay   Beauly   Culloden Moor   Rothes   Dufftown   Turriff   Peterhead
LEWIS   Eye Pen.   Findhorn   Huntly   Buchan Ness
WESTERN   Inverness   Grantown-on-Spey   GRAMPIAN
ISLES   Tarbert   Beauly   Inverurie   Elton
L. Seaforth   Aviemore   Alford   Aberdeen
HARRIS   HIGHLAND   Monadhliath Mts.   Cairn Gorm 1245   Tomintoul   Don   Girdle Ness
Rubha Hunish   Kingussie   Cairngorm Mts.   Ballater   Aboyne
North Uist   L. Gairloch   Trotternish   Newtonmore   Cairn Toul 1292   Cairn Macdhui 1311   Dee   Banchory
Lochmaddy   L. Maree   Braemar   Balmoral   Stonehaven
Monach Is.   Portree   Glen Affric   L. Oich   Badenoch   Lochnagar 1154   Braes of Angus   Laurencekirk
Benbecula   Raasay   Glen Moriston   Fort Augustus   Grampian Highlands   N. Esk   Inverbervie
South Uist   Ben More   Scalpay   Dornie   Glen Garry   Forest of Atholl   Tilt   Brechin
Lochboisdale   L. Bracadale   Kyle of Lochalsh   Glen Spean   Garry   Blair Atholl   Montrose
Barra   Cuillin Hills   L. Hourn   Pass of Killiecrankie   Kirriemuir   S. Esk
Barra Hd.   Cuillin Sound   Glen Fort   Pitlochry   Forfar   NORTH
Canna   Mallaig   L. Morar   L. Arkaig   L. Rannoch   L. Tummel   Alyth   SEA
Rhum   Arisaig   Fort William   Aberfeldy   Blairgowrie   Sidlaw Hills   Arbroath
Eigg   Ben Nevis 1343   Glen Coe   L. Tay   Dunkeld   Tay   Broughty Ferry
Muck   L. Moidart   L. Eil   Rannoch Moor   Ben Lawers 1214   S. Dundee
Pt. of Ardnamurchan   L. Smel   Ardgour   Ballachulish   Breadalbane   Scone   TAYSIDE   Firth of Tay
Coll   Loch Sunart   Killin   Crieff   FIFE   Tayport   St. Andrews
MORVERN   L. Linnhe   Ben Cruachan 1124   Ben More 1174   Perth   Fife Ness
Tobermory   Lismore   L. Earn   Ben Vorlich 983   Cupar   Anstruther
Tiree   Sound of Mull   Oban   B. Vorlich 942   Callander   Ochil Hills   Kinross   Leven
Staffa   Mull   Firth of Lorn   L. Katrine   Trossachs   L. Earn   Crieff   Cowdenbeath   Glenrothes   Buckhaven
Ben More 966   Inveraray   Ben Lomond 974   Dunblane   Alloa   Kirkcaldy
Iona   L. Awe   CENTRAL   Bannockburn   Dunfermline   Bass Rock
ATLANTIC   L. Fyne   L. Lomond   Stirling   Bo'ness   Rosyth   North Berwick   Dunbar
OCEAN   Colonsay   Forth   Grangemouth   Linlithgow   Firth of Forth   Prestonpans   St. Abbs Hd.
Lochgilphead   Helensburgh   Cumbernauld   Falkirk   Edinburgh   Leith   Eyemouth
Rubh a' Mhail   Crinan   Dunoon   Dumbarton   Bathgate   Livingston   LOTHIAN   Haddington
Greenock   Clydebank   Kirkintilloch   Dalkeith   Berwick-upon-Tweed
Port Glasgow   Renfrew   Glasgow   Airdrie   Penicuik   Holy I.
Islay   Rothesay   Bute   Paisley   Coatbridge   Lammermuir Hills   Duns
Bowmore   Johnstone   Largs   Rutherglen   Motherwell   Pentland Hills   Coldstream
Gigha   STRATHCLYDE   E. Kilbride   Wishaw   Peebles   Moorfoot Hills   Tweed   Galashiels
Port Ellen   Ardrossan   Kilbride   Hamilton   Carstairs   BORDERS   Kelso
Goat Fell 874   Saltcoats   Irvine   Kilmarnock   Lanark   Biggar   Melrose   Flodden   Till
Arran   Troon   Irvine   Tweed   Selkirk   Jedburgh   The Cheviot 816
Brodick   Prestwick   Ayr   Broad Law 840   Ettrick   Hawick   Coquet
Campbeltown   Ayr   Cumnock   SOUTHERN   Hawick   CHEVIOT   N. Tyne
Kintyre   Ailsa Craig   Girvan   Leadhills   UPLANDS   Moffat   HILLS
Mull of Kintyre   Doon   Sanquhar   Nith   Teviot   ENGLAND
Rathlin   Fair Hd.   Dalmellington   Esk   Langholm
Ballycastle   Merrick 843   DUMFRIES   Lockerbie
North   Ken   AND   Gretna Green
Channel   Newton Stewart   Dumfries   Annan   Hexham
Wigtown   Castle Douglas   Dalbeattie   Carlisle
NORTHERN   Stranraer   Gatehouse of Fleet   Kirkcudbright   HADRIAN'S WALL   S. Tyne   Wear
Portpatrick   Galloway   Solway Firth   Alston
IRELAND   Ballymena   Larne   Wigtown Bay   Derwent   Penrith
Whithorn   Workington   Skiddaw 931   Ullswater   Tees   Barnard Castle
Belfast   Bangor   Luce Bay   Mull of Galloway
Belfast Lough   Newtownards   Cumbrian Mts.

SHETLAND IS.
On same scale

Unst
Fetlar
Yell Sound   Yell
SHETLAND   Whalsay
Mainland   Bressay
Foula   Scalloway   Lerwick
Sumburgh Hd.

Projection: Conical with two standard parallels.

West from Greenwich

COPYRIGHT. GEORGE PHILIP & SON, LTD.

ft   m
3000   1000
1200   400
600   200
300   100
0   0
50   150
100   300
m   ft

1:2 000 000

10   0   10   20   30   40   50 miles
10   0   10   20   30   40   50   60   70   80 km

Towns underlined in Northern Ireland give their
names to the Districts in which they stand

The remaining Districts are:—

1 Fermanagh   5 Castlereagh
2 Moyle   6 Ards
3 Newtownabbey   7 Down
4 North Down   8 Newry & Mourne

1:4 000 000

20   0   20   40   60   80   100 miles
20   0   20   40   60   80   100   120   140   160 km

Orkney Is.
Westray   N. Ronaldsay
Mainland   Sanday
Stronsay
Hoy   Kirkwall
Pentland Firth   South Ronaldsay
Thurso
Wick

Shetland Is.
Unst
Yell
Mainland
Foula   Lerwick
Fair I.

ATLANTIC OCEAN

NORTH SEA

IRISH SEA

St. George's Channel

Bristol Channel

ENGLISH CHANNEL

SCOTLAND
North West Highlands
Grampian Mts.
Outer Hebrides
Inner Hebrides

Lewis
Stornoway
St. Kilda
Harris
North Uist
Benbecula
South Uist
Barra
Skye
Rhum
Eigg
Coll
Tiree
Staffa Iona
Mull
Colonsay
Jura
Islay
Kintyre
Arran

North Minch
Pentland Firth
Thurso
Wick
Golspie
Lairg
L. Shin
Ullapool
Kyle of Lochalsh
Dingwall
Nairn
Inverness
Invergordon
Elgin
Lossiemouth
Fraserburgh
Banff
Peterhead
Aberdeen
Stonehaven
Fort William
Ben Nevis 1343
Ballater
Balmoral
Blair Atholl
Forfar
Montrose
Arbroath
Dundee
Firth of Tay
St. Andrews
Perth
Crieff
Kinross
Cupar
Leven
Forth
Dunbar
Haddington
Edinburgh
Falkirk
Dunfermline
Kirkcaldy
Alloa
Stirling
Helensburgh
Greenock
Dumbarton
Paisley
Glasgow
Rothesay
Kilmarnock
Saltcoats
Prestwick
Ayr
Campbeltown
Berwick-on-Tweed
Galashiels
Selkirk
St. Boswells
Jedburgh
Peebles
Motherwell
Hamilton
Sanquhar
Nith
Moffat
Hawick
Cheviot Hills
Alnwick
Dumfries
Firth of Clyde
Firth of Lorn
Oban
Loch Linnhe
Lochgilphead
L. Lomond
L. Tay
L. Ness
Kingussie
Moray Firth

NORTHERN IRELAND
Derryveagh Mts.
Antrim Mts.
Mourne Mts.
Londonderry
Coleraine
Portrush
Larne
Ballymena
Ballymoney
Bangor
Belfast
Lisburn
Omagh
Enniskillen
Armagh
Downpatrick
Dundrum
Newry
Monaghan
Clones
L. Neagh
Malin Hd.
Tory I.
Aran I.
Letterkenny
Lifford

IRELAND
Donegal Bay
Killala Bay
Donegal
Sligo
Ballina
Westport
Castlebar
Connemara
Galway Bay
Galway
Athenry
Achill I.
Clare I.
Erris Hd.
Roscommon
Longford
Mullingar
Athlone
Tullamore
Birr
Nenagh
Ennis
Kilrush
Listowel
Tralee
Killarney
Macgillycuddy's Reeks 1040
Cahirciveen
Castletown Bere
Bantry
Bandon
Kinsale
Cork
Cobh
Cork Harbour
Youghal
Dungarvan
Fermoy
Mallow
Limerick
Golden Vale
Tipperary
Thurles
Clonmel
Carrick-on-Suir
Kilkenny
Carlow
Athy
Port Laoise
Kildare
Naas
Dublin (Baile Atha Cliath)
Dun Laoghaire
Bray
Wicklow Mts.
Wicklow
Arklow
Enniscorthy
New Ross
Waterford
Wexford
Rosslare
Carnsore Pt.
Drogheda
Balbriggan
Dundalk
Cavan
L. Mask
L. Corrib
L. Derg
Shannon
Loop Hd.

ENGLAND
WALES
Pennine Range
Cambrian Mts.
Cheviot Hills
Cumbrian Mts. 978
Cotswolds
Chiltern Hills
North Downs
South Downs
The Weald
The Fens
The Wash

Isle of Man
Douglas
Barrow
Morecambe Bay
Lancaster
Blackpool
Preston
Burnley
Blackburn
Bolton
Liverpool
St. Helens
Salford
Manchester
Stockport
Birkenhead
Macclesfield
Crewe
Chester
Wrexham
Stoke-on-Trent
Derby
Nottingham
Sheffield
Rotherham
Chesterfield
Mansfield
Lincoln
Leeds
Bradford
Halifax
Huddersfield
Wakefield
Barnsley
Scunthorpe
York
Hull
Grimsby
Spurn Hd.
Flamborough Hd.
Scarborough
Whitby
Middlesbrough
Darlington
Stockton
Hartlepool
Durham
Sunderland
Gateshead
South Shields
Tynemouth
Newcastle
Carlisle
Whitehaven
St. Bee's Hd.
Appleby
Kendal
Windermere
Ripon
Keighley
Beverley
Skegness
Boston
Sleaford
Grantham
Newark
Leicester
Oakham
Peterborough
Kings Lynn
Wisbech
Ely
Huntingdon
Northampton
Bedford
Cambridge
Bury St. Edmunds
Ipswich
Colchester
Harwich
Gt. Yarmouth
Norwich
Lowestoft
Coventry
Rugby
Corby
Leamington
Warwick
Stratford-on-Avon
Birmingham
Walsall
Wolverhampton
Kidderminster
Worcester
Hereford
Shrewsbury
Stafford
Burton-upon-Trent
Gloucester
Cheltenham
Monmouth
Oxford
Aylesbury
Luton
Hertford
Chelmsford
Buckingham
St. Albans
Watford
Slough
Windsor
Reading
London
Chatham
Gillingham
Maidstone
Margate
Canterbury
Ashford
Dover
Folkestone
Hastings
Eastbourne
Newhaven
Brighton
Worthing
Chichester
Portsmouth
Southampton
Winchester
Guildford
Aldershot
Reigate
Southend
Thames

Anglesey
Beaumaris
Holyhead
Caernarfon Bay
Caernarfon
Llandudno
Rhyl
Denbigh
Ruthin
Mold
Pwllheli
Dolgellau (Dolgelly)
Snowdon 1085
Cardigan Bay
Aberystwyth
Cardigan
Fishguard
St. David's Hd.
Haverfordwest
Milford Haven
Pembroke
Llanelli
Swansea
Port Talbot
Cardiff
Newport
Rhondda
Merthyr Tydfil
Brecon
Llandrindod Wells
Rhayader
Presteign
Welshpool
Montgomery
Llangollen
Newtown

Bristol
Bath
Trowbridge
Weston-super-Mare
Wells
Salisbury Plain
Salisbury
Wilton
Dorchester
Poole
Bournemouth
Weymouth
Needles
Newport
Isle of Wight
Exeter
Exmouth
Torquay
Dartmouth
Start Pt.
Plymouth
Devonport
St. Austell
Truro
Camborne
Penzance
Falmouth
Lizard
Land's End
Scilly Is.
Bude
Barnstaple
Ilfracombe
Lundy I.
Exmoor
Dartmoor
Taunton
Yeovil
Axminster
Swindon

West from Greenwich   East from Greenwich

Projection: Conical with two standard parallels

COPYRIGHT. GEORGE PHILIP & SON. LTD.

ft   m
3000 1000
1800   600
1200   400
600   200
300   100
0   0
100   300
200   600
400   1200
m   ft

1:2 500 000

10 0 10 20 30 40 50 miles
10 0 10 20 30 40 50 60 70 80 km

Projection: Conical with two standard parallels

East from Greenwich

COPYRIGHT. GEORGE PHILIP & SON LTD

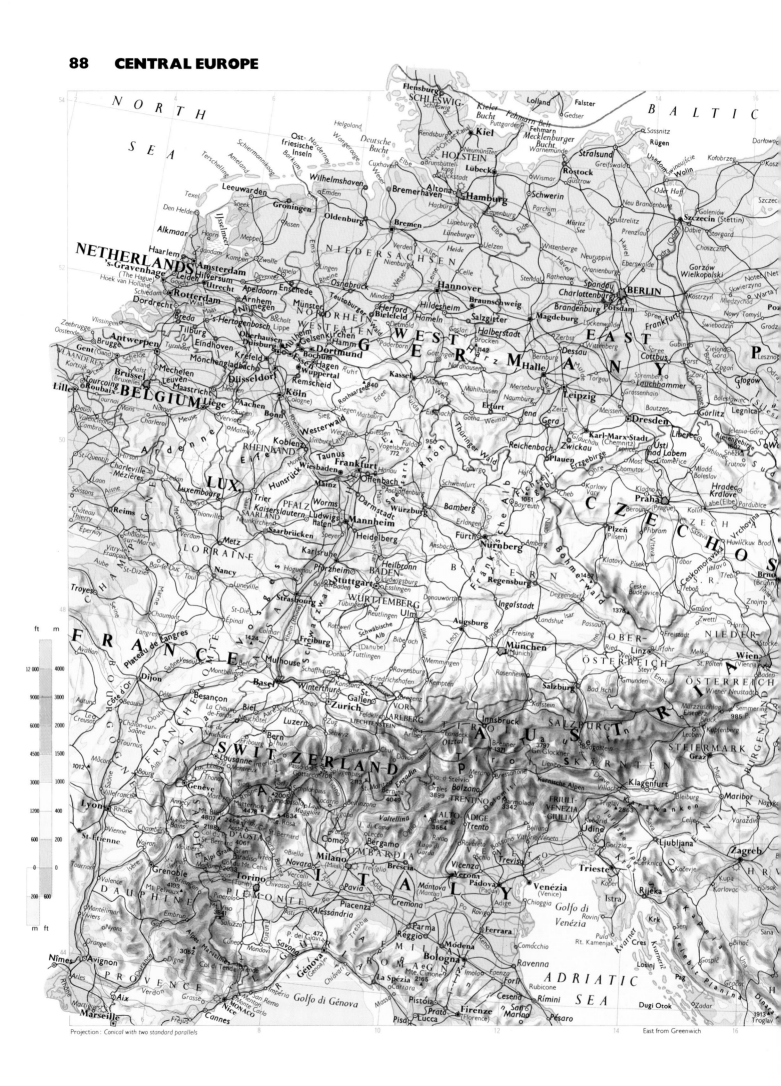

1:5 000 000

50   0   50   100 miles
50   0   50   100   150
km

**CENTRAL
EUROPE
POLITICAL**
1:25 000 000

DENMARK   København

NETH.   Berlin   POLAND   Warszawa   U.S.S.R.
WEST   EAST
BELGIUM   GERMANY
Brussel   Bonn   Praha
LUX.   CZECHOSLOVAKIA
FRANCE   Wien   Budapest
SWITZ.   AUSTRIA   HUNGARY   ROMANIA
Bern   LIECHT.

ITALY   Beograd   Bucureşti
MONACO   SAN MARINO   YUGOSLAVIA
Roma   BULGARIA
Sofiya

A

Zatoka
Gdańska

Zelenogradsk   Kaliningrad (Königsberg)   Chernyakhovsk   Vilnius   LITHUANIAN
Gdynia   Pregolya   S.S.R.
Sopot   R.   S.   F.   S.   R.   Gusev
Gdańsk   Braniewo   Lyna   ▲309   Suwałki   Alitus   Varena
(Danzig)   Elbląg   Kętrzyn   Gizycko   Augustów   Lida   Novogrudok
Malbork   Olsztyn   Grodno   Neman
Starogard   Kwidzyń   Ostróda   Pojezierze   Mazurski   Sokółka   ▲238   BYELORUSSIAN
Chełmno   Grudziądz   Iława   Mława   Ciechanów   Ostrów   Mazowiecka   Hajnówka   Bereza   S.S.R.
Toruń   Rypin   Lipno   Pułtusk   Brańsk   Czeremcha
Włocławek   Płock   Wkra   Bug   Zhabinka
Wisła (Vistula)   Warszawa   Mińsk   Mazowiecki   Siedlce   Biała   Brest
Kutno   Pruszków   (Warsaw)   Żyrardów   Otwock   Łuków   Podlaska
Koło   Łęczyca   Łowicz   Skierniewice   Grójec   Łuków   Międzyrzec   Podlaski
Konin   Kalisz   Zduńska   Łódź   Pilica   Kozienice   Włodawa
Wola   Tomaszów   Mazowiecki   Radom   Puławy   Chełm   Kovel
ostrów   Wieluń   Piotrków   Trybunalski   Końskie   Lublin   Vladimir   Volynskiy   Lutsk
Warta   Radomsko   Rádomsko   Ostrowiec   Świętokrzyski   Sandomierz   Krasnik   Zamość   Sokal   Rovno
Opole   Częstochowa   Kielce   Jędrzejów   Tarnobrzeg   390▲   San   Dubno   Ostróg
Tarnowskie   Góry   Zawiercie   Pinczów   Kamenka   Bugskaya   Radekhov   Brody
Zabrze   Bytom   Sosnowiec   Dąbrowa   Tarnowska   Przeworsk   Zolochev   Starokonstantinov
Gliwice   Chorzów   Katowice   Wisła (Vistula)   Jarosław   Rzeszów   Gorodok   Lvov   Ternopol
Kraków   Tarnów   Przemyśl   ▲471   Khmelnitskiy   ▲384
börz   Wieliczka   Nowy   Jasło   Sanok   Sambor   Dnestr   Buchach   Chortkov   Vinnitsa
Bielsko-   Sącz   Krosno   Drogobych   Stryi
Biała   Dukelský   Pr.   Borislav   Turka   Zhmerinka
Český   Cieszyn   1725   ▲502   Ivano-Frankovsk   Zaleshchiki   Kamenets-Podolskiy
Frýdek-   Západné   Beskydy   Tatry   Vychodné   Besky   Nadvornaya   Uman
Mistek   550   Žilina   Ružomberok   ▲2655   Prešov   ▲780   ▲1881   Kolomyya   Snyatyn   Khotin   Pervomaisk
Váh   SLOVAK   S.S.R.   Kosice   Uzhgorod   Per Yablonitse   Chernovtsy   Yedintsy   Soroki
Nizke   Tatry   Mukachevo   931▲   Storozhinets   Beltsy   Kotovsk
Kremnica   Slovenské   Rudohorie   Beregovo   2061▲   Dorohoi
Banská   Bystrica   Zvolen   Sátoraljaujhely   Khust   Sighetul   Rădăuti   Botoşani
Nitra   Banská   Štiavnica   Lučenec   Sajó   Tokaj   Pietrosul   2305▲   Vatra-Dornei   Suceava
N.   Hron   Miskolc   Nyiregyháza   Baia   Mare   Iaşi   ▲429   Kishinev
Zámky   Eger   Mezőkövesd   Satu   Mare   Someş   2102▲   Bistriţa   Roman   Bendery
Komárno   Gyöngyös   Hajdúböszörmény   Carei   Baia   Mare   Pietrosu   Piatra   Tiraspol
Esztergom   Vác   Hatvan   Jászberény   Dej   Bistriţa   Neamţ   Yaslu
Tatabánya   Hegysag   Karcag   Debrecen   Odessa
Székesfehérvár   Újpest   Cegléd   Szolnok   Mezőtúr   Oradea   Cluj   Turda   Praid   Bacău   Belgorod   Dnestrovskiy
BUDAPEST   Kecskemét   Körös   Negru   Tirgu   Aiud   Odorhelul   Secuiesc   Piatra   Neamţ
Dunaújváros   Kiskunfélegyháza   Salonta   Mureş   Miercurea   Ciuc   Birlad   Kagul
Dunaföldvár   Kalocsa   Békéscsaba   Gyula   Crişul   ▲1848   Abrud   Sighişoara   Bretcu
Kiskőrös   Szentes   Mţii Bihor   Transilvania   Medias   Focşani
Székszárd   Baja   Kiskunhalas   Hódmezővásárhely   Mákó   Brad   Alba-Iulia   Ozero
Bataszék   Szeged   Arad   Muresul   Deva   Sighişoara   Sibiu   Făgăraş   Galaţi   Sasyk
Pécs   Subotica   Senta   Kikinda   Simeria   Simeria   Braşov   Rimnicu   Sărat   Ismail   Kiliya
Mohács   Timişoara   Lugoj   Hunedoara   ROMANIA   Carpaţii   Meridionali   2535▲   2507▲   Braila   467▲   Tulcea   Sulina
Osijek   Novi   Sad   Banat   Caransebeş   Turnu   Roşu   Vt. Negoiul   Vt. Omul   Buzău   Reni   Bolgrad
bzok   Vinkovci   Zrenjanin   Reşiţa   Petroşeni   350   Cimpina   Buzău   Dunărea   (Danube)
Bosna   Sremska   Petrovaradin   Vršac   Bela   Crkva   Porta   Orientalis   2518   2509   Peleaga   Parîngul-Mare   Cimpulung   Tirgovişte   Ploieşti
Novi   Sad   Petrovaradin   Timişoara   Tirgu   Jiu   Rimnicu   Vilcea   Pitesti   Cernavodă   BLACK
Brčko   Bijeljina   Zemun   Pančevo   Mehadia   Portile   de   Fier   Ilu   Valahia   Bucureşti   Ialomiţa   Constanţa
Tuzla   Beograd   Orşova   Turnu-   (Bucharest)
Zemun   (Belgrade)   Smederevo   Severin   Pitesti   Slatina   Dîmbovita   Calaraşi   SEA
UNA   Pozarevac   Arges   Silistra
GOSLAVIA   1346   Craiova   Olteniţa   Mangalia
Sarajevo   Titovo   Užice   Čačak   Negotin   Caracal   Olt   Turnu   Giurgiu   Talbukhin
nik   Han Pijesak   Kragujevac   Bor   Timok   Măgurele   Ruse   (Ruschuk)   BULGARIA
Valjevo   Zaječar   Vidin   Corabia   Zimnicea   Sofiya
Bosna   Drina   Sava   Morava   Lom   Dunărea   (Danube)

COPYRIGHT. GEORGE PHILIP & SON. LTD.

1 : 5 000 000

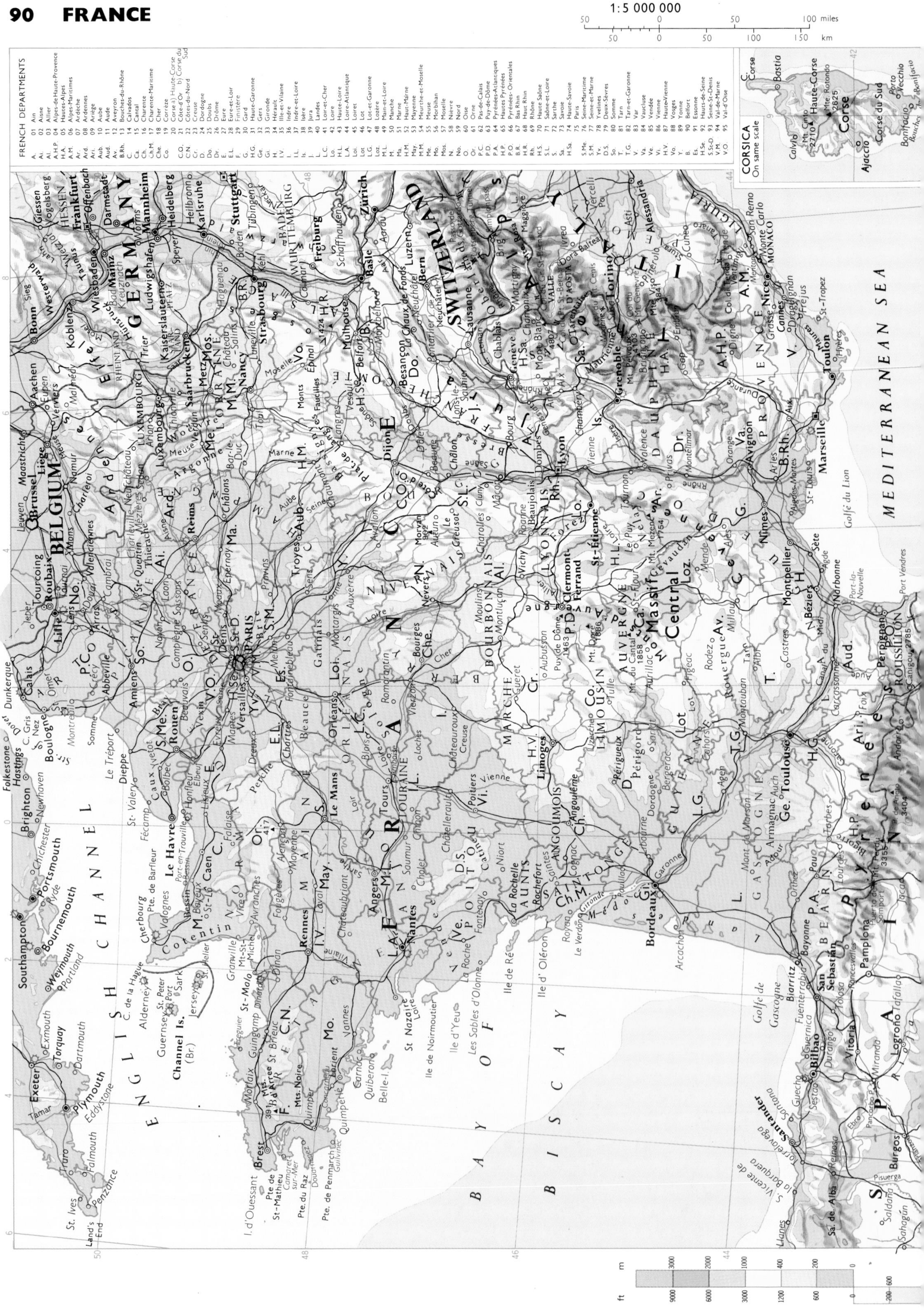

50   0   50   100 miles
50   0   50   100   150 km

FRENCH DEPARTMENTS

Abbr.	No.	Department
A.	01	Ain
Ai.	02	Aisne
Al.	03	Allier
B.A.	04	Alpes-de-Haute-Provence
H.A.	05	Hautes-Alpes
A.M.	06	Alpes-Maritimes
Ard.	07	Ardèche
	08	Ardennes
	09	Ariège
Au.	10	Aube
Aud.	11	Aude
Av.	12	Aveyron
B.Rh.	13	Bouches-du-Rhône
Ca.	14	Calvados
	15	Cantal
Ch.	16	Charente
Ch.M.	17	Charente-Maritime
Che.	18	Cher
Co.	19	Corrèze
	20	Corse a) Haute-Corse b) Corse du Sud
C.O.	21	Côte-d'Or
C.N.	22	Côtes-du-Nord
Cr.	23	Creuse
D.	24	Dordogne
Do.	25	Doubs
Dr.	26	Drôme
E.	27	Eure
E.L.	28	Eure-et-Loir
F.	29	Finistère
G.	30	Gard
H.G.	31	Haute-Garonne
Ge.	32	Gers
Gi.	33	Gironde
H.	34	Hérault
I.V.	35	Ille-et-Vilaine
I.	36	Indre
I.L.	37	Indre-et-Loire
Is.	38	Isère
J.	39	Jura
La.	40	Landes
L.C.	41	Loir-et-Cher
Lo.	42	Loire
H.L.	43	Haute-Loire
L.A.	44	Loire-Atlantique
Loi.	45	Loiret
L.	46	Lot
L.G.	47	Lot-et-Garonne
Loz.	48	Lozère
M.L.	49	Maine-et-Loire
Ma.	50	Manche
M.	51	Marne
H.M.	52	Haute-Marne
May.	53	Mayenne
M.M.	54	Meurthe-et-Moselle
Me.	55	Meuse
Mo.	56	Morbihan
Mos.	57	Moselle
N.	58	Nièvre
No.	59	Nord
O.	60	Oise
Or.	61	Orne
P.C.	62	Pas-de-Calais
P.D.	63	Puy-de-Dôme
P.A.	64	Pyrénées-Atlantiques
H.P.	65	Hautes Pyrénées
P.O.	66	Pyrénées-Orientales
B.R.	67	Bas-Rhin
H.R.	68	Haut-Rhin
Rh.	69	Rhône
H.S.	70	Haute-Saône
S.L.	71	Saône-et-Loire
Sa.	72	Sarthe
Sav.	73	Savoie
H.Sav.	74	Haute-Savoie
	75	Paris
S.Me.	76	Seine-Maritime
S.M.	77	Seine-et-Marne
Y.	78	Yvelines
D.S.	79	Deux-Sèvres
So.	80	Somme
T.	81	Tarn
T.G.	82	Tarn-et-Garonne
Va.	83	Var
V.	84	Vaucluse
Ve.	85	Vendée
Vi.	86	Vienne
H.V.	87	Haute-Vienne
Vo.	88	Vosges
Yo.	89	Yonne
B.	90	Belfort
Es.	91	Essonne
H.Se.	92	Hauts-de-Seine
S.St-D.	93	Seine-St-Denis
V.M.	94	Val-de-Marne
V.O.	95	Val-d'Oise

CORSICA
On same scale

Corse
Haute-Corse
Corse du Sud

m 3000 2000 1000 400 200 0
ft 9000 6000 3000 1200 600 0

1:5 000 000

50 0 50 100 miles

50 0 50 100 150 km

Projection: Conical with two standard parallels

COPYRIGHT GEORGE PHILIP & SON LTD

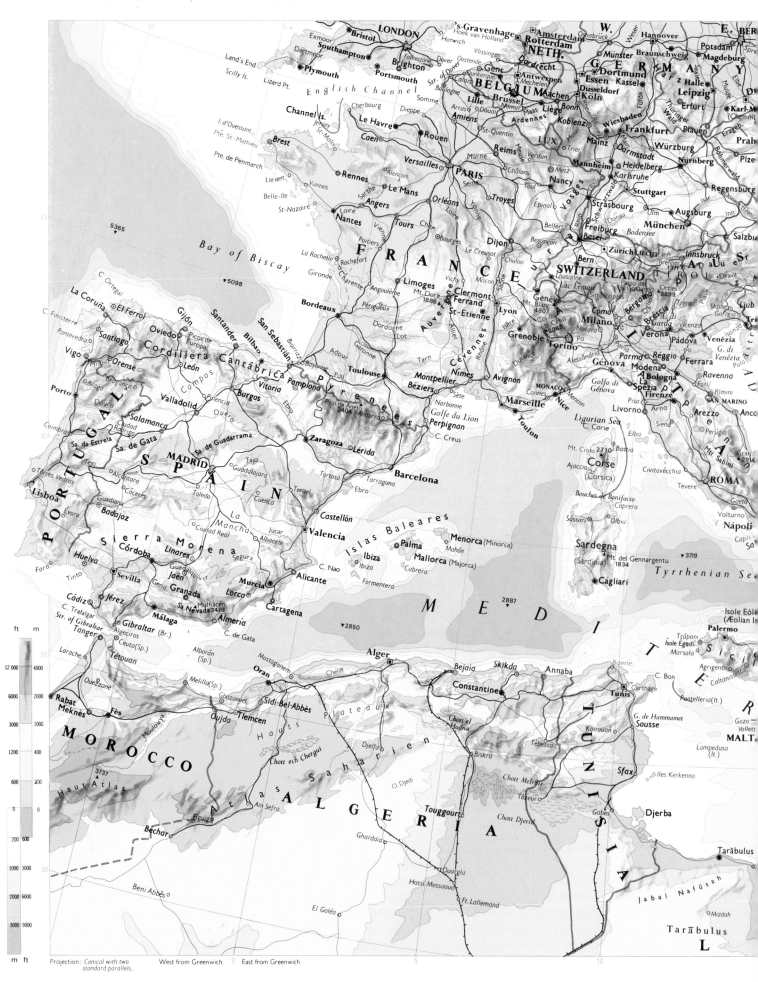

1:10 000 000

50   0   50   100   150   200 miles
50   0   100   200   300 km

POLAND
Poznań   Płock   Wisła (Vistula)   Warszawa   Pinsk   Polesye   Chernigov   Konotop   Sumy   Belgorod   Kozanskaya
Łódź   Brest   Pripyat   Pipyat   Nezhin   Kharkov   Volgograd
Wrocław   Radom   Lublin   Goryn   Kiyev   Pereyaslav-Khmelnitskiy   S.   S.   R.   Poltava   Voroshilovgrad (Lugansk)   Kamensk-Shakhtinskiy   Tsimlyanskoye   Vdkhr.
Chorzów   Kielce   Lutsk   Rovno   Zhitomir   Dnepr   Belaya Tserkov   Kremenchug   U   Artemovsk   Slavyansk   Vdkhr.
Ostrava   Kraków   Tarnów   Przemyśl   Lvov   Vinnitsa   U.   Berdichev   Kirovograd   Dneprodzerzhinsk   (Dnieper)   Pavlograd   Gorlovka   Makeyevka   Shakhty
Jablunkovsky Pr.   Tatry   Carpathian   Kamenets-Podol'skiy   Uman   S.   S.   Krivoy   Dnepropetrovsk   Zaporozhye   Donetsk   Novocherkassk
HOSLOVAKIA   550   2655   Prut   Mogilev-Podolskiy   Balta   Rog   Zhdanov (Mariupol)   Taganrog   Rostov
Košice   Chernovtsy   MOLDAVIAN   Dnestr   Pervomaysk   Voznesensk   S.   S.   R.   Azov   Manych
Bratislava   Miskolc   Vah   Hron   Tisza   Tokaj   Botoşani   Iaşi   Kishinev   Bendery   Balta   Nikolayev   Melitopol   Berdyansk   Oz. Manych Gudilo   Stavropol
Budapest   Debrecen   Sta. Maria   Pietrosul   2305   Kishinev   Tiraspol   Kherson   Perekop   Sea of Azov   Kerch   Tikhoretsk
HUNGARY   Oradea   Pietrosu   2102   S.   S.   R.   Odessa   Krasnodar   Armavir
Kecskemét   Cluj-Napoca   Belgorod-Dnestrovskiy   Karkinitskiy Zaliv   Krymskaya (Crimea)   Feodosiya   Kuban'   Maykop
Balaton   Hódmezővásárhely   Arad   ROMANIA   Sibiu   Negoiu   Braşov   Orasul Stalin   Ismail   Sulina   M. Tarkhankut   Yevpatoriya   Simferopol   1545   Novorossiysk   Tuapse
Szeged   2535   Meridionali   Galaţi   Sevastopol   Balaklava   Yalta
Subotica   Timişoara   Carpaţii   Portile   Piteşti   Brăila   BLACK   SEA   Sukhumi
Novi Sad   Petrovaradin   de Fier   Ploieşti   Constanţa   2211   Poti
Brod   Beograd   Orşova   Bucureşti   Silistra   İnce Burnu   Sinop   Batumi
Smederevo   Craiova   Dunărea (Danube)   Ruse   Tolbukhin   Batumi
Sarajevo   Kragujevac   Turnu-Severin   Vidin   Pleven   Tŭrnovo   Varna   İnebolu   Samsun   Giresun   Tirebolu   Trabzon   Rize
Mostar   Niš   Stara   Planina   Sliven   Burgas   Kastamonu   2565   Amasya   Kuzey   Anadolu   Dağları
Durmitor   2522   Sofiya   BULGARIA   Maritsa   Karadeniz Boğazı   Zonguldak   Kütahya   Çorum   Tokat   Sivas   Erzincan
Kotor   2764   Musala   Plovdiv   Edirne   (Bosporus)   Ereğli   Bolu   Ankara   Kızıl Irmak   Yozgat   Keban
Cetinje   2925   Rhodopi   Planina   İstanbul   Üsküdar   İzmit   Çankırı   Gürün   Malatya
Skopje   Strumica   Tekirdağ   Marmara   Üsküdar   İznik Gölü   Sakarya   Beypazarı   TURKEY   Kirşehir   Kayseri   Maraş
Tirana   Vardar   Sérrai   Kavalla   Denizi   Bursa   Bilecik   Eskişehir   Tuz   Erciyas   3770   Keban
Durrës   Bitola   Alexandroúpolis   Enez   Gelibolu   Bandırma   Çanakkale   Eskişehir   Gölü   Nigde   Gaziantep
Vlora   Athos   Gökçeada   (Gallipoli)   Troy   Balıkesir   Kütahya   Afyon Karahisar   Aksaray   Maraş   Osmaniye   Halab
Elbasani   2917   Límnos   Çanakkale Boğazı   Bolvadin   Karaman   Toroslar   Adana   Antakya   SYRIA
Thessaloníki   Notia   Pindhos   2033   Ayvalık   Çürüksu Çayı   Eğridir   Konya   Tarsus   Mersin   Dağları   İskenderun Körfezi   Al Lādhiqīyah   Hamah
GREECE   Lárisa   Vólos   Lésvos   Manisa   Aloşehir   Gölü   Beyşehir   Gölü   Silifke   Antakya   Hims
Kérkira   Vóriai Sporadhes   Évvoia   Khíos   İzmir   Aydın   İsparta   Elmalı   3086   Antalya   Baniyas   Tarabulus
Kefallinía   Athínai   Sámos   Muğla   Denizli   Burdur   Antalya   Körfezi   Nicosia   Famagusta   Tarābulus   Dimashq (Damascus)
Návpaktos   Piraiévs   Ikaría   Ródhos   Megiste   Morphou   LEBANON   2814   Jabal ad Durūz
Patrai   Kíklades   Síros   Andros   (Kastellórizon)   CYPRUS   Larnaca   Bayrūt (Beirut)   Jabal ad Durūz   Bosra
Pelopónnisos   Spárti   Náxos   Dhodhekánisos   Olympos   1951   Saydā   ash Shaykh
Olympia   Kalamáta   Mílos   Thíra   Ródhos   4486   Limassol   'Akko   Hefa (Haifa)   Jordan
Pílos   5121   los   Kárpathos   Tel Aviv-Yafo   Amman   JORDAN
Ákra Taínaron   Kithira   Khaniá   Íraklion   Gaza   Jerusalem   Dead Sea   Ma'ān
Andikíthira   Ídhi Óros   Rashid   Baḥra el Burullus   Dumyāt   Bur Sa'id   El 'Arish   Petra
Kríti   2456   El Mahalla   el Kubra   El Qantara   Ismā 'ilīya
Ionian   Sea   4135   Megiste   El Iskandarîya   Tanta   Gebel   el Tih   Al 'Aqabah
Zákinthos   Cyrene   Darnah   Khalīj Bōmba   Matrūh   El Suweis   Sinai   2637
C. Sta. Maria di Leuca   Al Marj (Barce)   Tubruq   Salūm   Khalīg el Salūm   Nile   El Faiyūm   Beni Suef
Sila   1929   Banghāzī   El 'Alamein   El QÂHIRA   EGYPT   Canal   Khalīj al 'Aqaba
Taranto   Khalīj Surt   Barqa   Salūm   Khalīj es Suweis
Brindisi   3174
Bari

MEDITERRANEAN   SEA

Golfo di Táranto
Srr. of Otranto

3083

COPYRIGHT. GEORGE PHILIP & SON, LTD.

– – – – – Division between Greeks
and Turks in Cyprus;
Turks to the north.

Passo del S. Gottardo
SWITZERLAND
Genève
Lyon
Brenner 1371
Merano
Bolzano
TRENTINO ALTO-ADIGE
Bressanone
Alpi Carniche
Villach
Klagenfurt
Bleiburg
Maribor
Mt. Blanc 4807
Matterhorn Mte. Rosa 4478 4634
Bernina 4049
P.so. di Stelvio 2757
Ortles
Marmolada 3342
Adamello 3554
Trento
Belluno
FRIULI VENEZIA GIULIA
Triglav 2863
Kobarid (Caporetto)
Udine
Gorízia
Ljubljana
Sava
Zagreb
Como
Bergamo
Lago di Garda
Rovereto
Schio
Vicenza
Treviso
Trieste
Novara
Milano (Milan)
Bréscia
Verona
Padova (Padua)
Venézia (Venice)
Golfo di Venézia
Pula (Pola)
Rijeka (Fiume)
Torino (Turin)
PIEMONTE
Pavia
Cremona
Mantova (Mantua)
Adige
Chióggia
Rovigo
Rovinj
Grenoble
Pinerolo
V. Pelvoux 4103
Asti
Alessándria
Piacenza
Parma
Ferrara
Krk
Cres
Losinj
DAUPHINÉ
Cuneo
P. dei Giovi 472
Réggio
Módena
Bologna
Ravenna
Comácchio
Pag
Avignon
PROVENCE
Savona
Genova (Genoa)
Carrara
Mte. Cimone 2165
Forlì
Cesena
Rimini
San Marino
Pésaro
Fano
Ancona
Aix
Marseille
Nice
Monaco
Riv. di Levante
La Spézia
Pistóia
Prato
Firenze (Florence)
Arezzo
Perúgia
Macerata
Toulon
Cannes
Côte d'Azur
San Remo
Golfo di Génova
Pisa
Livorno (Leghorn)
TOSCANA
Siena
UMBRIA
Ascoli Piceno
Teramo
Pescara
Îles d'Hyères
LIGURIAN SEA
C. Corse
Elba
Spoleto
Terni
Rieti
Gran Sasso 2914
L'Aquila
CORSE (CORSICA) (Fr.)
Mt. Cinto 2710
Aléria
ROMA (Rome)
Tivoli
MOLISE
Térmoli
Ajaccio
Sartène
Bonifacio
Civitavécchia
Ostia
Latina
Campobasso
Fóggia
G. di Manfredónia
Asinara
Golfo dell' Asinara
Maddalena
Caprera
Golfo Aranci
Olbia (Terranova)
BASILICATA
Sássari
Nuoro
SARDEGNA (SARDINIA)
Mte. Santo
3719
Napoli (Naples)
Salerno
Cágliari
Golfo di Cágliari
C. Spartivento
TYRRHENIAN SEA
Cosenza
Palermo
Messina
Réggio
Catánia
Siracusa (Syracuse)
Ragusa
MEDIT

MALTA
1:1 000 000
Gozo (Ghawdex)
Comino (Kemmuna)
Victoria (Rabat)
St. Pauls Bay
Valletta
Mdina
Rabat
Luqa
Zurrieq
Marsaxlokk
Birzebbuga

S.E. EUROPE
POLITICAL
1:25 000 000
FRANCE
SWITZ.
LIECHT.
AUSTRIA
Wien
Budapest
HUNGARY
U.S.S.R.
Bern
Venezia
Trieste
SAN MARINO
ITALY
Roma
Napoli
Corse (Fr.)
YUGOSLAVIA
ADRIATIC SEA
Beograd
ROMANIA
Bucuresti
Sofija
BULGARIA
ALBANIA
Tirana
Thessaloniki
GREECE
AEGEAN SEA
AFRICA
TURKEY
Sicilia
MALTA
Athinai
Kriti
MEDITERRANEAN SEA

1 : 5 000 000

95

ICELAND
on the same scale
as general map

Vadsø
Varangerfjorden
Kharlov
Nikel
Lotta
Kemijoki
Iisalmi
Kuopio
KUOPIO
Tangafjorden
Tana
Utsjoki
Ivalo
Inari 118
Rajoosseppo
Saariselkä
Pelkosenniemi
Kelloselkä
Kemijoki
KESKI-SUOMEN
Laksefjorden
Porsangen
Alta
Lakselv
Karasjok
Inari
Kittinen
Kitinen
Sodankylä
Rovaniemi
Kemijärvi
Simojärvi
Tervola
Oulu
Iijoki
Oulujärvi
Kajaani
N
Nordkapp
Hammerfest
Soroyunder
Sørøya
Seiland
Kvaløy
Masi
Enontekiö
Kautokeino
Ounasjoki
Kaukonen
Ylitornio
Tornio
Kemi
Haparanda
Hailuoto
Ylivieska
Raahe
VASA
Lopphavet
Kvænangen
Arnøy
326
Muonio älv
Kolari
Tornionjoki
Torne älv
Övertorneå
Råneå
Luleå
Byske
Kokkola (Gamlakarleby)
Jakobstad (Pietarsaari)
Nykarleby (Uusikaarlepyy)
Vaasa (Vasa)
Fugløysund
Vanna
Ringvassøy
Kvaløya
1681
Torne träsk
Kalix älv
Svappavaara
Malmberget
Gällivare
Råne älv
Boden
Piteå
Älvsbyn
Byske älv
Skellefteå
Hällnäs
Vindeln
Umeå
Kvarken
Holmsund
Ö
Tromsø
2117
Kiruna
Stora Lulevatten
Jokkmokk
Pite älv
Arvidsjaur
Skellefte älv
Örnsköldsvik
294
Senja
Narvik
Ofoti
2090
Sarektjåkko
Suitjelma
1913
Treggel-vas
Horna-vån
Uddjaur
Storavan
Arjeplog
Storuman
Stensele
Vojm-sjön
Lycksele
Angermanälven
NORRLAND
Kramfors
Andøy
Harstad
Frostisen
Tysfj
Fauske
1214
Nasa
Lønsdal
Malgoma
Vilhelmina
Ström-vattudal
Flåsjön
Hoting
Indals älv
Bräcke
Vesterålen
Langøy
Austvågøy
Hamarøy
Bodø
Saltfj
Svartisen 1699
Mo
Mosjøen
Vefsna
Resvatnet
1915
Börge-fjellet
1703
Ström-vattudal
Tåsjön
Ångermanälven
Östersund
Storsjön
Vestvågøy
Lofoten
Vestfjorden
Folda
Foldereid
Grong
Namsen
N-TRØNDELAG
Steinkjer
Hotagen
Kallsjön
766
Moskenstraumen
Moskenesøya
Værøy
Denna
Alsten
Vega
Vegali
Vikna
Folda
Namsos
Levanger
Verdalen
Storsjön
S-TRØNDELAG
Norway
Arctic Circle
Arctic Circle
Vega
Vegafj
Froan
Frøya
Hitra
Smøla
Trondheim
Trondheimsfjorden
Orkla
Orkanger
Gaula
Kristiansund
Molde
Ålesund

LAPLAND
TROMS
FINNMARK
NORRBOTTEN
VÄSTERBOTTEN
JÄMTLAND
FINLAND
VAASA
BOTTENVIKEN
LAPPI
OULU

Ifsafjördur
Arnarfjördur
Breidafjördur
Snæfellsjökull
Reykjavik
Keflavik
Hafnarfjördur
Reykjanes
Akranes
Faxaflói
Borgarnes
Langjökull
Hofsjökull
Eiríksjökull 1675
Vatnajökull
Drangajökull 925
Húnaflói
Siglufjördur
Akureyri
Skagafjördur
Eyjafjördur
Saudárkrókur
Vopnafjördur
Seydisfjördur
Héradsflói
Egilsstadir
Öræfajökull 2119
Mýrdalsjökull
Hekla 1491
Snæfell 1833
Vestmannaeyjar
Surtsey

NORWEGIAN SEA

West from Greenwich

1:5 000 000

20 10 0 20 40 60 80 100 miles
40 20 0 40 80 120 160 km

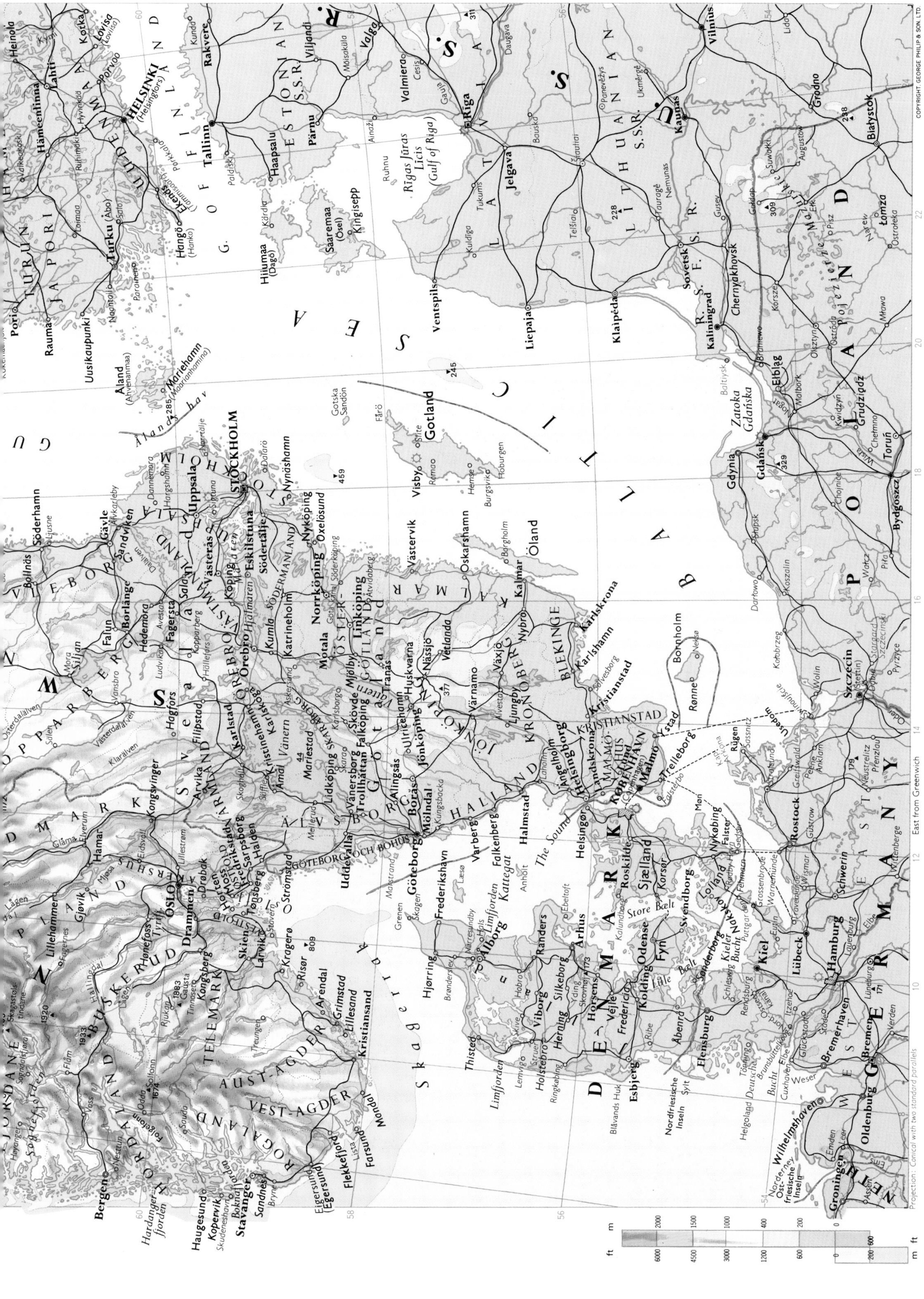

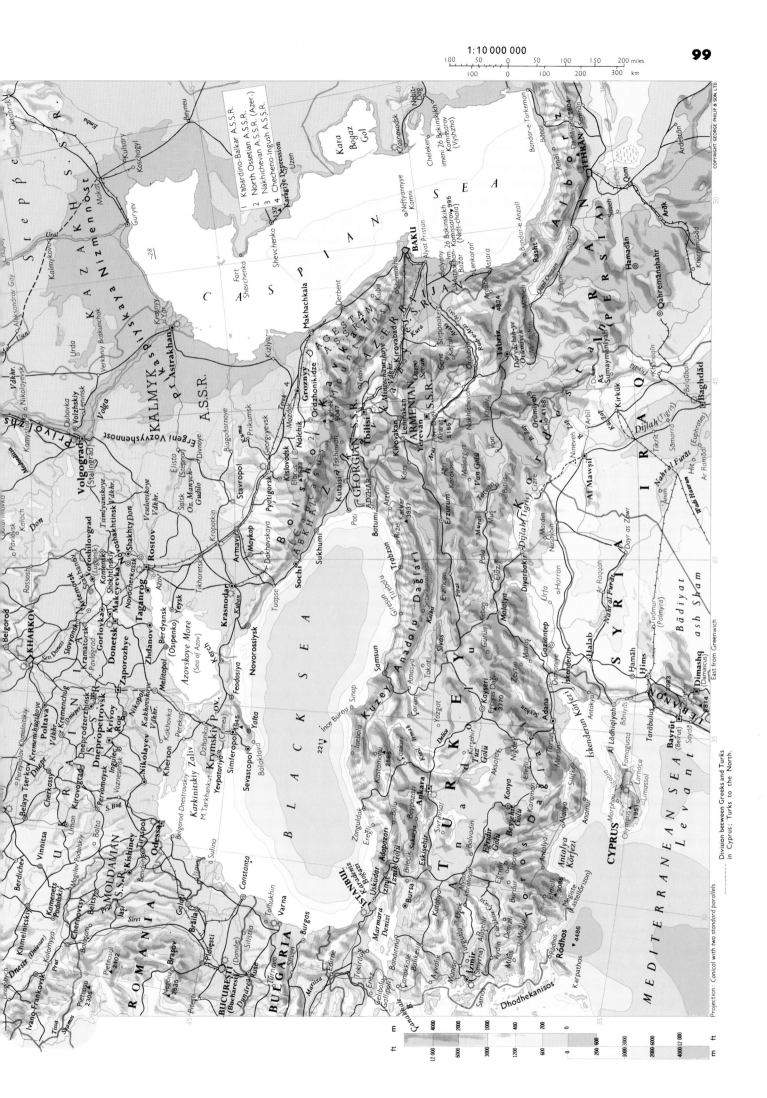

1 : 10 000 000

100   50   0   50   100   150   200 miles

100   0   100   200   300 km

COPYRIGHT. GEORGE PHILIP & SON LTD.

1 Kabardino-Balkar A.S.S.R.
2 North Ossetian A.S.S.R.
3 Nakhichevan A.S.S.R. (Azer.)
4 Checheno-Ingush A.S.S.R.

Karagiye Depression

Projection: Conical with two standard parallels

Division between Greeks and Turks
in Cyprus; Turks to the North.

East from Greenwich

m   ft
4000   12 000
2000   6000
1000   3000
400
200
0
0   ft
12 000
6000
3000
1200
600
200
0
m

CASPIAN SEA

BLACK SEA

MEDITERRANEAN SEA

KAZAKHSKAYA S.S.R.

UKRAINE

ROMANIA

BULGARIA

TURKEY

SYRIA

IRAQ

P E R S I A   (IRAN)

ARMENIAN S.S.R.

GEORGIAN S.S.R.

AZERBAYDZHAN S.S.R.

DAGESTAN A.S.S.R.

KALMYK A.S.S.R.

CYPRUS

LEBANON

BAKU

TEHRAN

Baghdad

Dimashq (Damascus)

Bayrūt (Beirut)

KHARKOV

Volgograd (Stalingrad)

Rostov

Odessa

ISTANBUL

Ankara

İzmir (Smyrna)

R.S.F.S.R.
1. Daghestan A.S.S.R.
2. Kabardino–Balkar A.S.S.R.
3. Mari A.S.S.R.
4. Mordovian A.S.S.R.
5. North Ossetian A.S.S.R.
6. Tatar A.S.S.R.
7. Udmurt A.S.S.R.
8. Chuvash A.S.S.R.
9. Checheno-Ingush A.S.S.R.
AZERBAIJAN
10. Nakhichevan A.S.S.R.
GEORGIA
11. Abkhaz A.S.S.R.
12. Adzhar A.S.S.R.

Projection: Conical Orthomorphic with two standard parallels

East from Greenwich

1:20 000 000

100 0 100 200 300 400 500 miles
100 0 200 400 600 800 km

Mys Dezhneva
(East C.)

St. Lawrence I.
(U.S.A.)

OCEAN

Laptev Sea

East Siberian Sea

Chukotskoye More

Ostrov Vrangelya

Severnaya Zemlya

Ostrov Shmidt

Ostrov Komsomolets

Ostrov Pioner

Ostrov Oktyabrskoy Revolyutsii

Ostrov Bolshevik

Proliv Vilkitskogo

Poluostrov Taymyr
Goro Byrranga

Oz. Taymyr

Nordvik

Novorybnoye

Pyasina

Iochanka

Kheta

Gory Putorana
1701

Khatanga

Kotuy

Anabar

Olenek

Tiksi

Verkhoyansk
2389

Khrebet Cherskogo
Gora Chen 2682

Yakutsk

YAKUT A. S. S. R.

Olekminsk

Okhotsk

Sea of Okhotsk

Poluostrov Kamchatka

Petropavlovsk-Kamchatskiy

Magadan

Bering Sea

Koryakskiy Khrebet

Okhotsko Kolymskoye

Sredinny

Sakhalin

Nikolayevsk-na-Am.

Komsomolsk

Khabarovsk

Sovetskaya Gavan

Yuzhno-Sakhalinsk

Birobidzhan

Krasnoyarsk

Bratsk

Nizhneudinsk

Irkutsk

Angarsk

Ulan Ude

Chita

Blagoveshchensk

Jiamusi

Hokkaido

Sapporo

Hakodate

MONGOLIA

Ulaanbaatar
(Ulan Bator)

Hangayn Nuruu

Edrengiyn Nuruu

Qiqihar

Harbin

Vladivostok

Nakhodka

Ussuriysk

Sea of Japan

JAPAN

Honshu

Niigata

Kanazawa

To-yama

Changchun

Jilin

Shenyang

Fushun

Anshan

Chongjin

Wonsan

NORTH KOREA

P'yongyang

SOUTH KOREA

Seoul

Pusan

Dalian

Beijing

Baotou

Zhangjiakou

Yingkou

REPUBLIC

GOBI

DESERT

Boundaries of U.S.S.R.
Boundaries of S.S.R.
Boundaries of A.S.S.R.

COPYRIGHT GEORGE PHILIP & SON LTD.

1:50 000 000

250   0   250   500   750   1000 miles

250   0   500   1000   1500 km

ARCTIC   OCEAN

PACIFIC   OCEAN

Aleutian Is.

Bering   Sea

C. Dezhnyov

Bering Str.

Kamchatka Peninsula

Sredinny Ra.

Gydan Ra. (Kolyma)

Sea of Okhotsk

Kuril Is.

Hokkaido

Sakhalin

Sikhote Alin Ra.

Sea of Japan

Japan

Honshu

Korea

Yellow Sea

East China Sea

Ryukyu Is.

Formosa

Bonin Is.

Caroline Is.

Guam

New Guinea

Philippine Is.

Luzon

Mindanao

Halmahera

Ceram

Banda Sea

Arafura Sea

Australia

Moluccas

Celebes Sea

Celebes

Sulu Sea

Palawan

Kinabalu

Borneo

Hainan

South China Sea

Malay Peninsula

G. of Thailand

Chao Phraya

Mekong

Si-kiang

Great Plain of China

Hwang

Yangtze

Koko Nor

Plateau of Mongolia

Nan Shan

Kunlun Shan

Plateau of Tibet

Everest 8848

Himalaya

Tsangpo

Brahmaputra

Irrawaddy

Salween

Bay of Bengal

Andaman Is.

Nicobar Is.

Ceylon

Polk Strait

Equator

INDIAN   OCEAN

Sunda Is.

Sumatra

Str. of Malacca

Java Sea

Macassar Strait

Bali

Timor

Flores

Eastern Ghats

Godavari

Krishna

India

Deccan

Western Ghats

Narmada

Tapti

Sutlej

Ganga

Thar Desert

Sulaiman Range

C. Comorin

Laccadive Is.

Maldive Is.

Chagos Arch.

Arabian Sea

G. of Oman

The Gulf

Socotra

Ras Asir (C. Guardafui)

G. of Aden

Somali Peninsula

Amirantes

Seychelles

Red Sea

Rub' al Khali

Arabia

Mesopotamia

Tigris

Euphrates

Syrian Desert

Dead Sea

Nile

Suez Canal

Cyprus

Anatolia

Taurus Mts.

Mediterranean Sea

Libyan Desert

Lake Victoria

Shatt al Arab

Plateau of Iran

Zagros

Elburz Mts.

Demavend 5604

Great Salt Desert

Caspian Sea

Caucasus

Elbrus 5633

Ararat 5165

Black Sea

Bosporus

Adriatic Sea

Rhine

Danube

Elbe

Oder

Vistula

Carpathians

North Sea

British Isles

Iceland

Greenland

Svalbard

Novaya Zemlya

Barents Sea

Kara Sea

Kola Pen.

White Sea

North Cape

Kolguyev I.

N. Dvina

Finland

Scandinavia

Baltic Sea

North European Plain

Russian Uplands

Central

Dnepr

Don

Volga

Ural

Steppe

Ural Mountains

1640

Narodnaya 1894

Tobol

Irtysh

West Siberian Plain

Ob

Turan Plain

Aral Sea

Syr Darya

Amu Darya

Turkmenistan

Helmand

Hamun

Hindu Kush

Pamir

Communism Pk. 7495

Karakoram Ra.

K2 8611

Tien Shan

L. Balkhash

Ili

Chu

Tarim

Takla Makan

Turfan Basin

Lop Nor

Altai

Belukha 4506

Sayan Mts.

Angara

Lower Tunguska

Yenisei

Central Siberian Plateau

Lena

Aldan

Stanovoy Ra.

Yablonovy Ra.

Amur

Great Khingan Mts.

Manchurian Plain

Sungari

Po Hai

Amga

Vitim

Verkhoyansk Range

Indigirka

Kolyma

New Siberian Is.

Chelyuskin

Taimyr Peninsula

Severnaya Zemlya

Laptev Sea

Olenek

Khatanga

Kotuy

Anabar

Wrangel I.

4750

4756

Sea of Japan

Sungari

Tropic of Cancer

Arctic Circle

60   50   40   30   20   10   0

60   80   100   120   140   160   180

m   6000   4000   2000   1000   400   200   0

ft   18 000   12 000   6000   3000   1200   600   0   200   600   2000   4000 12 000   6000 18 000   8000 24 000

1 : 50 000 000

250   0   250   500   750   1000 miles
250   0   500   1000   1500 km

COPYRIGHT. GEORGE PHILIP & SON. LTD.

Projection: Bonne

1:1 000 000

10   10   10   20 miles
10   0   10   20   30 km

1949–1974 Armistice lines between
Israel and the Arab States.

35   34 30   35   35 30

MEDITERRANEAN SEA

LEBANON

SYRIA

Sūr
(Tyre)

Nahariyya

'Akko
(Acre)

HEFA
(Haifa)

Tirat Karmel

'ATLIT

CAESAREA

Hadera

Netanya

S R A E L

TEL ARSHAF
Herzliyya
Ramat HaSharon
Bene
Beraq
TEL AVIV
YAFO
(Jaffa)
Ramat
Gan
Bat Yam
Holon

Rishon le Ziyyon

Nes Ziyyona
Ramla
Rehovot

TEL
GEZER

Ashdod

Ashqelon

Qiryat Gat

BET GUVRIN
TEL
LAKHISH

Gaza

**Gaza
Strip**

Khān
Yūnis

EGYPT

Be'er Sheva'

**H a g a l i l
(Galilee)**

HAZOR

Zefat

Nazerat
(Nazareth)

TEL
MEGIDDO

Yam Kinneret
(Sea of
Galilee)

Terverya
209

'Afula

'E m e q   Y i z r e' e l

Bet She'an

Janin

**S h o m r ō n
(Samaria)**

Tūlkarm

SAMARIA
SHECHEM
Nābulus
JACOB'S WELL

J O R D A N

As Salt

Rām Allāh
Al Birah

Arīḥā
(Jericho)

JERUSALEM
(Yerushalayim, Al Quds)
(Bethany)

Bayt Lahm (Bethlehem)
QUMRĀN

BIRAK SULAYMĀN
(SOLOMON'S POOLS)

Al Khalīl
(Hebron)

'AMMĀN

Az Zarqā'

D E A D   S E A

(BAHR EL MIYET)

MESADA

En Gedi

As Samū'

**Continuation
Southwards
1:2 500 000**

Al Khalīl
(Hebron)

Be'er Sheva'

Dimona

I S R A E L

H a   N e g e v

Mizpe Ramon

Makhtesh Ramon

E G Y P T

J O R D A N

PETRA

1727

Elat
Al
'Aqabah

Projection: Conical with two standard parallels

East from Greenwich

COPYRIGHT GEORGE PHILIP & SON, L.

ft   m
3000 1000
1200 400
600   200
0   0
200   600
m   ft

1:15 000 000

100   0   100   200   300   400 miles
100   0   100   200   300   400   500   600 km

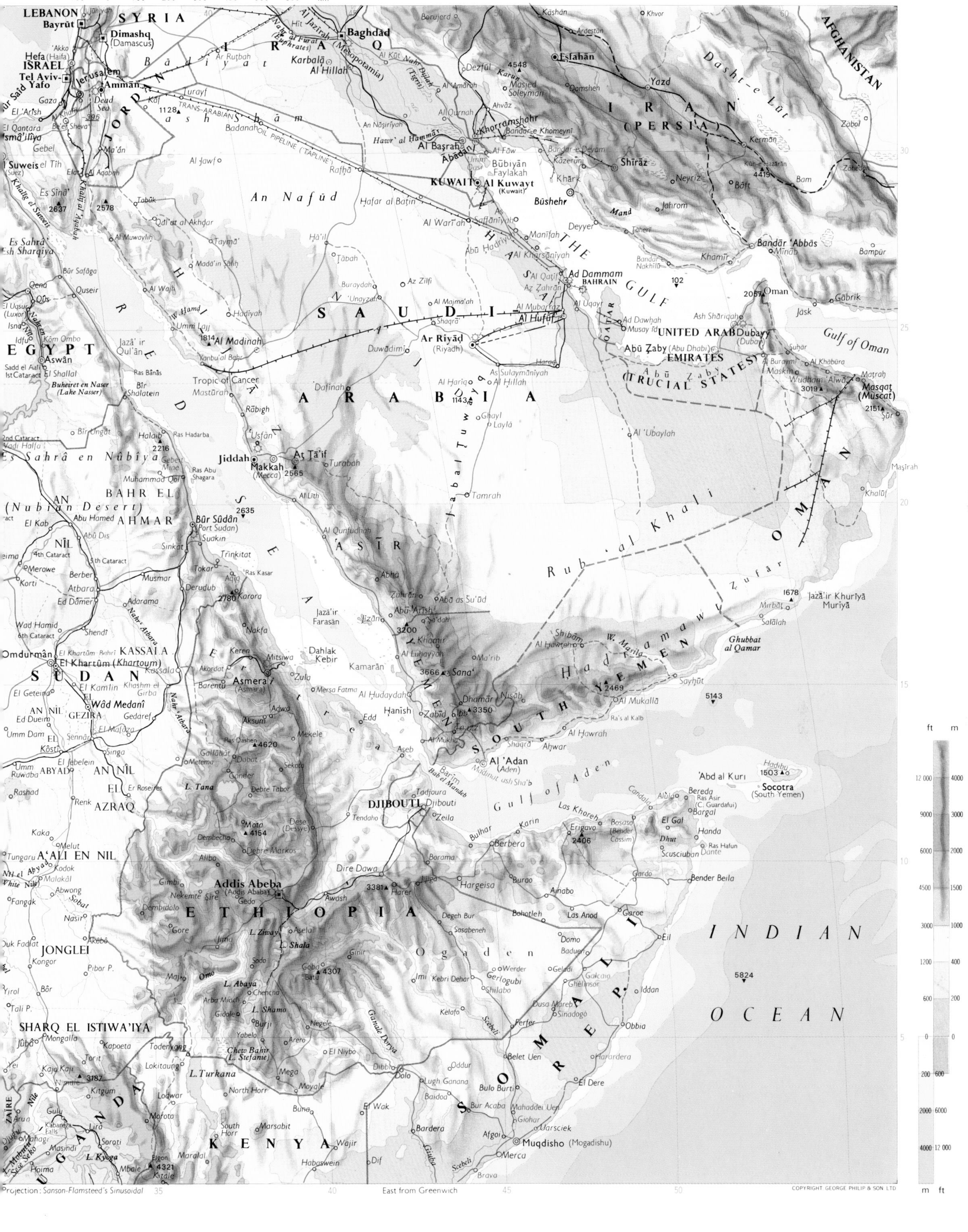

LEBANON
Bayrūt
Hefa (Haifa)
ISRAEL
Tel Aviv-Yafo
Jerusalem
Gaza
El 'Arîsh
Es Sahrā esh Sharqiya
Suweis (Suez)
el Tih
SYRIA
Dimashq (Damascus)
Akko
Amman
Dead Sea
Ma'ān
2637
2578
Tabūk
Qal'at al Akhḍar
JORDAN
Ḥā'il
IRAQ
Baghdād
Karbalā'
Al Ḥillah
Al Kūt
Al 'Amārah
An Nāṣirīyah
Al Qurnah
Hawr al Ḥammār
Al Baṣrah
Al Fāw
Ābādān
Khorramshahr
Dezfūl
4548
Eṣfahān
Qamsheh
Yazd
IRAN (PERSIA)
Dasht-e Lūt
Kermān
Bam
Zābol
AFGHANISTAN
Shīrāz
Bandar 'Abbās
Būshehr
Khārk
4419
Mināb
Bampūr
Gābrik
Jāsk
Gulf of Oman
Bandar Nakhīlū
Qatīf
Ad Dammām
BAHRAIN
Az Zahrān
102
2057
Oman
Suḥār
Al Khābūra
Maskat
3019
Masqaṭ (Muscat)
Sūr
2151
Maṣīrah
Khalūf

SAUDI ARABIA
An Nafūd
Ḥafar al Bāṭin
Al Jawf
Taymā'
Madd'in Sālih
Al Muwaylih
Al Wajh
Umm Lajj
Yanbu' al Bahr
1814 Al Madīnah
Rābigh
Jiddah
Makkah (Mecca)
2565
Aṣ Ṭā'if
Turabah
Tropic of Cancer
Buraydah
'Unayzah
Az Zilfī
Al Majma'ah
Shaqrā'
Ad Dawḥah
KUWAIT
AL Kuwayt (Kuwait)
Būbiyān
Faylakah
Umm Qaṣr
Safānīyah
Al Warī'ah
Abū Ḥadrīya
Al Qaṭīf
Al Mubarraz
Al Hufūf
Al 'Uqayr
Ar Riyād (Riyadh)
Duwādimi
As Sulaymānīyah
Al Hillah
Al Ḥarīq
1143
Dafīnah
Ghayl
Jabal Tuwayq
Layla
Al 'Ubaylah
UNITED ARAB EMIRATES (TRUCIAL STATES)
Abū Zaby (Abu Dhabi)
Ash Shāriqah
Dubayy (Dubai)
Abū Zaby
Al Buraymi
Wudām
Ḥareq
'ASĪR
Abhā
Abū 'Arīsh
Abū as Su'ūd
3200
Najrān
Khamīr
Sa'dah
Rub' al Khali
Shibām
Al Hudaydah
YEMEN
3666 Sana'
Dhamār
3350
Zabīd
6101
Nisāb
Hadramawt
2469
W. Marīb
Ghubbat al Qamar
Salālah
Mirbāt
1678
Jazā'ir Khurīyā Murīyā
OMAN
Zufār
W. Marīb

TRANS-ARABIAN OIL PIPELINE (TAPLINE)
Rafḥā
Badanah

EGYPT
Aswān
1st Cataract El Shallāl
Buheirat en Nâser (Lake Nasser)
Bûr Safâga
Quseir
Ras Bânâs
Bîr Shalatein
2nd Cataract
Wâdi Halfa
Es Sahrâ en Nûbiya (Nubian Desert)
El Kab
Abû Hamed
BAHR EL AHMAR
2216
Ras Hadarba
Ḥalaib
Muhammad Qōl
Bûr Sûdân (Port Sudan)
Sinkāt
Suakin
2635
Trinkitat
Ras Kasar
SUDAN
Omdurmân
El Khartûm Bahri
El Khartûm (Khartoum)
KASSALA
Kassala
Gedaref
Akordat
Keren
Asmera (Asmara)
Mitsiwa
Zula
Mersa Fatma
Edd
RED SEA
Dahlak Kebir
Kamarān
Al Luḥayyah
Al Ḥudaydah
Al Mukhā
Hanish
Jazā'ir Farasān
Yizān
Kamarān
Khamīr
ERITREA
Aksum
Adwa
Mekele
4620
Gonder
Debre Tabor
L. Tana
4154
Dese (Dessye)
Debre Markos
ETHIOPIA
Addis Abeba (Addis Ababa)
3381
Harer
Dire Dawa
Hargeisa
Āwash
Nekemte
Gimbi
Gore
Jīma
L. Ziway
L. Shala
Shala
4307
Soda
L. Abaya
Chencha
Arba Minch
L. Shamo
Burji
Negele
L. Stefanie (Chew Bahr)
Ogaden
Degeh Bur
Sasabeneh
Kebri Dehar
Ghellinsor
Shilabo
Kelafo
Ferfer
Dusa Mareb
Obbia
Sinadogo
5824
INDIAN OCEAN
Bulhar
Berbera
Karin
2406
Dhut
El Gal
Handa
Ras Hafun
Dante
Scusciuban
Bender Beila
Gardo
Eil
Garoe
Bohotleh
Las Anod
Iddan
Domo
Baduen
Werder
Gakcalo
Gelola
Bender Cassim (Bosaso)
Erigavo
Candala
Aluula
Bereda
Ras Asir (C. Guardafui)
Bargal
Socotra (South Yemen)
Hadibu
1503
'Abd al Kuri
Mūdīnut ush Sha'b
Al 'Adan (Aden)
Bāb el Mandeb
Shaqrā'
Aḥwar
Al Ḥawrah
Ra's al Kalb
5143
Al Mukallā
Sayḥūt
SOUTH YEMEN
DJIBOUTI
Djibouti
Tadjoura
Zeila
Las Khoreh
Gulf of Aden

SOMALI REP.
Burao
Ainabo
KENYA
L. Turkana
North Horr
Marsabit
Moyale
Mega
El Niybo
Buna
Wajir
El Wak
Baidoa
Bur Acaba
Mahaddei Uen
Giohar
Afgoi
Uarscieg
Muqdisho (Mogadishu)
Merca
Brava
Bardera
Lugh Ganana
Bulo Burti
El Dere
Harardera
Oddur
Belet Uen
Bur Burti
Gedo
Dif
Habaswein
Dolo
Dibbīl
Scebeli
Giumbo
ZAIRE
UGANDA
4321
L. Kyoga
Soroti
Mbale
Elgon
Masindi
Hoima
Lira
Gulu
Arua
Kabanega Falls
3187
Kitgum
Lodwar
Kapoeta
Todenyang
Lokitaung
South Horr
SHARQ EL ISTIWA'IYA
Jūba
Mongalla
Torit
Kajo Kaji
Yei
JONGLEI
Kongor
Bōr
Pibor P.
Yirol
Tali P.
A'ALI EN NIL
Malakāl
Abwong
Sobat
Nāsir
Fangak
AN NIL EL AZRAQ
Er Roseires
Renk
Kaka
Melut
Kodok
AN NIL EL ABYAD
Kosti
Ed Dueim
Um Ruwāba
Rashad
ABYAD
El Jebelein
Singa
Sennar
GEZIRA
Wâd Medanî
El Matana
El Hasaheisa
El Kamlin
AN NIL EL AZRAQ
El Geteina
Khashm el Girba
Gedaref
Nahr 'Atbara
2780
Karora
Nakfa
Barentū
Gallabat
Metema
Dabat
Sekota
Lalibela

Projection: Sanson-Flamsteed's Sinusoidal

East from Greenwich

35   40   45   50   20   15

COPYRIGHT GEORGE PHILIP & SON LTD

ft   m
12 000   4000
9000   3000
6000   2000
4500   1500
3000   1000
1200   400
600   200
0   0
200   600
2000   6000
4000   12 000
m   ft

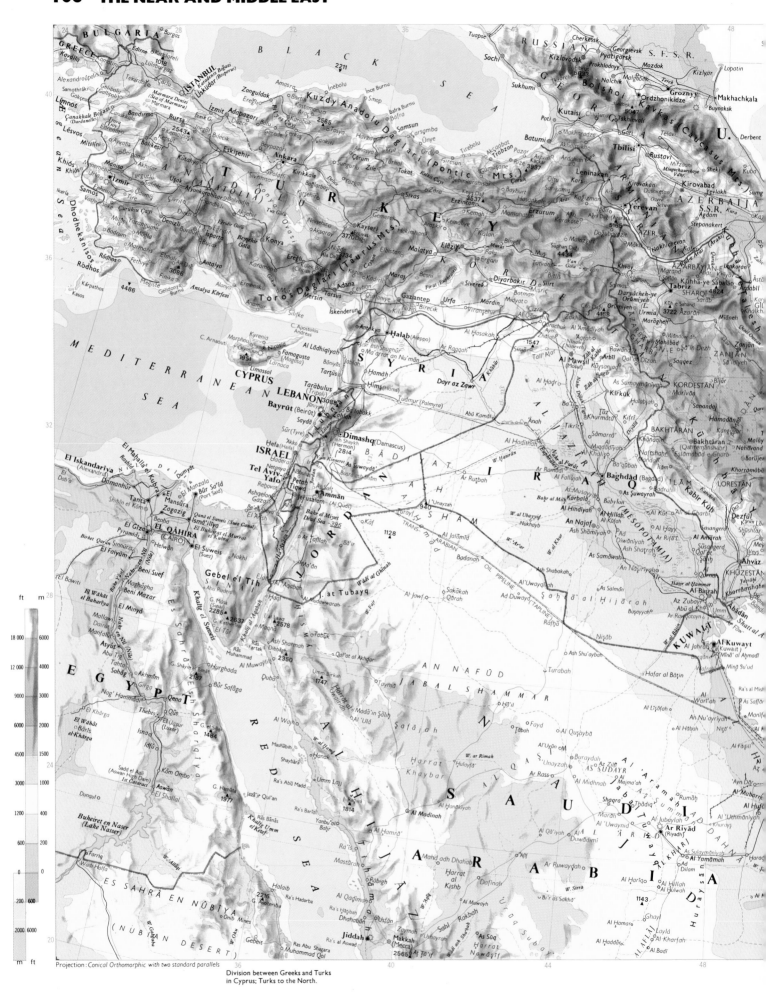

Projection: Conical Orthomorphic with two standard parallels

Division between Greeks and Turks
in Cyprus; Turks to the North.

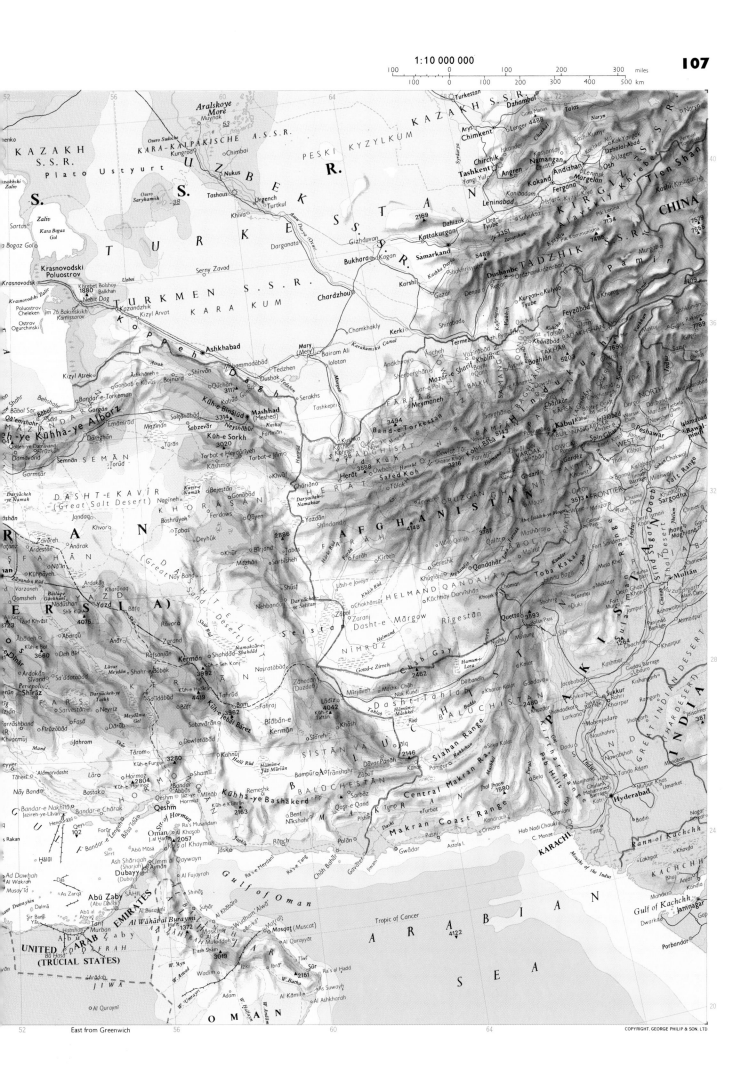

1:10 000 000

| 100 | 0 | 100 | 200 | 300 miles |

| 100 | 0 | 100 | 200 | 300 | 400 | 500 km |

KAZAKH S.S.R.

KAZAKH S.S.R.

KARA-KALPAKISCHE A.S.S.R.

Plato Ustyurt

PESKI KYZYLKUM

U Z B E K S.S.R.

Aralskoye More

Muynak 53

T U R K M E N S.S.R.

KARA KUM

KIRGIZ S.S.R.

Alayskiy Khrebet Tien Shan

CHINA

TADZHIK S.S.R.

Pamir

Tashkent

Samarkand

Bukhara

Dushanbe

Ashkhabad

Mashhad (Meshed)

H I N D U K U S H

A F G H A N I S T A N

BADAKHSHAN

Kabul

Peshawar

Islamabad
Rawalpindi

I R A N
(P E R S I A)

DASHT-E KAVIR
(Great Salt Desert)

KHORASAN

D A S H T - E - L U T
(Great Sand Desert)

HERAT

FARAH

ORUZGAN

Herāt

Kābul

KANDAHAR

HELMAND

Dasht-e Mārgow

Rigestān

Qandahār

Quetta

P A K I S T A N

GREAT INDIAN DESERT

SISTAN VA

BALUCHESTAN

NIMRUZ

Dasht-i-Tahlab

Zāhedān (Duzdab)

Kermān

Shīrāz

FARS

HORMOZ

Bandar-e ʿAbbās

Qeshm

Str. of Hormuz

Oman

Jal Ḥamm
2057

Abū Zaby
(Abu Dhabi)

UNITED ARAB EMIRATES
(TRUCIAL STATES)

Dubayy
(Dubai)

Ash Shāriqah
(Sharjah)

Gulf of Oman

Masqaṭ (Muscat)

Tropic of Cancer

A R A B I A N

S E A

O M A N

Central Makran Range

Makran Coast Range

BALUCHISTAN

KARACHI

Mouths of the Indus

I N D I A

Gulf of Kachchh

Rann of Kachchh

KACHCHH

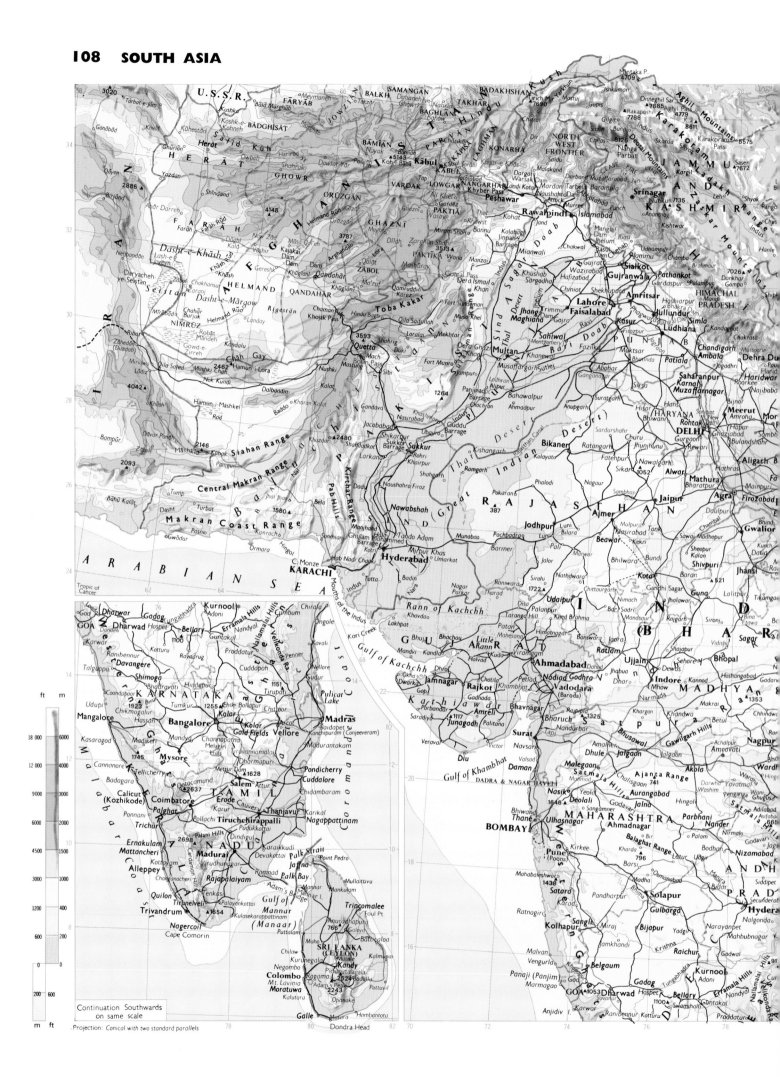

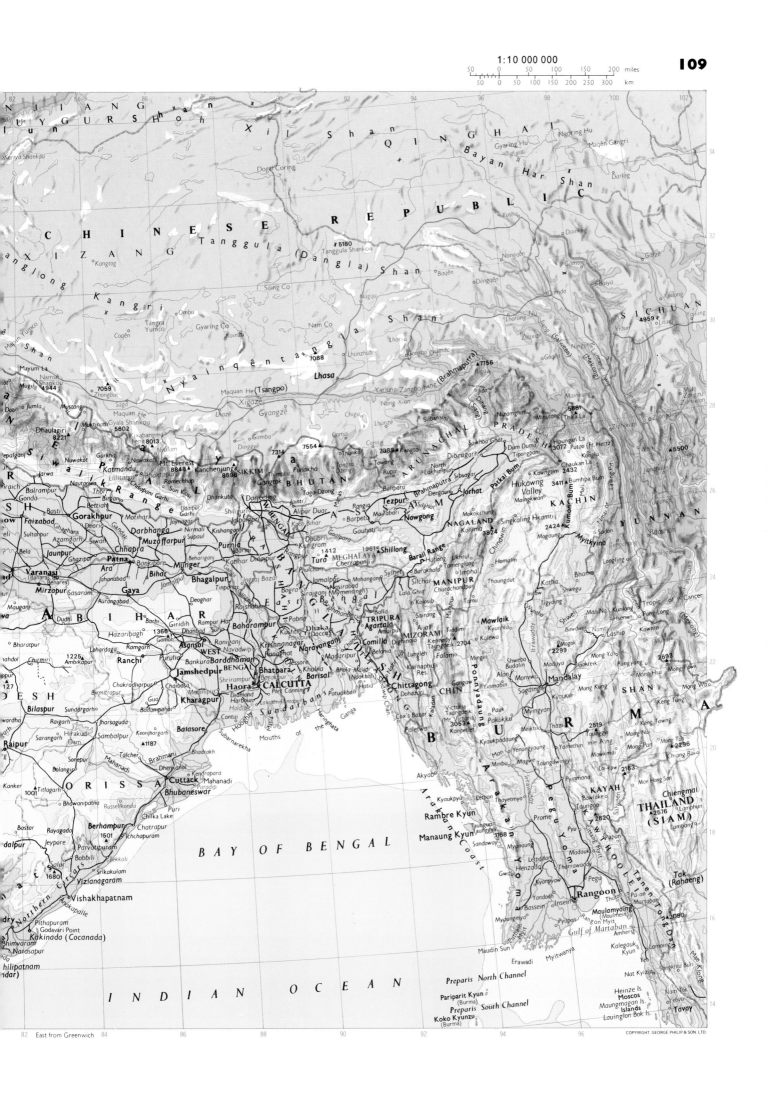

1:10 000 000

50   0   50   100   150   200 miles
50 0 50 100 150 200 250 300 km

N I A N G
U Y G U R S H   h'xan   h   h
o   Xil   Shan
Doger Coring

Q I N G H A I
Bayan   Har   Shan
Gyaring Hu   Ngoring Hu
Maqên Gangri
Darlog

34

C H I N E S E   R E P U B L I C

X I Z A N G   Tanggula (Dangla) Shan   5180
Yushu
Xinlong
Garzê

Kangtog
Siling Co
Nagqu
Dêngqên
Baiyu
S I C H U A N
4959

n g l o n g
K a n g r i
Tangra   Gyaring Co
Yumco
Ombu
Cogên
Nam Co
Lhari
Gongbo'gyamda
Zhxize
Nu (Salween)
Chang (Mekong)
Ningjing   Shan
Yidun   Litang
Zhag'yab

30

S h a n
Mayum La
Namse
Shankou   4944
Mugu
7059
Zhongba
Maquan He (Tsangpo)
Xigazê
Lhaze
Gyangzê
7088
Lhasa
Nyainqêntanglha Shan
Nang Xian
Yarlung Zangbo Jiang (Brahmaputra)
Riga
Gomo
Zhamog
Gêgên
Maikung
28

D0ti
Jumla
Dhaulagiri   8221
Mustang   Muktinath
5602   Gyala Shankou
Xixabangma
8013
7314   7554
Gomba   Dinggyê
Lhünzê
Chigu
Chona   Gomai
7089   Kangto
5881
Nizamghat
Huangan La   3072   Putao (Ft. Hertz)
5500
Zizhixian
Zizhixian

D H A U L A G I R I
e p a l g a n j
Jarwa
Nuwakot
Gurkha
Mt Everest   8848
Kanchenjunga   8598
SIKKIM
Gongtok
Punakha
Towang
Rupa
North Lakhimpur
Dibrugarh
A R U N A C H A L   P R A D E S H
Saikhoa Ghat
Dam Duma
Tipongpani
Konglu
7756
Chaukan La
Hkamti
4756

S   E
S i w a l i k
Katmandu   Lalitapur
Bhaktapur
Ramechhap
Sun Kosi
Dhankuta
Darjeeling
B E N G A L
Jainti
Tago-Dzong
B H U T A N
Balipara   Tezpur
Sibsagar
Jorhat
Mokokchung
K A C H I N
Hukawng   Valley
3411   Bumhpa Bum
Myitkyina
Sadon
Y U N N A N
Longling
24

R a n g e
Gorakhpur
Deoria
Motihari
Nautanwa
Thori
Jaynagar
Shiliguri
Jalpaiguri
Koch Bihar
Rangia
Gauhati
Barpeta
Mairabari
Nowgong
Shillong
N A G A L A N D
Kohima   3824
Singkaling Hkamti
2424
Mogaung
Baoshan
Tengchong

Faizabad
Ghaghara
Sultanpur
Azamgarh
Basti
Darbhanga
Muzaffarpur
Nirmali
Supaul
Purnia
Katihar
Dinajpur
Dhubri
Kurigram
Goalpara
Tura
1412
M E G H A L A Y A
1961
Cherrapunji
Sylhet
Barail Range
Haflong
Ukhrul
Tamenglong
Chindwin
Homalin
Thaungdut
Katha
Shwegu
Bhamo

Jaunpur
Ghazipur
Chhapra
Bankipore
Patna
Siwan
Bihar
Jahanabad
Munger
Behariganj
Barari
Katihar
Rajshahi
Bogra
E a s t
Sirajganj (Mymensingh)
Jamalpur
Mohanganj
Silchar
M A N I P U R
Churachandpur
Tamu
Tiddim
Tigyaing
Man Na
Kunlong
24

Varanasi (Banaras)
(Benares)
Mirzapur
Ara
Sasaram
Gaya
Aurangabad
Deoghar
Bhagalpur
Jamalpur
Tinpahar
Jangipur
Pabna
B E N G A L
Bhairab
Narsinghdi
Ballia
Lala Ghat
Sairang
MIZORAM
Kolasib
Aizal
Kennedy Peak
Taungdeik   2704
Kalewa
Alon
Shwebo
Budalin
Monywa   2299
Madaya
Gokteik
Lashio
Hsenwi
Mong Yai
Pangyang
2693
Mong Hsu
22

B I H A R
Dudhi
Hazaribagh
1366
Dhanbad
Giridih
Rampur Hat
Suri
Raniganj
TRIPURA
Agartala
Comilla
Belonia
Dimaghat
Lunglei
Falam
Mingin
Pauk
Pakokku
Kanpetlet
Mawlaik
Kyunhla
Ye-u
Kani
Myingyan
Mandalay
Kyaukse
Mong Kung
Keng Tung
Keng Tawng
Mong Nai
2576   Chiang Rai

Bharatpur
Lohardaga
Ramgarh
Chakradharpur
W E S T
B E N G A L
Asansol
Barddhaman
Bankura
Navadwip
Krishnanagar
Ranaghat
Jessore
Khulna
Madaripur
Bhola Majdir
(Noakhali)
Hatia
Chittagong
C H I N
Victoria   Taungdeik (Mt. Victoria)
3053
Karnaphuli   Res.
Kaladan
Minbu
Magwe
Yenangyaung
Taungdwingyi
Yamethin
Inle Aing
Meiktila
Thazi
Kyaukpadaung
2519
Mon
Pyinmana
Loi-kaw   2163
Mong Pan
2296   Chiang Rai
20

D E S H
Bilaspur
1225
Ambikapur
Raigarh
Ranchi
Purulia
Shrirampur
Haora
Diamond   Harbour
Port Canning
Barakpur
Bhatpara
CALCUTTA
Barisal
Sundarbans
Cox's Bazar
Akyab
Arakan   Coast
Palemyo
Kyaukpyu
Letbon
Thayetmyo
Prome
Pyu
Toungoo
Bawlake
2620
KAYAH
Papun
Mong Tön
Chiengmai
(SIAM)
Lamphun
2576
Lamphun

Jamshedpur
Kharagpur
Medinipur
Contai
Lakshmikantapur
Patuakhali
Sandwip Chan.
Dohazari
Sundargarh
Keonjhargarh
Balasore
Bhadrakh
Mouths   of   the   Ganga
Haringhata
Sandoway
Myanaung
Henzada
Tharrawaddy
Pegu
Yoma
Pyu
T H A I L A N D
Tak   (Rahaeng)
2080

vardha
Raipur
Sarangarh
Sambalpur
Hirakud   Dam
Talcher
Brahmani
Dhenkanal
Kendrapara
Mahanadi
Paradip
1187
O R I S S A
Cuttack
Bhubaneswar
Puri
Chilka Lake
Chatrapur
A r a k a n   Y o m a
Kyaukpyu
Rambre Kyun
Manaung Kyun
1168
Gwa
Bassein
Kyonpyaw
Yandoon
Rangon Myit
Maulamyaing (Moulmein)
Amherst
Martaban
Pa-an
Tanenthaung Dn
18

Kanker
Bolangir
Sonepur
Titlagarh
Bhawanipatna
Russellkonda
Berhampur
1501
Ichchapuram
Jeypore
Parvatipuram
Bobbili
Tekkali
Srikakulam
B A Y   O F   B E N G A L
Myaungmya
Rangoon
Inseim
Pyapon
Gulf of Martaban
Kalegauk Kyun
Singhla Buri
16

Bastar
dalpur
Salur
Rayagada
Jeypore
1680
Vizianagaram
Vishakhapatnam
Anakapalle
N o r t h e r n   C i r c a r s
Erawadi
Myitwanya
Maudin Sun
Preparis   North   Channel
Heinze Is.
Moscos
Nam Tok
14

dry
Godavari Point
Pithapuram
Kakinada (Cocanada)
himyaram
Narsapur
hilipatnam
ndar)
I N D I A N   O C E A N
Pariparit Kyun   (Burma)
Preparis   South   Channel
Preparis
Koko Kyunzu   (Burma)
Maungmagan Is.
Islands
Lauvington Bok Is.
Tavoy

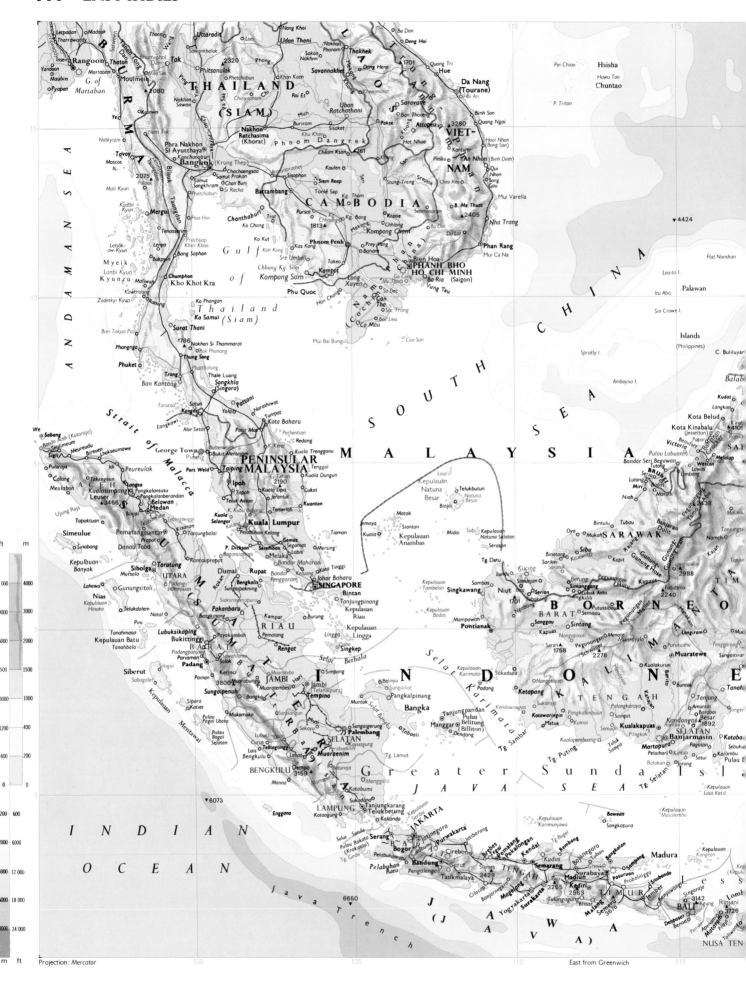

ft   m

12 000   4000

9000   3000

6000   2000

4500   1500

3000   1000

1200   400

600   200

0   0

200   600

2000   6000

4000   12 000

6000   18 000

8000   24 000

m ft

Projection: Mercator   East from Greenwich

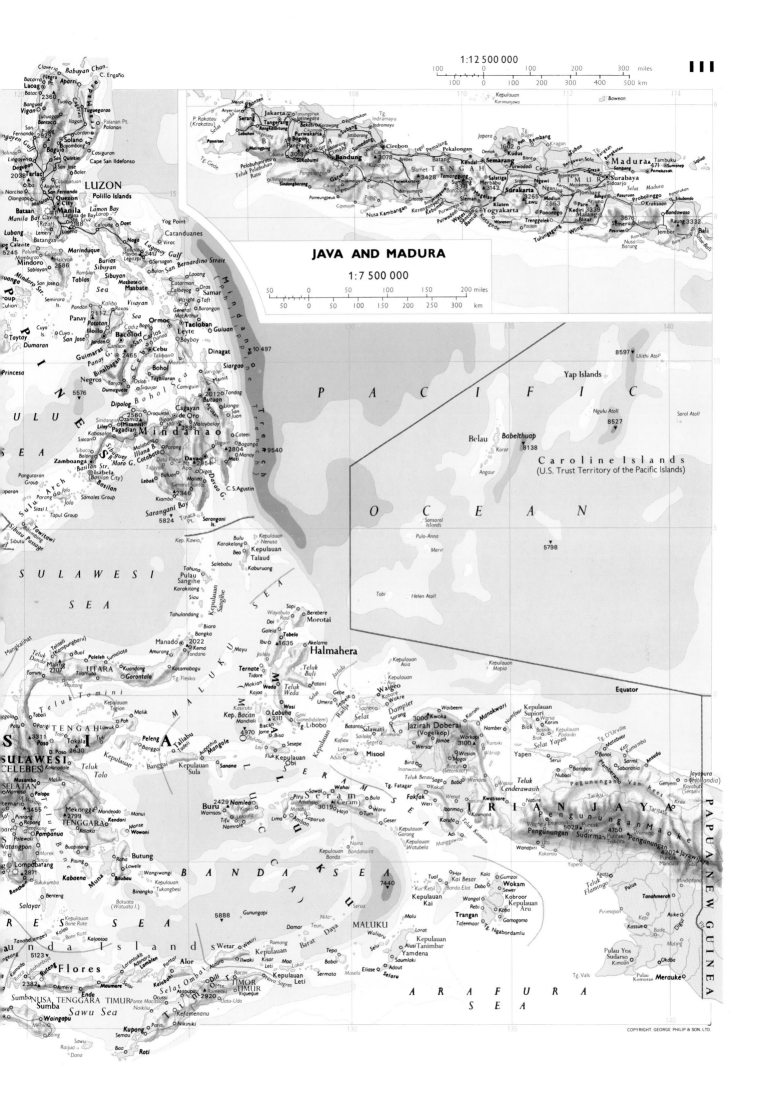

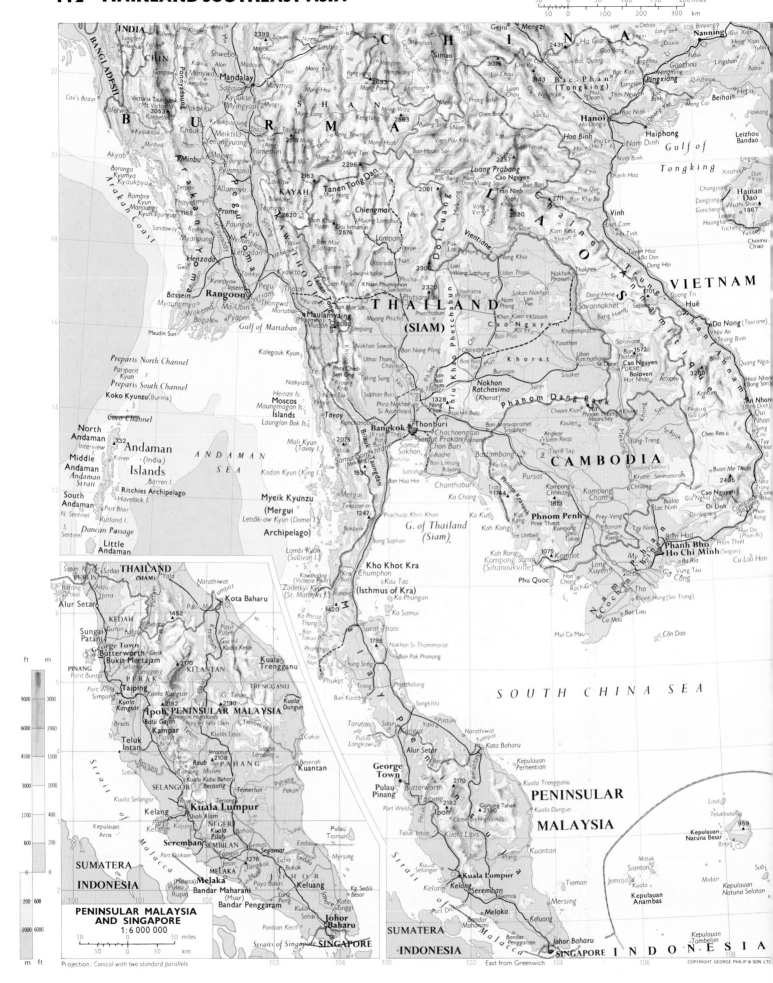

1:10 000 000

PENINSULAR MALAYSIA AND SINGAPORE
1:6 000 000

Projection: Conical with two standard parallels

East from Greenwich

COPYRIGHT. GEORGE PHILIP & SON. LTD

1:20 000 000

100   0   100   200   300   400 miles
100   0   100 200 300 400 500 600 km

COPYRIGHT GEORGE PHILIP & SON LTD

UNION OF SOVIET SOCIALIST REPUBLICS

KAZAKH S.S.R.

KIRGIZ S.S.R.

MONGOLIA

SINKIANG UYGUR (Aut. Reg.)

JAMMU & KASHMIR

TIBET (XIZANG)

QINGHAI

INDIA

NEPAL

BHUTAN

BANGLADESH

BURMA

THAILAND (SIAM)

LAOS

VIETNAM

C H I N A

YUNNAN

GUANGXI ZHUANG

GUANGDONG

GUIZHOU

HUNAN

JIANGXI

FUJIAN

HUBEI

HENAN

SHAANXI

NINGXIA HUIZU (Aut. Reg.)

SHANXI

HEBEI

SHANDONG

JIANGSU

ANHUI

ZHEJIANG

TAIWAN (FORMOSA)

HEILONGJIANG

JILIN

LIAONING

NORTH KOREA

SOUTH KOREA

JAPAN

PHILIPPINES

LUZON

BEIJING

SHANGHAI

TIANJIN

CHONGQING

Hong Kong

Macao

Kowloon

Batan Is.

Ryūkyū-Rettō

EAST CHINA SEA

YELLOW SEA

SOUTH CHINA SEA

BAY OF BENGAL

Korea Bay

Bo Hai

G. of Tonkin

Bashi Channel

East from Greenwich

Projection: Bonne

m 6000 4000 3000 2000 1500 1000 400 200 0
ft 18 000 12 000 9000 6000 4500 3000 1200 600 0
ft 4000 2000 6000 12 000 18 000
m 600 2000 4000 6000

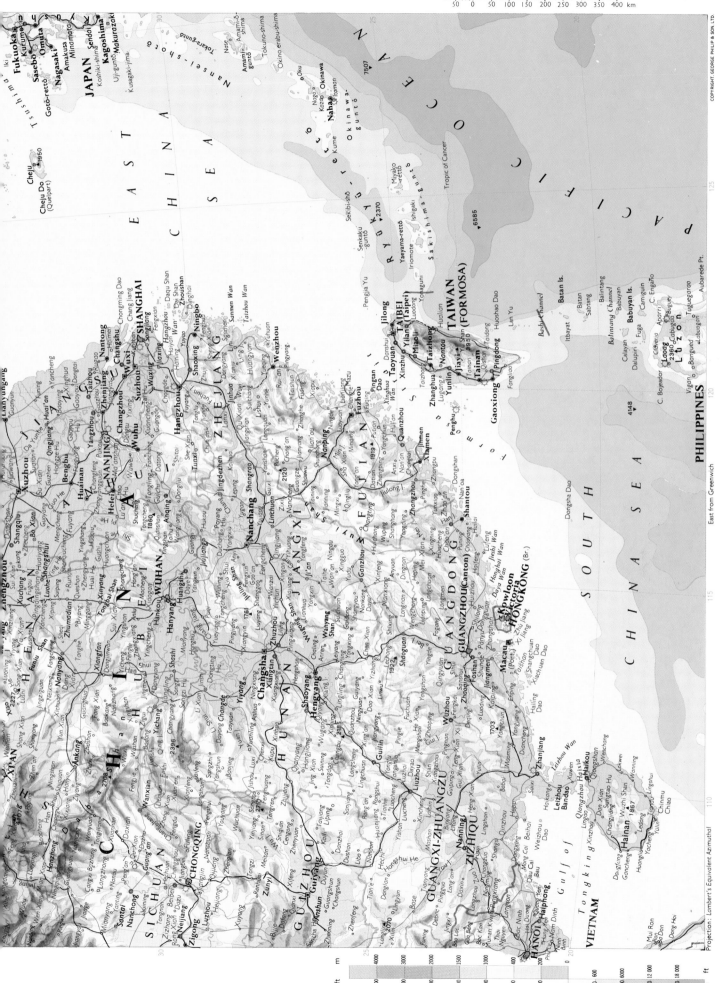

1:10 000 000

50   100   150   200   250 miles

50   0   50   100   150   200   250   300   350   400 km

COPYRIGHT. GEORGE PHILIP & SON, LTD.

PACIFIC OCEAN

NANSEI-SHOTO

EAST CHINA SEA

JAPAN

Fukuoka
Kurume
Sasebo
Nagasaki
Kagoshima
Omuta

Cheju
Cheju Do
(Quelpart)

Tropic of Cancer

Ryūkyū

TAIWAN (FORMOSA)

TAIBEI
(Taipei)

Gaoxiong

SHANGHAI

JIANGSU
ANHUI
ZHEJIANG
JIANGXI
FUJIAN
HUNAN
HUBEI
HENAN
SHAANXI
SICHUAN
GUIZHOU
GUANGXI-ZHUANGZU
GUANGDONG
HAINAN

WUHAN

NANJING
NANCHANG
Hangzhou
Changsha
Guiyang
Chongqing
Nanning
Guangzhou (Canton)
HONGKONG (Br.)
Macau (Port.)
Kowloon
Victoria

PHILIPPINES

Luzon

SOUTH CHINA SEA

Gulf of Tongking

VIETNAM

HANOI
Haiphong

Projection: Lambert's Equivalent Azimuthal

East from Greenwich

m
4000
3000
2000
1500
1000
400
200
0

ft
12 000
9000
6000
4500
3000
1200
600
0

ft
600
6000
12 000
18 000

m
200
2000
4000
6000

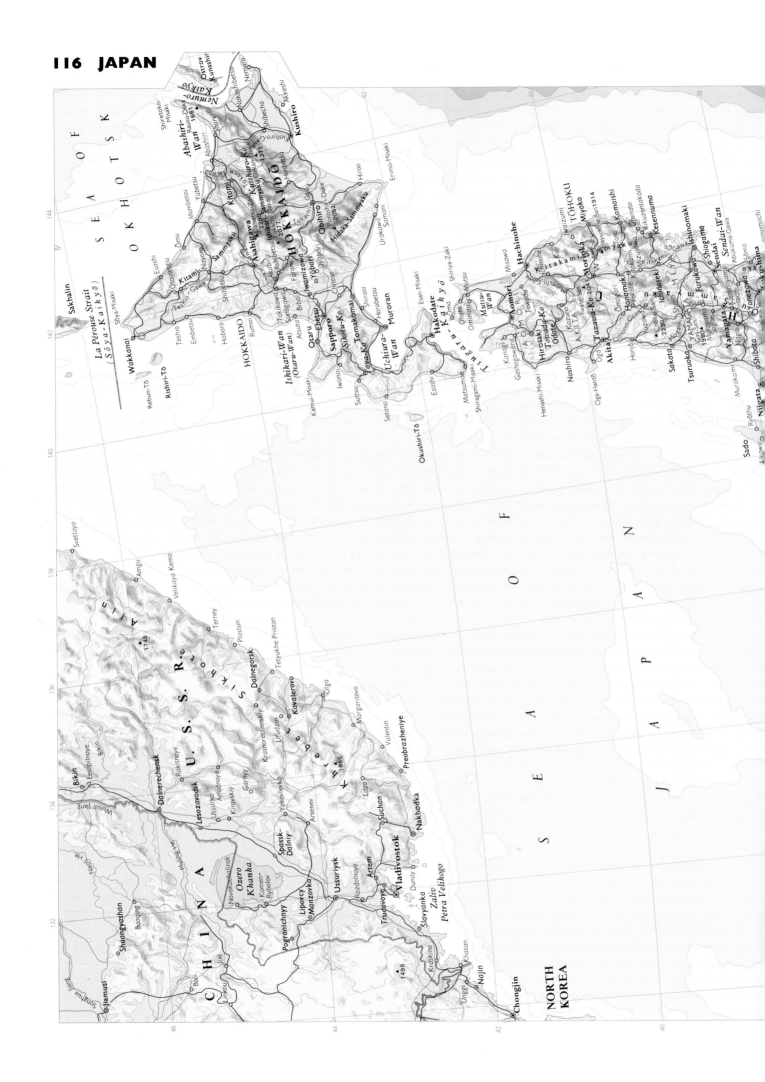

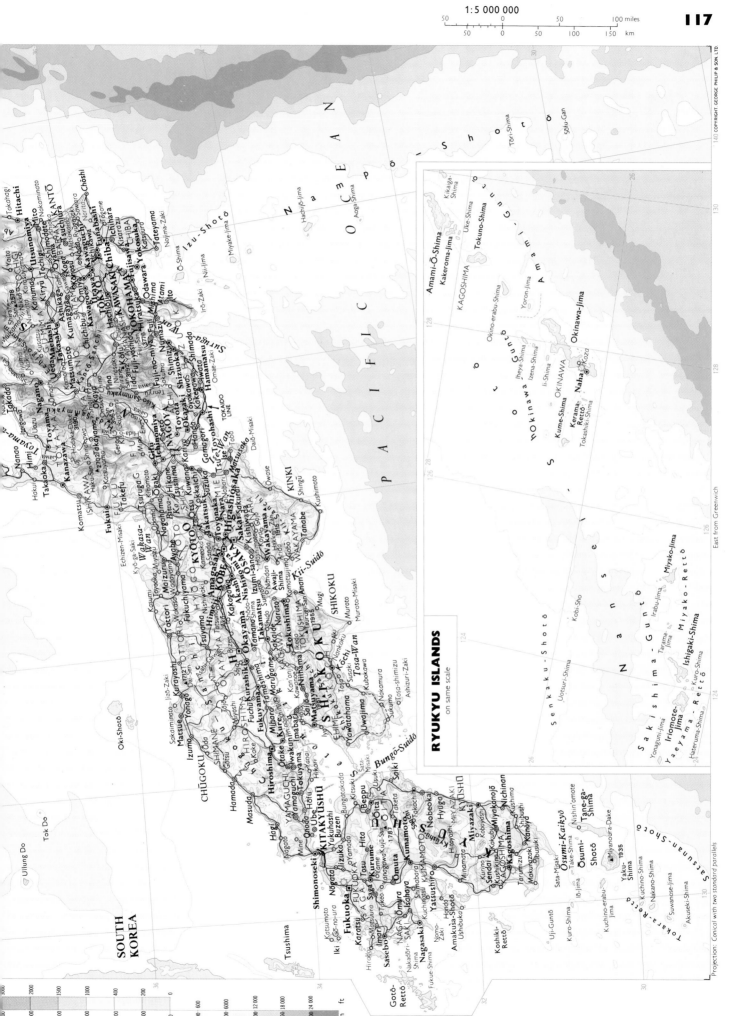

1 : 40 000 000

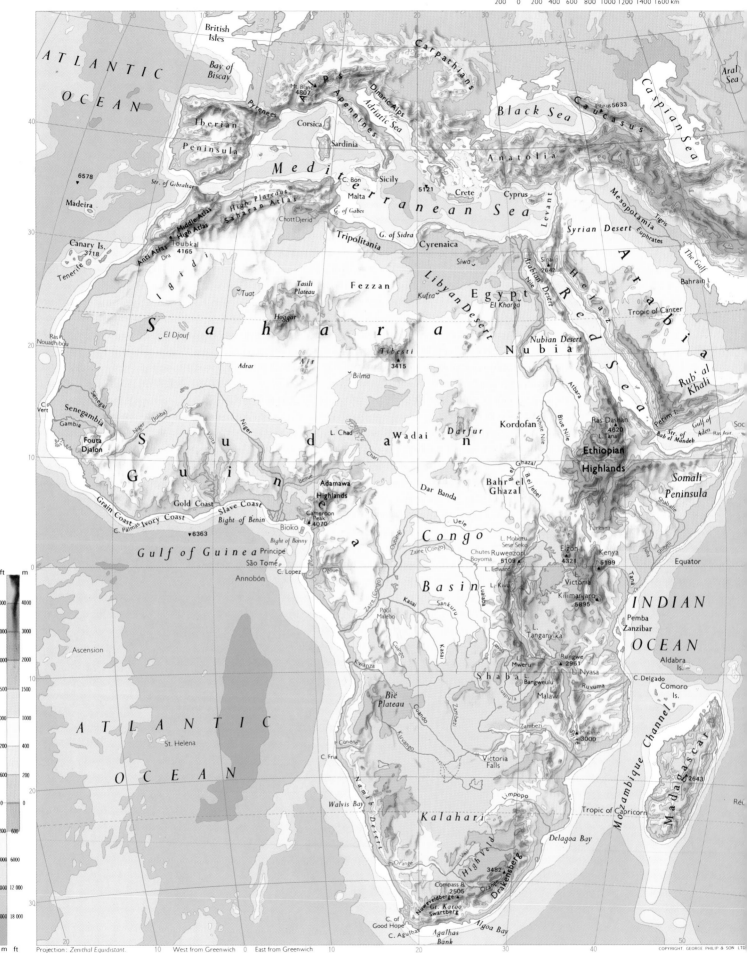

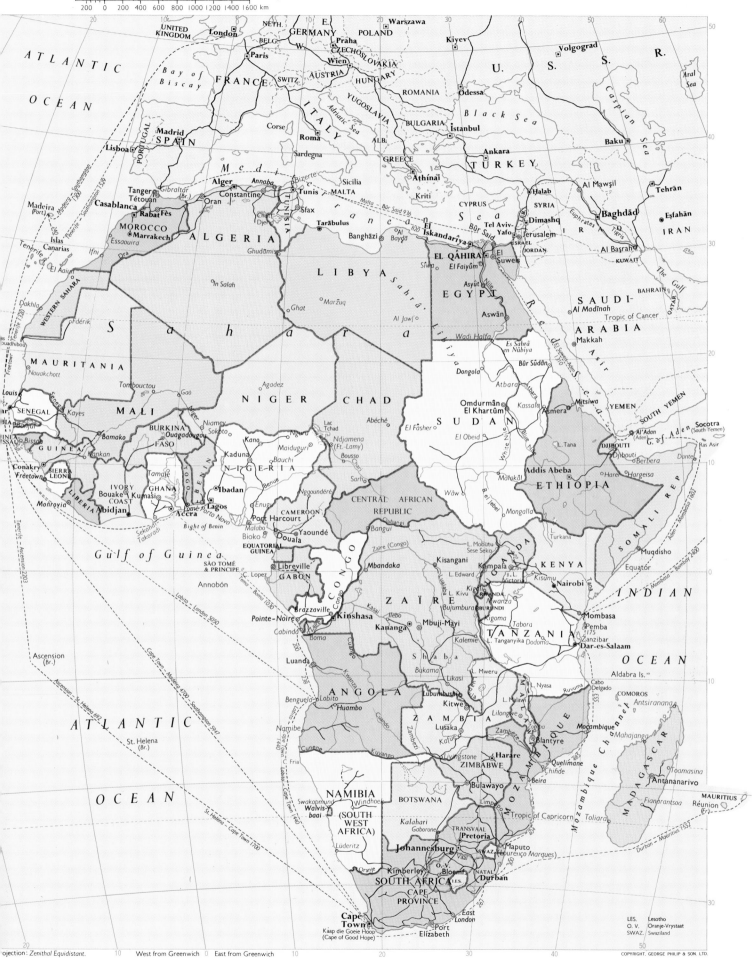

1:40 000 000

200 0   200   400   600   800   1000 miles
200 0 200 400 600 800 1000 1200 1400 1600 km

ATLANTIC

OCEAN

Madeira
(Port.)

Islas
Canarias

Tenerife

UNITED
KINGDOM   London

NETH.   GERMANY   POLAND   Warszawa

BELG.   W.   Praha   CZECHOSLOVAKIA   Kiyev

Paris   Wien   AUSTRIA   HUNGARY

FRANCE   SWITZ.   ITALY   YUGOSLAVIA   ROMANIA   Odessa

Bay of   Corse   BULGARIA   Istanbul
Biscay
                Roma   ALB.   GREECE   Athínai   TURKEY   Ankara

Madrid
SPAIN   Sardegna   Kriti   CYPRUS

Lisboa   Halab   Al Mawsil   Tehrān
PORTUGAL
                Sicilia   SYRIA   Dimashq   Baghdād   Esfahān

Tanger   Gibraltar   Alger   Annaba   Tunis   MALTA   Tel Aviv-   IRAQ   IRAN
Tétouan   (Br.)   Constantine   TUNISIA   Yafo   Jerusalem   Al Basrah
Casablanca   Oran   Sfax   ISRAEL   JORDAN   KUWAIT
Rabat Fès   The Gulf
MOROCCO   Marrakech   Tarābulus   El   El Iskandarîya   Bür Sa'id   SAUDI-   BAHRAIN   QATAR
Essaouira   Banghāzī   'Aqaba   EL QAHIRA   El Suweis   Al Madînah   ARABIA
Ifni   In Salah   El Faiyûm   Tropic of Cancer
El Aaiún   ALGERIA   LIBYA   Sahrā' Lībiya   EGYPT   Aswān   Makkah   Asir

WESTERN SAHARA   Ghadāmis   Marzūq   Makkah
Dakhla   S   a   h   a   r   a   Ghat   Al Jawf   Wâdi Halfa   Es Sahrā'
Nouadhibou   Dongola   en Nūbiya

MAURITANIA   Tombouctou   Agadez   SUDAN   Atbara
Nouakchott   Gaò   NIGER   CHAD   Abéché   El Fâsher   El Obeid   Omdurmân   Kassala   Mitsiwa   YEMEN
St-Louis   El Khartûm   Asmera   SOUTH YEMEN
SENEGAL   Kayes   MALI   Niamey   Sokoto   Kano   Ndjamena   Bousso   El Obeid   DJIBOUTI   Aden   Socotra
Banjul   Bamako   BURKINA   Maidugur   (Ft.-Lamy)   Malakal   Djibouti   (South Yemen)
GUINEA-   Kankan   FASO   Ouagadougou   Kaduna   Bauchi   Sarh   L. Tana   Harer   Berbera
BISSAU   NIGERIA   Benue   Ngaoundéré   Wâw   ETHIOPIA
Conakry   SIERRA   Tamale   GHANA   BENIN   Ibadan   Enugu   CAMEROON   CENTRAL AFRICAN   Bangui   Addis Abeba   SOMALI REP   Ras Asir
Freetown   LEONE   IVORY   Kumasi   TOGO   Lagos   Port Harcourt   REPUBLIC   Oubangui   Mongalla   Hargeisa
Monrovia   LIBERIA   Bouaké   Accra   Porto Novo   Malabo   Yaoundé   Zaire (Congo)   UGANDA   L. Turkana
Abidjan   COAST   Lomé   Bight of Benin   Bioko   Douala   GABON   Mbandaka   Kisangani   L. Mobutu   KENYA
Sekondi-   EQUATORIAL   Libreville   CONGO   Sese Seko   Kampala   Equator
Takoradi   GUINEA   SÃO TOMÉ   C. Lopez   ZAÏRE   L. Edward   L. Victoria   Kisumu   Nairobi
Gulf of Guinea   & PRINCIPE   Brazzaville   Kasai   L. Kivu   RWANDA   Mwanza   Mombasa
Annobón   Pointe-Noire   Kinshasa   Ilebo   Kigoma   BURUNDI   Bujumbura   Tabora   Pemba
                Cabinda   Boma   Mbuji-Mayi   Kananga   L. Tanganyika   Dodoma   TANZANIA   Zanzibar
Ascension   Luanda   Kalemie   Shaba   Dar-es-Salaam
(Br.)   Bukama   L. Mweru   INDIAN
St. Helena   ANGOLA   Likasi   Aldabra Is.   OCEAN
(Br.)   Benguela   Lobito   Lubumbashi   L. Nyasa   Cabo   COMOROS
ATLANTIC   Huambo   Kitwe   Kwe   MALAWI   Delgado   Antsiranana
                        Namibe   ZAMBIA   Lusaka   Lilongwe   Blantyre   Mahajanga   Moçambique
OCEAN   Cunene   Livingstone   Harare   Quelimane
                    NAMIBIA   BOTSWANA   ZIMBABWE   Chinde   MADAGASCAR
                    (SOUTH   Swakopmund   Windhoek   Bulawayo   Beira   Antananarivo
                    WEST   Kalahari   Gaborone   MOZAMBIQUE   MAURITIUS
                    AFRICA)   Lüderitz   TRANSVAAL   Pretoria   Fianarantsoa   Réunion (Fr.)
                    Walvis-   Johannesburg   Maputo   Toliara   Tropic of Capricorn
                    baai   Kimberley   O.V.   SWAZ.   (Lourenço Marques)
                        Oranje   Bloemf.   NATAL   Durban
                    SOUTH AFRICA   CAPE   LES.
                    Cape Town   PROVINCE   East London
                    Kaap die Goeie Hoop   Port Elizabeth
                    (Cape of Good Hope)

U. S. S. R.

Volgograd

Black Sea

Caspian Sea

Baku

Aral Sea

LES.   Lesotho
O.V.   Oranje-Vrystaat
SWAZ.   Swaziland

Projection: Zenithal Equidistant.   West from Greenwich   East from Greenwich   COPYRIGHT. GEORGE PHILIP & SON. LTD.

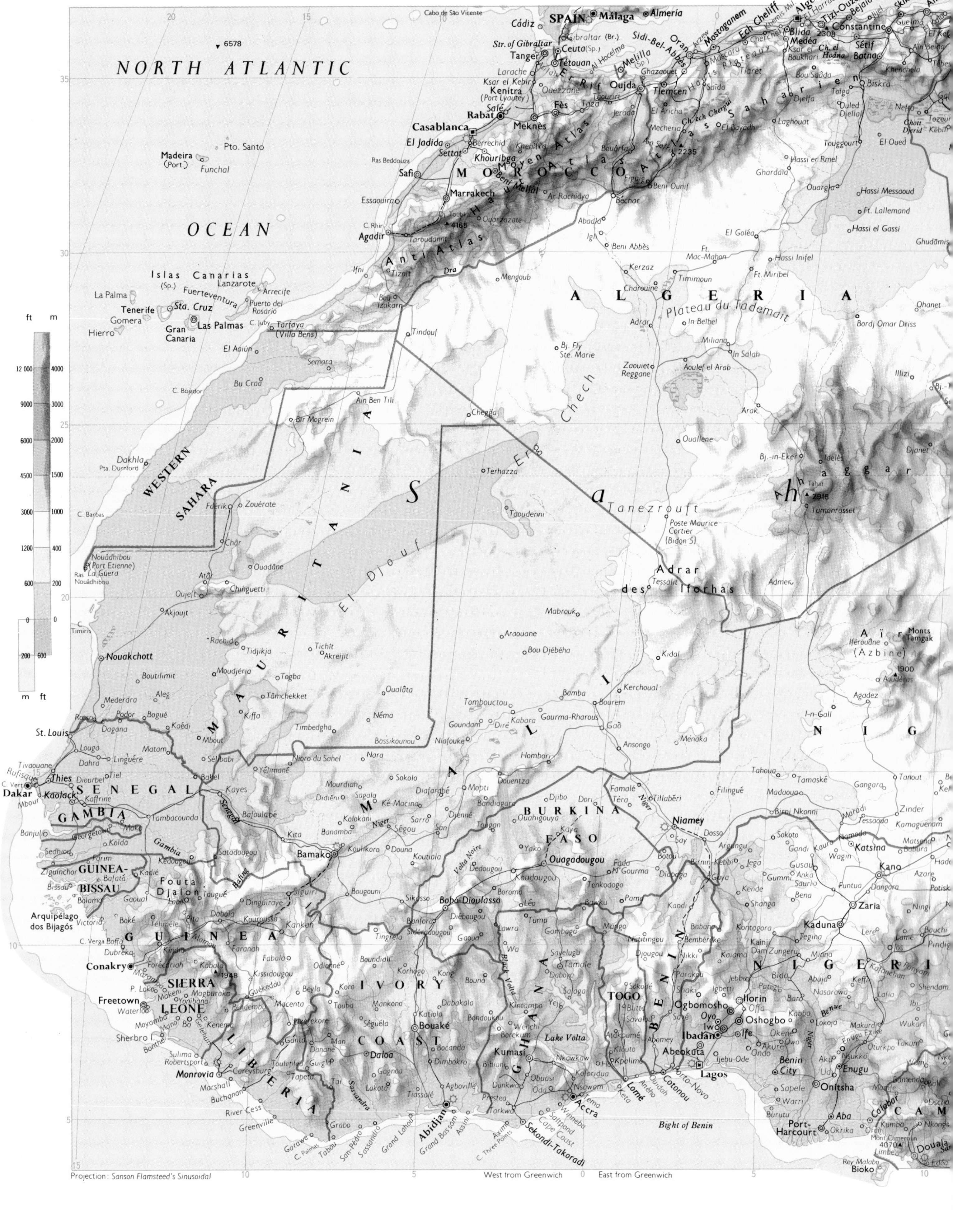

NORTH ATLANTIC

OCEAN

▼ 6578

SPAIN
Cádiz · Málaga · Almería
Gibraltar (Br.) · Sidi-Bel-Abbès
Str. of Gibraltar · Ceuta (Sp.) · Oran · Mostaganem · Ech Cheliff · Chemis Mil. · Alger (Algiers) · Harrach · Tizi-Ouzou · Bejaia · Jijel · Skikda · Annaba
Tanger · Tétouan · Al Hoceima · Ghazaouet · Tlemcen · Blida · Médéa · 2308 · Constantine · El Berd
Larache · Melilla (Sp.) · Oujda · Saida · Ksar el Hodna · Batna · Sétif · Khenchela
Ksar el Kebir · Ouezzane · Taourirt · Mecheria · El Bayadh · Djelfa · Tofga · Bou-Saâda · Biskra
Kenitra (Port Lyautey) · Fès · Taza · Jerada · Laghouat · Ouled Djellal · El Oued
Salé · Meknès · El Aricha · Chott Djerid · Touzeur
Rabat · Khenifra · Bouârfa · Ghardaïa · Touggourt · El Oued
Casablanca
El Jadida · Berrechid · Settat · Khouribga · Beni Mellal · Ar Rachidya · Béchar · Beni Ounif · 2235 · Hassi er Rmel · Hassi Messaoud
Safi · Marrakech · Abadla · Ouargla · Ft. Lallemand
Essaouira · Ouarzazate · Igli · Beni Abbès · Ghardaïa · Hassi el Gassi
C. Rhir · 4165 · Ighil · El Goléa · Hassi Inifel · Ghudāmis
Agadir · Taroudannt · Anti Atlas · Dra · Kerzaz · Ft. Mac-Mahon · Ft. Miribel
Ifni · Tiznit · Mengoub · Timimoun · In Salah · Ohanet

Madeira (Port.) · Funchal · Pto. Santo
Ras Beddouza

ALGERIA
Plateau du Tademaït

Islas Canarias (Sp.)
La Palma · Lanzarote
Tenerife · Fuerteventura · Arrecife
Gomera · Sta. Cruz · Puerto del Rosario
Hierro · Gran Canaria · Las Palmas · C. Juby · Tarfaya (Villa Bens)
El Aaiún · Semara · Tindouf · Bj. Fly · Ste. Marie · Miliana · Zaouiet Reggane · Aoulef el Arab · Illizi · Bj.
C. Bojador · Bu Craa · Aïn Ben Tili · Chegga · Arak · Bj.-in-Eker · Idelès · Djanet

WESTERN SAHARA
Dakhla · Pta. Durnford
C. Barbas · Fdérik · Zouérate · Terhazza · Tanezrouft · Ahaggar · Tahat · 2918 · Tamanrasset
Nouâdhibou (Port Etienne) · Châr · Taoudenni · Poste Maurice Cortier (Bidon 5)
Ras Nouâdhibou · La Güera · Ouadâne · Adrar des Iforhas · Tessalit · Admer

MAURITANIA
Atâr · Chinguetti · Mabrouk · Aïr · Monts Tamgak · (Azbine)
Oujeft · Akjoujt · Rachid · Tidjikja · Tichît · Araouane · Iférouâne · 1900 · Aoulelas
Timiris · Nouakchott · Boutilimit · Moudjéria · Togba · Akreijit · Bou Djébéha · Kidal · I-n-Gall · Agadez
Mederdra · Aleg · Tâmchekket · Oualâta · Tombouctou · Bamba · Kerchoual · Ménaka · NIGER
Rosso · Podor · Bogué · Kaêdi · Kiffa · Néma · Timbedgha · Goundam · Diré · Gourma-Rharous · Gaô · Ansongo · Tahoua · Tanout
St. Louis · Dagana · Mbout · Bôssikounou · Nara · Niafouké · Bourem · Homborí · Filingué · Madaoua · Gangara

MALI

SENEGAL
Louga · Tivaouane · Thiès · Matam · Linguère · Nioro du Sahel · Yélimané · Mourdiah · Sokolo · Diafarabé · Douentza · Djibo · Dori · Téra · Tillabéri · Birni Nkonni · Maradi · Zinder
Dakar · Kaolack · Kaffrine · Bakel · Kayes · Diéma · Didiéni · Ségou · Sarro · Djenné · Bandiagara · Famalé · Say · Niamey · Dosso · Argungu · Gandi · Kaura · Tessaoua · Kamugenam
GAMBIA · Mbour · Tambacounda · Bafoulabé · Kolokani · Banamba · Koulikoro · Mopti · BURKINA FASO · Botou · Birni-Kebbi · Jega · Gusau · Wagin · Katsina
Banjul · Georgetown · Kolda · Kita · Satadougou · Bamako · Douna · Koutiala · Ouahigouya · Yako · Ouagadougou · Fada N'Gourma · Diapaga · Goya · Kebbe · Gummi · Anka · Funtua · Dangora · Kano
Ziguinchor · Sédhiou · Farim · Bafatá · Gaoual · Tougué · Bougouni · Sikasso · Bobo-Dioulasso · Léo · Tenkodogo · Kende · Shanga · Bena · Azare · Potisk
GUINEA-BISSAU · Bolama · Victoria · Kindia · Dinguiraye · Kouroussa · Banfora · Diébougou · Boromo · Nikki · Kaiama · Kontagora · Lere · Kaduna · Zaria · Ningi · Bauchi
Bissau · Fouta Djalon · Dabola · Kankan · Tingrela · Sidéradougou · Gaoua · Wa · Gambaga · Babana · Kainji · Tegina · Pindig
Arquipélago dos Bijagós · Boké · Télimélé · Faranah · Fabola · Odienné · Korhogo · Kong · Bouna · Sayelugu · Djougou · Bembéréke · Zungeru · Lame
C. Verga · Dubreka · GUINEA · Kabala · Kissidougou · Beyla · Koro · Dabakala · Tamale · Dapoba · Natitingou · Nikki · Karaua · Kontagora · Dam · NIGERIA
Conakry · Forécariah · Mamou · IVORY COAST · Katiola · Kintampo · Yeji · Salaga · Parakou · Jebba · Bida · Nasarawa · Lafia · Keffi
SIERRA LEONE · 1948 · Guékédou · Touba · Mankona · Bondoukou · Wenchi · Sokode · Tchaki · Shaki · Ilorin · Offa · Kabba · Lokoja · Makurdi · Ibi · Wukari
Freetown · Makeni · Magburaka · Macenta · Séguéla · TOGO · Blitta · Savalou · Iseyin · Oyo · Oshogbo · Okene · Enugu · CAMEROON
Waterloo · Moyamba · Bo · Kenema · Zaukro · Bouaké · Bocanda · Dimbokro · Bibiani · Atakpamé · Abomey · Ogbomosho · Ife · Akure · Ondo · Onitsha
Sherbro · Bonthe · Sulima · Ganta · Man · Daloa · Bibiani · GHANA · Nkawkaw · Kpalimé · Cotonou · Porto-Novo · Ibadan · Abeokuta · Ijebu-Ode · Benin City · Sapele · Warri
Sumandu · Tapeta · Gagnoa · Kumasi · Lake Volta · Kpong · Lomé · Lagos · Sekondi-Takoradi · Aba · Port Harcourt · Calabar · Mont Cameroun 4070 · Douala
Monrovia · Marshall · Toulepleu · Guiglo · Agboville · Obuasi · Nsawam · Accra · Ikom · Okrika · Kumba · Bioko · Fako
LIBERIA · Buchanan · River Cess · Greenville · Tiassalé · Prestea · Tarkwa · Cape Coast · Bight of Benin · Rey Malaba · Limbe

Abidjan · Grand Bassam · Axim · C. Three Points

ft · m · 12000 · 4000 · 9000 · 3000 · 6000 · 2000 · 4500 · 1500 · 3000 · 1000 · 1200 · 400 · 600 · 200 · 0 · 0 · 200 · 600 · m · ft

West from Greenwich · East from Greenwich

1:15 000 000

100   0   100   200   300   400 miles

100   0   100   200   300   400   500   600 km

MEDITERRANEAN SEA

Pantelleria Sicily
(It.) Ragusa C. Passero
-Temime
Lampedusa MALTA
(It.)
erkenna

Pantelleria   Ragusa C. Passero
                        Iraklion
Ródhos   Karpathos
Krití

Antalya
Antalya Körfezi   TURKEY   İskenderun Körfezi İskenderun Al Mawṣil
                          Antalya   Halab   (Mosul)
                                  İskenderun Antakya
CYPRUS   Nicosia   SYRIA   Ḥamāh   Mesopotamia
         Limassol   Ḥimṣ
                    Tarabulus
                              LEBANON
                              Bayrūt   Dimashq
                                        (Damascus)   IRAQ
ISRAEL Ḥaifa   Ar Ruṭbah   Bādiyat
Tel Aviv- Jerusalem (Al Quds)
Yafo   Gazza Ammân JORDAN   ash Shām
          Dead Sea
          Al 'Aqabah   Al Jawf
                    Ma'ān
                                 An Nafūd
                         Tabūk
                              Madā'in Ṣāliḥ
                                      SAUDI
                         Taymā'
                                      ARABIA
                    Al Muwayliḥ
                         Al Wajh
                              Umm Lajj
                                   Al Madînah
Jiddah
Makkah
(Mecca)
Al Lith
Aṭ Ṭā'if

'are Tarābulus(Tripoli)
  Al Qaḍāḥ. Tājūra Al Khums Zlîtân
Al Qakabar Ghāryān Miṣrātah
Jū   968 Bani Walîd
    Mizdah
                    Banghāzī Barînā
                    (Benghazi) Suluq
                         Surt Zueitina
                         Ajdābiyah
Ra's Al-Unuf Marsa Brega
         Al' Uqaylah
Tarābulus

5121
Tūkrah
Tulmaythah(Cyrene) Marsā Susah (Apollonia)
Shahhāt Darnah
Al Bayḍā
878 Khalīj Bunbah
Tubruq (Tobruk)
Bardīa
Khalīj Surt
Sūfl Barrānî
Ras al Milh
El Iskandarîya
(Alexandria)
(Rosetta) Rashid
El Maḥalla el Kubra
Dumyāṭ
Damanhūr Tanṭa
El Mansūra
Būr Saʿīd
El 'Arîsh
Ismâ'îliya
Buheirat-Murrat-el-Kubra Gebel
El Suweis (Suez)
El Qanṭara
Khalīj es Suweis
Sinā
Khalīj el 'Aqaba

LIBYA
Fezzān
āwah Marzūq
ẓ

Suluq
Al Jaghbūb
Qārā
Munkhafeḍ el Qaṭṭāra
(Qaṭṭāra Depression)
Sîwa
El Faiyûm
El Minya
El Qâhira
(Cairo)
El Gîza
Helwân
Beni Suef
Benî Mazâr
Mallawî
Dairût
Asyûṭ
Abu Ṭîg
Qasr Farâfra
El Wâḥât el-Dakhla
El Qasr
Mût
El Wâḥât el-Khârga
Bârîs
El Khârga
Es Sahrâ'
Esh Sharqîya
Gebel el Tîh
Es Sinā
Ẓ
Bîr
Shalatein

Ḥūn
Marādah
Awjilah Al 'Irq
Zillah
1200
Al Jazirah
Rebiand
Al Jawf
Al Kufrah
Uweinat
1893
Ayn al 'Uwaynat

Sahrâ'
Cyrenaica
Lîbyegy a

Akhmîm
Sohâg Girga
Tahta
Qena Qûs
El Uqsur (Luxor)
Isnâ
Esna
1st Cataract
Aswân
Dunqul
Sadd el Aali
(Aswân High Dam)
Buheiret en Naser
(Lake Nasser)
Es Shallal

Būr Safâga
Quseir
Al Quṣayr
Ras Bânâs
Shalatein
Bîr Ungat
Halaib
Ras Hadarba

EGYPT

Tropic of Cancer

āwah Marzūq
arzûq Al Qaṭrūn
Toummo
ūma

r a

Toummo
Anzou
3150
Tarso Emissi
Bardaï
Émi Koussi
3415
Zouar
Gouri
Ounianga-Kébir
Ounianga Sérir
Depression du Mourdi
Nukheila
Bir 'Atrun
Laqiya Arba'in

2nd Cataract
Wadi Halfa
El Wâḥât el Selîma
Es Sahrâ en Nûbiya
Kosha
Abri
Delgo
(Nubian Desert)
3rd Cataract
Argo
Dongola
El Kab
Abu Hamed
Abū Dis
4th Cataract
Kareima
5th Cataract
Merowe
Korti
Ed Debba
Berber
Muhammad Qol
Gebeit
Mine
Ras Abu Shagara
Bûr Sûdân
(Port Sudan)
2635
Suakin
Sinkāt
Haiya Junction
Trinkitat
Agig
Ras Kasar
Karora
Tokar
Derudub
Musmar
Atbara
Ed Dâmer
Adarama

BAHR EL AHMAR

Tibesti
Wour
naye Bardaï
ma
Ain Galakka
Faya-Largeau
Fada
Ennedi
Borkou
Djourab

Oum Chalouba

SHAMÂL DÂRFÛR

Ed Debba
Korti
El Khandaq
Kareima
Berber
AN NÎL
ESH SHAMALÎYA

Wâd Hamid
Shendî
6th Cataract
Geili
Omdurmân El Khartûm Bahrî
El Khartûm
(Khartoum)
Kassala
Karora
Eritrea
Nakfa
Kerem
Mitsiwa
Asmera Zula

CHAD
Rig-Rig Zigey
Mao
Lac Tchad Bol
Massakory Yoo
Massaguet Bokoro
Ndjamena (Ft. Lamy)
Kousséri
Dikwa
Kondugo Massénya
Bitkine
Mongo
Kunduga
Chari
Madagali
Ati
Oum Hadjer
Am Dam
Abéché
Adré
Biltine
Arada
Tiné
Kutum
El Junaynah
Kabkâbîyah
El Fâsher
Marrah 3088
Zalingei
Iddal Ghanam
Nyâlâ
Mongororo
Goz Beïda
Guéréda
Tine
jigaibo
Malha
Hamrato esh Sheykh
Sodiri
Umm Keddâda
Umm Bel
Kâgmar
SHAMÂL KORDOFÂN
El Obeid
En Nahud
Abû Zabad
Ed Dueim
Umm Dam
Wad Banda
Toweisha
El Odaiya
Dilling
El Lagâwa
Abyad
ABYAD
Talodi
Kâding
Tungaru
Melut
Renk
AN NÎL EL AZRAQ
Karmuk
SUDAN

Kassala
el Girba
Khashm el Girba
Gedaref
Gedarif
AL GEZIRA
Wâd Medanî
El Managil
El Hasa
El Mafâza
Sennâr
Singa
Ed Damazin
Er Roseires
Kurmuk
Adi Ugri
Adwa
Aksum
Barentu
Mekele
4620
Adi Kwala
L. Tana
Gonder
Debre Tabor
Lalibela
Mekdela
Dembecha
Mota
Dessie

Makari
Marte
owa
Marua
Yagoua
Kélé
Bongor
Bousso
Melfi
ANUB DÂRFÛR
Rahad al Bardî
Buram
Abû Matariq
Muglâd
En Nahud
El Fula
KORDOFÂN
JANUB KORDOFÂN
Kodugli
Kadugli
Heiban
Kodok
Abwong
A'ALI EN NÎL
Malakal
Nasir

CENTRAL AFRICAN REPUBLIC
Bétaré Oya
Meiganga
Bocaranga
Bossangoa
Bozoum
Bouar
Baboua
Bouca
Bakala
Ippy
Bria
Yalinga
Grimari
Bambari
Kaga Bandoro
Bossembélé
Bali
Possel
Bangui
Damara
Carnot
Berbérati
Boda
Bimbo
Zongo
M'Baïki
Mobayi
Bambio
Mongoumba
Libenge

Iddal Ghanam
JANUB DÂRFÛR
Aoukalé
Birao
Songo
Ouanda Djallé
Kafia Kingi
Nyâmlêll
BAHR EL GHAZAL
Deim Zubeir
Wâw
Tonj
Sû'd
EL BUHEIRAT
Tainya
Rumbêk
Yirol
Tali P.
GHARB EL ISTIWA'IYA
Amâdi
Tombe
Maridî
Mongalla
Jûba
Kajo Kaji
Torit
Kapoeta
SHARQ EL ISTIWA'IYA
L. Turkana

ZAÏRE (CONGO)
Doruma
Dungu
Niangara
Ango
Bondo
Yakoma
Bambili
Buta
Amadi
Faradje
L. Albert
Gambela
Jimma
Dembidolo
Gore
Gimbi
Nekemte
L. Abaya
Soddo
Chencha
L. Shamo
4200
Gidole
Jarso
Yabelo
Mega
Chew Bahir
(L. Stefanie)
Todenyang
Lokitaung

ETHIOPIA
Addis Abeba
(Addis Ababa)
Addis Alem
Asela
Ziway
Gimbi

KENYA

BAHR EL AZRAQ

JONGLEI
Bôr
Pibor P.
Akobo
Kongor
Duk Fadiat
Bentiu
Fangak
Abwong
Kodok

COPYRIGHT. GEORGE PHILIP & SON. LTD.

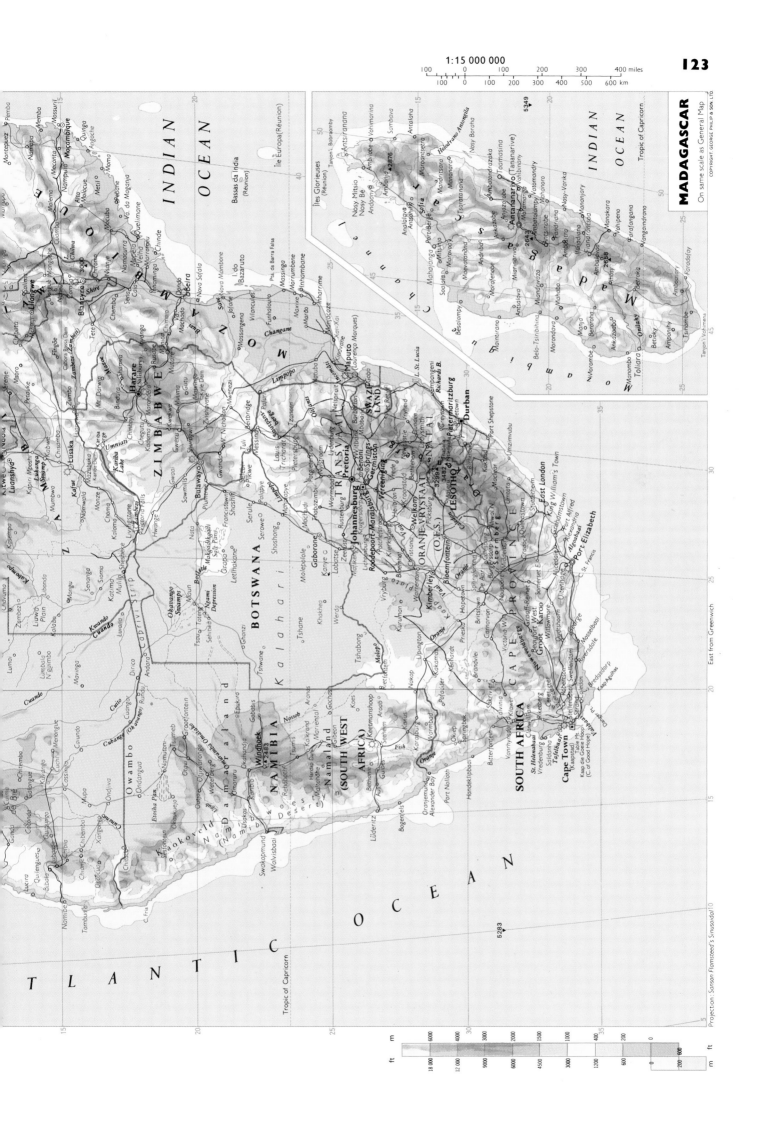

1:15 000 000

100   0   100   200   300   400 miles
100   0   100   200   300   400   500   600 km

MADAGASCAR
On same scale as General Map

COPYRIGHT GEORGE PHILIP & SON LTD

INDIAN OCEAN

INDIAN OCEAN

Tropic of Capricorn

Îles Glorieuses (Réunion)

Nosy Mitsio
Nosy Bé

5349

2643

2876

Antananarivo (Tananarive)

2658

Tropic of Capricorn

Ile Europa (Réunion)

Bassas da India (Reunion)

MOÇAMBIQUE

ZIMBABWE

Harare

Bulawayo

Beira

Lusaka

Victoria Falls

Livingstone

BOTSWANA

Kalahari

Okavango Swamps

NAMIBIA
(SOUTH WEST AFRICA)

Windhoek

Namib Desert

Limpopo

Maputo
(Lourenço Marques)

SWAZILAND

TRANSVAAL

Pretoria

Johannesburg

LESOTHO

ORANGE VRYSTAAT
(O.F.S.)

Bloemfontein

NATAL

Durban

Pietermaritzburg

Richards B.

East London

Port Elizabeth

Kimberley

CAPE PROVINCE

Karoo

SOUTH AFRICA

Cape Town
(Kaapstad)

Kaap die Goeie Hoop
(C. of Good Hope)

ATLANTIC OCEAN

INDIAN OCEAN

Tropic of Capricorn

5283

East from Greenwich

Projection Sanson Flamsteed's Sinusoidal 10

ft   m
18 000   6000
12 000   4000
         3000
9000   2000
6000   1500
4500   1000
3000   600
1200   400
600   200
0   0
m   ft

EUROPE

Leningrad

Moskva

Volga

Aral
Sea

Tashkent

Samarkand

AFGHANISTAN
Kabul
Srinagar
Lahore
PAKISTAN
Delhi
Agra
Kanpur

INDIA

Hyderabad

Madras

Sverdlovsk

Omsk

Novosibirsk

Barnaul

Semipalatinsk

Karaganda

L. Balkhash

Alma Ata

Ürümqi

U. S. S. R.

Tomsk

Yenisey

Irkutsk

Ozero
Baykal

Chita

Hovd

Ulyasutay

Ulaanbaatar

MONGOLIA

Ulan
Ude

Altai

A   S   I   A

Lena

Okhotsk

Blagoveshchensk
Amur

Khabarovsk

Manchuria

Harbin

Changchun

Shenyang

Beijing

Tianjin

N.
Dandong

KOREA

Lanzhou

CHINA

Xi'an

Chongqing

Wuhan

Changsha

Fuzhou

Wenzhou

Hangzhou

SHANGHAI

Nanjing

Kunlun Shan

XIZANG (TIBET)

Mt. Everest
8848

Lhasa

NEPAL

Brahmaputra

Ganges

Varanasi

Calcutta

BANGLA-
DESH

Chittagong

BURMA

Chiengmai

Mandalay

Myitkyina

Irrawaddy

Rangoon

THAILAND
(SIAM)

Bangkok

CAMBODIA

Mergui
Arch.

Isthmus of
Kra

Andaman Is.

Cuttack

Bay of
Bengal

SRI LANKA

Colombo

Nicobar Is.
1567

C. Camau

Gulf
of
Thailand

Phnom
Penh

Phanh Bho
Ho Chi Minh
(Saigon)

South
China
Sea

George Town

Kuala Lumpur

Melaka

PENINSULAR
MALAYSIA

SINGAPORE

Natuna

Nias

Sumatra

Bangka

Palembang

Sunda

INDO

Sunda Strait

Jakarta

Java Sea

Semarang

Surabaya

Java

Christmas I.
(Austral.)

Cocos (Keeling) Is.
(Austral.)

INDIAN

OCEAN

Amsterdam I.
(Fr.)

St. Paul I. (Fr.)

Mid

Oceanic

Ridge

Crozet Is.
(Fr.)

Kerguelen
(Fr.)

Heard Is. (Aust.)

Leningrad
Sea of Okhotsk

Kamchatka

Komandorskie Is.
(U.S.S.R.)

Near I.

Petropavlovsk

Gof Sakhalin

Sakhalin

La Perouse
Strait

Kuril Is.

Kuril Trench

Aleutian Tre

Aleutian Is.

Kiska

7822

7168

Vladivostok

Hakodate

Sea of
Japan

Sendai

Souls

Pusan

JAPAN

Kyōto

TOKYO

Yokohama

Kitakyūshū

Nagasaki

Osaka

Nagoya

Fujisan 3776

Qingdao

Yellow Sea

Jinan

Dalian

Huang Ho

Yangtze

Chang Jiang

Shikoku

Honshu Ridge

Japan Trench

10,554

Bonin Is.

Volcano Is.

Marcus I.

6603

Midway

Yomohama – Vancouver 4280

Emperor Seamount Chain

3389

KURO

Necker Ri

Wake I. (U.S.)

Marcus

Xiamen

Guangzhou

MACAU
(Port.)

HONG KONG

Taibei

Taiwan
(Formosa)

Hainan

Hanoi

VIETNAM

East
China
Sea

1066

Ryūkyū Is.

KURO SIWO

C. Engano

Manila

Mindoro

PHILIPPINES

Samar

10,497

Palawan

Sulu
Sea

Kinabalu

Labuan

SABAH

BRUNEI

SARAWAK

Borneo

Celebes

Ujung
Pandang

Celebes
Sea

Moluccas

Buru

Ceram

Amboina

Banda
Sea

Flores
Sea

Flores

Sumbawa

Lombok

Java
Trench

7450

Sumba

Timor

S   I   A

Tanimbar Is.

7440

5029

Aru Is.

Irian
Jaya

PAPUA
New
Guinea

Madang

Lae

New Britain

Port Moresby

NEW
GUINEA

9103

Rabaul

Arafura Sea

Torres Strait

Thursday I.
C. Arnhem

C. York

Darwin

Ashmore Is.

Larrimah

Wyndham

N.W.
Cape

Onslow

Northern
Territory

Newcastle
Waters

Mt. Isa

G. of
Carpentaria

AUSTRALIA

WESTERN AUSTRALIA

Shark Bay

Geraldton

Kalgoorlie-Boulder

Perth

Fremantle

Geographe Bay

Albany

K. George Sd.

Oodnadatta

L. Eyre

SOUTH AUSTRALIA

Alice Springs

Longreach

QUEENSLAND

Darling

Great
Australian Bight

F. - A. 1353

NEW SOUTH WALES

Cairns

Townsville

Rockhampton

Maryborough

Brisbane

Ipswich

Coral Sea
Islands
Territory

Coral Sea

Great Divide

Singapore 3772

Brisbane

VICTORIA

Ballarat

Geelong

Melbourne

Murray

Adelaide

Katoomba

Sydney

Newcastle

Wollongong

Canberra

Mt. Kosciusko 2230

Encounter
Bay

F. - A. 1353

Bass Strait

Launceston

TASMANIA

Hobart

AUSTRALIAN CURRENT

W. 1293

Tasman

Sea

Mt. Cook
3764

Auckland

Hamilton

Cook Strait

Nelson

Wellington

Christchurch

Oamaru

Dunedin

Invercargill

Stewart I.

NEW ZEA

Palmerston N.

Bounty

Antip

10,047

Norfolk I. (Aust.)

Lord Howe I. (Aust.)

S. - A. 1274

New
Caledonia
(Fr.)

Nouméa

Chesterfield
Is.

7570

VANUATU

Loyalty Is.

FIJI

Vanua Levu

Vitu Levu

Suva

Rotuma

Wallis
&
Futuna (Fr.)

Vanua Levu

644

SOLOMON
ISLANDS

Honiara

Guadalcanal

Louisiade
Arch.

9165

Sta. Cruz I.

TUVALU
(Ellice Is.)

Funafuti

NAURU

Banaba

Butaritari

Gilbert Is.

Baba

EQUATORIAL

Jaluit

Micronesia

Ponape

Truk

Fed. States of
Micronesia

Eniwetok
Atoll

Bikini
Atoll

Marshall Is.

U.S. TRUST TERR. OF THE
PACIFIC ISLANDS

Guam (U.S.)

11,022

Mariana Trench

Northern Marianas

Yap

Belau

Caroline Islands

Melanesia

Micronesia

P

PA

International Date Line

Kermadec

Auckland Is. (N.Z.)

Macquarie Is.
(Austral.)

Campbell I.
(N.Z.)

Mariana Trench

Admiralty Is.

New Ireland

Bismarck
Arch.

Dampier Strait

Halmahera

Kapul

India

Srinagar

Chengmai

Bband

Mindanao

Mindanao
Trench

4101

ft m

18 000   6000

12 000   4000

6000   2000

3000   1000

600   200

0   0

200   600

2000   6000

4000   12 000

6000   18 000

8000   24 000

m ft

60   East from Greenwich   120   140   160   180

South

Mid-

Indian

Ridge

East

Indian

Rise

Indian-Antarctic Ridge

Al 'Adan – Melbourne 6445

Colombo – Fremantle 3720

1772

1840

1580

5615

5814

5838

1233

1274

1140

1066

Fremantle

Cape Town - Fremantle 5615

Cape Town - Melbourne 5814

Cape Town - Hobart 5838

Amsterdam I.
(Fr.)

5615   Principal Shipping Routes
(Distances in Nautical Miles)

ALASKA
▲6050
Gulf of Alaska
Sitka
Juneau
Prince of Wales I.
Prince Rupert
Kitimat
Queen Charlotte Is.
Dawson Creek
L. Athabasca
Churchill
Lynn Lake
Prince Albert
Saskatoon
Edmonton
Medicine Hat
Regina
L. Winnipeg
Hudson Bay
James Bay
Belcher Is.
Scheffferville
Hamilton Inlet
GREENLAND
C. Farewell
NORTH
Labrador
Strait of Belle Isle
CANADA
NORTH AMERICA
Newfoundland
C. Race

Vancouver
Vancouver I.
Victoria
Seattle
Tacoma
Portland
Calgary
Winnipeg
Bismarck
Missouri
Duluth
L. Superior
Sault Ste. Marie
St. Lawrence
Montréal
Québec
Fredericton
Pr. Edward I.
C. Breton I.
Saint John
Sable I.
Anticosti
G. of St. Lawrence
Southampton 3091

C. Blanco
Spokane
Helena
Butte
Boise
ROCKY Mountains
Cheyenne
Des Moines
Minneapolis
St. Paul
Milwaukee
CHICAGO
L. Huron
L. Michigan
Toronto
Ottawa
L. Ontario
L. Erie
Buffalo
Detroit
Pittsburgh
Boston
NEW YORK
C. Sable
New York
ATLANTIC

Mendocino Seascarp
C. Mendocino
Sacramento
Oakland
San Francisco
4418
Salt Lake City
Colorado
Denver
Kansas City
St. Louis
UNITED STATES
Cincinnati
Indianapolis
Memphis
Appalachian Mts.
Richmond
Norfolk
Washington
Baltimore
Philadelphia
C. Hatteras
OCEAN

▼6741
2419
Murray Seascarp
2091
Los Angeles
San Diego
Santa Fé
Oklahoma
Little Rock
Dallas
Austin
El Paso
Atlanta
Savannah
Jacksonville
New York - Recife 3678
N.Y. 1972
Bermuda (U.K.)
Panamá - Liverpool 4530

CALIFORNIAN CURRENT
Guadalupe 6225
Pto. Eugenia
Ciudad Juárez
Torreón
SIERRA MADRE
Gulf of California
Houston
Galveston
New Orleans
San Antonio
Mobile
Tampa
Florida
Gulf of Mexico
Miami
Florida Strait
BAHAMAS

Tropic of Cancer
C.S. Lucas
Monterrey
Revilla Gigedo Is. (Mexico)
Aguascalientes
Guadalajara
San Luis Potosí
México
5700
Puebla
Veracruz
Tampico
Yucatan Channel
Mérida
La Habana
CUBA
West Indies
Hispaniola 9200
DOM. REP.
St. Thomas (U.S.)
Virgin Is.
Leeward Is.

Hawaiian Is. (U.S.A.)
Oahu
Honolulu
Hawaii
Clarion Fracture Zone
3277
Acapulco
▼7680
HAITI
JAMAICA
Santo Domingo
Kingston
PUERTO RICO
Guadeloupe (Fr.)
Martinique (Fr.)
BARBADOS

U.S.
IFIC
4711
Clipperton Fracture Zone
Clipperton I. (Fr.)
GUATEMALA
Guatemala
Salvador
EL SALVADOR
Tegucigalpa
HONDURAS
NICARAGUA
Managua
BELIZE
Caribbean Sea
Curaçao (Ne.)
Windward Is.
TRINIDAD & TOBAGO

3666
Zone
CENTRAL AMERICA
San José
COSTA RICA
Barranquilla
Colón
PANAMA
Panamá
Canal
Maracaibo
Caracas
VENEZUELA

CURRENT
Palmyra Is. (U.S.)
Cocos I.
835
Medellín
Bogotá
Cali
COLOMBIA
Orinoco

Teraina
Tabuaeran
Kiritimati
Jarvis I. (U.S.)
Equator
Galápagos (Ecuador)
C.S. Francisco
Quito
ECUADOR
Guayaquil
Cuenca
Chimborazo 6267
Iquitos
Manaus
Amazon

Island Ridge
Malden I.
Starbuck I.
Marquesas Is.
C. Pariñas
Lobos I.
Chiclayo
Trujillo
70b
BRAZIL
SOUTH

ATI
Tongareva
Penrhyn Is.
Manihiki
Suwarrow Is.
Caroline I.
Vostok
Flint I.
Leeward Is.
Society Is.
Tahiti - Panamá 4570
6369
Callao
PERU
Lima
Cuzco
AMERICA

Cook Islands (N.Z.)
1303
Windward Is.
Tahiti
FRENCH POLYNESIA
Tuamotu Archipelago
Tuamotu Ridge
Auckland - Panamá 6510
East Pacific Ridge
Southeast Pacific Basin
Arequipa
L. Titicaca
Illampu & Ancohuma 6550
La Paz
PERUVIAN CURRENT
8050
BOLIVIA

Austral
Rarotonga
Seamount Chain
Tubuai Is. (Austral Is.)
Rapa Iti
Tropic of Capricorn
Pitcairn I. (U.K.)
Ducie I.
Sala-y-Gomez (Chile)
San Félix (Chile)
San Ambrosio (Chile)
Easter Is. (Chile)
6866
Iquique
Chile
Antofagasta
Trench
PARAGUAY
Salta
Tucumán
Asunción
Corrientes
Pto. Alegre

Basin
Pacific - Antarctic Ridge
Arch. de Juan Fernández (Chile)
Alejandro Selkirk
Robinson Crusoe
Aconcagua 6960
Valparaíso
Santiago
Córdoba
Rosario
Santa Fe
Paysandú
URUGUAY
Montevideo
Río de la Plata
ANDES
ARGENTINA
La Plata
Buenos Aires
Mar del Plata
SOUTH

WEST WIND DRIFT
Pacific - Antarctic Basin
Concepción
Neuquén
PATAGONIA
P.A. Valparaíso
1414
Buenos Aires - Valparaíso
Buenos Aires - Montevideo
1355
1285
ATLANTIC
Argentine Basin 6212
OCEAN

CAPE HORN CURRENT
Chile Rise
Chonos Arch.
G. of Penas
P. Deseado
Wellington Is.
Sta. Cruz
Punta Arenas
Str. of Magellan
Tierra del Fuego
C. Horn
Falkland Is. (U.K.)
Stanley
South Georgia

Principal Air Routes

COPYRIGHT. GEORGE PHILIP & SON, LTD.

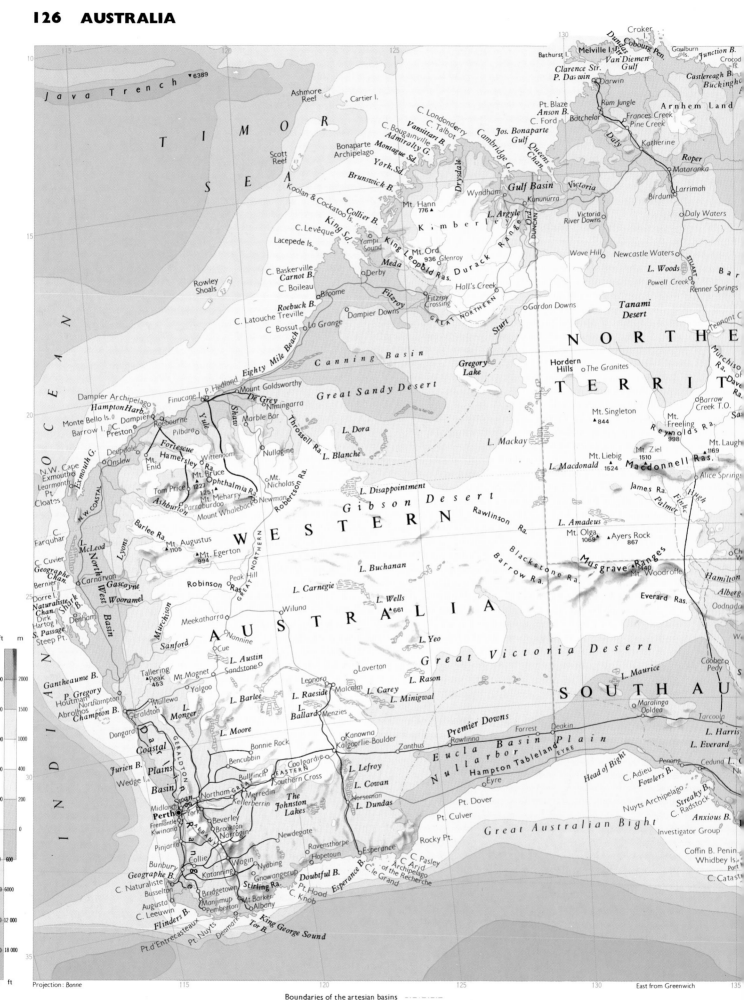

Projection: Bonne

Boundaries of the artesian basins - - - - -

East from Greenwich

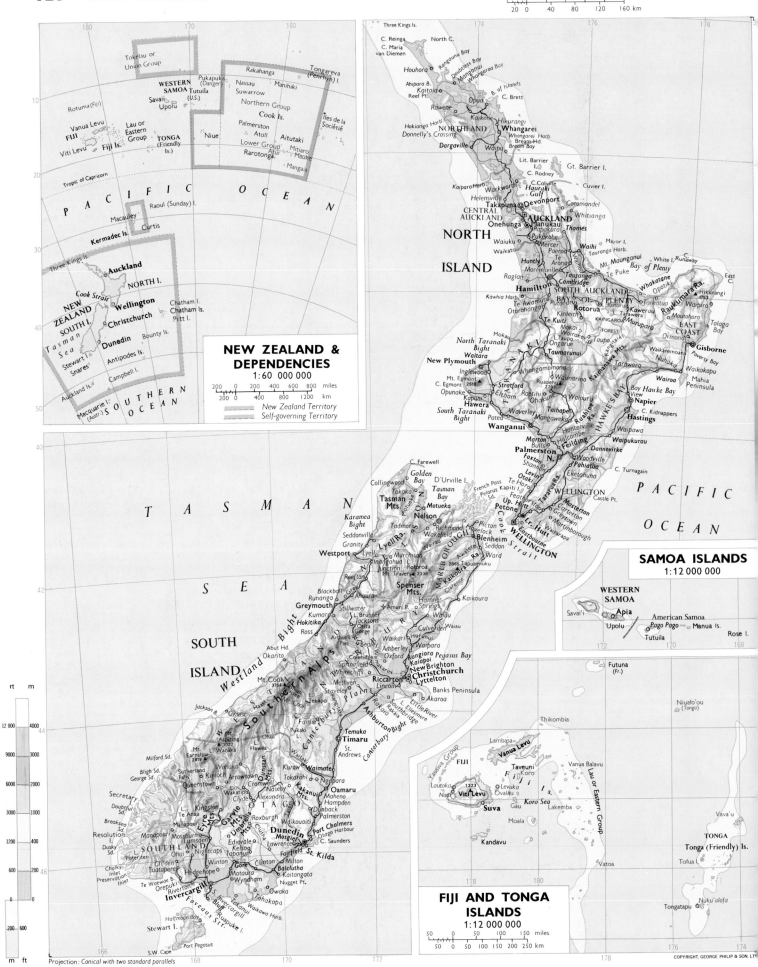

1:6 000 000

20 0   20 40 60 80   100 miles
20 0   40   80   120   160 km

NEW ZEALAND & DEPENDENCIES
1:60 000 000

200 0   200 400 600 800 miles
200 0   400   800   1200 km

New Zealand Territory
Self-governing Territory

SAMOA ISLANDS
1:12 000 000

WESTERN SAMOA

Savai'i

Apia

Upolu

American Samoa

Pago Pago Manua Is.

Tutuila

Rose I.

FIJI AND TONGA ISLANDS
1:12 000 000

50 0   50 100   150 miles
50 0 50 100 150 200 250 km

Projection: Conical with two standard parallels

COPYRIGHT. GEORGE PHILIP & SON. LTᴰ

INDEX

Introduction to Index

The number in bold type which follows each name in the index refers to the number of the map-page where that feature or place will be found. This is usually the largest scale on which the place or feature appears. Names in the U.S. are indexed to their state, which is not necessarily the largest scale.

The geographical co-ordinates which follow the place name are sometimes only approximate but are close enough for the place name to be located.

A solid square ■ follows the name of a country while an open square □ refers to a first order administrative area (states in the U.S.) A diamond ◇ refers to counties in the U.S. (parishes in Louisiana, census areas in Alaska).

Rivers have been indexed to their mouth or to where they join another river. All river names are followed by the symbol ⤳.

Abbreviations used

A.S.S.R. – *Autonomous Soviet Socialist Republic*
Ala. – *Alabama*
Ang. – *Angola*
Arch. – *Archipelago*
Arg. – *Argentina*
Ariz. – *Arizona*
Ark. – *Arkansas*
B. – *Baie, Bahia, Bay, Boca, Bucht, Bugt*
B.C. – *British Columbia*
Br. – *British*
C. – *Cabo, Cap, Cape*
C.H. – *Court House*
C. Prov. – *Cape Province*
Calif. – *California*
Chan. – *Channel*
Col. – *Colombia*
Colo. – *Colorado*
Conn. – *Connecticut*
Cord. – *Cordillera*
D.C. – *District of Columbia*
Del. – *Delaware*
Dep. – *Dependency*
Des. – *Desert*
Dist. – *District*
Dom. Rep. – *Dominican Republic*
E. – *East*
Eng. – *England*
Fd. – *Fjord*
Fed. – *Federal, Federation*
Fla. – *Florida*
Fr. – *France, French*
G. – *Golfe, Golfo, Gulf, Guba*
Ga. – *Georgia*
Gt. – *Great*
Hd. – *Head*
Hts. – *Heights*

I.(s) – *Ile, Ilha, Insel, Isla, Island(s)*
Ill. – *Illinois*
Ind. – *Indiana*
Ind. Res. – *Indian Reservation*
K. – *Kap, Kapp*
Kans. – *Kansas*
Kep. – *Kepulauan*
Kól. – *Kólpos*
Ky. – *Kentucky*
L. – *Lac, Lacul, Lago, Lagoa, Lake, Limni, Loch, Lough*
La. – *Louisiana*
Ld. – *Land*
Mad. P. – *Madhya Pradesh*
Man. – *Manitoba*
Mass. – *Massachusetts*
Md. – *Maryland*
Mich. – *Michigan*
Minn. – *Minnesota*
Miss. – *Mississippi*
Mo. – *Missouri*
Mont. – *Montana*
Mt.(s) – *Mont, Monta, Monti, Muntii, Montaña, Mount, Mountain(s)*
Mys. – *Mysore*
N. – *North, Northern*
N.B. – *New Brunswick*
N.C. – *North Carolina*
N. Dak. – *North Dakota*
N.H. – *New Hampshire*
N.Ire. – *Northern Ireland*
N.J. – *New Jersey*
N. Mex – *New Mexico*
N.S.W. – *New South Wales*
N.Y. – *New York*
N.Z. – *New Zealand*
Nat. For. – *National Forest*

Nat. Park – *National Park*
Nat. Rec. Area – *National Recreation Area*
Nebr. – *Nebraska*
Neth. – *Netherlands*
Nev. – *Nevada*
Newf. – *Newfoundland*
Nic. – *Nicaragua*
Nig. – *Nigeria*
O.F.S. – *Orange Free State*
Okla. – *Oklahoma*
Ont. – *Ontario*
Oreg. – *Oregon*
Oz. – *Ozero*
P. – *Pass, Passo, Pasul*
P.N.G. – *Papua New Guinea*
Pa. – *Pennsylvania*
Pak. – *Pakistan*
Pass. – *Passage*
Pen. – *Peninsula*
Pk. – *Peak*
Plat. – *Plateau*
Port. – *Portugal, Portuguese*
Prov. – *Province, Provincial*
Pt. – *Point*
Pta. – *Ponta, Punta*
Pte. – *Pointe*
Que. – *Quebec*
Queens. – *Queensland*
R. – *Rio, River*
R.I. – *Rhode Island*
R.S.F.S.R. – *Russian Soviet Federative Socialist Republic*
Ra.(s) – *Range(s)*
Reg. – *Region*
Rep. – *Republic*
Res. – *Reserve, Reservoir, Reservation*

S. – *South*
S. Africa – *South Africa*
S.C. – *South Carolina*
S. Dak – *South Dakota*
S. Leone – *Sierra Leone*
S.S.R. – *Soviet Socialist Republic*
Sa. – *Serra, Sierra*
Sask. – *Saskatchewan*
Scot. – *Scotland*
Sd. – *Sound*
Sp. – *Spain, Spanish*
Sprgs. – *Springs*
St. – *Saint*
Str. – *Strait, Stretto*
Switz. – *Switzerland*
Tanz. – *Tanzania*
Tas. – *Tasmania*
Tenn. – *Tennessee*
Terr. – *Territory*
Tex. – *Texas*
U.K. – *United Kingdom*
U.S.A. – *United States of America*
U.S.S.R. – *Union of Soviet Socialist Republics*
Ut. P. – *Uttar Pradesh*
Va. – *Virginia*
Ven. – *Venezuela*
Vic. – *Victoria*
Vt. – *Vermont*
Wash. – *Washington*
W. – *West*
W. Va. – *West Virginia*
Wis. – *Wisconsin*
Wyo. – *Wyoming*
Yug. – *Yugoslavia*

Alphabetical Order

The alphabetical order of names composed of two or more words is governed primarily by the first word and then by the second. This is an example of the rule:

> *East Tawas*
> *Eastbourne*
> *Easter Is.*
> *Eastern Ghats*
> *Eastmain* ↝

Physical features composed of a proper name (*Mexico*) and a description (*Gulf of*) are positioned alphabetically by the proper name. The description is positioned after the proper name and is usually abbreviated:

> *Mexico, G. of*
> *Michigan, L.*
> *Pacaraima, Sa.*

Where a description forms part of a settlement or administrative name however it is always written in full and put in its true alphabetic position:

> *Lake Placid*
> *Mount Vernon*
> *Sturgeon Bay*

Names composed of the definite article (*Le, La, Les, L'*) and a proper name are usually alphabetised by the proper name.

> *Havre, Le*
> *Spezia, La*
> *Wash, The*

This rule does not apply where foreign definite articles have become part of U.S. town names. For example:

> *La Grange*

Names beginning with M', Mc are all indexed as if they were spelled Mac. All names beginning St. are alphabetised under Saint, but Sankt, Sint, Sant', Santa and San are all spelt in full and are alphabetised accordingly.

If the same place name occurs two or more times in the index and all are in the same country, each is followed by the name of the administrative subdivision in which it is located. The names are placed in the alphabetical order of the subdivisions. For example:

> *Aberdeen, Ala.*
> *Aberdeen, Idaho*
> *Aberdeen, S. Dak.*
> *Aberdeen, Wash.*

If the same place name occurs twice or more in the index and the places are in different countries, they will be followed by the country names and the latter in alphabetical order.

> *Boston, U.K.*
> *Boston, U.S.A.*

If there is a mixture of these situations, the primary order is fixed by the alphabetical sequence of the countries and the secondary order by that of the country subdivisions. In the latter case the country names are omitted.

> *Bedford, Can.*
> *Bedford, U.K.*
> *Bedford, Ind., (U.S.A.)*
> *Bedford, Pa., (U.S.A.)*

Geographical Co-ordinates

In the index, each place name is followed by its geographical co-ordinates which allow the reader to find the place on the map. These co-ordinates give the latitude and the longitude of a particular place.

The unit of measurement for latitude and longitude is the degree, and it is subdivided into 60 minutes. An index entry states the position of a place in degrees and minutes, a space being left between the degrees and minutes. The latitude is followed by N(orth) or S(outh) and the longitude by E(ast) or W(est).

The diagrams below illustrate how the reader has to estimate the required distance from the nearest line of latitude or longitude. In the case of the first diagram, there is one degree, or 60 minutes between the lines and so to find the position of Newport an estimate has to be made. 28 parts of 60 north of the 41 degree latitude line and 19 parts of 60, or 19 minutes west of the 71 degree longitude line. In the case of the second diagram, it is a little more difficult to estimate since there are 10 degrees between the lines. In the example of Anchorage, the reader has to estimate 1 degree 13 minutes north of 60° and 9° 53 minutes west of 140°.

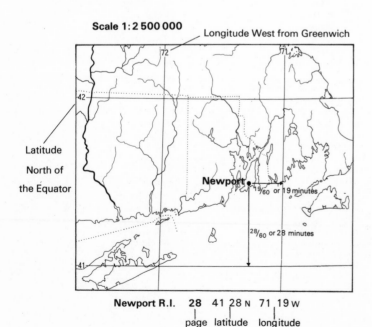

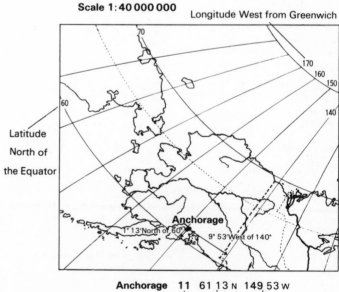

The latitude (or parallel) is the distance of a point north or south of the Equator measured as an angle with the center of the earth. The Equator is latitude 0°, the North Pole is 90°N, and the South Pole 90°S. On a globe, the lines could be drawn as concentric circles parallel to the Equator, decreasing in diameter from the Equator until they become a point at the poles. On the maps, these lines of latitude are usually represented as lines running across the map from East to West in smooth curves. They are numbered on the sides of the map. North of the Equator the numbers increase northwards, to the south they increase southwards. The degree interval between them depends on the scale of the map. On a large scale map (for example 1:2 500 000), the interval is one degree, but on a small scale map, (for example 1:40 000 000) the interval will be ten degrees.

Foreign Place Names

The atlas uses the local spellings for most place names, that is the name by which a place or feature is known within the country in which it occurs. For example:

> *Roma*
> *'s-Gravenhage*

The English conventional form is usually added in brackets on the map thus:

> *Roma (Rome)*
> *'s-Gravenhage (The Hague)*

In the index the English form is cross-referenced to the local spelling:

> *Rome = Roma*
> *Hague, The = 's-Gravenhage*

The Pronunciation of Foreign Place Names

English speaking people usually have no difficulty in reading and pronouncing correctly American and English place names. However, foreign place-name pronunciations may present many problems. Such problems can be minimised by following some simple rules. However, these rules cannot be applied to all situations, and there will be many exceptions.

1. In general, stress each syllable equally, unless your experience suggests otherwise.
2. Pronounce the letter 'a' as a broad 'a' as in 'arm'
3. Pronounce the letter 'e' as a short 'e' as in 'elm'
4. Pronounce the letter 'i' as a cross between a short 'i' and long 'e', as the two 'i's in 'California'.
5. Pronounce the letter 'o' as an intermediate 'o' as in 'soft'
6. Pronounce the letter 'u' as an intermediate 'u' as in 'sure'
7. Pronounce consonants hard, except in the Romance-language areas where 'g's are likely to be pronounced softly like 'j' in 'jam'; 'j' itself may be pronounced as 'y'; and 'x's may be pronounced as 'h'.

Moreover, English has no diacritical marks (accent and pronunciation signs), although some languages do. The following is a brief and general guide to the pronunciation of those most frequently used in the Western European languages.

		Pronunciation as in
French	é	d*a*y and shows that the e is to be pronounced e.g. Orléans.
	è	m*a*re
	î	used over any vowel and does not affect pronunciation; shows contraction of the name, usually ommission of 's' following a vowel.
	ç	's' before 'a', 'o' and 'u'
	¨	over 'e', 'i', and 'u' when they are used with another vowel and shows that each is to be pronounced.
German	ä	f*a*t
	ö	f*u*r
	ü	no English equivalent; like French 't*u*'
Italian	à, é	over vowels and indicates stress.
Portuguese	ã, õ	vowels pronounced nasally.
	ç	bo*ss*
	á	shows stress.
	ô	shows that a vowel has an 'i' or 'u' sound combined with it.
Spanish	ñ	ca*ny*on
	ü	pronounced as *w* and separately from adjoining vowels.
	á	usually indicates that this is a stressed vowel

Lines of longitude (or meridians) cut the latitude lines at right angles on the globe and intersect with one another at the poles. Longitude is measured by an angle at the center of the earth between it and the meridian of origin which runs through Greenwich (0°). It may be a measurement East or West of this line from 0° to 180° in each direction. The longitude line of 180° runs North – South through the Pacific Ocean. On a particular map, the interval between the lines of longitude is always the same as that between the lines of latitude. Normally, the meridians are drawn vertically. They are numbered in the top and bottom margins and a note states East or West from Greenwich.

Spellings of names are in the form given in the latest official lists and generally agree with the rules of the Permanent Committee on Geographical Names and the U.S. Board on Geographic Names.

Where languages do not use Roman alphabets these rules are used to transcribe these languages into Roman alphabet. These rules are based largely on pronunciation.

Swedish	å	l*aw*
	ä	f*a*t
	ö	f*u*r

The problem of place-name pronunciation is more difficult where the written form of the name is a transliteration (changing of a letter or letters of one alphabet into corresponding characters of another alphabet or language) from a non-Roman alphabet. Early English-speaking travelers and traders to such countries as China, Japan, and U.S.S.R. prepared written forms of the names that they heard there. Although no based upon a formal system, many of these written forms have become conventional place-name spelling.

More advanced study of particular languages has produced complex transliteration rules. These attempt to retain the nuances of the language concerned. One of the more difficult languages from the standpoint of both transliteration and pronunciation, is Chinese. Following are four examples of place names in three commonly used transliteration systems.

Chinese Postal System	Wade-Giles (pronunciation)	Pinyin
Peking	Pei-ching (ba-jing)	Beijing
Shanghai	Shang-hai (shäng-hi)	Shanghai
Canton	Kuang-chou (gwäng-jo)	Guangzhou

The Pinyin system, as developed by the Peking government, is the most recent system. It is the one adopted by the U.S. Board on Geographic Names and is used in this atlas. The Postal system contains the conventional place-name spellings and does not require diacritical markings. It is listed by the U.S. Board on Geographic Names as an alternative to the Pinyin system for many place-names in China.

The Chinese place-name problem is complicated further by actual changes in place-names over the years. For example, Mukden is now known as Shenyang.

In contrast to Chinese, Japanese romanization commonly employs only one diacritical mark, a line over 'o's and 'u's, which marks these as long vowels. Diacritical marks employed in the romanization of other languages not based on the Roman alphabet (such as Vietnamese and Hindi) are not commonly employed in general reference atlases as yet.

Aachen Ahome

A

Aachen 88 50 47N 6 4 E
A'âlâ en Nîl □ 121 8 50N 29 55 E
Aalsmeer 87 52 17N 4 43 E
Aalst, Belgium 87 50 56N 4 2 E
Aalst, Neth. 88 51 23N 5 29 E
Aalten 87 51 56N 6 35 E
Aarau 88 47 23N 8 4 E
Aare → 88 47 33N 8 14 E
Aarschot 87 50 59N 4 49 E
Aba 120 5 10N 7 19 E
Abacaxis → 71 3 54 S 58 47W
Ābādān 106 30 22N 48 20 E
Ābādeh 107 31 8N 52 40 E
Abadla 120 31 2N 2 45W
Abaeté 75 19 9 S 45 27W
Abaeté → 75 18 2 S 45 12W
Abaetetuba 74 1 40 S 48 50W
Abagnar Qi 114 43 52N 116 2 E
Abai 77 25 58 S 55 54W
Abajo Peak 52 37 51N 109 27W
Abakan 101 53 40N 91 10 E
Abancay 72 13 35 S 72 55W
Abapó 73 18 48 S 63 25W
Abariringa I. 124 2 50 S 171 40W
Abarqū 107 31 10N 53 20 E
'Abasān 104 31 19N 34 21 E
Abashiri 116 44 0N 144 15 E
Abashiri-Wan 116 44 0N 144 30 E
Abay 100 49 38N 72 53 E
Abaya, L. 121 6 30N 37 50 E
Abaza 100 52 39N 90 6 E
Abbay = Nîl el Azraq → 121 15 38N 32 31 E
Abbaye, Pt. 29 46 58N 88 8W
Abbeville, France 90 50 6N 1 49 E
Abbeville, Ala. 10 31 34N 85 15W
Abbeville, Ga. 18 31 59N 83 18W
Abbeville, La. 25 29 58N 92 8W
Abbeville, Miss. 31 34 30N 89 30W
Abbeville, S.C. 46 34 11N 82 23W
Abbeville County ◇ 46 34 15N 82 30W
Abbot Ice Shelf 5 73 0 S 92 0W
Abbotsford, Canada 62 49 5N 122 20W
Abbotsford, U.S.A. 55 44 57N 90 19W
Abbott, N. Mex. 38 36 18N 104 16W
Abbott, Tex. 51 31 53N 97 4W
Abbottabad 108 34 10N 73 15 E
Abd al Kūrī 105 12 5N 52 20 E
Abéché 121 13 50N 20 35 E
Åbenrå 97 55 3N 9 25 E
Abeokuta 120 7 3N 3 19 E
Aberaeron 83 52 15N 4 16W
Aberayron = Aberaeron 83 52 15N 4 16W
Abercorn = Mbala 122 8 46 S 31 24 E
Abercrombie 41 46 27N 96 44W
Aberdare 83 51 43N 3 27W
Aberdeen, Canada 63 52 20N 106 8W
Aberdeen, U.K. 84 57 9N 2 6W
Aberdeen, Idaho 20 42 57N 112 50W
Aberdeen, Ky. 48 37 15N 86 41W
Aberdeen, Md. 27 39 31N 76 10W
Aberdeen, Miss. 31 33 49N 88 33W
Aberdeen, N.C. 40 35 8N 79 26W
Aberdeen, S. Dak. 47 45 28N 98 29W
Aberdeen, Wash. 53 46 59N 123 50W
Aberdovey 83 52 33N 4 3W
Aberfeldy 84 56 37N 3 50W
Abergavenny 83 51 49N 3 1W
Abernant 10 33 17N 87 12W
Abernathy 50 33 50N 101 51W
Abert, L. 44 42 38N 120 14W
Aberystwyth 83 52 25N 4 6W
Abidjan 120 5 26N 3 58W
Abilene, Kans. 24 38 55N 97 13W
Abilene, Tex. 51 32 28N 99 43W
Abingdon, U.K. 83 51 40N 1 17W
Abingdon, Ill. 21 40 48N 90 24W
Abingdon, Va. 54 36 43N 81 59W
Abington, Conn. 28 41 52N 72 1W
Abington, Mass. 28 42 6N 70 57W
Abiquiu 38 36 13N 106 19W
Abiquiu Reservoir 38 36 16N 106 27W
Abita Springs 25 30 29N 90 2W
Abitau → 63 59 53N 109 3W
Abitau L. 63 60 27N 107 15W
Abitibi L. 60 48 40N 79 40W
Abkhaz A.S.S.R. □ 99 43 0N 41 0 E
Abkit 101 64 10N 157 10 E
Åbo 97 60 28N 22 15 E
Abohar 108 30 10N 74 10 E
Abomέy 120 7 10N 2 5 E
Abong-Mbang 122 4 0N 13 8 E
Abou-Deïa 121 11 20N 19 20 E
Aboyne 84 57 4N 2 48W
Abra Pampa 76 22 43 S 65 42W
Abrantes 91 39 24N 8 7W
Abreojos, Pta. 64 26 50N 113 40W
Abri 121 20 50N 30 27 E
Abrolhos, Banka 75 18 0 S 38 0W
Abrud 89 46 19N 23 5 E
Abruzzi □ 94 42 15N 14 0 E
Absaroka Range 56 44 45N 109 50W
Absarokee 33 45 31N 109 27W
Absecon 37 39 26N 74 30W
Abū al Khaşīb 106 30 25N 48 0 E
Abū 'Alī 106 27 20N 49 27 E
Abu 'Arīsh 105 16 53N 42 48 E
Abu Dhabi = Abū Ẓāby 107 24 28N 54 22 E
Abū Dīs, Jordan 104 31 47N 35 16 E
Abū Dis, Sudan 121 19 12N 33 38 E
Abū Ghaush 104 31 48N 35 6 E
Abu Hamed 121 19 32N 33 13 E
Abū Kamāl 106 34 30N 41 0 E
Abū Madd, Ra's 106 24 50N 37 7 E
Abu Matariq 121 10 59N 26 9 E
Abu Rudeis 106 28 54N 33 11 E
Abu Tig 121 27 4N 31 15 E
Abū Zabad 121 12 25N 29 10 E
Abū Ẓāby 107 24 28N 54 22 E
Abufari 73 5 25 S 62 59W
Abuja 120 9 16N 7 2 E
Abukuma-Gawa → 116 38 6N 140 52 E
Abukuma-Sammyaku 116 37 30N 140 45 E
Abunã 73 9 40 S 65 20W
Abunã → 73 9 41 S 65 20W
Abut Hd. 128 43 7 S 170 15 E
Abwong 121 9 2N 32 14 E
Acacías 70 3 59N 73 46W
Acadia National Park 26 44 20N 68 13W
Acadia Parish ◇ 25 30 13N 92 22W
Acajutla 66 13 36N 89 50W
Açailândia 74 5 0 S 47 50W
Acámbaro 64 20 0N 100 40W
Acaponeta 64 22 30N 105 20W
Acapulco 65 16 51N 99 56W
Acarai, Serra 71 1 50N 57 50W
Acaraú 74 2 53 S 40 7W
Acari, Brazil 74 6 31 S 36 38W
Acarí, Peru 72 15 25 S 74 36W
Acarigua 70 9 33N 69 12W
Acatlán 65 18 10N 98 3W
Acayucan 65 17 59N 94 58W
Accident 27 39 38N 79 19W
Accokeek 27 38 40N 77 2W
Accomac 54 37 43N 75 40W
Accomack County ◇ 54 37 45N 75 40W
Accra 120 5 35N 0 6W
Accrington 82 53 46N 2 22W
Acebal 76 33 20 S 60 50W
Aceh □ 110 4 15N 97 30 E
Achacachi 72 16 3 S 68 43W
Achaguas 70 7 46N 68 14W
Achalpur 108 21 22N 77 32 E
Achao 78 42 28 S 73 30W
Achill 85 53 56N 9 55W
Achill Hd. 85 53 59N 10 15W
Achill I. 85 53 58N 10 5W
Achill Sound 85 53 53N 9 55W
Achille 43 33 50N 96 23W
Achinsk 101 56 20N 90 20 E
Ackerman 31 33 19N 89 11W
Ackley 23 42 33N 93 3W
Acklins I. 67 22 30N 74 0W
Acland, Mt. 127 24 50 S 148 20 E
Acme, Canada 62 51 33N 113 30W
Acme, U.S.A. 25 31 17N 91 49W
Acobamba 72 12 52 S 74 35W
Acoma Indian Reservation 38 34 45N 107 30W
Acomayo 72 13 55 S 71 38W
Acomita 38 35 3N 107 34W
Aconcagua □, Argentina 76 32 50 S 70 0W
Aconcagua □, Chile 76 32 15 S 70 30W
Aconcagua, Cerro 76 32 39 S 70 0W
Aconquija, Mt. 76 27 0 S 66 0W
Acopiara 74 6 6 S 39 27W
Açores, Is. dos = Azores 2 38 44N 29 0W
Acorizal 73 15 12 S 56 22W
Acre = 'Akko 104 32 55N 35 4 E
Acre □ 72 9 1 S 71 0W
Acre → 72 8 45 S 67 22W
Açu 74 5 34 S 36 54W
Acushnet 28 41 41N 70 55W
Acworth 18 34 4N 84 41W
Ad Dahnā 106 24 30N 48 10 E
Ad Dammām 106 26 20N 50 5 E
Ad Dawhah 107 25 15N 51 35 E
Ad Dilam 106 23 55N 47 10 E
Ad Dīwānīyah 106 32 0N 45 0 E
Ada, Kans. 24 39 9N 97 53W
Ada, Minn. 30 47 18N 96 31W
Ada, Ohio 42 40 46N 83 49W
Ada, Okla. 43 34 46N 96 41W
Ada County ◇ 20 43 30N 116 15W
Adair, Iowa 23 41 30N 94 39W
Adair, Okla. 43 36 26N 95 16W
Adair County ◇, Iowa 23 41 20N 94 30W
Adair County ◇, Ky. 49 37 5N 85 20W
Adair County ◇, Mo. 32 40 10N 92 35W
Adair County ◇, Okla. 43 35 55N 94 45W
Adairsville 18 34 22N 84 56W
Adairville 48 36 40N 86 51W
Adaja → 91 41 32N 4 52W
Adak 11 51 45N 176 45W
Adak I. 11 51 45N 176 45W
Adam 107 22 15N 57 28 E
Adam, Mt. 78 51 34 S 60 4W
Adamantina 75 21 42 S 51 4W
Adamaoua, Massif de l' 121 7 20N 12 20 E
Adamawa Highlands = Adamaoua, Massif de l' 121 7 20N 12 20 E
Adamello, Mt. 94 46 10N 10 34 E
Adams, Ky. 49 38 3N 82 43W
Adams, Mass. 28 42 38N 73 7W
Adams, Minn. 30 43 34N 92 43W
Adams, N. Dak. 41 48 25N 98 5W
Adams, N.Y. 39 43 49N 76 1W
Adams, Nebr. 34 40 28N 96 31W
Adams, Okla. 43 36 45N 101 5W
Adams, Tenn. 48 36 35N 87 4W
Adams, Wis. 55 43 57N 89 49W
Adam's Bridge 108 9 15N 79 40 E
Adams Center 39 43 52N 76 0W
Adams County ◇, Colo. 16 39 50N 104 10W
Adams County ◇, Idaho 20 45 0N 116 30W
Adams County ◇, Ill. 21 40 0N 90 10W
Adams County ◇, Ind. 22 40 45N 85 0W
Adams County ◇, Iowa 23 41 0N 94 40W
Adams County ◇, Miss. 31 31 23N 91 24W
Adams County ◇, N. Dak. 41 46 0N 102 30W
Adams County ◇, Nebr. 34 40 30N 98 30W
Adams County ◇, Ohio 42 38 48N 83 33W
Adams County ◇, Pa. 45 39 50N 77 14W
Adams County ◇, Wash. 53 47 0N 118 30W
Adams County ◇, Wis. 55 43 0N 89 50W
Adams L. 62 51 10N 119 40W
Adams-Mcgill Reservoir 35 38 22N 115 7W
Adams Mt. 53 46 12N 121 30W
Adam's Peak 108 6 48N 80 30 E
Adamstown 45 40 15N 76 3W
Adamsville, Ohio 42 40 4N 81 53W
Adamsville, R.I. 28 41 30N 71 10W
Adamsville, Tenn. 48 35 14N 88 23W
Adamsville, Tex. 51 31 18N 98 10W
Adana 106 37 0N 35 16 E
Adapazarı 106 40 48N 30 25 E
Adarama 121 17 10N 34 52 E
Adare, C. 5 71 0 S 171 0 E
Adaut 111 8 8 S 131 7 E
Adavale 127 25 52 S 144 32 E
Adda → 94 45 8N 9 53 E
Addie 40 35 24N 83 10W
Addieville 21 38 23N 89 29W
Addington 43 34 15N 97 58W
Addis 25 30 21N 91 16W
Addis Ababa = Addis Abeba 121 9 2N 38 42 E
Addis Abeba 121 9 2N 38 42 E
Addis Alem 121 9 0N 38 17 E
Addison, Ala. 10 34 12N 87 11W
Addison, Ill. 21 41 55N 88 0W
Addison, N.Y. 39 42 1N 77 14W
Addison, Ohio 42 38 53N 82 9W
Addison, Vt. 36 44 8N 73 20W
Addison County ◇ 36 44 0N 73 15W
Addu Atoll 103 0 30 S 73 0 E
Addy 53 48 21N 117 50W
Adel, Ga. 18 31 8N 83 25W
Adel, Iowa 23 41 37N 94 1W
Adel, Oreg. 44 42 11N 119 54W
Adelaide, Australia 127 34 52 S 138 30 E
Adelaide, Bahamas 66 25 0N 77 31W
Adelaide I. 5 67 15 S 68 30W
Adelaide Pen. 58 68 15N 97 30W
Adelanto 15 34 35N 117 22W
Adélie, Terre 5 68 0 S 140 0 E
Adelphi 42 39 28N 82 45W
Adelphia 37 40 13N 74 15W
Aden = Al 'Adan 105 12 45N 45 0 E
Aden, G. of 105 13 0N 50 0 E
Adena 42 40 13N 80 53W
Adi 111 4 15 S 133 30 E
Adi Ugri 121 14 58N 38 48 E
Adieu, C. 126 32 0 S 132 10 E
Adige → 94 45 9N 12 20 E
Adilabad 108 19 33N 78 20 E
Adin 14 41 12N 120 57W
Adin Khel 107 32 45N 68 5 E
Adirondack Mts. 39 44 0N 74 0W
Adjud 95 46 7N 27 10 E
Adjuntas 57 18 10N 66 43W
Adlavik Is. 61 55 2N 57 45W
Admer 120 20 21N 5 27 E
Admiralty G. 126 14 20 S 125 55 E
Admiralty I. 11 57 30N 134 30W
Admiralty Inlet 53 48 8N 122 58W
Admiralty Is. 124 2 0 S 147 0 E
Adobe Creek Reservoir 16 38 14N 103 17W
Adonara 111 8 15 S 123 5 E
Adoni 108 15 33N 77 18W
Adour → 90 43 32N 1 32W
Adra 91 36 43N 3 3W
Adrano 94 37 40N 14 49 E
Adrar 120 27 51N 0 11W
Adré 121 13 40N 22 20 E
Adrī 121 27 32N 13 2 E
Adrian, Ga. 18 32 33N 82 35W
Adrian, Mich. 29 41 54N 84 2W
Adrian, Minn. 30 43 38N 95 56W
Adrian, Mo. 32 38 24N 94 21W
Adrian, Oreg. 44 43 45N 117 4W
Adrian, Tex. 50 35 16N 102 40W
Adriatic Sea 94 43 0N 16 0 E
Adua 111 1 45 S 129 50 E
Advance, Ind. 22 40 0N 86 40W
Advance, Mo. 32 37 6N 89 55W
Adwa 121 14 15N 38 52 E
Adzhar A.S.S.R. □ 99 42 0N 42 0 E
Ægean Sea 95 37 0N 25 0 E
Æolian Is. = Eólie, I. 94 38 30N 14 50 E
Aerht'ai Shan 113 46 40N 92 45 E
Aetna 24 37 5N 98 58W
Affton 32 38 33N 90 20W
Afghanistan ■ 107 33 0N 65 0 E
Afgoi 105 2 7N 44 59 E
'Afif 106 23 53N 42 56 E
Afogados da Ingàzeira 74 7 45 S 37 39W
Afognak I. 11 58 15N 152 30W
Africa 118 10 0N 20 0 E
Afton, Calif. 15 35 2N 116 23W
Afton, Iowa 23 41 2N 94 12W
Afton, N.Y. 39 42 14N 75 32W
Afton, Okla. 43 36 42N 94 58W
Afton, Wyo. 56 42 44N 110 56W
Afuá 74 0 15 S 50 20W
Afula 104 32 37N 35 17 E
Afyonkarahisar 106 38 45N 30 33 E
Agadès = Agadez 120 16 58N 7 59 E
Agadez 120 16 58N 7 59 E
Agadir 120 30 28N 9 35W
Agapa 101 71 27N 89 15 E
Agar 47 44 50N 100 5W
Agartala 109 23 50N 91 23 E
Ağaş 95 46 28N 26 15 E
Agassiz 62 49 14N 121 46W
Agassiz Pool 30 48 20N 95 59W
Agate 16 39 28N 103 57W
Agate Beach 44 44 41N 124 4W
Agate Fossil Beds National Monument 34 42 20N 103 50W
Agats 111 5 33 S 138 0 E
Agattu I. 11 52 25N 173 35W
Agawam, Mass. 28 42 5N 72 37W
Agawam, Mont. 33 48 0N 112 10W
Agboville 120 5 55N 4 15W
Agde 90 43 19N 3 28 E
Agen 90 44 12N 0 38 E
Agency 23 41 0N 92 18W
Agency L. 44 42 33N 121 58W
Agenda 24 39 43N 97 26W
Ages 49 36 52N 83 21W
Aghil Mts. 108 36 0N 77 0 E
Aginskoye 101 51 6N 114 32 E
Agnita 95 45 59N 24 40 E
Agra, India 108 27 17N 77 58 E
Agra, Kans. 24 39 46N 99 7W
Agra, Okla. 43 35 54N 96 53W
Agri → 94 40 13N 16 44 E
Ağri Daği 106 39 50N 44 15 E
Ağri Karakose 106 39 44N 43 3 E
Agricola 31 30 48N 88 31W
Agrigento 94 37 19N 13 33 E
Agrinion 95 38 37N 21 27 E
Água Branca 74 5 50 S 42 40W
Agua Caliente 64 26 30N 108 20W
Água Clara 73 20 25 S 52 45W
Agua Dulce 51 27 47N 97 55W
Agua Fria → 12 33 23N 112 22W
Agua Nueva 50 26 54N 98 36W
Agua Preta → 71 1 41 S 63 48W
Agua Prieta 64 31 20N 109 32W
Aguachica 70 8 19N 73 38W
Aguada 57 18 23N 67 11W
Aguada Cecilio 78 40 51 S 65 51W
Aguadas 70 5 40N 75 38W
Aguadilla 57 18 26N 67 10W
Aguadilla ◇ 57 18 20N 67 0W
Aguadilla, Bahía de 57 18 25N 67 10W
Aguadulce 66 8 15N 80 32W
Aguanaval → 64 23 45N 103 10W
Aguanish 61 50 14N 62 2W
Aguanus → 61 50 13N 62 5W
Aguapeí 73 16 12 S 59 43W
Aguapeí → 75 21 0 S 51 0W
Aguapey → 76 29 7 S 56 36W
Aguaray Guazú → 76 24 47 S 57 19W
Aguarico → 70 0 59 S 75 11W
Aguas Blancas 76 24 15 S 69 55W
Aguas Buenas 57 18 16N 66 6W
Aguas Calientes, Sierra de 76 25 26 S 66 40W
Águas Formosas 75 17 5 S 40 57W
Aguascalientes 64 21 53N 102 12W
Aguascalientes □ 64 22 0N 102 20W
Aguila 12 33 57N 113 11W
Aguila, Punta 57 17 57N 67 13W
Aguilar 16 37 24N 104 39W
Aguilares, Argentina 76 27 26 S 65 35W
Aguilares, U.S.A. 50 27 27N 99 5W
Aguilas 91 37 23N 1 35W
Aguja, C. de la 70 11 18N 74 12W
Agujereada, Pta. 57 18 30N 67 8W
Agulhas, Kaap 123 34 52 S 20 0 E
Agung 110 8 20 S 115 28 E
'Agur 104 31 42N 34 55 E
Agusan → 111 9 0N 125 30 E
Agustín Codazzi 70 10 2N 73 14W
Ahaggar 120 23 0N 6 30 E
Ahar 106 38 35N 47 0 E
Ahipara B. 128 35 5 S 173 5 E
Ahiri 108 19 30N 80 0 E
Ahmadabad 108 23 0N 72 40 E
Ahmadnagar 108 19 7N 74 46 E
Ahmadpur 108 29 12N 71 10 E
Ahmedabad = Ahmadabad 108 23 0N 72 40 E
Ahmednagar = Ahmadnagar 108 19 7N 74 46 E
Ahome 64 25 55N 109 11W

Ahoskie **Aleutian Range**

Ahoskie 40 36 17N 76 59W
Ahuachapán 66 13 54N 89 52W
Ahvāz 106 31 20N 48 40 E
Ahvenanmaa = Åland 97 60 15N 20 0 E
Ahwar 105 13 30N 46 40 E
Aiari → 70 1 22N 68 36W
Aibonito 57 18 9N 66 16W
Aichi □ 117 35 0N 137 15 E
Aiea 19 21 23N 157 56W
Aigua 77 34 13 S 54 46W
Aigues-Mortes 90 43 35N 4 12 E
Aihui 114 50 10N 127 30 E
Aija 72 9 50 S 77 45W
Aikawa 116 38 2N 138 15 E
Aiken 46 33 34N 81 43W
Aiken County ◇ 46 33 30N 81 40W
Ailey 18 32 11N 82 34W
Aillik 61 55 11N 59 18W
Ailsa Craig 84 55 15N 5 7W
'Ailūn 104 32 18N 35 47 E
Aim 101 59 0N 133 55 E
Aimere 111 8 45 S 121 3 E
Aimogasta 76 28 33 S 66 50W
Aimorés 75 19 30 S 41 4W
Ain □ 90 46 5N 5 20 E
Ain Banaiyan 107 23 0N 51 0 E
Aïn Beïda 120 35 50N 7 29 E
Aïn Ben Tili 120 25 59N 9 27W
Aïn Galakka 121 18 10N 18 30 E
Aïn-Sefra 120 32 47N 0 37W
Ainabo 105 9 0N 46 25 E
Ainsworth, Iowa 23 41 17N 91 33W
Ainsworth, Nebr. 34 42 33N 99 52W
Aipe 70 3 13N 75 15W
Aiquile 73 18 10 S 65 10W
Aïr 120 18 30N 8 0 E
Airão 71 1 56 S 61 22W
Airdrie 84 55 53N 3 57W
Aire → 82 53 42N 0 55W
Aisen □ 78 46 30 S 73 0W
Aisne □ 90 49 42N 3 40 E
Aisne → 90 49 26N 2 50 E
Aitkin 30 46 32N 93 42W
Aitkin County ◇ 30 46 30N 93 25W
Aiuaba 74 6 38 S 40 7W
Aiud 89 46 19N 23 44 E
Aix, Mt. 53 46 47N 121 15W
Aix-en-Provence 90 43 32N 5 27 E
Aix-la-Chapelle = Aachen 88 50 47N 6 4 E
Aiyansh 62 55 17N 129 2W
Aíyina 95 37 45N 23 26 E
Aiyion 95 38 15N 22 5 E
Aizawl 109 23 40N 92 44 E
Aizuwakamatsu 116 37 30N 139 56 E
Ajaccio 94 41 55N 8 40 E
Ajaju → 70 0 59N 72 20W
Ajalpan 65 18 22N 97 15W
Ajanta Ra. 108 20 28N 75 50 E
Ajdâbiyah 121 30 54N 20 4 E
'Ajmān 107 25 25N 55 30 E
Ajmer 108 26 28N 74 37 E
Ajo 12 32 22N 112 52W
Ak Dağ 106 36 30N 30 0 E
Akabira 116 43 33N 142 5 E
Akali L. 44 42 58N 120 2W
Akaroa 128 43 49 S 172 59 E
Akashi 117 34 45N 135 0 E
Akaska 47 45 20N 100 7W
Akelamo 111 1 35N 129 40 E
Akeley 30 47 0N 94 44W
Akershus fylke □ 97 60 0N 11 10 E
Aketi 122 2 38N 23 47 E
Akhelóös → 95 38 36N 21 14 E
Akhiok 11 56 57N 154 10W
Akhisar 106 38 56N 27 48 E
Akhmîm 121 26 31N 31 47 E
Akhtopol 95 42 6N 27 56 E
Aki 117 33 30N 133 54 E
Akiachak 11 60 55N 161 26W
Akiak 11 60 55N 161 13W
Akimiski I. 60 52 50N 81 30W
Akita 116 39 45N 140 7 E
Akita □ 116 39 40N 140 30 E
Akjoujt 120 19 45N 14 15W
Akkeshi 116 43 2N 144 51 E
'Akko 104 32 55N 35 4 E
Akkol 100 45 0N 75 39 E
Aklavik 58 68 12N 135 0W
Akō 117 34 45N 134 24 E
Akobo → 121 7 48N 33 3 E
Akola 108 20 42N 77 2 E
Akolmiut 11 60 55N 162 20W
Akordat 121 15 30N 37 40 E
Akpatok I. 59 60 25N 68 8W
Akra 41 48 47N 97 44W
Akranes 96 64 19N 21 58W
Akreïjit 120 18 19N 9 11W
Akron, Ala. 10 32 53N 87 45W
Akron, Colo. 16 40 10N 103 13W
Akron, Ind. 22 41 2N 86 1W
Akron, Iowa 23 42 50N 96 33W
Akron, N.Y. 39 43 1N 78 30W
Akron, Ohio 42 41 5N 81 31W
Akron, Pa. 45 40 9N 76 12W
Akrotíri, Ákra 95 40 26N 25 27 E
Aksai Chih 108 35 15N 79 55 E
Aksaray 106 38 25N 34 2 E
Aksarka 100 66 31N 67 50 E
Aksay 98 51 11N 53 0 E
Akşehir 106 38 18N 31 30 E
Aksenovo Zilovskoye 101 53 20N 117 40 E
Aksu 113 41 5N 80 10 E
Aksum 121 14 5N 38 40 E
Aktogay 100 46 57N 79 40 E
Aktyubinsk 99 50 17N 57 10 E
Aku 120 6 40N 7 18 E
Akun I. 11 54 11N 165 32W
Akure 120 7 15N 5 5 E
Akureyri 96 65 40N 18 6W
Akuseki-Shima 117 29 27N 129 37 E
Akutan 11 54 8N 165 46W
Akutan I. 11 54 7N 165 55W
Akutan Indian Reservation 11 54 10N 166 0W
Akyab = Sittwe 109 20 18N 92 45 E
Al 'Adan 105 12 45N 45 0 E
Al Aḩsā 106 25 50N 49 0 E
Al Amādīyah 106 37 5N 43 30 E
Al Amārah 106 31 55N 47 15 E
Al 'Aqabah 104 29 31N 35 0 E
Al 'Aramah 106 25 30N 46 0 E
Al Ashkhara 107 21 50N 59 30 E
Al 'Ayzarīyah 104 31 47N 35 15 E
Al Badī' 106 22 0N 46 35 E
Al Başrah 106 30 30N 47 50 E
Al Bāzūrīyah 104 33 15N 35 16 E
Al Bīrah 104 31 55N 35 12 E
Al Bu'ayrāt 121 31 24N 15 44 E
Al Buqay'ah 104 32 15N 35 30 E
Al Fallūjah 106 33 20N 43 55 E
Al Fāw 106 30 0N 48 30 E
Al Fujayrah 107 25 7N 56 18 E
Al Fuqaha 121 27 50N 16 22 E
Al Hābah 106 27 10N 47 0 E
Al Haddār 106 21 58N 45 57 E
Al Ḩadīthah 106 34 0N 41 13 E
Al Hāmad 106 31 30N 39 30 E
Al Ḩamar 106 22 23N 46 6 E
Al Ḩamrā' 106 24 2N 38 55 E
Al Ḩarīq 106 23 29N 46 27 E
Al Harīr, W. → 104 32 44N 35 59 E
Al Ḩasakah 106 36 35N 40 45 E
Al Ḩawrah 105 13 50N 47 35 E
Al Ḩawţah 105 16 5N 48 20 E
Al Ḩayy 106 32 5N 46 5 E
Al Ḩijāz 106 26 0N 37 30 E
Al Ḩillah, Iraq 106 32 30N 44 25 E
Al Ḩillah, Si. Arabia 106 23 35N 46 50 E
Al Hindīyah 106 32 30N 44 10 E
Al Ḩişnn 104 32 29N 35 52 E
Al Hoceïma 120 35 8N 3 58W
Al Ḩudaydah 105 14 50N 43 0 E
Al Hūfuf 106 25 25N 49 45 E
Al Ḩulwah 106 23 24N 46 48 E
Al Irq 121 29 5N 21 35 E
Al Ittihad = Madīnat ash Sha'b 105 12 50N 45 0 E
Al Jāfūrah 106 25 0N 50 15 E
Al Jaghbūb 121 29 42N 24 38 E
Al Jahrah 106 29 25N 47 40 E
Al Jalāmīd 106 31 20N 39 45 E
Al Jawf, Libya 121 24 10N 23 24 E
Al Jawf, Si. Arabia 106 29 55N 39 40 E
Al Jazirah, Asia 106 33 30N 44 0 E
Al Jazirah, Libya 121 26 10N 21 20 E
Al Jubayl 106 27 0N 49 50 E
Al Jubaylah 106 24 55N 46 25 E
Al Junaynah 121 13 27N 22 45 E
Al Khābūra 107 23 57N 57 5 E
Al Khalīl 104 31 32N 35 6 E
Al Khalūf 105 20 30N 58 13 E
Al Kharfah 106 22 0N 46 35 E
Al Kharj 106 24 0N 47 0 E
Al Kufrah 121 24 17N 23 15 E
Al Kūt 106 32 30N 46 0 E
Al Kuwayt 106 29 30N 47 30 E
Al Lādhiqīyah 106 35 30N 35 45 E
Al Lidām 105 20 33N 44 45 E
Al Lubban 104 32 9N 35 14 E
Al Luḩayyah 105 15 45N 42 40 E
Al Madīnah 106 24 35N 39 52 E
Al-Mafraq 104 32 17N 36 14 E
Al Majma'ah 106 25 57N 45 22 E
Al Manāmāh, Bahrain 107 26 10N 50 30 E
Al Marj 121 32 25N 20 30 E
Al Mawşil 106 36 15N 43 5 E
Al Mazra 104 31 16N 35 31 E
Al Midhnab 106 25 50N 44 18 E
Al Miqdādīyah 106 34 0N 45 0 E
Al Mish'āb 106 28 12N 48 36 E
Al Mubarraz 106 25 30N 49 40 E
Al Muḩarraq 107 26 15N 50 40 E
Al Mukallā 105 14 33N 49 2 E
Al Mukhā 105 13 18N 43 15 E
Al Musayyib 106 32 40N 44 25 E
Al Muwayliḩ 106 27 40N 35 30 E
Al Qaḑīmah 106 22 20N 39 13 E
Al Qāmishli 106 37 10N 41 10 E
Al Qaşabāt 121 32 39N 14 1 E
Al Qaţīf 106 26 35N 50 0 E
Al Qaţrūn 121 24 56N 15 3 E
Al Quaisūmah 106 28 10N 46 20 E
Al Quds = Jerusalem 104 31 47N 35 10 E
Al Qurayyāt 107 23 17N 58 53 E
Al Qurnah 106 31 1N 47 25 E
Al 'Ulā 106 26 35N 38 0 E
Al Uqaylah ash Sharqīgah 121 30 12N 19 10 E
Al Uqayr 106 25 40N 50 15 E
Al 'Uthmānīyah 106 25 5N 49 22 E
Al 'Uwaynid 106 24 50N 46 0 E
Al' 'Uwayqīlah 106 30 30N 42 10 E
Al 'Uyūn 106 26 30N 43 50 E
Al Wakrah 107 25 10N 51 40 E
Al Wari'āh 106 27 51N 47 25 E
Al Yamāmah 106 24 5N 47 30 E
Al Yāmūn 104 32 29N 35 14 E
Alabama □ 10 33 0N 87 0W
Alabama → 10 31 8N 87 57W
Alabaster 10 33 15N 86 49W
Alachua 17 29 47N 82 30W
Alachua County ◇ 17 29 45N 82 20W
Alagoa Grande 74 7 3 S 35 35W
Alagoas □ 74 9 0 S 36 0W
Alagoinhas 75 12 7 S 38 20W
Alajuela 66 10 2N 84 8W
Alakunuk 11 62 41N 164 37W
Alakurtti 98 67 0N 30 30 E
Alalakeiki Channel 19 20 30N 156 30W
Alalapura 71 2 20N 56 25W
Alalaú → 71 0 30 S 61 9W
Alamance County ◇ 40 36 0N 79 25W
Alameda, Calif. 14 37 46N 122 15W
Alameda, N. Mex. 38 35 11N 106 37W
Alameda County ◇ 14 37 40N 121 50W
Alamito → 50 29 45N 104 18W
Alamitos, Sierra de los 64 37 21N 115 10W
Alamo, Ga. 18 32 9N 82 47W
Alamo, N. Dak. 41 48 35N 103 28W
Alamo, Nev. 35 37 22N 115 10W
Alamo, Tenn. 48 35 47N 89 7W
Alamo Heights 51 29 28N 98 28W
Alamo Ind. Res. 38 34 20N 107 30W
Alamo L. 12 34 10N 113 35W
Alamogordo 38 32 54N 105 57W
Alamos 64 27 0N 109 0W
Alamosa 16 37 28N 105 52W
Alamosa → 16 37 22N 105 46W
Alamosa County ◇ 16 37 40N 105 40W
Åland 97 60 15N 20 0 E
Ålands hav 97 60 0N 19 30 E
Alandur 108 13 0N 80 15 E
Alanreed 50 35 13N 100 44W
Alanson 29 45 27N 84 47W
Alanya 106 36 38N 32 0 E
Alapaha 18 31 23N 83 13W
Alapayevsk 100 57 52N 61 42 E
Alarka 40 35 21N 83 27W
Alaşehir 99 38 23N 28 30 E
Alaska □ 11 64 0N 154 0W
Alaska, Gulf of 11 59 0N 146 0W
Alaska Highway 62 60 0N 130 0W
Alaska Peninsula 11 56 0N 159 0W
Alaska Range 11 62 0N 149 0W
Alataw Shankou 113 45 5N 81 57 E
Alatyr 98 54 45N 46 35 E
Alausi 70 2 0 S 78 50W
Alava, C. 53 48 10N 124 44W
Alba, Italy 94 44 41N 8 1 E
Alba, Mo. 32 37 14N 94 25W
Alba, Tex. 51 32 48N 95 38W
Alba □ 95 46 10N 23 30 E
Alba Iulia 89 46 8N 23 39 E
Albacete 91 39 0N 1 50W
Albania ■ 95 41 0N 20 0 E
Albany, Australia 126 35 1 S 117 58 E
Albany, Ga. 18 31 35N 84 10W
Albany, Ind. 22 40 18N 85 14W
Albany, Ky. 49 36 42N 85 8W
Albany, La. 25 30 30N 90 35W
Albany, Minn. 30 45 38N 94 34W
Albany, Mo. 32 40 15N 94 20W
Albany, N.Y. 39 42 39N 73 45W
Albany, Ohio 42 39 14N 82 12W
Albany, Okla. 43 33 53N 96 10W
Albany, Oreg. 44 44 38N 123 6W
Albany, Tex. 51 32 44N 99 18W
Albany, Vt. 36 44 43N 72 23W
Albany → 60 52 17N 81 31W
Albany County ◇, N.Y. 39 42 30N 74 0W
Albany County ◇, Wyo. 56 41 50N 105 40W
Albardón 76 31 20 S 68 30W
Albarracín, Sierra de 91 40 30N 1 30W
Albatross B. 127 12 45 S 141 30 E
Albemarle 40 35 21N 80 11W
Albemarle County ◇ 54 38 2N 78 30W
Albemarle Sd. 40 36 5N 76 0W
Alberche → 91 39 58N 4 46W
Alberdi 76 26 14 S 58 20W
Albert, Kans. 24 38 27N 99 1W
Albert, Okla. 43 35 14N 98 25W
Albert, Tex. 51 30 12N 98 36W
Albert, L. = Mobutu Sese Seko, L. 122 1 30N 31 0 E
Albert Canyon 62 51 8N 117 41W
Albert City 23 42 47N 94 57W
Albert Lea 30 43 39N 93 22W
Albert Nile → 122 3 36N 32 2 E
Albert Town 67 22 37N 74 33 E
Alberta, Ala. 10 32 14N 87 25W
Alberta, Va. 54 36 52N 77 53W
Alberta □ 62 54 40N 115 0W
Alberti 76 35 1 S 60 16W
Alberton, Canada 61 46 50N 64 0W
Alberton, U.S.A. 33 47 0N 114 29W
Albertville = Kalemie 122 5 55 S 29 9 E
Albertville, Ala. 10 34 16N 86 13W
Albertville, Minn. 30 45 14N 93 39W
Albi 90 43 56N 2 9 E
Albia 23 41 2N 92 48W
Albin 56 41 25N 104 6W
Albina 71 5 37N 54 15W
Albion, Calif. 14 39 14N 123 46W
Albion, Idaho 20 42 25N 113 35W
Albion, Ill. 21 38 23N 88 4W
Albion, Ind. 22 41 24N 85 25W
Albion, Iowa 23 42 7N 92 59W
Albion, Maine 26 44 32N 69 27W
Albion, Mich. 29 42 15N 84 45W
Albion, N.Y. 39 43 15N 78 12W
Albion, Nebr. 34 41 42N 98 0W
Albion, Okla. 43 34 40N 95 6W
Albion, Pa. 45 41 53N 80 22W
Albion, Wash. 53 46 48N 117 15W
Ålborg 97 57 2N 9 54 E
Alborz, Reshteh-ye Kūhhā-ye 107 36 0N 52 0 E
Albreda 62 52 35N 119 10W
Albright 54 39 30N 79 39W
Albuquerque, Brazil 73 19 23 S 57 26W
Albuquerque, U.S.A. 38 35 5N 106 39W
Albuquerque, Cayos de 66 12 10N 81 50W
Alburg 36 44 59N 73 18W
Alburnett 23 42 9N 91 37W
Alburquerque 91 39 15N 6 59W
Albury 127 36 3 S 146 56 E
Alcalá de Henares 91 40 28N 3 22W
Alcalá la Real 91 37 27N 3 57W
Alcalde 38 36 5N 106 3W
Alcamo 94 37 59N 12 55 E
Alcaníz 91 41 2N 0 8W
Alcântara, Brazil 74 2 20 S 44 30W
Alcántara, Spain 91 39 41N 6 57W
Alcantara L. 63 60 57N 108 9W
Alcaraz, Sierra de 91 38 40N 2 20W
Alcaudete 91 37 35N 4 5W
Alcázar de San Juan 91 39 24N 3 12W
Alcester 47 43 1N 96 38W
Alcira 91 39 9N 0 30W
Alco 13 35 53N 92 22W
Alcoa 49 35 48N 83 59W
Alcobaça 91 39 32N 9 0W
Alcolu 46 33 45N 80 13W
Alcoma 17 27 54N 81 29W
Alcona County ◇ 29 44 40N 83 40W
Alcorn 31 31 53N 91 8W
Alcorn County ◇ 31 34 56N 88 31W
Alcova 56 42 34N 106 43W
Alcoy 91 38 43N 0 30W
Alda 34 40 52N 98 28W
Aldabra Is. 3 9 22 S 46 28 E
Aldama 65 23 0N 98 4W
Aldan 101 58 40N 125 30 E
Aldan → 101 63 28N 129 35 E
Aldeburgh 83 52 9N 1 35 E
Alden, Iowa 23 42 31N 93 23W
Alden, Kans. 24 38 15N 98 19W
Alden, Minn. 30 43 40N 93 34W
Alden, N.Y. 39 42 54N 78 30W
Alder 33 45 19N 112 6W
Alderney 83 49 42N 2 12W
Aldershot 83 51 15N 0 43W
Alderson 54 37 44N 80 38W
Aldersyde 62 50 40N 113 53W
Aldine 51 29 56N 95 23W
Aledo, Ill. 21 41 12N 90 45W
Aledo, Tex. 51 32 42N 97 36W
Aleg 120 17 3N 13 55W
Alegre 75 20 50 S 41 30W
Alegrete 77 29 40 S 56 0W
Alegros Mt. 38 34 9N 108 11W
Aleisk 100 52 40N 83 0 E
Alejandro Selkirk, I. 125 33 50 S 80 15W
Aleknagik 11 59 17N 158 36W
Aleksandrovo 95 43 14N 24 51 E
Aleksandrovsk-Sakhaliniskiy 101 50 50N 142 20 E
Aleksandrovskiy Zavod 101 50 40N 117 50 E
Aleksandrovskoye 100 60 35N 77 50 E
Além Paraíba 75 21 52 S 42 41W
Alemania, Argentina 76 25 40 S 65 30W
Alemania, Chile 76 25 10 S 69 55W
Alençon 90 48 27N 0 4 E
Alentejo, Alto- 91 39 0N 7 40W
Alentejo, Baixo- 91 38 0N 8 30W
Alenuihaha Channel 19 20 30N 156 0W
Aleppo = Ḩalab 106 36 10N 37 15 E
Aléria 94 42 5N 9 26 E
Alert Bay 62 50 30N 126 55W
Alès 90 44 9N 4 5 E
Alesia 27 39 43N 76 51W
Alessándria 94 44 54N 8 37 E
Ålesund 96 62 28N 6 12 E
Aleutian Is. 11 52 0N 178 0W
Aleutian Islands ◇ 11 53 0N 176 0W
Aleutian Range 11 60 0N 154 0W

Aleutian Trench Amderma

Aleutian Trench 124 48 0N 180 0 E
Alex 43 34 55N 97 47W
Alexander, Ga. 18 33 1N 81 53W
Alexander, Iowa 23 42 48N 93 29W
Alexander, Kans. 24 38 28N 99 33W
Alexander, N. Dak. 41 47 51N 103 39W
Alexander, W. Va. 54 38 47N 80 13W
Alexander Archipelago 11 56 0N 136 0W
Alexander B. 123 28 36 S 16 33 E
Alexander City 10 32 56N 85 58W
Alexander County ◇, Ill. 21 37 10N 89 20W
Alexander County ◇, N.C. 40 35 50N 81 10W
Alexander I. 5 69 0 S 70 0W
Alexandra 128 45 14 S 169 25 E
Alexandra Falls 62 60 29N 116 18W
Alexandretta = İskenderun 106 36 32N 36 10 E
Alexandria = El Iskandarîya 121 31 0N 30 0 E
Alexandria, B.C., Canada 62 52 35N 122 27W
Alexandria, Ont., Canada 60 45 19N 74 38W
Alexandria, Romania 95 43 57N 25 24 E
Alexandria, S. Africa 123 33 38 S 26 28 E
Alexandria, Ind. 22 40 16N 85 41W
Alexandria, Ky. 49 38 58N 84 23W
Alexandria, La. 25 31 18N 92 27W
Alexandria, Minn. 30 45 53N 95 22W
Alexandria, Mo. 32 40 27N 91 28W
Alexandria, N.H. 36 43 37N 71 47W
Alexandria, Nebr. 34 40 15N 97 23W
Alexandria, Pa. 45 40 34N 78 6W
Alexandria, S. Dak. 47 43 39N 97 47W
Alexandria, Tenn. 48 36 5N 86 2W
Alexandria, Va. 54 38 48N 77 3W
Alexandria Bay 39 44 20N 75 55W
Alexandrina, L. 127 35 25 S 139 10 E
Alexandroúpolis 95 40 50N 25 54 E
Alexis 21 41 4N 90 33W
Alexis → 61 52 33N 56 8W
Alexis Creek 62 52 10N 123 20W
Alfalfa 43 35 13N 98 36W
Alfalfa County ◇ 43 36 45N 98 15W
Alfatar 95 43 59N 27 13 E
Alfenas 77 21 20 S 46 10W
Alford, U.K. 84 57 13N 2 42W
Alford, U.S.A. 17 30 42N 85 24W
Alfred, Maine 26 43 29N 70 43W
Alfred, N.Y. 39 42 16N 77 48W
Alfreton 82 53 6N 1 22W
Alga 100 49 53N 57 20 E
Algarve 91 36 58N 8 20W
Algeciras 91 36 9N 5 28W
Algemesí 91 39 11N 0 27W
Alger 120 36 42N 3 8 E
Alger County ◇ 29 46 20N 86 50W
Algeria ■ 120 35 10N 3 11 E
Alghero 94 40 34N 8 20 E
Algiers = Alger 120 36 42N 3 8 E
Algoabaai 123 33 50 S 25 45 E
Algodones 38 35 23N 106 29W
Algoma, Miss. 31 34 11N 89 2W
Algoma, Wis. 55 44 36N 87 26W
Algona 23 43 4N 94 14W
Algonac 29 42 37N 82 32W
Algonquin 21 42 10N 88 18W
Algood 49 36 12N 85 27W
Alhama de Murcia 91 37 51N 1 25W
Alhambra 15 34 8N 118 6W
Alhucemas = Al Hoceïma 120 35 8N 3 58W
'Alī al Gharbī 106 32 30N 46 45 E
Ali Khel 108 33 56N 69 35 E
Aliákmon → 95 40 30N 22 36 E
Alibo 121 9 52N 37 5 E
Alicante 91 38 23N 0 30W
Alice, N. Dak. 41 46 46N 97 33W
Alice, Tex. 51 27 45N 98 5W
Alice Arm 62 55 29N 129 31W
Alice Springs 126 23 40 S 133 50 E
Aliceville, Ala. 10 33 8N 88 9W
Aliceville, Kans. 24 38 9N 95 33W
Alicia 13 35 54N 91 5W
Alida 63 49 25N 101 55W
Aligarh 108 27 55N 78 10 E
Alīgūdarz 106 33 25N 49 45 E
Aline 43 36 31N 98 27W
Alingsås 97 57 56N 12 31 E
Alipur 108 29 25N 70 55 E
Alipur Duar 109 26 30N 89 35 E
Aliquippa 45 40 37N 80 15W
Aliwal North 123 30 45 S 26 45 E
Alix 62 52 24N 113 11W
Aljustrel 91 37 55N 8 10W
Alkali Flats 35 40 0N 115 58W
Alkali L. 35 41 42N 119 51W
Alkaline L. 41 46 40N 99 34W
Alkmaar 87 52 37N 4 45 E
Allagash 26 47 5N 69 3W
Allagash → 26 47 5N 69 3W
Allagash L. 26 46 18N 69 35W
Allahabad 109 25 25N 81 58 E
Allakaket 11 66 34N 152 39W
Allakh-Yun 101 60 50N 137 5 E
Allamakee County ◇ 23 43 15N 91 20W
Allamoore 50 31 5N 105 0W
Allan 63 51 53N 106 4W
Allanmyo 109 19 30N 95 17 E
Allanwater 60 50 14N 90 10W
Allardt 49 36 23N 84 53W
Allatoona L. 18 34 10N 84 44W
Allegan 29 42 32N 85 51W
Allegan County ◇ 29 42 35N 85 50W
Allegany, N.Y. 39 42 6N 78 30W
Allegany, Oreg. 44 43 26N 124 2W
Allegany County ◇, Md. 27 39 40N 78 40W
Allegany County ◇, N.Y. 39 42 15N 78 0W
Allegany Indian Reservation 39 42 6N 78 55W
Alleghany County ◇, N.C. 40 36 25N 81 10W
Alleghany County ◇, Va. 54 37 50N 80 0W
Allegheny → 45 40 27N 80 1W
Allegheny County ◇ 45 40 25N 80 0W
Allegheny Mts. 54 38 15N 80 10W
Allegheny National Forest 45 41 45N 79 5W
Allegheny Reservoir 45 41 50N 79 0W
Allemands, L. des 25 29 55N 90 35W
Allen, Argentina 78 38 58 S 67 50W
Allen, Kans. 24 38 39N 96 10W
Allen, Md. 27 38 17N 75 42W
Allen, Nebr. 34 42 25N 96 51W
Allen, Okla. 43 34 53N 96 25W
Allen, S. Dak. 47 43 17N 101 56W
Allen, Tex. 51 33 6N 96 40W
Allen, Bog of 85 53 15N 7 0W
Allen, L. 85 54 12N 8 5W
Allen County ◇, Ind. 22 41 5N 85 5W
Allen County ◇, Kans. 24 37 50N 95 15W
Allen County ◇, Ky. 48 36 45N 86 10W
Allen County ◇, Ohio 42 40 44N 84 6W
Allen Parish ◇ 25 30 37N 92 46W
Allenby Br. = Jisr al Ḩusayn 104 31 53N 35 33 E
Allendale, Ill. 21 38 32N 87 43W
Allendale, S.C. 46 33 1N 81 18W
Allendale County ◇ 46 33 0N 81 20W
Allende 64 28 20N 100 50W
Allenhurst 37 40 15N 73 59W
Allenspark 16 40 12N 105 32W
Allensville 48 36 43N 87 4W
Allentown, N.J. 37 40 11N 74 35W
Allentown, Pa. 45 40 37N 75 29W
Alleppey 108 9 30N 76 28 E
Allerton, Ill. 21 39 55N 87 56W
Allerton, Iowa 23 40 42N 93 22W
Alliance, Surinam 71 5 50N 54 50W
Alliance, Nebr. 34 42 6N 102 52W
Alliance, Ohio 42 40 55N 81 6W
Allier □ 90 46 25N 3 0 E
Allier → 90 46 57N 3 4 E
Alligator 31 34 6N 90 43W
Allison, Colo. 16 37 2N 107 29W
Allison, Iowa 23 42 45N 92 48W
Allison, Tex. 50 35 36N 100 6W
Alliston 60 44 9N 79 52W
Alloa 84 56 7N 3 49W
Allons 49 36 27N 85 21W
Allouez 55 44 27N 88 4W
Alloway 37 39 34N 75 22W
Allyn 53 47 23N 122 50W
Alma, Canada 61 48 35N 71 40W
Alma, Ark. 13 35 29N 94 13W
Alma, Colo. 16 39 17N 106 4W
Alma, Ga. 18 31 33N 82 28W
Alma, Kans. 24 39 1N 96 17W
Alma, Mich. 29 43 23N 84 39W
Alma, Mo. 32 39 6N 93 33W
Alma, Nebr. 34 40 6N 99 22W
Alma, Wis. 55 44 20N 91 55W
'Almā ash Sha'b 104 33 7N 35 9 E
Alma Ata 100 43 15N 76 57 E
Alma Center 55 44 26N 90 55W
Almada 91 38 40N 9 9W
Almadén 91 38 49N 4 52W
Almanor, L. 14 40 14N 121 9W
Almansa 91 38 51N 1 5W
Almanzor, Pico de 91 40 15N 5 18W
Almanzora → 91 37 14N 1 46W
Almas 75 11 33 S 47 9W
Almaş, Mţii. 95 44 49N 22 12 E
Almazán 91 41 30N 2 30W
Almeirim 71 1 30 S 52 34W
Almelo 87 52 22N 6 42 E
Almena 24 39 54N 99 43W
Almenara 75 16 11 S 40 42W
Almendralejo 91 38 41N 6 26W
Almería, Spain 91 36 52N 2 27W
Almeria, U.S.A. 34 41 50N 99 31W
Almira 53 47 43N 118 56W
Almirante 66 9 10N 82 30W
Almirante Montt, G. 78 51 52 S 72 50W
Almo 48 36 42N 88 16W
Almon 18 33 37N 83 56W
Almond, N.C. 40 35 22N 83 34W
Almond, Wis. 55 44 16N 89 25W
Almont, Colo. 16 38 40N 106 51W
Almont, Mich. 29 42 55N 83 3W
Almont, N. Dak. 41 46 44N 101 30W
Almora 108 29 38N 79 40 E
Almyra 13 34 24N 91 25W
Alnwick 82 55 25N 1 42W
Aloha 44 45 29N 122 52W
Alon 109 22 12N 95 5 E
Alonsa 63 50 50N 99 0W
Alor 111 8 15 S 124 30 E
Alor Setar 112 6 7N 100 22 E
Alpaugh 15 35 53N 119 29W
Alpena, Ark. 13 36 18N 93 18W
Alpena, Mich. 29 45 4N 83 27W
Alpena, S. Dak. 47 44 11N 98 22W
Alpena County ◇ 29 45 0N 83 40W
Alpercatas → 74 6 2 S 44 19W
Alpes-de-Haute-Provence □ 90 44 8N 6 10 E
Alpes-Maritimes □ 90 43 55N 7 10 E
Alpha, Australia 127 23 39 S 146 37 E
Alpha, Ill. 21 41 12N 90 23W
Alpha, Mich. 29 46 3N 88 23W
Alpha, N.J. 37 40 40N 75 9W
Alpine, Ariz. 12 33 51N 109 9W
Alpine, Ark. 13 34 14N 93 23W
Alpine, Tenn. 49 36 24N 85 13W
Alpine, Tex. 50 30 22N 103 40W
Alpine, Utah 52 40 27N 111 47W
Alpine, Wyo. 56 43 11N 111 3W
Alpine County ◇ 14 38 40N 119 50W
Alps 88 47 0N 8 0 E
Alsace 90 48 15N 7 25 E
Alsask 63 51 21N 109 59W
Alsásua 91 42 54N 2 10W
Alsea → 44 44 26N 124 5W
Alsen 41 48 38N 98 42W
Alsey 21 39 34N 90 26W
Alstead 36 43 10N 72 30W
Alsten 96 65 58N 12 40 E
Alta, Norway 96 69 57N 23 10 E
Alta, U.S.A. 23 42 40N 95 18W
Alta Gracia 76 31 40 S 64 30W
Alta Lake 62 50 10N 123 0W
Alta Vista, Iowa 23 43 12N 92 25W
Alta Vista, Kans. 24 38 52N 96 29W
Altaelva → 96 69 46N 23 45 E
Altafjorden 96 70 5N 23 5 E
Altagracia 70 10 45N 71 30W
Altagracia de Orituco 70 9 52N 66 23W
Altai = Aerht'ai Shan 113 46 40N 92 45 E
Altai Mts. 102 46 40N 92 45 E
Altair 51 29 34N 96 27W
Altamachi → 72 16 8 S 66 50W
Altamaha → 18 31 20N 81 20W
Altamira, Brazil 71 3 12 S 52 10W
Altamira, Chile 76 25 47 S 69 51W
Altamira, Colombia 70 2 3N 75 47W
Altamira, Mexico 65 22 24N 97 55W
Altamont, Ill. 21 39 4N 88 45W
Altamont, Kans. 24 37 12N 95 18W
Altamont, Mo. 32 39 53N 94 5W
Altamont, Oreg. 44 42 12N 121 44W
Altamont, S. Dak. 47 44 50N 96 42W
Altamont, Tenn. 49 35 26N 85 44W
Altamont, Utah 52 40 22N 110 17W
Altanbulag 113 50 16N 106 30 E
Altar 64 30 40N 111 50W
Altata 64 24 30N 108 0W
Altavista 54 37 6N 79 17W
Altay 113 47 48N 88 10 E
Altha 17 30 34N 85 8W
Altheimer 13 34 19N 91 51W
Altiplano 72 17 0 S 68 0W
Alto, Ga. 18 34 28N 83 35W
Alto, La. 25 32 22N 91 52W
Alto, N. Mex. 38 33 23N 105 41W
Alto, Tex. 51 31 39N 95 4W
Alto Adige = Trentino-Alto Adige □ 94 46 30N 11 0 E
Alto Araguaia 73 17 15 S 53 20W
Alto Cuchumatanes = Cuchumatanes, Sierra de los 66 15 35N 91 25W
Alto del Inca 76 24 10 S 68 10W
Alto Garças 73 16 56 S 53 32W
Alto Iriri → 73 8 50 S 53 25W
Alto Molocue 123 15 50 S 37 35 E
Alto Paraguai 73 14 30 S 56 31W
Alto Paraná □ 77 25 0 S 54 50W
Alto Parnaíba 74 9 6 S 45 57W
Alto Purús → 72 9 12 S 70 28W
Alto Río Senguerr 78 45 2 S 70 50W
Alto Santo 74 5 31 S 38 15W
Alto Sucuriú 73 19 19 S 52 47W
Alto Turi 74 2 54 S 45 38W
Alton, Ill. 21 38 53N 90 11W
Alton, Iowa 23 42 59N 96 1W
Alton, Kans. 24 39 28N 98 57W
Alton, Mo. 32 36 42N 91 24W
Alton, Utah 52 37 26N 112 29W
Alton Bay 36 43 27N 71 13W
Altona 88 53 32N 9 56 E
Altoona, Ala. 10 34 2N 86 20W
Altoona, Iowa 23 41 39N 93 28W
Altoona, Kans. 24 37 32N 95 40W
Altoona, Pa. 45 40 31N 78 24W
Altoona, Wis. 55 44 48N 91 26W
Altos 74 5 3 S 42 28W
Altun Shan 113 38 30N 88 0 E
Alturas 14 41 29N 120 32W
Altus 43 34 38N 99 20W
Altus, L. 43 34 53N 99 18W
Alùla 105 11 50N 50 45 E
Alum Bridge 54 39 2N 80 40W
Alusi 111 7 35 S 131 40 E
Alva, Ky. 49 36 44N 83 25W
Alva, Okla. 43 36 48N 98 40W
Alvarado, Mexico 65 18 40N 95 50W
Alvarado, Minn. 30 48 10N 97 0W
Alvarado, Tex. 51 32 24N 97 13W
Alvarães 71 3 12 S 64 50W
Alvaro Obregón, Presa 64 27 55N 109 52W
Alvaton 48 36 53N 86 21W
Alvear 76 29 5 S 56 30W
Alvesta 97 56 54N 14 35 E
Alvin, S.C. 46 33 22N 79 48W
Alvin, Tex. 51 29 26N 95 15W
Älvkarleby 97 60 34N 17 26 E
Alvo 34 40 52N 96 23W
Alvord, Iowa 23 43 21N 96 18W
Alvord, Tex. 51 33 22N 97 42W
Alvord Desert 44 42 30N 118 25W
Alvord L. 44 42 23N 118 36W
Älvsborgs län □ 97 58 30N 12 30 E
Älvsbyn 96 65 40N 21 0 E
Alwar 108 27 38N 76 34 E
Alxa Zuoqi 114 38 50N 105 40 E
Alyangula 127 13 55 S 136 30 E
Alyaskitovyy 101 64 45N 141 30 E
Alyata 99 39 58N 49 25 E
Alyth 84 56 38N 3 15W
Alzada 33 45 2N 104 25W
Am Dam 121 12 40N 20 35 E
Am Géréda 121 12 53N 21 14 E
Am-Timan 121 11 0N 20 10 E
Amacuro □ 71 8 50N 61 5W
Amadeus, L. 126 24 54 S 131 0 E
Amâdi, Sudan 121 5 29N 30 25 E
Amadi, Zaïre 122 3 40N 26 40 E
Amadjuak 59 64 0N 72 39W
Amadjuak L. 59 65 0N 71 8W
Amador County ◇ 14 38 25N 120 45W
Amagansett 39 40 59N 72 9W
Amagasaki 117 34 42N 135 20 E
Amakusa-Shotō 117 32 15N 130 10 E
Amalfi 70 6 55N 75 4W
Amalner 108 21 5N 75 5 E
Amambaí 77 23 5 S 55 13W
Amambaí → 77 23 22 S 53 56W
Amambay □ 77 23 0 S 56 0W
Amambay, Cordillera de 77 23 0 S 55 45W
Amami-Guntō 117 28 16N 129 21 E
Amami-Ō-Shima 117 28 0N 129 0 E
Amana 23 41 48N 91 52W
Amana → 71 9 45N 62 39W
Amaná, Lago 71 2 35 S 64 40W
Amanda 42 39 39N 82 45W
Amangeldy 100 50 10N 65 10 E
Amapá 74 2 5N 50 50W
Amapá □ 74 1 40N 52 0W
Amapari 71 0 37N 51 39W
Amarante 74 6 14 S 42 50W
Amarante do Maranhão 74 5 36 S 46 45W
Amaranth 63 50 36N 98 43W
Amargosa 75 13 2 S 39 36W
Amargosa → 15 36 14N 116 51W
Amargosa Range 15 36 20N 116 45W
Amarillo 50 35 13N 101 50W
Amaro, Mt. 94 42 5N 14 6 E
Amaro Leite 75 13 58 S 49 9W
Amasa 29 46 14N 88 27W
Amasra 106 41 45N 32 30 E
Amasya 106 40 40N 35 50 E
Amatauré 70 3 29 S 68 6W
Amatignak I. 11 51 16N 179 6W
Amatitlán 66 14 29N 90 38W
Amazon = Amazonas → 71 0 5 S 50 0W
Amazonas □, Brazil 72 4 0 S 62 0W
Amazonas □, Peru 72 5 0 S 78 0W
Amazonas □, Venezuela 70 3 30N 66 0W
Amazonas → 71 0 5 S 50 0W
Amazonia 32 39 53N 94 54W
Ambala 108 30 23N 76 56 E
Ambalavao 123 21 50 S 46 56 E
Ambam 122 2 20N 11 15 E
Ambanja 123 13 40 S 48 27 E
Ambarchik 101 69 40N 162 20 E
Ambartsevo 100 57 30N 83 52 E
Ambato 70 1 5 S 78 42W
Ambato, Sierra de 76 28 25 S 66 10W
Ambatolampy 123 19 20 S 47 35 E
Ambatondrazaka 123 17 55 S 48 28 E
Amber 43 35 10N 97 53W
Amberg 88 49 25N 11 52 E
Ambergris Cay 65 18 0N 88 0W
Amberley 128 43 9 S 172 44 E
Ambikapur 109 23 15N 83 15 E
Ambilobé 123 13 10 S 49 3 E
Ambler 11 67 5N 157 52W
Ambleside 82 54 26N 2 58W
Ambo 72 10 5 S 76 10W
Ambohitra 123 12 30 S 49 10 E
Ambon 111 3 35 S 128 20 E
Ambositra 123 20 31 S 47 25 E
Amboy, Calif. 15 34 33N 115 45W
Amboy, Ill. 21 41 44N 89 20W
Amboy, Minn. 30 43 53N 94 10W
Amboyna I. 110 7 50N 112 50 E
Ambridge 45 40 36N 80 14W
Ambriz 122 7 48 S 13 8 E
Ambrose, Ga. 18 31 36N 83 1W
Ambrose, N. Dak. 41 48 57N 103 29W
Ambrosia Lake 38 35 26N 107 54W
Amchitka I. 11 51 32N 179 0 E
Amderma 100 69 45N 61 30 E

Ameca **Antigo**

Ameca **64** 20 30N 104 0W
Ameca → **64** 20 40N 105 15W
Amecameca **65** 19 7N 98 46W
Ameland **87** 53 27N 5 45 E
Amelia, La. **25** 29 40N 91 6W
Amelia, Nebr. **34** 42 14N 98 55W
Amelia City **17** 30 35N 81 28W
Amelia County ◇ **54** 37 21N 77 59W
Amelia Court House **54** 37 21N 77 59W
Amelia I. **17** 30 40N 81 25W
Amen **101** 68 45N 180 0 E
American Corners **27** 38 47N 75 51W
American Falls **20** 42 47N 112 51W
American Falls Dam **20** 43 0N 113 0W
American Falls Reservoir **20** 42 47N 112 52W
American Fork **52** 40 23N 111 48W
American Highland **5** 73 0 S 75 0 E
American Samoa ■ **128** 14 20 S 170 40W
Americana **77** 22 45 S 47 20W
Americus, Ga. **18** 32 4N 84 14W
Americus, Kans. **24** 38 30N 96 16W
Americus, Mo. **32** 38 47N 91 34W
Amersfoort **87** 52 9N 5 23 E
Amery, Canada **63** 56 34N 94 3W
Amery, U.S.A. **55** 45 19N 92 22W
Amery Ice Shelf **5** 69 30 S 72 0 E
Ames, Iowa **23** 42 2N 93 37W
Ames, Okla. **43** 36 15N 98 11W
Ames, Tex. **51** 30 3N 94 45W
Amesbury **28** 42 51N 70 56W
Amesdale **63** 50 2N 92 55W
Amesville **42** 39 24N 81 57W
Amga **101** 60 50N 132 0 E
Amga → **101** 62 38N 134 32 E
Amgu **101** 45 45N 137 15 E
Amgun → **101** 52 56N 139 38 E
Amherst, Burma **109** 16 2N 97 20 E
Amherst, Canada **61** 45 48N 64 8W
Amherst, Colo. **16** 40 41N 102 10W
Amherst, Maine **26** 44 50N 68 22W
Amherst, Mass. **28** 42 23N 72 31W
Amherst, N.H. **36** 42 52N 71 38W
Amherst, N.Y. **39** 42 59N 78 48W
Amherst, Ohio **42** 41 24N 82 14W
Amherst, Tex. **50** 34 1N 102 25W
Amherst, Va. **54** 37 35N 79 3W
Amherst County ◇ **54** 37 38N 79 5W
Amherst Junction **55** 44 28N 89 19W
Amherstburg **60** 42 6N 83 6W
Amherstdale **54** 37 47N 81 49W
Amiata, Mte. **94** 42 54N 11 40 E
Amidon **41** 46 29N 103 19W
Amiens **90** 49 54N 2 16 E
Amirante Is. **3** 6 0 S 53 0 E
Amisk L. **63** 54 35N 102 15W
Amistad **38** 35 55N 103 9W
Amistad, Presa de la **64** 29 24N 101 0W
Amistad National Recreation Area **50** 29 32N 101 12W
Amistad Reservoir **50** 29 28N 101 4W
Amite **25** 30 44N 90 30W
Amite → **25** 30 18N 90 34W
Amite County ◇ **31** 31 10N 90 49W
Amity, Ark. **13** 34 16N 93 28W
Amity, Ind. **22** 39 26N 86 0W
Amity, Oreg. **44** 45 7N 123 12W
Amlia I. **11** 52 4N 173 30W
Amlwch **82** 53 24N 4 21W
'Ammān **104** 31 57N 35 52 E
Ammanford **83** 51 48N 4 0W
Ammi'ad **104** 32 55N 35 32 E
Ammon **20** 43 28N 111 58W
Ammonoonosuc → **36** 44 10N 72 2W
Amonate **54** 37 12N 81 38W
Amoret **32** 38 15N 94 35W
Amorgós **95** 36 50N 25 57 E
Amorita **43** 36 56N 98 18W
Amory **31** 33 59N 88 29W
Amos **60** 48 35N 78 5W
Amozoc **65** 19 2N 98 3W
Ampanihy **123** 24 40 S 44 45 E
Ampato, Nevado **72** 15 40 S 71 56W
Ampenan **110** 8 35 S 116 13 E
Amqa **104** 32 59N 35 10 E
Amqui **61** 48 28N 67 27W
Amraoti **108** 20 55N 77 45 E
Amreli **108** 21 35N 71 17 E
Amritsar **108** 31 35N 74 57 E
Amroha **108** 28 53N 78 30 E
Amsden **36** 43 25N 72 30W
Amsterdam, Neth. **87** 52 23N 4 54 E
Amsterdam, N.Y. **39** 42 56N 74 11W
Amsterdam, Ohio **42** 40 29N 80 56W
Amsterdam, I. **3** 37 30 S 77 30 E
Amudarya → **100** 43 40N 59 0 E
Amukta I. **11** 52 30N 171 16W
Amukta Pass **11** 52 0N 171 0W
Amund Ringnes I. **4** 78 20N 96 25W
Amundsen Gulf **58** 71 0N 124 0W
Amundsen Sea **5** 72 0 S 115 0W
Amuntai **110** 2 28 S 115 25 E
Amur → **101** 52 56N 141 10 E
Amurang **111** 1 5N 124 40 E
Amuri Pass **128** 42 31 S 172 11 E
Amursk **101** 50 14N 136 54 E
Amurzet **101** 47 50N 131 5 E
Amy **13** 33 44N 92 49W
An Nafūd **106** 28 15N 41 0 E
An Najaf **106** 32 3N 44 15 E
An Nāqūrah **104** 33 7N 35 8 E
An Nāṣirīyah **106** 31 0N 46 15 E
An Nhon **112** 13 55N 109 7 E
An Nîl □ **121** 19 30N 33 0 E
An Nîl el Abyad □ **121** 14 0N 32 15 E
An Nîl el Azraq □ **121** 12 30N 34 30 E
An Nu'ayrīyah **106** 27 30N 48 30 E
An Uaimh **85** 53 39N 6 40W
Anabar → **101** 73 8N 113 36 E
'Anabtā **104** 32 19N 35 7 E
Anacapa I. **15** 34 1N 119 26W
Anaco **71** 9 27N 64 28W
Anacoco **25** 31 15N 93 21W
Anaconda **33** 46 8N 112 57W
Anaconda Ra. **33** 45 30N 113 30W
Anacortes **53** 48 30N 122 37W
Anadarko **43** 35 4N 98 15W
Anadia **74** 9 42 S 36 18W
Anadolu **106** 38 0N 30 0 E
Anadyr **101** 64 35N 177 20 E
Anadyr → **101** 64 55N 176 5 E
Anadyrskiy Zaliv **101** 64 0N 180 0 E
'Ānah **106** 34 25N 42 0 E
Anahalu → **19** 21 37N 158 6W
Anaheim **15** 33 50N 117 55W
Anahim Lake **62** 52 28N 125 18W
Anahola **19** 22 9N 159 19W
Anáhuac, Mexico **64** 27 14N 100 9W
Anahuac, U.S.A. **51** 29 46N 94 41W
Anajás **74** 0 59 S 49 57W
Anajatuba **74** 3 16 S 44 37W
Anakapalle **109** 17 42N 83 6 E
Anaktuvuk Pass **11** 68 8N 151 45W
Analalava **123** 14 35 S 48 0 E
Anamã **71** 3 35 S 61 22W
Anambas, Kepulauan **110** 3 20N 106 30 E
Anamoose **41** 47 53N 100 15W
Anamosa **23** 42 7N 91 17W
Anamur **106** 36 8N 32 58 E
Anan **117** 33 54N 134 40 E
Anandale **25** 31 16N 92 27W
Anantnag **108** 33 45N 75 10 E
Anápolis **75** 16 15 S 48 50W
Anapu → **71** 1 53 S 50 53W
Anār **107** 30 55N 55 13 E
Anārak **107** 33 25N 53 40 E
Anasco **57** 18 17N 67 8W
Anatolia = Anadolu **106** 38 0N 30 0 E
Anatone **53** 46 8N 117 8W
Añatuya **76** 28 20 S 62 50W
Anauá → **71** 0 58N 61 21W
Anaunethad L. **63** 60 55N 104 25W
Anavilhanas, Arquipélago das **71** 2 42 S 60 45W
Anaye **121** 19 15N 12 50 E
Ancash □ **72** 9 30 S 77 45W
Anceney **33** 45 39N 111 21W
Ancho **38** 33 56N 105 45W
Ancho, Canal **78** 50 0 S 74 20W
Anchor **21** 40 34N 88 32W
Anchorage **11** 61 13N 149 54W
Anchorage ◇ **11** 61 0N 150 0W
Ancohuma, Nevada **72** 16 0 S 68 50W
Ancon, Panama **57** 8 56N 79 38W
Ancón, Peru **72** 11 50 S 77 10W
Ancona **94** 43 37N 13 30 E
Ancud **78** 42 0 S 73 50W
Ancud, G. de **78** 42 0 S 73 0W
Anda **114** 46 24N 125 19 E
Andacollo, Argentina **76** 37 10 S 70 42W
Andacollo, Chile **76** 30 5 S 71 10W
Andahuaylas **72** 13 40 S 73 25W
Andale **24** 37 48N 97 38W
Andalgalá **76** 27 40 S 66 30W
Åndalsnes **96** 62 35N 7 43 E
Andalucía □ **91** 37 35N 5 0W
Andalusia, Ala. **10** 31 18N 86 29W
Andalusia, Ill. **21** 41 26N 90 43W
Andalusia □ = Andalucía □ **91** 37 35N 5 0W
Andaman Is. **112** 12 30N 92 30 E
Andaman Sea **112** 13 0N 96 0 E
Andaman Str. **112** 12 15N 92 20 E
Andara **123** 18 2 S 21 9 E
Andaraí **75** 12 48 S 41 20W
Andenne **87** 50 30N 5 5 E
Anderson, Ala. **10** 34 55N 87 16W
Anderson, Alaska **11** 64 25N 149 15W
Anderson, Calif. **14** 40 27N 122 18W
Anderson, Ind. **22** 40 10N 85 41W
Anderson, Mo. **32** 36 39N 94 27W
Anderson, S.C. **46** 34 31N 82 39W
Anderson, Tex. **51** 30 29N 95 59W
Anderson → **58** 69 42N 129 0W
Anderson County ◇, Kans. **24** 38 15N 95 15W
Anderson County ◇, Ky. **49** 38 0N 85 0W
Anderson County ◇, S.C. **46** 34 30N 82 40W
Anderson County ◇, Tenn. **49** 36 6N 84 8W
Anderson County ◇, Tex. **51** 31 46N 95 38W
Anderson Ranch Reservoir **20** 43 22N 115 27W
Anderson Reservoir **14** 37 10N 121 38W
Andersonville **18** 32 12N 84 9W
Andes, Colombia **72** 5 40N 75 53W
Andes, U.S.A. **39** 42 12N 74 47W
Andes, Cord de los **72** 20 0 S 68 0W
Andes, L. **47** 43 11N 98 27W
Andfjorden **96** 69 10N 16 20 E
Andhra Pradesh □ **108** 16 0N 79 0 E
Andikíthira **95** 35 52N 23 15 E
Andizhan **100** 41 10N 72 0 E
Andkhvoy **107** 36 52N 65 8 E
Andoany **123** 13 25 S 48 16 E
Andoas **70** 2 55 S 76 25W
Andong **114** 36 40N 128 43 E
Andorra ■ **91** 42 30N 1 30 E
Andorra La Vella **91** 42 31N 1 32 E
Andover, U.K. **83** 51 13N 1 29W
Andover, Conn. **28** 41 44N 72 23W
Andover, Kans. **24** 37 43N 97 7W
Andover, Maine **26** 44 38N 70 45W
Andover, Mass. **28** 42 40N 71 8W
Andover, Minn. **30** 45 17N 93 21W
Andover, N.H. **36** 43 26N 71 49W
Andover, N.J. **37** 40 59N 74 45W
Andover, N.Y. **39** 42 10N 77 48W
Andover, Ohio **42** 41 36N 80 34W
Andover, S. Dak. **47** 45 25N 97 54W
Andradina **75** 20 54 S 51 23W
Andreanof Is. **11** 51 30N 176 0W
Andrew County ◇ **32** 40 0N 94 45W
Andrews, Ind. **22** 40 52N 85 36W
Andrews, Md. **27** 38 20N 76 10W
Andrews, N.C. **40** 35 12N 83 49W
Andrews, S.C. **46** 33 27N 79 34W
Andrews, Tex. **50** 32 19N 102 33W
Andrews County ◇ **50** 32 19N 102 33W
Ándria **94** 41 13N 16 17 E
Andriba **123** 17 30 S 46 58 E
Androka **123** 24 58 S 44 2 E
Andropov **98** 58 5N 38 50E
Andros **95** 37 50N 24 57E
Andros I. **66** 24 43N 77 47W
Androscoggin → **26** 43 58N 69 52W
Androscoggin County ◇ **26** 44 5N 70 10W
Andújar **91** 38 3N 4 5W
Anegada, Bahía **78** 40 20 S 62 20W
Anegada Passage **67** 18 15N 63 45W
Anegam **12** 32 22N 112 2W
Anécho **120** 6 12N 1 34 E
Añelo **78** 38 20 S 68 45W
Aneta **41** 47 41N 97 59W
Aneto, Pico de **91** 42 37N 0 40 E
Añez **73** 15 40 S 63 10W
Ang Thong **112** 14 35N 100 31 E
Angamos, Punta **76** 23 1 S 70 32W
Ang'angxi **114** 47 10N 123 48 E
Angara → **101** 58 30N 97 0 E
Angarsk **101** 52 30N 104 0 E
Ånge **96** 62 31N 15 35 E
Angel de la Guarda **64** 29 30N 113 30W
Angel Falls **71** 5 57N 62 30W
Angeles **111** 15 9N 120 33 E
Angeles National Forest **15** 33 15N 118 0W
Ängelholm **97** 56 15N 12 58 E
Angelina → **51** 30 54N 94 12W
Angelina County ◇ **51** 31 21N 94 44W
Angelina National Forest **51** 31 7N 94 15W
Angels Camp **14** 38 4N 120 32W
Angelus **24** 39 11N 100 41W
Ångermanälven → **96** 62 40N 18 0 E
Angers **90** 47 30N 0 35W
Ängesån → **96** 66 50N 22 15 E
Angical **75** 12 0 S 44 42W
Angie **25** 30 58N 89 49W
Angier **40** 35 31N 78 44W
Angikuni L. **63** 62 0N 100 0W
Angkor **112** 13 22N 103 50 E
Angle Inlet **30** 49 21N 95 4W
Anglesey **82** 53 17N 4 20W
Angleton **51** 29 10N 95 26W
Angmagssalik **4** 65 40N 37 20W
Ango **122** 4 10N 26 5 E
Angoche, I. **123** 16 20 S 39 50 E
Angol **76** 37 56 S 72 45W
Angola, Del. **27** 38 40N 75 10W
Angola, Ind. **22** 41 38N 85 0W
Angola, N.Y. **39** 42 38N 79 2W
Angola ■ **123** 12 0 S 18 0 E
Angoon **11** 57 30N 134 35W
Angora **34** 41 51N 103 8W
Angostura Reservoir **47** 43 21N 103 26W
Angoulême **90** 45 39N 0 10 E
Angoumois **90** 45 50N 0 25 E
Angra dos Reis **77** 23 0 S 44 10W
Angren **100** 41 1N 70 12 E
Anguilla, U.S.A. **31** 32 59N 90 50W
Anguilla, W. Indies **67** 18 14N 63 5W
Angus, Braes of **84** 56 51N 3 10W
Angwin **14** 38 34N 122 26W
Anhanduí → **77** 21 46 S 52 9W
Anholt **97** 56 42N 11 33 E
Anhua **115** 28 23N 111 12 E
Anhui □ **115** 32 0N 117 0 E
Anhwei □ = Anhui □ **115** 32 0N 117 0 E
Aniak **11** 61 35N 159 32W
Anicuns **75** 16 28 S 49 58W
Animas **38** 31 57N 108 48W
Animas → **38** 36 43N 108 13W
Animas Peak **38** 31 35N 108 47W
Anin **112** 15 36N 97 50 E
Anita **23** 41 27N 94 46W
Anjidiv I. **108** 14 40N 74 10 E
Anjou **90** 47 20N 0 15W
Anjozorobe **123** 18 22 S 47 52 E
Anju **114** 39 36N 125 40 E
Anka **120** 12 13N 5 58 E
Ankaboa, Tanjona **123** 21 58 S 43 20 E
Ankang **115** 32 40N 109 1 E
Ankara **106** 40 0N 32 54 E
Ankazoabo **123** 22 18 S 44 31 E
Ankazobe **123** 18 20 S 47 10 E
Ankeny **23** 41 44N 93 36W
Ankona **17** 27 21N 80 17W
Ankoro **122** 6 45 S 26 55 E
Anlu **115** 31 15N 113 45 E
Anmoore **54** 39 16N 80 18W
Ann, C. **28** 42 38N 70 35W
Ann Arbor **29** 42 17N 83 45W
Anna, Ill. **21** 37 28N 89 15W
Anna, Ohio **42** 40 24N 84 11W
Anna, Tex. **51** 33 21N 96 33W
Anna, L. **54** 38 4N 77 45W
Anna Regina **71** 7 10N 58 30W
Annaba **120** 36 50N 7 46 E
Annada **32** 39 16N 90 50W
Annalee → **85** 54 3N 7 15W
Annam = Trung-Phan **110** 16 0N 108 0 E
Annamitique, Chaîne **112** 17 0N 106 0 E
Annan **84** 55 0N 3 17W
Annan → **84** 54 58N 3 18W
Annandale, Minn. **30** 45 16N 94 8W
Annandale, Va. **54** 38 50N 77 12W
Annapolis, Md. **27** 38 59N 76 30W
Annapolis, Mo. **32** 37 22N 90 42W
Annapolis Royal **61** 44 44N 65 32W
Annawan **21** 41 24N 89 55W
Anne Arundel County ◇ **27** 39 0N 76 40W
Annecy **90** 45 55N 6 8 E
Annette I. **11** 55 9N 131 28W
Annette Island Indian Reservation **11** 55 5N 131 30W
Anning **113** 24 55N 102 26 E
Anniston, Ala. **10** 33 39N 85 50W
Anniston, Mo. **32** 36 50N 89 20W
Annobón = Pagalu **119** 1 25 S 5 36 E
Annona **51** 33 35N 94 55W
Annonciation, L' **60** 46 25N 74 55W
Annotto Bay **66** 18 17N 77 3W
Annville, Ky. **49** 37 19N 83 58W
Annville, Pa. **45** 40 20N 76 31W
Año Nuevo, Pt. **14** 37 7N 122 19W
Anoka, Minn. **30** 45 12N 93 23W
Anoka, Nebr. **34** 42 57N 98 50W
Anoka County ◇ **30** 45 15N 93 15W
Anqing **115** 30 30N 117 3 E
Anren **115** 26 43N 113 18 E
Ansāb **106** 29 11N 44 43 E
Ansai **114** 36 50N 109 20 E
Ansbach **88** 49 17N 10 34 E
Anse au Loup, L' **61** 51 32N 56 50W
Anselmo **34** 41 37N 99 52W
Anserma **70** 5 13N 75 48W
Anshan **114** 41 5N 122 58 E
Anshun **115** 26 18N 105 57 E
Ansirabe **123** 19 55 S 47 2 E
Ansley, La. **25** 32 24N 92 42W
Ansley, Nebr. **34** 41 18N 99 23W
Anson **51** 32 45N 99 54W
Anson B. **126** 13 20 S 130 6 E
Anson County ◇ **40** 35 0N 80 0W
Ansongo **120** 15 25N 0 35 E
Ansonia, Conn. **28** 41 21N 73 5W
Ansonia, Ohio **42** 40 13N 84 38W
Ansonville **40** 35 6N 80 7W
Ansted **54** 38 8N 81 6W
Anstruther **84** 56 14N 2 40W
Ansudu **111** 2 11 S 139 22 E
Antabamba **72** 14 40 S 73 0W
Antakya **106** 36 14N 36 10 E
Antalaha **123** 14 57 S 50 20 E
Antalya **106** 36 52N 30 45 E
Antalya Körfezi **106** 36 15N 31 30 E
Antananarivo **123** 18 55 S 47 31 E
Antarctic Pen. **5** 67 0 S 60 0W
Antarctica **5** 90 0 S 0 0 E
Antelope, Kans. **24** 38 26N 96 59W
Antelope, Oreg. **44** 44 55N 120 43W
Antelope County ◇ **34** 42 15N 98 0W
Antelope Cr. → **44** 42 28N 117 13W
Antelope Hills, Okla. **43** 35 55N 99 50W
Antelope Hills, Wyo. **56** 42 20N 108 25W
Antelope Range **35** 40 10N 114 30W
Antelope Reservoir **44** 42 54N 117 14W
Antenor Navarro **74** 6 44 S 38 27W
Antequera, Paraguay **76** 24 8 S 57 7W
Antequera, Spain **91** 37 5N 4 33W
Antero, Mt. **16** 38 41N 106 15W
Antero Reservoir **16** 38 56N 105 55W
Anthon **23** 42 23N 95 52W
Anthony, Fla. **17** 29 18N 82 7W
Anthony, Kans. **24** 37 9N 98 2W
Anthony, N. Mex. **38** 32 0N 106 36W
Anthoston **48** 37 46N 87 32W
Anti Atlas **120** 30 0N 8 30W
Anticosti, Î. d' **61** 49 30N 63 0W
Antigo **55** 45 9N 89 9W

Antigonish **Arklow**

Antigonish 61 45 38N 61 58W
Antigua, Guat. 66 14 34N 90 41W
Antigua, W. Indies 67 17 0N 61 50W
Antigua and Barbuda ■ 67 17 20N 61 48W
Antilla 66 20 40N 75 50W
Antimony 52 38 7N 112 0W
Antioch, Calif. 14 38 1N 121 48W
Antioch, Ill. 21 42 29N 88 6W
Antioch, Nebr. 34 42 4N 102 35W
Antioquia 70 6 40N 75 55W
Antioquia □ 70 7 0N 75 30W
Antipodes Is. 124 49 45 S 178 40 E
Antler 41 48 59N 101 17W
Antler → 63 49 8N 101 0W
Antlers 43 34 14N 95 37W
Antofagasta 76 23 50 S 70 30W
Antofagasta □ 76 24 0 S 69 0W
Antofagasta de la Sierra 76 26 5 S 67 20W
Antofalla 76 25 30 S 68 5W
Antofalla, Salar de 76 25 40 S 67 45W
Antoine 13 34 2N 93 25W
Anton, Colo. 16 39 45N 103 13W
Anton, Ky. 48 37 21N 87 24W
Anton, Tex. 50 33 49N 102 10W
Anton Chico 38 35 12N 105 9W
Antongila, Helodrano 123 15 30 S 49 50 E
Antonina 77 25 26 S 48 42W
Antonino 24 38 47N 99 24W
Antonito 16 37 5N 106 0W
Antrim 85 54 43N 6 13W
Antrim □ 85 54 55N 6 20W
Antrim, Mts. of 85 54 57N 6 8W
Antrim County ◇ 29 45 0N 85 10W
Antsalova 123 18 40 S 44 37 E
Antsiranana 123 12 25 S 49 20 E
Antsohihy 123 14 50 S 47 59 E
Antwerp = Antwerpen 87 51 13N 4 25 E
Antwerp, N.Y. 39 44 12N 75 37W
Antwerp, Ohio 42 41 11N 84 45W
Antwerpen 87 51 13N 4 25 E
Antwerpen □ 87 51 15N 4 40 E
Anupgarh 108 29 10N 73 10 E
Anuradhapura 108 8 22N 80 28 E
Anvers = Antwerpen 87 51 13N 4 25 E
Anvers I. 5 64 30 S 63 40W
Anvik 11 62 39N 160 13W
Anxi, Fujian, China 115 25 2N 118 12 E
Anxi, Gansu, China 113 40 30N 95 43 E
Anxious B. 126 33 24 S 134 45 E
Anyang 114 36 5N 114 21 E
Anyi, Jiangxi, China 115 28 49N 115 25 E
Anyi, Shanxi, China 115 35 2N 111 2 E
Anyuan 115 25 9N 115 21 E
Anza Borrego Desert State Park 15 33 0N 116 26W
'Anzah 104 32 22N 35 12 E
Anzhero-Sudzhensk 100 56 10N 86 0 E
Ánzio 94 41 28N 12 37 E
Anzoátegui □ 71 9 0N 64 30W
Aoga-Shima 117 32 28N 139 46 E
Aomori 116 40 45N 140 45 E
Aomori □ 116 40 45N 140 40 E
Aosta 94 45 43N 7 20 E
Aoudéras 120 17 45N 8 20 E
Aoulef el Arab 120 26 55N 1 2 E
Aozi 121 21 11N 18 34 E
Apa → 76 22 6 S 58 2W
Apache 43 34 54N 98 22W
Apache County ◇ 12 35 0N 109 30W
Apache Junction 12 33 25N 111 33W
Apache L. 12 33 36N 111 21W
Apache Mts. 50 31 12N 104 35W
Apache National Forest 12 33 30N 109 10W
Apache Sitgreaves National Forest 12 34 30N 110 30W
Apalachee B. 17 30 0N 84 0W
Apalachicola 17 29 43N 84 59W
Apalachicola → 17 29 43N 84 58W
Apalachicola B. 17 29 40N 85 0W
Apalachicola National Forest 17 30 10N 85 0W
Apaporis → 70 1 23 S 69 25W
Aparecida do Taboado 75 20 5 S 51 5W
Aparri 111 18 22N 121 38 E
Aparurén 71 5 6N 62 8W
Apàtity 98 67 34N 33 22 E
Apatzingán 64 19 0N 102 20W
Apeldoorn 87 52 13N 5 57 E
Apennines 80 44 20N 10 20 E
Apere → 73 13 44 S 65 18W
Apex 40 35 44N 78 51W
Apia 128 13 50 S 171 50W
Apiacás, Serra dos 73 9 50 S 57 0W
Apiaú → 71 2 39N 61 12W
Apiaú, Serra do 71 2 30N 62 0W
Apidiá → 73 11 39 S 61 11W
Apinajé 75 11 31 S 48 18W
Apishapa → 16 38 8N 103 57W
Apizaco 65 19 26N 98 9W
Aplao 72 16 0 S 72 40W
Apo, Mt. 111 6 53N 125 14 E
Apodi 74 5 39 S 37 48W
Apollonia = Marsá Susah 121 32 52N 21 59 E
Apolo 72 14 30 S 68 30W
Apónguao → 71 4 48N 61 36W
Apopka 17 28 40N 81 31W
Apopka L. 17 28 38N 81 38W
Aporé 73 18 58 S 52 1W
Aporé → 75 19 27 S 50 57W
Aporema 74 1 14N 50 49W
Apostle Is. 55 47 0N 90 40W
Apostle Islands Nat. Lakeshore 55 46 55N 91 0W
Apóstoles 77 28 0 S 56 0W
Apoteri 71 4 2N 58 32W
Appalachia 54 36 54N 82 47W
Appalachian Mts. 54 36 40N 81 45W
Appanoose County ◇ 23 40 45N 92 50W
Appennini 94 41 0N 15 0 E
Apple →, Ill. 21 42 11N 90 14W
Apple →, Wis. 55 45 9N 92 45W
Apple Creek 42 40 45N 81 51W
Apple Creek → 21 39 22N 90 37W
Apple Hill 83 45 13N 74 46W
Apple Valley 15 34 32N 117 14W
Appleby 82 54 35N 2 29W
Applegate, Mich. 29 43 21N 82 38W
Applegate, Oreg. 44 42 16N 123 10W
Appleton, Minn. 30 45 12N 96 1W
Appleton, Wis. 55 44 16N 88 25W
Appleton City 32 38 11N 94 2W
Appling 18 33 33N 82 19W
Appling County ◇ 18 31 45N 82 15W
Appomattox 54 37 21N 78 50W
Appomattox → 54 37 19N 77 17W
Appomattox County ◇ 54 37 21N 78 50W
Approuague 71 4 20N 52 0W
Approuague → 71 4 30N 51 57W
Apuaú 71 2 25 S 60 53W
Apucarana 77 23 55 S 51 33W
Apulia = Púglia □ 94 41 0N 16 30 E
Apure □ 70 7 10N 68 50W
Apure → 70 7 37N 66 25W
Apurímac □ 72 14 0 S 73 0W
Apurimac → 72 12 17 S 73 56W
Aqabah = Al 'Aqabah 104 29 31N 35 0 E
'Aqabah, Khalīj al 106 28 15N 33 20 E
Āqcheh 107 37 0N 66 5 E
Aqîq 121 18 14N 38 12 E
Aqrabā 104 32 9N 35 20 E
Aqrah 106 36 46N 43 45 E
Aquarius Mts. 12 34 45N 113 20W
Aquarius Plateau 52 38 0N 111 40W
Aquasco 27 38 35N 76 43W
Aquidauana 73 20 30 S 55 50W
Aquidauana → 73 19 44 S 56 50W
Áquila, L' 94 42 21N 13 24 E
Aquiles Serdán 64 28 37N 105 54W
Aquin 67 18 16N 73 24W
Ar Rachidiya 120 31 58N 4 20W
Ar Rafīd 104 32 57N 35 52 E
Ar Ramādī 106 33 25N 43 20 E
Ar Ramthā 104 32 34N 36 0 E
Ar Raqqah 106 36 0N 38 55 E
Ar Rass 106 25 50N 43 40 E
Ar Rifa'i 106 31 50N 46 10 E
Ar Riyāḑ 106 24 41N 46 42 E
Ar Rummān 104 32 9N 35 48 E
Ar Ruţbah 106 33 0N 40 15 E
Ar Ruwayḑah 106 23 40N 44 40 E
Ara 109 25 35N 84 32 E
Arab 10 34 19N 86 30W
'Arab, Bahr el → 121 18 0N 36 30 E
Arab, Shatt al 106 30 0N 48 31 E
Arabelo 71 4 55N 64 13W
Arabi 18 31 50N 83 44W
Arabia 102 25 0N 45 0 E
Arabian Gulf = The Gulf 107 27 0N 50 0 E
Arabian Sea 102 16 0N 65 0 E
Arac 106 41 15N 33 21 E
Aracaju 74 10 55 S 37 4W
Aracataca 70 10 38N 74 9W
Aracati 74 4 30 S 37 44W
Araçatuba 75 21 10 S 50 30W
Aracena 91 37 53N 6 38W
Araçuaí 75 16 52 S 42 4W
Araçuaí → 75 16 46 S 42 2W
'Arad, Israel 104 31 15N 35 12 E
Arad, Romania 97 46 10N 21 20 E
Arada 121 15 0N 20 20 E
Arafura Sea 111 9 0 S 135 0 E
Aragarças 73 15 55 S 52 15W
Aragon 18 34 2N 85 3W
Aragón □ 91 41 25N 1 0W
Aragón → 91 42 13N 1 44W
Aragua □ 70 10 0N 67 10W
Aragua de Barcelona 71 9 28N 64 49W
Araguacema 74 8 50 S 49 20W
Araguaçu 75 12 49 S 49 51W
Araguaia → 75 5 21 S 48 41W
Araguaiana 73 15 43 S 51 51W
Araguaína 74 7 12 S 48 12W
Araguari 75 18 38 S 48 11W
Araguari → 74 1 15N 49 55W
Araguatins 74 5 38 S 48 7W
Araioses 74 2 53 S 41 55W
Arak, Algeria 120 25 20N 3 45 E
Arāk, Iran 106 34 0N 49 40 E
Arakan Coast 109 19 0N 94 0 E
Arakan Yoma 109 20 0N 94 40 E
Araks = Aras, Rūd-e → 106 39 10N 47 10 E
Aral Sea = Aralskoye More 100 44 30N 60 0 E
Aralsk 100 46 50N 61 20 E
Aralskoye More 100 44 30N 60 0 E
Aramac 127 22 58 S 145 14 E
Aran I. 85 55 0N 8 30W
Aran Is. 85 53 5N 9 42W
Aranjuez 91 40 1N 3 40W
Aranos 123 24 9 S 19 7 E
Aransas County ◇ 51 28 5N 96 28W
Aransas Pass 51 27 55N 97 9W
Aranzazu 70 5 16N 75 30W
Araouane 120 18 55N 3 30W
Arapaho 43 35 34N 98 58W
Arapaho National Forest 16 39 30N 106 15W
Arapahoe, Colo. 16 38 51N 102 11W
Arapahoe, N.C. 40 35 2N 76 49W
Arapahoe, Nebr. 34 40 18N 99 54W
Arapahoe County ◇ 16 39 40N 104 15W
Arapari 74 5 34 S 49 15W
Arapey Grande → 76 30 55 S 57 49W
Arapiraca 74 9 45 S 36 39W
Arapkir 106 39 5N 38 30 E
Arapongas 77 23 29 S 51 28W
Araracuara 70 0 24 S 72 17W
Araranguá 77 29 0 S 49 30W
Araraquara 75 21 50 S 48 0W
Ararás, Serra das 77 25 0 S 53 10W
Ararat, Australia 127 37 16 S 143 0 E
Ararat, U.S.A. 54 36 36N 80 31W
Ararat, Mt. = Ağri Daği 106 39 50N 44 15 E
Arari 74 3 28 S 44 47W
Araripe, Chapada do 74 7 20 S 40 0W
Araripina 74 7 33 S 40 34W
Araruama, Lagoa de 75 22 53 S 42 12W
Araruna 74 6 52 S 35 44W
Aras, Rūd-e → 106 39 10N 47 10 E
Araticu 74 1 58 S 49 51W
Arauca 70 7 0N 70 40W
Arauca □ 70 6 40N 71 0W
Arauca → 70 7 24N 66 35W
Arauco 76 37 16 S 73 25W
Arauco □ 76 37 40 S 73 25W
Araújos 75 19 56 S 45 14W
Arauquita 70 7 2N 71 25W
Araure 70 9 34N 69 13W
Araxá 75 19 35 S 46 55W
Araya, Pen. de 71 10 40N 64 0W
Arbatax 94 39 57N 9 42 E
Arbaza 101 52 40N 92 30 E
Arbīl 106 36 15N 44 5 E
Arboletes 70 8 51N 76 26W
Arbon 20 42 27N 112 34W
Arborfield 63 53 6N 103 39W
Arborg 63 50 54N 97 13W
Arbroath 84 56 34N 2 35W
Arbuckle 14 39 1N 122 3W
Arbuckle L. 17 27 42N 81 24W
Arbuckle Mts. 43 34 20N 97 10W
Arc Dome 35 38 51N 117 22W
Arcachon 90 44 40N 1 10W
Arcade, Calif. 15 34 2N 118 15W
Arcade, Ga. 18 34 5N 83 34W
Arcade, N.Y. 39 42 32N 78 25W
Arcadia, Fla. 17 27 13N 81 52W
Arcadia, Ind. 22 40 11N 86 1W
Arcadia, Iowa 23 42 5N 95 3W
Arcadia, Kans. 24 37 38N 94 37W
Arcadia, La. 25 32 33N 92 55W
Arcadia, Mich. 29 44 30N 86 14W
Arcadia, Nebr. 34 41 25N 99 8W
Arcadia, Okla. 43 35 40N 97 20W
Arcadia, Pa. 45 40 47N 78 51W
Arcadia, Wis. 55 44 15N 91 30W
Arcanum 42 39 59N 84 33W
Arcata 14 40 52N 124 5W
Arcata B. 14 40 52N 124 5W
Archangel = Arkhangelsk 98 64 40N 41 0 E
Archbald 45 41 30N 75 32W
Archbold 42 41 31N 84 18W
Archdale 40 35 56N 79 57W
Archer, Fla. 17 29 32N 82 32W
Archer, Iowa 23 43 7N 95 45W
Archer, Nebr. 34 41 10N 98 8W
Archer → 127 13 28 S 141 41 E
Archer City 51 33 36N 98 38W
Archer County ◇ 51 33 35N 98 40W
Arches National Monument 52 38 45N 109 25W
Archibald 25 32 21N 91 47W
Archie, La. 25 31 35N 91 58W
Archie, Mo. 32 38 29N 94 21W
Archuleta County ◇ 16 37 10N 107 0W
Arcila = Asilah 120 35 29N 6 0W
Arco, Idaho 20 43 38N 113 18W
Arco, Minn. 30 44 23N 96 11W
Arcola, Canada 63 49 40N 102 30W
Arcola, Ill. 21 39 41N 88 19W
Arcola, Miss. 31 33 16N 90 53W
Arcola, Mo. 32 37 33N 93 53W
Arcos 91 41 12N 2 16W
Arcot 108 12 53N 79 20 E
Arcoverde 74 8 25 S 37 4W
Arctic Bay 59 73 1N 85 7W
Arctic Ocean 4 78 0N 160 0W
Arctic Red River 58 67 15N 134 0W
Arctic Village 11 68 8N 145 32W
Arda → 95 41 40N 26 29 E
Ardabīl 106 38 15N 48 18 E
Ardahan 106 41 7N 42 41 E
Ardakān = Sepīdān 107 30 20N 52 5 E
Ardèche □ 90 44 42N 4 16 E
Ardee 85 53 51N 6 32W
Arden 14 38 36N 121 33W
Ardennes 87 50 0N 5 10 E
Ardennes □ 90 49 35N 4 40 E
Ardenvoir 53 47 44N 120 22W
Ardestān 107 33 20N 52 25 E
Ardgour 84 56 45N 5 25W
Ardino 95 41 34N 25 9 E
Ardjuno 111 7 49 S 112 34 E
Ardmore, Ala. 10 34 59N 86 52W
Ardmore, Okla. 43 34 10N 97 8W
Ardmore, S. Dak. 47 43 1N 103 40W
Ardnacrusha 85 52 43N 8 38W
Ardnamurchan, Pt. of 84 56 44N 6 14W
Ardrossan 84 55 39N 4 50W
Ards □ 85 54 35N 5 30W
Ards Pen. 85 54 30N 5 25W
Arecibo 57 18 29N 66 43W
Arecibo ◇ 57 18 20N 66 35W
Aredale 23 42 50N 93 0W
Areia Branca 74 5 0 S 37 0W
Arena 55 43 10N 89 55W
Arena, Pt. 14 38 57N 123 44W
Arena de la Ventana, Punta 64 24 4N 109 52W
Arenac County ◇ 29 44 0N 83 55W
Arenales, Cerro 78 47 5 S 73 40W
Arenápolis 73 14 26 S 56 49W
Arendal 97 58 28N 8 46 E
Arenillas 70 3 33 S 80 10W
Arenzville 21 39 53N 90 22W
Arequipa 72 16 20 S 71 30W
Arequipa □ 72 16 0 S 72 50W
Arere 71 0 16 S 53 52W
Arero 121 4 41N 38 50 E
Arévalo 91 41 3N 4 43W
Arezzo 94 43 28N 11 50 E
Argenta, Canada 62 50 20N 116 55W
Argenta, U.S.A. 21 39 59N 88 49W
Argentário, Mte. 94 42 23N 11 11 E
Argentia 61 47 18N 53 58W
Argentina ■ 78 35 0 S 66 0W
Argentina Is. 5 66 0 S 64 0W
Argentino, L. 78 50 10 S 73 0W
Argeş □ 95 45 0N 24 45 E
Argeş → 89 44 30N 25 50 E
Arghandab → 108 31 30N 64 15 E
Argo 121 19 28N 30 30 E
Argolikós Kólpos 95 37 20N 22 52 E
Argonia 24 37 16N 97 46W
Argonne, France 90 49 0N 5 20 E
Argonne, U.S.A. 55 45 40N 88 53W
Árgos, Greece 95 37 40N 22 43 E
Argos, U.S.A. 22 41 14N 86 15W
Argostólion 95 38 12N 20 33 E
Arguello, Pt. 15 34 35N 120 39W
Argun → 101 53 20N 121 28 E
Argungu 120 12 40N 4 31 E
Argus Range 15 36 10N 117 40W
Argusville 41 47 3N 96 56W
Argyle, Minn. 30 48 20N 96 49W
Argyle, Wis. 55 42 42N 89 52W
Århus 97 56 8N 10 11 E
Ariadnoye 116 45 8N 134 25 E
Ariari → 70 2 35N 72 47W
Arica, Chile 72 18 32 S 70 20W
Arica, Colombia 70 2 0 S 71 50W
Arid, C. 126 34 1 S 123 10 E
Arida 117 34 5N 135 8 E
Aridh 106 25 0N 46 0 E
Ariège □ 90 42 56N 1 30 E
Ariel 53 45 57N 122 34W
Arieş → 95 46 24N 23 20 E
Arikaree → 34 40 1N 101 56W
Arima 67 10 38N 61 17W
Arimo 20 42 34N 112 10W
Arinos → 73 10 25 S 58 20W
Ario de Rosales 64 19 12N 102 0W
Arion 23 41 57N 95 27W
Aripuanã 73 9 25 S 60 30W
Aripuanã → 73 5 7 S 60 25W
Ariquemes 73 9 55 S 63 6W
Arisaig 84 56 55N 5 50W
Arismendi 70 8 29N 68 22W
Arispe 23 40 57N 94 13W
Aristazabal I. 62 52 40N 129 10W
Ariton 10 31 36N 85 43W
Arizaro, Salar de 76 24 40 S 67 50W
Arizona 76 35 45 S 65 25W
Arizona □ 12 34 0N 112 0W
Arizpe 64 30 20N 110 11W
Arjeplog 96 66 3N 18 2 E
Arjona 70 10 14N 75 22W
Arka 101 60 15N 142 0 E
Arkabutla L. 31 34 46N 90 8W
Arkadelphia 13 34 7N 93 4W
Arkaig, L. 84 56 58N 5 10W
Arkalyk 100 50 13N 66 50 E
Arkansas □ 13 35 0N 92 0W
Arkansas → 13 33 47N 91 4W
Arkansas City, Ark. 13 33 37N 91 12W
Arkansas City, Kans. 24 37 4N 97 2W
Arkansas County ◇ 13 34 18N 91 20W
Arkhangelsk 98 64 40N 41 0 E
Arklow 85 52 48N 6 10W

Arkoma **Atlantic Highlands**

Arkoma . . . 43 35 21N 94 26W
Arkport . . . 39 42 24N 77 42W
Arktícheskiy, Mys . . . 101 81 10N 95 0 E
Arlanzón → . . . 91 42 3N 4 17W
Arlberg Pass . . . 88 47 9N 10 12 E
Arlee . . . 33 47 10N 114 5W
Arles . . . 90 43 41N 4 40 E
Arley . . . 10 34 4N 87 13W
Arlington, Ariz. . . . 12 33 20N 112 46W
Arlington, Colo. . . . 16 38 20N 103 21W
Arlington, Ga. . . . 18 31 26N 84 44W
Arlington, Ill. . . . 21 41 29N 89 15W
Arlington, Iowa . . . 23 42 45N 91 40W
Arlington, Kans. . . . 24 37 54N 98 11W
Arlington, Ky. . . . 48 36 47N 89 1W
Arlington, Mass. . . . 28 42 25N 71 9W
Arlington, Minn. . . . 30 44 36N 94 5W
Arlington, N.Y. . . . 39 41 42N 73 54W
Arlington, Nebr. . . . 34 41 27N 96 21W
Arlington, Ohio . . . 42 40 54N 83 39W
Arlington, Oreg. . . . 44 45 43N 120 12W
Arlington, S. Dak. . . . 47 44 22N 97 8W
Arlington, Tenn. . . . 48 35 18N 89 40W
Arlington, Tex. . . . 51 32 44N 97 7W
Arlington, Va. . . . 54 38 53N 77 7W
Arlington, Vt. . . . 36 43 5N 73 9W
Arlington, Wash. . . . 53 48 12N 122 8W
Arlington, Wis. . . . 55 43 20N 89 23W
Arlington Heights . . . 21 42 5N 87 59W
Arlon . . . 87 49 42N 5 49 E
Arm . . . 31 31 30N 90 1W
Arma . . . 24 37 33N 94 42W
Armada . . . 29 42 51N 82 53W
Armagh . . . 85 54 22N 6 40W
Armagh □ . . . 85 54 18N 6 37W
Armagnac . . . 90 43 44N 0 10 E
Armavir . . . 99 45 2N 41 7 E
Armenia . . . 70 4 35N 75 45W
Armenian S.S.R. □ . . . 99 40 0N 44 0 E
Armidale . . . 127 30 30 S 151 40 E
Armijo . . . 38 35 4N 106 39W
Armona . . . 15 36 19N 119 42W
Armour . . . 47 43 19N 98 21W
Armourdale . . . 41 48 52N 99 23W
Armstrong, B.C., Canada . . . 62 50 25N 119 10W
Armstrong, Ont., Canada . . . 60 50 18N 89 4W
Armstrong, Iowa . . . 23 43 24N 94 29W
Armstrong, Mo. . . . 32 39 16N 92 42W
Armstrong, Tex. . . . 50 26 56N 97 47W
Armstrong County ◇, Pa. . . . 45 40 45N 79 25W
Armstrong County ◇, Tex. . . . 50 35 0N 101 20W
Arnaouti, C. . . . 106 35 6N 32 17 E
Arnarfjörður . . . 96 65 48N 23 40W
Arnaud → . . . 59 60 0N 70 0W
Arnaudville . . . 25 30 24N 91 56W
Arnegard . . . 41 47 49N 103 27W
Årnes . . . 96 66 1N 21 31W
Arnett . . . 43 36 8N 99 46W
Arnhem . . . 87 51 58N 5 55 E
Arnhem, C. . . . 127 12 20 S 137 30 E
Arnhem B. . . . 126 12 20 S 136 10 E
Arnhem Land . . . 126 13 10 S 134 30 E
Arno → . . . 94 43 41N 10 17 E
Arnold, Md. . . . 27 39 2N 76 30W
Arnold, Minn. . . . 30 46 53N 92 5W
Arnold, Mo. . . . 32 38 26N 90 23W
Arnold, Nebr. . . . 34 41 26N 100 12W
Arnolds Park . . . 23 43 22N 95 8W
Arnot . . . 63 55 56N 96 41W
Arnøy . . . 96 70 9N 20 40 E
Arnprior . . . 60 45 26N 76 21W
Aro → . . . 71 8 1N 64 11W
Aroab . . . 123 26 41 S 19 39 E
Arock . . . 44 42 55N 117 32W
Aroeiras . . . 74 7 31 S 35 41W
Aroma Park . . . 21 41 5N 87 48W
Aroostook → . . . 26 45 48N 67 45W
Aroostook County ◇ . . . 26 47 0N 69 0W
Arp . . . 51 32 14N 95 4W
Arpin . . . 55 44 33N 90 2W
Arque . . . 72 17 48 S 66 23W
Arraias . . . 75 12 56 S 46 57W
Arraias →, Mato Grosso, Brazil . . . 73 11 10 S 53 35W
Arraias →, Pará, Brazil . . . 74 7 30 S 49 20W
Arraijan . . . 57 8 56N 79 36W
Arran . . . 84 55 34N 5 12W
Arrandale . . . 62 54 57N 130 0W
Arras . . . 90 50 17N 2 46 E
Arrecife . . . 120 28 57N 13 37W
Arrecifes . . . 76 34 6 S 60 9W
Arrée, Mts. d' . . . 90 48 26N 3 55W
Arrey . . . 38 32 48N 107 19W
Arriaga, Chiapas, Mexico . . . 65 16 15N 93 52W
Arriaga, San Luis Potosí, Mexico . . . 64 21 55N 101 23W
Arriba . . . 16 39 17N 103 17W
Arrington . . . 24 39 28N 95 32W
Arrojado → . . . 75 13 24 S 44 20W
Arrow, L. . . . 85 54 3N 8 20W
Arrow Cr. → . . . 33 47 43N 109 50W
Arrow Rock . . . 32 39 4N 92 57W
Arrowhead . . . 62 50 40N 117 55W
Arrowhead, L. . . . 51 33 45N 98 25W
Arrowrock Reservoir . . . 20 43 36N 115 56W
Arrowsmith . . . 21 40 27N 88 38W
Arrowtown . . . 128 44 57 S 168 50 E
Arroyo . . . 57 17 58N 66 4W
Arroyo del Macho → . . . 38 33 49N 104 7W
Arroyo Grande . . . 15 35 7N 120 35W
Arroyo Hondo . . . 38 36 32N 105 40W
Arsenault L. . . . 63 55 6N 108 32W
Arsenev . . . 116 44 10N 133 15 E
Árta . . . 95 39 8N 21 2 E
Artas . . . 47 45 53N 99 49W
Arteaga . . . 64 18 50N 102 20W
Artemovsk, R.S.F.S.R., U.S.S.R. . . . 101 54 45N 93 35 E
Artemovsk, Ukraine S.S.R., U.S.S.R. . . . 99 48 35N 38 0 E
Arten . . . 116 43 22N 132 13 E
Artesia, Miss. . . . 31 33 25N 88 39W
Artesia, N. Mex. . . . 38 32 51N 104 24W
Artesia L. . . . 35 38 56N 119 22W
Artesia Wells . . . 51 28 17N 99 17W
Artesian . . . 47 44 1N 97 55W
Arthur, Ill. . . . 21 39 43N 88 28W
Arthur, N. Dak. . . . 41 47 6N 97 13W
Arthur, Nebr. . . . 34 41 35N 101 41W
Arthur, Tenn. . . . 49 36 33N 83 40W
Arthur County ◇ . . . 34 41 30N 101 40W
Arthur's Pass . . . 128 42 54 S 171 35 E
Arthur's Town . . . 67 24 38N 75 42W
Artigas . . . 76 30 20 S 56 30W
Artillery L. . . . 63 63 9N 107 52W
Artois, France . . . 90 50 20N 2 30 E
Artois, U.S.A. . . . 14 39 37N 122 12W
Artvin . . . 106 41 14N 41 44 E
Aru, Kepulauan . . . 111 6 0 S 134 30 E
Arua . . . 122 3 1N 30 58 E
Aruanã . . . 75 14 54 S 51 10W
Aruba . . . 67 12 30N 70 0W
Arumã . . . 71 4 44 S 62 8W
Arunachal Pradesh □ . . . 109 28 0N 95 0 E
Arusha . . . 122 3 20 S 36 40 E
Aruwimi → . . . 122 1 13N 23 36 E
Arvada, Colo. . . . 16 39 48N 105 5W
Arvada, Wyo. . . . 56 44 39N 106 8W
Arvayheer . . . 113 46 15N 102 48 E
Arvida . . . 61 48 25N 71 14W
Arvidsjaur . . . 96 65 35N 19 10 E
Arvika . . . 97 59 40N 12 36 E
Arvin . . . 15 35 12N 118 50W
Arxan . . . 114 47 11N 119 57 E
Arys . . . 100 42 26N 68 48 E
Arzamas . . . 98 55 27N 43 55 E
Arzew . . . 120 35 50N 0 23W
'As Saffānīyah . . . 106 28 5N 48 50 E
Aş Şāfī . . . 104 31 2N 35 28 E
As Salt . . . 104 32 2N 35 43 E
As Samāwah . . . 106 31 15N 45 15 E
As Samū' . . . 104 31 24N 35 4 E
As Sanamayn . . . 104 33 3N 36 10 E
As Sulaymānīyah . . . 106 24 9N 47 18 E
As Sumaymānīyah . . . 106 35 35N 45 29 E
As Summān . . . 106 25 0N 47 0 E
As Sūq . . . 106 21 58N 42 3 E
As Suwaydā' . . . 106 32 40N 36 30 E
As Suwayh . . . 107 22 10N 59 33 E
Aş Şuwayrah . . . 106 32 55N 45 0 E
Asahi-Gawa → . . . 117 34 36N 133 58 E
Asahigawa . . . 116 43 46N 142 22 E
Asansol . . . 109 23 40N 87 1 E
Asbestos . . . 61 45 47N 71 58W
Asbury . . . 32 37 16N 94 36W
Asbury Park . . . 37 40 13N 74 1W
Ascensión . . . 64 31 6N 107 59W
Ascensión, B. de la . . . 65 19 50N 87 20W
Ascension I. . . . 2 8 0 S 14 15W
Ascension Parish ◇ . . . 25 30 14N 90 55W
Aschaffenburg . . . 88 49 58N 9 8 E
Áscoli Piceno . . . 94 42 51N 13 34 E
Ascope . . . 72 7 46 S 79 8W
Ascotán . . . 76 21 45 S 68 17W
Ascutney . . . 36 43 24N 72 25W
Aseb . . . 105 13 0N 42 40 E
Asela . . . 121 8 0N 39 0 E
Asenovgrad . . . 95 42 1N 24 51 E
Ash Flat . . . 13 36 13N 91 37W
Ash Fork . . . 12 35 13N 112 29W
Ash Grove . . . 32 37 19N 93 35W
Ash Shām, Bādiyat . . . 106 32 0N 40 0 E
Ash Shāmīyah . . . 106 31 55N 44 35 E
Ash Shāriqah . . . 107 25 23N 55 26 E
Ash Shaţrah . . . 106 31 30N 46 10 E
Ash Shaykh, J. . . . 106 33 25N 35 50 E
Ash Shu'aybah . . . 106 27 53N 42 43 E
Ash Shu'bah . . . 106 28 54N 44 44 E
Ash Shūnah ash Shamālīyah . . . 104 32 37N 35 34 E
Asha . . . 98 55 0N 57 16 E
Ashaway . . . 28 41 25N 71 47W
Ashburn . . . 18 31 43N 83 39W
Ashburnham . . . 28 42 38N 71 55W
Ashburton . . . 128 43 53 S 171 48 E
Ashburton → . . . 126 21 40 S 114 56 E
Ashby, Minn. . . . 30 46 6N 95 49W
Ashby, Nebr. . . . 34 42 1N 101 56W
Ashby-de-la-Zouch . . . 82 52 45N 1 29W
Ashcroft . . . 62 50 40N 121 20W
Ashdod . . . 104 31 49N 34 35 E
Ashdot Yaaqov . . . 104 32 39N 35 35 E
Ashdown . . . 13 33 40N 94 8W
Ashe County ◇ . . . 40 36 25N 81 30W
Asheboro . . . 40 35 43N 79 49W
Asher . . . 43 34 59N 96 56W
Asherton . . . 51 28 27N 99 46W
Asherville . . . 24 39 24N 97 59W
Asheville . . . 40 35 36N 82 33W
Asheweig → . . . 60 54 17N 87 12W
Ashfield . . . 28 42 32N 72 48W
Ashford, U.K. . . . 83 51 8N 0 53 E
Ashford, Ala. . . . 10 31 11N 85 14W
Ashford, Wash. . . . 53 46 46N 122 2W
Ashibetsu . . . 116 43 31N 142 11 E
Ashikaga . . . 117 36 28N 139 29 E
Ashizuri-Zaki . . . 117 32 44N 133 0 E
Ashkhabad . . . 100 38 0N 57 50 E
Ashkum . . . 21 40 53N 87 57W
Ashland, Ala. . . . 10 33 16N 85 50W
Ashland, Ill. . . . 21 39 53N 90 1W
Ashland, Kans. . . . 24 37 11N 99 46W
Ashland, Ky. . . . 49 38 28N 82 38W
Ashland, La. . . . 25 32 9N 93 6W
Ashland, Maine . . . 26 46 38N 68 24W
Ashland, Miss. . . . 31 34 50N 89 11W
Ashland, Mo. . . . 32 38 47N 92 16W
Ashland, Mont. . . . 33 45 36N 106 16W
Ashland, N.H. . . . 36 43 42N 71 38W
Ashland, Nebr. . . . 34 41 3N 96 23W
Ashland, Ohio . . . 42 40 52N 82 19W
Ashland, Okla. . . . 43 34 46N 96 4W
Ashland, Oreg. . . . 44 42 12N 122 43W
Ashland, Va. . . . 54 37 46N 77 29W
Ashland, Wis. . . . 55 46 35N 90 53W
Ashland City . . . 48 36 17N 87 4W
Ashland County ◇, Ohio . . . 42 40 52N 82 19W
Ashland County ◇, Wis. . . . 55 46 35N 90 45W
Ashley, Ill. . . . 21 38 20N 89 11W
Ashley, Ind. . . . 22 41 32N 85 4W
Ashley, Mich. . . . 29 43 11N 84 29W
Ashley, N. Dak. . . . 41 46 2N 99 22W
Ashley, Ohio . . . 42 40 25N 82 57W
Ashley → . . . 52 40 20N 109 17W
Ashley County ◇ . . . 13 33 14N 91 48W
Ashley National Forest . . . 52 40 55N 110 0W
Ashmont . . . 62 54 7N 111 35W
Ashmore . . . 21 39 32N 88 1W
Ashmore Reef . . . 126 12 14 S 123 5 E
Ashokan Reservoir . . . 39 41 56N 74 13W
Ashq'elon . . . 104 31 42N 34 35 E
Ashtabula . . . 42 41 52N 80 47W
Ashtabula County ◇ . . . 42 41 40N 80 52W
Ashtabula L. . . . 41 47 2N 98 5W
Ashton, Idaho . . . 20 44 4N 111 27W
Ashton, Ill. . . . 21 41 52N 89 13W
Ashton, Iowa . . . 23 43 19N 95 47W
Ashton, Nebr. . . . 34 41 15N 98 48W
Ashton, R.I. . . . 28 41 56N 71 26W
Ashton, S. Dak. . . . 47 44 59N 98 31W
Ashton-under-Lyne . . . 82 53 30N 2 8W
Ashuanipi, L. . . . 61 52 45N 66 15W
Ashuelot → . . . 36 43 0N 72 29W
Ashville, Ala. . . . 10 33 50N 86 15W
Ashville, Fla. . . . 17 30 37N 83 39W
Ashville, Pa. . . . 45 40 34N 78 33W
Ashwood . . . 44 44 44N 120 45W
Asia . . . 102 45 0N 75 0 E
Asia, Kepulauan . . . 111 1 0N 131 13 E
Asidonhoppo . . . 71 3 50N 55 30W
Asifabad . . . 108 19 20N 79 24 E
Asike . . . 111 6 39 S 140 24 E
Asilah . . . 120 35 29N 6 0W
Asinara, G. dell' . . . 94 41 0N 8 30 E
Asinara I. . . . 94 41 5N 8 15 E
Asino . . . 100 57 0N 86 0 E
'Asīr □ . . . 105 18 40N 42 30 E
Asir, Ras . . . 105 11 55N 51 10 E
Askersund . . . 97 58 53N 14 55 E
Askewville . . . 40 36 7N 76 57W
Askja . . . 96 65 3N 16 48W
Askov . . . 30 46 12N 92 47W
Āsmār . . . 107 35 10N 71 27 E
Asmara = Asmera . . . 121 15 19N 38 55 E
Asmera . . . 121 15 19N 38 55 E
Asotin . . . 53 46 20N 117 3W
Asotin County ◇ . . . 53 46 8N 117 8W
Aspen . . . 16 39 11N 106 49W
Aspen Hill . . . 27 39 5N 77 5W
Aspermont . . . 50 33 8N 100 14W
Aspiring, Mt. . . . 128 44 23 S 168 46 E
Asquith . . . 63 52 8N 107 13W
Assam □ . . . 109 26 0N 93 0 E
Assaria . . . 24 38 41N 97 36W
Assateague I. . . . 27 38 15N 75 10W
Assateague Island National Seashore . . . 27 38 15N 75 10W
Assawompset Pond . . . 28 41 50N 70 55W
Asse . . . 87 50 24N 4 10 E
Assen . . . 87 53 0N 6 35 E
Assini . . . 120 5 9N 3 17W
Assiniboia . . . 63 49 40N 105 59W
Assiniboine → . . . 63 49 53N 97 8W
Assinippi . . . 28 42 10N 70 51W
Assis . . . 77 22 40 S 50 20W
Assisi . . . 94 43 4N 12 36 E
Assonet . . . 28 41 48N 71 4W
Assumption . . . 21 39 31N 89 3W
Assumption Parish ◇ . . . 25 30 0N 91 0W
Assynt, L. . . . 84 58 25N 5 15W
Astara . . . 99 38 30N 48 50 E
Astatula . . . 17 28 43N 81 44W
Asti . . . 94 44 54N 8 11 E
Astipálaia . . . 95 36 32N 26 22 E
Astorga . . . 91 42 29N 6 8W
Astoria, Ill. . . . 21 40 14N 90 21W
Astoria, Oreg. . . . 44 46 11N 123 50W
Astoria, S. Dak. . . . 47 44 34N 96 33W
Astrakhan . . . 99 46 25N 48 5 E
Astrakhan-Bazàr . . . 99 39 14N 48 30 E
Asturias □ . . . 91 43 15N 6 0W
Asunción . . . 76 25 10 S 57 30W
Asunción, La . . . 71 11 2N 63 53W
Aswân . . . 121 24 4N 32 57 E
Aswân High Dam = Sadd el Aali . . . 121 23 54N 32 54 E
Asyût . . . 121 27 11N 31 4 E
At Ţafīlah . . . 106 30 45N 35 30 E
At Ta'if . . . 105 21 5N 40 27 E
Aţ Ţur . . . 104 31 47N 35 14 E
Aţ Ţurrah . . . 104 32 39N 35 59 E
Atacama □ . . . 76 27 30 S 70 0W
Atacama, Desierto de . . . 76 24 0 S 69 20W
Atacama, Salar de . . . 76 23 30 S 68 20W
Ataco . . . 70 3 35N 75 23W
Atakpamé . . . 120 7 31N 1 13 E
Atalaya . . . 72 10 45 S 73 50W
Ataléia . . . 75 18 3 S 41 6W
Atami . . . 117 35 5N 139 4 E
Atapupu . . . 111 9 0 S 124 51 E
Atâr . . . 120 20 30N 13 5W
Atara . . . 101 63 10N 129 10 E
Atascadero . . . 15 35 29N 120 40W
Atascosa County ◇ . . . 51 28 55N 98 33W
Atasu . . . 100 48 30N 71 0 E
Atauro . . . 111 8 10 S 125 30 E
Atbara . . . 121 17 42N 33 59 E
'Atbara → . . . 121 17 40N 33 56 E
Atbasar . . . 100 51 48N 68 20 E
Atchafalaya → . . . 25 29 53N 91 28W
Atchafalaya B. . . . 25 29 25N 91 25W
Atchison . . . 24 39 34N 95 7W
Atchison County ◇, Kans. . . . 24 39 30N 95 15W
Atchison County ◇, Mo. . . . 32 40 25N 95 25W
Atco . . . 37 39 46N 74 53W
Ath . . . 87 50 38N 3 47 E
Athabasca . . . 62 54 45N 113 20W
Athabasca → . . . 63 58 40N 110 50W
Athabasca, L. . . . 63 59 15N 109 15W
Athboy . . . 85 53 37N 6 55W
Athena, Fla. . . . 17 29 59N 83 30W
Athena, Oreg. . . . 44 45 49N 118 30W
Athenry . . . 85 53 18N 8 45W
Athens = Athínai . . . 95 37 58N 23 46 E
Athens, Ala. . . . 10 34 48N 86 58W
Athens, Ga. . . . 18 33 57N 83 23W
Athens, Ill. . . . 21 39 58N 89 44W
Athens, La. . . . 25 32 39N 93 1W
Athens, Mich. . . . 29 42 5N 85 14W
Athens, N.Y. . . . 39 42 16N 73 49W
Athens, Ohio . . . 42 39 20N 82 6W
Athens, Pa. . . . 45 41 57N 76 31W
Athens, Tenn. . . . 49 35 27N 84 36W
Athens, Tex. . . . 51 32 12N 95 51W
Athens, Wis. . . . 55 45 2N 90 5W
Athens County ◇ . . . 42 39 20N 82 6W
Atherton . . . 127 17 17 S 145 30 E
Athínai . . . 95 37 58N 23 46 E
Athlone . . . 85 53 26N 7 57W
Athol, Idaho . . . 20 47 57N 116 42W
Athol, Mass. . . . 28 42 36N 72 14W
Athol, S. Dak. . . . 47 45 1N 98 36W
Atholl, Forest of . . . 84 56 51N 3 50W
Atholville . . . 61 47 59N 66 43W
Áthos . . . 95 40 9N 24 22 E
Athy . . . 85 53 0N 7 0W
Ati . . . 121 13 13N 18 20 E
Atico . . . 72 16 14 S 73 40W
Atikokan . . . 60 48 45N 91 37W
Atikonak L. . . . 61 52 40N 64 32W
Atka, U.S.A. . . . 11 52 12N 174 12W
Atka, U.S.S.R. . . . 101 60 50N 151 48 E
Atka I. . . . 11 52 7N 174 30W
Atkins . . . 13 35 14N 92 56W
Atkinson, Ga. . . . 18 31 13N 81 47W
Atkinson, Ill. . . . 21 41 25N 90 1W
Atkinson, N.C. . . . 40 34 32N 78 10W
Atkinson, Nebr. . . . 34 42 32N 98 59W
Atkinson County ◇ . . . 18 31 15N 82 50W
Atlanta, Ga. . . . 18 33 45N 84 23W
Atlanta, Idaho . . . 20 43 48N 115 8W
Atlanta, Ill. . . . 21 40 16N 89 14W
Atlanta, Ind. . . . 22 40 13N 86 2W
Atlanta, Kans. . . . 24 37 26N 96 46W
Atlanta, La. . . . 25 31 48N 92 45W
Atlanta, Mich. . . . 29 45 0N 84 9W
Atlanta, Mo. . . . 32 39 54N 92 29W
Atlanta, Nebr. . . . 34 40 22N 99 28W
Atlanta, Tex. . . . 51 33 7N 94 10W
Atlantic, Iowa . . . 23 41 24N 95 1W
Atlantic, N.C. . . . 40 34 54N 76 20W
Atlantic Beach . . . 17 30 20N 81 24W
Atlantic City . . . 37 39 21N 74 27W
Atlantic County ◇ . . . 37 39 30N 74 40W
Atlantic Highlands . . . 37 40 25N 74 3W

Atlantic Ocean **Baffin I.**

Atlantic Ocean **2** 0 0 20 0W
Atlantic Pk. **56** 42 37N 109 0W
Atlántico □ **70** 10 45N 75 0W
Atlin **62** 59 31N 133 41W
Atlin, L. **62** 59 26N 133 45W
'Atlit **104** 32 42N 34 56 E
Atmore **10** 31 2N 87 29W
Atoka **43** 34 23N 96 8W
Atoka County ◇ **43** 34 25N 96 0W
Atoka Reservoir **43** 34 27N 96 5W
Atomic City **20** 43 27N 112 49W
Atoyac → **65** 16 30N 97 31W
Atrak → **107** 37 50N 57 0 E
Atrato → **70** 8 17N 76 58W
Atsion **37** 39 44N 74 44W
Atsuta **116** 43 24N 141 26 E
Attala County ◇ **31** 33 4N 89 35W
Attalla **10** 34 1N 86 6W
Attapulgus **18** 30 45N 84 29W
Attawapiskat **60** 52 56N 82 24W
Attawapiskat → **60** 52 57N 82 18W
Attawapiskat, L. **60** 52 18N 87 54W
Attica, Ind. **22** 40 18N 87 15W
Attica, Kans. **24** 37 15N 98 13W
Attica, N.Y. **39** 42 52N 78 17W
Attica, Ohio **42** 41 4N 82 53W
Attikamagen L. **61** 55 0N 66 30W
'Attīl **104** 32 23N 35 4 E
Attleboro **28** 41 57N 71 17W
Attock **108** 33 52N 72 20 E
Attopeu **112** 14 48N 106 50 E
Attu **11** 52 56N 173 15 E
Attu I. **11** 52 55N 172 55 E
Attur **108** 11 35N 78 30 E
Atuel → **76** 36 17 S 66 50W
Åtvidaberg **97** 58 12N 16 0 E
Atwater, Calif. **14** 37 21N 120 37W
Atwater, Minn. **30** 45 8N 94 47W
Atwood, Colo. **16** 40 33N 103 16W
Atwood, Ill. **21** 39 48N 88 28W
Atwood, Kans. **24** 39 48N 101 3W
Atwood, Okla. **43** 34 57N 96 20W
Atwood, Tenn. **48** 35 59N 88 41W
Atwood L. **42** 40 33N 81 13W
Au Gres **29** 44 3N 83 42W
Au Sable **29** 44 25N 83 20W
Au Sable → **29** 44 25N 83 20W
Au Sable Forks **39** 44 27N 73 41W
Au Sable Pt., Mich. **29** 46 40N 86 8W
Au Sable Pt., Mich. **29** 44 20N 83 20W
Auau Channel **19** 20 50N 156 45W
Aube □ **90** 48 15N 4 0 E
Aube → **90** 48 34N 3 43 E
Aubrey **13** 34 43N 90 54W
Aubrey Cliffs **12** 35 45N 113 0W
Auburn, Ala. **10** 32 36N 85 29W
Auburn, Calif. **14** 38 54N 121 4W
Auburn, Ill. **21** 39 36N 89 45W
Auburn, Ind. **22** 41 22N 85 4W
Auburn, Iowa **23** 42 15N 94 53W
Auburn, Kans. **24** 38 54N 95 49W
Auburn, Ky. **48** 36 52N 86 43W
Auburn, Maine **26** 44 6N 70 14W
Auburn, Mass. **28** 42 12N 71 50W
Auburn, Mich. **29** 43 36N 84 4W
Auburn, Miss. **31** 31 22N 90 37W
Auburn, N.Y. **39** 42 56N 76 34W
Auburn, Nebr. **34** 40 23N 95 51W
Auburn, W. Va. **54** 39 6N 80 51W
Auburn, Wash. **53** 47 18N 122 14W
Auburndale, Fla. **17** 28 4N 81 48W
Auburndale, Wis. **55** 44 38N 90 0W
Auburntown **48** 35 57N 86 5W
Aubusson **90** 45 57N 2 11 E
Auch **90** 43 39N 0 36 E
Aucilla → **17** 30 5N 83 59W
Auckland **128** 36 52 S 174 46 E
Auckland Is. **124** 50 40 S 166 5 E
Aude □ **90** 43 8N 2 28 E
Aude → **90** 43 13N 3 14 E
Auden **60** 50 14N 87 53W
Audrain County ◇ **32** 39 10N 91 50W
Audubon, Iowa **23** 41 43N 94 56W
Audubon, Minn. **30** 46 52N 95 59W
Audubon County ◇ **23** 41 40N 94 50W
Aueti Paraná → **70** 1 51 S 65 37W
Augathella **127** 25 48 S 146 35 E
Auglaize County ◇ **42** 40 34N 84 12W
Augsburg **88** 48 22N 10 54 E
Augusta, Italy **94** 37 14N 15 12 E
Augusta, Ark. **13** 35 17N 91 22W
Augusta, Ga. **18** 33 28N 81 58W
Augusta, Ill. **21** 40 14N 90 57W
Augusta, Kans. **24** 37 41N 96 59W
Augusta, Ky. **49** 38 47N 84 0W
Augusta, Maine **26** 44 19N 69 47W
Augusta, Mo. **32** 38 34N 90 53W
Augusta, Mont. **33** 47 30N 112 24W
Augusta, N.J. **37** 41 8N 74 44W
Augusta, W. Va. **54** 39 18N 78 38W
Augusta, Wis. **55** 44 41N 91 7W
Augusta County ◇ **54** 38 9N 79 4W
Augustine I. **11** 59 22N 153 26W
Augustów **89** 53 51N 23 0 E
Augustus, Mt. **126** 24 20 S 116 50 E
Aulander **40** 36 14N 77 6W
Aullville **32** 39 1N 93 41W
Ault **16** 40 35N 104 44W
Aunis **90** 46 5N 0 50W
Auponhia **111** 1 58 S 125 27 E
Aurangabad, Bihar, India **109** 24 45N 84 18 E
Aurangabad, Maharashtra, India **108** 19 50N 75 23 E
Aurelia **23** 42 43N 95 26W
Aurilândia **75** 16 44 S 50 28W
Aurillac **90** 44 55N 2 26 E
Aurora, Colo. **16** 39 44N 104 52W
Aurora, Ill. **21** 41 45N 88 19W
Aurora, Ind. **22** 39 4N 84 54W
Aurora, Iowa **23** 42 37N 91 44W
Aurora, Kans. **24** 39 27N 97 32W
Aurora, Ky. **48** 36 47N 88 9W
Aurora, Maine **26** 44 51N 68 20W
Aurora, Minn. **30** 47 32N 92 14W
Aurora, Mo. **32** 36 58N 93 43W
Aurora, N.C. **40** 35 18N 76 47W
Aurora, N.Y. **39** 42 45N 76 42W
Aurora, Nebr. **34** 40 52N 98 0W
Aurora, S. Dak. **47** 44 17N 96 41W
Aurora, W. Va. **54** 39 19N 79 33W
Aurora County ◇ **47** 43 43N 98 29W
Aus **123** 26 35 S 16 12 E
Aust-Agder fylke □ **97** 58 55N 7 40 E
Austerlitz = Slavkov **88** 49 10N 16 52 E
Austin, Ark. **13** 35 0N 92 0W
Austin, Ind. **22** 38 45N 85 49W
Austin, Minn. **30** 43 40N 92 58W
Austin, Mont. **33** 46 39N 112 15W
Austin, Nev. **35** 39 30N 117 4W
Austin, Pa. **45** 41 38N 78 6W
Austin, Tex. **51** 30 17N 97 45W
Austin, L. **126** 27 40 S 118 0 E
Austin County ◇ **51** 29 57N 96 15W
Austintown **42** 41 6N 80 48W
Austinville **54** 36 51N 80 55W
Austral Downs **127** 20 30 S 137 45 E
Austral Is. = Tubuai Is. **125** 25 0 S 150 0W
Austral Seamount Chain **125** 24 0 S 150 0W
Australia ■ **124** 23 0 S 135 0 E
Australian Alps **127** 36 30 S 148 30 E
Australian Cap. Terr. □ **127** 35 30 S 149 0 E
Australian Dependency □ **5** 73 0 S 90 0 E
Austria ■ **88** 47 0N 14 0 E
Austvågøy **96** 68 20N 14 40 E
Austwell **51** 28 23N 96 51W
Autauga County ◇ **10** 32 26N 86 39W
Autaugaville **10** 32 26N 86 39W
Autazes **71** 3 35 S 59 8W
Autlán **64** 19 40N 104 30W
Autun **90** 46 58N 4 17 E
Auvergne **90** 45 20N 3 15 E
Auxerre **90** 47 48N 3 32 E
Auxvasse **32** 39 1N 91 54W
Auxvasse → **32** 38 41N 91 49W
Ava, Ill. **21** 37 53N 89 30W
Ava, Mo. **32** 36 57N 92 40W
Avallon **90** 47 30N 3 53 E
Avalon, Calif. **15** 33 21N 118 20W
Avalon, Miss. **31** 33 39N 90 5W
Avalon, N.J. **37** 39 6N 74 43W
Avalon, L. **38** 32 27N 104 15W
Avalon Pen. **61** 47 30N 53 20W
Avant **43** 36 29N 96 4W
Avaré **77** 23 4 S 48 58W
Avawatz Mts. **15** 35 40N 116 30W
Aveiro, Brazil **71** 3 10 S 55 5W
Aveiro, Portugal **91** 40 37N 8 38W
Āvej **106** 35 40N 49 15 E
Avellaneda **76** 34 50 S 58 10W
Avellino **94** 40 54N 14 46 E
Avenal **15** 36 0N 120 8W
Avenue **27** 38 16N 76 46W
Avera **18** 33 12N 82 32W
Aversa **94** 40 58N 14 11 E
Avery, Idaho **20** 47 15N 115 49W
Avery, Tex. **51** 33 33N 94 47W
Avery County ◇ **40** 36 5N 82 0W
Avery Island **25** 29 55N 91 54W
Aves, I. de **67** 15 45N 63 55W
Aves, Is. de **67** 12 0N 67 30W
Avesta **97** 60 9N 16 10 E
Aveyron □ **90** 44 22N 2 45 E
Aviá Terai **76** 26 45 S 60 50W
Avignon **90** 43 57N 4 50 E
Ávila **91** 40 39N 4 43W
Avilés **91** 43 35N 5 57W
Avilla, Ind. **22** 41 22N 85 14W
Avilla, Mo. **32** 37 8N 94 8W
Avinger **51** 32 54N 94 33W
Avis **45** 41 11N 77 19W
Avoca, Ireland **85** 52 52N 6 13W
Avoca, Iowa **23** 41 29N 95 20W
Avoca, Minn. **30** 43 57N 95 39W
Avoca, N.Y. **39** 42 25N 77 25W
Avoca, Nebr. **34** 40 48N 96 7W
Avoca, Tex. **51** 32 52N 99 43W
Avola **62** 51 45N 119 19W
Avon, Colo. **16** 39 38N 106 31W
Avon, Conn. **28** 41 49N 72 50W
Avon, Ill. **21** 40 40N 90 26W
Avon, Mont. **33** 46 36N 112 36W
Avon, N.C. **40** 35 21N 75 30W
Avon, N.Y. **39** 42 55N 77 45W
Avon, S. Dak. **47** 43 0N 98 4W
Avon □ **83** 51 30N 2 40W
Avon →, Avon, U.K. **83** 51 30N 2 43W
Avon →, Hants., U.K. **83** 50 44N 1 45W
Avon →, Warwick, U.K. **83** 52 0N 2 9W
Avon, Îles **127** 19 37 S 158 17 E
Avon Park **17** 27 36N 81 31W
Avondale, Ariz. **12** 33 26N 112 21W
Avondale, Colo. **16** 38 14N 104 21W
Avondale, Pa. **45** 39 50N 75 47W
Avonlea **63** 50 0N 105 0W
Avonmore **45** 40 32N 79 28W
Avonmouth **83** 51 30N 2 42W
Avoyelles Parish ◇ **25** 31 0N 92 0W
Avramov **95** 42 45N 26 38 E
Avranches **90** 48 40N 1 20W
Avrig **95** 45 43N 24 21 E
Awaji-Shima **117** 34 30N 134 50 E
'Awālī **107** 26 0N 50 30 E
'Awartā **104** 32 10N 35 17 E
Awash **105** 9 1N 40 10 E
Awatere → **128** 41 37 S 174 10 E
Awbārī **121** 26 46N 12 57 E
Awe, L. **84** 56 15N 5 15W
Awjilah **121** 29 8N 21 7 E
Axarfjörður **96** 66 15N 16 45W
Axel Heiberg I. **4** 80 0N 90 0W
Axial **16** 40 17N 107 47W
Axim **120** 4 51N 2 15W
Axinim **71** 4 2 S 59 22W
Axintele **95** 44 37N 26 47 E
Axioma **73** 6 45 S 64 31W
Axminster **83** 50 47N 3 1W
Axson **18** 31 17N 82 44W
Axtell, Kans. **24** 39 52N 96 15W
Axtell, Nebr. **34** 40 29N 99 8W
Ayabaca **72** 4 40 S 79 53W
Ayabe **117** 35 20N 135 20 E
Ayacucho, Argentina **76** 37 5 S 58 20W
Ayacucho, Peru **72** 13 0 S 74 0W
Ayaguz **100** 48 10N 80 0 E
Ayamonte **91** 37 12N 7 24W
Ayan **101** 56 30N 138 16 E
Ayapel **70** 8 19N 75 9W
Ayaviri **72** 14 50 S 70 35W
Āybak **107** 36 15N 68 5 E
Ayden **40** 35 28N 77 20W
Ayer **28** 42 34N 71 35W
Ayeritam **112** 5 24N 100 15 E
Ayers Rock **126** 25 23 S 131 5 E
Ayíos Evstrátios **95** 39 34N 24 58 E
Aykin **98** 62 15N 49 56 E
Aylesbury **83** 51 48N 0 49W
Aylmer L. **58** 64 0N 110 8W
'Ayn 'Arīk **104** 31 54N 35 8 E
Ayn Dār **106** 25 55N 49 10 E
Ayn Zālah **106** 36 45N 42 35 E
Aynor **46** 34 0N 79 12W
Ayolas **76** 27 10 S 56 59W
Ayon, Ostrov **101** 69 50N 169 0 E
Ayr, Australia **127** 19 35 S 147 25 E
Ayr, U.K. **84** 55 28N 4 37W
Ayr, N. Dak. **41** 47 3N 97 29W
Ayr, Nebr. **34** 40 26N 98 26W
Ayr → **84** 55 29N 4 40W
Ayre, Pt. of **82** 54 27N 4 21W
Ayshire **23** 43 2N 94 50W
Aytos **95** 42 42N 27 16 E
Aytoska Planina **95** 42 45N 27 30 E
Ayu, Kepulauan **111** 0 35N 131 5 E
Ayutla, Guat. **66** 14 40N 92 10W
Ayutla, Mexico **65** 16 58N 99 17W
Ayvalık **106** 39 20N 26 46 E
Az Ẓahrān **106** 26 10N 50 7 E
Az Zarqā **104** 32 5N 36 4 E
Az-Zilfī **106** 26 12N 44 52 E
Az Zubayr **106** 30 20N 47 50 E
Azamgarh **109** 26 5N 83 13 E
Azangaro **72** 14 55 S 70 13W
Āzarbāyjān-e Gharbī □ **106** 37 0N 44 30 E
Āzarbāyjān-e Sharqī □ **106** 37 20N 47 0 E
Azare **120** 11 55N 10 10 E
Azbine = Aïr **120** 18 30N 8 0 E
Azerbaijan S.S.R. □ **99** 40 20N 48 0 E
Aziscohos L. **26** 45 0N 71 0W
Azle **51** 32 54N 97 32W
Azogues **70** 2 35 S 78 0W
Azor **104** 32 2N 34 48 E
Azores **2** 38 44N 29 0W
Azov **99** 47 3N 39 25 E
Azov Sea = Azovskoye More **99** 46 0N 36 30 E
Azovskoye More **99** 46 0N 36 30 E
Azovy **100** 64 55N 64 35 E
Aztec, Ariz. **12** 32 49N 113 27W
Aztec, N. Mex. **38** 36 49N 107 59W
Aztec Peak **12** 33 49N 110 54W
Azúa de Compostela **67** 18 25N 70 44W
Azuaga **91** 38 16N 5 39W
Azuay □ **70** 2 55 S 79 0W
Azuero, Pen. de **66** 7 30N 80 30W
Azul **76** 36 42 S 59 43W
Azul, Serra **73** 14 50 S 54 50W
Azurduy **73** 19 59 S 64 29W
Azusa **15** 34 8N 117 52W

B

B. A. Steinhagen L. **51** 30 50N 94 15W
B. Everett Jordan L. **40** 35 30N 79 0W
Ba Don **112** 17 45N 106 26 E
Ba Ngoi = Cam Lam **112** 11 54N 109 10 E
Ba Ria **112** 10 30N 107 10 E
Ba Xian **114** 39 8N 116 22 E
Baa **111** 10 50 S 123 0 E
Baarle Nassau **87** 51 27N 4 56 E
Baarn **87** 52 12N 5 17 E
Bāb el Māndeb **105** 12 35N 43 25 E
Baba **95** 42 44N 23 59 E
Babaçulândia **74** 7 13 S 47 46W
Babadag **95** 44 53N 28 44 E
Babaeski **95** 41 26N 27 6 E
Babahoyo **70** 1 40 S 79 30W
Babana **120** 10 31N 3 46 E
Babar **111** 8 0 S 129 30 E
Babb **33** 48 51N 113 27W
Babbitt, Minn. **30** 47 41N 91 54W
Babbitt, Nev. **35** 38 32N 118 39W
Babbs **43** 34 57N 99 3W
Babine **62** 55 22N 126 37W
Babine → **62** 55 45N 127 44W
Babine L. **62** 54 48N 126 0W
Babo **111** 2 30 S 133 30 E
Bābol **107** 36 40N 52 50 E
Bābol Sar **107** 36 45N 52 45 E
Baboquivari Peak **12** 31 46N 111 36W
Baboua **122** 5 49N 14 58 E
Babson Park **17** 27 49N 81 32W
Babura **120** 12 51N 8 59 E
Babuyan Chan. **111** 18 40N 121 30 E
Babylon, Iraq **106** 32 40N 44 30 E
Babylon, U.S.A. **39** 40 42N 73 19W
Bac Kan **112** 22 5N 105 50 E
Bac Ninh **112** 21 13N 106 4 E
Bac Phan **112** 22 0N 105 0 E
Bac Quang **112** 22 30N 104 48 E
Baca County ◇ **16** 37 15N 102 30W
Bacabal **74** 4 15 S 44 45W
Bacajá → **71** 3 25 S 51 50W
Bacalar **65** 18 50N 87 27W
Bacan **111** 8 27 S 126 27 E
Bacan, Kepulauan **111** 0 35 S 127 30 E
Bacan, Pulau **111** 0 50 S 127 30 E
Bacarra **111** 18 15N 120 37 E
Bacău **89** 46 35N 26 55 E
Bacău □ **95** 46 30N 26 45 E
Bacerac **64** 30 18N 108 50W
Bachaquero **70** 9 56N 71 8W
Bachelina **100** 57 45N 67 20 E
Back → **58** 65 10N 104 0W
Back B. **54** 36 35N 75 57W
Backbone Mt. **27** 39 12N 79 28W
Backstairs Passage **127** 35 40 S 138 5 E
Backus **30** 46 49N 94 31W
Bacolod **111** 10 40N 122 57 E
Bacon County ◇ **18** 31 30N 82 30W
Baconton **18** 31 23N 84 10W
Bad → **47** 44 21N 100 22W
Bad Axe **29** 43 48N 83 0W
Bad Ischl **88** 47 44N 13 38 E
Bad River Indian Reservation **55** 46 30N 90 45W
Badagara **108** 11 35N 75 40 E
Badajós, L. **71** 3 15 S 62 50W
Badajoz **91** 38 50N 6 59W
Badakhshān □ **107** 36 30N 71 0 E
Badalona **91** 41 26N 2 15 E
Badalzai **108** 29 50N 65 35 E
Badampahar **109** 22 10N 86 10 E
Badanah **106** 30 58N 41 30 E
Badarinath **108** 30 45N 79 30 E
Badas **110** 4 33N 114 25 E
Badas, Kepulauan **110** 0 45N 107 5 E
Baddo → **107** 28 0N 64 20 E
Bade **111** 7 10 S 139 35 E
Baden, Austria **88** 48 1N 16 13 E
Baden, U.S.A. **45** 40 38N 80 14W
Baden-Baden **88** 48 45N 8 15 E
Baden-Württemberg □ **88** 48 40N 9 0 E
Badgastein **88** 47 7N 13 9 E
Badger, Canada **61** 49 0N 56 4W
Badger, Iowa **23** 42 37N 94 9W
Badger, Minn. **30** 48 47N 96 1W
Badger → **16** 40 17N 103 42W
Bādghīsāt □ **107** 35 0N 63 0 E
Badin, Pakistan **108** 24 38N 68 54 E
Badin, U.S.A. **40** 35 24N 80 6W
Badin L. **40** 35 25N 80 6W
Badlands **47** 43 55N 102 30W
Badlands National Park **47** 43 38N 102 56W
Badong **115** 31 1N 110 23 E
Baduen **105** 7 15N 47 40 E
Badulla **108** 7 1N 81 7 E
Badwater Cr. → **56** 43 17N 108 8W
Baeza, Ecuador **70** 0 25 S 77 53W
Baeza, Spain **91** 37 57N 3 25W
Bafatá **120** 12 8N 14 40W
Baffin B., Canada **4** 72 0N 64 0W
Baffin B., U.S.A. **50** 27 18N 97 30W
Baffin I. **59** 68 0N 75 0W

Bafia Banyo

Bafia 122 4 40N 11 10 E
Bafing → 120 13 49N 10 50W
Bafoulabé 120 13 50N 10 55W
Bāfq 107 31 40N 55 25 E
Bafra 106 41 34N 35 54 E
Bāft 107 29 15N 56 38 E
Bafwasende 122 1 3N 27 5 E
Bagamoyo 122 6 28 S 38 55 E
Baganga 111 7 34N 126 33 E
Bagansiapiapi 110 2 12N 100 50 E
Bagdad, Ariz. 12 34 34N 113 11W
Bagdad, Fla. 17 30 36N 87 2W
Bagdad, Ky. 49 38 16N 85 3W
Bagdarin 101 54 26N 113 36 E
Bagé 77 31 20 S 54 15W
Bagenalstown = Muine Bheag 85 52 42N 6 57W
Baggs 56 41 2N 107 39W
Baghdād 106 33 20N 44 30 E
Baghlān 107 36 12N 69 0 E
Baghlān □ 107 36 0N 68 30 E
Bagley 30 47 32N 95 24W
Bagotville 61 48 22N 70 54W
Bagua 72 5 35 S 78 22W
Baguio 111 16 26N 120 34 E
Bahama 40 36 10N 78 53W
Bahama, Canal Viejo de 66 22 10N 77 30W
Bahamas ■ 67 24 0N 75 0W
Baharampur 109 24 2N 88 27 E
Bahau 112 2 48N 102 26 E
Bahawalpur 108 29 24N 71 40 E
Bahía = Salvador 75 13 0 S 38 30W
Bahía □ 75 12 0 S 42 0W
Bahía, Islas de la 66 16 45N 86 15W
Bahía Blanca 76 38 35 S 62 13W
Bahía de Caráquez 70 0 40 S 80 27W
Bahía Honda 66 22 54N 83 10W
Bahía Laura 78 48 10 S 66 30W
Bahía Negra 73 20 5 S 58 5W
Bahr Aouk → 122 8 40N 19 0 E
Bahr el Ahmar □ 121 20 0N 35 0 E
Bahr el Ghazâl □ 121 7 0N 28 0 E
Bahr el Jebel → 121 7 30N 30 30 E
Bahr Salamat → 121 9 20N 18 0 E
Bahraich 109 27 38N 81 37 E
Bahrain ■ 107 26 0N 50 35 E
Bai Bung, Mui 112 8 38N 104 44 E
Baia Mare 89 47 40N 23 35 E
Baião 74 2 40 S 49 40W
Baïbokoum 121 7 46N 15 43 E
Baicheng 114 45 38N 122 42 E
Băicoi 95 45 3N 25 52 E
Baidoa 105 3 8N 43 30 E
Baie Comeau 61 49 12N 68 10W
Baie-St-Paul 61 47 28N 70 32W
Baie Trinité 61 49 25N 67 20W
Baie Verte 61 49 55N 56 12W
Ba'ījī 106 35 0N 43 30 E
Baikal, L. = Baykal, Oz. 101 53 0N 108 0 E
Baile Atha Cliath = Dublin 85 53 20N 6 18W
Băileşti 95 44 1N 23 20 E
Bailey 16 39 25N 105 29W
Bailey County ◇ 50 34 0N 102 55W
Baileys Harbor 55 45 4N 87 8W
Baileyton 49 36 20N 82 50W
Baileyville 24 39 51N 96 11W
Bailique, Ilha 74 1 2N 49 58W
Bailundo 123 12 10 S 15 50 E
Bainbridge, Ga. 18 30 55N 84 35W
Bainbridge, Ind. 22 39 46N 86 49W
Bainbridge, N.Y. 39 42 18N 75 29W
Bainbridge, Ohio 42 39 14N 83 16W
Baing 111 10 14 S 120 34 E
Bainville 33 48 8N 104 13W
Bā'ir 106 30 45N 36 55 E
Baird 51 32 24N 99 24W
Baird Mts. 11 67 0N 160 0W
Bairin Youqi 114 43 30N 118 35 E
Bairin Zuoqi 114 43 58N 119 15 E
Bairnsdale 127 37 48 S 147 36 E
Bairoil 56 42 15N 107 33W
Baitadi 109 29 35N 80 25 E
Baixa Grande 75 11 57 S 40 11W
Baiyin 114 36 45N 104 14 E
Baiyu Shan 114 37 15N 107 30 E
Baja 89 46 12N 18 59 E
Baja, Pta. 64 29 50N 116 0W
Baja California 64 31 10N 115 12W
Bajo Nuevo 66 15 40N 78 50W
Bakala 122 6 15N 20 20 E
Bakchav 100 57 1N 82 5 E
Bakel 120 14 56N 12 20W
Baker, Calif. 15 35 16N 116 4W
Baker, Fla. 17 30 48N 86 41W
Baker, Idaho 20 45 6N 113 44W
Baker, La. 25 30 35N 91 10W
Baker, Mont. 33 46 22N 104 17W
Baker, N. Dak. 41 48 10N 99 39W
Baker, Okla. 43 36 52N 101 1W
Baker, Oreg. 44 44 47N 117 50W
Baker, Canal 78 47 45 S 74 45W
Baker, L. 58 64 0N 96 0W
Baker, Mt. 53 48 47N 121 49W
Baker Butte 12 34 27N 111 22W
Baker County ◇, Fla. 17 30 20N 82 15W
Baker County ◇, Ga. 18 31 20N 84 30W
Baker County ◇, Oreg. 44 44 40N 117 50W
Baker Hill 10 31 47N 85 18W
Baker I. 124 0 10N 176 35W
Baker Lake 58 64 20N 96 3W
Baker's Dozen Is. 60 56 45N 78 45W
Bakersfield, Calif. 15 35 23N 119 1W
Bakersfield, Tex. 50 30 54N 102 18W
Bakersfield, Vt. 36 44 45N 72 48W
Bakhtārān 106 34 23N 47 30E
Bakinskikh Komissarov, im. 26 106 39 20N 49 15 E
Bakırköy 95 40 59N 28 53 E
Bakkafjörður 96 66 2N 14 48W
Bakkagerði 96 65 31N 13 49W
Bakony Forest = Bakony Hegység 89 47 10N 17 30 E
Bakony Hegység 89 47 10N 17 30 E
Bakouma 122 5 40N 22 56 E
Baku 99 40 25N 49 45 E
Bakutis Coast 5 74 0 S 120 0W
Bal'ā, Jordan 104 32 20N 35 6 E
Bala, U.S.A. 24 39 19N 96 57W
Bala, L. = Tegid, L. 82 52 53N 3 38W
Balabac, Str. 110 7 53N 117 5 E
Balabac I. 110 8 0N 117 0 E
Balabakk 106 34 0N 36 10 E
Balabalangan, Kepulauan 110 2 20 S 117 30 E
Bălăciţa 95 44 23N 23 8 E
Balaghat 108 21 49N 80 12 E
Balaghat Ra. 108 18 50N 76 30 E
Balaguer 91 41 50N 0 50 E
Balaklava 99 44 30N 33 30 E
Balakovo 98 52 4N 47 55 E
Balancán 65 17 48N 91 32W
Balashov 98 51 30N 43 10 E
Balasore = Baleshwar 109 21 35N 87 3 E
Balaton, Hungary 89 46 50N 17 40 E
Balaton, U.S.A. 30 44 14N 95 52W
Balboa, Panama 57 8 57N 79 34W
Balboa Hill 57 9 6N 79 44W
Balbriggan 85 53 35N 6 10W
Balcarce 76 38 0 S 58 10W
Balcarres 63 50 50N 103 35W
Balch Springs 51 32 43N 96 38W
Balchik 95 43 28N 28 11 E
Balclutha 128 46 15 S 169 45 E
Balcones Escarpment 50 29 30N 99 15W
Balcones Heights 51 29 26N 98 36W
Bald Creek 40 35 55N 82 25W
Bald Knob, Ark. 13 35 19N 91 34W
Bald Knob, Va. 54 37 56N 79 51W
Bald Knoll 56 42 22N 110 28W
Bald Mt. 44 43 16N 121 21W
Baldock L. 63 56 33N 97 57W
Baldwin, Fla. 17 30 18N 81 59W
Baldwin, Ga. 18 34 30N 83 32W
Baldwin, Ill. 21 38 11N 89 51W
Baldwin, La. 25 29 50N 91 33W
Baldwin, Mich. 29 43 54N 85 51W
Baldwin, N. Dak. 41 47 2N 100 45W
Baldwin, N.Y. 39 40 39N 73 36W
Baldwin, Pa. 45 40 23N 79 59W
Baldwin, Wis. 55 44 58N 92 22W
Baldwin City 24 38 47N 95 11W
Baldwin County ◇, Ala. 10 30 53N 87 46W
Baldwin County ◇, Ga. 18 33 5N 83 10W
Baldwinsville 39 43 10N 76 20W
Baldwinville 28 42 37N 72 5W
Baldwyn 31 34 31N 88 38W
Baldy Peak 12 33 54N 109 34W
Baldy Pk. 38 36 38N 105 13W
Baleares, Islas 91 39 30N 3 0 E
Balearic Is. = Baleares, Islas 91 39 30N 3 0 E
Baleia,Punta da 75 17 40 S 39 7W
Băleni 95 45 48N 27 51 E
Baler 111 15 46N 121 34 E
Baleshwar 109 21 35N 87 3 E
Balfate 66 15 48N 86 25W
Balfour 41 47 57N 100 32W
Balfouriyya 104 32 38N 35 18 E
Bali, Cameroon 120 5 54N 10 0 E
Bali, Indonesia 110 8 20 S 115 0 E
Bali □ 110 8 20 S 115 0 E
Bali, Selat 111 8 18 S 114 25 E
Balikesir 106 39 35N 27 58 E
Balikpapan 110 1 10 S 116 55 E
Balimbing 111 5 5N 119 58 E
Baling 112 5 41N 100 55 E
Balipara 109 26 50N 92 45 E
Baliza 73 16 0 S 52 20W
Balkan Mts. = Stara Planina 95 43 15N 23 0 E
Balkan Pen. 80 42 0N 22 0 E
Balkh 107 36 44N 66 47 E
Balkh □ 107 36 30N 67 0 E
Balkhash 100 46 50N 74 50 E
Balkhash, Ozero 100 46 0N 74 50 E
Balko 43 36 38N 100 41W
Ball 25 31 25N 92 25W
Ball Ground 18 34 20N 84 23W
Balla 109 24 10N 91 35 E
Ballachulish 84 56 40N 5 10W
Ballantine 33 45 57N 108 9W
Ballarat 127 37 33 S 143 50 E
Ballard, L. 126 29 20 S 120 10 E
Ballard County ◇ 48 37 0N 89 0W
Ballater 84 57 2N 3 2W
Ballenas, Canal de las 64 29 10N 113 45W
Balleny Is. 5 66 30 S 163 0 E
Ballina, Australia 127 28 50 S 153 31 E
Ballina, Mayo, Ireland 85 54 7N 9 10W
Ballina, Tipp., Ireland 85 52 49N 8 27W
Ballinasloe 85 53 20N 8 12W
Ballinger 51 31 45N 99 57W
Ballinrobe 85 53 36N 9 13W
Ballinskelligs B. 85 51 46N 10 11W
Ballston Spa 39 43 0N 73 51W
Balltown 23 42 38N 90 51W
Bally 45 40 24N 75 35W
Ballycastle 85 55 12N 6 15W
Ballymena 85 54 53N 6 18W
Ballymena □ 85 54 53N 6 18W
Ballymoney 85 55 5N 6 30W
Ballymoney □ 85 55 5N 6 23W
Ballyshannon 85 54 30N 8 10W
Balmaceda 78 46 0 S 71 50W
Balmoral 84 57 3N 3 13W
Balmorhea 50 30 59N 103 45W
Balonne → 127 28 47 S 147 56 E
Balrampur 109 27 30N 82 20 E
Balranald 127 34 38 S 143 33 E
Balş 95 44 22N 24 5 E
Balsam Lake 55 45 27N 92 27W
Balsapuerto 72 5 48 S 76 33W
Balsas 65 18 0N 99 40W
Balsas →, Goiás, Brazil 74 9 58 S 47 52W
Balsas →, Maranhão, Brazil 74 7 15 S 44 35W
Balsas →, Mexico 64 17 55N 102 10W
Balta, Romania 95 44 54N 22 38 E
Balta, U.S.A. 41 48 10N 100 2W
Balta, U.S.S.R. 99 48 2N 29 45 E
Baltic, Conn. 28 41 37N 72 5W
Baltic, Ohio 42 40 26N 81 42W
Baltic, S. Dak. 47 43 46N 96 44W
Baltic Sea 97 56 0N 20 0 E
Baltimore, Ireland 85 51 29N 9 22W
Baltimore, Md. 27 39 17N 76 37W
Baltimore, Ohio 42 39 51N 82 36W
Baltimore County ◇ 27 39 20N 76 40W
Baluchistan □ 107 27 30N 65 0 E
Balygychan 101 63 56N 154 12 E
Balzar 70 2 2 S 79 54W
Bam 107 29 7N 58 14 E
Bama 121 11 33N 13 41 E
Bamako 120 12 34N 7 55W
Bamba 120 17 5N 1 24W
Bambamarca 72 6 36 S 78 32W
Bambari 122 5 40N 20 35 E
Bamberg, Germany 88 49 54N 10 53 E
Bamberg, U.S.A. 46 33 18N 81 2W
Bamberg County ◇ 46 33 10N 81 0W
Bambili 122 3 40N 26 0 E
Bambuí 75 20 1 S 45 58W
Bamenda 120 5 57N 10 11 E
Bamfield 62 48 45N 125 10W
Bāmīān □ 107 35 0N 67 0 E
Bamiancheng 114 43 15N 124 2 E
Bampūr 107 27 15N 60 21 E
Ban Aranyaprathet 112 13 41N 102 30 E
Ban Ban 112 19 31N 103 30 E
Ban Bua Chum 112 15 11N 101 12 E
Ban Don = Surat Thani 112 9 6N 99 20 E
Ban Houei Sai 112 20 22N 100 32 E
Ban Khe Bo 112 19 10N 104 39 E
Ban Khun Yuam 112 18 49N 97 57 E
Ban Phai 112 16 4N 102 44 E
Ban Thateng 112 15 25N 106 27 E
Banaba 124 0 45 S 169 50 E
Banalia 122 1 32N 25 5 E
Banam 112 11 20N 105 17 E
Banamba 120 13 29N 7 22W
Bananal, I. do 75 11 30 S 50 30W
Banaras = Varanasi 109 25 22N 83 0 E
Banbridge 85 54 21N 6 17W
Banbridge □ 85 54 21N 6 16W
Banbury 83 52 4N 1 21W
Banchory 84 57 3N 2 30W
Bancroft, Canada 60 45 3N 77 51W
Bancroft, Idaho 20 42 43N 111 53W
Bancroft, Iowa 23 43 18N 94 13W
Bancroft, La. 25 30 34N 93 41W
Bancroft, Mich. 29 42 53N 84 4W
Bancroft, Nebr. 34 42 1N 96 34W
Band 95 46 30N 24 25 E
Band-e Torkestān 107 35 30N 64 0 E
Banda 108 25 30N 80 26 E
Banda, Kepulauan 111 4 37 S 129 50 E
Banda, La 76 27 45 S 64 10W
Banda Aceh 110 5 35N 95 20 E
Banda Elat 111 5 40 S 133 5 E
Banda Sea 111 6 0 S 130 0 E
Bandai-San 116 37 36N 140 4 E
Bandana 48 37 9N 88 56W
Bandanaira 111 4 32 S 129 54 E
Bandar = Machilipatnam 109 16 12N 81 8 E
Bandār 'Abbās 107 27 15N 56 15 E
Bandar-e Anzalī 106 37 30N 49 30 E
Bandar-e Chārak 107 26 45N 54 20 E
Bandar-e Deylam 106 30 5N 50 10 E
Bandar-e Khomeyni 106 30 30N 49 5 E
Bandar-e Lengeh 107 26 35N 54 58 E
Bandar-e Ma'shur 106 30 35N 49 10 E
Bandar-e Nakhīlū 107 26 58N 53 30 E
Bandar-e Rīg 107 29 29N 50 38 E
Bandar-e Torkeman 107 37 0N 54 10 E
Bandar Maharani 112 2 3N 102 34 E
Bandar Penggaram 110 1 50N 102 56 E
Bandar Seri Begawan 110 4 52N 115 0 E
Bandawe 123 11 58 S 34 5 E
Bandeira, Pico da 75 20 26 S 41 47W
Bandeirante 75 13 41 S 50 48W
Bandelier National Monument 38 35 50N 106 25W
Bandera, Argentina 76 28 55 S 62 20W
Bandera, U.S.A. 51 29 44N 99 5W
Bandera County ◇ 51 29 48N 99 15W
Banderas, Bahía de 64 20 40N 105 30W
Bandiagara 120 14 12N 3 29W
Bandırma 106 40 20N 28 0 E
Bandon, Ireland 85 51 44N 8 45W
Bandon, U.S.A. 44 43 7N 124 25W
Bandon → 85 51 40N 8 41W
Bandundu 122 3 15 S 17 22 E
Bandung 111 6 54 S 107 36 E
Băneasa 95 45 56N 27 55 E
Banes 67 21 0N 75 42W
Banff, Canada 62 51 10N 115 34W
Banff, U.K. 84 57 40N 2 32W
Banff Nat. Park 62 51 30N 116 15W
Banfora 120 10 40N 4 40W
Bang Hieng → 112 16 10N 105 10 E
Bang Lamung 112 13 3N 100 56 E
Bang Saphan 112 11 14N 99 28 E
Bangala Dam 123 21 7 S 31 25 E
Bangalore 108 12 59N 77 40 E
Bangassou 122 4 55N 23 7 E
Banggai 111 1 40 S 123 30 E
Banggi, P. 110 7 17N 117 12 E
Banghāzī 121 32 11N 20 3 E
Bangil 111 7 36 S 112 50 E
Bangka, Pulau, Sulawesi, Indonesia 111 1 50N 125 5 E
Bangka, Pulau, Sumatera, Indonesia 110 2 0 S 105 50 E
Bangka, Selat 110 2 30 S 105 30 E
Bangkalan 111 7 2 S 112 46 E
Bangkinang 110 0 18N 101 5 E
Bangko 110 2 5 S 102 9 E
Bangkok 112 13 45N 100 35 E
Bangladesh ■ 109 24 0N 90 0 E
Bangor, N. Ireland, U.K. 85 54 40N 5 40W
Bangor, Wales, U.K. 82 53 13N 4 9W
Bangor, Maine 26 44 48N 68 46W
Bangor, Mich. 29 42 18N 86 7W
Bangor, Pa. 45 40 52N 75 13W
Bangs 51 31 43N 99 8W
Bangs Mt. 12 36 48N 113 51W
Bangued 111 17 40N 120 37 E
Bangui 122 4 23N 18 35 E
Bangweulu, L. 122 11 0 S 30 0 E
Bani 67 18 16N 70 22W
Banī Na'īm 104 31 31N 35 10 E
Banī Suhaylah 104 31 21N 34 19 E
Banīnah 121 32 0N 20 12 E
Banister → 54 36 42N 78 48W
Bāniyās 106 35 10N 36 0 E
Banja Luka 94 44 49N 17 11 E
Banjar 111 7 24 S 108 30 E
Banjarmasin 110 3 20 S 114 35 E
Banjarnegara 111 7 24 S 109 42 E
Banjul 120 13 28N 16 40W
Bankipore 109 25 35N 85 10 E
Banks, Ala. 10 31 49N 85 51W
Banks, Ark. 13 33 35N 92 16W
Banks, Idaho 20 44 5N 116 8W
Banks, Miss. 31 34 50N 90 14W
Banks County ◇ 18 34 20N 83 30W
Banks I., B.C., Canada 62 53 20N 130 0W
Banks I., N.W.T., Canada 4 73 15N 121 30W
Banks I., Papua N. G. 127 10 10 S 142 15 E
Banks L., Ga. 18 31 2N 83 6W
Banks L., Wash. 53 47 47N 119 19W
Banks Pen. 128 43 45 S 173 15 E
Bankura 109 23 11N 87 18 E
Bann →, Down, U.K. 85 54 30N 6 31W
Bann →, Londonderry, U.K. 85 55 10N 6 34W
Bannack 33 45 10N 112 59W
Banner County ◇ 34 41 30N 103 40W
Banner Elk 40 36 10N 81 52W
Banner Hill 49 36 8N 82 25W
Bannertown 40 36 29N 80 35W
Banning 15 33 56N 116 53W
Banningville = Bandundu 122 3 15 S 17 22 E
Bannock County ◇ 20 42 30N 112 10W
Bannock Cr. → 20 42 53N 112 40W
Bannock Range 20 42 40N 112 30W
Bannockburn 84 56 5N 3 55W
Bannu 108 33 0N 70 18 E
Banská Bystrica 89 48 46N 19 14 E
Banská Štiavnica 89 48 25N 18 55 E
Bansko 95 41 52N 23 28 E
Banswara 108 23 32N 74 24 E
Banten 111 6 5 S 106 8 E
Bantry, Ireland 85 51 40N 9 28W
Bantry, U.S.A. 41 48 30N 100 37W
Bantry, B. 85 51 35N 9 50W
Bantul 111 7 55 S 110 19 E
Banu 108 35 35N 69 5 E
Banya 95 42 33N 24 50 E
Banyak, Kepulauan 110 2 10N 97 10 E
Banyo 120 6 52N 11 45 E

Banyumas Baxley

Banyumas 111 7 32 S 109 18 E
Banyuwangi 111 8 13 S 114 21 E
Banzare Coast 5 68 0 S 125 0 E
Banzyville = Mobayi 122 4 15N 21 8 E
Baocheng 115 33 12N 106 56 E
Baode 114 39 1N 111 5 E
Baoding 114 38 50N 115 28 E
Baoji 115 34 20N 107 5 E
Baojing 115 28 45N 109 41 E
Baokang 115 31 54N 111 12 E
Baoshan 113 25 10N 99 5 E
Baotou 114 40 32N 110 2 E
Baoying 115 33 17N 119 20 E
Bapatla 109 15 55N 80 30 E
Bapchule 12 33 12N 111 50W
Bāqa el Gharbīyya 104 32 25N 35 2 E
Ba'qūbah 106 33 45N 44 50 E
Baquedano 76 23 20 S 69 52W
Bar 95 42 8N 19 8 E
Bar Harbor 26 44 23N 68 13W
Bar-le-Duc 90 48 47N 5 10 E
Barabai 110 2 32 S 115 34 E
Barabinsk 100 55 20N 78 20 E
Baraboo 55 43 28N 89 45W
Baracoa 67 20 20N 74 30W
Barada 34 40 13N 95 35W
Baradero 76 33 52 S 59 29W
Baraga 29 46 47N 88 30W
Baraga County ◇ 29 46 40N 88 20W
Barahona 67 18 13N 71 7W
Barail Range 109 25 15N 93 20 E
Barakhola 109 25 0N 92 45 E
Barakpur 109 22 44N 88 30 E
Baralzon L. 63 60 0N 98 3W
Baramula 108 34 15N 74 20 E
Baran 108 25 9N 76 40 E
Baranoa 70 10 48N 74 55W
Baranof 11 57 5N 134 50W
Baranof I. 11 57 0N 135 0W
Baranovichi 98 53 10N 26 0 E
Barão de Cocais 75 19 56 S 43 28W
Barão de Grajaú 74 6 45 S 43 1W
Barão de Melgaço, Mato Grosso, Brazil 73 16 14 S 55 52W
Barão de Melgaço, Rondônia, Brazil 73 11 50 S 60 45W
Baraolt 95 46 5N 25 34 E
Barapasi 111 2 15 S 137 5 E
Barat Daya, Kepulauan 111 7 30 S 128 0 E
Barataria 25 29 44N 90 8W
Barataria B. 25 29 20N 89 55W
Baraya 70 3 10N 75 4W
Barbacena 75 21 15 S 43 56W
Barbacoas, Colombia 70 1 45N 78 0W
Barbacoas, Venezuela 70 9 29N 66 58W
Barbados ■ 67 13 0N 59 30W
Barbalha 74 7 19 S 39 17W
Barber County ◇ 24 37 15N 98 40W
Barbers Pt. 19 21 18N 158 7W
Barberton, S. Africa 123 25 42 S 31 2 E
Barberton, U.S.A. 42 41 0N 81 39W
Barberville 17 29 11N 81 26W
Barbosa 70 5 57N 73 37W
Barbour County ◇, Ala. 10 31 53N 85 27W
Barbour County ◇, W. Va. 54 39 0N 80 3W
Barboursville 54 38 24N 82 18W
Barbourville 49 36 52N 83 53W
Barbuda I. 67 17 30N 61 40W
Barca, La 64 20 20N 102 40W
Barcaldine 127 23 43 S 145 6 E
Barcelona, Spain 91 41 21N 2 10 E
Barcelona, Venezuela 71 10 10N 64 40W
Barceloneta 57 18 27N 66 32W
Barcelos 71 1 0 S 63 0W
Barclay 27 39 9N 75 52W
Barco 40 36 24N 75 59W
Barcoo → 127 25 30 S 142 50 E
Barda del Medio 78 38 45 S 68 11W
Bardas Blancas 76 35 49 S 69 45W
Barddhaman 109 23 14N 87 39 E
Bardera 105 2 20N 42 27 E
Bardi, Ra's 106 24 17N 37 31 E
Bardia 121 31 45N 25 0 E
Bardley 32 36 42N 91 7W
Bardsey I. 82 52 46N 4 47W
Bardstown 49 37 49N 85 28W
Bardwell 48 36 52N 89 1W
Bare Mt. 53 45 55N 122 4W
Bareilly 108 28 22N 79 27 E
Barents Sea 4 73 0N 39 0 E
Barentu 121 15 2N 37 35 E
Barga 113 30 40N 81 20 E
Bargal 105 11 25N 51 0 E
Bargersville 22 39 31N 86 10W
Barguzin 101 53 37N 109 37 E
Barhi 109 24 15N 85 25 E
Bari 94 41 6N 16 52 E
Bari Doab 108 30 20N 73 0 E
Barīm 105 12 39N 43 25 E
Barima → 71 8 33N 60 25W
Barinas 70 8 36N 70 15W
Barinas □ 70 8 10N 69 50W
Baring 32 40 15N 92 12W
Baring, C. 58 70 0N 117 30W
Baringo 122 0 47N 36 16 E
Baringo, L. 122 0 47N 36 16 E
Barinitas 70 8 45N 70 25W
Bariri 75 22 4 S 48 44W
Bārīs 121 24 42N 30 31 E
Barisal 109 22 45N 90 20 E
Barisan, Bukit 110 3 30 S 102 15 E
Barito → 110 4 0 S 114 50 E
Bark Pt. 55 46 53N 91 11W
Barkā' 107 23 40N 58 0 E
Barker 39 43 20N 78 33W
Barkhamsted Reservoir 28 41 53N 72 58W
Barkley, L. 48 37 1N 88 14W
Barkley Sound 62 48 50N 125 10W
Barkly Tableland 127 17 50 S 136 40 E
Barksdale 51 29 44N 100 2W
Barlee, L. 126 29 15 S 119 30 E
Barletta 94 41 20N 16 17 E
Barling 13 35 20N 94 18W
Barlow 48 37 3N 89 3W
Barlow L. 63 62 0N 103 0W
Barmer 108 25 45N 71 20 E
Barmouth 82 52 44N 4 3W
Barnard, Kans. 24 39 11N 98 3W
Barnard, Mo. 32 40 10N 94 50W
Barnard, Vt. 36 43 43N 72 38W
Barnard Castle 82 54 33N 1 55W
Barnaul 100 53 20N 83 40 E
Barnegat 37 39 45N 74 14W
Barnegat Bay 37 39 45N 74 10W
Barnegat Light 37 39 46N 74 6W
Barnes 24 39 43N 96 52W
Barnes City 23 41 31N 92 27W
Barnes County ◇ 41 47 0N 98 0W
Barnesboro 45 40 40N 78 47W
Barneston 34 40 5N 96 38W
Barnesville, Ga. 18 33 3N 84 9W
Barnesville, Md. 27 39 13N 77 23W
Barnesville, Minn. 30 46 39N 96 25W
Barnesville, Ohio 42 39 59N 81 11W
Barnet, U.K. 83 51 37N 0 15W
Barnet, U.S.A. 36 44 18N 72 3W
Barnett 32 38 23N 92 41W
Barneveld 87 52 7N 5 36 E
Barney 18 31 1N 83 31W
Barney, Mt. 127 28 17 S 152 44 E
Barnhart 50 31 8N 101 10W
Barnsdall 43 36 34N 96 10W
Barnsley 82 53 33N 1 29W
Barnstable 28 41 42N 70 18W
Barnstable County ◇ 28 41 40N 70 15W
Barnstaple 83 51 5N 4 3W
Barnstaple Harbor 28 41 43N 70 18W
Barnum 30 46 30N 92 42W
Barnwell 46 33 15N 81 23W
Barnwell County ◇ 46 33 15N 81 30W
Baro 120 8 35N 6 18 E
Baroda = Vadodara 108 22 20N 73 10 E
Baron 43 35 55N 94 36W
Barpeta 109 26 20N 91 10 E
Barques, Pt. Aux, Mich. 29 44 4N 82 58W
Barques, Pt. Aux, Mich. 29 45 48N 86 21W
Barquísimeto 70 10 4N 69 19W
Barra, Brazil 74 11 5 S 43 10W
Barra, U.K. 84 57 0N 7 30W
Barra, Sd. of 84 57 4N 7 25W
Barra da Estiva 75 13 38 S 41 19W
Barra de Navidad 64 19 12N 104 41W
Barra do Corda 74 5 30 S 45 10W
Barra do Mendes 75 11 43 S 42 4W
Barra do Piraí 75 22 30 S 43 50W
Barra Falsa, Pta. da 123 22 58 S 35 37 E
Barra Hd. 84 56 47N 7 40W
Barra Mansa 77 22 35 S 44 12W
Barracão do Barreto 73 8 48 S 58 24W
Barrackpur = Barakpur 109 22 44N 88 30 E
Barranca, Lima, Peru 72 10 45 S 77 50W
Barranca, Loreto, Peru 70 4 50 S 76 50W
Barrancabermeja 70 7 0N 73 50W
Barrancas, Colombia 70 10 57N 72 50W
Barrancas, Venezuela 71 8 55N 62 5W
Barrancos 91 38 10N 6 58W
Barranqueras 76 27 30 S 59 0W
Barranquilla 70 11 0N 74 50W
Barranquitas 57 18 11N 66 19W
Barras, Brazil 74 4 15 S 42 18W
Barras, Colombia 70 1 45 S 73 13W
Barraute 60 48 26N 77 38W
Barre, Mass. 28 42 25N 72 6W
Barre, Vt. 36 44 12N 72 30W
Barre do Bugres 73 15 0 S 57 11W
Barreal 76 31 33 S 69 28W
Barreiras 75 12 8 S 45 0W
Barreirinha 71 2 30 S 62 50W
Barreirinhas 74 2 30 S 42 50W
Barreiro 91 38 40N 9 6W
Barreiros 74 8 49 S 35 12W
Barren → 48 37 11N 86 37W
Barren County ◇ 48 37 0N 86 0W
Barren I., India 112 12 17N 93 50 E
Barren I., U.S.A. 11 58 55N 152 15W
Barren River L. 48 36 54N 86 8W
Barretos 75 20 30 S 48 35W
Barrett 30 45 55N 95 53W
Barrhead 62 54 10N 114 24W
Barrie 60 44 24N 79 40W
Barrier Ra. 127 31 0 S 141 30 E
Barrière 62 51 12N 120 7W
Barrineau Park 17 30 42N 87 26W
Barrington 28 41 44N 71 18W
Barrington L. 63 56 55N 100 15W
Barrington Tops 127 32 6 S 151 28 E
Barro do Garças 73 15 54 S 52 16W
Barron 55 45 24N 91 51W
Barron County ◇ 55 45 25N 91 50W
Barrow 11 71 18N 156 47W
Barrow → 85 52 10N 6 57W
Barrow County ◇ 18 34 0N 83 40W
Barrow Creek 126 21 30 S 133 55 E
Barrow I. 126 20 45 S 115 20 E
Barrow-in-Furness 82 54 8N 3 15W
Barrow Pt. 11 71 24N 156 29W
Barrow Ra. 126 26 0 S 127 40 E
Barrow Str. 4 74 20N 95 0W
Barry, U.K. 83 51 23N 3 19W
Barry, U.S.A. 21 39 42N 91 2W
Barry County ◇, Mich. 29 42 35N 85 25W
Barry County ◇, Mo. 32 36 45N 93 45W
Barry's Bay 60 45 29N 77 41W
Barryton 29 43 45N 85 9W
Barsi 108 18 10N 75 50 E
Barsoi 109 25 48N 87 57 E
Barstow, Calif. 15 34 54N 117 1W
Barstow, Tex. 50 31 28N 103 24W
Bartholomew County ◇ 22 39 10N 85 55W
Bartica 71 6 25N 58 40W
Bartin 106 41 38N 32 21 E
Bartle Frere, Mt. 127 17 27 S 145 50 E
Bartlesville 43 36 45N 95 59W
Bartlett, Kans. 24 37 3N 95 13W
Bartlett, N.H. 36 44 5N 71 17W
Bartlett, Nebr. 34 41 53N 98 33W
Bartlett, Tex. 51 30 48N 97 26W
Bartlett, L. 62 63 5N 118 20W
Bartlett Reservoir 12 33 49N 111 38W
Bartley 34 40 15N 100 18W
Barton, Ala. 10 34 44N 87 54W
Barton, Md. 27 39 34N 79 2W
Barton, N. Dak. 41 48 30N 100 11W
Barton, Vt. 36 44 45N 72 11W
Barton → 36 44 53N 72 13W
Barton County ◇, Kans. 24 38 30N 98 40W
Barton County ◇, Mo. 32 37 30N 94 20W
Barton-upon-Humber 82 53 41N 0 27W
Bartonville 21 40 39N 89 39W
Bartow, Fla. 17 27 54N 81 50W
Bartow, Ga. 18 32 53N 82 29W
Bartow County ◇ 18 34 20N 84 50W
Barú, I. de 70 10 15N 75 35W
Barú, Volcan 66 8 55N 82 35W
Barwick 18 30 54N 83 44W
Bas-Rhin □ 90 48 40N 7 30 E
Bâsa'idū 107 26 35N 55 20 E
Basalt, Colo. 16 39 22N 107 2W
Basalt, Idaho 20 43 19N 112 10W
Basankusa 122 1 5N 19 50 E
Basco 21 40 20N 91 12W
Bascuñán, C. 76 28 52 S 71 35W
Basel 88 47 35N 7 35 E
Bashkir A.S.S.R. □ 98 54 0N 57 0 E
Basilan 111 6 35N 122 0 E
Basilan Str. 111 6 50N 122 0 E
Basildon 83 51 34N 0 29 E
Basile 25 30 29N 92 36W
Basilicata □ 94 40 30N 16 0 E
Basim = Washim 108 20 3N 77 0 E
Basin, Mont. 33 46 16N 112 16W
Basin, Wyo. 56 44 23N 108 2W
Basinger 17 27 23N 81 2W
Basingstoke 83 51 15N 1 5W
Baskahegan L. 26 45 30N 67 48W
Baskatong, Rés. 60 46 46N 75 50W
Baskerville C. 126 17 10 S 122 15 E
Baskin 25 32 16N 91 45W
Basle = Basel 88 47 35N 7 35 E
Basoka 122 1 16N 23 40 E
Basongo 122 4 15 S 20 20 E
Basque Provinces = Vascongadas 91 42 50N 2 45W
Basra = Al Başrah 106 30 30N 47 50 E
Bass I. 42 41 40N 82 56W
Bass Lake 14 37 19N 119 33W
Bass Rock 84 56 5N 2 40W
Bass Str. 127 39 15 S 146 30 E
Bassano 62 50 48N 112 20W
Bassano del Grappa 94 45 45N 11 45 E
Bassas da India 123 22 0 S 39 0 E
Basse-Terre 67 16 0N 61 40W
Bassein 109 16 45N 94 30 E
Basseterre 67 17 17N 62 43W
Bassett, Nebr. 34 42 35N 99 32W
Bassett, Va. 54 36 46N 79 59W
Bassfield 31 31 30N 89 45W
Bassigny 90 48 0N 5 10 E
Bassikounou 120 15 55N 6 1W
Basswood L. 30 48 7N 91 34W
Bastain 54 37 9N 81 9W
Bastak 107 27 15N 54 25 E
Bastar 109 19 15N 81 40 E
Basti 109 26 52N 82 55 E
Bastia 94 42 40N 9 30 E
Bastogne 87 50 1N 5 43 E
Bastrop, La. 25 32 47N 91 55W
Bastrop, Tex. 51 30 7N 97 19W
Bastrop County ◇ 51 30 10N 97 20W
Bat Yam 104 32 2N 34 44 E
Bata 122 1 57N 9 50 E
Bataan 111 14 40N 120 25 E
Batabanó 66 22 40N 82 20W
Batabanó, G. de 66 22 30N 82 30W
Batac 111 18 3N 120 34 E
Batagoy 101 67 38N 134 38 E
Batak 95 41 57N 24 12 E
Batakan 110 4 5 S 114 38 E
Batalha 91 39 40N 8 50W
Batamay 101 63 30N 129 15 E
Batang, China 113 30 1N 99 0 E
Batang, Indonesia 111 6 55 S 109 45 E
Batangafo 122 7 25N 18 20 E
Batangas 111 13 35N 121 10 E
Batanta 111 0 55 S 130 40 E
Batatais 77 20 54 S 47 37W
Batavia, Ill. 21 41 51N 88 19W
Batavia, Iowa 23 41 0N 92 10W
Batavia, N.Y. 39 43 0N 78 11W
Batavia, Ohio 42 39 5N 84 11W
Batchelor 126 13 4 S 131 1 E
Batchtown 21 39 2N 90 43W
Bateman's B. 127 35 40 S 150 12 E
Bates, Ark. 13 34 55N 94 23W
Bates, Oreg. 44 44 36N 118 30W
Bates County ◇ 32 38 15N 94 20W
Batesburg 46 33 54N 81 33W
Batesland 47 43 8N 102 6W
Batesville, Ark. 13 35 46N 91 39W
Batesville, Ind. 22 39 18N 85 13W
Batesville, Miss. 31 34 19N 89 57W
Batesville, Tex. 51 28 58N 99 37W
Bath, U.K. 83 51 22N 2 22W
Bath, Ill. 21 40 11N 90 8W
Bath, Maine 26 43 55N 69 49W
Bath, N.C. 40 35 29N 76 49W
Bath, N.Y. 39 42 20N 77 19W
Bath, Pa. 45 40 44N 75 24W
Bath, S.C. 46 33 31N 81 51W
Bath, S. Dak. 47 45 28N 98 20W
Bath County ◇, Ky. 49 38 10N 83 45W
Bath County ◇, Va. 54 38 0N 79 50W
Bathgate, U.K. 84 55 54N 3 38W
Bathgate, U.S.A. 41 48 53N 97 29W
Bathurst = Banjul 120 13 28N 16 40W
Bathurst, Australia 127 33 25 S 149 31 E
Bathurst, Canada 61 47 37N 65 43W
Bathurst, C. 58 70 34N 128 0W
Bathurst B. 127 14 16 S 144 25 E
Bathurst I., Australia 126 11 30 S 130 10 E
Bathurst I., Canada 4 76 0N 100 30W
Bathurst In. 58 68 10N 108 50W
Bathurst Inlet 58 66 50N 108 1W
Batinah 107 24 0N 56 0 E
Batman 106 37 55N 41 5 E
Batna 120 35 34N 6 15 E
Baton Rouge 25 30 27N 91 11W
Batopilas 64 27 0N 107 45W
Batouri 122 4 30N 14 25 E
Batson 51 30 15N 94 40W
Battambang 112 13 7N 103 12 E
Batten Kill → 36 43 6N 73 35W
Batticaloa 108 7 43N 81 45 E
Battīr 104 31 44N 35 8 E
Battle, Canada 63 52 58N 110 52W
Battle, U.K. 83 50 55N 0 30 E
Battle →, Canada 63 52 43N 108 15W
Battle →, U.S.A. 14 40 21N 122 11W
Battle Creek, Iowa 23 42 19N 95 36W
Battle Creek, Mich. 29 42 19N 85 11W
Battle Creek, Nebr. 34 42 0N 97 36W
Battle Ground, Ind. 22 40 31N 86 50W
Battle Ground, Wash. 53 45 47N 122 32W
Battle Harbour 61 52 16N 55 35W
Battle Lake 30 46 17N 95 43W
Battle Mountain 35 40 38N 116 56W
Battle Mt. 56 41 2N 107 16W
Battleford 63 52 45N 108 15W
Batu 105 6 55N 39 45 E
Batu, Kepulauan 110 0 30 S 98 25 E
Batu Gajah 112 4 28N 101 3 E
Batu Pahat = Bandar Penggaram 110 1 50N 102 56 E
Batuata 111 6 12 S 122 42 E
Batumi 99 41 30N 41 30 E
Baturaja 110 4 11 S 104 15 E
Baturité 74 4 28 S 38 45W
Bau 110 1 25N 110 9 E
Baubau 111 5 25 S 122 38 E
Bauchi 120 10 22N 9 48 E
Baudette 30 48 43N 94 36W
Baures 73 13 35 S 63 35W
Bauru 75 22 10 S 49 0W
Baús 73 18 22 S 52 47W
Bautzen 88 51 11N 14 25 E
Bauxite 13 34 33N 92 30W
Bavaria = Bayern □ 88 49 7N 11 30 E
Bavaria 24 38 48N 97 45W
Bavispe → 64 29 30N 109 11W
Bawdwin 109 23 5N 97 20 E
Bawean 110 5 46 S 112 35 E
Bawku 120 11 3N 0 19W
Bawlake 109 19 11N 97 21 E
Baxley 18 31 47N 82 21W

Baxter Bellevue

Baxter, Iowa 23 41 49N 93 9W
Baxter, Minn. 30 46 21N 94 17W
Baxter, Tenn. 49 36 9N 85 38W
Baxter County ◇ 13 36 20N 92 23W
Baxter Springs 24 37 2N 94 44W
Baxterville 31 31 5N 89 36W
Bay 13 35 45N 90 34W
Bay, Laguna de 111 14 20N 121 11 E
Bay Bulls 61 47 19N 52 50W
Bay City, Mich. 29 43 36N 83 54W
Bay City, Oreg. 44 45 31N 123 53W
Bay City, Tex. 51 28 59N 95 58W
Bay County ◇, Fla. 17 30 20N 85 45W
Bay County ◇, Mich. 29 43 45N 84 5W
Bay de Verde 61 48 5N 52 54W
Bay Mills Indian Reservation 29 46 25N 84 15W
Bay Minette 10 30 53N 87 46W
Bay Port 29 43 51N 83 23W
Bay St. Louis 31 30 19N 89 20W
Bay Shore 39 40 43N 73 15W
Bay Springs 31 31 59N 89 17W
Bay View, N.Z. 128 39 25 S 176 50 E
Bay View, U.S.A. 27 39 39N 75 58W
Bayamo 66 20 20N 76 40W
Bayamon 57 18 24N 66 10W
Bayamon → 57 18 24N 66 9W
Bayan 114 46 5N 127 24 E
Bayan Har Shan 113 34 0N 98 0 E
Bayan Hot = Alxa Zuoqi 114 38 50N 105 40 E
Bayan Obo 114 41 52N 109 59 E
Bayanaul 100 50 45N 75 45 E
Bayanhongor 113 46 8N 102 43 E
Bayard, Iowa 23 41 51N 94 33W
Bayard, N. Mex. 38 32 46N 108 8W
Bayard, Nebr. 34 41 45N 103 20W
Bayard, W. Va. 54 39 16N 79 22W
Bayázeh 107 33 30N 54 40 E
Baybay 111 10 40N 124 55 E
Bayboro 40 35 9N 76 46W
Bayburt 106 40 15N 40 20 E
Bayern □ 88 49 7N 11 30 E
Bayeux 90 49 17N 0 42W
Bayfield, Colo. 16 37 14N 107 36W
Bayfield, Wis. 55 46 49N 90 49W
Bayfield County ◇ 55 46 25N 91 15W
Bayfield Ridge 55 46 45N 91 25W
Baykal, Oz. 101 53 0N 108 0 E
Baykit 101 61 50N 95 50 E
Baykonur 100 47 48N 65 50 E
Baylor County ◇ 51 33 35N 99 16W
Baymak 98 52 36N 58 19 E
Bayombong 111 16 30N 121 10 E
Bayonne, France 90 43 30N 1 28W
Bayonne, U.S.A. 37 40 40N 74 7W
Bayou Bartholomew → 25 32 43N 92 4W
Bayou Bodcau → 25 32 13N 93 30W
Bayou Cane 25 29 37N 90 45W
Bayou D'Arbonne L. 25 32 43N 92 21W
Bayou De View → 13 34 48N 91 18W
Bayou Dorcheat → 25 32 10N 93 25W
Bayou George 17 30 16N 85 33W
Bayou La Batre 10 30 24N 88 15W
Bayou Lafourche → 25 29 5N 90 14W
Bayou Macon → 25 31 55N 91 33W
Bayou Meto 13 34 13N 91 31W
Bayou Nepique → 25 30 11N 92 34W
Bayou Pierre → 31 31 55N 91 11W
Bayou Vista 25 29 41N 90 13W
Bayovar 72 5 50 S 81 0W
Bayport 17 28 32N 82 39W
Bayram-Ali 100 37 37N 62 10 E
Bayreuth 88 49 56N 11 35 E
Bayrūt 106 33 53N 35 31 E
Bayshore 17 26 43N 81 50W
Bayside 51 28 6N 97 13W
Bayside Beach 27 39 8N 76 27W
Bayt Awlá 104 31 37N 35 2 E
Bayt Fajjār 104 31 38N 35 9 E
Bayt Fūrīk 104 32 11N 35 20 E
Bayt Ḩānūn 104 31 32N 34 32 E
Bayt Jālā 104 31 43N 35 11 E
Bayt Lahm 104 31 43N 35 12 E
Bayt Rīma 104 32 2N 35 6 E
Bayt Sāḩūr 104 31 42N 35 13 E
Bayt Ummar 104 31 38N 35 7 E
Bayt 'ūr al Taḩtā 104 31 54N 35 5 E
Baytīn 104 31 56N 35 14 E
Baytown 51 29 43N 94 59W
Baytūniyā 104 31 54N 35 10 E
Bayview 20 47 59N 116 34W
Baza 91 37 30N 2 47W
Bazaar 24 38 16N 96 32W
Bazaruto, I. do 123 21 40 S 35 28 E
Bazhong 115 31 52N 106 46 E
Bazile Mills 34 42 31N 97 53W
Bazine 24 38 27N 99 42W
Beach 41 46 58N 104 0W
Beach City 42 40 39N 81 35W
Beach Haven 37 39 34N 74 14W
Beachville 27 38 8N 76 24W
Beachwood 37 39 56N 74 12W
Beachy Head 83 50 44N 0 16 E
Beacon, Iowa 23 41 17N 92 41W
Beacon, N.Y. 39 41 30N 73 58W
Beacon Hill 17 29 55N 85 23W
Beaconia 63 50 25N 96 31W
Beaconsfield 127 41 11 S 146 48 E
Beadle County ◇ 47 44 22N 98 13W
Beagle 24 38 25N 94 57W
Beagle, Canal 78 55 0 S 68 30W
Beallsville 42 39 51N 81 2W
Beals Branch → 50 32 10N 101 51W
Bear 27 39 38N 75 39W
Bear → 52 41 30N 112 8W
Bear Cr. →, Ala. 10 33 11N 88 5W
Bear Cr. →, Wyo. 56 41 41N 104 13W
Bear Creek 55 44 32N 88 44W
Bear I. 85 51 38N 9 50W
Bear L., B.C., Canada 62 56 10N 126 52W
Bear L., Man., Canada 63 55 8N 96 0W
Bear L., U.S.A. 52 41 59N 111 21W
Bear Lake 29 44 25N 86 9W
Bear Lake County ◇ 20 42 10N 111 15W
Bear Mt. 49 37 32N 84 16W
Bear Peak 56 43 4N 109 13W
Bear River City 52 41 37N 112 8W
Bear Tooth Pass 56 44 58N 109 28W
Bearden 13 33 43N 92 37W
Beardmore 60 49 36N 87 57W
Beardmore Glacier 5 84 30 S 170 0 E
Beardsley, Kans. 24 39 49N 101 14W
Beardsley, Minn. 30 45 33N 96 43W
Beardstown 21 40 1N 90 26W
Bearmouth 33 46 48N 113 20W
Béarn 90 43 8N 0 36W
Bearpaw Mts. 33 48 12N 109 30W
Bears Ears 52 37 38N 109 51W
Bearskin Lake 60 53 58N 91 2W
Beartooth Ra. 33 45 5N 109 40W
Beata, C. 67 17 40N 71 30W
Beata, I. 67 17 34N 71 31W
Beatrice, Ala. 10 31 44N 87 13W
Beatrice, Nebr. 34 40 16N 96 45W
Beatrice, C. 127 14 20 S 136 55 E
Beattie 24 39 52N 96 25W
Beatton → 62 56 15N 120 45W
Beatton River 62 57 26N 121 20W
Beatty, Nev. 35 36 54N 116 46W
Beatty, Oreg. 44 42 27N 121 16W
Beattyville 49 37 35N 83 42W
Beauce, Plaine de la 90 48 10N 1 45 E
Beauceville 61 46 13N 70 46W
Beauchêne, I. 78 52 55 S 59 15W
Beaufort, Malaysia 110 5 30N 115 40 E
Beaufort, N.C. 40 34 43N 76 40W
Beaufort, S.C. 46 32 26N 80 40W
Beaufort County ◇, N.C. 40 35 30N 76 50W
Beaufort County ◇, S.C. 46 32 20N 80 50W
Beaufort Sea 4 72 0N 140 0W
Beaufort West 123 32 18 S 22 36 E
Beauharnois 60 45 20N 73 52W
Beaulieu → 62 62 3N 113 11W
Beauly 84 57 29N 4 27W
Beauly → 84 57 26N 4 28W
Beaumaris 82 53 16N 4 7W
Beaumont, Calif. 15 33 56N 116 58W
Beaumont, Miss. 31 31 10N 88 55W
Beaumont, Tex. 51 30 5N 94 6W
Beaune 90 47 2N 4 50 E
Beauregard Parish ◇ 25 30 39N 93 25W
Beauséjour 63 50 5N 96 35W
Beauvais 90 49 25N 2 8 E
Beauval 63 55 9N 107 37W
Beaver, Alaska 11 66 22N 147 24W
Beaver, Kans. 24 38 38N 98 40W
Beaver, Ohio 42 39 2N 82 50W
Beaver, Okla. 43 36 49N 100 31W
Beaver, Oreg. 44 45 17N 123 49W
Beaver, Pa. 45 40 42N 80 19W
Beaver, Utah 52 38 17N 112 38W
Beaver, Wis. 55 45 8N 88 1W
Beaver →, B.C., Canada 62 59 52N 124 20W
Beaver →, Ont., Canada 60 55 55N 87 48W
Beaver →, Sask., Canada 63 55 26N 107 45W
Beaver →, U.S.A. 52 39 10N 112 57W
Beaver Bay 30 47 16N 91 18W
Beaver City 34 40 8N 99 50W
Beaver County ◇, Okla. 43 36 45N 100 25W
Beaver County ◇, Pa. 45 40 45N 80 20W
Beaver County ◇, Utah 52 38 20N 113 10W
Beaver Cr. →, Colo. 16 40 20N 103 33W
Beaver Cr. →, Mont. 33 48 27N 107 18W
Beaver Cr. →, N. Dak. 41 47 20N 103 39W
Beaver Cr. →, Nebr. 34 40 7N 99 29W
Beaver Cr. →, Tex. 51 33 53N 98 49W
Beaver Cr. →, Wyo. 56 42 58N 108 26W
Beaver Creek 30 43 37N 96 22W
Beaver Crossing 34 40 47N 97 17W
Beaver Dam, Ky. 48 37 24N 86 52W
Beaver Dam, Wis. 55 43 28N 88 50W
Beaver Dam L. 55 43 31N 88 53W
Beaver Falls 45 40 46N 80 20W
Beaver I. 29 45 40N 85 33W
Beaver L. 13 36 25N 93 51W
Beaverdam 42 40 50N 83 59W
Beaverhead → 33 45 31N 112 21W
Beaverhead County ◇ 33 45 5N 113 10W
Beaverhead Mts. 20 45 0N 113 20W
Beaverhill L., Alta., Canada 62 53 27N 112 32W
Beaverhill L., Man., Canada 63 54 5N 94 50W
Beaverhill L., N.W.T., Canada 63 63 2N 104 22W
Beaverlodge 62 55 11N 119 29W
Beavermouth 62 51 32N 117 23W
Beaverstone → 60 54 59N 89 25W
Beaverton, Mich. 29 43 53N 84 29W
Beaverton, Mont. 33 48 26N 107 15W
Beaverton, Oreg. 44 45 29N 122 48W
Beawar 108 26 3N 74 18 E
Bebe 51 29 25N 97 38W
Bebedouro 77 21 0 S 48 25W
Beccles 83 52 27N 1 33 E
Bečej 95 45 36N 20 3 E
Beceni 95 45 23N 26 48 E
Béchar 120 31 38N 2 18W
Becharof L. 11 57 56N 156 23W
Bechyn 30 44 39N 95 5W
Becker County ◇ 30 46 50N 95 50W
Beckham County ◇ 43 35 15N 99 40W
Beckley 54 37 47N 81 11W
Beckville 51 32 15N 92 27W
Beckwith Cr. → 25 30 13N 93 13W
Bedford, Canada 60 45 7N 72 59W
Bedford, S. Africa 123 32 40 S 26 10 E
Bedford, U.K. 83 52 8N 0 29W
Bedford, Ind. 22 38 52N 86 29W
Bedford, Iowa 23 40 40N 94 44W
Bedford, Ky. 49 38 36N 85 19W
Bedford, Mass. 28 42 29N 71 17W
Bedford, N.H. 36 42 55N 71 32W
Bedford, Ohio 42 41 23N 81 32W
Bedford, Pa. 45 40 1N 78 30W
Bedford, Va. 54 37 20N 79 31W
Bedford □ 83 52 4N 0 28W
Bedford, C. 127 15 14 S 145 21 E
Bedford County ◇, Pa. 45 40 0N 78 30W
Bedford County ◇, Tenn. 48 35 29N 86 28W
Bedford County ◇, Va. 54 37 20N 79 31W
Bedias 51 30 47N 95 57W
Bedourie 127 24 30 S 139 30 E
Bedrock 16 38 19N 108 54W
Bee 34 41 0N 97 4W
Bee County ◇ 51 28 24N 97 45W
Bee Ridge 17 27 17N 82 29W
Bee Springs 48 37 17N 86 17W
Beebe 13 35 4N 91 53W
Beech Bottom 54 40 14N 80 39W
Beech Creek 45 41 5N 77 36W
Beech Fork → 49 37 46N 85 41W
Beech Grove 22 39 44N 86 3W
Beecher 21 41 21N 87 38W
Beecher City 21 39 11N 88 47W
Beecher Falls 36 45 1N 71 31W
Beechgrove 48 35 38N 86 14W
Beechy 63 50 53N 107 24W
Beeler 24 38 26N 100 12W
Beemer 34 41 56N 96 48W
Be'er Sheva' 104 31 15N 34 48 E
Be'er Sheva' → 104 31 12N 34 40 E
Be'er Toviyya 104 31 44N 34 42 E
Be'eri 104 31 25N 34 30 E
Be'erotayim 104 32 19N 34 59 E
Beersheba = Be'er Sheva' 104 31 15N 34 48 E
Beersheba Springs 49 35 28N 85 39W
Beeston 82 52 55N 1 11W
Beeville 51 28 24N 97 45W
Befale 122 0 25N 20 45 E
Befandriana 123 21 55 S 44 0 E
Bega 127 36 41 S 149 51 E
Beggs 43 35 45N 96 4W
Behara 123 24 55 S 46 20 E
Behbehān 106 30 30N 50 15 E
Behshahr 107 36 45N 53 35 E
Bei Jiang → 115 23 2N 112 58 E
Bei'an 114 48 10N 126 20 E
Beibei 115 29 47N 106 22 E
Beihai 115 21 28N 109 6 E
Beijing 114 39 55N 116 20 E
Beijing □ 114 39 55N 116 20 E
Beilen 87 52 52N 6 27 E
Beira 123 19 50 S 34 52 E
Beira-Alta 91 40 35N 7 35W
Beira-Baixa 91 40 2N 7 30W
Beira-Litoral 91 40 5N 8 30W
Beirut = Bayrūt 106 33 53N 35 31 E
Beit Lāhiyah 104 31 32N 34 30 E
Beitaolaizhao 114 44 58N 125 58 E
Beitbridge 123 22 12 S 30 0 E
Beizhen 114 37 20N 118 2 E
Beja, Portugal 91 38 2N 7 53W
Béja, Tunisia 120 36 43N 9 12 E
Bejaia 120 36 42N 5 2 E
Bejestān 107 34 30N 58 5 E
Bekasi 111 6 14 S 106 59 E
Békéscsaba 89 46 40N 21 5 E
Bekok 112 2 20N 103 7 E
Bel Air 27 39 32N 76 21W
Bel Alton 27 38 28N 76 59W
Bela, India 109 25 50N 82 0 E
Bela, Pakistan 108 26 12N 66 20 E
Bela Crkva 95 44 55N 21 27 E
Bela Vista, Brazil 76 22 12 S 56 20W
Bela Vista, Mozam. 123 26 10 S 32 44 E
Belau Is. 124 7 30N 134 30 E
Belawan 110 3 33N 98 32 E
Belaya → 98 56 0N 54 32 E
Belaya Tserkov 99 49 45N 30 10 E
Belcamp 27 39 28N 76 14W
Belcher Is. 60 56 15N 78 45W
Belchertown 28 42 17N 72 24W
Belcourt 41 48 50N 99 45W
Belden 34 42 25N 97 13W
Belding 29 43 6N 85 14W
Belebey 98 54 7N 54 7 E
Belém 74 1 20 S 48 30W
Belém de São Francisco 74 8 46 S 38 58W
Belén, Argentina 76 27 40 S 67 5W
Belén, Colombia 70 1 26N 75 56W
Belén, Paraguay 76 23 30 S 57 6W
Belen, U.S.A. 38 34 40N 106 46W
Belene 95 43 39N 25 10 E
Belet Uen 105 4 30N 45 5 E
Belev 98 53 50N 36 5 E
Belews L. 40 36 15N 80 5W
Belfair 53 47 27N 122 50W
Belfast, S. Africa 123 25 42 S 30 2 E
Belfast, U.K. 85 54 35N 5 56W
Belfast, Maine 26 44 26N 69 1W
Belfast, N.Y. 39 42 21N 78 7W
Belfast, Tenn. 48 35 25N 86 42W
Belfast □ 85 54 35N 5 56W
Belfast, L. 85 54 40N 5 50W
Belfield 41 46 53N 103 12W
Belfort 90 47 38N 6 50 E
Belfort □ 90 47 38N 6 52 E
Belfry 33 45 9N 109 1W
Belgaum 108 15 55N 74 35 E
Belgium 55 43 30N 87 51W
Belgium ■ 87 50 30N 5 0 E
Belgorod 99 50 35N 36 35 E
Belgorod-Dnestrovskiy 99 46 11N 30 23 E
Belgrade = Beograd 95 44 50N 20 37 E
Belgrade, Maine 26 44 27N 69 50W
Belgrade, Minn. 30 45 27N 95 0W
Belgrade, Mont. 33 45 47N 111 11W
Belgrade, Nebr. 34 41 28N 98 4W
Belhaven 40 35 33N 76 37W
Beli Drim → 95 42 6N 20 25 E
Belinga 122 1 10N 13 2 E
Belington 54 39 2N 79 56W
Belinyu 110 1 35 S 105 50 E
Belitung 110 3 10 S 107 50 E
Belize ■ 65 17 0N 88 30W
Belize City 65 17 25N 88 0W
Belknap 21 37 19N 88 56W
Belknap County ◇ 36 43 30N 71 30W
Belkovskiy, Ostrov 101 75 32N 135 44 E
Bell 17 29 45N 82 52W
Bell → 60 49 48N 77 38W
Bell Buckle 48 35 35N 86 21W
Bell City, Ky. 48 36 31N 88 30W
Bell City, Mo. 32 37 1N 89 49W
Bell County ◇, Ky. 49 36 45N 83 40W
Bell County ◇, Tex. 51 31 3N 97 28W
Bell I. 61 50 46N 55 35W
Bell-Irving → 62 56 12N 129 5W
Bell Peninsula 59 63 50N 82 0W
Bell Ranch 38 35 32N 104 6W
Bell Ville 76 32 40 S 62 40W
Bella Bella 62 52 10N 128 10W
Bella Coola 62 52 25N 126 40W
Bella Flor 72 11 9 S 67 49W
Bella Unión 76 30 15 S 57 40W
Bella Vista, Corrientes, Argentina 76 28 33 S 59 0W
Bella Vista, Tucuman, Argentina 76 27 10 S 65 25W
Bellaire, Mich. 29 44 59N 85 13W
Bellaire, Ohio 42 40 1N 80 45W
Bellaire, Tex. 51 29 42N 95 28W
Bellamy 10 32 27N 88 8W
Bellary 108 15 10N 76 56 E
Belle, Mo. 32 38 17N 91 43W
Belle, W. Va. 54 38 14N 81 33W
Belle → 29 42 43N 82 30W
Belle Fourche 47 44 40N 103 51W
Belle Fourche → 47 44 26N 102 18W
Belle Fourche Reservoir 47 44 44N 103 41W
Belle Glade 17 26 41N 80 40W
Belle-Île 90 47 20N 3 10W
Belle Isle, Canada 61 51 57N 55 25W
Belle Isle, U.S.A. 17 28 27N 81 21W
Belle Isle, Str. of 61 51 30N 56 30W
Belle Plaine, Iowa 23 41 54N 92 17W
Belle Plaine, Kans. 24 37 24N 97 17W
Belle Plaine, Minn. 30 44 37N 93 46W
Belle Rive 21 38 14N 88 45W
Belle Valley 42 39 47N 81 33W
Bellechester 30 44 22N 92 31W
Belledune 61 47 55N 65 50W
Bellefontaine 42 40 22N 83 46W
Bellefonte, Del. 27 39 47N 75 30W
Bellefonte, Pa. 45 40 55N 77 47W
Bellemont 12 35 14N 111 50W
Belleoram 61 47 31N 55 25W
Belleplain 37 39 11N 74 46W
Belleview 17 29 4N 82 3W
Belleville, Canada 60 44 10N 77 23W
Belleville, Ill. 21 38 31N 89 59W
Belleville, Kans. 24 39 50N 97 38W
Belleville, N.J. 37 40 47N 74 9W
Belleville, Wis. 55 42 52N 89 32W
Bellevue, Canada 62 49 35N 114 22W
Bellevue, Idaho 20 43 28N 114 16W

Bellevue Bethpage

Bellevue, Iowa **23** 42 16N 90 26W
Bellevue, Md. **27** 38 42N 76 11W
Bellevue, Mich. **29** 42 27N 85 1W
Bellevue, Nebr. **34** 41 9N 95 54W
Bellevue, Ohio **42** 41 17N 82 51W
Bellevue, Tex. **51** 33 38N 98 1W
Bellevue, Wash. **53** 47 37N 122 12W
Bellflower, Ill. **21** 40 20N 88 32W
Bellflower, Mo. **32** 39 0N 91 21W
Bellin **59** 60 0N 70 0W
Bellingham, Mass. **28** 42 5N 71 28W
Bellingham, Minn. **30** 45 8N 96 17W
Bellingham, Wash. **53** 48 46N 122 29W
Bellingshausen **5** 62 0S 59 0W
Bellingshausen Sea **5** 66 0S 80 0W
Bellinzona **88** 46 11N 9 1E
Bellmawr **37** 39 52N 75 5W
Bellmead **51** 31 35N 97 6W
Bello **70** 6 20N 75 33W
Bellona Reefs **127** 21 26S 159 0E
Bellows Falls **36** 43 8N 72 27W
Bellport **39** 40 46N 72 56W
Bells, Tenn. **48** 35 43N 89 5W
Bells, Tex. **51** 33 37N 96 25W
Belltown **27** 38 45N 75 11W
Belluno **94** 46 8N 12 13E
Bellview **38** 34 49N 103 7W
Bellville, Ga. **18** 32 9N 81 59W
Bellville, Tex. **51** 29 57N 96 15W
Bellvue **16** 40 38N 105 10W
Bellwood, La. **25** 31 32N 93 12W
Bellwood, Nebr. **34** 41 21N 97 14W
Bellwood, Pa. **45** 40 36N 78 20W
Belmar **37** 40 11N 74 2W
Bélmez **91** 38 17N 5 17W
Belmond **23** 42 51N 93 37W
Belmont, Kans. **24** 37 32N 97 56W
Belmont, Miss. **31** 34 31N 88 13W
Belmont, N.C. **40** 35 14N 81 2W
Belmont, N.H. **36** 43 27N 71 29W
Belmont, N.Y. **39** 42 14N 78 2W
Belmont, Wis. **55** 42 44N 90 20W
Belmont County ◇ **42** 40 1N 81 4W
Belmonte **75** 16 0S 39 0W
Belmopan **65** 17 18N 88 30W
Belmore **42** 41 9N 83 56W
Belmullet **85** 54 13N 9 58W
Belo Horizonte **75** 19 55S 43 56W
Belo Jardim **74** 8 20S 36 26W
Belo-Tsiribihina **123** 19 40S 44 30E
Belogorsk **101** 51 0N 128 20E
Belogradets **95** 43 22N 27 18E
Beloit, Kans. **24** 39 28N 98 6W
Beloit, Wis. **55** 42 31N 89 2W
Belomorsk **98** 64 35N 34 30E
Belonia **109** 23 15N 91 30E
Beloretsk **98** 53 58N 58 24E
Belovo **100** 54 30N 86 0E
Beloye, Oz. **98** 60 10N 37 35E
Beloye More **98** 66 30N 38 0E
Belozem **95** 42 12N 25 2E
Belozersk **98** 60 0N 37 30E
Belpre, Kans. **24** 37 57N 99 6W
Belpre, Ohio **42** 39 17N 81 34W
Belt **33** 47 23N 110 55W
Belterra **71** 2 45S 55 0W
Belton, Mo. **32** 38 49N 94 32W
Belton, S.C. **46** 34 31N 82 30W
Belton, Tex. **51** 31 3N 97 28W
Beltrami **30** 47 33N 96 32W
Beltrami County ◇ **30** 47 45N 94 50W
Beltsville **27** 39 2N 76 54W
Beltsy **99** 47 48N 28 0E
Belturbet **85** 54 6N 7 28W
Belukha **100** 49 50N 86 50E
Beluran **110** 5 48N 117 35E
Belvidere, Ill. **21** 42 15N 88 50W
Belvidere, N.J. **37** 40 50N 75 5W
Belvidere, Nebr. **34** 40 15N 97 33W
Belvidere, S. Dak. **47** 43 50N 101 16W
Belvidere Mt. **36** 44 46N 72 33W
Belview **30** 44 36N 95 20W
Belvue **24** 39 13N 96 11W
Belyando → **127** 21 38S 146 50E
Belyy, Ostrov **100** 73 30N 71 0E
Belyy Yar **100** 58 26N 84 39E
Belzoni **31** 33 11N 90 29W
Bembéréke **120** 10 11N 2 43E
Bement **21** 39 55N 88 34W
Bemidji **30** 47 28N 94 53W
Bemis, Tenn. **48** 35 35N 88 49W
Bemis, W. Va. **54** 38 49N 79 45W
Ben 'Ammi **104** 33 0N 35 7E
Ben Cruachan **84** 56 26N 5 8W
Ben Dearg **84** 57 47N 4 58W
Ben Gardane **121** 33 11N 11 11E
Ben Hill County ◇ **18** 31 45N 83 10W
Ben Hope **84** 58 24N 4 36W
Ben Lawers **84** 56 33N 4 13W
Ben Lomond, Australia **127** 41 38S 147 42E
Ben Lomond, U.K. **84** 56 12N 4 39W
Ben Lomond, Ark. **13** 33 50N 94 7W
Ben Lomond, Calif. **14** 37 5N 122 5W
Ben Macdhui **84** 57 4N 3 40W
Ben Mhor **84** 57 16N 7 21W
Ben More, Central, U.K. **84** 56 23N 4 31W
Ben More, Strathclyde, U.K. **84** 56 26N 6 2W
Ben More Assynt **84** 58 7N 4 51W
Ben Nevis **84** 56 48N 5 0W
Ben Vorlich **84** 56 22N 4 15W
Ben Wyvis **84** 57 40N 4 35W
Bena, Nigeria **120** 11 20N 5 50E
Bena, U.S.A. **30** 47 21N 94 12W
Bena Dibele **122** 4 4S 22 50E
Benalla **127** 36 30S 146 0E
Benavides **50** 27 36N 98 25W
Benbecula **84** 57 26N 7 21W
Benbrook **51** 32 41N 97 28W
Benchley **51** 30 45N 96 27W
Bencubbin **126** 30 48S 117 52E
Bend **44** 44 4N 121 19W
Bender Beila **105** 9 30N 50 48E
Bendery **99** 46 50N 29 30E
Bendigo **127** 36 40S 144 15E
Benē Beraq **104** 32 6N 34 51E
Benedict, Kans. **24** 37 38N 95 45W
Benedict, Md. **27** 38 31N 76 41W
Benedict, Nebr. **34** 41 0N 97 36W
Beneditinos **74** 5 27S 42 22W
Benedito Leite **74** 7 13S 44 34W
Benevento **94** 41 7N 14 45E
Benevolence **18** 31 53N 84 44W
Benewah County ◇ **20** 47 5N 116 35W
Bengal, Bay of **109** 15 0N 90 0E
Bengbu **115** 32 58N 117 20E
Benghazi = Banghāzī **121** 32 11N 20 3E
Bengkalis **110** 1 30N 102 10E
Bengkulu **110** 3 50S 102 12E
Bengkulu □ **110** 3 48S 102 16E
Bengough **63** 49 25N 105 10W
Benguela **123** 12 37S 13 25E
Benham **49** 36 58N 82 57W
Beni **122** 0 30N 29 27E
Beni □ **73** 14 0S 65 0W
Beni → **73** 10 23S 65 24W
Beni Abbès **120** 30 5N 2 5W
Beni Mazâr **121** 28 32N 30 44E
Beni Mellal **120** 32 21N 6 21W
Beni Ounif **120** 32 0N 1 10W
Beni Suef **121** 29 5N 31 6E
Beni Ulid **121** 31 36N 13 53E
Beniah L. **62** 63 23N 112 17W
Benidorm **91** 38 33N 0 9W
Benin ■ **120** 10 0N 2 0E
Benin, Bight of **120** 5 0N 3 0E
Benin City **120** 6 20N 5 31E
Benjamin **51** 33 35N 99 48W
Benjamin Aceval **76** 24 58S 57 34W
Benjamin Constant **70** 4 40S 70 15W
Benjamin Hill **64** 30 10N 111 10W
Benkelman **34** 40 3N 101 32W
Benld **21** 39 6N 89 48W
Bennet **34** 40 41N 96 30W
Bennett, Canada **62** 59 56N 134 53W
Bennett, Colo. **16** 39 46N 104 26W
Bennett, Iowa **23** 41 43N 90 59W
Bennett, N.C. **40** 35 34N 79 33W
Bennett, N. Mex. **38** 32 4N 103 12W
Bennett, Ostrov **101** 76 21N 148 56E
Bennett County ◇ **47** 43 5N 101 45W
Bennettsville **46** 34 37N 79 41W
Bennington, Idaho **20** 42 24N 111 19W
Bennington, Kans. **24** 39 2N 97 36W
Bennington, N.H. **36** 43 0N 71 55W
Bennington, Nebr. **34** 41 22N 96 9W
Bennington, Okla. **43** 34 0N 96 2W
Bennington, Vt. **36** 42 53N 73 12W
Bennington County ◇ **36** 43 0N 73 10W
Benoa **110** 8 50S 115 20E
Benoit **31** 33 39N 91 1W
Benoni **123** 26 11S 28 18E
Benque Viejo **65** 17 5N 89 8W
Bens Run **54** 39 28N 81 6W
Benson, Ariz. **12** 31 58N 110 18W
Benson, Ill. **21** 40 51N 89 7W
Benson, La. **25** 31 52N 93 42W
Benson, Minn. **30** 45 19N 95 36W
Benson, N.C. **40** 35 23N 78 33W
Benson, Vt. **36** 43 42N 73 18W
Benson County ◇ **41** 48 5N 99 25W
Bent **107** 26 20N 59 31E
Bent County ◇ **16** 38 0N 103 0W
Benteng **111** 6 10S 120 30E
Bentinck I. **127** 17 3S 139 35E
Bentley **24** 37 54N 97 31W
Bentleyville **45** 40 7N 80 1W
Bento Gonçalves **77** 29 10S 51 31W
Benton, Ark. **13** 34 34N 92 35W
Benton, Calif. **14** 37 48N 118 32W
Benton, Ill. **21** 38 0N 88 55W
Benton, Iowa **23** 40 42N 94 22W
Benton, Kans. **24** 37 47N 97 6W
Benton, Ky. **48** 36 52N 88 21W
Benton, La. **25** 32 42N 93 44W
Benton, Miss. **31** 32 50N 90 16W
Benton, Mo. **32** 37 6N 89 34W
Benton, N.H. **36** 44 8N 71 55W
Benton, Pa. **45** 41 12N 76 23W
Benton, Tenn. **49** 35 10N 84 39W
Benton, Wis. **55** 42 34N 90 23W
Benton City, Mo. **32** 39 8N 91 46W
Benton City, Wash. **53** 46 16N 119 29W
Benton County ◇, Ark. **13** 36 22N 94 13W
Benton County ◇, Ind. **22** 40 35N 87 20W
Benton County ◇, Iowa **23** 42 0N 92 0W
Benton County ◇, Minn. **30** 45 45N 94 0W
Benton County ◇, Miss. **31** 34 50N 89 11W
Benton County ◇, Mo. **32** 38 20N 93 15W
Benton County ◇, Oreg. **44** 44 30N 123 20W
Benton County ◇, Tenn. **48** 36 4N 88 6W
Benton County ◇, Wash. **53** 46 25N 119 25W
Benton Harbor **29** 42 6N 86 27W
Benton Heights **29** 42 7N 86 24W
Benton L. **33** 47 40N 111 20W
Benton Ridge **42** 41 0N 83 48W
Bentonia **31** 32 38N 90 22W
Bentonite Spur **56** 44 52N 104 9W
Bentonville, Ark. **13** 36 22N 94 13W
Bentonville, Va. **54** 38 50N 78 19W
Bentung **112** 3 31N 101 55E
Benue → **120** 7 48N 6 46E
Benwood **54** 40 1N 80 44W
Benxi **114** 41 20N 123 48E
Benzdorp **71** 3 44N 54 5W
Benzie County ◇ **29** 44 40N 86 0W
Beo **111** 4 25N 126 50E
Beograd **95** 44 50N 20 37E
Beowawe **35** 40 35N 116 29W
Beppu **117** 33 15N 131 30E
Berau, Teluk **111** 2 30S 132 30E
Berber **121** 18 0N 34 0E
Berbera **105** 10 30N 45 2E
Berbérati **122** 4 15N 15 40E
Berbice □ **71** 4 0N 58 0W
Berbice → **71** 6 20N 57 32W
Berclair **51** 28 32N 97 36W
Berdichev **99** 49 57N 28 30E
Berdsk **100** 54 47N 83 2E
Berdyansk **99** 46 45N 36 50E
Berea, Ky. **49** 37 34N 84 17W
Berea, Nebr. **34** 42 13N 102 59W
Berebere **111** 2 25N 128 45E
Bereda **105** 11 45N 51 0E
Berekum **120** 7 29N 2 34W
Berens → **63** 52 25N 97 2W
Berens I. **63** 52 18N 97 18W
Berens River **63** 52 25N 97 0W
Beresford **47** 43 5N 96 47W
Bereşti **95** 46 6N 27 50E
Berezina → **98** 52 33N 30 14E
Berezniki **100** 59 24N 56 46E
Berezovo **100** 64 0N 65 0E
Bergama **106** 39 8N 27 15E
Bérgamo **94** 45 42N 9 40E
Bergen, Neth. **87** 52 40N 4 43E
Bergen, Norway **97** 60 23N 5 20E
Bergen, U.S.A. **39** 43 5N 77 57W
Bergen County ◇ **37** 41 0N 74 10W
Bergen-op-Zoom **87** 51 30N 4 18E
Bergenfield **37** 40 54N 73 58W
Berger **32** 38 41N 91 20W
Bergerac **90** 44 51N 0 30E
Bergland **29** 46 36N 89 34W
Bergoo **54** 38 29N 80 18W
Bergum **87** 53 13N 5 59E
Berhala, Selat **110** 1 0S 104 15E
Berhampore = Baharampur **109** 24 2N 88 27E
Berhampur **109** 19 15N 84 54E
Berheci → **95** 46 7N 27 19E
Bering Glacier **11** 60 20N 143 30W
Bering Sea **11** 60 0N 175 0W
Bering Strait **11** 65 30N 169 0W
Beringen **87** 51 3N 5 14E
Beringovskiy **101** 63 3N 179 19E
Berino **38** 32 4N 106 37W
Berisso **76** 34 56S 57 50W
Berja **91** 36 50N 2 56W
Berkeley, U.K. **83** 51 41N 2 28W
Berkeley, U.S.A. **14** 37 52N 122 16W
Berkeley County ◇, S.C. **46** 33 15N 80 0W
Berkeley County ◇, W. Va. **54** 39 27N 77 58W
Berkeley Springs **54** 39 38N 78 14W
Berkner I. **5** 79 30S 50 0W
Berkovitsa **95** 43 16N 23 8E
Berks County ◇ **45** 40 25N 76 0W
Berkshire □ **83** 51 30N 1 20W
Berkshire County ◇ **28** 42 25N 73 15W
Berkshire Hills **28** 42 20N 73 10W
Berland → **62** 54 0N 116 50W
Berlin, Germany **88** 52 32N 13 24E
Berlin, Ga. **18** 31 4N 83 37W
Berlin, Md. **27** 38 20N 75 13W
Berlin, N. Dak. **41** 46 23N 98 29W
Berlin, N.H. **36** 44 28N 71 11W
Berlin, N.J. **37** 39 48N 74 56W
Berlin, Okla. **43** 35 27N 99 36W
Berlin, Pa. **45** 39 55N 78 57W
Berlin, Wis. **55** 43 58N 88 57W
Berlin Heights **42** 41 20N 82 30W
Berlin L. **42** 41 3N 81 0W
Bermejo →, Formosa, Argentina **76** 26 51S 58 23W
Bermejo →, San Juan, Argentina **76** 32 30S 67 30W
Bermuda ■ **2** 32 45N 65 0W
Bern, Switz. **88** 46 57N 7 28E
Bern, U.S.A. **24** 39 58N 95 58W
Bernalillo **38** 35 18N 106 33W
Bernalillo County ◇ **38** 35 0N 106 45W
Bernam → **112** 3 45N 101 5E
Bernardo de Irigoyen **77** 26 15S 53 40W
Bernardo O'Higgins □ **76** 34 15S 70 45W
Bernardston **28** 42 40N 72 33W
Bernardsville **37** 40 43N 74 34W
Bernasconi **76** 37 55S 63 44W
Bernburg **88** 51 40N 11 42E
Berne = Bern **88** 46 57N 7 28E
Berne **22** 40 39N 84 57W
Bernice, La. **25** 32 49N 92 39W
Bernice, Okla. **43** 36 34N 94 57W
Bernie **32** 36 40N 89 58W
Bernier I. **126** 24 50S 113 12E
Beror Hayil **104** 31 34N 34 38E
Beroroha **123** 21 40S 45 10E
Beroun **88** 49 57N 14 5E
Berrechid **120** 33 18N 7 36W
Berrien County ◇, Ga. **18** 31 15N 83 10W
Berrien County ◇, Mich. **29** 42 0N 86 25W
Berrien Springs **29** 41 57N 86 20W
Berry, France **90** 47 0N 2 0E
Berry, Ala. **10** 33 40N 87 36W
Berry, Ky. **49** 38 31N 84 23W
Berry Is. **66** 25 40N 77 50W
Berrydale **17** 30 53N 87 3W
Berryessa L. **14** 38 31N 122 6W
Berryville, Ark. **13** 36 22N 93 34W
Berryville, Va. **54** 39 9N 77 59W
Bertha **30** 46 16N 95 4W
Berthold **41** 48 19N 101 44W
Berthoud **16** 40 19N 105 5W
Berthoud Pass **16** 39 48N 105 47W
Bertie County ◇ **40** 36 0N 77 0W
Bertoua **122** 4 30N 13 45E
Bertram, Iowa **23** 41 57N 91 32W
Bertram, Tex. **51** 30 45N 98 3W
Bertrand, Mich. **29** 41 47N 86 16W
Bertrand, Mo. **32** 36 55N 89 27W
Bertrand, Nebr. **34** 40 32N 99 38W
Berufjörður **96** 64 48N 14 29W
Beruri **71** 3 54S 61 22W
Berwick, Maine **26** 43 16N 70 52W
Berwick, N. Dak. **41** 48 22N 100 15W
Berwick, Pa. **45** 41 3N 76 14W
Berwick-upon-Tweed **82** 55 47N 2 0W
Berwyn, Ill. **21** 41 51N 87 47W
Berwyn, Nebr. **34** 41 21N 99 30W
Berwyn Mts. **82** 52 54N 3 26W
Beryl **52** 37 54N 113 40W
Besalampy **123** 16 43S 44 29E
Besançon **90** 47 15N 6 0E
Besar **110** 2 40S 116 0E
Beserah **112** 3 50N 103 21E
Besnard L. **63** 55 25N 106 0W
Besni **106** 37 41N 37 52E
Besor, N. → **104** 31 28N 34 22E
Bessemer, Ala. **10** 33 24N 86 58W
Bessemer, Mich. **29** 46 29N 90 3W
Bessemer, Pa. **45** 40 59N 80 30W
Bessemer City **40** 35 17N 81 17W
Bessie **43** 35 23N 98 59W
Best **50** 31 13N 101 37W
Bet Alfa **104** 32 31N 35 25E
Bet Dagan **104** 32 1N 34 49E
Bet Guvrin **104** 31 37N 34 54E
Bet Ha'Emeq **104** 32 58N 35 8E
Bet Hashitta **104** 32 31N 35 27E
Bet Qeshet **104** 32 41N 35 21E
Bet She'an **104** 32 30N 35 30E
Bet Shemesh **104** 31 44N 35 0E
Bet Yosef **104** 32 34N 35 33E
Betanzos **73** 19 34S 65 27W
Bétaré Oya **122** 5 40N 14 5E
Bethalto **21** 38 55N 90 2W
Bethanien **123** 26 31S 17 8E
Bethany = Al 'Ayzarīyah **104** 31 47N 35 15E
Bethany, Ill. **21** 39 39N 88 45W
Bethany, Mo. **32** 40 16N 94 2W
Bethany, Okla. **43** 35 31N 97 38W
Bethany Beach **27** 38 32N 75 5W
Bethel, Alaska **11** 60 48N 161 45W
Bethel, Conn. **28** 41 22N 73 25W
Bethel, Maine **26** 44 25N 70 47W
Bethel, Minn. **30** 45 24N 93 16W
Bethel, N.C. **40** 35 48N 77 22W
Bethel, Ohio **42** 38 58N 84 5W
Bethel, Okla. **43** 34 22N 94 51W
Bethel, Pa. **45** 40 28N 76 18W
Bethel, Vt. **36** 43 50N 72 38W
Bethel ◇ **11** 60 15N 163 0W
Bethel Acres **43** 35 22N 97 3W
Bethel Park **45** 40 20N 80 1W
Bethel Springs **48** 35 14N 88 36W
Bethera **46** 33 12N 79 47W
Bethesda, Md. **27** 38 59N 77 6W
Bethesda, N.C. **40** 35 57N 78 50W
Bethesda, Ohio **42** 40 1N 81 4W
Bethlehem = Bayt Lahm **104** 31 43N 35 12E
Bethlehem, S. Africa **123** 28 14S 28 18E
Bethlehem, Conn. **28** 41 38N 73 13W
Bethlehem, Md. **27** 38 45N 75 57W
Bethlehem, N.H. **36** 44 17N 71 41W
Bethlehem, Pa. **45** 40 37N 75 23W
Bethpage **39** 40 44N 73 30W

Bethulie
Bjargtangar

Bethulie **123** 30 30 S 25 59 E
Bethune, Colo. **16** 39 18N 102 26W
Bethune, S.C. **46** 34 25N 80 21W
Betijoque **70** 9 23N 70 44W
Betim **75** 19 58 S 44 7W
Betioky **123** 23 48 S 44 20 E
Betong **112** 5 45N 101 5 E
Betroka **123** 23 16 S 46 0 E
Betsiamites **61** 48 56N 68 40W
Betsiamites → **61** 48 56N 68 38W
Bettendorf **23** 41 32N 90 30W
Betterton **27** 39 22N 76 4W
Bettiah **109** 26 48N 84 33 E
Betul **108** 21 58N 77 59 E
Betung **110** 1 24N 111 31 E
Beuca **95** 44 14N 24 56 E
Beulah, Colo. **16** 38 5N 104 59W
Beulah, Mich. **29** 44 38N 86 6W
Beulah, N. Dak. **41** 47 16N 101 47W
Beulahville **40** 34 55N 77 46W
Beverley, Australia **126** 32 9 S 116 56 E
Beverley, U.K. **82** 53 52N 0 26W
Beverly, Kans. **24** 39 1N 97 58W
Beverly, Mass. **28** 42 33N 70 53W
Beverly, W. Va. **54** 38 51N 79 53W
Beverly, Wash. **53** 46 50N 119 56W
Beverly Beach **27** 38 53N 76 31W
Beverly Hills **15** 34 4N 118 25W
Beverwijk **87** 52 28N 4 38 E
Bevier **32** 39 45N 92 34W
Bexar **10** 34 11N 88 9W
Bexar County ◇ **51** 29 25N 98 30W
Bexley **42** 39 58N 82 56W
Beykoz **95** 41 8N 29 7 E
Beyla **120** 8 30N 8 38W
Beyneu **100** 45 10N 55 3 E
Beypazarı **106** 40 10N 31 56 E
Beyşehir Gölü **106** 37 40N 31 45 E
Bezet **104** 33 4N 35 8 E
Bezhitsa **98** 53 19N 34 17 E
Béziers **90** 43 20N 3 12 E
Bezwada = Vijayawada **109** 16 31N 80 39 E
Bhachau **108** 23 20N 70 16 E
Bhadrakh **109** 21 10N 86 30 E
Bhadravati **108** 13 49N 75 40 E
Bhagalpur **109** 25 10N 87 0 E
Bhakra Dam **108** 31 30N 76 45 E
Bhamo **109** 24 15N 97 15 E
Bhandara **108** 21 5N 79 42 E
Bhanrer Ra. **108** 23 40N 79 45 E
Bharat = India ■ **103** 20 0N 78 0 E
Bharatpur **108** 27 15N 77 30 E
Bhatpara **109** 22 50N 88 25 E
Bhaunagar = Bhavnagar **108** 21 45N 72 10 E
Bhavnagar **108** 21 45N 72 10 E
Bhawanipatna **109** 19 55N 80 10 E
Bhilsa = Vidisha **108** 23 28N 77 53 E
Bhilwara **108** 25 25N 74 38 E
Bhima → **108** 16 25N 77 17 E
Bhimavaram **109** 16 30N 81 30 E
Bhind **108** 26 30N 78 46 E
Bhiwandi **108** 19 20N 73 0 E
Bhiwani **108** 28 50N 76 9 E
Bhola **109** 22 45N 90 35 E
Bhopal **108** 23 20N 77 30 E
Bhubaneshwar **109** 20 15N 85 50 E
Bhuj **108** 23 15N 69 49 E
Bhumibol Dam **110** 17 15N 98 58 E
Bhusaval **108** 21 3N 75 46 E
Bhutan ■ **109** 27 25N 90 30 E
Biá → **70** 3 28 S 67 23W
Biafra, B. of = Bonny, Bight of **122** 3 30N 9 20 E
Biak **111** 1 10 S 136 6 E
Biała Podlaska **89** 52 4N 23 6 E
Białystok **89** 53 10N 23 10 E
Biaro **111** 2 5N 125 26 E
Biarritz **90** 43 29N 1 33W
Bibai **116** 43 19N 141 52 E
Bibala **123** 14 44 S 13 24 E
Bibb County ◇, Ala. **10** 32 57N 87 8W
Bibb County ◇, Ga. **18** 32 50N 83 45W
Bibby I. **63** 61 55N 93 0W
Biberach **88** 48 5N 9 49 E
Bibiani **120** 6 30N 2 8W
Bic **61** 48 20N 68 41W
Biche, La → **62** 59 57N 123 50W
Bicknell, Ind. **22** 38 47N 87 19W
Bicknell, Utah **52** 38 20N 111 33W
Bida **120** 9 3N 5 58 E
Bidar **108** 17 55N 77 35 E
Biddeford **26** 43 30N 70 28W
Biddiyā **104** 32 7N 35 4 E
Biddū **104** 31 50N 35 8 E
Bideford **83** 51 1N 4 13W
Bidon 5 = Poste Maurice Cortier **120** 22 14N 1 2 E
Bidor **112** 4 6N 101 15 E
Bié, Planalto de **123** 12 0 S 16 0 E
Bieber **14** 41 7N 121 8W
Biel **88** 47 8N 7 14 E
Bielé Karpaty **89** 49 5N 18 0 E
Bielefeld **88** 52 2N 8 31 E
Biella **94** 45 33N 8 3 E
Bielsko-Biała **89** 49 50N 19 2 E
Bien Hoa **112** 10 57N 106 49 E
Bienfait **63** 49 10N 102 50W
Bienne = Biel **88** 47 8N 7 14 E
Bienvenue **71** 3 0N 52 30W
Bienville **25** 32 22N 92 59W
Bienville, L. **60** 55 5N 72 40W
Bienville National Forest **31** 32 10N 89 25W
Bienville Parish ◇ **25** 32 20N 93 0W
Big →, Canada **61** 54 50N 58 55W
Big →, U.S.A. **32** 38 28N 90 37W
Big B. **61** 55 43N 60 35W
Big Baldy **20** 44 47N 115 13W
Big Bar **14** 40 45N 123 15W
Big Bay **29** 46 49N 87 44W
Big Bay de Noc **29** 45 45N 86 40W
Big Bear City **15** 34 16N 116 51W
Big Bear Lake **15** 34 15N 116 56W
Big Beaver **63** 49 10N 105 10W
Big Belt Mts. **33** 46 30N 111 25W
Big Bend, Calif. **14** 41 1N 121 55W
Big Bend, La. **25** 31 5N 91 48W
Big Bend Dam **47** 44 1N 99 23W
Big Bend National Park **50** 29 20N 103 5W
Big Black → **31** 32 3N 91 4W
Big Blue → **24** 39 35N 96 34W
Big Bow **24** 37 34N 101 34W
Big Cabin **43** 36 32N 95 14W
Big Canyon → **50** 29 45N 101 48W
Big Chino Wash → **12** 34 52N 112 28W
Big Clifty **48** 37 33N 86 9W
Big Cr. →, Canada **62** 51 42N 122 41W
Big Cr. →, U.S.A. **25** 32 10N 91 53W
Big Creek **20** 45 8N 115 20W
Big Creek L. **10** 30 43N 88 20W
Big Cypress Indian Reservation **17** 26 20N 81 10W
Big Cypress National Preserve **17** 26 0N 81 10W
Big Cypress Swamp **17** 26 15N 81 30W
Big Darby → **42** 39 37N 82 58W
Big Delta **11** 64 10N 145 51W
Big Eau Pleine Reservoir **55** 44 44N 89 46W
Big Falls, Minn. **30** 48 12N 93 48W
Big Falls, Wis. **55** 44 37N 89 1W
Big Flat **13** 36 1N 92 24W
Big Fork → **30** 48 31N 93 43W
Big Hatchet Peak **38** 31 38N 108 24W
Big Hole → **33** 45 34N 112 20W
Big Horn Basin **56** 44 15N 108 0W
Big Horn County ◇, Mont. **33** 45 25N 107 45W
Big Horn County ◇, Wyo. **56** 44 45N 108 0W
Big Island **54** 37 32N 79 22W
Big L., Calif. **14** 41 7N 121 25W
Big L., Maine **26** 45 11N 67 41W
Big L., Oreg. **44** 42 8N 120 2W
Big Lake, Alaska **11** 67 30N 149 27W
Big Lake, Minn. **30** 45 20N 93 45W
Big Lake, Tex. **50** 31 12N 101 28W
Big Lookout Mt. **44** 44 36N 117 17W
Big Lost → **20** 43 50N 112 44W
Big Muddy Cr. → **33** 48 8N 104 36W
Big Nemaha → **34** 40 1N 95 32W
Big Otter → **54** 37 7N 79 23W
Big Pine, Calif. **15** 37 10N 118 17W
Big Pine, Fla. **17** 24 40N 81 21W
Big Piney **56** 42 32N 110 7W
Big Quill L. **63** 51 55N 104 50W
Big Rapids **29** 43 42N 85 29W
Big Rib → **55** 44 56N 89 41W
Big River **63** 53 50N 107 0W
Big Rock **48** 36 35N 87 46W
Big Sable Pt. **29** 44 3N 86 1W
Big Sage Reservoir **14** 41 35N 120 38W
Big Sand L. **63** 57 45N 99 45W
Big Sandy, Mont. **33** 48 11N 110 7W
Big Sandy, Tenn. **48** 36 14N 88 5W
Big Sandy, Tex. **51** 32 35N 95 7W
Big Sandy → **12** 34 19N 113 31W
Big Sandy Cr. →, Colo. **16** 38 7N 102 29W
Big Sandy Cr. →, Mont. **33** 48 34N 109 48W
Big Sandy Cr. →, Nebr. **34** 40 13N 97 18W
Big Sandy L. **30** 46 46N 93 17W
Big Sandy Reservoir **56** 42 15N 109 26W
Big Satilla → **18** 31 27N 82 3W
Big Sheep Mt. **33** 47 10N 105 40W
Big Sioux → **47** 42 29N 96 27W
Big Smoky Valley **35** 38 40N 117 10W
Big Snowy Mts. **33** 46 45N 109 30W
Big Southern Butte **20** 43 23N 113 1W
Big Spring, Ky. **48** 37 48N 86 9W
Big Spring, Tex. **50** 32 15N 101 28W
Big Springs **34** 41 4N 102 5W
Big Stone City **47** 45 18N 96 28W
Big Stone County ◇ **30** 45 25N 96 15W
Big Stone Gap **54** 36 52N 82 47W
Big Sur **14** 36 15N 121 48W
Big Swamp → **40** 34 28N 78 57W
Big Timber **33** 45 50N 109 57W
Big Trout L. **60** 53 40N 90 0W
Big Wells **51** 28 34N 99 34W
Big Wood → **20** 42 52N 114 54W
Bigelow, Ark. **13** 35 0N 92 38W
Bigelow, Minn. **30** 43 30N 95 42W
Bigfork, Minn. **30** 47 45N 93 39W
Bigfork, Mont. **33** 48 4N 114 4W
Biggar, Canada **63** 52 4N 108 0W
Biggar, U.K. **84** 55 38N 3 31W
Biggs, Calif. **14** 39 25N 121 43W
Biggs, Oreg. **44** 45 40N 120 50W
Biggsville **21** 40 51N 90 52W
Bighorn **33** 46 10N 107 27W
Bighorn → **33** 46 10N 107 28W
Bighorn Canyon Nat. Rec. Area **33** 45 10N 108 0W
Bighorn L. **56** 44 55N 108 15W
Bighorn Mts. **56** 44 25N 107 0W
Bighorn National Forest **56** 44 50N 107 25W
Biglerville **45** 39 56N 77 15W
Bigorre **90** 43 6N 0 5 E
Bigpoint **31** 30 35N 88 29W
Bigstone L. **63** 53 42N 95 44W
Bihać **94** 44 49N 15 57 E
Bihar **109** 25 5N 85 40 E
Bihar □ **109** 25 0N 86 0 E
Bijagós, Arquipélago dos **120** 11 15N 16 10W
Bijapur, Karnataka, India **108** 16 50N 75 55 E
Bijapur, Mad. P., India **109** 18 50N 80 50 E
Bījār **106** 35 52N 47 35 E
Bijeljina **95** 44 46N 19 17 E
Bijie **115** 27 20N 105 16 E
Bijnor **108** 29 27N 78 11 E
Bijou Cr. → **16** 40 17N 104 0W
Bikaner **108** 28 2N 73 18 E
Bikin **101** 46 50N 134 20 E
Bikin → **116** 46 51N 134 2 E
Bikini Atoll **124** 12 0N 167 30 E
Bilara **108** 26 14N 73 53 E
Bilaspur **109** 22 2N 82 15 E
Bilauk Taung dan **112** 13 0N 99 0 E
Bilbao **91** 43 16N 2 56W
Bíldudalur **96** 65 41N 23 36W
Bilecik **106** 40 5N 30 5 E
Bilibino **101** 68 3N 166 20 E
Bilir **101** 65 40N 131 20 E
Bilk Creek Mts. **35** 41 50N 118 27W
Bill **56** 43 14N 105 16W
Bill Williams → **12** 34 18N 114 4W
Bill Williams Mts. **12** 35 12N 112 12W
Billerica **28** 42 34N 71 16W
Billingham **82** 54 36N 1 18W
Billings, Mo. **32** 37 4N 93 33W
Billings, Mont. **33** 45 47N 108 30W
Billings, Okla. **43** 36 32N 97 27W
Billings County ◇ **41** 47 0N 103 15W
Billiton Is = Belitung **110** 3 10 S 107 50 E
Billy Chinook, L. **44** 44 33N 121 20W
Bilma **121** 18 50N 13 30 E
Biloela **127** 24 24 S 150 31 E
Biloku **71** 1 50N 58 25W
Biloxi **31** 30 24N 88 53W
Biltine **121** 14 40N 20 50 E
Biltmore Forest **40** 35 34N 82 33W
Bima **111** 8 22 S 118 49 E
Bimbo **122** 4 15N 18 33 E
Bimini Is. **66** 25 42N 79 25W
Bin Xian **115** 35 2N 108 4 E
Bina-Etawah **108** 24 13N 78 14 E
Binalbagan **111** 10 12N 122 50 E
Bīnālūd, Kūh-e **107** 36 30N 58 30 E
Binatang **110** 2 10N 111 40 E
Binche **87** 50 26N 4 10 E
Bindura **123** 17 18 S 31 18 E
Binford **41** 47 34N 98 21W
Binger **43** 35 18N 98 21W
Bingham, Maine **26** 45 3N 69 53W
Bingham, N. Mex. **38** 33 55N 106 21W
Bingham, Nebr. **34** 42 1N 102 5W
Bingham Canyon **52** 40 32N 112 9W
Bingham County ◇ **20** 43 15N 112 30W
Binghamton **39** 42 6N 75 55W
Bingöl **106** 38 53N 40 29 E
Binh Dinh = An Nhon **112** 13 55N 109 7 E
Binh Son **112** 15 20N 108 40 E
Binjai **110** 3 20N 98 30 E
Binongko **111** 5 55 S 123 55 E
Binscarth **63** 50 37N 101 17W
Bint Jubayl **104** 33 8N 35 25 E
Bintan **110** 1 0N 104 0 E
Bintulu **110** 3 10N 113 0 E
Bintuni **111** 2 7 S 133 32 E
Binyamina **104** 32 32N 34 56 E
Binyang **115** 23 12N 108 47 E
Binzert = Bizerte **120** 37 15N 9 50 E
Bío Bío □ **76** 37 35 S 72 0W
Bioko **122** 3 30N 8 40 E
Biola **15** 36 48N 120 1W
Biq'at Bet Netofa **104** 32 49N 35 22 E
Bir **108** 19 0N 75 54 E
Bir Autrun **121** 18 15N 26 40 E
Bir Mogrein **120** 25 10N 11 25W
Bi'r Nabālā **104** 31 52N 35 12 E
Bîr Ungât **121** 22 8N 33 48 E
Bi'r Zayt **104** 31 59N 35 11 E
Bira **111** 2 3 S 132 2 E
Birak Sulaymān **104** 31 42N 35 7 E
Birao **121** 10 20N 22 47 E
Bîrca **95** 43 59N 23 36 E
Birch → **20** 43 51N 112 43W
Birch Hills **63** 52 59N 105 25W
Birch I. **63** 52 26N 99 54W
Birch L., N.W.T., Canada **62** 62 4N 116 33W
Birch L., Ont., Canada **60** 51 23N 92 18W
Birch L., U.S.A. **30** 47 45N 91 51W
Birch Mts. **62** 57 30N 113 10W
Birch Res. **43** 36 30N 96 27W
Birch River **63** 52 24N 101 6W
Birch Run **29** 43 15N 83 48W
Birch Tree **32** 36 59N 91 30W
Birchwood **55** 45 40N 91 33W
Bird **63** 56 30N 94 13W
Bird City **24** 39 45N 101 32W
Bird I. = Aves, I. de **67** 15 45N 63 55W
Bird I. **127** 22 10 S 155 28 E
Bird Island **30** 44 46N 94 54W
Birdlip **83** 51 50N 2 7W
Birds **21** 38 50N 87 40W
Birdseye **22** 38 19N 86 42W
Birdsville, Australia **127** 25 51 S 139 20 E
Birdsville, U.S.A. **27** 38 54N 76 36W
Birdum **126** 15 39 S 133 13 E
Birecik **106** 37 0N 38 0 E
Bireuen **110** 5 14N 96 39 E
Birigui **77** 21 18 S 50 16W
Birkenhead **82** 53 24N 3 1W
Bîrlad **89** 46 15N 27 38 E
Birmingham, U.K. **83** 52 30N 1 55W
Birmingham, Ala. **10** 33 31N 86 48W
Birmingham, Iowa **23** 40 53N 91 57W
Birmingham, Mich. **29** 42 33N 83 13W
Birmitrapur **109** 22 24N 84 46 E
Birnamwood **55** 44 56N 89 13W
Birni Nkonni **120** 13 55N 5 15 E
Birnin Kebbi **120** 12 32N 4 12 E
Birobidzhan **101** 48 50N 132 50 E
Birqīn **104** 32 27N 35 15 E
Birr **85** 53 7N 7 55W
Birsk **98** 55 25N 55 30 E
Birtle **63** 50 30N 101 5W
Birur **108** 13 30N 75 55 E
Bisa **111** 1 15 S 127 28 E
Bisbee, Ariz. **12** 31 27N 109 55W
Bisbee, N. Dak. **41** 48 37N 99 23W
Biscay **30** 44 50N 94 16W
Biscay, B. of **92** 45 0N 2 0W
Biscayne National Park **17** 25 25N 80 12W
Biscoe, Ark. **13** 34 49N 91 25W
Biscoe, N.C. **40** 35 22N 79 47W
Biscoe Bay **5** 77 0 S 152 0W
Biscoe I. **5** 66 0 S 67 0W
Biscostasing **60** 47 18N 82 9W
Biscucuy **70** 9 22N 69 59W
Bishop, Calif. **15** 37 22N 118 24W
Bishop, Ga. **18** 33 49N 83 26W
Bishop, Tex. **50** 27 35N 97 48W
Bishop Auckland **82** 54 40N 1 40W
Bishop Creek Reservoir **35** 41 15N 114 55W
Bishop's Falls **61** 49 2N 55 30W
Bishops Head **27** 38 16N 76 5W
Bishop's Stortford **83** 51 52N 0 11 E
Bishopville, Md. **27** 38 22N 75 12W
Bishopville, S.C. **46** 34 13N 80 15W
Biskra **120** 34 50N 5 44 E
Bislig **111** 8 15N 126 27 E
Bismarck, Ark. **13** 34 19N 93 10W
Bismarck, Ill. **21** 40 16N 87 37W
Bismarck, Mo. **32** 37 46N 90 38W
Bismarck, N. Dak. **41** 46 48N 100 47W
Bismarck Arch. **124** 2 30 S 150 0 E
Bison, Kans. **24** 38 31N 99 12W
Bison, Okla. **43** 36 12N 97 53W
Bison, S. Dak. **47** 45 31N 102 28W
Bispfors **96** 63 1N 16 37 E
Bissagos = Bijagós, Arquipélago dos **120** 11 15N 16 10W
Bissau **120** 11 45N 15 45W
Bissett **63** 51 2N 95 41W
Bistcho L. **62** 59 45N 118 50W
Bistineau, L. **25** 32 20N 93 25W
Bistreţu **95** 43 54N 23 23 E
Bistriţa **89** 47 9N 24 35 E
Bistriţa → **89** 46 30N 26 57 E
Bitam **122** 2 5N 11 25 E
Bitely **29** 43 45N 85 52W
Bithlo **17** 28 33N 81 6W
Bitkine **121** 11 59N 18 13 E
Bitlis **106** 38 20N 42 3 E
Bitola **95** 41 5N 21 10 E
Bitolj = Bitola **95** 41 5N 21 10 E
Bitter Cr. →, Utah **52** 39 59N 109 19W
Bitter Cr. →, Wyo. **56** 41 31N 109 27W
Bitter Creek **56** 41 33N 108 33W
Bitter L. = Buheirat-Murrat-el-Kubra **121** 30 15N 32 40 E
Bitter L. **47** 45 17N 97 19W
Bitterfontein **123** 31 0 S 18 32 E
Bitterroot → **33** 46 52N 114 7W
Bitterroot National Forest **20** 45 40N 114 30W
Bitterroot Range **20** 46 0N 114 20W
Bittinger **27** 39 37N 79 14W
Biu **121** 10 40N 12 3 E
Biwa-Ko **117** 35 15N 136 10 E
Biwabik **30** 47 32N 92 21W
Bixby, Mo. **32** 37 40N 91 7W
Bixby, Okla. **43** 35 57N 95 53W
Biyang **115** 32 38N 113 21 E
Biysk **100** 52 40N 85 0 E
Bizen **117** 34 43N 134 8 E
Bizerte **120** 37 15N 9 50 E
Bjargtangar **96** 65 30N 24 30W

Bjelovar Bojnūrd

Bjelovar 94 45 56N 16 49 E
Bjørnøya 4 74 30N 19 0 E
Black → = Da → 112 21 15N 105 20 E
Black →, Alaska 11 66 42N 144 42W
Black →, Ariz. 12 33 44N 110 13W
Black →, Ark. 13 35 38N 91 20W
Black →, La. 25 31 16N 91 50W
Black →, N.C. 40 34 35N 78 16W
Black →, N.Y. 39 43 59N 76 4W
Black →, S.C. 46 33 24N 79 15W
Black →, Wis. 55 43 57N 91 22W
Black →, Caledonia, Vt. 36 44 55N 72 13W
Black →, Mich. 29 45 39N 84 31W
Black →, Mich. 29 42 59N 82 27W
Black →, Windsor, Vt. 36 43 16N 72 27W
Black Bear Cr. → 43 36 25N 96 38W
Black Butte Reservoir 14 39 49N 122 20W
Black Canyon City 12 34 3N 112 5W
Black Canyon of the Gunnison National Monument 16 38 40N 107 35W
Black Cr. →, Ariz. 12 35 16N 109 14W
Black Cr. →, Miss. 31 30 39N 88 39W
Black Creek 55 44 29N 88 27W
Black Diamond, Canada 62 50 45N 114 14W
Black Diamond, U.S.A. 53 47 19N 122 0W
Black Earth 55 43 8N 89 45W
Black Forest = Schwarzwald 88 48 0N 8 0 E
Black Forest 16 39 0N 104 43W
Black Hawk 47 44 9N 103 19W
Black Hawk County ◇ 23 42 25N 92 20W
Black Hills 47 44 0N 103 45W
Black Hills National Forest 47 44 10N 103 50W
Black I. 63 51 12N 96 30W
Black Kettle National Grassland 43 35 45N 99 45W
Black L., Canada 63 59 12N 105 15W
Black L., Mich. 29 45 28N 84 16W
Black L., N.Y. 39 44 31N 75 36W
Black Mesa, Ariz. 12 36 30N 110 15W
Black Mesa, Okla. 43 36 58N 102 58W
Black Mt. = Mynydd Du 83 51 45N 3 45W
Black Mountain 40 35 37N 82 19W
Black Mt., Ky. 49 36 54N 82 54W
Black Mt., Oreg. 44 45 13N 119 17W
Black Mt., Tex. 50 29 38N 100 20W
Black Mts., U.K. 83 51 52N 3 5W
Black Mts., U.S.A. 12 35 30N 114 30W
Black Pine Pk. 20 42 8N 113 8W
Black Range 38 33 15N 107 50W
Black River, Jamaica 66 18 0N 77 50W
Black River, U.S.A. 39 44 1N 75 48W
Black River Falls 55 44 18N 90 51W
Black Rock, Ark. 13 36 7N 91 6W
Black Rock, N. Mex. 38 35 5N 108 47W
Black Rock Desert 35 41 10N 118 50W
Black Rock Range 35 41 20N 119 8W
Black Sea 93 43 30N 35 0 E
Black Springs 35 39 37N 119 51W
Black Squirrel Cr. → 16 38 14N 104 21W
Black Volta → 120 8 41N 1 33W
Black Warrior → 10 32 32N 87 51W
Blackall 127 24 25 S 145 45 E
Blackball 128 42 22 S 171 26 E
Blackbird 27 39 21N 75 40W
Blackburn, U.K. 82 53 44N 2 30W
Blackburn, Mo. 32 39 6N 93 29W
Blackburn, Okla. 43 36 23N 96 38W
Blackburn, Mt. 11 61 44N 143 26W
Blackduck 30 47 44N 94 33W
Blackfeet Indian Reservation 33 48 45N 113 0W
Blackfoot 20 43 11N 112 21W
Blackfoot →, Idaho 20 43 8N 112 30W
Blackfoot →, Mont. 33 46 52N 113 53W
Blackfoot River Reservoir 20 43 0N 111 43W
Blackford 48 37 27N 87 56W
Blackford County ◇ 22 40 30N 85 20W
Blackhall Mt. 56 41 2N 106 41W
Blackie 62 50 36N 113 37W
Blackman 17 30 56N 86 38W
Blackpool 82 53 48N 3 3W
Blacks Fork → 56 41 25N 109 37W
Blacks Harbour 61 45 3N 66 49W
Blacksburg, S.C. 46 35 7N 81 31W
Blacksburg, Va. 54 37 14N 80 25W
Blackshear 18 31 18N 82 14W
Blackshear L. 18 31 51N 83 56W
Blacksod B. 85 54 6N 10 0W
Blackstock 46 34 34N 81 8W
Blackstone, Mass. 28 42 1N 71 30W
Blackstone, Va. 54 37 4N 78 0W
Blackstone → 62 61 5N 122 55W
Blackstone Ra. 126 26 0 S 129 0 E
Blackville, Canada 61 46 44N 65 50W
Blackville, U.S.A. 46 33 22N 81 16W
Blackwater 32 38 59N 92 59W
Blackwater →, Ireland 85 51 55N 7 50W
Blackwater →, U.K. 85 54 31N 6 35W
Blackwater →, Fla. 17 30 36N 87 2W
Blackwater →, Md. 27 38 21N 76 1W
Blackwater →, Tex. 50 33 40N 100 47W
Blackwell, Okla. 43 36 48N 97 17W
Blackwell, Tex. 50 32 5N 100 19W
Blackwood 37 39 48N 75 4W
Bladen 34 40 19N 98 36W
Bladen County ◇ 40 34 30N 78 30W
Bladenboro 40 34 33N 78 48W
Bladsell 39 42 48N 78 50W
Blaenau Ffestiniog 82 53 0N 3 57W
Blagodarnoye 99 45 7N 43 37 E
Blagoveshchensk 101 50 20N 127 30 E
Blain 45 40 20N 77 31W
Blaine, Minn. 30 45 10N 93 13W
Blaine, Wash. 53 48 59N 122 45W
Blaine County ◇, Idaho 20 43 30N 114 0W
Blaine County ◇, Mont. 33 48 20N 109 0W
Blaine County ◇, Nebr. 34 42 0N 100 0W
Blaine County ◇, Okla. 43 35 50N 98 25W
Blaine Lake 63 52 51N 106 52W
Blair, Nebr. 34 41 33N 96 8W
Blair, Okla. 43 34 47N 99 20W
Blair, Wis. 55 44 18N 91 14W
Blair Athol 127 22 42 S 147 31 E
Blair Atholl 84 56 46N 3 50W
Blair County ◇ 45 40 30N 78 20W
Blairgowrie 84 56 36N 3 20W
Blairmore 62 49 40N 114 25W
Blairs 54 36 41N 79 23W
Blairsburg 23 42 29N 93 39W
Blairsden 14 39 47N 120 37W
Blairstown, Iowa 23 41 55N 92 5W
Blairstown, Mo. 32 38 34N 93 58W
Blairstown, N.J. 37 40 59N 74 57W
Blairsville, Ga. 18 34 53N 83 58W
Blairsville, Pa. 45 40 26N 79 16W
Blaj 95 46 10N 23 57 E
Blake Pt. 29 48 11N 88 25W
Blakely, Ga. 18 31 23N 84 56W
Blakely, Pa. 45 41 28N 75 37W
Blakeman 24 39 49N 101 7W
Blakesburg 23 40 58N 92 38W
Blakeslee 42 41 32N 84 44W
Blalock 44 45 42N 120 22W
Blanc, Mont 90 45 48N 6 50 E
Blanca 16 37 27N 105 31W
Blanca, Bahía 78 39 10 S 61 30W
Blanca, Sierra 50 31 15N 105 26W
Blanca Peak 16 37 35N 105 29W
Blanchard, Idaho 20 48 1N 116 59W
Blanchard, Iowa 23 40 35N 95 13W
Blanchard, N. Dak. 41 47 21N 97 13W
Blanchard, Okla. 43 35 8N 97 39W
Blanchard, Wash. 53 48 36N 122 25W
Blanchard → 42 41 2N 84 18W
Blanchardville 55 42 49N 89 52W
Blanche L., S. Austral., Australia 127 29 15 S 139 40 E
Blanche L., W. Austral., Australia 126 22 25 S 123 17 E
Blanchester 42 39 17N 83 59W
Blanco, N. Mex. 38 36 43N 107 50W
Blanco, Okla. 43 34 45N 95 46W
Blanco, Tex. 51 30 6N 98 25W
Blanco →, Argentina 76 30 20 S 68 42W
Blanco →, U.S.A. 51 29 51N 97 55W
Blanco, C., U.S.A. 44 42 51N 124 34W
Blanco, C., C. Rica 66 9 34N 85 8W
Blanco County ◇ 51 30 17N 98 25W
Bland, Mo. 32 38 18N 91 38W
Bland, Va. 54 37 6N 81 7W
Bland County ◇ 54 37 6N 81 7W
Blanda → 96 65 20N 19 40W
Blandford 28 42 11N 72 56W
Blandford Forum 83 50 52N 2 10W
Blanding 52 37 37N 109 29W
Blandinsville 21 40 33N 90 52W
Blaney Park 29 46 9N 85 55W
Blankenberge 87 51 20N 3 9 E
Blanket 51 31 49N 98 47W
Blanquilla, La 71 11 51N 64 37W
Blanquillo 77 32 53 S 55 37W
Blantyre 123 15 45 S 35 0 E
Blarney 85 51 57N 8 35W
Blatnitsa 95 43 41N 28 32 E
Blåvands Huk 97 55 33N 8 4 E
Blaydon 82 54 56N 1 47W
Blaze, Pt. 126 12 56 S 130 11 E
Bleckley County ◇ 18 32 25N 83 15W
Blednaya, Gora 100 76 20N 65 0 E
Bledsoe 50 33 38N 103 1W
Bledsoe County ◇ 49 35 36N 85 11W
Bleiburg 88 46 35N 14 49 E
Blejeşti 95 44 19N 25 27 E
Blekinge län □ 97 56 20N 15 20 E
Blencoe 23 41 56N 96 5W
Blenheim 128 41 38 S 173 57 E
Bletchley 83 51 59N 0 44W
Blewett Falls L. 40 35 3N 79 54W
Blida 120 36 30N 2 49 E
Bligh Sound 128 44 47 S 167 32 E
Blind River 60 46 10N 82 58W
Bliss 20 42 56N 114 57W
Blissfield, Mich. 29 41 50N 83 52W
Blissfield, Ohio 42 40 24N 81 58W
Blitar 111 8 5 S 112 11 E
Blitchton 18 32 12N 81 26W
Blitta 120 8 23N 1 6 E
Block I. 28 41 11N 71 35W
Block Island Sd. 28 41 15N 71 40W
Blocker 43 35 4N 95 34W
Blockton 23 40 37N 94 29W
Blodgett 32 37 0N 89 32W
Blodgett Iceberg Tongue 5 66 8 S 130 35 E
Bloemfontein 123 29 6 S 26 14 E
Bloemhof 123 27 38 S 25 32 E
Blois 90 47 35N 1 20 E
Blönduós 96 65 40N 20 12W
Bloodsworth I. 27 38 10N 76 3W
Bloodvein → 63 51 47N 96 43W
Bloody Foreland 85 55 10N 8 18W
Bloomer 55 45 6N 91 29W
Bloomfield, Ind. 22 39 1N 86 57W
Bloomfield, Iowa 23 40 45N 92 25W
Bloomfield, Ky. 49 37 55N 85 19W
Bloomfield, Mo. 32 36 53N 89 56W
Bloomfield, N.J. 37 40 48N 74 12W
Bloomfield, N. Mex. 38 36 43N 107 59W
Bloomfield, Nebr. 34 42 36N 97 39W
Blooming Grove 51 32 6N 96 43W
Blooming Prairie 30 43 52N 93 3W
Bloomingburg 42 39 36N 83 24W
Bloomingdale 49 36 34N 82 32W
Bloomington, Idaho 20 42 11N 111 24W
Bloomington, Ill. 21 40 28N 89 0W
Bloomington, Ind. 22 39 10N 86 32W
Bloomington, Minn. 30 44 50N 93 17W
Bloomington, Tex. 51 28 39N 96 54W
Bloomington, Wis. 55 42 53N 90 55W
Bloomsburg 45 41 0N 76 27W
Bloomsdale 32 38 1N 90 13W
Bloomville 42 41 3N 83 1W
Blora 111 6 57 S 111 25 E
Blossburg 45 41 41N 77 4W
Blossom 51 33 40N 95 23W
Blount County ◇, Ala. 10 33 57N 86 28W
Blount County ◇, Tenn. 49 35 46N 83 58W
Blountstown 17 30 27N 85 3W
Blountsville 10 34 5N 86 35W
Blountville 49 36 32N 82 19W
Bloxom 54 37 50N 75 38W
Blue → 22 38 11N 86 19W
Blue Cypress L. 17 27 44N 80 45W
Blue Diamond 35 36 3N 115 24W
Blue Earth 30 43 38N 94 6W
Blue Earth County ◇ 30 44 5N 94 0W
Blue Eye 32 36 30N 93 24W
Blue Hill, Maine 26 44 25N 68 35W
Blue Hill, Nebr. 34 40 20N 98 27W
Blue Knob 45 40 17N 78 34W
Blue Lake 14 40 53N 123 59W
Blue Mesa Reservoir 16 38 28N 107 20W
Blue Mound, Ill. 21 39 42N 89 7W
Blue Mound, Kans. 24 38 5N 95 0W
Blue Mountain, Colo. 16 40 15N 108 52W
Blue Mountain, Miss. 31 34 40N 89 2W
Blue Mountain L. 13 35 2N 93 53W
Blue Mts. 127 33 40 S 150 0 E
Blue Mt., Ark. 13 34 41N 94 3W
Blue Mt., N.H. 36 44 47N 71 28W
Blue Mt., Pa. 45 40 30N 76 20W
Blue Mts., Maine 26 44 50N 70 35W
Blue Mts., Oreg. 44 45 0N 118 20W
Blue Mud B. 127 13 30 S 136 0 E
Blue Nile = An Nîl el Azraq □ 121 12 30N 34 30 E
Blue Nile = Nîl el Azraq → 121 15 38N 32 31 E
Blue Rapids 24 39 41N 96 39W
Blue Ridge, Ga. 18 34 52N 84 20W
Blue Ridge, Va. 54 36 40N 80 50W
Blue Ridge L. 18 34 53N 84 17W
Blue River, Oreg. 44 44 9N 122 20W
Blue River, Wis. 55 43 11N 90 34W
Blue Springs, Mo. 32 39 1N 94 17W
Blue Springs, Nebr. 34 40 9N 96 40W
Blue Stack Mts. 85 54 46N 8 5W
Blueberry 55 46 35N 91 55W
Blueberry → 62 56 45N 120 49W
Bluefield, Va. 54 37 15N 81 17W
Bluefield, W. Va. 54 37 16N 81 13W
Bluefields 66 12 20N 83 50W
Bluejacket 43 36 48N 95 4W
Bluejoint L. 44 42 42N 119 38W
Bluestone L. 54 37 38N 80 53W
Bluewater 38 35 15N 107 59W
Bluff, N.Z. 128 46 37 S 168 20 E
Bluff, U.S.A. 52 37 17N 109 33W
Bluff City, Ark. 13 33 43N 93 8W
Bluff City, Kans. 24 37 5N 97 53W
Bluff City, Tenn. 49 36 28N 82 16W
Bluff Park 10 33 27N 86 47W
Bluffs 21 39 45N 90 32W
Bluffton, Ark. 13 34 54N 93 36W
Bluffton, Ga. 18 31 31N 84 52W
Bluffton, Ind. 22 40 44N 85 11W
Bluffton, Minn. 30 46 28N 95 14W
Bluffton, Ohio 42 40 54N 83 54W
Bluffton, S.C. 46 32 14N 80 52W
Bluford 21 38 20N 88 45W
Blumenau 77 27 0 S 49 0W
Blunt 47 44 31N 99 59W
Bly 44 42 24N 121 3W
Blyn 53 48 1N 123 0W
Blyth 82 55 8N 1 32W
Blythe, Calif. 15 33 37N 114 36W
Blythe, Ga. 18 33 17N 82 12W
Blytheville 13 35 56N 89 55W
Blythewood 46 34 13N 80 58W
Bo 120 7 55N 11 50W
Bo Duc 112 11 58N 106 50 E
Bo Hai 114 39 0N 120 0 E
Bo Xian 115 33 50N 115 45 E
Boa Esperança 71 3 21N 61 23W
Boa Nova 75 14 22 S 40 10W
Boa Viagem 74 5 7 S 39 44W
Boa Vista 71 2 48N 60 30W
Boaco 66 12 29N 85 35W
Boardman, Ohio 42 41 2N 80 40W
Boardman, Oreg. 44 45 51N 119 43W
Boaz, Ala. 10 34 12N 86 10W
Boaz, Wis. 55 43 20N 90 32W
Bobai 115 22 17N 109 59 E
Bobbili 109 18 35N 83 30 E
Bobcaygeon 60 44 33N 78 33W
Bobo-Dioulasso 120 11 8N 4 13W
Boboc 95 45 13N 26 59 E
Bobonaza → 70 2 36 S 76 38W
Bóbr → 88 52 4N 15 4 E
Bobraomby, Tanjon' i 123 12 40 S 49 10 E
Bobruysk 98 53 10N 29 15 E
Bobtown 45 39 46N 79 59W
Bobures 70 9 15N 71 11W
Boca de Drago 71 11 0N 61 50W
Boca de Uracoa 71 9 8N 62 20W
Bôca do Acre 72 8 50 S 67 27W
Bôca do Jari 71 1 7 S 51 58W
Bôca do Moaco 72 7 41 S 68 17W
Boca Grande, U.S.A. 17 26 45N 82 16W
Boca Grande, Venezuela 71 8 40N 60 40W
Boca Raton 17 26 21N 80 5W
Bocaiúva 75 17 7 S 43 49W
Bocanda 120 7 5N 4 31W
Bocaranga 122 7 0N 15 35 E
Bocas del Toro 66 9 15N 82 20W
Bocholt 88 51 50N 6 35 E
Bochum 88 51 28N 7 12 E
Bock 30 45 47N 93 33W
Boconó 70 9 15N 70 16W
Boconó → 70 8 43N 69 34W
Bocoyna 64 27 52N 107 35W
Boda 122 4 19N 17 26 E
Bodaybo 101 57 50N 114 0 E
Bodcaw 13 33 33N 93 25W
Bode 23 42 52N 94 17W
Bodega Bay 14 38 20N 123 3W
Boden 96 65 50N 21 42 E
Bodensee 88 47 35N 9 25 E
Bodhan 108 18 40N 77 44 E
Bodmin 83 50 28N 4 44W
Bodmin Moor 83 50 33N 4 36W
Bodoquena, Serra da 73 21 0 S 56 50W
Bodrog → 89 48 15N 21 35 E
Bodrum 106 37 5N 27 30 E
Boelus 34 41 5N 98 43W
Boende 122 0 24 S 21 12 E
Boerne 51 29 47N 98 44W
Boeuf → 25 30 36N 92 3W
Boffa 120 10 16N 14 3W
Bogalusa 25 30 47N 89 52W
Bogan → 127 29 59 S 146 17 E
Bogard 32 39 27N 93 32W
Bogata 51 33 28N 95 13W
Bogenfels 123 27 25 S 15 25 E
Boggeragh Mts. 85 52 2N 8 55W
Bognor Regis 83 50 47N 0 40W
Bogo 111 11 3N 124 0 E
Bogong, Mt. 127 36 47 S 147 17 E
Bogor 111 6 36 S 106 48 E
Bogorodskoye 101 52 22N 140 30 E
Bogota, Colombia 70 4 34N 74 0W
Bogota, U.S.A. 48 36 10N 89 26W
Bogotol 100 56 15N 89 50 E
Bogra 109 24 51N 89 22 E
Boguchany 101 58 40N 97 30 E
Bogué, Maurit. 120 16 45N 14 10W
Bogue, Kans. 24 39 22N 99 41W
Bogue, N.C. 40 34 42N 77 2W
Bogue Chitto 31 31 26N 90 27W
Bogue Chitto → 25 30 34N 89 50W
Bogue Hama Cr. → 31 31 10N 88 55W
Bohemian Forest = Böhmerwald 88 49 30N 12 40 E
Böhmerwald 88 49 30N 12 40 E
Bohol 111 9 50N 124 10 E
Bohol Sea 111 9 0N 124 0 E
Bohotleh 105 8 20N 46 25 E
Boi, Pta. de 77 23 55 S 45 15W
Boiaçu 71 0 27 S 61 46W
Boileau, C. 126 17 40 S 122 7 E
Boiling Springs 40 35 15N 81 40W
Boipeba, I. de 75 13 39 S 38 55W
Bois → 75 18 35 S 50 2W
Bois Blanc I. 29 45 46N 84 27W
Bois D'Arc 32 37 16N 93 30W
Bois de Sioux → 41 46 16N 96 36W
Boise 20 43 37N 116 13W
Boise → 20 43 49N 117 1W
Boise City 43 36 44N 102 31W
Boise County ◇ 20 44 0N 115 45W
Boise National Forest 20 44 5N 115 30W
Boissevain 63 49 15N 100 5W
Boistfort Pk. 53 46 29N 123 12W
Bojador C. 120 26 0N 14 30W
Bojana → 95 41 52N 19 22 E
Bojnūrd 107 37 30N 57 20 E

Bojonegoro Boyes

Bojonegoro 111 7 11 S 111 54 E
Bokchito 43 34 1N 96 9W
Boké 120 10 56N 14 17W
Boknafjorden 97 59 14N 5 40 E
Bokoro 121 12 25N 17 14 E
Bokoshe 43 35 11N 94 47W
Bokote 122 0 12 S 21 8 E
Bokpyin 112 11 18N 98 42 E
Bokungu 122 0 35 S 22 50 E
Bol 121 13 30N 15 0 E
Bolama 120 11 30N 15 30W
Bolan Pass 107 29 50N 67 20 E
Bolaños → 64 21 14N 104 8W
Bolbec 90 49 30N 0 30 E
Bolckow 32 40 7N 94 50W
Bold Spring 48 35 58N 87 41W
Boldeşti 95 45 3N 26 2 E
Bole 113 45 11N 81 37 E
Boles 13 34 47N 94 3W
Bolesławiec 88 51 17N 15 37 E
Boley 43 35 29N 96 29W
Boli 114 45 46N 130 31 E
Boligee 10 32 45N 88 2W
Bolinao C. 111 16 23N 119 55 E
Boling 51 29 16N 95 57W
Bolingbroke 18 32 57N 83 48W
Bolinger 25 32 57N 93 41W
Bolívar, Argentina 76 36 15 S 60 53W
Bolívar, Antioquía, Colombia 70 5 50N 76 1W
Bolívar, Cauca, Colombia 70 2 0N 77 0W
Bolívar, Peru 72 7 18 S 77 48W
Bolivar, Mo. 32 37 37N 93 25W
Bolivar, N.Y. 39 42 4N 78 10W
Bolivar, Tenn. 48 35 12N 89 0W
Bolívar □, Colombia 70 9 0N 74 40W
Bolívar □, Ecuador 70 1 15 S 79 5W
Bolívar □, Venezuela 71 6 20N 63 30W
Bolivar, Mt. 44 42 51N 123 56W
Bolivar County ◇ 31 33 50N 90 43W
Bolivar Peninsula 51 29 27N 94 39W
Bolivia 40 34 4N 78 9W
Bolivia ■ 73 17 6 S 64 0W
Bolivian Plateau 68 20 0 S 67 30W
Bolling 10 31 43N 86 42W
Bollinger County ◇ 32 37 20N 90 0W
Bollnäs 97 61 21N 16 24 E
Bolobo 122 2 6 S 16 20 E
Bologna 94 44 30N 11 20 E
Bologoye 98 57 55N 34 0 E
Bolomba 122 0 35N 19 0 E
Bolonchenticul 65 20 0N 89 49W
Bolong 111 7 6N 122 14 E
Boloven, Cao Nguyen 112 15 10N 106 30 E
Bolsena, L. di 94 42 35N 11 55 E
Bolshereche 100 56 4N 74 45 E
Bolshevik, Ostrov 101 78 30N 102 0 E
Bolshezemelskaya Tundra 98 67 0N 56 0 E
Bolshoi Kavkas 99 42 50N 44 0 E
Bolshoy Anyuy → 101 68 30N 160 49 E
Bolshoy Atlym 100 62 25N 66 50 E
Bolshoy Begichev, Ostrov 101 74 20N 112 30 E
Bolshoy Lyakhovskiy, Ostrov 101 73 35N 142 0 E
Bolsward 87 53 3N 5 32 E
Bolton, U.K. 82 53 35N 2 26W
Bolton, Miss. 31 32 21N 90 28W
Bolton, N.C. 40 34 20N 78 25W
Bolu 106 40 45N 31 35 E
Bolvadin 106 38 45N 31 4 E
Bolzano 94 46 30N 11 20 E
Bom Comércio 73 9 45 S 65 54W
Bom Conselho 74 9 10 S 36 41W
Bom Despacho 75 19 43 S 45 15W
Bom Jesus 74 9 4 S 44 22W
Bom Jesus da Gurguéia, Serra 74 9 0 S 43 0W
Bom Jesus da Lapa 75 13 15 S 43 25W
Boma, U.S.A. 49 36 8N 85 41W
Boma, Zaïre 122 5 50 S 13 4 E
Bomarton 51 33 31N 99 26W
Bomba, La 64 31 53N 115 2W
Bombala 127 36 56 S 149 15 E
Bombay, India 108 18 55N 72 50 E
Bombay, U.S.A. 39 44 56N 74 34W
Bomboma 122 2 25N 18 55 E
Bomili 122 1 45N 27 5 E
Bomongo 122 1 27N 18 21 E
Bomoseen, L. 36 43 39N 73 13W
Bomu → 122 4 40N 23 30 E
Bon, C. 121 37 1N 11 2 E
Bon Air, Tenn. 49 35 57N 85 22W
Bon Air, Va. 54 37 31N 77 34W
Bon Homme County ◇ 47 43 0N 97 50W
Bon Secour B. 10 30 15N 87 58W
Bonaire, Neth. Ant. 67 12 10N 68 15W
Bonaire, U.S.A. 18 32 33N 83 36W
Bonanza, Nic. 66 13 54N 84 35W
Bonanza, Colo. 16 38 18N 106 8W
Bonanza, Oreg. 44 42 12N 121 24W
Bonanza, Utah 52 40 1N 109 11W
Bonanza Pk. 53 48 14N 120 52W
Bonaparte 23 40 42N 91 48W
Bonaparte, Mt. 53 48 45N 119 8W
Bonaparte Archipelago 126 14 0 S 124 30 E
Bonaventure 61 48 5N 65 32W
Bonavista 61 48 40N 53 5W
Bonavista, C. 61 48 42N 53 5W
Bond, Colo. 16 39 53N 106 42W
Bond, Miss. 31 30 54N 89 10W
Bond County ◇ 21 38 50N 89 25W
Bond Falls Flowage, L. 29 46 30N 89 15W
Bondo 122 3 55N 23 53 E
Bondoukou 120 8 2N 2 47W
Bondowoso 111 7 55 S 113 49 E
Bondurant, Iowa 23 41 42N 93 28W
Bondurant, Ky. 48 36 31N 89 19W
Bondville 21 40 7N 88 22W
Bone, Teluk 111 4 10 S 120 50 E
Bone Gap 21 38 27N 88 0W
Bone Rate 111 7 25 S 121 5 E
Bone Rate, Kepulauan 111 6 30 S 121 10 E
Bo'ness 84 56 0N 3 38W
Bonetraill 41 48 26N 103 51W
Bong Son = Hoai Nhon 112 14 28N 109 1 E
Bongandanga 122 1 24N 21 3 E
Bongor 121 10 35N 15 20 E
Bonham 51 33 35N 96 11W
Bonifacio 94 41 24N 9 10 E
Bonifacio, Bouches de 94 41 12N 9 15 E
Bonifay 17 30 47N 85 41W
Bonilla 47 44 35N 98 30W
Bonin Is. 124 27 0N 142 0 E
Bonita 25 32 55N 91 40W
Bonita Springs 17 26 21N 81 47W
Bonlee 40 35 39N 79 25W
Bonn 88 50 43N 7 6 E
Bonne Terre 32 37 55N 90 33W
Bonneau 46 33 16N 79 58W
Bonner County ◇ 20 48 20N 116 30W
Bonners Ferry 20 48 42N 116 19W
Bonneville County ◇ 20 43 20N 111 20W
Bonneville Pk. 20 42 46N 112 8W
Bonneville Salt Flats 52 40 45N 113 50W
Bonnie 21 38 12N 88 54W
Bonnie Doone 40 35 5N 78 57W
Bonnie Rock 126 30 29 S 118 22 E
Bonnieville 49 37 23N 85 54W
Bonny, Bight of 122 3 30N 9 20 E
Bonny Reservoir 16 39 37N 102 11W
Bonnyville 63 54 20N 110 45W
Bono 13 35 55N 90 48W
Bonoi 111 1 45 S 137 41 E
Bontang 110 0 10N 117 30 E
Bonthain 111 5 34 S 119 56 E
Bonthe 120 7 30N 12 33W
Bontoc 111 17 7N 120 58 E
Book Cliffs 52 39 20N 109 0W
Booker 50 36 27N 100 32W
Boom 87 51 6N 4 20 E
Boomer 54 38 9N 81 17W
Boone, Colo. 16 38 15N 104 15W
Boone, Iowa 23 42 4N 93 53W
Boone, N.C. 40 36 13N 81 41W
Boone, Nebr. 34 41 38N 97 55W
Boone → 23 42 19N 93 56W
Boone County ◇, Ark. 13 36 14N 93 7W
Boone County ◇, Ill. 21 42 20N 89 50W
Boone County ◇, Ind. 22 40 5N 86 30W
Boone County ◇, Iowa 23 42 0N 94 0W
Boone County ◇, Ky. 49 38 55N 84 45W
Boone County ◇, Mo. 32 39 0N 92 20W
Boone County ◇, Nebr. 34 41 40N 98 0W
Boone County ◇, W. Va. 54 38 4N 81 49W
Boones Mill 54 37 7N 79 57W
Booneville, Ark. 13 35 8N 93 55W
Booneville, Ky. 49 37 29N 83 41W
Booneville, Miss. 31 34 39N 88 34W
Boonsboro 27 39 30N 77 39W
Boonton 37 40 54N 74 25W
Boonville, Calif. 14 39 1N 123 22W
Boonville, Ind. 22 38 3N 87 16W
Boonville, Mo. 32 38 58N 92 44W
Boonville, N.C. 40 36 14N 80 43W
Boonville, N.Y. 39 43 29N 75 20W
Boothbay Harbor 26 43 51N 69 38W
Boothia, Gulf of 59 71 0N 90 0W
Boothia Pen. 58 71 0N 94 0W
Boothville 25 29 20N 89 25W
Bootle, Cumbria, U.K. 82 54 17N 3 24W
Bootle, Merseyside, U.K. 82 53 28N 3 1W
Booué 122 0 5 S 11 55 E
Boqueron 57 18 2N 67 10W
Boquerón □ 73 21 30 S 60 0W
Boquete 66 8 46N 82 27W
Boquillas 50 29 11N 102 58W
Boquillas del Carmen 64 29 17N 102 53W
Bôr, Sudan 121 6 10N 31 40 E
Bor, Yugoslavia 95 44 8N 22 7 E
Borah Peak 20 44 8N 113 47W
Borama 105 9 55N 43 7 E
Borås 97 57 43N 12 56 E
Borāzjān 107 29 22N 51 10 E
Borba 71 4 12 S 59 34W
Borborema, Planalto da 74 7 0 S 37 0W
Bordeaux, France 90 44 50N 0 36W
Bordeaux, U.S.A. 48 36 12N 86 50W
Bordelonville 25 31 6N 91 55W
Borden 61 46 18N 63 47W
Borden County ◇ 50 32 46N 101 27W
Borden I. 4 78 30N 111 30W
Borden Springs 10 33 56N 85 28W
Bordentown 37 40 9N 74 43W
Borders □ 84 55 35N 2 50W
Bordertown 127 36 19 S 140 45 E
Borðeyri 96 65 12N 21 6W
Bordj Fly Ste. Marie 120 27 19N 2 32W
Bordj-in-Eker 120 24 9N 5 3 E
Bordj Omar Driss 120 28 10N 6 40 E
Bordulac 41 47 23N 98 58W
Borgarnes 96 64 32N 21 55W
Børgefjellet 96 65 20N 13 45 E
Borger, Neth. 87 52 54N 6 44 E
Borger, U.S.A. 50 35 39N 101 24W
Borgholm 97 56 52N 16 39 E
Borgne, L. 25 30 1N 89 42W
Borisoglebsk 99 51 27N 42 5 E
Borisov 98 54 17N 28 28 E
Borja 70 4 20 S 77 40W
Borkou 121 18 15N 18 50 E
Borkum I. 88 53 38N 6 41 E
Borlänge 97 60 29N 15 26 E
Borley, C. 5 66 15 S 52 30 E
Borneo 110 1 0N 115 0 E
Bornholm 97 55 10N 15 0 E
Borobudur 111 7 36 S 110 13 E
Borogontsy 101 62 42N 131 8 E
Boromo 120 11 45N 2 58W
Boron 15 35 0N 117 39W
Borongan 111 11 37N 125 26 E
Borovan 95 43 27N 23 45 E
Borovichi 98 58 25N 33 55 E
Borrego Springs 15 33 15N 116 23W
Borroloola 127 16 4 S 136 17 E
Borth 83 52 29N 4 3W
Borujerd 106 33 55N 48 50 E
Borup 30 47 11N 96 30W
Borzya 101 50 24N 116 31 E
Bosa 94 40 17N 8 32 E
Bosanska Gradiška 94 45 10N 17 15 E
Bosaso 105 11 12N 49 18 E
Boscastle 83 50 42N 4 42W
Boscawen 36 43 19N 71 37W
Bosco 25 32 17N 92 5W
Boscobel 55 43 8N 90 42W
Bose 115 23 53N 106 35 E
Boshan 114 36 28N 117 49 E
Boshrūyeh 107 33 50N 57 30 E
Bosler 56 41 35N 105 42W
Bosna → 95 45 4N 18 29 E
Bosna i Hercegovina □ 94 44 0N 18 0 E
Bosnik 111 1 5 S 136 10 E
Bosobolo 122 4 15N 19 50 E
Bosporus = Karadeniz Boğazı 106 41 10N 29 10 E
Bosque 38 34 34N 106 47W
Bosque County ◇ 51 31 56N 97 39W
Bossangoa 122 6 35N 17 30 E
Bossekop 96 69 57N 23 15 E
Bossembélé 121 5 25N 17 40 E
Bossier City 25 32 31N 93 44W
Bossier Parish ◇ 25 32 42N 93 44W
Bosso 121 13 43N 13 19 E
Bossut C. 126 18 42 S 121 35 E
Bosten Hu 113 41 55N 87 40 E
Boston, U.K. 82 52 59N 0 2W
Boston, Ga. 18 30 47N 83 47W
Boston, Mass. 28 42 22N 71 4W
Boston, Tex. 51 33 27N 94 25W
Boston Bar 62 49 52N 121 30W
Boston Bay 28 42 22N 70 54W
Boston Mts. 13 35 42N 93 15W
Bostwick, Fla. 17 29 46N 81 38W
Bostwick, Ga. 18 33 44N 83 31W
Boswell, Canada 62 49 28N 116 45W
Boswell, Ind. 22 40 31N 87 23W
Boswell, Okla. 43 34 2N 95 52W
Boswell, Pa. 45 40 10N 79 2W
Bosworth 32 39 28N 93 20W
Botetourt County ◇ 54 37 32N 79 41W
Botevgrad 95 42 55N 23 47 E
Bothnia, G. of 96 63 0N 20 0 E
Botijas 57 18 15N 66 22W
Botkins 42 40 28N 84 11W
Botletle → 123 20 10 S 23 15 E
Botoroaga 95 44 8N 25 32 E
Botoşani 89 47 42N 26 41 E
Botswana ■ 123 22 0 S 24 0 E
Bottineau 41 48 50N 100 27W
Bottineau County ◇ 41 48 55N 101 0W
Botucatu 77 22 55 S 48 30W
Botwood 61 49 6N 55 23W
Bou Djébéha 120 18 25N 2 45W
Bou Izakarn 120 29 12N 9 46W
Bouaké 120 7 40N 5 2W
Bouar 122 6 0N 15 40 E
Bouârfa 120 32 32N 1 58 E
Bouca 122 6 45N 18 25 E
Bouches-du-Rhône □ 90 43 37N 5 2 E
Bougainville C. 126 13 57 S 126 4 E
Bougie = Bejaia 120 36 42N 5 2 E
Bougouni 120 11 30N 7 20W
Bouillon 87 49 44N 5 3 E
Boulder, Colo. 16 40 1N 105 17W
Boulder, Mont. 33 46 14N 112 7W
Boulder, Utah 52 37 55N 111 25W
Boulder, Wyo. 56 42 45N 109 43W
Boulder City 35 35 59N 114 50W
Boulder County ◇ 16 40 10N 105 15W
Boulder Creek 14 37 7N 122 7W
Boulder L. 56 42 51N 109 40W
Boulder Peak 14 41 35N 123 5W
Boulia 127 22 52 S 139 51 E
Boulogne-sur-Mer 90 50 42N 1 36 E
Boultoum 120 14 45N 10 25 E
Bouna 120 9 10N 3 0W
Bound Brook 37 40 34N 74 32W
Boundary 11 64 4N 141 6W
Boundary County ◇ 20 48 45N 116 25W
Boundary Peak 35 37 51N 118 21W
Boundiali 120 9 30N 6 20W
Bountiful 52 40 53N 111 53W
Bounty I. 124 48 0 S 178 30 E
Bourbeuse → 32 38 24N 90 53W
Bourbon, Ind. 22 41 18N 86 7W
Bourbon, Mo. 32 38 9N 91 15W
Bourbon County ◇, Kans. 24 37 45N 94 45W
Bourbon County ◇, Ky. 49 38 10N 84 15W
Bourbonnais 90 46 28N 3 0 E
Bourem 120 17 0N 0 24W
Bourg-en-Bresse 90 46 13N 5 12 E
Bourges 90 47 9N 2 25 E
Bourgogne 90 47 0N 4 30 E
Bourke 127 30 8 S 145 55 E
Bournemouth 83 50 43N 1 53W
Bouse 12 33 56N 114 0W
Bouse Wash → 12 34 3N 114 20W
Bousso 121 10 34N 16 52 E
Boutilimit 120 17 45N 14 40W
Bouvet I. = Bouvetøya 2 54 26 S 3 24 E
Bouvetøya 2 54 26 S 3 24 E
Bovey 30 47 17N 93 25W
Bovigny 87 50 12N 5 55 E
Bovill 20 46 51N 116 24W
Bovina 50 34 31N 102 53W
Bow, N.H. 36 43 10N 71 34W
Bow, Wash. 53 48 34N 122 24W
Bow Island 62 49 50N 111 23W
Bowbells 41 48 48N 102 15W
Bowdle 47 45 27N 99 39W
Bowdoin L. 33 48 25N 107 41W
Bowdon, Ga. 18 33 32N 85 15W
Bowdon, N. Dak. 41 47 28N 99 43W
Bowdon Junction 18 33 40N 85 9W
Bowen, Australia 127 20 0 S 148 16 E
Bowen, U.S.A. 21 40 14N 91 4W
Bowens 27 38 30N 76 8W
Bowers 27 39 4N 75 24W
Bowersville, Ga. 18 34 22N 83 5W
Bowersville, Ohio 42 39 35N 83 44W
Bowie, Ariz. 12 32 19N 109 29W
Bowie, Colo. 16 38 55N 107 33W
Bowie, Md. 27 39 0N 76 47W
Bowie, Tex. 51 33 34N 97 51W
Bowie County ◇ 51 33 27N 94 25W
Bowie Cr. → 31 31 24N 89 27W
Bowland, Forest of 82 54 0N 2 30W
Bowlegs 43 35 9N 96 40W
Bowling Green, Fla. 17 27 38N 81 50W
Bowling Green, Ky. 48 36 59N 86 27W
Bowling Green, Mo. 32 39 21N 91 12W
Bowling Green, Ohio 42 41 23N 83 39W
Bowling Green, Va. 54 38 3N 77 21W
Bowling Green, C. 127 19 19 S 147 25 E
Bowlus 30 45 49N 94 24W
Bowman, Ga. 18 34 12N 83 2W
Bowman, N. Dak. 41 46 11N 103 24W
Bowman, S.C. 46 33 21N 80 41W
Bowman County ◇ 41 46 2N 103 30W
Bowman-Haley Reservoir 41 45 59N 103 14W
Bowman I. 5 65 0 S 104 0 E
Bowmanville 60 43 55N 78 41W
Bowmont 20 43 27N 116 32W
Bowmore 84 55 45N 6 18W
Bowral 127 34 26 S 150 27 E
Bowring 43 36 53N 96 7W
Bowron → 62 54 3N 121 50W
Bowser L. 62 56 30N 129 30W
Bowsman 63 52 14N 101 12W
Bowstring L. 30 47 33N 93 55W
Box Butte County ◇ 34 42 15N 103 0W
Box Elder 47 44 7N 103 4W
Box Elder County ◇ 52 41 30N 113 0W
Boxelder Cr. → 47 45 59N 103 57W
Boxford 28 42 40N 71 0W
Boxholm 23 42 10N 94 6W
Boxtel 87 51 36N 5 20 E
Boy River 30 47 10N 94 7W
Boyaca □ 70 5 30N 72 30W
Boyce, La. 25 31 23N 92 40W
Boyce, Va. 54 39 6N 78 4W
Boyceville 55 45 3N 92 2W
Boyd, Fla. 17 30 11N 83 37W
Boyd, Minn. 30 44 51N 95 54W
Boyd, Tex. 51 33 5N 97 34W
Boyd County ◇, Ky. 49 38 20N 82 40W
Boyd County ◇, Nebr. 34 42 50N 98 40W
Boydell 13 33 22N 91 29W
Boyden 23 43 12N 96 0W
Boydton 54 36 40N 78 24W
Boyer →, Canada 62 58 27N 115 57W
Boyer →, U.S.A. 23 41 27N 95 55W
Boyero 16 38 57N 103 16W
Boyertown 45 40 20N 75 38W
Boyes 33 45 16N 105 2W

Boyes Hot Springs **Brodhead**

Boyes Hot Springs 14 38 19N 122 29W
Boykin 18 31 6N 84 41W
Boykins 54 36 35N 77 12W
Boyle, Ireland 85 53 58N 8 19W
Boyle, U.S.A. 31 33 42N 90 44W
Boyle County ◇ 49 37 35N 84 55W
Boyne → 85 53 43N 6 15W
Boyne City 29 45 13N 85 1W
Boyne Falls 29 45 10N 84 55W
Boyni Qara 107 36 20N 67 0 E
Boynton 43 35 39N 95 39W
Boynton Beach 17 26 32N 80 4W
Boyoma, Chutes 118 0 35N 25 23 E
Boys Town 34 41 16N 96 8W
Boysen Reservoir 56 43 25N 108 11W
Bozeman 33 45 41N 111 2W
Bozen = Bolzano 94 46 30N 11 20 E
Bozman 27 38 46N 76 16W
Bozoum 122 6 25N 16 35 E
Bozovici 95 44 56N 22 1 E
Brabant □ 87 50 46N 4 30 E
Brabant L. 63 55 58N 103 43W
Brač 94 43 20N 16 40 E
Bracadale, L. 84 57 20N 6 30W
Bracciano, L. di 94 42 8N 12 11 E
Bracebridge 60 45 2N 79 19W
Brach 121 27 31N 14 20 E
Bräcke 96 62 45N 15 26 E
Bracken County ◇ 49 38 40N 84 5W
Brackettville 50 29 19N 100 25W
Brad 89 46 10N 22 50 E
Braddock 41 46 34N 100 6W
Braddock Heights 27 39 25N 77 30W
Braddyville 23 40 35N 95 2W
Bradenton 17 27 30N 82 34W
Bradford, U.K. 82 53 47N 1 45W
Bradford, Ark. 13 35 25N 91 27W
Bradford, Ill. 21 41 11N 89 39W
Bradford, N.H. 36 43 17N 71 56W
Bradford, Pa. 45 41 58N 78 38W
Bradford, R.I. 28 41 24N 71 45W
Bradford, Tenn. 48 36 5N 88 49W
Bradford, Vt. 36 43 59N 72 9W
Bradford County ◇, Fla. 17 30 0N 82 15W
Bradford County ◇, Pa. 45 41 50N 76 30W
Bradford Mt. 28 41 59N 73 18W
Bradfordsville 49 37 30N 85 9W
Bradgate 23 42 48N 94 25W
Bradley, Ark. 13 33 6N 93 39W
Bradley, Calif. 15 35 52N 120 48W
Bradley, Fla. 17 27 48N 81 59W
Bradley, Ill. 21 41 9N 87 52W
Bradley, Okla. 43 34 53N 97 42W
Bradley, S. Dak. 47 45 5N 97 39W
Bradley County ◇, Ark. 13 33 27N 92 10W
Bradley County ◇, Tenn. 49 35 10N 84 53W
Bradner 42 41 20N 83 26W
Bradore Bay 61 51 27N 57 18W
Bradshaw, Australia 127 15 21 S 130 16 E
Bradshaw, Nebr. 34 40 53N 97 45W
Bradshaw, Tex. 51 32 6N 99 54W
Bradshaw, W. Va. 54 37 21N 81 48W
Brady, Mont. 33 48 2N 111 51W
Brady, Nebr. 34 41 1N 100 22W
Brady, Tex. 51 31 9N 99 20W
Brady Cr. → 51 31 8N 98 59W
Braga 91 41 35N 8 25W
Bragado 76 35 2 S 60 27W
Bragança, Brazil 74 1 0 S 47 2W
Bragança, Portugal 91 41 48N 6 50W
Bragança Paulista 77 22 55 S 46 32W
Bragg City 32 36 16N 89 55W
Braggadocio 32 36 11N 89 50W
Braggs 43 35 40N 95 12W
Braham 30 45 44N 93 10W
Brahmanbaria 109 23 58N 91 15 E
Brahmani → 109 20 39N 86 46 E
Brahmaputra → 109 24 2N 90 59 E
Brahmaur 108 32 28N 76 32 E
Braich-y-pwll 82 52 47N 4 46W
Braidwood 21 41 16N 88 13W
Brăila 89 45 19N 27 59 E
Brăila □ 95 45 5N 27 30 E
Brainard 34 41 11N 97 0W
Brainerd 30 46 22N 94 12W
Braintree, U.K. 83 51 53N 0 34 E
Braintree, U.S.A. 28 42 13N 71 0W
Bralorne 62 50 50N 123 45W
Braman 43 36 56N 97 20W
Brampton, Canada 60 43 45N 79 45W
Brampton, U.S.A. 41 46 0N 97 52W
Bramwell 54 37 20N 81 19W
Branch 13 35 18N 93 57W
Branch County ◇ 29 41 50N 85 5W
Branchland 54 38 13N 82 12W
Branchville, N.J. 37 41 9N 74 45W
Branchville, S.C. 46 33 15N 80 49W
Branco → 71 1 20 S 61 50W
Branco, Cabo 74 7 9 S 34 47W
Brandenburg, Germany 88 52 24N 12 33 E
Brandenburg, U.S.A. 48 38 0N 86 10W
Brandon, Canada 63 49 50N 99 57W
Brandon, Colo. 16 38 27N 102 26W
Brandon, Fla. 17 27 56N 82 17W
Brandon, Iowa 23 42 19N 92 0W
Brandon, Minn. 30 45 58N 95 36W
Brandon, Miss. 31 32 16N 89 59W
Brandon, Nebr. 34 40 48N 101 55W
Brandon, S. Dak. 47 43 35N 96 35W
Brandon, Vt. 36 43 48N 73 6W
Brandon, Wis. 55 43 44N 88 47W
Brandon, Mt. 85 52 15N 10 15W
Brandon B. 85 52 17N 10 8W
Brandonville 54 39 40N 79 37W
Brandreth 39 43 56N 74 51W
Brandsen 76 35 10 S 58 15W
Brandsville 32 36 39N 91 42W
Brandt 47 44 40N 96 38W
Brandvlei 123 30 25 S 20 30 E
Brandy Pk. 44 42 36N 123 53W
Brandywine, Md. 27 38 42N 76 51W
Brandywine, W. Va. 54 38 38N 79 15W
Branford, Conn. 28 41 17N 72 49W
Branford, Fla. 17 29 58N 82 56W
Braniewo 89 54 25N 19 50 E
Bransfield Str. 5 63 0 S 59 0W
Brańsk 89 52 45N 22 50 E
Branson, Colo. 16 37 1N 103 53W
Branson, Mo. 32 36 39N 93 13W
Brantford, Canada 60 43 10N 80 15W
Brantford, U.S.A. 41 47 36N 98 55W
Brantley 10 31 35N 86 16W
Brantley County ◇ 18 31 10N 82 0W
Bras d'Or, L. 61 45 50N 60 50W
Brashear 32 40 9N 92 23W
Brasher Falls 39 44 49N 74 47W
Brasil, Planalto 68 18 0 S 46 30W
Brasiléia 72 11 0 S 68 45W
Brasília 75 15 47 S 47 55 E
Brasília Legal 71 3 49 S 55 36W
Braşov 89 45 38N 25 35 E
Braşov □ 95 45 45N 25 15 E
Brasschaat 87 51 19N 4 27 E
Brassey, Banjaran 110 5 0N 117 15 E
Brasstown Bald 18 34 53N 83 49W
Brassua L. 26 45 40N 69 55W
Bratan = Morozov 95 42 30N 25 10 E
Bratislava 88 48 10N 17 7 E
Bratsigovo 95 42 1N 24 22 E
Bratsk 101 56 10N 101 30 E
Bratt 17 30 58N 87 26W
Brattleboro 36 42 51N 72 34W
Braţul Chilia → 95 45 25N 29 20 E
Bratul Sfîntu Gheorghe → 95 45 0N 29 20 E
Braţul Sulina → 95 45 10N 29 20 E
Braunschweig 88 52 17N 10 28 E
Braunton 83 51 6N 4 9W
Brava 105 1 20N 44 8 E
Brave 45 39 44N 80 16W
Bravo del Norte → 64 25 57N 97 9W
Bravo del Norte, R. → = Grande, R. → 50 25 57N 97 9W
Brawley 15 32 59N 115 31W
Brawley Peaks 35 38 15N 118 55W
Brawley Wash → 12 32 34N 111 26W
Braxton 31 32 1N 89 58W
Braxton County ◇ 54 38 43N 80 39W
Bray 85 53 12N 6 6W
Bray-sur-Seine 90 48 25N 3 14 E
Braymer 32 39 35N 93 48W
Brayton 23 41 33N 94 56W
Brazeau → 62 52 55N 115 14W
Brazil 22 39 32N 87 8W
Brazil ■ 75 10 0 S 50 0W
Brazilian Highlands = Brasil, Planalto 68 18 0 S 46 30W
Brazo Sur → 76 25 21 S 57 42W
Brazoria 51 29 3N 95 34W
Brazoria County ◇ 51 29 10N 95 26W
Brazos → 51 28 53N 95 23W
Brazos County ◇ 51 30 40N 96 22W
Brazzaville 122 4 9 S 15 12 E
Brčko 95 44 54N 18 46 E
Brea 72 4 40 S 81 7W
Breadalbane 84 56 30N 4 15W
Breaksea Sd. 128 45 35 S 166 35 E
Bream Bay 128 35 56 S 174 28 E
Bream Head 128 35 51 S 174 36 E
Breas 76 25 29 S 70 24W
Breathitt County ◇ 49 37 30N 83 20W
Breaux Bridge 25 30 16N 91 54W
Brebes 111 6 52 S 109 3 E
Brechin 84 56 44N 2 40W
Breckenridge, Colo. 16 39 29N 106 3W
Breckenridge, Mich. 29 43 24N 84 29W
Breckenridge, Minn. 30 46 16N 96 35W
Breckenridge, Mo. 32 39 46N 93 48W
Breckenridge, Tex. 51 32 45N 98 54W
Breckinridge 43 36 26N 97 44W
Breckinridge County ◇ 48 37 45N 86 25W
Brecknock, Pen. 78 54 35 S 71 30W
Brecon 83 51 57N 3 23W
Brecon Beacons 83 51 53N 3 27W
Breda, Neth. 87 51 35N 4 45 E
Breda, U.S.A. 23 42 11N 94 59W
Bredasdorp 123 34 33 S 20 2 E
Breese 21 38 37N 89 32W
Bregenz 88 47 30N 9 45 E
Breiðafjörður 96 65 15N 23 15W
Brejinho de Nazaré 74 11 1 S 48 34W
Brejo 74 3 41 S 42 47W
Bremen, Germany 88 53 4N 8 47 E
Bremen, Ala. 10 33 59N 86 58W
Bremen, Ga. 18 33 43N 85 9W
Bremen, Ind. 22 41 27N 86 9W
Bremen, Ky. 48 37 22N 87 13W
Bremen, Ohio 42 39 42N 82 26W
Bremer County ◇ 23 42 50N 92 20W
Bremerhaven 88 53 34N 8 35 E
Bremerton 53 47 34N 122 38W
Bremond 51 31 10N 96 41W
Brenham 51 30 10N 96 24W
Brenner Pass 88 47 0N 11 30 E
Brent, Canada 60 46 2N 78 29W
Brent, U.K. 83 51 33N 0 18W
Brent, U.S.A. 10 32 56N 87 10W
Brentwood, U.K. 83 51 37N 0 19 E
Brentwood, Calif. 14 37 56N 121 42W
Brentwood, N.H. 36 42 58N 71 6W
Brentwood, N.Y. 39 40 47N 73 15W
Brentwood, Tenn. 48 36 2N 86 47W
Bréscia 94 45 33N 10 13 E
Breskens 87 51 23N 3 33 E
Breslau = Wrocław 88 51 5N 17 5 E
Bressanone 94 46 43N 11 40 E
Bressay I. 84 60 10N 1 5W
Bresse, Plaine de 90 46 50N 5 10 E
Brest, France 90 48 24N 4 31W
Brest, U.S.S.R. 98 52 10N 23 40 E
Bretagne 90 48 0N 3 0W
Bretçu 89 46 7N 26 18 E
Breton 62 53 7N 114 28W
Breton I. 25 29 13N 89 12W
Breton Sd. 25 29 35N 89 15W
Brett, C. 128 35 10 S 174 20 E
Brevard 40 35 14N 82 44W
Brevard County ◇ 17 28 20N 80 45W
Breves 74 1 40 S 50 29W
Brevig Mission 11 65 20N 166 29W
Brevort 29 46 1N 85 2W
Brewer 26 44 48N 68 46W
Brewerton 39 43 14N 76 9W
Brewster, Kans. 24 39 22N 101 23W
Brewster, Mass. 28 41 46N 70 5W
Brewster, Minn. 30 43 42N 95 28W
Brewster, Nebr. 34 41 56N 99 52W
Brewster, Ohio 42 40 43N 81 36W
Brewster, Wash. 53 48 6N 119 47W
Brewster, Kap 4 70 7N 22 0W
Brewster County ◇ 50 30 0N 103 0W
Brewton, Ala. 10 31 7N 87 4W
Brewton, Ga. 18 32 36N 82 48W
Brezhnev 100 55 42N 52 19 E
Brezovo 95 42 21N 25 5 E
Bria 122 6 30N 21 58 E
Brian Head 52 37 41N 112 50W
Briançon 90 44 54N 6 39 E
Briartown 43 35 18N 95 14W
Bribie I. 127 27 0 S 152 58 E
Briceland 14 40 7N 123 54W
Bricelyn 30 43 34N 93 49W
Briceville 49 36 11N 84 11W
Brickeys 13 34 52N 90 36W
Bridge, Idaho 20 42 8N 113 20W
Bridge, Oreg. 44 43 1N 124 0W
Bridge City 51 30 1N 93 51W
Bridgeboro 18 31 24N 83 59W
Bridgend 83 51 30N 3 35W
Bridgeport, Ala. 10 34 57N 85 43W
Bridgeport, Calif. 14 38 15N 119 14W
Bridgeport, Conn. 28 41 11N 73 12W
Bridgeport, Ill. 21 38 43N 87 46W
Bridgeport, Mich. 29 43 22N 83 53W
Bridgeport, Nebr. 34 41 40N 103 6W
Bridgeport, Okla. 43 35 33N 98 23W
Bridgeport, Tex. 51 33 13N 97 45W
Bridgeport, Wash. 53 48 0N 119 40W
Bridgeport, L. 51 33 13N 97 50W
Bridger 33 45 18N 108 55W
Bridger Peak 56 41 11N 107 2W
Bridger-Teton National Forest 56 43 5N 110 5W
Bridgeton, N.C. 40 35 7N 77 1W
Bridgeton, N.J. 37 39 26N 75 14W
Bridgetown, Australia 126 33 58 S 116 7 E
Bridgetown, Barbados 67 13 0N 59 30W
Bridgetown, Canada 61 44 55N 65 18W
Bridgetown, U.S.A. 27 39 2N 75 53W
Bridgeville, Calif. 14 40 25N 123 50W
Bridgeville, Del. 27 38 45N 75 36W
Bridgewater, Canada 61 44 25N 64 31W
Bridgewater, Conn. 28 41 32N 73 22W
Bridgewater, Iowa 23 41 15N 94 40W
Bridgewater, Maine 26 46 25N 67 51W
Bridgewater, Mass. 28 41 59N 70 58W
Bridgewater, N.Y. 39 42 53N 75 15W
Bridgewater, S. Dak. 47 43 33N 97 30W
Bridgewater, Va. 54 38 23N 78 59W
Bridgewater, Vt. 36 43 35N 72 38W
Bridgewater, C. 127 38 23 S 141 23 E
Bridgman 29 41 57N 86 33W
Bridgnorth 83 52 33N 2 25W
Bridgton 26 44 3N 70 42W
Bridgwater 83 51 7N 3 0W
Bridlington 82 54 6N 0 11W
Bridport, U.K. 83 50 43N 2 45W
Bridport, U.S.A. 36 43 58N 73 20W
Brie, Plaine de la 90 48 35N 3 10 E
Brier Cr. → 18 32 44N 81 26W
Brig 88 46 18N 7 59 E
Brigantine City 37 39 24N 74 22W
Brigg 82 53 33N 0 30W
Briggsdale 16 40 38N 104 20W
Briggsville 13 34 56N 93 30W
Brigham City 52 41 31N 112 1W
Brighton, Canada 60 44 2N 77 44W
Brighton, U.K. 83 50 50N 0 9W
Brighton, Colo. 16 39 59N 104 49W
Brighton, Fla. 17 27 14N 81 6W
Brighton, Ill. 21 39 2N 90 8W
Brighton, Iowa 23 41 10N 91 49W
Brighton, Mich. 29 42 32N 83 47W
Brighton, N.Y. 39 43 8N 77 34W
Brighton, Tenn. 48 35 29N 89 43W
Brighton Indian Reservation 17 27 0N 81 15W
Brightwood 40 36 10N 79 45W
Brilliant, Canada 62 49 19N 117 38W
Brilliant, U.S.A. 10 34 1N 87 46W
Brillion 55 44 11N 88 4W
Brimfield, Ill. 21 40 50N 89 53W
Brimfield, Mass. 28 42 7N 72 12W
Brimley 29 46 24N 84 34W
Brîndisi 95 40 39N 17 55 E
Brinkley 13 34 53N 91 12W
Brinnon 53 47 41N 122 54W
Brinsmade 41 48 11N 99 19W
Brinson 18 30 59N 84 44W
Brion, Î. 61 47 46N 61 26W
Brisbane 127 27 25 S 153 2 E
Briscoe 50 35 35N 100 17W
Briscoe County ◇ 50 34 28N 101 19W
Bristol, U.K. 83 51 26N 2 35W
Bristol, Colo. 16 38 7N 102 19W
Bristol, Conn. 28 41 40N 72 57W
Bristol, Fla. 17 30 26N 84 59W
Bristol, Ind. 22 41 43N 85 49W
Bristol, Md. 27 38 47N 76 40W
Bristol, N.H. 36 43 36N 71 44W
Bristol, Pa. 45 40 6N 74 51W
Bristol, R.I. 28 41 40N 71 16W
Bristol, S. Dak. 47 45 21N 97 45W
Bristol, Tenn. 49 36 36N 82 11W
Bristol, Va. 54 36 36N 82 11W
Bristol, Vt. 36 44 8N 73 5W
Bristol Bay 11 58 0N 159 0W
Bristol Bay ◇ 11 59 0N 156 30W
Bristol Channel 83 51 18N 4 30W
Bristol County ◇, Mass. 28 41 45N 71 0W
Bristol County ◇, R.I. 28 41 40N 71 20W
Bristol I. 5 58 45 S 28 0W
Bristol L. 15 34 28N 115 41W
Bristol Mts. 15 34 30N 115 50W
Bristow, Nebr. 34 42 51N 98 35W
Bristow, Okla. 43 35 50N 96 23W
British Antarctic Territory □ 5 66 0 S 45 0W
British Columbia □ 62 55 0N 125 15W
British Guiana = Guyana ■ 71 5 0N 59 0W
British Honduras = Belize ■ 65 17 0N 88 30W
British Isles 80 55 0N 4 0W
Britstown 123 30 37 S 23 30 E
Britt, Canada 60 45 46N 80 34W
Britt, U.S.A. 23 43 6N 93 48W
Brittany = Bretagne 90 48 0N 3 0W
Britton 47 45 48N 97 45W
Brlik 100 44 0N 74 5 E
Brno 88 49 10N 16 35 E
Broad →, Ga. 18 33 59N 82 39W
Broad →, S.C. 46 34 1N 81 4W
Broad B. 84 58 14N 6 16W
Broad Haven 85 54 20N 9 55W
Broad Law 84 55 30N 3 22W
Broad Sd. 127 22 0 S 149 45 E
Broadalbin 39 43 4N 74 12W
Broadbent 44 43 1N 124 0W
Broadhurst 18 31 28N 81 55W
Broadkill Beach 27 38 47N 75 10W
Broadmoor 16 38 50N 104 50W
Broads, The 82 52 45N 1 30 E
Broadsound Ra. 127 22 50 S 149 30 E
Broadus 33 45 27N 105 25W
Broadview, Canada 63 50 22N 102 35W
Broadview, Mont. 33 46 6N 108 53W
Broadview, N. Mex. 38 34 49N 103 13W
Broadwater 34 41 36N 102 51W
Broadwater County ◇ 33 46 25N 111 30W
Broadway 54 38 37N 78 48W
Broadwell 21 40 4N 89 27W
Brochet 63 57 53N 101 40W
Brochet, L. 63 58 36N 101 35W
Brock, Canada 63 51 26N 108 43W
Brock, U.S.A. 34 40 29N 95 58W
Brocken 88 51 48N 10 40 E
Brocket 41 48 13N 98 21W
Brockport 39 43 13N 77 56W
Brockton, Mass. 28 42 5N 71 1W
Brockton, Mont. 33 48 9N 104 55W
Brockville 60 44 35N 75 41W
Brockway, Mont. 33 47 18N 105 45W
Brockway, Pa. 45 41 15N 78 47W
Brocton, Ill. 21 39 43N 87 56W
Brocton, N.Y. 39 42 23N 79 26W
Brod 95 41 35N 21 17 E
Brodeur Pen. 59 72 30N 88 10W
Brodhead, Ky. 49 37 24N 84 25W

Brodhead Bunker Hill

Brodhead, Wis. 55 42 37N 89 22W
Brodick 84 55 34N 5 9W
Brodnax 54 36 43N 78 2W
Brogan. 44 44 15N 117 31W
Brokaw 55 45 2N 89 39W
Broken Arrow 43 36 3N 95 48W
Broken Bow, Nebr. 34 41 24N 99 38W
Broken Bow, Okla. 43 34 2N 94 44W
Broken Bow Lake 43 34 9N 94 40W
Broken Hill = Kabwe . . . . . . 123 14 30 S 28 29 E
Broken Hill . . . . 127 31 58 S 141 29 E
Brokopondo 71 5 3N 54 59W
Brokopondo □ 71 4 30N 55 30W
Bromfield 83 52 25N 2 45W
Bromide 43 34 24N 96 31W
Bromley . . . . 83 51 20N 0 5 E
Bronaugh 32 37 41N 94 28W
Brønderslev . . . . 97 57 16N 9 57 E
Bronson, Fla. 17 29 27N 82 39W
Bronson, Kans. 24 37 54N 95 4W
Bronson, Mich. 29 41 52N 85 12W
Bronson, Tex. 51 31 21N 94 1W
Bronte 50 31 53N 100 18W
Bronwood 18 31 50N 84 22W
Bronx County ◇ 39 40 50N 73 52W
Brook 22 40 52N 87 22W
Brook Park 42 41 24N 80 51W
Brooke County ◇ 54 40 16N 80 37W
Brookeland 51 31 10N 94 0W
Brookesmith 51 31 33N 99 7W
Brookfield, Mass. 28 42 13N 72 6W
Brookfield, Mo. 32 39 47N 93 4W
Brookfield, Vt. 36 44 4N 72 38W
Brookfield, Wis. 55 43 4N 88 9W
Brookhaven 31 31 35N 90 26W
Brookings, Oreg. 44 42 3N 124 17W
Brookings, S. Dak. 47 44 19N 96 48W
Brookings County ◇ 47 44 19N 96 48W
Brookland 13 35 54N 90 35W
Brooklet 18 32 23N 81 40W
Brookline, Mass. 28 42 20N 71 7W
Brookline, N.H. 36 42 44N 71 40W
Brooklyn, Ala. 10 31 16N 86 46W
Brooklyn, Conn. 28 41 47N 71 57W
Brooklyn, Ind. 22 39 32N 86 22W
Brooklyn, Iowa 23 41 44N 92 27W
Brooklyn, Mich. 29 42 7N 84 15W
Brooklyn, Miss. 31 31 3N 89 11W
Brooklyn, Wash. 53 46 47N 123 31W
Brooklyn Park, Md. 27 39 14N 76 37W
Brooklyn Park, Minn. 30 45 6N 93 23W
Brookmere 62 49 52N 120 53W
Brookneal 54 37 3N 78 57W
Brookport 21 37 8N 88 38W
Brooks, Canada 62 50 35N 111 55W
Brooks, Ky. 49 38 4N 85 43W
Brooks, Minn. 30 47 49N 96 0W
Brooks B. 62 50 15N 127 55W
Brooks County ◇, Ga. 18 30 50N 83 45W
Brooks County ◇, Tex. 50 27 0N 98 5W
Brooks L. 63 61 55N 106 35W
Brooks Range 11 68 0N 152 0W
Brookshire 51 29 47N 95 57W
Brookston, Ind. 22 40 36N 86 52W
Brookston, Minn. 30 46 52N 92 36W
Brooksville, Fla. 17 28 33N 82 23W
Brooksville, Ky. 49 38 41N 84 4W
Brooksville, Miss. 31 33 14N 88 35W
Brooksville, Okla. 43 35 12N 96 58W
Brookvale 16 39 38N 105 26W
Brookview 27 38 35N 75 48W
Brookville, Ind. 22 39 25N 85 1W
Brookville, Kans. 24 38 46N 97 52W
Brookville, N.J. 37 39 44N 74 18W
Brookville, Pa. 45 41 10N 79 5W
Brookville L. 22 39 28N 85 0W
Brookwood 10 33 17N 87 18W
Broom, L. 84 57 55N 5 15W
Broome . . . . 126 18 0 S 122 15 E
Broome County ◇ 39 42 5N 75 45W
Broomes Island 27 38 25N 76 33W
Broomfield 16 39 55N 105 5W
Brooten 30 45 30N 95 8W
Brora 84 58 0N 3 50W
Brora → 84 58 4N 3 52W
Broseley 32 36 40N 90 15W
Brosna → 85 53 8N 8 0W
Brotas de Macaúbas . . . . . . 75 12 0 S 42 38W
Brothers 44 43 49N 120 36W
Brotmanville 37 39 33N 75 3W
Broughton, Ill. 21 37 56N 88 27W
Broughton, Kans. 24 39 19N 97 3W
Broughton Island 59 67 33N 63 0W
Broughty Ferry 84 56 29N 2 50W
Broussard 25 30 9N 91 58W
Brouwershaven . . . . 87 51 45N 3 55 E
Broward County ◇ 17 26 15N 80 30W
Browerville 30 46 5N 94 52W
Brown City 29 43 13N 82 59W
Brown County ◇, Ill. 21 39 55N 90 45W
Brown County ◇, Ind. 22 39 10N 86 15W
Brown County ◇, Kans. . . . 24 39 45N 95 30W
Brown County ◇, Minn. . . . 30 44 10N 94 50W
Brown County ◇, Nebr. . . . 34 42 30N 100 0W
Brown County ◇, Ohio 42 38 55N 83 59W
Brown County ◇, S. Dak. . . 47 45 37N 98 19W
Brown County ◇, Tex. 51 31 43N 98 59W
Brown County ◇, Wis. 55 44 30N 88 0W
Brown Deer 55 43 10N 87 58W
Brown Willy 83 50 35N 4 34W
Brownell 24 38 38N 99 45W
Brownfield 50 33 11N 102 17W
Browning, Ill. 21 40 8N 90 22W
Browning, Mont. 33 48 34N 113 1W
Brownlee, Canada 63 50 43N 106 1W
Brownlee, U.S.A. 34 42 17N 100 37W
Brownlee Reservoir 20 44 50N 116 54W
Browns 21 38 23N 87 59W
Browns Mills 37 39 58N 74 34W
Browns Valley 30 45 36N 96 50W
Brownsburg 22 39 51N 86 24W
Brownsdale 30 43 45N 92 52W
Brownstown, Ill. 21 39 0N 88 57W
Brownstown, Ind. 22 38 53N 86 3W
Brownsville, Ky. 48 37 12N 86 16W
Brownsville, La. 25 32 29N 92 9W
Brownsville, Minn. 30 43 42N 91 17W
Brownsville, Oreg. 44 44 24N 122 59W
Brownsville, Pa. 45 40 1N 79 53W
Brownsville, Tenn. 48 35 36N 89 16W
Brownsville, Tex. 50 25 54N 97 30W
Brownsweg 71 5 5N 55 15W
Browntown 55 42 35N 89 48W
Brownville, Ala. 10 33 24N 87 52W
Brownville, Maine 26 45 18N 69 2W
Brownville, N.Y. 39 44 0N 75 59W
Brownville, Nebr. 34 40 24N 95 40W
Brownville Junction 26 45 21N 69 3W
Brownwood, Mo. 32 37 5N 89 57W
Brownwood, Tex. 51 31 43N 98 59W
Brownwood, L. 51 31 50N 99 0W
Broxton 18 31 38N 82 53W
Bruas . . . . 112 4 31N 100 46 E
Bruce, Fla. 17 30 28N 85 58W
Bruce, Miss. 31 33 59N 89 21W
Bruce, S. Dak. 47 44 26N 96 54W
Bruce, Wis. 55 45 28N 91 16W
Bruce, Mt. . . . . 126 22 37 S 118 8 E
Bruceton 48 36 3N 88 15W
Bruceton Mills 54 39 40N 79 38W
Bruceville, Ind. 22 38 46N 87 25W
Bruceville, Md. 27 38 40N 75 59W
Bruck an der Leitha . . . . 88 48 1N 16 47 E
Brue → 83 51 10N 2 59W
Bruges = Brugge . . . . 87 51 13N 3 13 E
Brugge . . . . 87 51 13N 3 13 E
Bruin Pt. 52 39 39N 110 21W
Brûlé, Canada 62 53 15N 117 58W
Brule, U.S.A. 34 41 6N 101 53W
Brule → 55 45 57N 88 12W
Brule County ◇ 47 43 45N 99 0W
Brule L. 30 46 58N 90 50W
Brumado . . . . 75 14 14 S 41 40W
Brumado → . . . . 75 14 13 S 41 40W
Brumley 32 38 5N 92 29W
Brundidge 10 31 43N 85 49W
Bruneau 20 42 53N 115 48W
Bruneau → 20 42 56N 115 57W
Brunei = Bandar Seri Begawan . . . . 110 4 52N 115 0 E
Brunei ■ . . . . 110 4 50N 115 0 E
Bruning 34 40 20N 97 34W
Brunner, L. . . . . 128 42 37 S 171 27 E
Bruno, Canada 63 52 20N 105 30W
Bruno, Minn. 30 46 17N 92 40W
Bruno, Nebr. 34 41 17N 96 58W
Brunsbüttelkoog . . . . 88 53 52N 9 13 E
Brunsville 23 42 49N 96 16W
Brunswick = Braunschweig . . 88 52 17N 10 28 E
Brunswick, Ga. 18 31 10N 81 30W
Brunswick, Maine 26 43 55N 69 58W
Brunswick, Md. 27 39 19N 77 38W
Brunswick, Mo. 32 39 26N 93 8W
Brunswick, Nebr. 34 42 20N 97 58W
Brunswick, Ohio 42 41 14N 81 51W
Brunswick, Pen. de . . . . 78 53 30 S 71 30W
Brunswick B. . . . . 126 15 15 S 124 50 E
Brunswick County ◇, N.C. . . 40 34 0N 78 20W
Brunswick County ◇, Va. . . . 54 36 46N 77 51W
Bruny I. . . . . 127 43 20 S 147 15 E
Brus Laguna 66 15 47N 84 35W
Brush 16 40 15N 103 37W
Brush Creek 48 36 7N 86 2W
Brushton 39 44 50N 74 31W
Brusly 25 30 23N 91 14W
Brusque . . . . 77 27 5 S 49 0W
Brussel . . . . 87 50 51N 4 21 E
Brussels = Bruxelles . . . . . . 87 50 51N 4 21 E
Brussels 55 44 44N 87 37W
Bruxelles . . . . 87 50 51N 4 21 E
Bryagovo . . . . 95 41 58N 25 8 E
Bryan, Ohio 42 41 28N 84 33W
Bryan, Tex. 51 30 40N 96 22W
Bryan County ◇, Ga. 18 32 0N 81 30W
Bryan County ◇, Okla. 43 34 0N 96 15W
Bryans Road 27 38 38N 77 4W
Bryansk . . . . 98 53 13N 34 25 E
Bryant, Ark. 13 34 36N 92 29W
Bryant, Ind. 22 40 32N 84 58W
Bryant, S. Dak. 47 44 35N 97 28W
Bryant Cr. → 32 36 36N 92 17W
Bryantown 27 38 36N 76 52W
Bryce Canyon National Park 52 37 30N 112 10W
Bryne . . . . 97 58 44N 5 38 E
Bryson 51 33 10N 98 23W
Bryson City 40 35 26N 83 27W
Bu Craa 120 26 45N 12 50W
Bua Yai . . . . 112 15 33N 102 26 E
Buabuq . . . . 121 31 29N 25 29 E
Buapinang . . . . 111 4 40 S 121 30 E
Buayan . . . . 111 6 3N 125 6 E
Bucak . . . . 106 37 28N 30 36 E
Bucaramanga 70 7 0N 73 0W
Buchan 84 57 32N 2 8W
Buchan Ness 84 57 29N 1 48W
Buchanan, Canada 63 51 40N 102 45W
Buchanan, Liberia 120 5 57N 10 2W
Buchanan, Ga. 18 33 48N 85 11W
Buchanan, Mich. 29 41 50N 86 22W
Buchanan, N. Dak. 41 47 4N 98 50W
Buchanan, Va. 54 37 32N 79 41W
Buchanan, L., Australia . . . 126 25 33 S 123 2 E
Buchanan, L., U.S.A. 51 30 45N 98 25W
Buchanan County ◇, Iowa . . 23 42 30N 91 50W
Buchanan County ◇, Mo. . . . 32 39 40N 94 50W
Buchanan County ◇, Va. . . . 54 37 17N 82 6W
Buchanan Dam 51 30 45N 98 25W
Buchans 61 48 50N 56 52W
Bucharest = Bucureşti . . . . 89 44 27N 26 10 E
Buchon, Pt. 15 35 15N 120 54W
Buck Grove 23 41 55N 95 23W
Buck I. 57 17 46N 64 37W
Buckatunna 31 31 32N 88 32W
Buckeye, Ariz. 12 33 22N 112 35W
Buckeye, Iowa 23 42 25N 93 23W
Buckeystown 27 39 20N 77 26W
Buckfield 26 44 17N 70 22W
Buckhannon 54 39 0N 80 8W
Buckhaven 84 56 10N 3 2W
Buckholts 51 30 52N 97 7W
Buckhorn, Ky. 49 37 21N 83 28W
Buckhorn, N. Mex. 38 33 2N 108 42W
Buckhorn L. 49 37 21N 83 28W
Buckie 84 57 40N 2 58W
Buckingham, Canada 60 45 37N 75 24W
Buckingham, U.K. 83 52 0N 0 59W
Buckingham, Colo. 16 40 37N 103 58W
Buckingham, Va. 54 37 33N 78 33W
Buckingham □ 83 51 50N 0 55W
Buckingham B. . . . . 127 12 10 S 135 40 E
Buckingham County ◇ 54 37 40N 78 40W
Buckland, Alaska 11 65 59N 161 8W
Buckland, Ohio 42 40 37N 84 16W
Buckland Newton 83 50 45N 2 25W
Buckley, Ill. 21 40 36N 88 2W
Buckley, Mich. 29 44 30N 85 41W
Buckley, Wash. 53 47 10N 122 2W
Bucklin, Kans. 24 37 33N 99 38W
Bucklin, Mo. 32 39 47N 92 53W
Buckman 30 45 54N 94 6W
Bucks County ◇ 45 40 15N 75 10W
Bucks L. 14 39 54N 121 12W
Bucksport 26 44 34N 68 47W
Bucktown 27 38 25N 76 3W
Bucoda 53 46 48N 122 52W
Buctouche 61 46 30N 64 45W
Bucureşti . . . . 89 44 27N 26 10 E
Bucyrus, Kans. 24 38 44N 94 44W
Bucyrus, N. Dak. 41 46 4N 102 47W
Bucyrus, Ohio 42 40 48N 82 59W
Buda, Ill. 21 41 20N 89 41W
Buda, Tex. 51 30 5N 97 51W
Budalin . . . . 109 22 20N 95 10 E
Budapest . . . . 89 47 29N 19 5 E
Budaun . . . . 108 28 5N 79 10 E
Budd Coast . . . . 5 68 0 S 112 0 E
Budd Lake 37 40 52N 74 44W
Budds Creek 27 38 23N 76 51W
Bude, U.K. 83 50 49N 4 33W
Bude, U.S.A. 31 31 28N 90 51W
Budeşti . . . . 95 44 13N 26 30 E
Búðareyri 96 65 2N 14 13W
Búðir 96 64 49N 23 23W
Budjala . . . . 122 2 50N 19 40 E
Buechel 49 38 12N 85 39W
Buena 37 39 31N 74 56W
Buena Vista, Bolivia . . . . . 73 17 27 S 63 40W
Buena Vista, Colo. 16 38 51N 106 8W
Buena Vista, Ga. 18 32 19N 84 31W
Buena Vista, Va. 54 37 44N 79 21W
Buena Vista County ◇ 23 42 45N 95 10W
Buena Vista L. 15 35 12N 119 18W
Buenaventura, Colombia . . . 70 3 53N 77 4W
Buenaventura, Mexico 64 29 50N 107 30W
Buenaventura, B. de 70 3 48N 77 17W
Buenópolis . . . . 75 17 54 S 44 11W
Buenos Aires, Argentina . . . 76 34 30 S 58 20W
Buenos Aires, Colombia . . . 70 1 36N 73 18W
Buenos Aires, C. Rica 66 9 10N 83 20W
Buenos Aires □ . . . . 76 36 30 S 60 0W
Buenos Aires, Lago . . . . 78 46 35 S 72 30W
Buesaco 70 1 23N 77 9W
Buffalo, Kans. 24 37 42N 95 42W
Buffalo, Minn. 30 45 10N 93 53W
Buffalo, Mo. 32 37 39N 93 6W
Buffalo, N. Dak. 41 46 55N 97 33W
Buffalo, N.Y. 39 42 53N 78 53W
Buffalo, Okla. 43 36 50N 99 38W
Buffalo, S.C. 46 34 43N 81 41W
Buffalo, S. Dak. 47 45 35N 103 33W
Buffalo, Tex. 51 31 28N 96 4W
Buffalo, W. Va. 54 38 37N 81 59W
Buffalo, Wyo. 56 44 21N 106 42W
Buffalo →, Canada 62 60 5N 115 5W
Buffalo →, Ark. 13 36 10N 92 26W
Buffalo →, Minn. 30 47 6N 96 49W
Buffalo →, Tenn. 48 36 0N 87 50W
Buffalo Bill Reservoir 56 44 30N 109 11W
Buffalo Center 23 43 23N 93 57W
Buffalo County ◇, Nebr. . . . 34 40 50N 99 0W
Buffalo County ◇, S. Dak. . . 47 44 0N 99 5W
Buffalo County ◇, Wis. . . . 55 44 20N 91 50W
Buffalo Cr. →, Okla. 43 36 47N 99 15W
Buffalo Cr. →, Wyo. 56 43 40N 106 30W
Buffalo Creek 16 39 23N 105 17W
Buffalo Gap, S. Dak. 47 43 30N 103 19W
Buffalo Gap, Tex. 51 32 17N 99 50W
Buffalo Head Hills 62 57 25N 115 55W
Buffalo L., Canada 62 52 27N 112 54W
Buffalo L., Tex. 50 34 52N 102 12W
Buffalo L., Wis. 55 43 47N 89 25W
Buffalo Narrows 63 55 51N 108 29W
Buffalo River National Park . 13 36 14N 92 36W
Buford 41 48 0N 103 59W
Bug →, Poland . . . . 99 52 31N 21 5 E
Bug →, U.S.S.R. . . . . 99 46 59N 31 58 E
Buga 70 4 0N 76 15W
Bugel, Tanjung . . . . 110 6 26 S 111 3 E
Bugsuk . . . . 110 8 15N 117 15 E
Bugt . . . . 114 48 47N 121 56 E
Bugulma . . . . 98 54 33N 52 48 E
Buguruslan . . . . 98 53 39N 52 26 E
Buheirat-Murrat-el-Kubra . . 121 30 15N 32 40 E
Buhl 20 42 36N 114 46W
Buhler 24 38 8N 97 46W
Buies Creek 40 35 25N 78 44W
Builth Wells 83 52 10N 3 26W
Buíque . . . . 74 8 37 S 37 9W
Buir Nur . . . . 113 47 50N 117 42 E
Bujumbura . . . . 122 3 16 S 29 18 E
Bukachacha . . . . 101 52 55N 116 50 E
Bukama . . . . 122 9 10 S 25 50 E
Bukavu . . . . 122 2 20 S 28 52 E
Bukene . . . . 122 4 15 S 32 48 E
Bukhara . . . . 100 39 48N 64 25 E
Bukittinggi . . . . 110 0 20 S 100 20 E
Bukoba . . . . 122 1 20 S 31 49 E
Bula . . . . 111 3 6 S 130 30 E
Buladean 40 36 7N 82 12W
Bulan . . . . 111 12 40N 123 52 E
Bulandshahr . . . . 108 28 28N 77 51 E
Bulawayo . . . . 123 20 7 S 28 32 E
Buldir I. . . . . 11 52 21N 175 56 E
Bulgan . . . . 113 48 45N 103 34 E
Bulgaria ■ . . . . 95 42 35N 25 30 E
Bulhar . . . . 105 10 25N 44 30 E
Buli, Teluk . . . . 111 1 5N 128 25 E
Buliluyan, C. . . . . 110 8 20N 117 15 E
Bulkley → 62 55 15N 127 40W
Bull L. 56 43 13N 109 3W
Bull Mts. 33 46 8N 109 0W
Bull Shoals L. 13 36 22N 92 35W
Bullard, Ga. 18 32 38N 83 30W
Bullard, Tex. 51 32 8N 95 19W
Buller → . . . . 128 41 44 S 171 36 E
Bullfinch . . . . 126 30 58 S 119 3 E
Bullhead 47 45 46N 101 5W
Bullion Mts. 15 34 40N 116 10W
Bullitt County ◇ 49 38 0N 85 40W
Bulloch County ◇ 18 32 20N 81 45W
Bullock County ◇ 10 32 9N 85 43W
Bulloo → . . . . 127 28 43 S 142 30 E
Bulls . . . . 128 40 10 S 175 24 E
Bulls B. 46 32 59N 79 35W
Bulls Gap 49 36 15N 83 5W
Bulnes . . . . 76 36 42 S 72 19W
Bulo Burti . . . . 105 3 50N 45 33 E
Bulsar = Valsad . . . . 108 20 40N 72 58 E
Bulu Karakelong . . . . 111 4 35N 126 50 E
Bulukumba . . . . 111 5 33 S 120 11 E
Bulun . . . . 101 70 37N 127 30 E
Bumba . . . . 122 2 13N 22 30 E
Bumhpa Bum . . . . 109 26 51N 97 14 E
Bumpus Mills 48 36 36N 87 50W
Buna, Kenya . . . . 122 2 58N 39 30 E
Buna, U.S.A. 51 30 26N 93 58W
Bunbah, Khalîj . . . . 121 32 20N 23 15 E
Bunbury . . . . 126 33 20 S 115 35 E
Bunceton 32 38 47N 92 48W
Bunch 43 35 41N 94 46W
Buncombe 21 37 27N 88 58W
Buncombe County ◇ 40 35 30N 82 30W
Buncrana 85 55 8N 7 28W
Bundaberg . . . . 127 24 54 S 152 22 E
Bundi . . . . 108 25 30N 75 35 E
Bundlicks Cr. → 25 30 36N 92 57W
Bundoran 85 54 24N 8 17W
Bungatakada . . . . 117 33 35N 131 25 E
Bungo-Suidō . . . . 117 33 0N 132 15 E
Bungun Shara . . . . 113 49 0N 104 0 E
Bunia . . . . 122 1 35N 30 20 E
Bunji . . . . 108 35 45N 74 40 E
Bunker 32 37 27N 91 13W
Bunker Hill, Ill. 21 39 3N 89 57W

Bunker Hill Caicó

Bunker Hill, Ind. 22 40 40N 86 6W
Bunker Hill, Kans. 24 38 53N 98 42W
Bunker Hill, Nev. 35 39 15N 117 8W
Bunker Hill, Oreg. 44 43 22N 124 12W
Bunkerville 35 36 46N 114 8W
Bunkie 25 30 57N 92 11W
Bunn 40 35 58N 78 15W
Bunnell 17 29 28N 81 16W
Buntok 110 1 40 S 114 58 E
Bunyu 110 3 35N 117 50 E
Buol 111 1 15N 121 32 E
Buon Me Thuot 112 12 40N 108 3 E
Buorkhaya, Mys 101 71 50N 132 40 E
Buqayq 106 26 0N 49 45 E
Buqei'a 104 32 58N 35 20 E
Bur Acaba 105 3 12N 44 20 E
Bûr Safâga 121 26 43N 33 57 E
Bûr Sa'îd 121 31 16N 32 18 E
Bûr Sûdân 121 19 32N 37 9 E
Bura 122 1 4 S 39 58 E
Burao 105 9 32N 45 32 E
Buras 25 29 22N 89 32W
Buraydah 106 26 20N 44 8 E
Buraymī, Al Wāhāt al 107 24 10N 55 43 E
Burbank, Calif. 15 34 11N 118 19W
Burbank, Okla. 43 36 42N 96 44W
Burbank, Wash. 53 46 12N 119 1W
Burchard 34 40 9N 96 21W
Burden 24 37 19N 96 45W
Burdett, Canada 62 49 50N 111 32W
Burdett, Kans. 24 38 12N 99 32W
Burdett, N.Y. 39 42 25N 76 51W
Burdick 24 38 34N 96 51W
Burdur 106 37 45N 30 22 E
Burdwan = Barddhaman 109 23 14N 87 39 E
Bure → 82 52 38N 1 45 E
Bureau County ◇ 21 41 25N 89 30W
Bureya → 101 49 27N 129 30 E
Burgas 95 42 33N 27 29 E
Burgaski Zaliv 95 42 30N 27 39 E
Burgaw 40 34 33N 77 56W
Burgenland □ 88 47 20N 16 20 E
Burgeo 61 47 37N 57 38W
Burgersdorp 123 31 0 S 26 20 E
Burgess Junction 56 44 46N 107 32W
Burgoon 42 41 16N 83 15W
Burgos 91 42 21N 3 41W
Burgsvik 97 57 3N 18 19 E
Burgundy = Bourgogne 90 47 0N 4 30 E
Burias 111 12 55N 123 5 E
Burica, Pta. 66 8 3N 82 51W
Burien 53 47 28N 122 21W
Burin, Canada 61 47 1N 55 14W
Būrīn, Jordan 104 32 11N 35 15 E
Buriram 112 15 0N 103 0 E
Buriti Alegre 75 18 9 S 49 3W
Buriti Bravo 74 5 50 S 43 50W
Buriti dos Lopes 74 3 10 S 41 52W
Burji 121 5 29N 37 51 E
Burkburnett 51 34 6N 98 34W
Burke, Idaho 20 47 31N 115 49W
Burke, S. Dak. 47 43 11N 99 18W
Burke County ◇, Ga. 18 33 0N 82 0W
Burke County ◇, N.C. 40 35 45N 81 40W
Burke County ◇, N. Dak. 41 48 55N 102 30W
Burkesville 49 36 48N 85 22W
Burketown 127 17 45 S 139 33 E
Burkett 51 32 0N 99 8W
Burkettsville 42 40 21N 84 39W
Burkeville, Tex. 51 31 0N 93 40W
Burkeville, Va. 54 37 11N 78 12W
Burkina Faso ■ 120 12 0N 1 0W
Burk's Falls 60 45 37N 79 24W
Burleigh County ◇ 41 47 0N 100 30W
Burleson 51 32 33N 97 19W
Burleson County ◇ 51 30 32N 96 42W
Burley 20 42 32N 113 48W
Burlingame, Calif. 14 37 35N 122 21W
Burlingame, Kans. 24 38 45N 95 50W
Burlington, Colo. 16 39 18N 102 16W
Burlington, Ill. 21 42 3N 88 33W
Burlington, Ind. 22 40 29N 86 24W
Burlington, Iowa 23 40 49N 91 14W
Burlington, Kans. 24 38 12N 95 45W
Burlington, Ky. 49 39 2N 84 43W
Burlington, Mass. 28 42 30N 71 12W
Burlington, N.C. 40 36 6N 79 26W
Burlington, N. Dak. 41 48 17N 101 26W
Burlington, N.J. 37 40 4N 74 51W
Burlington, Okla. 43 36 54N 98 25W
Burlington, Vt. 36 44 29N 73 12W
Burlington, Wash. 53 48 28N 122 20W
Burlington, Wis. 55 42 41N 88 17W
Burlington, Wyo. 56 44 27N 108 26W
Burlington County ◇ 37 39 50N 74 45W
Burlington Junction 32 40 27N 95 4W
Burlyu-Tyube 100 46 30N 79 10 E
Burma ■ 109 21 0N 96 30 E
Burna 48 37 15N 88 22W
Burnaby I. 62 52 25N 131 19W
Burnet 51 30 45N 98 14W
Burnet County ◇ 51 30 45N 98 15W
Burnett → 127 24 45 S 152 23 E
Burnett County ◇ 55 45 50N 92 20W
Burnettsville 22 40 46N 86 36W
Burney 14 40 53N 121 40W
Burnham, Maine 26 44 42N 69 26W
Burnham, Pa. 45 40 38N 77 34W
Burnie 127 41 4 S 145 56 E
Burning Springs 49 37 15N 83 49W
Burnley 82 53 47N 2 15W
Burns, Colo. 16 39 52N 106 53W
Burns, Kans. 24 38 5N 96 53W
Burns, Oreg. 44 43 35N 119 3W
Burns, Tenn. 48 36 3N 87 19W
Burns, Wyo. 56 41 12N 104 21W
Burns Flat 43 35 21N 99 10W
Burns Lake 62 54 20N 125 45W
Burnside 49 36 59N 84 36W
Burnside → 58 66 51N 108 4W
Burnsville, Ala. 10 32 28N 86 53W
Burnsville, Minn. 30 44 47N 93 17W
Burnsville, Miss. 31 34 51N 88 19W
Burnsville, N.C. 40 35 55N 82 18W
Burnsville, W. Va. 54 38 52N 80 40W
Burnt → 44 44 22N 117 14W
Burnt Corn 10 31 33N 87 10W
Burntfork 56 41 2N 109 59W
Burntwood → 63 56 8N 96 34W
Burntwood L. 63 55 22N 100 26W
Burqā 104 32 18N 35 11 E
Burqān 106 29 0N 47 57 E
Burqin 113 47 43N 87 0 E
Burr 34 40 33N 96 19W
Burr Oak, Kans. 24 39 52N 98 18W
Burr Oak, Mich. 29 41 51N 85 19W
Burra 127 33 40 S 138 55 E
Burro, Serranías del 64 29 0N 102 0W
Burrton 24 38 2N 97 41W
Burruyacú 76 26 30 S 64 40W
Burry Port 83 51 41N 4 17W
Bursa 106 40 15N 29 5 E
Burstall 63 50 39N 109 54W
Burt 23 43 12N 94 13W
Burt County ◇ 34 41 50N 96 15W
Burt L. 29 45 28N 84 40W
Burton, Nebr. 34 42 55N 99 35W
Burton, Tex. 51 30 11N 96 42W
Burton, L. 18 34 50N 83 33W
Burton L. 60 54 45N 78 20W
Burton-upon-Trent 82 52 48N 1 39W
Burtrum 30 45 52N 94 41W
Buru 111 3 30 S 126 30 E
Burundi ■ 122 3 15 S 30 0 E
Burung 110 0 24N 103 33 E
Burutu 120 5 20N 5 29 E
Burwell 34 41 47N 99 8W
Bury 82 53 36N 2 19W
Bury St. Edmunds 83 52 15N 0 42 E
Buryat A.S.S.R. □ 101 53 0N 110 0 E
Buşayyah 106 30 0N 46 10 E
Bush 25 30 36N 89 54W
Bush City 24 38 13N 95 9W
Būshehr 107 28 55N 50 55 E
Būshehr □ 107 28 20N 51 45 E
Bushell 63 59 31N 108 45W
Bushire = Būshehr 107 28 55N 50 55 E
Bushland 50 35 11N 102 4W
Bushnell, Fla. 17 28 40N 82 7W
Bushnell, Ill. 21 40 33N 90 31W
Bushnell, Nebr. 34 41 14N 103 54W
Bushong 24 38 39N 96 15W
Bushton 24 38 31N 98 24W
Bushwood 27 38 18N 76 47W
Bushy Head Mt. 43 36 2N 94 35W
Businga 122 3 16N 20 59 E
Buskerud fylke □ 97 60 13N 9 0 E
Busra ash Shām 106 32 30N 36 25 E
Busselton 126 33 42 S 115 15 E
Bussey 23 41 12N 92 53W
Bussum 87 52 16N 5 10 E
Bustamante, B. 78 45 5 S 66 18W
Bustard Hd. 127 24 0 S 151 48 E
Busto Arsizio 94 45 40N 8 50 E
Busu-Djanoa 122 1 43N 21 23 E
Busuanga 111 12 10N 120 0 E
Buta 122 2 50N 24 53 E
Butare 122 2 31 S 29 52 E
Butaritari 124 3 30N 174 0 E
Bute 84 55 48N 5 2W
Bute Inlet 62 50 40N 124 53W
Butembo 122 0 9N 29 18 E
Butha Qi 114 48 0N 122 32 E
Butiaba 122 1 50N 31 20 E
Butler, Ala. 10 32 5N 88 13W
Butler, Ga. 18 32 33N 84 14W
Butler, Ind. 22 41 26N 84 52W
Butler, Ky. 49 38 47N 84 22W
Butler, Md. 27 39 35N 76 45W
Butler, Mo. 32 38 16N 94 20W
Butler, N.J. 37 41 0N 74 20W
Butler, Okla. 43 35 38N 99 11W
Butler, Pa. 45 40 52N 79 54W
Butler County ◇, Ala. 10 31 50N 86 38W
Butler County ◇, Iowa 23 42 45N 92 45W
Butler County ◇, Kans. 24 37 45N 96 45W
Butler County ◇, Ky. 48 37 10N 86 45W
Butler County ◇, Mo. 32 36 45N 90 25W
Butler County ◇, Nebr. 34 41 15N 97 0W
Butler County ◇, Ohio 42 39 24N 84 34W
Butler County ◇, Pa. 45 41 0N 80 0W
Butner 40 36 8N 78 45W
Butte, Mont. 33 46 0N 112 32W
Butte, N. Dak. 41 47 50N 100 40W
Butte, Nebr. 34 42 58N 98 51W
Butte County ◇, Calif. 14 39 40N 121 45W
Butte County ◇, Idaho 20 43 50N 113 0W
Butte County ◇, S. Dak. 47 45 0N 103 30W
Butte Falls 44 42 33N 122 34W
Butte Mts. 35 39 50N 115 5W
Butterfield, Minn. 30 43 58N 94 48W
Butterfield, Mo. 32 36 45N 93 54W
Butternut 55 46 1N 90 30W
Butterworth 112 5 24N 100 23 E
Button B. 63 58 45N 94 23W
Buttonwillow 15 35 24N 119 28W
Butts County ◇ 18 33 20N 84 0W
Butuan 111 8 57N 125 33 E
Butung 111 5 0 S 122 45 E
Buturlinovka 99 50 50N 40 35 E
Buxton, Guyana 71 6 48N 58 2W
Buxton, U.K. 82 53 16N 1 54W
Buxton, N.C. 40 35 16N 75 32W
Buxton, N. Dak. 41 47 36N 97 6W
Buy 98 58 28N 41 28 E
Buyaga 101 59 50N 127 0 E
Büyük Çekmece 95 41 2N 28 35 E
Buzău 89 45 10N 26 50 E
Buzău □ 95 45 20N 26 30 E
Buzău → 89 45 10N 27 20 E
Buzău, Pasul 95 45 35N 26 12 E
Buzaymah 121 24 50N 22 2 E
Buzen 117 33 35N 131 5 E
Buzi → 123 19 50 S 34 43 E
Buzuluk 98 52 48N 52 12 E
Buzzards B. 28 41 30N 70 45W
Buzzards Bay 28 41 45N 70 37W
Byala, Ruse, Bulgaria 95 43 28N 25 44 E
Byala, Varna, Bulgaria 95 42 53N 27 55 E
Byala Slatina 95 43 26N 23 55 E
Byars 43 34 53N 97 3W
Bydgoszcz 89 53 10N 18 0 E
Byelorussian S.S.R. □ 98 53 30N 27 0 E
Byers, Colo. 16 39 43N 104 14W
Byers, Kans. 24 37 48N 98 52W
Byers, Tex. 51 34 4N 98 11W
Byesville 42 39 58N 81 32W
Byfield 28 42 46N 70 57W
Byhalia 31 34 52N 89 41W
Bylas 12 33 8N 110 7W
Bylot I. 59 73 13N 78 34W
Byng 43 34 50N 96 42W
Bynum 33 47 59N 112 19W
Byram 31 32 11N 90 15W
Byrd, C. 5 69 38 S 76 7W
Byrd Land 5 79 30 S 125 0W
Byrd Sub-Glacial Basin 5 82 0 S 120 0W
Byrdstown 49 36 34N 85 8W
Byron, Ga. 18 32 39N 83 46W
Byron, Ill. 21 42 8N 89 15W
Byron, Maine 26 44 43N 70 38W
Byron, Mich. 29 42 49N 83 57W
Byron, Minn. 30 44 2N 92 41W
Byron, Nebr. 34 40 0N 97 46W
Byron, Okla. 43 36 54N 98 19W
Byron, Wyo. 56 44 48N 108 30W
Byron, C. 127 28 38 S 153 40 E
Byrranga, Gory 101 75 0N 100 0 E
Byske 96 64 57N 21 11 E
Byske älv → 96 64 57N 21 13 E
Bytom 89 50 25N 18 54 E

C

C. J. Strike Reservoir 20 42 59N 115 58W
Ca Mau = Quan Long 112 9 7N 105 8 E
Ca Mau, Mui = Bai Bung, Mui 112 8 38N 104 44 E
Caacupé 76 25 23 S 57 5W
Caála 123 12 46 S 15 30 E
Caamano Sd. 62 52 55N 129 25W
Caapiranga 71 3 18 S 61 13W
Caazapá 76 26 8 S 56 19W
Caazapá □ 77 26 10 S 56 0W
Caballo Reservoir 38 32 54N 107 18W
Cabana 72 8 25 S 78 5W
Cabanaconde 72 15 38 S 71 58W
Cabanatuan 111 15 30N 120 58 E
Cabanillas 72 15 36 S 70 28W
Cabano 61 47 40N 68 56W
Cabarrus County ◇ 40 35 20N 80 30W
Cabazon 15 33 55N 116 47W
Cabedelo 74 7 0 S 34 50W
Cabell County ◇ 54 38 26N 82 8W
Cabery 21 41 0N 88 12W
Cabildo 76 32 30 S 71 5W
Cabimas 70 10 23N 71 25W
Cabinda 122 5 33 S 12 11 E
Cabinda □ 122 5 0 S 12 30 E
Cabinet Mts. 33 45 30N 115 0W
Cable 55 46 13N 91 17W
Cabo Blanco 78 47 15 S 65 47W
Cabo Frio 75 22 51 S 42 3W
Cabo Pantoja 70 1 0 S 75 10W
Cabo Raso 78 44 20 S 65 15W
Cabo Rojo 57 18 5N 67 9W
Cabonga, Réservoir 60 47 20N 76 40W
Cabool 32 37 7N 92 6W
Cabora Bassa Dam 123 15 20 S 32 50 E
Caborca 64 30 40N 112 10W
Cabot, Ark. 13 34 59N 92 1W
Cabot, Vt. 36 44 23N 72 18W
Cabot, Mt. 36 44 30N 71 25W
Cabot Strait 61 47 15N 59 40W
Cabrera, I. 91 39 8N 2 57 E
Cabri 63 50 35N 108 25W
Cabriel → 91 39 14N 1 3W
Cabrillo, Pt. 14 39 21N 123 50W
Cabruta 70 7 50N 66 10W
Çabuyaro 70 4 18N 72 49W
Čačak 95 43 54N 20 20 E
Cacao 71 4 33N 52 26W
Cacapon → 54 39 37N 78 16W
Cáceres, Brazil 73 16 5 S 57 40W
Cáceres, Colombia 70 7 35N 75 20W
Cáceres, Spain 91 39 26N 6 23W
Cache 43 34 38N 98 38W
Cache →, Ark. 13 34 43N 91 20W
Cache →, Ill. 21 37 4N 89 10W
Cache Bay 60 46 22N 80 0W
Cache County ◇ 52 41 40N 111 45W
Cache Cr. → 14 38 42N 121 42W
Cache la Poudre → 16 40 25N 104 36W
Cache National Forest 52 41 45N 111 29W
Cache Peak 20 42 11N 113 40W
Cachi 76 25 5 S 66 10W
Cachimbo 73 8 57 S 54 54W
Cachimbo, Serra do 73 9 30 S 55 0W
Cachoeira 75 12 30 S 39 0W
Cachoeira Alta 75 18 48 S 50 58W
Cachoeira de Itapemirim 75 20 51 S 41 7W
Cachoeira do Sul 77 30 3 S 52 53W
Cachoeiro do Arari 74 1 1 S 48 58W
Cachuela Esperanza 73 10 32 S 65 38W
Cacólo 122 10 9 S 19 21 E
Caconda 123 13 48 S 15 8 E
Cactus 50 36 4N 101 59W
Caçu 75 18 37 S 51 4W
Caculé 75 14 30 S 42 13W
Caddo, Okla. 43 34 7N 96 16W
Caddo, Tex. 51 32 43N 98 40W
Caddo → 13 34 10N 93 3W
Caddo County ◇ 43 35 10N 98 20W
Caddo Cr. → 43 34 14N 96 59W
Caddo Gap 13 34 24N 93 37W
Caddo L. 25 32 43N 93 55W
Caddo Mills 51 33 4N 96 14W
Caddo Parish ◇ 25 32 45N 93 58W
Caddoa 16 38 4N 102 56W
Cader Idris 82 52 43N 3 56W
Cades 46 33 47N 79 47W
Cadillac, Canada 60 48 14N 78 23W
Cadillac, U.S.A. 29 44 15N 85 24W
Cadiz, Phil. 111 10 57N 123 15 E
Cádiz, Spain 91 36 30N 6 20W
Cadiz, Ind. 22 39 57N 85 29W
Cadiz, Ky. 48 36 52N 87 50W
Cadiz, Ohio 42 40 22N 81 0W
Cádiz, G. de 91 36 40N 7 0W
Cadiz L. 15 34 18N 115 24W
Cadley 18 33 32N 82 40W
Cadomin 62 53 2N 117 20W
Cadott 55 44 57N 91 9W
Cadotte → 62 56 43N 117 10W
Cadwell 18 32 20N 83 4W
Caen 90 49 10N 0 22W
Caernarfon 82 53 8N 4 17W
Caernarfon B. 82 53 4N 4 40W
Caernarvon = Caernarfon 82 53 8N 4 17W
Caerphilly 83 51 34N 3 13W
Caesarea 104 32 30N 34 53 E
Caeté 75 19 55 S 43 40W
Caetité 75 13 50 S 42 32W
Cafayate 76 26 2 S 66 0W
Cafifi 70 5 13N 71 4W
Cagayan → 111 18 25N 121 42 E
Cagayan de Oro 111 8 30N 124 40 E
Cagles Mill L. 22 39 30N 86 53W
Cágliari 94 39 15N 9 6 E
Cágliari, G. di 94 39 8N 9 10 E
Caguán → 70 0 8 S 74 18W
Caguas 57 18 14N 66 2W
Caha Mts. 85 51 45N 9 40W
Cahaba → 10 32 20N 87 5W
Caher 85 52 23N 7 56W
Cahersiveen 85 51 57N 10 13W
Cahokia 21 38 34N 90 11W
Cahone 16 37 39N 108 49W
Cahore Pt. 85 52 34N 6 11W
Cahors 90 44 27N 1 27 E
Cahuapanas 72 5 15 S 77 0W
Cahuinari → 70 1 21 S 70 44W
Caia 123 17 51 S 35 24 E
Caiabis, Serra dos 73 11 30 S 56 30W
Caiapó, Serra do 73 17 0 S 52 0W
Caiapônia 73 16 57 S 51 49W
Caibarién 66 22 30N 79 30W
Caicara, Bolívar, Venezuela 70 7 38N 66 10W
Caicara, Monagas, Venezuela 71 9 52N 63 38W
Caicó 74 6 20 S 37 0W

Caicos Is. 67 21 40N 71 40W
Caicos Passage 67 22 45N 72 45W
Cailloma 72 15 9S 71 45W
Caillou B. 25 29 3N 91 0W
Caine → 73 18 23S 65 21W
Cains Store 49 37 8N 84 50W
Cainsville 32 40 26N 93 47W
Caird Coast 5 75 0S 25 0W
Cairn Gorm 84 57 7N 3 40W
Cairn Toul 84 57 3N 3 44W
Cairngorm Mts. 84 57 6N 3 42W
Cairns 127 16 57S 145 45 E
Cairo = El Qâhira 121 30 1N 31 14 E
Cairo, Ga. 18 30 52N 84 13W
Cairo, Ill. 21 37 0N 89 11W
Cairo, Ky. 48 37 42N 87 39W
Cairo, Mo. 32 39 31N 92 27W
Cairo, Nebr. 34 41 0N 98 36W
Cairo, Ohio 42 40 50N 84 5W
Cairo, W. Va. 54 39 13N 81 9W
Caithness, Ord of 84 58 9N 3 37W
Caiundo 123 15 50S 17 28 E
Caiza 73 20 2S 65 40W
Caja de Muertos, Isla 57 17 54N 66 31W
Cajabamba 72 7 38S 78 4W
Cajamarca 72 7 5S 78 28W
Cajamarca □ 72 6 15S 78 50W
Cajapió 74 2 58S 44 48W
Cajatambo 72 10 30S 77 2W
Cajàzeiras 74 6 52S 38 30W
Cajon Summit 15 34 21N 117 27W
Cal, La → 73 17 27S 58 15W
Calabar 120 4 57N 8 20 E
Calabozo 70 9 0N 67 28W
Calábria □ 94 39 24N 16 30 E
Calacota 72 17 16S 68 38W
Calafate 78 50 19S 72 15W
Calahorra 91 42 18N 1 59W
Calais, France 90 50 57N 1 56 E
Calais, U.S.A. 26 45 11N 67 17W
Calalaste, Cord. de 76 25 0S 67 0W
Calama, Brazil 73 8 0S 62 50W
Calama, Chile 76 22 30S 68 55W
Calamar, Bolívar, Colombia 70 10 15N 74 55W
Calamar, Vaupés, Colombia 70 1 58N 72 32W
Calamarca 72 16 55S 68 9W
Calamian Group 111 11 50N 119 55 E
Calamocha 91 40 50N 1 17W
Calamus → 34 41 48N 99 9W
Calang 110 4 37N 95 37 E
Calapan 111 13 25N 121 7 E
Calapooia → 44 44 38N 123 8W
Călăraşi 95 44 12N 27 20 E
Călăraşi □ 95 44 10N 27 0 E
Calatayud 91 41 20N 1 40W
Calauag 111 13 55N 122 15 E
Calaveras County ◇ 14 38 15N 120 40W
Calavite, Cape 111 13 26N 120 20 E
Calbayog 111 12 4N 124 38 E
Calca 72 13 22S 72 0W
Calcasieu → 25 30 5N 93 20W
Calcasieu L. 25 29 55N 93 18W
Calcasieu Parish ◇ 25 30 14N 93 23W
Calcutta 109 22 36N 88 24 E
Caldas □ 70 5 15N 75 30W
Caldas Novas 75 17 45S 48 38W
Calder → 82 53 44N 1 21W
Caldera 76 27 5S 70 55W
Caldwell, Ark. 13 35 5N 90 49W
Caldwell, Idaho 20 43 40N 116 41W
Caldwell, Kans. 24 37 2N 97 37W
Caldwell, Ohio 42 39 45N 81 31W
Caldwell, Tex. 51 30 32N 96 42W
Caldwell County ◇, Ky. 48 37 10N 87 50W
Caldwell County ◇, Mo. 32 39 40N 94 0W
Caldwell County ◇, N.C. 40 36 0N 81 30W
Caldwell County ◇, Tex. 51 29 53N 97 40W
Caldwell Parish ◇ 25 32 0N 92 0W
Caledon 123 34 14S 19 26 E
Caledon → 123 30 31S 26 5 E
Caledon B. 127 12 45S 137 0 E
Caledonia, Mich. 29 42 47N 85 31W
Caledonia, Minn. 30 43 38N 91 30W
Caledonia, Miss. 31 33 41N 88 20W
Caledonia, N. Dak. 41 47 28N 96 53W
Caledonia, N.Y. 39 42 58N 77 51W
Caledonia County ◇ 36 44 30N 72 10W
Calella 91 41 37N 2 40 E
Calera, Ala. 10 33 6N 86 45W
Calera, Okla. 43 33 52N 96 29W
Calera, La 76 32 50S 71 10W
Caleta Olivia 78 46 25S 67 25W
Calexico 15 32 40N 115 30W
Calf of Man 82 54 4N 4 48W
Calgary 62 51 0N 114 10W
Calhan 16 39 2N 104 18W
Calhoun, Ga. 18 34 30N 84 57W
Calhoun, Ill. 21 38 39N 88 3W
Calhoun, Ky. 48 37 32N 87 16W
Calhoun, Mo. 32 38 28N 93 38W
Calhoun, Tenn. 49 35 18N 84 45W
Calhoun City 31 33 51N 89 19W
Calhoun County ◇, Ala. 10 33 47N 86 0W
Calhoun County ◇, Ark. 13 33 35N 92 31W
Calhoun County ◇, Fla. 17 30 30N 85 15W
Calhoun County ◇, Ga. 18 31 30N 84 35W
Calhoun County ◇, Ill. 21 39 10N 90 40W
Calhoun County ◇, Iowa 23 42 25N 94 40W
Calhoun County ◇, Mich. 29 42 15N 85 0W
Calhoun County ◇, Miss. 31 33 56N 89 20W
Calhoun County ◇, S.C. 46 33 45N 80 50W
Calhoun County ◇, Tex. 51 28 37N 96 38W
Calhoun County ◇, W. Va. 54 38 55N 81 6W
Calhoun Falls 46 34 6N 82 36W
Cali 70 3 25N 76 35W
Calico Rock 13 36 7N 92 9W
Calicut 108 11 15N 75 43 E
Caliente, Calif. 15 35 17N 118 38W
Caliente, Nev. 35 37 37N 114 31W
Califon 37 40 42N 74 50W
California, Md. 27 38 18N 76 32W
California, Mo. 32 38 38N 92 34W
California, Pa. 45 40 4N 79 54W
California □ 14 37 30N 119 30W
California, Baja 64 32 10N 115 12W
California, Baja, T.N. □ 64 30 0N 115 0W
California, Baja, T.S. □ 64 25 50N 111 50W
California, Golfo de 64 27 0N 111 0W
California, Lr. = California, Baja 64 32 10N 115 12W
California Aqueduct 15 33 52N 117 12W
Călimăneşti 95 45 14N 24 20 E
Călineşti 95 45 21N 24 18 E
Calingasta 76 31 15S 69 30W
Calio 41 48 38N 98 56W
Calion 13 33 20N 92 32W
Calipatria 15 33 8N 115 31W
Calistoga 14 38 35N 122 35W
Calkiní 65 20 21N 90 3W
Callabonna, L. 127 29 40S 140 5 E
Callahan, Calif. 14 41 18N 122 48W
Callahan, Fla. 17 30 34N 81 50W
Callahan County ◇ 51 32 24N 99 24W
Callan 85 52 33N 7 25W
Callander 84 56 15N 4 14W
Callao, Peru 72 12 0S 77 0W
Callao, U.S.A. 52 39 54N 113 43W
Callaway, Fla. 17 30 8N 85 36W
Callaway, Minn. 30 46 59N 95 54W
Callaway, Nebr. 34 41 18N 99 56W
Callaway County ◇ 32 38 50N 91 50W
Callender 23 42 22N 94 17W
Calles 65 23 2N 98 42W
Callicoon 39 41 46N 75 3W
Calliham 51 28 29N 98 21W
Calling Lake 62 55 15N 113 12W
Calloway County ◇ 48 36 40N 88 15W
Calmar 23 43 11N 91 52W
Calne 82 51 26N 2 0W
Caloosahatchee → 17 26 31N 82 1W
Calpella 14 39 14N 123 12W
Calpine 14 39 40N 120 27W
Calstock 60 49 47N 84 9W
Caltagirone 94 37 13N 14 30 E
Caltanissetta 94 37 30N 14 3 E
Calulo 122 10 1S 14 56 E
Calumet, Iowa 23 42 57N 95 33W
Calumet, Mich. 29 47 14N 88 27W
Calumet, Minn. 30 47 19N 93 17W
Calumet, Okla. 43 35 36N 98 7W
Calumet City 21 41 37N 87 32W
Calumet County ◇ 55 44 5N 88 10W
Calunda 123 12 7S 23 36 E
Calvados □ 90 49 5N 0 15W
Calvert, Md. 27 39 42N 75 58W
Calvert, Tex. 51 30 59N 96 40W
Calvert City 48 37 2N 88 21W
Calvert County ◇ 27 38 30N 76 35W
Calvert I. 62 51 30N 128 0W
Calverton 27 39 3N 76 56W
Calvi 90 42 34N 8 45 E
Calvillo 64 21 51N 102 43W
Calvin, La. 25 31 58N 92 47W
Calvin, N. Dak. 41 48 51N 98 56W
Calvin, Okla. 43 34 58N 96 15W
Calvinia 123 31 28S 19 45 E
Calwa 15 36 42N 119 46W
Cam → 83 52 21N 0 16 E
Cam Lam 112 11 54N 109 10 E
Cam Ranh 112 11 54N 109 12 E
Camabatela 122 8 20S 15 26 E
Camacã 75 15 24S 39 30W
Camaçari 75 12 41S 38 18W
Camacho 64 24 25N 102 18W
Camacupa 123 11 58S 17 22 E
Camaguán 70 8 6N 67 36W
Camagüey 66 21 20N 78 0W
Camak 18 33 27N 82 39W
Camamu 75 13 57S 39 7W
Camaná 72 16 30S 72 50W
Camanche 23 41 47N 90 15W
Camanche Reservoir 14 38 14N 121 1W
Camano I. 53 48 0N 122 30W
Camaquã → 77 31 17S 51 47W
Camararé → 73 12 15S 58 55W
Camaret 90 48 16N 4 37W
Camargo, Bolivia 73 20 38S 65 15 E
Camargo, U.S.A. 43 36 1N 99 17W
Camarillo 15 34 13N 119 2W
Camarón, C. 66 16 0N 85 0W
Camarones 78 44 50S 65 40W
Camarones, B. 78 44 45S 65 35W
Camas, Idaho 20 44 0N 112 13W
Camas, Wash. 53 45 35N 122 24W
Camas County ◇ 20 43 30N 114 50W
Camas Valley 44 43 2N 123 40W
Cambará 77 23 2S 50 5W
Cambay = Khambhat 108 22 23N 72 33 E
Cambay, G. of 108 20 45N 72 30 E
Cambodia ■ 112 12 15N 105 0 E
Camborne 83 50 13N 5 18W
Cambrai 90 50 11N 3 14 E
Cambria, Calif. 15 35 34N 121 5W
Cambria, Wis. 55 43 33N 89 7W
Cambria County ◇ 45 40 30N 78 52W
Cambrian Mts. 83 52 25N 3 52W
Cambridge, Canada 60 43 23N 80 15W
Cambridge, Jamaica 66 18 18N 77 54W
Cambridge, N.Z. 128 37 54S 175 29 E
Cambridge, U.K. 83 52 13N 0 8 E
Cambridge, Idaho 20 44 34N 116 41W
Cambridge, Ill. 21 41 18N 90 12W
Cambridge, Iowa 23 41 54N 93 32W
Cambridge, Kans. 24 37 19N 96 40W
Cambridge, Mass. 28 42 22N 71 6W
Cambridge, Md. 27 38 34N 76 5W
Cambridge, Minn. 30 45 34N 93 13W
Cambridge, N.Y. 39 43 2N 73 22W
Cambridge, Nebr. 34 40 17N 100 10W
Cambridge, Ohio 42 40 2N 81 35W
Cambridge, Vt. 36 44 39N 72 53W
Cambridge Bay 58 69 10N 105 0W
Cambridge City 22 39 49N 85 10W
Cambridge Gulf 126 14 55S 128 15 E
Cambridge Springs 45 41 48N 80 4W
Cambridgeport 36 43 10N 72 35W
Cambridgeshire □ 83 52 12N 0 7 E
Cambuci 75 21 35S 41 55W
Camden, Ala. 10 31 59N 87 17W
Camden, Ark. 13 33 35N 92 50W
Camden, Del. 27 39 7N 75 33W
Camden, Ill. 21 40 9N 90 46W
Camden, Maine 26 44 13N 69 4W
Camden, Miss. 31 32 47N 89 50W
Camden, N.C. 40 36 20N 76 10W
Camden, N.J. 37 39 56N 75 7W
Camden, N.Y. 39 43 20N 75 45W
Camden, Ohio 42 39 38N 84 39W
Camden, S.C. 46 34 16N 80 36W
Camden, Tenn. 48 36 4N 88 6W
Camden, Tex. 51 30 55N 94 44W
Camden Bay 11 70 10N 145 15W
Camden County ◇, Ga. 18 31 0N 81 45W
Camden County ◇, Mo. 32 38 0N 92 45W
Camden County ◇, N.C. 40 36 20N 76 15W
Camden County ◇, N.J. 37 39 45N 75 0W
Camdenton 32 38 1N 92 45W
Camels Hump 36 44 19N 72 53W
Cameron, Ariz. 12 35 53N 111 25W
Cameron, La. 25 29 48N 93 20W
Cameron, Mo. 32 39 44N 94 14W
Cameron, Mont. 33 45 13N 111 41W
Cameron, N.C. 40 35 20N 79 15W
Cameron, Okla. 43 35 8N 94 32W
Cameron, S.C. 46 33 34N 80 43W
Cameron, Tex. 51 30 51N 96 59W
Cameron, W. Va. 54 39 50N 80 34W
Cameron, Wis. 55 45 25N 91 44W
Cameron County ◇, Pa. 45 41 30N 78 5W
Cameron County ◇, Tex. 50 26 12N 97 42W
Cameron Falls 60 49 8N 88 19W
Cameron Highlands 112 4 27N 101 22 E
Cameron Hills 62 59 48N 118 0W
Cameron Parish ◇ 25 29 58N 93 10W
Cameroon ■ 122 6 0N 12 30 E
Cameroun, Mt. 122 4 13N 9 10 E
Cametá 74 2 12S 49 30W
Camiguin, I. 111 8 55N 124 45 E
Camilla 18 31 14N 84 12W
Caminha 91 41 50N 8 50W
Camino 14 38 44N 120 41W
Camiranga 74 1 48S 46 17W
Camiri 73 20 3S 63 31W
Camissombo 122 8 7S 20 38 E
Camoa Mts. 71 1 30N 59 0W
Camocim 74 2 55S 40 50W
Camooweal 127 19 56S 138 7 E
Camopi 71 3 12N 52 17W
Camopi → 71 3 10N 52 20W
Camp County ◇ 51 33 0N 94 59W
Camp Creek 54 37 30N 81 6W
Camp Crook 47 45 33N 103 59W
Camp Douglas 55 43 55N 90 16W
Camp Hill, Ala. 10 32 48N 85 39W
Camp Hill, Pa. 45 40 14N 76 55W
Camp Houston 43 36 49N 99 7W
Camp Point 21 40 3N 91 4W
Camp Springs 27 38 48N 76 55W
Camp Verde 12 34 34N 111 51W
Camp Wood 51 29 40N 100 1W
Campagna 94 40 40N 15 5 E
Campaign 49 35 46N 85 38W
Campana 76 34 10S 58 55W
Campana, I. 78 48 20S 75 20W
Campania □ 94 40 50N 14 45 E
Campbell, Ala. 10 31 55N 87 59W
Campbell, Calif. 14 37 17N 121 57W
Campbell, Minn. 30 46 6N 96 24W
Campbell, Mo. 32 36 30N 90 4W
Campbell, Nebr. 34 40 18N 98 44W
Campbell, Ohio 42 41 5N 80 37W
Campbell County ◇, Ky. 49 38 55N 84 20W
Campbell County ◇, S. Dak. 47 45 55N 100 0W
Campbell County ◇, Tenn. 49 36 23N 84 7W
Campbell County ◇, Va. 54 37 15N 79 5W
Campbell County ◇, Wyo. 56 44 15N 105 30W
Campbell I. 124 52 30S 169 0 E
Campbell L. 63 63 14N 106 55W
Campbell River 62 50 5N 125 20W
Campbellsburg, Ind. 22 38 39N 86 16W
Campbellsburg, Ky. 49 38 31N 85 12W
Campbellsport 55 43 36N 88 17W
Campbellsville, Ky. 49 37 21N 85 20W
Campbellsville, Tenn. 48 35 20N 87 8W
Campbellton, Canada 61 47 57N 66 43W
Campbellton, U.S.A. 17 30 57N 85 24W
Campbeltown 84 55 25N 5 36W
Campeche 65 19 50N 90 32W
Campeche □ 65 19 50N 90 32W
Campeche, Bahía de 65 19 30N 93 0W
Camperville 63 51 59N 100 9W
Campina Grande 74 7 20S 35 47W
Campina Verde 75 19 31S 49 28W
Campinas 77 22 50S 47 0W
Campion 16 40 21N 105 5W
Campo, Cameroon 122 2 22N 9 50 E
Campo, U.S.A. 16 37 6N 102 35W
Campo Belo 75 20 52S 45 16W
Campo de Diauarum 73 11 12S 53 14W
Campo Flórido 75 19 47S 48 35W
Campo Formoso 74 10 30S 40 20W
Campo Grande 73 20 25S 54 40W
Campo Maíor 74 4 50S 42 12W
Campo Mourão 75 24 3S 52 22W
Campoalegre 70 2 41N 75 20W
Campobasso 94 41 34N 14 40 E
Campobello 46 35 7N 82 9W
Campos 75 21 50S 41 20W
Campos Altos 75 19 47S 46 10W
Campos Belos 75 13 10S 47 3W
Campos Novos 77 27 21S 51 50W
Campos Sales 74 7 4S 40 23W
Campti 25 31 54N 93 7W
Campton, Fla. 17 30 53N 86 31W
Campton, Ga. 18 33 52N 83 43W
Campton, Ky. 49 37 44N 83 33W
Camptonville 14 39 27N 121 3W
Campuya → 70 1 40S 73 30W
Campville 17 29 40N 82 7W
Camrose 62 53 0N 112 50W
Camsell Portage 63 59 37N 109 15W
Camuy 57 18 29N 66 51W
Camuy → 57 18 29N 66 51W
Can Tho 112 10 2N 105 46 E
Canaan, Conn. 28 42 2N 73 20W
Canaan, Miss. 31 34 56N 89 8W
Canaan, N.H. 36 43 40N 72 1W
Canada ■ 58 60 0N 100 0W
Cañada de Gómez 76 32 40S 61 30W
Canadian, Okla. 43 35 11N 95 39W
Canadian, Tex. 50 35 55N 100 23W
Canadian → 43 35 28N 95 3W
Canadian County ◇ 43 35 35N 98 0W
Canadys 46 33 3N 80 37W
Canajoharie 39 42 54N 74 35W
Çanakkale 106 40 8N 26 30 E
Çanakkale Boğazi 106 40 0N 26 0 E
Canal Flats 62 50 10N 115 48W
Canal Fulton 42 40 53N 81 36W
Canal Point 17 26 52N 80 38W
Canalejas 76 35 15S 66 34W
Canalou 32 36 46N 89 41W
Canals 76 33 35S 62 53W
Canandaigua 39 42 54N 77 17W
Canandaigua L. 39 42 47N 77 19W
Cananea 64 31 0N 110 20W
Cañar 70 2 33S 78 56W
Cañar □ 70 2 30S 79 0W
Canarias, Islas 120 28 30N 16 0W
Canarreos, Arch. de los 66 21 35N 81 40W
Canary Is. = Canarias, Islas 120 28 30N 16 0W
Canas, Rio → 57 18 3N 66 26W
Canaseraga 39 42 27N 77 45W
Canastra, Serra da 75 20 0S 46 20W
Canatlán 64 24 31N 104 47W
Canaveral, C. 17 28 27N 80 32W
Canaveral National Seashore 17 28 28N 80 34W
Canavieiras 75 15 39S 39 0W
Canberra 127 35 15S 149 8 E
Canby, Calif. 14 41 27N 120 52W
Canby, Minn. 30 44 43N 96 16W
Canby, Oreg. 44 45 16N 122 42W
Canchyuaya, Cordillera de 72 7 30S 74 0W
Candala 105 11 30N 49 58 E
Candarave 72 17 15S 70 13W
Candeias → 73 8 39S 63 31W
Candelaria, Argentina 77 27 29S 55 44W
Candelaria, U.S.A. 50 30 8N 104 41W
Candia = Iráklion 95 35 20N 25 12 E
Cândido de Abreu 75 24 35S 51 20W
Cândido Mendes 74 1 27S 45 43W
Candle 11 65 55N 161 56W
Candle L. 63 53 50N 105 18W
Candlemas I. 5 57 3S 26 40W

Candler County Carrauntoohill, Mt.

Candler County ◇ 18 32 30N 82 0W
Candlewood 37 40 9N 74 10W
Candlewood, L. 28 41 30N 73 27W
Cando 41 48 32N 99 12W
Candor 40 35 18N 79 45W
Candy Res. 43 36 32N 96 1W
Cane Bay 57 17 40N 64 50W
Cane Cr. → 52 38 35N 109 35W
Cane Valley 49 37 11N 85 19W
Canea = Khaniá 95 35 30N 24 4 E
Canela 74 10 15 S 48 25W
Canelones 77 34 32 S 56 17W
Cañete, Chile 76 37 50 S 73 30W
Cañete, Peru 72 13 8 S 76 30W
Caney, Kans. 24 37 1N 95 56W
Caney, Okla. 43 34 14N 96 13W
Caney Fork → 49 36 15N 85 57W
Caneyville 48 37 26N 86 29W
Canfield 13 33 11N 93 38W
Cangas 91 42 16N 8 47W
Canguaretama 74 6 20 S 35 5W
Canguçu 77 31 22 S 52 43W
Cangxi 115 31 47N 105 59 E
Cangzhou 114 38 19N 116 52 E
Canicado 123 24 2 S 33 2 E
Canim Lake 62 51 47N 120 54W
Canindé 74 4 22 S 39 19W
Canindé → 74 6 15 S 42 52W
Canipaan 110 8 33N 117 15 E
Canisteo 39 42 16N 77 36W
Canisteo → 39 42 7N 77 8W
Canistota 47 43 36N 97 18W
Cañitas 64 23 36N 102 43W
Canjilon 38 36 29N 106 26W
Çankırı 106 40 40N 33 37 E
Canmer 49 37 17N 85 46W
Canmore 62 51 7N 115 18W
Canna 84 57 3N 6 33W
Cannanore 108 11 53N 75 27 E
Cannel City 49 37 47N 83 17W
Cannelton 22 37 55N 86 45W
Cannes 90 43 32N 7 0 E
Canning Basin 126 19 50 S 124 0 E
Cannock 82 52 42N 2 2W
Cannon → 30 44 35N 92 33W
Cannon Ball 41 46 25N 100 38W
Cannon Beach 44 45 54N 123 58W
Cannon County ◇ 48 35 50N 86 4W
Cannon Falls 30 44 31N 92 54W
Cannonball → 41 46 26N 100 35W
Cannonsburg 49 38 23N 82 42W
Cannonsville Reservoir 39 42 4N 75 22W
Cannonville 52 37 34N 112 3W
Caño Colorado 70 2 18N 68 22W
Canobie Lake 36 42 49N 71 15W
Canoe L. 63 55 10N 108 15W
Canon 18 34 21N 83 7W
Canon City 16 38 27N 105 14W
Canon Largo → 38 36 43N 107 49W
Canoncito Indian Reservation 38 35 10N 107 0W
Canonsburg 45 40 16N 80 11W
Canoochee → 18 31 59N 81 19W
Canora 63 51 40N 102 30W
Canova 47 43 53N 97 30W
Canovanas 57 18 23N 65 54W
Canso 61 45 20N 61 0W
Canta 72 11 29 S 76 37W
Cantabria □ 91 43 10N 4 0W
Cantabrian Mts. = Cantábrica, Cordillera 91 43 0N 5 10W
Cantábrica, Cordillera 91 43 0N 5 10W
Cantal □ 90 45 4N 2 45 E
Cantaura 71 9 19N 64 21W
Canterbury, U.K. 83 51 17N 1 5 E
Canterbury, U.S.A. 28 41 41N 71 57W
Canterbury □ 128 43 45 S 171 19 E
Canterbury Bight 128 44 16 S 171 55 E
Canterbury Plains 128 43 55 S 171 22 E
Canto do Buriti 74 8 7 S 42 58W
Canton = Guangzhou, Guangdong, China 115 23 5N 113 10 E
Canton = Guangzhou, Guangdong, China 115 23 5N 113 10 E
Canton, Conn. 28 41 49N 72 54W
Canton, Ga. 18 34 14N 84 29W
Canton, Ill. 21 40 33N 90 2W
Canton, Kans. 24 38 23N 97 26W
Canton, Ky. 48 36 48N 87 58W
Canton, Mass. 28 42 9N 71 9W
Canton, Minn. 30 43 32N 91 56W
Canton, Miss. 31 32 37N 90 2W
Canton, Mo. 32 40 8N 91 32W
Canton, N.C. 40 35 32N 82 50W
Canton, N.Y. 39 44 36N 75 10W
Canton, Ohio 42 40 48N 81 23W
Canton, Okla. 43 36 3N 98 35W
Canton, Pa. 45 41 39N 76 51W
Canton, S. Dak. 47 43 18N 96 35W
Canton, Tex. 51 32 33N 95 52W
Canton L. 43 36 6N 98 35W
Cantonment 17 30 37N 87 20W
Cantril 23 40 39N 92 4W
Cantwell 11 63 24N 148 57W
Canudos 73 7 13 S 58 5W
Canumã, Amazonas, Brazil 71 4 2 S 59 4W
Canumã, Amazonas, Brazil 73 6 8 S 60 10W
Canumã → 73 3 55 S 59 10W
Canutama 73 6 30 S 64 20W
Canute 43 35 25N 99 17W
Canutillo 50 31 55N 106 36W
Canyon 50 34 59N 101 55W
Canyon City 44 44 23N 118 57W
Canyon County ◇ 20 43 35N 116 50W
Canyon Creek 33 46 49N 112 16W
Canyon De Chelly National Monument 12 36 10N 109 20W
Canyon Ferry L. 33 46 39N 111 44W
Canyon L. 51 29 52N 98 12W
Canyon Village 56 44 46N 110 32W
Canyonlands National Park 52 38 15N 110 0W
Canyonville 44 42 56N 123 17W
Cao Xian 115 34 50N 115 35 E
Caonillas, Lago 57 18 17N 66 39W
Cap-aux-Meules 61 47 23N 61 52W
Cap-Chat 61 49 6N 66 40W
Cap-de-la-Madeleine 60 46 22N 72 31W
Cap-Haïtien 67 19 40N 72 20W
Cap St.-Jacques = Vung Tau 112 10 21N 107 4 E
Capa 47 44 7N 100 59W
Capac 29 43 1N 82 56W
Capaia 122 8 27 S 20 13 E
Capanaparo → 70 7 1N 67 7W
Capanema 74 1 12 S 47 11W
Caparo →, Barinas, Venezuela 70 7 46N 70 23W
Caparo →, Bolívar, Venezuela 71 7 30N 64 0W
Capatárida 70 11 11N 70 37W
Cape Barren I. 127 40 25 S 148 15 E
Cape Breton Highlands Nat. Park 61 46 50N 60 40W
Cape Breton I. 61 46 0N 60 30W
Cape Canaveral 17 28 24N 80 36W
Cape Charles 54 37 16N 76 1W
Cape Coast 120 5 5N 1 15W
Cape Cod B. 28 41 50N 70 20W
Cape Cod National Seashore 28 41 56N 70 6W
Cape Coral 17 26 33N 81 57W
Cape Dorset 59 64 14N 76 32W
Cape Dyer 59 66 30N 61 22W
Cape Elizabeth 26 43 34N 70 12W
Cape Fear → 40 33 53N 78 1W
Cape Girardeau 32 37 19N 89 32W
Cape Girardeau County ◇ 32 37 25N 89 40W
Cape Hatteras National Seashore 40 35 30N 75 28W
Cape I. 46 33 2N 79 21W
Cape Lookout National Seashore 40 35 45N 76 25W
Cape May 37 38 56N 74 56W
Cape May County ◇ 37 39 10N 74 45W
Cape May Court House 37 39 5N 74 50W
Cape May Point 37 38 56N 74 58W
Cape Montague 61 46 5N 62 25W
Cape Pole 11 55 58N 133 48W
Cape Province □ 123 32 0 S 23 0 E
Cape St. Claire 27 39 3N 76 25W
Cape Tormentine 61 46 8N 63 47W
Cape Town 123 33 55 S 18 22 E
Cape Verde Is. ■ 2 17 10N 25 20W
Cape Vincent 39 44 8N 76 20W
Cape Yakataga 11 60 4N 142 26W
Cape York Peninsula 127 12 0 S 142 30 E
Capela 74 10 30 S 37 0W
Capela de Campo 74 4 40 S 41 55W
Capelinha 75 17 42 S 42 31W
Capernaum = Kefar Naḥum 104 32 54N 35 34 E
Capim 74 1 41 S 47 47W
Capim → 74 1 40 S 47 47W
Capinópolis 75 18 41 S 49 35W
Capinota 72 17 43 S 66 14W
Capitan 38 33 35N 105 35W
Capitán Aracena, I. 78 54 10 S 71 20W
Capitan Arturo Prat 5 63 0 S 60 15W
Capitán Pastene 78 38 13 S 73 1W
Capitan Pk. 38 33 36N 105 16W
Capitol Reef National Monument 52 38 15N 111 10W
Capitola 17 30 27N 84 5W
Capivara, Serra da 75 14 35 S 45 0W
Capoeira 73 5 37 S 59 33W
Capon Bridge 54 39 18N 78 26W
Capraia 94 43 2N 9 50 E
Capreol 60 46 43N 80 56W
Caprera 94 41 12N 9 28 E
Capri 94 40 34N 14 15 E
Capricorn, C. 127 23 30 S 151 13 E
Caprivi Strip 123 18 0 S 23 0 E
Caprock 38 33 24N 103 43W
Capron, Ill. 21 42 24N 88 44W
Capron, Okla. 43 36 54N 98 35W
Captain Cook 19 19 30N 155 55W
Captiva 17 26 31N 82 11W
Caquetá □ 70 1 0N 74 0W
Caquetá → 70 1 15 S 69 15W
Carabobo 70 10 2N 68 5W
Carabobo □ 70 10 10N 68 5W
Caracal 89 44 8N 24 22 E
Caracaraí 71 1 50N 61 8W
Caracas 70 10 30N 66 55W
Caracol 74 9 15 S 43 22W
Caracollo 72 17 39 S 67 10W
Carahue 78 38 43 S 73 12W
Caraí 75 17 12 S 41 42W
Carajás, Serra dos 74 6 0 S 51 30W
Caranapatuba 73 6 38 S 62 34W
Carandaiti 73 20 45 S 63 4W
Carangola 75 20 44 S 42 5W
Caransebeş 89 45 28N 22 18 E
Caraparaná → 70 1 45 S 73 13W
Caras 72 9 3 S 77 47W
Caratasca, Laguna 66 15 20N 83 40W
Caratinga 75 19 50 S 42 10W
Caratunk 26 45 8N 69 59W
Caraúbas 74 5 43 S 37 33W
Caravaca 91 38 8N 1 52W
Caravelas 75 17 45 S 39 15W
Caraveli 72 15 45 S 73 25W
Caraway 13 35 46N 90 19W
Caràzinho 77 28 16 S 52 46W
Carballo 91 43 13N 8 41W
Carberry 63 49 50N 99 25W
Carbó 64 29 42N 110 58W
Carbon, Canada 62 51 30N 113 9W
Carbon, Ind. 22 39 36N 87 6W
Carbon, Iowa 23 41 3N 94 50W
Carbon, Tex. 51 32 16N 98 50W
Carbon County ◇, Mont. 33 45 10N 109 0W
Carbon County ◇, Pa. 45 41 0N 75 50W
Carbon County ◇, Utah 52 39 40N 110 30W
Carbon County ◇, Wyo. 56 42 0N 107 0W
Carbon Hill 10 33 53N 87 32W
Carbonado 53 47 5N 122 3W
Carbonara, C. 94 39 8N 9 30 E
Carbondale, Colo. 16 39 24N 107 13W
Carbondale, Ill. 21 37 44N 89 13W
Carbondale, Kans. 24 38 49N 95 41W
Carbondale, Pa. 45 41 35N 75 30W
Carbonear 61 47 42N 53 13W
Carbonia 94 39 10N 8 30 E
Carcajou 62 57 47N 117 6W
Carcasse, C. 67 18 30N 74 28W
Carcassonne 90 43 13N 2 20 E
Carchi □ 70 0 45N 78 0W
Cardamom Hills 108 9 30N 77 15 E
Cárdenas, Cuba 66 23 0N 81 30W
Cárdenas, San Luis Potosí, Mexico 65 22 0N 99 41W
Cárdenas, Tabasco, Mexico 65 17 59N 93 21W
Cardiel, L. 78 48 55 S 71 10W
Cardiff, U.K. 83 51 28N 3 11W
Cardiff, U.S.A. 16 39 31N 107 19W
Cardigan 83 52 6N 4 41W
Cardigan, Mt. 36 43 40N 71 54W
Cardigan B. 83 52 30N 4 30W
Cardington 42 40 30N 82 54W
Cardón, Punta 70 11 37N 70 14W
Cardona, Spain 91 41 56N 1 40 E
Cardona, Uruguay 76 33 53 S 57 18W
Cardross 63 49 50N 105 40W
Cardston 62 49 15N 113 20W
Cardwell 32 36 3N 90 17W
Careen L. 63 57 0N 108 11W
Carefree 12 33 50N 111 55W
Carei 89 47 40N 22 29 E
Careiro 71 3 12 S 59 45W
Careme 111 6 55 S 108 27 E
Carencro 25 30 19N 92 3W
Carey, Idaho 20 43 19N 113 57W
Carey, Ohio 42 40 57N 83 23W
Carey, L. 126 29 0 S 122 15 E
Carey L. 63 62 12N 102 55W
Careysburg 120 6 34N 10 30W
Cargados Garajos 3 17 0 S 59 0 E
Carhuamayo 72 10 51 S 76 4W
Carhuas 72 9 15 S 77 39W
Carhué 76 37 10 S 62 50W
Caribbean Sea 67 15 0N 75 0W
Cariboo Mts. 62 53 0N 121 0W
Caribou 26 46 52N 68 1W
Caribou →, Man., Canada 63 59 20N 94 44W
Caribou →, N.W.T., Canada 62 61 27N 125 45W
Caribou County ◇ 20 42 50N 111 30W
Caribou I. 60 47 22N 85 49W
Caribou Is. 62 61 55N 113 15W
Caribou L., Man., Canada 63 59 21N 96 10W
Caribou L., Ont., Canada 60 50 25N 89 5W
Caribou Mts. 62 59 12N 115 40W
Caribou Nat. Forest 20 42 50N 111 5W
Caribou National Forest 20 42 40N 111 10W
Caribou Range 20 43 10N 111 15W
Carichic 64 27 56N 107 3W
Carillo 64 26 50N 103 55W
Carinhanha 75 14 15 S 44 46W
Carinhanha → 75 14 20 S 43 47W
Carinthia □ = Kärnten □ 88 46 52N 13 30 E
Caripito 71 10 8N 63 6W
Carite, Lago 57 18 5N 66 6W
Caritianas 73 9 20 S 63 6W
Carl Blackwell, L. 43 36 8N 97 11W
Carl Junction 32 37 11N 94 34W
Carleton, Mich. 29 42 4N 83 24W
Carleton, Nebr. 34 40 18N 97 41W
Carleton Place 60 45 8N 76 9W
Carlin 35 40 43N 116 7W
Carlingford, L. 85 54 0N 6 5W
Carlinville 21 39 17N 89 53W
Carlisle, U.K. 82 54 54N 2 55W
Carlisle, Ark. 13 34 47N 91 45W
Carlisle, Ind. 22 38 58N 87 24W
Carlisle, Iowa 23 41 30N 93 29W
Carlisle, Ky. 49 38 19N 84 1W
Carlisle, Pa. 45 40 12N 77 12W
Carlisle, S.C. 46 34 36N 81 28W
Carlisle, Wash. 53 47 10N 124 6W
Carlisle County ◇ 48 36 50N 89 0W
Carlock 21 40 35N 89 8W
Carlos, Minn. 30 45 58N 95 18W
Carlos, Tex. 51 30 36N 96 5W
Carlos Casares 76 35 32 S 61 20W
Carlos Chagas 75 17 43 S 40 45W
Carlos Tejedor 76 35 25 S 62 25W
Carlota, La 76 33 30 S 63 20W
Carlow 85 52 50N 6 58W
Carlow □ 85 52 43N 6 50W
Carlsbad, Calif. 15 33 10N 117 21W
Carlsbad, N. Mex. 38 32 25N 104 14W
Carlsbad, Tex. 50 31 36N 100 38W
Carlsbad Caverns National Park 38 32 10N 104 35W
Carlton, Minn. 30 46 40N 92 25W
Carlton, Oreg. 44 45 18N 123 11W
Carlton County ◇ 30 46 35N 92 50W
Carlyle, Canada 63 49 40N 102 20W
Carlyle, Ill. 21 38 37N 89 22W
Carlyle, Mont. 33 46 40N 104 4W
Carlyle L. 21 38 37N 89 21W
Carmacks 58 62 5N 136 16W
Carman 63 49 30N 98 0W
Carmangay 62 50 10N 113 10W
Carmanville 61 49 23N 54 19W
Carmarthen 83 51 52N 4 20W
Carmarthen B. 83 51 40N 4 30W
Carmel, Ind. 22 39 59N 86 8W
Carmel, N.Y. 39 41 26N 73 41W
Carmel-by-the-Sea 14 36 33N 121 55W
Carmel Mt. 104 32 45N 35 3 E
Carmel Valley 14 36 29N 121 43W
Carmelo 76 34 0 S 58 20W
Carmen, Bolivia 72 11 40 S 67 51W
Carmen, Colombia 70 9 43N 75 8W
Carmen, Paraguay 77 27 13 S 56 12W
Carmen, Idaho 20 45 15N 113 54W
Carmen, Okla. 43 36 35N 98 28W
Carmen → 64 30 42N 106 29W
Carmen, I. 64 26 0N 111 20W
Carmen de Patagones 78 40 50 S 63 0W
Carmensa 76 35 15 S 67 40W
Carmi 21 38 5N 88 10W
Carmichael 14 38 38N 121 19W
Carmona 91 37 28N 5 42W
Carnarvon, Australia 126 24 51 S 113 42 E
Carnarvon, S. Africa 123 30 56 S 22 8 E
Carnation 53 47 39N 121 55W
Carndonagh 85 55 15N 7 16W
Carnduff 63 49 10N 101 50W
Carnegie, Ga. 18 31 39N 84 47W
Carnegie, Okla. 43 35 6N 98 36W
Carnegie, Pa. 45 40 24N 80 5W
Carnegie, L. 126 26 5 S 122 30 E
Carneiro 24 38 44N 98 2W
Carnesville 18 34 22N 83 14W
Carney, Mich. 29 45 35N 87 34W
Carney, Okla. 43 35 48N 97 1W
Carneys Point 37 39 43N 75 28W
Carnic Alps = Karnische Alpen 88 46 36N 13 0 E
Carniche, Alpi 94 46 36N 13 0 E
Carnot 122 4 59N 15 56 E
Carnot B. 126 17 20 S 121 30 E
Carnsore Pt. 85 52 10N 6 20W
Caro 29 43 29N 83 24W
Carol City 17 25 56N 80 16W
Caroleen 40 35 17N 81 48W
Carolina, Brazil 74 7 10 S 47 30W
Carolina, Puerto Rico 57 18 23N 65 58W
Carolina, U.S.A. 28 41 28N 71 40W
Carolina, La 91 38 17N 3 38W
Carolina Beach 40 34 2N 77 54W
Caroline County ◇, Md. 27 38 50N 75 50W
Caroline County ◇, Va. 54 38 3N 77 21W
Caroline I. 125 9 15 S 150 3W
Caroline Is. 124 8 0N 150 0 E
Carollton 29 43 28N 83 55W
Caron 63 50 30N 105 50W
Caroni → 71 8 21N 62 43W
Carora 70 10 11N 70 5W
Carp 35 37 7N 114 29W
Carpathians, Mts. 89 49 50N 21 0 E
Carpaţii Meridionali 89 45 30N 25 0 E
Carpentaria, G. of 127 14 0 S 139 0 E
Carpenter, Iowa 23 43 25N 93 1W
Carpenter, Wyo. 56 41 3N 104 22W
Carpenterville 44 42 13N 124 17W
Carpina 74 7 51 S 35 15W
Carpinteria 15 34 24N 119 31W
Carr 16 40 54N 104 53W
Carr Mt. 36 43 52N 71 50W
Carrabassett 26 45 5N 70 13W
Carrabelle 17 29 51N 84 40W
Carrara 94 44 5N 10 7 E
Carrauntoohill, Mt. 85 52 0N 9 49W

Carretas, Punta
Cedar L.

Carretas, Punta 72 14 12 S 76 17W
Carrick-on-Shannon 85 53 57N 8 7W
Carrick-on-Suir 85 52 22N 7 30W
Carrickfergus 85 54 43N 5 50W
Carrickfergus □ 85 54 43N 5 49W
Carrickmacross 85 54 0N 6 43W
Carrier 43 36 29N 98 2W
Carrier Mills 21 37 41N 88 38W
Carriere 31 30 37N 89 39W
Carrigain, Mt. 36 44 6N 71 26W
Carrington 41 47 27N 99 8W
Carrizal Bajo 76 28 5 S 71 20W
Carrizalillo 76 29 5 S 71 30W
Carrizo Springs 51 28 31N 99 52W
Carrizozo 38 33 38N 105 53W
Carroll, Iowa 23 42 4N 94 52W
Carroll, Nebr. 34 42 17N 97 12W
Carroll, Ohio 42 39 48N 82 43W
Carroll County ◇, Ark. 13 36 22N 93 34W
Carroll County ◇, Ga. 18 33 30N 85 10W
Carroll County ◇, Ill. 21 42 0N 90 0W
Carroll County ◇, Ind. 22 40 35N 86 35W
Carroll County ◇, Iowa 23 42 0N 94 50W
Carroll County ◇, Ky. 49 38 40N 85 5W
Carroll County ◇, Md. 27 39 30N 77 0W
Carroll County ◇, Miss. 31 33 30N 89 55W
Carroll County ◇, Mo. 32 39 25N 93 30W
Carroll County ◇, N.H. 36 43 50N 71 45W
Carroll County ◇, Ohio 42 40 34N 81 5W
Carroll County ◇, Tenn. 48 36 0N 88 26W
Carroll County ◇, Va. 54 36 55N 80 50W
Carrolls 53 46 4N 122 52W
Carrollton, Ala. 10 33 16N 88 6W
Carrollton, Ga. 18 33 35N 85 5W
Carrollton, Ill. 21 39 18N 90 24W
Carrollton, Ky. 49 38 41N 85 11W
Carrollton, Miss. 31 33 30N 89 55W
Carrollton, Mo. 32 39 22N 93 30W
Carrollton, Ohio 42 40 34N 81 5W
Carrollton, Tex. 51 32 57N 96 55W
Carrolltown 45 40 36N 78 43W
Carron → 84 57 30N 5 30W
Carron, L. 84 57 22N 5 35W
Carrot → 63 53 50N 101 17W
Carrot River 63 53 17N 103 35W
Carruthers 63 52 52N 109 16W
Carry Falls Reservoir 39 44 31N 74 45W
Çarşamba 106 41 15N 36 45 E
Carse of Gowrie 84 56 30N 3 10W
Carson, Calif. 15 33 48N 118 17W
Carson, Iowa 23 41 14N 95 25W
Carson, N. Dak. 41 46 25N 101 34W
Carson, Wash. 53 45 44N 121 49W
Carson → 35 39 45N 118 40W
Carson City 35 39 10N 119 46W
Carson County ◇ 50 35 20N 101 25W
Carson L. 35 39 18N 118 43W
Carson National Forest 38 36 30N 106 15W
Carson Sink 35 39 50N 118 25W
Carstairs 84 55 42N 3 41W
Carta Valley 50 29 48N 100 41W
Cartagena, Colombia 70 10 25N 75 33W
Cartagena, Spain 91 37 38N 0 59W
Cartago, Colombia 70 4 45N 75 55W
Cartago, C. Rica 66 9 50N 85 52W
Cartago, U.S.A. 15 36 19N 118 2W
Carter, Ky. 49 38 26N 83 8W
Carter, Okla. 43 35 13N 99 30W
Carter, S. Dak. 47 43 23N 100 12W
Carter County ◇, Ky. 49 38 20N 83 0W
Carter County ◇, Mo. 32 37 0N 91 0W
Carter County ◇, Mont. 33 45 30N 104 30W
Carter County ◇, Okla. 43 34 15N 97 15W
Carter County ◇, Tenn. 49 36 17N 82 10W
Carter Lake 23 41 18N 95 54W
Carter Lake Reservoir 16 40 20N 105 13W
Carter Mt. 56 44 12N 109 25W
Carteret 37 40 34N 74 13W
Carteret County ◇ 40 34 50N 76 30W
Carters L. 18 34 37N 84 40W
Cartersville, Ga. 18 34 10N 84 48W
Cartersville, Va. 54 37 40N 78 6W
Carterton 128 41 2 S 175 31 E
Carterville 21 37 46N 89 5W
Carthage, Ark. 13 34 4N 92 33W
Carthage, Ill. 21 40 25N 91 8W
Carthage, Ind. 22 39 44N 85 34W
Carthage, Miss. 31 32 44N 89 32W
Carthage, Mo. 32 37 11N 94 19W
Carthage, N.C. 40 35 21N 79 25W
Carthage, N.Y. 39 43 59N 75 37W
Carthage, S. Dak. 47 44 10N 97 43W
Carthage, Tenn. 49 36 15N 85 57W
Carthage, Tex. 51 32 9N 94 20W
Cartier I. 126 12 31 S 123 29 E
Cartwright 61 53 41N 56 58W
Caruaru 74 8 15 S 35 55W
Carúpano 71 10 39N 63 15W
Carutapera 74 1 13 S 46 1W
Caruthersville 32 36 11N 89 39W
Carvalho 71 2 16 S 51 29W
Carver County ◇ 30 44 50N 93 45W
Carville 25 30 13N 91 6W
Carvoeiro 71 1 30 S 61 59W
Cary, Ill. 21 42 13N 88 14W
Cary, Miss. 31 32 49N 90 56W
Cary, N.C. 40 35 47N 78 46W
Caryville 49 36 18N 84 13W
Casa 13 35 2N 93 3W
Casa Blanca 38 35 3N 107 28W
Casa Branca 75 21 46 S 47 4W
Casa Grande 12 32 53N 111 45W
Casa Grande Ruins National
Monument 12 33 0N 111 30W
Casa Nova 74 9 25 S 41 5W
Casablanca, Chile 76 33 20 S 71 25W
Casablanca, Morocco 120 33 36N 7 36W
Casale Monferrato 94 45 8N 8 28 E
Casanare → 70 6 2N 69 51W
Casas Grandes 64 30 22N 108 0W
Cascade, Colo. 16 38 54N 104 58W
Cascade, Idaho 20 44 31N 116 2W
Cascade, Iowa 23 42 18N 91 1W
Cascade, Mont. 33 47 16N 111 42W
Cascade County ◇ 33 47 20N 111 30W
Cascade Head 44 45 3N 124 1W
Cascade Locks 44 45 40N 121 54W
Cascade Range 44 45 0N 121 45W
Cascade Reservoir 20 44 32N 116 3W
Cascadia 44 44 24N 122 29W
Casco, Maine 26 44 0N 70 31W
Casco, Wis. 55 44 34N 87 37W
Casco B. 26 43 45N 70 0W
Caserta 94 41 5N 14 20 E
Caseville 29 43 56N 83 16W
Casey, Ill. 21 39 18N 87 59W
Casey, Iowa 23 41 31N 94 32W
Casey County ◇ 49 37 20N 85 0W
Cash 13 35 48N 90 56W
Cashel 85 52 31N 7 53W
Cashie → 40 35 53N 76 49W
Cashiers 40 35 6N 83 6W
Cashion 43 35 48N 97 41W
Cashmere 53 47 31N 120 28W
Cashton 55 43 43N 90 47W
Casibare → 70 3 48N 72 18W
Casiguran 111 16 22N 122 7 E
Casilda 76 33 10 S 61 10W
Casimcea 95 44 45N 28 23 E
Casino 127 28 52 S 153 3 E
Casiquiare → 70 2 1N 67 7W
Casitas 72 3 54 S 80 39W
Caslan 62 54 38N 112 31W
Casma 72 9 30 S 78 20W
Casmalia 15 34 50N 120 32W
Casnovia 29 43 14N 85 48W
Cason 51 33 2N 94 49W
Caspe 91 41 14N 0 1W
Casper 56 42 51N 106 19W
Caspian 29 46 4N 88 38W
Caspian Sea 99 43 0N 50 0 E
Caspiana 25 32 17N 93 33W
Cass 54 38 24N 79 55W
Cass → 29 43 23N 83 59W
Cass City 29 43 36N 83 11W
Cass County ◇, Ill. 21 40 0N 90 15W
Cass County ◇, Ind. 22 40 45N 86 20W
Cass County ◇, Iowa 23 41 20N 94 55W
Cass County ◇, Mich. 29 41 50N 86 0W
Cass County ◇, Minn. 30 47 0N 94 10W
Cass County ◇, Mo. 32 38 40N 94 20W
Cass County ◇, N. Dak. 41 47 0N 97 0W
Cass County ◇, Nebr. 34 40 50N 96 10W
Cass County ◇, Tex. 51 33 1N 94 22W
Cass Lake 30 47 23N 94 37W
Cassadaga 39 42 20N 79 19W
Casselton 41 46 54N 97 13W
Cassia County ◇ 20 42 20N 113 30W
Cassiar 62 59 16N 129 40W
Cassiar Mts. 62 59 30N 130 30W
Cassilândia 73 19 9 S 51 45W
Cassinga 123 15 5 S 16 4 E
Cassoday 24 38 3N 96 38W
Cassopolis 29 41 55N 86 1W
Cassville, Mo. 32 36 41N 93 52W
Cassville, Pa. 45 40 18N 78 2W
Cassville, Wis. 55 42 43N 90 59W
Castaic L. 15 34 32N 118 37W
Castalia, Iowa 23 43 7N 91 41W
Castalia, Ohio 42 41 24N 82 49W
Castana 23 42 4N 95 55W
Castanhal 74 1 18 S 47 55W
Castella 14 41 9N 122 19W
Castellammare del Golfo 94 38 2N 12 53 E
Castellammare di Stábia 94 40 47N 14 29 E
Castelli 76 36 7 S 57 47W
Castellón de la Plana 91 39 58N 0 3W
Castelo 75 20 33 S 41 14 E
Castelo Branco 91 39 50N 7 31W
Castelo do Piauí 74 5 20 S 41 33W
Castelvetrano 94 37 40N 12 46 E
Castile 39 42 38N 78 3W
Castilla 72 5 12 S 80 38W
Castilla La Mancha 91 39 30N 3 30W
Castilla La Nueva 91 39 45N 3 20W
Castilla La Vieja 91 41 55N 4 0W
Castilla y Leon 91 42 0N 5 0 E
Castillón 64 28 20N 103 38W
Castillos 77 34 12 S 53 52W
Castle 43 35 28N 96 23W
Castle Dale 52 39 13N 111 1W
Castle Dome Peak 12 33 5N 114 9W
Castle Douglas 84 54 57N 3 57W
Castle Gate 52 39 44N 110 52W
Castle Hayne 40 34 21N 77 54W
Castle Hills 51 29 32N 98 31W
Castle Peak 16 39 1N 106 52W
Castle Pk. 20 44 1N 114 42W
Castle Point 128 40 54 S 176 15 E
Castle Rock, Colo. 16 39 22N 104 51W
Castle Rock, Wash. 53 46 17N 122 54W
Castle Rock Butte 47 45 0N 103 27W
Castle Rock L. 55 43 52N 89 57W
Castlebar 85 53 52N 9 17W
Castleberry 10 31 18N 87 1W
Castleblaney 85 54 7N 6 44W
Castleford 20 42 31N 114 52W
Castlegar 62 49 20N 117 40W
Castlemaine 127 37 2 S 144 12 E
Castlereagh 85 53 47N 8 30W
Castlereagh □ 85 54 33N 5 53W
Castlereagh → 127 30 12 S 147 32 E
Castlereagh B. 126 12 10 S 135 10 E
Castleton 36 43 37N 73 11W
Castleton-on-Hudson 39 42 32N 73 45W
Castletown 82 54 4N 4 40W
Castletown Bearhaven 85 51 40N 9 54W
Castlewood 47 44 44N 97 2W
Castolon 50 29 8N 103 31W
Castor, Canada 62 52 15N 111 50W
Castor, U.S.A. 25 32 15N 93 10W
Castor → 32 36 51N 89 44W
Castor Bayou → 25 31 47N 99 22W
Castres 90 43 37N 2 13 E
Castries 67 14 0N 60 50W
Castro, Brazil 77 24 45 S 50 0W
Castro, Chile 78 42 30 S 73 50W
Castro Alves 75 12 46 S 39 33W
Castro County ◇ 50 34 33N 102 19W
Castro del Río 91 37 41N 4 29W
Castro Valley 14 37 42N 122 4W
Castroville, Calif. 14 36 46N 121 45W
Castroville, Tex. 51 29 21N 98 53W
Castrovirreyna 72 13 20 S 75 18W
Casummit Lake 60 51 29N 92 22W
Caswell County ◇ 40 36 20N 79 20W
Cat Head Pt. 29 45 11N 85 37W
Cat I., Bahamas 67 24 30N 75 30W
Cat I., U.S.A. 31 30 14N 89 6W
Cat L. 60 51 40N 91 50W
Cat Spring 51 29 51N 96 20W
Catacamas 66 14 54N 85 56W
Catacáos 72 5 20 S 80 45W
Cataguases 75 21 23 S 42 39W
Catahoula L. 25 31 31N 92 7W
Catahoula Parish ◇ 25 31 35N 91 58W
Catalão 75 18 10 S 47 57W
Catalina, Canada 61 48 31N 53 4W
Catalina, U.S.A. 12 32 30N 110 50W
Catalonia = Cataluña □ 91 41 40N 1 15 E
Cataluña □ 91 41 40N 1 15 E
Catamarca 76 28 30 S 65 50W
Catamarca □ 76 27 0 S 65 50W
Catanduanes 111 13 50N 124 20 E
Catanduva 75 21 5 S 48 58W
Catánia 94 37 31N 15 4 E
Catano 57 18 27N 66 7W
Catanzaro 94 38 54N 16 38 E
Cataract L. 22 39 29N 86 55W
Catarina 51 28 21N 99 37W
Catarman 111 12 28N 124 35 E
Catastrophe C. 126 34 59 S 136 0 E
Cataula 18 32 39N 84 52W
Catawba 55 45 32N 90 32W
Catawba → 46 34 28N 80 53W
Catawba County ◇ 40 35 40N 81 10W
Catawissa 45 40 57N 76 28W
Cateel 111 7 47N 126 24 E
Catende 74 8 40 S 35 43W
Cathay 41 47 33N 99 25W
Cathedral City 15 33 47N 116 28W
Cathedral Mt. 50 30 11N 103 40W
Catherine, Ala. 10 32 11N 87 28W
Catherine, Kans. 24 38 56N 99 13W
Cathlamet 53 46 12N 123 23W
Catismiña 71 4 5N 63 40W
Catita 74 9 31 S 43 1W
Catlettsburg 49 38 25N 82 36W
Catlin 21 40 4N 87 42W
Catlow Valley 44 42 20N 119 5W
Cato I. 127 23 15 S 155 32 E
Catoche, C. 65 21 40N 87 8W
Catoctin Mts. 27 39 35N 77 30W
Catolé do Rocha 74 6 21 S 37 45W
Catonsville 27 39 17N 76 44W
Catoosa 43 36 11N 95 45W
Catoosa County ◇ 18 34 50N 85 10W
Catrima 51 28 21N 99 37W
Catrimani 71 0 27N 61 41W
Catrimani → 71 0 28N 61 44W
Catron County ◇ 38 34 0N 108 15W
Catskill 39 42 14N 73 52W
Catskill Mts. 39 42 10N 74 25W
Cattaraugus County ◇ 39 42 30N 78 45W
Cattaraugus Indian
Reservation 39 42 30N 79 0W
Catu 75 12 21 S 38 23W
Cauca □ 70 2 30N 76 50W
Cauca → 70 8 54N 74 28W
Caucaia 74 3 40 S 38 35W
Caucasia 70 8 0N 75 12W
Caucasus Mts. = Bolshoi
Kavkas 99 42 50N 44 0 E
Caucomgomoc L. 26 46 13N 69 36W
Caúngula 122 8 26 S 18 38 E
Cauquenes 76 36 0 S 72 22W
Caura → 71 7 38N 64 53W
Caurés → 71 1 21 S 62 20W
Causapscal 61 48 19N 67 12W
Causey 38 33 53N 103 8W
Cauthron 13 34 55N 94 18W
Cautín □ 78 39 0 S 72 30W
Cauvery → 108 11 9N 78 52 E
Caux, Pays de 90 49 38N 0 35 E
Cavalcante 75 13 48 S 47 30W
Cavalier 41 48 48N 97 37W
Cavalier County ◇ 41 48 55N 97 30W
Cavan 85 54 0N 7 22W
Cavan □ 85 53 58N 7 10W
Cave City, Ark. 13 35 57N 91 33W
Cave City, Ky. 49 37 8N 85 58W
Cave Creek 12 33 50N 111 57W
Cave in Rock 21 37 28N 88 10W
Cave Junction 44 42 10N 123 39W
Cave Run L. 49 38 5N 83 25W
Cave Spring 18 34 6N 85 20W
Caviana, I. 74 0 10N 50 10W
Cavite 111 14 29N 120 55 E
Cawker City 24 39 31N 98 26W
Cawnpore = Kanpur 108 26 28N 80 20 E
Caxias 74 4 55 S 43 20W
Caxias do Sul 77 29 10 S 51 10W
Caxito 122 8 30 S 13 30 E
Cay Sal Bank 66 23 45N 80 0W
Cayambe 70 0 3N 78 8W
Cayambe, Vol. 70 0 0N 77 59W
Cayce, Ky. 48 36 33N 89 2W
Cayce, S.C. 46 33 59N 81 4W
Cayenne 71 5 0N 52 18W
Cayenne □ 71 4 0N 53 0W
Cayes, Les 67 18 15N 73 46W
Cayey 57 18 7N 66 10W
Cayman Brac 66 19 43N 79 49W
Cayman Is. 66 19 40N 80 30W
Cayo Romano 67 22 0N 78 0W
Cayucos 15 35 27N 120 54W
Cayuga, Ind. 22 39 57N 87 28W
Cayuga, N. Dak. 41 46 4N 97 23W
Cayuga County ◇ 39 43 0N 76 35W
Cayuga Heights 39 42 28N 76 30W
Cayuga L. 39 42 41N 76 41W
Cayuse 44 45 41N 118 33W
Căzăneşti 95 44 36N 27 3 E
Cazenovia 39 42 56N 75 51W
Cazombo 123 11 54 S 22 56 E
Cazorla 70 8 1N 67 0W
Ceamurlia de Jos 95 44 43N 28 47 E
Ceanannus Mor 85 53 42N 6 53W
Ceará = Fortaleza 74 3 45 S 38 35W
Ceará □ 74 5 0 S 40 0W
Ceará Mirim 74 5 38 S 35 25W
Cearfoss 27 39 0N 77 0W
Ceauru, L. 95 44 58N 23 11 E
Cebaco, I. de 66 7 33N 81 9W
Cebollar 76 29 10 S 66 35W
Cebu 111 10 18N 123 54 E
Cecil, Ga. 18 31 3N 83 24W
Cecil, Oreg. 44 45 37N 119 58W
Cecil County ◇ 27 39 30N 76 0W
Cecilia 49 37 40N 85 57W
Cecilton 27 39 24N 75 52W
Cecilville 14 41 9N 123 8W
Cedar →, Iowa 23 41 17N 91 21W
Cedar →, Mich. 29 45 25N 87 26W
Cedar →, Nebr. 34 41 22N 97 56W
Cedar Bluff, Ala. 10 34 13N 85 37W
Cedar Bluff, Va. 54 37 5N 81 46W
Cedar Bluff Reservoir 24 38 47N 99 43W
Cedar Bluffs, Kans. 24 39 59N 100 34W
Cedar Bluffs, Nebr. 34 41 24N 96 37W
Cedar Breaks National
Monument 52 37 40N 112 50W
Cedar Brook 37 39 43N 74 54W
Cedar Butte 47 43 35N 101 1W
Cedar City, Mo. 32 38 36N 92 11W
Cedar City, Utah 52 37 41N 113 4W
Cedar County ◇, Iowa 23 41 45N 91 10W
Cedar County ◇, Mo. 32 37 45N 93 50W
Cedar County ◇, Nebr. 34 42 40N 97 15W
Cedar Cr. → 41 46 8N 101 19W
Cedar Creek, Ark. 13 34 47N 93 51W
Cedar Creek, Nebr. 34 41 2N 96 6W
Cedar Creek, Tex. 51 30 5N 97 30W
Cedar Creek Reservoir 51 32 11N 96 4W
Cedar Falls 23 42 32N 92 27W
Cedar Grove, Ind. 22 39 22N 84 56W
Cedar Grove, N.J. 37 40 51N 74 14W
Cedar Grove, W. Va. 54 38 13N 81 26W
Cedar Grove, Wis. 55 43 34N 87 49W
Cedar Hill, Mo. 32 38 21N 90 39W
Cedar Hill, N. Mex. 38 36 56N 107 53W
Cedar Hill, Tenn. 48 36 33N 87 0W
Cedar Key 17 29 8N 83 2W
Cedar L., Canada 63 53 10N 100 0W

Cedar L. Charlevoix, L.

Cedar L., Ill. 21 37 37N 89 18W
Cedar L., Tex. 50 32 49N 102 17W
Cedar Lake, Ind. 22 41 22N 87 26W
Cedar Lake, Tex. 51 28 54N 95 38W
Cedar Mills 30 44 57N 94 31W
Cedar Mts. 52 40 10N 112 30W
Cedar Park 51 30 30N 97 49W
Cedar Point 24 38 16N 96 49W
Cedar Rapids, Iowa 23 41 59N 91 40W
Cedar Rapids, Nebr. 34 41 34N 98 9W
Cedar Springs 29 43 13N 85 33W
Cedar Vale 24 37 6N 96 30W
Cedaredge 16 38 54N 107 56W
Cedartown 18 34 1N 85 15W
Cedarvale 62 55 1N 128 22W
Cedarville, Calif. 14 41 32N 120 10W
Cedarville, Ill. 21 42 23N 89 38W
Cedarville, Md. 27 38 40N 76 47W
Cedarville, N.J. 37 39 18N 75 12W
Cedarville, Ohio 42 39 44N 83 49W
Cedarwood 16 37 57N 104 37W
Cedral 64 23 50N 100 42W
Cedro 74 6 34 S 39 3W
Cedros, I. de 64 28 10N 115 20W
Ceduna 126 32 7 S 133 46 E
Cefalù 94 38 3N 14 1 E
Cegléd 89 47 11N 19 47 E
Cehegín 91 38 6N 1 48W
Ceiba 57 18 16N 65 39W
Ceiba, La 66 15 40N 86 50W
Celaya 64 20 31N 100 37W
Celbridge 85 53 20N 6 33W
Celebes = Sulawesi □ 111 2 0 S 120 0 E
Celebes Sea 111 3 0N 123 0 E
Celendín 72 6 52 S 78 10W
Celeste 51 33 18N 96 12W
Celica 70 4 7 S 79 59W
Celina, Ohio 42 40 33N 84 35W
Celina, Tenn. 49 36 33N 85 30W
Celina, Tex. 51 33 19N 96 47W
Celje 94 46 16N 15 18 E
Celle 88 52 37N 10 4 E
Cement 43 34 56N 98 8W
Cenepa → 70 4 40 S 78 10W
Cengong 115 27 13N 108 44 E
Centenário do Sul 75 22 48 S 51 36W
Centenary 46 34 2N 79 21W
Centennial Mts. 20 44 35N 111 55W
Centennial Wash → 12 33 17N 112 48W
Center, Colo. 16 37 45N 106 6W
Center, Ga. 18 34 3N 83 25W
Center, Mo. 32 39 30N 91 32W
Center, N. Dak. 41 47 7N 101 18W
Center, Nebr. 34 42 37N 97 53W
Center, Tex. 51 31 48N 94 11W
Center Barnstead 36 43 19N 71 15W
Center City 30 45 24N 92 49W
Center Cross 54 37 48N 76 47W
Center Harbor 36 43 42N 71 27W
Center Hill 17 28 38N 82 3W
Center Hill L. 49 36 6N 85 50W
Center Ossipee 36 43 45N 71 9W
Center Point, Ala. 10 33 38N 86 41W
Center Point, Ind. 22 39 25N 87 4W
Center Point, Iowa 23 42 12N 91 46W
Center Point, La. 25 31 15N 92 13W
Center Point, Tex. 51 29 57N 99 2W
Center Sandwich 36 43 39N 71 25W
Center Strafford 36 43 17N 71 10W
Centerburg 42 40 18N 82 42W
Centereach 39 40 52N 73 6W
Centerfield 52 39 8N 111 49W
Centerton 37 39 59N 75 0W
Centertown 32 38 38N 92 25W
Centerville, Ark. 13 35 7N 93 10W
Centerville, Calif. 15 36 44N 119 30W
Centerville, Del. 27 39 49N 75 37W
Centerville, Ind. 22 39 49N 85 0W
Centerville, Iowa 23 40 44N 92 52W
Centerville, Kans. 24 38 13N 95 1W
Centerville, La. 25 29 46N 91 26W
Centerville, Mo. 32 37 26N 90 58W
Centerville, N.C. 40 36 11N 78 6W
Centerville, N.Y. 39 42 29N 78 15W
Centerville, Ohio 42 39 38N 84 8W
Centerville, S. Dak. 47 43 7N 96 58W
Centerville, Tenn. 48 35 47N 87 28W
Centerville, Tex. 51 31 16N 95 59W
Centerville, Utah 52 40 55N 111 52W
Centerville, Pa. 45 41 44N 79 46W
Centerville, Pa. 45 40 3N 79 59W
Centrahoma 43 34 37N 96 21W
Central, Brazil 74 11 8 S 42 8W
Central, Alaska 11 65 35N 144 48W
Central, Mich. 29 47 25N 88 12W
Central, N. Mex. 38 32 47N 108 9W
Central, S.C. 46 34 44N 82 47W
Central, Utah 52 37 25N 113 38W
Central □ 84 56 10N 4 30W
Central, Cordillera, Bolivia 73 18 30 S 64 55W
Central, Cordillera, Colombia 70 5 0N 75 0W
Central, Cordillera, C. Rica 66 10 10N 84 5W
Central, Cordillera, Dom. Rep. 67 19 15N 71 0W
Central, Cordillera, Peru 72 7 0 S 77 30W
Central, Cordillera, Puerto Rico 57 18 8N 66 35W
Central African Republic ■ 122 7 0N 20 0 E
Central Aguirre 57 17 58N 66 14W
Central City, Colo. 16 39 48N 105 31W
Central City, Ill. 21 38 33N 89 8W
Central City, Iowa 23 42 12N 91 32W
Central City, Ky. 48 37 18N 87 7W
Central City, Nebr. 34 41 7N 98 0W
Central City, Pa. 45 40 7N 78 49W
Central City, S. Dak. 47 44 22N 103 46W
Central Falls 28 41 54N 71 23W
Central Islip 39 40 47N 73 12W
Central Lake 29 45 4N 85 16W
Central Makran Range 107 26 30N 64 15 E
Central Patricia 60 51 30N 90 9W
Central Point 44 42 23N 122 55W
Central Russian Uplands 80 54 0N 36 0 E
Central Siberian Plateau 101 65 0N 105 0 E
Central Square 39 43 17N 76 9W
Central Valley 14 40 41N 122 22W
Centralhatchee 18 33 22N 85 6W
Centralia, Ill. 21 38 32N 89 8W
Centralia, Kans. 24 39 44N 96 8W
Centralia, Mo. 32 39 13N 92 8W
Centralia, Okla. 43 36 48N 95 21W
Centralia, Wash. 53 46 43N 122 58W
Centre 10 34 9N 85 41W
Centre County ◇ 45 41 0N 78 0W
Centre Grove 37 39 20N 75 8W
Centreville, Ala. 10 32 57N 87 8W
Centreville, Md. 27 39 3N 76 4W
Centreville, Mich. 29 41 55N 85 32W
Centreville, Miss. 31 31 5N 91 4W
Century 17 30 58N 87 16W
Cephalonia = Kefallinía 95 38 20N 20 30 E
Ceptura 95 45 1N 26 21 E
Cepu 111 7 9 S 111 35 E
Ceram = Seram 111 3 10 S 129 0 E
Ceram Sea = Seram Sea 111 2 30 S 128 30 E
Cerbu 95 44 46N 24 46 E
Ceres, Argentina 76 29 55 S 61 55W
Ceres, Brazil 75 15 17 S 49 35W
Ceres, S. Africa 123 33 21 S 19 18 E
Ceres, U.S.A. 14 37 35N 120 57W
Ceresco 34 41 3N 96 39W
Cereté 70 8 53N 75 48W
Cerignola 94 41 17N 15 53 E
Cerigo = Kíthira 95 36 9N 23 0 E
Çerkeş 106 40 49N 32 52 E
Cerknica 94 45 48N 14 21 E
Cerna 95 45 4N 28 17 E
Cerna → 95 44 45N 24 0 E
Cernavodă 89 44 22N 28 3 E
Cerralvo 64 24 20N 109 45 E
Cerrillos 38 35 26N 106 8W
Cerritos 64 22 27N 100 20W
Cerro Gordo 21 39 53N 88 44W
Cerro Gordo County ◇ 23 43 5N 93 15W
Cerro Sombrero 78 52 45 S 69 15W
Cerro Vista Peak 38 36 14N 105 25W
Cervera 91 41 40N 1 16 E
Cervera del Río Alhama 91 42 2N 1 58W
César □ 70 9 0N 73 30W
Çesena 94 44 9N 12 14 E
České Budějovice 88 48 55N 14 25 E
Çeskomoravská Vrchovina 88 49 30N 15 40 E
Český Těšin 89 49 45N 18 39 E
Cessnock 127 32 50 S 151 21 E
Cetinje 95 42 23N 18 59 E
Ceuta 120 35 52N 5 18W
Cévennes 90 44 10N 3 50 E
Ceyhan 106 37 4N 35 47 E
Ceylon = Sri Lanka ■ 108 7 30N 80 50 E
Ceylon 30 43 32N 94 38W
Cha Pa 112 22 20N 103 47 E
Chablais 90 46 20N 6 36 E
Chacabuco 76 34 40 S 60 27W
Chachapoyas 72 6 15 S 77 50W
Chachasp 72 15 30 S 72 15W
Chachran 108 28 55N 70 30 E
Chaco □ 76 26 30 S 61 0W
Chaco → 38 36 46N 108 39W
Chaco Canyon National Monument 38 36 6N 108 0W
Chacuaco → 16 37 34N 103 38W
Chad ■ 121 15 0N 17 15 E
Chad, L. = Tchad, L. 121 13 30N 14 30 E
Chadan 101 51 17N 91 35 E
Chadbourn 40 34 19N 78 50W
Chadileuvú → 76 37 46 S 66 0W
Chadron 34 42 50N 103 0W
Chadwick 21 42 1N 89 53W
Chaffee, Mo. 32 37 11N 89 40W
Chaffee, N. Dak. 41 46 46N 97 21W
Chaffee County ◇ 16 38 45N 106 10W
Chagai Hills 108 29 30N 63 0 E
Chagda 101 58 45N 130 38 E
Chagos Arch. 102 6 0 S 72 0 E
Chagres → 57 9 10N 79 40W
Chāh Bahār 107 25 20N 60 40 E
Chāh Gay Hills 107 29 30N 64 0 E
Chahar Burjak 108 30 15N 62 0 E
Chahār Mahāll va Bakhtīarī □ 106 32 0N 49 0 E
Chaibasa 109 22 42N 85 49 E
Chaires 17 30 26N 84 7W
Chaitén 78 42 55 S 72 43W
Chajari 76 30 42 S 58 0W
Chakhānsūr 107 31 10N 62 0 E
Chakonipau, L. 61 56 18N 68 30W
Chakradharpur 109 22 45N 85 40 E
Chakwal 108 32 56N 72 53 E
Chala 72 15 48 S 74 20W
Chalcatongo 65 17 4N 97 34W
Chalchihuites 64 23 29N 103 53W
Chalcis = Khalkís 95 38 27N 23 42 E
Chaleur B. 61 47 55N 65 30W
Chalhuanca 72 14 15 S 73 15W
Chaling 115 26 58N 113 30 E
Chalisgaon 108 20 30N 75 10 E
Chalk Mts. 50 29 30N 103 18W
Chalky Inlet 128 46 3 S 166 31 E
Chalkyitsik 11 66 39N 143 43W
Challapata 72 18 53 S 66 50W
Challis 20 44 30N 114 14W
Challis National Forest 20 44 0N 113 40W
Chalmers 22 40 40N 86 52W
Chalmette 25 29 56N 89 58W
Châlons-sur-Marne 90 48 58N 4 20 E
Chama, Colo. 16 37 10N 105 23W
Chama, N. Mex. 38 36 54N 106 35W
Chaman 107 30 58N 66 25 E
Chamba, India 108 32 35N 76 10 E
Chamba, Tanzania 123 11 37 S 37 0 E
Chambal → 108 26 29N 79 15 E
Chamberino 38 32 3N 106 41W
Chamberlain 47 43 49N 99 20W
Chamberlain L. 26 46 14N 69 19W
Chambers, Ariz. 12 35 11N 109 26W
Chambers, Nebr. 34 42 12N 98 45W
Chambers County ◇, Ala. 10 32 54N 85 24W
Chambers County ◇, Tex. 51 29 47N 94 35W
Chambers I. 55 45 11N 87 22W
Chambersburg 45 39 56N 77 40W
Chambéry 90 45 34N 5 55 E
Chamblee 18 33 53N 84 18W
Chambord 61 48 25N 72 6W
Chamela 64 19 32N 105 5W
Chamical 76 30 22 S 66 27W
Chamisal 38 36 10N 105 44W
Chamois 32 38 41N 91 46W
Chamonix 90 45 55N 6 51 E
Champagne 62 60 49N 136 30W
Champagne, Plaine de 90 49 0N 4 30 E
Champaign 21 40 7N 88 15W
Champaign County ◇, Ill. 21 40 10N 88 10W
Champaign County ◇, Ohio 42 40 7N 83 45W
Champion, Mich. 29 46 31N 87 58W
Champion, Ohio 42 41 19N 80 51W
Champion B. 126 28 44 S 114 36 E
Champion Creek Reservoir 50 32 17N 100 52W
Champlain, Canada 60 46 27N 72 24W
Champlain, U.S.A. 39 44 59N 73 27W
Champlain, L. 39 44 40N 73 20W
Champlain Canal 39 43 30N 73 27W
Champotón 65 19 20N 90 50W
Chan Chan 72 8 7 S 79 0W
Chañaral 76 26 23 S 70 40W
Chancay 72 11 32 S 77 25W
Chancellor 47 43 22N 96 59W
Chandalar → 11 66 37N 146 0W
Chandeleur Is. 25 29 55N 88 57W
Chandeleur Sd. 25 29 55N 89 0W
Chandigarh 108 30 43N 76 47 E
Chandler, Canada 61 48 18N 64 46W
Chandler, Ariz. 12 33 18N 111 50W
Chandler, Ind. 22 38 3N 87 22W
Chandler, Minn. 30 43 56N 95 57W
Chandler, Okla. 43 35 42N 96 53W
Chandler, Tex. 51 32 18N 95 29W
Chandlerville 21 40 3N 90 9W
Chandless → 72 9 8 S 69 51W
Chandmani 113 45 22N 98 2 E
Chandpur 109 23 8N 90 45 E
Chandrapur 108 19 57N 79 25 E
Chang Jiang → 115 31 48N 121 10 E
Changanacheri 108 9 25N 76 31 E
Changane → 123 23 30 S 33 50 E
Changbai 114 41 25N 128 5 E
Changbai Shan 114 42 20N 129 0 E
Ch'angchou = Changzhou 115 31 47N 119 58 E
Changchun 114 43 57N 125 17 E
Changde 115 29 4N 111 35 E
Changfeng 115 32 28N 117 10 E
Changhai = Shanghai 115 31 15N 121 26 E
Changjiang 115 19 20N 108 55 E
Changjin-chŏsuji 114 40 30N 127 15 E
Changle 115 25 59N 119 27 E
Changli 114 39 40N 119 13 E
Changning 115 26 28N 112 22 E
Changping 114 40 14N 116 12 E
Changsha 115 28 12N 113 0 E
Changshou 115 29 51N 107 8 E
Changshu 115 31 38N 120 43 E
Changshun 115 26 3N 106 25 E
Changtai 115 24 35N 117 42 E
Changting 115 25 50N 116 22 E
Changyang 115 30 30N 111 10 E
Changzhi 114 36 10N 113 6 E
Changzhou 115 31 47N 119 58 E
Chanhassen 30 44 55N 93 32W
Channahon 21 41 26N 88 14W
Channapatna 108 12 40N 77 15 E
Channel Is., U.K. 83 49 30N 2 40W
Channel Is., U.S.A. 15 33 40N 119 15W
Channel Islands National Park 15 33 30N 119 0W
Channel-Port aux Basques 61 47 30N 59 9W
Channelview 51 29 47N 95 8W
Channing, Mich. 29 46 9N 88 5W
Channing, Tex. 50 35 41N 102 20W
Chantada 91 42 36N 7 46W
Chanthaburi 112 12 38N 102 12 E
Chantrey Inlet 58 67 48N 96 20W
Chanute 24 37 41N 95 27W
Chao Hu 115 31 30N 117 30 E
Chao Phraya → 112 13 32N 100 36 E
Chao'an 115 23 42N 116 32 E
Chaoyang, Guangdong, China 115 23 17N 116 30 E
Chaoyang, Liaoning, China 114 41 35N 120 22 E
Chapada dos Guimarães 73 15 26 S 55 45W
Chapala, Lago de 64 20 10N 103 20W
Chaparé → 73 15 58 S 64 42W
Chaparral 70 3 43N 75 28W
Chapayevo 99 50 25N 51 10 E
Chapayevsk 98 53 0N 49 40 E
Chapecó 77 27 14 S 52 41W
Chapel Hill, Ky. 48 36 43N 86 18W
Chapel Hill, N.C. 40 35 55N 79 4W
Chapel Hill, Tenn. 48 35 38N 86 41W
Chapin 21 39 46N 90 24W
Chapleau 60 47 50N 83 24W
Chaplin, Canada 63 50 28N 106 40W
Chaplin, U.S.A. 49 37 54N 85 13W
Chapman, Ala. 10 31 40N 86 43W
Chapman, Kans. 24 38 58N 97 1W
Chapman, Nebr. 34 41 2N 98 10W
Chapmanville 54 37 59N 82 1W
Chappaquiddick Island 28 41 22N 70 30W
Chappell 34 41 6N 102 28W
Chappell Hill 51 30 9N 96 15W
Chappells 46 34 11N 81 52W
Chaptico 27 38 21N 76 49W
Chār 120 21 32N 12 45 E
Chara 101 56 54N 118 20 E
Charadai 76 27 35 S 60 0W
Charagua 73 19 45 S 63 10W
Charalá 70 6 17N 73 10W
Charambirá, Punta 70 4 16N 77 32W
Charaña 72 17 30 S 69 25W
Charapita 70 0 37 S 74 21W
Charata 76 27 13 S 61 14W
Charcas 64 23 10N 101 20W
Charco 51 28 44N 97 37W
Charcoal L. 63 58 49N 102 22W
Chard 83 50 52N 2 59W
Chardara 100 41 16N 67 59 E
Chardon 42 41 35N 81 12W
Chardzhou 100 39 6N 63 34 E
Charente □ 90 45 50N 0 16 E
Charente-Maritime □ 90 45 30N 0 35W
Charenton 25 29 53N 91 32W
Chari → 121 12 58N 14 31 E
Chārīkār 107 35 0N 69 10 E
Charing 18 32 28N 84 22W
Chariton 23 41 1N 93 19W
Chariton → 32 39 19N 92 58W
Chariton County ◇ 32 39 30N 93 0W
Charity, Guyana 71 7 24N 58 36W
Charity, U.S.A. 32 37 31N 93 1W
Charity I. 29 44 2N 83 26W
Charlemont 28 42 38N 72 52W
Charleroi, Belgium 87 50 24N 4 27 E
Charleroi, U.S.A. 45 40 9N 79 57W
Charles 18 32 8N 84 50W
Charles → 28 42 22N 71 3W
Charles, C. 54 37 7N 75 58W
Charles City, Iowa 23 43 4N 92 41W
Charles City, Va. 54 37 21N 77 4W
Charles City County ◇ 54 37 21N 77 4W
Charles County ◇ 27 38 30N 77 0W
Charles L. 63 59 50N 110 33W
Charles M. Russell National Wildlife Refuge 33 47 45N 107 0W
Charles Mill L. 42 40 45N 82 22W
Charles Mix County ◇ 47 43 15N 98 42W
Charles Town 54 39 17N 77 52W
Charleston, Ark. 13 35 18N 94 5W
Charleston, Ill. 21 39 30N 88 10W
Charleston, Miss. 31 34 1N 90 4W
Charleston, Mo. 32 36 55N 89 21W
Charleston, S.C. 46 32 46N 79 56W
Charleston, Tenn. 49 35 17N 84 45W
Charleston, Utah 52 40 28N 111 28W
Charleston, W. Va. 54 38 21N 81 38W
Charleston County ◇ 46 32 50N 80 0W
Charleston Peak 35 36 16N 115 42W
Charlestown, Ind. 22 38 27N 85 40W
Charlestown, Md. 27 39 35N 75 59W
Charlestown, N.H. 36 43 14N 72 25W
Charlestown, R.I. 28 41 23N 71 45W
Charlesville 122 5 27 S 20 59 E
Charleville = Rath Luirc 85 52 21N 8 40W
Charleville 127 26 24 S 146 15 E
Charleville-Mézières 90 49 44N 4 40 E
Charlevoix 29 45 19N 85 16W
Charlevoix, L. 29 45 16N 85 8W

Charlevoix County Chilmark

Charlevoix County ◇ 29 45 15N 85 10W
Charlo 33 47 26N 114 10W
Charlotte, Iowa 23 41 58N 90 28W
Charlotte, Mich. 29 42 34N 84 50W
Charlotte, N.C. 40 35 13N 80 51W
Charlotte, Tenn. 48 36 11N 87 21W
Charlotte, Tex. 51 28 52N 98 43W
Charlotte Amalie, Virgin Is. 57 18 21N 64 56W
Charlotte County ◇, Fla. 17 26 50N 82 0W
Charlotte County ◇, Va. 54 37 0N 78 55W
Charlotte Court House 54 37 3N 78 39W
Charlotte Hall 27 38 28N 76 45W
Charlotte Harbor 17 26 50N 82 10W
Charlotte Waters 126 25 56 S 134 54 E
Charlottesville 54 38 2N 78 30W
Charlottetown 61 46 14N 63 8W
Charlton City 28 42 9N 71 58W
Charlton County ◇ 18 30 50N 82 10W
Charlton I. 60 52 0N 79 20W
Charny 61 46 43N 71 15W
Charolles 90 46 27N 4 16 E
Charouine 120 29 0N 0 15W
Charter Oak 23 42 4N 95 36W
Charters Towers 127 20 5 S 146 13 E
Chartres 90 48 29N 1 30 E
Chascomús 76 35 30 S 58 0W
Chase, Ala. 10 34 47N 86 33W
Chase, Kans. 24 38 21N 98 21W
Chase, Md. 27 39 22N 76 22W
Chase, Mich. 29 43 53N 85 38W
Chase City 54 36 48N 78 28W
Chase County ◇, Kans. 24 38 15N 96 45W
Chase County ◇, Nebr. 34 40 30N 101 40W
Chaseburg 55 43 40N 91 6W
Chaseley 41 47 27N 99 49W
Chasovnya-Uchurskaya 101 57 15N 132 50 E
Chataignier 25 30 34N 92 19W
Chatal Balkan = Udvoy Balkan 95 42 50N 26 50 E
Chatanika 11 65 7N 147 28W
Château-Salins 90 48 50N 6 30 E
Châteaubriant 90 47 43N 1 23W
Chateaugay 39 44 56N 74 5W
Châteauroux 90 46 50N 1 40 E
Châtellerault 90 46 50N 0 30 E
Chatfield, Ark. 13 35 0N 90 24W
Chatfield, Minn. 30 43 51N 92 11W
Chatfield, Ohio 42 40 57N 82 57W
Chatham, N.B., Canada 61 47 2N 65 28W
Chatham, Ont., Canada 60 42 24N 82 11W
Chatham, U.K. 83 51 22N 0 32 E
Chatham, Ill. 21 39 40N 89 42W
Chatham, La. 25 32 18N 92 27W
Chatham, Mass. 28 41 41N 69 58W
Chatham, Mich. 29 46 21N 86 56W
Chatham, N.J. 37 40 44N 74 23W
Chatham, N.Y. 39 42 21N 73 36W
Chatham, Va. 54 36 50N 79 24W
Chatham, I. 78 50 40 S 74 25W
Chatham County ◇, Ga. 18 32 0N 81 10W
Chatham County ◇, N.C. 40 35 45N 79 10W
Chatham Is. 124 44 0 S 176 40W
Chatom 10 31 28N 88 16W
Chatrapur 109 19 22N 85 2 E
Chatsworth, Ga. 18 34 46N 84 46W
Chatsworth, Ill. 21 40 45N 88 18W
Chatsworth, Iowa 23 42 55N 96 31W
Chatsworth, N.J. 37 39 49N 74 32W
Chattahoochee 17 30 42N 84 51W
Chattahoochee ➝ 18 30 54N 84 57W
Chattahoochee County ◇ 18 32 20N 84 50W
Chattahoochee National Forest 18 34 50N 84 0W
Chattanooga, Okla. 43 34 25N 98 39W
Chattanooga, Tenn. 49 35 3N 85 19W
Chattaroy 53 47 53N 117 21W
Chattooga County ◇ 18 34 30N 85 15W
Chauk 109 20 53N 94 49 E
Chaukan La 109 27 0N 97 15 E
Chaumont, France 90 48 7N 5 8 E
Chaumont, U.S.A. 39 44 4N 76 8W
Chauncey 42 39 24N 82 8W
Chautauqua 24 37 1N 96 11W
Chautauqua County ◇, Kans. 24 37 15N 96 15W
Chautauqua County ◇, N.Y. 39 42 20N 79 15W
Chautauqua L. 39 42 10N 79 24W
Chauvin, Canada 63 52 45N 110 10W
Chauvin, U.S.A. 25 29 26N 90 36W
Chaux-de-Fonds, La 88 47 7N 6 50 E
Chavantina 73 14 40 S 52 21W
Chaves, Brazil 74 0 15 S 49 55W
Chaves, Portugal 91 41 45N 7 32W
Chaves County ◇ 38 33 15N 104 30W
Chavies 49 37 21N 83 21W
Chavuma 123 13 4 S 22 40 E
Chaykovskiy 98 56 47N 54 9 E
Chazuta 72 6 30 S 76 0W
Chazy 39 44 53N 73 26W
Cheaha Mt. 10 33 29N 85 49W
Cheatham County ◇ 48 36 17N 87 4W
Cheb 88 50 9N 12 28 E
Chebanse 21 41 0N 87 54W
Cheboksary 98 56 8N 47 12 E
Cheboygan 29 45 39N 84 29W
Cheboygan County ◇ 29 45 20N 84 30W
Chech, Erg 120 25 0N 2 15W
Checheno-Ingush A.S.S.R. □ 99 43 30N 45 29 E
Checleset B. 62 50 5N 127 35W
Checotah 43 35 28N 95 31W
Chedabucto B. 61 45 25N 61 8W
Cheduba I. 109 18 45N 93 40 E
Cheektowaga 39 42 54N 78 45W
Cheesman L. 16 39 13N 105 16W
Chefornak 11 60 13N 164 12W
Chegdomyn 101 51 7N 133 1 E
Chegga 120 25 27N 5 40W
Chehalis 53 46 40N 122 58W
Chehalis ➝ 53 46 57N 123 50W
Cheju Do 115 33 29N 126 34 E
Chekiang = Zhejiang □ 115 29 0N 120 0 E
Chelan 53 47 51N 120 1W
Chelan, L. 53 48 11N 120 30W
Chelan County ◇ 53 48 0N 120 30W
Chelan Falls 53 47 48N 119 59W
Chelatchie 53 45 55N 122 25W
Cheleken 99 39 26N 53 7 E
Chelforó 78 39 0 S 66 33W
Chelkar 100 47 48N 59 39 E
Chelkar Tengiz, Solonchak 100 48 0N 62 30 E
Chełm 89 51 8N 23 30 E
Chełmno 89 53 20N 18 30 E
Chelmsford, U.K. 83 51 44N 0 29 E
Chelmsford, U.S.A. 28 42 36N 71 21W
Chełmża 89 53 10N 18 39 E
Chelsea, Iowa 23 41 55N 92 24W
Chelsea, Mich. 29 42 19N 84 1W
Chelsea, Okla. 43 36 32N 95 26W
Chelsea, Vt. 36 43 59N 72 27W
Cheltenham, U.K. 83 51 55N 2 5W
Cheltenham, U.S.A. 27 38 42N 76 50W
Chelyabinsk 100 55 10N 61 24 E
Chelyuskin, C. 102 77 30N 103 0 E
Chemainus 62 48 55N 123 42W
Chemehuevi Indian Reservation 15 34 30N 114 25W
Chemnitz = Karl-Marx-Stadt 88 50 50N 12 55 E
Chemquasabamticook L. 26 46 30N 69 37W
Chemung County ◇ 39 42 10N 76 45W
Chen, Gora 101 65 16N 141 50 E
Chen Xian 115 25 47N 113 1 E
Chenab ➝ 108 30 23N 71 2 E
Chenango ➝ 39 42 6N 75 55W
Chenango County ◇ 39 42 30N 75 40W
Chencha 121 6 15N 37 32 E
Chenchiang = Zhenjiang 115 32 11N 119 26 E
Chenes, Pointe aux 29 45 55N 84 54W
Cheney, Kans. 24 37 38N 97 47W
Cheney, Wash. 53 47 30N 117 35W
Cheney Reservoir 24 37 43N 97 48W
Cheneyville 25 31 1N 92 17W
Chengbu 115 26 18N 110 16 E
Chengcheng 115 35 8N 109 56 E
Chengchou = Zhengzhou 115 34 45N 113 34 E
Chengde 114 40 59N 117 58 E
Chengdu 113 30 38N 104 2 E
Chenggu 115 33 10N 107 21 E
Chengjiang 113 24 39N 103 0 E
Chengyang 114 36 18N 120 21 E
Chenkán 65 19 8N 90 58W
Chenoa 21 40 45N 88 43W
Chenoweth 44 45 37N 121 13W
Chenxi 115 28 2N 110 12 E
Cheo Reo 112 13 25N 108 28 E
Cheom Ksan 112 14 13N 104 56 E
Chepachet 28 41 55N 71 40W
Chepelare 95 41 44N 24 40 E
Chepén 72 7 15 S 79 23W
Chepes 76 31 20 S 66 35W
Chepo 66 9 10N 79 6W
Chequamegon National Forest 55 46 10N 91 0W
Chequamegon Pt. 55 46 42N 90 45W
Cher □ 90 47 10N 2 30 E
Cher ➝ 90 47 21N 0 29 E
Cheraw, Colo. 16 38 6N 103 31W
Cheraw, S.C. 46 34 42N 79 53W
Cherbourg 90 49 39N 1 40W
Cherchell 120 36 35N 2 12 E
Cherdyn 98 60 24N 56 29 E
Cheremkhovo 101 53 8N 103 1 E
Cherepanovo 100 54 15N 83 30 E
Cherepovets 98 59 5N 37 55 E
Chergui, Chott ech 120 34 21N 0 25 E
Cheriton 54 37 17N 75 58W
Cherkassy 99 49 27N 32 4 E
Cherlak 100 54 15N 74 55 E
Cherni 95 42 35N 23 18 E
Chernigov 98 51 28N 31 20 E
Chernikovsk 98 54 48N 56 8 E
Chernogorsk 101 53 49N 91 18 E
Chernovtsy 99 48 15N 25 52 E
Chernoye 101 70 30N 89 10 E
Chernyshovskiy 101 63 0N 112 30 E
Cherokee, Ala. 10 34 45N 87 58W
Cherokee, Iowa 23 42 45N 95 33W
Cherokee, Kans. 24 37 21N 94 49W
Cherokee, N.C. 40 35 29N 83 19W
Cherokee, Okla. 43 36 45N 98 21W
Cherokee, Tex. 51 30 59N 98 43W
Cherokee County ◇, Ala. 10 34 9N 85 41W
Cherokee County ◇, Ga. 18 34 20N 84 20W
Cherokee County ◇, Iowa 23 42 45N 95 35W
Cherokee County ◇, Kans. 24 37 15N 94 45W
Cherokee County ◇, N.C. 40 35 10N 84 10W
Cherokee County ◇, Okla. 43 36 0N 95 0W
Cherokee County ◇, S.C. 46 35 0N 81 40W
Cherokee County ◇, Tex. 51 31 58N 95 17W
Cherokee Falls 46 35 4N 81 32W
Cherokee Indian Reservation 40 35 30N 83 20W
Cherokee L. 49 36 10N 83 30W
Cherokee National Forest 49 36 0N 82 40W
Cherokees, Lake O' The 43 36 28N 95 2W
Cherquenco 78 38 35 S 72 0W
Cherrapunji 109 25 17N 91 47 E
Cherry ➝ 47 44 36N 101 30W
Cherry County ◇ 34 42 30N 101 0W
Cherry Cr. ➝ 16 39 45N 104 1W
Cherry Creek, Nev. 35 39 54N 114 53W
Cherry Creek, S. Dak. 47 44 36N 101 30W
Cherry Creek Lake 16 39 39N 104 52W
Cherry Hill 37 39 56N 75 2W
Cherry L. 14 37 59N 119 55W
Cherry Tree 45 40 44N 78 48W
Cherry Valley, Ark. 13 35 24N 90 45W
Cherry Valley, N.Y. 39 42 48N 74 45W
Cherryfield 26 44 36N 67 56W
Cherryvale 24 37 16N 95 33W
Cherryville 40 35 23N 81 23W
Cherskiy 101 68 45N 161 18 E
Cherskogo Khrebet 101 65 0N 143 0 E
Cherven-Bryag 95 43 17N 24 7 E
Cherwell ➝ 83 51 46N 1 18W
Chesaning 29 43 11N 84 7W
Chesapeake 54 36 50N 76 17W
Chesapeake B. 54 38 0N 76 10W
Chesapeake Beach 27 38 41N 76 32W
Chesapeake City 27 39 32N 75 49W
Chesaw 53 48 57N 119 3W
Chesdin, L. 54 37 20N 77 40W
Cheshire, Conn. 28 41 30N 72 54W
Cheshire, Mass. 28 42 34N 73 10W
Cheshire □ 82 53 14N 2 30W
Cheshire County ◇ 36 43 0N 72 15W
Cheshskaya Guba 98 67 20N 47 0 E
Chesilhurst 37 39 44N 74 52W
Cheslatta L. 62 53 49N 125 20W
Chesnee 46 35 9N 81 52W
Chester, U.K. 82 53 12N 2 53W
Chester, Ark. 13 35 41N 94 11W
Chester, Calif. 14 40 19N 121 14W
Chester, Ga. 18 32 24N 83 9W
Chester, Ill. 21 37 55N 89 49W
Chester, Mass. 28 42 17N 72 59W
Chester, Mont. 33 48 31N 110 58W
Chester, N.H. 36 42 55N 71 15W
Chester, N.J. 37 40 47N 74 42W
Chester, Okla. 43 36 13N 98 55W
Chester, Pa. 45 39 51N 75 22W
Chester, S.C. 46 34 43N 81 12W
Chester, S. Dak. 47 43 54N 96 56W
Chester, Va. 54 37 21N 77 27W
Chester, Vt. 36 43 16N 72 36W
Chester, W. Va. 54 40 37N 80 34W
Chester ➝ 27 39 3N 76 16W
Chester County ◇, Pa. 45 39 59N 75 50W
Chester County ◇, S.C. 46 34 30N 81 10W
Chester County ◇, Tenn. 48 35 20N 88 45W
Chesterfield, U.K. 82 53 14N 1 26W
Chesterfield, Ill. 21 39 15N 90 4W
Chesterfield, N.H. 36 42 52N 72 28W
Chesterfield, S.C. 46 34 44N 80 5W
Chesterfield, Va. 54 37 23N 77 31W
Chesterfield, Îles 124 19 52 S 158 15 E
Chesterfield County ◇, S.C. 46 34 30N 80 10W
Chesterfield County ◇, Va. 54 37 23N 77 31W
Chesterfield In. 58 63 25N 90 45W
Chesterfield Inlet 58 63 30N 90 45W
Chesterhill 42 39 29N 81 52W
Chestertown 27 39 13N 76 4W
Chesterville 27 39 17N 75 55W
Chestnut 25 32 3N 93 1W
Chestnut Mountain 18 34 10N 83 50W
Chesuncook L. 26 46 0N 69 21W
Cheswold 27 39 13N 75 35W
Chetco ➝ 44 42 3N 124 16W
Chetek 55 45 19N 91 39W
Chéticamp 61 46 37N 60 59W
Chetopa 24 37 2N 95 5W
Chetumal 65 18 30N 88 20W
Chetumal, Bahía de 65 18 40N 88 10W
Chetwynd 62 55 45N 121 36W
Chevak 11 61 32N 165 35W
Cheviot 42 39 10N 84 37W
Cheviot, The 82 55 29N 2 8W
Cheviot Hills 82 55 20N 2 30W
Chevy Chase 27 38 59N 77 5W
Chew Bahir 121 4 40N 36 50 E
Chewelah 53 48 17N 117 43W
Cheyenne, Okla. 43 35 37N 99 40W
Cheyenne, Wyo. 56 41 8N 104 49W
Cheyenne ➝ 47 44 41N 101 18W
Cheyenne Bottoms 24 38 27N 98 40W
Cheyenne County ◇, Colo. 16 38 50N 102 35W
Cheyenne County ◇, Kans. 24 39 45N 101 45W
Cheyenne County ◇, Nebr. 34 41 15N 103 0W
Cheyenne River Indian Reservation 47 45 0N 101 0W
Cheyenne Wells 16 38 49N 102 21W
Chhapra 109 25 48N 84 44 E
Chhatarpur 108 24 55N 79 35 E
Chhindwara 108 22 2N 78 59 E
Chhlong 112 12 15N 105 58 E
Chi ➝ 112 15 11N 104 43 E
Chiamis 111 7 20 S 108 21 E
Chiamussu = Jiamusi 114 46 40N 130 26 E
Chiang Mai 112 18 47N 98 59 E
Chiange 123 15 35 S 13 40 E
Chiapa ➝ 65 16 42N 93 0W
Chiapa de Corzo 65 16 42N 93 0W
Chiapas □ 65 17 0N 92 45W
Chiautla 65 18 18N 98 34W
Chiba 117 35 30N 140 7 E
Chibatu 111 7 6 S 107 59 E
Chibemba 123 15 48 S 14 8 E
Chibia 123 15 10 S 13 42 E
Chibougamau 60 49 56N 74 24W
Chibougamau L. 60 49 50N 74 20W
Chibuk 121 10 52N 12 50 E
Chic-Chocs, Mts. 61 48 55N 66 0W
Chicacole = Srikakulam 109 18 14N 83 58 E
Chicago 21 41 53N 87 38W
Chicago Heights 21 41 30N 87 38W
Chicamuxen 27 38 33N 77 15W
Chichagof I. 11 57 30N 135 30W
Chichén Itzá 65 20 40N 88 32W
Chichester 83 50 50N 0 47W
Chichibu 117 36 5N 139 10 E
Ch'ich'ihaerh = Qiqihar 114 47 26N 124 0 E
Chickahominy ➝ 54 37 14N 76 53W
Chickamauga 18 34 52N 85 18W
Chickamauga L. 49 35 6N 85 14W
Chickasaw 10 30 46N 88 5W
Chickasaw County ◇, Iowa 23 43 5N 92 20W
Chickasaw County ◇, Miss. 31 33 54N 89 0W
Chickasaw Nat. Rec. Area 43 34 26N 97 0W
Chickasawhay ➝ 31 30 59N 88 44W
Chickasha 43 35 3N 97 58W
Chicken 11 64 5N 141 56W
Chiclana de la Frontera 91 36 26N 6 9W
Chiclayo 72 6 42 S 79 50W
Chico, Calif. 14 39 44N 121 50W
Chico, Tex. 51 33 18N 97 48W
Chico ➝ 78 50 0 S 68 30W
Chicoa 123 15 35 S 32 20 E
Chicontepec 65 20 58N 98 10W
Chicopee, Ga. 18 34 15N 83 51W
Chicopee, Mass. 28 42 9N 72 37W
Chicopee ➝ 28 42 9N 72 37W
Chicora 31 31 34N 88 34W
Chicot 13 33 12N 91 17W
Chicot County ◇ 13 33 12N 91 17W
Chicoutimi 61 48 28N 71 5W
Chidambaram 108 11 20N 79 45 E
Chidester 13 33 42N 93 1W
Chidley C. 59 60 23N 64 26W
Chiefland 17 29 29N 82 52W
Chiengi 122 8 45 S 29 10 E
Chiese ➝ 94 45 8N 10 25 E
Chieti 94 42 22N 14 10 E
Chifeng 114 42 18N 118 58 E
Chignecto B. 61 45 30N 64 40W
Chignik 11 56 18N 158 24W
Chigorodó 70 7 41N 76 42W
Chiguana 76 21 0 S 67 58W
Chihuahua 64 28 40N 106 3W
Chihuahua □ 64 28 40N 106 3W
Chiili 100 44 20N 66 15 E
Chik Bollapur 108 13 25N 77 45 E
Chikaskia ➝ 43 36 37N 97 15W
Chikmagalur 108 13 15N 75 45 E
Chilac 65 18 20N 97 24W
Chilako ➝ 62 53 53N 122 57W
Chilapa 65 17 40N 99 11W
Chilas 108 35 25N 74 5 E
Chilaw 108 7 30N 79 50 E
Chilcotin ➝ 62 51 44N 122 23W
Childers 127 25 15 S 152 17 E
Childersburg 10 33 16N 86 21W
Childress 50 34 25N 100 13W
Childress County ◇ 50 34 25N 100 15W
Chile ■ 78 35 0 S 72 0W
Chile Chico 78 46 33 S 71 44W
Chile Rise 125 38 0 S 92 0W
Chilecito 76 29 10 S 67 30W
Chilete 72 7 10 S 78 50W
Chilhowee 32 38 36N 93 51W
Chilhowie 54 36 48N 81 41W
Chililabombwe 123 12 18 S 27 43 E
Chilili 38 34 53N 106 14W
Chilka L. 109 19 40N 85 25 E
Chilko ➝ 62 52 0N 123 40W
Chilko, L. 62 51 20N 124 10W
Chillagoe 127 17 7 S 144 33 E
Chillán 76 36 40 S 72 10W
Chillicothe, Ill. 21 40 55N 89 29W
Chillicothe, Iowa 23 41 5N 92 32W
Chillicothe, Mo. 32 39 48N 93 33W
Chillicothe, Ohio 42 39 20N 82 59W
Chillicothe, Tex. 51 34 15N 99 31W
Chilliwack 62 49 10N 121 54W
Chillum 27 38 56N 76 58W
Chilmark 28 41 21N 70 45W

Chilocco Claremont

Chilocco 43 36 59N 97 4W
Chiloé □ . . . . . . 78 43 0 S 73 0W
Chiloé, I. de . . . . . . 78 42 30 S 73 50W
Chiloquin 44 42 35N 121 52W
Chilpancingo 65 17 30N 99 30W
Chiltern Hills 83 51 44N 0 42W
Chilton 55 44 2N 88 10W
Chilton County ◇ 10 32 51N 86 38W
Chiluage . . . . . . 122 9 30 S 21 50 E
Chilwa, L. . . . . . . 123 15 15 S 35 40 E
Chimaltitán 64 21 46N 103 50W
Chimán 66 8 45N 78 40W
Chimay . . . . . . 87 50 3N 4 20 E
Chimayo 38 36 0N 105 56W
Chimbay . . . . . . 100 42 57N 59 47 E
Chimborazo . . . . . . 70 1 29 S 78 55W
Chimborazo □ . . . . . . 70 1 0 S 78 40W
Chimbote . . . . . . 72 9 0 S 78 35W
Chimishliya . . . . . . 95 46 34N 28 44 E
Chimkent . . . . . . 100 42 18N 69 36 E
Chimney Rock 16 37 13N 107 18W
Chimoio . . . . . . 123 19 4 S 33 30 E
Chin □ . . . . . . 109 22 0N 93 0 E
China, Mexico 65 25 40N 99 20W
China, U.S.A. 51 30 3N 94 20W
China ■ . . . . . . 113 30 0N 110 0 E
China Grove 40 35 34N 80 35W
Chinacates 64 25 0N 105 14W
Chinacota 70 7 37N 72 36W
Chinandega 66 12 35N 87 12W
Chinati Mts. 50 29 55N 104 30W
Chinati Peak 50 29 57N 104 29W
Chincha Alta . . . . . . 72 13 25 S 76 7W
Chinchón 91 40 9N 3 26W
Chinchorro, Banco 65 18 35N 87 20W
Chinchou = Jinzhou . . . . . . 114 41 5N 121 3 E
Chincoteague 54 37 56N 75 23W
Chincoteague Bay 27 38 15N 75 15W
Chinde . . . . . . 123 18 35 S 36 30 E
Chindwin → . . . . . . 109 21 26N 95 15 E
Chingola . . . . . . 123 12 31 S 27 53 E
Chinguetti 120 20 25N 12 24W
Chinhae . . . . . . 114 35 9N 128 47 E
Chinhoyi . . . . . . 123 17 20 S 30 8 E
Chiniot . . . . . . 108 31 45N 73 0 E
Chinipas 64 27 22N 108 32W
Chinju . . . . . . 114 35 12N 128 2 E
Chinle 12 36 9N 109 33W
Chinle Cr. → 52 37 12N 109 43W
Chinnampo . . . . . . 114 38 52N 125 10 E
Chino, Japan . . . . . . 117 35 59N 138 9 E
Chino, U.S.A. 15 34 1N 117 41W
Chino Valley 12 34 45N 112 27W
Chinon . . . . . . 90 47 10N 0 15 E
Chinook, Canada 63 51 28N 110 59W
Chinook, Mont. 33 48 35N 109 14W
Chinook, Wash. 53 46 16N 123 57W
Chinook Pass 53 46 52N 121 32W
Chinquapin 40 34 50N 77 49W
Chinsali . . . . . . 122 10 30 S 32 2 E
Chióggia . . . . . . 94 45 13N 12 15 E
Chíos = Khíos . . . . . . 95 38 27N 26 9 E
Chipata . . . . . . 123 13 38 S 32 28 E
Chipatujah . . . . . . 111 7 45 S 108 0 E
Chipewyan L. 63 58 0N 98 27W
Chipley 17 30 47N 85 32W
Chipman 61 46 6N 65 53W
Chipola → 17 30 1N 85 5W
Chippenham 83 51 27N 2 7W
Chippewa →, Mich. 29 43 35N 84 17W
Chippewa →, Minn. 30 44 56N 95 44W
Chippewa →, Wis. 55 44 25N 92 5W
Chippewa, L. 55 45 57N 91 12W
Chippewa County ◇, Mich. . 66 46 20N 84 40W
Chippewa County ◇, Minn. . 30 45 0N 95 35W
Chippewa County ◇, Wis. . . 55 45 5N 91 20W
Chippewa Falls 55 44 56N 91 24W
Chippewa National Forest . . . 30 47 45N 94 0W
Chiputneticook Lakes, Maine 26 45 35N 67 35W
Chiputneticook Lakes, Maine 26 45 43N 67 50W
Chiquián . . . . . . 72 10 10 S 77 0W
Chiquimula 66 14 51N 89 37W
Chiquinquira 70 5 37N 73 50W
Chiquitos, Llanos de . . . . . . 73 18 0 S 61 30W
Chirala . . . . . . 108 15 50N 80 26 E
Chirchik . . . . . . 100 41 29N 69 35 E
Chireno 51 31 30N 94 21W
Chirgua → 70 8 54N 67 58W
Chiricahua Mts. 12 32 0N 109 15W
Chiricahua National
Monument 12 32 0N 109 20W
Chiricahua Peak 12 31 51N 109 18W
Chiriquí, Golfo de 66 8 0N 82 10W
Chiriquí, Lago de 66 9 10N 82 0W
Chirmiri . . . . . . 109 23 15N 82 20 E
Chirnogi . . . . . . 95 44 7N 26 32 E
Chiromo . . . . . . 123 16 30 S 35 7 E
Chirpan . . . . . . 95 42 10N 25 19 E
Chirripó Grande, Cerro 66 9 29N 83 29W
Chisago County ◇ 30 45 30N 92 55W
Chisamba . . . . . . 123 14 55 S 28 20 E
Chisapani Garhi . . . . . . 109 27 30N 84 2 E
Chisholm, Canada 62 54 55N 114 10W
Chisholm, Maine 26 44 29N 70 12W
Chisholm, Minn. 30 47 29N 92 53W
Chisimaio . . . . . . 119 0 22 S 42 32 E
Chisos Mts. 50 29 5N 103 15W
Chistochina 11 62 34N 144 40W
Chistopol . . . . . . 98 55 25N 50 38 E
Chita, Colombia 70 6 11N 72 28W
Chita, U.S.S.R. . . . . . . 101 52 0N 113 35 E
Chitado . . . . . . 123 17 10 S 14 8 E
Chitembo . . . . . . 123 13 30 S 16 50 E
Chitina 11 61 31N 144 26W
Chitokoloki . . . . . . 123 13 50 S 23 13 E
Chitose . . . . . . 116 42 49N 141 39 E
Chitral . . . . . . 107 35 50N 71 56 E
Chitré 66 7 59N 80 27W
Chittagong . . . . . . 109 22 19N 91 48 E
Chittagong □ . . . . . . 109 24 5N 91 0 E
Chittaurgarh . . . . . . 108 24 52N 74 38 E
Chittenango 39 43 3N 75 52W
Chittenden 36 43 42N 72 55W
Chittenden County ◇ 36 44 30N 73 10W
Chittoor . . . . . . 108 13 15N 79 5 E
Chiusi . . . . . . 94 43 1N 11 58 E
Chivacoa 70 10 10N 68 54W
Chivasso . . . . . . 94 45 10N 7 52 E
Chivay . . . . . . 72 15 40 S 71 35W
Chivilcoy . . . . . . 76 34 55 S 60 0W
Chivington 16 38 26N 102 32W
Chkalov = Orenburg . . . . . . 98 51 45N 55 6 E
Chloride 12 35 25N 114 12W
Chocó □ 70 6 0N 77 0W
Chocolate Mts., Ariz. 12 33 15N 114 30W
Chocolate Mts., Calif. 15 33 15N 115 15W
Chocontá 70 5 9N 73 41W
Chocowinity 40 35 31N 77 6W
Choctaw 43 35 31N 97 17W
Choctaw Bluff 10 31 22N 87 46W
Choctaw County ◇, Ala. . . . 10 32 0N 88 10W
Choctaw County ◇, Miss. . . . 31 33 19N 89 11W
Choctaw County ◇, Okla. . . 43 34 0N 95 30W
Choctaw Indian Reservation . 31 32 48N 89 7W
Choctawatchee → 17 30 25N 86 8W
Choctawhatchee B. 17 30 20N 86 20W
Choele Choel . . . . . . 78 39 11 S 65 40W
Choix 64 26 40N 108 23W
Chojnice . . . . . . 89 53 42N 17 32 E
Chōkai-San . . . . . . 116 39 6N 140 3 E
Choke Canyon Res. 51 28 30N 98 20W
Chokio 30 45 34N 96 10W
Chokoloskee 17 25 49N 81 22W
Chokurdakh . . . . . . 101 70 38N 147 55 E
Cholet 90 47 4N 0 52W
Choluteca 66 13 20N 87 14W
Choluteca → 66 13 0N 87 20W
Choma . . . . . . 123 16 48 S 26 59 E
Chomutov . . . . . . 88 50 28N 13 23 E
Chon Buri . . . . . . 112 13 21N 101 1 E
Chonan . . . . . . 114 36 48N 127 9 E
Chone . . . . . . 70 0 40 S 80 0W
Chong'an . . . . . . 115 27 45N 118 0 E
Chongde . . . . . . 115 30 32N 120 26 E
Chŏngjin . . . . . . 114 41 47N 129 50 E
Chŏngju, N. Korea . . . . . . 114 39 40N 125 5 E
Chŏngju, S. Korea . . . . . . 114 36 39N 127 27 E
Chongli . . . . . . 114 40 58N 115 15 E
Chongoyape . . . . . . 72 6 35 S 79 25W
Chongqing . . . . . . 115 29 35N 106 25 E
Chongzuo . . . . . . 115 22 23N 107 20 E
Chŏnju . . . . . . 114 35 50N 127 4 E
Chonming Dao . . . . . . 115 31 40N 121 30 E
Chonos, Arch. de los . . . . . . 78 45 0 S 75 0W
Chopim → . . . . . . 77 25 35 S 53 5W
Choptank 27 38 41N 75 57W
Choptank → 27 38 38N 76 13W
Chorley 82 53 39N 2 39W
Chorolque, Cerro . . . . . . 76 20 59 S 66 5W
Chorrera, La . . . . . . 70 0 44 S 73 1W
Chŏrwŏn . . . . . . 114 38 15N 127 10 E
Chorzów . . . . . . 89 50 18N 18 57 E
Chos-Malal . . . . . . 76 37 20 S 70 15W
Chosan . . . . . . 114 40 50N 125 47 E
Choszczno . . . . . . 88 53 7N 15 25 E
Chota . . . . . . 72 6 33 S 78 39W
Choteau 33 47 49N 112 11W
Chotila . . . . . . 108 22 23N 71 15 E
Chouteau 43 36 11N 95 21W
Chouteau County ◇ 33 47 55N 110 30W
Chowan → 40 36 1N 76 40W
Chowan County ◇ 40 36 10N 76 40W
Chowchilla 14 37 7N 120 16W
Choybalsan . . . . . . 113 48 4N 114 30 E
Chrisman 21 39 48N 87 41W
Chrisney 22 38 1N 87 2W
Christchurch, N.Z. . . . . . . 128 43 33 S 172 47 E
Christchurch, U.K. 83 50 44N 1 33W
Christian County ◇, Ill. . . . 21 39 30N 89 15W
Christian County ◇, Ky. . . . 48 36 50N 87 30W
Christian County ◇, Mo. . . . 32 37 0N 93 10W
Christian Sd. 11 55 56N 134 40W
Christiana, S. Africa . . . . . . 123 27 52 S 25 8 E
Christiana, Del. 27 39 40N 75 40W
Christiana, Tenn. 48 35 43N 86 24W
Christiansburg, Ohio 42 40 3N 84 2W
Christiansburg, Va. 54 37 8N 80 25W
Christiansted, Virgin Is. 57 17 45N 64 42W
Christie 43 35 57N 94 42W
Christie B. 63 62 32N 111 10W
Christina → 63 56 40N 111 3W
Christine 41 46 35N 96 48W
Christmas I. = Kiritimati,
Pac. Oc. 125 1 58N 157 27W
Christmas I. = Kiritimati,
Pac. Oc. 125 1 58N 157 27W
Christmas I. . . . . . . 124 10 30 S 105 40 E
Christopher 21 37 59N 89 3W
Christoval 50 31 12N 100 30W
Chromo 16 37 2N 106 50W
Chrysler 10 31 18N 87 42W
Chu . . . . . . 100 43 36N 73 42 E
Chu → . . . . . . 112 19 53N 105 45 E
Chu Chua 62 51 22N 120 10W
Chualar 14 36 34N 121 31W
Ch'uanchou = Quanzhou . . . 115 24 55N 118 34 E
Chuathbaluk 11 61 40N 159 15W
Chubbuck 20 42 55N 112 28W
Chūbu □ . . . . . . 117 36 45N 137 30 E
Chubut □ . . . . . . 78 43 30 S 69 0W
Chubut → . . . . . . 78 43 20 S 65 5W
Chuchi L. 62 55 12N 124 30W
Chuckawalla Mts. 15 33 30N 115 20W
Chudskoye, Oz. . . . . . . 98 58 13N 27 30 E
Chugach Mts. 11 60 45N 147 0W
Chugach National Forest . . . 11 58 15N 152 45W
Chugiak 11 61 24N 149 29W
Chuginadak I. 11 52 50N 169 45W
Chūgoku □ . . . . . . 117 35 0N 133 0 E
Chūgoku-Sanchi . . . . . . 117 35 0N 133 0 E
Chugwater 56 41 46N 104 50W
Chukotskiy Khrebet . . . . . . 101 68 0N 175 0 E
Chukotskoye More 101 68 0N 175 0W
Chula, Ga. 18 31 33N 83 32W
Chula, Mo. 32 39 55N 93 29W
Chula, Va. 54 37 23N 77 54W
Chula Vista 15 32 39N 117 5W
Chulman . . . . . . 101 56 52N 124 52 E
Chulucanas . . . . . . 72 5 8 S 80 10W
Chulumani . . . . . . 72 16 24 S 67 31W
Chulym → . . . . . . 100 57 43N 83 51 E
Chuma . . . . . . 72 15 24 S 68 56W
Chumbicha . . . . . . 76 29 0 S 66 10W
Chumerna . . . . . . 95 42 45N 25 55 E
Chumikan . . . . . . 101 54 40N 135 10 E
Chumphon . . . . . . 112 10 35N 99 14 E
Chumpi . . . . . . 72 15 4 S 73 46W
Chuna → . . . . . . 101 57 47N 94 37 E
Chun'an . . . . . . 115 29 35N 119 3 E
Chunchŏn . . . . . . 114 37 58N 127 44 E
Chunchula 10 30 55N 88 12W
Chunky 31 32 20N 88 56W
Chunya . . . . . . 122 8 30 S 33 27 E
Chupadera Mesa 38 34 0N 106 0W
Chuquibamba . . . . . . 72 15 47 S 72 44W
Chuquibambilla . . . . . . 72 14 7 S 72 41W
Chuquicamata . . . . . . 76 22 15 S 69 0W
Chuquisaca □ . . . . . . 73 23 30 S 63 30W
Chur . . . . . . 88 46 52N 9 32 E
Churachandpur . . . . . . 109 24 20N 93 40 E
Church Creek 27 38 30N 76 10W
Church Hill, Md. 27 39 9N 75 59W
Church Hill, Tenn. 49 36 31N 82 43W
Church Point 25 30 24N 92 13W
Churchill 63 58 47N 94 11W
Churchill →, Man., Canada 63 58 47N 94 12W
Churchill →, Newf.,
Canada 61 53 19N 60 10W
Churchill, C. 63 58 46N 93 12W
Churchill County ◇ 35 39 30N 118 20W
Churchill Falls 61 53 36N 64 19W
Churchill L. 63 55 55N 108 20W
Churchill Pk. 62 58 10N 125 10W
Churchs Ferry 41 48 16N 99 12W
Churchville 27 39 34N 76 15W
Churdan 23 42 9N 94 29W
Churu . . . . . . 108 28 20N 74 50 E
Churubusco 22 41 14N 85 19W
Chushal . . . . . . 108 33 40N 78 40 E
Chuska Mts. 38 36 15N 108 50W
Chusovoy . . . . . . 98 58 15N 57 40 E
Chuvash A.S.S.R.□ . . . . . . 98 55 30N 47 0 E
Ci Xian . . . . . . 114 36 20N 114 25 E
Ciales 57 18 20N 66 28W
Cianjur . . . . . . 111 6 49 S 107 8 E
Cibadok . . . . . . 111 6 53 S 106 47 E
Cibatu . . . . . . 111 7 8 S 107 59 E
Cibola County ◇ 38 35 0N 108 0W
Cibola National Forest 38 35 10N 108 15W
Cicero, Ill. 21 41 51N 87 45W
Cicero, Ind. 22 40 8N 86 1W
Cícero Dantas . . . . . . 74 10 36 S 38 23W
Cidra 57 18 11N 66 10W
Cidra, Lago de 57 18 12N 66 8W
Ciechanów . . . . . . 89 52 52N 20 38 E
Ciego de Avila 66 21 50N 78 50W
Ciénaga 70 11 1N 74 15W
Ciénaga de Oro 70 8 53N 75 37W
Cienfuegos 66 22 10N 80 30W
Cieszyn . . . . . . 89 49 45N 18 35 E
Cieza 91 38 17N 1 23W
Cihuatlán 64 19 14N 104 35W
Cijulang . . . . . . 111 7 42 S 108 27 E
Cikajang . . . . . . 111 7 25 S 107 48 E
Cikampek . . . . . . 111 6 23 S 107 28 E
Cilacap . . . . . . 111 7 43 S 109 0 E
Cilician Gates P. . . . . . . 106 37 20N 34 52 E
Cîlnicu . . . . . . 95 44 54N 23 4 E
Cima 15 35 14N 115 30W
Cimahi . . . . . . 111 6 53 S 107 33 E
Cimarron, Kans. 24 37 48N 100 21W
Cimarron, N. Mex. 38 36 31N 104 55W
Cimarron → 43 36 10N 96 17W
Cimarron County ◇ 43 36 45N 102 30W
Cimone, Mte. . . . . . . 94 44 10N 10 40 E
Cîmpic Turzii . . . . . . 95 46 34N 23 53 E
Cîmpina . . . . . . 89 45 10N 25 45 E
Cîmpulung . . . . . . 89 45 17N 25 3 E
Cîmpuri . . . . . . 95 46 0N 26 50 E
Cinca → . . . . . . 91 41 26N 0 21 E
Cincinnati, Iowa 23 40 38N 92 56W
Cincinnati, Ohio 42 39 6N 84 31W
Cîndeşti . . . . . . 95 45 15N 26 42 E
Ciney . . . . . . 87 50 18N 5 5 E
Cinto, Mt. . . . . . . 94 42 24N 8 54 E
Ciorani . . . . . . 95 44 45N 26 25 E
Cipó . . . . . . 74 11 6 S 38 31W
Circle, Alaska 11 65 50N 144 4W
Circle, Mont. 33 47 25N 105 35W
Circleville, Kans. 24 39 31N 95 52W
Circleville, Ohio 42 39 36N 82 57W
Circleville, Utah 52 38 10N 112 16W
Circleville, W. Va. 54 38 40N 79 30W
Circleville Mt. 52 38 12N 112 24W
Cirebon . . . . . . 111 6 45 S 108 32 E
Cirencester 83 51 43N 1 59W
Cireşu . . . . . . 95 44 47N 22 31 E
Cisco, Ill. 21 40 1N 88 44W
Cisco, Tex. 51 32 23N 98 59W
Cisco, Utah 52 38 58N 109 19W
Cislău . . . . . . 95 45 14N 26 20 E
Cisnădie . . . . . . 95 45 42N 24 9 E
Cisne 21 38 31N 88 26W
Cisneros 70 6 33N 75 4W
Cissna Park 21 40 34N 87 54W
Cistern 51 29 49N 97 13W
Citaré → 71 1 11N 54 41W
Citlaltépetl 65 19 0N 97 20W
Citra 17 29 25N 82 7W
Citronelle 10 31 6N 88 14W
Citrus County ◇ 17 28 45N 82 30W
Citrus Heights 14 38 42N 121 17W
Citrus Springs 17 29 2N 82 27W
Ciuc, Munţii . . . . . . 95 46 25N 26 5 E
Ciucaş . . . . . . 95 45 31N 25 56 E
Ciudad Acuña 64 29 20N 100 58W
Ciudad Altamirano 64 18 20N 100 40W
Ciudad Bolívar 71 8 5N 63 36W
Ciudad Camargo 64 27 41N 105 10W
Ciudad de Valles 65 22 0N 99 0W
Ciudad del Carmen 65 18 38N 91 50W
Ciudad Delicias = Delicias . . 64 28 10N 105 30W
Ciudad Guayana 71 8 0N 62 30W
Ciudad Guerrero 64 28 33N 107 28W
Ciudad Guzmán 64 19 40N 103 30W
Ciudad Juárez 64 31 40N 106 28W
Ciudad Madero 65 22 19N 97 50W
Ciudad Mante 65 22 50N 99 0W
Ciudad Obregón 64 27 28N 109 59W
Ciudad Ojeda 70 10 12N 71 19W
Ciudad Real 91 38 59N 3 55W
Ciudad Rodrigo 91 40 35N 6 32W
Ciudad Trujillo = Santo
Domingo 67 18 30N 64 54W
Ciudad Victoria 65 23 41N 99 9W
Ciulniţa . . . . . . 95 44 26N 27 22 E
Civitanova Marche . . . . . . 94 43 18N 13 41 E
Civitavécchia . . . . . . 94 42 6N 11 46 E
Çivril . . . . . . 106 38 20N 29 43 E
Cizre . . . . . . 106 37 19N 42 10 E
Clackamas → 44 45 22N 122 36W
Clackamas County ◇ 44 45 15N 122 15W
Clacton-on-Sea . . . . . . 83 51 47N 1 10 E
Claflin 24 38 31N 98 32W
Claiborne, Ala. 10 31 33N 87 31W
Claiborne, Md. 27 38 50N 76 17W
Claiborne County ◇, Miss. . . 31 31 58N 90 59W
Claiborne County ◇, Tenn. . 49 36 27N 83 34W
Claiborne Parish ◇ 25 32 48N 93 4W
Clair Engle L. 14 40 48N 122 46W
Clair Haven 29 42 36N 82 49W
Claire, L. 62 58 35N 112 5W
Claire City 47 45 52N 97 6W
Clairton 45 40 18N 79 53W
Clallam Bay 53 48 15N 124 16W
Clallam County ◇ 53 48 0N 124 0W
Clam Gulch 11 60 15N 151 23W
Clan Alpine Mts. 35 39 40N 117 55W
Clancy 33 46 28N 111 59W
Clanton 10 32 51N 86 38W
Clanwilliam . . . . . . 123 32 11 S 18 52 E
Clara, Ireland 85 53 20N 7 38W
Clara, U.S.A. 31 31 35N 88 42W
Clara City 30 44 57N 95 22W
Clare, Iowa 23 42 35N 94 21W
Clare, Mich. 29 43 49N 84 46W
Clare □ 85 52 20N 9 0W
Clare → 85 53 22N 9 5W
Clare County ◇ 29 44 0N 84 50W
Clare I. 85 53 48N 10 0W
Claremont, Calif. 15 34 6N 117 43W
Claremont, Ill. 21 38 43N 87 58W
Claremont, N.H. 36 43 23N 72 20W

Claremont Cobre

aremont, S. Dak. 47 45 40N 98 1W
laremont, Va. 54 37 14N 76 58W
laremore 43 36 19N 95 36W
laremorris 85 53 45N 9 0W
larence, Iowa 23 41 53N 91 4W
larence, La. 25 31 49N 93 2W
larence, Mo. 32 39 45N 92 16W
larence →, Australia 127 29 25 S 153 22 E
larence →, N.Z. 128 42 10 S 173 56 E
larence, I. 78 54 0 S 72 0W
larence, Port 11 65 15N 166 40W
larence Cannon L. 32 39 28N 91 55W
larence I. 5 61 10 S 54 0W
larence Str. 126 12 0 S 131 0 E
larence Town 67 23 6N 74 59W
larendon, Ark. 13 34 42N 91 19W
larendon, Pa. 45 41 47N 79 6W
larendon, Tex. 50 34 56N 100 53W
larendon County ◇ 46 33 45N 80 10W
larenville 61 48 10N 54 1W
laresholm 62 50 0N 113 33W
lareton 56 43 42N 104 42W
larie Coast 5 68 0 S 135 0 E
larinda 23 40 44N 95 2W
larington 42 39 46N 80 52W
larion, Iowa 23 42 44N 93 44W
larion, Pa. 45 41 13N 79 23W
larion → 45 41 7N 79 41W
larion County ◇ 45 41 5N 79 40W
larion Fracture Zone 125 20 0N 120 0W
larissa 30 46 8N 94 57W
larita 43 34 29N 96 26W
lark, Mo. 32 39 17N 92 21W
lark, N.J. 37 40 38N 74 18W
lark, S. Dak. 47 44 53N 97 44W
lark County ◇, Ark. 13 33 55N 93 9W
lark County ◇, Idaho 20 44 15N 112 30W
lark County ◇, Ill. 21 39 20N 87 45W
lark County ◇, Ind. 22 38 30N 85 40W
lark County ◇, Kans. 24 37 15N 99 45W
lark County ◇, Ky. 49 38 0N 84 10W
lark County ◇, Mo. 32 40 25N 91 40W
lark County ◇, Nev. 35 36 10N 115 10W
lark County ◇, Ohio 42 39 55N 83 49W
lark County ◇, S. Dak. 47 44 50N 97 44W
lark County ◇, Wash. 53 45 55N 122 25W
lark County ◇, Wis. 55 44 40N 90 40W
lark Fork 20 48 9N 116 11W
lark Fork → 20 48 9N 116 15W
lark Hill L. 18 33 40N 82 12W
lark Mt. 15 35 32N 115 35W
lark National Forest 32 37 40N 92 10W
larkdale 12 34 46N 112 3W
larke, I. 127 40 32 S 148 10 E
larke City 61 50 12N 66 38W
larke County ◇, Ala. 10 31 42N 87 47W
larke County ◇, Ga. 18 34 0N 83 15W
larke County ◇, Iowa 23 41 0N 93 45W
larke County ◇, Miss. 31 32 2N 88 44W
larke County ◇, Va. 54 39 9N 77 59W
larke L. 63 54 24N 106 54W
larkesville 18 34 37N 83 31W
larkfield 30 44 48N 95 48W
larkia 20 47 1N 116 15W
larkrange 49 36 11N 85 1W
larks, La. 25 32 2N 92 8W
larks, Nebr. 34 41 13N 97 50W
larks Fork → 33 45 32N 108 50W
larks Grove 30 43 46N 93 20W
lark's Harbour 61 43 25N 65 38W
larks Hill 22 40 15N 86 43W
larks Point 11 58 51N 158 33W
larks Summit 45 41 30N 75 42W
larksburg, Calif. 14 38 25N 121 32W
larksburg, Mo. 32 38 40N 92 40W
larksburg, N.J. 37 40 12N 74 27W
larksburg, W. Va. 54 39 17N 80 30W
larksdale, Miss. 31 34 12N 90 35W
larksdale, Mo. 32 39 49N 94 33W
larkson, Ky. 48 37 30N 86 13W
larkson, Nebr. 34 41 43N 97 7W
larkston, Utah 52 41 55N 112 3W
larkston, Wash. 53 46 25N 117 3W
larksville, Ark. 13 35 28N 93 28W
larksville, Ind. 22 38 17N 85 45W
larksville, Iowa 23 42 47N 92 40W
larksville, Md. 27 39 12N 76 57W
larksville, Mich. 29 42 50N 85 15W
larksville, Mo. 32 39 22N 90 54W
larksville, Ohio 42 39 24N 83 59W
larksville, Tenn. 48 36 32N 87 21W
larksville, Tex. 51 33 37N 95 3W
larksville, Va. 54 36 37N 78 34W
larkton 40 34 29N 78 39W
laro → 75 19 8 S 50 40W
latonia 34 40 28N 96 51W
latskanie 44 46 6N 123 12W
latsop County ◇ 44 46 0N 123 40W
laude 50 35 7N 101 22W
laveria 111 18 37N 121 4 E
laxton 18 32 10N 81 55W
lay 54 38 28N 81 5W
lay Center, Kans. 24 39 23N 97 8W
lay Center, Nebr. 34 40 32N 98 3W
lay City, Ill. 21 38 41N 88 21W
lay City, Ind. 22 39 17N 87 7W
Clay City, Ky. 49 37 52N 83 55W
Clay County ◇, Ala. 10 33 16N 85 50W
Clay County ◇, Ark. 13 36 19N 90 36W
Clay County ◇, Fla. 17 30 0N 81 45W
Clay County ◇, Ga. 18 31 30N 85 0W
Clay County ◇, Ill. 21 38 45N 88 30W
Clay County ◇, Ind. 22 39 20N 87 10W
Clay County ◇, Iowa 23 43 5N 95 10W
Clay County ◇, Kans. 24 39 20N 97 10W
Clay County ◇, Ky. 49 37 10N 83 45W
Clay County ◇, Minn. 30 46 50N 96 30W
Clay County ◇, Miss. 31 33 36N 88 39W
Clay County ◇, Mo. 32 39 20N 94 20W
Clay County ◇, N.C. 40 35 5N 83 45W
Clay County ◇, Nebr. 34 40 30N 98 0W
Clay County ◇, S. Dak. 47 43 0N 97 0W
Clay County ◇, Tenn. 49 36 33N 85 30W
Clay County ◇, Tex. 51 33 49N 98 12W
Clay County ◇, W. Va. 54 38 28N 81 5W
Clay Springs 12 34 22N 110 18W
Claymont 27 39 48N 75 27W
Claypool, Ariz. 12 33 25N 110 51W
Claypool, Ind. 22 41 8N 85 53W
Claysville 45 40 7N 80 25W
Clayton, Ala. 10 31 53N 85 27W
Clayton, Del. 27 39 17N 75 38W
Clayton, Ga. 18 34 53N 83 23W
Clayton, Idaho 20 44 16N 114 24W
Clayton, Ill. 21 40 2N 90 54W
Clayton, Ind. 22 39 41N 86 31W
Clayton, Iowa 23 42 54N 91 9W
Clayton, Kans. 24 39 44N 100 11W
Clayton, La. 25 31 43N 91 33W
Clayton, Mo. 32 38 39N 90 20W
Clayton, N.C. 40 35 39N 78 28W
Clayton, N.J. 37 39 40N 75 6W
Clayton, N. Mex. 38 36 27N 103 11W
Clayton, N.Y. 39 44 14N 76 5W
Clayton, Okla. 43 34 35N 95 21W
Clayton, Wis. 55 45 20N 92 10W
Clayton County ◇, Ga. 18 33 30N 84 20W
Clayton County ◇, Iowa 23 42 50N 91 20W
Clayton Lake 26 46 36N 69 32W
Claytor L. 54 37 5N 80 35W
Cle Elum 53 47 12N 120 56W
Clear → 12 34 59N 110 38W
Clear, C. 85 51 26N 9 30W
Clear Boggy Cr. → 43 34 3N 95 47W
Clear Cr. → 56 44 53N 106 4W
Clear Creek County ◇ 16 39 40N 105 40W
Clear I. 85 51 26N 9 30W
Clear L., Calif. 14 39 2N 122 47W
Clear L., Iowa 23 43 8N 93 26W
Clear L., La. 25 31 53N 93 0W
Clear L., Utah 52 39 7N 112 38W
Clear Lake, Iowa 23 43 8N 93 23W
Clear Lake, Minn. 30 45 27N 94 0W
Clear Lake, Okla. 43 36 41N 100 16W
Clear Lake, S. Dak. 47 44 45N 96 41W
Clear Lake, Wis. 55 45 15N 92 16W
Clear Lake Reservoir 14 41 56N 121 5W
Clear Spring 27 39 39N 77 56W
Clearbrook 30 47 42N 95 26W
Clearco 54 38 6N 80 34W
Clearfield, Iowa 23 40 48N 94 29W
Clearfield, Pa. 45 41 2N 78 27W
Clearfield, Utah 52 41 7N 112 2W
Clearfield County ◇ 45 41 0N 78 35W
Clearlake Highlands 14 38 57N 122 38W
Clearmont, Mo. 32 40 31N 95 2W
Clearmont, Wyo. 56 44 38N 106 23W
Clearwater, Canada 62 51 38N 120 2W
Clearwater, Fla. 17 27 58N 82 48W
Clearwater, Kans. 24 37 30N 97 30W
Clearwater, Nebr. 34 42 10N 98 11W
Clearwater →, Alta., Canada 62 52 22N 114 57W
Clearwater →, Alta., Canada 63 56 44N 111 23W
Clearwater →, Idaho 20 46 31N 116 33W
Clearwater →, Minn. 30 47 54N 96 16W
Clearwater County ◇, Idaho 20 46 50N 115 30W
Clearwater County ◇, Minn. 30 47 30N 95 20W
Clearwater Cr. 62 61 36N 125 30W
Clearwater L. 32 37 8N 90 47W
Clearwater Mts. 20 46 5N 115 20W
Clearwater National Forest 20 46 40N 115 5W
Clearwater Prov. Park 63 54 0N 101 0W
Cleburne 51 32 21N 97 23W
Cleburne County ◇, Ala. 10 33 39N 85 35W
Cleburne County ◇, Ark. 13 35 30N 92 2W
Cleethorpes 82 53 33N 0 2W
Cleeve Cloud 83 51 56N 2 0W
Clem 18 33 32N 85 1W
Clements, Kans. 24 38 18N 96 44W
Clements, Md. 27 38 18N 76 43W
Clements, Minn. 30 44 23N 95 3W
Clemson 46 34 41N 82 50W
Clendenin 54 38 29N 81 21W
Cleo Springs 43 36 26N 98 29W
Clerks Rocks 5 56 0 S 34 30W
Clermont, Australia 127 22 49 S 147 39 E
Clermont, Fla. 17 28 33N 81 46W
Clermont, Iowa 23 43 0N 91 39W
Clermont, N.J. 37 39 59N 74 48W
Clermont County ◇ 42 39 5N 84 11W
Clermont-Ferrand 90 45 46N 3 4 E
Clervaux 87 50 4N 6 2 E
Cleveland, Ga. 18 34 36N 83 46W
Cleveland, Minn. 30 44 19N 93 50W
Cleveland, Miss. 31 33 45N 90 43W
Cleveland, N. Dak. 41 46 54N 99 6W
Cleveland, Ohio 42 41 30N 81 42W
Cleveland, Okla. 43 36 19N 96 28W
Cleveland, S.C. 46 35 4N 82 31W
Cleveland, Tenn. 49 35 10N 84 53W
Cleveland, Tex. 51 30 21N 95 5W
Cleveland, Utah 52 39 21N 110 51W
Cleveland, Va. 54 36 57N 82 9W
Cleveland, Wis. 55 43 55N 87 45W
Cleveland □ 82 54 35N 1 8 E
Cleveland, C. 127 19 11 S 147 1 E
Cleveland, Mt. 33 48 56N 113 51W
Cleveland County ◇, Ark. 13 33 58N 92 11W
Cleveland County ◇, N.C. 40 35 20N 81 40W
Cleveland County ◇, Okla. 43 35 10N 97 20W
Cleveland Heights 42 41 30N 81 34W
Cleveland National Forest 15 32 45N 116 40W
Clevelândia 77 26 24 S 52 23W
Clevelândia do Norte 71 3 49N 51 52W
Clever 32 37 2N 93 28W
Clew B. 85 53 54N 9 50W
Clewiston 17 26 45N 80 56W
Clifden, Ireland 85 53 30N 10 2W
Clifden, N.Z. 128 46 1 S 167 42 E
Clifford, Mich. 29 43 19N 83 11W
Clifford, N. Dak. 41 47 21N 97 24W
Cliffside 40 35 14N 81 46W
Clifftop 54 38 0N 80 56W
Clifton, Ariz. 12 33 3N 109 18W
Clifton, Colo. 16 39 7N 108 25W
Clifton, Idaho 20 42 11N 112 0W
Clifton, Ill. 21 40 56N 87 56W
Clifton, Kans. 24 39 34N 97 17W
Clifton, N.J. 37 40 53N 74 9W
Clifton, Tenn. 48 35 18N 88 1W
Clifton, Tex. 51 31 47N 97 35W
Clifton Forge 54 37 49N 79 50W
Clifton Springs 39 42 58N 77 8W
Clifty 13 36 14N 93 48W
Climax, Canada 63 49 10N 108 20W
Climax, Colo. 16 39 22N 106 11W
Climax, Ga. 18 30 53N 84 26W
Climax, Kans. 24 37 43N 96 13W
Climax, Mich. 29 42 14N 85 20W
Climax, Minn. 30 47 37N 96 49W
Clinch → 49 35 53N 84 29W
Clinch County ◇ 18 31 0N 82 45W
Clinchco 54 37 10N 82 22W
Cline 51 29 15N 100 5W
Clines Corners 38 35 1N 105 40W
Clingmans Dome 49 35 34N 83 30W
Clint 50 31 35N 106 14W
Clinton, B.C., Canada 62 51 6N 121 35W
Clinton, Ont., Canada 60 43 37N 81 32W
Clinton, N.Z. 128 46 12 S 169 23 E
Clinton, Ala. 10 32 58N 88 0W
Clinton, Ark. 13 35 36N 92 28W
Clinton, Conn. 28 41 17N 72 32W
Clinton, Ill. 21 40 9N 88 57W
Clinton, Ind. 22 39 40N 87 24W
Clinton, Iowa 23 41 51N 90 12W
Clinton, Ky. 48 36 40N 89 0W
Clinton, La. 25 30 52N 91 1W
Clinton, Maine 26 44 38N 69 30W
Clinton, Mass. 28 42 25N 71 41W
Clinton, Md. 27 38 46N 76 54W
Clinton, Mich. 29 42 4N 83 58W
Clinton, Minn. 30 45 28N 96 26W
Clinton, Miss. 31 32 20N 90 20W
Clinton, Mo. 32 38 22N 93 46W
Clinton, Mont. 33 46 46N 113 43W
Clinton, N.C. 40 35 0N 78 22W
Clinton, N.J. 37 40 38N 74 55W
Clinton, N.Y. 39 43 3N 75 23W
Clinton, Ohio 42 40 56N 81 38W
Clinton, Okla. 43 35 31N 98 58W
Clinton, S.C. 46 34 29N 81 53W
Clinton, Tenn. 49 36 6N 84 8W
Clinton, Wash. 53 47 59N 122 21W
Clinton, Wis. 55 42 34N 88 52W
Clinton Colden L. 58 63 58N 107 27W
Clinton County ◇, Ill. 21 38 35N 89 25W
Clinton County ◇, Ind. 22 40 20N 86 30W
Clinton County ◇, Iowa 23 41 55N 90 30W
Clinton County ◇, Ky. 49 36 45N 85 10W
Clinton County ◇, Mich. 29 42 55N 84 40W
Clinton County ◇, Mo. 32 39 35N 94 25W
Clinton County ◇, N.Y. 39 44 50N 73 40W
Clinton County ◇, Ohio 42 39 27N 83 50W
Clinton County ◇, Pa. 45 41 10N 77 50W
Clinton L. 21 40 15N 88 45W
Clintonville, W. Va. 54 37 54N 80 36W
Clintonville, Wis. 55 44 37N 88 46W
Clintwood 54 37 9N 82 28W
Clio, Ala. 10 31 37N 85 37W
Clio, Iowa 23 40 38N 93 27W
Clio, Mich. 29 43 11N 83 44W
Clio, S.C. 46 34 35N 79 33W
Clipperton, I. 125 10 18N 109 13W
Clipperton Fracture Zone 125 19 0N 122 0W
Clive L. 62 63 13N 118 54W
Cliza 73 17 36 S 65 56W
Cloates, Pt. 126 22 43 S 113 40 E
Clodomira 76 27 35 S 64 14W
Clonakilty 85 51 37N 8 53W
Clonakilty B. 85 51 33N 8 50W
Cloncurry 127 20 40 S 140 28 E
Clones 85 54 10N 7 13W
Clonmel 85 52 22N 7 42W
Clontarf 30 45 23N 95 40W
Cloquet 30 46 43N 92 28W
Cloquet → 30 46 52N 92 35W
Clorinda 76 25 16 S 57 45W
Cloud County ◇ 24 39 30N 97 45W
Cloud Peak 56 44 23N 107 11W
Cloudcroft 38 32 58N 105 45W
Clover, S.C. 46 35 7N 81 14W
Clover, Va. 54 36 50N 78 44W
Cloverdale, Ala. 10 34 56N 87 46W
Cloverdale, Calif. 14 38 48N 123 1W
Cloverdale, Ind. 22 39 31N 86 48W
Cloverdale, Ohio 42 41 1N 84 18W
Cloverleaf 51 29 46N 95 10W
Cloverport 48 37 50N 86 38W
Clovis, Calif. 15 36 49N 119 42W
Clovis, N. Mex. 38 34 24N 103 12W
Cluj-Napoca 89 46 47N 23 38 E
Cluny 90 46 26N 4 38 E
Clute 51 29 1N 95 24W
Clutha → 128 46 20 S 169 49 E
Clutier 23 42 4N 92 24W
Clwyd □ 82 53 5N 3 20W
Clwyd → 82 53 20N 3 30W
Clyattville 18 30 42N 83 19W
Clyde, N.Z. 128 45 12 S 169 20 E
Clyde, Kans. 24 39 36N 97 24W
Clyde, N.C. 40 35 32N 82 55W
Clyde, N.Y. 39 43 5N 76 52W
Clyde, Ohio 42 41 18N 82 59W
Clyde, Tex. 51 32 24N 99 30W
Clyde, Vt. 36 44 56N 73 0W
Clyde → 84 55 56N 4 29W
Clyde, Firth of 84 55 20N 5 0W
Clyde River 59 70 30N 68 30W
Clydebank 84 55 54N 4 25W
Clymer 45 40 40N 79 1W
Clyo 18 32 29N 81 16W
Co-Operative 49 36 42N 84 37W
Coachella 15 33 41N 116 10W
Coachella Canal 15 32 43N 114 57W
Coahoma 50 32 18N 101 18W
Coahoma County ◇ 31 34 12N 90 35W
Coahuayana → 64 18 41N 103 45W
Coahuayutla 64 18 19N 101 42W
Coahuila de Zaragoza □ 64 27 0N 103 0W
Coal → 62 59 39N 126 57W
Coal City 21 41 17N 88 17W
Coal County ◇ 43 34 40N 96 15W
Coal Grove 42 38 30N 82 39W
Coal Hill 13 35 26N 93 40W
Coalcomán 64 18 40N 103 10W
Coaldale, Canada 62 49 45N 112 35W
Coaldale, U.S.A. 16 38 22N 105 45W
Coalgate 43 34 32N 96 13W
Coaling 10 33 10N 87 20W
Coalinga 15 36 9N 120 21W
Coalmont, Colo. 16 40 34N 106 27W
Coalmont, Tenn. 49 35 20N 85 42W
Coalport 45 40 45N 78 32W
Coalville, U.K. 82 52 43N 1 21W
Coalville, U.S.A. 52 40 55N 111 24W
Coamo 57 18 5N 66 22W
Coaraci 75 14 38 S 39 32W
Coari 71 4 8 S 63 7W
Coari → 71 4 30 S 63 33W
Coari, L. de 71 4 15 S 63 22W
Coarsegold 14 37 16N 119 42W
Coast Mts. 62 55 0N 129 0W
Coast Ranges 44 44 0N 123 40W
Coastal Plains Basin 126 30 10 S 115 30 E
Coatbridge 84 55 52N 4 2W
Coatepec 65 19 27N 96 58W
Coatepeque 66 14 46N 91 55W
Coates 30 44 43N 93 2W
Coatesville 45 39 59N 75 50W
Coaticook 61 45 10N 71 46W
Coats, Kans. 24 37 31N 98 50W
Coats, N.C. 40 35 25N 78 40W
Coats I. 59 62 30N 83 0W
Coats Land 5 77 0 S 25 0W
Coatzacoalcos 65 18 7N 94 25W
Cobadin 95 44 5N 28 13 E
Cobalt, Canada 60 47 25N 79 42W
Cobalt, U.S.A. 20 45 6N 114 14W
Cobán 66 15 30N 90 21W
Cobar 127 31 27 S 145 48 E
Cobb 48 36 59N 87 47W
Cobb County ◇ 18 33 50N 84 40W
Cobb Island 27 38 16N 76 51W
Cobden, Ill. 21 37 32N 89 15W
Cobden, Minn. 30 44 17N 94 51W
Cóbh 85 51 50N 8 18W
Cobija 72 11 0 S 68 50W
Cobleskill 39 42 41N 74 29W
Cobourg 60 43 58N 78 10W
Cobourg Pen. 126 11 20 S 132 15 E
Cobre 35 41 7N 114 24W

enamed Mark Twain Lake
ow part of Mark Twain Nat. Forest

Cóbué Concepción

Cóbué 123 12 0 S 34 58 E
Coburg, Germany 88 50 15N 10 58 E
Coburg, U.S.A. 23 40 55N 95 16W
Coburn Mt. 26 45 28N 70 6W
Coca → 70 0 29 S 76 58W
Cocachacra 72 17 5 S 71 45W
Cocal 74 3 28 S 41 34W
Cocanada = Kakinada 109 16 57N 82 11 E
Cocha, La 76 27 50 S 65 40W
Cochabamba 73 17 26 S 66 10W
Coche, I. 71 10 47N 63 56W
Cochin 108 9 59N 76 22 E
Cochin China = Nam-Phan 112 10 30N 106 0 E
Cochise 12 32 7N 109 55W
Cochise County ◇ 12 32 0N 109 30W
Cochran 18 32 23N 83 21W
Cochran County ◇ 50 33 37N 102 48W
Cochrane, Alta., Canada 62 51 11N 114 30W
Cochrane, Ont., Canada 60 49 0N 81 0W
Cochrane, Ala. 10 33 4N 88 15W
Cochrane, Wis. 55 44 14N 91 50W
Cochrane → 63 59 0N 103 40W
Cochrane, L. 78 47 10 S 72 0W
Cochranton 45 41 31N 80 3W
Cockatoo I. 126 16 6 S 123 37 E
Cockburn, Canal 78 54 30 S 72 0W
Cockburn I. 60 45 55N 83 22W
Cocke County ◇ 49 35 58N 83 11W
Cockeysville 27 39 29N 76 39W
Coco → 66 15 0N 83 8W
Coco, Pta. 70 2 58N 77 43W
Coco Chan. 112 13 50N 93 25 E
Coco Solo 57 9 22N 79 53W
Cocoa 17 28 21N 80 44W
Cocoa Beach 17 28 19N 80 37W
Cocobeach 122 0 59N 9 34 E
Cocolalla 20 48 6N 116 37W
Coconino County ◇ 12 36 0N 112 0W
Coconino National Forest 12 34 45N 111 20W
Coconino Plateau 12 35 45N 112 40W
Cocora 95 44 45N 27 3 E
Côcos 75 14 10 S 44 33W
Côcos → 75 12 44 S 44 48W
Cocos I. 125 5 25N 87 55W
Cocos Is. 124 12 10 S 96 55 E
Cod, C. 28 42 5N 70 10W
Codajás 71 3 55 S 62 0W
Codera, C. 70 10 35N 66 4W
Coderre 63 50 11N 106 31W
Codington County ◇ 47 44 54N 97 7W
Codó 74 4 30 S 43 55W
Codpa 72 18 50 S 69 44W
Cody, Nebr. 34 42 56N 101 15W
Cody, Wyo. 56 44 32N 109 3W
Coe Hill 60 44 52N 77 50W
Coeburn 54 36 57N 82 28W
Coelemu 76 36 30 S 72 48W
Coelho Neto 74 4 15 S 43 0W
Coen 127 13 52 S 143 12 E
Coeroeni → 71 3 21N 57 31W
Coeur d' Alene 20 47 41N 116 46W
Coeur d' Alene Indian Reservation 20 47 10N 116 55W
Coeur d' Alene L. 20 47 32N 116 49W
Coeur d' Alene National Forest 20 47 55N 116 15W
Coeur d'Alene → 20 47 45N 116 0W
Coevorden 87 52 40N 6 44 E
Coffee County ◇, Ala. 10 31 23N 85 56W
Coffee County ◇, Ga. 18 31 30N 82 50W
Coffee County ◇, Tenn. 48 35 29N 86 5W
Coffeen 21 39 5N 89 24W
Coffeeville, Ala. 10 31 45N 88 5W
Coffeeville, Miss. 31 33 59N 89 41W
Coffey 32 40 6N 94 0W
Coffey County ◇ 24 38 15N 95 45W
Coffeyville 24 37 2N 95 37W
Coffs Harbour 127 30 16 S 153 5 E
Cofield 40 36 21N 76 54W
Cofre de Perote, Cerro 65 19 30N 97 10W
Cogar 43 35 20N 98 8W
Cogdell 18 31 10N 82 43W
Cogealac 95 44 36N 28 36 E
Coggon 23 42 17N 91 32W
Coghinas → 94 40 55N 8 48 E
Cognac 90 45 41N 0 20W
Cogswell 41 46 7N 97 47W
Cohagen 33 47 3N 106 37W
Cohansey 37 39 21N 75 22W
Cohasset 28 42 14N 70 48W
Cohocton → 39 42 9N 77 6W
Cohoes 39 42 46N 73 42W
Cohutta 18 34 58N 84 57W
Coiba, I. 66 7 30N 81 40W
Coig → 78 51 0 S 69 10W
Coihaique 78 45 30 S 71 45W
Coimbatore 108 11 2N 76 59 E
Coimbra, Brazil 72 19 55 S 57 48W
Coimbra, Portugal 91 40 15N 8 27W
Coín, Spain 91 36 40N 4 48W
Coin, U.S.A. 23 40 40N 95 14W
Coipasa, L. de 72 19 12 S 68 7W
Coipasa, Salar de 72 19 26 S 68 9W
Cojata 72 15 2 S 69 25W
Cojedes □ 70 9 20N 68 20W
Cojedes → 70 8 34N 68 5W
Cojimies 72 0 20N 80 0W
Cojutepequé 66 13 41N 88 54W
Cokato 30 45 5N 94 11W
Coke County ◇ 50 31 54N 100 29W
Coker 10 33 15N 87 41W
Cokeville 56 42 5N 110 57W
Colac 127 38 21 S 143 35 E
Colatina 75 19 32 S 40 37W
Colbeck, C. 5 77 6 S 157 48W
Colbert, Ga. 18 34 2N 83 13W
Colbert, Okla. 43 33 51N 96 30W
Colbert County ◇ 10 34 44N 87 42W
Colbourne 27 38 15N 75 26W
Colburn 20 48 24N 116 32W
Colby, Kans. 24 39 24N 101 3W
Colby, Wis. 55 44 55N 90 19W
Colchagua □ 76 34 30 S 71 0W
Colchester, U.K. 83 51 54N 0 55 E
Colchester, Conn. 28 41 35N 72 20W
Colchester, Ill. 21 40 25N 90 48W
Colcord 43 36 16N 94 42W
Cold Bay 11 55 12N 162 42W
Cold Mt. 40 35 25N 82 51W
Cold Spring, Minn. 30 45 27N 94 26W
Cold Spring, N.Y. 39 41 25N 73 57W
Cold Springs Cr. → 56 44 32N 104 6W
Coldspring 51 30 36N 95 8W
Coldstream 84 55 39N 2 14W
Coldwater, Kans. 24 37 16N 99 20W
Coldwater, Mich. 29 41 57N 85 0W
Coldwater, Miss. 31 34 41N 89 59W
Coldwater, Ohio 42 40 29N 84 38W
Coldwater → 31 34 10N 90 13W
Coldwater Cr. → 43 36 40N 101 10W
Cole 43 35 8N 97 33W
Cole Camp 32 38 28N 93 12W
Cole County ◇ 32 38 30N 92 15W
Colebrook 36 44 54N 71 30W
Coleman, Canada 62 49 40N 114 30W
Coleman, Fla. 17 28 48N 82 4W
Coleman, Ga. 18 31 40N 84 54W
Coleman, Mich. 29 43 46N 84 35W
Coleman, Okla. 43 34 16N 96 25W
Coleman, Tex. 51 31 50N 99 26W
Coleman, Wis. 55 45 4N 88 2W
Coleman → 127 15 6 S 141 38 E
Coleman County ◇ 51 31 50N 99 30W
Colerain 40 36 12N 76 46W
Coleraine, U.K. 85 55 8N 6 40 E
Coleraine, U.S.A. 30 47 17N 93 27W
Coleraine □ 85 55 8N 6 40 E
Coleridge, N.C. 40 35 39N 79 37W
Coleridge, Nebr. 34 42 30N 97 13W
Coleridge, L. 128 43 17 S 171 30 E
Coles 31 31 17N 91 2W
Coles County ◇ 21 39 30N 88 15W
Colesberg 123 30 45 S 25 5 E
Colesburg 23 42 38N 91 12W
Coleville 14 38 34N 119 30W
Colfax, Calif. 14 39 6N 120 57W
Colfax, Ill. 21 40 34N 88 37W
Colfax, Ind. 22 40 12N 86 40W
Colfax, Iowa 23 41 41N 93 14W
Colfax, La. 25 31 31N 92 42W
Colfax, N. Dak. 41 46 28N 96 53W
Colfax, Wash. 53 46 53N 117 22W
Colfax, Wis. 55 45 0N 91 44W
Colfax County ◇, N. Mex. 38 36 30N 104 30W
Colfax County ◇, Nebr. 34 41 30N 97 0W
Colgate 41 47 15N 97 39W
Colhué Huapi, L. 78 45 30 S 69 0W
Colima 64 19 10N 103 40W
Colima □ 64 19 10N 103 40W
Colima, Nevado de 64 19 35N 103 45W
Colina 76 33 13 S 70 45W
Colinas, Goiás, Brazil 75 14 15 S 48 2W
Colinas, Maranhão, Brazil 74 6 0 S 44 10W
Coll 84 56 40N 6 35W
Collaguasi 76 21 5 S 68 45W
Collbran 16 39 14N 107 58W
College 11 64 52N 147 49W
College Corner 42 39 34N 84 49W
College Heights 13 33 35N 91 48W
College Park, Fla. 17 29 53N 81 21W
College Park, Ga. 18 33 40N 84 27W
College Park, Md. 27 38 59N 76 56W
College Place 53 46 3N 118 23W
College Station 51 30 37N 96 21W
Collegedale 49 35 4N 85 3W
Collegeville 22 40 56N 87 9W
Colleton County ◇ 46 33 0N 80 40W
Collette 61 46 40N 65 30W
Collettsville 40 35 56N 81 41W
Colleyville 51 32 53N 97 9W
Collie 126 33 22 S 116 8 E
Collier B. 126 16 10 S 124 15 E
Collier County ◇ 17 26 0N 81 30W
Collierville 48 35 3N 89 40W
Collin County ◇ 51 33 6N 96 40W
Collingsworth County ◇ 50 35 0N 100 15W
Collingwood, Canada 60 44 29N 80 13W
Collingwood, N.Z. 128 40 41 S 172 40 E
Collins, Canada 60 50 17N 89 27W
Collins, Ark. 13 33 32N 91 34W
Collins, Ga. 18 32 11N 82 7W
Collins, Iowa 23 41 54N 93 18W
Collins, Miss. 31 31 39N 89 33W
Collins, Mo. 32 37 54N 93 37W
Collinston 25 32 41N 91 52W
Collinsville, Australia 127 20 30 S 147 56 E
Collinsville, Ala. 10 34 16N 85 52W
Collinsville, Conn. 28 41 49N 72 55W
Collinsville, Ill. 21 38 40N 89 59W
Collinsville, Miss. 31 32 30N 88 51W
Collinsville, Okla. 43 36 22N 95 51W
Collinsville, Tex. 51 33 34N 96 55W
Collinsville, Va. 54 36 43N 79 55W
Collinwood 48 35 10N 87 44W
Collipulli 76 37 55 S 72 30W
Collison 21 40 14N 87 48W
Collooney 85 54 11N 8 28W
Collyer 24 39 2N 100 7W
Colman 47 43 59N 96 49W
Colmar 90 48 5N 7 20 E
Colmesneil 51 30 54N 94 25W
Colne 82 53 51N 2 11W
Cologne = Köln 88 50 56N 6 58 E
Coloma, Calif. 14 38 48N 120 53W
Coloma, Mich. 29 42 11N 86 19W
Coloma, Wis. 55 44 2N 89 31W
Colomb-Béchar = Béchar 120 31 38N 2 18W
Colômbia 75 20 10 S 48 40W
Colombia ■ 70 3 45N 73 0W
Colombo 108 6 56N 79 58 E
Colome 47 43 16N 99 43W
Colón, Argentina 76 32 12 S 58 10W
Colón, Cuba 66 22 42N 80 54W
Colón, Panama 57 9 22N 79 54W
Colón, Peru 72 5 0 S 81 0W
Colon, Mich. 29 41 57N 85 19W
Colon, N.C. 40 35 32N 79 2W
Colon, Nebr. 34 41 18N 96 37W
Colona 16 38 20N 107 47W
Colonia 76 34 25 S 57 50W
Colonia Dora 76 28 34 S 62 59W
Colonial Beach 54 38 15N 76 58W
Colonial Heights 54 37 15N 77 25W
Colonie 39 42 43N 73 50W
Colonsay, Canada 63 51 59N 105 52W
Colonsay, U.K. 84 56 4N 6 12W
Colony, Kans. 24 38 4N 95 22W
Colony, Okla. 43 35 23N 98 41W
Colorado □ 16 39 30N 105 30W
Colorado →, Argentina 78 39 50 S 62 8W
Colorado →, Oreg. 44 44 0N 117 30W
Colorado →, Tex. 51 28 36N 95 59W
Colorado City, Ariz. 12 36 59N 112 59W
Colorado City, Tex. 50 32 24N 100 52W
Colorado County ◇ 51 29 42N 96 33W
Colorado I. 57 9 12N 79 50W
Colorado Plateau 12 37 0N 111 0W
Colorado River Aqueduct 15 33 50N 117 23W
Colorado River Ind. Res. 12 34 0N 114 25W
Colorado River Indian Reservation 12 33 50N 114 30W
Colorado Springs 16 38 50N 104 49W
Colotlán 64 22 6N 103 16W
Colquechaca 73 18 40 S 66 1W
Colquitt 18 31 10N 84 44W
Colquitt County ◇ 18 31 15N 83 50W
Colrain 28 42 41N 72 42W
Colstrip 33 45 53N 106 38W
Colt 13 35 8N 90 49W
Colter Peak 56 44 18N 110 7W
Colton, Calif. 15 34 4N 117 20W
Colton, N.Y. 39 44 33N 74 56W
Colton, S. Dak. 47 43 47N 96 56W
Colton, Wash. 53 46 34N 117 8W
Colts Neck 37 40 17N 74 11W
Columbia, Ala. 10 31 18N 85 7W
Columbia, Ill. 21 38 27N 90 12W
Columbia, Ky. 49 37 6N 85 18W
Columbia, La. 25 32 6N 92 5W
Columbia, Md. 27 39 14N 76 50W
Columbia, Miss. 31 31 15N 89 50W
Columbia, Mo. 32 38 57N 92 20W
Columbia, N.C. 40 35 55N 76 15W
Columbia, N.J. 37 40 56N 75 6W
Columbia, Pa. 45 40 2N 76 30W
Columbia, S.C. 46 34 0N 81 2W
Columbia, S. Dak. 47 45 37N 98 19W
Columbia, Tenn. 48 35 37N 87 2W
Columbia → 53 46 15N 124 5W
Columbia, C. 4 83 0N 70 0W
Columbia, Mt. 62 52 8N 117 20W
Columbia Basin 53 46 45N 119 5W
Columbia City, Ind. 22 41 10N 85 29W
Columbia City, Oreg. 44 45 53N 122 49W
Columbia County ◇, Ark. 13 33 16N 93 14W
Columbia County ◇, Fla. 17 30 15N 82 40W
Columbia County ◇, Ga. 18 33 30N 82 10W
Columbia County ◇, N.Y. 39 42 10N 73 40W
Columbia County ◇, Oreg. 44 45 55N 123 0W
Columbia County ◇, Pa. 45 41 10N 76 20W
Columbia County ◇, Wash. 53 46 19N 117 59W
Columbia County ◇, Wis. 55 43 30N 89 20W
Columbia Falls, Maine 26 44 39N 67 44W
Columbia Falls, Mont. 33 48 23N 114 11W
Columbia Heights 30 45 3N 93 15W
Columbia Road Reservoir 47 45 40N 98 18W
Columbiana, Ala. 10 33 11N 86 36W
Columbiana, Ohio 42 40 53N 80 42W
Columbiana County ◇ 42 40 46N 80 46W
Columbiaville 29 43 9N 83 25W
Columbine 16 40 56N 106 59W
Columbretes, Is. 91 39 50N 0 50 E
Columbus, Ga. 18 32 28N 84 59W
Columbus, Ind. 22 39 13N 85 55W
Columbus, Kans. 24 37 10N 94 50W
Columbus, Ky. 48 36 46N 89 6W
Columbus, Miss. 31 33 30N 88 25W
Columbus, Mont. 33 45 38N 109 15W
Columbus, N.C. 40 35 15N 82 12W
Columbus, N. Dak. 41 48 54N 102 47W
Columbus, N. Mex. 38 31 50N 107 38W
Columbus, Nebr. 34 41 26N 97 22W
Columbus, Ohio 42 39 58N 83 0W
Columbus, Tex. 51 29 42N 96 33W
Columbus, Wis. 55 43 21N 89 1W
Columbus County ◇ 40 34 15N 78 45W
Columbus Grove 42 40 55N 84 4W
Columbus Junction 23 41 17N 91 22W
Columbus Salt Marsh 35 38 5N 118 5W
Colusa 14 39 13N 122 1W
Colusa County ◇ 14 39 15N 122 15W
Colville 53 48 33N 117 54W
Colville →, Alaska 11 70 25N 150 30W
Colville →, Wash. 53 48 37N 118 5W
Colville, C. 128 36 29 S 175 21 E
Colville Indian Reservation 53 48 15N 119 0W
Colville National Forest 53 48 30N 117 15W
Colwell 23 43 9N 92 36W
Colwich 24 37 47N 97 32W
Colwyn Bay 82 53 17N 3 44W
Comácchio 94 44 41N 12 10 E
Comal County ◇ 51 29 53N 98 25W
Comalcalco 65 18 16N 93 13W
Comallo 78 41 0 S 70 5W
Comana 95 44 10N 26 10 E
Comanche, Okla. 43 34 22N 97 58W
Comanche, Tex. 51 31 54N 98 36W
Comanche County ◇, Kans. 24 37 15N 99 15W
Comanche County ◇, Okla. 43 34 40N 98 25W
Comanche County ◇, Tex. 51 31 55N 98 35W
Comanche National Grassland 16 37 20N 103 0W
Comandante Luis Piedrabuena 78 49 59 S 68 54W
Comăneşti 95 46 25N 26 26 E
Comarapa 73 17 54 S 64 29W
Comayagua 66 14 25N 87 37W
Comblain-au-Pont 87 50 29N 5 35 E
Comer, Ala. 10 32 2N 85 23W
Comer, Ga. 18 34 4N 83 8W
Comeragh Mts. 85 52 17N 7 35W
Comerio 57 18 13N 66 14W
Comfort 51 29 58N 98 55W
Comfrey 30 44 7N 94 54W
Comilla 109 23 28N 91 10 E
Comino 94 36 0N 14 20 E
Comitán 65 16 18N 92 9W
Commack 39 40 51N 73 18W
Commerce, Ga. 18 34 12N 83 28W
Commerce, Mo. 32 37 9N 89 27W
Commerce, Okla. 43 36 56N 94 53W
Commerce, Tex. 51 33 15N 95 54W
Commerce City 16 39 49N 104 56W
Commewijne □ 71 5 25N 54 45W
Committee B. 59 68 30N 86 30W
Commonwealth B. 5 67 0 S 144 0 E
Communism Pk. = Kommunizma, Pik 100 39 0N 72 2 E
Como, Italy 94 45 48N 9 5 E
Como, Colo. 16 39 19N 105 54W
Como, Miss. 31 34 31N 89 56W
Como, Tex. 51 33 3N 95 28W
Como, L. di 94 46 5N 9 17 E
Comobabi Mts. 12 32 0N 111 45W
Comodoro Rivadavia 78 45 50 S 67 40W
Comorin, C. 108 8 3N 77 40 E
Comoro Is. ■ 3 12 10 S 44 15 E
Comox 62 49 42N 124 55W
Compass Lake 17 30 36N 85 24W
Competition 32 37 29N 92 26W
Compiègne 90 49 24N 2 50 E
Compostela 64 21 15N 104 53W
Comprida, I. 77 24 50 S 47 42W
Comptche 14 39 16N 123 35W
Compton, Ark. 13 36 6N 93 18W
Compton, Calif. 15 33 54N 118 13W
Comstock, Minn. 30 46 40N 96 45W
Comstock, Nebr. 34 41 34N 99 15W
Comstock, Tex. 50 29 41N 101 10W
Comstock Park 29 43 2N 85 40W
Côn Dao 112 8 45N 106 45 E
Cona Niyeu 78 41 58 S 67 0W
Conakry 120 9 29N 13 49W
Conanicut I. 28 41 32N 71 21W
Conasauga → 18 34 33N 84 55W
Concan 51 29 30N 99 43W
Concarneau 90 47 52N 3 56W
Conceição 74 7 33 S 38 31W
Conceição da Barra 75 18 35 S 39 45W
Conceição do Araguaia 74 8 0 S 49 2W
Conceição do Canindé 74 7 54 S 41 34W
Concepción, Argentina 76 27 20 S 65 35W
Concepción, Bolivia 73 16 15 S 62 8W

Concepción Corumbá

Concepción, Chile 76 36 50S 73 0W
Concepción, Mexico 65 18 15N 90 5W
Concepción, Paraguay 76 23 22S 57 26W
Concepción, Peru 72 11 54S 75 19W
Concepción □ 76 37 0S 72 30W
Concepción → 64 30 32N 113 2W
Concepción, Est. de 78 50 30S 74 55W
Concepción, L. 73 17 20S 61 20W
Concepción, La 70 10 30N 71 50W
Concepción, Punta 64 26 55N 111 59W
Concepción del Oro 64 24 40N 101 30W
Concepción del Uruguay 76 32 35S 58 20W
Conception, Pt. 15 34 27N 120 28W
Conception B. 123 23 55S 14 22E
Conception I. 67 23 52N 75 9W
Conception Junction 32 40 16N 94 42W
Conchas → 38 35 23N 104 18W
Conchas Dam 38 35 22N 104 11W
Conchas Lake 38 35 23N 104 11W
Conche 61 50 55N 55 58W
Concho 12 34 28N 109 36W
Concho → 51 31 34N 99 43W
Concho County ◇ 51 31 13N 99 51W
Conchos →, Chihuahua, Mexico 64 29 32N 104 25W
Conchos →, Tamaulipas, Mexico 65 25 9N 98 35W
Conconully 53 48 34N 119 45W
Concord, Calif. 14 37 59N 122 2W
Concord, Ga. 18 33 5N 84 27W
Concord, Mass. 28 42 28N 71 21W
Concord, Md. 27 38 38N 75 48W
Concord, Mich. 29 42 11N 84 38W
Concord, Mo. 32 38 28N 90 23W
Concord, N.C. 40 35 25N 80 35W
Concord, N.H. 36 43 12N 71 32W
Concord, Tenn. 49 35 52N 84 8W
Concord, Vt. 36 44 26N 71 53W
Concordia, Argentina 76 31 20S 58 2W
Concórdia, Brazil 70 4 36S 66 36W
Concordia, Mexico 64 23 18N 106 2W
Concordia, Kans. 24 39 34N 97 40W
Concordia, Mo. 32 38 59N 93 34W
Concordia, La 65 16 8N 92 38W
Concordia Parish ◇ 25 31 38N 91 33W
Concrete 53 48 32N 121 45W
Conda 20 42 44N 111 32W
Condamine → 127 27 7S 149 48E
Conde, Brazil 75 11 49S 37 37W
Conde, U.S.A. 47 45 9N 98 6W
Condeúba 75 14 52S 42 0W
Condon, Mont. 33 47 34N 113 45W
Condon, Oreg. 44 45 14N 120 11W
Conecuh → 17 30 58N 87 13W
Conecuh County ◇ 10 31 26N 86 57W
Conecuh National Forest 10 31 2N 86 45W
Conejos, Mexico 64 26 14N 103 53W
Conejos, U.S.A. 16 37 5N 106 1W
Conejos → 16 37 18N 105 44W
Conejos County ◇ 16 37 10N 106 10W
Conesville 23 41 23N 91 21W
Confluence 45 39 49N 79 21W
Confusion Range 52 39 20N 113 40W
Confuso → 76 25 9S 57 34W
Congaree → 46 33 44N 80 38W
Conger 30 43 37N 93 32W
Congleton 82 53 10N 2 12W
Congo = Zaïre → 122 6 4S 12 24E
Congo 74 7 48S 36 40W
Congo (Kinshasa) ■ = Zaïre ■ 122 3 0S 23 0E
Congo ■ 122 1 0S 16 0E
Congo Basin 118 0 10S 24 30E
Congonhas 75 20 30S 43 52W
Congress, Ariz. 12 34 9N 112 51W
Congress, Ohio 42 40 56N 82 3W
Conifer 16 39 31N 105 18W
Coniston 60 46 29N 80 51W
Conjeeveram = Kanchipuram 108 12 52N 79 45E
Conklin, Canada 63 55 38N 111 5W
Conklin, U.S.A. 39 42 2N 75 49W
Conlen 50 36 14N 102 15W
Conn, L. 85 54 3N 9 15W
Connacht 85 53 23N 8 40W
Conneaut 42 41 57N 80 34W
Conneaut Lake 45 41 36N 80 18W
Conneautville 45 41 45N 80 22W
Connecticut □ 28 41 30N 72 45W
Connecticut → 28 41 16N 72 20W
Connell 53 46 40N 118 52W
Connellsville 45 40 1N 79 35W
Connemara 85 53 29N 9 45W
Connemaugh → 45 40 28N 79 19W
Conner 33 45 56N 114 7W
Connersville 22 39 39N 85 8W
Connerville 43 34 27N 96 38W
Conon → 84 57 33N 4 28W
Cononaco → 70 1 32S 75 35W
Cononbridge 84 57 32N 4 30W
Conover 40 35 42N 81 13W
Conowingo 27 39 40N 76 11W
Conquest 63 51 32N 107 14W
Conrad, Iowa 23 42 14N 92 52W
Conrad, Mont. 33 48 10N 111 57W
Conrath 55 45 22N 91 2W
Conroe 51 30 19N 95 27W
Conselheiro Lafaiete 75 20 40S 43 48W
Conselheiro Pena 75 19 10S 41 30W
Consort 63 52 1N 110 46W
Constance = Konstanz 88 47 39N 9 10E
Constance, L. = Bodensee 88 47 35N 9 25E
Constanța 89 44 14N 28 38E
Constanța □ 95 44 15N 28 15E
Constantina 91 37 51N 5 40W
Constantine, Algeria 120 36 25N 6 42E
Constantine, U.S.A. 29 41 50N 85 40W
Constantine, C. 11 58 24N 158 54W
Constitución, Chile 76 35 20S 72 30W
Constitución, Uruguay 76 42 0S 57 50W
Consul 63 49 20N 109 30W
Contact 35 41 46N 114 45W
Contai 109 21 54N 87 46E
Contamana 72 7 19S 74 55W
Contas → 75 14 17S 39 1W
Continental 42 41 6N 84 16W
Continental Divide 38 35 25N 108 19W
Continental L. 35 41 54N 118 43W
Contoocook → 36 43 27N 71 35W
Contra Costa County ◇ 14 37 50N 121 50W
Contreras 38 34 23N 106 49W
Controller B. 11 60 7N 144 15W
Contumaza 72 7 23S 78 57W
Convención 70 8 28N 73 21W
Convent 25 30 1N 90 50W
Converse, Ind. 22 40 35N 85 52W
Converse, La. 25 31 47N 93 42W
Converse County ◇ 56 43 0N 105 45W
Convoy 42 40 55N 84 43W
Conway = Conwy 82 53 17N 3 50W
Conway = Conwy → 82 53 18N 3 50W
Conway, Ark. 13 35 5N 92 26W
Conway, Kans. 24 38 22N 97 47W
Conway, Mo. 32 37 30N 92 49W
Conway, N.C. 40 36 26N 77 14W
Conway, N. Dak. 41 48 14N 97 41W
Conway, N.H. 36 43 59N 71 7W
Conway, S.C. 46 33 51N 79 3W
Conway, Tex. 50 35 13N 101 23W
Conway County ◇ 13 35 10N 92 38W
Conway L. 13 34 58N 92 25W
Conway Springs 24 37 24N 97 39W
Conwy 82 53 17N 3 50W
Conwy → 82 53 18N 3 50W
Conyers 18 33 40N 84 1W
Coober Pedy 126 29 1S 134 43E
Cooch Behar = Koch Bihar 109 26 22N 89 29E
Cook 34 40 31N 96 10W
Cook, Bahía 78 55 10S 70 0W
Cook, Mt. 128 43 36S 170 9E
Cook County ◇, Ga. 18 31 10N 83 25W
Cook County ◇, Ill. 21 41 50N 87 45W
Cook County ◇, Minn. 30 47 50N 90 30W
Cook Inlet 11 60 0N 152 0W
Cook Is. 125 17 0S 160 0W
Cook Strait 128 41 15S 174 29E
Cooke City 33 45 1N 109 56W
Cooke County ◇ 51 33 38N 97 8W
Cookes Peak 38 32 32N 107 44W
Cookeville 49 36 10N 85 30W
Cooks Hammock 17 29 56N 83 17W
Cookstown 85 54 40N 6 43W
Cookstown □ 85 54 40N 6 43W
Cooksville 21 40 33N 88 43W
Cooktown 127 15 30S 145 16E
Cool 51 32 49N 98 1W
Cooleemee 40 35 49N 80 33W
Coolgardie 126 30 55S 121 8E
Coolidge, Ariz. 12 32 59N 111 31W
Coolidge, Ga. 18 31 1N 83 52W
Coolidge, Kans. 24 38 3N 102 1W
Coolidge, Tex. 51 31 45N 96 39W
Coolidge Dam 12 33 0N 110 20W
Coolin 20 48 29N 116 51W
Cooma 127 36 12S 149 8E
Coon Rapids, Iowa 23 41 53N 94 41W
Coon Rapids, Minn. 30 45 9N 93 19W
Coon Valley 55 43 42N 91 1W
Coonamble 127 30 56S 148 27E
Coondapoor 108 13 42N 74 40E
Cooper, Ky. 49 36 46N 84 52W
Cooper, Tex. 51 33 23N 95 42W
Cooper →, S.C. 46 32 50N 79 56W
Cooper →, Va. 54 36 40N 82 44W
Cooper County ◇ 32 38 50N 92 45W
Cooperdale 42 40 13N 82 4W
Coopers Cr. → 127 28 29S 137 46E
Coopersburg 45 40 31N 75 23W
Cooperstown, N. Dak. 41 47 27N 98 8W
Cooperstown, N.Y. 39 42 42N 74 56W
Coopersville 29 43 4N 85 57W
Coorong, The 127 35 50S 139 20E
Coos Bay 44 43 22N 124 13W
Coos County ◇, N.H. 36 44 40N 71 15W
Coos County ◇, Oreg. 44 43 15N 124 0W
Coosa → 10 32 30N 86 16W
Coosa County ◇ 10 32 53N 86 13W
Coosawattee → 18 34 35N 84 55W
Cootamundra 127 34 36S 148 1E
Cootehill 85 54 5N 7 5W
Copahue Paso 76 37 49S 71 8W
Copainalá 65 17 8N 93 11W
Copalis Beach 53 47 7N 124 10W
Copán, Hond. 66 14 50N 89 9W
Copan, U.S.A. 43 36 54N 95 56W
Copan Res. 43 36 58N 95 57W
Copano B. 51 28 5N 97 5W
Copatana 70 2 48S 67 4W
Copco L. 14 41 59N 122 20W
Cope, Colo. 16 39 40N 102 51W
Cope, S.C. 46 33 23N 81 0W
Copeland, Fla. 17 25 57N 81 22W
Copeland, Idaho 20 48 54N 116 23W
Copeland, Kans. 24 37 33N 100 38W
Copenhagen = København 97 55 41N 12 34E
Copenhagen 39 43 54N 75 41W
Copiague 39 40 41N 73 24W
Copiah County ◇ 31 31 52N 90 24W
Copiapó 76 27 30S 70 20W
Copiapó → 76 27 19S 70 56W
Copp L. 62 60 14N 114 40W
Coppename → 71 5 48N 55 55W
Copper → 11 60 18N 145 3W
Copper Butte 53 48 42N 118 28W
Copper Center 11 61 58N 145 18W
Copper Cliff 60 46 28N 81 4W
Copper Harbor 29 47 28N 87 53W
Copperas Cove 51 31 8N 97 54W
Copperhill 49 35 0N 84 15W
Coppermine 58 67 50N 115 5W
Coppermine → 58 67 49N 116 4W
Coquet → 82 55 18N 1 45W
Coqui 57 17 59N 66 14W
Coquilhatville = Mbandaka 122 0 1N 18 18E
Coquille 44 43 11N 124 11W
Coquille → 44 43 7N 124 26W
Coquimbo 76 30 0S 71 20W
Coquimbo □ 76 31 0S 71 0W
Corabia 89 43 48N 24 30E
Coração de Jesus 75 16 43S 44 22W
Coracora 72 15 5S 73 45W
Coral Gables 17 25 45N 80 16W
Coral Harbour 59 64 8N 83 10W
Coral Sea 124 15 0S 150 0E
Coral Sea Islands Terr. 127 20 0S 155 0E
Coralville 23 41 40N 91 35W
Coralville L. 23 41 42N 91 33W
Coram, Mont. 33 48 25N 114 3W
Coram, N.Y. 39 40 52N 73 0W
Corantijn → 71 5 50N 57 8W
Coraopolis 45 40 31N 80 10W
Corato 94 41 12N 16 22E
Corbin, Kans. 24 37 8N 97 33W
Corbin, Ky. 49 36 57N 84 6W
Corbin, Mont. 33 46 23N 112 4W
Corby, Lincs., U.K. 83 52 49N 0 31W
Corby, Northants., U.K. 86 52 29N 0 41W
Corcoran 15 36 6N 119 33W
Corcubión 91 42 56N 9 12W
Cordele 18 31 58N 83 47W
Cordell 43 35 17N 98 59W
Cordisburgo 75 19 7S 44 21W
Córdoba, Argentina 76 31 20S 64 10W
Córdoba, Mexico 65 18 50N 97 0W
Córdoba, Spain 91 37 50N 4 50W
Córdoba □, Argentina 76 31 22S 64 15W
Córdoba □, Colombia 70 8 20N 75 40W
Córdoba, Sierra de 76 31 10S 64 25W
Cordon 111 16 42N 121 32E
Cordova, Ala. 10 33 46N 87 11W
Cordova, Alaska 11 60 33N 145 45W
Cordova, Ill. 21 41 41N 90 19W
Cordova, N. Mex. 38 36 1N 105 52W
Cordova, Nebr. 34 40 43N 97 21W
Cordova, S.C. 46 33 26N 80 55W
Core Banks 40 34 45N 76 15W
Coremas 74 7 1S 37 58W
Corentyne → 71 5 50N 57 8W
Corfu = Kérkira 95 39 38N 19 50E
Corfu 39 42 58N 78 24W
Corguinho 73 19 53S 54 52W
Corigliano Cálabro 94 39 36N 16 31E
Corinna 26 44 55N 69 16W
Corinne 52 41 33N 112 7W
Corinth = Kórinthos 95 37 56N 22 55E
Corinth, Ga. 18 33 14N 84 57W
Corinth, Ky. 49 38 30N 84 34W
Corinth, Miss. 31 34 56N 88 31W
Corinth, N.Y. 39 43 15N 73 49W
Corinth, W. Va. 54 39 25N 79 30W
Corinth, G. of = Korinthiakós Kólpos 95 38 16N 22 30E
Corinto, Brazil 75 18 20S 44 30W
Corinto, Nic. 66 12 30N 87 10W
Corj □ 95 45 5N 23 25E
Cork 85 51 54N 8 30W
Cork □ 85 51 50N 8 50W
Cork Harbour 85 51 46N 8 16W
Çorlu 95 41 11N 27 49E
Cormack L. 62 60 56N 121 37W
Cormorant 63 54 14N 100 35W
Cormorant L. 63 54 15N 100 50W
Corn 43 35 24N 98 48W
Corn Is. = Maiz, Islas del 66 12 15N 83 4W
Cornelia 18 34 31N 83 32W
Cornelio 64 29 55N 111 8W
Cornélio Procópio 77 23 7S 50 40W
Cornelius 40 35 29N 80 52W
Cornell, Ill. 21 41 0N 88 44W
Cornell, Wis. 55 45 10N 91 9W
Corner Brook 61 48 57N 57 58W
Corner Inlet 127 38 45S 146 20E
Cornersville 48 35 22N 86 50W
Cornerville 13 33 51N 91 56W
Corning, Ark. 13 36 25N 90 35W
Corning, Calif. 14 39 56N 122 11W
Corning, Iowa 23 40 59N 94 44W
Corning, Kans. 24 39 40N 96 2W
Corning, N.Y. 39 42 9N 77 3W
Corning, Ohio 42 39 36N 82 5W
Cornish 43 34 9N 97 36W
Cornlea 34 41 41N 97 34W
Cornucopia 44 45 0N 117 12W
Cornudas 50 31 47N 105 28W
Cornville 12 34 43N 111 55W
Cornwall, Canada 60 45 2N 74 44W
Cornwall, Conn. 28 41 50N 73 20W
Cornwall, Pa. 45 40 17N 76 25W
Cornwall, Vt. 36 43 56N 73 13W
Cornwall □ 83 50 26N 4 40W
Cornwall Bridge 28 41 49N 73 22W
Cornwallis I. 4 75 8N 95 0W
Cornwell, Fla. 17 27 23N 81 6W
Cornwell, S.C. 46 34 37N 81 10W
Coro 70 11 25N 69 41W
Coroaci 75 18 35S 42 17W
Coroatá 74 4 8S 44 0W
Corocoro 72 17 15S 68 28W
Corocoro, I. 71 8 30N 60 10W
Coroico 72 16 0S 67 50W
Coromandel, Brazil 75 18 28S 47 13W
Coromandel, N.Z. 128 36 45S 175 31E
Coromandel Coast 108 12 30N 81 0E
Corona, Calif. 15 33 53N 117 34W
Corona, N. Mex. 38 34 15N 105 36W
Corona, S. Dak. 47 45 20N 96 46W
Coronado 15 32 41N 117 11W
Coronado, Bahía de 66 9 0N 83 40W
Coronado Nat. Forest 12 32 10N 110 20W
Coronados, G. de los 78 41 40S 74 0W
Coronation 62 52 5N 111 27W
Coronation Gulf 58 68 25N 110 0W
Coronation I. 5 60 45S 46 0W
Coronda 76 31 58S 60 56W
Coronel 76 37 0S 73 10W
Coronel Bogado 76 27 11S 56 18W
Coronel Dorrego 76 38 40S 61 10W
Coronel Fabriciano 75 19 31S 42 38W
Coronel Murta 75 16 37S 42 11W
Coronel Oviedo 76 25 24S 56 30W
Coronel Ponce 73 15 34S 55 1W
Coronel Pringles 76 38 0S 61 30W
Coronel Suárez 76 37 30S 61 52W
Coronel Vidal 76 37 28S 57 45W
Corongo 72 8 30S 77 53W
Coronie □ 71 5 55N 56 20W
Coropuna, Nevado 72 15 30S 72 41W
Corozal, Belize 65 18 23N 88 23W
Corozal, Colombia 70 9 19N 75 18W
Corozal, Panama 57 8 59N 79 34W
Corozal, Puerto Rico 57 18 21N 66 19W
Corpus 77 27 10S 55 30W
Corpus Christi 51 27 47N 97 24W
Corpus Christi, L. 51 28 2N 97 52W
Corpus Christi B. 51 27 47N 97 22W
Corque 72 18 20S 67 41W
Corral, Chile 78 39 52S 73 26W
Corral, U.S.A. 20 43 21N 114 57W
Correctionville 23 42 29N 95 47W
Correll 30 45 14N 96 10W
Corrente 74 10 27S 45 10W
Corrente → 75 13 8S 43 28W
Correntes → 73 17 38S 55 8W
Correntina 75 13 20S 44 39W
Corrèze □ 90 45 20N 1 45E
Corrib, L. 85 53 5N 9 10W
Corrientes 76 27 30S 58 45W
Corrientes □ 76 28 0S 57 0W
Corrientes →, Argentina 76 30 42S 59 38W
Corrientes →, Peru 72 3 43S 74 35W
Corrientes, C., Colombia 70 5 30N 77 34W
Corrientes, C., Cuba 66 21 43N 84 30W
Corrientes, C., Mexico 64 20 25N 105 42W
Corrigan 51 31 0N 94 52W
Corriganville 27 39 45N 78 17W
Corry 45 41 55N 79 39W
Corryton 49 36 9N 83 47W
Corse 90 42 0N 9 0E
Corse, C. 94 43 1N 9 25E
Corse-du-Sud □ 90 41 45N 9 0E
Corsica = Corse 90 42 0N 9 0E
Corsica 47 43 25N 98 24W
Corsicana 51 32 6N 96 28W
Corson County ◇ 47 45 55N 101 0W
Cortez 16 37 21N 108 35W
Cortez Mts. 35 40 20N 116 20W
Cortland, N.Y. 39 42 36N 76 11W
Cortland, Nebr. 34 40 30N 96 42W
Cortland, Ohio 42 41 20N 80 44W
Cortland County ◇ 39 42 35N 76 5W
Cortona 94 43 16N 12 0E
Çorum, Turkey 106 40 30N 34 57E
Corum, U.S.A. 43 34 22N 98 6W
Corumbá 73 19 0S 57 30W

Corumbá Crown Cit

Corumbá → 75 18 19 S 48 55W
Corumbá de Goiás 75 16 0 S 48 50W
Corumbaíba 75 18 9 S 48 34W
Coruña, La 91 43 20N 8 25W
Corund 95 46 30N 25 13 E
Corunna = Coruña, La 91 43 20N 8 25W
Corunna 29 42 59N 84 7W
Corvallis, Mont. 33 46 19N 114 7W
Corvallis, Oreg. 44 44 34N 123 16W
Corvette, L. de la 60 53 25N 74 3W
Corwin 24 37 5N 98 18W
Corwith 23 42 59N 93 57W
Corydon, Ind. 22 38 13N 86 7W
Corydon, Iowa 23 40 46N 93 19W
Corydon, Ky. 48 37 44N 87 43W
Coryell County ◇ 51 31 26N 97 45W
Cosalá 64 24 28N 106 40W
Cosamaloapan 65 18 23N 95 50W
Cosenza 94 39 17N 16 14 E
Coşereni 95 44 38N 26 35 E
Coshocton 42 40 16N 81 51W
Coshocton County ◇ 42 40 16N 81 51W
Cosmopolis 53 46 57N 123 46W
Cosquín 76 31 15 S 64 30W
Cossatot → 13 33 48N 94 9W
Cost 51 29 26N 97 32W
Costa Blanca 91 38 25N 0 10W
Costa Brava 91 41 30N 3 0 E
Costa del Sol 91 36 30N 4 30W
Costa Dorada 91 40 45N 1 15 E
Costa Mesa 15 33 38N 117 55W
Costa Rica ■ 66 10 0N 84 0W
Costilla 38 36 59N 105 32W
Costilla County ◇ 16 37 15N 105 30W
Cosumnes → 14 38 16N 121 26W
Cotabato 111 7 14N 124 15 E
Cotacajes → 72 16 0 S 67 1W
Cotagaita 76 20 45 S 65 40W
Cotahuasi 72 15 12 S 72 50W
Cotati 14 38 20N 122 42W
Côte-d'Or □ 90 47 30N 4 50 E
Coteau des Prairies 47 44 20N 96 0W
Coteau du Missouri 41 47 0N 100 0W
Cotegipe 75 12 2 S 44 15W
Cotentin 90 49 30N 1 30W
Côtes-du-Nord □ 90 48 25N 2 40W
Cotesfield 34 41 22N 98 38W
Coto Laurel 57 18 3N 66 33W
Cotoca 73 17 49 S 63 3W
Cotonou 120 6 20N 2 25 E
Cotopaxi 16 38 22N 105 41W
Cotopaxi □ 70 0 5 S 78 55W
Cotopaxi, Vol. 72 0 40 S 78 30W
Cotswold Hills 83 51 42N 2 10W
Cottage Grove 44 43 48N 123 3W
Cottageville 46 32 56N 80 29W
Cottbus 88 51 44N 14 20 E
Cottle County ◇ 50 34 0N 100 18W
Cotton, Ga. 18 31 10N 84 4W
Cotton, Minn. 30 47 10N 92 28W
Cotton County ◇ 43 34 15N 98 20W
Cotton Plant 13 35 0N 91 15W
Cotton Valley 25 32 49N 93 25W
Cottondale, Ala. 10 33 11N 87 27W
Cottondale, Fla. 17 30 48N 85 23W
Cottonport 25 30 59N 92 3W
Cottonwood, Ala. 10 31 3N 85 18W
Cottonwood, Ariz. 12 34 45N 112 1W
Cottonwood, Calif. 14 40 23N 122 17W
Cottonwood, Idaho 20 46 3N 116 21W
Cottonwood, Minn. 30 44 37N 95 41W
Cottonwood, S. Dak. 47 43 58N 101 54W
Cottonwood → 30 44 17N 94 25W
Cottonwood County ◇ 30 44 0N 95 10W
Cottonwood Cr. → 50 31 23N 103 46W
Cottonwood Falls 24 38 22N 96 32W
Cottonwood Heights 52 40 38N 111 49W
Cottonwood Mts. 15 36 50N 117 40W
Cotuit 28 41 37N 70 26W
Cotulla 51 28 26N 99 14W
Couchwood 25 32 46N 93 23W
Couderay 55 45 48N 91 18W
Coudersport 45 41 46N 78 1W
Cougar 53 46 3N 122 18W
Coulee City 53 47 37N 119 17W
Coulee Dam 53 47 58N 118 58W
Coulee Dam Nat. Rec. Area 53 47 48N 119 45W
Coulman I. 5 73 35 S 170 0 E
Coulonge → 60 45 52N 76 46W
Coulterville, Calif. 14 37 43N 120 12W
Coulterville, Ill. 21 38 11N 89 36W
Counce 48 35 3N 88 16W
Council, Ga. 18 30 37N 82 31W
Council, Idaho 20 44 44N 116 26W
Council Bluffs 23 41 16N 95 52W
Council Grove 24 38 40N 96 29W
Council Grove Lake 24 38 41N 96 33W
Council Hill 43 35 31N 95 42W
Country Lake 37 39 55N 74 32W
Coupeville 53 48 13N 122 41W
Coupland 51 30 28N 97 23W
Courantyne → 72 5 55N 57 5W
Courtenay, Canada 62 49 45N 125 0W
Courtenay, U.S.A. 41 47 13N 98 34W
Courtland, Ala. 10 34 40N 87 19W
Courtland, Calif. 14 38 20N 121 34W
Courtland, Kans. 24 39 47N 97 54W
Courtland, Minn. 30 44 16N 94 20W
Courtland, Miss. 31 34 14N 89 57W
Courtland, Va. 54 36 43N 77 4W
Courtrai = Kortrijk 87 50 50N 3 17 E
Courtright Reservoir 15 37 5N 118 58W
Coushatta 25 32 1N 93 21W
Coutts 62 49 0N 111 57W
Covasna 95 45 50N 26 10 E
Covasna □ 95 45 50N 26 0 E
Cove, Ark. 13 34 26N 94 25W
Cove, Oreg. 44 45 18N 117 49W
Cove City 40 35 13N 77 19W
Cove Point 27 38 23N 76 24W
Covelo 14 39 48N 123 15W
Coveñas 70 9 24N 75 44W
Coventry, U.K. 83 52 25N 1 31W
Coventry, Conn. 28 41 48N 72 23W
Coventry, R.I. 28 41 41N 71 34W
Coventry L. 63 61 15N 106 15W
Coverdale 18 31 38N 83 58W
Covilhã 91 40 17N 7 31W
Covington, Ga. 18 33 36N 83 51W
Covington, Ind. 22 40 9N 87 24W
Covington, Ky. 49 39 5N 84 31W
Covington, La. 25 30 29N 90 6W
Covington, Mich. 29 46 33N 88 32W
Covington, Ohio 42 40 7N 84 21W
Covington, Okla. 43 36 18N 97 35W
Covington, Tenn. 48 35 34N 89 39W
Covington, Va. 54 37 47N 79 59W
Covington County ◇, Ala. 10 31 18N 86 29W
Covington County ◇, Miss. 31 31 39N 89 33W
Cow Cr. → 44 42 57N 123 22W
Cow Head L. 14 41 55N 120 2W
Cowal, L. 127 33 40 S 147 25 E
Cowan, Canada 63 52 5N 100 45W
Cowan, U.S.A. 48 35 10N 86 1W
Cowan, L. 126 31 45 S 121 45 E
Cowan L. 63 54 0N 107 15W
Coward 46 33 58N 79 45W
Cowden 21 39 15N 88 52W
Cowdenbeath 84 56 7N 3 20W
Cowdrey 16 40 52N 106 19W
Cowen 54 38 25N 80 34W
Cowes 83 50 45N 1 18W
Coweta 43 35 57N 95 39W
Coweta County ◇ 18 33 20N 84 50W
Cowles 34 40 10N 98 27W
Cowley 56 44 53N 108 28W
Cowley County ◇ 24 37 15N 96 45W
Cowlic 12 31 48N 111 59W
Cowlitz → 53 46 6N 122 55W
Cowlitz County ◇ 53 46 5N 122 50W
Cowpens 46 35 1N 81 48W
Cowra 127 33 49 S 148 42 E
Cox 18 31 27N 81 34W
Cox City 43 34 43N 97 44W
Coxim 73 18 30 S 54 55W
Coxim → 73 18 34 S 54 46W
Cox's Bazar 109 21 26N 91 59 E
Cox's Cove 61 49 7N 58 5W
Coxs Mills 54 39 3N 80 50W
Coxsackie 39 42 21N 73 48W
Coy 13 34 32N 91 53W
Coyame 64 29 28N 105 6W
Coyanosa Draw → 50 31 18N 103 6W
Coyle 43 35 57N 97 14W
Coyote 38 36 10N 106 37W
Coyote L. 15 35 4N 116 46W
Coyote Reservoir 14 37 7N 121 33W
Coyuca de Benítez 65 17 1N 100 8W
Coyuca de Catalan 64 18 18N 100 41W
Coyville 24 37 41N 95 54W
Cozad 34 40 52N 99 59W
Cozumel 65 20 31N 86 55W
Cozumel, Isla de 65 20 30N 86 40W
Crab Cr. → 53 46 49N 119 55W
Crab Orchard, Ky. 49 37 28N 84 30W
Crab Orchard, Nebr. 34 40 20N 96 25W
Crab Orchard L. 21 37 43N 89 9W
Crabtree 44 44 38N 122 54W
Cracow = Kraków 89 50 4N 19 57 E
Cradock 123 32 8 S 25 36 E
Craig, Alaska 11 55 29N 133 9W
Craig, Colo. 16 40 31N 107 33W
Craig, Iowa 23 42 54N 96 19W
Craig, Mo. 32 40 12N 95 23W
Craig, Mont. 33 47 5N 111 58W
Craig, Nebr. 34 41 47N 96 22W
Craig County ◇, Okla. 43 36 45N 95 10W
Craig County ◇, Va. 54 37 25N 80 5W
Craig Pass 56 44 26N 110 43W
Craigavon = Lurgan 85 54 28N 6 20W
Craighead County ◇ 13 35 50N 90 42W
Craigmont 20 46 15N 116 29W
Craigsville, Va. 54 38 5N 79 23W
Craigsville, W. Va. 54 38 20N 80 39W
Craiova 89 44 21N 23 48 E
Cranberry L. 39 44 11N 74 50W
Cranberry Portage 63 54 35N 101 23W
Cranbrook 62 49 30N 115 46W
Crandall 31 31 58N 88 32W
Crandon 55 45 34N 88 54W
Crane, Ind. 22 38 54N 86 54W
Crane, Mo. 32 36 54N 93 34W
Crane, Mont. 33 47 35N 104 16W
Crane, Oreg. 44 43 25N 118 35W
Crane, Tex. 50 31 24N 102 21W
Crane County ◇ 50 31 24N 102 21W
Crane Mt. 44 42 4N 120 13W
Cranfills Gap 51 31 46N 97 50W
Cranford 37 40 40N 74 18W
Cranston 28 41 47N 71 26W
Crapo 27 38 18N 76 9W
Crary 41 48 4N 98 38W
Crasna 95 46 32N 27 51 E
Crater L. 44 42 56N 122 6W
Crater Lake 44 42 54N 122 8W
Crater Lake National Park 44 42 55N 122 10W
Craters of the Moon National Monument 20 43 25N 113 30W
Crateús 74 5 10 S 40 39W
Crato 74 7 10 S 39 25W
Craven County ◇ 40 35 15N 77 10W
Cravo Norte 70 6 18N 70 12W
Cravo Norte → 70 6 18N 70 12W
Crawford, Ala. 10 32 27N 85 11W
Crawford, Colo. 16 38 42N 107 37W
Crawford, Miss. 31 33 18N 88 37W
Crawford, Nebr. 34 42 41N 103 25W
Crawford, Okla. 43 35 50N 99 48W
Crawford, Tex. 51 31 32N 97 27W
Crawford County ◇, Ark. 13 35 20N 94 18W
Crawford County ◇, Ga. 18 32 50N 84 0W
Crawford County ◇, Ill. 21 39 0N 87 45W
Crawford County ◇, Ind. 22 38 15N 86 25W
Crawford County ◇, Iowa 23 42 0N 95 20W
Crawford County ◇, Kans. 24 37 30N 94 45W
Crawford County ◇, Mich. 29 44 45N 84 40W
Crawford County ◇, Mo. 32 38 0N 91 20W
Crawford County ◇, Ohio 42 40 48N 82 59W
Crawford County ◇, Pa. 45 41 45N 80 0W
Crawford County ◇, Wis. 55 43 15N 90 50W
Crawfordsville, Ark. 13 35 14N 90 20W
Crawfordsville, Ind. 22 40 2N 86 54W
Crawfordsville, Iowa 23 41 12N 91 32W
Crawfordville, Fla. 17 30 11N 84 23W
Crawfordville, Ga. 18 33 33N 82 54W
Crawley 83 51 7N 0 10W
Crazy Mts. 33 46 12N 110 20W
Crazy Woman Cr. → 56 44 29N 106 8W
Creagerstown 27 39 37N 77 22W
Creal Springs 21 37 37N 88 50W
Crean L. 63 54 5N 106 9W
Crécy-en-Ponthieu 90 50 15N 1 53 E
Cree →, Canada 63 58 57N 105 47W
Cree →, U.K. 84 54 51N 4 24W
Cree L. 63 57 30N 106 30W
Creede 16 37 51N 106 56W
Creedmoor 40 36 7N 78 41W
Creek County ◇ 43 35 50N 96 20W
Creel 64 27 45N 107 38W
Creighton, Mo. 32 38 30N 94 4W
Creighton, Nebr. 34 42 28N 97 54W
Crellin 27 39 25N 79 25W
Cremona 94 45 8N 10 2 E
Crenshaw 31 34 30N 90 12W
Crenshaw County ◇ 10 31 43N 86 16W
Creole 25 29 49N 93 7W
Crepori → 73 5 42 S 57 8W
Cres 94 44 58N 14 25 E
Cresaptown 27 39 36N 78 50W
Cresbard 47 45 10N 98 57W
Crescent, Okla. 43 35 57N 97 36W
Crescent, Oreg. 44 43 28N 121 42W
Crescent Beach 17 29 46N 81 15W
Crescent City, Calif. 14 41 45N 124 12W
Crescent City, Fla. 17 29 26N 81 31W
Crescent L. 17 29 28N 81 30W
Cresco 23 43 22N 92 7W
Crespo 76 32 2 S 60 19W
Cresson 45 40 28N 78 36W
Crested Butte 16 38 52N 106 59W
Crestline, Calif. 15 34 14N 117 18W
Crestline, Ohio 42 40 47N 82 44W
Creston, Canada 62 49 10N 116 31W
Creston, Iowa 23 41 4N 94 22W
Creston, Wash. 53 47 46N 118 31W
Creston, Wyo. 56 41 42N 107 45W
Crestone 16 37 56N 105 47W
Crestview 17 30 46N 86 34W
Crestwood 49 38 19N 85 28W
Crestwood Village 37 39 56N 74 20W
Creswell, N.C. 40 35 53N 76 24W
Creswell, Oreg. 44 43 55N 123 1W
Crete = Kríti 95 35 15N 25 0 E
Crete, Ill. 21 41 27N 87 38W
Crete, Nebr. 34 40 38N 96 58W
Crete, I. 95 35 15N 25 0 E
Crete, La 62 58 11N 116 24W
Creus, C. 91 42 20N 3 19 E
Creuse □ 90 46 0N 2 0 E
Creuse → 90 47 0N 0 34 E
Creusot, Le 90 46 50N 4 24 E
Creve Coeur 21 40 39N 89 35W
Crewe, U.K. 82 53 6N 2 28W
Crewe, U.S.A. 54 37 10N 78 8W
Criciúma 77 28 40 S 49 23W
Cricket 40 36 11N 81 12W
Cricket Mts. 52 39 0N 112 0W
Crieff 84 56 22N 3 50W
Crimea = Krymskiy P-ov. 99 45 0N 34 0
Crinan 84 56 6N 5 34
Criner 43 34 58N 97 34
Cripple Creek 16 38 45N 105 11
Crisfield 27 37 59N 75 51
Crisp County ◇ 18 31 50N 83 50
Crisp Pt. 29 46 45N 85 16
Cristalândia 74 10 36 S 49 11
Cristino Castro 74 8 49 S 44 13
Cristobal 57 9 21N 79 55
Crişul Alb → 89 46 42N 21 17
Crişul Negru → 89 46 38N 22 26
Crittenden 49 38 47N 84 36
Crittenden County ◇, Ark. 13 35 14N 90 20
Crittenden County ◇, Ky. 48 37 20N 88 5
Crivitz 55 45 14N 88 1
Crixás 75 14 27 S 49 58
Crna Gora 95 42 10N 21 30
Crna Gora □ 95 42 40N 19 20
Crna Reka → 95 41 33N 21 59
Croaghpatrick 85 53 46N 9 40
Croatan National Forest 40 34 50N 77 5
Crocheron 27 38 15N 76 3
Crocker 32 37 57N 92 16
Crocker, Banjaran 110 5 40N 116 30
Crocker I. 126 11 12 S 132 32
Crockett 51 31 19N 95 27
Crockett County ◇, Tenn. 48 35 49N 89 14
Crockett County ◇, Tex. 50 30 45N 101 30
Crocodile Is. 126 12 3 S 134 58
Crofton, Ky. 48 37 3N 87 29
Crofton, Md. 27 39 1N 76 42
Crofton, Nebr. 34 42 44N 97 30
Croghan 39 43 54N 75 24
Croix, La, L. 60 48 20N 92 15
Cromarty, Canada 63 58 3N 94 9
Cromarty, U.K. 84 57 40N 4 2
Cromer 82 52 56N 1 18
Cromwell, N.Z. 128 45 3 S 169 14
Cromwell, Ala. 10 32 14N 88 17
Cromwell, Minn. 30 46 41N 92 53
Cromwell, Okla. 43 35 22N 96 29
Crook 16 40 52N 102 48
Crook County ◇, Oreg. 44 44 10N 120 20
Crook County ◇, Wyo. 56 44 44N 104 30
Crooked →, Canada 62 54 50N 122 54
Crooked →, U.S.A. 44 44 32N 121 16
Crooked Creek 11 61 52N 158 7
Crooked I. 67 22 50N 74 10
Crooked Island Passage 67 23 0N 74 30
Crooked L. 17 27 48N 81 35
Crooks 47 43 40N 96 49
Crookston, Minn. 30 47 47N 96 37
Crookston, Nebr. 34 42 56N 100 45
Crooksville 42 39 46N 82 6
Croom 27 38 45N 76 46
Cropsey 21 40 37N 88 29
Crosby, Minn. 30 46 29N 93 58
Crosby, Miss. 31 31 17N 91 4
Crosby, N. Dak. 41 48 55N 103 18
Crosby, Tex. 51 29 55N 95 4
Crosby, Mt. 56 43 52N 109 20
Crosby County ◇ 50 33 40N 101 14
Crosbyton 50 33 40N 101 14
Cross Anchor 46 34 39N 81 51
Cross City 17 29 38N 83 7
Cross County ◇ 13 35 14N 90 47
Cross Fell 82 54 44N 2 29
Cross Hill 46 34 18N 81 59
Cross L., Canada 63 54 45N 97 30
Cross L., U.S.A. 26 47 7N 68 20
Cross Lake 30 46 40N 94 7
Cross Plains, Tenn. 48 36 33N 86 42
Cross Plains, Tex. 51 32 8N 99 11
Cross Sound 11 56 0N 135 0
Cross Timbers 32 38 1N 93 14
Crossett 13 33 8N 91 58
Crossfield 62 51 25N 114 0
Crosshaven 85 51 48N 8 19
Crossroads 38 33 31N 103 20
Crossville, Ill. 21 38 10N 88 4
Crossville, Tenn. 49 35 57N 85 2
Croswell 29 43 16N 82 37
Crothersville 22 38 48N 85 50
Crotone 94 39 5N 17 6
Crouch 20 44 7N 115 58
Crouse 40 35 25N 81 18
Crow →, Canada 62 59 41N 124 20
Crow →, U.S.A. 16 40 23N 104 29
Crow Agency 33 45 36N 107 28
Crow Creek Indian Reservation 47 44 3N 99 25
Crow Hd. 85 51 34N 10 9
Crow Indian Reservation 33 45 25N 108 0
Crow Wing → 30 46 19N 94 20
Crow Wing County ◇ 30 46 30N 94 0
Crowder, Miss. 31 34 11N 90 8
Crowder, Okla. 43 35 7N 95 40
Crowell 51 33 59N 99 43
Crowley, Colo. 16 38 12N 103 51
Crowley, La. 25 30 13N 92 22
Crowley, Tex. 51 32 35N 97 22
Crowley, L. 14 37 35N 118 42
Crowley County ◇ 16 38 15N 103 45
Crowley Ridge 13 35 45N 90 45
Crown City 42 38 36N 82 17

Crown Point Dalmatia

Crown Point 22 41 25N 87 22W
Crownpoint 38 35 41N 108 9W
Crows Nest Pk. 47 44 3N 103 58W
Crowsnest Pass 62 49 40N 114 40W
Croydon, Australia 127 18 13 S 142 14 E
Croydon, U.K. 83 51 18N 0 5W
Croydon Flat 36 43 25N 72 12W
Crozet 54 38 4N 78 42W
Crozet Is. 3 46 27 S 52 0 E
Cruger 31 33 19N 90 14W
Crump L. 44 42 17N 119 50W
Crumpton 27 39 14N 75 55W
Cruz, C. 66 19 50N 77 50W
Cruz, La, C. Rica 66 11 4N 85 39W
Cruz, La, Mexico 64 23 55N 106 54W
Cruz Alta 77 28 45 S 53 40W
Cruz Bay 57 18 20N 64 48W
Cruz das Almas 75 12 0 S 39 6W
Cruz de Malta 74 8 15 S 40 20W
Cruz del Eje 76 30 45 S 64 50W
Cruzeiro 75 22 33 S 45 0W
Cruzeiro do Oeste 77 23 46 S 53 4W
Cruzeiro do Sul 72 7 35 S 72 35W
Cry L. 62 58 45N 129 0W
Crystal, Minn. 30 45 3N 93 22W
Crystal, N. Dak. 41 48 36N 97 40W
Crystal → 16 39 25N 107 14W
Crystal B. 17 28 50N 82 45W
Crystal Bay 35 39 15N 120 0W
Crystal Beach, Fla. 17 28 5N 82 47W
Crystal Beach, Md. 27 39 26N 75 59W
Crystal City, Mo. 32 38 13N 90 23W
Crystal City, Tex. 51 28 41N 99 50W
Crystal Falls 29 46 5N 88 20W
Crystal L. 29 44 40N 86 10W
Crystal Lake, Ill. 21 42 14N 88 19W
Crystal Lake, Iowa 23 43 13N 93 47W
Crystal River 17 28 54N 82 35W
Crystal Springs 31 31 59N 90 21W
Csongrád 89 46 43N 20 12 E
Cu Lao Hon 112 10 54N 108 18 E
Cuamba 123 14 45 S 36 22 E
Cuando → 123 14 0 S 19 30 E
Cuanza → 118 9 2 S 13 30 E
Cuarto → 76 33 25 S 63 2W
Cuatrociénegas 64 26 59N 102 5W
Cuauhtémoc 64 28 25N 106 52W
Cuba, Ala. 10 32 26N 88 23W
Cuba, Ill. 21 40 30N 90 12W
Cuba, Kans. 24 39 48N 97 27W
Cuba, Mo. 32 38 4N 91 24W
Cuba, N. Mex. 38 36 1N 107 4W
Cuba, N.Y. 39 42 13N 78 17W
Cuba ■ 66 22 0N 79 0W
Cuba City 55 42 36N 90 26W
Cubango → 123 18 50 S 22 25 E
Cubero 38 35 5N 107 31W
Cuchara, Pta. 57 17 57N 66 42W
Cucharas → 16 37 55N 104 32W
Cuchi 123 14 37 S 16 58 E
Cuchillo-Có 78 38 20 S 64 37W
Cuchivero → 70 7 40N 65 57W
Cuchumatanes, Sierra de los 66 15 35N 91 25W
Cucuí 70 1 12N 66 50W
Cucurpe 64 30 20N 110 43W
Cucurrupí 70 4 23N 76 56W
Cúcuta 70 7 54N 72 31W
Cudahy 55 42 58N 87 52W
Cudalbi 95 45 46N 27 41 E
Cuddalore 108 11 46N 79 45 E
Cuddapah 108 14 30N 78 47 E
Cuddeback L. 15 35 18N 117 29W
Cue 126 27 25 S 117 54 E
Cuenca, Ecuador 70 2 50 S 79 9W
Cuenca, Spain 91 40 5N 2 10W
Cuenca, Serranía de 91 39 55N 1 50W
Cuencamé 64 24 53N 103 41W
Cuernavaca 65 18 50N 99 20W
Cuero 51 29 6N 97 17W
Cuervo 38 35 2N 104 25W
Cuevas, Cerro 73 22 0 S 65 12W
Cuevas del Almanzora 91 37 18N 1 58W
Cuevo 72 20 15 S 63 30W
Cugir 95 45 48N 23 25 E
Cuiabá 73 15 30 S 56 0W
Cuiabá → 73 17 5 S 56 36W
Cuilco 66 15 24N 91 58W
Cuillin Hills 84 57 14N 6 15W
Cuillin Sd. 84 57 4N 6 20W
Cuiluan 114 47 51N 128 32 E
Cuima 123 13 25 S 15 45 E
Cuité 74 6 29 S 36 9W
Cuito → 123 18 1 S 20 48 E
Cuitzeo, L. de 64 19 55N 101 5W
Cuiuni → 71 0 45 S 63 7W
Cukai 110 4 13N 103 25 E
Culberson 40 35 0N 84 9W
Culberson County ◇ 50 31 30N 104 30W
Culbertson, Mont. 33 48 9N 104 31W
Culbertson, Nebr. 34 40 14N 100 50W
Culdesac 20 46 23N 116 40W
Culebra, Isla de 57 18 19N 65 18W
Culebra, Sierra de la 91 41 55N 6 20W
Culebrita, Isla 57 18 19N 65 14W
Culiacán 64 24 50N 107 23W
Culiacán → 64 24 30N 107 42W
Culion 111 11 54N 120 1 E
Culiseu → 73 12 14 S 53 17W
Cullen, U.K. 84 57 45N 2 50W
Cullen, U.S.A. 25 32 58N 93 27W
Cullera 91 39 9N 0 17W
Cullison 24 37 38N 98 54W
Cullman 10 34 11N 86 51W
Cullman County ◇ 10 34 11N 86 51W
Culloden 18 32 52N 84 6W
Culloden Moor 84 57 29N 4 7W
Cullom 21 40 53N 88 16W
Cullomburg 10 31 43N 88 18W
Cullowhee 40 35 19N 83 11W
Culp Creek 44 43 42N 122 50W
Culpeper 54 38 30N 78 0W
Culpeper County ◇ 54 38 28N 78 0W
Culuene → 73 12 56 S 52 51W
Culver, Ind. 22 41 13N 86 25W
Culver, Kans. 24 38 58N 97 46W
Culver, Oreg. 44 44 32N 121 13W
Culver, Pt. 126 32 54 S 124 43 E
Culverden 128 42 47 S 172 49 E
Culverton 18 33 19N 82 54W
Cumaná 71 10 30N 64 5W
Cumare 70 0 49N 72 32W
Cumari 75 18 16 S 48 11W
Cumberland, Canada 62 49 40N 125 0W
Cumberland, Iowa 23 41 16N 94 52W
Cumberland, Ky. 49 36 59N 82 59W
Cumberland, Md. 27 39 39N 78 46W
Cumberland, N.C. 40 35 0N 78 59W
Cumberland, N.J. 37 39 26N 75 14W
Cumberland, Ohio 42 39 51N 81 40W
Cumberland, Va. 54 37 30N 78 15W
Cumberland, Wis. 55 45 32N 92 1W
Cumberland → 48 37 9N 88 25W
Cumberland, L. 49 36 52N 85 9W
Cumberland City 48 36 23N 87 38W
Cumberland County ◇, Ill. 21 39 15N 88 15W
Cumberland County ◇, Ky. 49 36 45N 85 25W
Cumberland County ◇, Maine 26 43 50N 70 30W
Cumberland County ◇, N.C. 40 35 0N 78 45W
Cumberland County ◇, N.J. 37 39 20N 75 10W
Cumberland County ◇, Pa. 45 40 5N 77 10W
Cumberland County ◇, Tenn. 49 36 0N 85 0W
Cumberland County ◇, Va. 54 37 30N 78 15W
Cumberland Gap 49 36 36N 83 41W
Cumberland Gap Nat. Historic Park 49 36 36N 83 40W
Cumberland Hill 28 41 59N 71 28W
Cumberland I. 18 30 50N 81 25W
Cumberland I. Nat. Seashore 18 30 12N 81 24W
Cumberland Is. 127 20 35 S 149 10 E
Cumberland L. 63 54 3N 102 18W
Cumberland Pen. 59 67 0N 64 0W
Cumberland Plateau 49 36 0N 85 0W
Cumberland Pt. 29 47 51N 89 14W
Cumberland Sd. 59 65 30N 66 0W
Cumbria □ 82 54 35N 2 55W
Cumbrian Mts. 82 54 30N 3 0W
Cumbum 108 15 40N 79 10 E
Cumby 51 33 8N 95 50W
Cuminá → 71 1 30 S 56 0W
Cuminapanema → 71 1 9 S 54 54W
Cuming County ◇ 34 41 50N 96 40W
Cumming 18 34 12N 84 9W
Cummings 46 32 47N 80 59W
Cumnock 84 55 27N 4 18W
Cumpas 64 30 0N 109 48W
Cuncumén 76 31 53 S 70 38W
Cundiff 49 36 57N 85 15W
Cundinamarca □ 70 5 0N 74 0W
Cunene → 123 17 20 S 11 50 E
Cúneo 94 44 23N 7 32 E
Cunnamulla 127 28 2 S 145 38 E
Cunningham 24 37 39N 98 26W
Cupar, Canada 63 50 57N 104 10W
Cupar, U.K. 84 56 20N 3 0W
Cupertino 14 37 19N 122 2W
Cupica, Golfo de 70 6 25N 77 30W
Cuprum 20 45 5N 116 41W
Curaçá 74 8 59 S 39 54W
Curaçao 67 12 10N 69 0W
Curacautín 78 38 26 S 71 53W
Curahuara de Carangas 72 17 52 S 68 26W
Curanilahue 76 37 29 S 73 28W
Curaray → 70 2 20 S 74 5W
Curatabaca 71 6 19N 62 51W
Curecanti Nat. Rec. Area 16 38 24N 107 25W
Curepto 76 35 8 S 72 1W
Curiapo 72 8 33N 61 5W
Curicó 76 34 55 S 71 20W
Curicó □ 76 34 50 S 71 15W
Curicuriari → 70 0 14 S 66 48W
Curimatá 74 10 2 S 44 17W
Curiplaya 70 0 16N 74 52W
Curitiba 77 25 20 S 49 10W
Curlew, Iowa 23 42 59N 94 44W
Curlew, Wash. 53 48 53N 118 36W
Currais Novos 74 6 13 S 36 30W
Curralinho 74 1 45 S 49 46W
Current → 13 36 15N 90 55W
Currie, Minn. 30 44 3N 95 40W
Currie, N.C. 40 34 28N 78 6W
Currie, Nev. 35 40 16N 114 45W
Currituck 40 36 27N 76 1W
Currituck County ◇ 40 36 20N 76 0W
Currituck Sd. 40 36 20N 75 52W
Curry County ◇, N. Mex. 38 34 30N 103 15W
Curry County ◇, Oreg. 44 42 20N 124 20W
Curryville 32 39 21N 91 21W
Curtea de Argeş 95 45 12N 24 42 E
Curtin 44 43 43N 123 12W
Curtis, Ark. 13 34 0N 93 2W
Curtis, Nebr. 34 40 38N 100 31W
Curtis I. 127 23 35 S 151 10 E
Curuá →, Pará, Brazil 71 2 24 S 54 5W
Curuá →, Pará, Brazil 73 5 23 S 54 22W
Curuá, I. 74 0 48N 50 10W
Curuaés → 73 7 30 S 54 45W
Curuápanema → 71 2 25 S 55 2W
Curuçá 74 0 43 S 47 50W
Curuguaty 77 24 31 S 55 42W
Çürüksu Çayi → 99 37 27N 27 11 E
Curundu 57 8 59N 79 38W
Curup 110 4 26 S 102 13 E
Curupira, Serra 71 1 25N 64 30W
Cururu → 73 7 12 S 58 3W
Cururupu 74 1 50 S 44 50W
Curuzú Cuatiá 76 29 50 S 58 5W
Curvelo 75 18 45 S 44 27W
Cushing, Iowa 23 42 28N 95 41W
Cushing, Nebr. 34 41 19N 98 22W
Cushing, Okla. 43 35 59N 96 46W
Cushing, Tex. 51 31 49N 94 51W
Cushing, Mt. 62 57 35N 126 57W
Cushman, Ark. 13 35 53N 91 45W
Cushman, Oreg. 44 43 59N 124 3W
Cusick 53 48 20N 117 18W
Cusihuiriáchic 64 28 10N 106 50W
Cusseta 18 32 18N 84 47W
Custer, Mont. 33 46 8N 107 33W
Custer, S. Dak. 47 43 46N 103 36W
Custer, Wash. 53 48 55N 122 38W
Custer City 43 35 40N 98 53W
Custer County ◇, Colo. 16 38 10N 105 20W
Custer County ◇, Idaho 20 44 0N 114 0W
Custer County ◇, Mont. 33 46 25N 105 30W
Custer County ◇, Nebr. 34 41 30N 99 40W
Custer County ◇, Okla. 43 35 40N 99 0W
Custer County ◇, S. Dak. 47 43 50N 103 30W
Custer National Forest 33 45 15N 109 50W
Cut Bank 33 48 38N 112 20W
Cut Bank Cr. →, Mont. 33 48 29N 112 14W
Cut Bank Cr. →, N. Dak. 41 48 10N 100 45W
Cut Off 25 29 33N 90 20W
Cutervo 72 6 25 S 78 55W
Cuthbert 18 31 46N 84 48W
Cutler, Calif. 15 36 31N 119 17W
Cutler, Ill. 21 38 2N 89 34W
Cutler, Maine 26 44 40N 67 12W
Cutler Ridge 17 25 35N 80 20W
Cutlerville 29 42 50N 85 40W
Cutral-Có 78 38 58 S 69 15W
Cuttack 109 20 25N 85 57 E
Cuttyhunk I. 28 41 25N 70 56W
Cuvier, C. 126 23 14 S 113 22 E
Cuvier I. 128 36 27 S 175 50 E
Cuxhaven 88 53 51N 8 41 E
Cuyabeno 70 0 16 S 75 53W
Cuyahoga County ◇ 42 41 23N 81 43W
Cuyahoga Falls 42 41 8N 81 29W
Cuyo 111 10 50N 121 5 E
Cuyuma → 15 34 58N 120 38W
Cuyuna Range 30 46 25N 93 30W
Cuyuni → 71 6 23N 58 41W
Cuzco, Bolivia 72 20 0 S 66 50W
Cuzco, Peru 72 13 32 S 72 0W
Cuzco □ 72 13 31 S 71 59W
Cwmbran 83 51 39N 3 0W
Cyclades = Kikládhes 95 37 20N 24 30 E
Cyclone 45 41 50N 78 35W
Cygnes → 32 38 3N 94 17W
Cygnet 42 41 14N 83 39W
Cylinder 23 43 5N 94 33W
Cynthiana 49 38 23N 84 18W
Cypress 21 37 22N 89 1W
Cypress Hills 63 49 40N 109 30W
Cyprus ■ 106 35 0N 33 0 E
Cyrenaica 121 27 0N 23 0 E
Cyrene = Shaḥḥāt 121 32 48N 21 54 E
Cyril 43 34 54N 98 12W
Cyrus 30 45 37N 95 44W
Czar 63 52 27N 110 50W
Czechoslovakia ■ 88 49 0N 17 0 E
Czeremcha 89 52 32N 23 20 E
Częstochowa 89 50 49N 19 7 E

D

Da → 112 21 15N 105 20 E
Da Hinggan Ling 114 48 0N 121 0 E
Da Lat 112 11 56N 108 25 E
Da Nang 112 16 4N 108 13 E
Da Qaidam 113 37 50N 95 15 E
Da Yunhe, Jiangsu, China 115 34 25N 120 5 E
Da Yunhe, Zhejiang, China 115 30 45N 120 35 E
Da'an 114 45 30N 124 7 E
Daba Shan 115 32 0N 109 0 E
Dabajuro 70 11 2N 70 40W
Dabakala 120 8 15N 4 20W
Dabbūrīya 104 32 42N 35 22 E
Dabeiba 70 7 1N 76 16W
Dąbie 88 53 27N 14 45 E
Dabo 110 0 30 S 104 33 E
Dabola 120 10 50N 11 5W
Daboya 120 9 30N 1 20W
Dabrowa Tarnówska 89 50 10N 20 59 E
Dacca = Dhaka 109 23 43N 90 26 E
Dacca = Dhaka □ 109 24 25N 90 25 E
Dacoma 43 36 40N 98 34W
Dacula 18 33 59N 83 54W
Dadanawa 71 2 50N 59 30W
Dade City 17 28 22N 82 11W
Dade County ◇, Fla. 17 25 30N 80 30W
Dade County ◇, Ga. 18 35 30N 85 30W
Dade County ◇, Mo. 32 37 25N 93 50W
Dadeville, Ala. 10 32 50N 85 46W
Dadeville, Mo. 32 37 29N 93 41W
Dadra and Nagar Haveli □ 108 20 5N 73 0 E
Dadu 108 26 45N 67 45 E
Dăeni 95 44 51N 28 10 E
Daet 111 14 2N 122 55 E
Dafang 115 27 9N 105 39 E
Dagana 120 16 30N 15 35W
Dagestan A.S.S.R. □ 99 42 30N 47 0 E
Daggett County ◇ 52 40 55N 109 30W
Dagsboro 27 38 33N 75 15W
Dagupan 111 16 3N 120 20 E
Dahlak Kebir 105 15 50N 40 10 E
Dahlgren 21 38 12N 88 41W
Dahlonega 18 34 32N 83 59W
Dahlonega Plat. 18 34 10N 84 20W
Dahod 108 22 50N 74 15 E
Dahomey = Benin ■ 120 10 0N 2 0 E
Dahra 120 15 22N 15 30W
Dai-Sen 117 35 22N 133 32 E
Dai Shan 115 30 25N 122 10 E
Dai Xian 114 39 4N 112 58 E
Dailey 54 38 48N 79 54W
Daingean 85 53 18N 7 15W
Daingerfield 51 33 2N 94 44W
Daiō-Misaki 117 34 15N 136 45 E
Dairût 121 27 34N 30 43 E
Dairy 44 42 14N 121 31W
Daisetsu-Zan 116 43 30N 142 57 E
Daisetta 51 30 7N 94 39W
Daisy, Ark. 13 34 14N 93 45W
Daisy, Wash. 53 48 22N 118 10W
Dajarra 127 21 42 S 139 30 E
Dakar 120 14 34N 17 29W
Dakhla 120 23 50N 15 53W
Dakhla, El Wâhât el- 121 25 30N 28 50 E
Dakhovskaya 99 44 13N 40 13 E
Dakota, Ill. 21 42 23N 89 32W
Dakota, Minn. 30 43 55N 91 22W
Dakota City, Iowa 23 42 43N 94 12W
Dakota City, Nebr. 34 42 25N 96 25W
Dakota County ◇, Minn. 30 44 45N 93 0W
Dakota County ◇, Nebr. 34 42 30N 96 30W
Đakovica 95 42 22N 20 26 E
Dalachi 114 36 48N 105 0 E
Dalai Nur 114 43 20N 116 45 E
Dalälven 97 60 12N 16 43 E
Dalandzadgad 113 43 27N 104 30 E
Dalark 13 34 2N 92 53W
Dalarö 97 59 8N 18 24 E
Dālbandīn 107 29 0N 64 23 E
Dalbeattie 84 54 55N 3 50W
Dalby 127 27 10 S 151 17 E
Dale, Ind. 22 38 10N 86 59W
Dale, Okla. 43 35 24N 97 3W
Dale County ◇ 10 31 28N 85 39W
Dale Hollow L. 49 36 32N 85 27W
Daleville, Ala. 10 31 19N 85 43W
Daleville, Ind. 22 40 7N 85 33W
Daleville, Miss. 31 32 34N 88 41W
Dalhart 50 36 4N 102 31W
Dalhousie 61 48 5N 66 26W
Dali, Shaanxi, China 115 34 48N 109 58 E
Dali, Yunnan, China 113 25 40N 100 10 E
Dalian 114 38 50N 121 40 E
Dāliyat el Karmel 104 32 43N 35 2 E
Dalkeith, U.K. 84 55 54N 3 5W
Dalkeith, U.S.A. 17 30 0N 85 9W
Dallam County ◇ 50 36 15N 102 30W
Dallas, Ga. 18 33 55N 84 51W
Dallas, N.C. 40 35 19N 81 11W
Dallas, Oreg. 44 44 55N 123 19W
Dallas, Pa. 45 41 20N 75 58W
Dallas, S. Dak. 47 43 14N 99 31W
Dallas, Tex. 51 32 47N 96 49W
Dallas, Wis. 55 45 16N 91 51W
Dallas Center 23 41 41N 93 58W
Dallas City 21 40 38N 91 10W
Dallas County ◇, Ala. 10 32 25N 87 1W
Dallas County ◇, Ark. 13 33 59N 92 38W
Dallas County ◇, Iowa 23 41 40N 94 0W
Dallas County ◇, Mo. 32 37 40N 93 0W
Dallas County ◇, Tex. 51 32 50N 96 50W
Dalmacija □ 94 43 20N 17 0 E
Dalmatia = Dalmacija □ 94 43 20N 17 0 E

Dalmellington Dedéagach

Dalmellington **84** 55 20N 4 25W
Dalnegorsk **116** 44 32N 135 33 E
Dalneretchensk **101** 45 50N 133 40 E
Daloa **120** 7 0N 6 30W
Dalrymple, Mt. **127** 21 1 S 148 39 E
Dalton, Canada **60** 48 11N 84 1W
Dalton, Ga. **18** 34 46N 84 58W
Dalton, Mass. **28** 42 28N 73 11W
Dalton, Minn. **30** 46 10N 95 55W
Dalton, Nebr. **34** 41 25N 102 58W
Dalton, Ohio **42** 40 48N 81 42W
Dalton, Pa. **45** 41 32N 75 44W
Dalton Iceberg Tongue **5** 66 15 S 121 30 E
Dalvík **96** 65 58N 18 32W
Daly → **126** 13 35 S 130 19 E
Daly City **14** 37 42N 122 28W
Daly L. **63** 56 32N 105 39W
Daly Waters **126** 16 15 S 133 24 E
Daman **108** 20 25N 72 57 E
Damanhûr **121** 31 0N 30 30 E
Damar, Indonesia **111** 7 7 S 128 40 E
Damar, U.S.A. **24** 39 19N 99 35W
Damaraland **123** 21 0 S 17 0 E
Damascus = Dimashq **106** 33 30N 36 18 E
Damascus, Ark. **13** 35 22N 92 25W
Damascus, Ga. **18** 31 18N 84 43W
Damascus, Md. **27** 39 17N 77 12W
Damascus, Va. **54** 36 38N 81 47W
Damāvand **107** 35 47N 52 0 E
Damāvand, Qolleh-ye **107** 35 56N 52 10 E
Damba **122** 6 44 S 15 20 E
Dâmboviţa → **89** 44 40N 26 0 E
Dame Marie **67** 18 36N 74 26W
Dameron **27** 38 10N 76 22W
Dames Quarter **27** 38 11N 75 54W
Dāmghān **107** 36 10N 54 17 E
Damietta = Dumyât **121** 31 24N 31 48 E
Daming **114** 36 15N 115 6 E
Dāmīya **104** 32 6N 35 34 E
Damoh **108** 23 50N 79 28 E
Dampier **126** 20 41 S 116 42 E
Dampier, Selat **111** 0 40 S 131 0 E
Dampier Arch. **126** 20 38 S 116 32 E
Dampier Downs **126** 18 24 S 123 5 E
Dan → **54** 36 42N 78 50W
Dan Xian **115** 19 31N 109 33 E
Dana, Indonesia **111** 11 0 S 122 52 E
Dana, Ind. **22** 39 48N 87 30W
Dana, Iowa **23** 42 6N 94 14W
Dana, Lac **60** 50 53N 77 20W
Dana Point **15** 33 28N 117 42W
Danao **111** 10 31N 124 1 E
Danbury, Conn. **28** 41 24N 73 28W
Danbury, Iowa **23** 42 14N 95 43W
Danbury, N.C. **40** 36 25N 80 12W
Danbury, N.H. **36** 43 32N 71 52W
Danbury, Nebr. **34** 40 3N 100 25W
Danbury, Tex. **51** 29 14N 95 21W
Danby **36** 43 20N 72 59W
Danby L. **15** 34 13N 115 5W
Dandeldhura **109** 29 20N 80 35 E
Dandeli **108** 15 5N 74 30 E
Dandong **114** 40 10N 124 20 E
Dandridge **49** 36 1N 83 25W
Dane County ◇ **55** 43 0N 89 29W
Danforth, Ill. **21** 40 49N 87 59W
Danforth, Maine **26** 45 40N 67 52W
Danforth Hills **16** 40 15N 108 0W
Danger Pt. **123** 34 40 S 19 17 E
Dangora **120** 11 30N 8 7 E
Dangriga **65** 17 0N 88 13W
Dangshan **115** 34 27N 116 22 E
Dangtu **115** 31 32N 118 25 E
Dangyang **115** 30 52N 111 44 E
Daniel **56** 42 52N 110 4W
Daniel Boone National
Forest **49** 37 30N 84 0W
Daniels County ◇ **33** 48 40N 105 20W
Daniel's Harbour **61** 50 13N 57 35W
Daniel's Pass **52** 40 18N 111 10W
Danielson **28** 41 48N 71 53W
Danielsville **18** 34 8N 83 13W
Danilov **98** 58 16N 40 13 E
Dankhar Gompa **108** 32 10N 78 10 E
Danlí **66** 14 4N 86 35W
Dannebrog **34** 41 7N 98 33W
Dannemora, Sweden **97** 60 12N 17 51 E
Dannemora, U.S.A. **39** 44 43N 73 44W
Dannevirke **128** 40 12 S 176 8 E
Danshui **115** 25 12N 121 25 E
Dansville, Mich. **29** 42 34N 84 19W
Dansville, N.Y. **39** 42 34N 77 42W
Dante, Somalia **105** 10 25N 51 26 E
Dante, S. Dak. **47** 43 2N 98 11W
Dante, Va. **54** 36 59N 82 18W
Danube → = Donau → **88** 48 10N 17 0 E
Danube → **95** 45 20N 29 40 E
Danvers, Ill. **21** 40 32N 89 11W
Danvers, Mass. **28** 42 34N 70 56W
Danville, Ark. **13** 35 3N 93 24W
Danville, Calif. **14** 37 49N 122 0W
Danville, Ga. **18** 32 37N 83 15W
Danville, Ill. **21** 40 8N 87 37W
Danville, Ind. **22** 39 46N 86 32W
Danville, Iowa **23** 40 52N 91 19W
Danville, Kans. **24** 37 17N 97 54W
Danville, Ky. **49** 37 39N 84 46W
Danville, Ohio **42** 40 27N 82 16W
Danville, Pa. **45** 40 58N 76 37W
Danville, Va. **54** 36 36N 79 23W
Danville, Vt. **36** 44 25N 72 9W
Danville, W. Va. **54** 38 5N 81 50W
Danville, Wash. **53** 48 59N 118 30W
Danzhai **115** 26 11N 107 48 E
Danzig = Gdańsk **89** 54 22N 18 40 E
Dao **111** 10 30N 121 57 E
Dao Xian **115** 25 36N 111 31 E
Daoud = Aïn Beïda **120** 35 50N 7 29 E
Daphne **10** 30 36N 87 54W
Daqing Shan **114** 40 40N 111 0 E
Daqu Shan **115** 30 25N 122 20 E
Dar al Hamrā, Ad **106** 27 22N 37 43 E
Dar es Salaam **122** 6 50 S 39 12 E
Dar'ā **104** 32 36N 36 7 E
Dārāb **107** 28 50N 54 30 E
Daraj **120** 30 10N 10 28 E
Darband **108** 34 20N 72 50 E
Darbhanga **109** 26 15N 85 55 E
Darby **33** 46 1N 114 11W
Darby, C. **11** 64 19N 162 47W
Dardanelle, Ark. **13** 35 13N 93 9W
Dardanelle, Calif. **14** 38 20N 119 50W
Dardanelle L. **13** 35 14N 93 10W
Dardanelles = Çanakkale
Boğazi **106** 40 0N 26 0 E
Dare County ◇ **40** 35 45N 75 40W
Dârfûr, Sudan **121** 13 40N 24 0 E
Darfur, U.S.A. **30** 44 3N 94 50W
Dargai **108** 34 25N 71 55 E
Dargan Ata **100** 40 29N 62 10 E
Dargaville **128** 35 57 S 173 52 E
Darhan Muminggan Lianheqi **114** 41 40N 110 28 E
Darien, Panama **57** 9 7N 79 46W
Darien, Conn. **28** 41 5N 73 28W
Darien, Ga. **18** 31 23N 81 26W
Darien, Wis. **55** 42 36N 88 43W
Darién, G. del **70** 9 0N 77 0W
Darién, Serranía del **70** 8 30N 77 30W
Darjeeling = Darjiling **109** 27 3N 88 18 E
Darjiling **109** 27 3N 88 18 E
Dark Cove **61** 48 47N 54 13W
Darke County ◇ **42** 40 6N 84 38W
Darling → **127** 34 4 S 141 54 E
Darling, L. **41** 48 27N 101 35W
Darling Ra. **126** 32 30 S 116 0 E
Darlington, U.K. **82** 54 33N 1 33W
Darlington, Fla. **17** 30 57N 86 3W
Darlington, Ind. **22** 40 6N 86 47W
Darlington, La. **25** 30 53N 90 47W
Darlington, Md. **27** 39 38N 76 12W
Darlington, S.C. **46** 34 18N 79 52W
Darlington, Wis. **55** 42 41N 90 7W
Darlington County ◇ **46** 34 20N 80 0W
Darłowo **88** 54 25N 16 25 E
Dărmăneşti **95** 46 21N 26 33 E
Darmstadt **88** 49 51N 8 40 E
Darnah **121** 32 40N 22 35 E
Darnestown **27** 39 6N 77 18W
Darnley, C. **5** 68 0 S 69 0 E
Darnley B. **58** 69 30N 123 30W
Darr **34** 40 49N 99 53W
Darrington **53** 48 15N 121 36W
Darror → **105** 10 30N 50 0 E
Darrouzett **50** 36 27N 100 20W
Dart → **83** 50 24N 3 36W
Dart, C. **5** 73 6 S 126 20W
Dartmoor **83** 50 36N 4 0W
Dartmouth, Canada **61** 44 40N 63 30W
Dartmouth, U.K. **83** 50 21N 3 35W
Darvaza **100** 40 11N 58 24 E
Darvel, Teluk **111** 4 50N 118 20 E
Darwha **108** 20 15N 77 45 E
Darwin **126** 12 25 S 130 51 E
Darwin, Mt. **78** 0 10 S 69 55W
Dās **107** 25 20N 53 30 E
Dasher **18** 30 45N 83 13W
Dasht → **107** 25 10N 61 40 E
Dasht-e Kavīr **107** 34 30N 55 0 E
Dasht-e Lūt **107** 31 30N 58 0 E
Dasht-e Mārgow **107** 30 40N 62 30 E
Dassel **30** 45 5N 94 19W
Dateland **12** 32 48N 113 33W
Datia **108** 25 39N 78 27 E
Datian **115** 25 40N 117 50 E
Datil **38** 34 9N 107 51W
Datong, Anhui, China **115** 30 48N 117 44 E
Datong, Shanxi, China **114** 40 6N 113 18 E
Datu, Tanjung **110** 2 5N 109 39 E
Datu Piang **111** 7 2N 124 30 E
Daugava → **98** 57 4N 24 3 E
Daugavpils **98** 55 53N 26 32 E
Daule **70** 1 56 S 79 56W
Daule → **70** 2 10 S 79 52W
Daulpur **108** 26 45N 77 59 E
Dauphin, Canada **63** 51 9N 100 5W
Dauphin, U.S.A. **45** 40 22N 76 56W
Dauphin County ◇ **45** 40 20N 76 55W
Dauphin I. **10** 30 15N 88 11W
Dauphin Island **10** 30 15N 88 7W
Dauphin L. **63** 51 20N 99 45W
Dauphiné **90** 45 15N 5 25 E
Davangere **108** 14 25N 75 55 E
Davao **111** 7 0N 125 40 E
Davao, G. of **111** 6 30N 125 48 E
Dāvar Panāh **107** 27 25N 62 15 E
Davenport, Calif. **14** 37 1N 122 12W
Davenport, Fla. **17** 28 10N 81 36W
Davenport, Iowa **23** 41 32N 90 35W
Davenport, N. Dak. **41** 46 43N 97 4W
Davenport, N.Y. **39** 42 28N 74 51W
Davenport, Nebr. **34** 40 19N 97 49W
Davenport, Okla. **43** 35 42N 96 46W
Davenport, Wash. **53** 47 39N 118 9W
Davenport Ra. **126** 20 28 S 134 0 E
Davey **34** 40 59N 96 40W
David, Panama **66** 8 30N 82 30W
David, U.S.A. **49** 37 36N 82 54W
David City **34** 41 15N 97 8W
Davidson, Canada **63** 51 16N 105 59W
Davidson, N.C. **40** 35 30N 80 51W
Davidson, Okla. **43** 34 14N 99 5W
Davidson County ◇, N.C. **40** 35 45N 80 10W
Davidson County ◇, Tenn. **48** 36 10N 86 47W
Davidsonville **27** 38 55N 76 38W
Davie County ◇ **40** 35 50N 80 30W
Daviess County ◇, Ind. **22** 38 40N 87 5W
Daviess County ◇, Ky. **48** 38 40N 87 5W
Daviess County ◇, Mo. **32** 40 0N 94 0W
Davis, Antarct. **5** 68 34 S 17 55 E
Davis, Calif. **14** 38 33N 121 44W
Davis, Ill. **21** 42 25N 89 25W
Davis, N.C. **40** 34 48N 76 28W
Davis, Okla. **43** 34 30N 97 7W
Davis, S. Dak. **47** 43 16N 96 59W
Davis, W. Va. **54** 39 8N 79 28W
Davis, Mt. **45** 39 48N 79 10W
Davis City **23** 40 38N 93 49W
Davis County ◇, Iowa **23** 40 45N 92 25W
Davis County ◇, Utah **52** 41 0N 112 5W
Davis Creek **14** 41 44N 120 22W
Davis Dam **12** 35 11N 114 34W
Davis Inlet **61** 55 50N 60 59W
Davis Junction **21** 42 6N 89 6W
Davis Mts. **50** 30 50N 103 55W
Davis Sea **5** 66 0 S 92 0 E
Davis Str. **59** 65 0N 58 0W
Davisboro **18** 32 59N 82 36W
Davison **29** 43 2N 83 31W
Davison County ◇ **47** 43 43N 98 2W
Davisville **32** 37 49N 91 11W
Davos **88** 46 48N 9 49 E
Davy **54** 37 29N 81 39W
Davy Crockett National
Forest **51** 31 12N 95 2W
Davy L. **63** 58 53N 108 18W
Dawes County ◇ **34** 42 45N 103 0W
Dawn **50** 34 55N 102 12W
Dawson, Canada **58** 64 10N 139 30W
Dawson, Ga. **18** 31 46N 84 27W
Dawson, Minn. **30** 44 56N 96 3W
Dawson, N. Dak. **41** 46 52N 99 45W
Dawson, Nebr. **34** 40 8N 95 50W
Dawson, Oreg. **44** 44 22N 123 25W
Dawson, Tex. **51** 31 54N 96 43W
Dawson → **127** 23 25 S 149 45 E
Dawson, I. **78** 53 50 S 70 50W
Dawson County ◇, Ga. **18** 34 25N 84 10W
Dawson County ◇, Mont. **33** 47 15N 105 0W
Dawson County ◇, Nebr. **34** 40 50N 99 50W
Dawson County ◇, Tex. **50** 32 44N 101 58W
Dawson Creek **62** 55 45N 120 15W
Dawson Inlet **63** 61 50N 93 25W
Dawson Springs **48** 37 10N 87 41W
Dawsonville **18** 34 25N 84 7W
Daxian **115** 31 15N 107 23 E
Daxin **115** 22 50N 107 11 E
Daxue Shan **113** 30 30N 101 30 E
Day **17** 30 12N 83 17W
Day County ◇ **47** 45 20N 97 31W
Daye **115** 30 6N 114 58 E
Daykin **34** 40 21N 97 18W
Dayong **115** 29 11N 110 30 E
Dayr Abū Sa'īd **104** 32 30N 35 42 E
Dayr al-Ghuşūn **104** 32 21N 35 4 E
Dayr az Zawr **106** 35 20N 40 5 E
Dayr Dirwān **104** 31 55N 35 15 E
Daysland **62** 52 50N 112 20W
Dayton, Ala. **10** 32 21N 87 38W
Dayton, Mont. **33** 47 52N 114 17W
Dayton, Nev. **35** 39 14N 119 36W
Dayton, Ohio **42** 39 45N 84 12W
Dayton, Pa. **45** 40 53N 79 15W
Dayton, Tenn. **49** 35 30N 85 1W
Dayton, Tex. **51** 30 3N 94 54W
Dayton, Va. **54** 38 25N 78 56W
Dayton, Wash. **53** 46 19N 117 59W
Dayton, Wyo. **56** 44 53N 107 16W
Daytona Beach **17** 29 13N 81 1W
Dayu **115** 25 24N 114 22 E
Dayville **44** 44 28N 119 32W
Dazey **41** 47 11N 98 12W
Dazhu **115** 30 41N 107 15 E
Dazu **115** 29 40N 105 42 E
De Aar **123** 30 39 S 24 0 E
De Armanville **10** 33 38N 85 45W
De Baca County ◇ **38** 34 15N 104 30W
De Bary **17** 28 54N 81 18W
De Beque **16** 39 20N 108 13W
De Forest **55** 43 15N 89 20W
De Funiak Springs **17** 30 43N 86 7W
De Graff **30** 45 16N 95 28W
De Gray L. **13** 34 13N 93 7W
De Grey **126** 20 12 S 119 12 E
De Kalb, Ill. **21** 41 56N 88 46W
De Kalb, Miss. **31** 32 46N 88 39W
De Kalb, Tex. **51** 33 31N 94 37W
De Kalb County ◇, Ala. **10** 34 26N 85 43W
De Kalb County ◇, Ga. **18** 33 40N 84 10W
De Kalb County ◇, Ill. **21** 41 50N 88 45W
De Kalb County ◇, Ind. **22** 41 25N 85 0W
De Kalb County ◇, Mo. **32** 39 50N 94 25W
De Kalb County ◇, Tenn. **48** 36 0N 86 0W
De Kalb Junction **39** 44 30N 75 17W
De Land **17** 29 2N 81 18W
De Leon **51** 32 7N 98 32W
De Leon Springs **17** 29 7N 81 21W
De Long Mts. **11** 68 30N 163 0W
De Pere **55** 44 27N 88 4W
De Queen **13** 34 2N 94 21W
De Quincy **25** 30 27N 93 26W
De Ridder **25** 30 51N 93 17W
De Ruyter **39** 42 46N 75 53W
De Smet **47** 44 23N 97 33W
De Smet, L. **56** 44 29N 106 45W
De Soto, Ill. **21** 37 49N 89 14W
De Soto, Kans. **24** 38 59N 94 58W
De Soto, Miss. **31** 31 58N 88 43W
De Soto, Mo. **32** 38 8N 90 34W
De Soto, Wis. **55** 43 25N 91 12W
De Soto City **17** 27 27N 81 24W
De Soto County ◇, Fla. **17** 27 15N 81 45W
De Soto County ◇, Miss. **31** 34 53N 90 1W
De Soto National Forest **31** 31 0N 89 0W
De Soto Parish ◇ **25** 32 2N 93 43W
De Tour Village **29** 46 0N 83 56W
De Witt, Ark. **13** 34 18N 91 20W
De Witt, Ill. **21** 40 11N 88 47W
De Witt, Iowa **23** 41 49N 90 33W
De Witt, Mich. **29** 42 51N 84 34W
De Witt, Nebr. **34** 40 24N 96 55W
De Witt County ◇, Ill. **21** 40 10N 88 55W
De Witt County ◇, Tex. **51** 29 6N 97 17W
Dead L. **17** 30 10N 85 10W
Dead Sea **106** 31 30N 35 30 E
Deadhorse **11** 70 11N 148 27W
Deadman B. **17** 29 30N 83 30W
Deadwood **47** 44 23N 103 44W
Deadwood L. **62** 59 10N 128 30W
Deaf Smith County ◇ **50** 35 0N 102 30W
Deakin **126** 30 46 S 128 0 E
Deal **83** 51 13N 1 25 E
Deale **27** 38 47N 76 33W
Dean, Forest of **83** 51 50N 2 35W
Deán Funes **76** 30 20 S 64 20W
Dearborn, Mich. **29** 42 19N 83 11W
Dearborn, Mo. **32** 39 32N 94 46W
Dearborn County ◇ **22** 39 10N 85 0W
Deary **20** 46 48N 116 32W
Dease → **62** 59 56N 128 32W
Dease Inlet **11** 70 30N 155 0W
Dease L. **62** 58 40N 130 5W
Dease Lake **62** 58 25N 130 6W
Death Valley **15** 36 15N 116 50W
Death Valley Junction **14** 36 20N 110 25W
Death Valley National
Monument **15** 36 45N 117 15W
Deatsville **10** 32 37N 86 24W
Deaver **56** 44 54N 108 36W
Deba Habe **120** 10 14N 11 20 E
Debao **115** 23 21N 106 46 E
Debar **95** 41 31N 20 30 E
Debden **63** 53 30N 106 50W
Deblois **26** 44 45N 68 1W
Debolt **62** 55 12N 118 1W
Debre Markos **120** 10 20N 37 40 E
Debre Tabor **121** 11 50N 38 26 E
Debrecen **89** 47 33N 21 42 E
Decatur, Ala. **10** 34 36N 86 59W
Decatur, Ark. **13** 36 20N 94 28W
Decatur, Ga. **18** 33 47N 84 18W
Decatur, Ill. **21** 39 51N 88 57W
Decatur, Ind. **22** 40 50N 84 56W
Decatur, Mich. **29** 42 7N 85 58W
Decatur, Miss. **31** 32 26N 89 7W
Decatur, Nebr. **34** 42 0N 96 15W
Decatur, Tenn. **49** 35 31N 84 47W
Decatur, Tex. **51** 33 14N 97 35W
Decatur City **23** 40 45N 93 50W
Decatur County ◇, Ga. **18** 31 0N 84 30W
Decatur County ◇, Ind. **22** 39 15N 85 30W
Decatur County ◇, Iowa **23** 40 45N 93 45W
Decatur County ◇, Kans. **24** 39 45N 100 20W
Decatur County ◇, Tenn. **48** 35 35N 88 7W
Decaturville **48** 35 35N 88 7W
Deccan **108** 18 0N 79 0 E
Deception, Mt. **53** 47 49N 123 14W
Deception I. **5** 63 0 S 60 15W
Deception L. **63** 56 33N 104 13W
Decherd **48** 35 13N 86 5W
Deckerville **29** 43 32N 82 44W
Declo **20** 42 32N 113 40W
Decorah **23** 43 18N 91 48W
Dedéagach =
Alexandroúpolis **95** 40 50N 25 54 E

Dedham Diamond Head

Dedham, Iowa **23** 41 55N 94 49W
Dedham, Mass. **28** 42 15N 71 10W
Dédougou **120** 12 30N 3 25W
Dee →, Scotland, U.K. **84** 57 4N 2 7W
Dee →, Wales, U.K. **82** 53 15N 3 7W
Deefield **55** 43 3N 89 5W
Deep → **40** 35 36N 79 3W
Deep B. **62** 61 15N 116 35W
Deep Cr. → **42** 39 27N 83 0W
Deep Creek L. **27** 39 31N 79 24W
Deep Creek Range **52** 39 50N 113 50W
Deep Fork Canadian → **43** 35 28N 95 50W
Deep River, Conn. **28** 41 23N 72 26W
Deep River, Iowa **23** 41 35N 92 22W
Deep Springs L. **15** 37 20N 118 0W
Deepdale **126** 21 42 S 116 10 E
Deepstep **18** 33 1N 82 58W
Deepwater, Mo. **32** 38 16N 93 47W
Deepwater, N.J. **37** 39 41N 75 29W
Deer **13** 35 50N 93 13W
Deer → **63** 58 23N 94 13W
Deer Cr. →, Ind. **22** 40 34N 86 41W
Deer Cr. →, Md. **27** 39 40N 76 10W
Deer Creek, Ill. **21** 40 38N 89 20W
Deer Creek, Okla. **43** 36 48N 97 31W
Deer Grove **21** 41 37N 89 42W
Deer I., Alaska **11** 54 55N 162 18W
Deer I., Maine **26** 44 13N 68 41W
Deer Isle **26** 44 14N 68 41W
Deer Lake, Newf., Canada **61** 49 11N 57 27W
Deer Lake, Ont., Canada **63** 52 36N 94 20W
Deer Lodge **33** 46 24N 112 44W
Deer Lodge County ◇ **33** 46 0N 113 0W
Deer Park, Ala. **10** 31 13N 88 19W
Deer Park, Fla. **17** 28 6N 80 54W
Deer Park, Md. **27** 39 25N 79 18W
Deer Park, N.Y. **39** 40 46N 73 20W
Deer Park, Ohio **42** 39 13N 84 23W
Deer Park, Wash. **53** 47 57N 117 28W
Deer Park, Wis. **55** 45 11N 92 23W
Deer River **30** 47 20N 93 48W
Deer Trail **16** 39 37N 104 2W
Deerfield, Ill. **21** 42 10N 87 51W
Deerfield, Kans. **24** 37 59N 101 8W
Deerfield, Mo. **32** 37 50N 94 30W
Deerfield → **28** 42 35N 72 35W
Deerfield Beach **17** 26 19N 80 6W
Deering, Alaska **11** 66 4N 162 42W
Deering, N. Dak. **41** 48 24N 101 3W
Deerlodge National Forest **33** 46 20N 113 30W
Deersville **42** 40 18N 81 11W
Deerwood **30** 46 29N 93 54W
Deeth **35** 41 4N 115 17W
Defiance, Iowa **23** 41 49N 95 20W
Defiance, Ohio **42** 41 17N 84 22W
Defiance County ◇ **42** 41 23N 84 32W
Deganya **104** 32 43N 35 34 E
Degeh Bur **105** 8 11N 43 31 E
Deggendorf **88** 48 49N 12 59 E
Deh Bid **107** 30 39N 53 11 E
Dehi Titan **108** 33 45N 63 50 E
Dehibat **120** 32 0N 10 47 E
Dehkareqan **106** 37 43N 45 55 E
Dehra Dun **108** 30 20N 78 4 E
Dehui **114** 44 30N 125 40 E
Deinze **87** 50 59N 3 32 E
Dej **89** 47 10N 23 52 E
Dekese **122** 3 24 S 21 24 E
Del City **43** 35 26N 97 26W
Del Mar **15** 32 58N 117 16W
Del Norte **16** 37 41N 106 21W
Del Norte County ◇ **14** 41 40N 124 0W
Del Rio **50** 29 22N 100 54W
Delacroix **25** 29 46N 89 45W
Delafield **55** 43 4N 88 24W
Delanco **37** 40 3N 74 57W
Delano, Calif. **15** 35 46N 119 15W
Delano, Minn. **30** 45 2N 93 47W
Delano Peak **52** 38 22N 112 22W
Delaplaine **13** 36 14N 90 44W
Delavan, Ill. **21** 40 22N 89 33W
Delavan, Kans. **24** 38 40N 96 49W
Delavan, Wis. **55** 42 38N 88 39W
Delaware, Ark. **13** 35 17N 93 19W
Delaware, Ohio **42** 40 18N 83 4W
Delaware, Okla. **43** 36 47N 95 39W
Delaware □ **27** 39 0N 75 20W
Delaware → **27** 39 15N 75 20W
Delaware B. **27** 39 0N 75 10W
Delaware City **27** 39 35N 75 36W
Delaware County ◇, Ind. **22** 40 15N 85 25W
Delaware County ◇, Iowa **23** 42 30N 91 20W
Delaware County ◇, N.Y. **39** 42 15N 75 0W
Delaware County ◇, Ohio **42** 40 18N 83 4W
Delaware County ◇, Okla. **43** 36 25N 94 50W
Delaware County ◇, Pa. **45** 39 55N 75 23W
Delaware Cr. → **50** 32 2N 104 0W
Delaware Mts. **50** 31 45N 104 50W
Delaware Water Gap Nat. Rec. Area **37** 41 10N 74 55W
Delbarton **54** 37 43N 82 11W
Delcambre **25** 29 57N 91 58W
Delevan **39** 42 29N 78 29W
Delft **87** 52 1N 4 22 E
Delfzijl **87** 53 20N 6 55 E
Delgada, Pt. **14** 40 2N 124 5W
Delgado, C. **122** 10 45 S 40 40 E
Delgo **121** 20 6N 30 40 E
Delhi, India **108** 28 38N 77 17 E
Delhi, Calif. **14** 37 26N 120 46W
Delhi, Iowa **23** 42 26N 91 20W
Delhi, La. **25** 32 28N 91 30W
Delhi, N.Y. **39** 42 17N 74 55W
Delia, Canada **62** 51 38N 112 23W
Delia, U.S.A. **24** 39 15N 95 59W
Delice → **106** 39 45N 34 15 E
Delicias **64** 28 10N 105 30W
Delicias, Laguna **64** 28 7N 105 40W
Delight **13** 34 2N 93 31W
Dell **33** 44 44N 112 42W
Dell City **50** 31 56N 105 12W
Dell Rapids **47** 43 50N 96 43W
Delmar, Del. **27** 38 27N 75 35W
Delmar, Iowa **23** 42 0N 90 37W
Delmar, N.Y. **39** 42 37N 73 50W
Delmarva Peninsula **27** 38 45N 75 45W
Delmiro Gouveia **74** 9 24 S 38 6W
Delmont, N.J. **37** 39 13N 74 57W
Delmont, S. Dak. **47** 43 16N 98 10W
Deloit **23** 42 6N 95 19W
Delong, Ostrova **101** 76 40N 149 20 E
Deloraine **63** 49 15N 100 29W
Delorme, L. **61** 54 31N 69 52W
Delphi **22** 40 36N 86 41W
Delphos, Kans. **24** 39 17N 97 46W
Delphos, Ohio **42** 40 51N 84 21W
Delray Beach **17** 26 28N 80 4W
Delta, Ala. **10** 33 26N 85 42W
Delta, Colo. **16** 38 44N 108 4W
Delta, Mo. **32** 37 12N 89 44W
Delta, Ohio **42** 41 34N 84 0W
Delta, Utah **52** 39 21N 112 35W
Delta Amacuro □ **71** 8 30N 61 30W
Delta County ◇, Colo. **16** 38 50N 107 50W
Delta County ◇, Mich. **29** 46 0N 87 0W
Delta County ◇, Tex. **51** 33 23N 95 42W
Delta Junction **11** 64 2N 145 44W
Delta National Forest **31** 32 50N 90 55W
Deltona **17** 28 54N 81 16W
Demanda, Sierra de la **91** 42 15N 3 0W
Demba **122** 5 28 S 22 15 E
Dembecha **121** 10 32N 37 30 E
Dembidolo **121** 8 34N 34 50 E
Demer → **87** 50 57N 4 42 E
Demerara □ **71** 6 0N 58 30W
Deming, N. Mex. **38** 32 16N 107 46W
Deming, Wash. **53** 48 50N 122 13W
Demini → **71** 0 46 S 62 56W
Demopolis **10** 32 31N 87 50W
Demorest **18** 34 34N 83 33W
Demotte **22** 41 12N 87 12W
Dempo, Mt. **110** 4 2 S 103 15 E
Dempsey **43** 35 31N 99 49W
Den Burg **87** 53 3N 4 47 E
Den Haag = 's-Gravenhage **87** 52 7N 4 17 E
Den Helder **87** 52 57N 4 45 E
Den Oever **87** 52 56N 5 2 E
Denair **14** 37 32N 120 48W
Denau **100** 38 16N 67 54 E
Denbigh, U.K. **82** 53 12N 3 26W
Denbigh, U.S.A. **41** 48 19N 100 35W
Denbigh, C. **11** 64 23N 161 32W
Dendang **110** 3 7 S 107 56 E
Dendermonde **87** 51 2N 4 5 E
Dendron **54** 37 3N 76 56W
Deng Xian **115** 32 34N 112 4 E
Denham, Australia **126** 25 56 S 113 31 E
Denham, U.S.A. **30** 46 22N 92 57W
Denham Ra. **127** 21 55 S 147 46 E
Denham Springs **25** 30 29N 90 57W
Denhoff **41** 47 29N 100 16W
Denia **91** 38 49N 0 8 E
Deniliquin **127** 35 30 S 144 58 E
Denio **35** 41 59N 118 38W
Denison, Iowa **23** 42 1N 95 21W
Denison, Kans. **24** 39 24N 95 38W
Denison, Tex. **51** 33 45N 96 33W
Denison Range **127** 28 30 S 136 5 E
Denizli **106** 37 42N 29 2 E
Denman Glacier **5** 66 45 S 99 25 E
Denmark, Australia **126** 34 59 S 117 25 E
Denmark, Kans. **24** 39 5N 98 17W
Denmark, S.C. **46** 33 19N 81 9W
Denmark, Wis. **55** 44 21N 87 50W
Denmark ■ **97** 55 30N 9 0 E
Denmark Str. **4** 66 0N 30 0W
Dennard **13** 35 46N 92 31W
Dennehotso **12** 36 51N 109 51W
Dennis, Kans. **24** 37 21N 95 25W
Dennis, Miss. **31** 34 34N 88 14W
Dennis Port **28** 41 39N 70 8W
Dennison, Minn. **30** 44 25N 93 2W
Dennison, Ohio **42** 40 24N 81 19W
Dennisville **37** 39 12N 74 49W
Denpasar **110** 8 45 S 115 14 E
Dent **30** 46 33N 95 43W
Dent County ◇ **32** 37 35N 91 30W
Denton, Ga. **18** 31 44N 82 42W
Denton, Kans. **24** 39 44N 95 16W
Denton, Md. **27** 38 53N 75 50W
Denton, Mont. **33** 47 19N 109 57W
Denton, N.C. **40** 35 38N 80 6W
Denton, Nebr. **34** 40 44N 96 51W
Denton, Tex. **51** 33 13N 97 8W
Denton County ◇ **51** 33 15N 97 10W
Denton Cr. → **51** 32 58N 96 57W
D'Entrecasteaux Pt. **126** 34 50 S 115 57 E
Dentsville, Md. **27** 38 28N 76 51W
Dentsville, S.C. **46** 34 4N 80 58W
Denver, Colo. **16** 39 44N 104 59W
Denver, Ind. **22** 40 52N 86 5W
Denver, Iowa **23** 42 40N 92 20W
Denver, Pa. **45** 40 14N 76 8W
Denver City **50** 32 58N 102 50W
Denver County ◇ **16** 39 45N 105 0W
Deoghar **109** 24 30N 86 42 E
Deolali **108** 19 58N 73 50 E
Deora **16** 37 38N 102 56W
Deoria **109** 26 31N 83 48 E
Deosai Mts. **108** 35 40N 75 0 E
Depew **43** 35 48N 96 31W
Deping **114** 37 25N 116 58 E
Depoe Bay **44** 44 49N 124 4W
Deport **51** 33 32N 95 19W
Deposit **39** 42 4N 75 25W
Depue **21** 41 19N 89 19W
Deputatskiy **101** 69 18N 139 54 E
Dêqên **113** 28 34N 98 51 E
Deqing **115** 23 8N 111 42 E
Dera Ghazi Khan **108** 30 5N 70 43 E
Dera Ismail Khan **108** 31 50N 70 50 E
Derbent **99** 42 5N 48 15 E
Derby, Australia **126** 17 18 S 123 38 E
Derby, U.K. **82** 52 55N 1 28W
Derby, Conn. **28** 41 19N 73 5W
Derby, Iowa **23** 40 56N 93 27W
Derby, Kans. **24** 37 33N 97 16W
Derby, N.Y. **39** 42 41N 78 58W
Derby, Tex. **51** 28 46N 99 8W
Derby, Vt. **36** 44 57N 72 8W
Derby □ **82** 52 55N 1 28W
Derby Line **36** 45 0N 72 6W
Derg → **85** 54 42N 7 26W
Derg, L. **85** 53 0N 8 20W
Dergaon **109** 26 45N 94 0 E
Derma **31** 33 51N 89 17W
Dermantsi **95** 43 8N 24 17 E
Dermott, Ark. **13** 33 32N 91 26W
Dermott, Tex. **50** 32 51N 101 1W
Dernieres, Isles **25** 29 2N 90 50W
Derry = Londonderry **85** 55 0N 7 20W
Derry **36** 42 53N 71 19W
Derryveagh Mts. **85** 55 0N 8 40W
Derudub **121** 17 31N 36 7 E
Derwent **63** 53 41N 110 58W
Derwent →, Derby, U.K. **82** 52 53N 1 17W
Derwent →, N. Yorks., U.K. **82** 53 45N 0 57W
Derwentwater, L. **82** 54 35N 3 9W
Des Allemands **25** 29 49N 90 28W
Des Arc, Ark. **13** 34 58N 91 30W
Des Arc, Mo. **32** 37 17N 90 38W
Des Lacs **41** 48 16N 101 34W
Des Lacs → **41** 48 17N 100 20W
Des Moines, Iowa **23** 41 35N 93 37W
Des Moines, N. Mex. **38** 36 46N 103 50W
Des Moines → **23** 40 23N 91 25W
Des Moines County ◇ **23** 40 55N 91 10W
Des Plaines **21** 42 3N 87 52W
Des Plaines → **21** 41 23N 88 15W
Desaguadero →, Argentina **76** 34 30 S 66 46W
Desaguadero →, Bolivia **72** 18 24 S 67 5W
Desaguadero →, Peru **72** 16 35 S 69 5W
Desatoya Mts. **35** 39 20N 117 40W
Descanso **15** 32 51N 116 37W
Deschaillons **61** 46 32N 72 7W
Descharme → **63** 56 51N 109 13W
Deschutes → **44** 45 38N 120 55W
Deschutes County ◇ **44** 44 0N 121 30W
Deschutes National Forest **44** 43 40N 121 20W
Deschutes-Umatilla Plat. **44** 45 0N 119 40W
Desdemona **51** 32 16N 98 33W
Dese **105** 11 5N 39 40 E
Deseado, C. **78** 52 45 S 74 42W
Desecheo, Isla **57** 18 23N 67 29W
Desemboque **64** 30 30N 112 57W
Deseret **52** 39 17N 112 39W
Deseret Peak **52** 40 28N 112 38W
Desert Center **15** 33 43N 115 24W
Desert Hot Springs **15** 33 58N 116 30W
Desert Peak **52** 41 11N 113 22W
Desert Ranch Reservoir **35** 41 42N 116 33W
Desert Valley **35** 41 10N 118 5W
Desha **13** 35 44N 91 41W
Desha County ◇ **13** 33 48N 91 16W
Deshler, Nebr. **34** 40 9N 97 44W
Deshler, Ohio **42** 41 13N 83 54W
Désirade, I. **67** 16 18N 61 3W
Deskenatlata L. **62** 60 55N 112 3W
Desloge **32** 37 51N 90 32W
Desna → **98** 50 33N 30 32 E
Desnătui → **95** 44 15N 23 27 E
Desolación, I. **78** 53 0 S 74 0W
Despeñaperros, Paso **91** 38 24N 3 30W
Dessau **88** 51 49N 12 15 E
Dessye = Dese **105** 11 5N 39 40 E
Destin **17** 30 24N 86 30W
Detmold **88** 51 55N 8 50 E
Detroit, Mich. **29** 42 20N 83 3W
Detroit, Oreg. **44** 44 44N 122 9W
Detroit, Tex. **51** 33 40N 95 16W
Detroit → **29** 42 3N 83 9W
Detroit Beach **29** 41 56N 83 19W
Detroit Lakes **30** 46 49N 95 51W
Deuel County ◇, Nebr. **34** 41 10N 102 20W
Deuel County ◇, S. Dak. **47** 44 45N 96 41W
Deurne, Belgium **87** 51 12N 4 24 E
Deurne, Neth. **87** 51 27N 5 49 E
Deutsche Bucht **88** 54 10N 7 51 E
Deux-Sèvres □ **90** 46 35N 0 20W
Deva **89** 45 53N 22 55 E
Devakottai **108** 9 55N 78 45 E
Deventer **87** 52 15N 6 10 E
Devereux **18** 33 13N 83 5W
Deveron → **84** 57 40N 2 31W
Devesel **95** 44 28N 22 41 E
Devils Den **15** 35 46N 119 58W
Devils L., N. Dak. **41** 48 2N 98 58W
Devils L., Tex. **50** 29 34N 100 59W
Devils Lake **41** 48 7N 98 52W
Devils Paw **62** 58 47N 134 0W
Devils Playground **15** 35 0N 115 50W
Devils Tower National Monument **56** 44 48N 104 55W
Devin **95** 41 44N 24 24 E
Devine **51** 29 8N 98 54W
Devizes **83** 51 21N 2 0W
Devnya **95** 43 13N 27 33 E
Devol **43** 34 11N 98 35W
Devon, Canada **62** 53 24N 113 44W
Devon, Kans. **24** 37 55N 94 49W
Devon, Mont. **33** 48 28N 111 29W
Devon I. **4** 75 10N 85 0W
Devonport, Australia **127** 41 10 S 146 22 E
Devonport, N.Z. **128** 36 49 S 174 49 E
Devonport, U.K. **83** 50 23N 4 11W
Devonshire □ **83** 50 50N 3 40W
Dew **51** 31 36N 96 9W
Dewar **43** 35 28N 95 56W
Dewas **108** 22 59N 76 3 E
Deweese **34** 40 21N 98 8W
Dewey, Puerto Rico **57** 18 18N 65 18W
Dewey, Ariz. **12** 34 32N 112 15W
Dewey, Okla. **43** 36 48N 95 56W
Dewey Beach **27** 38 42N 75 5W
Dewey County ◇, Okla. **43** 36 0N 99 0W
Dewey County ◇, S. Dak. **47** 45 0N 101 0W
Dewey L. **49** 37 44N 82 44W
Deweyville **51** 30 18N 93 45W
Dewsbury **82** 53 42N 1 38W
Dewy Rose **18** 34 10N 82 57W
Dexter, Ga. **18** 32 27N 83 4W
Dexter, Kans. **24** 37 11N 96 43W
Dexter, Ky. **48** 36 44N 88 17W
Dexter, Maine **26** 45 1N 69 18W
Dexter, Mich. **29** 42 20N 83 53W
Dexter, Minn. **30** 43 43N 92 42W
Dexter, Mo. **32** 36 48N 89 57W
Dexter, N. Mex. **38** 33 12N 104 22W
Dexter City **42** 39 39N 81 28W
Deyhūk **107** 33 15N 57 30 E
Deyyer **107** 27 55N 51 55 E
Dezadeash L. **62** 60 28N 136 58W
Dezfūl **106** 32 20N 48 30 E
Dezhneva, Mys **101** 66 5N 169 40W
Dezhou **114** 37 26N 116 18 E
Dhafra **107** 23 20N 54 0 E
Dhahira **107** 23 40N 57 0 E
Dhahran = Aẓ Ẓahrān **106** 26 10N 50 7 E
Dhaka **109** 23 43N 90 26 E
Dhamtari **109** 20 42N 81 35 E
Dhanbad **109** 23 50N 86 30 E
Dhangarhi **109** 28 55N 80 40 E
Dhankuta **109** 26 55N 87 40 E
Dhar **108** 22 35N 75 26 E
Dharmapuri **108** 12 10N 78 10 E
Dharwad **108** 15 22N 75 15 E
Dharwar **108** 15 43N 75 1 E
Dhaulagiri **109** 28 39N 83 28 E
Dhenkanal **109** 20 45N 85 35 E
Dhidhimótikhon **95** 41 22N 26 29 E
Dhikti **95** 35 8N 25 22 E
Dhírfis **95** 38 40N 23 54 E
Dhodhekánisos **95** 36 35N 27 0 E
Dhrol **108** 22 33N 70 25 E
Dhubaibah **107** 23 25N 54 35 E
Dhuburi **109** 26 2N 89 59 E
Dhula **105** 15 10N 47 30 E
Dhule **108** 20 58N 74 50 E
Di Linh, Cao Nguyen **112** 11 30N 108 0 E
Diablo **53** 48 58N 121 8W
Diablo, Sierra **50** 31 15N 105 0W
Diablo Range **14** 37 20N 121 25W
Diafarabé **120** 14 9N 4 57W
Diagonal **23** 40 49N 94 20W
Diamante **76** 32 5 S 60 40W
Diamante → **76** 34 30 S 66 46W
Diamantina **75** 18 17 S 43 40W
Diamantina → **127** 26 45 S 139 10 E
Diamantino **73** 14 30 S 56 30W
Diamond **32** 36 59N 94 19W
Diamond, L. **44** 43 10N 122 9W
Diamond Harbour **109** 22 11N 88 14 E
Diamond Head **19** 21 16N 157 49W

Diamond Mts. Dot Lake

Diamond Mts. **35** 39 50N 115 30W
Diamond Pk., Colo. **16** 40 59N 108 50W
Diamond Pk., Idaho **20** 44 9N 113 5W
Diamond Springs **14** 38 42N 120 49W
Diamondville **56** 41 47N 110 32W
Diana **54** 38 34N 80 27W
Diancheng **115** 21 30N 111 4 E
Dianópolis **75** 11 38 S 46 50W
Diapaga **120** 12 5N 1 46 E
Dias Creek **37** 39 8N 74 53W
Dībā **107** 25 45N 56 16 E
Dibaya **122** 6 30 S 22 57 E
Dibaya-Lubue **122** 4 12 S 19 54 E
Dibbi **105** 4 10N 41 52 E
Dibble **43** 35 2N 97 38W
Dibble Glacier Tongue **5** 66 8 S 134 32 E
D'Iberville **31** 30 26N 88 54W
Diboll **51** 31 11N 94 47W
Dibrugarh **109** 27 29N 94 55 E
Dickens, Nebr. **34** 40 49N 101 2W
Dickens, Tex. **50** 33 37N 100 50W
Dickens County ◇ **50** 33 40N 100 50W
Dickenson County ◇ **54** 37 10N 82 22W
Dickey **41** 46 32N 98 27W
Dickey County ◇ **41** 46 2N 98 30W
Dickeyville **55** 42 38N 90 36W
Dickinson, N. Dak. **41** 46 53N 102 47W
Dickinson, Tex. **51** 29 28N 95 3W
Dickinson County ◇, Iowa **23** 43 20N 95 10W
Dickinson County ◇, Kans. **24** 38 50N 97 10W
Dickinson County ◇, Mich. **29** 46 0N 87 50W
Dickson, Okla. **43** 34 11N 96 59W
Dickson, Tenn. **48** 36 5N 87 23W
Dickson, U.S.S.R. **100** 73 40N 80 5 E
Dickson County ◇ **48** 36 11N 87 21W
Didiéni **120** 13 53N 8 6W
Didsbury **62** 51 35N 114 10W
Diébougou **120** 11 0N 3 15W
Diefenbaker L. **63** 51 0N 106 55W
Diego Garcia **3** 7 50 S 72 50 E
Diehlstadt **32** 36 58N 89 26W
Diekirch **87** 49 52N 6 10 E
Dien Bien **112** 21 20N 103 0 E
Dieppe **90** 49 54N 1 4 E
Dieren **87** 52 3N 6 6 E
Dierks **13** 34 7N 94 1W
Diest **87** 50 58N 5 4 E
Dieterich **21** 39 4N 88 23W
Dietrich **20** 42 55N 114 16W
Differdange **87** 49 31N 5 54 E
Difficult **49** 36 22N 85 54W
Digby **61** 44 38N 65 50W
Digges **63** 58 40N 94 0W
Digges Is. **59** 62 40N 77 50W
Dighinala **109** 23 15N 92 5 E
Dighton **24** 38 29N 100 28W
Digne **90** 44 5N 6 12 E
Digos **111** 6 45N 125 20 E
Digranes **96** 66 4N 14 44 E
Digul → **111** 7 7 S 138 42 E
Dihang → **109** 27 48N 95 30 E
Dijlah, Nahr → **106** 31 0N 47 25 E
Dijon **90** 47 20N 5 0 E
Diksmuide **87** 51 2N 2 52 E
Dikson = Dickson **100** 73 40N 80 5 E
Dikwa **121** 12 4N 13 30 E
Dili **111** 8 39 S 125 34 E
Dilia **38** 35 12N 105 4W
Dill City **43** 35 17N 99 8W
Dillard **18** 34 58N 83 23W
Diller **34** 40 7N 96 56W
Dilley **51** 28 40N 99 10W
Dilling **121** 12 3N 29 35 E
Dillingham **11** 59 3N 158 28W
Dillingham ◇ **11** 58 0N 157 0W
Dillon, Canada **63** 55 56N 108 35W
Dillon, Colo. **16** 39 37N 106 4W
Dillon, Mont. **33** 45 13N 112 38W
Dillon, S.C. **46** 34 25N 79 22W
Dillon → **63** 55 56N 108 56W
Dillon County ◇ **46** 34 20N 79 20W
Dillon L. **42** 40 1N 80 4W
Dillon Reservoir **16** 39 37N 106 3W
Dillsboro **22** 39 1N 85 4W
Dillsburg **45** 40 7N 77 2W
Dillwyn **54** 37 32N 78 27W
Dilolo **122** 10 28 S 22 18 E
Dimas **64** 23 43N 106 47W
Dimashq **106** 33 30N 36 18 E
Dimbokro **120** 6 45N 4 46W
Dîmboviţa □ **95** 45 0N 25 30 E
Dîmboviţa → **95** 44 14N 26 13 E
Dîmbovnic → **95** 44 28N 25 18 E
Dimitrovgrad, Bulgaria **95** 42 5N 25 35 E
Dimitrovgrad, U.S.S.R. **98** 54 14N 49 39 E
Dimmit County ◇ **51** 28 27N 99 46W
Dimmitt **50** 34 33N 102 19W
Dimock **47** 43 29N 97 59W
Dimona **104** 31 2N 35 1 E
Dinagat **111** 10 10N 125 40 E
Dinajpur **109** 25 33N 88 43 E
Dinan **90** 48 28N 2 2W
Dinant **87** 50 16N 4 55 E
Dinar **106** 38 5N 30 15 E
Dinara Planina **94** 44 0N 16 30 E
Dinard **90** 48 38N 2 6W
Dinaric Alps = Dinara Planina **94** 44 0N 16 30 E
Dindigul **108** 10 25N 78 0 E
Dinero **51** 28 14N 97 58W
Ding Xian **114** 38 30N 114 59 E
Dingbian **114** 37 35N 107 32 E
Dinghai **115** 30 1N 122 6 E
Dingle **85** 52 9N 10 17W
Dingle B. **85** 52 3N 10 20W
Dingnan **115** 24 45N 115 0 E
Dingtao **115** 35 5N 115 35 E
Dinguiraye **120** 11 18N 10 49W
Dingwall **84** 57 36N 4 26W
Dingxi **114** 35 30N 104 33 E
Dingxiang **114** 38 30N 112 58 E
Dinnebito Wash → **12** 35 29N 111 14W
Dinosaur **16** 40 15N 109 1W
Dinosaur National Monument **16** 40 30N 108 45W
Dinuba **15** 36 32N 119 23W
Dinwiddie **54** 37 5N 77 35W
Dinwiddie County ◇ **54** 37 5N 77 35W
Diomede **11** 65 47N 169 0W
Diourbel **120** 14 39N 16 12W
Dipolog **111** 8 36N 123 20 E
Dir **107** 35 8N 71 59 E
Diré **120** 16 20N 3 25W
Dire Dawa **105** 9 35N 41 45 E
Diriamba **66** 11 51N 86 19W
Dirico **123** 17 50 S 20 42 E
Dirk Hartog I. **126** 25 50 S 113 5 E
Dirranbandi **127** 28 33 S 148 17 E
Dirty Devil → **52** 37 58N 110 24W
Disa **108** 24 18N 72 10 E
Disappointment, C. **53** 46 18N 124 5W
Disappointment L. **126** 23 20 S 122 40 E
Disaster B. **127** 37 15 S 150 0 E
Disautel **53** 48 22N 119 14W
Discovery B. **127** 38 10 S 140 40 E
Dishman **53** 47 39N 117 17W
Disko **4** 69 45N 53 30W
Disko Bugt **4** 69 10N 52 0W
Dismal → **34** 41 50N 100 5W
Dismal Swamp **54** 36 40N 76 20W
Disney **43** 36 29N 95 1W
Disputanta **54** 37 8N 77 14W
Disteghil Sar **108** 36 20N 75 12 E
District of Columbia □ **27** 38 54N 77 1W
Distrito Federal □, Brazil **75** 15 45 S 47 45W
Distrito Federal □, Venezuela **70** 10 30N 66 55W
Diu **108** 20 45N 70 58 E
Divernon **21** 39 34N 89 39W
Diversion L. **51** 33 49N 98 56W
Divide **33** 45 45N 112 45W
Divide County ◇ **41** 48 55N 103 30W
Dividing Creek **37** 39 16N 75 6W
Divinópolis **75** 20 10 S 44 54W
Divisões, Serra dos **75** 17 0 S 51 0W
Divnoye **99** 45 55N 43 21 E
Dīwāl Kol **108** 34 23N 67 52 E
Dix, Ill. **21** 38 27N 88 56W
Dix, Nebr. **34** 41 14N 103 29W
Dix → **49** 37 49N 84 43W
Dix Hills **39** 40 49N 73 22W
Dixfield **26** 44 32N 70 28W
Dixie, Ala. **10** 31 9N 86 44W
Dixie, Ark. **13** 35 5N 91 22W
Dixie, Wash. **53** 46 8N 118 9W
Dixie County ◇ **17** 29 30N 83 15W
Dixie National Forest **52** 37 45N 112 15W
Dixie Union **18** 31 20N 82 28W
Dixmont **26** 44 41N 69 10W
Dixon, Calif. **14** 38 27N 121 49W
Dixon, Ill. **21** 41 50N 89 29W
Dixon, Iowa **23** 41 45N 90 47W
Dixon, Ky. **48** 37 31N 87 41W
Dixon, Mo. **32** 37 59N 92 6W
Dixon, Mont. **33** 47 19N 114 19W
Dixon, N. Mex. **38** 36 12N 105 53W
Dixon, Nebr. **34** 42 24N 97 2W
Dixon, Wyo. **56** 41 2N 107 32W
Dixon County ◇ **34** 42 30N 96 50W
Dixons Mills **10** 32 4N 87 47W
Dixonville **62** 56 32N 117 40W
Dixville Notch **36** 44 50N 71 18W
Diyarbakir **106** 37 55N 40 18 E
Diz Chah **107** 35 30N 55 30 E
Dizney **49** 36 51N 83 7W
Djado **121** 21 4N 12 14 E
Djakarta = Jakarta **111** 6 9 S 106 49 E
Djambala **122** 2 32 S 14 30 E
Djanet **120** 24 35N 9 32 E
Djawa = Jawa **111** 7 0 S 110 0 E
Djelfa **120** 34 40N 3 15 E
Djema **122** 6 3N 25 15 E
Djenné **120** 14 0N 4 30W
Djerid, Chott **120** 33 42N 8 30 E
Djibo **120** 14 9N 1 35W
Djibouti **105** 11 30N 43 5 E
Djibouti ■ **105** 12 0N 43 0 E
Djolu **122** 0 35N 22 5 E
Djougou **120** 9 40N 1 45 E
Djoum **122** 2 41N 12 35 E
Djourab **121** 16 40N 18 50 E
Djugu **122** 1 55N 30 35 E
Djúpivogur **96** 64 39N 14 17W
Dmitriya Lapteva, Proliv **101** 73 0N 140 0 E
Dneiper = Dnepr → **99** 46 30N 32 18 E
Dnepr → **99** 46 30N 32 18 E
Dneprodzerzhinsk **99** 48 32N 34 37 E
Dnepropetrovsk **99** 48 30N 35 0 E
Dnestr → **99** 46 18N 30 17 E
Dnestrovski = Belgorod **99** 50 35N 36 35 E
Dniester = Dnestr → **99** 46 18N 30 17 E
Doba **121** 8 40N 16 50 E
Dobbin **51** 30 22N 95 46W
Dobbs Ferry **39** 41 1N 73 52W
Dobbyn **127** 19 44 S 139 59 E
Doberai, Jazirah **111** 1 25 S 133 0 E
Doblas **76** 37 5 S 64 0W
Dobo **111** 5 45 S 134 15 E
Dobra **95** 44 52N 25 40 E
Dobrinishta **95** 41 49N 23 34 E
Dobruja **95** 44 30N 28 15 E
Dobson **40** 36 24N 80 43W
Doce → **75** 19 37 S 39 49W
Doctors Inlet **17** 30 6N 81 47W
Doddridge **13** 33 6N 93 55W
Doddridge County ◇ **54** 39 17N 80 44W
Dodecanese = Dhodhekánisos **95** 36 35N 27 0 E
Dodge, N. Dak. **41** 47 18N 102 12W
Dodge, Nebr. **34** 41 43N 96 53W
Dodge, Tex. **51** 30 45N 95 24W
Dodge Center **30** 44 2N 92 52W
Dodge City **24** 37 45N 100 1W
Dodge County ◇, Ga. **18** 33 10N 83 10W
Dodge County ◇, Minn. **30** 44 0N 92 50W
Dodge County ◇, Nebr. **34** 41 30N 96 40W
Dodge County ◇, Wis. **55** 43 20N 88 45W
Dodge L. **63** 59 50N 105 36W
Dodgeville **55** 42 58N 90 8W
Dodoma **122** 6 8 S 35 45 E
Dodsland **63** 51 50N 108 45W
Dodson, La. **25** 32 5N 92 39W
Dodson, Mont. **33** 48 24N 108 15W
Doe Run **32** 37 45N 90 30W
Doerun **18** 31 19N 83 55W
Doetinchem **87** 51 59N 6 18 E
Doftana **95** 45 11N 25 45 E
Dog Creek **62** 51 35N 122 14W
Dog I. **17** 29 48N 84 36W
Dog L., Man., Canada **63** 51 2N 98 31W
Dog L., Ont., Canada **60** 48 18N 89 30W
Dogger Bank **80** 54 50N 2 0 E
Dogi **108** 32 20N 62 50 E
Dohazari **109** 22 10N 92 5 E
Doi **111** 2 14N 127 49 E
Doi Luang **112** 18 30N 101 0 E
Doig → **62** 56 25N 120 40W
Dois Irmãos, Sa. **74** 9 0 S 42 30W
Dojran **95** 41 10N 22 45 E
Dokka **97** 60 49N 10 7 E
Dokkum **87** 53 20N 5 59 E
Doland **47** 44 54N 98 6W
Dolbeau **61** 48 53N 72 18W
Dole **90** 47 7N 5 31 E
Doles **18** 31 42N 83 53W
Dolgellau **82** 52 44N 3 53W
Dolgelley = Dolgellau **82** 52 44N 3 53W
Dolgeville **39** 43 6N 74 46W
Dolj □ **95** 44 10N 23 30 E
Dollart **87** 53 20N 7 10 E
Dolliver **23** 43 28N 94 37W
Dolna Banya **95** 42 18N 23 44 E
Dolni Dŭbnik **95** 43 24N 24 26 E
Dolomites = Dolomiti **94** 46 30N 11 40 E
Dolomiti **94** 46 30N 11 40 E
Dolores, Argentina **76** 36 20 S 57 40W
Dolores, Uruguay **76** 33 34 S 58 15W
Dolores, U.S.A. **16** 37 28N 108 30W
Dolores → **52** 38 49N 109 17W
Dolores County ◇ **16** 37 45N 108 30W
Dolphin and Union Str. **58** 69 5N 114 45W
Dolphin C. **78** 51 10 S 59 0W
Dolton **21** 41 38N 87 36W
Dom Joaquim **75** 18 57 S 43 16W
Dom Pedrito **77** 31 0 S 54 40W
Dom Pedro **74** 4 59 S 44 27W
Dombarovskiy **100** 50 46N 59 32 E
Dombås **97** 62 4N 9 8 E
Dombes **90** 46 3N 5 0 E
Domburg **87** 51 34N 3 30 E
Dome, The **36** 42 45N 73 12W
Domel I. = Letsôk-aw Kyun **112** 11 30N 98 25 E
Domeyko **76** 29 0 S 71 0W
Domeyko, Cordillera **76** 24 30 S 69 0W
Dominador **76** 24 21 S 69 20W
Dominica ■ **67** 15 20N 61 20W
Dominica Passage **67** 15 10N 61 20W
Dominican Rep. ■ **67** 19 0N 70 30W
Domo **105** 7 50N 47 10 E
Domodóssola **88** 46 6N 8 19 E
Don →, England, U.K. **82** 53 41N 0 51W
Don →, Scotland, U.K. **84** 57 14N 2 5W
Don →, U.S.S.R. **99** 47 4N 39 18 E
Don Benito **91** 38 53N 5 51W
Don Martín, Presa de **64** 27 30N 100 50W
Dona Ana **38** 32 23N 106 49W
Dona Ana County ◇ **38** 32 20N 107 0W
Dona Juana, Cerro **57** 18 0N 66 0W
Donaghadee **85** 54 38N 5 32W
Donahue **23** 41 42N 90 41W
Donalda **62** 52 35N 112 34W
Donalds **46** 34 23N 82 21W
Donaldson, Ark. **13** 34 14N 92 55W
Donaldson, Minn. **30** 48 35N 96 53W
Donaldsonville **25** 30 6N 90 59W
Donalsonville **18** 31 3N 84 53W
Donau → **88** 48 10N 17 0 E
Donauwörth **88** 48 42N 10 47 E
Doncaster, U.K. **82** 53 31N 1 9W
Doncaster, U.S.A. **27** 38 30N 77 15W
Dondo, Angola **122** 9 45 S 14 25 E
Dondo, Mozam. **123** 19 33 S 34 46 E
Dondo, Teluk **111** 0 29N 120 30 E
Dondra Head **108** 5 55N 80 40 E
Donegal **85** 54 39N 8 8W
Donegal □ **85** 54 53N 8 0W
Donegal B. **85** 54 30N 8 35W
Donets → **99** 47 33N 40 55 E
Donetsk **99** 48 0N 37 45 E
Dongara **126** 29 14 S 114 57 E
Dongfang **115** 18 50N 108 33 E
Donggala **111** 0 30 S 119 40 E
Donggou **114** 39 52N 124 10 E
Dongguan **115** 22 58N 113 44 E
Dongguang **114** 37 50N 116 30 E
Dongjingcheng **114** 44 0N 129 10 E
Donglan **115** 24 30N 107 21 E
Dongliu **115** 30 13N 116 55 E
Dongola **121** 19 9N 30 22 E
Dongou **122** 2 0N 18 5 E
Dongping **114** 35 55N 116 20 E
Dongshan **115** 23 43N 117 30 E
Dongsheng **114** 39 50N 110 0 E
Dongtai **115** 32 51N 120 21 E
Dongting Hu **113** 29 18N 112 45 E
Dongxing **115** 21 34N 108 0 E
Dongyang **115** 29 13N 120 15 E
Donie **51** 31 29N 96 13W
Doniphan, Kans. **24** 39 38N 95 5W
Doniphan, Mo. **32** 36 37N 90 50W
Doniphan, Nebr. **34** 40 46N 98 22W
Doniphan County ◇ **24** 39 45N 95 0W
Donley County ◇ **50** 35 0N 100 45W
Dønna, Norway **96** 66 6N 12 30 E
Donna, U.S.A. **50** 26 9N 98 4W
Donnaconna **61** 46 41N 71 41W
Donnan **23** 42 54N 91 53W
Donnelly, Idaho **20** 44 44N 116 5W
Donnelly, Minn. **30** 45 42N 96 1W
Donnelly's Crossing **128** 35 42 S 173 38 E
Donner Pass **14** 39 19N 120 20W
Donner und Blitzen → **44** 43 17N 118 49W
Donnybrook **41** 48 31N 101 53W
Donora **45** 40 11N 79 52W
Donovan **21** 40 53N 87 37W
Dooly County ◇ **18** 32 10N 83 50W
Doon **23** 43 17N 96 14W
Doon → **84** 55 26N 4 41W
Door County ◇ **55** 45 0N 87 15W
Door Peninsula **55** 44 45N 87 25W
Dor **104** 32 37N 34 55 E
Dora, Ala. **10** 33 44N 87 5W
Dora, Oreg. **44** 43 10N 123 59W
Dora, L. **126** 22 0 S 123 0 E
Dora Báltea → **94** 45 11N 8 5 E
Dorada, La **70** 5 30N 74 40W
Dorado **57** 18 28N 66 16W
Doran **30** 46 11N 96 29W
Doran L. **63** 61 13N 108 6W
Doraville **18** 33 54N 84 17W
Dorchester, U.K. **83** 50 42N 2 28W
Dorchester, N.H. **36** 43 44N 71 56W
Dorchester, Nebr. **34** 40 39N 97 7W
Dorchester, Wis. **55** 45 0N 90 20W
Dorchester, C. **59** 65 27N 77 27W
Dorchester County ◇, Md. **27** 38 20N 76 0W
Dorchester County ◇, S.C. **46** 33 10N 80 30W
Dordogne □ **90** 45 5N 0 40 E
Dordogne → **90** 45 2N 0 36W
Dordrecht **87** 51 48N 4 39 E
Dore, Mt. **90** 45 32N 2 50 E
Doré L. **63** 54 46N 107 17W
Doré Lake **63** 54 38N 107 36W
Dorena **44** 43 43N 122 52W
Dores do Indaiá **75** 19 27 S 45 36W
Dori **120** 14 3N 0 2W
Dorion **60** 45 23N 74 3W
Dornoch **84** 57 52N 4 0W
Dornoch Firth **84** 57 52N 4 0W
Dorohoi **89** 47 56N 26 30 E
Döröö Nuur **113** 48 0N 93 0 E
Dorrance **24** 38 51N 98 35W
Dorre I. **126** 25 13 S 113 12 E
Dorris **14** 41 58N 121 55W
Dorset **36** 43 15N 73 6W
Dorset □ **83** 50 48N 2 25W
Dortmund **88** 51 32N 7 28 E
Dorton **49** 37 17N 82 35W
Doruma **122** 4 42N 27 33 E
Dos Bahías, C. **78** 44 58 S 65 32W
Dos Bocas **57** 18 20N 66 40W
Dos Palos **14** 36 59N 120 37W
Dosso **120** 13 0N 3 13 E
Dot Lake **11** 63 40N 144 4W

Dothan Dusty

Dothan 10 31 13N 85 24W
Doty 53 46 38N 123 17W
Douai 90 50 21N 3 4 E
Douala 122 4 0N 9 45 E
Douarnenez 90 48 6N 4 21W
Douăzeci Şi Trei August 95 43 55N 28 40 E
Double Mountain Fork
Brazos → 50 33 16N 100 0W
Double Springs 10 34 9N 87 24W
Doubletop Pk. 56 43 21N 110 17W
Doubs □ 90 47 10N 6 20 E
Doubs → 90 46 53N 5 1 E
Doubtful Sd. 128 45 20 S 166 49 E
Doubtless B. 128 34 55 S 173 26 E
Douentza 120 14 58N 2 48W
Dougherty, Iowa 23 42 55N 93 3W
Dougherty, Okla. 43 34 24N 97 3W
Dougherty County ◇ 18 31 30N 84 15W
Douglas, U.K. 82 54 9N 4 29W
Douglas, Alaska 11 58 17N 134 24W
Douglas, Ariz. 12 31 21N 109 33W
Douglas, Ga. 18 31 31N 82 51W
Douglas, Mass. 28 42 6N 71 45W
Douglas, N. Dak. 41 47 51N 101 30W
Douglas, Nebr. 34 40 36N 96 23W
Douglas, Okla. 43 36 16N 97 40W
Douglas, Wyo. 56 42 45N 105 24W
Douglas C. 11 58 51N 153 15W
Douglas City 14 40 39N 122 57W
Douglas County ◇, Colo. 16 39 15N 105 0W
Douglas County ◇, Ga. 18 33 40N 84 45W
Douglas County ◇, Ill. 21 39 45N 88 15W
Douglas County ◇, Kans. 24 38 50N 95 15W
Douglas County ◇, Minn. 30 45 50N 95 20W
Douglas County ◇, Mo. 32 36 55N 92 30W
Douglas County ◇, Nebr. 34 41 15N 96 10W
Douglas County ◇, Nev. 35 38 55N 119 45W
Douglas County ◇, Oreg. 44 43 15N 123 0W
Douglas County ◇, S. Dak. 47 43 25N 98 24W
Douglas County ◇, Wash. 53 47 50N 119 45W
Douglas County ◇, Wis. 55 46 25N 91 55W
Douglas L. 49 35 58N 83 32W
Douglass, Kans. 24 37 31N 97 1W
Douglass, Tex. 51 31 40N 94 53W
Douglastown 61 48 46N 64 24W
Douglasville 18 33 45N 84 45W
Doumé 122 4 15N 13 25 E
Dounreay 84 58 34N 3 44W
Dourada, Serra 75 13 10 S 48 45W
Dourados 77 22 9 S 54 50W
Dourados → 77 21 58 S 54 18W
Douro → 91 41 8N 8 40W
Douro Litoral □ 91 41 10N 8 20W
Dousman 55 43 1N 88 29W
Dove → 82 52 51N 1 36W
Dove Creek 16 37 46N 108 54W
Dover, U.K. 83 51 7N 1 19 E
Dover, Ark. 13 35 24N 93 7W
Dover, Del. 27 39 10N 75 32W
Dover, Idaho 20 48 15N 116 36W
Dover, N.H. 36 43 12N 70 56W
Dover, N.J. 37 40 53N 74 34W
Dover, Ohio 42 40 32N 81 29W
Dover, Okla. 43 35 59N 97 55W
Dover, Tenn. 48 36 29N 87 50W
Dover, Pt. 126 32 32 S 125 32 E
Dover, Str. of 90 51 0N 1 30 E
Dover-Foxcroft 26 45 11N 69 13W
Dovey → 83 52 32N 4 0W
Dovrefjell 96 62 15N 9 33 E
Dow City 23 41 56N 95 30W
Dowa 123 13 38 S 33 58 E
Dowagiac 29 41 59N 86 6W
Dowlat Yār 107 34 30N 65 45 E
Dowlatābād 107 28 20N 56 40W
Dowling Park 17 30 15N 83 15W
Down □ 85 54 20N 6 0W
Downers Grove 21 41 48N 88 1W
Downey 20 42 26N 112 7W
Downham Market 83 52 36N 0 22 E
Downieville 14 39 34N 102 50W
Downing 32 40 29N 92 22W
Downpatrick 85 54 20N 5 43W
Downpatrick Hd. 85 54 20N 9 21W
Downs 21 40 24N 88 52W
Downs Mt. 56 43 18N 109 40W
Downsville 27 39 35N 77 48W
Dows 23 42 39N 93 30W
Dowshī 107 35 35N 68 43 E
Doylestown 55 43 25N 89 10W
Doyleville 16 38 25N 106 35W
Doyline 25 32 32N 93 25W
Dozier 10 31 10N 86 28W
Draa, Oued → 120 30 29N 6 1W
Drachten 87 53 7N 6 5 E
Dracut 28 42 40N 71 18W
Drăgăneşti 95 44 9N 24 32 E
Drăgăneşti-Viaşca 95 44 5N 25 33 E
Drăgăsani 95 44 39N 24 17 E
Dragerton 52 39 33N 110 25W
Dragoman, Prokhod 95 43 0N 22 53 E
Dragoon 12 32 2N 110 2W
Draguignan 90 43 30N 6 27 E
Drain 44 43 40N 123 19W
Drake, Ariz. 12 35 0N 112 20W
Drake, Colo. 16 40 40N 105 20W
Drake, N. Dak. 41 47 55N 100 23W
Drake Passage 5 58 0 S 68 0W
Drake Pk. 44 42 19N 120 7W
Drakensberg 123 31 0 S 28 0 E
Drakes Branch 54 36 59N 78 36W
Drakesboro 48 37 13N 87 3W
Drakesville 23 40 47N 92 31W
Dráma 95 41 9N 24 10 E
Drammen 97 59 42N 10 12 E
Drangajökull 96 66 9N 22 15W
Dranov, Ostrov 95 44 55N 29 30 E
Draper, S. Dak. 47 43 52N 100 30W
Draper, Utah 52 40 32N 111 52W
Drau = Drava → 89 45 33N 18 55 E
Drava → 89 45 33N 18 55 E
Drayden 27 38 11N 76 28W
Drayton Valley 62 53 12N 114 58W
Drenthe □ 87 52 52N 6 40 E
Dresden, Germany 88 51 2N 13 45 E
Dresden, Kans. 24 39 38N 100 26W
Dresden, N.Y. 39 42 41N 76 58W
Dresden, Tenn. 48 36 18N 88 42W
Dresser 55 45 20N 92 38W
Dreux 90 48 44N 1 23 E
Drew County ◇ 13 33 35N 91 40W
Drews Reservoir 44 42 7N 120 37W
Drexel, Mo. 32 38 29N 94 37W
Drexel, N.C. 40 35 45N 81 36W
Driffield 82 54 0N 0 25W
Driftwood 45 41 20N 78 8W
Driggs, Ark. 13 35 14N 93 46W
Driggs, Idaho 20 43 44N 111 6W
Drina → 95 44 53N 19 21 E
Drincea → 95 44 20N 22 55 E
Dripping Springs 51 30 12N 98 5W
Driscoll, N. Dak. 41 46 51N 100 9W
Driscoll, Tex. 50 27 41N 97 45W
Driskill Mt. 25 32 25N 92 54W
Drøbak 97 59 39N 10 39 E
Drogheda 85 53 45N 6 20W
Drogobych 99 49 20N 23 30 E
Droichead Nua 85 53 11N 6 50W
Droitwich 83 52 16N 2 10W
Drôme □ 90 44 38N 5 15 E
Dronning Maud Land 5 72 30 S 12 0 E
Drouzhba 95 43 15N 28 0 E
Drumheller 62 51 25N 112 40W
Drummond, Idaho 20 43 59N 111 20W
Drummond, Mont. 33 46 40N 113 9W
Drummond, Okla. 43 36 18N 98 2W
Drummond, Wis. 55 46 20N 91 15W
Drummond, L. 54 36 36N 76 28W
Drummond I. 29 46 1N 83 39W
Drummond Ra. 127 23 45 S 147 10 E
Drummondville 60 45 55N 72 25W
Drumright 43 35 59N 96 36W
Drury 27 38 48N 76 42W
Druzhina 101 68 14N 145 18 E
Dry Cr. → 56 44 31N 108 3W
Dry Creek 25 30 40N 93 3W
Dry Devils → 50 29 47N 100 59W
Dry Falls Dam 53 47 37N 119 19W
Dry L. 41 48 16N 98 59W
Dry Prong 25 31 35N 92 32W
Dry Ridge 49 38 41N 84 35W
Dryanovo 95 42 59N 25 28 E
Dryden, Canada 63 49 47N 92 50W
Dryden, N.Y. 39 42 30N 76 18W
Dryden, Tex. 50 30 3N 102 7W
Drygalski I. 5 66 0 S 92 0 E
Drysdale → 126 13 59 S 126 51 E
Dschang 122 5 32N 10 3 E
Du Bay, L. 55 44 40N 89 39W
Du Bois 34 40 2N 96 4W
Du Page County ◇ 21 41 50N 88 5W
Du Quoin 21 38 1N 89 14W
Ḍubā 106 27 10N 35 40 E
Dubach 25 32 42N 92 39W
Dubai = Dubayy 107 25 18N 55 20 E
Dubawnt → 63 64 33N 100 6W
Dubawnt, L. 63 63 4N 101 42W
Dubayy 107 25 18N 55 20 E
Dubbo 127 32 11 S 148 35 E
Dublin, Ireland 85 53 20N 6 18W
Dublin, Ga. 18 32 32N 82 54W
Dublin, Md. 27 39 39N 76 16W
Dublin, Miss. 31 34 4N 90 30W
Dublin, N.C. 40 34 39N 78 43W
Dublin, N.H. 36 42 52N 72 5W
Dublin, Tex. 51 32 5N 98 21W
Dublin, Va. 54 37 6N 80 41W
Dublin □ 85 53 24N 6 20W
Dublin B. 85 53 18N 6 5W
Dubois, Idaho 20 44 10N 112 14W
Dubois, Ind. 22 38 27N 86 48W
Dubois, Pa. 45 41 7N 78 46W
Dubois, Wyo. 56 43 33N 109 38W
Dubois County ◇ 22 38 20N 86 50W
Dubovka 99 49 5N 44 50 E
Dubréka 120 9 46N 13 31W
Dubrovnik 95 42 39N 18 6 E
Dubrovskoye 101 58 55N 111 10 E
Dubuque 23 42 30N 90 41W
Dubuque County ◇ 23 42 30N 90 50W
Dubuque Hills 21 42 15N 90 0W
Duchang 115 29 18N 116 12 E
Duchesne 52 40 10N 110 24W
Duchesne → 52 40 5N 109 41W
Duchesne County ◇ 52 40 20N 110 30W
Duchess 127 21 20 S 139 50 E
Ducie I. 125 24 40 S 124 48W
Duck → 48 36 2N 87 52W
Duck Hill 31 33 38N 89 43W
Duck Lake 63 52 50N 106 16W
Duck Mt. Prov. Parks 63 51 45N 101 0W
Duck River 48 35 43N 87 16W
Duck Valley Indian
Reservation 35 42 0N 116 10W
Ducktown 49 35 3N 84 23W
Duckwater 35 38 55N 115 40W
Dudhi 109 24 15N 83 10 E
Dudinka 101 69 30N 86 13 E
Dudley, U.K. 83 52 30N 2 5W
Dudley, Ga. 18 32 32N 83 5W
Dudley, Mo. 32 36 46N 90 8W
Dudley, Pa. 45 40 12N 78 10W
Dudleyville 12 32 54N 110 42W
Due West 46 34 20N 82 23W
Dueré 75 11 20 S 49 17W
Duero → 91 41 8N 8 40W
Duff Is. 124 9 53 S 167 8 E
Dufftown 84 57 26N 3 9W
Dufur 44 45 27N 121 8W
Dugdemona → 25 31 47N 92 22W
Dugger 22 39 4N 87 18W
Dugi Otok 94 44 0N 15 0 E
Duifken Pt. 127 12 33 S 141 38 E
Duisburg 88 51 27N 6 42 E
Duitama 70 5 50N 73 2W
Duke 43 34 40N 99 34W
Dukes County ◇ 28 41 23N 70 31W
Dukhān 107 25 25N 50 50 E
Duki 108 30 14N 68 25 E
Duku 120 10 43N 10 43 E
Dulac 25 29 23N 90 42W
Dulce 38 36 56N 107 0W
Dulce → 76 30 32 S 62 33W
Dulce, Golfo 66 8 40N 83 20W
Dŭlgopol 95 43 3N 27 22 E
Dulit, Banjaran 110 3 15N 114 30 E
Dulovo 95 43 48N 27 9 E
Duluth, Ga. 18 34 0N 84 9W
Duluth, Minn. 30 46 47N 92 6W
Dum Duma 109 27 40N 95 40 E
Dum Hadjer 121 13 18N 19 41 E
Dumaguete 111 9 17N 123 15 E
Dumai 110 1 35N 101 28 E
Dumaran 111 10 33N 119 50 E
Dumaring 111 1 46N 118 10 E
Dumas, Ark. 13 33 53N 91 29W
Dumas, Tex. 50 35 52N 101 58W
Dumbarton 84 55 58N 4 35W
Dumbrăveni 95 46 14N 24 34 E
Dumfries 84 55 4N 3 37W
Dumfries & Galloway □ 84 55 0N 4 0W
Dumoine → 60 46 13N 77 51W
Dumoine L. 60 46 55N 77 55W
Dumont 23 42 45N 92 58W
Dumyât 121 31 24N 31 48 E
Dun Laoghaire 85 53 17N 6 9W
Dunaföldvár 89 46 50N 18 57 E
Dunărea → 89 45 30N 8 15 E
Dunay 116 42 52N 132 22 E
Dunback 128 45 23 S 170 36 E
Dunbar, U.K. 84 56 0N 2 32W
Dunbar, Nebr. 34 40 38N 96 1W
Dunbar, Pa. 45 39 58N 79 37W
Dunbar, W. Va. 54 38 22N 81 45W
Dunbarton 36 43 8N 71 38W
Dunblane 84 56 10N 3 58W
Duncan, Canada 62 48 45N 123 40W
Duncan, Ariz. 12 32 43N 109 6W
Duncan, Nebr. 34 41 25N 97 30W
Duncan, Okla. 43 34 30N 97 57W
Duncan, L. 60 53 29N 77 58W
Duncan L. 62 62 51N 113 58W
Duncan Pass. 112 11 0N 92 30 E
Duncan Town 66 22 15N 75 45W
Duncannon 45 40 23N 77 2W
Duncanville 51 32 39N 96 55W
Duncombe 23 42 28N 94 0W
Dundalk, Ireland 85 54 1N 6 25W
Dundalk, U.S.A. 27 39 16N 76 32W
Dundalk Bay 85 53 55N 6 15W
Dundas, Canada 60 43 17N 79 59W
Dundas, Minn. 30 44 26N 93 12W
Dundas, Va. 54 36 55N 78 1W
Dundas, L. 126 32 35 S 121 50 E
Dundas I. 62 54 30N 130 50W
Dundas Str. 126 11 15 S 131 35 E
Dundee, S. Africa 123 28 11 S 30 15 E
Dundee, U.K. 84 56 29N 3 0W
Dundee, Iowa 23 42 35N 91 33W
Dundee, Ky. 48 37 34N 86 46W
Dundee, Mich. 29 41 57N 83 40W
Dundee, Minn. 30 43 51N 95 28W
Dundee, N.Y. 39 42 32N 76 59W
Dundrum 85 54 17N 5 50W
Dundrum B. 85 54 12N 5 40W
Dundy County ◇ 34 40 15N 101 45W
Dunedin, N.Z. 128 45 50 S 170 33 E
Dunedin, U.S.A. 17 28 1N 82 47W
Dunedin → 62 59 30N 124 5W
Dunfermline 84 56 5N 3 28W
Dungannon, U.K. 85 54 30N 6 47W
Dungannon, U.S.A. 54 36 50N 82 28W
Dungannon □ 85 54 30N 6 55W
Dungarvan 85 52 6N 7 40W
Dungarvan Bay 85 52 5N 7 35W
Dungeness, U.K. 83 50 54N 0 59 E
Dungeness, U.S.A. 53 48 9N 123 7W
Dungu 122 3 40N 28 32 E
Dunhua 114 43 20N 128 14 E
Dunhuang 113 40 8N 94 36 E
Dunkeld 84 56 34N 3 36W
Dunkerque 90 51 2N 2 20 E
Dunkerton 23 42 34N 92 10W
Dunkery Beacon 83 51 15N 3 37W
Dunkirk = Dunkerque 90 51 2N 2 20 E
Dunkirk, Ind. 22 40 23N 85 13W
Dunkirk, Mont. 33 48 29N 111 40W
Dunkirk, N.Y. 39 42 29N 79 20W
Dunkirk, Ohio 42 40 48N 83 39W
Dunklin County ◇ 32 36 20N 90 0W
Dunkwa 120 6 0N 1 47W
Dunlap, Ill. 21 40 52N 89 40W
Dunlap, Ind. 22 41 39N 85 56W
Dunlap, Iowa 23 41 51N 95 36W
Dunlap, Kans. 24 38 35N 96 22W
Dunlap, Tenn. 49 35 23N 85 23W
Dunlap, Tex. 50 34 8N 100 18W
Dúnleary = Dun Laoghaire 85 53 17N 6 9W
Dunlow 54 38 1N 82 26W
Dunmanus B. 85 51 31N 9 50W
Dunmor 48 37 4N 86 59W
Dunmore 45 41 25N 75 38W
Dunmore Hd. 85 52 10N 10 35W
Dunmore Town 66 25 30N 76 39W
Dunn, La. 25 32 28N 91 35W
Dunn, N.C. 40 35 19N 78 37W
Dunn Center 41 47 21N 102 37W
Dunn County ◇, N. Dak. 41 47 15N 102 35W
Dunn County ◇, Wis. 55 44 55N 91 50W
Dunnell 30 43 34N 94 47W
Dunnellon 17 29 3N 82 28W
Dunnet Hd. 84 58 38N 3 22W
Dunning 34 41 50N 100 6W
Dunnville 49 37 12N 85 1W
Dunoon 84 55 57N 4 56W
Dunqul 121 23 26N 31 37 E
Duns 84 55 47N 2 20W
Dunseith 41 48 50N 100 3W
Dunsmuir 14 41 13N 122 16W
Dunstable 83 51 53N 0 31W
Dunstan Mts. 128 44 53 S 169 35 E
Dunster 62 53 8N 119 50W
Dunvegan L. 63 60 8N 107 10W
Duolun 114 42 12N 116 28 E
Duplin County ◇ 40 34 50N 78 0W
Dupo 21 38 31N 90 13W
Dupont 22 38 53N 85 31W
Dupuyer 33 48 13N 112 30W
Duque de Caxias 75 22 45 S 43 19W
Duque de York, I. 78 50 37 S 75 25W
Dūrā 104 31 31N 35 1 E
Durack Range 126 16 50 S 127 40 E
Duran 38 34 28N 105 24W
Durance → 90 43 55N 4 45 E
Durand, Ga. 18 32 54N 84 51W
Durand, Ill. 21 42 26N 89 20W
Durand, Mich. 29 42 55N 83 59W
Durand, Wis. 55 44 38N 91 58W
Durango, Mexico 64 24 3N 104 39W
Durango, Spain 91 43 13N 2 40W
Durango, U.S.A. 16 37 16N 107 53W
Durango □ 64 25 0N 105 0W
Durant, Iowa 23 41 36N 90 54W
Durant, Miss. 31 33 4N 89 51W
Durant, Okla. 43 33 59N 96 25W
Durants Neck 40 36 8N 76 18W
Durazno 76 33 25 S 56 31W
Durazzo = Durrësi 95 41 19N 19 28 E
Durban 123 29 49 S 31 1 E
Durbin 54 38 33N 79 50W
Durg 109 21 15N 81 22 E
Durham, Canada 60 44 10N 80 49W
Durham, U.K. 82 54 47N 1 34W
Durham, Conn. 28 41 29N 72 41W
Durham, Kans. 24 38 30N 97 15W
Durham, N.C. 40 35 59N 78 54W
Durham, N.H. 36 43 8N 70 56W
Durham □ 82 54 42N 1 45W
Durham County ◇ 40 36 0N 78 55W
Durkee 44 44 35N 117 30W
Durmitor 92 43 10N 19 0 E
Durness 84 58 34N 4 45W
Durrësi 95 41 19N 19 28 E
D'Urville, Tanjung 111 1 28 S 137 54 E
D'Urville I. 128 40 50 S 173 55 E
Dusa Mareb 105 5 30N 46 15 E
Dushak 100 37 13N 60 1 E
Dushan 115 25 48N 107 30 E
Dushanbe 100 38 33N 68 48 E
Dushore 45 41 31N 76 24W
Dusky Sd. 128 45 47 S 166 30 E
Düsseldorf 88 51 15N 6 46 E
Dustin 43 35 12N 96 1W
Dusty 53 46 51N 117 38W

Dutch Harbor Edmonton

Dutch Harbor 11 53 53N 166 32W
Dutch John 52 40 55N 109 24W
Dutch Mills 13 35 52N 94 29W
Dutch Neck 37 40 17N 74 40W
Dutchess County ◇ 39 41 45N 73 45W
Dutchtown 32 37 18N 89 42W
Dutton 33 47 51N 111 43W
Duval County ◇, Fla. 17 30 30N 81 30W
Duval County ◇, Tex. 51 27 50N 98 30W
Duwādimi 106 24 35N 44 15 E
Duxbury 28 42 2N 70 40W
Duyun 115 26 18N 107 29 E
Duzce 106 40 50N 31 10 E
Duzdab = Zāhedān 107 29 30N 60 50 E
Dve Mogili 95 43 35N 25 55 E
Dvina, Sev. → 98 64 32N 40 30 E
Dvinsk = Daugavpils 98 55 53N 26 32 E
Dvinskaya Guba 98 65 0N 39 0 E
Dwarka 108 22 18N 69 8 E
Dwight, Ill. 21 41 5N 88 26W
Dwight, Kans. 24 38 50N 96 38W
Dwight, Nebr. 34 41 5N 97 1W
Dworshak Reservoir 20 46 48N 116 0W
Dyer 48 36 4N 88 59W
Dyer, C. 59 66 40N 61 0W
Dyer County ◇ 48 36 0N 89 25W
Dyer Plateau 5 70 45 S 65 30W
Dyersburg 48 36 3N 89 23W
Dyersville 23 42 29N 91 8W
Dyfed □ 83 52 0N 4 30W
Dysart, Canada 63 50 57N 104 2W
Dysart, U.S.A. 23 42 10N 92 18W
Dzamin Üüd 113 43 50N 111 58 E
Dzerzhinsk, Byelorussian S.S.R., U.S.S.R. 98 53 40N 27 1 E
Dzerzhinsk, R.S.F.S.R., U.S.S.R. 98 56 14N 43 30 E
Dzhalal-Abad 100 40 56N 73 0 E
Dzhalinda 101 53 26N 124 0 E
Dzhambul 100 42 54N 71 22 E
Dzhankoi 99 45 40N 34 20 E
Dzhardzhan 101 68 10N 124 10 E
Dzhelinde 101 70 0N 114 20 E
Dzhetygara 100 52 11N 61 12 E
Dzhezkazgan 100 47 44N 67 40 E
Dzhikimde 101 59 1N 121 47 E
Dzhizak 100 40 6N 67 50 E
Dzhugdzur, Khrebet 101 57 30N 138 0 E
Dzhungarskiye Vorota 100 45 0N 82 0 E
Dzibilchaltún 65 21 5N 89 36W
Dzilam de Bravo 65 21 24N 88 53W
Dzungarian Gates = Dzhungarskiye Vorota 100 45 0N 82 0 E
Dzuumod 113 47 45N 106 58 E

E

E. V. Spence Reservoir 50 31 58N 100 40W
Eabamet, L. 60 51 30N 87 46W
Eads, Colo. 16 38 29N 102 47W
Eads, Tenn. 48 35 12N 89 39W
Eagar 12 34 6N 109 17W
Eagle, Alaska 11 64 47N 141 12W
Eagle, Colo. 16 39 39N 106 50W
Eagle, Idaho 20 43 42N 116 21W
Eagle, Nebr. 34 40 49N 96 26W
Eagle, Wis. 55 42 53N 88 29W
Eagle →, Canada 61 53 36N 57 26W
Eagle →, U.S.A. 16 39 39N 107 4W
Eagle, Mt. 57 17 46N 64 49W
Eagle Bend 30 46 10N 95 2W
Eagle Butte 47 45 0N 101 10W
Eagle City 43 35 56N 98 35W
Eagle County ◇ 16 39 40N 106 50W
Eagle Cr. → 49 38 36N 85 4W
Eagle Grove 23 42 40N 93 54W
Eagle Harbor 27 38 35N 76 40W
Eagle L., Calif. 14 40 39N 120 45W
Eagle L., Maine 26 46 20N 69 22W
Eagle Lake, Maine 26 47 3N 68 36W
Eagle Lake, Minn. 30 44 10N 93 53W
Eagle Lake, Tex. 51 29 35N 96 20W
Eagle Mills 13 33 41N 92 43W
Eagle Mountain 15 33 49N 115 27W
Eagle Mountain L. 51 32 53N 97 28W
Eagle Nest 38 36 33N 105 16W
Eagle Nest Butte 47 43 27N 101 39W
Eagle Pass 50 28 43N 100 30W
Eagle Peak 14 41 17N 120 12W
Eagle Point 44 42 28N 122 48W
Eagle River 55 45 55N 89 15W
Eagle Rock 54 37 38N 79 48W
Eagletail Mts. 12 33 20N 113 30W
Eagletown 43 34 2N 94 34W
Eagleville, Calif. 14 41 19N 120 7W
Eagleville, Mo. 32 40 28N 93 59W
Eagleville, Tenn. 48 35 45N 86 39W
Eakly 43 35 18N 98 34W
Ealing 83 51 30N 0 19W
Earl, L. 14 41 50N 124 11W
Earl Grey 63 50 57N 104 43W
Earl Park 22 40 42N 87 25W
Earle 13 35 16N 90 28W
Earleville 27 39 24N 75 54W
Earlham 23 41 30N 94 7W
Earlimart 15 35 53N 119 16W
Earling 23 41 28N 95 46W
Earlington 48 37 16N 87 30W
Earlsboro 43 35 19N 96 47W
Earlville, Ill. 21 41 35N 88 55W
Earlville, N.Y. 39 42 44N 75 33W
Early, Iowa 23 42 28N 95 9W
Early, Tex. 51 31 46N 98 58W
Early Branch 46 32 45N 80 55W
Early County ◇ 18 31 20N 84 50W
Earn → 84 56 20N 3 19W
Earn, L. 84 56 23N 4 14W
Earnslaw, Mt. 128 44 32 S 168 27 E
Earth 50 34 14N 102 24W
Easley 46 34 50N 82 36W
East → 39 40 48N 73 48W
East Angus 61 45 30N 71 40W
East Arm Grand Traverse B. 29 44 50N 85 30W
East Aurora 39 42 46N 78 37W
East B., Fla. 17 30 5N 85 32W
East B., La. 25 29 0N 89 15W
East B., Tex. 51 29 30N 94 35W
East Barrington 36 43 12N 70 59W
East Baton Rouge Parish ◇ 25 30 30N 91 20W
East Bend 40 36 13N 80 31W
East Bengal 109 24 0N 90 0 E
East Berkshire 36 44 56N 72 42W
East Berlin 45 39 56N 76 59W
East Bernard 51 29 32N 96 4W
East Bernstadt 49 37 9N 84 12W
East Beskids = Vychodné Beskydy 89 49 30N 22 0 E
East Branch Clarion River L. 45 41 35N 78 35W
East Brewton 10 31 5N 87 4W
East Bridgewater 28 42 2N 70 58W
East Brunswick 37 40 25N 74 23W
East Canton 42 40 47N 81 17W
East C. 128 37 42 S 178 35 E
East Carbon 52 39 35N 110 25W
East Carroll Parish ◇ 25 32 45N 91 15W
East Charleston 36 44 49N 72 0W
East Chicago 22 41 38N 87 27W
East China Sea 113 30 5N 126 0 E
East Corinth 36 44 5N 72 12W
East Coulee 62 51 23N 112 27W
East Dorset 36 43 13N 73 0W
East Douglas 28 42 4N 71 43W
East Dublin 18 32 32N 82 52W
East Dubuque 21 42 30N 90 39W
East Ely 35 39 15N 114 53W
East Fairfield 36 44 47N 72 51W
East Falkland 78 51 30 S 58 30W
East Feliciana Parish ◇ 25 30 47N 91 8W
East Fork Bruneau → 20 42 34N 115 38W
East Fork Sevier → 52 38 14N 112 12W
East Fork White → 22 38 33N 87 14W
East Fultonham 42 39 51N 82 8W
East Germany ■ 88 52 0N 12 0 E
East Glacier Park 33 48 27N 113 13W
East Granby 28 41 57N 72 44W
East Grand Forks 30 47 56N 97 1W
East Grand Rapids 29 42 58N 85 37W
East Greenwich 28 41 40N 71 27W
East Haddam 28 41 27N 72 28W
East Hampton, Conn. 28 41 35N 72 31W
East Hampton, N.Y. 39 40 58N 72 11W
East Hartford 28 41 46N 72 39W
East Haven 28 41 17N 72 52W
East Haverhill 36 44 3N 71 58W
East Helena 33 46 35N 111 56W
East Holden 26 44 44N 68 38W
East Hope 20 48 14N 116 17W
East Indies 110 0 0 120 0 E
East Jordan 29 45 10N 85 7W
East Kilbride 84 55 46N 4 10W
East Kingston 36 42 54N 71 2W
East Lake, Mich. 29 44 15N 86 18W
East Lake, N.C. 40 35 53N 75 58W
East Lansing 29 42 44N 84 29W
East Las Vegas 35 36 6N 115 3W
East Lempster 36 43 13N 72 13W
East Liberty 42 40 20N 83 35W
East Liverpool 42 40 37N 80 35W
East London 123 33 0 S 27 55 E
East Longmeadow 28 42 4N 72 31W
East Lyme 28 41 22N 72 13W
East Lynn L. 54 38 10N 82 23W
East Lynne 32 38 40N 94 14W
East Main = Eastmain 60 52 10N 78 30W
East Meadow 39 40 43N 73 34W
East Middlebury 36 43 58N 73 6W
East Millinocket 26 45 38N 68 35W
East Moline 21 41 32N 90 26W
East Naples 17 26 8N 81 46W
East New Market 27 38 36N 75 56W
East Nishnabotna → 23 40 39N 95 38W
East Northport 39 40 53N 73 20W
East Norwich 39 40 51N 73 32W
East Olympia 53 46 58N 122 50W
East Orange 37 40 46N 74 13W
East Pacific Ridge 125 15 0 S 110 0W
East Pakistan = Bangladesh ■ 109 24 0N 90 0 E
East Palatka 17 29 39N 81 36W
East Palestine 42 40 50N 80 33W
East Park Reservoir 14 39 37N 122 31W
East Peoria 21 40 40N 89 34W
East Peru 23 41 14N 93 56W
East Petersburg 45 40 6N 76 21W
East Pine 62 55 48N 120 12W
East Pt. 61 46 27N 61 58W
East Point 18 33 41N 84 27W
East Portal 16 39 54N 105 39W
East Prairie 32 36 47N 89 23W
East Prospect 45 39 58N 76 32W
East Providence 28 41 49N 71 23W
East Pt. 57 17 45N 64 34W
East Randolph 36 43 57N 72 33W
East Range 35 40 30N 117 57W
East Retford 82 53 19N 0 55W
East Ridge 49 34 59N 85 13W
East Rochester 39 43 7N 77 29W
East Rupert 36 43 16N 73 8W
East St. Louis 21 38 37N 90 9W
East Schelde → = Oosterschelde 87 51 33N 4 0 E
East Siberian Sea 101 73 0N 160 0 E
East Spring Cr. → 16 39 30N 102 30W
East Sussex □ 83 51 0N 0 20 E
East Tavaputs Plateau 52 39 40N 109 40W
East Tawas 29 44 17N 83 29W
East Tohopekaliga Lake 17 28 18N 81 15W
East Troy 55 42 47N 88 24W
East Vineland 37 39 30N 74 55W
East Wallingford 36 43 25N 72 54W
East Wareham 28 41 46N 70 40W
East Wenatchee 53 47 25N 120 18W
Eastbourne, N.Z. 128 41 19 S 174 55 E
Eastbourne, U.K. 83 50 46N 0 18 E
Eastchester 39 40 57N 73 49W
Eastend 63 49 32N 108 50W
Easter Islands 125 27 0 S 109 0W
Eastern Bay 27 38 50N 76 15W
Eastern Ghats 108 14 0N 78 50 E
Eastern Group = Lau 128 17 0 S 178 30W
Eastern Shore 27 38 30N 75 50W
Easterville 63 53 8N 99 49W
Eastham 28 41 50N 69 58W
Easthampton 28 42 16N 72 40W
Eastlake 42 41 40N 81 26W
Eastland 51 32 24N 98 49W
Eastland County ◇ 51 32 25N 98 50W
Eastleigh 83 50 58N 1 21W
Eastmain 60 52 10N 78 30W
Eastmain → 60 52 27N 78 26W
Eastman, Ga. 18 32 12N 83 11W
Eastman, Wis. 55 43 10N 91 1W
Easton, Calif. 15 36 39N 119 47W
Easton, Conn. 28 41 15N 73 18W
Easton, Ill. 21 40 14N 89 50W
Easton, Kans. 24 39 21N 95 7W
Easton, Md. 27 38 47N 76 5W
Easton, Minn. 30 43 46N 93 54W
Easton, Mo. 32 39 43N 94 39W
Easton, Pa. 45 40 41N 75 13W
Easton, Wash. 53 47 14N 121 11W
Eastover 46 33 52N 80 41W
Eastpoint 17 29 44N 84 53W
Eastport, Idaho 20 48 59N 116 10W
Eastport, Maine 26 44 56N 67 0W
Eastsound 53 48 42N 122 55W
Eastville 54 37 21N 75 57W
Eaton, Colo. 16 40 32N 104 42W
Eaton, Ind. 22 40 21N 85 21W
Eaton, Ohio 42 39 45N 84 38W
Eaton County ◇ 29 42 35N 84 50W
Eaton Rapids 29 42 31N 84 39W
Eatonia 63 51 13N 109 25W
Eatons Neck Pt. 39 40 57N 73 24W
Eatonton 18 33 20N 83 23W
Eatontown 37 40 19N 74 4W
Eatonville 53 46 52N 122 16W
Eau Claire, Fr. Gui. 71 3 30N 53 40W
Eau Claire, Mich. 29 41 59N 86 18W
Eau Claire, Wis. 55 44 49N 91 30W
Eau Claire → 55 44 55N 89 35W
Eau Claire County ◇ 55 44 45N 91 20W
Eau Galle 55 44 42N 92 1W
Ebbw Vale 83 51 47N 3 12W
Ebeltoft 97 56 12N 10 41 E
Ebensburg 45 40 29N 78 44W
Eberswalde 88 52 49N 13 50 E
Ebetsu 116 43 7N 141 34 E
Eboli 94 40 39N 15 2 E
Ebolowa 122 2 55N 11 10 E
Ebony 54 36 37N 77 59W
Ebro → 91 40 43N 0 54 E
Eccles 54 37 47N 81 16W
Ech Cheliff 120 36 10N 1 20 E
Echechonnee → 18 32 39N 83 36W
Echigo-Sammyaku 117 36 50N 139 50 E
Echizen-Misaki 117 35 59N 135 57 E
Echo, Ala. 10 31 29N 85 28W
Echo, Minn. 30 44 37N 95 25W
Echo, Oreg. 44 45 45N 119 12W
Echo Bay, N.W.T., Canada 58 66 5N 117 55W
Echo Bay, Ont., Canada 60 46 29N 84 4W
Echo Cliffs 12 36 40N 111 35W
Echoing → 63 55 51N 92 5W
Echols County ◇ 18 30 45N 83 0W
Echternach 87 49 49N 6 25 E
Echuca 126 36 10 S 144 20 E
Ecija 91 37 30N 5 10W
Eckley 16 40 7N 102 29W
Eclectic 10 32 38N 86 2W
Econfina 17 30 22N 85 35W
Economy 22 39 59N 85 5W
Ecoporanga 75 18 23 S 40 50W
Ecru 31 34 21N 89 2W
Ector County ◇ 50 31 46N 102 31W
Ecuador ■ 70 2 0 S 78 0W
Ed Dâmer 121 17 27N 34 0 E
Ed Debba 121 18 0N 30 51 E
Ed Dueim 121 14 0N 32 10 E
Edam, Canada 63 53 11N 108 46W
Edam, Neth. 87 52 31N 5 3 E
Eday 84 59 11N 2 47W
Edcouch 50 26 18N 97 58W
Edd 105 14 0N 41 38 E
Eddiceton 31 31 30N 90 48W
Eddrachillis B. 84 58 16N 5 10W
Eddy County ◇, N. Dak. 41 47 50N 99 0W
Eddy County ◇, N. Mex. 38 32 30N 104 20W
Eddystone 83 50 11N 4 16W
Eddyville, Ill. 21 37 30N 88 35W
Eddyville, Iowa 23 41 9N 92 38W
Eddyville, Ky. 48 37 3N 88 4W
Eddyville, Nebr. 34 41 1N 99 38W
Ede 87 52 4N 5 40 E
Édea 122 3 51N 10 9 E
Edehon L. 63 60 25N 97 15W
Eden, Miss. 31 32 59N 90 20W
Eden, N.C. 40 36 29N 79 53W
Eden, S. Dak. 47 45 37N 97 25W
Eden, Tex. 51 31 13N 99 51W
Eden, Vt. 36 44 42N 72 33W
Eden, Wis. 55 43 42N 88 22W
Eden, Wyo. 56 42 3N 109 26W
Eden → 82 54 57N 3 2W
Eden L. 63 56 38N 100 15W
Eden Valley 30 45 19N 94 33W
Eden Valley Reservoir 56 42 14N 109 21W
Edenderry 85 53 21N 7 3W
Edenton 40 36 4N 76 39W
Edesville 27 39 9N 76 13W
Edgar, Nebr. 34 40 22N 97 58W
Edgar, Wis. 55 44 55N 89 59W
Edgar County ◇ 21 39 40N 87 45W
Edgar Springs 32 37 42N 91 52W
Edgard 25 30 3N 90 34W
Edgartown 28 41 23N 70 31W
Edge Hill 83 52 7N 1 28W
Edgecombe County ◇ 40 35 50N 77 30W
Edgefield 46 33 47N 81 56W
Edgefield County ◇ 46 33 50N 82 0W
Edgeley 41 46 22N 98 43W
Edgemere 27 39 14N 76 27W
Edgemont, Colo. 16 39 44N 105 8W
Edgemont, S. Dak. 47 43 18N 103 50W
Edgemoor 46 34 48N 81 1W
Edgeøya 4 77 45N 22 30 E
Edgerton, Kans. 24 38 46N 95 1W
Edgerton, Minn. 30 43 53N 96 8W
Edgerton, Mo. 32 39 30N 94 38W
Edgerton, Ohio 42 41 27N 84 45W
Edgerton, Wis. 55 42 50N 89 4W
Edgerton, Wyo. 56 43 25N 106 15W
Edgewater 17 28 59N 80 54W
Edgewater Park 37 40 4N 74 54W
Edgewood, Ill. 21 38 55N 88 40W
Edgewood, Ind. 22 39 41N 86 8W
Edgewood, Iowa 23 42 39N 91 24W
Edgewood, Md. 27 39 25N 76 18W
Edgewood, N. Mex. 38 35 4N 106 11W
Edgewood, Tex. 51 32 42N 95 53W
Edhessa 95 40 48N 22 5 E
Edievale 128 45 49 S 169 22 E
Edina, Minn. 30 44 53N 93 21W
Edina, Mo. 32 40 10N 92 11W
Edinboro 45 41 52N 80 8W
Edinburg, Ill. 21 39 39N 89 23W
Edinburg, Ind. 22 39 21N 85 58W
Edinburg, Miss. 31 32 48N 89 20W
Edinburg, N. Dak. 41 48 30N 97 52W
Edinburg, Tex. 50 26 18N 98 10W
Edinburg, Va. 54 38 49N 78 34W
Edinburgh 84 55 57N 3 12W
Edirne 95 41 40N 26 34 E
Edison, Ga. 18 31 34N 84 44W
Edison, N.J. 37 40 31N 74 25W
Edison, Nebr. 34 40 17N 99 47W
Edison, Ohio 42 40 33N 82 52W
Edisto → 46 32 29N 80 21W
Edisto Beach 46 32 29N 80 20W
Edisto I. 46 32 35N 80 20W
Edith 50 31 54N 100 37W
Edmond, Kans. 24 39 37N 99 50W
Edmond, Okla. 43 35 39N 97 29W
Edmonds 53 47 49N 122 23W
Edmondson 13 35 6N 90 19W
Edmonson 50 34 17N 101 54W
Edmonson County ◇ 48 37 10N 86 15W
Edmonton, Canada 62 53 30N 113 30W

Edmonton
Elliott

Edmonton, U.S.A. **49** 36 59N 85 37W
Edmore, Mich. **29** 43 25N 85 3W
Edmore, N. Dak. **41** 48 25N 98 27W
Edmund L. **63** 54 45N 93 17W
Edmunds County ◇ **47** 45 27N 99 20W
Edmundston **61** 47 23N 68 20W
Edna, Kans. **24** 37 4N 95 22W
Edna, Tex. **51** 28 59N 96 39W
Edon **42** 41 33N 84 46W
Edremit **106** 39 34N 27 0 E
Edroy **51** 27 59N 97 41W
Edsel Ford Ra. **5** 77 0 S 143 0W
Edson, Canada **62** 53 35N 116 28W
Edson, U.S.A. **24** 39 20N 101 33W
Eduardo Castex **76** 35 50 S 64 18W
Edwall **53** 47 30N 117 57W
Edward, L. **122** 0 25 S 29 40 E
Edward I. **60** 48 22N 88 37W
Edward VII Pen. **5** 80 0 S 150 0W
Edwards, Colo. **16** 39 39N 106 36W
Edwards, Miss. **31** 32 20N 90 36W
Edwards, N.Y. **39** 44 20N 75 15W
Edwards → **21** 41 9N 90 59W
Edwards County ◇, Ill. **21** 38 25N 88 5W
Edwards County ◇, Kans. **24** 37 50N 99 15W
Edwards County ◇, Tex. **50** 30 10N 100 13W
Edwards Plateau **50** 30 45N 101 20W
Edwardsburg **29** 41 48N 86 6W
Edwardsport **22** 38 49N 87 15W
Edwardsville **21** 38 49N 89 58W
Edzo **62** 62 49N 116 4W
Eek **11** 60 14N 162 2W
Eekloo **87** 51 11N 3 33 E
Eel →, Calif. **14** 40 38N 124 20W
Eel →, Ind. **22** 40 45N 86 22W
Eel →, Ind. **22** 39 7N 86 57W
Ef'e, Nahal **104** 31 9N 35 13 E
Effie **30** 47 50N 93 38W
Effingham, Ill. **21** 39 7N 88 33W
Effingham, Kans. **24** 39 31N 95 24W
Effingham, S.C. **46** 34 5N 79 46W
Effingham County ◇, Ga. **18** 32 20N 81 15W
Effingham County ◇, Ill. **21** 39 5N 88 35W
Effingham Falls **36** 43 47N 71 5W
Eforie Sud **95** 44 1N 28 37 E
Égadi, Ísole **94** 37 55N 12 16 E
Egan **47** 44 0N 96 37W
Egan Range **35** 39 35N 114 55W
Eganville **60** 45 32N 77 5W
Egegik **11** 58 13N 157 22W
Egeland **41** 48 38N 99 6W
Egenolf L. **63** 59 3N 100 0W
Eger = Cheb **88** 50 9N 12 28 E
Eger **89** 47 53N 20 27 E
Egersund **97** 58 26N 6 1 E
Egg Harbor **55** 45 3N 87 17W
Egg Harbor City **37** 39 32N 74 39W
Egg L. **63** 55 5N 105 30W
Egmont, C. **128** 39 16 S 173 45 E
Egmont, Mt. **128** 39 17 S 174 5 E
Egnar **16** 37 55N 108 56W
Eğridir **106** 37 52N 30 51 E
Eğridir Gölü **106** 37 53N 30 50 E
Éguas → **75** 13 26 S 44 14W
Egvekinot **101** 66 19N 179 50W
Egypt **31** 33 54N 88 44W
Egypt ■ **121** 28 0N 31 0 E
Ehime □ **117** 33 30N 132 40 E
Ehrenberg **12** 33 36N 114 31W
Ehrhardt **46** 33 6N 81 1W
Eidsvoll **97** 60 19N 11 14 E
Eifel **88** 50 10N 6 45 E
Eigg **84** 56 54N 6 10W
Eighty Mile Beach **126** 19 30 S 120 40 E
Eil **105** 8 0N 49 50 E
Eil, L. **84** 56 50N 5 15W
Eileen L. **63** 62 16N 107 37W
Einasleigh **127** 18 32 S 144 5 E
Eindhoven **87** 51 26N 5 30 E
Eire ■ **85** 53 0N 8 0W
Eiríksjökull **96** 64 46N 20 24W
Eirunepé **72** 6 35 S 69 53W
Eisenach **88** 50 58N 10 18 E
Eisenerz **88** 47 32N 14 54 E
Eitzen **30** 43 31N 91 28W
Ejutla **65** 16 34N 96 44W
Ekalaka **33** 45 53N 104 33W
Eketahuna **128** 40 38 S 175 43 E
Ekibastuz **100** 51 50N 75 10 E
Ekimchan **101** 53 0N 133 0W
Ekron **48** 37 56N 86 11W
Ekwan → **60** 53 12N 82 15W
Ekwan Pt. **60** 53 16N 82 7W
Ekwok **11** 59 22N 157 30W
El Aaiún **120** 27 9N 13 12W
El Aat **104** 32 50N 35 45 E
El Alamein **121** 30 48N 28 58 E
El Alto **72** 4 15 S 81 14W
El Aricha **120** 34 13N 1 10W
El Arīhā **104** 31 52N 35 27 E
El 'Arîsh **121** 31 8N 33 50 E
El Asnam = Ech Cheliff **120** 36 10N 1 20 E
El Banco **70** 9 0N 73 58W
El Baúl **70** 8 57N 68 17W
El Bawiti **121** 28 25N 28 45 E
El Bayadh **120** 33 40N 1 1 E
El Bluff **66** 11 59N 83 40W
El Bolsón **78** 41 55 S 71 30W
El Buheirat □ **121** 7 0N 30 0 E
El Caín **78** 41 38 S 68 19W
El Cajon **15** 32 48N 116 58W
El Callao **71** 7 18N 61 50W
El Campo **51** 29 12N 96 16W
El Capitan **33** 46 1N 114 23W
El Capitan Reservoir **15** 32 53N 116 49W
El Carmen, Bolivia **73** 13 40 S 63 55W
El Carmen, Venezuela **70** 1 16N 66 52W
El Centro **15** 32 48N 115 34W
El Cerrito **14** 37 55N 122 19W
El Cerro **73** 17 30 S 61 40W
El Cocuy **70** 6 25N 72 27W
El Corcovado **78** 43 25 S 71 35W
El Cuy **78** 39 55 S 68 25W
El Cuyo **65** 21 30N 87 40W
El Dere **105** 3 50N 47 8 E
El Díaz **65** 21 1N 87 17W
El Diviso **70** 1 22N 78 14W
El Djouf **120** 20 0N 11 30 E
El Dorado, Ark. **13** 33 12N 92 40W
El Dorado, Kans. **24** 37 49N 96 52W
El Dorado, Venezuela **71** 6 55N 61 37W
El Dorado County ◇ **14** 38 45N 120 40W
El Escorial **91** 40 35N 4 7W
El Faiyûm **121** 29 19N 30 50 E
El Fâsher **121** 13 33N 25 26 E
El Ferrol **91** 43 29N 8 15W
El Fuerte **64** 26 30N 108 40W
El Gal **105** 10 58N 50 20 E
El Geteina **121** 14 50N 32 27 E
El Gezira □ **121** 15 0N 33 0 E
El Gîza **121** 30 0N 31 10 E
El Goléa **120** 30 30N 2 50 E
El Harrache **120** 36 45N 3 5 E
El Indio **50** 28 31N 100 19W
El Iskandarîya **121** 31 0N 30 0 E
El Jadida **120** 33 11N 8 17W
El Jebelein **121** 12 40N 32 55 E
El Kab **121** 19 27N 32 46 E
El Kala **120** 36 50N 8 30 E
El Kamlin **121** 15 3N 33 11 E
El Kef **120** 36 12N 8 47 E
El Khandaq **121** 18 30N 30 30 E
El Khârga **121** 25 30N 30 33 E
El Khartûm **121** 15 31N 32 35 E
El Khartûm Bahrî **121** 15 40N 32 31 E
El Laqâwa **121** 11 25N 29 1 E
El Mafâza **121** 13 38N 34 30 E
El Mahalla el Kubra **121** 31 0N 31 0 E
El Maitén **78** 42 3 S 71 10W
El Mansûra **121** 31 0N 31 19 E
El Mantico **71** 7 38N 62 45W
El Miamo **71** 7 39N 61 46W
El Milagro **76** 30 59 S 65 59W
El Minyâ **121** 28 7N 30 33 E
El Mirage **12** 33 36N 112 19W
El Mirage L. **15** 34 39N 117 37W
El Nido **14** 37 8N 120 29W
El Obeid **121** 13 8N 30 10 E
El Odaiya **121** 12 8N 28 12 E
El Oro = Santa María del Oro **64** 25 58N 105 20W
El Oro **65** 19 48N 100 8W
El Oro □ **70** 3 30 S 79 50W
El Oued **120** 33 20N 6 58 E
El Palmar, Bolivia **73** 17 50 S 63 9W
El Palmar, Venezuela **71** 7 58N 61 53W
El Palmito, Presa **64** 25 40N 105 30W
El Paso, Ill. **21** 40 44N 89 1W
El Paso, Tex. **50** 31 45N 106 29W
El Paso County ◇, Colo. **16** 38 50N 104 30W
El Paso County ◇, Tex. **50** 31 55N 106 5W
El Portal **14** 37 41N 119 47W
El Porvenir, Mexico **64** 31 15N 105 51W
El Porvenir, U.S.A. **38** 35 43N 105 25W
El Progreso **66** 15 26N 87 51W
El Pueblito **64** 29 3N 105 4W
El Qâhira **121** 30 1N 31 14 E
El Qantara **121** 30 51N 32 20 E
El Qasr **120** 25 44N 28 42 E
El Reno **43** 35 32N 97 57W
El Rio **15** 34 14N 119 10W
El Rito **38** 36 21N 106 11W
El Salto **64** 23 47N 105 22W
El Salvador ■ **66** 13 50N 89 0W
El Sauce **66** 13 0N 86 40W
El Shallal **121** 24 0N 32 53 E
El Sombrero **70** 9 23N 67 3W
El Suweis **121** 29 58N 32 31 E
El Tigre **71** 8 44N 64 15W
El Tocuyo **70** 9 47N 69 48W
El Tofo **76** 29 22 S 71 18W
El Toro **57** 18 17N 65 50W
El Tránsito **76** 28 52 S 70 17W
El Turbio **78** 51 45 S 72 5W
El Uqsur **121** 25 41N 32 38 E
El Vado Reservoir **38** 36 36N 106 44W
El Vigía **70** 8 38N 71 39W
El Wak **122** 2 49N 40 56 E
El Wuz **121** 15 0N 30 7 E
El Yunque **57** 18 19N 65 50W
Elaine **13** 34 19N 90 51W
Elat **104** 29 30N 34 56 E
Elâzığ **106** 38 37N 39 14 E
Elba, Italy **94** 42 48N 10 15 E
Elba, Ala. **10** 31 25N 86 4W
Elba, Minn. **30** 44 5N 92 1W
Elba, Nebr. **34** 41 17N 98 34W
Elbasani **95** 41 9N 20 9 E
Elbe → **88** 53 50N 9 0 E
Elberfeld **22** 38 10N 87 27W
Elberon **23** 42 0N 92 19W
Elbert, Colo. **16** 39 13N 104 32W
Elbert, Tex. **51** 33 15N 99 0W
Elbert, Mt. **16** 39 7N 106 27W
Elbert County ◇, Colo. **16** 39 20N 104 15W
Elbert County ◇, Ga. **18** 34 10N 82 50W
Elberta **29** 44 37N 86 14W
Elberton **18** 34 7N 82 52W
Elbeuf **90** 49 17N 1 2 E
Elbidtan **106** 38 13N 37 12 E
Elbing = Elbląg **89** 54 10N 19 25 E
Elbing **24** 38 3N 97 8W
Elbląg **89** 54 10N 19 25 E
Elbow **63** 51 7N 106 35W
Elbow Lake **30** 45 59N 95 58W
Elbrus **99** 43 21N 42 30 E
Elburg **87** 52 26N 5 50 E
Elburz Mts. = Alborz, Reshteh-ye Kūhhā-ye **107** 36 0N 52 0 E
Elche **91** 38 15N 0 42W
Elcho **55** 45 26N 89 11W
Elcho I. **127** 11 55 S 135 45 E
Elderon **55** 44 47N 89 15W
Eldersburg **27** 39 24N 76 57W
Eldon, Iowa **23** 40 55N 92 13W
Eldon, Mo. **32** 38 21N 92 35W
Eldon, Wash. **53** 47 33N 123 3W
Eldora, Iowa **23** 42 22N 93 5W
Eldora, N.J. **37** 39 12N 74 52W
Eldorado, Argentina **77** 26 28 S 54 43W
Eldorado, Canada **63** 59 35N 108 30W
Eldorado, Mexico **64** 24 20N 107 22W
Eldorado, Ill. **21** 37 49N 88 26W
Eldorado, Md. **27** 38 37N 75 48W
Eldorado, Ohio **42** 39 54N 84 41W
Eldorado, Okla. **43** 34 28N 99 39W
Eldorado, Tex. **50** 30 52N 100 36W
Eldorado National Forest **35** 38 50N 120 20W
Eldorado Springs **32** 37 52N 94 1W
Eldorendo **18** 31 3N 84 39W
Eldoret **122** 0 30N 35 17 E
Eldred **45** 41 58N 78 23W
Eldridge, Ala. **10** 33 55N 87 37W
Eldridge, Iowa **23** 41 39N 90 35W
Eldridge, Mo. **32** 37 50N 92 45W
Eldridge, N. Dak. **41** 46 54N 98 51W
Eleanor **54** 38 32N 81 56W
Eleanor, L. **14** 37 59N 119 53W
Electra **51** 34 2N 98 55W
Electra L. **16** 37 33N 107 48W
Electric Mills **31** 32 46N 88 28W
Elefantes, G. **78** 46 28 S 73 49W
Elena **95** 42 55N 25 53 E
Elephant Butte Reservoir **38** 33 9N 107 11W
Elephant I. **5** 61 0 S 55 0W
Elesbão Veloso **74** 6 13 S 42 8W
Eleshnitsa **95** 41 52N 23 36 E
Eleuthera **66** 25 0N 76 20W
Eleva **55** 44 35N 91 28W
Eleven Point → **13** 36 9N 91 5W
Elevenmile Canyon Reservoir **16** 38 54N 105 29W
Elfers **17** 28 13N 82 43W
Elfin Cove **11** 58 12N 136 22W
Elfrida **12** 31 41N 109 41W
Elgin, Canada **61** 45 48N 65 10W
Elgin, U.K. **84** 57 39N 3 20W
Elgin, Ill. **21** 42 2N 88 17W
Elgin, Iowa **23** 42 57N 91 38W
Elgin, Kans. **24** 37 0N 96 17W
Elgin, Minn. **30** 44 8N 92 15W
Elgin, N. Dak. **41** 46 24N 101 51W
Elgin, Nebr. **34** 41 59N 98 5W
Elgin, Nev. **35** 37 21N 114 32W
Elgin, Okla. **43** 34 47N 98 18W
Elgin, Oreg. **44** 45 34N 117 55W
Elgin, S.C. **46** 34 10N 80 48W
Elgin, Tex. **51** 30 21N 97 22W
Elgon, Mt. **122** 1 10N 34 30 E
Eli **34** 42 57N 101 29W
Eliase **111** 8 21 S 130 48 E
Elida, N. Mex. **38** 33 57N 103 39W
Elida, Ohio **42** 40 47N 84 12W
Elim **11** 64 37N 162 15W
Elim Indian Reservation **11** 64 40N 162 0W
Elin Pelin **95** 42 40N 23 36 E
Eliot **26** 43 7N 70 47W
Elisabethville = Lubumbashi **123** 11 40 S 27 28 E
Eliseu Martins **74** 8 13 S 43 42W
Elista **99** 46 16N 44 14 E
Elizabeth, Australia **127** 34 42 S 138 41 E
Elizabeth, Colo. **16** 39 22N 104 36W
Elizabeth, Ill. **21** 42 19N 90 13W
Elizabeth, La. **25** 30 52N 92 48W
Elizabeth, Minn. **30** 46 23N 96 8W
Elizabeth, N.J. **37** 40 40N 74 13W
Elizabeth, W. Va. **54** 39 4N 81 24W
Elizabeth, C. **53** 47 21N 124 19W
Elizabeth City **40** 36 18N 76 14W
Elizabeth Islands **28** 41 27N 70 47W
Elizabethton **49** 36 21N 82 13W
Elizabethtown, Ill. **21** 37 27N 88 18W
Elizabethtown, Ky. **49** 37 42N 85 52W
Elizabethtown, N.C. **40** 34 38N 78 37W
Elizabethtown, N.Y. **39** 44 13N 73 36W
Elizabethtown, Pa. **45** 40 9N 76 36W
Elizabethville **45** 40 33N 76 49W
Elk **14** 39 8N 123 43W
Elk →, Ala. **10** 34 46N 87 16W
Elk →, Kans. **24** 37 15N 95 41W
Elk →, Md. **27** 39 26N 76 1W
Elk →, W. Va. **54** 38 21N 81 38W
Elk City, Idaho **20** 45 50N 115 26W
Elk City, Kans. **24** 37 18N 95 55W
Elk City, Okla. **43** 35 25N 99 25W
Elk City Lake **24** 37 17N 95 47W
Elk County ◇, Kans. **24** 37 30N 96 15W
Elk County ◇, Pa. **45** 41 35N 78 45W
Elk Cr. → **47** 44 15N 102 22W
Elk Creek, Calif. **14** 39 36N 122 32W
Elk Creek, Nebr. **34** 40 17N 96 8W
Elk Falls **24** 37 22N 96 11W
Elk Garden **54** 39 23N 79 9W
Elk Grove **14** 38 25N 121 22W
Elk Hill **45** 41 42N 75 32W
Elk Horn **23** 41 36N 95 3W
Elk Island Nat. Park **62** 53 35N 112 59W
Elk L. **29** 44 50N 85 20W
Elk Lake **60** 47 40N 80 25W
Elk Mound **55** 44 52N 91 42W
Elk Mountain **56** 41 41N 106 25W
Elk Mt. **56** 41 38N 106 32W
Elk Neck **27** 39 31N 75 57W
Elk Park **40** 36 10N 81 59W
Elk Point, Canada **63** 53 54N 110 55W
Elk Point, U.S.A. **47** 42 41N 96 41W
Elk Rapids **29** 44 54N 85 25W
Elk River, Idaho **20** 46 47N 116 11W
Elk River, Minn. **30** 45 18N 93 35W
Elk Springs **16** 40 21N 108 27W
Elk Valley **49** 36 29N 84 15W
Elkader **23** 42 51N 91 24W
Elkatawa **49** 37 34N 83 25W
Elkhart, Ill. **21** 40 1N 89 29W
Elkhart, Ind. **22** 41 41N 85 58W
Elkhart, Iowa **23** 41 48N 93 31W
Elkhart, Kans. **24** 37 0N 101 54W
Elkhart, Tex. **51** 31 38N 95 35W
Elkhart County ◇ **22** 41 35N 85 50W
Elkhart Lake **55** 43 50N 88 1W
Elkhorn, Canada **63** 49 59N 101 14W
Elkhorn, U.S.A. **55** 42 40N 88 33W
Elkhorn → **34** 41 8N 96 19W
Elkhorn City **49** 37 18N 82 21W
Elkhovo **95** 42 10N 26 40 E
Elkin **40** 36 15N 80 51W
Elkins, N. Mex. **38** 33 42N 104 4W
Elkins, W. Va. **54** 38 55N 79 51W
Elkland, Mo. **32** 37 27N 93 2W
Elkland, Pa. **45** 41 59N 77 19W
Elkmont **10** 34 56N 86 58W
Elko, Canada **62** 49 20N 115 10W
Elko, Ga. **18** 32 20N 83 42W
Elko, Minn. **30** 44 34N 93 19W
Elko, Nev. **35** 40 50N 115 46W
Elko County ◇ **35** 41 10N 115 20W
Elkol **56** 41 43N 110 37W
Elkridge **27** 39 13N 76 43W
Elkton, Ky. **48** 36 49N 87 9W
Elkton, Md. **27** 39 36N 75 50W
Elkton, Mich. **29** 43 49N 83 11W
Elkton, Minn. **30** 43 40N 92 42W
Elkton, Oreg. **44** 43 38N 123 34W
Elkton, S. Dak. **47** 44 14N 96 29W
Elkton, Va. **54** 38 25N 78 37W
Elkville **21** 37 55N 89 14W
Ella **55** 44 32N 92 3W
Ellaville **18** 32 14N 84 19W
Ellef Ringnes I. **4** 78 30N 102 2W
Ellenboro **54** 39 16N 81 3W
Ellenburg **39** 44 54N 73 48W
Ellendale, Del. **27** 38 48N 75 26W
Ellendale, Minn. **30** 43 52N 93 18W
Ellendale, N. Dak. **41** 46 0N 98 32W
Ellensburg **53** 46 59N 120 34W
Ellenton **18** 31 11N 83 35W
Ellenville **39** 41 43N 74 24W
Ellerbe **40** 35 4N 79 46W
Ellesmere I. **4** 79 30N 80 0W
Ellesworth Land **5** 76 0 S 89 0W
Ellettsville **22** 39 14N 86 38W
Ellice Is. = Tuvalu ■ **124** 8 0 S 178 0 E
Ellicott City **27** 39 16N 76 48W
Ellicottville **39** 42 17N 78 40W
Ellijay **18** 34 42N 84 29W
Ellington, Conn. **28** 41 54N 72 28W
Ellington, Mo. **32** 37 14N 90 58W
Ellington, N.Y. **39** 42 13N 79 7W
Ellinwood **24** 38 21N 98 35W
Elliot Lake **60** 46 25N 82 35W
Elliott, Iowa **23** 41 9N 95 10W
Elliott, Md. **27** 38 38N 75 59W
Elliott, Miss. **31** 33 41N 89 45W
Elliott, N. Dak. **41** 46 24N 97 49W

Elliott **Escoma**

Elliott, S.C. **46** 34 6N 80 10W
Elliott County ◇ **49** 38 5N 83 5W
Elliott Key **17** 25 27N 80 12W
Elliott Knob **54** 38 10N 79 19W
Ellis, Idaho **20** 44 42N 114 3W
Ellis, Kans. **24** 38 56N 99 34W
Ellis, Nebr. **34** 40 13N 96 53W
Ellis County ◇, Kans. **24** 38 45N 99 15W
Ellis County ◇, Okla. **43** 36 20N 99 50W
Ellis County ◇, Tex. **51** 32 24N 96 51W
Ellis Grove **21** 38 1N 89 55W
Elliston **33** 46 33N 112 26W
Ellisville **31** 31 36N 89 12W
Ellon **84** 57 21N 2 5W
Ellore = Eluru **109** 16 48N 81 8 E
Elloree **46** 33 32N 80 34W
Ells → **62** 57 18N 111 40W
Ellsinore **32** 36 56N 90 45W
Ellston **23** 40 51N 94 7W
Ellsworth, Kans. **24** 38 44N 98 14W
Ellsworth, Maine **26** 44 33N 68 25W
Ellsworth, Mich. **29** 45 10N 85 15W
Ellsworth, Minn. **30** 43 31N 96 1W
Ellsworth, Nebr. **34** 42 4N 102 17W
Ellsworth, Wis. **55** 44 44N 92 29W
Ellsworth County ◇ **24** 38 45N 98 15W
Ellsworth Land **5** 76 0 S 89 0W
Ellsworth Mts. **5** 78 30 S 85 0W
Ellwood City **45** 40 52N 80 17W
Ellzey **17** 29 19N 82 48W
Elm → **47** 44 21N 102 42W
Elm City **40** 35 48N 77 52W
Elm Cr. → **51** 28 42N 99 59W
Elm Creek **34** 40 43N 99 22W
Elm Fork **43** 34 53N 99 19W
Elm L. **47** 45 51N 98 42W
Elma, Canada **63** 49 52N 95 55W
Elma, Iowa **23** 43 15N 92 26W
Elma, Wash. **53** 47 0N 123 25W
Elmalı **106** 36 44N 29 56 E
Elmdale **24** 38 22N 96 39W
Elmer, Mo. **32** 39 57N 92 39W
Elmer, N.J. **37** 39 36N 75 10W
Elmer, Okla. **43** 34 29N 99 21W
Elmer City **53** 48 0N 118 58W
Elmhurst **21** 41 53N 87 56W
Elmira, Idaho **20** 48 29N 116 27W
Elmira, N.Y. **39** 42 6N 76 48W
Elmira Heights **39** 42 8N 76 50W
Elmo, Kans. **24** 38 41N 97 14W
Elmo, Mont. **33** 47 50N 114 21W
Elmo, Utah **52** 39 23N 110 49W
Elmodel **18** 31 21N 84 29W
Elmont **39** 40 43N 73 43W
Elmore, Ala. **10** 32 32N 86 19W
Elmore, Minn. **30** 43 30N 94 5W
Elmore City **43** 34 37N 97 24W
Elmore County ◇, Ala. **10** 32 32N 86 13W
Elmore County ◇, Idaho **20** 43 30N 115 30W
Elmwood, Ill. **21** 40 47N 89 58W
Elmwood, Nebr. **34** 40 50N 96 18W
Elmwood, Wis. **55** 44 47N 92 9W
Elmwood Park **21** 41 56N 87 49W
Elnora **22** 38 53N 87 5W
Elora **48** 35 1N 86 21W
Elorza **70** 7 3N 69 31W
Eloy **12** 32 45N 111 33W
Elrosa **30** 45 34N 94 57W
Elrose **63** 51 12N 108 0W
Elroy **55** 43 45N 90 16W
Elsa **50** 26 18N 97 59W
Elsah **21** 38 57N 90 22W
Elsas **60** 48 32N 82 55W
Elsberry **32** 39 10N 90 47W
Elsie, Mich. **29** 43 5N 84 23W
Elsie, Nebr. **34** 40 51N 101 23W
Elsie, Oreg. **44** 45 52N 123 36W
Elsinore = Helsingør **97** 56 2N 12 35 E
Elsinore **52** 38 41N 112 9W
Elsinore L. **15** 33 40N 117 21W
Elsinore Lake **15** 33 40N 117 20W
Elsmere, Del. **27** 39 44N 75 35W
Elsmere, Nebr. **34** 42 10N 100 11W
Elsmore **24** 37 48N 95 9W
Elsworth, L. **43** 34 49N 98 22W
Eltham **128** 39 26 S 174 19 E
Eltopia **53** 46 27N 119 1W
Eluru **109** 16 48N 81 8 E
Elvas **91** 38 50N 7 10W
Elverson **45** 40 9N 75 50W
Elverum **97** 60 53N 11 34 E
Elvins **32** 37 50N 90 32W
Elwood, Ill. **21** 41 24N 88 7W
Elwood, Ind. **22** 40 17N 85 50W
Elwood, Kans. **24** 39 45N 94 52W
Elwood, N.J. **37** 39 35N 74 43W
Elwood, Nebr. **34** 40 36N 99 52W
Elwood Reservoir **34** 40 42N 99 55W
Ely, U.K. **83** 52 24N 0 16 E
Ely, Iowa **23** 41 52N 91 35W
Ely, Minn. **30** 47 55N 91 51W
Ely, Nev. **35** 39 15N 114 54W
Elyashiv **104** 32 23N 34 55 E
Elyria, Kans. **24** 38 17N 97 38W
Elyria, Nebr. **34** 41 41N 99 0W
Elyria, Ohio **42** 41 22N 82 7W
Emāmrūd **107** 36 30N 55 0 E
Emanuel County ◇ **18** 32 40N 82 20W
Emba **100** 48 50N 58 8 E
Emba → **100** 46 38N 53 14 E
Embarcación **76** 23 10 S 64 0W
Embarras → **21** 38 39N 87 37W
Embarras Portage **63** 58 27N 111 28W
Embarrass **55** 44 40N 88 42W
Embetsu **116** 44 44N 141 47 E
Embira → **72** 7 19 S 70 15W
Embrun **90** 44 34N 6 30 E
Embu **122** 0 32 S 37 38 E
Emden, Germany **88** 53 22N 7 12 E
Emden, U.S.A. **21** 40 18N 89 29W
Emelle **10** 32 44N 88 19W
'Emeq Yizre'el **104** 32 35N 35 12 E
Emerado **41** 47 55N 97 22W
Emerald **127** 23 32 S 148 10 E
Emerson, Canada **63** 49 0N 97 10W
Emerson, Ark. **13** 33 6N 93 11W
Emerson, Ga. **18** 34 8N 84 45W
Emerson, Nebr. **34** 42 17N 96 44W
Emerson L. **15** 34 27N 116 23W
Emery, S. Dak. **47** 43 36N 97 37W
Emery, Utah **52** 38 55N 111 15W
Emery County ◇ **52** 39 0N 110 45W
Emigrant Gap **14** 39 19N 120 38W
Emilia-Romagna □ **94** 44 33N 10 40 E
Emily **30** 46 44N 93 58W
Emine, Nos **95** 42 40N 27 56 E
Eminece **32** 37 9N 91 21W
Eminence **49** 38 22N 85 11W
Emlenton **45** 41 11N 79 43W
Emmalane **18** 32 46N 82 0W
Emmaus **45** 40 32N 75 30W
Emmeloord **87** 52 44N 5 46 E
Emmen **87** 52 48N 6 57 E
Emmet, Ark. **13** 33 44N 93 28W
Emmet, Nebr. **34** 42 29N 98 49W
Emmet County ◇, Iowa **23** 43 20N 94 40W
Emmet County ◇, Mich. **29** 45 30N 84 55W
Emmetsburg **23** 43 7N 94 41W
Emmett, Idaho **20** 43 52N 116 30W
Emmett, Kans. **24** 39 19N 96 3W
Emmett, Mich. **29** 42 59N 82 46W
Emmitsburg **27** 39 42N 77 20W
Emmonak **11** 62 46N 164 30W
Emmons **30** 43 30N 93 29W
Emmons County ◇ **41** 46 20N 100 10W
Emmorton **27** 39 30N 76 20W
Emona **95** 42 43N 27 53 E
Emory **51** 32 52N 95 46W
Emory Peak **50** 29 15N 103 18W
Empalme **64** 28 1N 110 49W
Empangeni **123** 28 50 S 31 52 E
Empedrado **76** 28 0 S 58 46W
Emperor Seamount Chain **124** 40 0N 170 0 E
Empire, Calif. **14** 37 38N 120 54W
Empire, Colo. **16** 39 46N 105 41W
Empire, Ga. **18** 32 21N 83 18W
Empire, La. **25** 29 23N 89 36W
Empire, Mich. **29** 44 49N 86 4W
Empire, Nev. **35** 40 35N 119 21W
Empire City **43** 34 25N 98 2W
Empire Reservoir **16** 40 16N 104 12W
Emporia, Kans. **24** 38 25N 96 11W
Emporia, Va. **54** 36 42N 77 32W
Emporium **45** 41 31N 78 14W
Empress **63** 50 57N 110 0W
Ems → **88** 52 37N 9 26 E
Emu **114** 43 40N 128 6 E
En Gedi **104** 31 28N 35 25 E
En Gev **104** 32 47N 35 38 E
En Harod **104** 32 33N 35 22 E
'En Kerem **104** 31 47N 35 6 E
En Nahud **121** 12 45N 28 25 E
Ena **117** 35 25N 137 25 E
Enambú **70** 1 1N 70 17W
Enaratoli **111** 3 55 S 136 21 E
Enard B. **84** 58 5N 5 20W
Encampment **56** 41 12N 106 47W
Encantadas, Serra **77** 30 40 S 53 0W
Encanto, C. **111** 15 45N 121 38 E
Encarnación **77** 27 15 S 55 50W
Encarnación de Diaz **64** 21 30N 102 13W
Encinal **51** 28 2N 99 21W
Encinillas **64** 29 14N 106 18W
Encinitas **15** 33 3N 117 17W
Encino, N. Mex. **38** 34 39N 105 28W
Encino, Tex. **50** 26 56N 98 8W
Encontrados **70** 9 3N 72 14W
Encounter B. **127** 35 45 S 138 45 E
Encruzilhada **75** 15 31 S 40 54W
Endau **112** 2 40N 103 38 E
Endau → **112** 2 30N 103 30 E
Ende **111** 8 45 S 121 40 E
Endeavour **63** 52 10N 102 39W
Endeavour Str. **127** 10 45 S 142 0 E
Enderbury I. **124** 3 8 S 171 5W
Enderby **62** 50 35N 119 10W
Enderby Land **5** 66 0 S 53 0 E
Enderlin **41** 46 38N 97 36W
Enders **34** 40 27N 101 32W
Enders Reservoir **34** 40 25N 101 31W
Endicott, N.Y. **39** 42 6N 76 4W
Endicott, Nebr. **34** 40 5N 97 6W
Endicott, Wash. **53** 46 56N 117 41W
Endicott Mts. **11** 68 0N 152 0W
Endimari → **72** 8 46 S 66 7W
Endwell **39** 42 6N 76 2W
Ene → **72** 11 10 S 74 18W
Enez **99** 40 45N 26 5 E
Enfield, U.K. **83** 51 39N 0 4W
Enfield, Conn. **28** 41 58N 72 36W
Enfield, Ill. **21** 38 6N 88 20W
Enfield, N.C. **40** 36 11N 77 41W
Enfield, N.H. **36** 43 39N 72 9W
Enfield Center **36** 43 38N 72 8W
Engadin **88** 46 45N 10 10 E
Engaño, C., Dom. Rep. **67** 18 30N 68 20W
Engaño, C., Phil. **111** 18 35N 122 23 E
Engel **38** 33 4N 107 2W
Engelhard **40** 35 30N 75 58W
Engels **98** 51 28N 46 6 E
Engemann L. **63** 58 0N 106 55W
Enggano **110** 5 20 S 102 40 E
Enghien **87** 50 37N 4 2 E
Engkilili **110** 1 3N 111 42 E
England **13** 34 33N 91 58W
England □ **86** 53 0N 2 0W
Englebright L. **14** 39 14N 121 16W
Englee **61** 50 45N 56 5W
Englehart **60** 47 49N 79 52W
Engler L. **63** 59 8N 106 52W
Englewood, Colo. **16** 39 39N 104 59W
Englewood, Fla. **17** 26 58N 82 21W
Englewood, Kans. **24** 37 2N 99 59W
Englewood, Ohio **42** 39 53N 84 18W
Englewood, Tenn. **49** 35 26N 84 29W
English **22** 38 20N 86 28W
English → **63** 50 35N 93 30W
English Bazar = Ingraj Bazar **109** 24 58N 88 10 E
English Channel **86** 50 0N 2 0W
English Creek **37** 39 20N 74 42W
English River **60** 49 14N 91 0W
Englishtown **37** 40 18N 74 22W
Enid, Miss. **31** 34 7N 89 56W
Enid, Okla. **43** 36 24N 97 53W
Enid L. **31** 34 9N 89 54W
Eniwetok **124** 11 30N 162 15 E
Enka **40** 35 33N 82 39W
Enkhuizen **87** 52 42N 5 17 E
Enloe **51** 33 26N 95 39W
Enna **94** 37 34N 14 15 E
Ennadai **63** 61 8N 100 53W
Ennadai L. **63** 61 0N 101 0W
Ennedi **121** 17 15N 22 0 E
Ennis, Ireland **85** 52 51N 8 59W
Ennis, Mont. **33** 45 21N 111 44W
Ennis, Tex. **51** 32 20N 96 38W
Enniscorthy **85** 52 30N 6 35W
Enniskillen **85** 54 20N 7 40W
Ennistimon **85** 52 56N 9 18W
Enns → **88** 48 14N 14 32 E
Eno → **40** 36 5N 78 50W
Enoch **52** 37 47N 113 2W
Enochs **50** 33 52N 102 46W
Enola **34** 41 54N 97 28W
Enontekiö **96** 68 23N 23 37 E
Enoree → **46** 34 26N 81 25W
Enosburg Falls **36** 44 55N 72 48W
Enping **115** 22 16N 112 21 E
Enriquillo, L. **67** 18 20N 72 5W
Enschede **87** 52 13N 6 53 E
Ensenada, Argentina **76** 34 55 S 57 55W
Ensenada, Mexico **64** 31 50N 116 50W
Ensenada, Puerto Rico **57** 17 58N 66 56W
Ensenada, U.S.A. **38** 36 44N 106 32W
Ensenada, La **78** 41 12 S 72 33W
Enshi **115** 30 18N 109 29 E
Ensign **24** 37 39N 100 14W
Ensley **17** 30 31N 87 16W
Entebbe **122** 0 4N 32 28 E
Enterprise, Canada **62** 60 47N 115 45W
Enterprise, Ala. **10** 31 19N 85 51W
Enterprise, Calif. **14** 40 30N 122 22W
Enterprise, Kans. **24** 38 54N 97 7W
Enterprise, La. **25** 31 54N 91 53W
Enterprise, Miss. **31** 32 10N 88 49W
Enterprise, Oreg. **44** 45 25N 117 17W
Enterprise, Utah **52** 37 34N 113 43W
Entiat **53** 47 40N 120 13W
Entre Ríos, Bolivia **76** 21 30 S 64 25W
Entre Rios, Bahia, Brazil **75** 11 56 S 38 5W
Entre Rios, Pará, Brazil **73** 5 24 S 54 21W
Entre Ríos □ **76** 30 30 S 58 30W
Entrecasteaux, Pt. d' **128** 34 50 S 115 56 E
Enugu **120** 6 20N 7 30 E
Enugu Ezike **120** 7 0N 7 29 E
Enumclaw **53** 47 12N 121 59W
Envigado **70** 6 10N 75 35W
Enville **48** 35 23N 88 26W
Envira **72** 7 18 S 70 13W
Eolia **32** 39 14N 91 1W
Eólie, I. **94** 38 30N 14 50 E
Eoline **10** 32 59N 87 8W
Epe **87** 52 21N 5 59 E
Épernay **90** 49 3N 3 56 E
Epes **10** 32 42N 88 7W
Ephesus **106** 37 50N 27 33 E
Ephraim **52** 39 22N 111 35W
Ephrata, Pa. **45** 40 11N 76 11W
Ephrata, Wash. **53** 47 19N 119 33W
Épinal **90** 48 10N 6 27 E
Epira **71** 5 5N 57 20W
Epleys **48** 36 56N 86 56W
Epping, U.K. **83** 51 42N 0 8 E
Epping, N. Dak. **41** 48 17N 103 21W
Epping, N.H. **36** 43 2N 71 4W
Epps **25** 32 36N 91 29W
Epukiro **123** 21 40 S 19 9 E
Equality **21** 37 44N 88 20W
Equatorial Guinea ■ **122** 2 0 S 8 0 E
Equeipa **71** 5 22N 62 43W
Equinox Mt. **36** 43 11N 73 9W
Er Rahad **121** 12 45N 30 32 E
Er Rif **120** 35 1N 4 1W
Er Roseires **121** 11 55N 34 30 E
Erath **25** 29 58N 92 2W
Erath County ◇ **51** 32 13N 98 12W
Erāwadī Myit → = Irrawaddy → **109** 15 50N 95 6 E
Erbacon **54** 38 31N 80 35W
Ercha **101** 69 45N 147 20 E
Erciyaş Dağı **106** 38 30N 35 30 E
Erdao Jiang → **114** 43 0N 127 0 E
Erebato → **71** 5 54N 64 16W
Erebus, Mt. **5** 77 35 S 167 0 E
Erechim **77** 27 35 S 52 15W
Ereğli, Turkey **106** 41 15N 31 30 E
Ereğli, Turkey **106** 37 31N 34 4 E
Erenhot **114** 43 48N 111 59 E
Eresma → **91** 41 26N 40 45W
Erewadi Myitwanya **109** 15 30N 95 0 E
Erfurt **88** 50 58N 11 2 E
Ergani **106** 38 17N 39 49 E
Ergene → **95** 41 1N 26 22 E
Ergeni Vozyshennost **99** 47 0N 44 0 E
Ergun Zuoqi **114** 50 47N 121 31 E
Erhard **30** 46 29N 96 6W
Eriboll, L. **84** 58 28N 4 41W
Érice **94** 38 4N 12 34 E
Erick **43** 35 13N 99 52W
Ericson **34** 41 47N 98 41W
Eridu **17** 30 18N 83 45W
Erie, Colo. **16** 40 3N 105 3W
Erie, Ill. **21** 41 39N 90 5W
Erie, Kans. **24** 37 34N 95 15W
Erie, N. Dak. **41** 47 7N 97 23W
Erie, Pa. **45** 42 8N 80 5W
Erie Canal **39** 43 5N 78 43W
Erie County ◇, N.Y. **39** 42 50N 78 45W
Erie County ◇, Ohio **42** 41 24N 82 33W
Erie County ◇, Pa. **45** 42 0N 80 0W
Erie L. **42** 41 50N 82 0W
Erigavo **105** 10 35N 47 20 E
Eriksdale **63** 50 52N 98 7W
Erímanthos **95** 37 57N 21 50 E
Erimo-misaki **116** 41 50N 143 15 E
Erin **48** 36 19N 87 42W
Eritrea □ **121** 14 0N 41 0 E
Erlangen **88** 49 35N 11 0 E
Erlanger **49** 39 1N 84 36W
Erling, L. **13** 33 3N 93 32W
Ermelo **87** 52 18N 5 35 E
Ermenak **106** 36 38N 33 0 E
Ermoúpolis = Síros **95** 37 28N 24 57 E
Ernakulam = Cochin **108** 9 59N 76 22 E
Erne → **85** 54 30N 8 16W
Erne, Lough **85** 54 26N 7 46W
Ernul **40** 35 15N 77 4W
Erode **108** 11 24N 77 45 E
Erramala Hills **108** 15 30N 78 15 E
Errigal, Mt. **85** 55 2N 8 8W
Erris Hd. **85** 54 19N 10 0W
Errol **36** 44 47N 71 8W
Erskine **30** 47 40N 96 0W
Erwin, N.C. **40** 35 20N 78 41W
Erwin, S. Dak. **47** 44 29N 97 27W
Erwin, Tenn. **49** 36 9N 82 25W
Erwinville **25** 30 32N 91 24W
Erzgebirge **88** 50 25N 13 0 E
Erzin **101** 50 15N 95 10 E
Erzincan **106** 39 46N 39 30 E
Erzurum **106** 39 57N 41 15 E
Es Sahrâ' Esh Sharqîya **121** 26 0N 33 30 E
Es Sînâ' **121** 29 0N 34 0 E
Esan-Misaki **116** 41 40N 141 10 E
Esashi, Hokkaidō, Japan **116** 44 56N 142 35 E
Esashi, Hokkaidō, Japan **116** 41 52N 140 7 E
Esbjerg **97** 55 29N 8 29 E
Esbon **24** 39 49N 98 26W
Escada **74** 8 22 S 35 8W
Escalante **52** 37 47N 111 36W
Escalante → **52** 37 24N 110 57W
Escalante Desert **52** 37 50N 113 20W
Escalón, Mexico **64** 26 46N 104 20W
Escalon, U.S.A. **14** 37 48N 121 0W
Escambia → **17** 30 32N 87 15W
Escambia County ◇, Ala. **10** 31 7N 87 4W
Escambia County ◇, Fla. **17** 30 30N 87 30W
Escanaba **29** 45 45N 87 4W
Escanaba → **29** 45 47N 87 3W
Escatawpa → **31** 30 26N 88 33W
Escatawpu → **31** 30 25N 88 35W
Esch-sur-Alzette **87** 49 32N 6 0 E
Escobal **57** 9 9N 79 58W
Escoma **72** 15 40 S 69 8W

Escondida, La Fajardo

Escondida, La 64 24 6N 99 55W
Escondido 15 33 7N 117 5W
Escuinapa 64 22 50N 105 50W
Escuintla 66 14 20N 90 48W
Eşfahān 107 33 0N 53 0 E
Esh Sham = Dimashq 106 33 30N 36 18 E
Esh Shamâlîya □ 121 19 0N 29 0 E
Eshta' ol 104 31 47N 35 0 E
Esk →, Dumf. & Gall., U.K. 84 54 58N 3 4W
Esk →, N. Yorks., U.K. 82 54 27N 0 36W
Eskifjörður 96 65 3N 13 55W
Eskilstuna 97 59 22N 16 32 E
Eskimo Pt. 63 61 10N 94 15W
Eskişehir 106 39 50N 30 35 E
Eskridge 24 38 52N 96 6W
Esla → 91 41 29N 6 3W
Eslāmābād-e Gharb 106 34 10N 46 30 E
Esmeralda, I. 78 48 55 S 75 25W
Esmeralda, La 76 22 16 S 62 33W
Esmeralda County ◇ 35 37 50N 117 45W
Esmeraldas 70 1 0N 79 40W
Esmeraldas □ 70 0 40N 79 30W
Esmeraldas → 70 0 58N 79 38W
Esmond 41 48 2N 99 46W
Esmont 54 37 50N 78 37W
Esom Hill 18 33 57N 85 23W
Espada, Pta. 70 12 5N 71 7W
Espanola, Canada 60 46 15N 81 46W
Espanola, Fla. 17 29 31N 81 19W
Espanola, N. Mex. 38 35 59N 106 5W
Esparta 66 9 59N 84 40W
Esparto 14 38 42N 122 1W
Espenberg, C. 11 66 33N 163 36W
Esperança 74 7 1 S 35 51W
Esperance 126 33 45 S 121 55 E
Esperance B. 126 33 48 S 121 55 E
Esperantinópolis 74 4 53 S 44 53W
Esperanza, Antarct. 5 65 0 S 55 0W
Esperanza, Santa Cruz, Argentina 78 51 1 S 70 49W
Esperanza, Santa Fe, Argentina 76 31 29 S 61 3W
Esperanza, Puerto Rico 57 18 6N 65 28W
Esperanza, La, Argentina 78 40 26 S 68 32W
Esperanza, La, Cuba 66 22 46N 83 44W
Esperanza, La, Hond. 66 14 15N 88 10W
Espichel, C. 91 38 22N 9 16W
Espigão, Serra do 77 26 35 S 50 30W
Espinal 70 4 9N 74 53W
Espinar 72 14 51 S 71 24W
Espinazo, Sierra del = Espinhaço, Serra do 75 17 30 S 43 30W
Espinhaço, Serra do 75 17 30 S 43 30W
Espinilho, Serra do 77 28 30 S 55 0W
Espino 70 8 34N 66 1W
Espírito Santo □ 75 20 0 S 40 45W
Espíritu Santo, B. del 65 19 15N 87 0W
Espíritu Santo, I. 64 24 30N 110 23W
Espita 65 21 1N 88 19W
Esplanada 75 11 47 S 37 57W
Espungabera 123 20 29 S 32 45 E
Esquel 78 42 55 S 71 20W
Esquina 76 30 0 S 59 30W
Essaouira 120 31 32N 9 42W
Essen, Belgium 87 51 28N 4 28 E
Essen, Germany 88 51 28N 6 59 E
Essequibo □ 71 7 0N 59 0W
Essequibo → 71 6 50N 58 30W
Essex, Calif. 15 34 44N 115 15W
Essex, Conn. 28 41 21N 72 24W
Essex, Ill. 21 41 11N 88 11W
Essex, Iowa 23 40 50N 95 18W
Essex, Md. 27 39 19N 76 29W
Essex, Mo. 32 36 50N 89 8W
Essex, Mont. 33 48 17N 113 37W
Essex, N.Y. 39 44 19N 73 21W
Essex □ 83 51 48N 0 30 E
Essex County ◇, Mass. 28 42 35N 70 50W
Essex County ◇, N.J. 37 40 45N 74 15W
Essex County ◇, N.Y. 39 44 0N 73 40W
Essex County ◇, Va. 54 37 56N 76 52W
Essex County ◇, Vt. 36 44 45N 71 45W
Essex Junction 36 44 29N 73 7W
Essexville 29 43 37N 83 50W
Esslingen 88 48 43N 9 19 E
Essonne □ 90 48 30N 2 20 E
Estacada 44 45 17N 122 20W
Estados, I. de Los 78 54 40 S 64 30W
Estância, Brazil 74 11 16 S 37 26W
Estancia, U.S.A. 38 34 46N 106 4W
Este, Cabo 57 18 5N 67 51W
Este, Punta 57 18 8N 65 16W
Estelí 66 13 9N 86 22W
Estelline, S. Dak. 47 44 35N 96 54W
Estelline, Tex. 50 34 33N 100 26W
Estellville 37 39 23N 74 45W
Esterhazy 63 50 37N 102 5W
Estero 17 26 26N 81 49W
Estes Park 16 40 23N 105 31W
Estevan 63 49 10N 102 59W
Estevan Group 62 53 3N 129 38W
Estherville 23 43 24N 94 50W
Estherwood 25 30 11N 92 28W
Estill 46 32 45N 81 15W
Estill County ◇ 49 37 40N 84 0W
Estill Springs 48 35 16N 86 8W
Eston 63 51 8N 108 40W
Estonian S.S.R. □ 98 58 30N 25 30 E
Estoril 91 38 42N 9 23W
Estrada, La 91 42 43N 8 27W
Estrêla, Serra da 91 40 10N 7 45W
Estremadura 91 39 0N 9 0W
Estrondo, Serra do 74 7 20 S 48 0W
Esztergom 89 47 47N 18 44 E
Eṭ Ṭîra 104 32 14N 34 56 E
Etamamu 61 50 18N 59 59W
Etawah 108 26 48N 79 6 E
Etawney L. 63 57 50N 96 50W
Etchison 27 39 15N 77 8W
Ethan 47 43 33N 97 59W
Ethel, La. 25 30 47N 91 8W
Ethel, Miss. 31 33 7N 89 28W
Ethel, Mo. 32 39 54N 92 45W
Ethelbert 63 51 32N 100 25W
Ethelsville 10 33 25N 88 13W
Ethiopia ■ 105 8 0N 40 0 E
Ethiopian Highlands 118 10 0N 37 0 E
Ethridge, Mont. 33 48 34N 112 8W
Ethridge, Tenn. 48 35 19N 87 18W
Etive, L. 84 56 30N 5 12W
Etna, Italy 94 37 45N 15 0 E
Etna, Calif. 14 41 27N 122 54W
Etna, Maine 26 44 49N 69 7W
Etna, Utah 52 41 40N 113 58W
Etolin Strait 11 60 20N 165 15W
Eton 18 34 50N 84 46W
Etosha Pan 123 18 40 S 16 30 E
Etowah 49 35 20N 84 32W
Etowah County ◇ 10 34 0N 86 0W
Étroits, Les 61 47 24N 68 54W
Etropole 95 42 50N 24 0 E
Etter 50 36 3N 101 59W
Ettrick 55 44 10N 91 16W
Ettrick Water 84 55 31N 2 55W
Etzatlán 64 20 48N 104 5W
Etzná 65 19 35N 90 15W
Eubank 49 37 17N 84 40W
Euboea = Évvoia 95 38 30N 24 0 E
Eucla Basin 126 31 19 S 126 9 E
Euclid 42 41 34N 81 32W
Euclides da Cunha 74 10 31 S 39 1W
Eudora, Ark. 13 33 7N 91 16W
Eudora, Kans. 24 38 57N 95 6W
Eufaula, Ala. 10 31 54N 85 9W
Eufaula, Okla. 43 35 17N 95 35W
Eufaula L. 43 35 18N 95 21W
Eugene, Mo. 32 38 21N 92 24W
Eugene, Oreg. 44 44 5N 123 4W
Eugenia, Punta 64 27 50N 115 5W
Euless 51 32 50N 97 5W
Eulonia 18 31 32N 81 26W
Eunice, La. 25 30 30N 92 25W
Eunice, N. Mex. 38 32 26N 103 10W
Eupen 87 50 37N 6 3 E
Euphrates = Furāt, Nahr al → 106 31 0N 47 25 E
Eupora 31 33 32N 89 16W
Eurcka Springs 13 36 24N 93 44W
Eure □ 90 49 6N 1 0 E
Eure-et-Loir □ 90 48 22N 1 30 E
Eureka, Canada 4 80 0N 85 56W
Eureka, Calif. 14 40 47N 124 9W
Eureka, Ill. 21 40 43N 89 16W
Eureka, Kans. 24 37 49N 96 17W
Eureka, Mo. 32 38 30N 90 38W
Eureka, Mont. 33 48 53N 115 3W
Eureka, Nev. 35 39 31N 115 58W
Eureka, S.C. 46 33 42N 81 46W
Eureka, S. Dak. 47 45 46N 99 38W
Eureka, Utah 52 39 58N 112 7W
Eureka, Wash. 53 46 18N 118 37W
Eureka County ◇ 35 40 0N 116 10W
Europa, Île 123 22 20 S 40 22 E
Europa, Picos de 91 43 10N 4 49W
Europa, Pta. de 91 36 3N 5 21W
Europa Pt. = Europa, Pta. de 91 36 3N 5 21W
Europe 80 50 0N 20 0 E
Europoort 87 51 57N 4 10 E
Eustis, Fla. 17 28 51N 81 41W
Eustis, Maine 26 45 13N 70 29W
Eustis, Nebr. 34 40 40N 100 2W
Eustis, L. 17 28 50N 81 44W
Eutaw 10 32 50N 87 53W
Eutawville 46 33 24N 80 21W
Eutsuk L. 62 53 20N 126 45W
Eva, Brazil 71 3 9 S 59 56W
Eva, U.S.A. 10 34 20N 86 46W
Evadale 51 30 21N 94 5W
Eval 104 32 15N 35 15 E
Evan 30 44 21N 94 50W
Evangeline 25 30 16N 92 34W
Evangeline Parish ◇ 25 30 47N 92 25W
Evans, Colo. 16 40 23N 104 41W
Evans, La. 25 30 59N 93 30W
Evans, W. Va. 54 38 49N 81 47W
Evans, Mt. 16 39 35N 105 39W
Evans City 45 40 46N 80 4W
Evans County ◇ 18 32 10N 81 55W
Evans L. 60 50 50N 77 0W
Evansdale 23 42 30N 92 17W
Evanston, Ill. 21 42 3N 87 41W
Evanston, Ky. 49 37 28N 83 2W
Evanston, Wyo. 56 41 16N 110 58W
Evansville, Ark. 13 35 48N 94 30W
Evansville, Ill. 21 38 5N 89 56W
Evansville, Ind. 22 37 58N 87 35W
Evansville, Minn. 30 46 0N 95 41W
Evansville, Wis. 55 42 47N 89 18W
Evansville, Wyo. 56 42 52N 106 16W
Evant 51 31 29N 98 9W
Evart 29 43 54N 85 2W
Evarts 49 36 52N 83 12W
Eveleth 30 47 28N 92 32W
Evelyn 25 31 59N 93 27W
Even Yahuda 104 32 16N 34 53 E
Evening Shade 13 36 4N 91 37W
Evensk 101 62 12N 159 30 E
Evensville 49 35 34N 84 57W
Everard, L. 126 31 30 S 135 0 E
Everard Ras. 126 27 5 S 132 28 E
Everest 24 39 41N 95 26W
Everest, Mt. 109 28 5N 86 58 E
Everett, Ga. 18 31 24N 81 38W
Everett, Mass. 28 42 24N 71 4W
Everett, Pa. 45 40 1N 78 23W
Everett, Wash. 53 47 59N 122 12W
Everglades, The 17 25 50N 81 0W
Everglades City 17 25 52N 81 23W
Everglades National Park 17 25 30N 81 0W
Evergreen, Ala. 10 31 26N 86 57W
Evergreen, Colo. 16 39 38N 105 19W
Evergreen, N.C. 40 34 25N 78 54W
Evergreen Park 21 41 43N 87 41W
Everly 23 43 10N 95 19W
Everton 32 37 21N 93 42W
Evesham 83 52 6N 1 57W
Evinayong 122 1 26N 10 35 E
Évora 91 38 33N 7 57W
Évreux 90 49 0N 1 8 E
Évvoia 95 38 30N 24 0 E
Évvoia □ 95 38 40N 23 40 E
Ewa 19 21 20N 158 3W
Ewa Beach 19 21 19N 158 1W
Ewan 53 47 7N 117 44W
Ewe, L. 84 57 49N 5 38W
Ewen 29 46 32N 89 17W
Ewing, Ky. 49 38 26N 83 52W
Ewing, Mo. 32 40 6N 91 43W
Ewing, N.J. 37 40 15N 74 48W
Ewing, Nebr. 34 42 16N 98 21W
Ewing, Va. 54 36 38N 83 26W
Ewo 122 0 48 S 14 45 E
Exaltación 73 13 10 S 65 20W
Excello 32 39 38N 92 29W
Excelsior Mts. 35 38 15N 118 10W
Excelsior Springs 32 39 20N 94 13W
Exe → 83 50 38N 3 27W
Exell 50 35 38N 101 59W
Exeter, U.K. 83 50 43N 3 31W
Exeter, Calif. 15 36 18N 119 9W
Exeter, Maine 26 44 58N 69 9W
Exeter, Mo. 32 36 40N 93 56W
Exeter, N.H. 36 42 59N 70 57W
Exeter, Nebr. 34 40 39N 97 27W
Exeter, R.I. 28 41 35N 71 32W
Exira 23 41 35N 94 52W
Exmoor 83 51 10N 3 59W
Exmore 54 37 32N 75 50W
Exmouth, Australia 126 21 54 S 114 10 E
Exmouth, U.K. 83 50 37N 3 26W
Exmouth G. 126 22 15 S 114 15 E
Expedition Range 127 24 30 S 149 12 E
Extremadura □ 91 39 30N 6 5W
Exuma Sound 66 24 30N 76 20W
Eyak 11 60 32N 145 36W
Eyasi, L. 122 3 30 S 35 0 E
Eyeberry L. 63 63 8N 104 43W
Eyemouth 84 55 53N 2 5W
Eyjafjörður 96 66 15N 18 30W
Eyota 30 43 59N 92 14W
Eyrarbakki 96 63 52N 21 9W
Eyre 126 32 15 S 126 18 E
Eyre (North), L. 127 28 30 S 137 20 E
Eyre, L. 127 29 30 S 137 26 E
Eyre Cr. → 127 26 40 S 139 0 E
Eyre Mts. 128 45 25 S 168 25 E
Eyre Pen. 126 33 30 S 137 17 E

F

Fabens 50 31 30N 106 10W
Fabius 39 42 50N 75 59W
Fabriano 94 43 20N 12 52 E
Făcăeni 95 44 32N 27 53 E
Facatativá 70 4 49N 74 22W
Faceville 18 30 45N 84 38W
Fachi 120 18 6N 11 34 E
Fada 121 17 13N 21 34 E
Fada-n-Gourma 120 12 10N 0 30 E
Faddeyevskiy, Ostrov 101 76 0N 150 0 E
Fāḍilī 106 26 55N 49 10 E
Faenza 94 44 17N 11 53 E
Făgăras 89 45 48N 24 58 E
Făgăras, Munţii 95 45 40N 24 40 E
Fagernes 97 60 59N 9 14 E
Fagersta 97 60 1N 15 46 E
Fagnano, L. 78 54 30 S 68 0W
Fahraj 107 29 0N 59 0 E
Fahūd 107 22 18N 56 28 E
Fair Bluff 40 34 19N 79 2W
Fair Grove 32 37 23N 93 9W
Fair Haven, N.J. 37 40 22N 74 2W
Fair Haven, Vt. 36 43 36N 73 16W
Fair Hd. 85 55 14N 6 10W
Fair Isle 86 59 30N 1 40W
Fair Oaks 43 36 17N 95 50W
Fair Plain 29 42 5N 86 27W
Fair Play, Mo. 32 37 38N 93 35W
Fair Play, S.C. 46 34 31N 82 59W
Fairbank, Ariz. 12 31 43N 110 11W
Fairbank, Iowa 23 42 38N 92 3W
Fairbank, Md. 27 38 41N 76 20W
Fairbanks, Alaska 11 64 51N 147 43W
Fairbanks, Fla. 17 29 44N 82 16W
Fairbanks North Star ◇ 11 65 0N 147 0W
Fairborn 42 39 49N 84 2W
Fairburn, Ga. 18 33 34N 84 35W
Fairburn, S. Dak. 47 43 41N 103 13W
Fairbury, Ill. 21 40 45N 88 31W
Fairbury, Nebr. 34 40 8N 97 11W
Fairchance 45 39 49N 79 45W
Fairchild 55 44 36N 90 58W
Fairdale, Ky. 49 38 6N 85 46W
Fairdale, N. Dak. 41 48 30N 98 14W
Fairfax, Ala. 10 32 48N 85 11W
Fairfax, Calif. 14 37 59N 122 35W
Fairfax, Iowa 23 41 55N 91 47W
Fairfax, Minn. 30 44 32N 94 43W
Fairfax, Mo. 32 40 20N 95 24W
Fairfax, Okla. 43 36 34N 96 42W
Fairfax, S.C. 46 32 59N 81 15W
Fairfax, S. Dak. 47 43 2N 98 54W
Fairfax, Va. 54 38 51N 77 18W
Fairfax, Vt. 36 44 40N 73 1W
Fairfax County ◇ 54 38 51N 77 18W
Fairfield, Ala. 10 33 29N 86 55W
Fairfield, Calif. 14 38 15N 122 3W
Fairfield, Conn. 28 41 9N 73 16W
Fairfield, Idaho 20 43 21N 114 44W
Fairfield, Ill. 21 38 23N 88 22W
Fairfield, Iowa 23 40 56N 91 57W
Fairfield, Ky. 49 37 56N 85 23W
Fairfield, Mont. 33 47 37N 111 59W
Fairfield, N.C. 40 35 32N 76 14W
Fairfield, N. Dak. 41 47 11N 103 14W
Fairfield, Nebr. 34 40 26N 98 6W
Fairfield, Pa. 45 39 47N 77 22W
Fairfield, Tex. 51 31 44N 96 10W
Fairfield County ◇, Conn. 28 41 15N 73 20W
Fairfield County ◇, Ohio 42 39 43N 82 36W
Fairfield County ◇, S.C. 46 34 25N 81 10W
Fairford 63 51 37N 98 38W
Fairgrove 29 43 32N 83 33W
Fairhaven, Mass. 28 41 39N 70 55W
Fairhaven, Md. 27 38 45N 76 34W
Fairhope 10 30 31N 87 54W
Fairland, Ind. 22 39 35N 85 52W
Fairland, Okla. 43 36 45N 94 51W
Fairlee, Md. 27 39 13N 76 10W
Fairlee, Vt. 36 43 54N 72 9W
Fairlie 128 44 5 S 170 49 E
Fairmont, Minn. 30 43 39N 94 28W
Fairmont, N.C. 40 34 30N 79 7W
Fairmont, Nebr. 34 40 38N 97 35W
Fairmont, Okla. 43 36 21N 97 43W
Fairmont, W. Va. 54 39 29N 80 9W
Fairmont Hot Springs 62 50 20N 115 56W
Fairmount, Ga. 18 34 26N 84 42W
Fairmount, Ill. 21 40 3N 87 56W
Fairmount, Ind. 22 40 25N 85 39W
Fairmount, Md. 27 38 6N 75 48W
Fairmount, N. Dak. 41 46 3N 96 36W
Fairmount, N.Y. 39 43 5N 76 12W
Fairplains 40 36 12N 81 9W
Fairplay 16 39 15N 106 2W
Fairport 39 43 6N 77 27W
Fairport Harbor 42 41 45N 81 17W
Fairview, Canada 62 56 5N 118 25W
Fairview, Ill. 21 40 38N 90 10W
Fairview, Kans. 24 39 50N 95 44W
Fairview, Mich. 29 44 44N 84 3W
Fairview, Mont. 33 47 51N 104 3W
Fairview, N.J. 37 40 23N 74 5W
Fairview, Okla. 43 36 16N 98 29W
Fairview, Pa. 45 42 2N 80 15W
Fairview, S. Dak. 47 43 13N 96 29W
Fairview, Tenn. 48 35 59N 87 7W
Fairview, Utah 52 39 38N 111 26W
Fairview, W. Va. 54 39 36N 80 15W
Fairview Park 22 39 41N 87 25W
Fairweather, Mt. 11 58 55N 137 32W
Faisalabad 108 31 30N 73 5 E
Faison 40 35 7N 78 8W
Faith 47 45 2N 102 2W
Faizabad 109 26 45N 82 10 E
Fajardo 57 18 20N 65 39W

Fajardo Fisher B.

Fajardo → 57 18 20N 65 39W
Fakfak 111 3 0S 132 15 E
Fakiya 95 42 10N 27 6 E
Faku 114 42 32N 123 21 E
Falaise 90 48 54N 0 12W
Falam 109 23 0N 93 45 E
Fălciu 95 46 17N 28 7 E
Falcon, Colo. 16 38 56N 104 37W
Falcon, N.C. 40 35 11N 78 39W
Falcón □ 70 11 0N 69 50W
Falcon, C. 44 45 46N 123 59W
Falcon Reservoir 50 26 34N 99 10W
Falfurrias 50 27 14N 98 9W
Falher 62 55 44N 117 15W
Falkenberg 97 56 54N 12 30 E
Falkirk 84 56 0N 3 47W
Falkland, East, I. 78 51 40 S 58 30W
Falkland, West, I. 78 51 40 S 60 0W
Falkland Is. 78 51 30 S 59 0W
Falkland Is. Dependency □ 5 57 0 S 40 0W
Falkland Sd. 78 52 0 S 60 0W
Falkner 31 34 51N 88 56W
Falköping 97 58 12N 13 33 E
Falkville 10 34 22N 86 55W
Fall → 24 37 24N 95 40W
Fall Branch 49 36 25N 82 37W
Fall Creek 55 44 46N 91 17W
Fall River, Kans. 24 37 36N 96 2W
Fall River, Mass. 28 41 43N 71 10W
Fall River, Wis. 55 43 23N 89 3W
Fall River County ◇ 47 43 10N 103 30W
Fall River Lake 24 37 39N 96 4W
Fall River Mills 14 41 3N 121 26W
Fallbrook 15 33 23N 117 15W
Fallon, Mont. 33 46 50N 105 8W
Fallon, Nev. 35 39 28N 118 47W
Fallon County ◇ 33 46 20N 104 30W
Fallon Indian Reservation 35 39 25N 118 45W
Falls Church 54 38 53N 77 10W
Falls City, Nebr. 34 40 3N 95 36W
Falls City, Oreg. 44 44 52N 123 26W
Falls City, Tex. 51 28 59N 98 1W
Falls County ◇ 51 31 18N 96 54W
Falls Creek 45 41 9N 78 48W
Fallsburg 49 38 11N 82 40W
Fallston, Md. 27 39 31N 76 25W
Fallston, N.C. 40 35 26N 81 30W
Falmouth, Jamaica 66 18 30N 77 40W
Falmouth, U.K. 83 50 9N 5 5W
Falmouth, Fla. 17 30 21N 83 8W
Falmouth, Ky. 49 38 41N 84 20W
Falmouth, Maine 26 43 44N 70 14W
Falmouth, Mass. 28 41 33N 70 37W
Falmouth, Mich. 29 44 15N 85 5W
Falmouth, Va. 54 38 20N 77 28W
False Pass 11 54 51N 163 25W
Falso, C. 66 15 12N 83 21W
Falster 97 54 45N 11 55 E
Falsterbo 97 55 23N 12 50 E
Falun, Sweden 97 60 37N 15 37 E
Falun, U.S.A. 24 38 40N 97 46W
Famagusta 106 35 8N 33 55 E
Famatina, Sierra de 76 27 30 S 68 0W
Family L. 63 51 54N 95 27W
Fan Xian 114 35 55N 115 38 E
Fancy Farm 48 36 48N 88 47W
Fandriana 123 20 14 S 47 21 E
Fang Xian 115 32 3N 110 40 E
Fangchang 115 31 5N 118 4 E
Fangcheng 115 33 18N 112 59 E
Fangliao 115 22 22N 120 38 E
Fangzheng 114 49 50N 128 48 E
Fanjiatun 114 43 40N 125 0 E
Fannich, L. 84 57 40N 5 0W
Fannin County ◇, Ga. 18 34 50N 84 15W
Fannin County ◇, Tex. 51 33 35N 96 11W
Fanny Bay 62 49 27N 124 48W
Fano 94 43 50N 13 0 E
Fanshawe 43 34 57N 94 55W
Fao = Al Fāw 106 30 0N 48 30 E
Faradje 122 3 50N 29 45 E
Faradofay 123 25 2 S 47 0 E
Farafangana 123 22 49 S 47 50 E
Farāh 107 32 20N 62 7 E
Farāh □ 107 32 25N 62 10 E
Farallon Is. 14 37 45N 123 10W
Faranah 120 10 3N 10 45W
Farasān, Jazā'ir 105 16 45N 41 55 E
Fareham 83 50 52N 1 11W
Farewell 11 62 31N 153 54W
Farewell, C. 128 40 29 S 172 43 E
Farewell C. = Farvel, Kap 4 59 48N 43 55W
Fargo, Ga. 18 30 41N 82 34W
Fargo, N. Dak. 41 46 53N 96 48W
Fargo, Okla. 43 36 22N 99 37W
Fari'a → 104 32 12N 35 27 E
Faribault 30 44 18N 93 16W
Faribault County ◇ 30 43 45N 94 0W
Farim 120 12 27N 15 9W
Farīmān 107 35 40N 59 49 E
Farina 21 38 50N 88 46W
Farinha → 74 6 51 S 47 30W
Farley 23 42 27N 91 0W
Farmer City 21 40 15N 88 39W
Farmers Branch 51 32 56N 96 54W
Farmersburg 22 39 15N 87 23W
Farmersville, Calif. 15 36 18N 119 12W
Farmersville, Ill. 21 39 27N 89 39W
Farmersville, Tex. 51 33 10N 96 22W
Farmerville 25 32 47N 92 24W
Farmingdale 37 40 12N 74 10W
Farmington, Ark. 13 36 3N 94 15W
Farmington, Calif. 14 37 55N 120 59W
Farmington, Del. 27 38 52N 75 35W
Farmington, Ga. 18 33 47N 83 26W
Farmington, Ill. 21 40 42N 90 0W
Farmington, Iowa 23 40 38N 91 44W
Farmington, Maine 26 44 40N 70 9W
Farmington, Md. 27 39 42N 76 4W
Farmington, Minn. 30 44 38N 93 8W
Farmington, Mo. 32 37 47N 90 25W
Farmington, Mont. 33 47 53N 112 10W
Farmington, N.C. 40 36 1N 80 32W
Farmington, N.H. 36 43 24N 71 4W
Farmington, N. Mex. 38 36 44N 108 12W
Farmington, Utah 52 40 59N 111 53W
Farmington, Wash. 53 47 5N 117 3W
Farmington → 28 41 51N 72 38W
Farmville, N.C. 40 35 36N 77 35W
Farmville, Va. 54 37 18N 78 24W
Farnam 34 40 42N 100 13W
Farnborough 83 51 17N 0 46W
Farne Is. 82 55 38N 1 37W
Farner 49 35 9N 84 19W
Farnsworth 50 36 19N 100 58W
Faro, Brazil 71 2 10 S 56 39W
Faro, Portugal 91 37 2N 7 55W
Fårö, Sweden 97 57 55N 19 5 E
Faroe Is. 80 62 0N 7 0W
Farquhar, C. 126 23 50 S 113 36 E
Farragut 23 40 43N 95 29W
Farrar → 84 57 30N 4 30W
Farrāshband 107 28 57N 52 5 E
Farrell 45 41 13N 80 30W
Farrukhabad-cum-Fatehgarh 108 27 30N 79 32 E
Fars □ 107 29 30N 55 0 E
Fársala 95 39 17N 22 23 E
Farsund 97 58 5N 6 55 E
Fartak, Râs 106 28 5N 34 34 E
Fartura, Serra da 77 26 21 S 52 52W
Farvel, Kap 4 59 48N 43 55W
Farwell, Mich. 29 43 50N 84 52W
Farwell, Minn. 30 45 45N 95 37W
Farwell, Nebr. 34 41 13N 98 38W
Farwell, Tex. 50 34 23N 103 2W
Faryab 108 28 7N 57 14 E
Fāryāb □ 107 36 0N 65 0 E
Fasā 107 29 0N 53 39 E
Fastnet Rock 85 51 22N 9 37W
Fatagar, Tanjung 111 2 46 S 131 57 E
Fatehgarh 108 27 25N 79 35 E
Fatehpur, Raj., India 108 28 0N 74 40 E
Fatehpur, Ut. P., India 109 25 56N 81 13 E
Fatima 61 47 24N 61 53W
Faucett 32 39 36N 94 48W
Faucilles, Monts 90 48 5N 5 50 E
Faulk County ◇ 47 45 0N 99 0W
Faulkner County ◇ 13 35 10N 92 16W
Faulkton 47 45 2N 99 8W
Fauquier County ◇ 54 38 43N 77 48W
Făurei 95 45 6N 27 19 E
Fauresmith 123 29 44 S 25 17 E
Fauske 96 67 17N 15 25 E
Faust 52 40 11N 112 24W
Favara 94 37 19N 13 39 E
Favignana 94 37 56N 12 18 E
Favourable Lake 60 52 50N 93 39W
Fawn → 60 52 22N 88 20W
Faxaflói 96 64 29N 23 0W
Faxon 43 34 28N 98 35W
Fay 43 35 49N 98 39W
Faya-Largeau 121 17 58N 19 6 E
Fayd 106 27 1N 42 52 E
Fayette, Ala. 10 33 41N 87 50W
Fayette, Iowa 23 42 51N 91 48W
Fayette, Miss. 31 31 43N 91 4W
Fayette, Mo. 32 39 9N 92 41W
Fayette, N.Y. 39 42 49N 76 49W
Fayette, Ohio 42 41 40N 84 20W
Fayette, Utah 52 39 14N 111 51W
Fayette County ◇, Ala. 10 33 41N 87 50W
Fayette County ◇, Ga. 18 33 25N 84 30W
Fayette County ◇, Ill. 21 39 0N 89 0W
Fayette County ◇, Ind. 22 39 35N 85 10W
Fayette County ◇, Iowa 23 42 50N 91 50W
Fayette County ◇, Ky. 49 38 0N 84 30W
Fayette County ◇, Ohio 42 39 32N 83 26W
Fayette County ◇, Pa. 45 40 0N 79 40W
Fayette County ◇, Tenn. 48 35 15N 89 21W
Fayette County ◇, Tex. 51 29 54N 96 52W
Fayette County ◇, W. Va. 54 37 59N 81 9W
Fayetteville, Ark. 13 36 4N 94 10W
Fayetteville, Ga. 18 33 27N 84 27W
Fayetteville, N.C. 40 35 3N 78 53W
Fayetteville, N.Y. 39 43 2N 76 0W
Fayetteville, Tenn. 48 35 9N 86 34W
Fayetteville, Tex. 51 29 54N 96 41W
Fayetteville, W. Va. 54 38 3N 81 6W
Faywood 38 32 32N 108 1W
Fazenda Nova 75 16 11 S 50 48W
Fazilka 108 30 27N 74 2 E
Fdérik 120 22 40N 12 45W
Fé, La 66 22 2N 84 15W
Feale → 85 52 26N 9 40W
Fear, C. 40 33 50N 77 58W
Feather → 14 38 47N 121 36W
Feather Falls 14 39 36N 121 16W
Featherston 128 41 6 S 175 20 E
Fécamp 90 49 45N 0 22 E
Federación 76 31 0 S 57 55W
Federal Dam 30 47 15N 94 14W
Federal Heights 16 39 52N 105 1W
Federal Way 53 47 18N 122 19W
Federalsburg 27 38 42N 75 47W
Feeding Hills 28 42 4N 72 41W
Fehmarn 88 54 26N 11 10 E
Fehmarn Bælt 88 54 35N 11 20 E
Fei Xian 115 35 18N 117 59 E
Feijó 72 8 9 S 70 21W
Feilding 128 40 13 S 175 35 E
Feira de Santana 75 12 15 S 38 57W
Felch 29 46 0N 87 50W
Felda 17 26 34N 81 26W
Feldkirch 88 47 15N 9 37 E
Felicity 42 38 51N 84 6W
Felipe Carrillo Puerto 65 19 38N 88 3W
Felixlândia 75 18 47 S 44 55W
Felixstowe 83 51 58N 1 22 E
Fellsmere 17 27 46N 80 36W
Felt, Idaho 20 43 52N 111 11W
Felt, Okla. 43 36 34N 102 48W
Felton, Del. 27 39 1N 75 35W
Felton, Minn. 30 47 5N 96 30W
Felton, Pa. 45 39 51N 76 34W
Femunden 96 62 10N 11 53 E
Fen He → 114 35 36N 110 42 E
Fence Lake 38 34 40N 108 40W
Feng Xian, Jiangsu, China 115 34 43N 116 35 E
Feng Xian, Shaanxi, China 115 33 54N 106 40 E
Fengcheng, Jiangxi, China 115 28 12N 115 48 E
Fengcheng, Liaoning, China 114 40 28N 124 5 E
Fengdu 115 29 55N 107 41 E
Fengfeng 114 36 28N 114 8 E
Fenghua 115 29 40N 121 25 E
Fenghuang 115 27 57N 109 29 E
Fengjie 115 31 5N 109 36 E
Fengkai 115 23 24N 111 30 E
Fengle 115 31 29N 112 29 E
Fengning 114 41 10N 116 33 E
Fengtai 114 39 50N 116 18 E
Fengxian 115 30 55N 121 26 E
Fengxiang 115 34 29N 107 25 E
Fengxin 115 28 41N 115 18 E
Fengyang 115 32 51N 117 29 E
Fengzhen 114 40 25N 113 2 E
Fenit 85 52 17N 9 51W
Fenn 20 45 58N 116 16W
Fennimore 55 42 59N 90 39W
Fennville 29 42 36N 86 6W
Fenoarivo Atsinanana 123 17 22 S 49 25 E
Fens, The 82 52 45N 0 2 E
Fenton, Iowa 23 43 13N 94 26W
Fenton, La. 25 30 22N 92 55W
Fenton, Mich. 29 42 48N 83 42W
Fentress 51 29 45N 97 47W
Fentress County ◇ 49 36 25N 85 0W
Fenwood 55 44 52N 90 1W
Fenyang 114 37 18N 111 48 E
Feodosiya 99 45 2N 35 28 E
Ferdinand, Idaho 20 46 9N 116 24W
Ferdinand, Ind. 22 38 14N 86 52W
Ferdows 107 33 58N 58 2 E
Ferfer 105 5 4N 45 9 E
Fergana 100 40 23N 71 19 E
Fergus 60 43 43N 80 24W
Fergus County ◇ 33 47 30N 109 10W
Fergus Falls 30 46 17N 96 4W
Ferguson, Ky. 48 37 3N 84 36W
Ferguson, Mo. 32 38 45N 90 18W
Ferland 60 50 19N 88 27W
Fermanagh □ 85 54 21N 7 40W
Fermoy 85 52 4N 8 18W
Fern Creek 49 38 9N 85 36W
Fern Ridge L. 44 44 7N 123 18W
Fernández 76 27 55 S 63 50W
Fernandina Beach 17 30 40N 81 27W
Fernando de Noronha 74 4 0 S 33 10W
Fernando Póo = Bioko 122 3 30N 8 40 E
Fernandópolis 75 20 16 S 50 14W
Ferndale, Calif. 14 40 35N 124 16W
Ferndale, Md. 27 39 11N 76 39W
Ferndale, Wash. 53 48 51N 122 36W
Fernie 62 49 30N 115 5W
Fernley 35 39 36N 119 15W
Fernwood, Idaho 20 47 7N 116 24W
Fernwood, Miss. 31 31 11N 90 27W
Fernwood, N.Y. 39 43 16N 73 40W
Ferozepore = Firozpur 108 30 55N 74 40 E
Ferrara 94 44 50N 11 36 E
Ferrellsburg 54 38 2N 82 6W
Ferreñafe 72 6 42 S 79 50W
Ferriday 25 31 38N 91 33W
Ferris, Ill. 21 40 28N 91 10W
Ferris, Tex. 51 32 32N 96 40W
Ferrisburg 36 44 12N 73 15W
Ferrol, Pen. de 72 9 10 S 78 35W
Ferron 52 39 5N 111 8W
Ferros 75 19 14 S 43 2W
Ferrum 54 36 55N 80 1W
Ferry County ◇ 53 48 30N 118 30W
Ferryland 61 47 2N 52 53W
Ferrysburg 29 43 5N 86 13W
Ferryville 55 43 21N 91 6W
Fertile, Iowa 23 43 16N 93 25W
Fertile, Minn. 30 47 32N 96 17W
Fès 120 34 0N 5 0W
Feshi 122 6 8 S 18 10 E
Fessenden 41 47 39N 99 38W
Festus 32 38 13N 90 24W
Feteşti 95 44 22N 27 51 E
Fethiye 106 36 36N 29 10 E
Fetlar 84 60 36N 0 52W
Feuilles → 59 58 47N 70 4W
Feyzābād 107 37 7N 70 33 E
Fezzan 121 27 0N 15 0 E
Ffestiniog 82 52 58N 3 56W
Fiambalá 76 27 45 S 67 37W
Fianarantsoa 123 21 26 S 47 5 E
Fianga 121 9 55N 15 9 E
Fichtelgebirge 88 50 10N 12 0 E
Ficksburg 123 28 51 S 27 53 E
Field, Canada 60 46 31N 80 1W
Field, U.S.A. 49 36 54N 83 36W
Fieldon 21 39 7N 90 30W
Fields 25 30 32N 93 35W
Fields Landing 14 40 44N 124 13W
Fierro 38 32 51N 108 5W
Fife 51 31 24N 99 22W
Fife □ 84 56 13N 3 2W
Fife Lake 29 44 35N 85 21W
Fife Ness 84 56 17N 2 35W
Fifield 55 45 53N 90 25W
Figeac 90 44 37N 2 2 E
Figueira da Foz 91 40 7N 8 54W
Figueras 91 42 18N 2 58 E
Figuig 120 32 5N 1 11W
Fiji ■ 128 17 20 S 179 0 E
Filadelfia, Bolivia 72 11 20 S 68 46W
Filadélfia, Brazil 74 7 21 S 47 30W
Filer 20 42 34N 114 37W
Filey 82 54 13N 0 18W
Filiaşi 95 44 32N 23 31 E
Filiatrá 95 37 9N 21 35 E
Filipstad 97 59 43N 14 9 E
Fillmore, Canada 63 49 50N 103 25W
Fillmore, Calif. 15 34 24N 118 55W
Fillmore, Utah 52 38 58N 112 20W
Fillmore County ◇, Minn. 30 43 40N 92 0W
Fillmore County ◇, Nebr. 34 40 30N 97 40W
Filyos → 106 41 35N 32 10 E
Fincastle 54 37 30N 79 53W
Findhorn → 84 57 38N 3 38W
Findlay, Ill. 21 39 31N 88 45W
Findlay, Ohio 42 41 2N 83 39W
Fine 39 44 15N 75 8W
Fingal 41 46 46N 97 47W
Finger 48 35 22N 88 36W
Finger L. 63 53 33N 124 18W
Finger Lakes 39 42 40N 76 30W
Fîngoè 123 15 12 S 31 50 E
Finike 106 36 21N 30 10 E
Finistère □ 90 48 20N 4 0W
Finisterre, C. 91 42 50N 9 19W
Finke → 126 27 0 S 136 10 E
Finksburg 27 39 30N 76 54W
Finland ■ 98 63 0N 27 0 E
Finland, G. of 98 60 0N 26 0 E
Finlay → 62 57 0N 125 10W
Finley, N. Dak. 41 47 31N 97 50W
Finley, Okla. 43 34 20N 95 30W
Finn → 85 54 50N 7 55W
Finney County ◇ 24 38 0N 100 40W
Finnmark fylke □ 96 69 30N 25 0 E
Finucane I. 126 20 19 S 118 30 E
Fiora → 94 42 20N 11 35 E
Fiq 104 32 46N 35 41 E
Fire I. 39 40 40N 73 11W
Fire Island National Seashore 39 40 38N 73 8W
Fire River 60 48 47N 83 21W
Firebag → 63 57 45N 111 21W
Firebaugh 15 36 52N 120 27W
Firedrake L. 63 61 25N 104 30W
Firenze 94 43 47N 11 15 E
Firozabad 108 27 10N 78 25 E
Firozpur 108 30 55N 74 40 E
First Connecticut L. 36 45 5N 71 15W
Firth, Idaho 20 43 18N 112 11W
Firth, Nebr. 34 40 33N 96 37W
Fīrūzābād 107 28 52N 52 35 E
Fīrūzkūh 107 35 50N 52 50 E
Firvale 62 52 27N 126 13W
Fischer 51 29 58N 98 16W
Fish → 123 28 7 S 17 45 E
Fish L. 52 38 33N 111 42W
Fish Lake Reservoir 30 46 57N 92 17W
Fish Pt. 29 43 44N 83 31W
Fish River L. 26 46 50N 68 47W
Fisheating Cr. → 17 26 57N 81 7W
Fisher, Ark. 13 35 30N 90 58W
Fisher, Ill. 21 40 19N 88 21W
Fisher, La. 25 31 30N 93 28W
Fisher, Minn. 30 47 48N 96 48W
Fisher → 33 48 22N 115 19W
Fisher B. 63 51 35N 97 13W

Fisher County Fort Oglethorpe

Fisher County ◇ **50** 32 45N 100 23W
Fishers **22** 39 57N 86 1W
Fishers I. **39** 41 15N 72 0W
Fishers Peak **16** 37 6N 104 28W
Fishguard **83** 51 59N 4 59W
Fishing Bridge **56** 44 29N 110 22W
Fishing Creek **27** 38 20N 76 14W
Fishing L. **63** 52 10N 95 24W
Fishlake National Forest **52** 38 40N 112 20W
Fishtrap L. **49** 37 25N 82 26W
Fisk **32** 36 47N 90 12W
Fiskdale **28** 42 7N 72 7W
Fitchburg **28** 42 35N 71 48W
Fitri, L. **121** 12 50N 17 28 E
Fittstown **43** 34 37N 96 38W
Fitz Roy **78** 47 0 S 67 0W
Fitzgerald, Canada **62** 59 51N 111 36W
Fitzgerald, U.S.A. **18** 31 43N 83 15W
Fitzhugh **13** 35 22N 91 19W
Fitzroy → **126** 17 31 S 123 35 E
Fitzroy Crossing **126** 18 9 S 125 38 E
Fiume = Rijeka **94** 45 20N 14 21 E
Fizi **122** 4 17 S 28 55 E
Flagler **16** 39 18N 103 4W
Flagler Beach **17** 29 29N 81 8W
Flagler County ◇ **17** 29 30N 81 20W
Flagstaff **12** 35 12N 111 39W
Flagstaff L., Maine **26** 45 12N 70 19W
Flagstaff L., Oreg. **44** 42 35N 119 45W
Flaherty **48** 37 50N 86 4W
Flaherty I. **60** 56 15N 79 15W
Flåm **97** 60 50N 7 7 E
Flambeau → **55** 45 18N 91 14W
Flamborough Hd. **82** 54 8N 0 4W
Flaming Gorge Dam **52** 40 55N 109 25W
Flaming Gorge National
Recreation Area **56** 41 10N 109 25W
Flaming Gorge Reservoir **56** 41 10N 109 25W
Flamingo **17** 25 8N 80 57W
Flamingo, Teluk **111** 5 30 S 138 0 E
Flanagan **21** 40 53N 88 52W
Flanders = Flandres **87** 51 10N 3 15 E
Flandre Occidental □ **87** 51 0N 3 0 E
Flandre Orientale □ **87** 51 0N 4 0 E
Flandreau **47** 44 3N 96 36W
Flandres **87** 51 10N 3 15 E
Flandres, Plaines des **87** 51 10N 3 15 E
Flannan Is. **86** 58 9N 7 52W
Flasher **41** 46 27N 101 14W
Flåsjön **96** 64 5N 15 40 E
Flat **11** 62 28N 158 1W
Flat →, Canada **62** 61 51N 128 0W
Flat →, Mich. **29** 42 56N 85 20W
Flat →, N.C. **40** 36 5N 78 49W
Flat Lick **49** 36 50N 83 46W
Flat River **32** 37 51N 90 31W
Flat River Res. **28** 41 42N 71 37W
Flat Rock, Ala. **10** 34 46N 85 42W
Flat Rock, Ill. **21** 38 54N 87 40W
Flat Rock, Mich. **29** 42 6N 83 17W
Flat Top Mt. **52** 40 22N 112 11W
Flat Woods **48** 35 29N 87 50W
Flatey, Barðastrandarsýsla,
Iceland **96** 66 10N 17 52W
Flatey, Suður-þingeyjarsýsla,
Iceland **96** 65 22N 22 56W
Flathead → **33** 47 22N 114 47W
Flathead County ◇ **33** 48 15N 113 30W
Flathead Indian Reservation **33** 47 35N 114 30W
Flathead L. **33** 47 51N 114 8W
Flathead National Forest **33** 47 45N 113 10W
Flatonia **51** 29 41N 97 7W
Flatrock → **22** 39 12N 85 56W
Flattery, C. **53** 48 23N 124 29W
Flatwillow Cr. → **33** 46 56N 107 55W
Flatwoods, Ky. **48** 38 31N 82 43W
Flatwoods, La. **25** 31 24N 92 52W
Flatwoods, W. Va. **54** 38 43N 80 39W
Flaxton **41** 48 54N 102 24W
Flaxville **33** 48 48N 105 11W
Fleetwood, U.K. **82** 53 55N 3 1W
Fleetwood, U.S.A. **45** 40 27N 75 49W
Fleischmanns **39** 42 10N 74 32W
Flekkefjord **97** 58 18N 6 39 E
Fleming **16** 40 41N 102 50W
Fleming County ◇ **49** 38 20N 83 40W
Flemingsburg **49** 38 25N 83 45W
Flemington, N.J. **37** 40 31N 74 52W
Flemington, W. Va. **54** 39 16N 80 8W
Flensburg **30** 45 57N 94 32W
Flesko, Tanjung **111** 0 29N 124 30 E
Fletcher, N.C. **40** 35 26N 82 30W
Fletcher, Okla. **43** 34 50N 98 15W
Fletcher Pond **29** 45 1N 83 47W
Fletton **83** 52 34N 0 13W
Flin Flon **63** 54 46N 101 53W
Flinders → **127** 17 36 S 140 36 E
Flinders B. **126** 34 19 S 115 19 E
Flinders I. **127** 40 0 S 148 0 E
Flinders Ranges **127** 31 30 S 138 30 E
Flint, U.K. **82** 53 15N 3 7W
Flint, U.S.A. **29** 43 1N 83 41W
Flint →, Ala. **10** 34 30N 86 30W
Flint →, Ga. **18** 30 57N 84 34W
Flint, I. **125** 11 26 S 151 48W
Flint Hills **24** 38 0N 96 40W
Flintstone **27** 39 42N 78 34W
Flippin **13** 36 17N 92 36W
Flodden **82** 55 37N 2 8W
Flomaton **10** 31 0N 87 16W
Flomot **50** 34 14N 100 59W
Flora, Ill. **21** 38 40N 88 29W
Flora, Ind. **22** 40 33N 86 31W
Flora, Miss. **31** 32 33N 90 19W
Flora, Oreg. **44** 45 54N 117 19W
Flora Vista **38** 36 48N 108 3W
Florahome **17** 29 44N 81 54W
Floral **13** 35 36N 91 45W
Floral City **17** 28 45N 82 17W
Florala **10** 31 0N 86 20W
Florânia **74** 6 8 S 36 49W
Florence = Firenze **94** 43 47N 11 15 E
Florence, Ala. **10** 34 48N 87 41W
Florence, Ariz. **12** 33 2N 111 23W
Florence, Ark. **13** 33 46N 91 39W
Florence, Colo. **16** 38 23N 105 8W
Florence, Kans. **24** 38 15N 96 56W
Florence, Ky. **49** 39 0N 84 38W
Florence, Md. **27** 39 20N 77 8W
Florence, Miss. **31** 32 9N 90 8W
Florence, Mo. **32** 38 35N 92 59W
Florence, Mont. **33** 46 38N 114 5W
Florence, Oreg. **44** 43 58N 124 7W
Florence, S.C. **46** 34 12N 79 46W
Florence, S. Dak. **47** 45 3N 97 20W
Florence, Tex. **51** 30 51N 97 48W
Florence, Wis. **55** 45 56N 88 15W
Florence County ◇, S.C. **46** 34 0N 79 45W
Florence County ◇, Wis. **55** 45 50N 88 20W
Florennes **87** 50 15N 4 35 E
Florenville **87** 49 40N 5 19 E
Flores, Brazil **74** 7 51 S 37 59W
Flores, Guat. **66** 16 59N 89 50W
Flores, Indonesia **111** 8 35 S 121 0 E
Flores I. **62** 49 20N 126 10W
Flores Sea **110** 6 30 S 124 0 E
Floresta **74** 8 40 S 37 26W
Floresville **51** 29 8N 98 10W
Florey **50** 32 27N 102 36W
Florham Park **37** 40 47N 74 23W
Floriano **74** 6 50 S 43 0W
Florianópolis **77** 27 30 S 48 30W
Florida, Cuba **66** 21 32N 78 14W
Florida, Puerto Rico **57** 18 22N 66 34W
Florida, Uruguay **77** 34 7 S 56 10W
Florida □ **17** 28 0N 82 0W
Florida B. **17** 25 0N 80 45W
Florida City **17** 25 27N 80 29W
Florida Keys **17** 24 40N 81 0W
Florida Ridge **17** 27 38N 80 24W
Florien **25** 31 27N 93 28W
Floris **23** 40 52N 92 20W
Florissant, Colo. **16** 38 57N 105 17W
Florissant, Mo. **32** 38 48N 90 20W
Florissant National
Monument **16** 38 54N 105 17W
Florø **97** 61 35N 5 1 E
Flower's Cove **61** 51 14N 56 46W
Floyd, Iowa **23** 43 8N 92 44W
Floyd, N. Mex. **38** 34 13N 103 35W
Floyd, Va. **54** 36 55N 80 19W
Floyd → **23** 42 29N 96 23W
Floyd County ◇, Ga. **18** 34 15N 85 10W
Floyd County ◇, Ind. **22** 38 20N 85 55W
Floyd County ◇, Iowa **23** 43 5N 92 45W
Floyd County ◇, Ky. **49** 37 30N 82 45W
Floyd County ◇, Tex. **50** 34 0N 101 15W
Floyd County ◇, Va. **54** 36 58N 80 25W
Floydada **50** 33 59N 101 20W
Fluk **111** 1 42 S 127 44 E
Flushing = Vlissingen **87** 51 26N 3 34 E
Flushing, Mich. **29** 43 4N 83 51W
Flushing, Ohio **42** 40 9N 81 4W
Fluvanna County ◇ **54** 37 52N 78 16W
Fly → **124** 8 25 S 143 0 E
Flying Fish, C. **5** 72 6 S 102 29W
Flying H **38** 33 2N 105 8W
Flynn **51** 31 9N 96 8W
Foam Lake **63** 51 40N 103 32W
Foard City **51** 33 53N 99 48W
Foard County ◇ **51** 33 59N 99 43W
Focşani **95** 45 41N 27 15 E
Fogang **115** 23 52N 113 30 E
Fóggia **94** 41 28N 15 31 E
Fogo **61** 49 43N 54 17W
Fogo I. **61** 49 40N 54 5W
Foix **90** 42 58N 1 38 E
Folda, Nord-Trøndelag,
Norway **96** 64 41N 10 50 E
Folda, Nordland, Norway **96** 67 38N 14 50 E
Foley, Ala. **10** 30 24N 87 41W
Foley, Fla. **17** 30 4N 83 32W
Foley, Minn. **30** 45 40N 93 55W
Foleyet **60** 48 15N 82 25W
Folgefonn **97** 60 3N 6 23 E
Folkestone **83** 51 5N 1 11 E
Folkston **18** 30 50N 82 0W
Follett **50** 36 26N 100 8W
Folsom, La. **25** 30 38N 90 11W
Folsom, N.J. **37** 39 38N 74 51W
Folsom, N. Mex. **38** 36 51N 103 55W
Folsom, W. Va. **54** 39 28N 80 31W
Folsom L. **14** 38 42N 121 9W
Fond-du-Lac, Canada **63** 59 19N 107 12W
Fond du Lac, U.S.A. **55** 43 47N 88 27W
Fond-du-Lac → **63** 59 17N 106 0W
Fond du Lac County ◇ **55** 43 40N 88 30W
Fond du Lac Indian
Reservation **30** 46 45N 92 40W
Fonda, Iowa **23** 42 35N 94 51W
Fonda, N.Y. **39** 42 57N 74 22W
Fonde **49** 36 36N 83 53W
Fonseca, G. de **66** 13 10N 87 40W
Fontainebleau **90** 48 24N 2 40 E
Fontana, Calif. **15** 34 6N 117 26W
Fontana, Kans. **24** 38 25N 94 51W
Fontana, Wis. **55** 42 33N 88 35W
Fontana, L. **78** 44 55 S 71 30W
Fontana L. **40** 35 27N 83 48W
Fontana Village **40** 35 26N 83 50W
Fontanelle **23** 41 17N 94 34W
Fontas → **62** 58 14N 121 48W
Fonte Boa **70** 2 33 S 66 0W
Fontenay-le-Comte **90** 46 28N 0 48W
Fontenelle Reservoir **56** 42 1N 110 3W
Fontur **96** 66 23N 14 32W
Foochow = Fuzhou **115** 26 5N 119 16 E
Foosland **21** 40 22N 88 26W
Footville **55** 42 40N 89 12W
Foping **115** 33 41N 108 0 E
Forada **30** 45 48N 95 21W
Foraker **43** 36 52N 96 34W
Foraker, Mt. **11** 62 58N 151 24W
Forbes, Australia **127** 33 22 S 148 0 E
Forbes, U.S.A. **41** 45 57N 98 47W
Forbing **25** 32 24N 93 44W
Ford **24** 37 38N 99 45W
Ford → **29** 45 41N 87 9W
Ford City, Calif. **15** 35 9N 119 27W
Ford City, Pa. **45** 40 46N 79 32W
Ford County ◇, Ill. **21** 40 30N 88 10W
Ford County ◇, Kans. **24** 37 45N 100 0W
Ford Dry L. **15** 33 37N 114 59W
Ford I. **19** 21 22N 157 58W
Fordland **32** 37 9N 92 57W
Fordoche **25** 30 36N 91 37W
Fordsville **48** 37 38N 86 43W
Fordville **41** 48 13N 97 48W
Fordyce, Ark. **13** 33 49N 92 25W
Fordyce, Nebr. **34** 42 42N 97 22W
Forécariah **120** 9 28N 13 10W
Forel, Mt. **4** 66 52N 36 55W
Foreman **13** 33 43N 94 24W
Foremost **62** 49 26N 111 34W
Forest, La. **25** 32 47N 91 25W
Forest, Miss. **31** 32 22N 89 29W
Forest, Ohio **42** 40 48N 83 31W
Forest → **41** 48 21N 97 9W
Forest Acres **46** 34 1N 80 58W
Forest Center **30** 47 48N 91 19W
Forest City, Iowa **23** 43 16N 93 39W
Forest City, N.C. **40** 35 20N 81 52W
Forest City, Pa. **45** 41 39N 75 28W
Forest County ◇, Pa. **45** 41 30N 79 10W
Forest County ◇, Wis. **55** 45 35N 88 45W
Forest Dale **36** 43 48N 73 4W
Forest Grove **44** 45 31N 123 7W
Forest Hill, La. **25** 31 3N 92 32W
Forest Hill, Md. **27** 39 35N 76 23W
Forest Home **10** 31 52N 86 50W
Forest Lake **30** 45 17N 92 59W
Forest Park **18** 33 37N 84 22W
Forest River **41** 48 13N 97 28W
Forestburg **62** 52 35N 112 1W
Foresthill **14** 39 1N 120 49W
Foreston, Minn. **30** 45 44N 93 43W
Foreston, S.C. **46** 33 38N 80 4W
Forestville, Canada **61** 48 48N 69 2W
Forestville, Md. **27** 38 51N 76 52W
Forestville, Mich. **29** 43 40N 82 37W
Forestville, N.Y. **39** 42 28N 79 10W
Forestville, Wis. **55** 44 41N 87 29W
Forez, Mts. du **90** 45 40N 3 50 E
Forfar **84** 56 40N 2 53W
Forgan **43** 36 54N 100 32W
Forge Village **28** 42 35N 71 29W
Fork Union **54** 37 46N 78 16W
Forked Deer → **48** 35 56N 89 35W
Forked River **37** 39 50N 74 12W
Forkland **10** 32 39N 87 53W
Forks **53** 47 57N 124 23W
Forks of Salmon **14** 41 16N 123 19W
Forkville **31** 32 28N 89 40W
Forlì **94** 44 14N 12 2 E
Forman **41** 46 7N 97 38W
Formby Pt. **82** 53 33N 3 7W
Formentera **91** 38 43N 1 27 E
Formiga **75** 20 27 S 45 25W
Formosa = Taiwan ■ **115** 23 30N 121 0 E
Formosa, Argentina **76** 26 15 S 58 10W
Formosa, Brazil **75** 15 32 S 47 20W
Formosa □ **76** 25 0 S 60 0W
Formosa, Serra **73** 12 0 S 55 0W
Formosa Bay **122** 2 40 S 40 20 E
Formoso → **75** 10 34 S 49 56W
Forres **84** 57 37N 3 38W
Forrest, Ill. **21** 40 45N 88 25W
Forrest, N. Mex. **38** 34 48N 103 36W
Forrest City **13** 35 1N 90 47W
Forrest County ◇ **31** 31 10N 89 13W
Forreston **21** 42 8N 89 35W
Forsayth **127** 18 33 S 143 34 E
Forsyth, Ga. **18** 33 2N 83 56W
Forsyth, Mo. **32** 36 41N 93 6W
Forsyth, Mont. **33** 46 16N 106 41W
Forsyth County ◇, Ga. **18** 34 15N 84 5W
Forsyth County ◇, N.C. **40** 36 10N 80 15W
Fort Adams **31** 31 5N 91 33W
Fort Albany **60** 52 15N 81 35W
Fort Amador **57** 8 56N 79 32W
Fort Apache Indian
Reservation **12** 33 45N 110 0W
Fort Assiniboine **62** 54 20N 114 45W
Fort Atkinson, Iowa **23** 43 9N 91 56W
Fort Atkinson, Wis. **55** 42 56N 88 50W
Fort Augustus **84** 57 9N 4 40W
Fort Barnwell **40** 35 18N 77 20W
Fort Belknap Agency **33** 48 29N 108 45W
Fort Belknap Indian
Reservation **33** 48 20N 108 40W
Fort Bend County ◇ **51** 29 34N 95 49W
Fort Benton **33** 47 49N 110 40W
Fort Berthold Indian
Reservation **41** 47 45N 102 15W
Fort Bidwell **14** 41 52N 120 9W
Fort Bragg **14** 39 26N 123 48W
Fort Branch **22** 38 15N 87 35W
Fort Bridger **56** 41 19N 110 23W
Fort Calhoun **34** 41 27N 96 2W
Fort Chimo **59** 58 6N 68 15W
Fort Chipewyan **63** 58 42N 111 8W
Fort Clayton **57** 9 0N 79 35W
Fort Cobb **43** 35 6N 98 26W
Fort Cobb Reservoir **43** 35 10N 98 27W
Fort Collins **16** 40 35N 105 5W
Fort-Coulonge **60** 45 50N 76 45W
Fort Davis, Panama **57** 9 17N 79 56W
Fort Davis, Ala. **10** 32 15N 85 43W
Fort Davis, Tex. **50** 30 35N 103 54W
Fort-de-France **67** 14 36N 61 2W
Fort de Possel = Possel **122** 5 5N 19 10 E
Fort Defiance **12** 35 45N 109 5W
Fort Deposit **10** 31 59N 86 35W
Fort Dick **14** 41 52N 124 9W
Fort Dodge **23** 42 30N 94 11W
Fort Drum **17** 27 32N 80 48W
Fort Duchesne **52** 40 17N 109 52W
Fort Edward **39** 43 16N 73 35W
Fort Fairfield **26** 46 46N 67 50W
Fort Frances **63** 48 36N 93 24W
Fort Franklin **58** 65 10N 123 30W
Fort Gaines **18** 31 36N 85 3W
Fort Garland **16** 37 26N 105 26W
Fort Gay **54** 38 7N 82 36W
Fort George **60** 53 50N 79 0W
Fort Gibson **43** 35 48N 95 15W
Fort Gibson L. **43** 35 52N 95 14W
Fort Good-Hope **58** 66 14N 128 40W
Fort Hall **20** 43 2N 112 26W
Fort Hall Indian Reservation **20** 43 2N 112 5W
Fort Hancock **50** 31 18N 105 51W
Fort Hertz = Putao **109** 27 28N 97 30 E
Fort Hope **60** 51 30N 88 0W
Fort Jameson = Chipata **123** 13 38 S 32 28 E
Fort Jennings **42** 40 54N 84 18W
Fort Jesup **25** 31 37N 93 24W
Fort Jones **14** 41 36N 122 51W
Fort Kent **26** 47 15N 68 36W
Fort Klamath **44** 42 42N 122 0W
Fort Knox **49** 37 54N 85 57W
Fort Lallemand **120** 31 13N 6 17 E
Fort-Lamy = Ndjamena **121** 12 10N 14 59 E
Fort Laramie **56** 42 13N 104 31W
Fort Lauderdale **17** 26 7N 80 8W
Fort Lawn **46** 34 42N 80 54W
Fort Liard **62** 60 14N 123 30W
Fort Liberté **67** 19 42N 71 51W
Fort Loudoun L. **49** 35 47N 84 15W
Fort Lupton **16** 40 5N 104 49W
Fort McDermitt Ind. Res. **44** 42 0N 117 42W
Fort McDowell Indian
Reservation **12** 33 40N 111 50W
Fort Mackay **62** 57 12N 111 41W
Fort McKenzie **61** 57 20N 69 0W
Fort Macleod **62** 49 45N 113 30W
Fort MacMahon **120** 29 43N 1 45 E
Fort McMurray **62** 56 44N 111 7W
Fort McPherson **58** 67 30N 134 55W
Fort Madison **23** 40 38N 91 27W
Fort Meade **17** 27 45N 81 48W
Fort Mill **46** 35 2N 80 57W
Fort Miribel **120** 29 25N 2 55 E
Fort Mitchell, Ala. **10** 32 20N 85 1W
Fort Mitchell, Ky. **49** 39 2N 84 34W
Fort Mitchell, Va. **54** 36 55N 78 29W
Fort Mohave Ind. Res. **12** 34 55N 114 35W
Fort Morgan **16** 40 15N 103 48W
Fort Motte **46** 33 44N 80 42W
Fort Myers **17** 26 39N 81 52W
Fort Myers Villas **17** 26 34N 81 52W
Fort Nelson **62** 58 50N 122 44W
Fort Nelson → **62** 59 32N 124 0W
Fort Norman **58** 64 57N 125 30W
Fort Oglethorpe **18** 34 57N 85 16W

Fort Payne Friesland

Fort Payne **10** 34 26N 85 43W
Fort Peck **33** 48 1N 106 27W
Fort Peck Dam **33** 48 0N 106 26W
Fort Peck Indian Reservation **33** 48 30N 105 30W
Fort Peck L. **33** 48 0N 106 26W
Fort Pierce **17** 27 27N 80 20W
Fort Pierre **47** 44 21N 100 22W
Fort Plain **39** 42 56N 74 37W
Fort Portal **122** 0 40N 30 20 E
Fort Providence **62** 61 3N 117 40W
Fort Qu'Appelle **63** 50 45N 103 50W
Fort Randall Dam **47** 43 4N 98 34W
Fort Ransom **41** 46 31N 97 56W
Fort Recovery **42** 40 25N 84 47W
Fort Resolution **62** 61 10N 113 40W
Fort Ripley **30** 46 10N 94 22W
Fort Robinson **34** 42 40N 103 28W
Fort Roseberry = Mansa **122** 11 13 S 28 55 E
Fort Rupert **60** 51 30N 78 40W
Fort St. James **62** 54 30N 124 10W
Fort St. John **62** 56 15N 120 50W
Fort Sandeman **108** 31 20N 69 31 E
Fort Saskatchewan **62** 53 40N 113 15W
Fort Scott **24** 37 50N 94 42W
Fort Severn **60** 56 0N 87 40W
Fort Shawnee **42** 40 42N 84 7W
Fort Sherman **57** 9 22N 79 56W
Fort Shevchenko **99** 43 40N 51 20 E
Fort-Sibut **122** 5 46N 19 10 E
Fort Simpson **62** 61 45N 121 15W
Fort Smith, Canada **62** 60 0N 111 51W
Fort Smith, U.S.A. **13** 35 23N 94 25W
Fort Stanton **38** 33 30N 105 31W
Fort Stockton **50** 30 53N 102 53W
Fort Sumner **38** 34 28N 104 15W
Fort Supply **43** 36 35N 99 35W
Fort Thomas **49** 39 5N 84 27W
Fort Thompson **47** 44 3N 99 26W
Fort Totten **41** 47 59N 99 0W
Fort Totten Indian
Reservation **41** 47 58N 99 0W
Fort Towson **43** 34 0N 95 10W
Fort Trinquet = Bir Mogrein **120** 25 10N 11 25W
Fort Valley **18** 32 33N 83 53W
Fort Vermilion **62** 58 24N 116 0W
Fort Walton Beach **17** 30 25N 86 36W
Fort Washakie **56** 43 0N 108 53W
Fort Washington **27** 38 42N 77 3W
Fort Wayne **22** 41 4N 85 9W
Fort White **17** 29 55N 82 44W
Fort William **84** 56 48N 5 8W
Fort Worth **51** 32 45N 97 18W
Fort Yates **41** 46 5N 100 38W
Fort Yukon **11** 66 34N 145 16W
Fort Yuma Indian
Reservation **15** 32 45N 114 35W
Fortaleza, Bolivia **72** 12 6 S 66 49W
Fortaleza, Brazil **74** 3 45 S 38 35W
Forteau **61** 51 28N 56 58W
Fortescue **37** 39 12N 75 12W
Forth, Firth of **84** 56 5N 2 55W
Fortín Coronel Eugenio
Garay **73** 20 31 S 62 8W
Fortín Garrapatal **73** 21 27 S 61 30W
Fortín General Pando **73** 19 45 S 59 47W
Fortín Madrejón **73** 20 45 S 59 52W
Fortín Uno **78** 38 50 S 65 18W
Fortine **33** 48 46N 114 54W
Fortrose **84** 57 35N 4 10W
Fortsonia **18** 34 1N 82 47W
Fortuna, Calif. **14** 40 36N 124 9W
Fortuna, Mo. **32** 38 34N 92 48W
Fortuna, N. Dak. **41** 48 55N 103 47W
Fortuna Ledge **11** 61 53N 162 5W
Fortune B. **61** 47 30N 55 22W
Fortville **22** 39 56N 85 51W
Forūr **107** 26 20N 54 30 E
Foshan **115** 23 4N 113 5 E
Foss Reservoir **43** 35 33N 99 11W
Fossil **44** 45 0N 120 9W
Fossil Butte Nat. Mon. **56** 41 50N 110 27W
Fossil L. **44** 43 19N 120 25W
Fosston **30** 47 35N 95 45W
Foster, Ky. **49** 38 48N 84 13W
Foster, Nebr. **34** 42 16N 97 40W
Foster, Oreg. **44** 44 25N 122 40W
Foster, R.I. **28** 41 47N 71 44W
Foster ➛ **63** 55 47N 105 49W
Foster County ◇ **41** 47 30N 99 0W
Foster L. **44** 42 59N 119 15W
Fosters **10** 33 6N 87 41W
Fostoria, Iowa **23** 43 15N 95 9W
Fostoria, Kans. **24** 39 26N 96 30W
Fostoria, Ohio **42** 41 10N 83 25W
Fougamou **122** 1 16 S 10 30 E
Fougères **90** 48 21N 1 14W
Fouke **13** 33 16N 93 53W
Foul Pt. **108** 8 35N 81 18 E
Foula, I. **86** 60 10N 2 5W
Foulness I. **83** 51 36N 0 55 E
Foulness Pt. **83** 51 36N 0 59 E
Foumban **120** 5 45N 10 50 E
Fount **49** 36 59N 83 50W
Fountain, Colo. **16** 38 41N 104 42W
Fountain, Fla. **17** 30 29N 85 25W
Fountain, Mich. **29** 44 3N 86 11W
Fountain, Minn. **30** 43 45N 92 8W
Fountain, N.C. **40** 35 41N 77 38W
Fountain City, Ind. **22** 39 57N 84 55W
Fountain City, Wis. **55** 44 8N 91 43W
Fountain County ◇ **22** 40 5N 87 15W
Fountain Cr. ➛ **16** 38 15N 104 36W
Fountain Green **52** 39 38N 111 38W
Fountain Head **27** 39 42N 77 42W
Fountain Hill **13** 33 21N 91 51W
Fountain Inn **46** 34 42N 82 12W
Fountain Run **48** 36 18N 85 56W
Four Mountains, Is. of **11** 53 0N 170 0W
Four Oaks **40** 35 27N 78 26W
Four Town **30** 48 17N 95 20W
Fourchu **61** 45 43N 60 17W
Fourteen Mile Pt. **29** 47 0N 89 10W
Fouta Djalon **120** 11 20N 12 10W
Foux, Cap-à- **67** 19 43N 73 27W
Foveaux Str. **128** 46 42 S 168 10 E
Fowblesburg **27** 39 34N 76 50W
Fowey **83** 50 20N 4 39W
Fowler, Calif. **15** 36 38N 119 41W
Fowler, Colo. **16** 38 8N 104 2W
Fowler, Ind. **22** 40 37N 87 19W
Fowler, Kans. **24** 37 23N 100 12W
Fowler, Mich. **29** 43 0N 84 45W
Fowlerton, Ind. **22** 40 25N 85 34W
Fowlerton, Tex. **51** 28 28N 98 48W
Fowlerville **29** 42 40N 84 4W
Fowlstown **18** 30 48N 84 33W
Fownhope **83** 52 0N 2 37W
Fox **43** 34 22N 97 30W
Fox ➛, Canada **63** 56 3N 93 18W
Fox ➛, Ill. **21** 41 21N 88 50W
Fox ➛, Wis. **55** 44 32N 88 0W
Fox Is. **11** 54 0N 168 0W
Fox Lake, Ill. **21** 42 24N 88 11W
Fox Lake, Wis. **55** 43 34N 88 55W
Fox Valley **63** 50 30N 109 25W
Foxboro **28** 42 4N 71 16W
Foxe Basin **59** 66 0N 77 0W
Foxe Chan. **59** 65 0N 80 0W
Foxe Pen. **59** 65 0N 76 0W
Foxpark **56** 41 5N 106 9W
Foxton **128** 40 29 S 175 18 E
Foyil **43** 36 26N 95 31W
Foyle, Lough **85** 55 6N 7 8W
Foynes **85** 52 37N 9 5W
Foz do Gregório **72** 6 47 S 70 44W
Foz do Iguaçu **77** 25 30 S 54 30W
Foz do Riosinho **72** 7 11 S 71 50W
Frackville **45** 40 47N 76 14W
Framingham **28** 42 17N 71 25W
Franca **75** 20 33 S 47 30W
Francavilla Fontana **95** 40 32N 17 35 E
France ■ **90** 47 0N 3 0 E
Frances **53** 46 33N 123 30W
Frances ➛ **62** 60 16N 129 10W
Frances, L. **33** 48 16N 112 13W
Frances L. **62** 61 23N 129 30W
Francés Viejo, C. **67** 19 40N 70 0W
Francestown **36** 42 58N 71 49W
Francesville **22** 40 59N 86 53W
Franceville **122** 1 40 S 13 32 E
Franche-Comté **90** 46 30N 5 50 E
Francis, Mont. **33** 46 9N 111 5W
Francis, Okla. **43** 34 52N 96 36W
Francis, Utah **52** 40 37N 111 17W
Francis, L. **36** 45 2N 71 20W
Francis Case, L. **47** 43 4N 98 34W
Francis Creek **55** 44 12N 87 44W
Francis Marion National
Forest **46** 33 10N 79 40W
Francisco de Orellana **70** 0 28 S 76 58W
Francisco I. Madero,
Coahuila, Mexico **64** 25 48N 103 18W
Francisco I. Madero,
Durango, Mexico **64** 24 32N 104 22W
Francisco Sáo **75** 16 28 S 43 30W
Francistown **123** 21 7 S 27 33 E
François, Canada **61** 47 35N 56 45W
François, Mart. **67** 14 38N 60 57W
François L. **62** 54 0N 125 30W
Franconia, Ariz. **12** 34 44N 114 17W
Franconia, N.H. **36** 44 14N 71 44W
Francs Pk. **56** 43 58N 109 18W
Franeker **87** 53 12N 5 33 E
Frankenmuth **29** 43 20N 83 44W
Frankewing **48** 35 12N 86 51W
Frankford, Del. **27** 38 31N 75 14W
Frankford, Mo. **32** 39 29N 91 19W
Frankford, W. Va. **54** 37 56N 80 23W
Frankfort, Ind. **22** 40 17N 86 31W
Frankfort, Kans. **24** 39 42N 96 25W
Frankfort, Ky. **49** 38 12N 84 52W
Frankfort, Maine **26** 44 37N 68 53W
Frankfort, Mich. **29** 44 38N 86 14W
Frankfort, Ohio **42** 39 24N 83 11W
Frankfort, S. Dak. **47** 44 53N 98 18W
Frankfurt am Main **88** 50 7N 8 40 E
Frankfurt an der Oder **88** 52 50N 14 31 E
Fränkische Alb **88** 49 20N 11 30 E
Franklin, Ariz. **12** 32 41N 109 5W
Franklin, Ga. **18** 33 17N 85 6W
Franklin, Idaho **20** 42 1N 111 48W
Franklin, Ill. **21** 39 37N 90 3W
Franklin, Ind. **22** 39 29N 86 3W
Franklin, Kans. **24** 37 32N 94 42W
Franklin, Ky. **48** 36 43N 86 35W
Franklin, La. **25** 29 48N 91 30W
Franklin, Maine **26** 44 35N 68 14W
Franklin, Mass. **28** 42 5N 71 24W
Franklin, Minn. **30** 47 32N 92 32W
Franklin, N.C. **40** 35 11N 83 23W
Franklin, N.H. **36** 43 27N 71 39W
Franklin, N.J. **37** 41 7N 74 35W
Franklin, N.Y. **39** 42 21N 75 10W
Franklin, Nebr. **34** 40 6N 98 57W
Franklin, Ohio **42** 39 34N 84 18W
Franklin, Pa. **45** 41 24N 79 50W
Franklin, Tenn. **48** 35 55N 86 52W
Franklin, Tex. **51** 31 2N 96 29W
Franklin, Va. **54** 36 41N 76 56W
Franklin, W. Va. **54** 38 39N 79 20W
Franklin, Pt. **11** 70 55N 158 48W
Franklin B. **58** 69 45N 126 0W
Franklin County ◇, Ala. **10** 34 21N 87 42W
Franklin County ◇, Ark. **13** 35 29N 93 50W
Franklin County ◇, Fla. **17** 29 50N 84 45W
Franklin County ◇, Ga. **18** 34 20N 83 10W
Franklin County ◇, Idaho **20** 42 10N 111 50W
Franklin County ◇, Ill. **21** 38 0N 89 0W
Franklin County ◇, Ind. **22** 39 25N 85 5W
Franklin County ◇, Iowa **23** 42 45N 93 25W
Franklin County ◇, Kans. **24** 38 30N 95 15W
Franklin County ◇, Ky. **49** 38 15N 84 55W
Franklin County ◇, Maine **26** 45 0N 70 30W
Franklin County ◇, Mass. **28** 42 30N 72 35W
Franklin County ◇, Miss. **31** 31 28N 90 54W
Franklin County ◇, Mo. **32** 38 25N 91 0W
Franklin County ◇, N.C. **40** 36 0N 78 20W
Franklin County ◇, N.Y. **39** 44 30N 74 15W
Franklin County ◇, Nebr. **34** 40 15N 99 0W
Franklin County ◇, Ohio **42** 40 0N 83 4W
Franklin County ◇, Pa. **45** 39 56N 77 40W
Franklin County ◇, Tenn. **48** 35 10N 86 1W
Franklin County ◇, Tex. **51** 33 11N 95 13W
Franklin County ◇, Va. **54** 37 0N 80 0W
Franklin County ◇, Vt. **36** 44 50N 72 50W
Franklin County ◇, Wash. **53** 46 30N 119 0W
Franklin D. Roosevelt L. **53** 48 18N 118 9W
Franklin Grove **21** 41 51N 89 18W
Franklin I. **5** 76 10 S 168 30 E
Franklin L. **35** 40 25N 115 22W
Franklin Mts. **58** 65 0N 125 0W
Franklin Parish ◇ **25** 32 10N 91 43W
Franklin Square **39** 40 43N 73 41W
Franklin Str. **58** 72 0N 96 0W
Franklinton, La. **25** 30 51N 90 9W
Franklinton, N.C. **40** 36 6N 78 27W
Franklinville, N.J. **37** 39 37N 75 5W
Franklinville, N.Y. **39** 42 20N 78 27W
Frankston **51** 32 3N 95 30W
Frankton **22** 40 13N 85 46W
Frankville **10** 31 39N 88 9W
Frannie **56** 44 58N 108 37W
Frantsa Iosifa, Zemlya **100** 82 0N 55 0 E
Franz **60** 48 25N 84 30W
Franz Josef Land = Frantsa
Iosifa, Zemlya **100** 82 0N 55 0 E
Fraser **16** 39 57N 105 49W
Fraser ➛, B.C., Canada **62** 49 7N 123 11W
Fraser ➛, Newf., Canada **61** 56 39N 62 10W
Fraser I. **127** 25 15 S 153 10 E
Fraser Lake **62** 54 0N 124 50W
Fraserburgh **84** 57 41N 2 0W
Fraserdale **60** 49 55N 81 37W
Fray Bentos **76** 33 10 S 58 15W
Frazee **30** 46 44N 95 42W
Frazer **33** 48 3N 106 2W
Frazeysburg **42** 40 7N 82 7W
Frazier Park **15** 34 49N 118 56W
Fred **51** 30 34N 94 10W
Freda **41** 46 21N 101 10W
Frederic, Mich. **29** 44 47N 84 45W
Frederic, Wis. **55** 45 40N 92 28W
Frederica **27** 39 1N 75 28W
Fredericia **97** 55 34N 9 45 E
Frederick, Colo. **16** 40 6N 104 56W
Frederick, Md. **27** 39 25N 77 25W
Frederick, Okla. **43** 34 23N 99 1W
Frederick, S. Dak. **47** 45 50N 98 31W
Frederick County ◇, Md. **27** 39 30N 77 25W
Frederick County ◇, Va. **54** 39 5N 78 13W
Frederick Reef **127** 20 58 S 154 23 E
Fredericksburg, Iowa **23** 42 58N 92 12W
Fredericksburg, Tex. **51** 30 16N 98 52W
Fredericksburg, Va. **54** 38 18N 77 28W
Fredericktown, Mo. **32** 37 34N 90 18W
Fredericktown, Ohio **42** 40 29N 82 33W
Fredericton **61** 45 57N 66 40W
Fredericton Junc. **61** 45 41N 66 40W
Frederika **23** 42 53N 92 19W
Frederikshavn **97** 57 28N 10 31 E
Frederiksted, Virgin Is. **57** 17 43N 64 53W
Fredonia, Ariz. **12** 36 57N 112 32W
Fredonia, Kans. **24** 37 32N 95 49W
Fredonia, Ky. **48** 37 12N 88 4W
Fredonia, N. Dak. **41** 46 20N 99 6W
Fredonia, N.Y. **39** 42 26N 79 20W
Fredonia, Pa. **45** 41 19N 80 16W
Fredrikstad **97** 59 13N 10 57 E
Freeborn County ◇ **30** 43 40N 93 15W
Freeburg, Ill. **21** 38 26N 89 55W
Freeburg, Mo. **32** 38 19N 91 56W
Freedom **43** 36 46N 99 7W
Freehold **37** 40 16N 74 17W
Freel Peak **35** 38 52N 119 54W
Freeland **45** 41 1N 75 54W
Freeling, Mt. **126** 22 35 S 133 6 E
Freels, C. **61** 49 15N 53 30W
Freeman, Mo. **32** 38 37N 94 30W
Freeman, S. Dak. **47** 43 21N 97 26W
Freeman L. **22** 40 42N 86 45W
Freeport, Bahamas **66** 26 30N 78 47W
Freeport, Canada **61** 44 15N 66 20W
Freeport, Fla. **17** 30 30N 86 8W
Freeport, Ill. **21** 42 17N 89 36W
Freeport, Kans. **24** 37 12N 97 51W
Freeport, Maine **26** 43 52N 70 6W
Freeport, Mich. **29** 42 46N 85 19W
Freeport, Minn. **30** 45 40N 94 42W
Freeport, N.Y. **39** 40 39N 73 35W
Freeport, Pa. **45** 40 41N 79 41W
Freeport, Tex. **51** 28 57N 95 21W
Freer **51** 27 53N 98 37W
Freesoil **29** 44 7N 86 14W
Freestone County ◇ **51** 31 44N 96 10W
Freetown **120** 8 30N 13 17W
Freeville **39** 42 31N 76 21W
Frégate, L. **60** 53 15N 74 45W
Freiberg **88** 50 55N 13 20 E
Freire **78** 38 54 S 72 38W
Freirina **76** 28 30 S 71 10W
Freising **88** 48 24N 11 47 E
Freistadt **88** 48 30N 14 30 E
Freistatt **32** 37 1N 93 54W
Fréjus **90** 43 25N 6 44 E
Fremantle **126** 32 7 S 115 47 E
Fremont, Calif. **14** 37 32N 121 57W
Fremont, Ind. **22** 41 44N 84 56W
Fremont, Iowa **23** 41 13N 92 26W
Fremont, Ky. **48** 36 58N 88 37W
Fremont, Mich. **29** 43 28N 85 57W
Fremont, N.C. **40** 35 33N 77 58W
Fremont, Nebr. **34** 41 26N 96 30W
Fremont, Ohio **42** 41 21N 83 7W
Fremont, Utah **52** 38 27N 111 37W
Fremont, Wis. **55** 44 16N 88 52W
Fremont ➛ **52** 38 24N 110 42W
Fremont County ◇, Colo. **16** 38 30N 105 30W
Fremont County ◇, Idaho **20** 44 15N 111 20W
Fremont County ◇, Iowa **23** 40 45N 95 35W
Fremont County ◇, Wyo. **56** 43 0N 108 30W
Fremont L. **56** 42 57N 109 48W
Fremont National Forest **44** 42 20N 120 50W
French ➛ **45** 45 56N 80 54W
French Broad ➛, N.C. **40** 35 57N 83 51W
French Broad ➛, Tenn. **49** 35 58N 83 51W
French Camp, Calif. **14** 37 53N 121 16W
French Camp, Miss. **31** 33 18N 89 24W
French Frigate Shoals **19** 23 45N 166 10W
French Guiana ■ **71** 4 0N 53 0W
French Gulch **14** 40 42N 122 38W
French Lick **22** 38 33N 86 37W
French Meadows Res. **14** 39 10N 120 40W
French River **30** 46 54N 91 54W
French Terr. of Afars & Issas
= Djibouti ■ **105** 12 0N 43 0 E
Frenchboro **26** 44 7N 68 22W
Frenchburg **49** 37 57N 83 38W
Frenchglen **44** 42 50N 118 55W
Frenchman Butte **63** 53 35N 109 38W
Frenchman Cr. ➛, Mont. **33** 48 31N 107 10W
Frenchman Cr. ➛, Nebr. **34** 40 14N 100 50W
Frenchman L., Calif. **14** 39 54N 120 11W
Frenchman L., Nev. **35** 36 48N 115 56W
Frenchtown, Mont. **33** 47 1N 114 14W
Frenchtown, N.J. **37** 40 32N 75 4W
Frenchville **26** 47 17N 68 23W
Fresco ➛ **73** 7 15 S 51 30W
Freshfield, C. **5** 68 25 S 151 10 E
Fresnillo **64** 23 10N 103 0W
Fresno **15** 36 44N 119 47W
Fresno County ◇ **15** 36 40N 120 0W
Fresno Reservoir **33** 48 36N 109 57W
Frewsburg **39** 42 3N 79 10W
Freycinet Pen. **127** 42 10 S 148 25 E
Fria, C. **123** 18 0 S 12 0 E
Fría, La **70** 8 13N 72 15W
Friant **15** 36 59N 119 43W
Friars Point **31** 34 22N 90 38W
Frías **76** 28 40 S 65 5W
Fribourg **88** 48 0N 7 52 E
Friday Harbor **53** 48 32N 123 1W
Fridley **30** 45 5N 93 16W
Friedrichshafen **88** 47 39N 9 29 E
Friend, Kans. **24** 38 16N 100 55W
Friend, Nebr. **34** 40 38N 97 17W
Friendly **27** 38 42N 76 59W
Friendly, Is. = Tonga ■ **128** 19 50 S 174 30W
Friendship, N.Y. **39** 42 12N 78 8W
Friendship, Tenn. **48** 35 55N 89 14W
Friendship, Wis. **55** 43 58N 89 49W
Friendsville **27** 39 40N 79 24W
Fries **54** 36 43N 80 59W
Friesland **55** 43 35N 89 4W

Friesland — Garfield County

Friesland □ **87** 53 5N 5 50 E
Frijoles **57** 9 11N 79 48W
Frio → **51** 28 26N 98 11W
Frio County ◇ **51** 28 54N 99 6W
Frio Draw → **50** 34 50N 102 19W
Friona **50** 34 38N 102 43W
Frisco **16** 39 35N 106 6W
Frisco City **10** 31 26N 87 24W
Frisco Peak **52** 38 31N 113 17W
Frissell, Mt. **28** 42 3N 73 28W
Fritch **50** 35 38N 101 36W
Friuli-Venezia Giulia □ **94** 46 0N 13 0 E
Frobisher B. **59** 62 30N 66 0W
Frobisher Bay **59** 63 44N 68 31W
Frobisher L. **63** 56 20N 108 15W
Frohavet **96** 63 50N 9 35 E
Froid **33** 48 20N 104 30W
Fromberg **33** 45 24N 108 54W
Frome **83** 51 16N 2 17W
Frome, L. **127** 30 45 S 139 45 E
Front Range **16** 40 25N 105 45W
Front Royal **54** 38 55N 78 12W
Fronteiras **74** 7 5 S 40 37W
Frontenac **24** 37 27N 94 42W
Frontera **65** 18 30N 92 40W
Frontier **56** 41 49N 110 32W
Frontier County ◇ **34** 40 30N 100 30W
Frosinone **94** 41 38N 13 20 E
Frost, Minn. **30** 43 35N 93 56W
Frost, Tex. **51** 32 5N 96 49W
Frostburg **27** 39 39N 78 56W
Frostisen **96** 68 14N 17 10 E
Frostproof **17** 27 45N 81 32W
Frøya **96** 63 43N 8 40 E
Fruita **16** 39 9N 108 44W
Fruitdale, Ala. **10** 31 21N 88 25W
Fruitdale, S. Dak. **47** 44 40N 103 42W
Fruithurst **10** 33 44N 85 26W
Fruitland, Idaho **20** 44 0N 116 55W
Fruitland, Iowa **23** 41 21N 91 8W
Fruitland, Md. **27** 38 19N 75 37W
Fruitland, Mo. **32** 37 27N 89 38W
Fruitland, N. Mex. **38** 36 44N 108 24W
Fruitland Park **17** 28 51N 81 54W
Fruitport **29** 43 7N 86 9W
Fruitvale, Colo. **16** 39 5N 108 30W
Fruitvale, Idaho **20** 44 49N 116 26W
Fruitvale, Wash. **53** 46 37N 120 33W
Frumoasa **95** 46 28N 25 48 E
Frunze **100** 42 54N 74 46 E
Frutal **75** 20 0 S 49 0W
Frýdek-Místek **89** 49 40N 18 20 E
Fryeburg **26** 44 1N 70 59W
Fu Xian, Liaoning, China **114** 39 38N 121 58 E
Fu Xian, Shaanxi, China **114** 36 0N 109 20 E
Fucheng **114** 37 50N 116 10 E
Fuchū **117** 34 34N 133 14 E
Fuchuan **115** 24 50N 111 5 E
Fuchun Jiang → **115** 30 5N 120 5 E
Fuding **115** 27 20N 120 12 E
Fuente Ovejuna **91** 38 15N 5 25W
Fuentes de Oñoro **91** 40 33N 6 52W
Fuerte → **64** 25 50N 109 25W
Fuerte Olimpo **76** 21 0 S 57 51W
Fuerteventura **120** 28 30N 14 0W
Fugløysund **96** 70 15N 20 20 E
Fugou **115** 34 3N 114 25 E
Fuhai **113** 47 2N 87 25 E
Fuji **117** 35 9N 138 39 E
Fuji-no-miya **117** 35 10N 138 40 E
Fuji-San **117** 35 22N 138 44 E
Fuji-yoshida **117** 35 30N 138 46 E
Fujian □ **115** 26 0N 118 0 E
Fujin **114** 47 16N 132 1 E
Fujisawa **117** 35 22N 139 29 E
Fukien = Fujian □ **115** 26 0N 118 0 E
Fukuchiyama **117** 35 19N 135 9 E
Fukue-Shima **117** 32 40N 128 45 E
Fukui **117** 36 0N 136 10 E
Fukui □ **117** 36 0N 136 12 E
Fukuoka **117** 33 39N 130 21 E
Fukuoka □ **117** 33 30N 131 0 E
Fukushima, Japan **116** 37 44N 140 28 E
Fukushima, Japan **116** 37 45N 140 28 E
Fukushima □ **116** 37 30N 140 15 E
Fukuyama **117** 34 35N 133 20 E
Fulda, Germany **88** 50 32N 9 41 E
Fulda, U.S.A. **30** 43 53N 95 36W
Fulda → **88** 51 27N 9 40 E
Fuling **115** 29 40N 107 20 E
Fullerton, Calif. **15** 33 53N 117 56W
Fullerton, N. Dak. **41** 46 10N 98 26W
Fullerton, Nebr. **34** 41 22N 97 58W
Fulton, Ala. **10** 31 47N 87 44W
Fulton, Ark. **13** 33 37N 93 49W
Fulton, Ill. **21** 41 52N 90 11W
Fulton, Kans. **24** 38 1N 94 43W
Fulton, Ky. **48** 36 30N 88 53W
Fulton, Miss. **31** 34 16N 88 25W
Fulton, Mo. **32** 38 52N 91 57W
Fulton, N.Y. **39** 43 19N 76 25W
Fulton, Ohio **42** 40 28N 82 50W
Fulton, S. Dak. **47** 43 44N 97 49W
Fulton, Tex. **51** 28 4N 97 2W
Fulton County ◇, Ark. **13** 36 22N 91 50W
Fulton County ◇, Ga. **18** 33 40N 84 40W
Fulton County ◇, Ill. **21** 40 30N 90 10W
Fulton County ◇, Ind. **22** 41 5N 86 15W
Fulton County ◇, Ky. **48** 36 32N 89 10W
Fulton County ◇, N.Y. **39** 43 10N 74 30W
Fulton County ◇, Ohio **42** 41 33N 84 8W
Fulton County ◇, Pa. **45** 39 55N 78 5W
Fultondale **10** 33 37N 86 48W
Fults **21** 38 10N 90 13W
Funabashi **117** 35 45N 140 0 E
Funafuti **124** 8 30 S 179 0 E
Funchal **120** 32 38N 16 54W
Fundación **70** 10 31N 74 11W
Fundão, Brazil **75** 19 55 S 40 24W
Fundão, Portugal **91** 40 8N 7 30W
Fundy, B. of, Canada **61** 45 0N 66 0W
Fundy, B. of, U.S.A. **26** 44 30N 66 30W
Funing, Jiangsu, China **115** 33 45N 119 50 E
Funing, Yunnan, China **115** 23 35N 105 45 E
Funiu Shan **115** 33 30N 112 20 E
Funk **34** 40 28N 99 15W
Funston **18** 31 12N 83 52W
Funtua **120** 11 30N 7 18 E
Fuping **114** 38 48N 114 12 E
Fuqing **115** 25 41N 119 21 E
Fuquay-Varina **40** 35 35N 78 48W
Furano **116** 43 21N 142 23 E
Furāt, Nahr al → **106** 31 0N 47 25 E
Furbero **65** 20 22N 97 31W
Furman **46** 32 41N 81 11W
Furnas, Represa de **75** 20 50 S 45 0W
Furnas County ◇ **34** 40 15N 100 0W
Furneaux Group **127** 40 10 S 147 50 E
Furness, Pen. **82** 54 12N 3 10W
Fürth **88** 49 29N 11 0 E
Furukawa **116** 38 34N 140 58 E
Fury and Hecla Str. **59** 69 56N 84 0W
Fusagasuga **70** 4 21N 74 22W
Fushan **114** 37 30N 121 15 E
Fushun **114** 41 50N 123 56 E
Fusong **114** 42 20N 127 15 E
Fusui **115** 22 40N 107 56 E
Futrono **78** 40 8 S 72 24W
Futuna **124** 14 25 S 178 20 E
Fuxin **114** 42 5N 121 48 E
Fuyang, Anhui, China **115** 33 0N 115 48 E
Fuyang, Zhejiang, China **115** 30 5N 119 57 E
Fuyu **114** 45 12N 124 43 E
Fuyuan **114** 48 20N 134 5 E
Fuzhou **115** 26 5N 119 16 E
Fwaka **123** 12 5 S 29 25 E
Fylde **82** 53 50N 2 58W
Fyn **97** 55 20N 10 30 E
Fyne, L. **84** 56 0N 5 20W

G

Gabbettville **18** 32 57N 85 8W
Gabbs **35** 38 52N 117 55W
Gabbs Valley Range **35** 38 34N 118 0W
Gabela **122** 11 0 S 14 24 E
Gabès **120** 33 53N 10 2 E
Gabès, Golfe de **121** 34 0N 10 30 E
Gabilan Range **15** 36 30N 121 15W
Gabon ■ **122** 0 10 S 10 0 E
Gaborone **123** 24 45 S 25 57 E
Gabrovo **95** 42 52N 25 19 E
Gachsārān **107** 30 15N 50 45 E
Gackle **41** 46 38N 99 9W
Gadag **108** 15 30N 75 45 E
Gadarwara **108** 22 50N 78 50 E
Gadhada **108** 22 0N 71 35 E
Gadsden, Ala. **10** 34 1N 86 1W
Gadsden, Ariz. **12** 32 33N 114 47W
Gadsden, S.C. **46** 33 51N 80 46W
Gadsden County ◇ **17** 30 30N 84 45W
Gadwal **108** 16 10N 77 50 E
Găeşti **95** 44 48N 25 19 E
Gaffney **46** 35 5N 81 39W
Gafsa **120** 32 24N 8 43 E
Gage **43** 36 19N 99 45W
Gage County ◇ **34** 40 20N 96 45W
Gagetown **61** 45 46N 66 10W
Gagnoa **120** 6 56N 5 16W
Gagnon **61** 51 50N 68 5W
Gagnon, L. **63** 62 3N 110 27W
Gai Xian **114** 40 22N 122 20 E
Gail **50** 32 46N 101 27W
Gaillard, L. **28** 41 21N 72 46W
Gaimán **78** 43 10 S 65 25W
Gaines County ◇ **50** 32 43N 102 39W
Gainesboro **49** 36 21N 85 39W
Gainesville, Fla. **17** 29 40N 82 20W
Gainesville, Ga. **18** 34 18N 83 50W
Gainesville, Mo. **32** 36 36N 92 26W
Gainesville, Tex. **51** 33 38N 97 8W
Gainsborough **82** 53 23N 0 46W
Gairdner L. **126** 31 30 S 136 0 E
Gairloch, L. **84** 57 43N 5 45W
Gaithersburg **27** 39 8N 77 12W
Gakona **11** 62 18N 145 18W
Galán, Cerro **76** 25 55 S 66 52W
Galangue **123** 13 42 S 16 9 E
Galápagos **125** 0 0 89 0W
Galas → **112** 4 55N 101 57 E
Galashiels **84** 55 37N 2 50W
Galaţi **89** 45 27N 28 2 E
Galaţi □ **95** 45 45N 27 30 E
Galatia, Ill. **21** 37 51N 88 37W
Galatia, Kans. **24** 38 38N 98 58W
Galatina **95** 40 10N 18 10 E
Galax **54** 36 40N 80 56W
Galcaio **105** 6 30N 47 30 E
Galdhøpiggen **97** 61 38N 8 18 E
Galeana **64** 24 50N 100 4W
Galela **111** 1 50N 127 49 E
Galena, Alaska **11** 64 44N 156 56W
Galena, Ill. **21** 42 25N 90 26W
Galena, Kans. **24** 37 4N 94 38W
Galena, Md. **27** 39 21N 75 53W
Galena, Mo. **32** 36 48N 93 28W
Galena Park **51** 29 44N 95 14W
Galera, Pta. **78** 39 59 S 73 43W
Galera Point **67** 10 8N 61 0W
Galesburg, Ill. **21** 40 57N 90 22W
Galesburg, Kans. **24** 37 28N 95 21W
Galesburg, Mich. **29** 42 17N 85 26W
Galesburg, N. Dak. **41** 47 16N 97 24W
Galestown **27** 38 35N 75 42W
Galesville **55** 44 5N 91 21W
Galeton, Colo. **16** 40 31N 104 35W
Galeton, Pa. **45** 41 44N 77 39W
Galheirão → **75** 12 23 S 45 5W
Galheiros **75** 13 18 S 46 25W
Galicea Mare **95** 44 4N 23 19 E
Galich **98** 58 23N 42 12 E
Galiche **95** 43 34N 23 50 E
Galicia □ **91** 42 43N 7 45W
Galilee = Hagalil **104** 32 53N 35 18 E
Galion **42** 40 44N 82 47W
Galiuro Mts. **12** 32 30N 110 20W
Gallabat **121** 12 58N 36 11 E
Gallatin, Mo. **32** 39 55N 93 58W
Gallatin, Tenn. **48** 36 24N 86 27W
Gallatin, Tex. **51** 31 54N 95 9W
Gallatin → **33** 45 56N 111 30W
Gallatin County ◇, Ill. **21** 37 45N 88 15W
Gallatin County ◇, Ky. **49** 38 45N 84 55W
Gallatin County ◇, Mont. **33** 45 55N 111 15W
Gallatin Gateway **33** 45 35N 111 12W
Gallatin National Forest **33** 45 15N 111 15W
Galle **108** 6 5N 80 10 E
Gállego → **91** 41 39N 0 51W
Gallegos → **78** 51 35 S 69 0W
Galley Hd. **85** 51 32N 8 56W
Gallia County ◇ **42** 38 49N 82 12W
Galliano **25** 29 26N 90 18W
Gallinas, Pta. **70** 12 28N 71 40W
Gallion **10** 32 30N 87 43W
Gallipoli = Gelibolu **95** 40 28N 26 43 E
Gallípoli **95** 40 8N 18 0 E
Gallipolis **42** 38 49N 82 12W
Gällivare **96** 67 9N 20 40 E
Gallman **31** 31 56N 90 23W
Gallo Mts. **38** 34 5N 108 35W
Galloo I. **39** 43 55N 76 25W
Galloway **84** 55 0N 4 25W
Galloway, Mull of **84** 54 38N 4 50W
Gallup **38** 35 32N 108 45W
Gal'on **104** 31 38N 34 51 E
Galoya **108** 8 10N 80 55 E
Galt, Calif. **14** 38 15N 121 18W
Galt, Iowa **23** 42 42N 93 36W
Galt, Mo. **32** 40 8N 93 23W
Galty Mts. **85** 52 22N 8 10W
Galtymore **85** 52 22N 8 12W
Galva, Ill. **21** 41 10N 90 3W
Galva, Iowa **23** 42 30N 95 25W
Galvarino **78** 38 24 S 72 47W
Galveston, Ind. **22** 40 35N 86 11W
Galveston, Tex. **51** 29 18N 94 48W
Galveston B. **51** 29 36N 94 50W
Galveston County ◇ **51** 29 28N 95 5W
Galveston I. **51** 29 16N 94 51W
Gálvez **76** 32 0 S 61 14W
Galway **85** 53 16N 9 4W
Galway □ **85** 53 16N 9 3W
Galway B. **85** 53 10N 9 20W
Gamagori **117** 34 50N 137 14 E
Gamaliel, Ark. **13** 36 27N 92 14W
Gamaliel, Ky. **49** 36 38N 85 48W
Gambaga **120** 10 30N 0 28W
Gambela **121** 8 14N 34 38 E
Gambell **11** 63 47N 171 45W
Gamber **27** 39 28N 76 56W
Gambia ■ **120** 13 25N 16 0W
Gambia → **120** 13 28N 16 34W
Gamboa **57** 9 7N 79 42W
Gamboma **122** 1 55 S 15 52 E
Gamerco **38** 35 34N 108 46W
Gamlakarleby = Kokkola **96** 63 50N 23 8 E
Gammon → **63** 51 24N 95 44W
Gan Gan **78** 42 30 S 68 10W
Gan Jiang → **113** 29 15N 116 0 E
Gan Shemu'el **104** 32 28N 34 56 E
Gan Yavne **104** 31 48N 34 42 E
Ganado, Ariz. **12** 35 43N 109 33W
Ganado, Tex. **51** 29 2N 96 31W
Gananoque **60** 44 20N 76 10W
Ganaveh **107** 29 35N 50 35 E
Gancheng **115** 18 51N 108 37 E
Gand = Gent **87** 51 2N 3 42 E
Ganda **123** 13 3 S 14 35 E
Gandak → **109** 25 39N 85 13 E
Gandava **108** 28 32N 67 32 E
Gandeeville **54** 38 42N 81 25W
Gander **61** 48 58N 54 35W
Gander L. **61** 48 58N 54 35W
Gandhi Sagar **108** 24 40N 75 40 E
Gandi **120** 12 55N 5 49 E
Gandu **75** 13 45 S 39 30W
Ganedidalem = Gani **111** 0 48 S 128 14 E
Ganga → **109** 23 20N 90 30 E
Ganganagar **108** 29 56N 73 56 E
Gangara **120** 14 35N 8 29 E
Gangaw **109** 22 5N 94 5 E
Gangdisê Shan **109** 31 20N 81 0 E
Ganges = Ganga → **109** 23 20N 90 30 E
Gangtok **109** 27 20N 88 37 E
Gani **111** 0 48 S 128 14 E
Gannett **20** 43 22N 114 11W
Gannett Peak **56** 43 11N 109 39W
Gannvalley **47** 44 2N 98 59W
Ganquan **114** 36 20N 109 20 E
Gans **43** 35 23N 94 42W
Gansu □ **114** 36 0N 104 0 E
Ganta **120** 7 15N 8 59W
Gantheaume B. **126** 27 40 S 114 10 E
Gantt **10** 31 25N 86 29W
Ganyem **111** 2 46 S 140 12 E
Ganyu **115** 34 50N 119 8 E
Ganzhou **115** 25 51N 114 56 E
Gao Bang **112** 22 37N 106 18 E
Gao'an **115** 28 26N 115 17 E
Gaomi **114** 36 20N 119 42 E
Gaoping **114** 35 45N 112 55 E
Gaoua **120** 10 20N 3 8W
Gaoual **120** 11 45N 13 25W
Gaoxiong **115** 22 38N 120 18 E
Gaoyou **115** 32 47N 119 26 E
Gaoyou Hu **115** 32 45N 119 20 E
Gaoyuan **114** 37 8N 117 58 E
Gap **90** 44 33N 6 5 E
Gar **113** 32 10N 79 58 E
Gar Dzong **108** 32 20N 79 55 E
Garachiné **66** 8 0N 78 12W
Garanhuns **74** 8 50 S 36 30W
Garawe **120** 4 35N 8 0W
Garber **43** 36 26N 97 35W
Garberville **14** 40 6N 123 48W
Garça **75** 22 14 S 49 37W
Garças → **74** 8 43 S 39 41W
Garças, Rio das → **73** 15 54 S 52 16W
Garcia **16** 37 0N 105 32W
Garcias **73** 20 34 S 52 13W
Gard **105** 9 30N 49 6 E
Gard □ **90** 44 2N 4 10 E
Garda, L. di **94** 45 40N 10 40 E
Gardala **121** 5 40N 37 25 E
Gardar **41** 48 35N 97 53W
Garde L. **63** 62 50N 106 13W
Garden **29** 45 47N 86 33W
Garden City, Ala. **10** 34 1N 86 45W
Garden City, Ga. **18** 32 6N 81 9W
Garden City, Idaho **20** 43 38N 116 16W
Garden City, Kans. **24** 37 58N 100 53W
Garden City, Mo. **32** 38 34N 94 12W
Garden City, S. Dak. **47** 44 57N 97 35W
Garden City, Tex. **50** 31 52N 101 29W
Garden City, Utah **52** 41 57N 111 24W
Garden County ◇ **34** 41 30N 102 15W
Garden Grove, Calif. **15** 33 47N 117 55W
Garden Grove, Iowa **23** 40 50N 93 36W
Garden I. **29** 45 49N 85 30W
Garden Island B. **25** 29 0N 89 0W
Garden Lakes **18** 34 19N 85 17W
Garden Plain **24** 37 40N 97 41W
Garden Valley **20** 44 6N 115 57W
Gardena **20** 43 58N 116 12W
Gardendale **10** 33 39N 86 49W
Gardēz **107** 33 37N 69 9 E
Gardi **18** 31 32N 81 48W
Gardiner, Maine **26** 44 14N 69 47W
Gardiner, Oreg. **44** 43 44N 124 7W
Gardiners B. **39** 41 5N 72 5W
Gardiners I. **39** 41 6N 72 6W
Gardner, Colo. **16** 37 47N 105 10W
Gardner, Fla. **17** 27 21N 81 48W
Gardner, Kans. **24** 38 49N 94 56W
Gardner, Mass. **28** 42 34N 71 59W
Gardner Canal **62** 53 27N 128 8W
Gardner L. **26** 44 45N 67 20W
Gardner Pinnacles **19** 25 0N 167 55W
Gardnerville **35** 38 56N 119 45W
Gare Tigre **71** 4 58N 53 9W
Gareloi I. **11** 51 48N 178 48W
Garfield, Ark. **13** 36 27N 93 58W
Garfield, Kans. **24** 38 5N 99 14W
Garfield, Minn. **30** 45 56N 95 30W
Garfield, N.J. **37** 40 52N 74 6W
Garfield, N. Mex. **38** 32 46N 107 16W
Garfield, Wash. **53** 47 1N 117 9W
Garfield County ◇, Colo. **16** 39 30N 108 0W

Garfield County Gifu

Garfield County ◇, Mont. 33 47 15N 107 0W
Garfield County ◇, Nebr. 34 41 50N 99 0W
Garfield County ◇, Okla. 43 36 20N 97 45W
Garfield County ◇, Utah 52 37 50N 111 20W
Garfield County ◇, Wash. 53 46 28N 117 36W
Garfield Heights 42 41 26N 81 37W
Garfield Mt. 33 44 31N 112 37W
Gargano, Mte. 94 41 43N 15 43 E
Garibaldi 44 45 34N 123 55W
Garibaldi Prov. Park 62 49 50N 122 40W
Garies 123 30 32 S 17 59 E
Garigliano → 94 41 13N 13 44 E
Garland, Ala. 10 31 33N 86 50W
Garland, Ark. 13 33 22N 93 43W
Garland, Kans. 24 37 44N 94 37W
Garland, N.C. 40 34 47N 78 24W
Garland, Nebr. 34 40 57N 96 59W
Garland, Tex. 51 32 55N 96 38W
Garland, Utah 52 41 45N 112 10W
Garland County ◇ 13 34 34N 93 10W
Garm 100 39 0N 70 20 E
Garmsār 107 35 20N 52 25 E
Garnavillo 23 42 52N 91 14W
Garner, Iowa 23 43 6N 93 36W
Garner, N.C. 40 35 43N 78 37W
Garnett 24 38 17N 95 14W
Garoe 105 8 25N 48 33 E
Garonne → 90 45 2N 0 36W
Garoua 121 9 19N 13 21 E
Garrard County ◇ 49 37 35N 84 30W
Garretson 47 43 43N 96 30W
Garrett 22 41 21N 85 8W
Garrett County ◇ 27 39 30N 79 20W
Garrison, Iowa 23 42 9N 92 8W
Garrison, Ky. 49 38 36N 83 10W
Garrison, Minn. 30 46 18N 93 50W
Garrison, Mont. 33 46 31N 112 49W
Garrison, N. Dak. 41 47 40N 101 25W
Garrison, Nebr. 34 41 11N 97 10W
Garrison, Tex. 51 31 49N 94 30W
Garrison, Utah 52 38 56N 114 2W
Garrison Dam 41 47 30N 101 25W
Garry → 84 56 47N 3 47W
Garry L. 58 65 58N 100 18W
Garsen 122 2 20 S 40 5 E
Garson → 63 56 20N 110 1W
Garson L. 63 56 19N 110 2W
Garut 111 7 14 S 107 53 E
Garvie Mts. 128 45 30 S 168 50 E
Garvin 43 33 57N 94 56W
Garvin County ◇ 43 34 45N 97 20W
Garwa = Garoua 121 9 19N 13 21 E
Garwin 23 42 6N 92 41W
Garwood 51 29 27N 96 24W
Gary, Ind. 22 41 36N 87 20W
Gary, Minn. 30 47 22N 96 16W
Gary, S. Dak. 47 44 48N 96 27W
Gary, Tex. 51 32 2N 94 22W
Gary, W. Va. 54 37 22N 81 33W
Garza County ◇ 50 33 12N 101 23W
Garza-Little Elm Reservoir 51 33 4N 96 59W
Garzê 113 31 39N 99 58 E
Garzón 70 2 10N 75 40W
Gas City 22 40 29N 85 37W
Gas-San 116 38 32N 140 1 E
Gasan Kuli 100 37 40N 54 20 E
Gascogne 90 43 45N 0 20 E
Gascogne, G. de 90 44 0N 2 0W
Gascon 38 35 53N 105 27W
Gasconade 32 38 40N 91 34W
Gasconade → 32 38 41N 91 33W
Gasconade County ◇ 32 38 25N 91 30W
Gascony = Gascogne 90 43 45N 0 20 E
Gascoyne 41 46 7N 103 5W
Gascoyne → 126 24 52 S 113 37 E
Gashaka 120 7 20N 11 29 E
Gasparilla I. 17 26 46N 82 16W
Gaspé 61 48 52N 64 30W
Gaspé, C. 61 48 48N 64 7W
Gaspé, Pén. de 61 48 45N 65 40W
Gaspésie, Parc Prov. de la 61 48 55N 65 50W
Gasquet 14 41 51N 123 58W
Gassaway 54 38 41N 80 47W
Gaston, Ind. 22 40 19N 85 31W
Gaston, N.C. 40 36 30N 77 39W
Gaston, S.C. 46 33 49N 81 5W
Gaston, L. 40 36 30N 77 49W
Gaston County ◇ 40 31 15N 81 10W
Gastonia 40 35 16N 81 11W
Gastre 78 42 20 S 69 15W
Gata, C. de 91 36 41N 2 13W
Gata, Sierra de 91 40 20N 6 45W
Gataga → 62 58 35N 126 59W
Gate 43 36 51N 100 4W
Gate City 54 36 38N 82 35W
Gates, N.C. 40 36 30N 76 46W
Gates, N.Y. 39 43 9N 77 42W
Gates, Oreg. 44 44 45N 122 25W
Gates, Tenn. 48 35 50N 89 24W
Gates County ◇ 40 36 25N 76 40W
Gateshead 82 54 57N 1 37W
Gatesville, N.C. 40 36 24N 76 45W
Gatesville, Tex. 51 31 26N 97 45W
Gateway 16 38 41N 108 59W
Gatico 76 22 29 S 70 20W
Gâtinais 90 48 5N 2 40 E
Gatineau → 60 45 27N 75 42W
Gatineau, Parc de la 60 45 40N 76 0W
Gatliff 49 36 41N 84 1W
Gatlinburg 49 35 43N 83 31W
Gato 16 37 3N 107 12W
Gatooma 123 18 20 S 29 52 E
Gatun 57 9 16N 79 55W
Gatun, L. 66 9 7N 79 56W
Gatun Dam 57 9 16N 79 55W
Gatun Locks 57 9 16N 79 55W
Gau 128 18 2 S 179 18 E
Gauer L. 63 57 0N 97 50W
Gauhati 109 26 10N 91 45 E
Gaula → 96 63 21N 10 14 E
Gauley → 54 38 10N 81 12W
Gauley Bridge 54 38 10N 81 12W
Gausta, Mt. 97 59 48N 8 40 E
Gautier 31 30 23N 88 37W
Gavāter 107 25 10N 61 31 E
Gavins Point Dam 47 42 51N 97 29W
Gaviota 15 34 29N 120 13W
Gävleborgs län □ 97 61 30N 16 15 E
Gawilgarh Hills 108 21 15N 76 45 E
Gawler 127 34 30 S 138 42 E
Gawler Ranges 126 32 30 S 135 45 E
Gaxun Nur 113 42 22N 100 30 E
Gay, Ga. 18 33 6N 84 35W
Gay, Mich. 29 47 14N 88 10W
Gay, U.S.S.R. 98 51 27N 58 27 E
Gaya, India 109 24 47N 85 4 E
Gaya, Niger 120 11 52N 3 28 E
Gaylord, Kans. 24 39 39N 98 51W
Gaylord, Mich. 29 45 2N 84 41W
Gaylord, Minn. 30 44 33N 94 13W
Gaylordsville 28 41 39N 73 29W
Gayndah 127 25 35 S 151 32 E
Gays Mills 55 43 19N 90 51W
Gayville 47 42 53N 97 10W
Gaza 104 31 30N 34 28 E
Gaza Strip 104 31 29N 34 25 E
Gazelle 14 41 31N 122 31W
Gaziantep 106 37 6N 37 23 E
Gazli 100 40 14N 63 24 E
Gdańsk 89 54 22N 18 40 E
Gdańska, Zatoka 89 54 30N 19 20 E
Gdov 98 58 48N 27 55 E
Gdynia 89 54 35N 18 33 E
Ge'a 104 31 38N 34 37 E
Gearhart 44 46 1N 123 55W
Gearhart Mt. 44 42 30N 120 53W
Geary 43 35 38N 98 19W
Geary County ◇ 24 39 0N 96 45W
Geauga County ◇ 42 41 35N 81 12W
Gebe 111 0 5N 129 25 E
Gebeit Mine 121 21 3N 36 29 E
Gebel Mûsa 106 28 32N 33 59 E
Gedaref 121 14 2N 35 28 E
Geddes 47 43 15N 98 42W
Gede, Tanjung 110 6 46 S 105 12 E
Gedera 104 31 49N 34 46 E
Gedser 97 54 35N 11 55 E
Geelong 127 38 10 S 144 22 E
Geidam 121 12 57N 11 57 E
Geiger 10 32 52N 88 18W
Geikie → 63 57 45N 103 52W
Geili 121 16 1N 32 37 E
Geistown 45 40 18N 78 52W
Geita 122 2 48 S 32 12 E
Gejiu 113 23 20N 103 10 E
Gela 94 37 6N 14 18 E
Geladi 105 6 59N 46 30 E
Gelderland □ 87 52 5N 6 10 E
Geldermalsen 87 51 53N 5 17 E
Geldrop 87 51 25N 5 32 E
Geleen 87 50 57N 5 49 E
Gelehun 120 8 20N 11 40W
Gelibolu 95 40 28N 26 43 E
Gelsenkirchen 88 51 30N 7 5 E
Gem 24 39 26N 100 54W
Gem County ◇ 20 44 0N 116 25W
Gemas 112 2 37N 102 36 E
Gembloux 87 50 34N 4 43 E
Gemena 122 3 13N 19 48 E
Gemerek 106 39 15N 36 10 E
Gen He → 114 50 16N 119 32 E
Gendringen 87 51 52N 6 21 E
Gene Autry 43 34 19N 97 2W
General Acha 76 37 20 S 64 38W
General Alvear,
Buenos Aires, Argentina 76 36 0 S 60 0W
General Alvear, Mendoza,
Argentina 76 35 0 S 67 40W
General Artigas 76 26 52 S 56 16W
General Belgrano 76 36 35 S 58 47W
General Cabrera 76 32 53 S 63 52W
General Carrera, L. 78 46 35 S 72 0W
General Cepeda 64 25 23N 101 27W
General Conesa 78 40 6 S 64 25W
General Guido 76 36 40 S 57 50W
General Juan Madariaga 76 37 0 S 57 0W
General La Madrid 76 37 17 S 61 20W
General Lorenzo Vintter 78 40 45 S 64 26W
General MacArthur 111 11 18N 125 28 E
General Martin Miguel de
Güemes 76 24 35 S 65 0W
General Paz 76 27 45 S 57 36W
General Pico 76 35 45 S 63 50W
General Pinedo 76 27 15 S 61 20W
General Pinto 76 34 45 S 61 50W
General Sampaio 74 4 2 S 39 29W
General Santos 111 6 5N 125 14 E
General Toshevo 95 43 42N 28 6 E
General Trevino 65 26 14N 99 29W
General Trías 64 28 21N 106 22W
General Viamonte 76 35 1 S 61 3W
General Villegas 76 35 0 S 63 0W
General Vintter, L. 78 43 55 S 71 40W
Genesee 20 46 33N 116 56W
Genesee → 39 43 16N 77 36W
Genesee County ◇, Mich. 29 43 0N 83 40W
Genesee County ◇, N.Y. 39 43 0N 78 10W
Geneseo, Ill. 21 41 27N 90 9W
Geneseo, Kans. 24 38 31N 98 10W
Geneseo, N.Y. 39 42 48N 77 49W
Geneva = Genève 88 46 12N 6 9 E
Geneva, Ala. 10 31 2N 85 52W
Geneva, Ga. 18 32 35N 84 33W
Geneva, Ill. 21 41 53N 88 18W
Geneva, Ind. 22 40 36N 84 58W
Geneva, Iowa 23 42 41N 93 8W
Geneva, Minn. 30 43 49N 93 16W
Geneva, N.Y. 39 42 52N 76 59W
Geneva, Nebr. 34 40 32N 97 36W
Geneva, Ohio 42 41 48N 80 57W
Geneva, L. = Léman, Lac 88 46 26N 6 30 E
Geneva County ◇ 10 31 6N 85 42W
Genève 88 46 12N 6 9 E
Genil → 91 37 42N 5 19W
Genk 87 50 58N 5 32 E
Gennargentu, Mti. del 94 40 0N 9 10 E
Gennep 87 51 41N 5 59 E
Genoa = Génova 94 44 24N 8 56 E
Genoa, Colo. 16 39 17N 103 30W
Genoa, Ill. 21 42 6N 88 42W
Genoa, Nebr. 34 41 27N 97 44W
Genoa, Ohio 42 41 31N 83 22W
Genoa, Wis. 55 43 35N 91 13W
Genoa → 78 44 55 S 70 5W
Genoa City 55 42 30N 88 20W
Genola 30 45 58N 94 7W
Génova 94 44 24N 8 56 E
Génova, Golfo di 94 44 0N 9 0 E
Gent 87 51 2N 3 42 E
Gentio do Ouro 74 11 25 S 42 30W
Gentry, Ark. 13 36 16N 94 29W
Gentry, Mo. 32 40 20N 94 25W
Gentry County ◇ 32 40 10N 94 25W
Geographe B. 126 33 30 S 115 15 E
Geographe Chan. 126 24 30 S 113 0 E
Georga, Zemlya 100 80 30N 49 0 E
George, S. Africa 123 33 58 S 22 29 E
George, Iowa 23 43 21N 96 0W
George, Wash. 53 47 5N 119 53W
George → 61 58 49N 66 10W
George, L., Uganda 122 0 5N 30 10 E
George, L., Fla. 17 29 17N 81 36W
George, L., Mich. 29 46 27N 84 8W
George, L., N.Y. 39 43 37N 73 33W
George County ◇ 31 30 56N 88 35W
George River = Port
Nouveau-Québec 59 58 30N 65 59W
George Sound 128 44 52 S 167 25 E
George Town, Bahamas 66 23 33N 75 47W
George Town, Malaysia 112 5 25N 100 15 E
George V Coast 5 69 0 S 148 0 E
George VI Sound 5 71 0 S 68 0W
George Washington National
Forest 54 38 0N 79 50W
George West 51 28 20N 98 7W
Georgetown, Australia 127 18 17 S 143 33 E
Georgetown, Ont., Canada 60 43 40N 79 56W
Georgetown, P.E.I., Canada 61 46 13N 62 24W
Georgetown, Cayman Is. 66 19 20N 81 24W
Georgetown, Gambia 120 13 30N 14 47W
Georgetown, Guyana 71 6 50N 58 12W
Georgetown, Calif. 14 38 54N 120 50W
Georgetown, Colo. 16 39 42N 105 42W
Georgetown, Del. 27 38 41N 75 23W
Georgetown, Fla. 17 29 23N 81 38W
Georgetown, Ga. 18 31 53N 85 6W
Georgetown, Idaho 20 42 29N 111 22W
Georgetown, Ill. 21 39 59N 87 38W
Georgetown, Ky. 49 38 13N 84 33W
Georgetown, La. 25 31 46N 92 23W
Georgetown, Mass. 28 42 44N 70 59W
Georgetown, Miss. 31 31 52N 90 10W
Georgetown, Ohio 42 38 52N 83 54W
Georgetown, S.C. 46 33 23N 79 17W
Georgetown, Tex. 51 30 38N 97 41W
Georgetown County ◇ 46 33 30N 79 15W
Georgi Dimitrov 95 42 15N 23 54 E
Georgi Dimitrov, Yazovir 95 42 37N 25 18 E
Georgia □ 18 32 50N 83 15W
Georgia, Str. of 62 49 25N 124 0W
Georgia, Strait of 53 49 20N 124 0W
Georgia Center 36 44 42N 73 9W
Georgian B. 60 45 15N 81 0W
Georgian S.S.R. □ 99 42 0N 43 0 E
Georgiana 10 31 38N 86 44W
Georgievsk 99 44 12N 43 28 E
Georgina → 127 23 30 S 139 47 E
Georgiu-Dezh 99 51 3N 39 30 E
Gera 88 50 53N 12 11 E
Geraardsbergen 87 50 45N 3 53 E
Geral, Serra, Bahia, Brazil 75 14 0 S 41 0W
Geral, Serra, Goiás, Brazil 74 11 15 S 46 30W
Geral, Serra, Sta. Catarina,
Brazil 77 26 25 S 50 0W
Geral de Goiás, Serra 75 12 0 S 46 0W
Geral do Paraná Serra 75 15 0 S 47 30W
Gerald 32 38 24N 91 20W
Geraldine 33 47 36N 110 16W
Geraldton, Australia 126 28 48 S 114 32 E
Geraldton, Canada 60 49 44N 86 59W
Gerber 14 40 4N 122 9W
Gerber Reservoir 44 42 12N 121 8W
Gerdine, Mt. 11 61 35N 152 27W
Gerede 106 40 45N 32 10 E
Gereshk 107 31 47N 64 35 E
Gerik 112 5 25N 101 0 E
Gering 34 41 50N 103 40W
Gerizim 104 32 13N 35 15 E
Gerlach 35 40 39N 119 21W
Gerlogubi 105 6 53N 45 3 E
Germansen Landing 62 55 43N 124 40W
Germantown, Ill. 21 38 33N 89 32W
Germantown, Ohio 42 39 38N 84 22W
Germantown, Tenn. 48 35 5N 89 49W
Germantown, Wis. 55 43 14N 88 6W
Germany, East ■ 88 52 0N 12 0 E
Germany, West ■ 88 52 0N 9 0 E
Germiston 123 26 15 S 28 10 E
Gero 117 35 48N 137 14 E
Gerona 91 41 58N 2 46 E
Geronimo 43 34 29N 98 23W
Gerrard 62 50 30N 117 17W
Gers □ 90 43 35N 0 38 E
Gerty 43 34 50N 96 17W
Geser 111 3 50 S 130 54 E
Gethsémani 61 50 13N 60 40W
Gettysburg, Pa. 45 39 50N 77 14W
Gettysburg, S. Dak. 47 45 1N 99 57W
Getz Ice Shelf 5 75 0 S 130 0W
Geuda Springs 24 37 7N 97 9W
Gévaudan 90 44 40N 3 40 E
Geyser 33 47 16N 110 30W
Geyserville 14 38 42N 122 54W
Geysir 96 64 19N 20 18W
Ghaghara → 109 25 45N 84 40 E
Ghana ■ 120 6 0N 1 0W
Ghanzi 123 21 50 S 21 34 E
Gharb el Istiwa'iya □ 121 5 0N 30 0 E
Ghardaïa 120 32 20N 3 37 E
Gharyān 121 32 10N 13 0 E
Ghat 120 24 59N 10 11 E
Ghawdex = Gozo 94 36 0N 14 13 E
Ghayl 106 21 40N 46 20 E
Ghazal, Bahr el →, Chad 121 15 0N 17 0 E
Ghazâl, Bahr el →, Sudan 121 9 31N 30 25 E
Ghazaouet 120 35 8N 1 50W
Ghaziabad 108 28 42N 77 26 E
Ghazipur 109 25 38N 83 35 E
Ghaznī 108 33 30N 68 28 E
Ghaznī □ 107 32 10N 68 20 E
Ghèlinsor 105 6 28N 46 39 E
Ghent = Gent 87 51 2N 3 42 E
Ghent, Ky. 49 38 44N 85 4W
Ghent, Minn. 30 44 31N 95 54W
Gheorghe Gheorghiu-Dej 95 46 17N 26 47 E
Ghergani 95 44 37N 25 37 E
Ghizao 108 33 20N 65 44 E
Ghowr □ 107 34 0N 64 20 E
Ghugus 108 19 58N 79 12 E
Ghūriān 107 34 17N 61 25 E
Gia Lai = Pleiku 112 13 57N 108 0 E
Gia Nghia 112 12 0N 107 42 E
Gian 111 5 45N 125 20 E
Giant's Causeway 85 55 15N 6 30W
Giarabub = Al Jaghbūb 121 29 42N 24 38 E
Giarre 94 37 44N 15 10 E
Gibara 66 21 9N 76 11W
Gibbon, Nebr. 34 40 45N 98 51W
Gibbon, Oreg. 44 45 42N 118 21W
Gibbonsville 20 45 33N 113 56W
Gibbstown 37 39 50N 75 18W
Gibeon 123 25 7 S 17 45 E
Gibraltar 91 36 7N 5 22W
Gibraltar, Str. of 91 35 55N 5 40W
Gibsland 25 32 33N 93 3W
Gibson, Ga. 18 33 14N 82 36W
Gibson, La. 25 29 41N 90 59W
Gibson City 21 40 28N 88 22W
Gibson County ◇, Ind. 22 38 20N 87 35W
Gibson County ◇, Tenn. 48 36 0N 89 0W
Gibson Des. 126 24 0 S 126 0 E
Gibsons 62 49 24N 123 32W
Gibsonton 17 27 51N 82 23W
Giddings 51 30 11N 96 56W
Gideon 32 36 27N 89 55W
Giessen 88 50 34N 8 40 E
Gifford, Fla. 17 27 40N 80 25W
Gifford, Iowa 23 42 17N 93 5W
Gifford, Wash. 53 48 18N 118 9W
Gifford Pinchot National
Forest 53 46 15N 121 55W
Gifu 117 35 30N 136 45 E
Gifu □ 117 35 40N 137 0 E

Giganta, Sa. de la **Goodlettsville**

Giganta, Sa. de la	**64**	25 30N	111 30W
Gigen	**95**	43 40N	24 28 E
Gigha	**84**	55 42N	5 45W
Gijón	**91**	43 32N	5 42W
Gil I.	**62**	53 12N	129 15W
Gila	**38**	32 58N	108 38W
Gila →	**12**	32 43N	114 33W
Gila Bend	**12**	32 57N	112 43W
Gila Bend Indian Reservation	**12**	33 0N	112 30W
Gila Bend Mts.	**12**	33 10N	113 0W
Gila Cliff Dwelings National Monument	**38**	33 2N	108 16W
Gila County ◇	**12**	33 30N	110 45W
Gila Mts.	**12**	33 10N	109 50W
Gila National Forest	**38**	33 30N	108 30W
Gila River Indian Reservation	**12**	33 15N	112 0W
Gīlān □	**106**	37 0N	50 0 E
Gilbert, Ariz.	**12**	33 21N	111 47W
Gilbert, Iowa	**23**	42 7N	93 39W
Gilbert, La.	**25**	32 3N	91 40W
Gilbert, Minn.	**30**	47 29N	92 28W
Gilbert, S.C.	**46**	33 56N	81 24W
Gilbert, W. Va.	**54**	37 37N	81 52W
Gilbert →	**127**	16 35 S	141 15 E
Gilbert Is. = Kiribati ■	**124**	1 0N	176 0 E
Gilbert Pk.	**53**	46 29N	121 25W
Gilbert Plains	**63**	51 9N	100 28W
Gilbertown	**10**	31 53N	88 19W
Gilbertville	**28**	42 19N	72 12W
Gilboa	**42**	41 1N	83 55W
Gilbués	**74**	9 50 S	45 21W
Gilby	**41**	48 5N	97 28W
Gilchrist, Oreg.	**44**	43 29N	121 41W
Gilchrist, Tex.	**51**	29 31N	94 29W
Gilchrist County ◇	**17**	29 45N	82 45W
Gildford	**33**	48 34N	110 18W
Gilead, Maine	**26**	44 24N	70 59W
Gilead, Nebr.	**34**	40 9N	97 25W
Giles County ◇, Tenn.	**48**	35 10N	86 0W
Giles County ◇, Va.	**54**	37 20N	80 44W
Gilford I.	**62**	50 40N	126 30W
Gilford Park	**37**	39 58N	74 8W
Gilgandra	**127**	31 43 S	148 39 E
Gilgit	**108**	35 50N	74 15 E
Gill	**16**	40 27N	104 33W
Gillam	**63**	56 20N	94 40W
Gillespie	**21**	39 8N	89 49W
Gillespie County ◇	**51**	30 16N	98 52W
Gillett, Ark.	**13**	34 7N	91 23W
Gillett, Wis.	**55**	44 54N	88 19W
Gillett Grove	**23**	43 1N	95 2W
Gillette	**56**	44 18N	105 30W
Gillham	**13**	34 10N	94 19W
Gilliam	**25**	32 50N	93 51W
Gilliam County ◇	**44**	47 20N	120 10W
Gillingham	**83**	51 23N	0 34 E
Gillis	**25**	30 22N	93 12W
Gillis Range	**35**	38 42N	118 21W
Gillsville	**18**	34 18N	83 38W
Gilman, Colo.	**16**	39 32N	106 24W
Gilman, Ill.	**21**	40 46N	88 0W
Gilman, Iowa	**23**	41 53N	92 47W
Gilman, Vt.	**36**	44 23N	71 42W
Gilman, Wis.	**55**	45 10N	90 48W
Gilman City	**32**	40 8N	93 53W
Gilmanton	**36**	43 55N	71 25W
Gilmer	**51**	32 44N	94 57W
Gilmer County ◇, Ga.	**18**	34 40N	84 30W
Gilmer County ◇, W. Va.	**54**	38 56N	80 50W
Gilmore	**13**	35 25N	90 17W
Gilmore City	**23**	42 44N	94 27W
Gilmour	**60**	44 48N	77 37W
Gilort →	**95**	44 38N	23 32 E
Gilpin	**49**	37 15N	84 53W
Gilpin County ◇	**16**	39 50N	105 40W
Gilroy	**14**	37 1N	121 34W
Gilsum	**36**	43 3N	72 16W
Giltner	**34**	40 47N	98 9W
Gimbi	**121**	9 3N	35 42 E
Gimli	**63**	50 40N	97 0W
Gimzo	**104**	31 56N	34 56 E
Gîngiova	**95**	43 54N	23 50 E
Ginir	**105**	7 6N	40 40 E
Giohar	**105**	2 48N	45 30 E
Gióna, Óros	**95**	38 38N	22 14 E
Gippsland	**127**	37 45 S	147 15 E
Girard, Ga.	**18**	33 3N	81 43W
Girard, Ill.	**21**	39 27N	89 47W
Girard, Kans.	**24**	37 31N	94 51W
Girard, Ohio	**42**	41 9N	80 42W
Girard, Pa.	**45**	42 0N	80 19W
Girard, Tex.	**50**	33 22N	100 40W
Girardot	**70**	4 18N	74 48W
Girdle Ness	**84**	57 9N	2 2W
Girdletree	**27**	38 6N	75 24W
Giresun	**106**	40 55N	38 30 E
Girga	**121**	26 17N	31 55 E
Giridih	**109**	24 10N	86 21 E
Gironde □	**90**	44 45N	0 30W
Gironde →	**90**	45 32N	1 7W
Girvan	**84**	55 15N	4 50W
Girvin	**50**	31 5N	102 24W
Gisborne	**128**	38 39 S	178 5 E
Gisenyi	**122**	1 41 S	29 15 E
Gitega	**122**	3 26 S	29 56 E
Giuba →	**105**	1 30N	42 35 E
Giurgeni	**95**	44 45N	27 48 E
Giurgiu	**89**	43 52N	25 57 E
Giv'at Brenner	**104**	31 52N	34 47 E
Giv'atayim	**104**	32 4N	34 49 E
Giza = El Gîza	**121**	30 0N	31 10 E
Gizhiga	**101**	62 3N	160 30 E
Gizhiginskaya, Guba	**101**	61 0N	158 0 E
Giżycko	**89**	54 2N	21 48 E
Gjirokastra	**95**	40 7N	20 10 E
Gjoa Haven	**58**	68 20N	96 8W
Gjøvik	**97**	60 47N	10 43 E
Glace Bay	**61**	46 11N	59 58W
Glacier	**53**	48 53N	121 57W
Glacier Bay	**11**	58 40N	136 0W
Glacier Bay National Park	**11**	58 45N	136 30W
Glacier County ◇	**33**	48 50N	112 50W
Glacier Nat. Park	**62**	51 15N	117 30W
Glacier Peak	**53**	48 7N	121 7W
Gladbrook	**23**	42 11N	92 43W
Glade	**24**	39 41N	99 19W
Glade Spring	**54**	36 47N	81 47W
Glades County ◇	**17**	26 50N	81 15W
Gladewater	**51**	32 33N	94 56W
Gladstone, Canada	**63**	50 13N	98 57W
Gladstone, Mich.	**29**	45 51N	87 1W
Gladstone, Mo.	**32**	39 13N	94 35W
Gladstone, N. Dak.	**41**	46 52N	102 34W
Gladstone, N.J.	**37**	40 43N	74 40W
Gladstone, N. Mex.	**38**	36 18N	103 58W
Gladstone, Oreg.	**44**	45 23N	122 36W
Gladwin	**29**	43 59N	84 29W
Gladwin County ◇	**29**	44 0N	84 25W
Glady	**54**	38 48N	79 43W
Gladys L.	**62**	59 50N	133 0W
Gláma	**96**	65 48N	23 0W
Glåma →	**97**	59 12N	10 57 E
Glamis	**15**	32 55N	115 0W
Glasco	**24**	39 22N	97 50W
Glascock County ◇	**18**	33 15N	82 40W
Glasford	**21**	40 34N	89 49W
Glasgow, U.K.	**84**	55 52N	4 14W
Glasgow, Del.	**27**	39 38N	75 45W
Glasgow, Ky.	**49**	37 0N	85 55W
Glasgow, Mo.	**32**	39 14N	92 51W
Glasgow, Mont.	**33**	48 12N	106 38W
Glasgow, Va.	**54**	37 38N	79 27W
Glass Mts.	**50**	30 30N	103 10W
Glassboro	**37**	39 42N	75 7W
Glasscock County ◇	**50**	31 52N	101 29W
Glastonbury, U.K.	**83**	51 9N	2 42W
Glastonbury, U.S.A.	**28**	41 43N	72 37W
Glauchau	**88**	50 50N	12 33 E
Glazier	**50**	36 1N	100 16W
Glazov	**98**	58 9N	52 40 E
Gleason	**48**	36 13N	88 37W
Gleiwitz = Gliwice	**89**	50 22N	18 41 E
Glen, Mont.	**33**	45 28N	112 43W
Glen, N.H.	**36**	44 7N	71 11W
Glen Affric	**84**	57 15N	5 0W
Glen Allan	**31**	33 2N	91 2W
Glen Alpine	**40**	35 44N	81 47W
Glen Burnie	**27**	39 10N	76 37W
Glen Campbell	**45**	40 49N	78 50W
Glen Canyon	**52**	37 30N	110 40W
Glen Canyon Dam	**12**	36 57N	111 29W
Glen Canyon National Recreation Area	**52**	37 15N	111 0W
Glen Coe	**82**	56 40N	5 0W
Glen Cove	**39**	40 52N	73 38W
Glen Dean	**48**	37 39N	86 32W
Glen Elder	**24**	39 30N	98 18W
Glen Flora	**51**	29 21N	96 12W
Glen Garry	**84**	57 3N	5 7W
Glen Haven	**16**	40 27N	105 27W
Glen Innes	**127**	29 44 S	151 44 E
Glen Lyon	**45**	41 10N	76 5W
Glen Mor	**84**	57 12N	4 37 E
Glen Moriston	**84**	57 10N	4 58W
Glen Orchy	**84**	56 27N	4 52W
Glen Rock	**45**	39 48N	76 44W
Glen Rose	**51**	32 14N	97 45W
Glen Spean	**84**	56 53N	4 40W
Glen Ullin	**41**	46 49N	101 50W
Glenallen	**32**	37 19N	90 2W
Glenburn	**41**	48 31N	101 13W
Glencliff	**36**	43 58N	71 53W
Glencoe, Ala.	**10**	33 57N	85 56W
Glencoe, Ky.	**49**	38 43N	84 49W
Glencoe, Minn.	**30**	44 46N	94 9W
Glencoe, Okla.	**43**	36 14N	96 56W
Glendale, Ariz.	**12**	33 32N	112 11W
Glendale, Calif.	**15**	34 9N	118 15W
Glendale, Fla.	**17**	30 52N	86 7W
Glendale, Ky.	**49**	37 36N	85 54W
Glendale, Oreg.	**44**	42 44N	123 26W
Glendale, Utah	**52**	37 19N	112 36W
Glendale L.	**45**	40 42N	78 32W
Glendevey	**16**	40 48N	105 56W
Glendive	**33**	47 7N	104 43W
Glendo	**56**	42 30N	105 2W
Glendo Reservoir	**56**	42 29N	104 57W
Glendora, Miss.	**31**	33 50N	90 18W
Glendora, N.J.	**37**	39 50N	75 4W
Glengarriff	**85**	51 45N	9 33W
Glenham	**47**	45 32N	100 16W
Glenmont	**42**	40 31N	82 6W
Glenmora	**25**	30 59N	92 35W
Glenn, Calif.	**14**	39 31N	122 1W
Glenn, Mich.	**29**	42 31N	86 14W
Glenn County ◇	**14**	39 40N	122 20W
Glennallen	**11**	62 7N	145 33W
Glenns Ferry	**20**	42 57N	115 18W
Glennville	**18**	31 56N	81 56W
Glenoma	**53**	46 31N	122 10W
Glenpool	**43**	35 58N	96 1W
Glenrock	**56**	42 52N	105 52W
Glenrothes	**84**	56 12N	3 11W
Glens Falls	**39**	43 19N	73 39W
Glenside	**45**	40 6N	75 9W
Glenties	**85**	54 48N	8 18W
Glenville, Minn.	**30**	43 34N	93 17W
Glenville, N.C.	**40**	35 10N	83 8W
Glenville, Nebr.	**34**	40 30N	98 15W
Glenville, W. Va.	**54**	38 56N	80 50W
Glenwood, Alta., Canada	**62**	49 21N	113 31W
Glenwood, Newf., Canada	**61**	49 0N	54 58W
Glenwood, Ala.	**10**	31 40N	86 10W
Glenwood, Ark.	**13**	34 20N	93 33W
Glenwood, Ga.	**18**	32 11N	82 40W
Glenwood, Hawaii	**19**	19 29N	155 9W
Glenwood, Ill.	**21**	41 33N	87 37W
Glenwood, Ind.	**22**	39 37N	85 18W
Glenwood, Iowa	**23**	41 3N	95 45W
Glenwood, Minn.	**30**	45 39N	95 23W
Glenwood, N. Mex.	**38**	33 19N	108 53W
Glenwood, Oreg.	**44**	45 39N	123 16W
Glenwood, Utah	**52**	38 46N	111 59W
Glenwood, Wash.	**53**	46 1N	121 17W
Glenwood City	**55**	45 4N	92 10W
Glenwood Springs	**16**	39 33N	107 19W
Glidden	**23**	42 4N	94 44W
Glide	**44**	43 18N	123 6W
Gliwice	**89**	50 22N	18 41 E
Globe	**12**	33 24N	110 47W
Glodeanu Siliştea	**95**	44 50N	26 48 E
Głogów	**88**	51 37N	16 5 E
Gloria, La	**70**	8 37N	73 48W
Glorieta	**38**	35 35N	105 46W
Glorieuses, Îles	**123**	11 30 S	47 20 E
Glossop	**82**	53 27N	1 56W
Gloster	**31**	31 12N	91 1W
Gloucester, U.K.	**83**	51 52N	2 15W
Gloucester, Mass.	**28**	42 37N	70 40W
Gloucester, N.J.	**37**	39 54N	75 8W
Gloucester, Va.	**54**	37 25N	76 32W
Gloucester County ◇, N.J.	**37**	39 40N	75 15W
Gloucester County ◇, Va.	**54**	37 25N	76 32W
Gloucestershire □	**83**	51 44N	2 10W
Glover, Mo.	**32**	37 29N	90 42W
Glover, Vt.	**36**	44 42N	72 12W
Gloversville	**39**	43 3N	74 21W
Glovertown	**61**	48 40N	54 3W
Glŭbovo	**95**	42 8N	25 55 E
Glückstadt	**88**	53 46N	9 28 E
Glynn County ◇	**18**	31 10N	81 30W
Gmünd	**88**	48 45N	15 0 E
Gmunden	**88**	47 55N	13 48 E
Gnadenhutten	**42**	40 22N	81 26W
Gniezno	**89**	52 30N	17 35 E
Gnowangerup	**126**	33 58 S	117 59 E
Go Cong	**112**	10 22N	106 40 E
Gō-no-ura	**117**	33 44N	129 40 E
Goa	**108**	15 33N	73 59 E
Goa □	**108**	15 33N	73 59 E
Goalpara	**109**	26 10N	90 40 E
Goat Fell	**84**	55 37N	5 11W
Goba, Ethiopia	**105**	7 1N	39 59 E
Goba, Mozam.	**123**	26 15 S	32 13 E
Gobabis	**123**	22 30 S	19 0 E
Gobernador Gregores	**78**	48 46 S	70 15W
Gobi	**114**	44 0N	111 0 E
Gobles	**29**	42 22N	85 53W
Gobō	**117**	33 53N	135 10 E
Gochas	**123**	24 59 S	18 55 E
Godavari →	**109**	16 25N	82 18 E
Godavari Point	**109**	17 0N	82 20 E
Godbout	**61**	49 20N	67 38W
Goddard	**24**	37 39N	97 34W
Goderich	**60**	43 45N	81 41W
Godfrey, Ga.	**18**	33 27N	83 30W
Godfrey, Ill.	**21**	38 58N	90 11W
Godhavn	**4**	69 15N	53 38W
Godhra	**108**	22 49N	73 40 E
Godoy Cruz	**76**	32 56 S	68 52W
Gods →	**63**	56 22N	92 51W
Gods L.	**63**	54 40N	94 15W
Godthåb	**4**	64 10N	51 35W
Godwin Austen = K2	**108**	35 58N	76 32 E
Goehner	**34**	40 50N	97 13W
Goeie Hoop, Kaap die	**123**	34 24 S	18 30 E
Goéland, L. au	**60**	49 50N	76 48W
Goeree	**87**	51 50N	4 0 E
Goes	**87**	51 30N	3 55 E
Goessel	**24**	38 15N	97 21W
Goff →	**43**	36 43N	101 29W
Goffs, Calif.	**15**	34 55N	115 4W
Goffs, Kans.	**24**	39 40N	95 56W
Goffstown	**36**	43 1N	71 36W
Gogama	**60**	47 35N	81 43W
Gogebic, L.	**29**	46 30N	89 35W
Gogebic County ◇	**29**	46 25N	89 45W
Gogebic Range	**55**	46 20N	90 20W
Gogra = Ghaghara →	**109**	25 45N	84 40 E
Goiana	**74**	7 33 S	34 59W
Goianésia	**75**	15 18 S	49 7W
Goiânia	**75**	16 43 S	49 20W
Goiás	**75**	15 55 S	50 10W
Goiás □	**74**	12 10 S	48 0W
Goiatuba	**75**	18 1 S	49 23W
Gojō	**117**	34 21N	135 42 E
Gojra	**108**	31 10N	72 40 E
Gokteik	**109**	22 26N	97 0 E
Golan Heights = Hagolan	**104**	33 0N	35 45 E
Golchikha	**4**	71 45N	83 30 E
Golconda, Ill.	**21**	37 22N	88 29W
Golconda, Nev.	**35**	40 58N	117 30W
Gold Beach	**44**	42 25N	124 25W
Gold Coast	**118**	4 0N	1 40W
Gold Creek	**11**	62 46N	149 41W
Gold Hill	**44**	42 26N	123 3W
Gold Point	**35**	37 21N	117 22W
Gold River	**62**	49 46N	126 3 E
Goldcreek	**33**	46 35N	112 55W
Golden, Canada	**62**	51 20N	117 59W
Golden, Ill.	**21**	40 7N	91 1W
Golden, Mo.	**32**	36 31N	93 39W
Golden, N. Mex.	**38**	35 16N	106 13W
Golden, Okla.	**43**	34 2N	94 54W
Golden Bay	**128**	40 40 S	172 50 E
Golden City	**32**	37 24N	94 5W
Golden Gate	**21**	38 22N	88 12W
Golden Gate National Recreation Area	**14**	37 49N	122 31W
Golden Hinde	**62**	49 40N	125 44W
Golden Meadow	**25**	29 24N	90 16W
Golden Prairie	**63**	50 13N	109 37W
Golden Vale	**85**	52 33N	8 17W
Golden Valley	**41**	47 17N	102 4W
Golden Valley County ◇, Mont.	**33**	46 30N	109 15W
Golden Valley County ◇, N. Dak.	**41**	47 0N	103 58W
Goldendale	**53**	45 49N	120 50W
Goldfield, Iowa	**23**	42 44N	93 55W
Goldfield, Nev.	**35**	37 42N	117 14W
Goldfields	**63**	59 28N	108 29W
Goldonna	**25**	32 1N	92 54W
Goldsand L.	**63**	57 2N	101 8W
Goldsboro, Md.	**27**	39 2N	75 47W
Goldsboro, N.C.	**40**	35 23N	77 59W
Goldsby	**43**	35 9N	97 28W
Goldsmith	**50**	31 59N	102 37W
Goldston	**40**	35 36N	79 20W
Goldthwaite	**51**	31 27N	98 34W
Golęniów	**88**	53 35N	14 50 E
Goleta	**15**	34 27N	119 50W
Golfito	**66**	8 41N	83 5W
Goliad	**51**	28 40N	97 23W
Goliad County ◇	**51**	28 45N	97 25W
Golovin	**11**	64 33N	163 2W
Golspie	**84**	57 58N	3 58W
Goltry	**43**	36 32N	98 9W
Golva	**41**	46 44N	103 59W
Golyam Perelik	**95**	41 36N	24 33 E
Golyama Kamchiya →	**95**	43 10N	27 55 E
Goma	**122**	2 11 S	29 18 E
Gomel	**98**	52 28N	31 0 E
Gomera	**120**	28 7N	17 14W
Gómez Palacio	**64**	25 40N	104 0W
Gomogomo	**111**	6 39 S	134 43 E
Gomoh	**109**	23 52N	86 10 E
Gompa = Ganta	**120**	7 15N	8 59W
Gonābād	**107**	34 15N	58 45 E
Gonaïves	**67**	19 20N	72 42W
Gonâve, G. de la	**67**	19 29N	72 42W
Gonâve, Î. de la	**67**	18 45N	73 0W
Gonbab-e Kāvūs	**107**	37 20N	55 25 E
Gonda	**109**	27 9N	81 58 E
Gonder	**121**	12 39N	37 30 E
Gondia	**108**	21 23N	80 10 E
Gonghe	**113**	36 18N	100 32 E
Goniri	**121**	11 30N	12 15 E
Gonvick	**30**	47 44N	95 31W
Gonzales, Calif.	**14**	36 30N	121 26W
Gonzales, La.	**25**	30 14N	90 55W
Gonzales, Tex.	**51**	29 30N	97 27W
Gonzales County ◇	**51**	29 26N	97 32W
González Chaves	**76**	38 2 S	60 5W
Goochland	**54**	37 41N	77 53W
Goochland County ◇	**54**	37 41N	77 53W
Good Hope	**21**	40 33N	90 41W
Good Hope, C. of = Goeie Hoop, Kaap die	**123**	34 24 S	18 30 E
Good Thunder	**30**	44 0N	94 4W
Goodell	**23**	42 55N	93 37W
Gooderham	**60**	44 54N	78 21W
Goodeve	**63**	51 4N	103 10W
Goodhue	**30**	44 24N	92 37W
Goodhue County ◇	**30**	44 25N	92 45W
Gooding	**20**	42 56N	114 43W
Gooding County ◇	**20**	43 0N	115 0W
Goodland, Ind.	**22**	40 46N	87 18W
Goodland, Kans.	**24**	39 21N	101 43W
Goodlett	**51**	34 20N	99 53W
Goodlettsville	**48**	36 19N	86 43W

Goodman Grass

Goodman, Miss. 31 32 58N 89 55W
Goodman, Mo. 32 36 44N 94 25W
Goodman, Wis. 55 45 38N 88 21W
Goodnews Bay 11 59 7N 161 35W
Goodnight 50 35 2N 101 11W
Goodrich, Colo. 16 40 20N 104 7W
Goodrich, N. Dak. 41 47 29N 100 8W
Goodrich, Tex. 51 30 36N 94 57W
Goodridge 30 48 9N 95 48W
Goodsoil 63 54 24N 109 13W
Goodsprings 35 35 50N 115 26W
Goodwater 10 33 4N 86 3W
Goodwell 43 36 36N 101 38W
Goodyear 12 33 26N 112 21W
Goole 82 53 42N 0 52W
Goondiwindi 127 28 30 S 150 21 E
Goor 87 52 13N 6 33 E
Goose →, Canada 61 53 20N 60 35W
Goose →, U.S.A. 41 47 28N 96 52W
Goose Bay 61 53 15N 60 20W
Goose Creek 46 32 59N 80 2W
Goose L. 14 41 56N 120 26W
Gop 108 22 5N 69 50 E
Gorakhpur 109 26 47N 83 23 E
Gorda, Punta, Nic. 66 14 20N 83 10W
Gorda, Punta, U.S.A. 14 40 16N 124 22W
Gordo 10 33 19N 87 54W
Gordon, Ga. 18 32 54N 83 20W
Gordon, Nebr. 34 42 48N 102 12W
Gordon, Ohio 42 39 56N 84 31W
Gordon, Tex. 51 32 33N 98 22W
Gordon, Wis. 55 46 15N 91 48W
Gordon, I. 78 54 55 S 69 30W
Gordon County 18 34 30N 84 50W
Gordon Cr. → 34 42 49N 100 44W
Gordon Downs 126 18 48 S 128 33 E
Gordon L., Alta., Canada 63 56 30N 110 25W
Gordon L., N.W.T., Canada 62 63 5N 113 11W
Gordonsville 54 38 9N 78 11W
Gordonville, Mo. 32 37 19N 89 41W
Gordonville, Tex. 51 33 48N 96 51W
Goré, Chad 121 7 59N 16 31 E
Gore, Ethiopia 121 8 12N 35 32 E
Gore, N.Z. 128 46 5 S 168 58 E
Gore, U.S.A. 43 35 32N 95 7W
Gore Bay 60 45 57N 82 28W
Gore Mt. 36 44 55N 71 48W
Goree 51 33 28N 99 31W
Goreville 21 37 33N 88 58W
Gorey 85 52 41N 6 18W
Gorgān 107 36 55N 54 30 E
Gorgona, I. 72 3 0N 78 10W
Gorham, Ill. 21 37 43N 89 29W
Gorham, Kans. 24 38 53N 99 1W
Gorham, Maine 26 43 41N 70 26W
Gorham, N.H. 36 44 23N 71 10W
Gorin 32 40 22N 92 1W
Gorinchem 87 51 50N 4 59 E
Gorinhatã 75 19 15 S 49 45W
Gorízia 94 45 56N 13 37 E
Gorki = Gorkiy 98 56 20N 44 0 E
Gorkiy 98 56 20N 44 0 E
Gorkovskoye Vdkhr. 98 57 2N 43 4 E
Görlitz 88 51 10N 14 59 E
Gorlovka 99 48 19N 38 5 E
Gorman 51 32 12N 98 41W
Gorna Oryakhovitsa 95 43 7N 25 40 E
Gorno Ablanovo 95 43 37N 25 43 E
Gorno-Altaysk 100 51 50N 86 5 E
Gorno Slinkino 100 60 5N 70 0 E
Gornyatski 98 67 32N 64 3 E
Gornyi 116 44 57N 133 59 E
Gorontalo 111 0 35N 123 5 E
Gort 85 53 4N 8 50W
Gortner 27 39 20N 79 24W
Gorum 25 31 26N 92 56W
Gorzów Wielkopolski 88 52 43N 15 15 E
Goshen, Calif. 15 36 21N 119 25W
Goshen, Conn. 28 41 50N 73 14W
Goshen, Ind. 22 41 35N 85 50W
Goshen, N.J. 37 39 8N 74 51W
Goshen, N.Y. 39 41 24N 74 20W
Goshen, Oreg. 44 43 58N 123 2W
Goshen, Utah 52 39 57N 111 54W
Goshen County ◇ 56 42 0N 104 10W
Goshogawara 116 40 48N 140 27 E
Goshute Indian Reservation 35 39 50N 114 5W
Goshute L. 35 40 9N 114 42W
Goshute Mts. 35 40 15N 114 19W
Goshute Valley 35 40 45N 114 20W
Goslar 88 51 55N 10 23 E
Gosnell 13 35 58N 89 58W
Gosper County ◇ 34 40 30N 99 50W
Gospič 94 44 35N 15 23 E
Gosport, U.K. 83 50 48N 1 8W
Gosport, U.S.A. 22 39 21N 86 40W
Goss 31 31 21N 89 53W
Gossville 36 43 12N 71 22W
Göta kanal 97 58 50N 13 58 E
Gotebo 43 35 4N 98 53W
Göteborg 97 57 43N 11 59 E
Göteborgs och Bohus län □ 97 58 30N 11 30 E
Gotha 88 50 56N 10 42 E
Gotham 55 43 13N 90 18W
Gothenburg 34 40 56N 100 10W
Gotland 97 57 30N 18 33 E
Gotse Delchev 95 41 43N 23 46 E
Gotska Sandön 97 58 24N 19 15 E
Gōtsu 117 35 0N 132 14 E
Göttingen 88 51 31N 9 55 E
Gottwaldov 89 49 14N 17 40 E
Goubangzi 114 41 20N 121 52 E
Gouda 87 52 1N 4 42 E
Gough 18 33 6N 82 14W
Gough I. 2 40 10 S 9 45W
Gouin Rés. 60 48 35N 74 40W
Goulburn 127 34 44 S 149 44 E
Goulburn Is. 126 11 40 S 133 20 E
Gould, Ark. 13 33 59N 91 34W
Gould, Okla. 43 34 40N 99 47W
Gould City 29 46 6N 85 42W
Goulds 17 25 33N 80 23W
Gounou-Gaya 121 9 38N 15 31 E
Gouri 121 19 36N 19 36 E
Gourma Rharous 120 16 55N 1 50W
Gouvêa 75 18 27 S 43 44W
Gouverneur 39 44 20N 75 28W
Govan, Canada 63 51 20N 105 0W
Govan, U.S.A. 46 33 13N 81 11W
Gove, Australia 127 12 25 S 136 55 E
Gove, U.S.A. 24 38 58N 100 29W
Gove County ◇ 24 38 50N 100 30W
Governador Valadares 75 18 15 S 41 57W
Governor's Harbour 66 25 10N 76 14W
Gowanda 39 42 28N 78 56W
Gowd-e Zirreh 107 29 45N 62 0 E
Gower 32 39 37N 94 36W
Gower, The 83 51 35N 4 10W
Gowna, L. 85 53 52N 7 35W
Gowrie 23 42 17N 94 17W
Gowrie, Carse of 84 56 30N 3 10W
Goya 76 29 10 S 59 10W
Goyllarisquisga 72 10 31 S 76 24W
Goz Beïda 121 12 10N 21 20 E
Gozo 94 36 0N 14 13 E
Graaff-Reinet 123 32 13 S 24 32 E
Gračac 94 44 18N 15 57 E
Grace 20 42 35N 111 44W
Gracemont 43 35 11N 98 16W
Graceville, Fla. 17 30 58N 85 31W
Graceville, Minn. 30 45 34N 96 26W
Gracewood 18 33 22N 82 2W
Gracey 48 36 53N 87 40W
Gracias a Dios, C. 66 15 0N 83 10W
Gradaús 74 7 43 S 51 11W
Gradaús, Serra dos 74 8 0 S 50 45W
Gradets 95 42 46N 26 30 E
Grado 91 43 23N 6 4W
Grady, Ala. 10 31 59N 86 3W
Grady, Ark. 13 34 5N 91 42W
Grady, N. Mex. 38 34 49N 103 19W
Grady County ◇, Ga. 18 30 50N 84 15W
Grady County ◇, Okla. 43 35 0N 97 50W
Gradyville 49 37 4N 85 25W
Graeca, Lacul 95 44 5N 26 10 E
Graénalon, L. 96 64 10N 17 20W
Graettinger 23 43 14N 94 45W
Graford 51 32 56N 98 14W
Grafton, Australia 127 29 38 S 152 58 E
Grafton, Ill. 21 38 58N 90 26W
Grafton, Iowa 23 43 20N 93 4W
Grafton, Mass. 28 42 12N 71 41W
Grafton, N. Dak. 41 48 25N 97 25W
Grafton, N.H. 36 43 34N 71 57W
Grafton, Ohio 42 41 16N 82 4W
Grafton, Vt. 36 43 10N 72 37W
Grafton, W. Va. 54 39 21N 80 2W
Grafton, Wis. 55 43 19N 87 57W
Grafton, C. 127 16 51 S 146 0 E
Grafton County ◇ 36 43 50N 71 45W
Graham, Canada 60 49 20N 90 30W
Graham, Ga. 18 31 50N 82 30W
Graham, N.C. 40 36 5N 79 25W
Graham, Tex. 51 33 6N 98 35W
Graham → 62 56 31N 122 17W
Graham, Mt. 12 32 42N 109 52W
Graham Bell, Os. 100 80 5N 70 0 E
Graham County ◇, Ariz. 12 33 0N 110 0W
Graham County ◇, Kans. 24 39 20N 99 45W
Graham County ◇, N.C. 40 35 20N 83 50W
Graham I. 62 53 40N 132 30W
Graham L. 26 44 39N 68 24W
Graham Land 5 65 0 S 64 0W
Grahamdale 63 51 23N 98 30W
Grahamstown 123 33 19 S 26 31 E
Grain Coast 118 4 20N 10 0W
Grainfield 24 39 7N 100 28W
Grainger County ◇ 49 36 17N 83 31W
Grainola 43 36 57N 96 39W
Grajaú 74 5 50 S 46 4W
Grajaú → 74 3 41 S 44 48W
Grambling 25 32 32N 92 43W
Gramercy 25 30 4N 90 42W
Grampian 45 40 58N 78 37W
Grampian □ 84 57 0N 3 0W
Grampian Mts. 84 56 50N 4 0W
Gran → 71 4 1N 55 30W
Gran Altiplanicie Central 78 49 0 S 69 30W
Gran Canaria 120 27 55N 15 35W
Gran Chaco 76 25 0 S 61 0W
Gran Paradiso 94 45 33N 7 17 E
Gran Sabana, La 71 5 30N 61 30W
Gran Sasso d'Italia 94 42 25N 13 30 E
Granada, Nic. 66 11 58N 86 0W
Granada, Spain 91 37 10N 3 35W
Granada, Colo. 16 38 4N 102 19W
Granada, Minn. 30 43 42N 94 21W
Granard 85 53 47N 7 30W
Granbury 51 32 27N 97 47W
Granby, Canada 60 45 25N 72 45W
Granby, Colo. 16 40 5N 105 56W
Granby, Conn. 28 41 57N 72 47W
Granby, Mo. 32 36 55N 94 15W
Granby, L. 16 40 9N 105 52W
Grand →, Mich. 29 43 4N 86 15W
Grand →, Mo. 32 39 23N 93 7W
Grand →, S. Dak. 47 45 40N 100 45W
Grand Bahama 66 26 40N 78 30W
Grand Bank 61 47 6N 55 48W
Grand Bassam 120 5 10N 3 49W
Grand Bay 10 30 29N 88 21W
Grand Blanc 29 42 56N 83 38W
Grand-Bourge 67 15 53N 61 19W
Grand Cane 25 32 5N 93 49W
Grand Canyon 12 36 3N 112 9W
Grand Canyon National Park 12 36 15N 112 30W
Grand Cayman 66 19 20N 81 20W
Grand Chenier 25 29 46N 92 58W
Grand Coulee 53 47 57N 119 0W
Grand Coulee Dam 53 47 57N 118 59W
Grand County ◇, Colo. 16 40 10N 106 15W
Grand County ◇, Utah 52 39 0N 109 30W
Grand Falls 61 48 56N 55 40W
Grand Forks, Canada 62 49 0N 118 30W
Grand Forks, U.S.A. 41 47 55N 97 3W
Grand Forks County ◇ 41 47 55N 97 22W
Grand Haven 29 43 4N 86 13W
Grand I., La. 25 29 10N 90 0W
Grand I., Mich. 29 46 31N 86 40W
Grand Island 34 40 55N 98 21W
Grand Isle, La. 25 29 14N 90 0W
Grand Isle, Vt. 36 44 43N 73 18W
Grand Isle County ◇ 36 44 57N 73 17W
Grand Junction, Colo. 16 39 4N 108 33W
Grand Junction, Iowa 23 42 2N 94 14W
Grand L., N.B., Canada 61 45 57N 66 7W
Grand L., Newf., Canada 61 49 0N 57 30W
Grand L., Newf., Canada 61 53 40N 60 30W
Grand L., La. 25 29 55N 92 47W
Grand L., Maine 26 45 40N 67 50W
Grand L., Ohio 42 40 32N 84 25W
Grand Lac Victoria 60 47 35N 77 35W
Grand Lahou 120 5 10N 5 0W
Grand Lake, Colo. 16 40 15N 105 49W
Grand Lake, La. 25 30 2N 93 17W
Grand Lake Matagamon 26 46 12N 68 47W
Grand Lake Seboeis 26 46 18N 68 39W
Grand Ledge 29 42 45N 84 45W
Grand Manan Channel 26 44 40N 67 0W
Grand Manan I. 61 44 45N 66 52W
Grand Marais, Canada 60 47 45N 90 25W
Grand Marais, Mich. 29 46 40N 85 59W
Grand Marais, Minn. 30 47 45N 90 20W
Grand Meadow 30 43 42N 92 34W
Grand Mère 60 46 36N 72 40W
Grand Mesa 16 39 0N 108 15W
Grand Mesa National Forest 16 39 20N 107 50W
Grand Portage 30 47 58N 89 41W
Grand Portage Indian
Reservation 30 47 55N 89 50W
Grand Prairie 51 32 47N 97 0W
Grand Rapids, Canada 63 53 12N 99 19W
Grand Rapids, Mich. 29 42 58N 85 40W
Grand Rapids, Minn. 30 47 14N 93 31W
Grand Rapids, Ohio 42 41 25N 83 52W
Grand Ridge, Fla. 17 30 43N 85 1W
Grand Ridge, Ill. 21 41 14N 88 50W
Grand River 23 40 49N 93 58W
Grand Rivers 48 37 1N 88 14W
Grand Ronde 44 45 4N 123 37W
Grand Rounde → 53 46 5N 116 59W
Grand Saline 51 32 41N 95 43W
Grand Santi 71 4 20N 54 24W
Grand Teton Mt. 56 43 44N 110 48W
Grand Teton National Park 56 43 50N 110 50W
Grand Tower 21 37 38N 89 30W
Grand Traverse B. 29 45 5N 85 35W
Grand Traverse County ◇ 29 44 40N 85 35W
Grand Valley 16 39 27N 108 3W
Grand View, Canada 63 51 10N 100 42W
Grand View, U.S.A. 20 42 59N 116 6W
Grand Wash Cliffs 12 36 0N 113 50W
Grande →, Jujuy,
Argentina 76 24 20 S 65 2W
Grande →, Mendoza,
Argentina 76 36 52 S 69 45W
Grande →, Bolivia 73 15 51 S 64 39W
Grande →, Bahia, Brazil 74 11 30 S 44 30W
Grande →, Minas Gerais,
Brazil 75 20 6 S 51 4W
Grande →, Venezuela 71 8 36N 61 39W
Grande, B. 78 50 30 S 68 20W
Grande, Coxilha 77 28 18 S 51 30W
Grande, I. 75 23 9 S 44 14W
Grande, Rio → 50 25 58N 97 9W
Grande, Serra, Goiás, Brazil 74 11 15 S 46 30W
Grande, Serra, Piauí, Brazil 74 8 0 S 45 0W
Grande Baie 61 48 19N 70 52W
Grande Baleine, R. de la → 60 55 16N 77 47W
Grande Cache 62 53 53N 119 8W
Grande de Anasco, Rio → 57 18 16N 67 11W
Grande de Arecibo, Rio → 57 18 29N 66 43W
Grande de Loiza, Rio → 57 18 26N 65 53W
Grande de Manati, Rio → 57 18 29N 66 32W
Grande de Santiago → 64 21 20N 105 50W
Grande-Entrée 61 47 30N 61 40W
Grande Prairie 62 55 10N 118 50W
Grande-Rivière 61 48 26N 64 30W
Grande Ronde → 44 46 5N 116 59W
Grande-Vallée 61 49 14N 65 8W
Grandes-Bergeronnes 61 48 16N 69 35W
Grandfalls 50 31 20N 102 51W
Grandfield 43 34 14N 98 41W
Grandin, Mo. 32 36 50N 90 50W
Grandin, N. Dak. 41 47 14N 97 0W
Grandoe Mines 62 56 29N 129 54W
Grandview, Iowa 23 41 16N 91 11W
Grandview, Mo. 32 38 53N 94 32W
Grandview, Tex. 51 32 16N 97 11W
Grandview, Wash. 53 46 15N 119 54W
Grandville 29 42 54N 85 46W
Graneros 76 34 5 S 70 45W
Grangemouth 84 56 1N 3 43W
Granger, Iowa 23 41 46N 93 49W
Granger, Tex. 51 30 43N 97 26W
Granger, Wash. 53 46 21N 120 11W
Granger, Wyo. 56 41 35N 109 58W
Grangeville 20 45 56N 116 7W
Granite, Colo. 16 39 3N 106 16W
Granite, Okla. 43 34 58N 99 23W
Granite City 21 38 42N 90 9W
Granite County ◇ 33 46 25N 113 30W
Granite Falls, Minn. 30 44 49N 95 33W
Granite Falls, N.C. 40 35 48N 81 26W
Granite Falls, Wash. 53 48 5N 121 58W
Granite Mts., Ariz. 12 32 20N 113 20W
Granite Mts., Wyo. 56 42 45N 107 40W
Granite Pass 56 44 38N 107 30W
Granite Peak, Mont. 33 45 10N 109 48W
Granite Peak, Nev. 35 41 40N 117 35W
Granite Pt. 29 46 47N 87 36W
Granite Quarry 40 35 37N 80 26W
Granite Range 35 40 55N 119 25W
Graniteville, S.C. 46 33 34N 81 49W
Graniteville, Vt. 36 44 8N 72 29W
Granity 128 41 39 S 171 51 E
Granja 74 3 7 S 40 50W
Granja de Torrehermosa 91 38 19N 5 35W
Grannis 13 34 14N 94 20W
Grano 41 48 37N 101 35W
Granollers 91 41 39N 2 18 E
Grant, Colo. 16 39 28N 105 40W
Grant, Fla. 17 27 56N 80 32W
Grant, Iowa 23 41 9N 94 59W
Grant, La. 25 30 47N 92 57W
Grant, Mich. 29 43 20N 85 51W
Grant, Mont. 33 45 1N 113 4W
Grant, Nebr. 34 40 50N 101 43W
Grant, Okla. 43 33 57N 95 31W
Grant, Mt. 35 38 34N 118 48W
Grant City 32 40 29N 94 25W
Grant County ◇, Ark. 13 34 19N 92 24W
Grant County ◇, Ind. 22 40 30N 85 40W
Grant County ◇, Kans. 24 37 30N 101 15W
Grant County ◇, Ky. 49 38 35N 84 35W
Grant County ◇, Minn. 30 45 55N 96 0W
Grant County ◇, N. Dak. 41 46 15N 101 30W
Grant County ◇, N. Mex. 38 33 0N 108 30W
Grant County ◇, Nebr. 34 41 50N 101 45W
Grant County ◇, Okla. 43 36 50N 97 45W
Grant County ◇, Oreg. 44 44 30N 119 0W
Grant County ◇, S. Dak. 47 45 12N 96 47W
Grant County ◇, W. Va. 54 39 4N 79 4W
Grant County ◇, Wash. 53 47 10N 119 30W
Grant County ◇, Wis. 55 42 50N 90 45W
Grant Parish ◇ 25 31 32N 92 25W
Grant Park 21 41 14N 87 39W
Grant Range 35 38 30N 115 25W
Grantham, U.K. 82 52 55N 0 39W
Grantham, U.S.A. 36 43 29N 72 8W
Grantown-on-Spey 84 57 19N 3 36W
Grants 38 35 9N 107 52W
Grants Pass 44 42 26N 123 19W
Grantsburg 55 45 47N 92 41W
Grantsdale 33 46 12N 114 9W
Grantsville, Md. 27 39 42N 79 12W
Grantsville, Utah 52 40 36N 112 28W
Grantsville, W. Va. 54 38 55N 81 6W
Grantville 18 33 14N 84 50W
Granville, France 90 48 50N 1 35W
Granville, Ill. 21 41 16N 89 14W
Granville, Mass. 28 42 4N 72 52W
Granville, N. Dak. 41 48 16N 100 47W
Granville, N.Y. 39 43 24N 73 16W
Granville, Ohio 42 40 4N 82 31W
Granville, Vt. 36 43 58N 72 51W
Granville County ◇ 40 36 20N 78 40W
Granville L. 63 56 18N 100 30W
Grapeland 51 31 30N 95 29W
Grapevine L. 51 32 58N 97 4W
Gras, L. de 58 64 30N 110 30W
Grasmere 20 42 23N 115 53W
Grasonville 27 38 57N 76 13W
Grass → 63 56 3N 96 33W

Grass Creek Grundy

Grass Creek 56 43 56N 108 39W
Grass Lake 29 42 15N 84 13W
Grass River Prov. Park 63 54 40N 100 50W
Grass Valley, Calif. 14 39 13N 121 4W
Grass Valley, Oreg. 44 45 22N 120 47W
Grasse 90 43 38N 6 56 E
Grassrange 33 47 2N 108 48W
Grasston 30 45 48N 93 9W
Grassy Butte 41 47 24N 103 15W
Gratiot 55 42 35N 90 1W
Gratiot County ◇ 29 43 15N 84 40W
Gratz 49 38 28N 84 57W
Gravatá 74 8 10 S 35 29W
Gravelbourg 63 49 50N 106 35W
Gravelly 13 34 53N 93 41W
's-Gravenhage 87 52 7N 4 17 E
Graves County ◇ 48 36 45N 88 40W
Gravesend 83 51 25N 0 22 E
Gravette 13 36 25N 94 27W
Gravity 23 40 46N 94 45W
Gravois, Pointe-à- 67 16 15N 73 56W
Gravois Mills 32 38 19N 92 49W
Gray, Ga. 18 33 1N 83 32W
Gray, Iowa 23 41 49N 94 59W
Gray, Ky. 49 36 57N 84 0W
Gray, Okla. 43 36 34N 100 49W
Gray County ◇, Kans. 24 37 40N 100 20W
Gray County ◇, Tex. 50 35 26N 100 48W
Gray Court 46 34 36N 82 7W
Gray Hawk 49 37 24N 83 56W
Grayland 53 46 49N 124 6W
Grayling, Alaska 11 62 57N 160 3W
Grayling, Mich. 29 44 40N 84 43W
Grayling → 62 59 21N 125 0W
Grays Harbor 53 46 59N 124 1W
Grays Harbor County ◇ 53 47 15N 123 45W
Grays L. 20 43 4N 111 26W
Grays River 53 46 21N 123 37W
Grayslake 21 42 21N 88 2W
Grayson, Canada 63 50 45N 102 40W
Grayson, Ky. 49 38 20N 82 57W
Grayson, Okla. 43 35 32N 95 51W
Grayson County ◇, Ky. 48 37 25N 86 20W
Grayson County ◇, Tex. 51 33 38N 96 36W
Grayson County ◇, Va. 54 36 40N 81 10W
Graysville 49 35 27N 85 8W
Grayton 27 38 26N 77 13W
Grayville 21 38 16N 88 0W
Graz 88 47 4N 15 27 E
Greasy L. 62 62 55N 122 12W
Great Abaco I. 66 26 25N 77 10W
Great Australia Basin 127 26 0 S 140 0 E
Great Australian Bight 126 33 30 S 130 0 E
Great B. 36 43 5N 70 53W
Great Bahama Bank 66 23 15N 78 0W
Great Barrier I. 128 36 11 S 175 25 E
Great Barrier Reef 127 18 0 S 146 50 E
Great Barrington 28 42 12N 73 22W
Great Basin 35 40 0N 117 0W
Great Bay 37 39 30N 74 25W
Great Bear → 58 65 0N 124 0W
Great Bear L. 58 65 30N 120 0W
Great Bend, Kans. 24 38 22N 98 46W
Great Bend, N. Dak. 41 46 9N 96 48W
Great Bend, Pa. 45 41 58N 75 45W
Great Blasket I. 85 52 5N 10 30W
Great Central 62 49 20N 125 10W
Great Divide Basin 56 42 0N 108 0W
Great Dividing Ra. 127 23 0 S 146 0 E
Great Egg Harbor → 37 39 18N 74 40W
Great Exuma I. 66 23 30N 75 50W
Great Falls, Canada 63 50 27N 96 1W
Great Falls, Mont. 33 47 30N 111 17W
Great Falls, S.C. 46 34 34N 80 54W
Great Guana Cay 66 24 0N 76 20W
Great Harbour Deep 61 50 25N 56 32W
Great I. 63 58 53N 96 35W
Great Inagua I. 67 21 0N 73 20W
Great Indian Desert = Thar Desert 108 28 0N 72 0 E
Great L. 40 34 49N 77 2W
Great Lake 127 41 50 S 146 40 E
Great Miama → 42 39 7N 84 49W
Great Mills 27 38 14N 76 30W
Great Neck 39 40 48N 73 44W
Great Orme's Head 82 53 20N 3 52W
Great Ouse → 82 52 47N 0 22 E
Great Plains 6 47 0N 105 0W
Great Plains Reservoir 16 38 15N 102 43W
Great Pond 26 44 57N 68 19W
Great Pt. 28 41 24N 70 3W
Great Quitticas Pond 28 41 48N 70 54W
Great Ruaha → 122 7 56 S 37 52 E
Great Saint Bernard P. 88 45 50N 7 10 E
Great Salt L. 52 41 15N 112 40W
Great Salt Lake Desert 52 40 50N 113 30W
Great Salt Plains L. 43 36 45N 98 8W
Great Sand Dunes National Monument 16 37 48N 105 45W
Great Sandy Desert, Australia 126 21 0 S 124 0 E
Great Sandy Desert, U.S.A. 44 43 35N 120 15W
Great Sitkin I. 11 52 3N 176 6W
Great Slave L. 62 61 23N 115 38W
Great Smoky Mts. 49 35 40N 83 40W
Great Smoky Mts. Nat. Pk. 49 35 40N 83 40W
Great South Bay 39 40 40N 73 15W
Great Stour = Stour → 83 51 15N 1 20 E
Great Stour → 83 51 15N 1 20 E
Great Victoria Des. 126 29 30 S 126 30 E
Great Wall 114 38 30N 109 30 E
Great Wass I. 26 44 29N 67 36W
Great Whernside 82 54 9N 1 59W
Great Yarmouth 82 52 40N 1 45 E
Greater Antilles 67 17 40N 74 0W
Greater London □ 83 51 30N 0 5W
Greater Manchester □ 82 53 30N 2 15W
Greater Sunda Is. 110 7 0 S 112 0 E
Gredos, Sierra de 91 40 20N 5 0W
Greece 39 43 13N 77 41W
Greece ■ 95 40 0N 23 0 E
Greeley, Colo. 16 40 25N 104 42W
Greeley, Iowa 23 42 35N 91 21W
Greeley, Kans. 24 38 22N 95 8W
Greeley, Nebr. 34 41 33N 98 32W
Greeley County ◇, Kans. 24 38 30N 101 45W
Greeley County ◇, Nebr. 34 41 30N 98 30W
Greeleyville 46 33 40N 79 59W
Green 24 39 26N 97 0W
Green →, Ill. 21 41 28N 90 23W
Green →, Ky. 48 37 54N 87 30W
Green →, Utah 52 38 11N 109 53W
Green B. 55 46 0N 87 30W
Green Bank, N.J. 37 39 40N 74 36W
Green Bank, W. Va. 54 38 25N 79 50W
Green Bay 55 44 31N 88 0W
Green Camp 42 40 32N 83 13W
Green City 32 40 16N 92 57W
Green County ◇, Ky. 49 37 15N 85 35W
Green County ◇, Wis. 55 42 45N 89 40W
Green Cove Springs 17 29 59N 81 42W
Green Creek 37 39 3N 74 54W
Green Forest 13 36 20N 93 26W
Green Island, N.Z. 128 45 55 S 170 26 E
Green Island, U.S.A. 23 42 9N 90 20W
Green Isle 30 44 41N 94 1W
Green L., Minn. 30 45 15N 94 54W
Green L., Wis. 55 43 49N 89 0W
Green Lake 55 43 51N 88 58W
Green Lake County ◇ 55 43 45N 89 0W
Green Mountain National Forest 36 44 0N 73 0W
Green Mountain Reservoir 16 39 53N 106 20W
Green Mts. 36 43 45N 72 45W
Green Peter L. 44 44 26N 122 37W
Green Pond 46 32 44N 80 37W
Green Ridge 32 38 37N 93 25W
Green River, Utah 52 38 59N 110 10W
Green River, Wyo. 56 41 32N 109 28W
Green River L. 49 37 15N 85 15W
Green Sea 46 34 8N 78 59W
Green Swamp 40 34 15N 78 25W
Green Valley, Ariz. 12 31 52N 110 56W
Green Valley, Ill. 21 40 24N 89 38W
Greenacres City 17 26 38N 80 7W
Greenback 49 35 40N 84 10W
Greenbelt 27 39 0N 76 53W
Greenbrier, Ark. 13 35 14N 92 23W
Greenbrier, Tenn. 48 36 26N 86 48W
Greenbrier → 54 37 39N 80 53W
Greenbrier County ◇ 54 37 56N 80 23W
Greenbrier Estates 40 35 42N 78 38W
Greenbush 30 48 42N 96 11W
Greencastle, Ind. 22 39 38N 86 52W
Greencastle, Pa. 45 39 47N 77 44W
Greendale 22 39 7N 84 52W
Greene, Iowa 23 42 54N 92 48W
Greene, Maine 26 44 12N 70 8W
Greene, N.Y. 39 42 20N 75 46W
Greene County ◇, Ala. 10 32 50N 87 53W
Greene County ◇, Ark. 13 36 3N 90 29W
Greene County ◇, Ga. 18 33 30N 83 5W
Greene County ◇, Ill. 21 39 20N 90 20W
Greene County ◇, Ind. 22 39 0N 87 0W
Greene County ◇, Iowa 23 42 0N 94 25W
Greene County ◇, Miss. 31 31 10N 88 45W
Greene County ◇, Mo. 32 37 15N 93 20W
Greene County ◇, N.C. 40 35 30N 77 40W
Greene County ◇, N.Y. 39 42 20N 74 0W
Greene County ◇, Ohio 42 39 41N 83 56W
Greene County ◇, Pa. 45 39 55N 80 5W
Greene County ◇, Tenn. 49 36 10N 82 50W
Greene County ◇, Va. 54 38 18N 78 26W
Greeneville 49 36 10N 82 50W
Greenfield, Calif. 15 36 19N 121 15W
Greenfield, Ill. 21 39 21N 90 12W
Greenfield, Ind. 22 39 47N 85 46W
Greenfield, Iowa 23 41 18N 94 28W
Greenfield, Mass. 28 42 35N 72 36W
Greenfield, Mo. 32 37 25N 93 51W
Greenfield, N.H. 36 42 55N 71 51W
Greenfield, Ohio 42 39 21N 83 23W
Greenfield, Okla. 43 35 44N 98 23W
Greenfield, Tenn. 48 36 9N 88 48W
Greenhills 42 39 16N 84 32W
Greenland, Mich. 29 46 47N 89 6W
Greenland, N.H. 36 43 4N 70 50W
Greenland □ 4 66 0N 45 0W
Greenland Sea 4 73 0N 10 0W
Greenleaf 24 39 44N 96 59W
Greenlee County ◇ 12 33 0N 109 15W
Greenock 84 55 57N 4 46W
Greenore 85 54 2N 6 8W
Greenore Pt. 85 52 15N 6 20W
Greenough 33 46 55N 113 25W
Greenport 39 41 6N 72 22W
Greens Pk. 12 34 5N 109 33W
Greensboro, Ala. 10 32 42N 87 36W
Greensboro, Fla. 17 30 34N 84 45W
Greensboro, Ga. 18 33 35N 83 11W
Greensboro, Md. 27 38 58N 75 48W
Greensboro, N.C. 40 36 4N 79 48W
Greensboro, Vt. 36 44 36N 72 18W
Greensburg, Ind. 22 39 20N 85 29W
Greensburg, Kans. 24 37 36N 99 18W
Greensburg, Ky. 49 37 16N 85 30W
Greensburg, La. 25 30 50N 90 40W
Greensburg, Pa. 45 40 18N 79 33W
Greensville County ◇ 54 36 42N 77 32W
Greentown 22 40 29N 85 58W
Greenup, Ill. 21 39 15N 88 10W
Greenup, Ky. 49 38 35N 82 50W
Greenup County ◇ 49 38 30N 83 0W
Greenview 21 40 5N 89 44W
Greenville, Liberia 120 5 1N 9 6W
Greenville, Ala. 10 31 50N 86 38W
Greenville, Calif. 14 40 8N 120 57W
Greenville, Fla. 17 30 28N 83 38W
Greenville, Ga. 18 33 2N 84 43W
Greenville, Ill. 21 38 53N 89 25W
Greenville, Ky. 48 37 12N 87 11W
Greenville, Maine 26 45 28N 69 35W
Greenville, Mich. 29 43 11N 85 15W
Greenville, Miss. 31 33 24N 91 4W
Greenville, Mo. 32 37 8N 90 27W
Greenville, N.C. 40 35 37N 77 23W
Greenville, N.H. 36 42 46N 71 49W
Greenville, Ohio 42 40 6N 84 38W
Greenville, Pa. 45 41 24N 80 23W
Greenville, S.C. 46 34 51N 82 24W
Greenville, Tex. 51 33 8N 96 7W
Greenville, Wis. 55 44 18N 88 32W
Greenville County ◇ 46 34 50N 82 20W
Greenwald 30 45 36N 94 52W
Greenwater Lake Prov. Park 63 52 32N 103 30W
Greenway 13 36 21N 90 13W
Greenwich, U.K. 83 51 28N 0 0 E
Greenwich, Conn. 28 41 2N 73 38W
Greenwich, N.J. 37 39 24N 75 21W
Greenwich, N.Y. 39 43 5N 73 30W
Greenwich, Ohio 42 41 2N 82 31W
Greenwood, Canada 62 49 10N 118 40W
Greenwood, Ark. 13 35 13N 94 16W
Greenwood, Del. 27 38 49N 75 35W
Greenwood, Fla. 17 30 52N 85 10W
Greenwood, Ind. 22 39 37N 86 7W
Greenwood, Ky. 49 36 53N 84 30W
Greenwood, La. 25 32 27N 93 58W
Greenwood, Miss. 31 33 31N 90 11W
Greenwood, Nebr. 34 40 58N 96 27W
Greenwood, S.C. 46 34 12N 82 10W
Greenwood, Wis. 55 44 46N 90 36W
Greenwood County ◇, Kans. 24 37 45N 96 15W
Greenwood County ◇, S.C. 46 34 10N 82 5W
Greenwood L. 46 34 11N 81 54W
Greer, Idaho 20 46 24N 116 11W
Greer, Mo. 32 36 46N 91 21W
Greer, S.C. 46 34 56N 82 14W
Greer County ◇ 43 35 0N 99 35W
Greers Ferry L. 13 35 32N 92 10W
Greeson L. 13 34 9N 93 43W
Gregg County ◇ 51 32 30N 94 44W
Gregório → 72 6 50 S 70 46W
Gregory, Ark. 13 35 9N 91 21W
Gregory, Mich. 29 42 28N 84 5W
Gregory, S. Dak. 47 43 14N 99 26W
Gregory, Tex. 51 27 56N 97 18W
Gregory, L. 127 28 55 S 139 0 E
Gregory County ◇ 47 43 11N 99 18W
Gregory Lake 126 20 10 S 127 30 E
Gregory Ra. 127 19 30 S 143 40 E
Greifswald 88 54 6N 13 23 E
Gremikha 98 67 50N 39 40 E
Grenada, Calif. 14 41 39N 122 31W
Grenada, Miss. 31 33 47N 89 49W
Grenada ■ 67 12 10N 61 40W
Grenada County ◇ 31 33 47N 89 49W
Grenada L. 31 33 50N 89 47W
Grenadines, The 67 12 40N 61 20W
Grenen 97 57 44N 10 40 E
Grenfell 63 50 30N 102 56W
Grenoble 90 45 12N 5 42 E
Grenola 24 37 21N 96 27W
Grenora 41 48 37N 103 56W
Grenville, N. Mex. 38 36 36N 103 37W
Grenville, S. Dak. 47 45 28N 97 23W
Grenville, C. 127 12 0 S 143 13 E
Grenville Chan. 62 53 40N 129 46W
Gres, Pt. au 29 43 59N 83 41W
Gresham, Nebr. 34 41 2N 97 24W
Gresham, Oreg. 44 45 30N 122 26W
Gresham, S.C. 46 33 56N 79 25W
Gresik 111 7 13 S 112 38 E
Gressitt 54 37 29N 76 43W
Gresston 18 32 17N 83 15W
Gretna, Fla. 17 30 37N 84 40W
Gretna, La. 25 29 55N 90 4W
Gretna, Nebr. 34 41 8N 96 15W
Gretna, Va. 54 36 57N 79 22W
Gretna Green 84 55 0N 3 3W
Grevenmacher 87 49 41N 6 26 E
Grey → 128 42 27 S 171 12 E
Grey, C. 127 13 0 S 136 35 E
Grey Eagle 30 45 50N 94 45W
Grey Range 127 27 0 S 143 30 E
Grey Res. 61 48 20N 56 30W
Greybull 56 44 30N 108 3W
Greybull → 56 44 28N 108 3W
Greylock, Mt. 28 42 38N 73 10W
Greymouth 128 42 29 S 171 13 E
Greystone 16 40 37N 108 41W
Greytown, N.Z. 128 41 5 S 175 29 E
Greytown, S. Africa 123 29 1 S 30 36 E
Gribbell I. 62 53 23N 129 0W
Gridley, Calif. 14 39 22N 121 42W
Gridley, Ill. 21 40 45N 88 53W
Gridley, Kans. 24 38 6N 95 53W
Griffin, Ga. 18 33 15N 84 16W
Griffin, Ind. 22 38 12N 87 55W
Griffin, L. 17 28 52N 81 51W
Griffith, Australia 127 34 18 S 146 2 E
Griffith, U.S.A. 22 41 34N 87 26W
Griffithsville 54 38 14N 81 59W
Grifton 40 35 23N 77 26W
Griggs County ◇ 41 47 34N 98 21W
Griggsville 21 39 43N 90 43W
Grim, C. 127 40 45 S 144 45 E
Grimari 122 5 43N 20 6 E
Grimes 23 41 41N 93 47W
Grimes County ◇ 51 30 29N 95 59W
Grimesland 40 35 34N 77 11W
Grimsby 82 53 35N 0 5W
Grímsey 96 66 33N 18 0W
Grimshaw 62 56 10N 117 40W
Grimsley 49 36 16N 84 59W
Grimstad 97 58 22N 8 35 E
Grindu 95 44 44N 26 50 E
Grinnell, Iowa 23 41 45N 92 43W
Grinnell, Kans. 24 39 6N 100 38W
Gris Nez, C. 90 50 52N 1 35 E
Griswold 23 41 14N 95 8W
Grita, La 70 8 8N 71 59W
Groais I. 61 50 55N 55 35W
Grodno 98 53 42N 23 52 E
Grodzisk Wielkopolski 88 52 15N 16 22 E
Groesbeck 51 30 48N 96 31W
Grójec 89 51 50N 20 58 E
Grong 96 64 25N 12 8 E
Groningen, Neth. 87 53 15N 6 35 E
Groningen, Surinam 71 5 48N 55 28W
Groningen □ 87 53 16N 6 40 E
Groom 50 35 12N 101 6W
Groom L. 35 37 17N 115 48W
Groot-Brakrivier 123 34 2 S 22 18 E
Groot Karoo 123 32 35 S 23 0 E
Groote Eylandt 127 14 0 S 136 40 E
Grootfontein 123 19 31 S 18 6 E
Gros C. 62 61 59N 113 32W
Gros Ventre Range 56 43 12N 110 22W
Gross 34 42 57N 98 34W
Gross Glockner 88 47 5N 12 40 E
Grosse Pointe 29 42 24N 82 56W
Grosse Tete 25 30 25N 91 26W
Grossenhain 88 51 17N 13 32 E
Grosseto 94 42 45N 11 7 E
Groswater B. 61 54 20N 57 40W
Groton, Conn. 28 41 21N 72 5W
Groton, Mass. 28 42 37N 71 34W
Groton, N.Y. 39 42 36N 76 22W
Groton, S. Dak. 47 45 27N 98 6W
Groton, Vt. 36 44 12N 72 12W
Grottoes 54 38 16N 78 50W
Grouard Mission 62 55 33N 116 9W
Groundhog → 60 48 45N 82 58W
Grouse 20 43 41N 113 37W
Grouse Creek 52 41 42N 113 53W
Grouse Creek Mts. 52 41 30N 113 50W
Grovania 18 32 22N 83 40W
Grove 43 36 36N 94 46W
Grove City, Ohio 42 39 53N 83 6W
Grove City, Pa. 45 41 10N 80 5W
Grove Hill 10 31 42N 87 47W
Grove Place 57 17 43N 64 49W
Groveland, Calif. 14 37 50N 120 14W
Groveland, Fla. 17 28 34N 81 51W
Groveland, Mass. 28 42 46N 71 2W
Groveport 42 39 51N 82 53W
Grover, Colo. 16 40 52N 104 14W
Grover, S.C. 46 33 6N 80 36W
Grover, Utah 52 38 14N 111 21W
Grover City 15 35 7N 120 37W
Grover Hill 42 41 1N 84 29W
Groves 51 29 57N 93 54W
Grovespring 32 37 24N 92 37W
Groveton, N.H. 36 44 36N 71 31W
Groveton, Tex. 51 31 4N 95 8W
Grovetown 18 33 27N 82 12W
Growler Mts. 12 32 15N 113 0W
Groznyy 99 43 20N 45 45 E
Grudovo 95 42 21N 27 10 E
Grudziądz 89 53 30N 18 47 E
Grulla 50 26 16N 98 39W
Grünau 123 27 45 S 18 26 E
Grundy 54 37 17N 82 6W

Grundy Center Hajdúböszörmény

Grundy Center 23 42 22N 92 47W
Grundy County ◇, Ill. 21 41 20N 88 25W
Grundy County ◇, Iowa 23 42 25N 92 45W
Grundy County ◇, Mo. 32 40 5N 93 30W
Grundy County ◇, Tenn. 49 35 26N 85 44W
Gruver, Iowa 23 43 24N 94 42W
Gruver, Tex. 50 36 16N 101 24W
Gryazi 98 52 30N 39 58 E
Grygla 30 48 18N 95 37W
Grytviken 5 53 50 S 37 10W
Gu Achi 12 32 20N 112 2W
Gua 109 22 18N 85 20 E
Guacanayabo, G. de 66 20 40N 77 20W
Guacara 70 10 14N 67 53W
Guachípas → 76 25 40 S 65 30W
Guachiría → 70 5 27N 70 36W
Guadalajara, Mexico 64 20 40N 103 20W
Guadalajara, Spain 91 40 37N 3 12W
Guadalcanal 124 9 32 S 160 12 E
Guadales 76 34 30 S 67 55W
Guadalete → 91 36 35N 6 13W
Guadalhorce → 91 36 41N 4 27W
Guadalquivir → 91 36 47N 6 22W
Guadalupe = Guadeloupe ■ 67 16 20N 61 40W
Guadalupe, Brazil 74 6 44 S 43 47W
Guadalupe, U.S.A. 12 33 25N 111 55W
Guadalupe → 51 28 27N 96 47W
Guadalupe, Sierra de 91 39 28N 5 30W
Guadalupe Bravos 64 31 20N 106 10W
Guadalupe County ◇, N. Mex. 38 35 0N 104 45W
Guadalupe County ◇, Tex. 51 29 34N 97 58W
Guadalupe de los Reyes 64 24 10N 106 0W
Guadalupe I. 125 29 0N 118 50W
Guadalupe Mts. 38 32 15N 105 0W
Guadalupe Mts. Nat. Pk. 50 32 0N 104 30W
Guadalupe Peak 50 31 50N 104 52W
Guadalupe y Calvo 64 26 6N 106 58W
Guadalupita 38 36 8N 105 14W
Guadarrama, Sierra de 91 41 0N 4 0W
Guadeloupe ■ 67 16 20N 61 40W
Guadeloupe Passage 67 16 50N 62 15W
Guadiana → 91 37 14N 7 22W
Guadix 91 37 18N 3 11W
Guafo, Boca del 78 43 35 S 74 0W
Guafo, I. 78 43 35 S 74 50W
Guainía □ 70 2 30N 69 0W
Guainía → 70 2 1N 67 7W
Guaíra 77 24 5 S 54 10W
Guaira, La 70 10 36N 66 56W
Guaitecas, Islas 78 44 0 S 74 30W
Guajará-Mirim 73 10 50 S 65 20W
Guajataca, Lago de 57 18 24N 66 56W
Guajira □ 70 11 30N 72 30W
Guajira, La □ 70 11 30N 72 30W
Guajira, Pen. de la 70 12 0N 72 0W
Gualaceo 70 2 54 S 78 47W
Gualala 14 38 46N 123 32W
Gualán 66 15 8N 89 22W
Gualeguay 76 33 10 S 59 14W
Gualeguaychú 76 33 3 S 59 31W
Gualicho, Salina 78 40 25 S 65 20W
Gualjaina 78 42 45 S 70 30W
Guam 124 13 27N 144 45 E
Guamá 74 1 37 S 47 29W
Guamá → 74 1 29 S 48 30W
Guamblin, I. 78 44 50 S 75 0W
Guaminí 76 37 1 S 62 28W
Guamote 70 1 56 S 78 43W
Guampí, Sierra de 71 6 0N 65 35W
Guamúchil 64 25 25N 108 3W
Guan Xian 113 31 2N 103 38 E
Guanabacoa 66 23 8N 82 18W
Guanacaste, Cordillera del 66 10 40N 85 4W
Guanaceví 64 25 40N 106 0W
Guanahani = San Salvador 67 24 0N 74 40W
Guanajay 66 22 56N 82 42W
Guanajibo, Punta 57 18 10N 67 11W
Guanajuato 64 21 0N 101 20W
Guanajuato □ 64 20 40N 101 20W
Guanambi 75 14 13 S 42 47W
Guanare 70 8 42N 69 12W
Guanare → 70 8 13N 67 46W
Guandacol 76 29 30 S 68 40W
Guane 66 22 10N 84 7W
Guang'an 115 30 28N 106 35 E
Guangde 115 30 54N 119 25 E
Guangdong □ 115 23 0N 113 0 E
Guanghua 115 32 22N 111 38 E
Guangshun 115 26 8N 106 21 E
Guangxi Zhuangzu Zizhiqu □ 115 24 0N 109 0 E
Guangyuan 115 32 26N 105 51 E
Guangze 115 27 30N 117 12 E
Guangzhou 115 23 5N 113 10 E
Guanhães 75 18 47 S 42 57W
Guanica 57 17 59N 66 55W
Guanica, Laguna de 57 17 58N 66 0W
Guanipa → 71 9 56N 62 26W
Guano L. 44 42 11N 119 32W
Guanta 71 10 14N 64 36W
Guantánamo 67 20 10N 75 14W
Guantao 114 36 42N 115 25 E
Guanyun 115 34 20N 119 18 E
Guapí 70 2 36N 77 54W
Guápiles 66 10 10N 83 46W
Guaporé → 73 11 55 S 65 4W
Guaqui 72 16 41 S 68 54W
Guarabira 74 6 51 S 35 29W
Guaranda 70 1 36 S 79 0W
Guarapari 75 20 40 S 40 30W
Guarapuava 77 25 20 S 51 30W
Guaratinguetá 77 22 49 S 45 9W
Guaratuba 77 25 53 S 48 38W
Guarda 91 40 32N 7 20W
Guardafui, C. = Asir, Ras 105 11 55N 51 10 E
Guaria □ 76 25 45 S 56 30W
Guárico □ 70 8 40N 66 35W
Guarrojo → 70 4 6N 70 42W
Guarujá 77 24 2 S 46 25W
Guarus 75 21 44 S 41 20W
Guasave 64 25 34N 108 27W
Guascama, Pta. 70 2 32N 8 24W
Guasdualito 70 7 15N 70 44W
Guasipati 71 7 28N 61 54W
Guatemala 66 14 40N 90 22W
Guatemala ■ 66 15 40N 90 30W
Guatire 70 10 28N 66 32W
Guaviare → 70 4 3N 67 44W
Guaxupé 75 21 10 S 47 5W
Guayabero → 70 2 36N 72 47W
Guayama 57 17 59N 66 7W
Guayama ◇ 57 18 10N 66 15W
Guayaneco, Arch. 78 47 45 S 75 10W
Guayanilla 57 18 1N 66 47W
Guayanilla, Bahia de 57 17 55N 66 50W
Guayaquil 70 2 15 S 79 52W
Guayaquil, G. de 70 3 10 S 81 0W
Guayaramerín 73 10 48 S 65 23W
Guayas → 70 1 23N 74 50W
Guaymas 64 27 59N 110 54W
Guaynabo 57 18 22N 66 7W
Guazhou 115 32 17N 119 21 E
Guchil 112 5 35N 102 10 E
Gudbrandsdalen 97 61 33N 10 0 E
Guddu Barrage 108 28 30N 69 50 E
Gudivada 109 16 30N 81 3 E
Gudur 108 14 12N 79 55 E
Guecho 91 43 21N 2 59W
Guékédou 120 8 40N 10 5W
Guelma 120 36 25N 7 29 E
Guelph 60 43 35N 80 20W
Güepi 70 0 9 S 75 10W
Güer Aike 78 51 39 S 69 35W
Güera, La 120 20 51N 17 0W
Guéréda 121 14 31N 22 5 E
Guéret 90 46 11N 1 51 E
Guerneville 14 38 30N 123 0W
Guernica 91 43 19N 2 40W
Guernsey, Chan. Is. 83 49 30N 2 35W
Guernsey, Iowa 23 41 39N 92 21W
Guernsey, Wyo. 56 42 16N 104 45W
Guernsey County ◇ 42 40 2N 81 35W
Guernsey Reservoir 56 42 17N 104 46W
Guerra 50 26 53N 98 54W
Guerrero □ 65 17 30N 100 0W
Gueydan 25 30 2N 92 31W
Guffey 16 38 45N 105 31W
Guffy Peak 56 43 29N 107 54W
Gui Jiang → 115 23 30N 111 15 E
Gui Xian 115 23 8N 109 35 E
Guia Lopes da Laguna 77 21 26 S 56 7W
Guichi 115 30 39N 117 27 E
Guide Rock 34 40 4N 98 20W
Guidong 115 26 7N 113 57 E
Guiglo 120 6 45N 7 30W
Guilarte, Monte 57 18 9N 66 46W
Guildford 83 51 14N 0 34W
Guildhall 36 44 34N 71 34W
Guilford, Conn. 28 41 17N 72 41W
Guilford, Maine 26 45 10N 69 23W
Guilford County ◇ 40 36 10N 79 45W
Guilin 115 25 18N 110 15 E
Guilvinec 90 47 48N 4 17W
Guimarães 74 2 9 S 44 42W
Guimaras 111 10 35N 122 37 E
Guin 10 33 58N 87 55W
Guinda 14 38 50N 122 12W
Guinea ■ 120 10 20N 10 0W
Guinea, Gulf of 118 3 0N 2 30 E
Guinea-Bissau ■ 120 12 0N 15 0W
Güines 66 22 50N 82 0W
Guingamp 90 48 34N 3 10W
Guion 13 35 56N 91 57W
Guiping 115 23 21N 110 2 E
Guiratinga 73 16 21 S 53 45W
Güiria 71 10 32N 62 18W
Guiuan 111 11 5N 125 55 E
Guixi 115 28 16N 117 15 E
Guiyang, Guizhou, China 115 26 32N 106 40 E
Guiyang, Hunan, China 115 25 46N 112 42 E
Guizhou □ 115 27 0N 107 0 E
Gujarat □ 108 23 20N 71 0 E
Gujranwala 108 32 10N 74 12 E
Gujrat 108 32 40N 74 2 E
Gulbarga 108 17 20N 76 50 E
Gulf Basin 126 15 20 S 129 0 E
Gulf Breeze 17 30 22N 87 9W
Gulf County ◇ 17 29 50N 85 15W
Gulf Hammock 17 29 15N 82 43W
Gulf Islands National Seashore 17 30 10N 87 10W
Gulf Shores 10 30 17N 87 41W
Gulfport, Fla. 17 27 44N 82 43W
Gulfport, Miss. 31 30 22N 89 6W
Gulkana 11 62 16N 145 23W
Gull L. 30 46 25N 94 21W
Gull Lake 63 50 10N 108 29W
Gullivan B. 17 25 45N 81 40W
Gulshad 100 46 45N 74 25 E
Gulu 122 2 48N 32 17 E
Gumboro 27 38 28N 75 22W
Gumma □ 117 36 30N 138 20 E
Gummi 120 12 4N 5 9 E
Gümüsane 106 40 30N 39 30 E
Gumzai 111 5 28 S 134 42 E
Gun L. 29 42 36N 85 31W
Guna 108 24 40N 77 19 E
Gundih 111 7 10 S 110 56 E
Gungu 122 5 43 S 19 20 E
Gunisao → 63 53 56N 97 53W
Gunisao L. 63 53 33N 96 15W
Gunnedah 127 30 59 S 150 15 E
Gunnison, Colo. 16 38 33N 106 56W
Gunnison, Miss. 31 33 57N 90 57W
Gunnison, Utah 52 39 9N 111 49W
Gunnison → 16 39 4N 108 35W
Gunnison County ◇ 16 38 40N 107 0W
Gunnison National Forest 16 38 30N 107 0W
Gunnison Peak 16 38 49N 107 23W
Gunpowder → 27 39 20N 76 20W
Guntakal 108 15 11N 77 27 E
Guntersville 10 34 21N 86 18W
Guntersville L. 10 34 25N 86 23W
Guntown 31 34 27N 88 40W
Guntur 109 16 23N 80 30 E
Gunungapi 111 6 45 S 126 30 E
Gunungsitoli 110 1 15N 97 30 E
Gunza 122 10 50 S 13 50 E
Guo He → 115 32 59N 117 10 E
Guoyang 115 33 32N 116 12 E
Gupis 108 36 15N 73 20 E
Gura-Teghii 95 45 30N 26 25 E
Gurabo 57 18 16N 65 58W
Gürchañ 106 34 55N 49 25 E
Gurdaspur 108 32 5N 75 31 E
Gurdon 13 33 55N 93 9W
Gurgaon 108 28 27N 77 1 E
Gurguéia → 74 6 50 S 43 24W
Guri Dam 71 7 50N 62 52W
Gurkha 109 28 5N 84 40 E
Gurley 34 41 19N 102 58W
Gurnee 21 42 22N 87 55W
Gurnet Point 28 42 1N 70 34W
Gurun 112 5 49N 100 27 E
Gurupá 74 1 25 S 51 35W
Gurupá, I. Grande de 71 1 25 S 51 45W
Gurupi 75 11 43 S 49 4W
Gurupi → 74 1 13 S 46 6W
Gurupi, Serra do 74 5 0 S 47 30W
Guryev 99 47 5N 52 0 E
Gusau 120 12 12N 6 40 E
Gushan 114 39 50N 123 35 E
Gushi 115 32 11N 115 41 E
Gustavus 11 58 25N 135 44W
Gustine, Calif. 14 37 16N 121 0W
Gustine, Tex. 51 31 51N 98 24W
Güstrow 88 53 47N 12 12 E
Guthrie, Ky. 48 36 39N 87 10W
Guthrie, Okla. 43 35 53N 97 25W
Guthrie, Tex. 50 33 37N 100 19W
Guthrie Center 23 41 41N 94 30W
Guthrie County ◇ 23 41 40N 94 30W
Gutiérrez 73 19 25 S 63 34W
Guttenberg 23 42 47N 91 6W
Guyana ■ 71 5 0N 59 0W
Guyandotte → 54 38 25N 82 25W
Guyanes → 57 18 6N 65 50W
Guyang 114 41 0N 110 5 E
Guyenne 90 44 30N 0 40 E
Guymon 43 36 41N 101 29W
Guyton 18 32 20N 81 24W
Guyuan 114 36 0N 106 20 E
Guzhen 115 33 22N 117 18 E
Guzmán, Laguna de 64 31 25N 107 25W
Gwa 109 17 36N 94 34 E
Gwaai 123 19 15 S 27 45 E
Gwādar 107 25 10N 62 18 E
Gwalior 108 26 12N 78 10 E
Gwanda 123 20 55 S 29 0 E
Gweebarra B. 85 54 52N 8 21W
Gweedore 85 55 4N 8 15W
Gwent □ 83 51 45N 2 55W
Gweru 123 19 28 S 29 45 E
Gwinn 29 46 19N 87 27W
Gwinner 41 46 14N 97 40W
Gwinnett County ◇ 18 34 0N 84 0W
Gwydir → 127 29 27 S 149 48 E
Gwynedd □ 82 53 0N 4 0W
Gyaring Hu 113 34 50N 97 40 E
Gydanskiy P-ov. 100 70 0N 78 0 E
Gympie 127 26 11 S 152 38 E
Gyöngyös 89 47 48N 20 0 E
Győr 89 47 41N 17 40 E
Gypsum, Colo. 16 39 39N 106 57W
Gypsum, Kans. 24 38 42N 97 26W
Gypsum Pt. 62 61 53N 114 35W
Gypsumville 63 51 45N 98 40W

H

Ha 'Arava 104 30 50N 35 20 E
Haakon County ◇ 47 44 25N 101 35W
Haapamäki 96 62 18N 24 28 E
Haarlem 87 52 23N 4 39 E
Haast → 128 43 50 S 169 2 E
Hab Nadi Chauki 108 25 0N 66 50 E
Habana, La 66 23 8N 82 22W
Habaswein 122 1 2N 39 30 E
Habay 62 58 50N 118 44W
Habersham 18 34 36N 83 34W
Habersham County ◇ 18 34 40N 83 30W
Haboro 116 44 22N 141 42 E
Hachijō-Jima 117 33 5N 139 45 E
Hachinohe 116 40 30N 141 29 E
Hachiōji 117 35 40N 139 20 E
Hachita 38 31 55N 108 19W
Hackberry, Ariz. 12 35 22N 113 44W
Hackberry, La. 25 30 0N 93 17W
Hackensack, Minn. 30 46 56N 94 31W
Hackensack, N.J. 37 40 53N 74 3W
Hackett 13 35 11N 94 25W
Hackettstown 37 40 51N 74 50W
Hackleburg 10 34 17N 87 50W
Hadarba, Ras 121 22 4N 36 51 E
Hadd, Ras al 107 22 35N 59 50 E
Haddam 24 39 52N 97 18W
Haddington 84 55 57N 2 48W
Haddock 18 33 2N 83 26W
Hadejia 120 12 30N 10 5 E
Hadera 104 32 27N 34 55 E
Hadera, N. → 104 32 28N 34 52 E
Hadhramaut = Hadramawt 105 15 30N 49 30 E
Hadlock 53 48 2N 122 45W
Hadlyme 28 41 25N 72 25W
Hadramawt 105 15 30N 49 30 E
Hadrians Wall 82 55 0N 2 30W
Haeju 114 38 3N 125 45 E
Haena 19 22 14N 159 34W
Haerhpin = Harbin 114 45 48N 126 40 E
Hafar al Bāţin 106 28 25N 46 0 E
Hafizabad 108 32 5N 73 40 E
Haflong 109 25 10N 93 5 E
Hafnarfjörður 96 64 4N 21 57W
Haft-Gel 106 31 30N 49 32 E
Hafun, Ras 105 10 29N 51 30 E
Hagalil 104 32 53N 35 18 E
Hagemeister I. 11 58 39N 160 54W
Hagen 88 51 21N 7 29 E
Hagerhill 49 37 42N 82 48W
Hagerman, Idaho 20 42 49N 114 54W
Hagerman, N. Mex. 38 33 7N 104 20W
Hagerstown, Ind. 22 39 55N 85 10W
Hagerstown, Md. 27 39 39N 77 43W
Hagfors 97 60 3N 13 45 E
Hagi, Iceland 96 65 28N 23 25W
Hagi, Japan 117 34 30N 131 22 E
Hagolan 104 33 0N 35 45 E
Hags Hd. 85 52 57N 9 30W
Hague, N. Dak. 41 46 2N 99 59W
Hague, N.Y. 39 43 45N 73 30W
Hague, C. de la 90 49 44N 1 56W
Hague, The = 's-Gravenhage 87 52 7N 4 17 E
Haguenau 90 48 49N 7 47 E
Hahira 18 30 59N 83 22W
Hahnville 25 29 59N 90 25W
Haicheng 114 40 50N 122 45 E
Haifa = Hefa 104 32 46N 35 0 E
Haifeng 115 22 58N 115 10 E
Haig 34 41 53N 103 45W
Haigler 34 40 1N 101 56W
Haikang 115 20 52N 110 8 E
Haikou 115 20 1N 110 16 E
Ḩā'il 106 27 28N 41 45 E
Hailar 114 49 10N 119 38 E
Hailar He → 114 49 30N 117 50 E
Hailey 20 43 31N 114 19W
Haileybury 60 47 30N 79 38W
Hailin 114 44 37N 129 30 E
Hailing Dao 115 21 35N 111 47 E
Hailong 114 42 32N 125 40 E
Hailun 114 47 28N 126 50 E
Hailuoto 96 65 3N 24 45 E
Haimen 115 31 52N 121 10 E
Hainan 115 19 0N 110 0 E
Hainan Dao 115 19 0N 109 30 E
Hainaut □ 87 50 30N 4 0 E
Haines, Alaska 11 59 14N 135 26W
Haines, Oreg. 44 44 55N 117 56W
Haines ◇ 11 57 0N 135 30W
Haines City 17 28 7N 81 38W
Haines Junction 62 60 45N 137 30W
Hainesport 37 39 59N 74 50W
Haining 115 30 28N 120 40 E
Haiphong 112 20 47N 106 41 E
Haiti ■ 67 19 0N 72 30W
Haiwee Reservoir 15 36 8N 117 57W
Haiya Junction 121 18 20N 36 21 E
Haiyan 115 30 28N 120 58 E
Haiyang 114 36 47N 121 9 E
Haiyuan 114 36 35N 105 52 E
Haja 111 3 19 S 129 37 E
Hajar Bangar 121 10 40N 22 45 E
Hajdúböszörmény 89 47 40N 21 30 E

Hajnówka Harman

Hajnówka 89 52 45N 23 32 E
Hajr 107 24 0N 56 34 E
Hakken-Zan 117 34 10N 135 54 E
Hakodate 116 41 45N 140 44 E
Haku-San 117 36 9N 136 46 E
Hakui 117 36 53N 136 47 E
Hala 108 25 43N 68 20 E
Ḩalab 106 36 10N 37 15 E
Ḩalabjah 106 35 10N 45 58 E
Halaib 121 22 12N 36 30 E
Halalii L. 19 21 52N 160 11W
Halawa, C. 19 21 10N 156 43W
Halawa Heights 19 21 23N 157 55W
Halberstadt 88 51 53N 11 2 E
Halbur 23 42 0N 94 59W
Halcombe 128 40 8 S 175 30 E
Halcon, Mt. 111 13 0N 121 30 E
Haldeman 49 38 15N 83 19W
Halden 97 59 9N 11 23 E
Haldia 109 22 5N 88 3 E
Haldwani 108 29 31N 79 30 E
Hale, Colo. 16 39 38N 102 9W
Hale, Mo. 32 39 36N 93 20W
Hale Center 50 34 4N 101 51W
Hale County ◇, Ala. 10 32 42N 87 36W
Hale County ◇, Tex. 50 34 0N 101 55W
Haleakala Crater 19 20 43N 156 16W
Haleakala National Park 19 20 40N 156 15W
Haleiwa 19 21 36N 158 6W
Halethorpe 27 39 15N 76 42W
Haley 41 45 58N 103 7W
Haleyville, Ala. 10 34 14N 87 37W
Haleyville, N.J. 37 39 17N 75 2W
Half Way 32 37 37N 93 15W
Halfmoon Landing 18 31 42N 81 16W
Halfway 27 39 37N 77 46W
Halfway → 62 56 12N 121 32W
Ḩalḩul 104 31 35N 35 7 E
Hali 105 18 30N 41 30 E
Haliburton 60 45 3N 78 30W
Halifax, Canada 61 44 38N 63 35W
Halifax, U.K. 82 53 43N 1 51W
Halifax, Mass. 28 41 59N 70 52W
Halifax, N.C. 40 36 20N 77 35W
Halifax, Va. 54 36 46N 78 56W
Halifax B. 127 18 50 S 147 0 E
Halifax County ◇, N.C. 40 36 15N 77 40W
Halifax County ◇, Va. 54 36 55N 79 0W
Halīl → 107 27 40N 58 30 E
Halkett, C. 11 70 48N 152 11W
Hall 33 46 35N 113 12W
Hall Beach 59 68 46N 81 12W
Hall County ◇, Ga. 18 34 15N 83 50W
Hall County ◇, Nebr. 34 40 45N 98 30W
Hall County ◇, Tex. 50 34 30N 100 35W
Hall I. 11 60 40N 173 6W
Hall Summit 25 32 11N 93 18W
Hallam 34 40 32N 96 47W
Hallandale 17 25 59N 80 8W
Hallands län □ 97 56 50N 12 50 E
Halle, Belgium 87 50 44N 4 13 E
Halle, Germany 88 51 29N 12 0 E
Halleck 35 40 57N 115 27W
Hällefors 97 59 47N 14 31 E
Hallett 43 36 19N 96 35W
Hallettsville 51 29 27N 96 57W
Halley 13 33 32N 91 20W
Halley Bay 5 75 31 S 26 36W
Halliday 41 47 21N 102 20W
Halliday L. 63 61 21N 108 56W
Halligan Reservoir 16 40 53N 105 20W
Hallingdal → 97 60 34N 9 12 E
Hällnäs 96 64 19N 19 36 E
Hallock 30 48 47N 96 57W
Halls, Ga. 18 34 18N 84 56W
Halls, Tenn. 48 35 53N 89 24W
Halls Creek 126 18 16 S 127 38 E
Halls Summit 24 38 21N 95 41W
Hallstead 45 41 58N 75 45W
Hallsville, Mo. 32 39 7N 92 13W
Hallsville, Tex. 51 32 30N 94 35W
Halltown 32 37 12N 93 38W
Hallwood 54 37 53N 75 36W
Halma 30 48 40N 96 36W
Halmahera 111 0 40N 128 0 E
Halmstad 97 56 41N 12 52 E
Halq el Oued 121 36 53N 10 18 E
Hals 97 56 59N 10 18 E
Halsey, Nebr. 34 41 54N 100 16W
Halsey, Oreg. 44 44 23N 123 7W
Hälsingborg = Helsingborg 97 56 3N 12 42 E
Halstad 30 47 21N 96 50W
Halstead 24 38 0N 97 31W
Haltom City 51 32 48N 97 16W
Halul 107 25 40N 52 40 E
Hamada 117 34 56N 132 4 E
Hamadān 106 34 52N 48 32 E
Hamadān □ 106 35 0N 49 0 E
Hamāh 106 35 5N 36 40 E
Hamamatsu 117 34 45N 137 45 E
Hamar 97 60 48N 11 7 E
Hamarøy 96 68 5N 15 38 E
Hambantota 108 6 10N 81 10 E
Hamber Prov. Park 62 52 20N 118 0W
Hamberg 41 47 46N 99 31W
Hamblen County ◇ 49 36 13N 83 18W
Hambleton 54 39 5N 79 39W
Hamburg, Germany 88 53 32N 9 59 E
Hamburg, Ark. 13 33 14N 91 48W
Hamburg, Calif. 14 41 47N 123 4W
Hamburg, Conn. 28 41 23N 72 21W
Hamburg, Ill. 21 39 14N 90 43W
Hamburg, Iowa 23 40 36N 95 39W
Hamburg, Minn. 30 44 44N 93 58W
Hamburg, Miss. 31 31 35N 91 4W
Hamburg, N.J. 37 41 9N 74 35W
Hamburg, N.Y. 39 42 43N 78 50W
Hamburg, Pa. 45 40 33N 75 59W
Hamden 28 41 23N 72 54W
Hame 97 61 30N 24 0 E
Hämeenlinna 96 61 0N 24 28 E
Hameln 88 52 7N 9 24 E
Hamer 20 43 56N 112 12W
Hamersley Ra. 126 22 0 S 117 45 E
Hamersville 42 38 55N 83 59W
Hamhung 114 39 54N 127 30 E
Hami 113 42 55N 93 25 E
Hamilton, Australia 127 37 45 S 142 2 E
Hamilton, Canada 60 43 15N 79 50W
Hamilton, N.Z. 128 37 47 S 175 19 E
Hamilton, U.K. 84 55 47N 4 2W
Hamilton, Ala. 10 34 9N 87 59W
Hamilton, Alaska 11 62 54N 163 53W
Hamilton, Colo. 16 40 22N 107 37W
Hamilton, Ga. 18 32 45N 84 53W
Hamilton, Ill. 21 40 24N 91 21W
Hamilton, Kans. 24 37 59N 96 10W
Hamilton, Mich. 29 42 41N 86 0W
Hamilton, Mo. 32 39 45N 94 0W
Hamilton, Mont. 33 46 15N 114 10W
Hamilton, N.C. 40 35 57N 77 12W
Hamilton, N. Dak. 41 48 48N 97 24W
Hamilton, N.Y. 39 42 50N 75 33W
Hamilton, Ohio 42 39 24N 84 34W
Hamilton, Oreg. 44 44 44N 119 18W
Hamilton, Tex. 51 31 42N 98 7W
Hamilton, L. 13 34 26N 93 2W
Hamilton City 14 39 45N 122 1W
Hamilton County ◇, Fla. 17 30 30N 83 0W
Hamilton County ◇, Ill. 21 38 5N 88 30W
Hamilton County ◇, Ind. 22 40 5N 86 5W
Hamilton County ◇, Iowa 23 42 20N 93 40W
Hamilton County ◇, Kans. 24 38 0N 101 45W
Hamilton County ◇, N.Y. 39 43 30N 74 30W
Hamilton County ◇, Nebr. 34 40 45N 98 0W
Hamilton County ◇, Ohio 42 39 13N 84 33W
Hamilton County ◇, Tenn. 49 35 17N 85 10W
Hamilton County ◇, Tex. 51 31 40N 98 8W
Hamilton Dome 56 43 46N 108 35W
Hamilton Inlet 61 54 0N 57 30W
Hamiota 63 50 11N 100 38W
Hamler 42 41 14N 84 2W
Hamlet, Ind. 22 41 23N 86 35W
Hamlet, N.C. 40 34 53N 79 42W
Hamlet, Nebr. 34 40 23N 101 14W
Hamlin, Tex. 50 32 53N 100 8W
Hamlin, W. Va. 54 38 17N 82 6W
Hamlin County ◇ 47 44 40N 97 13W
Hamlin L. 29 44 3N 86 28W
Hamm 88 51 40N 7 49 E
Hammerfest 96 70 39N 23 41 E
Hammon 43 35 38N 99 23W
Hammond, Ill. 21 39 48N 88 36W
Hammond, Ind. 22 41 38N 87 30W
Hammond, La. 25 30 30N 90 28W
Hammond, Minn. 30 44 13N 92 23W
Hammond, N.Y. 39 44 27N 75 42W
Hammond, Oreg. 44 46 12N 123 57W
Hammondsport 39 42 25N 77 13W
Hammonton 37 39 39N 74 48W
Hampden, N.Z. 128 45 18 S 170 50 E
Hampden, Maine 26 44 44N 68 51W
Hampden, N. Dak. 41 48 32N 98 40W
Hampden County ◇ 28 42 10N 72 35W
Hampden Sydney 54 37 14N 78 28W
Hampshire, Ill. 21 42 6N 88 32W
Hampshire, Tenn. 48 35 36N 87 18W
Hampshire □ 83 51 3N 1 20W
Hampshire County ◇, Mass. 28 42 15N 72 35W
Hampshire County ◇, W. Va. 54 39 18N 78 38W
Hampshire Downs 83 51 10N 1 10W
Hampstead, Md. 27 39 37N 76 51W
Hampstead, N.C. 40 34 22N 77 44W
Hampstead, N.H. 36 42 51N 71 10W
Hampton, Ark. 13 33 32N 92 28W
Hampton, Conn. 28 41 47N 72 3W
Hampton, Fla. 17 29 52N 82 8W
Hampton, Ga. 18 33 23N 84 17W
Hampton, Iowa 23 42 45N 93 13W
Hampton, Minn. 30 44 37N 93 0W
Hampton, N.H. 36 42 57N 70 50W
Hampton, N.J. 37 40 42N 74 58W
Hampton, Nebr. 34 40 53N 97 53W
Hampton, Oreg. 44 43 40N 120 14W
Hampton, S.C. 46 32 52N 81 7W
Hampton, Tenn. 49 36 17N 82 10W
Hampton, Va. 54 37 2N 76 21W
Hampton Bays 39 40 53N 72 30W
Hampton County ◇ 46 32 50N 81 10W
Hampton Harbour 126 20 30 S 116 30 E
Hampton Springs 17 30 5N 83 40W
Hampton Tableland 126 32 0 S 127 0 E
Hamrat esh Sheykh 121 14 38N 27 55 E
Hams → 56 41 35N 109 57W
Hams Bluff 57 17 46N 64 52W
Han Jiang → 115 23 25N 116 40 E
Han Pijesak 95 44 0N 19 0 E
Han Shui → 115 30 35N 114 18 E
Hana 19 20 45N 155 59W
Hanaford 21 37 57N 88 50W
Hanahan 46 32 55N 80 0W
Hanalei 19 22 12N 159 30W
Hanamaki 116 39 23N 141 7 E
Hanamaulu 19 21 59N 159 22W
Hanapepe 19 21 55N 159 35W
Hanau 88 50 8N 8 56 E
Hanauma B. 19 21 15N 157 40W
Hanceville 10 34 4N 86 46W
Hancheng 114 35 31N 110 25 E
Hancock, Iowa 23 41 24N 95 21W
Hancock, Md. 27 39 42N 78 11W
Hancock, Mich. 29 47 8N 88 35W
Hancock, Minn. 30 45 30N 95 48W
Hancock, N.H. 36 42 57N 71 58W
Hancock, N.Y. 39 41 57N 75 17W
Hancock, Vt. 36 43 56N 72 51W
Hancock, Wis. 55 44 8N 89 31W
Hancock, Mt. 56 44 9N 110 25W
Hancock County ◇, Ga. 18 33 20N 83 0W
Hancock County ◇, Ill. 21 40 25N 91 10W
Hancock County ◇, Ind. 22 39 50N 85 45W
Hancock County ◇, Iowa 23 43 5N 93 45W
Hancock County ◇, Ky. 48 37 50N 86 45W
Hancock County ◇, Maine 26 44 30N 68 30W
Hancock County ◇, Miss. 31 30 17N 89 23W
Hancock County ◇, Ohio 42 41 2N 83 39W
Hancock County ◇, Tenn. 49 36 32N 83 13W
Hancock County ◇, W. Va. 54 40 30N 80 35W
Hancocks Bridge 37 39 31N 75 28W
Hand County ◇ 47 44 31N 99 59W
Handa, Japan 117 34 53N 137 0 E
Handa, Somalia 105 10 37N 51 2 E
Handan 114 36 35N 114 28 E
Handeni 122 5 25 S 38 2 E
Hanegev 104 30 50N 35 0 E
Haney 62 49 12N 122 40W
Hanford, Calif. 15 36 20N 119 39W
Hanford, Wash. 53 46 37N 119 19W
Hangang → 114 37 50N 126 30 E
Hangayn Nuruu 113 47 30N 100 0 E
Hangchou = Hangzhou 115 30 18N 120 11 E
Hanggin Houqi 114 40 58N 107 4 E
Hangö 97 59 50N 22 57 E
Hangu 114 39 18N 117 53 E
Hangzhou 115 30 18N 120 11 E
Hangzhou Wan 115 30 15N 120 45 E
Ḩanīsh J. 105 13 45N 42 46 E
Hanita 104 33 5N 35 10 E
Hankinson 41 46 4N 96 54W
Hanko 97 59 59N 22 57 E
Hankou 115 30 35N 114 30 E
Hanksville 52 38 22N 110 43W
Hanle 108 32 42N 79 4 E
Hanley Falls 30 44 42N 95 37W
Hanmer Springs 128 42 32 S 172 50 E
Hann, Mt. 126 16 0 S 126 0 E
Hanna, Canada 62 51 40N 111 54W
Hanna, Ind. 22 41 25N 86 47W
Hanna, La. 25 31 58N 93 21W
Hanna, Okla. 43 35 12N 95 53W
Hanna, Utah 52 40 26N 110 48W
Hanna, Wyo. 56 41 52N 106 34W
Hanna City 21 40 42N 89 48W
Hannaford 41 47 19N 98 11W
Hannah 41 48 58N 98 42W
Hannah B. 60 51 40N 80 0W
Hannibal, Mo. 32 39 42N 91 22W
Hannibal, N.Y. 39 43 19N 76 35W
Hannover, Germany 88 52 23N 9 43 E
Hannover, U.S.A. 41 47 7N 101 26W
Hanoi 112 21 5N 105 55 E
Hanover = Hannover 88 52 23N 9 43 E
Hanover, Ill. 21 42 15N 90 17W
Hanover, Ind. 22 38 43N 85 28W
Hanover, Kans. 24 39 54N 96 53W
Hanover, Mass. 28 42 7N 70 49W
Hanover, Mich. 29 42 6N 84 33W
Hanover, Minn. 30 45 10N 93 40W
Hanover, Mont. 33 47 7N 109 33W
Hanover, N.H. 36 43 42N 72 17W
Hanover, N. Mex. 38 32 48N 108 6W
Hanover, Ohio 42 40 4N 82 16W
Hanover, Pa. 45 39 48N 76 59W
Hanover, Va. 54 37 46N 77 22W
Hanover, I. 78 51 0 S 74 50W
Hanover County ◇ 54 37 46N 77 29W
Hanoverton 42 40 45N 80 56W
Hans Lollik I. 57 18 24N 64 53W
Hansboro 41 48 57N 99 23W
Hansen 20 42 32N 114 18W
Hansford County ◇ 50 36 10N 101 30W
Hansi 108 29 10N 75 57 E
Hanska 30 44 9N 94 30W
Hanson, Fla. 17 30 34N 83 21W
Hanson, Ky. 48 37 25N 87 29W
Hanson County ◇ 47 43 39N 97 47W
Hanson Range 126 27 0 S 136 30 E
Hanston 24 38 7N 99 43W
Hanyang 115 30 35N 114 2 E
Hanyin 115 32 54N 108 28 E
Hanzhong 115 33 10N 107 1 E
Hanzhuang 115 34 33N 117 23 E
Haora 109 22 37N 88 20 E
Haparanda 96 65 52N 24 8 E
Hapeville 18 33 40N 84 25W
Happy 50 34 45N 101 52W
Happy Camp 14 41 48N 123 23W
Happy Jack 12 34 45N 111 24W
Happy Valley 61 53 15N 60 20W
Hapur 108 28 45N 77 45 E
Ḩaql 106 29 10N 35 0 E
Haquira 72 14 14 S 72 12W
Har 111 5 16 S 133 14 E
Har Hu 113 38 20N 97 38 E
Har Us Nuur 113 48 0N 92 0 E
Har Yehuda 104 31 35N 34 57 E
Ḩaraḑ 106 24 22N 49 0 E
Harahan 25 29 56N 90 11W
Haraisan Plateau 106 23 0N 47 40 E
Haralson 18 33 14N 84 34W
Haralson County ◇ 18 33 45N 85 10W
Haranomachi 116 37 38N 140 58 E
Harardera 105 4 33N 47 38 E
Harare 123 17 43 S 31 2 E
Harazé 121 14 20N 19 12 E
Harbeson 27 38 43N 75 17W
Harbin 114 45 48N 126 40 E
Harbor Beach 29 43 51N 82 39W
Harbor Springs 29 45 26N 85 0W
Harbour Breton 61 47 29N 55 50W
Harbour Grace 61 47 40N 53 22W
Harburg 88 53 27N 9 58 E
Harcourt 23 42 16N 94 11W
Harcuvar Mts. 12 34 0N 113 30W
Hardangerfjorden 97 60 15N 6 0 E
Hardap Dam 123 24 32 S 17 50 E
Hardee County ◇ 17 27 30N 81 45W
Hardeeville 46 32 17N 81 5W
Hardeman County ◇, Tenn. 48 35 6N 89 0W
Hardeman County ◇, Tex. 51 34 20N 99 50W
Hardenberg 87 52 34N 6 37 E
Harderwijk 87 52 21N 5 38 E
Hardesty 43 36 37N 101 12W
Hardin, Ill. 21 39 10N 90 37W
Hardin, Ky. 48 36 46N 88 18W
Hardin, Mo. 32 39 16N 93 50W
Hardin, Mont. 33 45 44N 107 37W
Hardin, Tex. 51 30 9N 94 44W
Hardin County ◇, Ill. 21 37 30N 88 15W
Hardin County ◇, Iowa 23 42 25N 93 15W
Hardin County ◇, Ky. 48 37 40N 86 0W
Hardin County ◇, Ohio 42 40 40N 83 47W
Hardin County ◇, Tenn. 48 35 14N 88 15W
Hardin County ◇, Tex. 51 30 22N 94 19W
Harding, S. Africa 123 30 35 S 29 55 E
Harding, U.S.A. 30 46 7N 94 2W
Harding, L. 10 32 40N 85 5W
Harding County ◇, N. Mex. 38 36 0N 104 0W
Harding County ◇, S. Dak. 47 45 30N 103 30W
Hardinsburg, Ind. 22 38 28N 86 17W
Hardinsburg, Ky. 48 37 47N 86 28W
Hardisty 62 52 40N 111 18W
Hardman 44 45 10N 119 41W
Hardoi 108 27 26N 80 6 E
Hardtner 24 37 1N 98 39W
Hardwar = Haridwar 108 29 58N 78 9 E
Hardwick, Ga. 18 33 4N 83 14W
Hardwick, Mass. 28 42 21N 72 12W
Hardwick, Minn. 30 43 47N 96 12W
Hardwick, Vt. 36 44 30N 72 22W
Hardy, Ark. 13 36 19N 91 29W
Hardy, Mont. 33 47 12N 111 47W
Hardy, Nebr. 34 40 1N 97 56W
Hardy, Pen. 78 55 30 S 68 20W
Hardy County ◇ 54 39 0N 78 50W
Hardy Dam Pond 29 43 30N 85 37W
Hare B. 61 51 15N 55 45W
Hare Gilboa 104 32 31N 35 25 E
Hare Meron 104 32 59N 35 24 E
Harer 105 9 20N 42 8 E
Harford County ◇ 27 39 35N 76 25W
Hargeisa 105 9 30N 44 2 E
Harghita □ 95 46 30N 25 30 E
Harghita, Mţii 95 46 25N 25 35 E
Hargill 50 26 27N 98 1W
Hargshamn 97 60 12N 18 30 E
Hari → 110 1 16 S 104 5 E
Haridwar 108 29 58N 78 9 E
Haringhata → 109 22 0N 89 58 E
Harīrūd 107 35 0N 61 0 E
Harīrūd → 107 34 20N 62 30 E
Harker Heights 51 31 5N 97 40W
Harkers Island 40 34 42N 76 34W
Harlan, Iowa 23 41 39N 95 19W
Harlan, Kans. 24 39 36N 98 46W
Harlan, Ky. 49 36 51N 83 19W
Harlan County ◇, Ky. 49 36 50N 83 15W
Harlan County ◇, Nebr. 34 40 15N 99 20W
Harlan County Lake 34 40 4N 99 13W
Harlech 82 52 52N 4 7W
Harlem, Ga. 18 33 25N 82 19W
Harlem, Mont. 33 48 32N 108 47W
Harleyville 46 33 13N 80 27W
Harlingen, Neth. 87 53 11N 5 25 E
Harlingen, U.S.A. 50 26 12N 97 42W
Harlowton 33 46 26N 109 50W
Harman 54 38 55N 79 32W

Harmon Heber

Harmon **21** 41 43N 89 33W
Harmon County ◇ **43** 34 45N 99 50W
Harmony, Ind. **22** 39 32N 87 4W
Harmony, Maine **26** 44 58N 69 33W
Harmony, Md. **27** 38 47N 75 53W
Harmony, Minn. **30** 43 33N 92 1W
Harmony, N.C. **40** 35 58N 80 46W
Harnett County ◇ **40** 35 20N 78 50W
Harney **27** 39 44N 77 13W
Harney, L. **17** 28 45N 81 3W
Harney Basin **44** 43 0N 119 30W
Harney County ◇ **44** 45 0N 119 0W
Harney L. **44** 43 14N 119 8W
Harney Peak **47** 43 52N 103 32W
Härnösand **96** 62 38N 18 0 E
Haro, C. **64** 27 50N 110 55W
Harold, Fla. **17** 30 40N 86 53W
Harold, Ky. **49** 37 32N 82 38W
Harp L. **61** 55 5N 61 50W
Harper, Iowa **23** 41 22N 92 3W
Harper, Kans. **24** 37 17N 98 1W
Harper, Oreg. **44** 43 52N 117 37W
Harper, Tex. **51** 30 18N 99 15W
Harper, Mt. **11** 64 14N 143 51W
Harper County ◇, Kans. **24** 37 15N 98 0W
Harper County ◇, Okla. **43** 36 50N 99 40W
Harper L. **15** 35 2N 117 17W
Harpers Ferry, Iowa **23** 43 12N 91 9W
Harpers Ferry, W. Va. **54** 39 20N 77 44W
Harpersville **10** 33 21N 86 26W
Harpeth → **48** 36 18N 87 10W
Harqualala Mts. **12** 33 45N 113 20W
Harrah, Okla. **43** 35 29N 97 10W
Harrah, Wash. **53** 46 24N 120 33W
Ḩarrat al Kishb **106** 22 30N 40 15 E
Ḩarrat al 'Uwairidh **106** 26 50N 38 0 E
Harrell **13** 33 31N 92 24W
Harrellsville **40** 36 18N 76 48W
Harriman **49** 35 56N 84 33W
Harriman Reservoir **36** 42 48N 72 55W
Harrington, Del. **27** 38 56N 75 35W
Harrington, Maine **26** 44 37N 67 49W
Harrington, Wash. **53** 47 29N 118 15W
Harrington Harbour **61** 50 31N 59 30W
Harris, U.K. **84** 57 50N 6 55W
Harris, Kans. **24** 38 19N 95 26W
Harris, Minn. **30** 45 35N 92 58W
Harris, Mo. **32** 40 18N 93 21W
Harris, Okla. **43** 33 45N 94 44W
Harris, L. **17** 28 47N 81 49W
Harris, Sd. of **84** 57 44N 7 6W
Harris County ◇, Ga. **18** 32 40N 84 50W
Harris County ◇, Tex. **51** 29 46N 95 22W
Harris L. **126** 31 10 S 135 10 E
Harrisburg, Ark. **13** 35 34N 90 43W
Harrisburg, Ill. **21** 37 44N 88 32W
Harrisburg, Mo. **32** 39 9N 92 28W
Harrisburg, N.C. **40** 35 19N 80 39W
Harrisburg, Nebr. **34** 41 33N 103 44W
Harrisburg, Oreg. **44** 44 16N 123 10W
Harrisburg, Pa. **45** 40 16N 76 53W
Harrisburg, S. Dak. **47** 43 26N 96 42W
Harrison, Ark. **13** 36 14N 93 7W
Harrison, Ga. **18** 32 50N 82 43W
Harrison, Idaho **20** 47 27N 116 47W
Harrison, Mich. **29** 44 1N 84 48W
Harrison, Mont. **33** 45 42N 111 47W
Harrison, Nebr. **34** 42 41N 103 53W
Harrison, C. **61** 54 55N 57 55W
Harrison Bay **11** 70 40N 151 0W
Harrison County ◇, Ind. **22** 38 10N 86 10W
Harrison County ◇, Iowa **23** 41 40N 95 50W
Harrison County ◇, Ky. **49** 38 25N 84 20W
Harrison County ◇, Miss. **31** 30 30N 89 7W
Harrison County ◇, Mo. **32** 40 20N 94 0W
Harrison County ◇, Ohio **42** 40 18N 81 11W
Harrison County ◇, Tex. **51** 32 33N 94 23W
Harrison County ◇, W. Va. **54** 39 17N 80 30W
Harrison L. **62** 49 33N 121 50W
Harrisonburg, La. **25** 31 46N 91 49W
Harrisonburg, Va. **54** 38 27N 78 52W
Harrisonville **32** 38 39N 94 21W
Harriston, Canada **60** 43 57N 80 53W
Harriston, U.S.A. **31** 31 44N 91 2W
Harrisville, Mich. **29** 44 39N 83 17W
Harrisville, N.Y. **39** 44 9N 75 19W
Harrisville, R.I. **28** 41 58N 71 41W
Harrisville, W. Va. **54** 39 13N 81 3W
Harrod **42** 40 43N 83 56W
Harrodsburg **49** 37 46N 84 51W
Harrogate, U.K. **82** 53 59N 1 32W
Harrogate, U.S.A. **49** 36 35N 83 40W
Harrold **47** 44 31N 99 44W
Harrow **83** 51 35N 0 15W
Harry S. Truman Reservoir **32** 38 16N 93 24W
Harry Strunk L. **34** 40 23N 100 13W
Harstad **96** 68 48N 16 30 E
Hart, Mich. **29** 43 42N 86 22W
Hart, Tex. **50** 34 23N 102 7W
Hart County ◇, Ga. **18** 34 15N 83 0W
Hart County ◇, Ky. **49** 37 20N 85 50W
Hart L. **44** 42 25N 119 51W
Hart Mt. **44** 42 23N 119 53W
Hartfield **54** 37 33N 76 27W
Hartford, Ala. **10** 31 6N 85 42W
Hartford, Ark. **13** 35 1N 94 23W
Hartford, Conn. **28** 41 46N 72 41W
Hartford, Ga. **18** 32 17N 83 28W
Hartford, Iowa **23** 41 28N 93 24W
Hartford, Ky. **48** 37 27N 86 55W
Hartford, Mich. **29** 42 13N 86 10W
Hartford, S. Dak. **47** 43 38N 96 57W
Hartford, Tenn. **49** 35 49N 83 9W
Hartford, Wis. **55** 43 19N 88 22W
Hartford City **22** 40 27N 85 22W
Hartford County ◇ **28** 41 45N 72 45W
Hartington **34** 42 37N 97 16W
Hartland, Canada **61** 46 20N 67 32W
Hartland, Maine **26** 44 53N 69 27W
Hartland, Minn. **30** 43 48N 93 29W
Hartland, Vt. **36** 43 32N 72 24W
Hartland, Wis. **55** 43 6N 88 21W
Hartland Pt. **83** 51 2N 4 32W
Hartlepool **82** 54 42N 1 11W
Hartley, Iowa **23** 43 11N 95 29W
Hartley, Tex. **50** 35 53N 102 24W
Hartley, Zimbabwe **123** 18 10 S 30 14 E
Hartley Bay **62** 53 25N 129 15W
Hartley County ◇ **50** 35 50N 102 30W
Hartline **53** 47 41N 119 6W
Hartly **27** 39 10N 75 43W
Hartman **16** 38 7N 102 13W
Hartney **63** 49 30N 100 35W
Hartsburg **32** 38 42N 92 19W
Hartsel **16** 39 1N 105 48W
Hartselle **10** 34 27N 86 56W
Hartshorne **43** 34 51N 95 34W
Hartsville, S.C. **46** 34 23N 80 4W
Hartsville, Tenn. **48** 36 24N 86 10W
Hartville, Mo. **32** 37 15N 92 31W
Hartville, Ohio **42** 40 58N 81 20W
Hartville, Wyo. **56** 42 20N 104 44W
Hartwell **18** 34 21N 82 56W
Hartwell L. **46** 34 21N 82 49W
Hartwick **23** 41 47N 92 21W
Harvard, Idaho **20** 46 55N 116 44W
Harvard, Ill. **21** 42 25N 88 37W
Harvard, Nebr. **34** 40 37N 98 6W
Harvard, Mt. **16** 38 56N 106 19W
Harvey, Ark. **13** 34 51N 93 47W
Harvey, Ill. **21** 41 36N 87 50W
Harvey, N. Dak. **41** 47 47N 99 56W
Harvey Cedars **37** 39 43N 74 11W
Harvey County ◇ **24** 38 0N 97 30W
Harveyville **24** 38 47N 95 58W
Harwich, U.K. **83** 51 56N 1 18 E
Harwich, U.S.A. **28** 41 41N 70 5W
Harwinton **28** 41 46N 73 4W
Harwood, Mo. **32** 37 57N 94 9W
Harwood, Tex. **51** 29 40N 97 30W
Haryana □ **108** 29 0N 76 10 E
Harz **88** 51 40N 10 40 E
Hasa **106** 26 0N 49 0 E
Hasharon **104** 32 12N 34 49 E
Hashefela **104** 31 30N 34 43 E
Hashimoto **117** 34 19N 135 37 E
Haskell, Ark. **13** 34 30N 92 38W
Haskell, Okla. **43** 35 50N 95 40W
Haskell, Tex. **51** 33 10N 99 44W
Haskell County ◇, Kans. **24** 37 30N 100 45W
Haskell County ◇, Okla. **43** 35 10N 95 10W
Haskell County ◇, Tex. **51** 33 12N 99 45W
Haskins **42** 41 28N 83 42W
Haslet **51** 32 59N 97 21W
Hassayampa → **12** 33 19N 112 42W
Hasselt **87** 50 56N 5 21 E
Hassi Inifel **120** 29 50N 3 41 E
Hassi Messaoud **120** 31 43N 6 8 E
Hastings, N.Z. **128** 39 39 S 176 52 E
Hastings, U.K. **83** 50 51N 0 36 E
Hastings, Fla. **17** 29 43N 81 31W
Hastings, Iowa **23** 41 1N 95 30W
Hastings, Mich. **29** 42 39N 85 17W
Hastings, Minn. **30** 44 44N 92 51W
Hastings, Nebr. **34** 40 35N 98 23W
Hastings, Okla. **43** 34 14N 98 7W
Hasty **16** 38 7N 102 58W
Haswell **16** 38 27N 103 10W
Hat Nhao **112** 14 46N 106 32 E
Hatch, N. Mex. **38** 32 40N 107 9W
Hatch, Utah **52** 37 39N 112 26W
Hatches Creek **126** 20 56 S 135 12 E
Hatchet L. **63** 58 36N 103 40W
Hatchie → **48** 35 35N 89 53W
Hatchineha, L. **17** 28 2N 81 25W
Haţeg, Mţii. **95** 45 25N 23 0 E
Hateruma-Shima **117** 24 3N 123 47 E
Hatfield, Ark. **13** 34 29N 94 23W
Hatfield, Ind. **22** 37 54N 87 14W
Hatfield, Mass. **28** 42 22N 72 36W
Hatfield, Minn. **30** 43 58N 96 12W
Hatfield, Pa. **45** 40 17N 75 18W
Hatgal **113** 50 26N 100 9 E
Hathras **108** 27 36N 78 6 E
Hatia **109** 22 30N 91 5 E
Hatillo **57** 18 29N 66 50W
Hato de Corozal **70** 6 11N 71 45W
Hato Mayor **67** 18 46N 69 15W
Hatteras **40** 35 13N 75 42W
Hatteras, C. **40** 35 14N 75 32W
Hatteras I. **40** 35 30N 75 28W
Hattiesburg **31** 31 20N 89 17W
Hatton, Ala. **10** 34 34N 87 25W
Hatton, N. Dak. **41** 47 38N 97 27W
Hatton, Wash. **53** 46 47N 118 50W
Hatvan **89** 47 40N 19 45 E
Hau Bon = Cheo Reo **112** 13 25N 108 28 E
Haubstadt **22** 38 12N 87 34W
Haugan **33** 47 23N 115 24W
Haugen **55** 45 37N 91 46W
Haugesund **97** 59 23N 5 13 E
Haultain → **63** 55 51N 106 46W
Hauppauge **39** 40 50N 73 12W
Hauraki Gulf **128** 36 35 S 175 5 E
Hauran **104** 32 50N 36 15 E
Hauser **44** 43 30N 124 13W
Haut, I. au **26** 44 3N 68 38W
Haut Atlas **120** 32 30N 5 0W
Haut-Rhin □ **90** 48 0N 7 15 E
Hautah, Wahāt al **106** 23 40N 47 0 E
Haute-Corse □ **90** 42 30N 9 30 E
Haute-Garonne □ **90** 43 28N 1 30 E
Haute-Loire □ **90** 45 5N 3 50 E
Haute-Marne □ **90** 48 10N 5 20 E
Haute-Saône □ **90** 47 45N 6 10 E
Haute-Savoie □ **90** 46 0N 6 20 E
Haute-Vienne □ **90** 45 50N 1 10 E
Hauterive **61** 49 10N 68 16W
Hautes-Alpes □ **90** 44 42N 6 20 E
Hautes-Pyrénées □ **90** 43 0N 0 10 E
Hauts-de-Seine □ **90** 48 52N 2 15 E
Hauts Plateaux **120** 34 14N 1 0 E
Hauula **19** 21 37N 157 55W
Havana = Habana, La **66** 23 8N 82 22W
Havana, Ark. **13** 35 7N 93 32W
Havana, Fla. **17** 30 37N 84 25W
Havana, Ill. **21** 40 18N 90 4W
Havana, Kans. **24** 37 6N 95 57W
Havana, N. Dak. **41** 45 57N 97 37W
Havant **86** 50 51N 0 59W
Havasu Cr. → **12** 36 19N 112 46W
Havasu L. **12** 34 18N 114 8W
Havasupai Indian Reservation **12** 36 15N 112 35W
Havel → **88** 52 40N 12 15 E
Havelange **87** 50 23N 5 15 E
Havelock, N.B., Canada **61** 46 2N 65 24W
Havelock, Ont., Canada **60** 44 26N 77 53W
Havelock, N.Z. **128** 41 17 S 173 48 E
Havelock, N.C. **40** 34 53N 76 54W
Havelock, N. Dak. **41** 46 29N 102 45W
Havelock I. **112** 11 55N 93 2 E
Haven **24** 37 54N 97 47W
Havensville **24** 39 31N 96 5W
Haverfordwest **83** 51 48N 4 59W
Haverhill, Fla. **17** 26 42N 80 7W
Haverhill, Mass. **28** 42 47N 71 5W
Haverhill, N.H. **36** 44 3N 72 4W
Havering **83** 51 33N 0 20 E
Havertown **45** 39 58N 75 18W
Haviland **24** 37 37N 99 6W
Havlíčkův Brod **88** 49 36N 15 33 E
Havre **33** 48 33N 109 41W
Havre, Le **90** 49 30N 0 5 E
Havre-Aubert **61** 47 12N 61 56W
Havre de Grace **27** 39 33N 76 6W
Havre-St.-Pierre **61** 50 18N 63 33W
Havza **106** 41 0N 35 35 E
Haw → **40** 35 36N 79 3W
Haw Knob **40** 35 19N 84 2W
Hawaii **19** 19 30N 155 30W
Hawaii □ **19** 20 0N 157 45W
Hawaii County ◇ **19** 19 30N 155 30W
Hawaii Volcanoes National Park **19** 19 23N 155 17W
Hawaiian Is. **125** 20 30N 156 0W
Hawaiian Ridge **125** 24 0N 165 0W
Hawarden, Canada **63** 51 25N 106 36W
Hawarden, U.S.A. **23** 43 0N 96 29W
Hawea Lake **128** 44 28 S 169 19 E
Hawera **128** 39 35 S 174 19 E
Hawesville **48** 37 54N 86 45W
Hawi **19** 20 14N 155 50W
Hawick **84** 55 25N 2 48W
Hawk Junction **60** 48 5N 84 38W
Hawk Point **32** 38 58N 91 8W
Hawk Springs **56** 41 47N 104 16W
Hawke B. **128** 39 25 S 177 20 E
Hawker **127** 31 59 S 138 22 E
Hawke's Bay □ **128** 39 45 S 176 35 E
Hawkesbury **60** 45 37N 74 37W
Hawkesbury → **127** 33 30 S 151 10 E
Hawkesbury I. **62** 53 37N 129 3W
Hawkeye **23** 42 56N 91 57W
Hawkins, Tex. **51** 32 35N 95 12W
Hawkins, Wis. **55** 45 31N 90 43W
Hawkins County ◇ **49** 36 24N 83 1W
Hawkinsville **18** 32 17N 83 28W
Hawks **29** 45 18N 83 53W
Hawksbill **54** 38 34N 78 27W
Hawksbill Mt. **40** 35 55N 81 53W
Hawley, Minn. **30** 46 53N 96 19W
Hawley, Pa. **45** 41 28N 75 11W
Hawley, Tex. **51** 32 37N 99 49W
Haworth **43** 33 51N 94 39W
Hawrān **104** 32 45N 36 15 E
Hawthorne, Fla. **17** 29 36N 82 5W
Hawthorne, Nev. **35** 38 32N 118 38W
Haxtun **16** 40 39N 102 38W
Hay, Australia **127** 34 30 S 144 51 E
Hay, U.K. **83** 52 4N 3 9W
Hay, U.S.A. **53** 46 41N 117 55W
Hay →, Australia **127** 25 14 S 138 0 E
Hay →, Canada **62** 60 50N 116 26W
Hay →, U.S.A. **55** 44 59N 91 51W
Hay L. **62** 58 50N 118 50W
Hay Lakes **62** 53 12N 113 2W
Hay River **62** 60 51N 115 44W
Hay Springs **34** 42 41N 102 41W
Hayachine-San **116** 39 34N 141 29 E
Hayden, Ariz. **12** 33 0N 110 47W
Hayden, Colo. **16** 40 30N 107 16W
Hayden, Idaho **20** 47 46N 116 47W
Hayden, N. Mex. **38** 35 59N 103 16W
Hayden Peak **20** 42 59N 116 40W
Hayes, La. **25** 30 7N 92 55W
Hayes, S. Dak. **47** 44 23N 101 1W
Hayes → **63** 57 3N 92 12W
Hayes, Mt. **11** 63 37N 146 43W
Hayes Center **34** 40 31N 101 1W
Hayes County ◇ **34** 40 30N 101 0W
Hayesville, Iowa **23** 41 16N 92 15W
Hayesville, N.C. **40** 35 3N 83 49W
Hayfield **30** 43 53N 92 51W
Hayfork **14** 40 33N 123 11W
Haylow **18** 30 50N 82 54W
Haymarket **54** 38 49N 77 38W
Haynes, Ark. **13** 34 54N 90 47W
Haynes, N. Dak. **41** 45 59N 102 28W
Haynesville, La. **25** 32 58N 93 8W
Haynesville, Maine **26** 45 50N 67 59W
Hayneville, Ala. **10** 32 11N 86 35W
Hayneville, Ga. **18** 32 23N 83 37W
Hays, Canada **62** 50 6N 111 48W
Hays, U.S.A. **24** 38 53N 99 20W
Hays County ◇ **51** 29 59N 97 53W
Haysi **54** 37 12N 82 18W
Haystack Peak **52** 39 50N 113 55W
Haysville **24** 37 34N 97 21W
Hayti, Mo. **32** 36 14N 89 44W
Hayti, S. Dak. **47** 44 40N 97 13W
Hayward, Calif. **14** 37 40N 122 5W
Hayward, Minn. **30** 43 39N 93 15W
Hayward, Wis. **55** 46 1N 91 29W
Hayward's Heath **83** 51 0N 0 5W
Haywood **40** 35 37N 79 4W
Haywood County ◇, N.C. **40** 35 30N 83 0W
Haywood County ◇, Tenn. **48** 35 36N 89 16W
Hazard, Ky. **49** 37 15N 83 12W
Hazard, Nebr. **34** 41 6N 99 9W
Hazaribag **109** 23 58N 85 26 E
Hazel, Ky. **48** 36 30N 88 20W
Hazel, S. Dak. **47** 44 46N 97 23W
Hazel → **54** 38 33N 77 51W
Hazel Green **55** 42 32N 90 26W
Hazel Run **30** 44 45N 95 43W
Hazelton, Canada **62** 55 20N 127 42W
Hazelton, Idaho **20** 42 36N 114 8W
Hazelton, Kans. **24** 37 5N 98 24W
Hazelton, N. Dak. **41** 46 29N 100 17W
Hazelton Peak **56** 44 6N 107 3W
Hazelwood **40** 35 28N 83 0W
Hazen, Ark. **13** 34 47N 91 35W
Hazen, N. Dak. **41** 47 18N 101 38W
Hazen, Nev. **35** 39 34N 119 3W
Hazlehurst, Ga. **18** 31 52N 82 36W
Hazlehurst, Miss. **31** 31 52N 90 24W
Hazlet **37** 40 25N 74 12W
Hazleton, Ind. **22** 38 29N 87 33W
Hazleton, Iowa **23** 42 37N 91 54W
Hazleton, Pa. **45** 40 57N 75 59W
Hazlettville **27** 39 9N 75 40W
Ḩaẕor **104** 33 2N 35 32 E
He Devil **20** 45 21N 116 33W
He Xian **115** 24 27N 111 30 E
Head of Bight **126** 31 30 S 131 25 E
Headland **10** 31 21N 85 21W
Headquarters **20** 46 38N 115 48W
Headrick **43** 34 38N 99 9W
Healdsburg **14** 38 37N 122 52W
Healdton **43** 34 14N 97 29W
Healdville **36** 43 25N 72 45W
Healy, Alaska **11** 63 52N 148 58W
Healy, Kans. **24** 38 36N 100 37W
Heanor **82** 53 1N 1 20W
Heard County ◇ **18** 33 15N 85 0W
Heard I. **3** 53 0 S 74 0 E
Hearne **51** 30 53N 96 36W
Hearne B. **63** 60 10N 99 10W
Hearne L. **62** 62 20N 113 10W
Hearst **60** 49 40N 83 41W
Heart → **41** 46 46N 100 50W
Heart L. **56** 44 16N 110 29W
Heart's Content **61** 47 54N 53 27W
Heartwell **34** 40 34N 98 47W
Heath → **72** 12 31 S 68 38W
Heath Pt. **61** 49 8N 61 40W
Heath Springs **46** 34 36N 80 40W
Heath Steele **61** 47 17N 66 5W
Heathsville **54** 37 55N 76 29W
Heavener **43** 34 53N 94 36W
Hebbardsville **48** 37 47N 87 23W
Hebbronville **50** 27 18N 98 41W
Hebei □ **114** 39 0N 116 0 E
Heber, Ariz. **12** 34 26N 110 36W
Heber, Calif. **15** 32 44N 115 32W

Heber City Hillsboro

Heber City 52 40 31N 111 25W
Heber Springs 13 35 30N 92 2W
Hebert 63 50 30N 107 10W
Hebgen L. 33 44 52N 111 20W
Hebi 114 35 57N 114 7 E
Hebo 44 45 14N 123 52W
Hebrides 84 57 30N 7 0W
Hebrides, Inner Is. 84 57 20N 6 40W
Hebrides, Outer Is. 84 57 30N 7 40W
Hebron = Al Khalīl 104 31 32N 35 6 E
Hebron, Canada 59 58 5N 62 30W
Hebron, Conn. 28 41 39N 72 22W
Hebron, Ill. 21 42 28N 88 26W
Hebron, Ind. 22 41 19N 87 12W
Hebron, Md. 27 38 25N 75 41W
Hebron, N. Dak. 41 46 54N 102 3W
Hebron, N.H. 36 43 42N 71 48W
Hebron, Nebr. 34 40 10N 97 35W
Hebron, Tex. 51 33 2N 96 52W
Hecate Str. 62 53 10N 130 30W
Hechi 115 24 40N 108 2 E
Hechuan 115 30 2N 106 12 E
Hecla 47 45 53N 98 9W
Hecla I. 63 51 10N 96 43W
Hector, Ark. 13 35 28N 92 59W
Hector, Minn. 30 44 45N 94 43W
Hede 96 62 23N 13 30 E
Hedemora 97 60 18N 15 58 E
Hedgesville 54 39 31N 77 58W
Hedley 50 34 52N 100 39W
Hedrick 23 41 11N 92 19W
Heemstede 87 52 22N 4 37 E
Heerde 87 52 24N 6 2 E
Heerenveen 87 52 57N 5 55 E
Heerlen 87 50 55N 6 0 E
Ḥefa 104 32 46N 35 0 E
Hefei 115 31 52N 117 18 E
Heflin 10 33 39N 85 35W
Hefner, L. 43 35 35N 97 36W
Hegang 114 47 20N 130 19 E
Heiberger 10 32 46N 87 17W
Heidelberg, Germany 88 49 23N 8 41 E
Heidelberg, Minn. 30 44 30N 93 38W
Heidelberg, Miss. 31 31 53N 88 59W
Heidrick 49 36 52N 83 54W
Heilbron 123 27 16 S 27 59 E
Heilbronn 88 49 8N 9 13 E
Heilongjiang □ 114 48 0N 126 0 E
Heilunkiang = Heilongjiang □ 114 48 0N 126 0 E
Heinola 97 61 13N 26 2 E
Heinze Is. 112 14 25N 97 45 E
Heizer 24 38 25N 98 53W
Hejaz = Al Ḥijāz 106 26 0N 37 30 E
Hejian 114 38 25N 116 5 E
Hejiang 115 28 43N 105 46 E
Hekimhan 106 38 50N 38 0 E
Hekla 96 63 56N 19 35W
Hekou 113 22 30N 103 59 E
Helan Shan 114 39 0N 105 55 E
Helemano → 19 21 35N 158 7W
Helen 27 38 22N 76 42W
Helena, Ala. 10 33 18N 86 51W
Helena, Ark. 13 34 32N 90 36W
Helena, Calif. 14 40 47N 123 8W
Helena, Ga. 18 32 5N 82 55W
Helena, Mont. 33 46 36N 112 2W
Helena National Forest 33 46 30N 111 30W
Helensburgh 84 56 0N 4 44W
Helensville 128 36 41 S 174 29 E
Ḥeleẓ 104 31 36N 34 39 E
Helgoland 88 54 10N 7 51 E
Heligoland = Helgoland 88 54 10N 7 51 E
Helix 44 45 51N 118 39W
Hell Cr. → 16 39 30N 102 30W
Hellendoorn 87 52 24N 6 27 E
Hellertown 45 40 35N 75 21W
Hellevoetsluis 87 51 50N 4 8 E
Hellín 91 38 31N 1 40W
Hells Canyon 44 45 10N 116 50W
Hells Canyon Nat. Rec. Area 44 45 30N 117 45W
Helmand □ 107 31 20N 64 0 E
Helmand → 107 31 12N 61 34 E
Helmand, Hamun 107 31 15N 61 15 E
Helmond 87 51 29N 5 41 E
Helmsdale 84 58 7N 3 40W
Helmville 33 46 52N 112 58W
Helotes 51 29 35N 98 41W
Helper 52 39 41N 110 51W
Helsingborg 97 56 3N 12 42 E
Helsingfors 97 60 15N 25 3 E
Helsingør 97 56 2N 12 35 E
Helsinki 97 60 15N 25 3 E
Helston 83 50 7N 5 17W
Helton 49 36 58N 83 24W
Helvellyn 82 54 31N 3 1W
Helwân 121 29 50N 31 20 E
Hematite 32 38 12N 90 29W
Hemet 15 33 45N 116 58W
Hemingford 34 42 19N 103 4W
Hemingway 46 33 45N 79 27W
Hemphill 51 31 20N 93 51W
Hemphill County ◇ 50 35 55N 100 15W
Hempstead, N.Y. 39 40 43N 73 38W
Hempstead, Tex. 51 30 6N 96 5W
Hempstead County ◇ 13 33 40N 93 36W
Hemse 97 57 15N 18 22 E
Henagar 10 34 38N 85 46W
Henan □ 115 34 0N 114 0 E
Henares → 91 40 24N 3 30W
Henashi-Misaki 116 40 37N 139 51 E
Henderson, Argentina 76 36 18 S 61 43W
Henderson, Ga. 18 32 21N 83 47W
Henderson, Iowa 23 41 8N 95 26W
Henderson, Ky. 48 37 50N 87 35W
Henderson, Md. 27 39 6N 75 47W
Henderson, N.C. 40 36 20N 78 25W
Henderson, Nebr. 34 40 47N 97 49W
Henderson, Nev. 35 36 2N 114 59W
Henderson, Tenn. 48 35 26N 88 38W
Henderson, Tex. 51 32 9N 94 48W
Henderson County ◇, Ill. 21 40 50N 90 55W
Henderson County ◇, Ky. 48 37 45N 87 35W
Henderson County ◇, N.C. 40 35 15N 82 30W
Henderson County ◇, Tenn. 48 35 39N 88 24W
Henderson County ◇, Tex. 50 32 12N 95 51W
Hendersonville, N.C. 40 35 19N 82 28W
Hendersonville, S.C. 46 32 48N 80 43W
Hendersonville, Tenn. 48 36 18N 86 37W
Hendley 34 40 8N 99 58W
Hendorf 95 46 4N 24 55 E
Hendricks 30 44 30N 96 25W
Hendricks County ◇ 22 39 45N 86 30W
Hendrum 30 47 16N 96 49W
Hendry County ◇ 17 26 30N 81 20W
Henefer 52 41 1N 111 30W
Heng Xian 115 22 40N 109 17 E
Hengdaohezi 114 44 52N 129 0 E
Hengelo 87 52 3N 6 19 E
Hengshan, Hunan, China 115 27 16N 112 45 E
Hengshan, Shaanxi, China 114 37 58N 109 5 E
Hengshui 114 37 41N 115 40 E
Hengyang 115 26 52N 112 33 E
Henlopen, C. 27 38 48N 75 6W
Hennepin, Ill. 21 41 15N 89 21W
Hennepin, Okla. 43 34 31N 97 21W
Hennepin County ◇ 30 45 0N 93 30W
Hennessey 43 36 6N 97 54W
Henniker 36 43 11N 71 50W
Henning, Ill. 21 40 18N 87 42W
Henning, Minn. 30 46 19N 95 27W
Henning, Tenn. 48 35 41N 89 34W
Henrico County ◇ 54 37 33N 77 20W
Henrietta 51 33 49N 98 12W
Henrietta, Ostrov 101 77 6N 156 30 E
Henrietta Maria C. 60 55 9N 82 20W
Henriette 30 45 53N 93 7W
Henrieville 52 37 30N 112 0W
Henry, Ill. 21 41 7N 89 22W
Henry, Nebr. 34 41 58N 104 4W
Henry, S. Dak. 47 44 53N 97 28W
Henry, Tenn. 48 36 12N 88 25W
Henry, C. 54 36 56N 76 1W
Henry County ◇, Ala. 10 31 34N 85 15W
Henry County ◇, Ga. 18 33 25N 84 5W
Henry County ◇, Ill. 21 41 20N 90 10W
Henry County ◇, Ind. 22 39 55N 85 25W
Henry County ◇, Iowa 23 41 0N 91 30W
Henry County ◇, Ky. 49 38 25N 85 10W
Henry County ◇, Mo. 32 38 25N 93 45W
Henry County ◇, Ohio 42 41 19N 84 2W
Henry County ◇, Tenn. 48 36 18N 88 19W
Henry County ◇, Va. 54 36 50N 79 56W
Henry Mts. 52 38 0N 110 50W
Henryetta 43 35 27N 95 59W
Henrys Fork → 20 41 0N 109 39W
Henrys Lake 20 44 36N 111 21W
Henshaw 48 37 37N 88 3W
Henshaw L. 15 33 15N 116 45W
Hensler 41 47 16N 101 5W
Hentiyn Nuruu 113 48 30N 108 30 E
Henzada 109 17 38N 95 26 E
Hepburn 23 40 51N 95 1W
Hephzibah 18 33 19N 82 6W
Heping 115 24 29N 115 0 E
Hepler 24 37 40N 94 58W
Heppner 44 45 21N 119 33W
Hepu 115 21 40N 109 12 E
Héraðsflói 96 65 42N 14 12W
Héraðsvötn → 96 65 45N 19 25W
Herāt 107 34 20N 62 7 E
Herāt □ 107 35 0N 62 0 E
Hérault □ 90 43 34N 3 15 E
Herbert I. 11 52 45N 170 7W
Hercegnovi 95 42 30N 18 33 E
Hercegovina = Bosna i Hercegovina □ 94 44 0N 18 0 E
Herculaneum 32 38 16N 90 23W
Herðubreið 96 65 11N 16 21W
Hereford, U.K. 83 52 4N 2 42W
Hereford, Ariz. 12 31 26N 110 6W
Hereford, Colo. 16 40 57N 104 18W
Hereford, Md. 27 39 35N 76 40W
Hereford, Tex. 50 34 49N 102 24W
Hereford and Worcester □ 83 52 10N 2 30W
Herentals 87 51 12N 4 51 E
Herford 88 52 7N 8 40 E
Herington 24 38 40N 96 57W
Herjehogna 97 61 43N 12 7 E
Herkimer, Kans. 24 39 54N 96 43W
Herkimer, N.Y. 39 43 2N 74 59W
Herkimer County ◇ 39 43 0N 75 0W
Herman, Minn. 30 45 49N 96 9W
Herman, Nebr. 34 41 40N 96 13W
Hermann 32 38 42N 91 27W
Hermansville 29 45 42N 87 36W
Hermantown 30 46 50N 92 15W
Hermanville 31 31 58N 90 50W
Hermiston 44 45 51N 119 17W
Hermitage, N.Z. 128 43 44 S 170 5 E
Hermitage, Ark. 13 33 27N 92 10W
Hermitage, Mo. 32 37 56N 93 19W
Hermite, I. 78 55 50 S 68 0W
Hermleigh 50 32 38N 100 46W
Hermon 39 44 28N 75 14W
Hermon, Mt. = Ash Shaykh, J. 106 33 25N 35 50 E
Hermosa 47 43 50N 103 12W
Hermosillo 64 29 10N 111 0W
Hernad → 89 47 56N 21 8 E
Hernandarias 77 25 20 S 54 40W
Hernando, Argentina 76 32 28 S 63 40W
Hernando, Fla. 17 28 54N 82 23W
Hernando, Miss. 31 34 50N 90 0W
Hernando County ◇ 17 28 35N 82 30W
Herndon, Kans. 24 39 55N 100 47W
Herndon, Ky. 48 36 44N 87 34W
Herndon, Pa. 45 40 43N 76 51W
Herndon, Va. 54 38 58N 77 23W
Herne Bay 83 51 22N 1 8 E
Herning 97 56 8N 8 58 E
Herod 18 31 42N 84 26W
Heroica = Caborca 64 30 40N 112 10W
Heroica Nogales = Nogales 64 31 20N 110 56W
Heron 33 48 3N 115 57W
Heron Bay 60 48 40N 86 25W
Heron Lake 30 43 48N 95 19W
Herreid 47 45 50N 100 4W
Herrera 91 37 26N 4 55W
Herrick 47 43 7N 99 11W
Herrin 21 37 48N 89 2W
Herrington L. 49 37 45N 84 44W
Herscher 21 41 3N 88 6W
Hersey 29 43 51N 85 27W
Hershey 34 41 10N 101 0W
Herstal 87 50 40N 5 38 E
Hertford, U.K. 83 51 47N 0 4W
Hertford, U.S.A. 40 36 11N 76 28W
Hertford □ 83 51 51N 0 5W
Hertford County ◇ 40 36 20N 77 0W
's-Hertogenbosch 87 51 42N 5 17 E
Hervey B. 127 25 0 S 152 52 E
Herzliyya 104 32 10N 34 50 E
Hesperia, Calif. 15 34 25N 117 18W
Hesperia, Mich. 29 43 34N 86 3W
Hesperus 16 37 17N 108 2W
Hesse = Hessen □ 88 50 40N 9 20 E
Hessel 29 46 0N 84 26W
Hessen □ 88 50 40N 9 20 E
Hessmer 25 31 3N 92 8W
Hesston 24 38 8N 97 26W
Hetch Hetchy Aqueduct 14 37 29N 122 19W
Hetch Hetchy Reservoir 14 37 57N 119 47W
Hettinger 41 46 0N 102 42W
Hettinger County ◇ 41 46 25N 102 30W
Heuvelton 39 44 37N 75 25W
Hevron → 104 31 12N 34 42 E
Hewett, C. 59 70 16N 67 45W
Hewins 24 37 3N 96 25W
Hewitt 30 46 20N 95 5W
Hewlett 54 37 55N 77 35W
Hexham 82 54 58N 2 7W
Hexigten Qi 114 43 18N 117 30 E
Hext 51 30 52N 99 32W
Heyburn, L. 43 35 57N 96 18W
Heysham 82 54 5N 2 53W
Heyworth 21 40 19N 88 59W
Hialeah 17 25 50N 80 17W
Hiattville 24 37 43N 94 52W
Hiawassee 18 34 58N 83 46W
Hiawatha, Kans. 24 39 51N 95 32W
Hiawatha, Utah 52 39 29N 111 1W
Hiawatha National Forest 29 46 15N 86 40W
Hibbing 30 47 25N 92 56W
Hickman, Del. 27 38 50N 75 42W
Hickman, Ky. 48 36 34N 89 11W
Hickman, Nebr. 34 40 37N 96 38W
Hickman County ◇, Ky. 48 36 40N 89 0W
Hickman County ◇, Tenn. 48 35 47N 87 28W
Hickok 24 37 34N 101 14W
Hickory, Ky. 48 36 48N 88 40W
Hickory, N.C. 40 35 44N 81 21W
Hickory, L. 40 35 49N 81 12W
Hickory County ◇ 32 37 55N 93 15W
Hickory Grove 46 34 59N 81 25W
Hickory Plains 13 34 59N 91 44W
Hickory Ridge 13 35 24N 90 58W
Hickory Valley 48 35 9N 89 8W
Hicks Pt. 127 37 49 S 149 17 E
Hicksville, N.Y. 39 40 46N 73 32W
Hicksville, Ohio 42 41 18N 84 46W
Hico 51 31 59N 98 2W
Hida-Gawa → 117 35 26N 137 3 E
Hida-Sammyaku 117 36 30N 137 40 E
Hidaka-Sammyaku 116 42 35N 142 45 E
Hidalgo, Mexico 65 24 15N 99 26W
Hidalgo, Ill. 21 39 9N 88 9W
Hidalgo, Tex. 50 26 6N 98 16W
Hidalgo □ 65 20 30N 99 10W
Hidalgo, Presa M. 64 26 30N 108 35W
Hidalgo County ◇, N. Mex. 38 32 0N 108 45W
Hidalgo County ◇, Tex. 50 26 25N 98 10W
Hidalgo del Parral 64 26 58N 105 40W
Hidrolândia 75 17 0 S 49 15W
Hierro 120 27 44N 18 0 E
Higashiajima-San 116 37 40N 140 10 E
Higashiōsaka 117 34 40N 135 37 E
Higbee 32 39 19N 92 31W
Higgins 50 36 7N 100 2W
Higgins L. 29 44 29N 84 43W
Higginsport 42 38 47N 83 58W
Higginsville 32 39 4N 93 43W
High Atlas = Haut Atlas 120 32 30N 5 0W
High Bridge 37 40 40N 74 54W
High Hill 32 38 53N 91 23W
High I., Canada 61 56 40N 61 10W
High I., U.S.A. 29 45 44N 85 41W
High Island 51 29 34N 94 24W
High Level 62 58 31N 117 8W
High Point 40 35 57N 80 0W
High Prairie 62 55 30N 116 30W
High Pt., N.J. 37 41 19N 74 40W
High Pt., Wyo. 56 41 37N 107 43W
High River 62 50 30N 113 50W
High Rock L., N.C. 40 35 36N 80 14W
High Rock L., Nev. 35 41 17N 119 17W
High Rolls 38 32 57N 105 50W
High Springs 17 29 50N 82 36W
High Wycombe 83 51 37N 0 45W
Highgate Center 36 44 56N 73 3W
Highland, Calif. 15 34 8N 117 13W
Highland, Ill. 21 38 44N 89 41W
Highland, Ind. 22 41 33N 87 28W
Highland, Kans. 24 39 52N 95 16W
Highland, N.Y. 39 41 43N 73 58W
Highland, Wis. 55 43 5N 90 22W
Highland □ 84 57 30N 5 0W
Highland Beach 27 38 56N 76 28W
Highland City 17 27 58N 81 53W
Highland County ◇, Ohio 42 39 12N 83 37W
Highland County ◇, Va. 54 38 25N 79 35W
Highland Hills 21 41 51N 88 1W
Highland Home 10 31 57N 86 19W
Highland Lakes 37 41 11N 74 28W
Highland Mills 18 33 17N 84 28W
Highland Park 21 42 11N 87 48W
Highland Springs 54 37 33N 77 20W
Highland View 17 29 50N 85 19W
Highlands, N.C. 40 35 3N 83 12W
Highlands, N.J. 37 40 24N 73 59W
Highlands County ◇ 17 27 20N 81 20W
Highmore 47 44 31N 99 27W
Highpoint 31 33 11N 89 9W
Highrock L. 63 57 5N 105 32W
Hightstown 37 40 16N 74 31W
Highwood 21 42 12N 87 48W
Highwood Mts. 33 47 30N 110 30W
Higüay 67 18 37N 68 42W
Higuero, Punta 57 18 22N 67 16W
Hiiumaa 98 58 50N 22 45 E
Ḥijārah, Şaḥrā' al 106 30 25N 44 30 E
Hijo = Tagum 111 7 33N 125 53 E
Hikari 117 33 58N 131 58 E
Hiko 35 37 32N 115 14W
Hikone 117 35 15N 136 10 E
Hiland 56 43 7N 107 21W
Hilda 46 33 16N 81 15W
Hildesheim 88 52 9N 9 55 E
Hildreth 34 40 20N 99 3W
Hilgard 44 45 21N 118 14W
Hill City, Idaho 20 43 18N 115 3W
Hill City, Kans. 24 39 22N 99 51W
Hill City, Minn. 30 46 59N 93 36W
Hill City, S. Dak. 47 43 56N 103 35W
Hill County ◇, Mont. 33 48 40N 110 0W
Hill County ◇, Tex. 51 32 1N 97 8W
Hill Cr. → 52 39 55N 109 40W
Hill Island L. 63 60 30N 109 50W
Hillcrest Center 15 35 23N 118 57W
Hillcrest Heights 27 38 50N 76 57W
Hillegom 87 52 18N 4 35 E
Hilliard, Fla. 17 30 41N 81 55W
Hilliard, Ohio 42 40 2N 83 10W
Hilliards 45 41 5N 79 50W
Hillingdon 83 51 33N 0 29W
Hillister 51 30 40N 94 23W
Hillman, Mich. 29 45 4N 83 54W
Hillman, Minn. 30 46 0N 93 53W
Hillmond 63 53 26N 109 41W
Hillrose 16 40 20N 103 31W
Hills, Iowa 23 41 33N 91 32W
Hills, Minn. 30 43 32N 96 21W
Hills Creek L. 44 43 43N 122 26W
Hillsboro, Ga. 18 33 11N 83 38W
Hillsboro, Ill. 21 39 9N 89 29W
Hillsboro, Kans. 24 38 21N 97 12W
Hillsboro, Md. 27 38 55N 75 50W
Hillsboro, Mo. 32 38 14N 90 34W
Hillsboro, N. Dak. 41 47 26N 97 3W
Hillsboro, N.H. 36 43 7N 71 54W
Hillsboro, N. Mex. 38 32 55N 107 34W
Hillsboro, Ohio 42 39 12N 83 37W
Hillsboro, Oreg. 44 45 31N 122 59W
Hillsboro, Tex. 51 32 1N 97 8W

Hillsboro Hopkins

Hillsboro, W. Va. 54 38 8N 80 13W
Hillsboro, Wis. 55 43 39N 90 21W
Hillsboro Canal 17 26 30N 80 15W
Hillsboro Upper Village 36 43 9N 71 58W
Hillsborough, U.S.A. 40 36 5N 79 7W
Hillsborough, W. Indies 67 12 28N 61 28W
Hillsborough County ◇, Fla. 17 27 50N 82 20W
Hillsborough County ◇, N.H. 36 42 50N 71 45W
Hillsdale, Ill. 21 41 37N 90 11W
Hillsdale, Kans. 24 38 40N 94 51W
Hillsdale, Mich. 29 41 56N 84 38W
Hillsdale, Okla. 43 36 34N 97 59W
Hillsdale County ◇ 29 41 50N 84 40W
Hillside, Ariz. 12 34 25N 112 55W
Hillside, N.J. 37 40 42N 74 13W
Hillsmere Shore 27 38 56N 76 32W
Hillsport 60 49 27N 85 34W
Hillston 127 33 30 S 145 31 E
Hillsville 54 36 46N 80 44W
Hilltonia 18 32 53N 81 40W
Hillview 49 38 5N 85 49W
Hilo 19 19 44N 155 5W
Hilo B. 19 19 45N 155 5W
Hilt 14 41 50N 122 37W
Hilton 39 43 17N 77 48W
Hilton Head I. 46 32 13N 80 45W
Hilversum 87 52 14N 5 10 E
Himachal Pradesh □ 108 31 30N 77 0 E
Himalaya, Mts. 109 29 0N 84 0 E
Himatnagar 108 23 37N 72 57 E
Himeji 117 34 50N 134 40 E
Himi 117 36 50N 137 0 E
Ḥimş 106 34 40N 36 45 E
Hinako, Kepulauan 110 0 50N 97 20 E
Hinchcliff 31 34 19N 90 17W
Hinche 67 19 9N 72 1W
Hinchinbrook I. 127 18 20 S 146 15 E
Hinckley, U.K. 83 52 33N 1 21W
Hinckley, Ill. 21 41 46N 88 38W
Hinckley, Minn. 30 46 1N 92 56W
Hinckley, Utah 52 39 20N 112 40W
Hinckley Reservoir 39 43 19N 75 7W
Hindman 49 37 20N 82 59W
Hinds County ◇ 31 32 16N 90 25W
Hindsboro 21 39 41N 88 8W
Hindu Kush 107 36 0N 71 0 E
Hindubagh 108 30 56N 67 57 E
Hindupur 108 13 49N 77 32 E
Hines, Fla. 17 29 45N 83 14W
Hines, Oreg. 44 43 34N 119 5W
Hines Creek 62 56 20N 118 40W
Hinesburg 36 44 18N 73 6W
Hineston 25 31 9N 92 46W
Hinesville 18 31 51N 81 36W
Hinganghat 108 20 30N 78 52 E
Hingham, Mass. 28 42 15N 70 53W
Hingham, Mont. 33 48 33N 110 25W
Hingoli 108 19 41N 77 15 E
Hinlopenstretet 4 79 35N 18 40 E
Hinna = Imi 105 6 28N 42 10 E
Hinsdale, Md. 27 42 26N 73 8W
Hinsdale, Mont. 33 48 24N 107 5W
Hinsdale, N.H. 36 42 47N 72 29W
Hinsdale County ◇ 16 37 50N 107 20W
Hinson 17 30 39N 84 25W
Hinton, Canada 62 53 26N 117 34W
Hinton, Iowa 23 42 38N 96 18W
Hinton, Okla. 43 35 28N 98 21W
Hinton, W. Va. 54 37 40N 80 54W
Hippolytushoef 87 52 54N 4 58 E
Hirado 117 33 22N 129 33 E
Hirakud Dam 109 21 32N 83 45 E
Hiram 42 41 19N 81 9W
Hiratsuka 117 35 19N 139 21 E
Hiroo 116 42 17N 143 19 E
Hirosaki 116 40 34N 140 28 E
Hiroshima 117 34 24N 132 30 E
Hiroshima □ 117 34 50N 133 0 E
Hîrşova 95 44 40N 27 59 E
Hisar 108 29 12N 75 45 E
Hispaniola 67 19 0N 71 0W
Hita 117 33 20N 130 58 E
Hitachi 117 36 36N 140 39 E
Hitchcock, Okla. 43 35 58N 98 21W
Hitchcock, S. Dak. 47 44 38N 98 25W
Hitchcock, Tex. 51 29 21N 95 1W
Hitchcock County ◇ 34 40 15N 101 0W
Hitchin 83 51 57N 0 16W
Hitchins 49 38 17N 82 55W
Hitchita 43 35 31N 95 44W
Hitoyoshi 117 32 13N 130 45 E
Hitra 96 63 30N 8 45 E
Hitterdal 30 46 59N 96 16W
Hiwannee 31 31 49N 88 41W
Hiwassee 54 36 58N 80 43W
Hiwassee → 49 35 19N 84 47W
Hiwassee L. 40 35 9N 84 11W
Hixton 55 44 23N 91 1W
Ḥiyyon, N. → 104 30 25N 35 10 E
Hjalmar L. 63 61 33N 109 25W
Hjälmaren 97 59 18N 15 40 E
Hjørring 97 57 29N 9 59 E
Hńak 4 70 40N 52 10W
Ho 120 6 37N 0 27 E
Ho Chi Minh, Phanh Bho 112 10 58N 106 40 E
Ho Chi Minh City = Phanh Bho Ho Chi Minh, Vietnam 112 10 58N 106 40 E
Ho Chi Minh City = Phanh Bho Ho Chi Minh, Vietnam 112 10 58N 106 40 E
Hoa Binh 112 20 50N 105 20 E
Hoai Nhon 112 14 28N 109 1 E
Hoare B. 59 65 17N 62 30W
Hobart, Australia 127 42 50 S 147 21 E
Hobart, Ind. 22 41 32N 87 15W
Hobart, N.Y. 39 42 22N 74 40W
Hobart, Okla. 43 35 1N 99 6W
Hobbs 38 32 42N 103 8W
Hobbs Coast 5 74 50 S 131 0W
Hobe Sound 17 27 4N 80 8W
Hoberg 32 37 4N 93 51W
Hobgood 40 36 2N 77 24W
Hobo 70 2 35N 75 30W
Hoboken, Belgium 87 51 11N 4 21 E
Hoboken, U.S.A. 18 31 11N 82 8W
Hobro 97 56 39N 9 46 E
Hobson, Ky. 49 37 25N 85 22W
Hobson, Mont. 33 47 0N 109 52W
Hobucken 40 35 15N 76 34W
Hoburgen 97 56 55N 18 7 E
Hochheim 51 29 19N 97 17W
Hockessin 27 39 47N 75 42W
Hocking 42 39 12N 81 45W
Hocking County ◇ 42 39 32N 82 25W
Hockley County ◇ 50 33 35N 102 23W
Hodaka-Dake 117 36 17N 137 39 E
Hodge 25 32 17N 92 43W
Hodgeman County ◇ 24 38 0N 100 0W
Hodgenville 49 37 34N 85 44W
Hodges 46 34 17N 82 15W
Hodgson 63 51 13N 97 36W
Hódmezövásárhely 89 46 28N 20 22 E
Hodna, Chott el 120 35 30N 5 0 E
Hodonín 88 48 50N 17 10 E
Hoehne 16 37 17N 104 23W
Hoek van Holland 87 52 0N 4 7 E
Hof, Germany 88 50 18N 11 55 E
Hof, Iceland 96 64 33N 14 40W
Höfðakaupstaður 96 65 50N 20 19W
Hoffman, Ill. 21 38 32N 89 16W
Hoffman, Minn. 30 45 50N 95 48W
Hoffman, N.C. 40 35 2N 79 33W
Hoffman, Okla. 43 35 29N 95 51W
Hofsjökull 96 64 49N 18 48W
Hofsós 96 65 53N 19 26W
Hōfu 117 34 3N 131 34 E
Hog I., Mich. 29 45 48N 85 22W
Hog I., Va. 54 37 26N 75 42W
Hogansville 18 33 10N 84 55W
Hogback Mt., Mont. 33 44 54N 112 7W
Hogback Mt., Nebr. 34 41 44N 103 42W
Hogeland 33 48 51N 108 40W
Hogsty Reef 67 21 41N 73 48W
Hoh → 53 47 45N 124 29W
Hoh Xil Shan 113 35 0N 89 0 E
Hohe Venn 87 50 30N 6 5 E
Hohenwald 48 35 33N 87 33W
Hohhot 114 40 52N 111 40 E
Hoi An 112 15 30N 108 19 E
Hoi Xuan 112 20 25N 105 9 E
Hoisington 24 38 31N 98 47W
Hōjō 117 33 58N 132 46 E
Hokah 30 43 46N 91 21W
Hoke County ◇ 40 35 0N 79 15W
Hokianga Harbour 128 35 31 S 173 22 E
Hokitika 128 42 42 S 171 0 E
Hokkaidō □ 116 43 30N 143 0 E
Holbrook, Ariz. 12 34 54N 110 10W
Holbrook, Idaho 20 42 10N 112 39W
Holbrook, Mass. 28 42 9N 71 1W
Holbrook, N.Y. 39 40 49N 73 5W
Holbrook, Nebr. 34 40 18N 100 1W
Holcomb, Kans. 24 37 59N 100 59W
Holcomb, Mo. 32 36 24N 90 2W
Holcomb, N.Y. 39 42 54N 77 25W
Holden, Canada 62 53 13N 112 11W
Holden, Mass. 28 42 21N 71 52W
Holden, Mo. 32 38 43N 94 1W
Holden, Utah 52 39 6N 112 16W
Holdenville 43 35 5N 96 24W
Holder 17 28 58N 82 25W
Holderness, U.K. 82 53 45N 0 5W
Holderness, U.S.A. 36 43 43N 71 37W
Holdfast 63 50 58N 105 25W
Holdich 78 45 57 S 68 13W
Holdingford 30 45 44N 94 28W
Holdrege 34 40 26N 99 23W
Holgate, N.J. 37 39 33N 74 15W
Holgate, Ohio 42 41 15N 84 8W
Holguín 66 20 50N 76 20W
Holladay, Tenn. 48 35 52N 88 9W
Holladay, Utah 52 40 40N 111 50W
Hollams Bird I. 123 24 40 S 14 30 E
Holland, Ark. 13 35 10N 92 16W
Holland, Ga. 18 34 21N 85 22W
Holland, Iowa 23 42 24N 92 48W
Holland, Mich. 29 42 47N 86 7W
Holland, Minn. 30 44 6N 96 11W
Holland, Mo. 32 36 3N 89 52W
Holland, Tex. 51 30 53N 97 24W
Holland Patent 39 43 15N 75 15W
Hollandale, Minn. 30 43 46N 93 12W
Hollandale, Miss. 31 33 10N 90 51W
Hollandale, Wis. 55 42 53N 89 56W
Hollansburg 42 39 59N 84 50W
Hollenberg 24 39 58N 96 59W
Holley, Fla. 17 30 27N 86 54W
Holley, N.Y. 39 43 14N 78 2W
Holley, Oreg. 44 44 21N 122 47W
Hollick Kenyon Plateau 5 82 0 S 110 0W
Holliday 51 33 49N 98 42W
Hollidaysburg 45 40 26N 78 24W
Hollis, Ark. 13 34 52N 93 7W
Hollis, Kans. 24 39 38N 97 33W
Hollis, Okla. 43 34 41N 99 55W
Hollister, Calif. 14 36 51N 121 24W
Hollister, Idaho 20 42 21N 114 35W
Hollister, Mo. 32 36 38N 93 12W
Hollister, N.C. 40 36 15N 77 56W
Hollister, Okla. 43 34 21N 98 52W
Holliston 28 42 12N 71 26W
Hollow Rock 48 36 2N 88 16W
Holloway 30 45 15N 95 55W
Holly, Colo. 16 38 3N 102 7W
Holly, Mich. 29 42 48N 83 38W
Holly Grove 13 34 36N 91 12W
Holly Hill, Fla. 17 29 16N 81 3W
Holly Hill, S.C. 46 33 19N 80 25W
Holly Pond 10 34 10N 86 37W
Holly Ridge 40 34 30N 77 33W
Holly Springs, Ga. 18 34 10N 84 30W
Holly Springs, Miss. 31 34 46N 89 27W
Holly Springs, N.C. 40 35 39N 78 50W
Holly Springs National Forest 31 34 40N 89 5W
Hollywood, Ala. 10 34 44N 85 59W
Hollywood, Fla. 17 26 1N 80 9W
Hollywood, Md. 27 38 21N 76 34W
Hollywood, Miss. 31 34 45N 90 22W
Holman 38 36 2N 105 23W
Holman Island 58 70 42N 117 41W
Hólmavík 96 65 42N 21 40W
Holmen 55 43 58N 91 15W
Holmes → 17 30 30N 85 50W
Holmes, Mt. 56 44 49N 110 51W
Holmes Beach 17 27 31N 82 43W
Holmes County ◇, Fla. 17 30 50N 85 45W
Holmes County ◇, Miss. 31 33 7N 90 3W
Holmes County ◇, Ohio 42 40 33N 81 55W
Holmesville 42 40 38N 81 56W
Holmsund 96 63 41N 20 20 E
Holon 104 32 2N 34 47 E
Holopaw 17 28 8N 81 5W
Holroyd → 127 14 10 S 141 36 E
Holstebro 97 56 22N 8 37 E
Holstein, Iowa 23 42 29N 95 33W
Holstein, Nebr. 34 40 28N 98 39W
Holston → 49 35 58N 83 51W
Holsworthy 83 50 48N 4 21W
Holt, Iceland 96 63 33N 19 48W
Holt, Fla. 17 30 43N 86 45W
Holt, Mich. 29 42 39N 84 31W
Holt, Minn. 30 48 18N 96 11W
Holt, Mo. 32 39 27N 94 21W
Holt County ◇, Mo. 32 40 5N 95 10W
Holt County ◇, Nebr. 34 42 30N 98 45W
Holton, Canada 61 54 31N 57 12W
Holton, Ind. 22 39 5N 85 23W
Holton, Kans. 24 39 28N 95 44W
Holtville 15 32 49N 115 23W
Holualoa 19 19 37N 155 57W
Holwerd 87 53 22N 5 54 E
Holy Cross 11 62 12N 159 46W
Holy I., England, U.K. 82 55 42N 1 48W
Holy I., Wales, U.K. 82 53 17N 4 37W
Holyhead 82 53 18N 4 38W
Holyoke, Colo. 16 40 35N 102 18W
Holyoke, Mass. 28 42 12N 72 37W
Holyrood, Canada 61 47 27N 53 8W
Holyrood, U.S.A. 24 38 35N 98 25W
Homalin 109 24 55N 95 0 E
Hombori 120 15 20N 1 38W
Home 24 39 51N 96 31W
Home B. 59 68 40N 67 10W
Home Hill 127 19 43 S 147 25 E
Homedale 20 43 37N 116 56W
Homeland 18 30 51N 82 1W
Homer, Alaska 11 59 39N 151 33W
Homer, Ga. 18 34 20N 83 30W
Homer, La. 25 32 48N 93 4W
Homer, Mich. 29 42 9N 84 49W
Homer, N.Y. 39 42 38N 76 11W
Homer, Nebr. 34 42 19N 96 29W
Homer City 45 40 32N 79 10W
Homer Youngs Pk. 33 45 19N 113 41W
Homerville 18 31 2N 82 45W
Homestead, Fla. 17 25 28N 80 29W
Homestead, Oreg. 44 45 2N 116 51W
Homewood, Ala. 10 33 29N 86 47W
Homewood, Ill. 21 41 34N 87 40W
Hominy 43 36 25N 96 24W
Homochitto National Forest 31 31 15N 91 20W
Homorod 95 46 5N 25 15 E
Homosassa Springs 17 28 48N 82 35W
Homs = Ḥimş 106 34 40N 36 45 E
Hon 13 34 56N 94 11W
Hon Chong 112 10 25N 104 30 E
Honaker 54 37 1N 81 59W
Honan = Henan □ 115 34 0N 114 0 E
Honaunau 19 19 26N 155 55W
Honbetsu 116 43 7N 143 37 E
Honda 70 5 12N 74 45W
Hondeklipbaai 123 30 19 S 17 17 E
Hondo, Japan 117 32 27N 130 12 E
Hondo, N. Mex. 38 33 24N 105 16W
Hondo, Tex. 51 29 21N 99 9W
Hondo → 65 18 25N 88 21W
Honduras ■ 66 14 40N 86 30W
Honduras, Golfo de 66 16 50N 87 0W
Honea Path 46 34 27N 82 24W
Hønefoss 97 60 10N 10 18 E
Honesdale 45 41 34N 75 16W
Honey Grove 51 33 35N 95 55W
Honey Island 51 30 24N 94 27W
Honey L. 14 40 15N 120 19W
Honeyville, Fla. 17 30 3N 85 11W
Honeyville, Utah 52 41 38N 112 4W
Honfleur 90 49 25N 0 13 E
Hong Kong ■ 115 22 11N 114 14 E
Honga 27 38 19N 76 14W
Hong'an 115 31 20N 114 40 E
Hongha → 112 22 0N 104 0 E
Honghai Wan 115 22 40N 115 0 E
Honghu 115 29 50N 113 30 E
Hongjiang 115 27 7N 109 59 E
Hongshui He → 115 23 48N 109 30 E
Hongtong 114 36 16N 111 40 E
Honguedo, Détroit d' 61 49 15N 64 0W
Hongze Hu 115 33 15N 118 35 E
Honiara 124 9 27 S 159 57 E
Honiton 83 50 48N 3 11W
Honjō 116 39 23N 140 3 E
Honokaa 19 20 5N 155 28W
Honokahua 19 21 0N 156 40W
Honolulu 19 21 19N 157 52W
Honolulu County ◇ 19 21 20N 157 50W
Honomu 19 19 52N 155 7W
Honor 29 44 40N 86 1W
Honouliuli 19 21 22N 158 2W
Honshū 117 36 0N 138 0 E
Honuapo B. 19 19 5N 155 33W
Hood, Mt. 44 45 23N 121 42W
Hood, Pt. 126 34 23 S 119 34 E
Hood Canal 53 47 35N 123 0W
Hood County ◇ 51 32 27N 97 47W
Hood River 44 45 43N 121 31W
Hood River County ◇ 44 45 30N 121 20W
Hoodoo Peak 53 48 15N 120 19W
Hoodsport 53 47 24N 123 9W
Hoogeveen 87 52 44N 6 30 E
Hoogezand 87 53 11N 6 45 E
Hooghly → = Hughli → 109 21 56N 88 4 E
Hook Hd. 85 52 8N 6 57W
Hook of Holland = Hoek van Holland 87 52 0N 4 7 E
Hooker 43 36 52N 101 13W
Hooker County ◇ 34 41 50N 101 0W
Hooks 51 33 28N 94 16W
Hoolehua 19 21 10N 157 5W
Hoonah 11 58 7N 135 27W
Hoopa 14 41 3N 123 41W
Hoopa Valley Indian Reservation 14 41 10N 123 45W
Hooper, Colo. 16 37 45N 105 53W
Hooper, Nebr. 34 41 37N 96 33W
Hooper, Wash. 53 46 45N 118 9W
Hooper Bay 11 61 32N 166 6W
Hooper Str. 27 38 15N 76 5W
Hoopersville 27 38 16N 76 11W
Hoopeston 21 40 28N 87 40W
Hoople 41 48 32N 97 38W
Hoorn 87 52 38N 5 4 E
Hoosac Range 28 42 45N 73 2W
Hoosick Falls 39 42 54N 73 21W
Hoosier National Forest, Ind. 22 38 30N 86 35W
Hoosier National Forest, Ind. 22 39 0N 86 10W
Hoover Dam 12 36 1N 114 44W
Hoover Reservoir 42 40 7N 82 53W
Hooversville 45 40 9N 78 55W
Hop Bottom 45 41 42N 75 46W
Hopatcong 37 40 55N 74 40W
Hopatcong, L. 37 40 57N 74 38W
Hope, Canada 62 49 25N 121 25 E
Hope, Ark. 13 33 40N 93 36W
Hope, Ind. 22 39 18N 85 46W
Hope, Kans. 24 38 41N 97 5W
Hope, N. Dak. 41 47 19N 97 43W
Hope, N. Mex. 38 32 49N 104 44W
Hope, R.I. 28 41 44N 71 34W
Hope Mills 40 34 59N 78 57W
Hope Town 66 26 35N 76 57W
Hope Valley 28 41 30N 71 43W
Hopedale, Canada 61 55 28N 60 13W
Hopedale, U.S.A. 21 40 25N 89 25W
Hopei = Hebei □ 114 39 0N 116 0 E
Hopelchén 65 19 46N 89 50W
Hopeton 43 36 41N 98 40W
Hopetoun 126 33 57 S 120 7 E
Hopetown 123 29 34 S 24 3 E
Hopewell, Miss. 31 31 57N 90 13W
Hopewell, Va. 54 37 18N 77 17W
Hopi Indian Reservation 12 36 15N 110 30W
Hopkins, Mich. 29 42 37N 85 46W

Hopkins | Hungry Horse Reservoir

Hopkins, Mo. 32 40 33N 94 49W
Hopkins, S.C. 46 33 54N 80 53W
Hopkins County ◇, Ky. 48 37 20N 87 30W
Hopkins County ◇, Tex. 51 33 8N 95 36W
Hopkinsville 48 36 52N 87 29W
Hopkinton, Iowa 23 42 21N 91 15W
Hopkinton, Mass. 28 42 14N 71 31W
Hopkinton, N.H. 36 43 12N 71 41W
Hopkinton, R.I. 28 41 28N 71 48W
Hopland 14 38 58N 123 7W
Hoquiam 53 46 59N 123 53W
Horace, Kans. 24 38 29N 101 47W
Horace, N. Dak. 41 46 45N 96 54W
Horatio, Ark. 13 33 56N 94 21W
Horatio, S.C. 46 34 1N 80 33W
Hordaland fylke □ . . . . . 97 60 25N 6 15 E
Horden Hills . . . . . 126 20 40 S 130 20 E
Hordville 34 41 5N 97 53W
Horezu . . . . . 95 45 6N 24 0 E
Horicon 55 43 27N 88 38W
Horlick Mts. . . . . 5 84 0 S 102 0W
Hormigueros 57 18 8N 67 8W
Hormoz . . . . . 107 27 35N 55 0 E
Hormoz, Jaz. ye . . . . . 107 27 8N 56 28 E
Hormozgān □ . . . . . 107 27 30N 56 0 E
Hormuz Str. . . . . 107 26 30N 56 30 E
Horn, Austria . . . . . 88 48 39N 15 40 E
Horn, Ísafjarðarsýsla, Iceland 96 66 28N 22 28W
Horn, Suður-Múlasýsla, Iceland 96 65 10N 13 31W
Horn → 62 61 30N 118 1W
Horn, Cape = Hornos, Cabo de . . . . . 78 55 50 S 67 30W
Horn Head 85 55 13N 8 0W
Horn I. 31 30 14N 88 39W
Horn Lake 31 34 58N 90 2W
Horn Mts. 62 62 15N 119 15W
Hornavan . . . . . 96 66 15N 17 30 E
Hornbeak 48 36 20N 89 18W
Hornbeck 25 31 20N 93 24W
Hornbrook 14 41 55N 122 33W
Horncastle 82 53 13N 0 8W
Hornell 39 42 20N 77 40W
Hornell L. 62 62 20N 119 25W
Hornepayne 60 49 14N 84 48W
Hornersville 32 36 3N 90 7W
Hornick 23 42 14N 96 6W
Hornitos 14 37 30N 120 14W
Hornos, Cabo de . . . . . 78 55 50 S 67 30W
Hornsby 48 35 14N 88 50W
Hornsea 82 53 55N 0 10W
Horobetsu . . . . . 116 42 24N 141 6 E
Horqin Youyi Qianqi . . . . . 114 46 5N 122 3 E
Horqueta . . . . . 76 23 15 S 56 55W
Horqueta, La 71 7 55N 60 20W
Horry County ◇ 46 33 50N 79 0W
Horse → 16 38 5N 103 19W
Horse Branch 48 37 28N 86 41W
Horse Cave 49 37 11N 85 54W
Horse Cr. →, Fla. 17 27 6N 81 58W
Horse Cr. →, Mo. 32 37 46N 93 53W
Horse Cr. →, Wyo. 56 41 57N 103 58W
Horse Creek 56 41 25N 105 11W
Horse Creek Reservoir 16 38 10N 103 24W
Horse Heaven Hills 53 46 3N 119 30W
Horse Is. 61 50 15N 55 50W
Horse L. 14 40 40N 120 31W
Horsefly L. 62 52 25N 121 0W
Horsehead L. 41 47 3N 99 47W
Horseheads 39 42 10N 76 49W
Horsens . . . . . 97 55 52N 9 51 E
Horseshoe Bend 20 43 55N 116 12W
Horseshoe Reservoir 12 33 59N 111 42W
Horsetooth Reservoir 16 40 36N 105 10W
Horsham, Australia . . . . . 127 36 44 S 142 13 E
Horsham, U.K. 83 51 4N 0 20W
Horten . . . . . 97 59 25N 10 32 E
Hortense 18 31 20N 81 57W
Horton 24 39 40N 95 32W
Horton → 58 69 56N 126 52W
Hortonville 55 44 20N 88 38W
Horwood, L. 60 48 5N 82 20W
Hose, Gunung-Gunung . . . . . 110 2 5N 114 6 E
Hosford 17 30 23N 84 48W
Hoshangabad . . . . . 108 22 45N 77 45 E
Hoshiarpur . . . . . 108 31 30N 75 58 E
Hoskins, Nebr. 34 42 7N 97 18W
Hoskins, Oreg. 44 44 41N 123 28W
Hoskinston 49 37 5N 83 24W
Hosmer 47 45 34N 99 28W
Hospers 23 43 4N 95 54W
Hospet . . . . . 108 15 15N 76 20 E
Hospitalet de Llobregat . . . . . 91 41 21N 2 6 E
Hoste, I. . . . . . 78 55 0 S 69 0W
Hot . . . . . 112 18 8N 98 29 E
Hot Creek Range 35 38 40N 116 20W
Hot Spring County ◇ 13 34 14N 92 55W
Hot Springs, Ark. 13 34 31N 93 3W
Hot Springs, Mont. 33 47 37N 114 40W
Hot Springs, N.C. 40 35 54N 82 50W
Hot Springs, S. Dak. 47 43 26N 103 29W
Hot Springs, Va. 54 38 0N 79 50W
Hot Springs County ◇ 56 43 55N 108 30W
Hot Sulphur Springs 16 40 4N 106 6W
Hotagen . . . . . 96 63 50N 14 30 E
Hotan . . . . . 113 37 25N 79 55 E
Hotchkiss 16 38 48N 107 43W
Hotevilla 12 35 56N 110 41W
Hoting . . . . . 96 64 8N 16 15 E
Hotte, Massif de la 67 18 30N 73 45W
Houck 12 35 20N 109 10W
Houffalize . . . . . 87 50 8N 5 48 E
Houghton, Mich. 29 47 7N 88 34W
Houghton, N.Y. 39 42 25N 78 10W
Houghton County ◇ 29 47 0N 88 45W
Houghton L. 29 44 21N 84 44W
Houghton Lake 29 44 18N 84 45W
Houghton-le-Spring 82 54 51N 1 28W
Houhora . . . . . 128 34 49 S 173 9 E
Houlka 31 34 2N 89 1W
Houlton 26 46 8N 67 51W
Houma 25 29 36N 90 43W
Housatonic 28 42 16N 73 22W
Housatonic → 28 41 10N 73 7W
House 38 34 39N 103 54W
House Range 52 39 30N 113 20W
Houston, Canada 62 54 25N 126 39W
Houston, Ark. 13 35 2N 92 42W
Houston, Fla. 17 30 15N 82 54W
Houston, Minn. 30 43 46N 91 34W
Houston, Miss. 31 33 54N 89 0W
Houston, Mo. 32 37 22N 91 58W
Houston, Tex. 51 29 46N 95 22W
Houston → 25 30 16N 93 13W
Houston, L. 51 29 55N 95 8W
Houston County ◇, Ala. 10 31 11N 85 14W
Houston County ◇, Ga. 18 32 20N 83 45W
Houston County ◇, Minn. 30 43 35N 91 30W
Houston County ◇, Tenn. 48 36 19N 87 42W
Houston County ◇, Tex. 51 31 19N 95 27W
Houston County L. 51 31 25N 95 35W
Houstonia 32 38 54N 93 22W
Houtman Abrolhos . . . . . 126 28 43 S 113 48 E
Hovd . . . . . 113 48 2N 91 37 E
Hove 83 50 50N 0 10W
Hoven 47 45 15N 99 47W
Hovenweep National Monument 16 37 20N 109 0W
Hovland 30 47 51N 89 58W
Hövsgöl Nuur . . . . . 113 51 0N 100 30 E
Howard, Colo. 16 38 27N 105 50W
Howard, Ga. 18 32 36N 84 23W
Howard, Kans. 24 37 28N 96 16W
Howard, Pa. 45 41 1N 77 40W
Howard, S. Dak. 47 44 1N 97 32W
Howard, Wis. 55 44 33N 88 4W
Howard City 29 43 24N 85 28W
Howard County ◇, Ark. 13 34 7N 94 1W
Howard County ◇, Ind. 22 40 30N 86 10W
Howard County ◇, Iowa 23 43 20N 92 20W
Howard County ◇, Md. 27 39 15N 77 0W
Howard County ◇, Mo. 32 39 10N 92 40W
Howard County ◇, Nebr. 34 41 15N 98 30W
Howard County ◇, Tex. 50 32 15N 101 28W
Howard Draw → 50 30 10N 101 35W
Howard Hanson Reservoir . . 53 47 17N 121 47W
Howard L. 63 62 15N 105 57W
Howard Lake 30 45 4N 94 4W
Howe, Idaho 20 43 48N 113 0W
Howe, Ind. 22 41 43N 85 25W
Howe, Okla. 43 34 57N 94 38W
Howe, Tex. 51 33 30N 96 37W
Howe, C. . . . . . 127 37 30 S 150 0 E
Howell, Mich. 29 42 36N 83 56W
Howell, Utah 52 41 48N 112 27W
Howell County ◇ 32 36 45N 91 50W
Howes 47 44 37N 102 3W
Howes Mill 32 37 38N 91 16W
Howison 31 30 40N 89 8W
Howland 26 45 14N 68 40W
Howley 61 49 12N 57 2W
Howrah = Haora . . . . . 109 22 37N 88 20 E
Howth Hd. 85 53 21N 6 0W
Hoxie, Ark. 13 36 3N 90 59W
Hoxie, Kans. 24 39 21N 100 26W
Hoy I. 84 58 50N 3 15W
Høyanger . . . . . 97 61 13N 6 4 E
Hoyleton 21 38 27N 89 16W
Hoyt, Colo. 16 40 1N 104 5W
Hoyt, Kans. 24 39 15N 95 43W
Hpungan Pass . . . . . 109 27 30N 96 55 E
Hrádec Králové . . . . . 88 50 15N 15 50 E
Hron → . . . . . 89 47 49N 18 45 E
Hrvatska . . . . . 94 45 20N 16 0 E
Hsenwi . . . . . 109 23 22N 97 55 E
Hsiamen = Xiamen . . . . . 114 24 25N 118 4 E
Hua Hin . . . . . 112 12 34N 99 58 E
Hua Xian, Henan, China . . . . . 115 35 30N 114 30 E
Hua Xian, Shaanxi, China . . . 115 34 30N 109 48 E
Huacaya . . . . . 73 20 45 S 63 43W
Huacheng . . . . . 115 24 4N 115 37 E
Huachinera 64 30 9N 108 55W
Huacho . . . . . 72 11 10 S 77 35W
Huachón . . . . . 72 10 35 S 76 0W
Huachuan . . . . . 114 46 50N 130 21 E
Huachuca City 12 31 34N 110 21W
Huade . . . . . 114 41 55N 113 59 E
Huadian . . . . . 114 43 0N 126 40 E
Huai He → . . . . . 115 33 0N 118 30 E
Huai'an . . . . . 115 33 30N 119 10 E
Huaide . . . . . 114 43 30N 124 40 E
Huainan . . . . . 115 32 38N 116 58 E
Huaiyang . . . . . 115 33 40N 114 52 E
Huaiyuan . . . . . 115 24 31N 108 22 E
Huajianzi . . . . . 114 41 23N 125 20 E
Huajuapan de Leon 65 17 50N 97 48W
Hualalai 19 19 42N 155 52W
Hualapai Indian Reservation 12 35 45N 113 20W
Hualapai Mts. 12 34 45N 113 45W
Hualapai Peak 12 35 5N 113 54W
Hualian . . . . . 115 23 59N 121 37 E
Huallaga → . . . . . 72 5 0 S 75 30W
Huallanca . . . . . 72 8 50 S 77 56W
Huamachuco . . . . . 72 7 50 S 78 5W
Huambo . . . . . 123 12 42 S 15 54 E
Huan Jiang → . . . . . 114 34 28N 109 0 E
Huan Xian . . . . . 114 36 33N 107 7 E
Huancabamba . . . . . 72 5 10 S 79 15W
Huancane . . . . . 72 15 10 S 69 44W
Huancapi . . . . . 72 13 40 S 74 0W
Huancavelica . . . . . 72 12 50 S 75 5W
Huancavelica □ . . . . . 72 13 0 S 75 0W
Huancayo . . . . . 72 12 5 S 75 12W
Huanchaca . . . . . 72 20 15 S 66 40W
Huanchaca, Serranía de . . . . . 73 14 30 S 60 39W
Huang He → . . . . . 114 37 55N 118 50 E
Huangchuan . . . . . 115 32 15N 115 10 E
Huangliu . . . . . 115 18 20N 108 50 E
Huanglong . . . . . 114 35 30N 109 59 E
Huangshi . . . . . 115 30 10N 115 3 E
Huangyan . . . . . 115 28 38N 121 19 E
Huanta . . . . . 72 12 55 S 74 20W
Huánuco . . . . . 72 9 55 S 76 15W
Huánuco □ . . . . . 72 9 55 S 76 14W
Huanuni . . . . . 72 18 16 S 66 51W
Huanzo, Cordillera de . . . . . 72 14 35 S 73 20W
Huaral . . . . . 72 11 32 S 77 13W
Huaraz . . . . . 72 9 30 S 77 32W
Huari . . . . . 72 9 14 S 77 14W
Huarmey . . . . . 72 10 5 S 78 5W
Huarochiri . . . . . 72 12 9 S 76 15W
Huarocondo . . . . . 72 13 26 S 72 14W
Huasamota 64 22 30N 104 30W
Huascarán . . . . . 72 9 8 S 77 36W
Huascarán, Nevado . . . . . 72 9 7 S 77 37W
Huasco . . . . . 76 28 30 S 71 15W
Huasco → . . . . . 76 28 27 S 71 13W
Huatabampo 64 26 50N 109 50W
Huauchinango 65 20 11N 98 3W
Huautla de Jiménez 65 18 8N 96 51W
Huay Namota 64 21 56N 104 30W
Huayllay . . . . . 72 11 3 S 76 21W
Hubbard, Iowa 23 42 18N 93 18W
Hubbard, Nebr. 34 42 23N 96 36W
Hubbard, Oreg. 44 45 11N 122 48W
Hubbard, Tex. 51 31 51N 96 48W
Hubbard County ◇ 30 47 10N 94 50W
Hubbard Creek L. 51 32 50N 98 58W
Hubbard L. 29 44 48N 83 34W
Hubbardton 36 43 42N 73 12W
Hubbart Pt. 63 59 21N 94 41W
Hubbell, Mich. 29 47 11N 88 26W
Hubbell, Nebr. 34 40 1N 97 29W
Hubei □ . . . . . 115 31 0N 112 0 E
Hubli-Dharwad = Dharwad . 108 15 22N 75 15 E
Huddersfield 82 53 38N 1 49W
Huddy 49 37 36N 82 17W
Hudiksvall . . . . . 97 61 43N 17 10 E
Hudson, Canada 63 50 6N 92 9W
Hudson, Colo. 16 40 4N 104 39W
Hudson, Fla. 17 28 22N 82 42W
Hudson, Iowa 23 42 24N 92 28W
Hudson, Kans. 24 38 6N 98 40W
Hudson, Maine 26 45 0N 68 53W
Hudson, Mass. 28 42 23N 71 34W
Hudson, Md. 27 38 36N 76 15W
Hudson, Mich. 29 41 51N 84 21W
Hudson, N.C. 40 35 51N 81 30W
Hudson, N.H. 36 42 46N 71 26W
Hudson, N.Y. 39 42 15N 73 46W
Hudson, S. Dak. 47 43 8N 96 27W
Hudson, Wis. 55 44 58N 92 45W
Hudson, Wyo. 56 42 54N 108 35W
Hudson → 39 40 42N 74 2W
Hudson, L. 43 36 14N 95 11W
Hudson Bay 59 52 51N 102 23W
Hudson County ◇ 37 40 45N 74 5W
Hudson Falls 39 43 18N 73 35W
Hudson Hope 62 56 0N 121 54W
Hudson Mts. . . . . . 5 74 32 S 99 20W
Hudson Str. 59 62 0N 70 0W
Hudsonville 29 42 52N 85 52W
Hudspeth County ◇ 50 31 30N 105 30W
Hue . . . . . 112 16 30N 107 35 E
Huechucuicui, Pta. . . . . . 78 41 48 S 74 2W
Hueco Mts. 50 31 53N 105 58W
Huehuetenango 66 15 20N 91 28W
Huejúcar 64 22 21N 103 13W
Huelva 91 37 18N 6 57W
Huentelauquén . . . . . 76 31 38 S 71 33W
Huerfano → 16 38 14N 104 15W
Huerfano County ◇ 16 37 40N 104 50W
Huerta, Sa. de la . . . . . 76 31 10 S 67 30W
Huesca 91 42 8N 0 25W
Huetamo 64 18 36N 100 54W
Huffman 51 30 1N 95 6W
Huger 46 33 6N 79 48W
Hugh → . . . . . 126 25 1 S 134 1 E
Hugh Butler L. 34 40 21N 100 39W
Hughenden . . . . . 127 20 52 S 144 10 E
Hughes, Alaska 11 66 3N 154 15W
Hughes, Ark. 13 34 57N 90 28W
Hughes County ◇, Okla. 43 35 0N 96 15W
Hughes County ◇, S. Dak. . . 47 44 30N 100 0W
Hughes Springs 51 33 0N 94 38W
Hughesville, Md. 27 38 32N 76 47W
Hughesville, Mo. 32 38 50N 93 18W
Hughesville, Pa. 45 41 14N 76 44W
Hughli → . . . . . 109 21 56N 88 4 E
Hughson 14 37 36N 120 52W
Hugo, Colo. 16 39 8N 103 28W
Hugo, Okla. 43 34 1N 95 31W
Hugo L. 43 34 3N 95 27W
Hugoton 24 37 11N 101 21W
Hui Xian . . . . . 114 35 27N 113 12 E
Hui'an . . . . . 115 25 1N 118 43 E
Huichang . . . . . 115 25 32N 115 45 E
Huichapán 65 20 24N 99 40W
Huihe . . . . . 114 48 12N 119 17 E
Huila □ 70 2 30N 75 45W
Huila, Nevado del 70 3 0N 76 0W
Huilai . . . . . 115 23 0N 116 18 E
Huimin . . . . . 114 37 27N 117 28 E
Huinan . . . . . 114 42 40N 126 2 E
Huinca Renancó . . . . . 76 34 51 S 64 22W
Huining . . . . . 114 35 38N 105 0 E
Huinong . . . . . 114 39 5N 106 35 E
Huixtla 65 15 9N 92 28W
Huize . . . . . 113 26 24N 103 15 E
Huizhou . . . . . 115 23 0N 114 23 E
Hukawng Valley . . . . . 109 26 30N 96 30 E
Hukou . . . . . 115 29 45N 116 21 E
Hulah L. 43 36 56N 96 5W
Hulan . . . . . 114 46 1N 126 37 E
Ḩulayfā' . . . . . 106 25 58N 40 45 E
Hulbert, Mich. 29 46 21N 85 9W
Hulbert, Okla. 43 35 56N 95 9W
Huld . . . . . 113 45 5N 105 30 E
Ḩulda . . . . . 104 31 50N 34 51 E
Hulen 49 36 47N 83 31W
Hulett 56 44 41N 104 36W
Hulin . . . . . 114 45 48N 132 59 E
Hull, Canada 60 45 25N 75 44W
Hull, U.K. 82 53 45N 0 20W
Hull, Fla. 17 27 7N 81 56W
Hull, Ill. 21 39 43N 91 13W
Hull, Iowa 23 43 11N 96 8W
Hull, Mass. 28 42 18N 70 55W
Hull → 82 53 43N 0 25W
Hulst . . . . . 87 51 17N 4 2 E
Hulun Nur . . . . . 114 49 0N 117 30 E
Huma . . . . . 114 51 43N 126 38 E
Huma He → . . . . . 114 51 42N 126 42 E
Humacao 57 18 9N 65 50W
Humacao ◇ 57 18 15N 65 45W
Humahuaca . . . . . 76 23 10 S 65 25W
Humaitá, Brazil . . . . . 73 7 35 S 63 1W
Humaitá, Paraguay . . . . . 76 27 2 S 58 31W
Humansville 32 37 48N 93 35W
Humber → 82 53 40N 0 10W
Humberside □ 82 53 50N 0 30W
Humble 51 30 0N 95 18W
Humboldt, Canada 63 52 15N 105 9W
Humboldt, Ariz. 12 34 30N 112 14W
Humboldt, Ill. 21 39 36N 88 19W
Humboldt, Iowa 23 42 44N 94 13W
Humboldt, Kans. 24 37 49N 95 26W
Humboldt, Nebr. 34 40 10N 95 57W
Humboldt, S. Dak. 47 43 39N 97 5W
Humboldt, Tenn. 48 35 50N 88 55W
Humboldt → 35 39 59N 118 36W
Humboldt B. 14 40 45N 124 10W
Humboldt County ◇, Calif. . 14 40 50N 124 0W
Humboldt County ◇, Iowa . . 23 42 50N 94 10W
Humboldt County ◇, Nev. . . 35 41 20N 118 10W
Humboldt Gletscher 4 79 30N 62 0W
Humboldt National Forest . . . 35 41 45N 115 30W
Humboldt Peak 16 37 59N 105 33W
Humboldt Range 35 40 20N 118 10W
Humboldt Sink 35 40 1N 118 38W
Humbolt Salt Marsh 35 39 50N 117 55W
Hume 32 38 6N 94 34W
Hume, L. . . . . . 127 36 0 S 147 0 E
Humeston 23 40 52N 93 30W
Humnoke 13 34 33N 91 45W
Humphrey, Ark. 13 34 25N 91 43W
Humphrey, Nebr. 34 41 42N 97 29W
Humphreys 43 34 33N 99 14W
Humphreys, Mt. 15 37 17N 118 40W
Humphreys County ◇, Miss. 31 33 6N 90 30W
Humphreys County ◇, Tenn. 48 36 5N 87 48W
Humphreys Peak 12 35 21N 111 41W
Hūn . . . . . 121 29 2N 16 0 E
Húnaflói 96 65 50N 20 50W
Hunan □ . . . . . 115 27 30N 112 0 E
Hunchun . . . . . 114 42 52N 130 28 E
Hundred 54 39 41N 80 28W
Hundred Mile House 62 51 38N 121 18W
Hunedoara . . . . . 89 45 40N 22 50 E
Hungary ■ . . . . . 89 47 20N 19 20 E
Hungary, Plain of . . . . . 80 47 0N 20 0 E
Hŭngnam . . . . . 114 39 49N 127 45 E
Hungry Horse 33 48 23N 114 4W
Hungry Horse Reservoir 33 48 21N 114 1W

Hunnewell Indian Cr.

Hunnewell, Kans. 24 37 1N 97 25W
Hunnewell, Mo. 32 39 40N 91 52W
Hunsrück 88 49 30N 7 0 E
Hunstanton 82 52 57N 0 30 E
Hunt 51 30 4N 99 20W
Hunt County ◇ 51 33 8N 96 7W
Hunt Mt. 56 44 55N 107 59W
Hunter, Ark. 13 35 3N 91 8W
Hunter, Kans. 24 39 14N 98 24W
Hunter, N. Dak. 41 47 12N 97 13W
Hunter, N.Y. 39 42 13N 74 13W
Hunter, Okla. 43 36 34N 97 40W
Hunter I., Australia 127 40 30 S 144 45 E
Hunter I., Canada 62 51 55N 128 0W
Hunterdon County ◇ 37 40 30N 75 0W
Hunters 53 48 7N 118 12W
Huntersville 40 35 25N 80 51W
Huntertown 22 41 14N 85 10W
Hunterville 128 39 56 S 175 35 E
Huntingburg 22 38 18N 86 57W
Huntingdon, Canada 60 45 6N 74 10W
Huntingdon, U.K. 83 52 20N 0 11W
Huntingdon, Pa. 45 40 30N 78 1W
Huntingdon, Tenn. 48 36 0N 88 26W
Huntingdon County ◇ 45 40 15N 78 0W
Huntington, Ark. 13 35 5N 94 16W
Huntington, Ind. 22 40 53N 85 30W
Huntington, Mass. 28 42 14N 72 53W
Huntington, N.Y. 39 40 52N 73 26W
Huntington, Oreg. 44 44 21N 117 16W
Huntington, Tex. 51 31 17N 94 34W
Huntington, Utah 52 39 20N 110 58W
Huntington, Vt. 36 44 22N 72 58W
Huntington, W. Va. 54 38 25N 82 27W
Huntington →, Nev. 35 40 37N 115 43W
Huntington →, Utah 52 39 9N 110 55W
Huntington Beach 15 33 40N 118 5W
Huntington County ◇ 22 40 50N 85 30W
Huntington Station 39 40 51N 73 25W
Huntingtown 27 38 37N 76 37W
Huntland 48 35 3N 86 16W
Huntley, Ill. 21 42 10N 88 26W
Huntley, Mont. 33 45 54N 108 19W
Huntley, Nebr. 34 40 13N 99 18W
Huntly, N.Z. 128 37 34 S 175 11 E
Huntly, U.K. 84 57 27N 2 48W
Huntsville, Canada 60 45 20N 79 14W
Huntsville, Ala. 10 34 44N 86 35W
Huntsville, Ark. 13 36 5N 93 44W
Huntsville, Ky. 48 37 10N 86 53W
Huntsville, Mo. 32 39 26N 92 33W
Huntsville, Ohio 42 40 26N 83 48W
Huntsville, Tenn. 49 36 25N 84 29W
Huntsville, Tex. 51 30 43N 95 33W
Huntsville, Utah 52 41 16N 111 46W
Huo Xian 114 36 36N 111 42 E
Huonville 127 43 0 S 147 5 E
Huoqiu 115 32 20N 116 12 E
Huoshao Dao 115 22 40N 121 30 E
Hupeh □ = Hubei □ 115 31 0N 112 0 E
Hure Qi 114 42 45N 121 45 E
Hurezani 95 44 49N 23 40 E
Hurley, Miss. 31 30 40N 88 30W
Hurley, Mo. 32 36 56N 93 30W
Hurley, N. Mex. 38 32 42N 108 8W
Hurley, N.Y. 39 41 55N 74 4W
Hurley, S. Dak. 47 43 17N 97 5W
Hurley, Wis. 55 46 27N 90 11W
Hurlock 27 38 38N 75 52W
Huron, Calif. 15 36 12N 120 6W
Huron, Kans. 24 39 38N 95 21W
Huron, Ohio 42 41 24N 82 33W
Huron, S. Dak. 47 44 22N 98 13W
Huron → 29 42 2N 83 11W
Huron, L. 29 44 30N 82 40W
Huron Beach 29 45 30N 84 6W
Huron County ◇, Mich. 29 43 50N 83 0W
Huron County ◇, Ohio 42 41 15N 82 37W
Huron Mts. 29 46 50N 88 0W
Huron National Forest 29 44 30N 84 0W
Hurricane 52 37 11N 113 17W
Hurricane Cliffs 12 36 45N 113 20W
Hurst 51 32 49N 97 9W
Hurstboro 10 32 15N 85 25W
Hurstville 23 42 6N 90 41W
Hurunui → 128 42 54 S 173 18 E
Húsavík 96 66 3N 17 21W
Huskvarna 97 57 47N 14 15 E
Huslia 11 65 41N 156 24W
Hussar 62 51 3N 112 41W
Hustisford 55 43 21N 88 36W
Husum 53 45 48N 121 29W
Hutch Mt. 12 34 47N 111 22W
Hutchinson, Kans. 24 38 5N 97 56W
Hutchinson, Minn. 30 44 54N 94 22W
Hutchinson County ◇, S. Dak. 47 43 25N 97 48W
Hutchinson County ◇, Tex. 50 35 50N 101 30W
Hutou 114 45 58N 133 38 E
Hutsonville 21 39 7N 87 40W
Huttig 13 33 2N 92 11W
Hutto 51 30 33N 97 33W
Hutton 27 39 25N 79 28W
Huttonsville 54 38 43N 79 59W
Ḩuwwārah 104 32 9N 35 15 E
Huxford 10 31 13N 87 28W
Huxley 23 41 54N 93 36W
Huy 87 50 31N 5 15 E
Huyett 27 39 40N 77 20W
Hvammur 96 65 13N 21 49W
Hvar 94 43 11N 16 28 E
Hvítá 96 64 40N 21 5W
Hvítá → 96 64 0N 20 58W
Hvítárvatn 96 64 37N 19 50W
Hwang Ho = Huang He → 114 37 55N 118 50 E
Hwange 123 18 18 S 26 30 E
Hyak 53 47 24N 121 24W
Hyannis, Mass. 28 41 39N 70 17W
Hyannis, Nebr. 34 42 0N 101 46W
Hyargas Nuur 113 49 0N 93 0 E
Hyattsville 27 38 57N 76 56W
Hyattville 56 44 15N 107 36W
Hybart 10 31 50N 87 23W
Hyco L. 40 36 31N 79 3W
Hydaburg 11 55 12N 132 50W
Hyde County ◇, N.C. 40 35 30N 76 20W
Hyde County ◇, S. Dak. 47 44 31N 99 27W
Hyde Park, Guyana 71 6 30N 58 16W
Hyde Park, U.S.A. 36 44 36N 72 37W
Hyden 49 37 10N 83 22W
Hyderabad, India 108 17 22N 78 29 E
Hyderabad, Pakistan 108 25 23N 68 24 E
Hydes 27 39 30N 76 29W
Hydro 43 35 33N 98 39W
Hyères 90 43 8N 6 9 E
Hyesan 114 41 20N 128 10 E
Hygiene 16 40 11N 105 11W
Hyland → 62 59 52N 128 12W
Hymera 22 39 11N 87 18W
Hyndman 45 39 49N 78 43W
Hyndman Peak 20 43 45N 114 8W
Hyōgo □ 117 35 15N 135 0 E
Hyrum 52 41 38N 111 51W
Hysham 33 46 18N 107 14W
Hythe 83 51 4N 1 5 E
Hyūga 117 32 25N 131 35 E
Hyvinge = Hyvinkää 97 60 38N 24 50 E
Hyvinkää 97 60 38N 24 50 E

I

I-n-Gall 120 16 51N 7 1 E
Iaco → 72 9 3 S 68 34W
Iaçu 75 12 45 S 40 13W
Iaeger 54 37 28N 81 49W
Ialomiţa □ 95 44 30N 27 30 E
Ialomiţa → 95 44 42N 27 51 E
Iamonia L. 17 30 38N 84 14W
Ianca 95 45 6N 27 29 E
Iara 95 46 31N 23 35 E
Iaşi 89 47 10N 27 40 E
Iatan 32 39 29N 94 59W
Iatt L. 25 31 35N 92 40W
Iauaretê 70 0 36N 69 12W
Iba 111 15 22N 120 0 E
Ibadan 120 7 22N 3 58 E
Ibagué 70 4 20N 75 20W
Ibaiti 75 23 50 S 50 10W
Ibapah 52 40 2N 113 59W
Ibar → 95 43 43N 20 45 E
Ibaraki □ 117 36 10N 140 10 E
Ibarra 70 0 21N 78 7W
Ibera, Laguna 76 28 30 S 57 9W
Iberia 32 38 5N 92 18W
Iberia Parish ◇ 25 30 1N 91 49W
Iberian Peninsula 80 40 0N 5 0W
Iberville 60 45 19N 73 17W
Iberville, Lac d' 60 55 55N 73 15W
Iberville Parish ◇ 25 30 17N 91 14W
Ibi 120 8 15N 9 44 E
Ibiá 75 19 30 S 46 30W
Ibicaraí 75 14 51 S 39 36W
Ibicuí 75 14 51 S 39 59W
Ibicuy 76 33 55 S 59 10W
Ibioapaba, Sa. da 74 4 0 S 41 30W
Ibipetuba 74 11 0 S 44 32W
Ibitiara 75 12 39 S 42 13W
Ibiza 91 38 54N 1 26 E
Ibo 123 12 22 S 40 40 E
Ibonma 111 3 29 S 133 31 E
Ibotirama 75 12 13 S 43 12W
Ibu 111 1 35N 127 33 E
Ibusuki 117 31 12N 130 40 E
Icá 72 14 0 S 75 48W
Ica □ 72 14 20 S 75 30W
Içá → 72 2 55 S 67 58W
Icabarú 71 4 20N 61 45W
Icabarú → 71 4 45N 62 15W
Içana 70 0 21N 67 19W
Içana → 70 0 26N 67 19W
Icatu 74 2 46 S 44 4W
Ice Harbor Dam 53 46 15N 118 53W
Iceland ■ 96 65 0N 19 0W
Icha 101 55 30N 156 0 E
Ich'ang = Yichang 115 30 40N 111 20 E
Ichchapuram 109 19 10N 84 40 E
Ichihara 117 35 28N 140 5 E
Ichikawa 117 35 44N 139 55 E
Ichilo → 73 15 57 S 64 50W
Ichinohe 116 40 13N 141 17 E
Ichinomiya 117 35 18N 136 48 E
Ichinoseki 116 38 55N 141 8 E
Icó 74 6 24 S 38 51W
Icoraci 74 1 18 S 48 28W
Icy C. 11 70 20N 161 52W
Ida 29 41 55N 83 34W
Ida County ◇ 23 42 25N 95 30W
Ida Grove 23 42 21N 95 28W
Idabel 43 33 54N 94 50W
Idaho □ 20 45 0N 115 0W
Idaho City 20 43 50N 115 50W
Idaho County ◇ 20 45 35N 115 30W
Idaho Falls 20 43 30N 112 2W
Idaho Springs 16 39 45N 105 31W
Idalia 16 39 42N 102 18W
Idalou 50 33 40N 101 41W
Idana 24 39 22N 97 16W
Idanha 44 44 42N 122 5W
Idd el Ghanam 121 11 30N 24 19 E
Iddan 105 6 10N 48 55 E
Ideal 47 43 33N 99 54W
Idehan 121 27 10N 11 30 E
Idehan Marzūq 121 24 50N 13 51 E
Idelès 120 23 50N 5 53 E
Idfû 121 25 0N 32 49 E
Ídhi Óros 95 35 15N 24 45 E
Ídhra 95 37 20N 23 28 E
Idi 110 5 2N 97 37 E
Idiofa 122 4 55 S 19 42 E
Idlip 106 35 55N 36 38 E
Idna 104 31 34N 34 58 E
Idria 15 36 25N 120 41W
Idutywa 123 32 8 S 28 18 E
Ieper 87 50 51N 2 53 E
Ierápetra 95 35 0N 25 44 E
Ierzu 94 39 48N 9 32 E
Ifanadiana 123 21 19 S 47 39 E
Ife 120 7 30N 4 31 E
Ifni 120 29 29N 10 12W
Iforas, Adrar des 120 19 40N 1 40 E
Igara Paraná → 70 2 9 S 71 47W
Igarapava 75 20 3 S 47 47W
Igarapé Açu 74 1 4 S 47 33W
Igarapé-Mirim 74 1 59 S 48 58W
Igarka 101 67 30N 86 33 E
Igatimi 77 24 5 S 55 40W
Igbetti 120 8 44N 4 8 E
Iggesund 97 61 39N 17 10 E
Igiugig 11 59 20N 155 55W
Iglésias 94 39 19N 8 27 E
Igli 120 30 25N 2 19W
Igloolik 59 69 20N 81 49W
Ignace 60 49 30N 91 40W
Ignacio 16 37 7N 107 38W
Iguaçu → 77 25 36 S 54 36W
Iguaçu, Cat. del 77 25 41 S 54 26W
Iguala 65 18 20N 99 40W
Igualada 91 41 37N 1 37 E
Iguape 75 24 43 S 47 33W
Iguassu = Iguaçu → 77 25 36 S 54 36W
Iguatu 74 6 20 S 39 18W
Iguéla 122 2 0 S 9 16 E
Iheya-Shima 117 27 4N 127 58 E
Ihlen 30 43 55N 96 22W
Ihosy 123 22 24 S 46 8 E
Ii 96 65 19N 25 22 E
Ii-Shima 117 26 43N 127 47 E
Iida 117 35 35N 137 50 E
Iijoki → 96 65 20N 25 20 E
Iisalmi 96 63 32N 27 10 E
Iiyama 117 36 51N 138 22 E
Iizuka 117 33 38N 130 42 E
Ijebu-Ode 120 6 47N 3 58 E
IJmuiden 87 52 28N 4 35 E
IJssel → 87 52 35N 5 50 E
IJsselmeer 87 52 45N 5 20 E
Ijuí → 77 27 58 S 55 20W
Ikaría 95 37 35N 26 10 E
Ikeda 117 34 1N 133 48 E
Ikela 122 1 6 S 23 6 E
Ikhtiman 95 42 27N 23 48 E
Iki 117 33 45N 129 42 E
Ilagan 111 17 7N 121 53 E
Īlām 106 33 0N 46 0 E
Ilanskiy 101 56 14N 96 3 E
Île-à-la Crosse 63 55 27N 107 53W
Île-à-la-Crosse, Lac 63 55 40N 107 45W
Île-de-France 90 49 0N 2 20 E
Ilebo 122 4 17 S 20 55 E
Ilek 100 51 32N 53 21 E
Ilek → 98 51 30N 53 22 E
Ilfeld 38 35 25N 105 34W
Ilford 63 56 4N 95 35W
Ilfov □ 95 44 20N 26 0 E
Ilfracombe, Australia 127 23 30 S 144 30 E
Ilfracombe, U.K. 83 51 13N 4 8W
Ilha Grande 71 0 27 S 65 2W
Ilha Grande, Baía da 75 23 9 S 44 30W
Ilhéus 75 14 49 S 39 2W
Iliamna 11 59 45N 154 55W
Iliamna L. 11 59 30N 155 0W
Ilich 100 40 50N 68 27 E
Iliff 16 40 45N 103 4W
Iligan 111 8 12N 124 13 E
Ilio Pt. 19 21 13N 157 16W
Iliodhrómia 95 39 12N 23 50 E
Ilion 39 43 1N 75 2W
Ilkeston 82 52 59N 1 19W
Illana B. 111 7 35N 123 45 E
Illapel 76 32 0 S 71 10W
'Illār 104 32 23N 35 7 E
Ille-et-Vilaine □ 90 48 10N 1 30W
Iller → 88 48 23N 9 58 E
Illimani 72 16 30 S 67 50W
Illinois □ 21 41 0N 89 0W
Illinois →, Ark. 13 35 30N 95 5W
Illinois →, Ill. 21 38 58N 90 28W
Illinois →, Oreg. 44 42 33N 124 3W
Illiopolis 21 39 51N 89 15W
Illium = Troy 106 39 57N 26 12 E
Illmo 32 37 13N 89 30W
Ilmen, Oz. 98 58 15N 31 10 E
Ilo 72 17 40 S 71 20W
Iloilo 111 10 45N 122 33 E
Ilorin 120 8 30N 4 35 E
Ilwaco 53 46 19N 124 3W
Ilwaki 111 7 55 S 126 30 E
Imabari 117 34 4N 133 0 E
Imandra, Oz. 98 67 30N 33 0 E
Imari 117 33 15N 129 52 E
Imbabura □ 70 0 30N 78 45W
Imbaimadai 71 5 44N 60 17W
Imbler 44 45 28N 117 58W
Imboden 13 36 12N 91 11W
imeni 26 Bakinskikh Komissarov, Azerbaijan, U.S.S.R. 99 39 19N 49 12 E
imeni 26 Bakinskikh Komissarov, Turkmen S.S.R., U.S.S.R. 99 39 22N 54 10 E
Imeni Poliny Osipenko 101 52 30N 136 29 E
Imeri, Serra 70 0 50N 65 25W
Imi 105 6 28N 42 10 E
Imlay 35 40 40N 118 9W
Imlay City 29 43 2N 83 5W
Immingham 82 53 37N 0 12W
Immokalee 17 26 25N 81 25W
Imnaha → 44 45 49N 116 46W
Imogene 23 40 53N 95 29W
Imola 94 44 20N 11 42 E
Imperatriz, Amazonas, Brazil 72 5 18 S 67 11W
Imperatriz, Maranhão, Brazil 74 5 30 S 47 29W
Impéria 94 43 52N 8 0 E
Imperial, Canada 63 51 21N 105 28W
Imperial, Peru 72 13 4 S 76 21W
Imperial, Calif. 15 32 51N 115 34W
Imperial, Nebr. 34 40 31N 101 39W
Imperial, Pt. 12 36 15N 111 57W
Imperial Beach 15 32 35N 117 8W
Imperial County ◇ 15 33 0N 115 20W
Imperial Dam 12 32 55N 114 25W
Imperial Reservoir 12 32 53N 114 28W
Imperial Valley 15 33 0N 115 30W
Impfondo 122 1 40N 18 0 E
Imphal 109 24 48N 93 56 E
Imuruan B. 111 10 40N 119 10 E
In Belbel 120 27 55N 1 12 E
In Salah 120 27 10N 2 32 E
Ina, Japan 117 35 50N 138 0 E
Ina, U.S.A. 21 38 9N 88 54W
Inajá 74 8 54 S 37 49W
Inangahua Junc. 128 41 52 S 171 59 E
Inanwatan 111 2 10 S 132 14 E
Iñapari 72 11 0 S 69 40W
Inari 96 68 54N 27 5 E
Inarijärvi 96 69 0N 28 0 E
Inawashiro-Ko 116 37 29N 140 6 E
Inca 91 39 43N 2 54 E
Incaguasi 76 29 12 S 71 5W
İnce-Burnu 106 42 7N 34 56 E
Inchon 114 37 27N 126 40 E
Incline Village 35 39 10N 119 58W
Incomáti → 123 25 46 S 32 43 E
Indalsälven → 96 62 36N 17 30 E
Indaw 109 24 15N 96 5 E
Independence, Calif. 15 36 48N 118 12W
Independence, Iowa 23 42 28N 91 54W
Independence, Kans. 24 37 14N 95 42W
Independence, Ky. 49 38 57N 84 33W
Independence, La. 25 30 38N 90 30W
Independence, Mo. 32 39 6N 94 25W
Independence, Oreg. 44 44 51N 123 11W
Independence, Va. 54 36 37N 81 9W
Independence, Wis. 55 44 22N 91 25W
Independence County ◇ 13 35 46N 91 39W
Independence Cr. → 50 30 27N 101 44W
Independence Fjord 4 82 10N 29 0W
Independence Mts. 35 41 20N 116 0W
Independence Pass 16 39 7N 106 33W
Independência 74 5 23 S 40 19W
Independencia, La 65 16 31N 91 47W
Independenţa 95 45 25N 27 42 E
Index 53 47 50N 121 33W
India ■ 103 20 0N 78 0 E
Indiahoma 43 34 37N 98 45W
Indialantic 17 28 6N 80 34W
Indian → 17 27 10N 80 10W
Indian-Antarctic Ridge 124 49 0 S 120 0 E
Indian Cabins 62 59 52N 117 40W
Indian Cr. → 47 44 39N 103 19W

Indian Harbour **Itajubá**

Indian Harbour 61 54 27N 57 13W
Indian Harbour Beach 17 28 10N 80 35W
Indian Head, Canada 63 50 30N 103 41W
Indian Head, U.S.A. 27 38 38N 77 12W
Indian Heights 22 40 26N 86 10W
Indian L., Mich. 29 45 59N 86 20W
Indian L., N.Y. 39 43 42N 74 19W
Indian L., Ohio 42 40 30N 83 53W
Indian Lake 39 43 47N 74 16W
Indian Mills 37 39 48N 74 46W
Indian Ocean 3 5 0S 75 0E
Indian Peak 52 38 16N 113 53W
Indian River 29 45 25N 84 37W
Indian River Bay 27 38 36N 75 4W
Indian River County ◇ 17 27 40N 80 45W
Indian Rock 53 45 59N 120 49W
Indian Rocks Beach 17 27 53N 82 51W
Indian Springs 35 36 35N 115 40W
Indian Village 24 37 5N 95 38W
Indiana 45 40 37N 79 9W
Indiana □ 22 40 0N 86 0W
Indiana County ◇ 45 40 45N 79 0W
Indiana Dunes Nat. Lakeshore 22 41 40N 87 0W
Indianapolis 22 39 46N 86 9W
Indianola, Iowa 23 41 22N 93 34W
Indianola, Miss. 31 33 27N 90 39W
Indianola, Nebr. 34 40 14N 100 25W
Indianola, Okla. 43 35 10N 95 46W
Indiantown 17 27 1N 80 28W
Indiapora 75 19 57S 50 17W
Indiga 98 67 50N 48 50E
Indigirka → 101 70 48N 148 54E
Indio 15 33 43N 116 13W
Indonesia ■ 110 5 0S 115 0E
Indore 108 22 42N 75 53E
Indramayu 111 6 20S 108 19E
Indravati → 109 19 20N 80 20E
Indre □ 90 46 50N 1 39E
Indre-et-Loire □ 90 47 12N 0 40E
Indrio 17 27 31N 80 21W
Indus → 108 24 20N 67 47E
Industry, Ill. 21 40 20N 90 36W
Industry, Kans. 24 39 8N 97 10W
Industry, Tex. 51 29 58N 96 30W
İnebolu 106 41 55N 33 40E
İnegöl 106 40 5N 29 31E
Inés, Mt. 78 48 30S 69 40W
Inez 49 37 52N 82 32W
Infiernillo, Presa del 64 18 9N 102 0W
Ingalls, Ark. 13 33 23N 92 9W
Ingalls, Kans. 24 37 50N 100 27W
Ingapirca 74 2 38S 78 56W
Ingende 122 0 12S 18 57E
Ingeniero Jacobacci 78 41 20S 69 36W
Ingenio Santa Ana 76 27 25S 65 40W
Ingham 127 18 43S 146 10E
Ingham County ◇ 29 42 35N 84 30W
Ingleborough 82 54 11N 2 23W
Ingleside, Md. 27 39 6N 75 53W
Ingleside, Tex. 51 27 53N 97 13W
Inglewood, N.Z. 128 39 9S 174 14E
Inglewood, U.S.A. 15 33 58N 118 21W
Inglis 17 29 2N 82 40W
Ingólfshöfði 96 63 48N 16 39W
Ingolstadt 88 48 45N 11 26E
Ingomar 33 46 35N 107 23W
Ingonish 61 46 42N 60 18W
Ingraj Bazar 109 24 58N 88 10E
Ingram, Tex. 51 30 5N 99 14W
Ingram, Wis. 55 45 31N 90 49W
Ingrid Christensen Coast 5 69 30S 76 0E
Ingulec 99 47 42N 33 14E
Inhambane 123 23 54S 35 30E
Inhambupe 75 11 47S 38 21W
Inhaminga 123 18 26S 35 0E
Inharrime 123 24 30S 35 0E
Inhuma 74 6 40S 41 42W
Inhumas 75 16 22S 49 30W
Inini □ 71 4 0N 53 0W
Inírida → 70 3 55N 67 52W
Inishbofin 85 53 35N 10 12W
Inishmore 85 53 8N 9 45W
Inishowen 85 55 14N 7 15W
Injune 127 25 53S 148 32E
Inklin 62 58 56N 133 5W
Inklin → 62 58 50N 133 10W
Inkom 20 42 48N 112 15W
Inkster, Mich. 29 42 18N 83 19W
Inkster, N. Dak. 41 48 9N 97 39W
Inland L. 10 33 50N 86 30W
Inle L. 109 20 30N 96 58E
Inlet 39 43 45N 74 48W
Inman, Kans. 24 38 14N 97 47W
Inman, Nebr. 34 42 23N 98 32W
Inman, S.C. 46 35 3N 82 5W
Inn → 88 48 35N 13 28E
Inner Hebrides 84 57 0N 6 30W
Inner Mongolia = Nei Monggol Zizhiqu □ 114 42 0N 112 0E
Inner Sound 84 57 30N 5 55W
Innetalling I. 60 56 0N 79 0W
Innisfail, Australia 127 17 33S 146 5E
Innisfail, Canada 62 52 0N 113 57W
In'no-shima 117 34 19N 133 10E
Innsbruck 88 47 16N 11 23E
Inny → 85 53 30N 7 50W
Inocência 75 19 47S 51 48W
Inola 43 36 9N 95 31W
Inongo 122 1 55S 18 30E
Inoucdjouac 59 58 25N 78 15W
Inowrocław 89 52 50N 18 12E
Inquisivi 72 16 50S 67 10W
Insein 109 16 50N 96 5E
Însurăței 95 44 50N 27 40E
Inta 98 66 5N 60 8E
Intendente Alvear 76 35 12S 63 32W
Intercession City 17 28 16N 81 31W
Interior 47 43 44N 101 59W
Interlachen 17 29 37N 81 53W
Interlaken 39 42 37N 76 44W
International Falls 30 48 36N 93 25W
Intervale 36 44 6N 71 8W
Interview I. 112 12 55N 92 42E
Inthanon, Doi 112 18 35N 98 29E
Intiyaco 76 28 43S 60 5W
Intracoastal City 25 29 47N 92 9W
Intutu 70 3 32S 74 48W
Inútil, B. 78 53 30S 70 15W
Inuvik 58 68 16N 133 40W
Inver Grove Heights 30 44 51N 93 1W
Inveraray 84 56 13N 5 5W
Inverbervie 84 56 50N 2 17W
Invercargill 128 46 24S 168 24E
Inverell 127 29 45S 151 8E
Invergordon 84 57 41N 4 10W
Invermere 62 50 30N 116 2W
Inverness, Canada 61 46 15N 61 19W
Inverness, U.K. 84 57 29N 4 12W
Inverness, Ala. 10 32 1N 85 45W
Inverness, Calif. 14 38 6N 122 51W
Inverness, Fla. 17 28 50N 82 20W
Inverness, Miss. 31 33 21N 90 35W
Inverurie 84 57 15N 2 21W
Investigator Group 126 34 45S 134 20E
Investigator Str. 127 35 30S 137 0E
Inwood 23 43 19N 96 26W
Inya 100 50 28N 86 37E
Inyo County ◇ 15 36 30N 117 40W
Inyo Mts. 15 36 40N 118 0W
Inyo National Forest 15 37 30N 118 15W
Inyokern 15 35 39N 117 49W
Inza 98 53 55N 46 25E
Iō-Jima 117 30 48N 130 18E
Ioánnina □ 95 39 39N 20 57E
Iola, Ill. 21 38 50N 88 38W
Iola, Kans. 24 37 55N 95 24W
Iola, Wis. 55 44 30N 89 8W
Ion Corvin 95 44 7N 27 50E
Iona, U.K. 84 56 20N 6 25W
Iona, Idaho 20 43 32N 111 56W
Iona, Minn. 30 43 55N 95 47W
Iona, S. Dak. 47 43 33N 99 26W
Ione, Calif. 14 38 21N 120 56W
Ione, Oreg. 44 45 30N 119 50W
Ione, Wash. 53 48 45N 117 25W
Ionia, Iowa 23 43 2N 92 27W
Ionia, Kans. 24 39 40N 98 21W
Ionia, Mich. 29 42 59N 85 4W
Ionia, Mo. 32 38 30N 93 19W
Ionia County ◇ 29 42 55N 85 5W
Ionian Is. = Iónioi Nísoi 95 38 40N 20 0E
Ionian Sea 95 37 30N 17 30E
Iónioi Nísoi 95 38 40N 20 0E
Íos 95 36 41N 25 20E
Iosco County ◇ 29 44 20N 83 40W
Iota 25 30 20N 92 30W
Iowa 25 30 14N 93 1W
Iowa □ 23 42 15N 93 15W
Iowa → 23 41 10N 91 1W
Iowa City 23 41 40N 91 32W
Iowa County ◇, Iowa 23 41 40N 92 0W
Iowa County ◇, Wis. 55 43 0N 90 10W
Iowa Falls 23 42 31N 93 16W
Iowa Park 51 33 57N 98 40W
Ipameri 75 17 44S 48 9W
Ipariá 72 9 17S 74 29W
Ipava 21 40 21N 90 19W
Ipiales 70 0 50N 77 37W
Ipiaú 75 14 8S 39 44W
Ipin = Yibin 113 28 45N 104 32E
Ipirá 75 12 10S 39 44W
Ipiranga 70 3 13S 65 57W
Ípiros □ 95 39 30N 20 30E
Ipixuna 72 7 0S 71 40W
Ipixuna →, Amazonas, Brazil 72 7 11S 71 51W
Ipixuna →, Amazonas, Brazil 73 5 45S 63 2W
Ipoh 112 4 35N 101 5E
Iporá 75 11 23S 50 40W
Ippy 122 6 5N 21 7E
Ipswich, Australia 127 27 35S 152 40E
Ipswich, U.K. 83 52 4N 1 9E
Ipswich, Mass. 28 42 41N 70 50W
Ipswich, S. Dak. 47 45 27N 99 2W
Ipswich B. 28 42 41N 70 42W
Ipu 74 4 23S 40 44W
Ipueiras 74 4 33S 40 43W
Ipupiara 75 11 49S 42 37W
Iquique 72 20 19S 70 5W
Iquitos 70 3 45S 73 10W
Ira 50 32 35N 101 0W
Iraan 50 30 55N 101 54W
Irabu-Jima 117 24 50N 125 10E
Iracoubo 71 5 30N 53 10W
Iráklion 95 35 20N 25 12E
Irala 77 25 55S 54 35W
Iran ■ 107 33 0N 53 0E
Iran, Gunung-Gunung 110 2 20N 114 50E
Īrānshahr 107 27 15N 60 40E
Irapa 71 10 34N 62 35W
Irapuato 64 20 40N 101 30W
Iraq ■ 106 33 0N 44 0E
Irasburg 36 44 18N 73 47W
Irati 77 25 25S 50 38W
Irbid 104 32 35N 35 48E
Irebu 122 0 40S 17 46E
Irecê 74 11 18S 41 52W
Iredell 51 31 59N 97 52W
Iredell County ◇ 40 35 45N 80 50W
Ireland ■ 85 53 0N 8 0W
Ireland's Eye 85 53 25N 6 4W
Ireng → 71 3 33N 59 51W
Iret 101 60 3N 154 20E
Ireton 23 42 58N 96 19W
Iri 114 35 59N 127 0E
Irian Jaya □ 111 4 0S 137 0E
Iringa 122 7 48S 35 43E
Iriomote-Jima 117 24 19N 123 48E
Irion County ◇ 50 31 15N 101 0W
Iriona 66 15 57N 85 11W
Iriri → 71 3 52S 52 37W
Iriri Novo → 73 8 46S 53 22W
Irish Sea 82 54 0N 5 0W
Irkineyeva 101 58 30N 96 49E
Irkutsk 101 52 18N 104 20E
Irma 63 52 55N 111 14W
Irō-Zaki 117 34 36N 138 51E
Iron Belt 55 46 24N 90 19W
Iron City, Ga. 18 31 1N 84 49W
Iron City, Tenn. 48 35 1N 87 35W
Iron County ◇, Mich. 29 46 15N 88 35W
Iron County ◇, Mo. 32 37 30N 90 40W
Iron County ◇, Utah 52 37 50N 113 20W
Iron County ◇, Wis. 55 46 15N 90 15W
Iron Gate = Portile de Fier 89 44 42N 22 30E
Iron Junction 30 47 25N 92 36W
Iron Knob 127 32 46S 137 8E
Iron Mountain, Mich. 29 45 49N 88 4W
Iron Mountain, Mo. 32 37 42N 90 39W
Iron Mts. 54 36 40N 81 45W
Iron Ridge 55 43 24N 88 32W
Iron River, Mich. 29 46 6N 88 39W
Iron River, Wis. 55 46 34N 91 24W
Ironbridge 83 52 38N 2 29W
Irondale, Ala. 10 33 32N 86 42W
Irondale, Mo. 32 37 50N 90 41W
Irondale, Ohio 42 40 34N 80 44W
Irondequoit 39 43 13N 77 35W
Ironside 44 44 19N 117 57W
Ironsides 27 38 30N 77 12W
Ironton, Minn. 30 46 28N 93 59W
Ironton, Mo. 32 37 36N 90 38W
Ironton, Ohio 42 38 32N 82 41W
Ironwood 29 46 27N 90 9W
Iroquois, Ill. 21 40 50N 87 35W
Iroquois, S. Dak. 47 44 22N 97 51W
Iroquois → 22 41 5N 87 49W
Iroquois County ◇ 21 40 45N 87 50W
Iroquois Falls 60 48 46N 80 41W
Irrawaddy □ 109 17 0N 95 0E
Irrawaddy → 109 15 50N 95 6E
Irrigon 44 45 54N 119 30W
Irtysh → 100 61 4N 68 52E
Irumu 122 1 32N 29 53E
Irún 91 43 20N 1 52W
Irvine, Canada 63 49 57N 110 16W
Irvine, U.K. 84 55 37N 4 40W
Irvine, Calif. 15 33 41N 117 46W
Irvine, Ky. 49 37 42N 83 58W
Irvinestown 85 54 28N 7 38W
Irving, Ill. 21 39 12N 89 24W
Irving, Tex. 51 32 49N 96 56W
Irvington, Ill. 21 38 26N 89 10W
Irvington, Ky. 48 37 53N 86 17W
Irvona 45 40 46N 78 33W
Irwin 23 41 47N 95 12W
Irwin County ◇ 18 31 40N 83 15W
Irwinton 18 32 49N 83 10W
Irwinville 18 31 39N 83 23W
Isaac → 127 22 55S 149 20E
Isabel, Kans. 24 37 28N 98 33W
Isabel, S. Dak. 47 45 24N 101 26W
Isabel Segunda 57 18 9N 65 27W
Isabela, Phil. 111 6 40N 122 10E
Isabela, Puerto Rico 57 18 30N 67 2W
Isabela, I. 64 21 51N 105 55W
Isabela, La 67 19 58N 71 2W
Isabella, Cord. 66 13 30N 85 25W
Isabella County ◇ 29 43 40N 84 50W
Isabella L. 15 35 39N 118 28W
Isabelle, Pt. 29 47 21N 87 56W
Ísafjarðardjúp 96 66 10N 23 0W
Ísafjörður 96 66 5N 23 9W
Isahaya 117 32 52N 130 2E
Isana → 70 0 26N 67 19W
Isangi 122 0 52N 24 10E
Isanti 30 45 29N 93 15W
Isanti County ◇ 30 45 30N 93 15W
Isaquah 53 47 32N 122 2W
Isar → 88 48 49N 12 58E
Isbiceni 95 43 45N 24 40E
Iscayachi 73 21 31S 65 3W
Íschia 94 40 45N 13 51E
Iscuandé 70 2 28N 77 59W
Ise 117 34 25N 136 45E
Ise-Wan 117 34 43N 136 43E
Isère □ 90 45 15N 5 40E
Isère → 90 44 59N 4 51E
Isherton 71 2 20N 59 25W
Ishigaki-Shima 117 24 20N 124 10E
Ishikari-Gawa → 116 43 15N 141 23E
Ishikari-Sammyaku 116 43 30N 143 0E
Ishikari-Wan 116 43 25N 141 1E
Ishikawa □ 117 36 30N 136 30E
Ishim 100 56 10N 69 30E
Ishim → 100 57 45N 71 10E
Ishinomaki 116 38 32N 141 20E
Ishioka 117 36 11N 140 16E
Ishkuman 108 36 30N 73 50E
Ishpeming 29 46 29N 87 40W
Isil Kul 100 54 55N 71 16E
Isiolo 122 0 24N 37 33E
Isiro 122 2 53N 27 40E
İskenderun 106 36 32N 36 10E
İskenderun Körfezi 99 36 40N 35 50E
Iskŭr → 95 43 45N 24 25E
Iskŭr, Yazovir 95 42 23N 23 30E
Iskut → 62 56 45N 131 49W
Isla → 84 56 32N 3 20W
Isla Vista 15 34 25N 119 53W
Islamabad 108 33 40N 73 10E
Islamorada 17 24 56N 80 37W
Island → 62 60 25N 121 12W
Island County ◇ 53 48 10N 122 35W
Island Creek 27 38 27N 76 35W
Island Falls, Canada 60 49 35N 81 20W
Island Falls, U.S.A. 26 46 1N 68 16W
Island Heights 37 39 57N 74 9W
Island L. 63 53 47N 94 25W
Island Lake Res. 30 47 48N 94 19W
Island Park 20 44 24N 111 19W
Island Park Reservoir 20 44 25N 111 24W
Island Pond 36 44 49N 71 53W
Islands, B. of 61 49 11N 58 15W
Islay 84 55 46N 6 10W
Isle 30 46 8N 93 28W
Isle aux Morts 61 47 35N 59 0W
Isle La Motte 36 44 52N 73 18W
Isle of Hope 18 31 58N 81 5W
Isle of Wight 54 36 54N 76 43W
Isle of Wight □ 83 50 40N 1 20W
Isle of Wight Bay 27 38 22N 75 6W
Isle of Wight County ◇ 54 36 54N 76 43W
Isle Royale 29 48 0N 88 54W
Isle Royale National Park 29 48 0N 88 55W
Islesboro I. 26 44 19N 68 54W
Isleta 38 34 55N 106 42W
Isleta Indian Reservation 38 34 55N 106 45W
Isleton 14 38 10N 121 37W
Ismail 99 45 22N 28 46E
Ismâ'ilîya 121 30 37N 32 18E
Ismay 33 46 30N 104 48W
Isna 121 25 17N 32 30E
Isola 31 33 16N 90 35W
İsparta 106 37 47N 30 30E
Isperikh 95 43 43N 26 50E
Íspica 94 36 47N 14 53E
Israel ■ 104 32 0N 34 50E
Israel → 36 44 29N 71 35W
Issano 71 5 49N 59 26W
Issaquena County ◇ 31 32 54N 91 3W
Issue 27 38 16N 76 53W
Issyk-Kul, Ozero 100 42 25N 77 15E
İstanbul 106 41 0N 29 0E
Istmina 70 5 10N 76 39W
Isto, Mt. 11 69 12N 143 48W
Istokpoga, L. 17 27 23N 81 17W
Istra 94 45 10N 14 0E
Istranca Dağları 95 41 48N 27 30E
Istria = Istra 94 45 10N 14 0E
Itá 76 25 29S 57 21W
Itabaiana, Paraíba, Brazil 74 7 18S 35 19W
Itabaiana, Sergipe, Brazil 74 10 41S 37 37W
Itabaianinha 74 11 16S 37 47W
Itaberaba 75 12 32S 40 18W
Itaberaí 75 16 2S 49 48W
Itabira 75 19 37S 43 13W
Itabirito 75 20 15S 43 48W
Itaboca 71 4 50S 62 40W
Itabuna 75 14 48S 39 16W
Itacajá 74 8 19S 47 46W
Itacaunas → 74 5 21S 49 8W
Itacoatiara 71 3 8S 58 25W
Itacuaí → 72 4 20S 70 12W
Itaguaçu 75 19 48S 40 51W
Itaguari → 75 14 11S 44 40W
Itaguatins 74 5 47S 47 29W
Itaim → 74 7 2S 42 2W
Itainópolis 74 7 24S 41 31W
Itaituba 71 4 10S 55 50W
Itajaí 77 27 50S 48 39W
Itajubá 75 22 24S 45 30W

Itajuípe Javier, I.

Itajuípe **75** 14 41 S 39 22W
Italy **51** 32 11N 96 53W
Italy ■ **94** 42 0N 13 0 E
Itamataré **74** 2 16 S 46 24W
Itambacuri **75** 18 1 S 41 42W
Itambé **75** 15 15 S 40 37W
Itanhauã → **71** 4 45 S 63 48W
Itanhém **75** 17 9 S 40 20W
Itapaci **75** 14 57 S 49 34W
Itapagé **74** 3 41 S 39 34W
Itaparica, I. de **75** 12 54 S 38 42W
Itapebi **75** 15 56 S 39 32W
Itapecuru-Mirim **74** 3 24 S 44 20W
Itaperuna **75** 21 10 S 41 54W
Itapetinga **75** 15 15 S 40 15W
Itapetininga **77** 23 36 S 48 7W
Itapeva **77** 23 59 S 48 59W
Itapicuru →, Bahia, Brazil **74** 11 47 S 37 32W
Itapicuru →, Maranhão, Brazil **74** 2 52 S 44 12W
Itapinima **73** 5 25 S 60 44W
Itapipoca **74** 3 30 S 39 35W
Itapiranga **71** 2 45 S 58 1W
Itapiúna **74** 4 33 S 38 57W
Itaporanga **74** 7 18 S 38 0W
Itapuá □ **77** 26 40 S 55 40W
Itapuranga **75** 15 40 S 49 59W
Itaquari **75** 20 20 S 40 25W
Itaquatiara **72** 2 58 S 58 30W
Itaquí **76** 29 8 S 56 30W
Itararé **77** 24 6 S 49 23W
Itarumã **75** 18 42 S 51 25W
Itasca **51** 32 10N 97 9W
Itasca County ◇ **30** 47 25N 93 25W
Itatí **76** 27 16 S 58 15W
Itatira **74** 4 30 S 39 37W
Itatuba **73** 5 46 S 63 20W
Itatupa **71** 0 37 S 51 12W
Itaueira **74** 7 36 S 43 2W
Itaueira → **74** 6 41 S 42 55W
Itaúna **75** 20 4 S 44 34W
Itawamba County ◇ **31** 34 16N 88 25W
Itchen → **83** 50 57N 1 20W
Ite **72** 17 55 S 70 57W
Ithaca = Itháki **88** 38 25N 20 40 E
Ithaca, Mich. **29** 43 18N 84 36W
Ithaca, N.Y. **39** 42 27N 76 30W
Ithaca, Nebr. **34** 41 10N 96 33W
Itháki **88** 38 25N 20 40 E
Itinga **75** 16 36 S 41 47W
Itiquira **73** 17 12 S 54 7W
Itiquira → **73** 17 18 S 56 44W
Itiruçu **75** 13 31 S 40 9W
Itiúba **74** 10 43 S 39 51W
Itkilik → **11** 70 9N 150 56W
Ito **117** 34 58N 139 5 E
Itoigawa **117** 37 2N 137 51 E
Itonamas → **72** 12 28 S 64 24W
Itta Bena **31** 33 30N 90 20W
Itu **77** 23 17 S 47 15W
Ituaçu **75** 13 50 S 41 18W
Ituango **70** 7 4N 75 45W
Ituiutaba **75** 19 0 S 49 25W
Itumbiara **75** 18 20 S 49 10W
Ituna **63** 51 10N 103 24W
Ituni **71** 5 28N 58 15W
Itupiranga **74** 5 9 S 49 20W
Iturama **75** 19 44 S 50 11W
Iturbe **76** 23 0 S 65 25W
Iturup, Ostrov **101** 45 0N 148 0 E
Ituverava **75** 20 20 S 47 47W
Ituxi → **73** 7 18 S 64 51W
Ituyuro → **76** 22 40 S 63 50W
Iuka, Kans. **24** 37 44N 98 44W
Iuka, Miss. **31** 34 49N 88 12W
Iva **46** 34 19N 82 40W
Ivaí → **77** 23 18 S 53 42W
Ivalo **96** 68 38N 27 35 E
Ivalojoki → **96** 68 40N 27 40 E
Ivan **13** 33 55N 92 26W
Ivanhoe, Australia **127** 32 56 S 144 20 E
Ivanhoe, Calif. **15** 36 23N 119 13W
Ivanhoe, Minn. **30** 44 28N 96 15W
Ivanhoe, Va. **54** 36 50N 80 58W
Ivanhoe L. **63** 60 25N 106 30W
Ivano-Frankovsk **99** 48 40N 24 40 E
Ivanof Bay **11** 55 54N 159 29W
Ivanovo **98** 57 5N 41 0 E
Ivaylovgrad **95** 41 32N 26 8 E
Ivdel **98** 60 42N 60 24 E
Ivesdale **21** 39 57N 88 28W
Ivinheima → **77** 23 14 S 53 42W
Iviza = Ibiza **91** 38 54N 1 26 E
Ivolândia **75** 16 34 S 50 51W
Ivor **54** 36 54N 76 54W
Ivory Coast ■ **120** 7 30N 5 0W
Ivrea **94** 45 30N 7 52 E
Ivugivik **59** 62 24N 77 55W
Ivydale **54** 38 32N 81 2W
Ivywild **16** 38 49N 104 51W
Iwahig **110** 8 36N 117 32 E
Iwaizumi **116** 39 50N 141 45 E
Iwaki **117** 37 4N 140 55 E
Iwakuni **117** 34 15N 132 8 E
Iwamizawa **116** 43 12N 141 46 E
Iwanai **116** 42 58N 140 30 E
Iwata **117** 34 42N 137 51 E
Iwate □ **116** 39 30N 141 30 E
Iwate-San **116** 39 51N 141 0 E
Iwo **120** 7 39N 4 9 E
Ixiamas **72** 13 50 S 68 5W
Ixtepec **65** 16 32N 95 10W
Ixtlán de Juárez **65** 17 23N 96 28W
Ixtlán del Río **64** 21 5N 104 21W
Iyo **117** 33 45N 132 45 E
Izabel, L. de **66** 15 30N 89 10W
Izamal **65** 20 56N 89 1W
Izard County ◇ **13** 36 4N 91 54W
Izegem **87** 50 55N 3 12 E
Izena-Shima **117** 26 56N 127 56 E
Izgrev **95** 43 36N 26 58 E
Izhevsk = Ustinov **98** 56 51N 53 14 E
İzmir **99** 38 25N 27 8 E
İzmit **106** 40 45N 29 50 E
Izozog, Bañados de **73** 18 48 S 62 10W
Izra **104** 32 51N 36 15 E
Iztochni Rodopi **95** 41 45N 25 30 E
Izu-Shotō **117** 34 30N 140 0 E
Izumi-sano **117** 34 23N 135 18 E
Izumo **117** 35 20N 132 46 E

J

J. B. Thomas, L. **50** 32 36N 101 8W
J.F. Rodrigues **74** 2 55 S 50 20W
J. Percy Priest Reservoir **48** 36 9N 86 37W
Jaba' **104** 32 20N 35 13 E
Jabalpur **108** 23 9N 79 58 E
Jabālyah **104** 31 32N 34 27 E
Jablah **106** 35 20N 36 0 E
Jablanica **95** 41 20N 20 30 E
Jablonec **88** 50 43N 15 10 E
Jaboatão **74** 8 7 S 35 1W
Jaboticabal **77** 21 15 S 48 17W
Jaburu **73** 5 30 S 64 0W
Jaca **91** 42 35N 0 33W
Jacala **65** 21 1N 99 11W
Jacaré → **74** 10 3 S 42 13W
Jacareí **77** 23 20 S 46 0W
Jacarèzinho **77** 23 5 S 50 0W
Jaciara **73** 15 59 S 54 57W
Jacinto **75** 16 10 S 40 17W
Jacinto City **51** 29 46N 95 13W
Jaciparaná **73** 9 15 S 64 23W
Jack County ◇ **51** 33 13N 98 10W
Jackman Station **26** 45 37N 70 15W
Jackpot **35** 41 59N 114 40W
Jacks Fork → **32** 37 12N 91 18W
Jacksboro, Tenn. **49** 36 20N 84 11W
Jacksboro, Tex. **51** 33 13N 98 10W
Jackson, Ala. **10** 31 31N 87 53W
Jackson, Calif. **14** 38 21N 120 46W
Jackson, Ga. **18** 33 20N 83 57W
Jackson, Ky. **49** 37 33N 83 23W
Jackson, La. **25** 30 50N 91 13W
Jackson, Mich. **29** 42 15N 84 24W
Jackson, Minn. **30** 43 37N 95 1W
Jackson, Miss. **31** 32 18N 90 12W
Jackson, Mo. **32** 37 23N 89 40W
Jackson, Mont. **33** 45 23N 113 28W
Jackson, N.C. **40** 36 23N 77 25W
Jackson, N.H. **36** 44 10N 71 11W
Jackson, N.J. **37** 40 6N 74 23W
Jackson, Nebr. **34** 42 27N 96 34W
Jackson, Ohio **42** 39 3N 82 39W
Jackson, S.C. **46** 33 20N 81 47W
Jackson, Tenn. **48** 35 37N 88 49W
Jackson, Wis. **55** 43 19N 88 10W
Jackson, Wyo. **56** 43 29N 110 46W
Jackson Bay **128** 43 58 S 168 42 E
Jackson County ◇, Ala. **10** 34 40N 86 2W
Jackson County ◇, Ark. **13** 35 37N 91 16W
Jackson County ◇, Colo. **16** 40 45N 106 20W
Jackson County ◇, Fla. **17** 30 45N 85 15W
Jackson County ◇, Ga. **18** 34 10N 83 34W
Jackson County ◇, Ill. **21** 37 45N 89 25W
Jackson County ◇, Ind. **22** 38 55N 86 0W
Jackson County ◇, Iowa **23** 42 10N 90 35W
Jackson County ◇, Kans. **24** 39 20N 95 45W
Jackson County ◇, Ky. **49** 37 25N 84 0W
Jackson County ◇, Mich. **29** 42 15N 84 30W
Jackson County ◇, Minn. **30** 43 40N 95 10W
Jackson County ◇, Miss. **31** 30 32N 88 42W
Jackson County ◇, Mo. **32** 39 0N 94 20W
Jackson County ◇, N.C. **40** 35 20N 83 10W
Jackson County ◇, Ohio **42** 39 3N 82 39W
Jackson County ◇, Okla. **43** 34 30N 99 25W
Jackson County ◇, Oreg. **44** 42 20N 122 45W
Jackson County ◇, S. Dak. **47** 43 45N 101 45W
Jackson County ◇, Tenn. **49** 36 21N 85 39W
Jackson County ◇, Tex. **51** 28 59N 96 39W
Jackson County ◇, W. Va. **54** 38 49N 81 43W
Jackson County ◇, Wis. **55** 44 20N 90 45W
Jackson Junction **23** 43 7N 92 2W
Jackson L., Fla. **17** 30 30N 84 17W
Jackson L., Ga. **18** 33 19N 83 50W
Jackson L., Wyo. **56** 43 52N 110 36W
Jackson Mts. **35** 41 10N 118 30W
Jackson Parish ◇ **25** 32 15N 92 43W
Jackson Reservoir **16** 40 22N 104 6W
Jacksons **128** 42 46 S 171 32 E
Jacksonville, Ala. **10** 33 49N 85 46W
Jacksonville, Ark. **13** 34 52N 92 7W
Jacksonville, Fla. **17** 30 20N 81 39W
Jacksonville, Ga. **18** 31 49N 82 59W
Jacksonville, Ill. **21** 39 44N 90 14W
Jacksonville, N.C. **40** 34 45N 77 26W
Jacksonville, Ohio **42** 39 29N 82 5W
Jacksonville, Oreg. **44** 42 19N 122 57W
Jacksonville, Tex. **51** 31 58N 95 17W
Jacksonville, Vt. **36** 42 47N 72 49W
Jacksonville Beach **17** 30 17N 81 24W
Jacmel **67** 18 14N 72 32W
Jacob Lake **12** 36 43N 112 13W
Jacobabad **108** 28 20N 68 29 E
Jacobina **74** 11 11 S 40 30W
Jacob's Well **104** 32 13N 35 13 E
Jacobsville **27** 39 7N 76 31W
Jacques-Cartier, Mt. **61** 48 57N 66 0W
Jacuí → **77** 30 2 S 51 15W
Jacumba **15** 32 37N 116 11W
Jacundá → **74** 1 57 S 50 26W
Jadotville = Likasi **122** 10 55 S 26 48 E
Jādū **121** 32 0N 12 0 E
Jaén, Peru **72** 5 25 S 78 40W
Jaén, Spain **91** 37 44N 3 43W
Jaffa = Tel Aviv-Yafo **104** 32 4N 34 48 E
Jaffna **108** 9 45N 80 2 E
Jaffrey **36** 42 49N 72 2W
Jagadhri **108** 30 10N 77 20 E
Jagdalpur **109** 19 3N 82 0 E
Jagersfontein **123** 29 44 S 25 27 E
Jagraon **108** 30 50N 75 25 E
Jagtial **108** 18 50N 79 0 E
Jaguaquara **75** 13 32 S 39 58W
Jaguariaíva **77** 24 10 S 49 50W
Jaguaribe **74** 5 53 S 38 37W
Jaguaribe → **74** 4 25 S 37 45W
Jaguaruana **74** 4 50 S 37 47W
Jagüey Grande **66** 22 35N 81 7W
Jahrom **107** 28 30N 53 31 E
Jaicoa, Cord. **57** 18 25N 67 5W
Jaicós **74** 7 21 S 41 8W
Jailolo **111** 1 5N 127 30 E
Jailolo, Selat **111** 0 5N 129 5 E
Jaipur **108** 27 0N 75 50 E
Jakarta **111** 6 9 S 106 49 E
Jakin **18** 31 6N 84 59W
Jakobstad **96** 63 40N 22 43 E
Jal **38** 32 7N 103 12W
Jalai Nur **114** 49 27N 117 42 E
Jalalabad **108** 34 30N 70 29 E
Jalapa, Guat. **66** 14 39N 89 59W
Jalapa, Mexico **65** 19 30N 96 56W
Jalas, Jabal al **106** 27 30N 36 30 E
Jales **75** 20 10 S 50 33W
Jalgaon, Maharashtra, India **108** 21 2N 76 31 E
Jalgaon, Maharashtra, India **108** 21 0N 75 42 E
Jalisco □ **64** 20 0N 104 0W
Jalna **108** 19 48N 75 38 E
Jalón → **91** 41 47N 1 4W
Jalpa **64** 21 38N 102 58W
Jalpaiguri **109** 26 32N 88 46 E
Jalq **107** 27 35N 62 46 E
Jaluit I. **124** 6 0N 169 30 E
Jamaica, Iowa **23** 41 51N 94 18W
Jamaica, Vt. **36** 43 13N 72 46W
Jamaica ■ **66** 18 10N 77 30W
Jamalpur, Bangla. **109** 24 52N 89 56 E
Jamalpur, India **109** 25 18N 86 28 E
Jamanxim → **73** 4 43 S 56 18W
Jamari **73** 8 45 S 63 27W
Jamari → **73** 8 27 S 63 30W
Jambe **111** 1 15 S 132 10 E
Jambi **110** 1 38 S 103 30 E
Jambi □ **110** 1 30 S 102 30 E
James **18** 32 58N 83 29W
James →, Mo. **32** 36 45N 93 30W
James →, S. Dak. **47** 42 52N 97 18W
James →, Va. **54** 36 56N 76 27W
James, L. **40** 35 44N 81 54W
James B. **60** 51 30N 80 0W
James City **40** 35 5N 77 2W
James City County ◇ **54** 37 16N 76 40W
James Range **126** 24 10 S 132 30 E
James Ross I. **5** 63 58 S 57 50W
Jamesburg **37** 40 21N 74 27W
Jamesport **32** 39 58N 93 48W
Jamestown, Australia **127** 33 10 S 138 32 E
Jamestown, Calif. **14** 37 57N 120 25W
Jamestown, Ind. **22** 39 56N 86 38W
Jamestown, Kans. **24** 39 36N 97 52W
Jamestown, Ky. **49** 36 59N 85 4W
Jamestown, La. **25** 32 21N 93 13W
Jamestown, N. Dak. **41** 46 54N 98 42W
Jamestown, N.Y. **39** 42 6N 79 14W
Jamestown, Ohio **42** 39 39N 83 33W
Jamestown, Pa. **45** 41 29N 80 27W
Jamestown, R.I. **28** 41 30N 71 22W
Jamestown, S.C. **46** 33 17N 79 42W
Jamestown, Tenn. **49** 36 26N 84 56W
Jamestown, Va. **54** 37 13N 76 47W
Jamestown Reservoir **41** 46 56N 98 43W
Jamesville **40** 35 49N 76 54W
Jamieson **44** 44 11N 117 26W
Jamiltepec **65** 16 17N 97 49W
Jamison **34** 43 0N 99 18W
Jamkhaudi **108** 16 30N 75 15 E
Jammā'īn **104** 32 8N 35 12 E
Jammu **108** 32 43N 74 54 E
Jammu & Kashmir □ **108** 34 25N 77 0 E
Jamnagar **108** 22 30N 70 6 E
Jamrud **108** 33 59N 71 24 E
Jamshedpur **109** 22 44N 86 12 E
Jämtlands län □ **96** 62 40N 13 50 E
Jan L. **63** 54 56N 102 55W
Jan Mayen Is. **4** 71 0N 9 0W
Janaúba **75** 15 48 S 43 19W
Janaucu, I. **74** 0 30N 50 10W
Jand **108** 33 30N 72 6 E
Jandaia **75** 17 6 S 50 7W
Jandaq **107** 34 3N 54 22 E
Jandiatuba → **70** 3 28 S 68 42W
Jane **32** 36 33N 94 18W
Jane Lew **54** 39 7N 80 25W
Janesville, Calif. **14** 40 18N 120 32W
Janesville, Iowa **23** 42 39N 92 28W
Janesville, Minn. **30** 44 7N 93 42W
Janesville, Wis. **55** 42 41N 89 1W
Jangeru **110** 2 20 S 116 29 E
Jango **73** 20 27 S 55 29W
Janīn **104** 32 28N 35 18 E
Janinà = Ioánnina □ **95** 39 39N 20 57 E
Janos **64** 30 45N 108 10W
Jansen, Colo. **16** 37 9N 104 32W
Jansen, Nebr. **34** 40 11N 97 5W
Januária **75** 15 25 S 44 25W
Janub Dârfûr □ **121** 11 0N 25 0 E
Janub Kordofân □ **121** 12 0N 30 0 E
Jaora **108** 23 40N 75 10 E
Japan ■ **117** 36 0N 136 0 E
Japan, Sea of **116** 40 0N 135 0 E
Japan Trench **124** 32 0N 142 0 E
Japen = Yapen **111** 1 50 S 136 0 E
Japurá → **70** 3 8 S 64 46W
Jaque **70** 7 27N 78 8W
Jaraguá **75** 15 45 S 49 20W
Jaraguari **73** 20 9 S 54 35W
Jarama → **91** 40 2N 3 39W
Jaramillo **78** 47 10 S 67 7W
Jarash **104** 32 17N 35 54 E
Jarauçu → **71** 1 48 S 52 22W
Jardim **76** 21 28 S 56 2W
Jardines de la Reina, Is. **66** 20 50N 78 50W
Jargalant = Hovd **113** 48 2N 91 37 E
Jari → **71** 1 9 S 51 54W
Jarosław **89** 50 2N 22 42 E
Jarratt **54** 36 48N 77 28W
Jarrettsville **27** 39 36N 76 29W
Jarso **121** 5 15N 37 30 E
Jaru **73** 10 26 S 62 27W
Jaru → **73** 10 5 S 61 59W
Jarvis I. **125** 0 15 S 159 55W
Jarvisburg **40** 36 9N 75 52W
Jarwa **109** 27 38N 82 30 E
Jasin **112** 2 20N 102 26 E
Jāsk **107** 25 38N 57 45 E
Jasło **89** 49 45N 21 30 E
Jason, Is. **78** 51 0 S 61 0W
Jasonville **22** 39 10N 87 12W
Jasper, Canada **62** 52 55N 118 5W
Jasper, Ala. **10** 33 50N 87 17W
Jasper, Ark. **13** 36 1N 93 11W
Jasper, Fla. **17** 30 31N 82 57W
Jasper, Ga. **18** 34 28N 84 26W
Jasper, Ind. **22** 38 24N 86 56W
Jasper, Minn. **30** 43 51N 96 24W
Jasper, Mo. **32** 37 20N 94 18W
Jasper, Tenn. **49** 35 5N 85 38W
Jasper, Tex. **51** 30 56N 94 1W
Jasper County ◇, Ga. **18** 33 20N 83 45W
Jasper County ◇, Ill. **21** 39 0N 88 10W
Jasper County ◇, Ind. **22** 41 0N 87 5W
Jasper County ◇, Iowa **23** 41 40N 93 0W
Jasper County ◇, Miss. **31** 32 2N 89 2W
Jasper County ◇, Mo. **32** 37 10N 94 20W
Jasper County ◇, S.C. **46** 32 30N 81 0W
Jasper County ◇, Tex. **51** 30 40N 93 54W
Jasper Nat. Park **62** 52 50N 118 8W
Jassy = Iaşi **89** 47 10N 27 40 E
Jászberény **89** 47 30N 19 55 E
Jataí **75** 17 58 S 51 48W
Jatapu → **71** 2 13 S 58 17W
Jatibarang **111** 6 28 S 108 18 E
Jatinegara **111** 6 13 S 106 52 E
Játiva **91** 39 0N 0 32W
Jatobal **74** 4 35 S 49 33W
Jatt **104** 32 24N 35 2 E
Jaú **75** 22 10 S 48 30W
Jaú → **71** 1 54 S 61 26W
Jauaperí → **71** 1 26 S 61 35W
Jauja **72** 11 45 S 75 15W
Jaunpur **109** 25 46N 82 44 E
Jauru → **73** 16 22 S 57 46W
Java = Jawa **111** 7 0 S 110 0 E
Java **47** 45 30N 99 53W
Java Sea **110** 4 35 S 107 15 E
Java Trench **124** 10 0 S 110 0 E
Javhlant = Ulyasutay **113** 47 56N 97 28 E
Javier, I. **78** 47 5 S 74 25W

Jawa Joseph

Jawa 111 7 0 S 110 0 E
Jay, Fla. 17 30 57N 87 9W
Jay, Maine 26 44 30N 70 13W
Jay, N.Y. 39 44 20N 73 45W
Jay, Okla. 43 36 25N 94 48W
Jay County ◇ 22 40 25N 85 0W
Jay Peak 36 44 55N 72 32W
Jaya, Puncak 111 3 57 S 137 17 E
Jayanca 72 6 24 S 79 50W
Jayanti 109 26 45N 89 40 E
Jayapura 111 2 28 S 140 38 E
Jayawijaya, Pegunungan 111 5 0 S 139 0 E
Jaynagar 109 26 43N 86 9 E
Jayton 50 33 15N 100 34W
Jayuya 57 18 14N 66 36W
Jazminal 64 24 56N 101 25W
Jean, Nev. 35 35 47N 115 20W
Jean, Tex. 51 33 18N 98 37W
Jean Marie River 58 61 32N 120 38W
Jean Rabel 67 19 50N 73 5W
Jeanerette 25 29 55N 91 40W
Jeanette, Ostrov 101 76 43N 158 0 E
Jebba 120 9 9N 4 48 E
Jebel, Bahr el ⟶ 121 15 38N 32 31 E
Jeberos 72 5 15 S 76 10W
Jedburgh 84 55 28N 2 33W
Jędrzejów 89 50 35N 20 15 E
Jedway 62 52 17N 131 14W
Jeff Davis County ◇, Ga. 18 31 50N 82 45W
Jeff Davis County ◇, Tex. 50 30 50N 104 5W
Jeffers 30 44 3N 95 12W
Jefferson, Colo. 16 39 23N 105 48W
Jefferson, Ga. 18 34 7N 83 35W
Jefferson, Iowa 23 42 1N 94 23W
Jefferson, Maine 26 44 13N 69 27W
Jefferson, Md. 27 39 22N 77 32W
Jefferson, N.C. 40 36 25N 81 28W
Jefferson, Ohio 42 41 44N 80 46W
Jefferson, Okla. 43 36 43N 97 48W
Jefferson, Oreg. 44 44 43N 123 1W
Jefferson, S.C. 46 34 39N 80 23W
Jefferson, S. Dak. 47 42 36N 96 34W
Jefferson, Tex. 51 32 46N 94 21W
Jefferson, Wis. 55 43 0N 88 48W
Jefferson ⟶ 33 45 56N 111 31W
Jefferson, Mt. 44 44 41N 121 48W
Jefferson City, Mo. 32 38 34N 92 10W
Jefferson City, Tenn. 49 36 7N 83 30W
Jefferson County ◇, Ala. 10 33 31N 86 48W
Jefferson County ◇, Ark. 13 34 13N 92 1W
Jefferson County ◇, Colo. 16 39 40N 105 15W
Jefferson County ◇, Fla. 17 30 20N 84 0W
Jefferson County ◇, Ga. 18 33 10N 82 25W
Jefferson County ◇, Idaho 20 43 50N 112 20W
Jefferson County ◇, Ill. 21 38 20N 88 55W
Jefferson County ◇, Ind. 22 43 50N 85 25W
Jefferson County ◇, Iowa 23 41 0N 92 0W
Jefferson County ◇, Kans. 24 39 15N 95 30W
Jefferson County ◇, Ky. 49 38 10N 85 40W
Jefferson County ◇, Miss. 31 31 43N 91 4W
Jefferson County ◇, Mo. 32 38 15N 90 30W
Jefferson County ◇, Mont. 33 46 8N 112 0W
Jefferson County ◇, N.Y. 39 44 0N 76 0W
Jefferson County ◇, Nebr. 34 40 15N 97 10W
Jefferson County ◇, Ohio 42 40 25N 80 54W
Jefferson County ◇, Okla. 43 34 10N 97 50W
Jefferson County ◇, Oreg. 44 44 40N 121 10W
Jefferson County ◇, Pa. 45 41 5N 79 0W
Jefferson County ◇, Tenn. 49 36 7N 83 30W
Jefferson County ◇, Tex. 51 29 55N 94 15W
Jefferson County ◇, W. Va. 54 39 17N 77 52W
Jefferson County ◇, Wash. 53 47 50N 123 45W
Jefferson County ◇, Wis. 55 43 0N 88 45W
Jefferson Davis County ◇ 31 31 36N 89 52W
Jefferson Davis Parish ◇ 25 30 14N 92 49W
Jefferson Mt. 35 38 46N 116 55W
Jefferson National Forest 54 37 10N 81 15W
Jefferson Parish ◇ 25 29 44N 90 8W
Jeffersonton 54 38 38N 77 55W
Jeffersontown 49 38 12N 85 35W
Jeffersonville, Ga. 18 32 41N 83 20W
Jeffersonville, Ind. 22 38 17N 85 44W
Jeffersonville, Ky. 49 37 59N 83 51W
Jeffersonville, Ohio 42 39 39N 83 34W
Jeffersonville, Vt. 36 44 40N 72 50W
Jeffrey City 56 42 30N 107 49W
Jeffrey Reservoir 34 40 58N 100 24W
Jega 120 12 15N 4 23 E
Jekyll I. 18 31 4N 81 25W
Jelenia Góra 88 50 50N 15 45 E
Jelgava 98 56 41N 23 49 E
Jellico 49 36 53N 84 8W
Jellicoe 60 49 40N 87 30W
Jemaja 110 3 5N 105 45 E
Jember 111 8 11 S 113 41 E
Jembongan 110 6 45N 117 20 E
Jemeppe 87 50 37N 5 30 E
Jemez Indian Reservation 38 35 40N 106 50W
Jemez Mts. 38 35 45N 106 30W
Jemez Pueblo 38 35 37N 106 44W
Jemez Springs 38 35 46N 106 42W
Jemison 10 32 58N 86 45W
Jena, Germany 88 50 56N 11 33 E
Jena, Fla. 17 29 40N 83 22W
Jena, La. 25 31 41N 92 8W
Jenison 29 42 54N 85 47W
Jenkins, Ky. 49 37 10N 82 38W
Jenkins, Minn. 30 46 39N 94 20W
Jenkins, N.J. 37 39 42N 74 32W
Jenkins County ◇ 18 32 45N 82 0W
Jenks 43 36 1N 95 58W
Jenner 14 38 27N 123 7W
Jennings, Fla. 17 30 36N 83 6W
Jennings, Kans. 24 39 41N 100 18W
Jennings, La. 25 30 13N 92 40W
Jennings, Mo. 32 38 43N 90 16W
Jennings, Okla. 43 36 11N 96 34W
Jennings ⟶ 62 59 38N 132 5W
Jennings County ◇ 22 39 0N 85 40W
Jensen 52 40 22N 109 20W
Jensen Beach 17 27 15N 80 14W
Jequié 75 13 51 S 40 5W
Jequitaí ⟶ 75 17 4 S 44 50W
Jequitinhonha 75 16 30 S 41 0W
Jequitinhonha ⟶ 75 15 51 S 38 53W
Jerada 120 34 17N 2 10W
Jerantut 112 3 56N 102 22 E
Jerauld County ◇ 47 44 0N 98 45W
Jérémie 67 18 40N 74 10W
Jeremoabo 74 10 4 S 38 21W
Jeremy Point 28 41 53N 70 4W
Jerez, Punta 65 22 58N 97 40W
Jerez de García Salinas 64 22 39N 103 0W
Jerez de la Frontera 91 36 41N 6 7W
Jerez de los Caballeros 91 38 20N 6 45W
Jericho = El Arīhā 104 31 52N 35 27 E
Jerico Springs 32 37 37N 94 1W
Jerimoth Hill 28 41 51N 71 47W
Jermyn 51 33 16N 98 23W
Jerome, Ariz. 12 34 45N 112 7W
Jerome, Ark. 13 33 24N 91 28W
Jerome, Idaho 20 42 44N 114 31W
Jerome County ◇ 20 42 42N 114 15W
Jerrobert 63 51 56N 109 8W
Jerry City 42 41 15N 83 36W
Jersey, Ark. 13 33 26N 92 19W
Jersey, Ga. 18 33 43N 83 47W
Jersey, I. 83 49 13N 2 7W
Jersey City 37 40 44N 74 4W
Jersey County ◇ 21 39 5N 90 20W
Jersey Shore 45 41 12N 77 15W
Jersey Village 51 29 53N 95 34W
Jerseyville 21 39 7N 90 20W
Jerusalem, Asia 104 31 47N 35 10 E
Jerusalem, U.S.A. 18 30 58N 81 50W
Jervis B. 127 35 8 S 150 46 E
Jessamine County ◇ 49 37 50N 84 35W
Jesselton = Kota Kinabalu 110 6 0N 116 4 E
Jessieville 13 34 42N 93 4W
Jessore 109 23 10N 89 10 E
Jessup L. 17 28 43N 81 14W
Jesup, Ga. 18 31 36N 81 53W
Jesup, Iowa 23 42 29N 92 4W
Jesús 72 7 15 S 78 25W
Jesús Carranza 65 17 28N 95 1W
Jesús María 76 30 59 S 64 5W
Jet 43 36 40N 98 11W
Jetmore 24 38 4N 99 54W
Jewell, Iowa 23 42 20N 93 39W
Jewell, Kans. 24 39 40N 98 10W
Jewell County ◇ 24 39 45N 98 10W
Jewell Valley 54 37 15N 81 48W
Jewett, Ill. 21 39 13N 88 15W
Jewett, Ohio 42 40 22N 81 2W
Jewett, Tex. 51 31 22N 96 9W
Jewett City 28 41 36N 72 0W
Jeypore 109 18 50N 82 38 E
Jhal Jhao 107 26 20N 65 35 E
Jhalawar 108 24 40N 76 10 E
Jhang Maghiana 108 31 15N 72 22 E
Jhansi 108 25 30N 78 36 E
Jharsaguda 109 21 50N 84 5 E
Jhelum 108 33 0N 73 45 E
Jhelum ⟶ 108 31 20N 72 10 E
Jhunjhunu 108 28 10N 75 30 E
Ji Xian 114 36 7N 110 40 E
Jia Xian 114 38 12N 110 28 E
Jiamusi 114 46 40N 130 26 E
Ji'an 115 27 6N 114 59 E
Jianchuan 113 26 38N 99 55 E
Jiande 115 29 23N 119 15 E
Jiangbei 115 29 40N 106 34 E
Jiange 115 32 4N 105 32 E
Jiangjin 115 29 14N 106 14 E
Jiangling 115 30 25N 112 12 E
Jiangmen 115 22 32N 113 0 E
Jiangshan 115 28 40N 118 37 E
Jiangsu □ 115 33 0N 120 0 E
Jiangxi □ 115 27 30N 116 0 E
Jiangyin 115 31 54N 120 17 E
Jiangyong 115 25 20N 111 22 E
Jiangyou 115 31 44N 104 43 E
Jianning 115 26 50N 116 50 E
Jian'ou 115 27 3N 118 17 E
Jianshi 115 30 37N 109 38 E
Jianshui 113 23 36N 102 43 E
Jianyang 115 27 20N 118 5 E
Jiao Xian 114 36 18N 120 1 E
Jiaohe 114 38 2N 116 20 E
Jiaozhou Wan 114 36 5N 120 10 E
Jiaozuo 115 35 16N 113 12 E
Jiawang 115 34 28N 117 26 E
Jiaxing 115 30 49N 120 45 E
Jiayi 115 23 30N 120 24 E
Jibão, Serra do 75 14 48 S 45 0W
Jibuti = Djibouti ■ 105 12 0N 43 0 E
Jicarilla Indian Reservation 38 36 45N 107 0W
Jicarón, I. 66 7 10N 81 50W
Jiddah 105 21 29N 39 10 E
Jido 109 29 2N 94 58 E
Jifnā 104 31 58N 35 13 E
Jigger 25 32 2N 91 45W
Jihlava 88 49 28N 15 35 E
Jihlava ⟶ 88 48 55N 16 36 E
Jijel 120 36 52N 5 50 E
Jijiga 105 9 20N 42 50 E
Jilin 114 43 44N 126 30 E
Jilin □ 114 44 0N 124 0 E
Jiloca ⟶ 91 41 21N 1 39W
Jilong 115 25 8N 121 42 E
Jim Hogg County ◇ 50 27 0N 98 45W
Jim Thorpe 45 40 52N 75 44W
Jim Wells County ◇ 51 28 0N 98 0W
Jima 121 7 40N 36 47 E
Jiménez 64 27 10N 104 54W
Jimo 114 36 23N 120 30 E
Jin Xian 114 38 55N 121 42 E
Jinan 114 36 38N 117 1 E
Jincheng 114 35 29N 112 50 E
Jing He ⟶ 115 34 27N 109 4 E
Jing Xian 115 26 33N 109 40 E
Jingchuan 114 35 20N 107 20 E
Jingdezhen 115 29 20N 117 11 E
Jinggu 113 23 35N 100 41 E
Jinghai 114 38 55N 116 55 E
Jingle 114 38 20N 111 55 E
Jingmen 115 31 0N 112 10 E
Jingning 114 35 30N 105 43 E
Jingshan 115 31 1N 113 7 E
Jingtai 114 37 10N 104 6 E
Jingxi 115 23 8N 106 27 E
Jingyu 114 42 25N 126 45 E
Jingyuan 114 36 30N 104 40 E
Jingziguan 115 33 15N 111 0 E
Jinhe 114 51 18N 121 32 E
Jinhua 115 29 8N 119 38 E
Jining, Nei Mongol Zizhiqu, China 114 41 5N 113 0 E
Jining, Shandong, China 115 35 22N 116 34 E
Jinja 122 0 25N 33 12 E
Jinmen Dao 115 24 25N 118 25 E
Jinnah Barrage 107 32 58N 71 33 E
Jinotega 66 13 6N 85 59W
Jinotepe 66 11 50N 86 10W
Jinshi 115 29 40N 111 50 E
Jinxiang 115 35 5N 116 22 E
Jinzhou 114 41 5N 121 3 E
Jiparaná ⟶ 73 8 3 S 62 52W
Jipijapa 70 1 0 S 80 40W
Jiquilpan 64 19 57N 102 42W
Jishou 115 28 21N 109 43 E
Jisr al Ḩusayn 104 31 53N 35 33 E
Jisr ash Shughūr 106 35 49N 36 18 E
Jitra 112 6 16N 100 25 E
Jiu ⟶ 89 44 40N 23 25 E
Jiudengkou 114 39 56N 106 40 E
Jiujiang 115 29 42N 115 58 E
Jiuling Shan 115 28 40N 114 40 E
Jiuquan 113 39 50N 98 20 E
Jixi 114 45 20N 130 50 E
Jizō-Zaki 117 35 34N 133 20 E
Jo Daviess County ◇ 21 42 20N 90 10W
Joaçaba 77 27 5 S 51 31W
Joaíma 75 16 39 S 41 2W
Joanna 46 34 25N 81 49W
João 74 2 46 S 50 59W
João Amaro 75 12 46 S 40 22W
João Câmara 74 5 32 S 35 48W
João Pessoa 74 7 10 S 34 52W
João Pinheiro 75 17 45 S 46 10W
Joaquim Távora 75 23 30 S 49 58W
Joaquin 51 31 58N 94 3W
Joaquín V. González 76 25 10 S 64 0W
Jobos 57 17 58N 66 10W
Jobos, Bahía de 57 17 59N 66 14W
Jocassee, L. 46 34 58N 82 56W
Jodhpur 108 26 23N 73 8 E
Joensuu 98 62 37N 29 49 E
Joes 16 39 39N 102 41W
Jofane 123 21 15 S 34 18 E
Joggins 61 45 42N 64 27W
Jogjakarta = Yogyakarta 111 7 49 S 110 22 E
Johannesburg, S. Africa 123 26 10 S 28 2 E
Johannesburg, U.S.A. 15 35 22N 117 38W
John Day 44 44 25N 118 57W
John Day ⟶ 44 45 44N 120 39W
John Day Dam 53 45 43N 120 41W
John Day Fossil Buttes Nat. Mon. 44 44 43N 120 21W
John H. Kerr Reservoir 40 36 36N 78 18W
John Martin Reservoir 16 38 4N 102 56W
John o' Groats 84 58 39N 3 3W
John Redmond Reservoir 24 38 14N 95 46W
John W. Flanagan Reservoir 54 37 15N 82 22W
Johns I. 46 32 40N 80 10W
Johns Island 46 32 47N 80 7W
Johnson, Kans. 24 37 34N 101 45W
Johnson, Vt. 36 44 38N 72 41W
Johnson City, N.Y. 39 42 7N 75 58W
Johnson City, Tenn. 49 36 19N 82 21W
Johnson City, Tex. 51 30 17N 98 25W
Johnson County ◇, Ark. 13 35 28N 93 28W
Johnson County ◇, Ga. 18 32 45N 82 40W
Johnson County ◇, Ill. 21 37 30N 88 50W
Johnson County ◇, Ind. 22 39 30N 86 5W
Johnson County ◇, Iowa 23 41 40N 91 35W
Johnson County ◇, Kans. 24 38 45N 94 45W
Johnson County ◇, Ky. 49 37 50N 82 50W
Johnson County ◇, Mo. 32 38 45N 93 45W
Johnson County ◇, Nebr. 34 40 20N 96 15W
Johnson County ◇, Tenn. 49 36 29N 81 48W
Johnson County ◇, Tex. 51 32 21N 97 23W
Johnson County ◇, Wyo. 56 44 0N 106 35W
Johnson Draw ⟶ 50 30 8N 101 7W
Johnson Reservoir 34 40 42N 99 49W
Johnsonburg, N.J. 37 40 58N 74 53W
Johnsonburg, Pa. 45 41 29N 78 41W
Johnsondale 15 35 58N 118 32W
Johnson's Crossing 62 60 29N 133 18W
Johnsonville 46 33 49N 79 27W
Johnston, R.I. 28 41 50N 71 30W
Johnston, S.C. 46 33 50N 81 48W
Johnston, L. 126 32 25 S 120 30 E
Johnston City 21 37 49N 88 56W
Johnston County ◇, N.C. 40 35 30N 78 20W
Johnston County ◇, Okla. 43 34 20N 96 40W
Johnston Falls = Mambilima Falls 122 10 31 S 28 45 E
Johnston I. 125 17 10N 169 8W
Johnstone Str. 62 50 28N 126 0W
Johnstown, Colo. 16 40 20N 104 54W
Johnstown, N.Y. 39 43 0N 74 22W
Johnstown, Nebr. 34 42 34N 100 3W
Johnstown, Ohio 42 40 9N 82 41W
Johnstown, Pa. 45 40 20N 78 55W
Johor □ 112 2 5N 103 20 E
Johor Baharu 112 1 28N 103 46 E
Joice 23 43 22N 93 27W
Joiner 13 35 31N 90 9W
Joinvile 77 26 15 S 48 55 E
Joinville I. 5 65 0 S 55 30W
Jojutla 65 18 37N 99 11W
Jokkmokk 96 66 35N 19 50 E
Jökulsá á Dal ⟶ 96 65 40N 14 16W
Jökulsá Fjöllum ⟶ 96 66 10N 16 30W
Joliet, Ill. 21 41 32N 88 5W
Joliet, Mont. 33 45 29N 108 58W
Joliette 60 46 3N 73 24W
Jolley 23 42 29N 94 43W
Jolo 111 6 0N 121 0 E
Jombang 111 7 33 S 112 14 E
Jome 111 1 16 S 127 30 E
Jones 25 32 58N 91 39W
Jones County ◇, Ga. 18 33 0N 83 30W
Jones County ◇, Iowa 23 42 5N 91 5W
Jones County ◇, Miss. 31 31 36N 89 12W
Jones County ◇, N.C. 40 35 0N 77 30W
Jones County ◇, S. Dak. 47 44 0N 100 50W
Jones County ◇, Tex. 51 32 45N 99 54W
Jones Sound 4 76 0N 85 0W
Jonesboro, Ark. 13 35 50N 90 42W
Jonesboro, Ga. 18 33 31N 84 22W
Jonesboro, Ill. 21 37 27N 89 16W
Jonesboro, Ind. 22 40 29N 85 38W
Jonesboro, La. 25 32 15N 92 43W
Jonesboro, Tenn. 49 36 18N 82 29W
Jonesboro, Tex. 51 31 37N 97 53W
Jonesburg 32 38 51N 91 18W
Jonesport 26 44 32N 67 37W
Jonestown, Miss. 31 34 19N 90 27W
Jonestown, Pa. 45 40 25N 76 29W
Jonesville, La. 25 31 38N 91 49W
Jonesville, Mich. 29 41 59N 84 40W
Jonesville, N.C. 40 36 14N 80 51W
Jonesville, S.C. 46 34 50N 81 41W
Jonesville, Va. 54 36 41N 83 7W
Jonglei □ 121 7 30N 32 30 E
Jönköping 97 57 45N 14 10 E
Jönköpings län □ 97 57 30N 14 30 E
Jonquière 61 48 27N 71 14W
Joplin, Mo. 32 37 6N 94 31W
Joplin, Mont. 33 48 34N 110 46W
Joppa 21 37 12N 88 51W
Jordan, Phil. 111 10 41N 122 38 E
Jordan, Minn. 30 44 40N 93 38W
Jordan, Mont. 33 47 19N 106 55W
Jordan, N.Y. 39 43 4N 76 29W
Jordan ■ 106 31 0N 36 0 E
Jordan ⟶, Asia 104 31 48N 35 32 E
Jordan ⟶, U.S.A. 52 40 49N 112 8W
Jordan Valley 44 42 59N 117 3W
Jordânia 75 15 55 S 40 11W
Jorge, C. 78 51 40 S 75 35W
Jorhat 109 26 45N 94 12 E
Jorm 107 36 50N 70 52 E
Jörn 96 65 4N 20 1 E
Jornado del Muerto 38 33 15N 106 50W
Jorong 110 3 58 S 114 56 E
Jorquera ⟶ 76 28 3 S 69 58W
Jos 120 9 53N 8 51 E
José Batlle y Ordóñez 77 33 20 S 55 10W
José de San Martín 78 44 4 S 70 26W
Joseph, Oreg. 44 45 21N 117 14W
Joseph, Utah 52 38 38N 112 13W

Joseph Kanawha County

Joseph → 53 46 3N 117 1W
Joseph, L. 61 52 45N 65 18W
Joseph Bonaparte G. 126 14 35 S 128 50 E
Joseph City 12 34 57N 110 20W
Josephine County ◇ 44 42 20N 123 40W
Joshua 51 32 28N 97 23W
Joshua Tree 15 34 8N 116 19W
Joshua Tree National Monument 15 33 55N 116 0W
Jostedal 97 61 35N 7 15 E
Jotunheimen 97 61 35N 8 25 E
Jourdanton 51 28 55N 98 33W
Joussard 62 55 22N 115 50W
Jovellanos 66 22 40N 81 10W
Jowzjān □ 107 36 10N 66 0 E
Joy 21 41 12N 90 53W
Joya, La 72 16 43 S 71 52W
Joyce 53 48 8N 123 44W
Ju Xian 115 36 35N 118 20 E
Juab County ◇ 52 39 40N 113 0W
Juan Aldama 64 24 20N 103 23W
Juan Bautista Alberdi 76 34 26 S 61 48W
Juan de Fuca, Str of 53 48 18N 124 0W
Juan de Nova 123 17 3 S 43 45 E
Juan Fernández, Arch. de 125 33 50 S 80 0W
Juan José Castelli 76 25 27 S 60 57W
Juan L. Lacaze 76 34 26 S 57 25W
Juana Diaz 57 18 3N 66 31W
Juanjuí 72 7 10 S 76 45W
Juárez, Argentina 76 37 40 S 59 43W
Juárez, Mexico 64 27 37N 100 44W
Juárez, Sierra de 64 32 0N 116 0W
Juatinga, Ponta de 75 23 17 S 44 30W
Juàzeiro 74 9 30 S 40 30W
Juàzeiro do Norte 74 7 10 S 39 18W
Jubbulpore = Jabalpur 108 23 9N 79 58 E
Juby, C. 120 28 0N 12 59W
Júcar → 91 39 5N 0 10W
Júcaro 66 21 37N 78 51W
Juchitán 65 16 27N 95 5W
Jud 41 46 32N 98 54W
Judaea = Har Yehuda 104 31 35N 34 57 E
Judith → 33 47 44N 109 39W
Judith, Pt. 28 41 22N 71 29W
Judith Basin County ◇ 33 46 55N 110 10W
Judith Gap 33 46 41N 109 45W
Judith Mts. 33 47 15N 109 20W
Judsonia 13 35 16N 91 38W
Jufari → 71 1 13 S 62 0W
Jugoslavia = Yugoslavia ■ 95 44 0N 20 0 E
Juigalpa 66 12 6N 85 26W
Juiz de Fora 75 21 43 S 43 19W
Jujuy □ 76 23 20 S 65 40W
Julesburg 16 40 59N 102 16W
Julesburg Reservoir 16 40 56N 102 38W
Juli 72 16 10 S 69 25W
Julia Creek 127 20 39 S 141 44 E
Juliaca 72 15 25 S 70 10W
Julian, N.C. 40 35 54N 79 39W
Julian, Nebr. 34 40 31N 95 52W
Julianatop 71 3 40N 56 30W
Julianehåb 4 60 43N 46 0W
Juliette, L 18 33 2N 83 50W
Julimes 64 28 25N 105 27W
Jullundur 108 31 20N 75 40 E
Julu 114 37 15N 115 2 E
Jumentos Cays 67 23 0N 75 40 E
Jumet 87 50 27N 4 25 E
Jumilla 91 38 28N 1 19W
Jumla 109 29 15N 82 13 E
Jumna = Yamuna → 109 25 30N 81 53 E
Jump → 55 45 17N 91 5W
Junagadh 108 21 30N 70 30 E
Juncos 57 18 14N 65 55W
Junction, Tex. 51 30 29N 99 46W
Junction, Utah 52 38 14N 112 13W
Junction B. 126 11 52 S 133 55 E
Junction City, Ga. 18 32 36N 84 28W
Junction City, Kans. 24 39 2N 96 50W
Junction City, Ky. 49 37 35N 84 48W
Junction City, La. 25 33 0N 92 43W
Junction City, Oreg. 44 44 13N 123 12W
Junction City, Wis. 55 44 35N 89 46W
Jundah 127 24 46 S 143 2 E
Jundiaí 77 24 30 S 47 0W
June Lake 14 37 47N 119 4W
Juneau, Alaska 11 58 18N 134 25W
Juneau, Wis. 55 43 24N 88 42W
Juneau ◇ 11 58 30N 134 0W
Juneau County ◇ 55 43 50N 90 10W
Junee 127 34 53 S 147 35 E
Junggar Pendi 113 44 30N 86 0 E
Juniata 34 40 35N 98 30W
Juniata → 45 40 24N 77 1W
Juniata County ◇ 45 40 45N 77 5W
Junín, Argentina 76 34 33 S 60 57W
Junín, Peru 72 11 12 S 76 0W
Junín □ 72 11 30 S 75 0W
Junín de los Andes 78 39 45 S 71 0W
Junior 54 38 59N 79 57W
Juniper 18 32 32N 84 36W
Juniper Mts. 12 35 10N 113 0W
Jūniyah 106 33 59N 35 38 E
Juno 50 30 9N 101 7W
Juno Beach 17 26 52N 80 3W
Juntura 44 43 45N 118 5W
Juparanã, Lagoa 75 19 16 S 40 8W
Jupiter 17 26 57N 80 6W
Jupiter → 61 49 29N 63 37W
Juquiá 75 24 19 S 47 38W
Jur, Nahr el → 121 8 45N 29 15 E
Jura 84 56 0N 5 50W
Jura □ 90 46 47N 5 45 E
Jura, Mts. 90 46 40N 6 5 E
Jura, Sd. of 84 55 57N 5 45W
Jurado 70 7 7N 77 46W
Jurilovca 95 44 46N 28 52 E
Juruá → 70 2 37 S 65 44W
Juruena 73 13 0 S 58 10W
Juruena → 73 7 20 S 58 3W
Juruti 71 2 9 S 56 4W
Justice 54 37 35N 81 50W
Justin 51 33 5N 97 18W
Justo Daract 76 33 52 S 65 12W
Jutaí 72 5 11 S 68 54W
Jutaí → 70 2 43 S 66 57W
Juticalpa 66 14 40N 86 12W
Jutland = Jylland 97 56 25N 9 30 E
Juventud, I. de la 66 21 40N 82 40W
Juwain 107 31 45N 61 30 E
Jylland 97 56 25N 9 30 E
Jyväskylä 110 62 14N 25 50 E

K

K2 108 35 58N 76 32 E
Ka Lae 19 18 55N 155 41W
Kaaawa 19 21 33N 157 51W
Kaala 19 21 31N 158 9W
Kaalasin 112 16 26N 103 30 E
Kaalualu B. 19 18 58N 155 37W
Kaap die Goeie Hoop 123 34 24 S 18 30 E
Kaap Plato 123 28 30 S 24 0 E
Kaapkruis 123 21 43 S 14 0 E
Kaapstad = Cape Town 123 33 55 S 18 22 E
Kabaena 111 5 15 S 122 0 E
Kabala 120 9 38N 11 37W
Kabale 122 1 15 S 30 0 E
Kabalo 122 6 0 S 27 0 E
Kabambare 122 4 41 S 27 39 E
Kabanjahe 110 3 6N 98 30 E
Kabara 120 16 40N 2 50W
Kabardino-Balkar-A.S.S.R. □ 99 43 30N 43 30 E
Kabare 111 0 4 S 130 58 E
Kabarega Falls 122 2 15N 31 30 E
Kabasalan 111 7 47N 122 44 E
Kabba 120 7 50N 6 3 E
Kabetogama L. 30 48 28N 93 1W
Kabi 121 13 30N 12 35 E
Kabinakagami L. 60 48 54N 84 25W
Kabīr, Zab al 106 36 0N 43 0 E
Kabīr Kūh 106 33 0N 47 30 E
Kabkabīyah 121 13 50N 24 0 E
Kabompo → 123 14 10 S 23 11 E
Kabongo 122 7 22 S 25 33 E
Kabūd Gonbad 107 37 5N 59 45 E
Kābul 107 34 28N 69 11 E
Kābul □ 107 34 30N 69 0 E
Kabul → 108 33 55N 72 14 E
Kaburuang 111 3 50N 126 30 E
Kabwe 123 14 30 S 28 29 E
Kachchh, Gulf of 108 22 50N 69 15 E
Kachchh, Rann of 108 24 0N 70 0 E
Kachin □ 109 26 0N 97 30 E
Kachiry 100 53 10N 75 50 E
Kackar 106 40 45N 41 10 E
Kackley 24 39 42N 97 51W
Kadan Kyun 110 12 30N 98 20 E
Kadina 127 34 0 S 137 43 E
Kadirli 106 37 23N 36 5 E
Kadiyevka = Stakhanov 99 48 35N 38 40 E
Kadoka 47 43 50N 101 31W
Kâdugli 121 11 0N 29 45 E
Kaduna 120 10 30N 7 21 E
Kaédi 120 16 9N 13 28W
Kaelé 121 10 7N 14 27 E
Kaena Pt. 19 21 35N 158 17W
Kaesŏng 114 37 58N 126 35 E
Kâf 106 31 25N 37 29 E
Kafakumba 122 9 38 S 23 46 E
Kafan 99 39 18N 46 15 E
Kafanchan 120 9 40N 8 20 E
Kaffrine 120 14 8N 15 36W
Kafia Kingi 121 9 20N 24 25 E
Kafirévs, Ákra 95 38 9N 24 38 E
Kafr 'Ayn 104 32 3N 35 7 E
Kafr Kammā 104 32 44N 35 26 E
Kafr Kannā 104 32 45N 35 20 E
Kafr Mālik 104 32 0N 35 18 E
Kafr Mandā 104 32 49N 35 15 E
Kafr Quaddūm 104 32 14N 35 7 E
Kafr Rā'ī 104 32 23N 35 9 E
Kafr Şīr 104 33 19N 35 23 E
Kafr Yāsīf 104 32 58N 35 10 E
Kafue → 123 15 30 S 26 0 E
Kafulwe 122 9 0 S 29 1 E
Kaga Bandoro 122 7 0N 19 10 E
Kagamil I. 11 53 0N 169 43W
Kagan 100 39 43N 64 33 E
Kagawa □ 117 34 15N 134 0 E
Kağizman 106 40 5N 43 10 E
Kagoshima 117 31 35N 130 33 E
Kagoshima □ 117 31 30N 130 30 E
Kahaluu 19 21 28N 157 50W
Kahama 122 4 8 S 32 30 E
Kahana 19 21 34N 157 53W
Kahana B. 19 21 35N 157 50W
Kahayan → 110 3 40 S 114 0 E
Kahemba 122 7 18 S 18 55 E
Kahlotus 53 46 39N 118 33W
Kahniah → 62 58 15N 120 55W
Kahnūj 107 27 55N 57 40 E
Kahoka 32 40 25N 91 44W
Kahoolawe 19 20 33N 156 37W
Kahuku 19 21 41N 157 57W
Kahuku Pt. 19 21 43N 157 59W
Kahului 19 20 54N 156 28W
Kai, Kepulauan 111 5 55 S 132 45W
Kai Besar 111 5 35 S 133 0 E
Kai-Ketil 111 5 45 S 132 40 E
Kaiama 120 9 36N 4 1 E
Kaiapoi 128 42 24 S 172 40 E
Kaibab 12 36 54N 112 44W
Kaibab Indian Reservation 12 36 55N 112 40W
Kaibab National Forest 12 36 35N 112 15W
Kaibab Plateau 12 36 45N 112 15W
Kaibito Plateau 12 36 30N 111 15W
Kaieteur Falls 71 5 1N 59 10W
Kaifeng 115 34 48N 114 21 E
Kaihua 115 29 12N 118 20 E
Kaikohe 128 35 25 S 173 49 E
Kaikoura 128 42 25 S 173 43 E
Kaikoura Pen. 128 42 25 S 173 43 E
Kaikoura Ra. 128 41 59 S 173 41 E
Kaili 115 26 33N 107 59 E
Kailu 114 43 38N 121 18 E
Kailua, Hawaii 19 21 24N 157 44W
Kailua, Hawaii 19 21 24N 157 45W
Kailua B. 19 21 25N 157 40W
Kailua Kona 19 19 39N 155 59W
Kaimana 111 3 39 S 133 45 E
Kaimanawa Mts. 128 39 15 S 175 56 E
Kaimuki 19 21 17N 157 48W
Kaingaroa Forest 128 38 24 S 176 30 E
Kainji Res. 120 10 1N 4 40 E
Kaipara Harbour 128 36 25 S 174 14 E
Kaiparowits Plateau 52 37 30N 111 20W
Kaiping 115 22 23N 112 42 E
Kaipokok B. 61 54 54N 59 47W
Kaironi 111 0 47 S 133 40 E
Kairouan 120 35 45N 10 5 E
Kaiserslautern 88 49 30N 7 43 E
Kaitaia 128 35 8 S 173 17 E
Kaitangata 128 46 17 S 169 51 E
Kaiwi Channel 19 21 15N 157 30W
Kaiyuan 114 42 28N 124 1 E
Kaiyuh Mts. 11 64 30N 158 0W
Kajaani 96 64 17N 27 46 E
Kajabbi 127 20 0 S 140 1 E
Kajana = Kajaani 96 64 17N 27 46 E
Kajang 112 2 59N 101 48 E
Kajo Kaji 121 3 58N 31 40 E
Kaka 121 10 38N 32 10 E
Kaka Pt. 19 20 31N 156 33W
Kakabeka Falls 60 48 24N 89 37W
Kakamas 123 28 45 S 20 33 E
Kakamega 122 0 20N 34 46 E
Kakanui Mts. 128 45 10 S 170 30 E
Kake, Japan 117 34 36N 132 19 E
Kake, U.S.A. 11 56 59N 133 57W
Kakegawa 117 34 45N 138 1 E
Kakeroma-Jima 117 28 8N 129 14 E
Kakhonak 11 59 26N 154 51W
Kakhovka 99 46 40N 33 15 E
Kakhovskoye Vdkhr. 99 47 5N 34 16 E
Kakinada 109 16 57N 82 11 E
Kakisa → 62 61 3N 118 10W
Kakisa L. 62 60 56N 117 43W
Kakogawa 117 34 46N 134 51 E
Kaktovik 11 70 8N 143 38W
Kakwa → 62 54 37N 118 28W
Kalabagh 108 33 0N 71 28 E
Kalabahi 111 8 13 S 124 31 E
Kalabáka 95 39 42N 21 39 E
Kalabo 123 14 58 S 22 40 E
Kalach 99 50 22N 41 0 E
Kaladan → 109 20 20N 93 5 E
Kalahari 123 24 0 S 21 30 E
Kalaheo 19 21 56N 159 32W
Kalakan 101 55 15N 116 45 E
Kalama 53 46 1N 122 51W
Kalamata 95 37 3N 22 10 E
Kalamazoo 29 42 17N 85 35W
Kalamazoo → 29 42 40N 86 10W
Kalamazoo County ◇ 29 42 15N 85 30W
Kalan 106 39 7N 39 32 E
Kalao 111 7 21 S 121 0 E
Kalaotoa 111 7 20 S 121 50 E
Kalapana 19 19 21N 154 59W
Kalasin 112 16 26N 103 30 E
Kalat 107 29 8N 66 31 E
Kalaupapa 19 21 12N 156 59W
Kalegauk Kyun 109 15 33N 97 35 E
Kalemie 122 5 55 S 29 9 E
Kaleva 29 44 22N 86 1W
Kalewa 109 23 10N 94 15 E
Kálfafellsstaður 96 64 11N 15 53W
Kalgan = Zhangjiakou 114 40 48N 114 55 E
Kalgoorlie-Boulder 126 30 40 S 121 22 E
Kaliakra, Nos 95 43 21N 28 30 E
Kalianda 110 5 50 S 105 45 E
Kalibo 111 11 43N 122 22 E
Kalida 42 40 59N 84 12W
Kalihi 19 21 20N 157 53W
Kalima 122 2 33 S 26 32 E
Kalimantan Barat □ 110 0 0 110 30 E
Kalimantan Selatan □ 110 2 30 S 115 30 E
Kalimantan Tengah □ 110 2 0 S 113 30 E
Kalimantan Timur □ 110 1 30N 116 30 E
Kálimnos 95 37 0N 27 0 E
Kalinin 98 56 55N 35 55 E
Kaliningrad 98 54 42N 20 32 E
Kalipetrovo 95 44 5N 27 14 E
Kalispell 33 48 12N 114 19W
Kalisz 89 51 45N 18 8 E
Kaliua 122 5 5 S 31 48 E
Kalix → 96 65 50N 23 11 E
Kalkaska 29 44 44N 85 11W
Kalkaska County ◇ 29 44 45N 85 5W
Kalkrand 123 24 1 S 17 35 E
Kallia 104 31 46N 35 30 E
Kallsjön 96 63 38N 13 0 E
Kalmar 97 56 40N 16 20 E
Kalmyk A.S.S.R. □ 99 46 5N 46 1 E
Kalmykovo 99 49 0N 51 47 E
Kalocsa 89 46 32N 19 0 E
Kalofer 95 42 37N 24 59 E
Kalohi Channel 19 21 0N 157 0W
Kalomo 123 17 0 S 26 30 E
Kalona 23 41 29N 91 43W
Kaltag 11 64 20N 158 43W
Kaluga 98 54 35N 36 10 E
Kalundborg 97 55 41N 11 5 E
Kalutara 108 6 35N 80 0 E
Kalvesta 24 38 4N 100 18W
Kalya 98 60 15N 59 59 E
Kam Keut 112 18 20N 104 48 E
Kama → 98 55 45N 52 0 E
Kamaishi 116 39 16N 141 53 E
Kamakou 19 21 7N 156 52W
Kamananui → 19 21 38N 158 4W
Kamandorskiye Ostrava 101 55 0N 167 0 E
Kamaran 105 15 21N 42 35 E
Kamas 52 40 38N 111 17W
Kambarka 98 56 15N 54 11 E
Kamchatka, P-ov. 101 57 0N 160 0 E
Kamehameha Heights 19 21 21N 157 52W
Kamela 44 45 26N 118 24W
Kamen 100 53 50N 81 30 E
Kamen-Rybolov 116 44 46N 132 2 E
Kamenets-Podolskiy 99 48 45N 26 10 E
Kamenjak, Rt. 94 44 47N 13 55 E
Kamenka 98 65 58N 44 0 E
Kameno 95 42 34N 27 18 E
Kamensk-Shakhtinskiy 99 48 23N 40 20 E
Kamensk Uralskiy 100 56 25N 62 2 E
Kamenskoye 101 62 45N 165 30 E
Kamenyak 95 43 24N 26 57 E
Kameoka 117 35 0N 135 35 E
Kamiah 20 46 14N 116 2W
Kamilukuak, L. 63 62 22N 101 40W
Kamina 122 8 45 S 25 0 E
Kaminak L. 63 62 10N 95 0W
Kaminoyama 116 38 9N 140 17 E
Kamishak Bay 11 59 15N 153 45W
Kamloops 62 50 40N 120 20W
Kamloops L. 62 50 45N 120 40W
Kamo 116 37 39N 139 3 E
Kamooloa 19 21 34N 158 7W
Kampala 122 0 20N 32 30 E
Kampar 112 4 18N 101 9 E
Kampar → 110 0 30N 103 8 E
Kampen 87 52 33N 5 53 E
Kampot 112 10 36N 104 10 E
Kampsville 21 39 18N 90 37W
Kampuchea = Cambodia ■ 112 12 15N 105 0 E
Kampung → 111 5 44 S 138 24 E
Kampungbaru = Tolitoli 111 1 5N 120 50 E
Kamrar 23 42 24N 93 44W
Kamrau, Teluk 111 3 30 S 133 36 E
Kamsack 63 51 34N 101 54W
Kamskoye Vdkhr. 98 58 0N 56 0 E
Kamuchawie L. 63 56 18N 101 59W
Kamuela 19 20 1N 155 41W
Kamui-Misaki 116 43 20N 140 21 E
Kamyshin 99 50 10N 45 24 E
Kanaaupscow 60 54 2N 76 30W
Kanab 52 37 3N 112 32W
Kanab → 12 36 24N 112 38W
Kanabec County ◇ 30 45 55N 93 20W
Kanaga I. 11 51 45N 177 22W
Kanagi 116 40 54N 140 27 E
Kanairiktok → 61 55 2N 60 18W
Kananga 122 5 55 S 22 18 E
Kanarraville 52 37 32N 113 11W
Kanash 98 55 30N 47 32 E
Kanawha 23 42 56N 93 48W
Kanawha → 54 38 50N 82 9W
Kanawha County ◇ 54 38 21N 81 38W

Kanazawa Kelibia

Kanazawa 117 36 30N 136 38 E
Kanchanaburi 112 14 2N 99 31 E
Kanchenjunga 109 27 50N 88 10 E
Kanchipuram 108 12 52N 79 45 E
Kanda Kanda 122 6 52 S 23 48 E
Kandalaksha 98 67 9N 32 30 E
Kandalakshkiy Zaliv 98 66 0N 35 0 E
Kandalu 108 29 55N 63 20 E
Kandangan 110 2 50 S 115 20 E
Kandi 120 11 7N 2 55 E
Kandiyohi County ◇ 30 45 10N 95 0W
Kandla 108 23 0N 70 10 E
Kandy 108 7 18N 80 43 E
Kane, Ill. 21 39 11N 90 21W
Kane, Pa. 45 41 40N 78 49W
Kane, Wyo. 56 44 51N 108 12W
Kane Bassin 4 79 30N 68 0W
Kane County ◇, Ill. 21 41 50N 88 25W
Kane County ◇, Utah 52 37 15N 112 0W
Kaneilio Pt. 19 21 27N 158 12W
Kaneohe 19 21 25N 157 48W
Kaneohe B. 19 21 30N 157 50W
Kangar 112 6 27N 100 12 E
Kangaroo I. 127 35 45 S 137 0 E
Kangavar 106 34 40N 48 0 E
Kangean, Kepulauan 110 6 55 S 115 23 E
Kangerdlugsuak 4 68 10N 32 20W
Kanggyee 114 41 0N 126 35 E
Kangnŭng 114 37 45N 128 54 E
Kango 122 0 11N 10 5 E
Kangto 109 27 50N 92 35 E
Kaniapiskau → 61 56 40N 69 30W
Kaniapiskau L. 61 54 10N 69 55W
Kaniksu National Forest 20 48 50N 116 30W
Kanin, P-ov. 98 68 0N 45 0 E
Kanin Nos, Mys 98 68 45N 43 20 E
Kankakee 21 41 7N 87 52W
Kankakee → 21 41 23N 88 15W
Kankakee County ◇ 21 41 10N 87 50W
Kankan 120 10 23N 9 15W
Kanker 109 20 10N 81 40 E
Kankunskiy 101 57 37N 126 8 E
Kannapolis 40 35 30N 80 37W
Kannauj 108 27 3N 79 56 E
Kannod 108 22 45N 76 40 E
Kano 120 12 2N 8 30 E
Kan'onji 117 34 7N 133 39 E
Kanopolis 24 38 43N 98 9W
Kanopolis Lake 24 38 37N 97 58W
Kanorado 24 39 20N 102 2W
Kanosh 52 38 48N 112 26W
Kanowit 110 2 14N 112 20 E
Kanowna 126 30 32 S 121 31 E
Kanoya 117 31 25N 130 50 E
Kanpetlet 109 21 10N 93 59 E
Kanpur 108 26 28N 80 20 E
Kansas, Ill. 21 39 33N 87 56W
Kansas, Okla. 43 36 12N 94 48W
Kansas □ 24 38 30N 99 0W
Kansas → 24 39 7N 94 37W
Kansas City, Kans. 24 39 7N 94 38W
Kansas City, Mo. 32 39 6N 94 35W
Kansk 101 56 20N 95 37 E
Kansu = Gansu □ 114 36 0N 104 0 E
Kantang 112 7 25N 99 31 E
Kantishna → 11 64 45N 149 58W
Kantō □ 117 36 15N 139 30 E
Kantō-Sanchi 117 35 59N 138 50 E
Kanturk 85 52 10N 8 55W
Kanuma 117 36 34N 139 42 E
Kanye 123 25 0 S 25 28 E
Kaohsiung = Gaoxiong 115 22 38N 120 18 E
Kaoko Otavi 123 18 12 S 13 45 E
Kaolack 120 14 5N 16 8W
Kapaa 19 22 5N 159 19W
Kapahulu 19 21 0N 157 0W
Kapanga 122 8 30 S 22 40 E
Kapapa I. 19 21 29N 157 48W
Kapchagai 100 43 50N 77 10 E
Kapela 94 44 40N 15 40 E
Kapfenberg 88 47 26N 15 18 E
Kapiri Mposhi 123 13 59 S 28 43 E
Kāpīsā □ 107 35 0N 69 20 E
Kapiskau → 60 52 47N 81 55W
Kapit 110 2 0N 112 55 E
Kapiti I. 128 40 50 S 174 56 E
Kaplan 25 30 0N 92 17W
Kapoeta 121 4 50N 33 35 E
Kaposvár 89 46 25N 17 47 E
Kapowsin 53 46 59N 122 13W
Kapuas → 110 0 25 S 109 20 E
Kapuas Hulu, Pegunungan 110 1 30N 113 30 E
Kapuskasing 60 49 25N 82 30W
Kapuskasing → 60 49 49N 82 0W
Kaputir 122 2 5N 35 28 E
Kara 100 69 10N 65 0 E
Kara Bogaz Gol, Zaliv 99 41 0N 53 30 E
Kara Kalpak A.S.S.R. □ 100 43 0N 60 0 E
Kara Sea 100 75 0N 70 0 E
Karabük 106 41 12N 32 37 E
Karabutak 100 49 59N 60 14 E
Karachi 108 24 53N 67 0 E
Karad 108 17 15N 74 10 E
Karadeniz Boğazı 106 41 10N 29 10 E
Karaganda 100 49 50N 73 10 E
Karagayly 100 49 26N 76 0 E
Karaginskiy, Ostrov 101 58 45N 164 0 E
Karagiye Depression 99 43 27N 51 45 E
Karaikal 108 10 59N 79 50 E
Karaikkudi 108 10 0N 78 45 E
Karaj 107 35 48N 51 0 E
Karakas 100 48 20N 83 30 E
Karakitang 111 3 14N 125 28 E
Karakoram Pass 108 35 33N 77 50 E
Karakoram Ra. 108 35 30N 77 0 E
Karakum, Peski 100 39 30N 60 0 E
Karalon 101 57 5N 115 50 E
Karaman 106 37 14N 33 13 E
Karamay 113 45 30N 84 58 E
Karambu 110 3 53 S 116 6 E
Karamea Bight 128 41 22 S 171 40 E
Karanganyar 111 7 38 S 109 37 E
Karasburg 123 28 0 S 18 44 E
Karasino 100 66 50N 86 50 E
Karasjok 96 69 27N 25 30 E
Karasuk 100 53 44N 78 2 E
Karasuyama 117 36 39N 140 9 E
Karatau 100 43 10N 70 28 E
Karatau, Khrebet 100 43 30N 69 30 E
Karawanken 94 46 30N 14 40 E
Karazhal 100 48 2N 70 49 E
Karbalā 106 32 36N 44 3 E
Karcag 89 47 19N 20 57 E
Karda 101 55 0N 103 16 E
Kardhítsa 95 39 23N 21 54 E
Kareeberge 123 30 50 S 22 0 E
Karelian A.S.S.R. □ 98 65 30N 32 30 E
Karen 112 12 49N 92 53 E
Kargānrūd 106 37 55N 49 0 E
Kargasok 100 59 3N 80 53 E
Kargat 100 55 10N 80 15 E
Kargil 108 34 32N 76 12 E
Kargopol 98 61 30N 38 58 E
Kariba Dam 123 16 30 S 28 35 E
Kariba Gorge 123 16 30 S 28 50 E
Kariba Lake 123 16 40 S 28 25 E
Karibib 123 21 0 S 15 56 E
Karimata, Kepulauan 110 1 25 S 109 0 E
Karimata, Selat 110 2 0 S 108 40 E
Karimnagar 108 18 26N 79 10 E
Karimunjawa, Kepulauan 110 5 50 S 110 30 E
Karin 105 10 50N 45 52 E
Kariya 117 34 58N 137 1 E
Karkaralinsk 100 49 26N 75 30 E
Karkinitskiy Zaliv 99 45 56N 33 0 E
Karkur 104 32 29N 34 57 E
Karl-Marx-Stadt 88 50 50N 12 55 E
Karlovac 94 45 31N 15 36 E
Karlovy Vary 88 50 13N 12 51 E
Karlsborg 97 58 33N 14 33 E
Karlshamn 97 56 10N 14 51 E
Karlskoga 97 59 22N 14 33 E
Karlskrona 97 56 10N 15 35 E
Karlsruhe, Germany 88 49 3N 8 23 E
Karlsruhe, U.S.A. 41 48 6N 100 37W
Karlstad, Sweden 97 59 23N 13 30 E
Karlstad, U.S.A. 30 48 35N 96 31W
Karluk 11 57 34N 154 28W
Karluk Indian Reservation 11 57 35N 154 20W
Karnack 51 32 40N 94 10W
Karnak 21 37 18N 88 58W
Karnal 108 29 42N 77 2 E
Karnali → 109 29 0N 83 20 E
Karnaphuli Res. 109 22 40N 92 20 E
Karnataka □ 108 13 15N 77 0 E
Karnes City 51 28 53N 97 54W
Karnes County ◇ 51 28 49N 97 51W
Karnische Alpen 88 46 36N 13 0 E
Kärnten □ 88 46 52N 13 30 E
Karonga 122 9 57 S 33 55 E
Karora 121 17 44N 38 15 E
Kárpathos 95 35 37N 27 10 E
Karpinsk 98 59 45N 60 1 E
Karpogory 98 63 59N 44 27 E
Kars 106 40 40N 43 5 E
Karsakpay 100 47 55N 66 40 E
Karshi 100 38 53N 65 48 E
Karsun 98 54 14N 46 57 E
Kartaly 100 53 3N 60 40 E
Karufa 111 3 50 S 133 20 E
Karungu 122 0 50 S 34 10 E
Karur 108 10 59N 78 2 E
Karval 16 38 44N 103 32W
Karwar 108 14 55N 74 13 E
Kas Kong 112 11 27N 102 12 E
Kasaan 11 55 32N 132 24W
Kasai → 122 3 30 S 16 10 E
Kasama 122 10 16 S 31 9 E
Kasanga 122 8 30 S 31 10 E
Kasangulu 122 4 33 S 15 15 E
Kasaragod 108 12 30N 74 58 E
Kasba L. 63 60 20N 102 10W
Kasempa 123 13 30 S 25 44 E
Kasenga 122 10 20 S 28 45 E
Kashabowie 60 48 40N 90 26W
Kāshān 107 34 5N 51 30 E
Kashi 113 39 30N 76 2 E
Kashiwazaki 117 37 22N 138 33 E
Kashk-e Kohneh 107 34 55N 62 30 E
Kāshmar 107 35 16N 58 26 E
Kashmir 108 34 0N 76 0 E
Kashun Noerh = Gaxun Nur 113 42 22N 100 30 E
Kasilof 11 60 23N 151 18W
Kasimov 98 54 55N 41 20 E
Kasiruta 111 0 25 S 127 12 E
Kaskaskia → 21 37 58N 89 57W
Kaskattama → 63 57 3N 90 4W
Kaskinen 96 62 22N 21 15 E
Kaskö 96 62 22N 21 15 E
Kaslo 62 49 55N 116 55W
Kasmere L. 63 59 34N 101 10W
Kasongo 122 4 30 S 26 33 E
Kasongo Lunda 122 6 35 S 16 49 E
Kásos 95 35 20N 26 55 E
Kaspichan 95 43 18N 27 11 E
Kassala 121 16 0N 36 0 E
Kassalâ □ 121 15 20N 36 26 E
Kassel 88 51 19N 9 32 E
Kasson 30 44 2N 92 45W
Kassue 111 6 58 S 139 21 E
Kastamonu 106 41 25N 33 43 E
Kastellorizon = Megiste 93 36 8N 29 34 E
Kastoría 95 40 30N 21 19 E
Kasulu 122 4 37 S 30 5 E
Kasumi 117 35 38N 134 38 E
Kasur 108 31 5N 74 25 E
Kata 101 58 46N 102 40 E
Katahdin, Mt. 26 45 54N 68 56W
Katako Kombe 122 3 25 S 24 20 E
Katalla 11 60 12N 144 31W
Katangi 108 21 56N 79 50 E
Katangli 101 51 42N 143 14 E
Katanning 126 33 40 S 117 33 E
Katha 109 24 10N 96 30 E
Katherine 126 14 27 S 132 20 E
Kathiawar 108 22 20N 71 0 E
Kathleen 17 28 7N 82 2W
Kathryn 41 46 41N 97 58W
Katiet 110 2 21 S 99 54 E
Katihar 109 25 34N 87 36 E
Katima Mulilo 123 17 28 S 24 13 E
Katingan = Mendawai → 110 3 30 S 113 0 E
Katiola 120 8 10N 5 10W
Katmai National Monument 11 58 20N 155 0W
Katmandu 109 27 45N 85 20 E
Katompe 122 6 2 S 26 23 E
Katoomba 127 33 41 S 150 19 E
Katowice 89 50 17N 19 5 E
Katrine, L. 84 56 15N 4 30W
Katrineholm 97 59 9N 16 12 E
Katsumoto 117 33 51N 129 42 E
Katsuura 117 35 10N 140 20 E
Katsuyama 117 36 3N 136 30 E
Kattegatt 97 57 0N 11 20 E
Katwijk-aan-Zee 87 52 12N 4 24 E
Katy 51 29 47N 95 49W
Kauai 19 22 3N 159 30W
Kauai Channel 19 21 45N 158 50W
Kauai County ◇ 19 22 0N 159 30W
Kaufman 51 32 35N 96 19W
Kaufman County ◇ 51 32 35N 96 20W
Kauhola Pt. 19 20 15N 155 47W
Kaukauna 55 44 17N 88 17W
Kaukonahua → 19 21 35N 158 7W
Kaukonen 96 67 31N 24 53 E
Kaula I. 19 21 40N 160 33W
Kaulakahi Channel 19 22 0N 159 55W
Kauliranta 96 66 27N 23 41 E
Kaumalapau 19 20 47N 156 59W
Kauna Pt. 19 19 2N 155 53W
Kaunakakai 19 21 6N 157 1W
Kaunas 98 54 54N 23 54 E
Kaupo 19 20 38N 156 8W
Kaura Namoda 120 12 37N 6 33 E
Kautokeino 96 69 0N 23 4 E
Kavacha 101 60 16N 169 51 E
Kavalerovo 116 44 15N 135 4 E
Kavali 108 14 55N 80 1 E
Kavála 95 40 57N 24 28 E
Kavarna 95 43 26N 28 22 E
Kavkaz, Bolshoi 99 42 50N 44 0 E
Kaw 71 4 30N 52 15W
Kaw City 43 36 46N 96 50W
Kaw L. 43 36 50N 96 55W
Kawagoe 117 35 55N 139 29 E
Kawaguchi 117 35 52N 139 45 E
Kawaihae 19 20 3N 155 50W
Kawaihae B. 19 20 0N 155 50W
Kawaihoa Pt. 19 21 47N 160 12W
Kawaikimi 19 22 5N 159 29W
Kawailoa Beach 19 21 37N 158 5W
Kawambwa 122 9 48 S 29 3 E
Kawanoe 117 34 1N 133 34 E
Kawardha 109 22 0N 81 17 E
Kawasaki 117 35 35N 139 42 E
Kaweah, L. 15 36 28N 118 52W
Kawela 19 21 42N 158 1W
Kawene 60 48 45N 91 15W
Kawerau 128 38 7 S 176 42 E
Kawhia Harbour 128 38 5 S 174 51 E
Kawio, Kepulauan 111 4 30N 125 30 E
Kawkawlin 29 43 39N 83 57W
Kawnro 109 22 48N 99 8 E
Kawthaung 112 10 5N 98 36 E
Kawthoolei □ = Kawthule □ 109 18 0N 97 30 E
Kawthule □ 109 18 0N 97 30 E
Kay County ◇ 43 36 50N 97 5W
Kaya 120 13 4N 1 10W
Kayah □ 109 19 15N 97 15 E
Kayak I. 11 59 56N 144 23W
Kayan → 110 2 55N 117 35 E
Kaycee 56 43 43N 106 38W
Kayeli 111 3 20 S 127 10 E
Kayenta 12 36 44N 110 15W
Kayes 120 14 25N 11 30W
Kaylor 47 43 11N 97 50W
Kayoa 111 0 1N 127 28 E
Kayseri 106 38 45N 35 30 E
Kaysville 52 41 2N 111 56W
Kayuagung 110 3 24 S 104 50 E
Kazachinskoye 101 56 16N 107 36 E
Kazachye 101 70 52N 135 58 E
Kazakh S.S.R. □ 100 50 0N 70 0 E
Kazan 98 55 48N 49 3 E
Kazanlúk 95 42 38N 25 20 E
Kāzerūn 107 29 38N 51 40 E
Kazumba 122 6 25 S 22 5 E
Kazuno 116 40 10N 140 45 E
Kazym → 100 63 54N 65 50 E
Ké-Macina 120 13 58N 5 22W
Kéa 95 37 35N 24 22 E
Keaau 19 19 37N 155 2W
Keahi Pt. 19 21 19N 157 59W
Keahole Pt. 19 19 44N 156 4W
Kealaikahiki Channel 19 20 35N 156 50W
Kealaikahiki Pt. 19 20 32N 156 42W
Kealakekua 19 19 31N 155 55W
Kealia 19 19 24N 155 53W
Keams Canyon 12 35 49N 110 12W
Keansburg 37 40 27N 74 8W
Kearney, Mo. 32 39 22N 94 22W
Kearney, Nebr. 34 40 42N 99 5W
Kearney County ◇ 34 40 30N 99 0W
Kearneysville 54 39 23N 77 53W
Kearns 52 40 39N 112 0W
Kearny, Ariz. 12 33 3N 110 55W
Kearny, N.J. 37 40 46N 74 9W
Kearny County ◇ 24 38 0N 101 15W
Kearsarge, Mt. 36 43 22N 71 50W
Keatchie 25 32 11N 93 54W
Keating 44 44 53N 117 35W
Keats 24 39 14N 96 43W
Keau 19 19 38N 155 2W
Keawakapu 19 20 43N 156 27W
Keban 99 38 50N 38 50 E
Kebnekaise 96 67 53N 18 33 E
Kebri Dehar 105 6 45N 44 17 E
Kebumen 111 7 42 S 109 40 E
Kechika → 62 59 41N 127 12W
Kecskemét 89 46 57N 19 42 E
Kedah □ 112 5 50N 100 40 E
Keddie 14 40 1N 120 58W
Kedgwick 61 47 40N 67 20W
Kediri 111 7 51 S 112 1 E
Kédougou 120 12 35N 12 10W
Keedysville 27 39 29N 77 40W
Keefers 62 50 0N 121 40W
Keefeton 43 35 36N 95 21W
Keehi Lagoon 19 21 20N 157 54W
Keeley L. 63 54 54N 108 8W
Keeling Is. = Cocos Is. 124 12 10 S 96 55 E
Keene, N. Dak. 41 47 56N 102 56W
Keene, N.H. 36 42 56N 72 17W
Keene, Tex. 51 32 24N 97 20W
Keenesburg 16 40 7N 104 31W
Keensburg 21 38 21N 87 52W
Keeper Hill 85 52 46N 8 17W
Keer-Weer, C. 127 14 0 S 141 32 E
Keetmanshoop 123 26 35 S 18 8 E
Keewatin 30 47 24N 93 5W
Keewatin □ 63 63 20N 95 0W
Keewatin → 63 56 29N 100 46W
Kefallinía 95 38 20N 20 30 E
Kefamenanu 111 9 28 S 124 29 E
Kefar 'Eqron 104 31 52N 34 49 E
Kefar Ḥasīdim 104 32 47N 35 5 E
Kefar Naḥum 104 32 54N 35 34 E
Kefar Sava 104 32 11N 34 54 E
Kefar Szold 104 33 11N 35 39 E
Kefar Vitkin 104 32 22N 34 53 E
Kefar Yehezqel 104 32 34N 35 22 E
Kefar Yona 104 32 20N 34 54 E
Kefar Zekharya 104 31 43N 34 57 E
Kefar Zetim 104 32 48N 35 27 E
Keffi 120 8 55N 7 43 E
Keflavík 96 64 2N 22 35W
Keg River 62 57 54N 117 55W
Kegahka 61 50 9N 61 18W
Keighley 82 53 52N 1 54W
Keikiwaha Pt. 19 19 31N 155 58W
Keith 84 57 33N 2 58W
Keith Arm 58 64 20N 122 15W
Keith County ◇ 34 41 15N 101 40W
Keithsburg 21 41 6N 90 56W
Keizer 44 44 57N 123 1W
Kekaha 19 21 58N 159 43W
Kekri 108 26 0N 75 10 E
Kël 101 69 30N 124 10 E
Kelan 114 38 43N 111 31 E
Kelang 112 3 2N 101 26 E
Kelantan □ 112 5 10N 102 0 E
Kelantan → 112 6 13N 102 14 E
Kelibia 121 36 50N 11 3 E

Kell Kildare

Kell 21 38 30N 88 54W
Kellé 122 0 8S 14 38 E
Keller, Ga. 18 31 50N 81 15W
Keller, Wash. 53 48 5N 118 41W
Kellerberrin 126 31 36S 117 38 E
Kellerton 23 40 43N 94 3W
Kellerville 50 35 22N 100 30W
Kellett C. 4 72 0N 126 0W
Kelley 23 41 57N 93 40W
Kelleys I. 42 41 36N 82 42W
Kelliher 30 47 57N 94 27W
Kellogg, Idaho 20 47 32N 116 7W
Kellogg, Iowa 23 41 43N 92 54W
Kellogg, Minn. 30 44 18N 91 59W
Kelloselkä 96 66 56N 28 53 E
Kells = Ceanannus Mor 85 53 42N 6 53W
Kelly 48 36 58N 87 29W
Kellyville 43 35 57N 96 13W
Kélo 121 9 10N 15 45 E
Kelowna 62 49 50N 119 25W
Kelsey Bay 62 50 25N 126 0W
Kelseyville 14 38 59N 122 50W
Kelso, N.Z. 128 45 54S 169 15 E
Kelso, U.K. 84 55 36N 2 27W
Kelso, Ark. 13 33 48N 91 16W
Kelso, Wash. 53 46 9N 122 54W
Keluang 112 2 3N 103 18 E
Kelvington 63 52 10N 103 30W
Kem 98 65 0N 34 38 E
Kem → 98 64 57N 34 41 E
Kema 111 1 22N 125 8 E
Kemah, Turkey 106 39 32N 39 5 E
Kemah, U.S.A. 51 29 33N 95 1W
Kemano 62 53 35N 128 0W
Kemenets-Podolskiy 99 48 40N 26 40 E
Kemerovo 100 55 20N 86 5 E
Kemi 96 65 44N 24 34 E
Kemi älv = Kemijoki → 96 65 47N 24 32 E
Kemijärvi 96 66 43N 27 22 E
Kemijoki → 96 65 47N 24 32 E
Kemmerer 56 41 48N 110 32W
Kemmuna = Comino 94 36 0N 14 20 E
Kemp 51 32 26N 96 14W
Kemp, L. 51 33 46N 99 9W
Kemp Coast 5 69 0S 55 0 E
Kemper County ◇ 31 32 46N 88 39W
Kempsey 127 31 1S 152 50 E
Kempt, L. 60 47 25N 74 22W
Kempten 88 47 42N 10 18 E
Kempton, Ill. 21 40 56N 88 14W
Kempton, Ind. 22 40 17N 86 14W
Kemptown 27 39 20N 77 13W
Kemptville 60 45 0N 75 38W
Kenai 11 60 33N 151 16W
Kenai Mts. 11 60 0N 150 0W
Kenai Peninsula 11 60 0N 151 0W
Kenai Peninsula ◇ 11 59 30N 151 0W
Kenansville, Fla. 17 27 53N 80 59W
Kenansville, N.C. 40 34 58N 77 58W
Kenbridge 54 36 58N 78 8W
Kendal, Indonesia 110 6 56S 110 14 E
Kendal, U.K. 82 54 19N 2 44W
Kendall, Fla. 17 25 41N 80 19W
Kendall, Kans. 24 37 56N 101 33W
Kendall, Wis. 55 43 48N 90 21W
Kendall County ◇, Ill. 21 41 35N 88 25W
Kendall County ◇, Tex. 51 29 57N 98 48W
Kendall Park 37 40 25N 74 34W
Kendallville 22 41 27N 85 16W
Kendari 111 3 50S 122 30 E
Kendawangan 110 2 32S 110 17 E
Kende 120 11 30N 4 12 E
Kendleton 51 29 26N 96 0W
Kendrapara 109 20 35N 86 30 E
Kendrick, Fla. 17 29 15N 82 10W
Kendrick, Idaho 20 46 37N 116 39W
Kendrick, Okla. 43 35 47N 96 46W
Kenedy 51 28 49N 97 51W
Kenedy County ◇ 50 27 0N 97 40W
Kenefic 43 34 9N 96 22W
Kenefick 51 30 7N 94 52W
Kenema 120 7 50N 11 14W
Kenesaw 34 40 37N 98 39W
Keng Tawng 109 20 45N 98 18 E
Keng Tung 109 21 0N 99 30 E
Kenge 122 4 50S 17 4 E
Kenhardt 123 29 19S 21 12 E
Kenitra 120 34 15N 6 40W
Kenly 40 35 36N 78 7W
Kenmare, Ireland 85 51 52N 9 35W
Kenmare, U.S.A. 41 48 41N 102 5W
Kenmare → 85 51 40N 10 0W
Kenmore 39 42 58N 78 52W
Kenn Reef 127 21 12S 155 46 E
Kenna, N. Mex. 38 33 51N 103 46W
Kenna, W. Va. 54 38 41N 81 40W
Kennaday Peak 56 41 27N 106 31W
Kennard, Nebr. 34 41 28N 96 12W
Kennard, Tex. 51 31 22N 95 11W
Kennebec 47 43 54N 99 52W
Kennebec → 26 43 45N 69 46W
Kennebec County ◇ 26 44 20N 69 50W
Kennebunk 26 43 23N 70 33W
Kennebunkport 26 43 21N 70 28W
Kennedy, Ala. 10 33 35N 87 59W
Kennedy, Minn. 30 48 39N 96 54W
Kennedy Taungdeik 109 23 15N 93 45 E
Kennedyville 27 39 18N 75 58W
Kenner 25 29 59N 90 15W
Kennesaw 18 34 1N 84 37W
Kennet → 83 51 24N 0 58W
Kennett 32 36 14N 90 3W
Kennett Square 45 39 51N 75 43W
Kennewick 53 46 12N 119 7W
Kenney 21 40 6N 89 5W
Keno 44 42 8N 121 56W
Kénogami 61 48 25N 71 15W
Kenogami → 60 51 6N 84 28W
Kenora 63 49 47N 94 29W
Kenosha 55 42 35N 87 49W
Kenosha County ◇ 55 42 35N 87 50W
Kenova 54 38 24N 82 35W
Kensal 41 47 18N 98 44W
Kensett, Ark. 13 35 14N 91 40W
Kensett, Iowa 23 43 21N 93 13W
Kensington, Canada 61 46 28N 63 34W
Kensington, Conn. 28 41 38N 72 46W
Kensington, Kans. 24 39 46N 99 2W
Kensington, Md. 27 39 2N 77 5W
Kensington, Minn. 30 45 47N 95 42W
Kent, Conn. 28 41 44N 73 29W
Kent, Iowa 23 40 57N 94 28W
Kent, Minn. 30 46 26N 96 41W
Kent, Ohio 42 41 9N 81 22W
Kent, Oreg. 44 45 12N 120 42W
Kent, Tex. 50 31 4N 104 13W
Kent, Wash. 53 47 23N 122 14W
Kent □ 83 51 12N 0 40 E
Kent City 29 43 12N 85 45W
Kent County ◇, Del. 27 39 10N 75 30W
Kent County ◇, Md. 27 39 15N 76 0W
Kent County ◇, Mich. 29 43 0N 85 35W
Kent County ◇, R.I. 28 41 35N 71 40W
Kent County ◇, Tex. 50 33 10N 100 45W
Kent I. 27 38 52N 76 18W
Kent Pen. 58 68 30N 107 0W
Kentau 100 43 32N 68 36 E
Kentland 22 40 46N 87 27W
Kentmore Park 27 39 22N 75 58W
Kenton, Del. 27 39 14N 75 40W
Kenton, Mich. 29 46 28N 88 54W
Kenton, Ohio 42 40 39N 83 37W
Kenton, Okla. 43 36 54N 102 58W
Kenton, Tenn. 48 36 12N 89 1W
Kenton County ◇ 49 38 55N 84 32W
Kentucky □ 49 37 0N 84 0W
Kentucky → 49 38 41N 85 11W
Kentucky L. 48 37 1N 88 16W
Kentville 61 45 6N 64 29W
Kentwood 25 30 56N 90 31W
Kenya ■ 122 1 0N 38 0 E
Kenya, Mt. 122 0 10S 37 18 E
Kenyon 30 44 16N 92 59W
Keo 13 34 36N 92 1W
Keokea 19 20 43N 156 22W
Keokuk 23 40 24N 91 24W
Keokuk County ◇ 23 41 20N 92 10W
Keosauqua 23 40 44N 91 58W
Keota, Colo. 16 40 42N 104 5W
Keota, Iowa 23 41 22N 91 57W
Keota, Okla. 43 35 15N 94 55W
Keowee L. 46 34 30N 82 55W
Kepi 111 6 32S 139 19 E
Keppel B. 127 23 21S 150 55 E
Kepsut 106 39 40N 28 9 E
Kepuhi Pt. 19 21 29N 158 14W
Kerala □ 108 11 0N 76 15 E
Kerama-Rettō 117 26 5N 127 15 E
Kerang 127 35 40S 143 55 E
Kerby 44 42 12N 123 39W
Kerch 99 45 20N 36 20 E
Kerchoual 120 17 12N 0 20 E
Kerem Maharal 104 32 39N 34 59 E
Keren 121 15 45N 38 28 E
Kerens 51 32 8N 96 14W
Kerguelen 3 48 15S 69 10 E
Kericho 122 0 22S 35 15 E
Kerinci 110 1 40S 101 15 E
Kerkhoven 30 45 12N 95 19W
Kerki 100 37 50N 65 12 E
Kérkira 95 39 38N 19 50 E
Kerkrade 87 50 53N 6 4 E
Kermadec Is. 124 30 0S 178 15W
Kermadec Trench 124 30 30S 176 0W
Kermān, Iran 107 30 15N 57 1 E
Kerman, U.S.A. 15 36 43N 120 4W
Kermān □ 107 30 0N 57 0 E
Kermānshāh = Qahremānshahr 106 34 23N 47 0 E
Kermen 95 42 30N 26 16 E
Kermit, Tex. 50 31 52N 103 6W
Kermit, W. Va. 54 37 50N 82 24W
Kern → 15 35 16N 119 18W
Kern County ◇ 15 35 20N 118 30W
Kernersville 40 36 7N 80 5W
Kernville 15 35 45N 118 26W
Kerr County ◇ 51 27 53N 97 13W
Kerrick, Minn. 30 46 20N 92 35W
Kerrick, Tex. 50 36 30N 102 15W
Kerrobert 63 52 0N 109 11W
Kerrville 51 30 3N 99 8W
Kerry □ 85 52 7N 9 35W
Kerry Hd. 85 52 26N 9 56W
Kersey 16 40 23N 104 34W
Kershaw 46 34 33N 80 35W
Kershaw County ◇ 46 34 20N 80 40W
Kertosono 111 7 38S 112 9 E
Kerulen → 113 48 48N 117 0 E
Kerzaz 120 29 29N 1 37W
Kesagami → 60 51 40N 79 45W
Kesagami L. 60 50 23N 80 15W
Kesennuma 116 38 54N 141 35 E
Keshena 55 44 53N 88 39W
Keski-Suomen lääni □ 96 62 0N 25 30 E
Kestenga 98 66 0N 31 50 E
Keswick 82 54 35N 3 9W
Ket → 100 58 55N 81 32 E
Keta 120 5 49N 1 0 E
Ketapang 110 1 55S 110 0 E
Ketchikan 11 55 21N 131 39W
Ketchikan Gateway ◇ 11 55 30N 131 0W
Ketchum, Idaho 20 43 41N 114 22W
Ketchum, Okla. 43 36 32N 95 1W
Kettering, U.K. 83 52 24N 0 44W
Kettering, U.S.A. 42 39 41N 84 10W
Kettle →, Canada 63 56 40N 89 34W
Kettle →, U.S.A. 30 45 52N 92 46W
Kettle Cr. → 45 41 18N 77 51W
Kettle Falls 53 48 37N 118 3W
Kettle River 30 46 29N 92 53W
Kettle River Range 53 48 30N 118 40W
Kettleman City 15 36 1N 119 58W
Keuka L. 39 42 30N 77 9W
Kevin 33 48 45N 111 58W
Kewanee 21 41 14N 89 56W
Kewanna 22 41 1N 86 25W
Kewaskum 55 43 31N 88 14W
Kewaunee 55 44 27N 87 31W
Kewaunee County ◇ 55 44 30N 87 40W
Keweenaw B. 29 47 0N 88 15W
Keweenaw County ◇ 29 47 20N 88 5W
Keweenaw Peninsula 29 47 15N 88 15W
Keweenaw Pt. 29 47 25N 87 43W
Key 50 32 44N 101 48W
Key Biscayne 17 25 42N 80 10W
Key Colony Beach 17 24 45N 80 57W
Key Harbour 60 45 50N 80 45W
Key Largo 17 25 5N 80 27W
Key West 17 24 33N 81 48W
Keya Paha → 34 42 54N 99 0W
Keya Paha County ◇ 34 42 50N 99 40W
Keyapaha 47 43 7N 100 8W
Keyes 43 36 49N 102 15W
Keyesport 21 38 45N 89 17W
Keyhole Reservior 56 44 21N 104 51W
Keymar 27 39 38N 77 16W
Keyport 37 40 26N 74 12W
Keyser 54 39 26N 78 59W
Keystone, Iowa 23 42 0N 92 12W
Keystone, Nebr. 34 41 13N 101 35W
Keystone, S. Dak. 47 43 54N 103 25W
Keystone L. 43 36 15N 96 25W
Keystone Peak 12 31 53N 111 13W
Keysville, Ga. 18 33 14N 82 14W
Keysville, Va. 54 37 2N 78 29W
Keytesville 32 39 26N 92 56W
Kezar Falls 26 43 48N 70 53W
Kezhma 101 58 59N 101 9 E
Khabarovo 100 69 30N 60 30 E
Khabarovsk 101 48 30N 135 5 E
Khābūr → 106 35 0N 40 30 E
Khairpur 108 27 32N 68 49 E
Khakhea 123 24 48S 23 22 E
Khalkhāl 106 37 37N 48 32 E
Khalkís 95 38 27N 23 42 E
Khalmer-Sede = Tazovskiy 100 67 30N 78 44 E
Khalmer Yu 100 67 58N 65 1 E
Khalturin 98 58 40N 48 50 E
Khambhat 108 22 23N 72 33 E
Khamir 105 16 0N 44 0 E
Khān Yūnis 104 31 21N 34 18 E
Khānābād 107 36 45N 69 5 E
Khānaqīn 106 34 23N 45 25 E
Khandwa 108 21 49N 76 22 E
Khandyga 101 62 42N 135 35 E
Khanewal 108 30 20N 71 55 E
Khaniá 95 35 30N 24 4 E
Khanion Kólpos 95 35 33N 23 55 E
Khanka, Ozero 101 45 0N 132 24 E
Khanty-Mansiysk 100 61 0N 69 0 E
Khapcheranga 101 49 42N 112 24 E
Kharagpur 109 22 20N 87 25 E
Kharan Kalat 107 28 34N 65 21 E
Kharānaq 107 32 20N 54 45 E
Kharda 108 18 40N 75 34 E
Khârga, El Wâhât el 121 25 10N 30 35 E
Khargon 108 21 45N 75 35 E
Khārk, Jazireh 106 29 15N 50 28 E
Kharkov 99 49 58N 36 20 E
Kharmanli 95 41 55N 25 55 E
Kharovsk 98 59 56N 40 13 E
Kharsānīya 106 27 10N 49 10 E
Khartoum = El Khartûm 121 15 31N 32 35 E
Khasab 107 26 14N 56 15 E
Khasan 116 42 25N 130 40 E
Khāsh 108 28 15N 61 15 E
Khashm el Girba 121 14 59N 35 58 E
Khaskovo 95 41 56N 25 30 E
Khatanga 101 72 0N 102 20 E
Khatanga → 101 72 55N 106 0 E
Khatangskiy, Zaliv 4 66 0N 112 0 E
Khatyrka 101 62 3N 175 15 E
Khaybar, Harrat 106 25 45N 40 0 E
Khed Brahma 108 24 7N 73 5 E
Khemmarat 112 16 10N 105 15 E
Khenchela 120 35 28N 7 11 E
Khenifra 120 32 58N 5 46W
Kherson 99 46 35N 32 35 E
Kheta → 101 71 54N 102 6 E
Khilok 101 51 30N 110 45 E
Khíos 95 38 27N 26 9 E
Khíos, I. 95 38 20N 26 0 E
Khisar-Momina Banya 95 42 30N 24 44 E
Khiuma = Hiiumaa 98 58 50N 22 45 E
Khiva 100 41 30N 60 18 E
Khīyāv 106 38 30N 47 45 E
Khlebarovo 95 43 37N 26 15 E
Khlong → 112 15 30N 98 50 E
Khmelnitskiy 99 49 23N 27 0 E
Khmer Rep. = Cambodia ■ 112 12 15N 105 0 E
Khojak P. 107 30 55N 66 30 E
Kholm, Afghan. 107 36 45N 67 40 E
Kholm, U.S.S.R. 98 57 10N 31 15 E
Kholmsk 101 47 40N 142 5 E
Khomayn 106 33 40N 50 7 E
Khon Kaen 112 16 30N 102 47 E
Khong 112 14 5N 105 56 E
Khong → 112 15 0N 106 50 E
Khonu 101 66 30N 143 12 E
Khoper → 98 49 30N 42 20 E
Khorāsān □ 107 34 0N 58 0 E
Khorat = Nakhon Ratchasima 112 14 59N 102 12 E
Khorat, Cao Nguyen 112 15 30N 102 50 E
Khorog 100 37 30N 71 36 E
Khorramābād 106 33 30N 48 25 E
Khorrāmshahr 106 30 29N 48 15 E
Khouribga 120 32 58N 6 57W
Khowai 109 24 5N 91 40 E
Khu Khan 112 14 42N 104 12 E
Khugiani 108 31 28N 66 14 E
Khulna 109 22 45N 89 34 E
Khulna □ 109 22 25N 89 35 E
Khūr 107 32 55N 58 18 E
Khurayş 106 24 55N 48 5 E
Khūrīyā Mūrīyā, Jazā 'ir 105 17 30N 55 58 E
Khush 108 32 55N 62 10 E
Khushab 108 32 20N 72 20 E
Khuzdar 108 27 52N 66 30 E
Khūzestān □ 106 31 0N 49 0 E
Khvor 107 33 45N 55 0 E
Khvormūj 107 28 40N 51 30 E
Khvoy 106 38 35N 45 0 E
Khyber Pass 108 34 10N 71 8 E
Kiamba 111 6 2N 124 46 E
Kiamichi → 43 33 58N 95 14W
Kiamichi Mt. 43 34 38N 94 35W
Kiana 11 66 58N 160 26W
Kiangsi = Jiangxi □ 115 27 30N 116 0 E
Kiangsu = Jiangsu □ 115 33 0N 120 0 E
Kibangou 122 3 26S 12 22 E
Kibombo 122 3 57S 25 53 E
Kibondo 122 3 35S 30 45 E
Kibwesa 122 6 30S 29 58 E
Kibwezi 122 2 27S 37 57 E
Kichiga 101 59 50N 163 5 E
Kickapoo → 55 43 5N 90 53W
Kickapoo, L. 51 33 40N 98 47W
Kickapoo Indian Reservation 24 39 40N 95 50W
Kicking Horse Pass 62 51 28N 116 16W
Kidal 120 18 26N 1 22 E
Kidder 32 39 47N 94 6W
Kidder County ◇ 41 47 0N 99 55W
Kidderminster 83 52 24N 2 13W
Kidnappers, C. 128 39 38S 177 5 E
Kief 41 47 51N 100 31W
Kiel, Germany 88 54 16N 10 8 E
Kiel, U.S.A. 55 43 55N 88 2W
Kiel Canal = Nord-Ostsee Kanal 88 54 15N 9 40 E
Kielce 89 50 52N 20 42 E
Kieler Bucht 88 54 30N 10 30 E
Kiester 30 43 32N 93 43W
Kiev = Kiyev 99 50 30N 30 28 E
Kifār 'Aşyūn 104 31 39N 35 7 E
Kiffa 120 16 37N 11 24W
Kifrī 106 34 45N 45 0 E
Kigali 122 1 59S 30 4 E
Kigoma-Ujiji 122 4 55S 29 36 E
Kihei 19 20 47N 156 28W
Kiholo B. 19 19 50N 155 55W
Kii-Sanchi 117 34 20N 136 0 E
Kii-Suidō 117 33 40N 135 0 E
Kikaiga-Shima 117 28 19N 129 59 E
Kikinda 95 45 50N 20 30 E
Kikládhes 95 37 20N 24 30 E
Kikládhes □ 95 37 0N 25 0 E
Kikwit 122 5 5S 18 45 E
Kila 33 48 7N 114 27W
Kilauea 19 22 13N 159 25W
Kilauea Crater 19 19 25N 155 17W
Kilbourne, Ill. 21 40 9N 90 1W
Kilbourne, La. 25 33 0N 91 20W
Kildare, Ireland 85 53 10N 6 50W

Kildare Knox, C.

Kildare, Ga. 18 32 32N 81 27W
Kildare, Okla. 43 36 48N 97 3W
Kildare □ 85 53 10N 6 50W
Kildeer 41 47 22N 102 45W
Kilgore, Idaho 20 44 24N 111 54W
Kilgore, Nebr. 34 42 56N 100 57W
Kilgore, Tex. 51 32 23N 94 53W
Kilimanjaro 122 3 7S 37 20E
Kilindini 122 4 4S 39 40E
Kilis 106 36 50N 37 10E
Kilju 114 40 57N 129 25E
Kilkee 85 52 41N 9 40W
Kilkenny, Ireland 85 52 40N 7 17W
Kilkenny, U.S.A. 30 44 19N 93 34W
Kilkenny □ 85 52 35N 7 15W
Kilkieran B. 85 53 18N 9 45W
Kill Devil Hills 40 36 1N 75 39W
Killala 85 54 13N 9 12W
Killala B. 85 54 20N 9 12W
Killaloe 85 52 48N 8 28W
Killam 62 52 47N 111 51W
Killarney, Canada 60 45 55N 81 30W
Killarney, Ireland 85 52 2N 9 30W
Killarney, Lakes of 85 52 0N 9 30W
Killary Harbour 85 53 38N 9 52W
Killbuck 42 40 30N 81 59W
Killbuck → 42 40 30N 81 59W
Killdeer 63 49 6N 106 22W
Killeen 51 31 7N 97 44W
Killen 10 34 52N 87 32W
Killiecrankie, Pass of 84 56 44N 3 46W
Killin 84 56 28N 4 20W
Killingly 28 41 0N 71 0W
Killingworth 28 41 21N 72 30W
Killini 95 37 54N 22 25E
Killybegs 85 54 38N 8 26W
Kilmarnock, U.K. 84 55 36N 4 30W
Kilmarnock, U.S.A. 54 37 43N 76 23W
Kilmichael 31 33 27N 89 34W
Kilosa 122 6 48S 37 0E
Kilrush 85 52 39N 9 30W
Kilwa Kisiwani 122 8 58S 39 32E
Kilwa Kivinje 122 8 45S 39 25E
Kim 16 37 15N 103 21W
Kimaam 111 7 58S 138 53E
Kimba 127 33 8S 136 23E
Kimball, Nebr. 34 41 14N 103 40W
Kimball, S. Dak. 47 43 45N 98 57W
Kimball, W. Va. 54 37 26N 81 30W
Kimball County ◇ 34 41 15N 103 40W
Kimballton 23 41 38N 95 4W
Kimberley, Australia 126 16 20S 127 0E
Kimberley, Canada 62 49 40N 115 59W
Kimberley, S. Africa 123 28 43S 24 46E
Kimberly, Idaho 20 42 32N 114 22W
Kimberly, Oreg. 44 44 46N 119 39W
Kimble County ◇ 51 30 29N 99 46W
Kimbolton 42 40 9N 81 34W
Kimbrough 10 32 2N 87 34W
Kimchaek 114 40 40N 129 10E
Kimchŏn 114 36 11N 128 4E
Kimry 98 56 55N 37 15E
Kimsquit 62 52 45N 126 57W
Kinabalu 110 6 0N 116 0E
Kinard 17 30 16N 85 15W
Kinards 46 34 23N 81 46W
Kinaskan L. 62 57 38N 130 8W
Kincaid, Canada 63 49 40N 107 0W
Kincaid, Ill. 21 39 35N 89 25W
Kincaid, Kans. 24 38 5N 95 9W
Kincaid, L. 21 39 39N 89 29W
Kincardine 60 44 10N 81 40W
Kinchafoonee Cr. → 18 31 38N 84 10W
Kinde 29 43 56N 83 0W
Kinder 25 30 29N 92 51W
Kindersley 63 51 30N 109 10W
Kindia 120 10 0N 12 52W
Kindred 41 46 39N 97 1W
Kindu 122 2 55S 25 50E
Kineshma 98 57 30N 42 5E
King 40 36 17N 80 22W
King and Queen County ◇ 54 37 40N 76 53W
King and Queen Court House 54 37 40N 76 53W
King City, Calif. 15 36 13N 121 8W
King City, Mo. 32 40 3N 94 31W
King County ◇, Tex. 50 33 37N 100 19W
King County ◇, Wash. 53 47 25N 121 40W
King Cove 11 55 3N 162 19W
King Frederick VI Land = Kong Frederik VI.s Kyst 4 63 0N 43 0W
King George 54 38 16N 77 11W
King George B. 78 51 30S 60 30W
King George County ◇ 54 38 16N 77 11W
King George I. 5 60 0S 60 0W
King George Is. 59 57 20N 80 30W
King George Sd. 126 35 5S 118 0E
King I. = Kadan Kyun 110 12 30N 98 20E
King I., Australia 127 39 50S 144 0E
King I., Canada 62 52 10N 127 40W
King Leopold Ranges 126 17 30S 125 45E
King of Prussia 45 40 5N 75 23W
King Salmon 11 58 42N 156 40W
King Sd. 126 16 50S 123 20E
King William 54 37 41N 77 1W
King William County ◇ 54 37 41N 77 1W
King William I. 58 69 10N 97 25W
King William's Town 123 32 51S 27 22E
Kingaroy 127 26 32S 151 51E
Kingfield 26 44 58N 70 9W
Kingfisher 43 35 52N 97 56W
Kingfisher County ◇ 43 36 0N 98 0W
Kingman, Ariz. 12 35 12N 114 4W
Kingman, Kans. 24 37 39N 98 7W
Kingman County ◇ 24 37 30N 98 0W
Kings →, Ark. 13 36 30N 93 35W
Kings →, Calif. 15 36 3N 119 50W
Kings →, Utah 52 41 31N 118 8W
Kings Canyon National Park 15 36 50N 118 40W
Kings County ◇, Calif. 15 36 0N 119 50W
Kings County ◇, N.Y. 39 40 37N 73 55W
King's Lynn 82 52 45N 0 25E
Kings Mountain 40 35 15N 81 20W
Kings Peak 52 40 46N 110 23W
Kings Valley 44 44 42N 123 26W
Kingsbridge 83 50 17N 3 46W
Kingsburg 15 36 31N 119 33W
Kingsbury County ◇ 47 44 23N 97 33W
Kingscourt 85 53 55N 6 48W
Kingsdown 24 37 32N 99 46W
Kingsford 29 45 48N 88 4W
Kingsland, Ark. 13 33 52N 92 18W
Kingsland, Ga. 18 30 48N 81 41W
Kingsland, Tex. 51 30 40N 98 26W
Kingsley, Iowa 23 42 35N 95 58W
Kingsley, Mich. 29 44 35N 85 32W
Kingsmill 50 35 29N 101 4W
Kingsport 49 36 33N 82 33W
Kingston, Canada 60 44 14N 76 30W
Kingston, Jamaica 66 18 0N 76 50W
Kingston, N.Z. 128 45 20S 168 43E
Kingston, Ark. 13 36 3N 93 31W
Kingston, Ga. 18 34 14N 84 57W
Kingston, Ky. 49 37 39N 84 15W
Kingston, Mass. 28 42 0N 70 43W
Kingston, Md. 27 38 5N 75 46W
Kingston, Mich. 29 43 25N 83 11W
Kingston, Minn. 30 45 12N 94 19W
Kingston, Mo. 32 39 39N 94 2W
Kingston, N.H. 36 42 56N 71 3W
Kingston, N.Y. 39 41 56N 73 59W
Kingston, Ohio 42 39 28N 82 55W
Kingston, Okla. 43 33 59N 96 45W
Kingston, Pa. 45 41 16N 75 54W
Kingston, Tenn. 49 35 52N 84 31W
Kingston, Utah 52 38 13N 112 11W
Kingston, Wis. 55 43 42N 89 8W
Kingston South East 127 36 51S 139 55E
Kingston Springs 48 36 6N 87 7W
Kingston-upon-Thames 83 51 23N 0 20W
Kingstown 67 13 10N 61 10W
Kingstree 46 33 40N 79 50W
Kingsville, Canada 60 42 2N 82 45W
Kingsville, Md. 27 39 27N 76 25W
Kingsville, Mo. 32 38 45N 94 4W
Kingsville, Tex. 50 27 31N 97 52W
Kingussie 84 57 5N 4 2W
Kingwood 54 39 28N 79 41W
Kinistino 63 52 57N 105 2W
Kinkaid L. 21 37 40N 89 25W
Kinkala 122 4 18S 14 49E
Kinki □ 117 33 30N 136 0E
Kinleith 128 38 20S 175 56E
Kinmundy 21 38 46N 88 51W
Kinnaird 62 49 17N 117 39W
Kinnairds Hd. 84 57 40N 2 0W
Kinnelon 37 41 0N 74 22W
Kinneret 104 32 44N 35 34E
Kinneret, Yam 104 32 45N 35 35E
Kinney 30 47 31N 92 44W
Kinney County ◇ 50 29 19N 100 25W
Kino 64 28 45N 111 59W
Kinoje → 60 52 8N 81 25W
Kinomoto 117 35 30N 136 13E
Kinross 84 56 13N 3 25W
Kinsale, Ireland 85 51 42N 8 31W
Kinsale, U.S.A. 54 38 2N 76 35W
Kinsale, Old Hd. of 85 51 37N 8 32W
Kinshasa 122 4 20S 15 15E
Kinsley 24 37 55N 99 25W
Kinston, Ala. 10 31 13N 86 10W
Kinston, N.C. 40 35 16N 77 35W
Kinta 43 35 8N 95 14W
Kintampo 120 8 5N 1 41W
Kintap 110 3 51S 115 13E
Kintyre 84 55 30N 5 35W
Kintyre, Mull of 84 55 17N 5 55W
Kinushseo → 60 55 15N 83 45W
Kinuso 62 55 20N 115 25W
Kinwood 51 29 55N 95 19W
Kinzua 44 44 59N 120 3W
Kiosk 60 46 6N 78 53W
Kiowa, Colo. 16 39 21N 104 28W
Kiowa, Kans. 24 37 1N 98 29W
Kiowa, Okla. 43 34 43N 95 54W
Kiowa → 43 36 46N 99 55W
Kiowa County ◇, Colo. 16 38 25N 102 50W
Kiowa County ◇, Kans. 24 37 30N 99 15W
Kiowa County ◇, Okla. 43 35 0N 99 0W
Kiowa Cr. → 16 40 20N 104 5W
Kipahigan L. 63 55 20N 101 55W
Kipapa → 19 21 24N 158 1W
Kiparissía 95 37 15N 21 40E
Kiparissiakós Kólpos 95 37 25N 21 25E
Kipembawe 122 7 38S 33 27E
Kipili 122 7 28S 30 32E
Kipling 63 50 6N 102 38W
Kipnuk 11 59 56N 164 3W
Kipp 24 38 47N 97 27W
Kippure 85 53 11N 6 23W
Kipushi 123 11 48S 27 12E
Kirby, Ark. 13 34 15N 93 39W
Kirby, Tex. 51 29 28N 98 23W
Kirby, Wyo. 56 43 48N 108 11W
Kirbyville 51 30 40N 93 54W
Kirensk 101 57 50N 107 55E
Kirgiz S.S.R. □ 100 42 0N 75 0E
Kirgiziya Steppe 99 50 0N 55 0E
Kiri 122 1 29S 19 0E
Kiribati ■ 124 1 0N 176 0E
Kırıkkale 106 39 51N 33 32E
Kirillov 98 59 51N 38 14E
Kirin = Jilin 114 43 44N 126 30E
Kirin □ = Jilin □ 114 44 0N 124 0E
Kiritimati 125 1 58N 157 27W
Kirk, Colo. 16 39 37N 102 36W
Kirk, Oreg. 44 42 45N 121 50W
Kirkcaldy 84 56 7N 3 10W
Kirkcudbright 84 54 50N 4 3W
Kirkee 108 18 34N 73 56E
Kirkenes 96 69 40N 30 5E
Kirkintilloch 84 55 57N 4 10W
Kirkjubœjarklaustur 96 63 47N 18 4W
Kirkland, Ariz. 12 34 25N 112 43W
Kirkland, Ill. 21 42 6N 88 51W
Kirkland, Tex. 51 34 23N 100 4W
Kirkland, Wash. 53 47 41N 122 13W
Kirkland Junction 12 34 22N 112 40W
Kirkland Lake 60 48 9N 80 2W
Kırklareli 95 41 44N 27 15E
Kirklin 22 40 12N 86 22W
Kirkman 23 41 44N 95 16W
Kirkmansville 48 37 1N 87 15W
Kirksey 48 36 42N 88 24W
Kirksville 32 40 12N 92 35W
Kirkūk 106 35 30N 44 21E
Kirkwall 84 58 59N 2 59W
Kirkwood, Del. 27 39 34N 75 42W
Kirkwood, Ill. 21 40 52N 90 45W
Kirkwood, Mo. 32 38 35N 90 24W
Kiron 23 42 12N 95 20W
Kirov 100 58 35N 49 40E
Kirovabad 99 40 45N 46 20E
Kirovakan 99 40 48N 44 30E
Kirovograd 99 48 35N 32 20E
Kirovsk, R.S.F.S.R., U.S.S.R. 98 67 48N 33 50E
Kirovsk, Turkmen S.S.R., U.S.S.R. 100 37 42N 60 23E
Kirovskiy, R.S.F.S.R., U.S.S.R. 101 54 27N 155 42E
Kirovskiy, R.S.F.S.R., U.S.S.R. 116 45 7N 133 30E
Kirriemuir, Canada 63 51 56N 110 20W
Kirriemuir, U.K. 84 56 41N 3 0W
Kirsanov 98 52 35N 42 40E
Kırşehir 106 39 14N 34 5E
Kirteh 107 32 15N 63 0E
Kirthar Range 108 27 0N 67 0E
Kirtland 38 36 44N 108 21W
Kiruna 96 67 52N 20 15E
Kirundu 122 0 50S 25 35E
Kirwin 24 39 40N 99 7W
Kirwin Reservoir 24 39 40N 99 8W
Kiryū 117 36 24N 139 20E
Kisalaya 66 14 40N 84 3W
Kisangani 122 0 35N 25 15E
Kisar 111 8 5S 127 10E
Kisaran 110 3 0N 99 37E
Kisarazu 117 35 23N 139 55E
Kisatchie 25 31 25N 93 10W
Kisatchie National Forest 25 31 45N 92 30W
Kiselevsk 100 54 5N 86 39E
Kishanganj 109 26 3N 88 14E
Kishangarh 108 27 50N 70 30E
Kishinev 99 47 0N 28 50E
Kishiwada 117 34 28N 135 22E
Kishon 104 32 49N 35 2E
Kishtwar 108 33 20N 75 48E
Kisii 122 0 40S 34 45E
Kisiju 122 7 23S 39 19E
Kiska I. 11 51 59N 177 30E
Kiskatinaw → 62 56 8N 120 10W
Kiskittogisu L. 63 54 13N 98 20W
Kiskőrös 89 46 37N 19 20E
Kiskunfelégyháza 89 46 42N 19 53E
Kiskunhalas 89 46 28N 19 37E
Kislovodsk 99 43 50N 42 45E
Kismet 24 37 12N 100 42W
Kiso-Gawa → 117 35 20N 136 45E
Kiso-Sammyaku 117 35 45N 137 45E
Kisofukushima 117 35 52N 137 43E
Kissidougou 120 9 5N 10 0W
Kissimmee 17 28 18N 81 24W
Kissimmee → 17 27 9N 80 52W
Kissimmee, L. 17 27 55N 81 17W
Kississing L. 63 55 10N 101 20W
Kisumu 122 0 3S 34 45E
Kit Carson 16 38 46N 102 48W
Kit Carson County ◇ 16 39 15N 102 30W
Kita 120 13 5N 9 25W
Kitab 100 39 7N 66 52E
Kitaibaraki 117 36 50N 140 45E
Kitakami 116 39 20N 141 10E
Kitakami-Gawa → 116 38 25N 141 19E
Kitakami-Sammyaku 116 39 30N 141 30E
Kitakata 116 37 39N 139 52E
Kitakyūshū 117 33 50N 130 50E
Kitale 122 1 0N 35 0E
Kitami 116 43 48N 143 54E
Kitami-Sammyaku 116 44 22N 142 43E
Kitchener 60 43 27N 80 29W
Kitega = Gitega 122 3 26S 29 56E
Kitgum 122 3 17N 32 52E
Kíthira 95 36 9N 23 0E
Kíthnos 95 37 26N 24 27E
Kitikmeot □ 58 70 0N 110 0W
Kitimat 62 54 3N 128 38W
Kitinen → 96 67 34N 26 40E
Kitsap County ◇ 53 47 30N 122 45W
Kitsuki 117 33 25N 131 37E
Kittanning 45 40 49N 79 31W
Kittery, Maine 26 43 5N 70 45W
Kittery, N.H. 36 43 5N 70 45W
Kittitas 53 46 59N 120 25W
Kittitas County ◇ 53 47 10N 120 30W
Kitts Hummock 27 39 8N 75 25W
Kittson County ◇ 30 48 50N 96 50W
Kitui 122 1 17S 38 0E
Kitwe 123 12 54S 28 13E
Kitzmiller 27 39 23N 79 10W
Kivalina 11 67 44N 164 33W
Kivalo 96 66 18N 26 0E
Kivu, L. 122 1 48S 29 0E
Kiyev 99 50 30N 30 28E
Kiyevskoye Vdkhr. 99 51 0N 30 0E
Kizel 98 59 3N 57 40E
Kızıl Irmak → 99 39 15N 36 0E
Kizlyar 99 43 51N 46 40E
Kizyl-Arvat 100 38 58N 56 15E
Kladno 88 50 10N 14 7E
Klagenfurt 88 46 38N 14 20E
Klaipeda 98 55 43N 21 10E
Klamath 14 41 32N 124 2W
Klamath → 14 41 33N 124 5W
Klamath County ◇ 44 42 40N 121 40W
Klamath Falls 44 42 13N 121 46W
Klamath Marsh 44 43 0N 121 40W
Klamath Mts. 14 41 50N 123 20W
Klamath National Forest 14 41 30N 123 20W
Klamath River 14 41 52N 122 50W
Klappan → 62 58 0N 129 43W
Klarälven → 97 59 23N 13 32E
Klaten 111 7 43S 110 36E
Klatovy 88 49 23N 13 18E
Klawer 123 31 44S 18 36E
Klawock 11 55 33N 133 6W
Kleberg County ◇ 50 27 31N 97 52W
Kleena Kleene 62 52 0N 124 59W
Klein 33 46 24N 108 33W
Klemme 23 43 1N 93 36W
Klemtu 62 52 35N 128 55W
Klerksdorp 123 26 51S 26 38E
Klickitat 53 45 49N 121 9W
Klickitat County ◇ 53 45 55N 120 30W
Klinaklini → 62 51 21N 125 40W
Kline 46 33 8N 81 21W
Klipplaat 123 33 0S 24 22E
Klisura 95 42 40N 24 28E
Kłodzko 88 50 28N 16 38E
Klondike 58 64 0N 139 26W
Klouto 120 6 57N 0 44E
Kluane L. 58 61 15N 138 40W
Klukwan 11 59 24N 135 54W
Klyuchevskaya, Guba 101 55 50N 160 30E
Knapp 55 44 57N 92 5W
Knaresborough 82 54 1N 1 29W
Knee L., Man., Canada 63 55 3N 94 45W
Knee L., Sask., Canada 63 55 51N 107 0W
Kneeland 14 40 45N 123 59W
Knezha 95 43 30N 24 5E
Knierim 23 42 27N 94 27W
Knife → 41 47 17N 101 20W
Knife River 30 46 57N 91 47W
Knight I. 11 60 21N 147 45W
Knight Inlet 62 50 45N 125 40W
Knighton 83 52 21N 3 2W
Knights Landing 14 38 48N 121 43W
Knightstown 22 39 48N 85 32W
Knob, C. 126 34 32S 119 16E
Knob Lick, Ky. 49 37 5N 85 42W
Knob Lick, Mo. 32 37 41N 90 22W
Knob Noster 32 38 46N 93 33W
Knobel 13 36 19N 90 36W
Knockmealdown Mts. 85 52 16N 8 0W
Knokke 87 51 20N 3 17E
Knossos 95 35 16N 25 10E
Knott County ◇ 49 37 20N 83 0W
Knotts Island 40 36 31N 75 56W
Knowles 43 36 53N 100 12W
Knox, Ind. 22 41 18N 86 37W
Knox, N. Dak. 41 48 20N 99 41W
Knox, Pa. 45 41 14N 79 32W
Knox, C. 62 54 11N 133 5W

Knox City

Kūhpāyeh

Knox City, Mo. 32 40 9N 92 1W
Knox City, Tex. 51 33 25N 99 49W
Knox Coast 5 66 30 S 108 0 E
Knox County ◇, Ill. 21 40 55N 90 10W
Knox County ◇, Ind. 22 38 40N 87 25W
Knox County ◇, Ky. 49 36 55N 83 50W
Knox County ◇, Maine 26 44 5N 69 5W
Knox County ◇, Mo. 32 40 10N 92 10W
Knox County ◇, Nebr. 34 42 40N 97 50W
Knox County ◇, Ohio 42 40 23N 82 29W
Knox County ◇, Tenn. 49 36 0N 83 0W
Knox County ◇, Tex. 51 33 35N 99 48W
Knoxville, Ga. 18 32 47N 83 59W
Knoxville, Ill. 21 40 55N 90 17W
Knoxville, Iowa 23 41 19N 93 6W
Knoxville, Pa. 45 41 57N 77 27W
Knoxville, Tenn. 49 35 58N 83 55W
Ko Chang 112 12 0N 102 20 E
Ko Kut 112 11 40N 102 32 E
Ko Phra Thong 112 9 6N 98 15 E
Ko Tao 112 10 6N 99 48 E
Koartac 59 60 55N 69 40W
Koba, Aru, Indonesia 111 6 37 S 134 37 E
Koba, Bangka, Indonesia 110 2 26 S 106 14 E
Kobarid 94 46 15N 13 30 E
Kobayashi 117 31 56N 130 59 E
Kōbe 117 34 45N 135 10 E
København 97 55 41N 12 34 E
Kōbi-Sho 117 25 56N 123 41 E
Koblenz 88 50 21N 7 36 E
Kobroor, Kepulauan 111 6 10 S 134 30 E
Kobuk 11 66 55N 156 52W
Kobuk ◇ 11 66 0N 160 0W
Kobuk → 11 66 54N 160 38W
Kočani 95 41 55N 22 25 E
Kočevje 94 45 39N 14 50 E
Koch Bihar 109 26 22N 89 29 E
Kocheya 101 52 32N 120 42 E
Kōchi 117 33 30N 133 35 E
Kōchi □ 117 33 40N 133 30 E
Kochiu = Gejiu 113 23 20N 103 10 E
Kodiak 11 57 47N 152 24W
Kodiak I. 11 57 20N 154 0W
Kodiak Island ◇ 11 57 30N 154 0W
Kodiang 112 6 21N 100 18 E
Koehn Dry L. 15 35 20N 117 53W
Koes 123 26 0 S 19 15 E
Kofa Mts. 12 33 15N 113 40W
Kofiau 111 1 11 S 129 50 E
Koforidua 120 6 3N 0 17W
Kōfu 117 35 40N 138 30 E
Koga 117 36 11N 139 43 E
Kogaluk → 61 56 12N 61 44W
Koh-i-Bābā 107 34 30N 67 0 E
Kohala Mts. 19 20 5N 155 45W
Kohat 108 33 40N 71 29 E
Kohima 109 25 35N 94 10 E
Kohkīlūyeh va Būyer Aḥmadi □ 107 31 30N 50 30 E
Kohler Ra. 5 77 0 S 110 0W
Kokand 100 40 30N 70 57 E
Kokanee Glacier Prov. Park 62 49 47N 117 10W
Kokas 111 2 42 S 132 26 E
Kokchetav 100 53 20N 69 25 E
Kokemäenjoki 97 61 32N 21 44 E
Kokerite 71 7 12N 59 35W
Kokkola 96 63 50N 23 8 E
Koko Head 19 21 16N 157 43W
Koko Kyunzu 112 14 10N 93 25 E
Kokomo, Ind. 22 40 29N 86 8W
Kokomo, Miss. 31 31 12N 90 0W
Kokonau 111 4 43 S 136 26 E
Koksoak → 59 58 30N 68 10W
Kokstad 123 30 32 S 29 29 E
Kokubu 117 31 44N 130 46 E
Kokuora 101 71 35N 144 50 E
Kola, Indonesia 111 5 35 S 134 30 E
Kola, U.S.S.R. 98 68 45N 33 8 E
Kola Pen. = Kolskiy Poluostrov 98 67 30N 38 0 E
Kolaka 111 4 3 S 121 46 E
Kolar 108 13 12N 78 15 E
Kolar Gold Fields 108 12 58N 78 16 E
Kolari 96 67 20N 23 48 E
Kolarovgrad 95 43 18N 26 55 E
Kolayat 108 27 50N 72 50 E
Kolda 120 12 55N 14 57W
Kolding 97 55 30N 9 29 E
Kole 122 3 16 S 22 42 E
Kolepom = Yos Sudarso, Pulau 111 8 0 S 138 30 E
Kolguyev, Ostrov 98 69 20N 48 30 E
Kolhapur 108 16 43N 74 15 E
Koliganek 11 59 48N 157 25W
Kolín 88 50 2N 15 9 E
Köln 88 50 56N 6 58 E
Koło 89 52 14N 18 40 E
Koloa 19 21 55N 159 28W
Kołobrzeg 88 54 10N 15 35 E
Kolokani 120 13 35N 7 45W
Kolomna 98 55 8N 38 45 E
Kolomyya 99 48 31N 25 2 E
Kolonodale 111 2 3 S 121 25 E
Kolosib 109 24 15N 92 45 E
Kolpashevo 100 58 20N 83 5 E
Kolskiy Poluostrov 98 67 30N 38 0 E
Kolskiy Zaliv 98 69 23N 34 0 E
Kolwezi 122 10 40 S 25 25 E
Kolyma → 101 69 30N 161 0 E
Kolymskoye, Okhotsko 101 63 0N 157 0 E
Komárno 89 47 49N 18 5 E
Komatsu 117 36 25N 136 30 E
Komatsujima 117 34 0N 134 35 E
Komi A.S.S.R. □ 98 64 0N 55 0 E
Kommunizma, Pik 100 39 0N 72 2 E
Komodo 111 8 37 S 119 20 E
Komono 122 3 10 S 13 20 E
Komoran, Pulau 111 8 18 S 138 45 E
Komoro 117 36 19N 138 26 E
Komotini 95 41 9N 25 26 E
Kompong Cham 112 12 0N 105 30 E
Kompong Chhnang 112 12 20N 104 35 E
Kompong Som 110 10 38N 103 30 E
Kompong Speu 112 11 26N 104 32 E
Kompong Thom 112 12 35N 104 51 E
Komsomolets, Ostrov 101 80 30N 95 0 E
Komsomolsk 101 50 30N 137 0 E
Konarhá □ 107 35 30N 71 3 E
Konawa 43 34 58N 96 45W
Konch 108 26 0N 79 10 E
Kondakovo 101 69 36N 152 0 E
Kondoa 122 4 55 S 35 50 E
Kondopaga 98 62 12N 34 17 E
Kondratyevo 101 57 22N 98 15 E
Konduga 121 11 35N 13 26 E
Konevo 98 62 8N 39 20 E
Kong 120 8 54N 4 36W
Kong, Koh 112 11 20N 103 0 E
Kong Christian IX.s Land 4 68 0N 36 0W
Kong Christian X.s Land 4 74 0N 29 0W
Kong Franz Joseph Fd. 4 73 20N 24 30W
Kong Frederik IX.s Land 4 67 0N 52 0W
Kong Frederik VI.s Kyst 4 63 0N 43 0W
Kong Frederik VIII.s Land 4 78 30N 26 0W
Kong Oscar Fjord 4 72 20N 24 0W
Kongju 114 36 30N 127 0 E
Konglu 109 27 13N 97 57 E
Kongolo 122 5 22 S 27 0 E
Kongor 121 7 1N 31 27 E
Kongsberg 97 59 39N 9 39 E
Kongsvinger 97 60 12N 12 2 E
Königsberg = Kaliningrad 98 54 42N 20 32 E
Konin 89 52 12N 18 15 E
Konjic 95 43 42N 17 58 E
Konosha 98 61 0N 40 5 E
Kōnosu 117 36 3N 139 31 E
Konotop 99 51 12N 33 7 E
Konqi He → 113 40 45N 90 10 E
Końskie 89 51 15N 20 23 E
Konstanz 88 47 39N 9 10 E
Kontagora 120 10 23N 5 27 E
Kontum 112 14 24N 108 0 E
Konya 106 37 52N 32 35 E
Konya Ovasi 106 38 30N 33 0 E
Konza 122 1 45 S 37 7 E
Koochiching County ◇ 30 48 15N 93 50W
Koolan I. 126 16 0 S 123 45 E
Koolau Range 19 21 35N 158 0W
Koosharem 52 38 31N 111 53W
Kooskia 20 46 9N 115 59W
Koostatak 63 51 26N 97 26W
Kootenai → 20 49 0N 116 30W
Kootenai County ◇ 20 47 45N 116 30W
Kootenai National Forest 33 48 30N 115 40W
Kootenay L. 62 49 45N 116 50W
Kootenay Nat. Park 62 51 0N 116 0W
Kopaonik Planina 95 43 10N 21 50 E
Kópavogur 96 64 6N 21 55W
Koper 94 45 31N 13 44 E
Kopervik 97 59 17N 5 17 E
Kopeysk 100 55 7N 61 37 E
Köping 97 59 31N 16 3 E
Kopparberg 97 59 52N 15 0 E
Kopparbergs län □ 97 61 20N 14 15 E
Koppeh Dāgh 107 38 0N 58 0 E
Kopperston 54 37 45N 81 35W
Koprivlen 95 41 36N 23 53 E
Koprivshtitsa 95 42 40N 24 19 E
Korab 95 41 44N 20 40 E
Korça 95 40 37N 20 50 E
Korčula 94 42 57N 17 8 E
Kordestan 106 35 30N 42 0 E
Kordestān □ 106 36 0N 47 0 E
Korea Bay 114 39 0N 124 0 E
Korea Strait 102 34 0N 129 30 E
Korhogo 120 9 29N 5 28W
Korim 111 0 58 S 136 10 E
Korinthiakós Kólpos 95 38 16N 22 30 E
Kórinthos 95 37 56N 22 55 E
Kōriyama 116 37 24N 140 23 E
Koro, Fiji 128 17 19 S 179 23 E
Koro, Ivory C. 120 8 32N 7 30W
Koro, Mali 120 14 1N 2 58W
Koro Sea 128 17 30 S 179 45W
Korogwe 122 5 5 S 38 25 E
Korona 17 29 25N 81 12W
Koror 112 7 20N 134 28 E
Körös → 89 46 43N 20 12 E
Korsakov 101 46 36N 142 42 E
Korshunovo 101 58 37N 110 10 E
Korsör 97 55 20N 11 9 E
Kortes Dam 56 42 12N 106 52W
Korti 121 18 6N 31 33 E
Kortrijk 87 50 50N 3 17 E
Koryakskiy Khrebet 101 61 0N 171 0 E
Kos 95 36 50N 27 15 E
Koschagyl 99 46 40N 54 0 E
Kościan 88 52 5N 16 40 E
Kosciusko 31 33 4N 89 35W
Kosciusko, Mt. 127 36 27 S 148 16 E
Kosciusko County ◇ 22 41 15N 85 50W
Kosha 121 20 50N 30 30 E
K'oshih = Kashi 113 39 30N 76 2 E
Koshiki-Rettō 117 31 45N 129 49 E
Koshkonong 32 36 36N 91 39W
Koshkonong L. 55 42 52N 88 58W
Košice 89 48 42N 21 15 E
Koslan 98 63 28N 48 52 E
Kosŏng 114 38 40N 128 22 E
Kosovska-Mitrovica 95 42 54N 20 52 E
Kosse 51 31 18N 96 38W
Kossuth County ◇ 23 43 15N 94 10W
Kostamuksa 98 62 34N 32 44 E
Kostenets 95 42 15N 23 52 E
Kôstî 121 13 8N 32 43 E
Kostroma 98 57 50N 40 58 E
Kostrzyn 88 52 24N 17 14 E
Koszalin 88 53 50N 16 8 E
Kota 108 25 14N 75 49 E
Kota Baharu 112 6 7N 102 14 E
Kota Belud 110 6 21N 116 26 E
Kota Kinabalu 110 6 0N 116 4 E
Kota Tinggi 112 1 44N 103 53 E
Kotaagung 110 5 38 S 104 29 E
Kotabaru 110 3 20 S 116 20 E
Kotabumi 110 4 49 S 104 54 E
Kotagede 111 7 54 S 110 26 E
Kotamobagu 111 0 57N 124 31 E
Kotaneelee → 62 60 11N 123 42W
Kotawaringin 110 2 28 S 111 27 E
Kotcho L. 62 59 7N 121 12W
Kotel 95 42 52N 26 26 E
Kotelnich 98 58 20N 48 10 E
Kotelnyy, Ostrov 101 75 10N 139 0 E
Kotka 97 60 28N 26 58 E
Kotlas 98 61 15N 47 0 E
Kotlenska Planina 95 42 56N 26 30 E
Kotli 108 33 30N 73 55 E
Kotlik 11 63 2N 163 33W
Kotor 95 42 25N 18 47 E
Kotri 108 25 22N 68 22 E
Kottayam 108 9 35N 76 33 E
Kotturu 108 14 45N 76 10 E
Kotuy → 101 71 54N 102 6 E
Kotzebue 11 66 53N 162 39W
Kotzebue Sound 11 66 20N 163 0W
Kouango 122 5 0N 20 10 E
Koudougou 120 12 10N 2 20W
Kouilou → 122 4 10 S 12 5 E
Kouki 122 7 22N 17 3 E
Koula Moutou 122 1 15 S 12 25 E
Koulen 112 13 50N 104 40 E
Koulikoro 120 12 40N 7 50W
Koumra 121 8 50N 17 35 E
Kounradskiy 100 46 59N 75 0 E
Kountze 51 30 22N 94 19W
Kourou 71 5 9N 52 39W
Kouroussa 120 10 45N 9 45W
Kousseri 121 12 0N 14 55 E
Koutiala 120 12 25N 5 23W
Kouts 22 41 19N 87 2W
Kovdor 98 67 34N 30 24 E
Kovel 98 51 10N 24 20 E
Kovrov 98 56 25N 41 25 E
Kowkash 60 50 20N 87 12W
Kowloon 115 22 20N 114 15 E
Koyabuti 111 2 36 S 140 37 E
Koyuk 11 64 56N 161 9W
Koyukuk 11 64 53N 157 42W
Koyukuk → 11 64 55N 157 32W
Koza 117 26 19N 127 46 E
Kozan 106 37 35N 35 50 E
Kozáni 95 40 19N 21 47 E
Kozhikode = Calicut 108 11 15N 75 43 E
Kozhva 98 65 10N 57 0 E
Kozloduy 95 43 45N 23 42 E
Kozlovets 95 43 30N 25 20 E
Kpalimé 120 6 57N 0 44 E
Kra, Isthmus of = Kra, Kho Khot 112 10 15N 99 30 E
Kra, Kho Khot 112 10 15N 99 30 E
Kra Buri 112 10 22N 98 46 E
Kragan 111 6 43 S 111 38 E
Kragerø 97 58 52N 9 25 E
Kragujevac 95 44 2N 20 56 E
Krakatau = Rakata, Pulau 110 6 10 S 105 20 E
Kraków 89 50 4N 19 57 E
Kraksaan 111 7 43 S 113 23 E
Kraljevo 95 43 44N 20 41 E
Kramatorsk 99 48 50N 37 30 E
Kramer 41 48 42N 100 43W
Kramfors 96 62 55N 17 48 E
Kranzburg 47 44 54N 96 55W
Krasavino 98 60 58N 46 29 E
Kraskino 101 42 44N 130 48 E
Kraśnik 89 50 55N 22 5 E
Krasnodar 99 45 5N 39 0 E
Krasnokamsk 98 58 4N 55 48 E
Krasnorechenskiy 116 44 41N 135 14 E
Krasnoselkupsk 100 65 20N 82 10 E
Krasnoturinsk 100 59 46N 60 12 E
Krasnoufimsk 98 56 57N 57 46 E
Krasnouralsk 98 58 21N 60 3 E
Krasnovishersk 98 60 23N 57 3 E
Krasnovodsk 99 40 0N 52 52 E
Krasnoyarsk 101 56 8N 93 0 E
Krasnyy Yar 99 46 43N 48 23 E
Kratie 112 12 32N 106 10 E
Krau 111 3 19 S 140 5 E
Kravanh, Chuor Phnum 112 12 0N 103 32 E
Krawang 111 6 19N 107 18 E
Krebs 43 34 56N 95 43W
Krefeld 88 51 20N 6 32 E
Kremenchug 99 49 5N 33 25 E
Kremenchugskoye Vdkhr. 99 49 20N 32 30 E
Kremikovtsi 95 42 46N 23 28 E
Kremlin 43 36 33N 97 50W
Kremmling 16 40 4N 106 24W
Kremnica 89 48 45N 18 50 E
Kress 50 34 22N 101 45W
Kribi 122 2 57N 9 56 E
Krichem 95 42 8N 24 28 E
Krishna → 109 15 57N 80 59 E
Krishnanagar 109 23 24N 88 33 E
Kristiansand 97 58 9N 8 1 E
Kristianstad 97 56 2N 14 9 E
Kristianstads län □ 97 56 15N 14 0 E
Kristiansund 96 63 7N 7 45 E
Kristiinankaupunki 96 62 16N 21 21 E
Kristinehamn 97 59 18N 14 13 E
Kristinestad 96 62 16N 21 21 E
Kríti 95 35 15N 25 0 E
Krivoy Rog 99 47 51N 33 20 E
Krk 94 45 8N 14 40 E
Kronobergs län □ 97 56 45N 14 30 E
Kronprins Olav Kyst 5 69 0 S 42 0 E
Kronprinsesse Märtha Kyst 5 73 30 S 10 0 E
Kronshtadt 98 60 5N 29 45 E
Kroonstad 123 27 43 S 27 19 E
Kropotkin, R.S.F.S.R., U.S.S.R. 101 59 0N 115 30 E
Kropotkin, R.S.F.S.R., U.S.S.R. 99 45 28N 40 28 E
Krosno 89 49 42N 21 46 E
Krotoszyn 89 51 42N 17 23 E
Krotz Springs 25 30 32N 91 45W
Krugersdorp 123 26 5 S 27 46 E
Krum 51 33 16N 97 14W
Krumovgrad 95 41 29N 25 38 E
Krung Thep = Bangkok 112 13 45N 100 35 E
Krusenstern, C. 11 67 8N 163 45W
Kruševac 95 43 35N 21 28 E
Krymskiy P-ov. 99 45 0N 34 0 E
Ksar el Boukhari 120 35 51N 2 52 E
Ksar el Kebir 120 35 0N 6 0W
Ksar es Souk = Ar Rachidiya 120 31 58N 4 20W
Ku Tree Reservoir 19 21 30N 157 59W
Kuala 110 2 55N 105 47 E
Kuala Kangsar 112 4 46N 100 56 E
Kuala Kerai 112 5 30N 102 12 E
Kuala Kubu Baharu 112 3 34N 101 39 E
Kuala Lipis 112 4 10N 102 3 E
Kuala Lumpur 112 3 9N 101 41 E
Kuala Sedili Besar 112 1 55N 104 5 E
Kuala Terengganu 110 5 20N 103 8 E
Kualakapuas 110 2 55 S 114 20 E
Kualakurun 110 1 10 S 113 50 E
Kualapembuang 110 3 14 S 112 38 E
Kualapuu 19 21 10N 157 2W
Kualasimpang 110 4 17N 98 3 E
Kualoa Pt. 19 21 31N 157 50W
Kuandang 111 0 56N 123 1 E
Kuandian 114 40 45N 124 45 E
Kuangchou = Guangzhou 115 23 5N 113 10 E
Kuantan 112 3 49N 103 20 E
Kuapa Pond 19 21 17N 157 43W
Kuba 99 41 21N 48 32 E
Kubak 107 27 10N 63 10 E
Kuban → 99 45 20N 37 30 E
Kubokawa 117 33 12N 133 8 E
Kubrat 95 43 49N 26 31 E
Kuchino-eruba-Jima 117 30 28N 130 12 E
Kuchino-Shima 117 29 57N 129 55 E
Kuchinotsu 117 32 36N 130 11 E
Kucing 110 1 33N 110 25 E
Kuda 108 23 10N 71 15 E
Kudat 110 6 55N 116 55 E
Kudus 111 6 48 S 110 51 E
Kudymkar 100 59 1N 54 39 E
Kueiyang = Guiyang 115 26 32N 106 40 E
Kufrinjah 104 32 20N 35 41 E
Kufstein 88 47 35N 12 11 E
Kugong I. 60 56 18N 79 50W
Kūh-e 'Alijūq 107 31 30N 51 41 E
Kūh-e Dīnār 107 30 40N 51 0 E
Kūh-e-Hazārām 107 29 35N 57 20 E
Kūh-e-Jebāl Bārez 107 29 0N 58 0 E
Kūh-e Sorkh 107 35 30N 58 45 E
Kūh-e Taftān 107 28 40N 61 0 E
Kūhak 107 27 12N 63 10 E
Kūhhā-ye-Bashākerd 107 26 45N 59 0 E
Kūhhā-ye Sabalān 106 38 15N 47 45 E
Kūhpāyeh 107 32 44N 52 20 E

Kuile He Lake Alfred

Kuile He → 114 49 32N 124 42 E
Kuito 123 12 22 S 16 55 E
Kuiu I. 11 57 45N 134 10W
Kuji 116 40 11N 141 46 E
Kujū-San 117 33 5N 131 15 E
Kukawa 121 12 58N 13 27 E
Kukuihaele 19 20 5N 155 35W
Kulai 112 1 44N 103 35 E
Kulasekarappattinam 108 8 20N 78 0 E
Kuldja = Yining 113 43 58N 81 10 E
Kulm 41 46 18N 98 57W
Kulsary 100 46 59N 54 1 E
Kulunda 100 52 35N 78 57 E
Kulyab 100 37 55N 69 50 E
Kum Tekei 100 43 10N 79 30 E
Kuma → 99 44 55N 47 0 E
Kumagaya 117 36 9N 139 22 E
Kumai 110 2 44 S 111 43 E
Kumamba, Kepulauan 111 1 36 S 138 45 E
Kumamoto 117 32 45N 130 45 E
Kumamoto □ 117 32 55N 130 55 E
Kumanovo 95 42 9N 21 42 E
Kumara 128 42 37 S 171 12 E
Kumasi 120 6 41N 1 38W
Kumba 122 4 36N 9 24 E
Kume-Shima 117 26 20N 126 47 E
Kumertau 98 52 46N 55 47 E
Kumla 97 59 8N 15 10 E
Kumo 120 10 1N 11 12 E
Kumon Bum 109 26 30N 97 15 E
Kumukahi, C. 19 19 31N 154 49W
Kuna 20 43 30N 116 25W
Kunashir, Ostrov 101 44 0N 146 0 E
Kunghit I. 62 52 6N 131 3W
Kungrad 100 43 6N 58 54 E
Kungsbacka 97 57 30N 12 5 E
Kungur 98 57 25N 56 57 E
Kunia 19 21 28N 158 4W
Kuningan 111 6 59 S 108 29 E
Kunlong 109 23 20N 98 50 E
Kunlun Shan 109 36 0N 86 30 E
Kunming 113 25 1N 102 41 E
Kunsan 114 35 59N 126 45 E
Kunshan 115 31 22N 120 58 E
Kununurra 126 15 40 S 128 50 E
Kunya-Urgenoh 100 42 19N 59 10 E
Kuopio 96 62 53N 27 35 E
Kuopion lääni □ 96 63 25N 27 10 E
Kupa → 94 45 28N 16 24 E
Kupang 111 10 19 S 123 39 E
Kupreanof I. 11 56 50N 133 30W
Kuqa 113 41 35N 82 30 E
Kura → 99 39 50N 49 20 E
Kurashiki 117 34 40N 133 50 E
Kurayoshi 117 35 26N 133 50 E
Kürdzhali 95 41 38N 25 21 E
Kure 117 34 14N 132 32 E
Kure I. 19 28 25N 178 25W
Kurgaldzhino 100 50 35N 70 20 E
Kurgan 100 55 26N 65 18 E
Kuria Maria Is. = Khūrīyā Mūrīyā, Jazā 'ir 105 17 30N 55 58 E
Kurigram 109 25 49N 89 39 E
Kuril Is. = Kurilskiye Ostrova 101 45 0N 150 0 E
Kuril Trench 124 44 0N 153 0 E
Kurilsk 101 45 14N 147 53 E
Kurilskiye Ostrova 101 45 0N 150 0 E
Kurino 117 31 57N 130 43 E
Kurmuk 121 10 33N 34 21 E
Kurnool 108 15 45N 78 0 E
Kuro-Shima, Japan 117 30 50N 129 57 E
Kuro-Shima, Japan 117 24 14N 124 1 E
Kurow 128 44 44 S 170 29 E
Kursk 98 51 42N 36 11 E
Kuršumlija 95 43 9N 21 19 E
Kurthwood 25 31 20N 93 10W
Kurtistown 19 19 36N 155 4W
Kuruktag 113 41 0N 89 0 E
Kuruman 123 27 28 S 23 28 E
Kurume 117 33 15N 130 30 E
Kurunegala 108 7 30N 80 23 E
Kurupukari 71 4 43N 58 37W
Kurya 101 61 15N 108 10 E
Kusatsu 117 36 37N 138 36 E
Kusawa L. 62 60 20N 136 13W
Kushikino 117 31 44N 130 16 E
Kushima 117 31 29N 131 14 E
Kushimoto 117 33 28N 135 47 E
Kushiro 116 43 0N 144 25 E
Kushiro → 116 42 59N 144 23 E
Kushka 100 35 20N 62 18 E
Kushtia 109 23 55N 89 5 E
Kushva 98 58 18N 59 45 E
Kuskokwim → 11 60 5N 162 25W
Kuskokwim B. 11 59 45N 162 25W
Kuskokwim Mts. 11 62 30N 156 0W
Kussharo-Ko 116 43 38N 144 21 E
Kustanay 100 53 10N 63 35 E
Kütahya 106 39 30N 30 2 E
Kutaisi 99 42 19N 42 40 E
Kutaraja = Banda Aceh 110 5 35N 95 20 E
Kutch, Gulf of = Kachchh, Gulf of 108 22 50N 69 15 E
Kutch, Rann of = Kachchh, Rann of 108 24 0N 70 0 E
Kutno 89 52 15N 19 23 E
Kuttawa 48 37 4N 88 7W
Kutu 122 2 40 S 18 11 E
Kutum 121 14 10N 24 40 E
Kutztown 45 40 31N 75 47W
Kuwait = Al Kuwayt 106 29 30N 47 30 E
Kuwait ■ 106 29 30N 47 30 E
Kuwana 117 35 0N 136 43 E
Kuybyshev, R.S.F.S.R., U.S.S.R. 100 55 27N 78 19 E
Kuybyshev, R.S.F.S.R., U.S.S.R. 98 53 8N 50 6 E
Kuybyshevskoye Vdkhr. 98 55 2N 49 30 E
Küysanjaq 106 36 5N 44 38 E
Kuyto, Oz. 98 64 40N 31 0 E
Kuyumba 101 60 58N 96 59 E
Kuzey Anadolu Dağlari 106 41 30N 35 0 E
Kuzitrin → 11 65 10N 165 25W
Kuznetsk 98 53 12N 46 40 E
Kuzomen 98 66 22N 36 50 E
Kvænangen 96 70 5N 21 15 E
Kvarner 94 44 50N 14 10 E
Kvarnerič 94 44 43N 14 37 E
Kvichak B. 11 58 48N 157 30W
Kwadacha → 62 57 28N 125 38W
Kwakoegron 71 5 12N 55 25W
Kwamouth 122 3 9 S 16 12 E
Kwando → 123 18 27 S 23 32 E
Kwangju 114 35 9N 126 54 E
Kwangsi-Chuang = Guangxi Zhuangzu Zizhiqu □ 115 24 0N 109 0 E
Kwangtung = Guangdong □ 115 23 0N 113 0 E
Kwataboahegan → 60 51 9N 80 50W
Kwatisore 111 3 18 S 134 50 E
Kweichow = Guizhou □ 115 27 0N 107 0 E
Kwekwe 123 18 58 S 29 48 E
Kwethluk 11 60 49N 161 26W
Kwigillingok 11 59 51N 163 8W
Kwiguk 11 62 46N 164 30W
Kwinana New Town 126 32 15 S 115 47 E
Kwoka 111 0 31 S 132 27 E
Kyabé 121 9 30N 19 0 E
Kyaikto 112 17 20N 97 3 E
Kyakhta 101 50 30N 106 25 E
Kyangin 109 18 20N 95 20 E
Kyaukpadaung 109 20 52N 95 8 E
Kyaukpyu 109 19 28N 93 30 E
Kyaukse 109 21 36N 96 10 E
Kyburz 14 38 47N 120 18W
Kyle, S. Dak. 47 43 26N 102 10W
Kyle, Tex. 51 29 59N 97 53W
Kyle Dam 123 20 15 S 31 0 E
Kyle of Lochalsh 84 57 17N 5 43W
Kyō-ga-Saki 117 35 45N 135 15 E
Kyoga, L. 122 1 35N 33 0 E
Kyongju 114 35 51N 129 14 E
Kyongpyaw 109 17 12N 95 10 E
Kyōto 117 35 0N 135 45 E
Kyōto □ 117 35 15N 135 45 E
Kyren 101 51 45N 101 45 E
Kyrenia 106 35 20N 33 20 E
Kystatyam 101 67 20N 123 10 E
Kytal Ktakh 101 65 30N 123 40 E
Kyulyunken 101 64 10N 137 5 E
Kyunhla 109 23 25N 95 15 E
Kyuquot 62 50 3N 127 25W
Kyūshū 117 33 0N 131 0 E
Kyūshū □ 117 33 0N 131 0 E
Kyūshū-Sanchi 117 32 35N 131 17 E
Kyustendil 95 42 16N 22 41 E
Kyusyur 101 70 39N 127 15 E
Kyzyl 101 51 50N 94 30 E
Kyzyl-Kiya 100 40 16N 72 8 E
Kyzylkum, Peski 100 42 30N 65 0 E
Kzyl-Orda 100 44 48N 65 28 E

L

La Barge 56 42 16N 110 12W
La Belle, Fla. 17 26 46N 81 26W
La Belle, Mo. 32 40 7N 91 55W
La Center 48 37 4N 88 58W
La Chorrera 57 8 53N 79 47W
La Conner 53 48 23N 122 30W
La Crescent 30 43 50N 91 18W
La Croix L. 30 48 20N 92 10W
La Crosse, Fla. 17 29 51N 82 24W
La Crosse, Kans. 24 38 32N 99 18W
La Crosse, Va. 54 36 42N 78 6W
La Crosse, Wash. 53 46 49N 117 53W
La Crosse, Wis. 55 43 48N 91 15W
La Crosse County ◇ 55 44 0N 91 0W
La Cygne 24 38 21N 94 46W
La Esperanza 57 18 23N 66 45W
La Farge 55 43 35N 90 38W
La Fayette, Ga. 18 34 42N 85 17W
La Fayette, Ky. 48 36 40N 87 40W
La Feria 50 26 9N 97 50W
La Follette 49 36 23N 84 7W
La Fontaine 22 40 40N 85 43W
La Garita 16 37 50N 106 15W
La Grande 44 45 20N 118 5W
La Grange, Ark. 13 34 39N 90 44W
La Grange, Ga. 18 33 2N 85 2W
La Grange, Ky. 49 38 25N 85 23W
La Grange, Mo. 32 40 3N 91 35W
La Grange, N.C. 40 35 19N 77 47W
La Grange, Tenn. 48 35 3N 89 15W
La Grange, Tex. 51 29 54N 96 52W
La Grange, Wyo. 56 41 38N 104 10W
La Harpe, Ill. 21 40 35N 90 58W
La Harpe, Kans. 24 37 55N 95 18W
La Jara, Colo. 16 37 16N 105 58W
La Jara, N. Mex. 38 36 5N 106 58W
La Joya 50 26 14N 98 27W
La Junta 16 37 59N 103 33W
La Luz 38 32 59N 105 57W
La Madera 38 36 23N 106 3W
La Marque 51 29 23N 94 58W
La Mesa, Calif. 15 32 46N 117 3W
La Mesa, N. Mex. 38 32 7N 106 42W
La Moille 21 41 32N 89 17W
La Moine → 21 39 59N 90 31W
La Monte 32 38 46N 93 26W
La Moure 41 46 21N 98 18W
La Moure County ◇ 41 46 23N 98 29W
La Palma 12 32 53N 111 31W
La Pine 44 43 40N 121 30W
La Place 25 30 4N 90 29W
La Plant 47 45 9N 100 39W
La Plata, Md. 27 38 32N 76 59W
La Plata, Mo. 32 40 2N 92 29W
La Plata, N. Mex. 38 36 56N 108 12W
La Plata County ◇ 16 37 15N 107 50W
La Porte 22 41 36N 86 43W
La Porte City 23 42 19N 92 12W
La Porte County ◇ 22 41 30N 86 45W
La Pryor 51 28 57N 99 51W
La Puente 38 36 42N 106 36W
La Push 53 47 55N 124 38W
La Sal 52 38 20N 109 15W
La Sal Mts. 52 38 30N 109 10W
La Salle, Colo. 16 40 21N 104 42W
La Salle, Ill. 21 41 20N 89 6W
La Salle, Minn. 30 44 4N 94 33W
La Salle County ◇, Ill. 21 41 20N 88 50W
La Salle County ◇, Tex. 51 28 26N 99 14W
La Salle Parish ◇ 25 31 41N 92 8W
La Santa, Cerro 57 18 7N 66 4W
La Union 38 31 57N 106 40W
La Vale 27 39 40N 78 48W
La Valle 55 43 35N 90 8W
La Vergne 48 36 1N 86 35W
La Verkin 52 37 12N 113 16W
La Vernia 51 29 21N 98 7W
La Veta 16 37 31N 105 0W
La Veta Pass 16 37 36N 105 13W
Laau Pt. 19 21 6N 157 19W
Labadieville 25 29 50N 90 57W
Labak 111 6 32N 124 5 E
Labé 120 11 24N 12 16W
Laberge, L. 62 61 11N 135 12W
Labette 24 37 14N 95 11W
Labette County ◇ 24 37 15N 95 15W
Labis 112 2 22N 103 2 E
Laboulaye 76 34 10 S 63 30W
Labrador, Coast of □ 59 53 20N 61 0W
Labrador City 61 52 57N 66 55W
Lábrea 73 7 15 S 64 51W
Labuan, Pulau 110 5 21N 115 13 E
Labuha 111 0 30 S 127 30 E
Labuhan 111 6 22 S 105 50 E
Labuhanbaja 111 8 28 S 120 1 E
Labuk, Telok 110 6 10N 117 50 E
Labytnangi 100 66 39N 66 21 E
Lac Allard 61 50 33N 63 24W
Lac Bouchette 61 48 16N 72 11W
Lac Courte Oreilles Indian Reservation 55 45 50N 91 15W
Lac du Flambeau 55 45 58N 89 53W
Lac du Flambeau Indian Reservation 55 46 0N 89 50W
Lac Édouard 60 47 40N 72 16W
Lac la Biche 62 54 45N 111 58W
Lac la Martre 58 63 8N 117 16W
Lac-Mégantic 61 45 35N 70 53W
Lac qui Parle County ◇ 30 44 55N 96 0W
Lac Seul 63 50 28N 92 0W
Lacantúm → 65 16 36N 90 40W
Laccadive Is. = Lakshadweep Is. 102 10 0N 72 30 E
Lacepede Is. 126 16 55 S 122 0 E
Lacey 53 47 7N 122 49W
Lachay, Pta. 72 11 17 S 77 44W
Lachine 60 45 30N 73 40W
Lachlan → 127 34 22 S 143 55 E
Lachute 60 45 39N 74 21W
Lackawanna 39 42 50N 78 50W
Lackawanna County ◇ 45 41 30N 75 50W
Laclede County ◇ 32 37 40N 92 35W
Lacombe, Canada 62 52 30N 113 44W
Lacombe, U.S.A. 25 30 19N 89 56W
Lacon 21 41 2N 89 24W
Lacona, Iowa 23 41 12N 93 23W
Lacona, N.Y. 39 43 39N 76 10W
Laconia, Ind. 22 38 2N 86 5W
Laconia, N.H. 36 43 32N 71 28W
Lacoochee 17 28 28N 82 11W
Ladakh Ra. 108 34 0N 78 0 E
Ladário 73 19 1 S 57 35W
Ladd 21 41 23N 89 13W
Laddonia 32 39 15N 91 39W
Ladelle 13 33 28N 91 48W
Lādīz 107 28 55N 61 15 E
Ladoga 22 39 55N 86 48W
Ladoga, L. = Ladozhskoye Ozero 98 61 15N 30 30 E
Ladonia 51 33 25N 95 57W
Ladozhskoye Ozero 98 61 15N 30 30 E
Ladrillero, G. 78 49 20 S 75 35W
Ladson 46 32 59N 80 6W
Lady Grey 123 30 43 S 27 13 E
Lady Lake 17 28 55N 81 55W
Ladysmith, Canada 62 49 0N 123 49W
Ladysmith, S. Africa 123 28 32 S 29 46 E
Ladysmith, U.S.A. 55 45 28N 91 12W
Lae 124 6 40 S 147 2 E
Læsø 97 57 15N 10 53 E
Lafayette, Ala. 10 32 54N 85 24W
Lafayette, Calif. 14 37 53N 122 7W
Lafayette, Colo. 16 39 58N 105 12W
Lafayette, Ind. 22 40 25N 86 54W
Lafayette, La. 25 30 14N 92 1W
Lafayette, Minn. 30 44 27N 94 24W
Lafayette, Ohio 42 40 46N 83 57W
Lafayette, Oreg. 44 45 15N 123 7W
Lafayette, Tenn. 48 36 31N 86 2W
Lafayette, Mt. 36 44 10N 71 38W
Lafayette County ◇, Ark. 13 33 22N 93 43W
Lafayette County ◇, Fla. 17 30 0N 83 0W
Lafayette County ◇, Miss. 31 34 22N 89 31W
Lafayette County ◇, Mo. 32 39 5N 93 45W
Lafayette County ◇, Wis. 55 42 35N 90 10W
Lafayette Parish ◇ 25 30 14N 92 1W
Laferte → 62 61 53N 117 44W
Lafia 120 8 30N 8 34 E
Lafitte 25 29 40N 90 6W
Lafleche 63 49 45N 106 40W
Lafontaine 24 37 24N 95 51W
Lafourche Parish ◇ 25 29 34N 90 23W
Lagan → 85 54 35N 5 55W
Lagarfljót → 96 65 40N 14 18W
Lagarto 74 10 54 S 37 41W
Lågen → 97 61 8N 10 25 E
Laghmān □ 107 34 20N 70 0 E
Laghouat 120 33 50N 2 59 E
Lago Posadas 78 47 30 S 71 40W
Lago Ranco 78 40 19 S 72 30W
Lagonoy Gulf 111 13 50N 123 50 E
Lagos, Nigeria 120 6 25N 3 27 E
Lagos, Portugal 91 37 5N 8 41W
Lagos de Moreno 64 21 21N 101 55W
Lagrange, Australia 126 18 45 S 121 43 E
Lagrange, Ind. 22 41 39N 85 25W
Lagrange, Maine 26 45 11N 68 54W
Lagrange, Ohio 42 41 14N 82 7W
Lagrange County ◇ 22 41 35N 85 25W
Laguna, Brazil 77 28 30 S 48 50W
Laguna, U.S.A. 38 35 2N 107 25W
Laguna Beach 15 33 33N 117 47W
Laguna Indian Reservation 38 35 0N 107 20W
Laguna Limpia 76 26 32 S 59 45W
Laguna Mts. 15 33 0N 116 40W
Lagunas, Chile 76 21 0 S 69 45W
Lagunas, Peru 72 5 10 S 75 35W
Lagunillas 73 19 38 S 63 43W
Laha 114 48 12N 124 35 E
Lahad Datu 111 5 0N 118 20 E
Lahaina 19 20 53N 156 41W
Lahat 110 3 45 S 103 30 E
Lahewa 110 1 22N 97 12 E
Lahijan 106 37 10N 50 6 E
Lahilahi Pt. 19 21 28N 158 13W
Lahn → 88 50 52N 8 35 E
Laholm 97 56 30N 13 2 E
Lahoma 43 36 23N 98 5W
Lahontan Reservoir 35 39 28N 119 4W
Lahore 108 31 32N 74 22 E
Lahti 97 60 58N 25 40 E
Lahtis = Lahti 97 60 58N 25 40 E
Laï 121 9 25N 16 18 E
Lai Chau 112 22 5N 103 3 E
Laibin 115 23 42N 109 14 E
Laie 19 21 39N 157 56W
Laifeng 115 29 27N 109 20 E
Laingsburg 29 42 54N 84 21W
Lair 49 38 20N 84 18W
Lairg 84 58 1N 4 24W
Lais 110 3 35 S 102 0 E
Laiyang 114 36 59N 120 45 E
Laizhou Wan 114 37 30N 119 30 E
Laja → 64 20 55N 100 46W
Lajas 57 18 3N 67 4W
Lajere 120 11 58N 11 25 E
Lajes, Rio Grande d. N., Brazil 74 5 41 S 36 14W
Lajes, Sta. Catarina, Brazil 77 27 48 S 50 20W
Lajinha 75 20 9 S 41 37W
Lajitas 50 29 16N 103 46W
Lajoya 38 34 21N 106 51W
Lakar 111 8 15 S 128 17 E
Lake, Miss. 31 32 21N 89 20W
Lake, Wyo. 56 44 33N 110 24W
Lake Alfred 17 28 6N 81 44W

Lake Andes Las Termas

Lake Andes 47 43 9N 98 32W
Lake Arthur, La. 25 30 5N 92 41W
Lake Arthur, N. Mex. 38 33 0N 104 22W
Lake Benton 30 44 15N 96 17W
Lake Bird 17 30 14N 83 37W
Lake Bronson 30 48 44N 96 40W
Lake Butler 17 30 1N 82 21W
Lake Cargelligo 127 33 15 S 146 22 E
Lake Charles 25 30 14N 93 13W
Lake Chelan National Recreation Area 53 48 25N 120 52W
Lake City, Ark. 13 35 49N 90 26W
Lake City, Calif. 14 41 39N 120 13W
Lake City, Colo. 16 38 2N 107 19W
Lake City, Fla. 17 30 11N 82 38W
Lake City, Iowa 23 42 16N 94 44W
Lake City, Kans. 24 37 21N 98 49W
Lake City, Mich. 29 44 20N 85 13W
Lake City, Minn. 30 44 27N 92 16W
Lake City, Pa. 45 42 1N 80 21W
Lake City, S.C. 46 33 52N 79 45W
Lake City, S. Dak. 47 45 44N 97 25W
Lake City, Tenn. 49 36 13N 84 9W
Lake Clarke Shores 17 26 39N 80 5W
Lake Clear Junction 39 44 22N 74 14W
Lake County ◇, Calif. 14 39 5N 122 45W
Lake County ◇, Colo. 16 39 10N 106 20W
Lake County ◇, Fla. 17 28 45N 81 45W
Lake County ◇, Ill. 21 42 20N 88 0W
Lake County ◇, Ind. 22 41 25N 87 25W
Lake County ◇, Mich. 29 44 0N 85 50W
Lake County ◇, Minn. 30 47 30N 91 20W
Lake County ◇, Mont. 33 47 40N 114 10W
Lake County ◇, Ohio 42 41 40N 81 21W
Lake County ◇, Oreg. 44 44 45N 120 20W
Lake County ◇, S. Dak. 47 44 0N 97 7W
Lake County ◇, Tenn. 48 36 23N 89 29W
Lake Crystal 30 44 6N 94 13W
Lake Delton 55 43 35N 89 47W
Lake Forest 21 42 15N 87 50W
Lake Fork 20 44 50N 116 5W
Lake Fork Cr. → 52 40 13N 110 7W
Lake Geneva 55 42 36N 88 26W
Lake George, Colo. 16 38 59N 105 22W
Lake George, Mich. 29 43 58N 84 57W
Lake George, Minn. 30 47 12N 94 59W
Lake George, N.Y. 39 43 26N 73 43W
Lake Harbor 17 26 42N 80 48W
Lake Harbour 59 62 50N 69 50W
Lake Havasu City 12 34 27N 114 22W
Lake Helen 17 28 59N 81 14W
Lake Hughes 15 34 41N 118 26W
Lake Isabella 15 35 38N 118 28W
Lake Jackson 51 29 3N 95 27W
Lake Lenore 63 52 24N 104 59W
Lake Lillian 30 44 57N 94 53W
Lake Linden 29 47 11N 88 24W
Lake Louise 62 51 30N 116 10W
Lake Lure 40 35 25N 82 12W
Lake Mead National Recreation Area 12 36 15N 114 30W
Lake Meredith National Recreation Area 50 35 50N 101 50W
Lake Mills, Iowa 23 43 25N 93 32W
Lake Mills, Wis. 55 43 5N 88 55W
Lake Mohawk 37 41 1N 74 39W
Lake Monroe 17 28 50N 81 19W
Lake Nebagamon 55 46 31N 91 42W
Lake Norden 47 44 35N 97 13W
Lake Odessa 29 42 47N 85 8W
Lake of the Woods County ◇ 30 48 40N 94 50W
Lake Orion 29 42 47N 83 14W
Lake Oswego 44 45 25N 122 40W
Lake Ozark 32 38 12N 92 38W
Lake Park, Fla. 17 26 48N 80 3W
Lake Park, Ga. 18 30 41N 83 11W
Lake Park, Iowa 23 43 27N 95 19W
Lake Park, Minn. 30 46 53N 96 6W
Lake Placid, Fla. 17 27 18N 81 22W
Lake Placid, N.Y. 39 44 17N 73 59W
Lake Pleasant 39 43 28N 74 25W
Lake Preston 47 44 22N 97 23W
Lake Providence 25 32 48N 91 10W
Lake Range 35 40 10N 119 20W
Lake River 60 54 30N 82 31W
Lake Ronkonkoma 39 40 50N 73 6W
Lake Shore 27 39 7N 76 29W
Lake Stevens 53 48 1N 122 4W
Lake Superior Prov. Park 60 47 45N 84 45W
Lake Toxaway 40 35 8N 82 56W
Lake View, Iowa 23 42 18N 95 3W
Lake View, S.C. 46 34 21N 79 10W
Lake Villa 21 42 25N 88 5W
Lake Village 13 33 20N 91 17W
Lake Wales 17 27 54N 81 35W
Lake Wilson 30 43 59N 95 57W
Lake Worth 17 26 37N 80 3W
Lake Zurich 21 42 12N 88 5W
Lakecreek 44 42 26N 122 37W
Lakefield, Canada 60 44 25N 78 16W
Lakefield, U.S.A. 30 43 41N 95 10W
Lakehurst 37 40 1N 74 19W
Lakeland, Fla. 17 28 3N 81 57W
Lakeland, Ga. 18 31 2N 83 4W
Lakemba 128 18 13 S 178 47W
Lakemont 45 40 28N 78 24W
Lakemount 18 34 47N 83 25W
Lakeport, Calif. 14 39 3N 122 55W
Lakeport, Mich. 29 43 7N 82 30W
Lakeshore, Calif. 15 37 15N 119 12W
Lakeshore, Miss. 31 30 15N 89 26W
Lakeside, Ariz. 12 34 9N 109 58W
Lakeside, Calif. 15 32 52N 116 55W
Lakeside, Nebr. 34 42 3N 102 26W
Lakeside, Oreg. 44 43 35N 124 11W
Lakeside, Va. 54 37 37N 77 28W
Laketon 50 35 33N 100 38W
Laketown 52 41 49N 111 19W
Lakeview, Mont. 33 44 36N 111 49W
Lakeview, Ohio 42 40 29N 83 56W
Lakeview, Oreg. 44 42 11N 120 21W
Lakeview, Tex. 50 34 40N 100 42W
Lakeview, Mich. 29 42 17N 85 12W
Lakeview, Mich. 29 43 27N 85 17W
Lakeville, Conn. 28 41 58N 73 26W
Lakeville, Ind. 22 41 31N 86 16W
Lakeville, Mass. 28 41 50N 70 55W
Lakeville, Minn. 30 44 39N 93 14W
Lakewood, Colo. 16 39 44N 105 5W
Lakewood, N.J. 37 40 6N 74 13W
Lakewood, N. Mex. 38 32 38N 104 23W
Lakewood, N.Y. 39 42 6N 79 19W
Lakewood, Ohio 42 41 29N 81 48W
Lakewood, Wash. 53 48 9N 122 13W
Lakewood, Wis. 55 45 18N 88 31W
Lakewood Center 53 47 11N 122 32W
Laki 96 64 4N 18 14W
Lakin 24 37 57N 101 15W
Lakitusaki → 60 54 21N 82 25W
Lakonikós Kólpos 95 36 40N 22 40 E
Lakota, Ivory C. 120 5 50N 5 30W
Lakota, Iowa 23 43 23N 94 6W
Lakota, N. Dak. 41 48 2N 98 21W
Laksefjorden 96 70 45N 26 50 E
Lakselv 96 70 2N 24 56 E
Lakshadweep Is. 102 10 0N 72 30 E
Lala Ghat 109 24 30N 92 40 E
Lalibela 121 12 2N 39 2 E
Lalin, China 114 45 12N 127 0 E
Lalín, Spain 91 42 40N 8 5W
Lalitapur = Patan 109 27 40N 85 20 E
Lamaing 109 15 25N 97 53 E
Lamar, Ark. 13 35 27N 93 23W
Lamar, Colo. 16 38 5N 102 37W
Lamar, Mo. 32 37 30N 94 16W
Lamar, Nebr. 34 40 34N 101 59W
Lamar, Okla. 43 35 6N 96 8W
Lamar, S.C. 46 34 10N 80 4W
Lamar County ◇, Ala. 10 33 45N 88 7W
Lamar County ◇, Ga. 18 33 5N 84 10W
Lamar County ◇, Miss. 31 31 9N 89 25W
Lamar County ◇, Tex. 51 33 40N 95 33W
Lamarque 78 39 24 S 65 40W
Lamas 72 6 28 S 76 31W
Lamb County ◇ 50 34 0N 102 15W
Lambaréné 122 0 41 S 10 12 E
Lambasa 128 16 30 S 179 10 E
Lambay I. 85 53 30N 6 0W
Lambayeque □ 72 6 45 S 80 0W
Lambert, Miss. 31 34 12N 90 17W
Lambert, Mont. 33 47 41N 104 37W
Lambert Glacier 5 71 0 S 70 0 E
Lamberton 30 44 14N 95 16W
Lambertville, Mich. 29 41 46N 83 35W
Lambertville, N.J. 37 40 22N 74 57W
Lambi Kyun 112 10 50N 98 20 E
Lame 120 45 35N 106 40W
Lame Deer 33 45 37N 106 40W
Lamego 91 41 5N 7 52W
Lamèque 61 47 45N 64 38W
Lamesa 50 32 44N 101 58W
Lamía 95 38 55N 22 26 E
Lamine → 32 38 59N 92 51W
Lamison 10 32 7N 87 34W
Lammermuir Hills 84 55 50N 2 40W
Lamoille → 36 44 38N 73 13W
Lamoille County ◇ 36 44 40N 72 40W
Lamon Bay 111 14 30N 122 20 E
Lamona 53 47 22N 118 29W
Lamoni 23 40 37N 93 56W
Lamont, Canada 62 53 46N 112 50W
Lamont, Calif. 15 35 15N 118 55W
Lamont, Fla. 17 30 23N 83 49W
Lamont, Kans. 24 38 7N 96 2W
Lamont, Miss. 31 33 32N 91 5W
Lamont, Okla. 43 36 42N 97 30W
Lamont, Wash. 53 47 12N 117 54W
Lamont, Wyo. 56 42 13N 107 29W
Lampa 72 15 22 S 70 22W
Lampang 112 18 16N 99 32 E
Lampasas 51 31 4N 98 11W
Lampasas → 51 30 59N 97 24W
Lampasas County ◇ 51 31 5N 98 10W
Lampazos de Naranjo 64 27 2N 100 32W
Lampedusa 94 35 36N 12 40 E
Lampeter 83 52 6N 4 6W
Lampman 63 49 25N 102 50W
Lamprey 63 58 33N 94 8W
Lampung □ 110 5 30 S 104 30 E
Lamu 122 2 16 S 40 55 E
Lamud 72 6 10 S 77 57W
Lamut, Tg. 110 3 50 S 105 58 E
Lamy 38 35 29N 105 53W
Lan Xian 114 38 15N 111 35 E
Lan Yu 115 22 5N 121 35 E
Lanagan 32 36 37N 94 27W
Lanai 19 20 50N 156 55W
Lanai City 19 20 50N 156 55W
Lanaihale 19 20 49N 156 53W
Lanak La 108 34 27N 79 32 E
Lanak'o Shank'ou = Lanak La 108 34 27N 79 32 E
Lanao, L. 111 7 52N 124 15 E
Lanark, U.K. 84 55 40N 3 48W
Lanark, U.S.A. 21 42 6N 89 50W
Lanark Village 17 29 53N 84 36W
Lancashire □ 82 53 40N 2 30W
Lancaster, U.K. 82 54 3N 2 48W
Lancaster, Calif. 15 34 42N 118 8W
Lancaster, Kans. 24 39 34N 95 18W
Lancaster, Ky. 49 37 37N 84 35W
Lancaster, Minn. 30 48 52N 96 48W
Lancaster, Mo. 32 40 31N 92 32W
Lancaster, N.H. 36 44 29N 71 34W
Lancaster, N.Y. 39 42 54N 78 40W
Lancaster, Ohio 42 39 43N 82 36W
Lancaster, Pa. 45 40 2N 76 19W
Lancaster, S.C. 46 34 43N 80 46W
Lancaster, Tex. 51 32 35N 96 45W
Lancaster, Va. 54 37 46N 76 28W
Lancaster, Wis. 55 42 51N 90 43W
Lancaster County ◇, Nebr. 34 40 45N 96 45W
Lancaster County ◇, Pa. 45 40 0N 76 19W
Lancaster County ◇, S.C. 46 34 40N 80 40W
Lancaster County ◇, Va. 54 37 45N 76 30W
Lancaster Sd. 4 74 13N 84 0W
Lance Creek 56 43 2N 104 39W
Lancer 63 50 48N 108 53W
Lanchow = Lanzhou 114 36 1N 103 52 E
Lanciano 94 42 15N 14 22 E
Lanco 78 39 24 S 72 46W
Lancones 72 4 30 S 80 30W
Land Between The Lakes 48 36 25N 88 0W
Land Between the Lakes Rec. Area 48 36 55N 88 5W
Landa 41 48 54N 100 55W
Lándana 122 5 11 S 12 5 E
Landeck 88 47 9N 10 34 E
Landen 87 50 45N 5 5 E
Lander 56 42 50N 108 44W
Lander County ◇ 35 40 0N 117 0W
Landes □ 90 43 57N 0 48W
Landes, Les 90 44 20N 1 0W
Landi Kotal 108 34 7N 71 6 E
Landis 40 35 33N 80 37W
Landisburg 45 40 21N 77 19W
Lando 46 34 46N 81 1W
Landrum 46 35 11N 82 11W
Land's End 83 50 4N 5 43W
Landshut 88 48 31N 12 10 E
Landskrona 97 55 53N 12 50 E
Lane, Kans. 24 38 26N 95 5W
Lane, S.C. 46 33 32N 79 53W
Lane, S. Dak. 47 44 4N 98 26W
Lane County ◇, Kans. 24 38 30N 100 30W
Lane County ◇, Oreg. 44 44 0N 123 0W
Lanesboro, Iowa 23 42 11N 94 41W
Lanesboro, Mass. 28 42 31N 73 14W
Lanesboro, Minn. 30 43 43N 91 58W
Lanett 10 32 52N 85 12W
Lang Bay 62 49 45N 124 21W
Lang Shan 114 41 0N 106 30 E
Lang Son 112 21 52N 106 42 E
La'nga Co 109 30 45N 81 15 E
Langara I. 62 54 14N 133 1W
Langatabbetje 71 4 59N 54 28W
Langdon, Kans. 24 37 51N 98 19W
Langdon, N. Dak. 41 48 45N 98 22W
Langenburg 63 50 51N 101 43W
Langford 47 45 36N 97 50W
Langholm 84 55 9N 2 59W
Langjökull 96 64 39N 20 12W
Langkawi, P. 112 6 25N 99 45 E
Langkon 111 6 30N 116 40 E
Langlade 61 46 50N 56 20W
Langlade County ◇ 55 45 15N 89 10W
Langley, Ark. 13 34 19N 93 51W
Langley, Ky. 49 37 32N 82 47W
Langley, Okla. 43 36 28N 95 3W
Langlois 44 42 56N 124 27W
Langøya 96 68 45N 14 50 E
Langres 90 47 52N 5 20 E
Langres, Plateau de 90 47 45N 5 3 E
Langsa 110 4 30N 97 57 E
Langston 43 35 59N 97 18W
Langtry 50 29 49N 101 34W
Languedoc 90 43 58N 4 0 E
L'Anguille → 13 34 44N 90 40W
Langxiangzhen 114 39 43N 116 8 E
Langzhong 115 31 38N 105 58 E
Lanier County ◇ 18 31 0N 83 5W
Lanigan 63 51 51N 105 2W
Lankao 115 34 48N 114 50 E
Lankin 41 48 19N 97 55W
Lansdale 45 40 14N 75 17W
Lansdowne 27 39 15N 76 40W
Lansdowne House 60 52 14N 87 53W
L'Anse 29 46 45N 88 27W
L'Anse Indian Reservation 29 46 45N 88 20W
Lansford, N. Dak. 41 48 38N 101 23W
Lansford, Pa. 45 40 50N 75 53W
Lansing, Ill. 21 41 34N 87 33W
Lansing, Iowa 23 43 22N 91 13W
Lansing, Kans. 24 39 15N 94 54W
Lansing, Mich. 29 42 44N 84 33W
Lantana 17 26 35N 80 3W
Lanus 76 34 44 S 58 27W
Lanxi 115 29 13N 119 28 E
Lanzarote 120 29 0N 13 40W
Lanzhou 114 36 1N 103 52 E
Lao Cai 112 22 30N 103 57 E
Laoag 111 18 7N 120 34 E
Laoang 111 12 32N 125 8 E
Laoha He → 114 43 25N 120 35 E
Laois □ 85 53 0N 7 20W
Laon 90 49 33N 3 35 E
Laona 55 45 34N 88 40W
Laos ■ 112 17 45N 105 0 E
Lapa 77 25 46 S 49 44W
Laparan 111 6 0N 120 0 E
Lapeer 29 43 3N 83 19W
Lapeer County ◇ 29 43 5N 83 15W
Lapel 22 40 4N 85 51W
Lapi □ 96 67 0N 27 0 E
Lapland = Lappland 96 68 7N 24 0 E
Laporte, Colo. 16 40 38N 105 8W
Laporte, Minn. 30 47 13N 94 45W
Laporte, Pa. 45 41 25N 76 30W
Lappans 27 39 33N 77 43W
Lappland 96 68 7N 24 0 E
Laprida 76 37 34 S 60 45W
Laptev Sea 101 76 0N 125 0 E
Lapwai 20 46 24N 116 48W
Lār 107 27 40N 54 14 E
Lara □ 70 10 10N 69 50W
Larache 120 35 10N 6 5W
Laramie 56 41 19N 105 35W
Laramie → 56 42 13N 104 33W
Laramie County ◇ 56 41 15N 104 40W
Laramie Mts. 56 42 0N 105 30W
Laramie Pk. 56 42 17N 105 27W
Laranjeiras 74 10 48 S 37 10W
Laranjeiras do Sul 77 25 23 S 52 23W
Larantuka 111 8 21 S 122 55 E
Larap 111 14 18N 122 39 E
Larat 111 7 0 S 132 0 E
Larchwood 23 43 27N 96 26W
Larder Lake 60 48 5N 79 40W
Laredo, Mo. 32 40 2N 93 27W
Laredo, Tex. 50 27 30N 99 30W
Laredo Sd. 62 52 30N 128 53W
Lares 57 18 18N 66 53W
Larga, L. 51 27 30N 97 25W
Largo 17 27 55N 82 47W
Largo Key 17 25 15N 80 15W
Largs 84 55 48N 4 51W
Lariang 111 1 26 S 119 17 E
Larimer County ◇ 16 40 40N 105 20W
Larimore 41 47 54N 97 38W
Lárisa 95 39 49N 22 28 E
Lark, N. Dak. 41 46 27N 101 24W
Lark, Tex. 50 35 12N 101 14W
Larkspur 16 39 14N 104 53W
Larnaca 106 35 0N 33 35 E
Larne 85 54 52N 5 50W
Larned 24 38 11N 99 6W
Larose 25 29 34N 90 23W
Larrabee 23 42 52N 95 33W
Larrimah 126 15 35 S 133 12 E
Larsen Bay 11 57 32N 153 59W
Larsen Ice Shelf 5 67 0 S 62 0W
Larson 41 48 53N 102 52W
Larue 42 40 35N 83 23W
Larue County ◇ 49 37 30N 85 40W
Larvik 97 59 4N 10 0 E
Laryak 100 61 15N 80 0 E
Las Animas 16 38 4N 103 13W
Las Animas County ◇ 16 37 15N 104 0W
Las Anod 105 8 26N 47 19 E
Las Brenãs 76 27 5 S 61 7W
Las Cascadas 57 9 5N 79 41W
Las Coloradas 78 39 34 S 70 36W
Las Cruces 38 32 19N 106 47W
Las Flores 76 36 10 S 59 7W
Las Heras 76 32 51 S 68 49W
Las Horquetas 78 48 14 S 71 11W
Las Khoreh 105 11 10N 48 20 E
Las Lajas 78 38 30 S 70 25W
Las Lomas 72 4 40 S 80 10W
Las Lomitas 76 24 43 S 60 35W
Las Marias 57 18 15N 66 59W
Las Mercedes 70 9 7N 66 24W
Las Nutrias 38 34 28N 106 46W
Las Palmas, Argentina 76 27 8 S 58 45W
Las Palmas, Canary Is. 120 28 7N 15 26W
Las Palmas □ 120 28 10N 15 28W
Las Piedras, Puerto Rico 57 18 11N 65 52W
Las Piedras, Uruguay 77 34 44 S 56 14W
Las Pipinas 76 35 30 S 57 19W
Las Plumas 78 43 40 S 67 15W
Las Rosas 76 32 30 S 61 35W
Las Tablas 66 7 49N 80 14W
Las Termas 76 27 29 S 64 52W

Las Tunas, Pta. Leona

Las Tunas, Pta. 57 18 30N 66 38W
Las Varillas 76 31 50 S 62 50W
Las Vegas, N. Mex. 38 35 36N 105 13W
Las Vegas, Nev. 35 36 10N 115 9W
Lascano 77 33 35 S 54 12W
Lashburn 63 53 10N 109 40W
Lashio 109 22 56N 97 45 E
Lassance 75 17 54 S 44 34W
Lassen County ◇ 14 40 45N 120 30W
Lassen National Forest 14 40 30N 121 15W
Lassen Peak 14 40 29N 121 30W
Lassen Volcanic National Park 14 40 30N 121 20W
Last Chance 16 39 44N 103 36W
Last Mountain L. 63 51 5N 105 14W
Lastoursville 122 0 55 S 12 38 E
Lastovo 94 42 46N 16 55 E
Lastrup 30 46 2N 94 4W
Latacunga 70 0 50 S 78 35W
Latah County ◇ 20 46 45N 116 50W
Latakia = Al Lādhiqīyah 106 35 30N 35 45 E
Latchford 60 47 20N 79 50W
Latham, Ill. 21 39 58N 89 10W
Latham, Kans. 24 37 32N 96 38W
Lathrop, Calif. 14 37 49N 121 16W
Lathrop, Mo. 32 39 33N 94 20W
Lathrop Wells 35 36 39N 116 24W
Latimer, Iowa 23 42 46N 93 22W
Latimer, Kans. 24 38 44N 96 51W
Latimer County ◇ 43 34 50N 95 10W
Latina 94 41 26N 12 53 E
Latium = Lazio □ 94 42 10N 12 30 E
Laton 15 36 26N 119 41W
Latouche Treville, C. 126 18 27 S 121 49 E
Latrobe 45 40 19N 79 23W
Latrun 104 31 50N 34 58 E
Latta 46 34 21N 79 26W
Latvian S.S.R. □ 98 56 50N 24 0 E
Lau 128 17 0 S 178 30W
Lauca → 72 19 9 S 68 10W
Lauchhammer 88 51 35N 13 48 E
Lauderdale 31 32 31N 88 31W
Lauderdale County ◇, Ala. 10 34 56N 87 46W
Lauderdale County ◇, Miss. 31 32 22N 88 42W
Lauderdale County ◇, Tenn. 48 35 45N 89 23W
Lauenburg 88 53 23N 10 33 E
Laugarbakki 96 65 20N 20 55W
Laughing Fish Pt. 29 46 32N 87 1W
Laughlin Pk. 38 36 40N 104 10W
Launceston, Australia 127 41 24 S 147 8 E
Launceston, U.K. 83 50 38N 4 21W
Laune → 85 52 5N 9 40W
Launglon Bok 112 13 50N 97 54 E
Laura, Australia 127 15 32 S 144 32 E
Laura, U.S.A. 42 39 59N 84 22W
Laurel, Del. 27 38 33N 75 34W
Laurel, Fla. 17 27 8N 82 27W
Laurel, Iowa 23 41 53N 92 55W
Laurel, Md. 27 39 6N 76 51W
Laurel, Miss. 31 31 41N 89 8W
Laurel, Mont. 33 45 40N 108 46W
Laurel, Nebr. 34 42 26N 97 6W
Laurel, Wash. 53 45 57N 121 23W
Laurel Bay 46 32 27N 80 47W
Laurel County ◇ 49 37 5N 84 10W
Laurel Hill 40 34 49N 79 33W
Laurel River L. 49 36 57N 84 10W
Laureldale, N.J. 37 39 30N 74 41W
Laureldale, Pa. 45 40 23N 75 56W
Laurelville 42 39 28N 82 44W
Laurencekirk 84 56 50N 2 30W
Laurens, Iowa 23 42 51N 94 52W
Laurens, S.C. 46 34 30N 82 1W
Laurens County ◇, Ga. 18 32 30N 83 0W
Laurens County ◇, S.C. 46 34 30N 82 0W
Laurentian Plat. 61 52 0N 70 0W
Laurentides, Parc Prov. des 61 47 45N 71 15W
Laurie L. 63 56 35N 101 57W
Laurinburg 40 34 47N 79 28W
Laurium 29 47 14N 88 27W
Lausanne 88 46 32N 6 38 E
Laut 110 4 45N 108 0 E
Laut Ketil, Kepulauan 110 4 45 S 115 40 E
Lautaro 78 38 31 S 72 27W
Lautoka 128 17 37 S 177 27 E
Lauzon 61 46 48N 71 10W
Lava Beds National Monument 14 41 40N 121 30W
Lava Hot Springs 20 42 37N 112 1W
Lavaca 13 35 20N 94 10W
Lavaca → 51 28 41N 96 35W
Lavaca County ◇ 51 29 27N 96 57W
Laval 90 48 4N 0 48W
Lavalle 76 28 15 S 65 15W
Lavallette 37 39 58N 74 4W
Laverendrye Prov. Park 60 46 15N 17 15W
Laverne 43 36 43N 99 54W
Laverton 126 28 44 S 122 29 E
Lavi 104 32 47N 35 25 E
Lavic L. 15 34 40N 116 21W
Lavina 33 46 18N 108 56W
Lavon L. 51 33 2N 96 28W
Lavonia 18 34 26N 83 6W
Lavras 75 21 20 S 45 0W
Lavrentiya 101 65 35N 171 0W
Lávrion 95 37 40N 24 4 E
Lawas 110 4 55N 115 25 E
Lawele 111 5 16 S 123 3 E
Lawen 44 43 27N 118 48W
Lawler 23 43 4N 92 9W
Lawn 51 32 8N 99 45W
Lawndale 40 35 25N 81 34W
Lawng Pit 109 25 30N 97 25 E
Lawrence, Ind. 22 39 50N 86 2W
Lawrence, Kans. 24 38 58N 95 14W
Lawrence, Mass. 28 42 43N 71 10W
Lawrence, Mich. 29 42 13N 86 3W
Lawrence, Nebr. 34 40 18N 98 16W
Lawrence County ◇, Ala. 10 34 29N 87 18W
Lawrence County ◇, Ark. 13 36 0N 91 0W
Lawrence County ◇, Ill. 21 38 45N 87 45W
Lawrence County ◇, Ind. 22 38 50N 86 30W
Lawrence County ◇, Ky. 49 38 5N 82 45W
Lawrence County ◇, Miss. 31 31 33N 90 7W
Lawrence County ◇, Mo. 32 37 10N 93 50W
Lawrence County ◇, Ohio 42 38 32N 82 41W
Lawrence County ◇, Pa. 45 41 0N 80 15W
Lawrence County ◇, S. Dak. 47 44 23N 103 44W
Lawrence County ◇, Tenn. 48 35 14N 87 20W
Lawrenceburg, Ind. 22 39 6N 84 52W
Lawrenceburg, Ky. 49 38 2N 84 54W
Lawrenceburg, Tenn. 48 35 14N 87 20W
Lawrenceville, Ga. 18 33 57N 83 59W
Lawrenceville, Ill. 21 38 44N 87 41W
Lawrenceville, N.J. 37 40 18N 74 44W
Lawrenceville, Pa. 45 41 59N 77 8W
Lawrenceville, Va. 54 36 46N 77 51W
Lawson 32 39 26N 94 12W
Lawtey 17 30 3N 82 5W
Lawton, Mich. 29 42 10N 85 50W
Lawton, N. Dak. 41 48 18N 98 22W
Lawton, Okla. 43 34 37N 98 25W
Lawu 111 7 40 S 111 13 E
Laxford, L. 84 58 25N 5 10W
Lay 16 40 32N 107 53W
Laylá 106 22 10N 46 40 E
Laysan I., Pac. Oc. 125 25 30N 167 0W
Laysan I., U.S.A. 19 25 50N 171 50W
Layton, Fla. 17 24 50N 80 47W
Layton, N.J. 37 41 13N 74 50W
Layton, Utah 52 41 4N 111 58W
Laytonsville 27 39 13N 77 9W
Laytonville 14 39 41N 123 29W
Lazear 16 38 47N 107 47W
Lazio □ 94 42 10N 12 30 E
Lazo 116 43 25N 133 55 E
Le Center 30 44 23N 93 44W
Le Claire 23 41 36N 90 21W
Le Flore County ◇ 43 35 0N 94 45W
Le Grand, Calif. 14 37 14N 120 15W
Le Grand, Iowa 23 42 0N 92 47W
Le Loup 24 38 42N 95 10W
Le Mars 23 42 47N 96 10W
Le Moyen 25 30 48N 92 4W
Le Roy, Ill. 21 40 21N 88 46W
Le Roy, Kans. 24 38 5N 95 38W
Le Roy, Mich. 29 44 2N 85 27W
Le Roy, Minn. 30 43 31N 92 30W
Le Roy, N.Y. 39 42 58N 78 0W
Le Roy, Pa. 45 41 41N 76 43W
Le Sueur 30 44 28N 93 55W
Le Sueur County ◇ 30 44 20N 93 45W
Lea → 83 51 30N 0 10W
Lea County ◇ 38 32 50N 103 30W
Leachville 13 35 56N 90 16W
Lead 47 44 21N 103 46W
Lead Hill, Ark. 13 36 25N 92 55W
Lead Hill, Mo. 32 37 6N 92 38W
Leadbetter Pt. 53 46 39N 124 3W
Leader 63 50 50N 109 30W
Leadhills 84 55 25N 3 47W
Leadore 20 44 41N 113 21W
Leadpoint 53 48 55N 117 35W
Leadville 16 39 15N 106 18W
Leadwood 32 37 52N 90 36W
Leaf 31 31 2N 88 48W
Leaf → 31 30 59N 88 44W
League City 51 29 31N 95 6W
Leake County ◇ 31 32 42N 89 38W
Leakesville 31 31 9N 88 33W
Leakey 51 29 44N 99 46W
Leamington, Canada 60 42 3N 82 36W
Leamington, U.K. 83 52 18N 1 32W
Leamington, U.S.A. 52 39 32N 112 17W
Leandro Norte Alem 77 27 34 S 55 15W
Learmonth 126 22 13 S 114 10 E
Leary 18 31 29N 84 31W
Leasburg, Mo. 32 38 5N 91 18W
Leasburg, N.C. 40 36 24N 79 10W
Leask 63 53 5N 106 45W
Leatherwood 49 37 2N 83 11W
Leavenworth, Ind. 22 38 12N 86 21W
Leavenworth, Kans. 24 39 19N 94 55W
Leavenworth, Wash. 53 47 36N 120 40W
Leavenworth County ◇ 24 39 15N 95 0W
Leavittsburg 42 41 14N 80 53W
Leawood 24 38 58N 94 37W
Lebam 53 46 34N 123 33W
Lebanon, Conn. 28 41 38N 72 13W
Lebanon, Ind. 22 40 3N 86 28W
Lebanon, Kans. 24 39 49N 98 33W
Lebanon, Ky. 49 37 34N 85 15W
Lebanon, Mo. 32 37 41N 92 40W
Lebanon, N.H. 36 43 39N 72 15W
Lebanon, Nebr. 34 40 3N 100 17W
Lebanon, Ohio 42 39 26N 84 13W
Lebanon, Okla. 43 33 59N 96 55W
Lebanon, Oreg. 44 44 32N 122 55W
Lebanon, Pa. 45 40 20N 76 26W
Lebanon, S. Dak. 47 45 4N 99 46W
Lebanon, Tenn. 48 36 12N 86 18W
Lebanon, Va. 54 36 54N 82 5W
Lebanon ■ 106 34 0N 36 0 E
Lebanon County ◇ 45 40 20N 76 25W
Lebanon Junction 49 37 50N 85 44W
Lebanon State Forest 37 39 53N 74 30W
Lebec 15 34 50N 118 52W
Lebo 24 38 25N 95 51W
Lebrija 91 36 53N 6 5W
Lebu 76 37 40 S 73 47W
Lecce 95 40 20N 18 10 E
Lecco 94 45 50N 9 27 E
Lechang 115 25 10N 113 20 E
Lecompte 25 31 6N 92 24W
Łeczyca 89 52 5N 19 15 E
Ledbury 83 52 3N 2 25W
Ledong 115 18 41N 109 5 E
Leduc 62 53 15N 113 30W
Ledyard 23 43 25N 94 10W
Lee, Fla. 17 30 25N 83 18W
Lee, Ill. 21 41 48N 88 56W
Lee, Maine 26 45 22N 68 17W
Lee, Mass. 28 42 19N 73 15W
Lee → 85 51 50N 8 30W
Lee City 49 37 44N 83 20W
Lee County ◇, Ala. 10 32 39N 85 23W
Lee County ◇, Ark. 13 34 46N 90 46W
Lee County ◇, Fla. 17 26 30N 81 45W
Lee County ◇, Ga. 18 31 45N 84 5W
Lee County ◇, Ill. 21 41 45N 89 20W
Lee County ◇, Iowa 23 40 40N 91 30W
Lee County ◇, Ky. 49 37 35N 83 45W
Lee County ◇, Miss. 31 34 16N 88 43W
Lee County ◇, N.C. 40 35 30N 79 10W
Lee County ◇, S.C. 46 34 10N 80 15W
Lee County ◇, Tex. 51 30 17N 96 58W
Lee County ◇, Va. 54 36 45N 83 5W
Lee Vining 14 37 58N 119 7W
Leech L. 30 47 10N 94 24W
Leech Lake Indian Reservation 30 47 20N 94 10W
Leedey 43 35 52N 99 21W
Leeds, U.K. 82 53 48N 1 34W
Leeds, Ala. 10 33 33N 86 33W
Leeds, Maine 26 44 18N 70 7W
Leeds, N. Dak. 41 48 17N 99 27W
Leeds, Utah 52 37 14N 113 22W
Leek 82 53 7N 2 2W
Leektown 37 39 38N 74 26W
Leelanau County ◇ 29 44 55N 85 50W
Leelanau L. 29 44 55N 85 43W
Lees Summit 32 38 55N 94 23W
Leesburg, Fla. 17 28 49N 81 53W
Leesburg, Ga. 18 31 44N 84 10W
Leesburg, N.J. 37 39 15N 74 59W
Leesburg, Ohio 42 39 21N 83 33W
Leesburg, Va. 54 39 7N 77 34W
Leesport 45 40 27N 75 58W
Leesville, La. 25 31 9N 93 16W
Leesville, Ohio 42 40 27N 81 13W
Leesville L. 54 37 5N 79 25W
Leeton 127 34 33 S 146 23 E
Leeuwarden 87 53 15N 5 48 E
Leeuwin, C. 126 34 20 S 115 9 E
Leeville 25 29 15N 90 12W
Leeward Is., Atl. Oc. 67 16 30N 63 30W
Leeward Is., Pac. Oc. 125 16 0 S 147 0W
Leflore 43 34 54N 94 59W
Leflore County ◇ 31 33 30N 90 20W
Lefors 50 35 26N 100 48W
Lefroy, L. 126 31 21 S 121 40 E
Legal 62 53 55N 113 35W
Legazpi 111 13 10N 123 45 E
Leggett, Calif. 14 39 52N 123 43W
Leggett, Tex. 51 30 49N 94 52W
Leghorn = Livorno 94 43 32N 10 18 E
Legnica 88 51 12N 16 10 E
Leh 108 34 9N 77 35 E
Lehi 52 40 24N 111 51W
Lehigh, Iowa 23 42 22N 94 3W
Lehigh, Kans. 24 38 22N 97 18W
Lehigh, Okla. 43 34 28N 96 13W
Lehigh → 45 40 41N 75 12W
Lehigh Acres 17 26 36N 81 39W
Lehigh County ◇ 45 40 40N 75 50W
Lehighton 45 40 50N 75 43W
Lehliu 95 44 29N 26 20 E
Lehr 41 46 17N 99 21W
Lehua I. 19 22 1N 160 6W
Leicester, U.K. 83 52 39N 1 9W
Leicester, Mass. 28 42 15N 71 55W
Leicester, Vt. 36 43 50N 73 8W
Leicester □ 83 52 40N 1 10W
Leichhardt → 127 17 35 S 139 48 E
Leiden 87 52 9N 4 30 E
Leidy, Mt. 56 43 44N 110 24W
Leie → 87 51 2N 3 45 E
Leigh 34 41 42N 97 14W
Leighton, Ala. 10 34 42N 87 32W
Leighton, Iowa 23 41 20N 92 47W
Leine → 88 52 20N 9 50 E
Leinster □ 85 53 0N 7 10W
Leinster, Mt. 85 52 38N 6 47W
Leipsic, Del. 27 39 14N 75 31W
Leipsic, Ohio 42 41 6N 83 59W
Leipzig 88 51 20N 12 23 E
Leiria 91 39 46N 8 53W
Leitchfield 48 37 29N 86 18W
Leitersburg 27 39 42N 77 37W
Leith, U.K. 84 55 59N 3 10W
Leith, U.S.A. 41 46 22N 101 38W
Leith Hill 83 51 10N 0 23W
Leitrim 85 54 0N 8 5W
Leitrim □ 85 54 8N 8 0W
Leiyang 115 26 27N 112 45 E
Leizhou Bandao 115 21 0N 110 0 E
Leizhou Wan 115 20 50N 110 20 E
Lek → 87 52 0N 6 0 E
Leksula 111 3 46 S 126 31 E
Lela 50 35 14N 100 21W
Leland, Ill. 21 41 37N 88 48W
Leland, Iowa 23 43 20N 93 38W
Leland, Mich. 29 45 1N 85 45W
Leland, Miss. 31 33 24N 90 54W
Leland, Oreg. 44 42 38N 123 27W
Leland, Wash. 53 47 53N 122 53W
Leland Lakes 63 60 0N 110 59W
Leleiwi Pt. 19 19 44N 155 0W
Leleque 78 42 28 S 71 0W
Lelia Lake 50 34 54N 100 46W
Lelystad 87 52 30N 5 25 E
Léman, Lac 88 46 26N 6 30 E
Lemay 32 38 32N 90 16W
Lemery 111 13 51N 120 56 E
Lemeta 11 64 52N 147 44W
Lemhi 20 44 52N 113 38W
Lemhi → 20 45 12N 113 53W
Lemhi County ◇ 20 45 0N 114 0W
Lemhi Range 20 44 0N 113 0W
Lemington 36 44 51N 71 36W
Lemitar 38 34 10N 106 55W
Lemmer 87 52 51N 5 43 E
Lemmon 47 45 57N 102 10W
Lemon Grove 15 32 45N 117 2W
Lemoore 15 36 18N 119 46W
Lemoyne 34 41 17N 101 49W
Lempster 36 43 15N 72 12W
Lemvig 97 56 33N 8 20 E
Lena, Ill. 21 42 23N 89 49W
Lena, Miss. 31 32 36N 89 36W
Lena → 101 72 52N 126 40 E
Lena, Mt. 52 40 50N 109 20W
Lenapah 43 36 51N 95 38W
Lenawee County ◇ 29 41 50N 84 5W
Lençóis 75 12 35 S 41 24W
Lengau de Vaca, Pta. 76 30 14 S 71 38W
Lenggong 112 5 6N 100 58 E
Leninabad 100 40 17N 69 37 E
Leninakan 99 40 47N 43 50 E
Leningrad 98 59 55N 30 20 E
Leningradskaya 5 69 50 S 160 0 E
Leninogorsk 100 50 20N 83 30 E
Leninsk 99 48 40N 45 15 E
Leninsk-Kuznetskiy 100 54 44N 86 10 E
Leninskoye 101 47 56N 132 38 E
Lenkoran 99 39 45N 48 50 E
Lenmalu 111 1 45 S 130 15 E
Lennep 33 46 25N 110 33W
Lennox 47 43 21N 96 53W
Lennox, I. 78 55 18 S 66 50W
Lenoir 40 35 55N 81 32W
Lenoir City 49 35 48N 84 16W
Lenoir County ◇ 40 35 10N 77 40W
Lenora 24 39 37N 100 0W
Lenore 20 46 31N 116 33W
Lenore L. 63 52 30N 104 59W
Lenox, Ga. 18 31 16N 83 28W
Lenox, Iowa 23 40 53N 94 34W
Lenox, Mass. 28 42 22N 73 17W
Lenox, Mo. 32 37 39N 91 46W
Lens 90 50 26N 2 50 E
Lensk 101 60 48N 114 55 E
Lentini 94 37 18N 15 0 E
Lenwood 15 34 53N 117 7W
Leoben 88 47 22N 15 5 E
Leola, Ark. 13 34 10N 92 35W
Leola, S. Dak. 47 45 43N 98 56W
Leoma 48 35 10N 87 21W
Leominster, U.K. 83 52 15N 2 43W
Leominster, U.S.A. 28 42 32N 71 46W
León, Mexico 64 21 7N 101 30W
León, Nic. 66 12 20N 86 51W
León, Spain 91 42 38N 5 34W
Leon, Iowa 23 40 44N 93 45W
Leon, Kans. 24 37 42N 96 46W
Leon, Okla. 43 33 53N 97 26W
León □ 91 42 40N 5 55W
Leon → 51 31 14N 97 28W
León, Montañas de 91 42 30N 6 18W
Leon County ◇, Fla. 17 30 30N 84 15W
Leon County ◇, Tex. 51 31 16N 95 59W
Leon Valley 51 29 28N 98 38W
Leona, Kans. 24 39 47N 95 19W
Leona, Tex. 51 31 9N 95 58W

Leona Lineville

Leona → 51 28 45N 99 11W
Leonard, Minn. 30 47 39N 95 16W
Leonard, N. Dak. 41 46 39N 97 15W
Leonard, Tex. 51 33 23N 96 15W
Leonardtown 27 38 17N 76 38W
Leonardville 24 39 22N 96 51W
Leonia 17 30 55N 86 1W
Leonora 126 28 49 S 121 19 E
Léopold II, Lac = Mai-Ndombe, L. 122 2 0 S 18 20 E
Leopoldina 75 21 28 S 42 40W
Leopoldo Bulhões 75 16 37 S 48 46W
Leopoldsburg 87 51 7N 5 13 E
Léopoldville = Kinshasa 122 4 20 S 15 15 E
Leoti 24 38 29N 101 21W
Leoville 63 53 39N 107 33W
Lepanto 13 35 37N 90 20W
Lepel 98 54 50N 28 40 E
Lepikha 101 64 45N 125 55 E
Leping 115 28 47N 117 7 E
Leraysville 45 41 51N 76 11W
Lerdo 64 25 32N 103 32W
Léré 121 9 39N 14 13 E
Lérida 91 41 37N 0 39 E
Lerna 21 39 25N 88 17W
Lerwick 84 60 10N 1 10W
Lesbos, I. = Lésvos 95 39 10N 26 20 E
Leshukonskoye 98 64 54N 45 46 E
Leskov I. 5 56 0 S 28 0W
Leskovac 95 43 0N 21 58 E
Leslie, Ark. 13 35 50N 92 34W
Leslie, Ga. 18 31 57N 84 5W
Leslie, Mich. 29 42 27N 84 26W
Leslie County ◇ 49 37 5N 83 25W
Lesopilnoye 116 46 44N 134 20 E
Lesotho ■ 123 29 40 S 28 0 E
Lesozavodsk 101 45 30N 133 29 E
Lesse → 87 50 15N 4 54 E
Lesser Antilles 67 15 0N 61 0W
Lesser Slave L. 62 55 30N 115 25W
Lessines 87 50 42N 3 50 E
Lessley 31 31 10N 91 25W
Lester 54 37 44N 81 18W
Lesterville 47 43 2N 97 35W
Lestock 63 51 19N 103 59W
Lésvos 95 39 10N 26 20 E
Leszno 88 51 50N 16 30 E
Letart Falls 42 38 54N 81 56W
Letcher 47 43 54N 98 8W
Letcher County ◇ 49 37 5N 82 55W
Letchworth 83 51 58N 0 13W
Letea, Ostrov 95 45 18N 29 20 E
Letha 20 43 54N 116 39W
Lethbridge 62 49 45N 112 45W
Lethem 71 3 20N 59 50W
Leti, Kepulauan 111 8 10 S 128 0 E
Leticia 70 4 9 S 70 0W
Leting 114 39 23N 118 55 E
Letohatchee 10 32 8N 86 29W
Letpadan 109 17 45N 95 45 E
Letpan 109 19 28N 94 10 E
Letsôk-aw Kyun 112 11 30N 98 25 E
Letterkenny 85 54 57N 7 42W
Letts 23 41 20N 91 14W
Leu 95 44 10N 24 0 E
Leucadia 15 33 4N 117 18W
Leupp Corner 12 35 5N 110 52W
Leuser, G. 110 3 46N 97 12 E
Leuven 87 50 52N 4 42 E
Leuze, Hainaut, Belgium 87 50 36N 3 37 E
Leuze, Namur, Belgium 87 50 33N 4 54 E
Levan 52 39 33N 111 52W
Levanger 96 63 45N 11 19 E
Levelland 50 33 35N 102 23W
Levelock 11 59 7N 156 51W
Leven 84 56 12N 3 0W
Leven, L. 84 56 12N 3 22W
Leveque C. 126 16 20 S 123 0 E
Levering 29 45 38N 84 47W
Levin 128 40 37 S 175 18 E
Lévis 61 46 48N 71 9W
Levis, L. 62 62 37N 117 58W
Levisa Fork → 49 38 8N 82 37W
Levittown, N.Y. 39 40 44N 73 31W
Levittown, Pa. 45 40 9N 74 51W
Levka 95 41 52N 26 15 E
Levkás 95 38 40N 20 43 E
Levkôsia = Nicosia 106 35 10N 33 25 E
Levski 95 43 21N 25 10 E
Levskigrad 95 42 38N 24 47 E
Levy County ◇ 17 29 15N 82 45W
Lewellen 34 41 20N 102 9W
Lewes, U.K. 83 50 53N 0 2 E
Lewes, U.S.A. 27 38 46N 75 9W
Lewis, U.K. 84 58 10N 6 40W
Lewis, Colo. 16 37 30N 108 40W
Lewis, Iowa 23 41 18N 95 5W
Lewis, Kans. 24 37 56N 99 15W
Lewis → 53 45 51N 122 48W
Lewis, Butt of 84 58 30N 6 12W
Lewis and Clark County ◇ 33 47 25N 112 35W
Lewis And Clark L. 34 42 51N 97 29W
Lewis and Clark National Forest 33 47 0N 111 0W
Lewis County ◇, Idaho 20 46 15N 116 29W
Lewis County ◇, Ky. 49 38 30N 83 25W
Lewis County ◇, Mo. 32 40 5N 91 40W
Lewis County ◇, N.Y. 39 43 45N 75 30W
Lewis County ◇, Tenn. 48 35 33N 87 33W
Lewis County ◇, W. Va. 54 39 2N 80 28W
Lewis County ◇, Wash. 53 46 30N 122 0W
Lewis L. 56 44 18N 110 38W
Lewis Range 33 48 5N 113 5W
Lewis Run 45 41 52N 78 40W
Lewis Smith, L. 10 33 56N 87 6W
Lewisburg, Ky. 48 36 59N 86 57W
Lewisburg, Ohio 42 39 51N 84 33W
Lewisburg, Pa. 45 40 58N 76 54W
Lewisburg, Tenn. 48 35 27N 86 48W
Lewisburg, W. Va. 54 37 48N 80 27W
Lewisport 48 37 56N 86 54W
Lewisporte 61 49 15N 55 3W
Lewiston, Calif. 14 40 43N 122 48W
Lewiston, Idaho 20 46 25N 117 1W
Lewiston, Maine 26 44 6N 70 13W
Lewiston, Mich. 29 44 53N 84 18W
Lewiston, Minn. 30 43 59N 91 52W
Lewiston, N.C. 40 36 7N 77 10W
Lewiston, N.Y. 39 43 11N 79 3W
Lewiston, Nebr. 34 40 14N 96 25W
Lewiston, Utah 52 41 59N 111 51W
Lewistown, Ill. 21 40 24N 90 9W
Lewistown, Md. 27 39 32N 77 25W
Lewistown, Mo. 32 40 5N 91 49W
Lewistown, Mont. 33 47 4N 109 26W
Lewistown, Pa. 45 40 36N 77 34W
Lewisville, Ark. 13 33 22N 93 35W
Lewisville, Ohio 42 39 46N 81 13W
Lewisville, Tex. 51 33 5N 97 0W
Lexington, Ala. 10 34 58N 87 22W
Lexington, Ga. 18 33 52N 83 7W
Lexington, Ill. 21 40 39N 88 47W
Lexington, Ky. 49 38 3N 84 30W
Lexington, Mich. 29 43 16N 82 32W
Lexington, Miss. 31 33 7N 90 3W
Lexington, Mo. 32 39 11N 93 52W
Lexington, N.C. 40 35 49N 80 15W
Lexington, Nebr. 34 40 47N 99 45W
Lexington, Ohio 42 40 41N 82 35W
Lexington, Okla. 43 35 1N 97 20W
Lexington, Oreg. 44 45 27N 119 42W
Lexington, S.C. 46 33 59N 81 11W
Lexington, Tenn. 48 35 39N 88 24W
Lexington, Tex. 51 30 25N 97 1W
Lexington, Va. 54 37 47N 79 27W
Lexington, Wash. 53 46 11N 122 54W
Lexington County ◇ 46 33 50N 81 10W
Lexington Park 27 38 16N 76 27W
Leyte 111 11 0N 125 0 E
Lhasa 113 29 25N 90 58 E
Lhazê 113 29 5N 87 38 E
Lhokseumawe 110 5 10N 97 10 E
Lhuntsi Dzong 109 27 39N 91 10 E
Li Shui → 115 29 24N 112 1 E
Li Xian, Gansu, China 115 34 10N 105 5 E
Li Xian, Hunan, China 115 29 36N 111 42 E
Lianga 111 8 38N 126 6 E
Liangdang 115 33 56N 106 18 E
Lianhua 115 27 3N 113 54 E
Lianjiang 115 26 12N 119 27 E
Lianping 115 24 26N 114 30 E
Lianshanguan 114 40 53N 123 43 E
Lianyungang 115 34 40N 119 11 E
Liao He → 114 41 0N 121 50 E
Liaocheng 114 36 28N 115 58 E
Liaodong Bandao 114 40 0N 122 30 E
Liaodong Wan 114 40 20N 121 10 E
Liaoning □ 114 42 0N 122 0 E
Liaoyang 114 41 15N 122 58 E
Liaoyuan 114 42 58N 125 2 E
Liaozhong 114 41 23N 122 50 E
Liard → 62 61 51N 121 18W
Líbano 70 4 55N 75 4W
Libau = Liepaja 98 56 30N 21 0 E
Libby 33 48 23N 115 33W
Libenge 122 3 40N 18 55 E
Liberal, Kans. 24 37 3N 100 55W
Liberal, Mo. 32 37 34N 94 31W
Liberdade 72 10 5 S 70 20W
Liberdade → 73 9 40 S 52 17W
Liberec 88 50 47N 15 7 E
Liberia 66 10 40N 85 30W
Liberia ■ 120 6 30N 9 30W
Libertad 70 8 20N 69 37W
Libertad, La 66 16 47N 90 7W
Libertad, La □ 72 8 0 S 78 30W
Liberty, Ill. 21 39 53N 91 6W
Liberty, Ind. 22 39 38N 84 56W
Liberty, Kans. 24 37 9N 95 36W
Liberty, Ky. 49 37 19N 84 56W
Liberty, Maine 26 44 24N 69 18W
Liberty, Miss. 31 31 10N 90 49W
Liberty, Mo. 32 39 15N 94 25W
Liberty, N.C. 40 35 51N 79 34W
Liberty, N.Y. 39 41 48N 74 45W
Liberty, Nebr. 34 40 5N 96 29W
Liberty, Pa. 45 41 34N 77 6W
Liberty, S.C. 46 34 48N 82 42W
Liberty, Tex. 51 30 3N 94 48W
Liberty, Wash. 53 47 14N 120 42W
Liberty Center 42 41 27N 84 1W
Liberty County ◇, Fla. 17 30 15N 85 0W
Liberty County ◇, Ga. 18 31 50N 81 30W
Liberty County ◇, Mont. 33 48 40N 111 0W
Liberty County ◇, Tex. 51 30 7N 94 52W
Liberty Hill, S.C. 46 34 29N 80 48W
Liberty Hill, Tex. 51 30 40N 97 55W
Liberty Lake 53 47 39N 117 5W
Libertytown, Md. 27 39 30N 77 15W
Libertytown, Md. 27 38 18N 75 18W
Libertyville, Ill. 21 42 18N 87 57W
Libertyville, Iowa 23 40 57N 92 3W
Libo 115 25 22N 107 53 E
Libobo, Tanjung 111 0 54 S 128 28 E
Libonda 123 14 28 S 23 12 E
Libourne 90 44 55N 0 14W
Libramont 87 49 55N 5 23 E
Libreville 122 0 25N 9 26 E
Libya ■ 121 27 0N 17 0 E
Libyan Desert 118 25 0N 25 0 E
Licantén 76 35 55 S 72 0W
Licata 94 37 6N 13 55 E
Lichfield 82 52 40N 1 50W
Lichtenburg 123 26 8 S 26 8 E
Lichuan 115 30 18N 108 57 E
Licking 32 37 30N 91 54W
Licking → 49 39 6N 84 30W
Licking County ◇ 42 40 3N 82 24W
Lida 35 37 28N 117 30W
Lidderdale 23 42 8N 94 47W
Lidgerwood 41 46 5N 97 9W
Lidköping 97 58 31N 13 14 E
Liebenthal 24 38 39N 99 19W
Liechtenstein ■ 88 47 8N 9 35 E
Liège 87 50 38N 5 35 E
Liège □ 87 50 32N 5 35 E
Liegnitz = Legnica 88 51 12N 16 10 E
Lienyünchiangshih = Lianyungang 115 34 40N 119 11 E
Lienz 88 46 50N 12 46 E
Liepaja 98 56 30N 21 0 E
Lier 87 51 7N 4 34 E
Liesta 95 45 38N 27 34 E
Lièvre → 60 45 31N 75 26W
Liffey → 85 53 21N 6 20W
Lifford 85 54 50N 7 30W
Lifudzin 116 44 21N 134 58 E
Lighthouse Point 17 26 15N 80 7W
Lighthouse Pt. 17 29 54N 84 21W
Lightning → 56 43 11N 104 44W
Lignite 41 48 53N 102 34W
Ligon 49 37 22N 82 41W
Ligonier, Ind. 22 41 28N 85 35W
Ligonier, Pa. 45 40 15N 79 14W
Ligua, La 76 32 30 S 71 16W
Liguria □ 94 44 30N 9 0 E
Ligurian Sea 94 43 20N 9 0 E
Lihou Reefs and Cays 127 17 25 S 151 40 E
Lihue 19 21 59N 159 23W
Lijiang 113 26 55N 100 20 E
Likasi 122 10 55 S 26 48 E
Likati 122 3 20N 24 0 E
Likely 14 41 14N 120 30W
Lilbourn 32 36 36N 89 37W
Liling 115 27 42N 113 29 E
Lille 90 50 38N 3 3 E
Lille Bælt 97 55 20N 9 45 E
Lillehammer 97 61 8N 10 30 E
Lillesand 97 58 15N 8 23 E
Lilleshall 83 52 45N 2 22W
Lillestrøm 97 59 58N 11 5 E
Lillie 25 32 56N 92 39W
Lillington 40 35 24N 78 49W
Lillooet → 62 49 15N 121 57W
Lilly 45 40 26N 78 37W
Lilongwe 123 14 0 S 33 48 E
Liloy 111 8 4N 122 39 E
Lily 47 45 11N 97 41W
Lima, Indonesia 111 3 37 S 128 4 E
Lima, Peru 72 12 0 S 77 0W
Lima, Ill. 21 40 11N 91 23W
Lima, Mont. 33 44 38N 112 36W
Lima, N.Y. 39 42 55N 77 37W
Lima, Ohio 42 40 44N 84 6W
Lima, Okla. 43 35 10N 96 36W
Lima □ 72 12 3 S 77 3W
Lima, Punta 57 18 11N 65 42W
Limassol 106 34 42N 33 1 E
Limavady 85 55 3N 6 58W
Limavady □ 85 55 0N 6 55W
Limay → 78 39 0 S 68 0W
Limay Mahuida 76 37 10 S 66 45W
Limbang 110 4 42N 115 6 E
Limbe 122 4 1N 9 10 E
Limburg □, Belgium 87 51 2N 5 25 E
Limburg □, Neth. 87 51 20N 5 55 E
Lime 44 44 24N 117 19W
Lime Ridge 55 43 28N 90 9W
Lime Springs 23 43 27N 92 17W
Lime Village 11 61 21N 155 28W
Limeira 77 22 35 S 47 28W
Limerick, Ireland 85 52 40N 8 38W
Limerick, U.S.A. 26 43 41N 70 48W
Limerick □ 85 52 30N 8 50W
Limestone, Maine 26 46 55N 67 50W
Limestone, N.Y. 39 42 2N 78 38W
Limestone, Tenn. 49 36 14N 82 38W
Limestone → 63 56 31N 94 7W
Limestone, L. 50 31 25N 96 22W
Limestone County ◇, Ala. 10 34 48N 86 58W
Limestone County ◇, Tex. 51 31 39N 96 31W
Limfjorden 97 56 55N 9 0 E
Limia → 91 41 41N 8 50W
Limmen Bight 126 14 40 S 135 35 E
Límnos 95 39 50N 25 5 E
Limoeiro 74 7 52 S 35 27W
Limoeiro do Norte 74 5 5 S 38 0W
Limoges 90 45 50N 1 15 E
Limón, C. Rica 66 10 0N 83 2W
Limon, U.S.A. 16 39 16N 103 41W
Limon B. 57 9 22N 79 56W
Limousin 90 46 0N 1 0 E
Limpopo → 123 25 15 S 33 30 E
Limuru 122 1 2 S 36 35 E
Linares, Chile 76 35 50 S 71 40W
Linares, Colombia 70 1 23N 77 31W
Linares, Mexico 65 24 50N 99 40W
Linares, Spain 91 38 10N 3 40W
Linares □ 76 36 0 S 71 0W
Linch 56 43 37N 106 12W
Lincheng 114 37 25N 114 30 E
Linchuan 115 27 57N 116 15 E
Lincoln, Argentina 76 34 55 S 61 30W
Lincoln, N.Z. 128 43 38 S 172 30 E
Lincoln, U.K. 82 53 14N 0 32W
Lincoln, Ark. 13 35 57N 94 25W
Lincoln, Calif. 14 38 54N 121 17W
Lincoln, Del. 27 38 52N 75 25W
Lincoln, Ill. 21 40 9N 89 22W
Lincoln, Iowa 23 42 16N 92 42W
Lincoln, Kans. 24 39 3N 98 9W
Lincoln, Maine 26 45 22N 68 30W
Lincoln, Mich. 29 44 41N 83 25W
Lincoln, Mo. 32 38 23N 93 20W
Lincoln, Mont. 33 46 58N 112 41W
Lincoln, N.H. 36 44 3N 71 40W
Lincoln, N. Mex. 38 33 30N 105 23W
Lincoln, Nebr. 34 40 49N 96 41W
Lincoln, Wash. 53 47 50N 118 25W
Lincoln □ 82 53 14N 0 32W
Lincoln City 44 44 57N 124 1W
Lincoln County ◇, Ark. 13 33 56N 91 51W
Lincoln County ◇, Colo. 16 39 0N 103 20W
Lincoln County ◇, Ga. 18 33 45N 82 20W
Lincoln County ◇, Idaho 20 43 0N 114 0W
Lincoln County ◇, Kans. 24 39 0N 98 10W
Lincoln County ◇, Ky. 49 37 25N 84 40W
Lincoln County ◇, Maine 26 44 0N 69 30W
Lincoln County ◇, Minn. 30 44 25N 96 10W
Lincoln County ◇, Miss. 31 31 35N 90 26W
Lincoln County ◇, Mo. 32 39 0N 91 0W
Lincoln County ◇, Mont. 33 48 45N 115 30W
Lincoln County ◇, N.C. 40 35 30N 81 10W
Lincoln County ◇, N. Mex. 38 33 40N 105 30W
Lincoln County ◇, Nebr. 34 41 0N 101 0W
Lincoln County ◇, Nev. 35 37 20N 115 0W
Lincoln County ◇, Okla. 43 35 40N 96 50W
Lincoln County ◇, Oreg. 44 44 40N 123 50W
Lincoln County ◇, S. Dak. 47 43 21N 96 53W
Lincoln County ◇, Tenn. 48 35 9N 86 34W
Lincoln County ◇, W. Va. 54 38 14N 81 59W
Lincoln County ◇, Wash. 53 47 45N 118 30W
Lincoln County ◇, Wis. 55 45 20N 89 40W
Lincoln County ◇, Wyo. 56 42 0N 110 30W
Lincoln National Forest 38 32 45N 105 40W
Lincoln Parish ◇ 25 32 32N 92 38W
Lincoln Park, Colo. 16 38 25N 105 10W
Lincoln Park, Ga. 18 32 52N 84 20W
Lincoln Park, Mich. 29 42 15N 83 11W
Lincoln Sea 4 84 0N 55 0W
Lincoln Wolds 82 53 20N 0 5W
Lincolnton, Ga. 18 33 48N 82 29W
Lincolnton, N.C. 40 35 29N 81 16W
Lincolnville, Kans. 24 38 30N 96 58W
Lincolnville, Maine 26 44 17N 69 1W
Lind 53 46 58N 118 37W
Linda 14 39 8N 121 34W
Lindale, Ga. 18 34 11N 85 11W
Lindale, Tex. 51 32 31N 95 25W
Linden, Guyana 72 6 0N 58 10W
Linden, Ala. 10 32 18N 87 48W
Linden, Calif. 14 38 1N 121 5W
Linden, Ind. 22 40 11N 86 54W
Linden, Mich. 29 42 49N 83 47W
Linden, N.J. 37 40 38N 74 15W
Linden, Tenn. 48 35 37N 87 50W
Linden, Tex. 51 33 1N 94 22W
Linden, Wis. 55 42 55N 90 16W
Lindenhurst 39 40 41N 73 23W
Lindenwold 37 39 49N 74 59W
Lindi 122 9 58 S 39 38 E
Lindian 114 47 11N 124 52 E
Lindley 39 42 1N 77 8W
Lindon 16 39 44N 103 24W
Lindsay, Canada 60 44 22N 78 43W
Lindsay, Calif. 15 36 12N 119 5W
Lindsay, Nebr. 34 41 42N 97 42W
Lindsay, Okla. 43 34 50N 97 38W
Lindsborg 24 38 35N 97 40W
Lindy 34 42 44N 97 44W
Línea de la Concepción, La 91 36 15N 5 23W
Linesville 45 41 39N 80 26W
Lineville, Ala. 10 33 19N 85 45W
Lineville, Iowa 23 40 35N 93 32W

Linfen **Lomié**

Linfen 114 36 3N 111 30 E
Ling Xian 114 37 22N 116 30 E
Lingao 115 19 56N 109 42 E
Lingayen 111 16 1N 120 14 E
Lingayen G. 111 16 10N 120 15 E
Lingchuan 115 25 26N 110 21 E
Lingen 88 52 32N 7 21 E
Lingga 110 0 12 S 104 37 E
Lingga, Kepulauan 110 0 10 S 104 30 E
Lingle 56 42 8N 104 21W
Lingling 115 26 17N 111 37 E
Lingshan 115 22 25N 109 18 E
Lingshi 114 36 48N 111 48 E
Lingshui 115 18 27N 110 0 E
Lingtai 115 35 0N 107 40 E
Linguéré 120 15 25N 15 5W
Lingyuan 114 41 10N 119 15 E
Lingyun 115 25 2N 106 35 E
Linh Cam 112 18 31N 105 31 E
Linhai 115 28 50N 121 8 E
Linhares 75 19 25 S 40 4W
Linhe 114 40 48N 107 20 E
Linjiang 114 41 50N 127 0 E
Linköping 97 58 28N 15 36 E
Linkou 114 45 15N 130 18 E
Linlithgow 84 55 58N 3 38W
Linn, Kans. 24 39 41N 97 5W
Linn, Mo. 32 38 29N 91 51W
Linn, Tex. 50 26 34N 98 7W
Linn County ◇, Iowa 23 42 5N 91 35W
Linn County ◇, Kans. 24 38 15N 94 45W
Linn County ◇, Mo. 32 39 50N 93 10W
Linn County ◇, Oreg. 44 44 30N 122 20W
Linn Creek 32 38 2N 92 43W
Linn Grove 23 42 53N 95 15W
Linneus, Maine 26 46 3N 67 52W
Linneus, Mo. 32 39 53N 93 11W
Linnhe, L. 84 56 36N 5 25W
Lino Lakes 30 45 12N 93 6W
Linqing 114 36 50N 115 42 E
Lins 77 21 40 S 49 44W
Lintao 114 35 18N 103 52 E
Lintlaw 63 52 4N 103 14W
Linton, Canada 61 47 15N 72 16W
Linton, Ind. 22 39 2N 87 10W
Linton, N. Dak. 41 46 16N 100 14W
Linville 40 36 4N 81 52W
Linwood, Ala. 10 31 56N 85 52W
Linwood, Kans. 24 39 0N 95 2W
Linwood, N.J. 37 39 21N 74 34W
Linwood, Nebr. 34 41 25N 96 56W
Linwu 115 25 19N 112 31 E
Linxi 114 43 36N 118 2 E
Linxia 113 35 36N 103 10 E
Linyi 115 35 5N 118 21 E
Linz, Austria 88 48 18N 14 18 E
Linz, Germany 88 50 33N 7 18 E
Lion, G. du 90 43 0N 4 0 E
Lion's Head 60 44 58N 81 15W
Lípari, Is. 94 38 30N 14 50 E
Lipetsk 98 52 37N 39 35 E
Liping 115 26 15N 109 7 E
Lipovcy Manzovka 116 44 12N 132 26 E
Lippe → 88 51 39N 6 38 E
Lipscomb 50 36 14N 100 16W
Lipscomb County ◇ 50 36 15N 100 15W
Lira 122 2 17N 32 57 E
Liria 91 39 37N 0 35W
Lisala 122 2 12N 21 38 E
Lisboa 91 38 42N 9 10W
Lisbon = Lisboa 91 38 42N 9 10W
Lisbon, Ill. 21 41 29N 88 29W
Lisbon, Maine 26 44 2N 70 6W
Lisbon, Md. 27 39 20N 77 4W
Lisbon, N. Dak. 41 46 27N 97 41W
Lisbon, N.H. 36 44 13N 71 55W
Lisbon, N.Y. 39 44 44N 75 19W
Lisbon, Ohio 42 40 46N 80 46W
Lisbon Falls 26 44 0N 70 4W
Lisburn 85 54 30N 6 9W
Lisburne, C. 11 68 53N 166 13W
Liscannor, B. 85 52 57N 9 24W
Lisco 34 41 30N 102 37W
Liscomb 23 42 11N 93 0W
Lishi 114 37 31N 111 8 E
Lishui 115 28 28N 119 54 E
Lisianski I., Pac. Oc. 124 26 2N 174 0W
Lisianski I., U.S.A. 19 26 2N 174 0W
Lisieux 90 49 10N 0 12 E
Lismore, Australia 127 28 44 S 153 21 E
Lismore, Ireland 85 52 8N 7 58W
Lismore, U.S.A. 30 43 45N 95 57W
Lisse 87 52 16N 4 33 E
Lista, Norway 97 58 7N 6 39 E
Lista, Sweden 97 59 19N 16 16 E
Lister, Mt. 5 78 0 S 162 0 E
Listowel, Canada 60 43 44N 80 58W
Listowel, Ireland 85 52 27N 9 30W
Litang, China 115 23 12N 109 8 E
Litang, Malaysia 111 5 27N 118 31 E
Litani →, Lebanon 104 33 20N 35 14 E
Litani →, Surinam 104 3 40N 54 0W
Litchfield, Conn. 28 41 45N 73 11W
Litchfield, Ill. 21 39 11N 89 39W
Litchfield, Mich. 29 42 3N 84 46W
Litchfield, Minn. 30 45 8N 94 32W
Litchfield, Nebr. 34 41 10N 99 9W
Litchfield County ◇ 28 41 40N 73 15W
Litchfield Park 12 33 30N 112 22W
Litchville 41 46 39N 98 12W
Lithgow 127 33 25 S 150 8 E
Líthinon, Ákra 95 34 55N 24 44 E
Lithuanian S.S.R. □ 98 55 30N 24 0 E
Lititz 45 40 9N 76 18W
Litoměřice 88 50 33N 14 10 E
Little →, Ark. 13 33 45N 94 3W
Little →, Ky. 48 36 51N 87 58W
Little →, N.C. 40 35 18N 78 42W
Little →, Tex. 51 30 51N 96 41W
Little Abaco I. 66 26 50N 77 30W
Little Andaman I. 112 10 40N 92 15 E
Little Barrier I. 128 36 12 S 175 8 E
Little Belt Mts. 33 46 40N 110 45W
Little Bighorn → 33 45 44N 107 34W
Little Blue → 24 39 42N 96 41W
Little Cadotte → 62 56 41N 117 6W
Little Cayman, I. 66 19 41N 80 3W
Little Churchill → 63 57 30N 95 22W
Little Chute 55 44 17N 88 16W
Little City 43 34 5N 96 36W
Little Colorado → 12 36 12N 111 48W
Little Creek 27 39 10N 75 27W
Little Current 60 45 55N 82 0W
Little Current → 60 50 57N 84 36W
Little Diomede I. 11 65 45N 168 56W
Little Eagle 47 45 40N 100 49W
Little Egg Harbor → 37 39 35N 74 18W
Little Falls, Minn. 30 45 59N 94 22W
Little Falls, N.J. 37 40 53N 74 14W
Little Falls, N.Y. 39 43 3N 74 51W
Little Fork → 30 48 31N 93 35W
Little Grand Rapids 63 52 0N 95 29W
Little Haw Cr. → 17 29 23N 81 24W
Little Humboldt → 35 41 1N 117 43W
Little Inagua I. 67 21 40N 73 50W
Little Kanawha → 54 39 16N 81 34W
Little Lake 15 35 56N 117 55W
Little Lost → 20 43 46N 112 58W
Little Minch 84 57 35N 6 45W
Little Missouri →, Ark. 13 33 49N 92 54W
Little Missouri →, N. Dak. 41 47 36N 102 25W
Little Missouri Badlands 41 47 5N 103 45W
Little Ouse → 83 52 25N 0 50 E
Little Pee Dee → 46 33 42N 79 11W
Little Powder → 33 45 28N 105 20W
Little Red → 13 35 11N 91 27W
Little River, N.Z. 128 43 45 S 172 49 E
Little River, U.S.A. 24 38 24N 98 1W
Little River County ◇ 13 33 40N 94 8W
Little Rock, Ark. 13 34 45N 92 17W
Little Rock, S.C. 46 34 29N 79 24W
Little Rocky Mts. 33 47 55N 108 30W
Little Sable Pt. 29 43 38N 86 33W
Little Salt L. 52 37 55N 112 53W
Little Sioux → 23 41 48N 96 4W
Little Sitkin 11 51 57N 178 31 E
Little Smoky → 62 54 44N 117 11W
Little Snake → 16 40 27N 108 26W
Little Tallapoosa → 18 33 18N 85 34W
Little Tennessee →, N.C. 40 35 47N 84 15W
Little Tennessee →, Tenn. 49 35 47N 84 16W
Little Traverse B. 29 45 25N 85 10W
Little Valley 39 42 15N 78 48W
Little White → 47 43 40N 100 40W
Little Wood → 20 42 57N 114 21W
Little York, Ill. 21 41 1N 90 45W
Little York, Ind. 22 38 42N 85 54W
Littlefield, Ariz. 12 36 53N 113 56W
Littlefield, Tex. 50 33 55N 102 20W
Littlefork 30 48 24N 93 34W
Littlehampton 83 50 48N 0 32W
Littlerock, Calif. 15 34 31N 117 59W
Littlerock, Wash. 53 46 54N 123 1W
Littlestown 45 39 45N 77 5W
Littleton, Colo. 16 39 37N 105 0W
Littleton, Ill. 21 40 14N 90 37W
Littleton, Maine 26 46 14N 67 51W
Littleton, N.C. 40 36 26N 77 54W
Littleton, N.H. 36 44 18N 71 46W
Littleton, W. Va. 54 39 42N 80 32W
Littleton Common 28 42 33N 71 28W
Littleville 10 34 36N 87 41W
Liuba 115 33 38N 106 55 E
Liucheng 115 24 38N 109 14 E
Liukang Tenggaja 111 6 45 S 118 50 E
Liuwa Plain 123 14 20 S 22 30 E
Liuyang 115 28 10N 113 37 E
Liuzhou 115 24 22N 109 22 E
Live Oak, Calif. 14 39 17N 121 40W
Live Oak, Fla. 17 30 18N 82 59W
Live Oak County ◇ 51 28 20N 98 7W
Livengood 11 65 32N 148 33W
Livermore, Calif. 14 37 41N 121 47W
Livermore, Colo. 16 40 47N 105 16W
Livermore, Iowa 23 42 52N 94 11W
Livermore, Ky. 48 37 29N 87 8W
Livermore, Mt. 50 30 38N 104 11W
Livermore Falls 26 44 29N 70 11W
Liverpool, Australia 127 33 54 S 150 58 E
Liverpool, Canada 61 44 5N 64 41W
Liverpool, U.K. 82 53 25N 3 0W
Liverpool, U.S.A. 39 43 6N 76 13W
Liverpool Plains 127 31 15 S 150 15 E
Liverpool Ra. 127 31 50 S 150 30 E
Livia 48 37 34N 87 6W
Livingston, Guat. 66 15 50N 88 50W
Livingston, Ala. 10 32 35N 88 11W
Livingston, Calif. 14 37 23N 120 43W
Livingston, Ill. 21 38 58N 89 46W
Livingston, Ky. 49 37 17N 84 13W
Livingston, La. 25 30 30N 90 45W
Livingston, Mont. 33 45 40N 110 34W
Livingston, N.J. 37 40 48N 74 19W
Livingston, Tenn. 49 36 23N 85 19W
Livingston, Tex. 51 30 43N 94 56W
Livingston, Wis. 55 42 54N 90 26W
Livingston, L. 51 30 50N 95 10W
Livingston County ◇, Ill. 21 40 55N 88 50W
Livingston County ◇, Ky. 48 37 10N 88 20W
Livingston County ◇, Mich. 29 42 35N 83 55W
Livingston County ◇, Mo. 32 39 50N 93 30W
Livingston County ◇, N.Y. 39 42 40N 77 45W
Livingston Manor 39 41 54N 74 50W
Livingston Parish ◇ 25 30 30N 90 45W
Livingstone 123 17 46 S 25 52 E
Livingstonia 122 10 38 S 34 5 E
Livny 98 52 30N 37 30 E
Livonia, Ind. 22 38 33N 86 17W
Livonia, La. 25 30 34N 91 33W
Livonia, Mich. 29 42 23N 83 23W
Livonia, Mo. 32 40 30N 92 42W
Livonia, N.Y. 39 42 49N 77 40W
Livorno 94 43 32N 10 18 E
Livramento 77 30 55 S 55 30W
Livramento do Brumado 75 13 39 S 41 50W
Liwale 122 9 48 S 37 58 E
Lizard Cr. → 23 42 30N 94 14W
Lizard Pt. 83 49 57N 5 11W
Lizarda 74 9 36 S 46 41W
Lizella 18 32 48N 83 49W
Lizemores 54 38 20N 81 11W
Ljubljana 94 46 4N 14 33 E
Ljungan → 96 62 18N 17 23 E
Ljungby 97 56 49N 13 55 E
Ljusdal 97 61 46N 16 3 E
Ljusnan → 97 61 12N 17 8 E
Ljusne 97 61 13N 17 7 E
Llamellín 72 9 0 S 76 54W
Llancanelo, Salina 76 35 40 S 69 8W
Llandeilo 83 51 53N 4 0W
Llandovery 83 51 59N 3 49W
Llandrindod Wells 83 52 15N 3 23W
Llandudno 82 53 19N 3 51W
Llanelli 83 51 41N 4 11W
Llanes 91 43 25N 4 50W
Llangollen 82 52 58N 3 10W
Llanidloes 83 52 28N 3 31W
Llano 51 30 45N 98 41W
Llano → 51 30 39N 98 26W
Llano County ◇ 51 30 45N 98 41W
Llano Estacado 38 33 30N 102 40W
Llanos 72 5 0N 71 35W
Llanquihue □ 78 41 30 S 73 0W
Llanquihue, L. 78 41 10 S 75 50W
Llera 65 23 19N 99 1W
Llica 72 19 52 S 68 16W
Llico 76 34 46 S 72 5W
Llobregat → 91 41 19N 2 9 E
Lloret de Mar 91 41 41N 2 53 E
Lloyd L. 63 57 22N 108 57W
Lloydminster 63 53 17N 110 0W
Lloyds 27 38 36N 76 12W
Llullaillaco, Volcán 76 24 43 S 68 30W
Loa 52 38 24N 111 39W
Loa → 76 21 26 S 70 41W
Loami 21 39 40N 89 51W
Lobatse 123 25 12 S 25 40 E
Lobelville 48 35 46N 87 47W
Lobería 76 38 10 S 58 40W
Lobito 123 12 18 S 13 35 E
Lobos 76 35 10 S 59 0W
Lobos, I. 64 27 15N 110 30W
Lobos, Is. 68 6 57 S 80 45W
Lobos de Tierra, I. 72 6 27 S 80 52W
Lobstick L. 61 54 0N 65 0W
Loc Binh 112 21 46N 106 54 E
Loc Ninh 112 11 50N 106 34 E
Locarno 88 46 10N 8 47 E
Loch Raven 27 39 26N 76 33W
Lochaber 84 56 55N 5 0W
Lochcarron 84 57 25N 5 30W
Loche, La 63 56 29N 109 26W
Lochearn 27 39 21N 76 43W
Lochem 87 52 9N 6 26 E
Loches 90 47 7N 1 0 E
Lochgelly 84 56 7N 3 18W
Lochgilphead 84 56 2N 5 37W
Lochinver 84 58 9N 5 15W
Lochloosa L. 17 29 30N 82 7W
Lochnagar 84 56 57N 3 14W
Lochsa → 20 46 9N 115 36W
Lochy → 84 56 52N 5 3W
Lock Haven 45 41 8N 77 28W
Lock Springs 32 39 51N 93 47W
Lockeford 14 38 10N 121 9W
Lockeport 61 43 47N 65 4W
Lockerbie 84 55 7N 3 21W
Lockesburg 13 33 58N 94 10W
Lockhart, S.C. 46 34 47N 81 28W
Lockhart, Tex. 51 29 53N 97 40W
Lockington 42 40 12N 84 14W
Lockney 50 34 7N 101 27W
Lockport, Ill. 21 41 35N 88 3W
Lockport, La. 25 29 39N 90 33W
Lockport, N.Y. 39 43 10N 78 42W
Lockridge 23 40 59N 91 45W
Lockwood 32 37 23N 93 57W
Loco 43 34 50N 97 38W
Locust 40 35 15N 80 25W
Locust Cr. → 32 39 40N 93 17W
Locust Fork → 10 33 33N 87 11W
Locust Grove, Ga. 18 33 21N 84 7W
Locust Grove, Okla. 43 36 12N 95 10W
Lod 104 31 57N 34 54 E
Loda 21 40 31N 88 4W
Lodeinoye Pole 98 60 44N 33 33 E
Lodge Grass 33 45 19N 107 22W
Lodgepole, Nebr. 34 41 9N 102 38W
Lodgepole, S. Dak. 47 45 48N 102 40W
Lodgepole → 34 41 2N 102 10W
Lodgepole Cr. → 16 40 57N 102 23W
Lodhran 108 29 32N 71 30 E
Lodi, Calif. 14 38 8N 121 16W
Lodi, Wis. 55 43 19N 89 32W
Lodja 122 3 30 S 23 23 E
Lodwar 122 3 10N 35 40 E
Łódź 89 51 45N 19 27 E
Lofoten 96 68 30N 15 0 E
Logan, Iowa 23 41 39N 95 47W
Logan, Kans. 24 39 40N 99 34W
Logan, N. Mex. 38 35 22N 103 25W
Logan, Ohio 42 39 32N 82 25W
Logan, Utah 52 41 44N 111 50W
Logan, W. Va. 54 37 51N 81 59W
Logan County ◇, Ark. 13 35 18N 93 44W
Logan County ◇, Colo. 16 40 45N 103 0W
Logan County ◇, Ill. 21 41 10N 89 20W
Logan County ◇, Kans. 24 39 0N 101 0W
Logan County ◇, Ky. 48 36 50N 86 50W
Logan County ◇, N. Dak. 41 46 28N 99 25W
Logan County ◇, Nebr. 34 41 30N 100 30W
Logan County ◇, Ohio 42 40 22N 83 46W
Logan County ◇, Okla. 43 36 0N 97 30W
Logan County ◇, W. Va. 54 37 58N 82 0W
Logan Martin Reservoir 10 33 26N 86 20W
Logandale 35 36 36N 114 29W
Logansport, Ind. 22 40 45N 86 22W
Logansport, La. 25 31 58N 94 0W
Loganton 45 41 2N 77 19W
Loganville, Ga. 18 33 50N 83 54W
Loganville, Wis. 55 43 27N 90 2W
Logroño 91 42 28N 2 27W
Lohardaga 109 23 27N 84 45 E
Lohrville 23 42 17N 94 33W
Loi-kaw 109 19 40N 97 17 E
Loimaa 97 60 50N 23 5 E
Loir → 90 47 33N 0 32W
Loir-et-Cher □ 90 47 40N 1 20 E
Loire □ 90 45 40N 4 5 E
Loire → 90 47 16N 2 10W
Loire-Atlantique □ 90 47 25N 1 40W
Loiret □ 90 47 58N 2 10 E
Loíza 57 18 26N 65 53W
Loíza, Lago 57 18 17N 66 0W
Loja, Ecuador 72 3 59 S 79 16W
Loja, Spain 91 37 10N 4 10W
Loja □ 70 4 0 S 79 13W
Loji 111 1 38 S 127 28 E
Lokandu 122 2 30 S 25 45 E
Lokeren 87 51 6N 3 59 E
Lokitaung 122 4 12N 35 48 E
Lokka 96 67 49N 27 45 E
Løkken Verk 96 63 7N 9 43 E
Lokoja 120 7 47N 6 45 E
Lokolama 122 2 35 S 19 50 E
Lokwei 115 19 5N 110 31 E
Lola 48 37 19N 88 18W
Lola, Mt. 14 39 26N 120 22W
Loliondo 122 2 2 S 35 39 E
Lolita 51 28 50N 96 33W
Lolland 97 54 45N 11 30 E
Lolo 33 46 45N 114 5W
Lolo Hot Springs 33 46 44N 114 32W
Lolo National Forest 33 47 8N 114 40W
Lolo Peak 33 46 41N 114 14W
Lom 95 43 48N 23 12 E
Loma, Colo. 16 39 12N 108 49W
Loma, Mont. 33 47 56N 110 30W
Loma, N. Dak. 41 48 38N 98 32W
Loma Prieta 14 37 6N 121 50W
Lomami → 122 0 46N 24 16 E
Loman 30 48 31N 93 49W
Lomas de Zamóra 76 34 45 S 58 25W
Lomax 21 40 41N 91 4W
Lombard 21 41 53N 88 1W
Lombardia □ 94 45 35N 9 45 E
Lombardy = Lombardia □ 94 45 35N 9 45 E
Lomblen 111 8 30 S 123 32 E
Lombok 110 8 45 S 116 30 E
Lomé 120 6 9N 1 20 E
Lomela 122 2 19 S 23 15 E
Lomela → 122 1 30 S 22 50 E
Lometa 51 31 13N 98 24W
Lomié 122 3 13N 13 38 E

Lomond Lucerne

Lomond 62 50 24N 112 36W
Lomond, L. 84 56 8N 4 38W
Lompobatang 111 5 24S 119 56E
Lompoc 15 34 38N 120 28W
Łomza 89 53 10N 22 2E
Lonaconing 27 39 34N 78 59W
Loncoche 78 39 20S 72 50W
Loncopuè 78 38 4S 70 37W
Londa 108 15 30N 74 30E
London, Canada 60 42 59N 81 15W
London, U.K. 83 51 30N 0 5W
London, Ark. 13 35 20N 93 15W
London, Ky. 49 37 8N 84 5W
London, Ohio 42 39 53N 83 27W
London, Greater □ 83 51 30N 0 5W
London Mills 21 40 43N 90 11W
Londonderry, U.K. 85 55 0N 7 20W
Londonderry, Ohio 42 39 16N 82 48W
Londonderry, Vt. 36 43 14N 72 48W
Londonderry □ 85 55 0N 7 20W
Londonderry, C. 126 13 45S 126 55E
Londonderry, I. 78 55 0S 71 0W
Londontowne 27 38 55N 76 33W
Londrina 77 23 18S 51 10W
Lone Grove 43 34 11N 97 14W
Lone Mountain 49 36 24N 83 35W
Lone Mt. 47 45 23N 103 44W
Lone Oak, Ky. 48 37 2N 88 40W
Lone Oak, Tex. 51 33 0N 95 57W
Lone Pine 15 36 36N 118 4W
Lone Star 51 32 55N 94 43W
Lone Wolf 43 34 59N 99 15W
Lonejack 32 38 52N 94 10W
Lonepine 33 47 42N 114 38W
Lonerock 44 45 5N 119 53W
Long B. 46 33 35N 78 45W
Long Beach, Calif. 15 33 47N 118 11W
Long Beach, Miss. 31 30 21N 89 9W
Long Beach, N.Y. 39 40 35N 73 39W
Long Beach, Wash. 53 46 21N 124 3W
Long Branch 37 40 18N 74 0W
Long Branch L. 32 39 50N 92 30W
Long County ◇ 18 31 45N 81 45W
Long Creek 44 44 43N 119 6W
Long Eaton 82 52 54N 1 16W
Long I., Bahamas 67 23 20N 75 10W
Long I., U.S.A. 39 40 45N 73 30W
Long Island 24 39 57N 99 32W
Long Island Sd. 28 41 10N 73 0W
Long L., Canada 60 49 30N 86 50W
Long L., Mich. 29 45 13N 83 29W
Long L., N. Dak. 41 46 44N 100 6W
Long L., N.Y. 39 44 1N 74 24W
Long L., Wash. 53 47 50N 117 51W
Long L., Maine 26 47 13N 68 15W
Long L., Maine 26 46 43N 69 23W
Long Lake 39 43 58N 74 25W
Long Mt. 32 36 43N 92 31W
Long Pine 34 42 32N 99 42W
Long Pt. 61 48 47N 58 46W
Long Point 21 41 0N 88 54W
Long Pond 28 41 48N 70 56W
Long Prairie 30 45 59N 94 52W
Long Prairie → 30 46 20N 94 36W
Long Pt 30 48 59N 94 59W
Long Range Mts. 61 49 30N 57 30W
Long Ridge 49 38 35N 84 49W
Long Str. 4 70 0N 175 0E
Long Xian 115 34 55N 106 55E
Long Xuyen 112 10 19N 105 28E
Long'an 115 23 10N 107 40E
Longboat Key 17 27 23N 82 39W
Longbranch 53 47 13N 122 46W
Longchuan 115 24 5N 115 17E
Longdale 43 36 8N 98 33W
Longde 114 35 30N 106 20E
Longford, Ireland 85 53 43N 7 50W
Longford, U.S.A. 24 39 10N 97 20W
Longford □ 85 53 42N 7 45W
Longhua 114 41 18N 117 45E
Longiram 110 0 5S 115 45E
Longjiang 114 47 20N 123 12E
Longkou 114 37 40N 120 18E
Longlac 60 49 45N 86 25W
Longlin 115 24 47N 105 20E
Longmeadow 28 42 3N 72 34W
Longmen 115 23 40N 114 18E
Longmont 16 40 10N 105 6W
Longnan 115 24 55N 114 47E
Longnawan 110 1 51N 114 55E
Longone → 121 10 0N 15 40E
Longquan 115 28 7N 119 10E
Longreach 127 23 28S 144 14E
Longridge 27 38 16N 75 37W
Longshan 115 29 29N 109 25E
Longsheng 115 25 48N 110 0E
Longstreet 25 32 6N 93 57W
Longton 24 37 23N 96 5W
Longtown, U.K. 83 51 58N 2 59W
Longtown, U.S.A. 32 37 40N 89 47W
Longview, Canada 62 50 32N 114 10W
Longview, Ill. 21 39 53N 88 4W
Longview, Miss. 31 33 24N 88 55W
Longview, N.C. 40 35 44N 81 23W
Longview, Tex. 51 32 30N 94 44W
Longview, Wash. 53 46 8N 122 57W
Longville, La. 25 30 36N 93 14W
Longville, Minn. 30 46 59N 94 13W
Longwood 17 28 42N 81 21W
Longwoods 27 38 52N 76 5W
Longxi 114 34 53N 104 40E
Longzhou 115 22 22N 106 50E
Lonoke 13 34 47N 91 54W
Lonoke County ◇ 13 34 47N 91 54W
Lonquimay 78 38 26S 71 14W
Lons-le-Saunier 90 46 40N 5 31E
Lonsdale 30 44 29N 93 26W
Loogootee 22 38 41N 86 55W
Lookeba 43 35 22N 98 22W
Looking Glass → 29 42 52N 84 54W
Lookout 14 41 13N 121 9W
Lookout, C., N.C. 40 34 35N 76 32W
Lookout, C., Oreg. 44 45 20N 124 1W
Lookout, C., Canada 60 55 18N 83 56W
Lookout, Pt. 29 44 3N 83 35W
Lookout Mountain 49 34 59N 85 21W
Lookout Mt., Ala. 10 34 20N 85 45W
Lookout Mt., Oreg. 44 45 21N 121 31W
Loomis, Nebr. 34 40 29N 99 31W
Loomis, Wash. 53 48 49N 119 38W
Loon →, Alta., Canada 62 57 8N 115 3W
Loon →, Man., Canada 63 55 53N 101 59W
Loon Lake, Canada 63 54 2N 109 10W
Loon Lake, U.S.A. 53 48 4N 117 38W
Loop Hd. 85 52 34N 9 55W
Loose Creek 32 38 31N 91 57W
Lop Nor = Lop Nur 113 40 20N 90 10E
Lop Nur 113 40 20N 90 10E
Lopatina, G. 101 50 47N 143 10E
Lopez, C. 122 0 47S 8 40E
Lopez Pt. 15 36 1N 121 34W
Lopphavet 96 70 27N 21 15E
Lora → 107 32 0N 67 15E
Lora, Hamun-i- 107 29 38N 64 58E
Lorain 42 41 28N 82 11W
Lorain County ◇ 42 41 14N 82 7W
Loraine, Ill. 21 40 9N 91 13W
Loraine, Tex. 50 32 25N 100 43W
Loralai 108 30 20N 68 41E
Lorca 91 37 41N 1 42W
Lord Howe I. 124 31 33S 159 6E
Lord Howe Ridge 124 30 0S 162 30E
Lordsburg 38 32 21N 108 43W
Lore City 42 39 59N 81 28W
Loreauville 25 30 3N 91 44W
Lorenzo, Idaho 20 43 44N 111 52W
Lorenzo, Tex. 50 33 40N 101 32W
Loreto, Bolivia 73 15 13S 64 40W
Loreto, Brazil 74 7 5S 45 10W
Loreto, Italy 94 43 26N 13 36E
Loreto, Mexico 64 26 1N 111 21W
Loreto □ 70 5 0S 75 0W
Loretta 24 38 39N 99 12W
Loretto 48 35 5N 87 26W
Lorica 70 9 14N 75 49W
Lorient 90 47 45N 3 23W
Lorimor 23 41 8N 94 3W
Loris 46 34 4N 78 53W
Loristān □ 106 33 20N 47 0E
Lorman 31 31 49N 91 3W
Lorn 84 56 26N 5 10W
Lorn, Firth of 84 56 20N 5 40W
Lorraine, France 90 49 0N 6 0E
Lorraine, U.S.A. 24 38 34N 98 19W
Lorrainville 60 47 21N 79 23W
Lorton 34 40 35N 96 1W
Los Alamos, Calif. 15 34 44N 120 17W
Los Alamos, N. Mex. 38 35 53N 106 19W
Los Alamos County ◇ 38 35 55N 106 15W
Los Altos 14 37 23N 122 7W
Los Andes 76 32 50S 70 40W
Los Angeles, Chile 76 37 28S 72 23W
Los Angeles, U.S.A. 15 34 4N 118 15W
Los Angeles Aqueduct 15 35 22N 118 5W
Los Angeles County ◇ 15 34 20N 118 10W
Los Antiguos 78 46 35S 71 40W
Los Banos 14 37 4N 120 51W
Los Blancos 76 23 40S 62 30W
Los Fresnos 50 26 4N 97 29W
Los Gatos 14 37 14N 121 59W
Los Hermanos 71 11 45N 84 25W
Los Lagos 78 39 51S 72 50W
Los Lamentos 64 30 36N 105 50W
Los Lomas 72 4 40S 80 10W
Los Lunas 38 34 48N 106 44W
Los Menucos 78 40 50S 68 10W
Los Mochis 64 25 45N 109 5W
Los Molinos 14 40 1N 122 6W
Los Monos 78 46 1S 69 36W
Los Olivos 15 34 40N 120 7W
Los Padillas 38 34 57N 106 42W
Los Padres National Forest 15 34 40N 119 40W
Los Palacios 66 22 35N 83 15W
Los Pinas → 16 36 56N 107 36W
Los Pinos 38 36 59N 106 3W
Los Reyes 64 19 34N 102 30W
Los Ríos □ 70 1 30S 79 25W
Los Roques 70 11 50N 66 45W
Los Teques 70 10 21N 67 2W
Los Testigos 71 11 23N 63 6W
Los Vilos 76 32 10S 71 30W
Losada → 70 2 12N 73 55W
Losantville 22 40 2N 85 11W
Loshkalakh 101 62 45N 147 20E
Lošinj 94 44 30N 14 30E
Lossiemouth 84 57 43N 3 17W
Lost →, Ind. 22 38 33N 86 49W
Lost →, Oreg. 44 41 56N 121 30W
Lost Chance Cr. → 40 38 32N 110 55W
Lost Creek 54 39 10N 80 21W
Lost Hills 15 35 37N 119 41W
Lost Nation 23 41 58N 90 49W
Lost Peak 52 37 29N 113 55W
Lost River Range 20 44 8N 113 47W
Lost Springs, Kans. 24 38 34N 96 58W
Lost Springs, Wyo. 56 42 46N 104 56W
Lostwood 41 48 29N 102 25W
Lot □ 90 44 39N 1 40E
Lot → 90 44 18N 0 20E
Lot-et-Garonne □ 90 44 22N 0 30E
Lota 76 37 5S 73 10W
Lothair 33 48 28N 111 14W
Lothian □ 84 55 50N 3 0W
Lott 51 31 12N 97 2W
Loubomo 122 4 9S 12 47E
Loudon, N.H. 36 43 16N 71 27W
Loudon, Tenn. 49 35 45N 84 20W
Loudon County ◇ 49 35 45N 84 20W
Loudonville 42 40 38N 82 14W
Loudoun County ◇ 54 39 5N 77 50W
Louga 120 15 45N 16 5W
Loughborough 82 52 46N 1 11W
Loughman 17 28 14N 81 34W
Loughrea 85 53 11N 8 33W
Loughros More B. 85 54 48N 8 30W
Louin 31 32 4N 89 16W
Louis Trichardt 123 23 0S 29 43E
Louis XIV, Pte. 60 54 37N 79 45W
Louisa, Ky. 49 38 7N 82 36W
Louisa, Va. 54 38 1N 78 0W
Louisa County ◇, Iowa 23 41 15N 91 15W
Louisa County ◇, Va. 54 38 1N 78 0W
Louisana □ 25 31 0N 93 0W
Louisbourg 61 45 55N 60 0W
Louisburg, Kans. 24 38 37N 94 41W
Louisburg, Minn. 30 45 10N 96 10W
Louisburg, Mo. 32 37 46N 93 8W
Louisburg, N.C. 40 36 6N 78 18W
Louise, Miss. 31 32 59N 90 35W
Louise, Tex. 51 29 6N 96 24W
Louise I. 62 52 55N 131 50W
Louiseville 60 46 20N 72 56W
Louisiade Arch. 124 11 10S 153 0E
Louisiana 32 39 27N 91 3W
Louisville, Ala. 10 31 47N 85 33W
Louisville, Colo. 16 39 59N 105 8W
Louisville, Ga. 18 33 0N 82 25W
Louisville, Ill. 21 38 46N 88 30W
Louisville, Kans. 24 39 15N 96 18W
Louisville, Ky. 49 38 15N 85 46W
Louisville, Miss. 31 33 7N 89 3W
Louisville, Nebr. 34 41 0N 96 10W
Louisville, Ohio 42 40 50N 81 16W
Loulé 91 37 9N 8 0W
Lount L. 63 50 10N 94 20W
Loup → 34 41 24N 97 19W
Loup City 34 41 17N 98 58W
Loup County ◇ 34 41 50N 99 30W
Lourdes 90 43 6N 0 3W
Lourdes-du-Blanc-Sablon 61 51 24N 57 12W
Lourenço 71 2 30N 51 40W
Lourenço-Marques = Maputo 123 25 58S 32 32E
Louth, Ireland 85 53 47N 6 33W
Louth, U.K. 82 53 23N 0 0E
Louth □ 85 53 55N 6 30W
Louvain = Leuven 87 50 52N 4 42E
Louvale 18 32 10N 84 50W
Louvière, La 87 50 27N 4 10E
Louviers 16 39 28N 105 1W
Love 63 53 29N 104 10W
Love County ◇ 43 34 0N 97 15W
Love Point 27 39 2N 76 19W
Lovech 95 43 8N 24 42E
Lovelady 51 31 8N 95 27W
Loveland, Colo. 16 40 24N 105 5W
Loveland, Ohio 42 39 16N 84 16W
Loveland, Okla. 43 34 18N 98 46W
Loveland Pass 16 39 40N 105 53W
Lovell, Maine 26 44 7N 70 54W
Lovell, Wyo. 56 44 50N 108 24W
Lovelock 35 40 11N 118 28W
Loves Park 21 42 19N 89 3W
Lovett 18 32 38N 82 46W
Loviisa = Lovisa 97 60 28N 26 12E
Lovilia 23 41 8N 92 55W
Loving 38 32 17N 104 6W
Loving County ◇ 50 31 42N 103 36W
Lovingston 54 37 46N 78 52W
Lovington, Ill. 21 39 43N 88 38W
Lovington, N. Mex. 38 32 57N 103 21W
Lovisa 97 60 28N 26 12E
Low Rocky Pt. 127 42 59S 145 29E
Lowa 122 1 25S 25 47E
Lowden 23 41 52N 90 56W
Lowell, Ark. 13 36 15N 94 8W
Lowell, Fla. 17 29 20N 82 12W
Lowell, Ind. 22 41 18N 87 25W
Lowell, Mass. 28 42 38N 71 19W
Lowell, N.C. 40 35 16N 81 6W
Lowell, Oreg. 44 43 55N 122 47W
Lowell, Vt. 36 44 48N 72 27W
Lowell, L. 20 43 35N 116 44W
Lower Arrow L. 62 49 40N 118 5W
Lower Brule 47 44 5N 99 34W
Lower Brule Indian Reservation 47 44 5N 100 0W
Lower Gilmanton 36 43 24N 71 24W
Lower Granite L. 53 46 26N 117 14W
Lower Hutt 128 41 10S 174 55E
Lower Kalskag 11 61 31N 160 22W
Lower Klamath L. 14 41 57N 121 42W
Lower L. 14 41 16N 120 2W
Lower Lake 14 38 55N 122 37W
Lower Marlboro 27 38 39N 76 41W
Lower Monumental Dam 53 46 32N 118 33W
Lower Neguac 61 47 20N 65 10W
Lower New York B. 37 40 33N 74 5W
Lower Paia 19 20 55N 156 23W
Lower Post 62 59 58N 128 30W
Lower Red L. 30 47 58N 95 0W
Lowes 48 36 53N 88 46W
Lowes Crossroads 27 38 34N 75 24W
Lowestoft 83 52 29N 1 44E
Lowgap 40 36 32N 80 52W
Łowicz 89 52 6N 19 55E
Lowland 40 35 18N 76 35W
Lowman 20 44 5N 115 37W
Lowmoor 54 37 47N 79 53W
Lowndes County ◇, Ala. 10 32 11N 86 35W
Lowndes County ◇, Ga. 18 30 50N 83 15W
Lowndes County ◇, Miss. 31 33 30N 88 25W
Lowndesboro 10 32 17N 86 37W
Lowndesville 46 34 13N 82 39W
Lowry, Minn. 30 45 42N 95 31W
Lowry, S. Dak. 47 45 20N 99 59W
Lowry City 32 38 8N 93 44W
Lowrys 46 34 47N 81 14W
Lowville 39 43 47N 75 29W
Lowyar □ 107 34 0N 69 0E
Loxley 10 30 37N 87 45W
Loxton 127 34 28S 140 31E
Loyal, Okla. 43 35 59N 98 6W
Loyal, Wis. 55 44 44N 90 30W
Loyal Valley 51 30 35N 99 0W
Loyall 49 36 51N 83 22W
Loyalton, Calif. 14 39 41N 120 14W
Loyalton, S. Dak. 47 45 17N 99 17W
Loyalty Is. = Loyauté, Is. 124 21 0S 167 30E
Loyang = Luoyang 115 34 40N 112 26E
Loyauté, Is. 124 21 0S 167 30E
Lozère □ 90 44 35N 3 30E
Lua Makiki 19 20 33N 156 37W
Luachimo 122 7 23S 20 48E
Luacono 122 11 15S 21 37E
Lualaba → 122 0 26N 25 20E
Lu'an 115 31 45N 116 29E
Luan Chau 112 21 38N 103 24E
Luan Xian 114 39 40N 118 40E
Luanda 122 8 50S 13 15E
Luang Prabang 112 19 52N 102 10E
Luangwa 123 15 35S 30 16E
Luangwa → 123 14 25S 30 25E
Luanping 114 40 53N 117 23E
Luanshya 123 13 3S 28 28E
Luapula → 122 9 26S 28 33E
Luarca 91 43 32N 6 32W
Luashi 122 10 50S 23 36E
Luau 122 10 40S 22 10E
Lubalo 122 9 10S 19 15E
Lubang Is. 111 13 50N 120 12E
Lubbock 50 33 35N 101 51W
Lubbock County ◇ 50 33 35N 101 50W
Lubec 26 44 52N 66 59W
Lübeck 88 53 52N 10 41E
Lubefu 122 4 47S 24 27E
Lubero = Luofu 122 0 10S 29 15E
Lubicon L. 62 56 23N 115 56W
Lublin, Poland 89 51 12N 22 38E
Lublin, U.S.A. 55 45 5N 90 43W
Lubran 106 34 0N 36 0E
Lubuagan 111 17 21N 121 10E
Lubuk Antu 110 1 3N 111 50E
Lubuklinggau 110 3 15S 102 55E
Lubuksikaping 110 0 10N 100 15E
Lubumbashi 123 11 40S 27 28E
Lubutu 122 0 45S 26 30E
Lucama 40 35 39N 78 0W
Lucapa 122 8 20S 21 45E
Lucas, Kans. 24 39 4N 98 32W
Lucas, Ky. 48 36 53N 86 2W
Lucas, Ohio 42 40 42N 82 25W
Lucas County ◇, Iowa 23 41 0N 93 20W
Lucas County ◇, Ohio 42 41 31N 83 48W
Lucasville 42 38 53N 82 59W
Lucca 94 43 50N 10 30E
Luce Bay 84 54 45N 4 48W
Luce County ◇ 29 46 30N 85 30W
Lucea 66 18 25N 78 10W
Lucedale 31 30 56N 88 35W
Lucena, Phil. 111 13 56N 121 37E
Lucena, Spain 91 37 27N 4 31W
Lučenec 89 48 18N 19 42E
Lucerne = Luzern 88 47 3N 8 18E

Lucerne McGehee

Lucerne 14 39 6N 122 48W
Lucerne L. 15 34 31N 116 58W
Lucerne Valley 15 34 27N 116 57W
Lucero 64 30 49N 106 30W
Lucero, L. 38 32 42N 106 27W
Lucie → 71 13 51 S 12 35 E
Lucile 20 45 32N 116 18W
Lucira 123 14 0 S 12 35 E
Luck 55 45 35N 92 29W
Luckenwalde 88 52 5N 13 11 E
Luckey 42 41 27N 83 29W
Lucknow 109 26 50N 81 0 E
Lüda = Dalian 114 38 50N 121 40 E
Luda Kamchiya → 95 43 3N 27 29 E
Ludden 41 46 1N 98 7W
Ludell 24 39 52N 100 58W
Lüderitz 123 26 41 S 15 8 E
Ludhiana 108 30 57N 75 56 E
Ludington 29 43 57N 86 27W
Ludlow, U.K. 83 52 23N 2 42W
Ludlow, Calif. 15 34 43N 116 10W
Ludlow, Colo. 16 37 20N 104 35W
Ludlow, Ill. 21 40 23N 88 8W
Ludlow, Mass. 28 42 10N 72 29W
Ludlow, Miss. 31 32 34N 89 43W
Ludlow, Mo. 32 39 39N 93 42W
Ludlow, Vt. 36 43 24N 72 42W
Ludowici 18 31 43N 81 45W
Ludus 95 46 29N 24 5 E
Ludvika 97 60 8N 15 14 E
Ludwigsburg 88 48 53N 9 11 E
Ludwigshafen 88 49 27N 8 27 E
Luebo 122 5 21 S 21 23 E
Lueders 51 32 48N 99 37W
Luepa 71 5 43N 61 31W
Lüeyang 115 33 22N 106 10 E
Lufeng 115 22 57N 115 38 E
Lufira → 122 9 30 S 27 0 E
Lufkin 51 31 21N 94 44W
Luga 98 58 40N 29 55 E
Lugang 115 24 4N 120 23 E
Lugano 88 46 0N 8 57 E
Lugansk = Voroshilovgrad 99 48 38N 39 15 E
Lugh Ganana 105 3 48N 42 34 E
Lugnaquilla 85 52 58N 6 28W
Lugo 91 43 2N 7 35W
Lugoff 46 34 13N 80 40W
Lugoj 89 45 42N 21 57 E
Lugovoye 100 42 55N 72 43 E
Luiana 123 17 25 S 22 59 E
Luis 64 26 36N 109 11W
Luís Correia 74 3 0 S 41 35W
Luís Gonçalves 74 5 37 S 50 25W
Luis Lopez 38 33 59N 106 53W
Luitpold Coast 5 78 30 S 32 0W
Luiza 122 7 40 S 22 30 E
Luján 76 34 45 S 59 5W
Lukachukai 12 36 25N 109 15W
Lukanga Swamps 123 14 30 S 27 40 E
Luke 27 39 30N 79 5W
Lukenie → 122 3 0 S 18 50 E
Lukeville 12 31 53N 112 49W
Lŭki 95 41 50N 24 43 E
Lukolela 122 1 10 S 17 12 E
Lukovit 95 43 13N 24 11 E
Łuków 89 51 58N 22 22 E
Lula, Ga. 18 34 23N 83 40W
Lula, Miss. 31 34 27N 90 29W
Lule älv → 96 65 35N 22 10 E
Luleå 96 65 35N 22 10 E
Lüleburgaz 95 41 23N 27 22 E
Luling 51 29 41N 97 39W
Lulong 114 39 53N 118 51 E
Lulonga → 122 1 0N 19 0 E
Lulu 17 30 7N 82 29W
Lulua → 122 6 30 S 22 50 E
Luluabourg = Kananga 122 5 55 S 22 18 E
Lumai 123 13 13 S 21 25 E
Lumajang 111 8 8 S 113 13 E
Lumbala N'guimbo 123 14 18 S 21 18 E
Lumber → 40 34 12N 79 10W
Lumber City 18 31 56N 82 41W
Lumberton, Miss. 31 31 0N 89 27W
Lumberton, N.C. 40 34 37N 79 0W
Lumberton, N. Mex. 38 36 56N 106 56W
Lumby 62 50 10N 118 50W
Lummi Indian Reservation 53 48 52N 122 32W
Lumpkin 18 32 3N 84 48W
Lumpkin County ◇ 18 34 40N 84 0W
Lumsden 128 45 44 S 168 27 E
Lumut 112 4 13N 100 37 E
Luna County ◇ 38 32 15N 107 45W
Lund, Nev. 35 38 52N 115 0W
Lund, Utah 52 38 0N 113 26W
Lundazi 123 12 20 S 33 7 E
Lundu 110 1 40N 109 50 E
Lundy 83 51 10N 4 41W
Lune → 82 54 0N 2 51W
Lüneburg 88 53 15N 10 23 E
Lüneburg Heath = Lüneburger Heide 88 53 0N 10 0 E
Lüneburger Heide 88 53 0N 10 0 E
Lunenburg, Canada 61 44 22N 64 18W
Lunenburg, Va. 54 36 58N 78 16W
Lunenburg, Vt. 36 44 26N 71 42W
Lunenburg County ◇ 54 36 58N 78 16W
Lunéville 90 48 36N 6 30 E
Lunglei 109 22 55N 92 45 E
Luni 108 26 0N 73 6 E
Lūni → 108 24 41N 71 14 E
Luning 35 38 30N 118 11W
Luo He → 115 34 35N 110 20 E
Luobei 114 47 35N 130 50 E
Luocheng 115 24 48N 108 53 E
Luochuan 114 35 45N 109 26 E
Luoding 115 22 45N 111 40 E
Luodong 115 24 41N 121 46 E
Luofu 122 0 10 S 29 15 E
Luoning 115 34 35N 111 40 E
Luoyang 115 34 40N 112 26 E
Luoyuan 115 26 28N 119 30 E
Luozi 122 4 54 S 14 0 E
Lupeni 95 45 21N 23 13 E
Łupków 89 49 15N 22 4 E
Lupton 12 35 21N 109 4W
Lupus 32 38 51N 92 27W
Luqa 94 35 48N 14 27 E
Luque 76 25 19 S 57 25W
Luquillo 57 18 23N 65 43W
Luquillo, Sierra de 57 18 20N 65 47W
Luray, Kans. 24 39 7N 98 41W
Luray, Mo. 32 40 27N 91 53W
Luray, S.C. 46 32 49N 81 14W
Luray, Va. 54 38 40N 78 28W
Luremo 122 8 30 S 17 50 E
Lurgan 85 54 28N 6 20W
Luribay 72 17 6 S 67 39W
Lurin 72 12 17 S 76 52W
Lusaka 123 15 28 S 28 16 E
Lusambo 122 4 58 S 23 28 E
Lusby 27 38 22N 76 26W
Luseland 63 52 5N 109 24W
Lushan 115 33 45N 112 55 E
Lushih 115 34 3N 111 3 E
Lushoto 122 4 47 S 38 20 E
Lushton 34 40 43N 97 44W
Lüshun 114 38 45N 121 15 E
Lusk 56 42 46N 104 27W
Lussanvira 75 20 42 S 51 7W
Luta = Lüda 114 38 50N 121 40 E
Lutcher 25 30 2N 90 42W
Lutesville 32 37 18N 89 59W
Luther, Iowa 23 41 58N 93 49W
Luther, Mich. 29 44 2N 85 41W
Luther, Okla. 43 35 40N 97 12W
Luthersville 18 33 13N 84 45W
Lutherville-Timonium 27 39 25N 76 38W
Lutie 50 35 1N 100 13W
Luton 83 51 53N 0 24W
Lutong 110 4 30N 114 0 E
Lutsen 30 47 39N 90 41W
Lutsk 98 50 50N 25 15 E
Luttrell 49 36 12N 83 45W
Lutts 48 35 9N 87 56W
Lutz 17 28 9N 82 28W
Lützow Holmbukta 5 69 10 S 37 30 E
Luverne, Ala. 10 31 43N 86 16W
Luverne, Iowa 23 42 55N 94 5W
Luverne, Minn. 30 43 39N 96 13W
Luverne, N. Dak. 41 47 16N 97 55W
Luwuk 111 0 56 S 122 47 E
Luxembourg 87 49 37N 6 9 E
Luxembourg □ 87 49 58N 5 30 E
Luxembourg ■ 87 50 0N 6 0 E
Luxemburg, Iowa 23 42 36N 91 5W
Luxemburg, Wis. 55 44 33N 87 42W
Luxi 115 28 20N 110 7 E
Luxor = El Uqsur 121 25 41N 32 38 E
Luxora 13 35 45N 89 56W
Luza 98 60 39N 47 10 E
Luzern 88 47 3N 8 18 E
Luzerne County ◇ 45 41 10N 76 0W
Luzhai 115 24 29N 109 42 E
Luzhou 115 28 52N 105 20 E
Luziânia 75 16 20 S 48 0W
Luzilândia 74 3 28 S 42 22W
Luzon 111 16 0N 121 0 E
Lvov 99 49 50N 24 0 E
Lyakhovskiye, Ostrova 101 73 40N 141 0 E
Lyallpur = Faisalabad 108 31 30N 73 5 E
Lyaskovets 95 43 6N 25 44 E
Lycan 16 37 37N 102 12W
Lycksele 96 64 38N 18 40 E
Lycoming County ◇ 45 41 20N 77 0W
Lydda = Lod 104 31 57N 34 54 E
Lydenburg 123 25 10 S 30 29 E
Lydia 46 34 17N 80 7W
Lyell 128 41 48 S 172 4 E
Lyell I. 62 52 40N 131 35W
Lyell Range 128 41 38 S 172 20 E
Lyerly 18 34 24N 85 24W
Lyford 50 26 25N 97 48W
Lykens 45 40 34N 76 42W
Lyle 30 43 30N 92 57W
Lyles 48 35 55N 87 21W
Lyman, Miss. 31 30 30N 89 7W
Lyman, Nebr. 34 41 55N 104 2W
Lyman, Wash. 53 48 32N 122 4W
Lyman, Wyo. 56 41 20N 110 18W
Lyman County ◇ 47 44 0N 100 0W
Lyman L. 12 34 22N 109 23W
Lyme 36 43 48N 72 12W
Lyme Regis 83 50 44N 2 57W
Lymington 83 50 46N 1 32W
Lyna → 89 54 17N 21 0 E
Lynch, Ky. 49 36 58N 82 54W
Lynch, Nebr. 34 42 50N 98 28W
Lynch Station 54 37 9N 79 18W
Lynchburg, Ohio 42 39 15N 83 48W
Lynchburg, S.C. 46 34 3N 80 4W
Lynchburg, Tenn. 48 35 17N 86 22W
Lynchburg, Va. 54 37 25N 79 9W
Lynches → 46 33 50N 79 22W
Lynd 30 44 23N 95 54W
Lynden 53 48 57N 122 27W
Lyndon, Ill. 21 41 43N 89 56W
Lyndon, Kans. 24 38 37N 95 41W
Lyndon B. Johnson, L. 51 30 33N 98 20W
Lyndon Station 55 43 43N 89 54W
Lyndonville, N.Y. 39 43 20N 78 23W
Lyndonville, Vt. 36 44 31N 72 1W
Lynn, Ala. 10 34 3N 87 33W
Lynn, Ind. 22 40 3N 84 56W
Lynn, Mass. 28 42 28N 70 57W
Lynn, Utah 52 41 53N 113 45W
Lynn Canal 11 58 50N 135 15W
Lynn County ◇ 50 33 10N 101 48W
Lynn Garden 49 36 35N 82 34W
Lynn Haven 17 30 15N 85 39W
Lynn Lake 63 56 51N 101 3W
Lynndyl 52 39 31N 112 22W
Lynne 17 29 12N 81 55W
Lynnville, Ky. 48 36 34N 88 34W
Lynnville, Tenn. 48 35 23N 87 0W
Lynnwood 53 47 49N 122 19W
Lynton 83 51 14N 3 50W
Lynx L. 63 62 25N 106 15W
Lynxville 55 43 15N 91 2W
Lyon, France 90 45 46N 4 50 E
Lyon, U.S.A. 31 34 13N 90 33W
Lyon County ◇, Iowa 23 43 20N 96 10W
Lyon County ◇, Kans. 24 38 30N 96 10W
Lyon County ◇, Ky. 48 37 0N 88 5W
Lyon County ◇, Minn. 30 44 25N 95 50W
Lyon County ◇, Nev. 35 38 45N 119 10W
Lyon Mountain 39 44 43N 73 55W
Lyonnais 90 45 45N 4 15 E
Lyons = Lyon 90 45 46N 4 50 E
Lyons, Colo. 16 40 14N 105 16W
Lyons, Ga. 18 32 12N 82 19W
Lyons, Ind. 22 38 59N 87 5W
Lyons, Kans. 24 38 21N 98 12W
Lyons, N.Y. 39 43 5N 77 0W
Lyons, Nebr. 34 41 56N 96 28W
Lyons, Ohio 42 41 42N 84 4W
Lyons, Oreg. 44 44 47N 122 37W
Lyons, Tex. 51 30 23N 96 34W
Lyons Falls 39 43 37N 75 22W
Lysva 98 58 7N 57 49 E
Lytle 51 29 14N 98 48W
Lyttelton 128 43 35 S 172 44 E
Lytton, Canada 62 50 13N 121 31W
Lytton, U.S.A. 23 42 25N 94 51W
Lyubimets 95 41 50N 26 5 E

M

Mā'ad 104 32 37N 35 36 E
Ma'alah 106 26 31N 47 20 E
Ma'ān 106 30 12N 35 44 E
Ma'anshan 115 31 44N 118 29 E
Maarianhamina 97 60 5N 19 55 E
Ma'arrat un Nu'man 106 35 38N 36 40 E
Maas → 87 51 45N 4 32 E
Maaseik 87 51 6N 5 45 E
Maassluis 87 51 56N 4 16 E
Maastricht 87 50 50N 5 40 E
Mabank 51 32 22N 96 6W
Mabaruma 71 8 10N 59 50W
Mabel 30 43 32N 91 46W
Mabel L. 62 50 35N 118 43W
Maben 54 37 38N 81 23W
Mablethorpe 82 53 21N 0 14 E
Mableton 18 33 49N 84 35W
Mabrouk 120 19 29N 1 15W
Mabton 53 46 13N 120 0W
Mac Nutt 63 51 5N 101 36W
Macachín 76 37 10 S 63 43W
McAdoo 45 40 55N 75 59W
Macaé 75 22 20 S 41 43W
Macaíba 74 5 51 S 35 21W
Macajuba 75 12 9 S 40 22W
McAlester 43 34 56N 95 46W
McAlister 38 34 42N 103 47W
McAllen 50 26 12N 98 14W
McAlpin 17 30 8N 82 57W
Macamic 60 48 45N 79 0W
Macao = Macau ■ 115 22 16N 113 35 E
Macapá 71 0 5N 51 4W
Macará 70 4 23 S 79 57W
Macarani 75 15 33 S 40 24W
Macarena, Serranía de la 70 2 45N 73 55W
McArthur, Calif. 14 41 3N 121 24W
McArthur, Ohio 42 39 15N 82 29W
McArthur → 127 15 54 S 136 40 E
McArthur River 127 16 27 S 136 7 E
Macas 70 2 19 S 78 7W
Macate 72 8 48 S 78 7W
Macau 74 5 0 S 36 40W
Macau ■ 115 22 16N 113 35 E
Macaúbas 75 13 2 S 42 42W
Macaya → 70 0 59N 72 20W
McBain 29 44 12N 85 13W
McBee 46 34 28N 80 15W
McBride, Canada 62 53 20N 120 19W
McBride, Mo. 32 37 50N 89 50W
McBride, Okla. 43 33 54N 96 36W
McBrides 29 43 21N 85 2W
McCall 20 44 55N 116 6W
McCallsburg 23 42 10N 93 23W
McCamey 50 31 8N 102 14W
McCammon 20 42 39N 112 12W
McCarthy 11 61 26N 142 56W
McCartys 38 35 4N 107 41W
McCauley I. 62 53 40N 130 15W
McCaysville 18 34 59N 84 23W
McClain County ◇ 43 35 0N 97 30W
McClave 16 38 8N 102 51W
McCleary 53 47 3N 123 16W
McClelland 23 41 20N 95 41W
McClellanville 46 33 5N 79 28W
Macclenny 17 30 17N 82 7W
Macclesfield, U.K. 82 53 16N 2 9W
Macclesfield, U.S.A. 40 35 45N 77 40W
McClintock 63 57 50N 94 10W
McCloud 14 41 15N 122 8W
McClure, Ohio 42 41 22N 83 57W
McClure, Pa. 45 40 42N 77 19W
McClure, L. 14 37 35N 120 16W
McClure Str. 4 75 0N 119 0W
McClusky 41 47 29N 100 27W
McColl 46 34 40N 79 33W
McComb, Miss. 31 31 15N 90 27W
McComb, Ohio 42 41 7N 83 48W
McConaughy, L. 34 41 14N 101 40W
McCone County ◇ 33 47 40N 105 50W
McConnells 46 34 52N 81 14W
McConnellsburg 45 39 56N 77 59W
McConnelsville 42 39 39N 81 51W
McCook 34 40 12N 100 38W
McCook County ◇ 47 43 44N 97 23W
McCool 31 33 12N 89 21W
McCool Junction 34 40 45N 97 36W
McCormick 46 33 55N 82 17W
McCormick County ◇ 46 33 50N 82 15W
McCoy 16 39 55N 106 44W
McCracken 24 38 36N 99 33W
McCracken County ◇ 48 37 5N 88 45W
McCreary County ◇ 49 37 45N 84 30W
McCrory 13 35 16N 91 12W
McCulloch County ◇ 51 31 9N 99 20W
McCune 24 37 21N 95 1W
McCurtain 43 35 9N 94 58W
McCurtain County ◇ 43 34 10N 94 45W
McCusker → 63 55 32N 108 39W
McDade 51 30 17N 97 14W
McDame 62 59 44N 128 59W
McDavid 17 30 52N 87 19W
McDermitt 35 41 59N 117 43W
Macdoel 14 41 50N 122 0W
McDonald, Kans. 24 39 47N 101 22W
McDonald, N. Mex. 38 33 9N 103 19W
McDonald, L. 33 48 35N 113 56W
McDonald County ◇ 32 36 40N 94 20W
McDonald Is. 3 54 0 S 73 0 E
Macdonald L. 126 23 30 S 129 0 E
Macdonnell Ranges 126 23 40 S 133 0 E
McDonough 18 33 27N 84 9W
McDonough County ◇ 21 40 30N 90 40W
McDougal 13 36 26N 90 23W
McDougall, Mt. 56 42 54N 110 36W
Macdougall L. 58 66 0N 98 27W
McDowell 54 38 20N 79 29W
McDowell County ◇, N.C. 40 35 40N 82 0W
McDowell County ◇, W. Va. 54 37 22N 81 33W
MacDowell L. 60 52 15N 92 45W
Macduff 84 57 40N 2 30W
McDuffie County ◇ 18 33 20N 82 25W
Macedo de Cavaleiros 122 11 25 S 16 45 E
Macedonia = Makedhonía □ 95 40 39N 22 0 E
Macedonia = Makedonija □ 95 41 53N 21 40 E
Macedonia, Ill. 21 38 3N 88 42W
Macedonia, Iowa 23 41 12N 95 25W
Macedonia, Ohio 42 41 19N 81 31W
Maceió 74 9 40 S 35 41W
Macenta 120 8 35N 9 32W
Maceo 48 37 51N 87 0W
Macerata 94 43 19N 13 28 E
McEwen 48 36 7N 87 38W
McFadden 56 41 39N 106 8W
McFaddin 51 28 33N 97 1W
McFall 32 40 7N 94 13W
McFarland, Calif. 15 35 41N 119 14W
McFarland, Kans. 24 39 3N 96 14W
McFarland, Wis. 55 43 1N 89 17W
McFarlane → 63 59 12N 107 58W
Macfarlane, L. 127 32 0 S 136 40 E
McGee Creek Res. 43 34 22N 95 38W
McGehee 13 33 38N 91 24W

McGill Majari

McGill 35 39 23N 114 47W
Macgillycuddy's Reeks 85 52 2N 9 45W
McGrath 11 62 58N 155 36W
McGraw 39 42 36N 76 8W
MacGregor 63 49 57N 98 48W
McGregor, Iowa 23 43 1N 91 11W
McGregor, N. Dak. 41 48 36N 102 56W
McGregor, Tex. 51 31 27N 97 24W
McGregor → 62 55 10N 122 0W
McGrew 34 41 45N 103 25W
McGuffey 42 40 42N 83 47W
Mach 107 29 50N 67 20 E
Machacalis 75 17 5 S 40 45W
Machado = Jiparanā → 73 8 3 S 62 52W
Machagai 76 26 56 S 60 2W
Machakos 122 1 30 S 37 15 E
Machala 70 3 20 S 79 57W
Machattie, L. 127 24 50 S 139 48 E
Macheng 115 31 12N 115 2 E
McHenry, Ill. 21 42 21N 88 16W
McHenry, Md. 27 39 36N 79 22W
McHenry, Miss. 31 30 43N 89 8W
McHenry, N. Dak. 41 47 35N 98 35W
McHenry County ◇, Ill. 21 42 20N 88 25W
McHenry County ◇, N. Dak. 41 48 20N 100 45W
Machevna 101 61 20N 172 20 E
Machias 26 44 43N 67 28W
Machias → 26 44 43N 67 22W
Machichi → 63 57 3N 92 6W
Machilipatnam 109 16 12N 81 8 E
Machiques 70 10 4N 72 34W
Machupicchu 72 13 8 S 72 30W
Machynlleth 83 52 36N 3 51W
McIlwraith Ra. 127 13 50 S 143 20 E
Măcin 95 45 16N 28 8 E
McIntire 23 43 26N 92 36W
McIntosh, Ala. 10 31 16N 88 2W
McIntosh, Minn. 30 47 38N 95 53W
McIntosh, N. Mex. 38 34 52N 106 3W
McIntosh, S. Dak. 47 45 55N 101 21W
McIntosh County ◇, Ga. 18 31 30N 81 25W
McIntosh County ◇, N. Dak. 41 46 2N 99 20W
McIntosh County ◇, Okla. 43 35 20N 95 40W
McIntosh L. 63 55 45N 105 0W
Macintyre → 127 28 37 S 150 47 E
Mack 16 39 13N 108 52W
Mackay, Australia 127 21 8 S 149 11 E
Mackay, U.S.A. 20 43 55N 113 37W
Mackay → 62 57 10N 111 38W
Mackay, L. 126 22 30 S 129 0 E
McKean County ◇ 45 41 50N 78 45W
McKee 49 37 25N 84 0W
McKee City 37 39 26N 74 37W
McKee Cr. → 21 39 46N 90 36W
McKeesport 45 40 21N 79 52W
McKenney 54 36 59N 77 43W
Mackenzie, Canada 62 55 20N 123 5W
Mackenzie, Guyana 71 6 0N 58 17W
McKenzie, Ala. 10 31 33N 86 43W
McKenzie, N. Dak. 41 46 50N 100 25W
McKenzie, Tenn. 48 36 8N 88 31W
Mackenzie →, Australia 127 23 38 S 149 46 E
Mackenzie →, Canada 58 69 10N 134 20W
McKenzie → 44 44 7N 123 6W
McKenzie Bridge 44 44 11N 122 10W
Mackenzie City = Linden 72 6 0N 58 10W
McKenzie County ◇ 41 47 55N 103 30W
Mackenzie Highway 62 58 0N 117 15W
Mackenzie Mts. 58 64 0N 130 0W
Mackeys 40 35 56N 76 37W
McKibben 50 36 8N 101 20W
Mackinac, Straits of 29 45 50N 84 40W
Mackinac County ◇ 29 46 5N 85 0W
Mackinac Island 29 45 51N 84 37W
Mackinaw 21 40 32N 89 21W
Mackinaw → 21 40 33N 89 44W
Mackinaw City 29 45 47N 84 44W
McKinley, Mt. 11 63 4N 151 0W
McKinley County ◇ 38 35 30N 108 0W
McKinley Park 11 63 44N 148 55W
McKinley Sea 4 84 0N 10 0W
McKinleyville 14 40 57N 124 6W
McKinney 51 33 12N 96 37W
McKinney Mt. 50 29 50N 103 47W
McKinnon 18 31 25N 81 56W
McKittrick 32 38 44N 91 27W
Macksburg 23 41 13N 94 11W
Macksville 24 37 58N 98 58W
McLain 31 31 7N 88 50W
McLaughlin 47 45 49N 100 49W
McLaurin 31 31 10N 89 13W
Maclean 127 29 26 S 153 16 E
McLean, Ill. 21 40 19N 89 10W
McLean, Nebr. 34 42 23N 97 28W
McLean, Tex. 50 35 14N 100 36W
McLean County ◇, Ill. 21 40 30N 88 50W
McLean County ◇, Ky. 48 37 30N 87 15W
McLean County ◇, N. Dak. 41 47 30N 101 0W
McLeansboro 21 38 6N 88 32W
Maclear 123 31 2 S 28 23 E
Macleay → 127 30 56 S 153 0 E
McLennan 62 55 42N 116 50W
McLennan County ◇ 51 31 33N 97 9W
McLeod 41 46 24N 97 18W
MacLeod, B. 63 62 53N 110 0W
McLeod County ◇ 30 44 50N 94 15W
McLeod L. 128 24 9 S 113 47 E
MacLeod Lake 62 54 58N 123 0W
M'Clintock Chan. 58 72 0N 102 0W
McLoud 43 35 26N 97 6W
McLoughlin, Mt. 44 42 27N 122 19W
McLouth 24 39 12N 95 13W
McLure 62 51 2N 120 13W
McMillan, L. 38 32 36N 104 21W
McMinn County ◇ 49 35 27N 84 36W
McMinnville, Oreg. 44 45 13N 123 12W
McMinnville, Tenn. 49 35 41N 85 46W
McMorran 63 51 19N 108 42W
McMullen County ◇ 51 28 28N 98 33W
McMurdo Sd. 5 77 0 S 170 0 E
McMurray = Fort McMurray 62 56 44N 111 7W
McMurray 53 48 19N 122 14W
McNab 13 33 40N 93 50W
McNairy County ◇ 48 35 10N 88 36W
McNary, Ariz. 12 34 4N 109 51W
McNary, Tex. 50 31 15N 105 48W
*McNaughton L. 62 52 0N 118 10W
McNeal 12 31 36N 109 40W
McNeil 13 33 21N 93 13W
McNeill 31 30 40N 89 38W
Macomb, Ill. 21 40 27N 90 40W
Macomb, Okla. 43 35 10N 97 0W
Macomb County ◇ 29 42 40N 83 0W
Mâcon, France 90 46 19N 4 50 E
Macon, Ga. 18 32 51N 83 38W
Macon, Ill. 21 39 43N 89 0W
Macon, Miss. 31 33 7N 88 34W
Macon, Mo. 32 39 44N 92 28W
Macon, Nebr. 34 40 13N 98 55W
Macon County ◇, Ala. 10 32 25N 85 42W
Macon County ◇, Ga. 18 32 20N 84 0W
Macon County ◇, Ill. 21 39 50N 89 0W
Macon County ◇, Mo. 32 39 50N 92 30W
Macon County ◇, N.C. 40 35 15N 83 30W
Macon County ◇, Tenn. 48 36 31N 86 2W
Macondo 123 12 37 S 23 46 E
Macoun L. 63 56 32N 103 40W
Macoupin County ◇ 21 39 20N 89 55W
McPherson 24 38 22N 97 40W
McPherson County ◇, Kans. 24 38 20N 97 40W
McPherson County ◇, Nebr. 34 41 30N 101 0W
McPherson County ◇, S. Dak. 47 45 46N 99 0W
McQuady 48 37 42N 86 31W
Macquarie → 127 30 5 S 147 30 E
Macquarie Harbour 127 42 15 S 145 23 E
Macquarie Is. 124 54 36 S 158 55 E
McRae, Ark. 13 35 7N 91 49W
McRae, Ga. 18 32 4N 82 54W
McRoberts 49 37 12N 82 40W
MacRobertson Land 5 71 0 S 64 0 E
Macroom 85 51 54N 8 57W
Macujer 70 0 24N 73 10W
Macusani 72 14 4 S 70 29W
Macuspana 65 17 46N 92 36W
Mácuzari, Presa 64 27 10N 109 10W
McVeigh 49 37 32N 82 15W
McVeytown 45 40 30N 77 45W
McVille 41 47 46N 98 11W
Macwahoc 26 45 38N 68 16W
Macy 34 42 7N 96 21W
Mad →, Calif. 14 40 57N 124 7W
Mad →, Ohio 42 39 46N 84 12W
Mad →, Vt. 36 44 18N 72 41W
Madagali 121 10 56N 13 33 E
Madagascar ■ 123 20 0 S 47 0 E
Madā'in Sālih 106 26 46N 37 57 E
Madama 121 22 0N 13 40 E
Madame I. 61 45 30N 60 58W
Madan 95 41 30N 24 57 E
Madang 124 5 12 S 145 49 E
Madaoua 120 14 5N 6 27 E
Madaripur 109 23 19N 90 15 E
Madauk 109 17 56N 96 52 E
Madawaska 26 47 21N 68 20W
Madawaska → 60 45 27N 76 21W
Madaya 109 22 12N 96 10 E
Maddalena 94 41 15N 9 23 E
Madden Dam 57 9 13N 79 37W
Madden L. 57 9 15N 79 35W
Maddock 41 47 58N 99 32W
Maddox 27 38 20N 76 48W
Madeira 120 32 50N 17 0W
Madeira → 71 3 22 S 58 45W
Madeira Beach 17 27 48N 82 48W
Madeleine, Îs. de la 61 47 30N 61 40W
Madelia 30 44 3N 94 25W
Madeline 14 41 3N 120 28W
Madeline I. 55 46 49N 90 42W
Madera 15 36 57N 120 3W
Madera County ◇ 14 37 15N 119 35W
Madha 108 18 0N 75 30 E
Madhya Pradesh □ 108 21 50N 81 0 E
Madidi → 72 12 32 S 66 52W
Madikeri 108 12 30N 75 45 E
Madill 43 34 6N 96 46W
Madimba 122 5 0 S 15 0 E
Madīnat ash Sha'b 105 12 50N 45 0 E
Madingou 122 4 10 S 13 33 E
Madison, Ala. 10 34 42N 86 45W
Madison, Ark. 13 35 1N 90 43W
Madison, Fla. 17 30 28N 83 25W
Madison, Ga. 18 33 36N 83 28W
Madison, Ind. 22 38 44N 85 23W
Madison, Kans. 24 38 8N 96 8W
Madison, Maine 26 44 48N 69 53W
Madison, Md. 27 38 30N 76 13W
Madison, Minn. 30 45 1N 96 11W
Madison, Miss. 31 32 28N 90 7W
Madison, Mo. 32 39 28N 92 13W
Madison, N.C. 40 36 23N 79 58W
Madison, N.J. 37 40 46N 74 25W
Madison, Nebr. 34 41 50N 97 27W
Madison, Ohio 42 41 46N 81 3W
Madison, S. Dak. 47 44 0N 97 7W
Madison, Tenn. 48 36 16N 86 42W
Madison, Va. 54 38 23N 78 15W
Madison, W. Va. 54 38 4N 81 49W
Madison, Wis. 55 43 4N 89 24W
Madison → 33 45 56N 111 31W
Madison County ◇, Ala. 10 34 44N 86 35W
Madison County ◇, Ark. 13 36 5N 93 44W
Madison County ◇, Fla. 17 30 30N 83 30W
Madison County ◇, Ga. 18 34 10N 83 10W
Madison County ◇, Idaho 20 43 55N 111 50W
Madison County ◇, Ill. 21 38 50N 89 55W
Madison County ◇, Ind. 22 40 10N 85 45W
Madison County ◇, Iowa 23 41 20N 94 0W
Madison County ◇, Ky. 49 37 40N 84 20W
Madison County ◇, Miss. 31 32 37N 90 2W
Madison County ◇, Mo. 32 37 30N 90 20W
Madison County ◇, Mont. 33 45 12N 112 0W
Madison County ◇, N.C. 40 35 50N 82 50W
Madison County ◇, N.Y. 39 43 0N 75 45W
Madison County ◇, Nebr. 34 41 50N 97 30W
Madison County ◇, Ohio 42 39 53N 83 27W
Madison County ◇, Tenn. 48 35 37N 88 49W
Madison County ◇, Tex. 51 31 0N 96 0W
Madison County ◇, Va. 54 38 23N 78 15W
Madison Heights 54 37 25N 79 8W
Madison Lake 30 44 12N 93 49W
Madison Mills 42 39 39N 83 20W
Madison Parish ◇ 25 32 25N 91 11W
Madisonville, Ky. 48 37 20N 87 30W
Madisonville, La. 25 30 24N 90 10W
Madisonville, Tenn. 49 35 31N 84 22W
Madisonville, Tex. 51 30 57N 95 55W
Madiun 111 7 38 S 111 32 E
Madley 83 52 3N 2 51W
Madras = Tamil Nadu □ 108 11 0N 77 0 E
Madras, India 108 13 8N 80 19 E
Madras, U.S.A. 44 44 38N 121 8W
Madre, Laguna, Mexico 65 25 0N 97 30W
Madre, Laguna, U.S.A. 50 27 0N 97 30W
Madre, Sierra, Mexico 65 16 0N 93 0W
Madre, Sierra, Phil. 111 17 0N 122 0 E
Madre de Dios □ 72 12 0 S 70 15W
Madre de Dios → 72 10 59 S 66 8W
Madre de Dios, I. 78 50 20 S 75 10W
Madre del Sur, Sierra 65 17 30N 100 0W
Madre Occidental, Sierra 64 27 0N 107 0W
Madre Oriental, Sierra 64 25 0N 100 0W
Madrid, Spain 91 40 25N 3 45W
Madrid, Ala. 10 31 2N 85 24W
Madrid, Iowa 23 41 53N 93 49W
Madrid, N. Mex. 38 35 24N 106 9W
Madrid, N.Y. 39 44 45N 75 8W
Madrid, Nebr. 34 40 51N 101 33W
Madura, Selat 111 7 30 S 113 20 E
Madurai 108 9 55N 78 10 E
Madurantakam 108 12 30N 79 50 E
Mae Hong Son 112 19 16N 98 1 E
Mae Sot 112 16 43N 98 34 E
Maebashi 117 36 24N 139 4 E
Măeruş 95 45 53N 25 31 E
Maeser 52 40 28N 109 35W
Maesteg 83 51 36N 3 40W
Maestra, Sierra 66 20 15N 77 0W
Maestrazgo, Mts. del 91 40 30N 0 25W
Maevatanana 123 16 56N 46 49 E
Maeystown 21 38 13N 90 14W
Mafeking 63 52 40N 101 10W
Mafia 122 7 45 S 39 50 E
Mafikeng 123 25 50 S 25 38 E
Mafra, Brazil 77 26 10 S 50 0W
Mafra, Portugal 91 38 55N 9 20W
Magadan 101 59 38N 150 50 E
Magadi 122 1 54 S 36 19 E
Magallanes □ 78 52 0 S 72 0W
Magallanes, Estrecho de 78 52 30 S 75 0W
Magangué 70 9 14N 74 45W
Magazine 13 35 9N 93 48W
Magazine Mt. 13 35 10N 93 41W
Magburaka 120 8 47N 12 0W
Magdalena, Argentina 76 35 5 S 57 30W
Magdalena, Bolivia 73 13 13 S 63 57W
Magdalena, Malaysia 110 4 25N 117 55 E
Magdalena, Mexico 64 30 50N 112 0W
Magdalena, U.S.A. 38 34 7N 107 15W
Magdalena □ 70 10 0N 74 0W
Magdalena →, Colombia 70 11 6N 74 51W
Magdalena →, Mexico 64 30 40N 112 25W
Magdalena, B. 64 24 30N 112 10W
Magdalena, I., Chile 78 44 40 S 73 0W
Magdalena, I., Mexico 64 24 40N 112 15W
Magdalena, Llano de la 64 25 0N 111 30W
Magdalena Mts. 38 33 45N 107 15W
Magdeburg 88 52 8N 11 36 E
Magdi'el 104 32 10N 34 54 E
Magee 31 31 52N 89 44W
Magee, I. 85 54 48N 5 44W
Magelang 111 7 29 S 110 13 E
Magellan's Str. = Magallanes, Estrecho de 78 52 30 S 75 0W
Maggiore, L. 94 46 0N 8 35 E
Maghār 104 32 54N 35 24 E
Magherafelt 85 54 44N 6 37W
Magic Reservoir 20 43 15N 114 22W
Magna 52 40 42N 112 6W
Magnet 34 42 27N 97 28W
Magnetic Pole (North) 4 76 12N 100 12W
Magnetic Pole (South) 5 68 48 S 139 30 E
Magnitogorsk 98 53 27N 59 4 E
Magnolia, Ark. 13 33 16N 93 14W
Magnolia, Del. 27 39 4N 75 29W
Magnolia, Iowa 23 41 42N 95 52W
Magnolia, Ky. 49 37 27N 85 45W
Magnolia, Miss. 31 31 9N 90 28W
Magnolia, Ohio 42 40 39N 81 18W
Magnolia, Tex. 51 30 13N 95 45W
Magoffin County ◇ 49 37 45N 83 5W
Magog 61 45 18N 72 9W
Magosa = Famagusta 106 35 8N 33 55 E
Magpie L. 61 51 0N 64 41W
Magrath 62 49 25N 112 50W
Maguarinho, C. 74 0 15 S 48 30W
Maguse L. 63 61 40N 95 10W
Maguse Pt. 63 61 20N 93 50W
Magwe 109 20 10N 95 0 E
Mahābād 106 36 50N 45 45 E
Mahabo 123 20 23 S 44 40 E
Mahaffey 45 40 53N 78 44W
Mahagi 122 2 20N 31 0 E
Mahaicony 71 6 36N 57 48W
Mahajamba, Helodranon' i 123 15 24 S 47 5 E
Mahakam → 110 0 35 S 117 17 E
Mahalapye 123 23 1 S 26 51 E
Maḩallāt 107 33 55N 50 30 E
Mahanadi → 109 20 20N 86 25 E
Mahanoro 123 19 54 S 48 48 E
Mahanoy City 45 40 49N 76 9W
Maharashtra □ 108 20 30N 75 30 E
Mahaska 24 39 59N 97 20W
Mahaska County ◇ 23 41 20N 92 40W
Mahbubnagar 108 16 45N 77 59 E
Mahdia, Guyana 71 5 13N 59 8W
Mahdia, Tunisia 121 35 28N 11 0 E
Mahenge 122 8 45 S 36 41 E
Maheno 128 45 10 S 170 50 E
Mahesana 108 23 39N 72 26 E
Mahia Pen. 128 39 9 S 177 55 E
Mahmudia 95 45 5N 29 5 E
Mahnomen 30 47 19N 95 58W
Mahnomen County ◇ 30 47 20N 95 45W
Mahomet 21 40 12N 88 24W
Mahón 91 39 53N 4 16 E
Mahone Bay 61 44 30N 64 20W
Mahoning County ◇ 42 41 6N 80 48W
Mahtowa 30 46 34N 92 38W
Mai-Ndombe, L. 122 2 0 S 18 20 E
Maicao 70 11 23N 72 13W
Maici → 73 6 30 S 61 43W
Maicurú → 71 2 14 S 54 17W
Maiden 40 35 35N 81 13W
Maiden Rock 55 44 34N 92 18W
Maidenhead 83 51 31N 0 42W
Maidstone, Canada 63 53 5N 109 20W
Maidstone, U.K. 83 51 16N 0 31 E
Maiduguri 121 12 0N 13 20 E
Maigualida, Sierra 71 5 30N 65 10W
Maijdi 109 22 48N 91 10 E
Maikala Ra. 109 22 0N 81 0 E
Maili 19 21 25N 158 11W
Maili Pt 19 21 24N 158 11W
Main →, Germany 88 50 0N 8 18 E
Main →, U.K. 85 54 49N 6 20W
Main Centre 63 50 35N 107 21W
Maine 90 48 0N 0 0 E
Maine □ 26 45 15N 69 15W
Maine → 85 52 10N 9 40W
Maine-et-Loire □ 90 47 31N 0 30W
Maingkwan 109 26 15N 96 37 E
Mainit, L. 111 9 31N 125 30 E
Mainland, Orkney, U.K. 84 59 0N 3 10W
Mainland, Shetland, U.K. 84 60 15N 1 22W
Maintirano 123 18 3 S 44 1 E
Mainz 88 50 0N 8 17 E
Maipú 76 36 52 S 57 50W
Maiquetía 70 10 36N 66 57W
Mairabari 109 26 30N 92 22 E
Maire, Le, Est. de 78 54 50 S 65 0W
Mairipotaba 75 17 18 S 49 28W
Maisí 67 20 17N 74 9W
Maisi, Pta. de 67 20 10N 74 10W
Maitland, Australia 127 32 33 S 151 36 E
Maitland, Maine 26 40 12N 95 5W
Maitland, Mo. 32 40 12N 95 5W
Maiz, Islas del 66 12 15N 83 4W
Maizuru 117 35 25N 135 22 E
Majagual 70 8 33N 74 38W
Majalengka 111 6 55 S 108 14 E
Majari → 71 3 29N 60 58W

*Renamed Kinbasket L.

Majd el Kurūm | Mantalingajan, Mt.

Majd el Kurūm 104 32 56N 35 15 E
Majene 111 3 38 S 118 57 E
Majes → 72 16 40 S 72 44W
Maji 121 6 12N 35 30 E
Major 63 51 52N 109 37W
Major County ◇ 43 36 15N 98 30W
Majorca, I. = Mallorca 91 39 30N 3 0 E
Majunga 123 15 40 S 46 25 E
Majuriā 73 7 30 S 64 55W
Maka 120 13 40N 14 10W
Makah Indian Reservation 53 48 23N 124 29W
Makaha 19 21 29N 158 13W
Makahoa Pt. 19 21 41N 157 56W
Makahuena Pt. 19 21 52N 159 27W
Makakilo City 19 21 22N 158 5W
Makale 111 3 6 S 119 51 E
Makanda 21 37 37N 89 13W
Makapuu Pt. 19 21 19N 157 39W
Makari 122 12 35N 14 28 E
Makarikari = Makgadikgadi Salt Pans 123 20 40 S 25 45 E
Makarovo 101 57 40N 107 45 E
Makasar = Ujung Pandang 111 5 10 S 119 20 E
Makasar, Selat 111 1 0 S 118 20 E
Makat 100 47 39N 53 19 E
Makawao 19 20 52N 156 17W
Makedhonía □ 95 40 39N 22 0 E
Makedonija □ 95 41 53N 21 40 E
Makeni 120 8 55N 12 5W
Makeyevka 99 48 0N 38 0 E
Makgadikgadi Salt Pans 123 20 40 S 25 45 E
Makhachkala 99 43 0N 47 30 E
Makian 111 0 20N 127 20 E
Makindu 122 2 18 S 37 50 E
Makinsk 100 52 37N 70 26 E
Makkah 106 21 30N 39 54 E
Makkovik 61 55 10N 59 10W
Maklakovo 101 58 16N 92 29 E
Makó 89 46 14N 20 33 E
Makokou 122 0 40N 12 50 E
Makoti 41 47 58N 101 48W
Makoua 122 0 5 S 15 50 E
Makrai 108 22 2N 77 0 E
Makran 107 26 13N 61 30 E
Makran Coast Range 107 25 40N 64 0 E
Maksimkin Yar 100 58 42N 86 50 E
Mākū 106 39 15N 44 31 E
Makumbi 122 5 50 S 20 43 E
Makurazaki 117 31 15N 130 20 E
Makurdi 121 7 43N 8 35 E
Makushin Volcano 11 53 53N 166 55W
Mal B. 85 52 50N 9 30W
Mala 72 12 40 S 76 38W
Mala, Pta. 66 7 28N 80 2W
Malabang 111 7 36N 124 3 E
Malabar 17 28 0N 80 34W
Malabar Coast 108 11 0N 75 0 E
Malacca, Str. of 112 3 0N 101 0 E
Malad City 20 42 12N 112 15W
Malae Pt. 19 20 7N 155 53W
Málaga, Colombia 70 6 42N 72 44W
Málaga, Spain 91 36 43N 4 23W
Malaga, N. Mex. 38 32 14N 104 4W
Malaga, Ohio 42 39 51N 81 9W
Málaga □ 91 36 38N 4 58W
Malakâl 121 9 33N 31 40 E
Malakand 108 34 40N 71 55 E
Malakoff 51 32 10N 96 1W
Malamyzh 101 50 0N 136 50 E
Malang 111 7 59 S 112 45 E
Malanje 122 9 36 S 16 17 E
Mälaren 97 59 30N 17 10 E
Malargüe 76 35 32 S 69 30W
Malartic 60 48 9N 78 9W
Malaspina Glacier 11 59 50N 140 30W
Malatya 106 38 25N 38 20 E
Malawi ■ 123 13 0 S 34 0 E
Malawi, L. 123 12 30 S 34 30 E
Malay Pen. 112 7 25N 100 0 E
Malaybalay 111 8 5N 125 7 E
Malāyer 106 34 19N 48 51 E
Malaysia ■ 110 5 0N 110 0 E
Malazgirt 106 39 10N 42 33 E
Malbaie, La 61 47 40N 70 10W
Malbork 89 54 3N 19 1 E
Malcolm, Australia 126 28 51 S 121 25 E
Malcolm, U.S.A. 34 40 54N 96 52W
Malcom 23 41 43N 92 33W
Maldegem 87 51 14N 3 26 E
Malden, Ill. 21 41 25N 89 22W
Malden, Mass. 28 42 26N 71 4W
Malden, Mo. 32 36 34N 89 57W
Malden I. 125 4 3 S 155 1W
Maldives ■ 102 7 0N 73 0 E
Maldonado 77 35 0 S 55 0W
Maldonado, Punta 65 16 19N 98 35W
Malé Karpaty 88 48 30N 17 20 E
Maléa, Ákra 95 36 28N 23 7 E
Malebo, Pool 118 4 17 S 15 20 E
Malegaon 108 20 30N 74 38 E
Malema 123 14 57 S 37 20 E
Malesus 48 35 33N 88 50W
Malgomaj 96 64 40N 16 30 E
Malha 121 15 8N 25 10 E
Malhão, Sa. do 91 37 25N 8 0W
Malheur → 44 44 4N 116 59W
Malheur County ◇ 44 45 15N 117 45W
Malheur L. 44 43 20N 118 48W
Malheur National Forest 44 44 10N 119 15W
Mali ■ 120 15 0N 2 0W
Mali → 109 25 40N 97 40 E
Mali Kyun 112 13 0N 98 20 E
Malibu 15 34 2N 118 41W
Malih → 104 32 20N 35 34 E
Malik 111 0 39 S 123 16 E
Malili 111 2 42 S 121 6 E
Malin 44 42 1N 121 24W
Malinau 110 3 35N 116 40 E
Malindi 122 3 12 S 40 5 E
Malines = Mechelen 87 51 2N 4 29 E
Maling 111 1 0N 121 0 E
Malinta 42 41 19N 84 2W
Malita 111 6 19N 125 39 E
Maljamar 38 32 51N 103 46W
Malko Tŭrnovo 95 41 59N 27 31 E
Mallacoota Inlet 127 37 34 S 149 40 E
Mallaig 84 57 0N 5 50W
Mallard 23 42 56N 94 41W
Mallawi 121 27 44N 30 44 E
Malleco □ 78 38 10 S 72 20W
Mallorca 91 39 30N 3 0 E
Mallow 85 52 8N 8 40W
Malmberget 96 67 11N 20 40 E
Malmédy 87 50 25N 6 2 E
Malmö, Sweden 97 55 36N 12 59 E
Malmo, U.S.A. 34 41 16N 96 43W
Malmöhus län □ 97 55 45N 13 30 E
Malnaş 95 46 2N 25 49 E
Malo Konare 95 42 12N 24 24 E
Maloca 71 0 43N 55 57W
Malolos 111 14 50N 120 49 E
Malomir 95 42 16N 26 30 E
Malone, Fla. 17 30 57N 85 10W
Malone, N.Y. 39 44 51N 74 18W
Malone, L. 48 37 5N 87 2W
Maloney, L. 34 41 3N 100 48W
Malorad 95 43 28N 23 41 E
Malott 53 48 17N 119 42W
Maloy 23 40 40N 94 25W
Malozemelskaya Tundra 98 67 0N 50 0 E
Malpelo 72 4 3N 81 35W
Malta, Brazil 74 6 54 S 37 31W
Malta, Idaho 20 42 18N 113 22W
Malta, Ill. 21 41 56N 88 52W
Malta, Mont. 33 48 21N 107 52W
Malta ■ 94 35 50N 14 30 E
Malta Bend 32 39 12N 93 22W
Maltahöhe 123 24 55 S 17 0 E
Malton 82 54 9N 0 48W
Maluku 111 1 0 S 127 0 E
Maluku □ 111 3 0 S 128 0 E
Maluku, Kepulauan 111 3 0 S 128 0 E
Malvan 108 16 2N 73 30 E
Malvern, U.K. 83 52 7N 2 19W
Malvern, Ark. 13 34 22N 92 49W
Malvern, Iowa 23 41 0N 95 35W
Malvern, Ohio 42 40 42N 81 11W
Malvern Hills 83 52 0N 2 19W
Malvinas, Is. = Falkland Is. 78 51 30 S 59 0W
Malyy Lyakhovskiy, Ostrov 101 74 7N 140 36 E
Mama 101 58 18N 112 54 E
Mamahatun 106 39 50N 40 23 E
Mamaia 89 44 18N 28 37 E
Mamala B. 19 21 15N 157 55W
Mamanguape 74 6 50 S 35 4W
Mamaroneck 39 40 57N 73 44W
Mamasa 111 2 55 S 119 20 E
Mamayes 57 18 22N 65 46W
Mamberamo → 111 2 0 S 137 50 E
Mambilima Falls 122 10 31 S 28 45 E
Mamburao 111 13 13N 120 39 E
Mameigwess L. 60 52 35N 87 50W
Mamfe 120 5 50N 9 15 E
Mamiña 72 20 5 S 69 14W
Mammoth 12 32 43N 110 39W
Mammoth Cave National Park 48 37 8N 86 13W
Mammoth Hot Springs 56 44 59N 110 42W
Mammoth Lakes 14 37 39N 118 59W
Mammoth Pool Reservoir 14 37 20N 119 19W
Mammoth Spring 13 36 30N 91 33W
Mamoré → 73 10 23 S 65 53W
Mamou, Guinea 120 10 15N 12 0W
Mamou, U.S.A. 25 30 38N 92 25W
Mampawah 110 0 30N 109 5 E
Mamuil Malal, Paso 78 39 35 S 71 28W
Mamuju 111 2 41 S 118 50 E
Man, Ivory C. 120 7 30N 7 40W
Man, U.S.A. 54 37 45N 81 53W
Man, I. of 82 54 15N 4 30W
Man Na 109 23 27N 97 19 E
Mana, Fr. Gui. 71 5 45N 53 55W
Mana, U.S.A. 19 22 2N 159 47W
Mana → 71 5 45N 53 55W
Manaar, Gulf of = Mannar, G. of 108 8 30N 79 0 E
Manabí □ 70 0 40 S 80 5W
Manacacías → 70 4 23N 72 4W
Manacapuru 71 3 16 S 60 37W
Manacapuru → 71 3 18 S 60 37W
Manacor 91 39 34N 3 13 E
Manado 111 1 29N 124 51 E
Managua 66 12 6N 86 20W
Managua, L. 66 12 20N 86 30W
Manahawkin 37 39 42N 74 16W
Manakara 123 22 8 S 48 1 E
Manana I. 19 21 20N 157 40W
Mananara 123 16 10 S 49 46 E
Mananjary 123 21 13 S 48 20 E
Manantenina 123 24 17 S 47 19 E
Manaos = Manaus 71 3 0 S 60 0W
Manapire → 70 7 42N 66 7W
Manapouri 128 45 34 S 167 39 E
Manapouri, L. 128 45 32 S 167 32 E
Manas 113 44 17N 85 56 E
Manas → 109 26 12N 90 40 E
Manasir 107 24 30N 51 10 E
Manasquan 37 40 8N 74 3W
Manasquan → 37 40 6N 74 2W
Manassa 16 37 11N 105 56W
Manassas 54 38 45N 77 29W
Manatee County ◇ 17 27 30N 82 30W
Manati 57 18 26N 66 30W
Manaung 109 18 45N 93 40 E
Manaus 71 3 0 S 60 0W
Manawa 55 44 28N 88 55W
Manawan L. 63 55 24N 103 14W
Manay 111 7 17N 126 33 E
Mancelona 29 44 54N 85 4W
Mancha, La 91 39 10N 2 54W
Manche □ 90 49 10N 1 20W
Manchegorsk 98 67 40N 32 40 E
Manchester, U.K. 82 53 30N 2 15W
Manchester, Calif. 14 38 58N 123 41W
Manchester, Conn. 28 41 47N 72 31W
Manchester, Ga. 18 32 51N 84 37W
Manchester, Iowa 23 42 29N 91 27W
Manchester, Kans. 24 39 6N 97 19W
Manchester, Ky. 49 37 9N 83 46W
Manchester, Mass. 28 42 35N 70 46W
Manchester, Md. 27 39 40N 76 53W
Manchester, Mich. 29 42 9N 84 2W
Manchester, N.H. 36 42 59N 71 28W
Manchester, Ohio 42 38 41N 83 36W
Manchester, Tenn. 48 35 29N 86 5W
Manchester, Vt. 36 43 10N 73 4W
Manchester L. 63 61 28N 107 29W
Mancora, Pta. 72 4 9 S 81 1W
Mancos 16 37 21N 108 18W
Mand → 107 28 20N 52 30 E
Manda 122 10 30 S 34 40 E
Mandabé 123 21 0 S 44 55 E
Mandaguari 77 23 32 S 51 42W
Mandal 97 58 2N 7 25 E
Mandalay 109 22 0N 96 4 E
Mandale = Mandalay 109 22 0N 96 4 E
Mandalī 106 33 43N 45 28 E
Mandan 41 46 50N 100 54W
Mandar, Teluk 111 3 35 S 119 15 E
Mandaree 41 47 43N 102 41W
Mandasor = Mandsaur 108 24 3N 75 8 E
Manderson 56 44 16N 107 58W
Mandeville 25 30 22N 90 4W
Mandi 108 31 39N 76 58 E
Mandimba 123 14 20 S 35 40 E
Mandioli 111 0 40 S 127 20 E
Mandioré, L. 73 18 8 S 57 33W
Mandla 109 22 39N 80 30 E
Mandritsara 123 15 50 S 48 49 E
Mandsaur 108 24 3N 75 8 E
Mandvi 108 22 51N 69 22 E
Mandya 108 12 30N 77 0 E
Manfalût 121 27 20N 30 52 E
Manfredónia 94 41 40N 15 55 E
Manga 75 14 46 S 43 56W
Mangabeiras, Chapada das 74 10 0 S 46 30W
Mangaia 128 21 55 S 157 55W
Mangalia 89 43 50N 28 35 E
Mangalore 108 12 55N 74 47 E
Manggar 110 2 50 S 108 10 E
Manggawitu 111 4 8 S 133 32 E
Mangham 25 32 19N 91 47W
Mangkalihat, Tanjung 111 1 2N 118 59 E
Mangla Dam 108 33 9N 73 44 E
Manglares, C. 70 1 36N 79 2W
Mangnai 113 37 52N 91 43 E
Mango 120 10 20N 0 30 E
Mangoche 123 14 25 S 35 16 E
Mangole 111 1 50 S 125 55 E
Mangonia Park 17 26 45N 80 4W
Mangonui 128 35 1 S 173 32 E
Mangueigne 121 10 30N 21 15 E
Mangueira, Lagoa da 77 33 0 S 52 50W
Mangum 43 34 53N 99 30W
Manhasset 39 40 48N 73 42W
Manhattan, Kans. 24 39 11N 96 35W
Manhattan, Mont. 33 45 51N 111 20W
Manhattan, N.Y. 39 40 45N 73 59W
Manhuaçu 75 20 15 S 42 2W
Manhumirim 75 20 22 S 41 57W
Maní 70 4 49N 72 17W
Manicoré 73 5 48 S 61 16W
Manicoré → 73 5 51 S 61 19W
Manicouagan → 61 49 30N 68 30W
Manicouagan L. 61 51 25N 68 15W
Manīfah 106 27 44N 49 0 E
Manifest 25 31 43N 91 58W
Manigotagan 63 51 6N 96 18W
Manigotagan L. 63 50 52N 95 37W
Manihiki 125 10 24 S 161 1W
Manila, Phil. 111 14 40N 121 3 E
Manila, Ark. 13 35 53N 90 10W
Manila, Utah 52 40 59N 109 43W
Manila B. 111 14 0N 120 0 E
Manilla 23 41 53N 95 14W
Manipur □ 109 25 0N 94 0 E
Manipur → 109 23 45N 94 20 E
Manisa 106 38 38N 27 30 E
Manistee 29 44 15N 86 19W
Manistee → 29 44 15N 86 21W
Manistee County ◇ 29 44 20N 86 10W
Manistee National Forest 29 44 0N 86 0W
Manistique 29 45 57N 86 15W
Manistique → 29 45 57N 86 15W
Manistique L. 29 46 15N 85 46W
Manito 21 40 26N 89 47W
Manito L. 63 52 43N 109 43W
Manitoba □ 63 55 30N 97 0W
Manitoba, L. 63 51 0N 98 45W
Manitou, Canada 63 49 15N 98 32W
Manitou, U.S.A. 43 34 30N 98 59W
Manitou Beach 29 41 58N 84 19W
Manitou I. 29 47 25N 87 37W
Manitou L., Ont., Canada 63 49 15N 93 0W
Manitou L., Qué., Canada 61 50 55N 65 17W
Manitou Springs 16 38 52N 104 55W
Manitoulin I. 60 45 40N 82 30W
Manitowaning 60 45 46N 81 49W
Manitowish 55 46 8N 90 1W
Manitowish Waters 55 46 9N 89 53W
Manitowoc 55 44 5N 87 40W
Manitowoc County ◇ 55 44 10N 87 50W
Manitsauá-Missu → 73 10 58 S 53 20W
Manizales 70 5 5N 75 32W
Manja 123 21 26 S 44 20 E
Manjacaze 123 24 45 S 34 0 E
Manjhand 108 25 50N 68 10 E
Manjil 106 36 46N 49 30 E
Manjimup 126 34 15 S 116 6 E
Manjra → 108 18 49N 77 52 E
Mankato, Kans. 24 39 47N 98 13W
Mankato, Minn. 30 44 10N 94 0W
Mankono 120 8 1N 6 10W
Mankota 63 49 25N 107 5W
Manley 34 40 55N 96 10W
Manley Hot Springs 11 65 0N 150 38W
Manlius 21 41 27N 89 40W
Manly 23 43 17N 93 12W
Manmad 108 20 18N 74 28 E
Manna 110 4 25 S 102 55 E
Mannar 108 9 1N 79 54 E
Mannar, G. of 108 8 30N 79 0 E
Mannar I. 108 9 5N 79 45 E
Mannford 43 36 8N 96 24W
Mannheim 88 49 28N 8 29 E
Manning, Canada 62 56 53N 117 39W
Manning, Ark. 13 34 1N 92 48W
Manning, Iowa 23 41 55N 95 3W
Manning, N. Dak. 41 47 14N 102 46W
Manning, S.C. 46 33 42N 80 13W
Manning Prov. Park 62 49 5N 120 45W
Mannington, Ky. 48 37 8N 87 28W
Mannington, W. Va. 54 39 32N 80 21W
Manns Harbor 40 35 53N 75 46W
Mannsville, N.Y. 39 43 43N 76 4W
Mannsville, Okla. 43 34 11N 96 53W
Mano 120 8 3N 12 2W
Manoa 73 9 40 S 65 27W
Manokin 27 38 5N 75 55W
Manokotak 11 58 58N 159 3W
Manokwari 111 0 54 S 134 0 E
Manombo 123 22 57 S 43 28 E
Manono 122 7 15 S 27 25 E
Manouane L. 61 50 45N 70 45W
Manresa 91 41 48N 1 50 E
Mans, Le 90 48 0N 0 10 E
Mansa 122 11 13 S 28 55 E
Mansel I. 59 62 0N 80 0W
Mansfield, U.K. 82 53 8N 1 12W
Mansfield, Ark. 13 35 4N 94 15W
Mansfield, Ga. 18 33 31N 83 44W
Mansfield, Ill. 21 40 13N 88 31W
Mansfield, La. 25 32 2N 93 43W
Mansfield, Mass. 28 42 2N 71 13W
Mansfield, Mo. 32 37 6N 92 35W
Mansfield, Ohio 42 40 45N 82 31W
Mansfield, Pa. 45 41 48N 77 5W
Mansfield, S. Dak. 47 45 15N 98 34W
Mansfield, Tenn. 48 36 11N 88 17W
Mansfield, Tex. 51 32 34N 97 9W
Mansfield, Wash. 53 47 49N 119 38W
Mansfield, Mt. 36 44 33N 72 49W
Mansfield Hollow L. 28 41 45N 72 11W
Mansfield L. 22 39 43N 87 4W
Mansidão 74 10 43 S 44 2W
Manso → 75 13 50 S 47 0W
Manson, Iowa 23 42 32N 94 32W
Manson, Wash. 53 47 53N 120 9W
Manson Creek 62 55 37N 124 32W
Mansura 25 31 4N 92 3W
Manta 70 1 0 S 80 40W
Manta, B. de 70 0 54 S 80 44W
Mantador 41 46 10N 96 59W
Mantalingajan, Mt. 110 8 55N 117 45 E

Manteca
Marshville

Manteca 14 37 48N 121 13W
Mantecal 70 7 34N 69 17W
Mantee 31 33 44N 89 3W
Mantena 75 18 47S 40 59W
Manteno 21 41 15N 87 50W
Manteo 40 35 55N 75 40W
Manter 24 37 31N 101 53W
Mantes-la-Jolie 90 49 0N 1 41 E
Manthani 108 18 40N 79 35 E
Manti 52 39 16N 111 38W
Manti-la Sal National Forest 52 37 50N 109 50W
Mantiqueira, Serra da 75 22 0S 44 0W
Mantoloking 37 40 4N 74 4W
Manton 29 44 25N 85 24W
Mantorville 30 44 5N 92 45W
Mántova 94 45 20N 10 42 E
Mänttä 96 62 0N 24 40 E
Mantua = Mántova 94 45 20N 10 42 E
Mantua, Ohio 42 41 17N 81 14W
Mantua, Utah 52 41 30N 111 57W
Manu 72 12 10S 70 51W
Manu → 72 12 16S 70 55W
Manua Is. 128 14 13S 169 35W
Manuae 125 19 30S 159 0W
Manuel Alves → 75 11 19S 48 28W
Manuel Alves Grande → 74 7 27S 47 35W
Manuel Urbano 72 8 53S 69 18W
Manuelito 38 35 24N 109 0W
Manui 111 3 35S 123 5 E
Manuripi → 72 11 6S 67 36W
Manvel 41 48 5N 97 11W
Manville, N.J. 37 40 33N 74 35W
Manville, Wyo. 56 42 47N 104 37W
Many 25 31 34N 93 29W
Manyara, L. 122 3 40S 35 50 E
Manych-Gudilo, Oz. 99 46 24N 42 38 E
Manyoni 122 5 45S 34 55 E
Manzai 108 32 12N 70 15 E
Manzanares 91 39 0N 3 22W
Manzanillo, Cuba 66 20 20N 77 31W
Manzanillo, Mexico 64 19 0N 104 20W
Manzanillo, Pta. 66 9 30N 79 40W
Manzanita 44 45 43N 123 56W
Manzano Mts. 38 34 40N 106 20W
Manzanola 16 38 6N 103 52W
Manzhouli 114 49 35N 117 25 E
Mao 121 14 4N 15 19 E
Maoke, Pegunungan 111 3 40S 137 30 E
Maoming 115 21 50N 110 54 E
Mapam Yumco 113 30 45N 81 28 E
Mapastepec 65 15 26N 92 54W
Mapia, Kepulauan 111 0 50N 134 20 E
Mapimí 64 25 50N 103 50W
Mapimí, Bolsón de 64 27 30N 104 15W
Mapire 71 7 45N 64 42W
Maple →, Iowa 23 42 0N 95 59W
Maple →, Mich. 29 42 59N 84 57W
Maple →, N. Dak. 41 46 56N 96 55W
Maple →, S. Dak. 47 45 48N 98 38W
Maple Creek 63 49 55N 109 29W
Maple Falls 53 48 56N 122 5W
Maple Hill, Kans. 24 39 5N 96 2W
Maple Hill, N.C. 40 34 40N 77 42W
Maple Rapids 29 43 6N 84 42W
Maple Shade 37 39 57N 74 58W
Maplesville 10 32 47N 86 52W
Mapleton, Iowa 23 42 10N 95 47W
Mapleton, Kans. 24 38 1N 94 53W
Mapleton, Minn. 30 43 56N 93 57W
Mapleton, Oreg. 44 44 2N 123 52W
Mapleton, Utah 52 40 8N 111 35W
Mapuera → 71 1 5S 57 2W
Maputo 123 25 58S 32 32 E
Maqnā 106 28 25N 34 50 E
Maquela do Zombo 122 6 0S 15 15 E
Maquinchao 78 41 15S 68 50W
Maquoketa 23 42 4N 90 40W
Maquoketa → 23 42 11N 90 19W
Maquon 21 40 48N 90 10W
Mar, Serra do 77 25 30S 49 0W
Mar Chiquita, L. 76 30 40S 62 50W
Mar del Plata 76 38 0S 57 30W
Mara 71 6 0N 57 36W
Maraā 70 1 52S 65 25W
Marabá 74 5 20S 49 5W
Maracá, I. de 74 2 10N 50 30W
Maracaibo 70 10 40N 71 37W
Maracaibo, Lago de 70 9 40N 71 30W
Maracaju 77 21 38S 55 9W
Maracajú, Serra de 73 23 57S 55 1W
Maracanã 74 0 46S 47 27W
Maracás 75 13 26S 40 18W
Maracay 70 10 15N 67 28W
Marādah 121 29 15N 19 15 E
Maradi 120 13 29N 8 10 E
Marāgheh 106 37 30N 46 12 E
Maragogipe 75 12 46S 38 55W
Marāh 106 25 0N 45 35 E
Marais des Cygnes → 24 38 2N 94 14W
Marajó, B. de 74 1 0S 48 30W
Marajó, Ilha de 74 1 0S 49 30W
Maralal 122 1 0N 36 38 E
Maralinga 126 30 13S 131 32 E
Maramec 43 36 15N 96 41W
Marampa 120 8 45N 12 28W
Marana 12 32 27N 111 13W
Marand 106 38 30N 45 45 E
Maranguape 74 3 55S 38 50W
Maranhão = São Luís 74 2 39S 44 15W
Maranhão □ 74 5 0S 46 0W
Maranoa → 127 27 50S 148 37 E
Marañón → 72 4 30S 73 35W
Marão 123 24 18S 34 2 E
Marapi → 71 0 37N 55 58W
Marari 72 5 43S 67 47W
Maraş 106 37 37N 36 53 E
Mărăşeşti 95 45 52N 27 14 E
Marathon, Canada 60 48 44N 86 23W
Marathón, Greece 95 38 11N 23 58 E
Marathon, Fla. 17 24 43N 81 5W
Marathon, Iowa 23 42 52N 94 59W
Marathon, N.Y. 39 42 27N 76 2W
Marathon, Tex. 50 30 12N 103 15W
Marathon, Wis. 55 44 56N 89 50W
Marathon County ◇ 55 44 50N 89 45W
Maratua 111 2 10N 118 35 E
Maraú 75 14 6S 39 0W
Maravatío 64 19 51N 100 25W
Maravillas Cr. → 50 29 34N 102 47W
Marbella 91 36 30N 4 57W
Marble, Ark. 13 36 8N 93 35W
Marble, Colo. 16 39 4N 107 12W
Marble, N.C. 40 35 10N 83 55W
Marble Bar 126 21 9S 119 44 E
Marble Canyon 12 36 49N 111 38W
Marble City 43 35 35N 94 49W
Marble Falls 51 30 35N 98 16W
Marble Hill 32 37 18N 89 58W
Marble Rock 23 42 58N 92 52W
Marblehead 28 42 30N 70 51W
Marblemount 53 48 32N 121 26W
Marbleton 56 42 34N 110 7W
Marburg 88 50 49N 8 36 E
Marbury 27 38 35N 77 10W
Marcapata 72 13 31S 70 52W
Marceline 32 39 43N 92 57W
Marcellus, Mich. 29 42 2N 85 49W
Marcellus, N.Y. 39 42 59N 76 20W
Marcellus, Wash. 53 47 14N 118 24W
March 83 52 33N 0 5 E
Marché 90 46 0N 1 20 E
Marche □ 94 43 22N 13 10 E
Marche-en-Famenne 87 50 14N 5 19 E
Marches = Marche □ 94 43 22N 13 10 E
Marco 17 25 58N 81 44W
Marcola 44 44 10N 122 52W
Marcona 72 15 10S 75 0W
Marcos Juárez 76 32 42S 62 5W
Marcus, Pac. Oc. 124 24 0N 153 45 E
Marcus, U.S.A. 23 42 50N 95 48W
Marcus Baker, Mt. 11 61 26N 147 45W
Marcus Necker Ridge 124 20 0N 175 0 E
Marcy, Mt. 39 44 7N 73 56W
Mardan 108 34 20N 72 0 E
Mardela Springs 27 38 28N 75 45W
Mardin 106 37 20N 40 43 E
Marechal Deodoro 74 9 43S 35 54W
Maree L. 84 57 40N 5 30W
Mareeba 127 16 59S 145 28 E
Marek = Stanke Dimitrov 95 42 17N 23 9 E
Marek 111 4 41S 120 24 E
Maremma 94 42 45N 11 15 E
Marengo, Ill. 21 42 15N 88 37W
Marengo, Ind. 22 38 22N 86 21W
Marengo, Iowa 23 41 48N 92 4W
Marengo, Ohio 42 40 24N 82 49W
Marengo, Wash. 53 47 1N 118 12W
Marengo County ◇ 10 32 18N 87 48W
Marenisco 29 46 23N 89 45W
Marfa 50 30 19N 104 1W
Margaret Bay 62 51 20N 126 35W
Margaret L. 62 58 56N 115 25W
Margaretville 39 42 9N 74 39W
Margarita 57 9 20N 79 55W
Margarita, Isla de 71 11 0N 64 0W
Margaritovo 116 43 25N 134 45 E
Margate, U.K. 83 51 23N 1 24 E
Margate, U.S.A. 17 26 15N 80 12W
Margate City 37 39 20N 74 30W
Marguerite 62 52 30N 122 25W
Mari A.S.S.R. □ 98 56 30N 48 0 E
María Elena 76 22 18S 69 40W
María Grande 76 31 45S 59 55W
Maria I. 126 14 52S 135 45 E
Maria van Diemen, C. 128 34 29S 172 40 E
Marian, L. 17 27 53N 81 6W
Marian L. 62 63 0N 116 15W
Mariana Trench 124 13 0N 145 0 E
Marianao 66 23 8N 82 24W
Marianna, Ark. 13 34 46N 90 46W
Marianna, Fla. 17 30 46N 85 14W
Marianna, Pa. 45 40 2N 80 6W
Marias → 33 47 56N 110 30W
Mariato, Punta 66 7 12N 80 52W
Ma'rib 105 15 25N 45 21 E
Maribor 94 46 36N 15 40 E
Maricao 57 18 11N 66 59W
Maricopa, Ariz. 12 33 4N 112 3W
Maricopa, Calif. 15 35 4N 119 24W
Maricopa County ◇ 12 33 15N 112 30W
Maricopa Indian Reservation 12 33 0N 112 10W
Maricopa Mts. 12 32 0N 112 30W
Marîdî 121 4 55N 29 25 E
Marié → 70 0 27S 66 26W
Marie-Galante 67 15 56N 61 16W
Mariecourt 59 61 30N 72 0W
Mariehamn 97 60 5N 19 55 E
Marienberg 87 52 30N 6 35 E
Marienbourg 87 50 6N 4 31 E
Mariental 123 24 36S 18 0 E
Marienthal 24 38 29N 101 13W
Marienville 45 41 28N 79 8W
Maries → 32 38 30N 92 1W
Maries County ◇ 32 38 10N 91 55W
Mariestad 97 58 43N 13 50 E
Marietta, Ga. 18 33 57N 84 33W
Marietta, Miss. 31 34 30N 88 28W
Marietta, Ohio 42 39 25N 81 27W
Marietta, Okla. 43 33 56N 97 7W
Marietta, S.C. 46 35 1N 82 30W
Mariinsk 100 56 10N 87 20 E
Marília 75 22 13S 50 0W
Marín 91 42 23N 8 42W
Marin County ◇ 14 38 0N 122 45W
Marina 14 36 41N 121 48W
Marinduque 111 13 25N 122 0 E
Marine 21 38 47N 89 47W
Marine City 29 42 43N 82 30W
Marine on St. Croix 30 45 12N 92 46W
Marinel, Le 122 10 25S 25 17 E
Marineland 17 29 40N 81 13W
Marinette 55 45 6N 87 38W
Marinette County ◇ 55 45 25N 88 10W
Maringá 77 23 26S 52 2W
Maringouin 25 30 29N 91 31W
Marion, Ala. 10 32 38N 87 19W
Marion, Ark. 13 35 13N 90 12W
Marion, Ill. 21 37 44N 88 56W
Marion, Ind. 22 40 32N 85 40W
Marion, Iowa 23 42 2N 91 36W
Marion, Kans. 24 38 21N 97 1W
Marion, Ky. 48 37 20N 88 5W
Marion, La. 25 32 54N 92 15W
Marion, Mass. 28 41 42N 70 46W
Marion, Mich. 29 44 6N 85 9W
Marion, Miss. 31 32 25N 88 39W
Marion, Mont. 33 48 6N 114 40W
Marion, N.C. 40 35 41N 82 1W
Marion, N. Dak. 41 46 37N 98 20W
Marion, Nebr. 34 40 1N 100 29W
Marion, Ohio 42 40 35N 83 8W
Marion, S.C. 46 34 11N 79 24W
Marion, S. Dak. 47 43 25N 97 16W
Marion, Va. 54 36 50N 81 31W
Marion, Wis. 55 44 39N 88 54W
Marion, L. 46 33 28N 80 10W
Marion County ◇, Ala. 10 34 9N 87 59W
Marion County ◇, Ark. 13 36 14N 92 41W
Marion County ◇, Fla. 17 29 15N 82 0W
Marion County ◇, Ga. 18 32 25N 84 35W
Marion County ◇, Ill. 21 38 40N 88 55W
Marion County ◇, Ind. 22 39 45N 86 10W
Marion County ◇, Iowa 23 41 20N 93 5W
Marion County ◇, Kans. 24 38 20N 97 0W
Marion County ◇, Ky. 49 37 30N 85 15W
Marion County ◇, Miss. 31 31 15N 89 50W
Marion County ◇, Mo. 32 39 50N 91 35W
Marion County ◇, Ohio 42 40 35N 83 8W
Marion County ◇, Oreg. 44 44 50N 122 50W
Marion County ◇, S.C. 46 34 10N 79 20W
Marion County ◇, Tenn. 49 35 5N 85 38W
Marion County ◇, Tex. 51 32 46N 94 21W
Marion County ◇, W. Va. 54 39 29N 80 9W
Marion Junction 10 32 26N 87 14W
Marion Lake 24 38 22N 97 5W
Marion Reef 127 19 10S 152 17 E
Marion Station 27 38 2N 75 46W
Marionville 32 37 0N 93 38W
Maripa 71 7 26N 65 9W
Maripasoula 71 3 40N 54 4W
Mariposa 14 37 29N 119 58W
Mariposa County ◇ 14 37 30N 120 0W
Mariscal Estigarribia 76 22 3S 60 40W
Marissa 21 38 15N 89 45W
Maritsa 95 42 1N 25 50 E
Maritsa → 95 42 15N 24 0 E
Marīvān 106 35 30N 46 25 E
Mark Twain National Forest 32 36 50N 92 0W
Markazī □ 107 35 0N 49 30 E
Marked Tree 13 35 32N 90 25W
Marken 87 52 26N 5 12 E
Markesan 55 43 42N 88 59W
Market Drayton 82 52 55N 2 30W
Market Harborough 83 52 29N 0 55W
Markham 51 28 58N 96 4W
Markham I. 4 84 0N 0 45W
Markham L. 63 62 30N 102 35W
Markham Mt. 5 83 0S 164 0 E
Markle 22 40 50N 85 20W
Markleeville 14 38 42N 119 47W
Markleville 22 39 59N 85 37W
Markleysburg 45 39 44N 79 27W
Markovo 101 64 40N 169 40 E
Marks, U.S.A. 31 34 16N 90 16W
Marks, U.S.S.R. 98 51 45N 46 50 E
Marks Butte 16 40 53N 102 23W
Marksville 25 31 8N 92 4W
Marland 43 36 34N 97 9W
Marlboro, N.J. 37 40 19N 74 15W
Marlboro, N.Y. 39 41 36N 73 59W
Marlboro County ◇ 46 34 40N 79 40W
Marlborough, Conn. 28 41 8N 72 27W
Marlborough, Mass. 28 42 21N 71 33W
Marlborough, N.H. 36 42 54N 72 13W
Marlborough □ 128 41 45S 173 33 E
Marlborough Downs 83 51 25N 1 55W
Marlette 29 43 20N 83 5W
Marlin, Tex. 51 31 18N 96 54W
Marlin, Wash. 53 47 25N 118 59W
Marlinton 54 38 13N 80 6W
Marlow, Ga. 18 32 16N 81 23W
Marlow, N.H. 36 43 9N 72 12W
Marlow, Okla. 43 34 39N 97 58W
Marlton 37 39 54N 74 55W
Marmaduke 13 36 11N 90 23W
Marmagao 108 15 25N 73 56 E
Marmara 95 40 35N 27 38 E
Marmara, Sea of = Marmara Denizi 106 40 45N 28 15 E
Marmara Denizi 106 40 45N 28 15 E
Marmaris 106 36 50N 28 14 E
Marmarth 41 46 18N 103 54W
Marmelos → 73 6 6S 61 46W
Marmion L. 60 48 55N 91 20W
Marmolada, Mte. 94 46 25N 11 55 E
Marmora, Canada 60 44 28N 77 41W
Marmora, U.S.A. 37 39 16N 74 39W
Marne 23 41 27N 95 6W
Marne □ 90 49 0N 4 10 E
Marne → 90 8 23N 18 36 E
Maro Reef 19 25 25N 170 35W
Maroa, U.S.A. 21 40 2N 88 57W
Maroa, Venezuela 70 2 43N 67 33W
Maroantsetra 123 15 26S 49 44 E
Marondera 123 18 5S 31 42 E
Maroni → 71 4 0N 52 0W
Maroua 121 10 40N 14 20 E
Marovoay 123 16 6S 46 39 E
Marowijne □ 71 4 0N 55 0W
Marowijne → 71 5 45N 53 58W
Marquand 32 37 26N 90 10W
Marquesas Is. 125 9 30S 140 0W
Marquesas Keys 17 24 35N 82 10W
Marquette, Iowa 23 43 3N 91 11W
Marquette, Kans. 24 38 33N 97 50W
Marquette, Mich. 29 46 33N 87 24W
Marquette County ◇, Mich. 29 46 20N 87 30W
Marquette County ◇, Wis. 55 43 50N 89 25W
Marquette I. 29 45 58N 84 24W
Marquez 51 31 14N 96 15W
Marra, Gebel 121 7 20N 27 35 E
Marrakech 120 31 9N 8 0W
Marrecas, Serra das 74 9 0S 41 0W
Marree 127 29 39S 138 1 E
Marrero 25 29 54N 90 6W
Marromeu 123 18 40S 36 25 E
Marrowbone 49 36 50N 85 30W
Marrupa 123 13 8S 37 30 E
Mars 45 40 42N 80 1W
Mars Hill, Maine 26 46 31N 67 52W
Mars Hill, N.C. 40 35 50N 82 33W
Marsá Susah 121 32 52N 21 59 E
Marsabit 122 2 18N 38 0 E
Marsala 94 37 48N 12 25 E
Marsaxlokk 94 35 47N 14 32 E
Marseille 90 43 18N 5 23 E
Marseilles = Marseille 90 43 18N 5 23 E
Marseilles 21 41 20N 88 43W
Marsh I. 25 29 34N 91 53W
Marsh Pass 12 36 36N 110 35W
Marsh Peak 52 40 43N 109 50W
Marshall = Fortuna Ledge 11 61 53N 162 5W
Marshall, Liberia 120 6 8N 10 22W
Marshall, Ark. 13 35 55N 92 38W
Marshall, Ill. 21 39 23N 87 42W
Marshall, Ind. 22 39 51N 87 11W
Marshall, Mich. 29 42 16N 84 58W
Marshall, Mo. 32 39 7N 93 12W
Marshall, N.C. 40 35 48N 82 41W
Marshall, Okla. 43 36 9N 97 38W
Marshall, Tex. 51 32 33N 94 23W
Marshall County ◇, Ala. 10 34 21N 86 18W
Marshall County ◇, Ill. 21 41 0N 89 20W
Marshall County ◇, Ind. 22 41 20N 86 15W
Marshall County ◇, Iowa 23 42 0N 93 0W
Marshall County ◇, Kans. 24 39 45N 96 30W
Marshall County ◇, Ky. 48 36 55N 88 20W
Marshall County ◇, Minn. 30 48 15N 96 15W
Marshall County ◇, Miss. 31 34 46N 89 27W
Marshall County ◇, Okla. 43 34 0N 96 50W
Marshall County ◇, S. Dak. 47 45 48N 97 45W
Marshall County ◇, Tenn. 48 35 27N 86 48W
Marshall County ◇, W. Va. 54 39 50N 80 34W
Marshall Is. 124 9 0N 171 0 E
Marshallberg 40 34 44N 76 31W
Marshallton 27 39 44N 75 39W
Marshalltown 23 42 3N 92 55W
Marshallville, Ga. 18 32 27N 83 56W
Marshallville, Ohio 42 40 54N 81 44W
Marshfield, Mo. 32 37 15N 92 54W
Marshfield, Vt. 36 44 20N 72 20W
Marshfield, Wis. 55 44 40N 90 10W
Marshfield Hills 28 42 9N 70 44W
Marshville 40 35 0N 80 25W

Marshyhope Mazīnān

Marshyhope → **27** 38 32N 75 45W
Marsing **20** 43 33N 116 48W
Marston **32** 36 31N 89 37W
Marstrand **97** 57 53N 11 35 E
Mart **51** 31 33N 96 50W
Martaban **109** 16 30N 97 35 E
Martaban, G. of **109** 16 5N 96 30 E
Martapura, Kalimantan, Indonesia **110** 3 22 S 114 47 E
Martapura, Sumatera, Indonesia **110** 4 19 S 104 22 E
Marte **121** 12 23N 13 46 E
Martelange **87** 49 49N 5 43 E
Martelle **23** 42 1N 91 22W
Martensdale **23** 41 23N 93 45W
Martha's Vineyard **28** 41 25N 70 38W
Marthasville **32** 38 38N 91 4W
Marthaville **25** 31 44N 93 24W
Martin, Mich. **29** 42 32N 85 39W
Martin, N. Dak. **41** 47 50N 100 7W
Martin, S. Dak. **47** 43 11N 101 44W
Martin, Tenn. **48** 36 21N 88 51W
Martin County ◇, Fla. **17** 27 10N 80 20W
Martin County ◇, Ind. **22** 38 40N 86 50W
Martin County ◇, Ky. **49** 37 45N 82 30W
Martin County ◇, Minn. **30** 43 40N 94 30W
Martin County ◇, N.C. **40** 35 45N 77 0W
Martin County ◇, Tex. **50** 32 18N 101 58W
Martin L. **10** 32 41N 85 55W
Martin Pt. **11** 70 8N 143 16W
Martinborough **128** 41 14 S 175 29 E
Martinez **14** 38 1N 122 8W
Martinez L. **12** 32 59N 114 29W
Martinho Campos **75** 19 20 S 45 13W
Martinique **67** 14 40N 61 0W
Martinique Passage **67** 15 15N 61 0W
Martinópolis **77** 22 11 S 51 12W
Martins Ferry **42** 40 6N 80 44W
Martinsburg, Md. **27** 39 10N 77 28W
Martinsburg, Mo. **32** 39 6N 91 39W
Martinsburg, Nebr. **34** 42 30N 96 50W
Martinsburg, Ohio **42** 40 16N 82 21W
Martinsburg, Pa. **45** 40 19N 78 20W
Martinsburg, W. Va. **54** 39 27N 77 58W
Martinsville, Ill. **21** 39 20N 87 53W
Martinsville, Ind. **22** 39 26N 86 25W
Martinsville, Va. **54** 36 41N 79 52W
Martinton **21** 40 55N 87 44W
Marton **128** 40 4 S 175 23 E
Martos **91** 37 44N 3 58W
Marudi **110** 4 10N 114 19 E
Ma'ruf **107** 31 30N 67 6 E
Marugame **117** 34 15N 133 40 E
Maruim **74** 10 45 S 37 5W
Marvel **16** 37 7N 108 8W
Marvell **13** 34 33N 90 55W
Marvin **47** 45 16N 96 55W
Marvine, Mt. **52** 38 40N 111 39W
Marwar **108** 25 43N 73 45 E
Mary **100** 37 40N 61 50 E
Mary Frances L. **63** 63 19N 106 13W
Mary Kathleen **127** 20 44 S 139 48 E
Maryborough = Port Laoise **85** 53 2N 7 20W
Maryborough, Queens., Australia **127** 25 31 S 152 37 E
Maryborough, Vic., Australia **127** 37 0 S 143 44 E
Marydel **27** 39 7N 75 45W
Maryfield **63** 49 50N 101 35W
Maryhill **53** 45 41N 120 49W
Maryland □ **27** 39 0N 76 30W
Maryland City **27** 39 6N 76 50W
Maryland Line **27** 39 43N 76 40W
Maryland Point **27** 38 22N 77 14W
Maryneal **50** 32 14N 100 27W
Maryport **82** 54 43N 3 30W
Marys → **35** 41 4N 115 16W
Marys Corner **53** 46 33N 122 49W
Mary's Harbour **61** 52 18N 55 51W
Marys Pk. **44** 44 30N 123 33W
Marystown **61** 47 10N 55 10W
Marysvale **52** 38 27N 112 14W
Marysville, Canada **62** 49 35N 116 0W
Marysville, Calif. **14** 39 9N 121 35W
Marysville, Kans. **24** 39 51N 96 39W
Marysville, Mich. **29** 42 54N 82 29W
Marysville, Ohio **42** 40 14N 83 22W
Marysville, Pa. **45** 40 21N 76 56W
Marysville, Wash. **53** 48 3N 122 11W
Maryville, Mo. **32** 40 21N 94 52W
Maryville, Tenn. **49** 35 46N 83 58W
Marzo, Punta **70** 6 50N 77 42W
Marzūq **121** 25 53N 13 57 E
Masada = Mesada **104** 31 20N 35 19 E
Masaka **122** 0 21 S 31 45 E
Masalembo, Kepulauan **110** 5 35 S 114 30 E
Masalima, Kepulauan **110** 5 4 S 117 5 E
Masamba **111** 2 30 S 120 15 E
Masan **114** 35 11N 128 32 E
Masandam, Ras **107** 26 30N 56 30 E
Masardis **26** 46 30N 68 22W
Masaryktown **17** 28 27N 82 27W
Masasi **122** 10 45 S 38 52 E
Masaya **66** 12 0N 86 7W
Masbate **111** 12 21N 123 36 E
Mascara **120** 35 26N 0 6 E
Mascot **49** 36 4N 83 45W
Mascota **64** 20 30N 104 50W
Mascoutah **21** 38 29N 89 48W
Masela **111** 8 9 S 129 51 E
Maseru **123** 29 18 S 27 30 E
Mashābih **106** 25 35N 36 30 E
Mashan **115** 23 40N 108 11 E
Mashhad **107** 36 20N 59 35 E
Mashkel, Hamun-i- **107** 28 30N 63 0 E
Mashki Chāh **107** 29 5N 62 30 E
Mashulaville **31** 33 5N 88 45W
Masi **96** 69 26N 23 40 E
Masi Manimba **122** 4 40 S 17 54 E
Masindi **122** 1 40N 31 43 E
Masisea **72** 8 35 S 74 22W
Masjed Soleyman **106** 31 55N 49 18 E
Mask, L. **85** 53 36N 9 24W
Maskell **34** 42 41N 96 59W
Maslen Nos **95** 42 18N 27 48 E
Masoala, Tanjon' i **123** 15 59 S 50 13 E
Masohi **111** 3 2 S 128 15 E
Mason, Ill. **21** 38 57N 88 38W
Mason, Mich. **29** 42 35N 84 27W
Mason, N.H. **36** 42 45N 71 47W
Mason, Ohio **42** 39 22N 84 19W
Mason, Tenn. **48** 35 25N 89 32W
Mason, Tex. **51** 30 45N 99 14W
Mason, W. Va. **54** 39 1N 82 2W
Mason, Wis. **55** 46 26N 91 4W
Mason City, Ill. **21** 40 12N 89 42W
Mason City, Iowa **23** 43 9N 93 12W
Mason City, Nebr. **34** 41 13N 99 18W
Mason County ◇, Ill. **21** 40 15N 89 50W
Mason County ◇, Ky. **49** 38 35N 83 50W
Mason County ◇, Mich. **29** 44 0N 86 15W
Mason County ◇, Tex. **51** 30 45N 99 15W
Mason County ◇, W. Va. **54** 38 50N 82 8W
Mason County ◇, Wash. **53** 47 20N 123 10W
Mason Springs **27** 38 36N 77 10W
Masontown **54** 39 33N 79 48W
Masonville, Colo. **16** 40 29N 105 13W
Masonville, Iowa **23** 42 29N 91 36W
Masqat **107** 23 37N 58 36 E
Massa **94** 44 2N 10 7 E
Massabesic L. **36** 43 0N 71 23W
Massac County ◇ **21** 37 15N 88 45W
Massachusetts □ **28** 42 30N 72 0W
Massachusetts B. **28** 42 20N 70 50W
Massacre L. **35** 41 39N 119 36W
Massada **104** 33 41N 35 36 E
Massaguet **121** 12 28N 15 26 E
Massakory **121** 13 0N 15 49 E
Massangena **123** 21 34 S 33 0 E
Massapê **74** 3 31 S 40 19W
Massapequa **39** 40 41N 73 29W
Massawa = Mitsiwa **121** 15 35N 39 25 E
Massena, Iowa **23** 41 15N 94 46W
Massena, N.Y. **39** 44 56N 74 54W
Massénya **121** 11 21N 16 9 E
Masset **62** 54 2N 132 10W
Massey **27** 39 18N 75 49W
Massif Central **90** 45 30N 2 21 E
Massillon **42** 40 48N 81 32W
Massinga **123** 23 15 S 35 22 E
Masson I. **5** 66 10 S 93 20 E
Mastanli = Momchilgrad **95** 41 33N 25 23 E
Masten's Corner **27** 38 57N 75 37W
Masters **16** 40 18N 104 15W
Masterton **128** 40 56 S 175 39 E
Mastic **39** 40 47N 72 54W
Mastuj **108** 36 20N 72 36 E
Mastung **107** 29 50N 66 56 E
Masuda **117** 34 40N 131 51 E
Masvingo **123** 20 8 S 30 49 E
Mata de São João **75** 12 31 S 38 17W
Mataboor **111** 1 41 S 138 3 E
Matachewan **60** 47 56N 80 39W
Matacuni → **71** 3 2N 65 16W
Matad **113** 47 11N 115 27 E
Matadi **122** 5 52 S 13 31 E
Matador **50** 34 1N 100 49W
Matagalpa **66** 13 0N 85 58W
Matagami **60** 49 45N 77 34W
Matagami, L. **60** 49 50N 77 40W
Matagorda **51** 28 42N 95 58W
Matagorda B. **51** 28 40N 96 0W
Matagorda County ◇ **51** 29 0N 96 0W
Matagorda I. **51** 28 15N 96 30W
Matagorda Peninsula **51** 28 38N 96 0W
Matak, P. **110** 3 18N 106 16 E
Matalaque **72** 16 26 S 70 49W
Matam **120** 15 34N 13 17W
Matamoros, Campeche, Mexico **65** 18 50N 90 50W
Matamoros, Coahuila, Mexico **64** 25 33N 103 15W
Matamoros, Puebla, Mexico **65** 18 2N 98 17W
Matamoros, Tamaulipas, Mexico **65** 25 50N 97 30W
Ma'ṭan as Sarra **121** 21 45N 22 0 E
Matane **61** 48 50N 67 33W
Matanuska-Susitna ◇ **11** 62 30N 150 0W
Matanzas **66** 23 0N 81 40W
Matapan, C. = Taínaron, Ákra **95** 36 22N 22 27 E
Matapédia **61** 48 0N 66 59W
Matara **108** 5 58N 80 30 E
Mataram **110** 8 41 S 116 10 E
Matarani **72** 17 0 S 72 10W
Mataranka **126** 14 55 S 133 4 E
Mataura **128** 46 11 S 168 51 E
Matawan **37** 40 25N 74 14W
Mategua **73** 13 1 S 62 48W
Matehuala **64** 23 40N 100 40W
Mateira **75** 18 54 S 50 30W
Matera **94** 40 40N 16 37 E
Matewan **54** 37 37N 82 10W
Matfield Green **24** 38 9N 96 31W
Matheson **16** 39 10N 103 59W
Matheson Island **63** 51 45N 96 56W
Mathews **54** 37 26N 76 19W
Mathews, L. **15** 33 51N 117 27W
Mathews County ◇ **54** 37 26N 76 19W
Mathias **54** 38 53N 78 52W
Mathis **51** 28 6N 97 50W
Mathiston **31** 33 32N 89 7W
Mathura **108** 27 30N 77 40 E
Mati **111** 6 55N 126 15 E
Matías Romero **65** 16 53N 95 2W
Matinicus **26** 43 52N 68 54W
Matlock, U.K. **82** 53 8N 1 32W
Matlock, U.S.A. **23** 43 15N 95 56W
Matmata **120** 33 37N 9 59 E
Mato → **71** 7 9N 65 7W
Mato, Serrania de **70** 6 25N 65 25W
Mato Grosso □ **73** 14 0 S 55 0W
Mato Grosso, Planalto do **73** 15 0 S 59 57W
Matoaka **54** 37 25N 81 15W
Matochkin Shar **100** 73 10N 56 40 E
Matosinhos **91** 41 11N 8 42W
Matrah **107** 23 37N 58 30 E
Matrûh **121** 31 19N 27 9 E
Matsue **117** 35 25N 133 10 E
Matsumae **116** 41 26N 140 7 E
Matsumoto **117** 36 15N 138 0 E
Matsusaka **117** 34 34N 136 32 E
Matsuura **117** 33 20N 129 49 E
Matsuyama **117** 33 45N 132 45 E
Mattagami → **60** 50 43N 81 29W
Mattamuskeet, L. **40** 35 30N 76 12W
Mattancheri **108** 9 50N 76 15 E
Mattapoisett **28** 41 40N 70 49W
Mattaponi → **54** 37 31N 76 47W
Mattawa **60** 46 20N 78 45W
Mattawamkeag **26** 45 32N 68 21W
Matterhorn, Switz. **88** 45 58N 7 39 E
Matterhorn, U.S.A. **35** 41 49N 115 23W
Matthew Town **67** 20 57N 73 40W
Matthews, Ind. **22** 40 23N 85 30W
Matthews, Md. **27** 38 49N 75 57W
Matthews, Mo. **32** 36 46N 89 35W
Matthews, N.C. **40** 35 7N 80 43W
Matthew's Ridge **71** 7 37N 60 10W
Mattice **60** 49 40N 83 20W
Mattituck **39** 40 59N 72 32W
Mattole → **14** 40 18N 124 21W
Mattoon, Ill. **21** 39 29N 88 23W
Mattoon, Wis. **55** 45 1N 89 2W
Mattson **31** 34 6N 90 31W
Matua **110** 2 58 S 110 46 E
Matucana **72** 11 55 S 76 25W
Matun **108** 33 22N 69 58 E
Matunuck **28** 41 23N 71 32W
Maturín **71** 9 45N 63 11W
Mau Ranipur **108** 25 16N 79 8 E
Maud, Okla. **43** 35 8N 96 46W
Maud, Tex. **51** 33 20N 94 21W
Maudheim **5** 71 5 S 11 0W
Maudin Sun **109** 16 0N 94 30 E
Maués **71** 3 20 S 57 45W
Mauganj **109** 24 50N 81 55 E
Maui **19** 20 48N 156 20W
Maui County ◇ **19** 20 45N 156 20W
Mauke **128** 20 9 S 157 20W
Maulamyaing **109** 16 30N 97 40 E
Mauldin **46** 34 47N 82 19W
Maule □ **76** 36 5 S 72 30W
Maullín **78** 41 38 S 73 37W
Maumee **42** 41 34N 83 39W
Maumee → **42** 41 42N 83 28W
Maumelle, L. **13** 34 51N 92 29W
Maumere **111** 8 38 S 122 13 E
Maun **123** 20 0 S 23 26 E
Mauna Kea **19** 19 50N 155 28W
Mauna Loa **19** 19 30N 155 35W
Maunabo **57** 18 1N 65 54W
Maunaloa **19** 21 8N 157 13W
Maunalua B. **19** 21 15N 157 45W
Maunawili **19** 21 23N 157 46W
Maungmagan Kyunzu **112** 14 0N 97 48 E
Maunie **21** 38 2N 88 3W
Maupin **44** 45 11N 121 5W
Maurepas, L. **25** 30 15N 90 30W
Maures **90** 43 15N 6 15 E
Maurice → **37** 39 13N 75 2W
Maurice L. **126** 29 30 S 131 0 E
Mauriceville **51** 30 12N 93 52W
Mauritania ■ **120** 20 50N 10 0W
Mauritius ■ **3** 20 0 S 57 0 E
Maury **40** 35 29N 77 35W
Maury → **54** 37 50N 79 25W
Maury City **48** 35 49N 89 14W
Maury County ◇ **48** 35 37N 87 2W
Mauston **55** 43 48N 90 5W
Mavaca → **71** 2 31N 65 11W
Maverick County ◇ **50** 28 55N 100 8W
Mavinga **123** 15 50 S 20 21 E
Mavisdale **54** 37 12N 81 59W
Mavqi'im **104** 31 38N 34 32 E
Mawk Mai **109** 20 14N 97 37 E
Mawlaik **109** 23 40N 94 26 E
Mawson Base **5** 67 30 S 62 53 E
Mawson Coast **5** 68 30 S 63 0 E
Max **41** 47 49N 101 18W
Maxbass **41** 48 43N 101 9W
Maxcanú **65** 20 40N 92 0W
Maxeys **18** 33 45N 83 11W
Maxhamish L. **62** 59 50N 123 17W
Maxinkuckee, L. **22** 41 12N 86 24W
Maxixe **123** 23 54 S 35 17 E
Maxton **40** 34 44N 79 21W
Maxville **33** 46 28N 113 14W
Maxwell, Calif. **14** 39 17N 122 11W
Maxwell, Iowa **23** 41 53N 93 24W
Maxwell, N. Mex. **38** 36 32N 104 33W
Maxwell, Nebr. **34** 41 5N 100 31W
May, Idaho **20** 44 36N 113 55W
May, Okla. **43** 36 37N 99 45W
May, C. **37** 38 56N 74 58W
May Pen **66** 17 58N 77 15W
Maya → **101** 54 31N 134 41 E
Maya Mts. **65** 16 30N 89 0W
Mayaguana **67** 22 30N 72 44W
Mayaguez **57** 18 13N 67 9W
Mayaguez ◇ **57** 18 10N 67 0W
Mayaguez, Bahia de **57** 18 15N 67 15W
Mayapán **65** 20 28N 89 27W
Mayarí **67** 20 40N 75 41W
Maybell **16** 40 31N 108 5W
Maybeury **54** 37 22N 81 22W
Mayenne **90** 48 20N 0 38W
Mayenne □ **90** 48 10N 0 40W
Mayer **12** 34 24N 112 14W
Mayersville **31** 32 54N 91 3W
Mayerthorpe **62** 53 57N 115 8W
Mayes County ◇ **43** 36 15N 95 10W
Mayesville **46** 34 0N 80 12W
Mayetta, Kans. **24** 39 20N 95 43W
Mayetta, N.J. **37** 39 40N 74 18W
Mayfield, Ga. **18** 33 21N 82 48W
Mayfield, Idaho **20** 43 25N 115 54W
Mayfield, Kans. **24** 37 16N 97 33W
Mayfield, Ky. **48** 36 44N 88 38W
Mayfield, Utah **52** 39 7N 111 43W
Mayflower **13** 34 57N 92 26W
Mayhill **38** 32 53N 105 29W
Maykop **99** 44 35N 40 25 E
Maymyo **112** 22 2N 96 28 E
Maynard, Ark. **13** 36 25N 90 54W
Maynard, Iowa **23** 42 47N 91 53W
Maynard, Mass. **28** 42 26N 71 27W
Maynardville **49** 36 15N 83 48W
Maynooth **85** 53 22N 6 38W
Mayo, Canada **58** 63 38N 135 57W
Mayo, Fla. **17** 30 3N 83 10W
Mayo, S.C. **46** 35 5N 81 52W
Mayo □ **85** 53 47N 9 7W
Mayo →, Argentina **78** 45 45 S 69 45W
Mayo →, Mexico **64** 26 45N 109 47W
Mayo →, Peru **72** 6 38 S 76 15W
Mayodan **40** 36 25N 79 58W
Mayon Volcano **111** 13 15N 123 41 E
Mayor I. **128** 37 16 S 176 17 E
Mays Landing **37** 39 27N 74 44W
Mays Lick **48** 38 31N 83 50W
Mayson L. **63** 57 55N 107 10W
Maysville, Ky. **49** 38 39N 83 46W
Maysville, Mo. **32** 39 53N 94 22W
Maysville, N.C. **40** 34 54N 77 14W
Maysville, Okla. **43** 34 49N 97 24W
Maythalūn **104** 32 21N 35 16 E
Mayu **111** 1 30N 126 30 E
Mayview **32** 39 3N 93 50W
Mayville, Mich. **29** 43 20N 83 21W
Mayville, N. Dak. **41** 47 30N 97 20W
Mayville, N.Y. **39** 42 15N 79 30W
Mayville, Wis. **55** 43 30N 88 33W
Maywood **34** 40 39N 100 37W
Mayya **101** 61 44N 130 18 E
Maza **41** 48 22N 99 12W
Mazabuka **123** 15 52 S 27 44 E
Mazagán = El Jadida **120** 33 11N 8 17W
Mazagão **71** 0 7 S 51 16W
Mazama **53** 48 36N 120 24W
Mazán **70** 3 30 S 73 0W
Māzandarān □ **107** 36 30N 52 0 E
Mazapil **64** 24 38N 101 34W
Mazar-e Sharīf **107** 36 41N 67 0 E
Mazarredo **78** 47 10 S 66 50W
Mazarrón **91** 37 38N 1 19W
Mazaruni → **71** 6 25N 58 35W
Mazatán **64** 29 0N 110 8W
Mazatenango **66** 14 35N 91 30W
Mazatlán **64** 23 10N 106 30W
Mazatzal Mts. **12** 34 0N 111 30W
Māzhān **107** 32 30N 59 0 E
Mazie, Ky. **49** 38 2N 82 58W
Mazie, Okla. **43** 36 6N 95 22W
Mazīnān **107** 36 19N 56 56 E

Mazoe Merrick County

Mazoe → 123 16 45 S 32 30 E
Mazomanie 55 43 11N 89 48W
Mazon 21 41 14N 88 25W
Mazu Dao 115 26 10N 119 55 E
Mbabane 123 26 18 S 31 6 E
Mbaïki 122 3 53N 18 1 E
Mbala 122 8 46 S 31 24 E
Mbale 122 1 8N 34 12 E
Mbalmayo 122 3 33N 11 33 E
Mbamba Bay 122 11 13 S 34 49 E
Mbandaka 122 0 1N 18 18 E
Mbanza Congo 122 6 18 S 14 16 E
Mbanza Ngungu 122 5 12 S 14 53 E
Mbarara 122 0 35 S 30 40 E
Mbeya 122 8 54 S 33 29 E
Mbini □ 122 1 30N 10 0 E
Mbour 120 14 22N 16 54W
Mbout 120 16 1N 12 38W
Mbuji-Mayi 122 6 9 S 23 40 E
Mbulu 122 3 45 S 35 30 E
Mburucuyá 76 28 1 S 58 14W
Mchinji 123 13 47 S 32 58 E
Mdina 94 35 51N 14 25 E
Meacham 44 45 31N 118 25W
Mead, Nebr. 34 41 14N 96 29W
Mead, Okla. 43 34 0N 96 31W
Mead, Wash. 53 47 46N 117 21W
Mead, L. 12 36 1N 114 44W
Meade 24 37 17N 100 20W
Meade → 11 70 52N 155 55W
Meade County ◇, Kans. 24 37 15N 100 20W
Meade County ◇, Ky. 48 37 55N 86 10W
Meade County ◇, S. Dak. 47 44 30N 102 30W
Meade River 11 70 28N 157 24W
Meadow, S. Dak. 47 45 32N 102 13W
Meadow, Tex. 50 33 20N 102 12W
Meadow, Utah 52 38 53N 112 24W
Meadow → 54 38 12N 80 57W
Meadow Bridge 54 37 52N 80 51W
Meadow Grove 34 42 2N 97 44W
Meadow Lake 63 54 10N 108 26W
Meadow Lake Prov. Park 63 54 27N 109 0W
Meadow Valley Wash → 35 36 40N 114 34W
Meadow Vista 14 39 6N 121 1W
Meadowlands 30 47 4N 92 44W
Meadows 36 44 21N 71 28W
Meadowview 54 36 40N 81 52W
Meadville, Miss. 31 31 28N 90 54W
Meadville, Mo. 32 39 47N 93 18W
Meadville, Pa. 45 41 39N 80 9W
Meaford 60 44 36N 80 35W
Meagher County ◇ 33 46 40N 111 0W
Mealy Mts. 61 53 10N 58 0W
Meander River 62 59 2N 117 42W
Meansville 18 33 3N 84 18W
Mearim → 74 3 4 S 44 35W
Meath □ 85 53 32N 6 40W
Meath Park 63 53 27N 105 22W
Meaux 90 48 58N 2 50 E
Mebane 40 36 6N 79 16W
Mebechi-Gawa → 116 40 31N 141 31 E
Mecaya → 70 0 29N 75 11W
Mecca = Makkah 106 21 30N 39 54 E
Mecca 15 33 34N 116 5W
Mechanic Falls 26 44 7N 70 24W
Mechanicsburg, Ill. 21 39 49N 89 24W
Mechanicsburg, Ohio 42 40 4N 83 33W
Mechanicsburg, Pa. 45 40 13N 77 1W
Mechanicsville, Iowa 23 41 54N 91 16W
Mechanicsville, Md. 27 38 26N 76 44W
Mechanicsville, Va. 54 37 36N 77 22W
Mechanicville 39 42 54N 73 41W
Mechelen 87 51 2N 4 29 E
Mecheria 120 33 35N 0 18W
Mecklenburg County ◇, N.C. 40 35 10N 80 50W
Mecklenburg County ◇, Va. 54 36 55N 78 20W
Mecklenburger Bucht 88 54 20N 11 40 E
Meckling 47 42 51N 97 4W
Meconta 123 14 59 S 39 50 E
Mecosta 29 43 37N 85 14W
Mecosta County ◇ 29 43 35N 85 20W
Meda → 126 17 20 S 123 50 E
Medan 110 3 40N 98 38 E
Medanales 38 36 11N 106 11W
Médanos 78 38 50 S 62 42W
Medanosa, Pta. 78 48 8 S 66 0W
Medart 17 30 5N 84 23W
Medaryville 22 41 5N 86 55W
Medéa 120 36 12N 2 50 E
Medeiros Neto 75 17 20 S 40 14W
Medellín 70 6 15N 75 35W
Medemblik 87 52 46N 5 8 E
Mederdra 120 17 0N 15 38W
Medfield 28 42 11N 71 18W
Medford, Mass. 28 42 25N 71 7W
Medford, Minn. 30 44 11N 93 15W
Medford, N.J. 37 39 54N 74 50W
Medford, Okla. 43 36 48N 97 44W
Medford, Oreg. 44 42 19N 122 52W
Medford, Wis. 55 45 9N 90 20W
Medford Lakes 37 39 52N 74 48W
Medgidia 95 44 15N 28 19 E
Media 45 39 55N 75 23W
Media Agua 76 31 58 S 68 25W
Media Luna 76 34 45 S 66 44W
Mediapolis 23 41 0N 91 10W
Mediaş 89 46 9N 24 22 E
Medical Lake 53 47 34N 117 41W
Medicine Bow 56 41 54N 106 12W
Medicine Bow → 56 42 0N 106 40W
Medicine Bow Mts. 16 40 40N 106 0W
Medicine Bow National Forest 56 42 20N 105 38W
Medicine Cr. →, Mo. 32 39 43N 93 24W
Medicine Cr. →, Nebr. 34 40 17N 100 10W
Medicine Hat 63 50 0N 110 45W
Medicine L. 33 48 28N 104 24W
Medicine Lake 33 48 30N 104 30W
Medicine Lodge 24 37 17N 98 35W
Medicine Lodge → 24 36 49N 98 20W
Medina = Al Madīnah 106 24 35N 39 52 E
Medina, Brazil 75 16 15 S 41 29W
Medina, Colombia 70 4 30N 73 21W
Medina, N. Dak. 41 46 54N 99 18W
Medina, N.Y. 39 43 13N 78 23W
Medina, Ohio 42 41 8N 81 52W
Medina, Tenn. 48 35 48N 88 46W
Medina, Tex. 51 29 48N 99 15W
Medina → 51 29 16N 98 29W
Medina County ◇, Ohio 42 41 8N 81 52W
Medina County ◇, Tex. 51 29 21N 99 9W
Medina del Campo 91 41 18N 4 55W
Medina L. 51 29 32N 98 56W
Medina-Sidonia 91 36 28N 5 57W
Medinipur 109 22 25N 87 21 E
Medio Mundo, Punta 57 18 16N 65 37W
Mediterranean Sea 92 35 0N 15 0 E
Medley 63 54 25N 110 16W
Médoc 90 45 10N 0 56W
Medora, Ill. 21 39 11N 90 9W
Medora, Ind. 22 38 49N 86 10W
Medora, N. Dak. 41 46 55N 103 31W
Medport = Marsaxlokk 94 35 47N 14 32 E
Medstead 63 53 19N 108 5W
Medveditsa → 99 49 35N 42 41 E
Medvezhi, Ostrava 101 71 0N 161 0 E
Medvezhyegorsk 98 63 0N 34 25 E
Medway 28 42 8N 71 24W
Medway → 83 51 28N 0 45 E
Meekatharra 126 26 32 S 118 29 E
Meeker, Colo. 16 40 2N 107 55W
Meeker, Okla. 43 35 30N 96 54W
Meeker County ◇ 30 45 10N 94 30W
Meeks Bay 14 39 2N 120 8W
Meerut 108 29 1N 77 42 E
Meeteetse 56 44 9N 108 52W
Mega 121 3 57N 38 19 E
Mégara 95 37 58N 23 22 E
Megargel 51 33 27N 98 56W
Meghalaya □ 109 25 50N 91 0 E
Megiddo 104 32 36N 35 11 E
Mégiscane, L. 60 48 35N 75 55W
Megiste 93 36 8N 29 34 E
Mehadia 89 44 56N 22 23 E
Meharry, Mt. 126 22 59 S 118 35 E
Meherrin → 54 36 26N 76 57W
Mei Jiang → 115 24 25N 116 35 E
Mei Xian 115 24 16N 116 6 E
Meia Ponte → 75 18 32 S 49 36W
Meiganga 122 6 30N 14 25 E
Meigs 18 31 4N 84 6W
Meigs County ◇, Ohio 42 39 3N 82 8W
Meigs County ◇, Tenn. 49 35 31N 84 47W
Meiktila 109 20 53N 95 54 E
Meio → 75 13 36 S 44 7W
Me'ir Shefeya 104 32 35N 34 58 E
Meiss L. 14 41 52N 122 4W
Meissen 88 51 10N 13 29 E
Meitan 115 27 45N 107 29 E
Mejillones 76 23 10 S 70 30W
Mékambo 122 1 2N 13 50 E
Mekdela 121 11 24N 39 10 E
Mekhtar 108 30 30N 69 15 E
Mekinock 41 48 1N 97 22W
Meknès 120 33 57N 5 33W
Mekong → 112 9 30N 106 15 E
Mekongga 111 3 39 S 121 15 E
Mekoryuk 11 60 23N 166 11W
Melagiri Hills 108 12 20N 77 30 E
Melaka 112 2 15N 102 15 E
Melaka □ 112 2 20N 102 15 E
Melalap 110 5 10N 116 5 E
Melanesia 124 4 0 S 155 0 E
Melba 20 43 23N 116 32W
Melbourne, Australia 127 37 50 S 145 0 E
Melbourne, Ark. 13 36 4N 91 54W
Melbourne, Fla. 17 28 5N 80 37W
Melbourne, Iowa 23 41 57N 93 6W
Melcher 23 41 14N 93 15W
Melchor Múzquiz 64 27 50N 101 30W
Melchor Ocampo 64 24 52N 101 40W
Mélèzes → 59 57 30N 71 0W
Melfa 54 37 39N 75 45W
Melfi 121 11 0N 17 59 E
Melfort 63 52 50N 104 37W
Melilla 120 35 21N 2 57W
Melilot 104 31 22N 34 37 E
Melipilla 76 33 42 S 71 15W
Melissa 51 33 17N 96 34W
Melita 63 49 15N 101 0W
Melitopol 99 46 50N 35 22 E
Melitota 27 39 16N 76 9W
Melk 88 48 13N 15 20 E
Mellansel 96 63 25N 18 17 E
Mellen 55 46 20N 90 40W
Mellerud 97 58 41N 12 28 E
Mellette 47 45 9N 98 30W
Mellette County ◇ 47 43 35N 101 0W
Mellish Reef 127 17 25 S 155 50 E
Mellizo Sur, Cerro 78 48 33 S 73 10W
Mellott 22 40 10N 87 9W
Mellwood 13 34 12N 90 56W
Melnik 95 41 30N 23 25 E
Melo 77 32 20 S 54 10W
Melolo 111 9 53 S 120 40 E
Melrose, U.K. 84 53 35N 2 44W
Melrose, Iowa 23 40 59N 93 3W
Melrose, Mass. 28 42 27N 71 4W
Melrose, Minn. 30 45 40N 94 49W
Melrose, Mont. 33 45 38N 112 41W
Melrose, N. Mex. 38 34 26N 103 38W
Melrose, Wis. 55 44 8N 91 1W
Melstone 33 46 36N 107 52W
Melton Mowbray 82 52 46N 0 52W
Melun 90 48 32N 2 39 E
Melut 121 10 30N 32 13 E
Melvern 24 38 30N 95 38W
Melvern Lake 24 38 30N 95 50W
Melville, Canada 63 50 55N 102 50W
Melville, U.S.A. 25 30 42N 91 45W
Melville, C. 127 14 11 S 144 30 E
Melville, L. 61 53 30N 60 0W
Melville B. 127 12 0 S 136 45 E
Melville I., Australia 126 11 30 S 131 0 E
Melville I., Canada 4 75 30N 112 0W
Melville Pen. 59 68 0N 84 0W
Melvin, Ala. 10 31 56N 88 28W
Melvin, Ill. 21 40 34N 88 15W
Melvin, Tex. 51 31 12N 99 35W
Melvin → 62 59 11N 117 31W
Melvin Village 36 43 42N 71 28W
Melvina 55 43 48N 90 47W
Memba 123 14 11 S 40 30 E
Memboro 111 9 30 S 119 30 E
Memel = Klaipeda 98 55 43N 21 10 E
Memmingen 88 47 59N 10 12 E
Memphis, Fla. 17 27 32N 82 34W
Memphis, Mich. 29 42 54N 82 46W
Memphis, Mo. 32 40 28N 92 10W
Memphis, Nebr. 34 41 6N 96 26W
Memphis, Tenn. 48 35 8N 90 3W
Memphis, Tex. 50 34 44N 100 33W
Memphis Junction 48 36 57N 86 29W
Memphremagog, L. 36 45 0N 72 12W
Mena 13 34 35N 94 15W
Menahga 30 46 45N 95 6W
Menai Strait 82 53 14N 4 10W
Ménaka 120 15 59N 2 18 E
Menan = Chao Phraya → 112 13 32N 100 36 E
Menan 20 43 43N 111 59W
Menard, Mont. 33 45 59N 111 10W
Menard, Tex. 51 30 55N 99 47W
Menard County ◇, Ill. 21 40 0N 89 50W
Menard County ◇, Tex. 51 30 55N 99 45W
Menasha 55 44 13N 88 26W
Menate 110 0 12 S 113 3 E
Mendawai → 110 3 30 S 113 0 E
Mende 90 44 31N 3 30 E
Mendenhall 31 31 58N 89 52W
Mendenhall, C. 11 59 45N 166 10W
Menderes → 106 37 25N 28 45 E
Mendez 65 25 7N 98 34W
Mendham 37 40 47N 74 36W
Mendip Hills 83 51 17N 2 40W
Mendocino 14 39 19N 123 48W
Mendocino, C. 14 40 26N 124 25W
Mendocino, L. 14 39 12N 123 11W
Mendocino County ◇ 14 39 20N 123 20W
Mendocino National Forest 14 39 45N 122 50W
Mendocino Seascarp 125 41 0N 140 0W
Mendon, Mich. 29 42 0N 85 27W
Mendon, Mo. 32 39 36N 93 8W
Mendon, Ohio 42 40 40N 84 31W
Mendon, Vt. 36 43 40N 72 54W
Mendota, Calif. 15 36 45N 120 23W
Mendota, Ill. 21 41 33N 89 7W
Mendota, L. 55 43 7N 89 25W
Mendoza 76 32 50 S 68 52W
Mendoza □ 76 33 0 S 69 0W
Mene Grande 70 9 49N 70 56W
Menemen 106 38 34N 27 3 E
Menen 87 50 47N 3 7 E
Menéndez, L. 78 42 40 S 71 51W
Menfi 94 37 36N 12 57 E
Mengcheng 115 33 18N 116 31 E
Menggala 110 4 30 S 105 15 E
Mengshan 115 24 14N 110 55 E
Mengzi 113 23 20N 103 22 E
Menifee County ◇ 49 37 55N 83 35W
Menihek L. 61 54 0N 67 0W
Menin = Menen 87 50 47N 3 7 E
Menindee 127 32 20 S 142 25 E
Menlo, Ga. 18 34 29N 85 29W
Menlo, Iowa 23 41 31N 94 24W
Menlo, Kans. 24 39 21N 100 43W
Menlo, Wash. 53 46 38N 123 39W
Menlo Park 14 37 27N 122 12W
Menno 47 43 14N 97 34W
Meno 43 36 23N 98 11W
Menominee 29 45 6N 87 37W
Menominee → 55 45 6N 87 36W
Menominee County ◇, Mich. 29 45 30N 87 40W
Menominee County ◇, Wis. 55 45 0N 88 45W
Menominee Ind. Reservation 55 45 0N 88 45W
Menominee Ra. 29 46 0N 88 10W
Menomonee Falls 55 43 11N 88 7W
Menomonie 55 44 53N 91 55W
Menongue 123 14 48 S 17 52 E
Menorca 91 40 0N 4 0 E
Mentasta Lake 11 62 55N 143 45W
Mentawai, Kepulauan 110 2 0 S 99 0 E
Mentmore 38 35 31N 108 51W
Menton 90 43 50N 7 29 E
Mentone, Ind. 22 41 10N 86 2W
Mentone, Tex. 50 31 42N 103 36W
Mentor, Minn. 30 47 42N 96 9W
Mentor, Ohio 42 41 40N 81 21W
Mentor-on-the-Lake 42 41 43N 81 22W
Menzelinsk 98 55 53N 53 1 E
Menzies 126 29 40 S 120 58 E
Me'ona 104 33 1N 35 15 E
Meoqui 64 28 17N 105 29W
Meppel 87 52 42N 6 12 E
Mequon 55 43 14N 87 59W
Mer Rouge 25 32 47N 91 48W
Merabéllou, Kólpos 95 35 10N 25 50 E
Meramec → 32 38 24N 90 21W
Meran = Merano 94 46 40N 11 10 E
Merano 94 46 40N 11 10 E
Merauke 111 8 29 S 140 24 E
Merbabu 111 7 30 S 110 40 E
Merca 105 1 48N 44 50 E
Merced 14 37 18N 120 29W
Merced → 14 37 21N 120 59W
Merced County ◇ 14 37 15N 120 30W
Mercedes, Buenos Aires, Argentina 76 34 40 S 59 30W
Mercedes, Corrientes, Argentina 76 29 10 S 58 5W
Mercedes, San Luis, Argentina 76 33 40 S 65 21W
Mercedes, Uruguay 76 33 12 S 58 0W
Mercedes, U.S.A. 50 26 9N 97 55W
Mercedita 76 28 20 S 70 35W
Mercer, N.Z. 128 37 16 S 175 5 E
Mercer, Maine 26 44 41N 69 56W
Mercer, Mo. 32 40 31N 93 32W
Mercer, N. Dak. 41 47 29N 100 43W
Mercer, Pa. 45 41 14N 80 15W
Mercer, Tenn. 48 35 29N 89 2W
Mercer, Wis. 55 46 10N 90 4W
Mercer County ◇, Ill. 21 41 15N 90 40W
Mercer County ◇, Ky. 49 37 50N 84 50W
Mercer County ◇, Mo. 32 40 25N 93 30W
Mercer County ◇, N. Dak. 41 47 15N 102 0W
Mercer County ◇, N.J. 37 40 15N 74 40W
Mercer County ◇, Ohio 42 40 33N 84 35W
Mercer County ◇, Pa. 45 41 15N 80 10W
Mercer County ◇, W. Va. 54 37 22N 81 6W
Mercer Island 53 47 35N 122 15W
Mercersburg 45 39 50N 77 54W
Mercerville 37 40 14N 74 41W
Mercier 72 10 42 S 68 5W
Mercury 51 31 28N 99 10W
Mercy C. 59 65 0N 63 30W
Meredith, Colo. 16 39 22N 106 44W
Meredith, N.H. 36 43 39N 71 30W
Meredith, L. 50 35 43N 101 33W
Meredith C. 78 52 15 S 60 40W
Meredith L. 16 38 12N 103 43W
Meredosia 21 39 50N 90 34W
Merei 95 45 7N 26 43 E
Merga = Nukheila 121 19 1N 26 21 E
Mergui Arch. = Myeik Kyunzu 112 11 30N 97 30 E
Mérida, Mexico 65 20 9N 89 40W
Mérida, Spain 91 38 55N 6 25W
Mérida, Venezuela 70 8 24N 71 8W
Mérida □ 70 8 30N 71 10W
Mérida, Cord. de 68 9 0N 71 0W
Meriden, Conn. 28 41 32N 72 48W
Meriden, Iowa 23 42 48N 95 38W
Meriden, Kans. 24 39 11N 95 34W
Meriden, N.H. 36 43 36N 72 16W
Meridian, Ga. 18 31 27N 81 23W
Meridian, Idaho 20 43 37N 116 24W
Meridian, Miss. 31 32 22N 88 42W
Meridian, Okla. 43 35 48N 97 15W
Meridian, Tex. 51 31 56N 97 39W
Merigold 31 33 50N 90 43W
Meriruma 71 1 15N 54 50W
Meriwether County ◇ 18 33 0N 84 40W
Merkel 51 32 28N 100 1W
Merksem 87 51 16N 4 25 E
Merlin 44 42 31N 123 25W
Mermentau 25 30 12N 92 35W
Merna 34 41 29N 99 46W
Merowe 121 18 29N 31 46 E
Merredin 126 31 28 S 118 18 E
Merrick, U.K. 84 55 8N 4 30W
Merrick, U.S.A. 39 40 40N 73 33W
Merrick County ◇ 34 41 15N 98 0W

Merricourt Millstone

Merricourt 41 46 12N 98 46W
Merrill, Iowa 23 42 43N 96 15W
Merrill, Mich. 29 43 25N 84 20W
Merrill, Miss. 31 30 59N 88 43W
Merrill, Oreg. 44 42 1N 121 36W
Merrill, Wis. 55 45 11N 89 41W
Merrillan 55 44 27N 90 50W
Merrillville, Ga. 18 30 57N 83 53W
Merrillville, Ind. 22 41 29N 87 20W
Merrimac, Ky. 49 37 25N 85 8W
Merrimac, Mass. 28 42 50N 71 0W
Merrimac, Wis. 55 43 22N 89 37W
Merrimack 36 42 49N 70 49W
Merrimack → 28 42 49N 70 49W
Merrimack County ◇ 36 43 15N 71 45W
Merriman 34 42 55N 101 42W
Merrimon 40 34 57N 76 38W
Merritt, Canada 62 50 10N 120 45W
Merritt, U.S.A. 53 47 47N 120 50W
Merritt Island 17 28 21N 80 42W
Merritt Reservoir 34 42 38N 100 53W
Merry I. 60 55 29N 77 31W
Merryville 25 30 45N 93 33W
Mersa Fatma 105 14 57N 40 17 E
Mersch 87 49 44N 6 7 E
Merseburg 88 51 20N 12 0 E
Mersey → 82 53 20N 2 56W
Merseyside □ 82 53 25N 2 55W
Mershon 18 31 28N 82 15W
Mersin 106 36 51N 34 36 E
Mersing 112 2 25N 103 50 E
Merthyr Tydfil 83 51 45N 3 23W
Mértola 91 37 40N 7 40 E
Mertzon 50 31 16N 100 49W
Meru 122 0 3N 37 40 E
Merwin, L. 53 45 57N 122 33W
Mesa, Ariz. 12 33 25N 111 50W
Mesa, Colo. 16 39 10N 108 8W
Mesa, Wash. 53 46 35N 119 0W
Mesa County ◇ 16 39 0N 108 30W
Mesa Verde 16 37 15N 108 45W
Mesa Verde National Park 16 37 11N 108 29W
Mesabi Range 30 47 40N 92 45W
Mesada 104 31 20N 35 19 E
Mescalero 38 33 9N 105 46W
Mescalero Indian Reservation 38 33 12N 105 40W
Meservey 23 42 55N 93 29W
Mesgouez, L. 60 51 20N 75 0W
Meshed = Mashhad 107 36 20N 59 35 E
Meshra er Req 121 8 25N 29 18 E
Mesick 29 44 24N 85 43W
Mesilinka → 62 56 6N 124 30W
Mesilla 38 32 16N 106 48W
Mesita 16 37 6N 105 36W
Mesolóngion 95 38 21N 21 28 E
Mesopotamia = Al Jazirah 106 33 30N 44 0 E
Mesquite, N. Mex. 38 32 10N 106 42W
Mesquite, Tex. 51 32 46N 96 36W
Mesquite L. 15 35 43N 115 35W
Mess Cr. → 62 57 55N 131 14W
Messier, Canal 78 48 20 S 74 33W
Messina, Italy 94 38 10N 15 32 E
Messina, S. Africa 123 22 20 S 30 0 E
Messina, Str. di 94 38 5N 15 35 E
Messíni 95 37 4N 22 1 E
Messiniakós, Kólpos 95 36 45N 22 5 E
Mesta → 95 41 30N 24 0 E
Mestre, Espigão 75 12 30 S 46 10W
Meta 32 38 19N 92 10W
Meta □ 70 3 30N 73 0W
Meta → 70 6 12N 67 28W
Metairie 25 29 58N 90 10W
Metaline Falls 53 48 52N 117 22W
Metamora, Ill. 21 40 47N 89 22W
Metamora, Mich. 29 42 57N 83 17W
Metán 76 25 30 S 65 0W
Metangula 123 12 40 S 34 50 E
Metcalf, Ga. 18 30 43N 83 59W
Metcalf, Ill. 21 39 48N 87 48W
Metcalfe County ◇ 49 37 0N 85 40W
Metema 121 12 56N 36 13 E
Methow 53 48 8N 120 0W
Methow → 53 48 5N 119 55W
Methuen 28 42 44N 71 11W
Methven 128 43 38 S 171 40 E
Methy L. 63 56 28N 109 30W
Metil 123 16 24 S 39 0 E
Metkovets 95 43 37N 23 10 E
Metlakatla 11 55 8N 131 35W
Metolius 44 44 35N 121 11W
Metropolis 21 37 9N 88 44W
Metter 18 32 24N 82 3W
Mettur Dam 108 11 45N 77 45 E
Metuchen 37 40 32N 74 22W
Metulla 104 33 17N 35 34 E
Metz, France 90 49 8N 6 10 E
Metz, U.S.A. 32 37 59N 94 27W
Meulaboh 110 4 11N 96 3 E
Meureudu 110 5 19N 96 10 E
Meurthe-et-Moselle □ 90 48 52N 6 0 E
Meuse □ 90 49 8N 5 25 E
Meuse → 87 50 45N 5 41 E
Mexborough 82 53 29N 1 18W
Mexia 51 31 41N 96 29W
Mexiana, I. 74 0 0 49 30W
Mexicali 64 32 40N 115 30W
Mexican Hat 52 37 9N 109 52W
Mexican Springs 38 35 47N 108 50W
México, Mexico 65 19 20N 99 10W
Mexico, Maine 26 44 34N 70 33W
Mexico, Mo. 32 39 10N 91 53W
México □ 64 19 20N 99 10W
Mexico ■ 64 20 0N 100 0W
Mexico, G. of 65 25 0N 90 0W
Mexico B. 39 43 35N 76 20W
Mexico Beach 17 29 57N 85 25W
Meyers Chuck 11 55 45N 132 15W
Meyersdale 45 39 49N 79 2W
Meymaneh 107 35 53N 64 38 E
Mezdra 95 43 12N 23 42 E
Mezen 98 65 50N 44 20 E
Mezen → 98 66 11N 43 59 E
Mezökövesd 89 47 49N 20 35 E
Mezötúr 89 47 0N 20 41 E
Mezquital 64 23 29N 104 23W
Mhow 108 22 33N 75 50 E
Miahuatlán 65 16 21N 96 36W
Miami, Ariz. 12 33 24N 110 52W
Miami, Fla. 17 25 47N 80 11W
Miami, Mo. 32 39 19N 93 14W
Miami, N. Mex. 38 36 21N 104 48W
Miami, Okla. 43 36 53N 94 53W
Miami, Tex. 50 35 42N 100 38W
Miami Beach 17 25 47N 80 8W
Miami Canal 17 26 30N 80 45W
Miami County ◇, Ind. 22 40 45N 86 0W
Miami County ◇, Kans. 24 38 30N 94 45W
Miami County ◇, Ohio 42 40 9N 84 15W
Miami Shores 17 25 52N 80 12W
Miami Springs 17 25 49N 80 17W
Miamisburg 42 39 38N 84 17W
Mian Xian 115 33 10N 106 32 E
Mianchi 115 34 48N 111 48 E
Mīāndow āb 106 37 0N 46 5 E
Miandrivazo 123 19 31 S 45 29 E
Mīāneh 106 37 30N 47 40 E
Mianwali 108 32 38N 71 28 E
Mianyang, Hubei, China 115 30 25N 113 25 E
Mianyang, Sichuan, China 115 31 22N 104 47 E
Miaoli 115 24 37N 120 49 E
Miarinarivo 123 18 57 S 46 55 E
Miass 98 54 59N 60 6 E
Micanopy 17 29 30N 82 17W
Micăsasa 95 46 7N 24 7 E
Micaville 40 35 55N 82 13W
Miccasukee, L. 17 30 33N 83 53W
Micco 17 27 53N 80 30W
Miccosukee 17 30 36N 84 3W
Michie 48 35 3N 88 26W
Michigamme, L. 29 46 32N 88 5W
Michigamme Res. 29 46 10N 88 10W
Michigan 41 48 1N 98 7W
Michigan □ 29 44 0N 85 0W
Michigan Center 29 42 14N 84 20W
Michigan City 22 41 43N 86 54W
Michigan I. 55 46 53N 90 29W
Michigan L. 29 44 0N 87 0W
Michigantown 22 40 20N 86 24W
Michipicoten 60 47 55N 84 55W
Michipicoten I. 60 47 40N 85 40W
Michoacan □ 64 19 0N 102 0W
Michurin 95 42 9N 27 51 E
Michurinsk 98 52 58N 40 27 E
Mico, Pta. 66 12 0N 83 30W
Micronesia 124 11 0N 160 0 E
Mid Glamorgan □ 83 51 40N 3 25W
Mid-Indian Ridge 124 40 0 S 75 0 E
Mid-Oceanic Ridge 124 42 0 S 90 0 E
Midai, P. 110 3 0N 107 47 E
Midale 63 49 25N 103 20W
Middelburg, Neth. 87 51 30N 3 36 E
Middelburg, S. Africa 123 31 30 S 25 0 E
Middle Alkali L. 14 41 27N 120 5W
Middle Andaman I. 112 12 30N 92 30 E
Middle Concho → 50 31 27N 100 25W
Middle Fork Feather → 14 38 33N 121 30W
Middle Fork John Day → 44 44 45N 119 38W
Middle Fork Salmon → 20 45 18N 114 36W
Middle Fork Sappa Cr. → 24 39 42N 100 51W
Middle Loup → 34 41 17N 98 24W
Middle Pease → 50 34 15N 100 7W
Middle Point 42 40 51N 84 27W
Middle River, Md. 27 39 20N 76 27W
Middle River, Minn. 30 48 26N 96 10W
Middleberg 43 35 6N 97 44W
Middleboro 28 41 54N 70 55W
Middlebourne 54 39 30N 80 54W
Middleburg, Fla. 17 30 4N 81 52W
Middleburg, N.Y. 39 42 36N 74 20W
Middleburg, Pa. 45 40 47N 77 3W
Middleburg, Va. 54 38 58N 77 44W
Middlebury, Conn. 28 41 32N 73 7W
Middlebury, Ind. 22 41 41N 85 42W
Middlebury, Vt. 36 44 1N 73 10W
Middlefield, Mass. 28 42 20N 73 2W
Middlefield, Ohio 42 41 28N 81 5W
Middleport, N.Y. 39 43 13N 78 29W
Middleport, Ohio 42 39 0N 82 3W
Middlesboro 49 36 36N 83 43W
Middlesbrough 82 54 35N 1 14W
Middlesex, Belize 66 17 2N 88 31W
Middlesex, U.S.A. 40 35 47N 78 12W
Middlesex County ◇, Conn. 28 41 25N 72 30W
Middlesex County ◇, Mass. 28 42 20N 71 15W
Middlesex County ◇, N.J. 37 40 30N 74 25W
Middlesex County ◇, Va. 54 37 36N 76 36W
Middleton, Canada 61 44 57N 65 4W
Middleton, Idaho 20 43 42N 116 37W
Middleton, Mass. 28 42 36N 71 1W
Middleton, Mich. 29 43 11N 84 43W
Middleton, Tenn. 48 35 4N 88 53W
Middleton, Wis. 55 43 6N 89 30W
Middleton I. 11 59 26N 146 20W
Middletown, Calif. 14 38 45N 122 37W
Middletown, Conn. 28 41 34N 72 39W
Middletown, Del. 27 39 27N 75 43W
Middletown, Ill. 21 40 11N 89 35W
Middletown, Ind. 22 40 3N 85 32W
Middletown, Md. 27 39 27N 77 33W
Middletown, Mo. 32 39 8N 91 25W
Middletown, N.J. 37 40 24N 74 8W
Middletown, N.Y. 39 41 27N 74 25W
Middletown, Ohio 42 39 31N 84 24W
Middletown, Pa. 45 40 12N 76 44W
Middletown, R.I. 28 41 32N 71 17W
Middletown, Va. 54 39 2N 78 17W
Middletown Springs 36 43 28N 73 8W
Middleville, Mich. 29 42 43N 85 28W
Middleville, N.Y. 39 43 8N 74 58W
Midi, Canal du 90 43 45N 1 21 E
Midland, Canada 60 44 45N 79 50W
Midland, Calif. 15 33 52N 114 48W
Midland, Md. 27 39 37N 78 55W
Midland, Mich. 29 43 37N 84 14W
Midland, Oreg. 44 42 8N 121 49W
Midland, S. Dak. 47 44 4N 101 10W
Midland, Tex. 50 32 0N 102 3W
Midland County ◇, Mich. 29 43 35N 84 20W
Midland County ◇, Tex. 50 32 0N 102 0W
Midleton 85 51 52N 8 12W
Midlothian, Md. 27 39 40N 78 58W
Midlothian, Tex. 51 32 30N 97 0W
Midnight 31 33 3N 90 35W
Midvale, Idaho 20 44 28N 116 44W
Midvale, Ohio 42 40 26N 81 23W
Midvale, Utah 52 40 37N 111 54W
Midville 18 32 49N 82 14W
Midway, Ala. 10 32 5N 85 31W
Midway, Fla. 17 30 30N 84 27W
Midway, Ky. 49 38 9N 84 41W
Midway, Tex. 51 31 2N 95 45W
Midway, Utah 52 40 31N 111 28W
Midway Is., Pac. Oc. 124 28 13N 177 22W
Midway Is., U.S.A. 19 28 13N 177 22W
Midway Park 40 34 44N 77 21W
Midwest 56 43 25N 106 16W
Midwest City 43 35 27N 97 24W
Midyat 106 37 25N 41 23 E
Mie □ 117 34 30N 136 10 E
Międzychód 88 52 35N 15 53 E
Międzyrzec Podlaski 89 51 58N 22 45 E
Miercurea Ciuc 89 46 21N 25 48 E
Mieres 91 43 18N 5 48W
Mieville 30 44 36N 92 49W
Mifflintown 45 40 34N 77 24W
Mifflin 42 40 46N 82 22W
Mifflin County ◇ 45 40 45N 77 45W
Mifflinburg 45 40 55N 77 3W
Migdāl 104 32 51N 35 30 E
Migdal Afeq 104 32 5N 34 58 E
Miguel Alemán, Presa 65 18 15N 96 40W
Miguel Alves 74 4 11 S 42 55W
Miguel Calmon 74 11 26 S 40 36W
Mihara 117 34 24N 133 5 E
Mikhaylovgrad 95 43 27N 23 16 E
Mikínai 95 37 43N 22 46 E
Mikindani 122 10 15 S 40 2 E
Mikkalo 44 45 28N 120 14W
Mikkeli 97 61 43N 27 15 E
Mikkeli □ 96 62 0N 28 0 E
Mikkwa → 62 58 25N 114 46W
Míkonos 95 37 30N 25 25 E
Mikun 98 62 20N 50 0 E
Milaca 30 45 45N 93 39W
Milagro 70 2 11 S 79 36W
Milam 51 31 26N 93 51W
Milam County ◇ 51 30 51N 96 59W
Milan = Milano 94 45 28N 9 10 E
Milan, Ga. 18 32 1N 83 4W
Milan, Ill. 21 41 27N 90 34W
Milan, Ind. 22 39 7N 85 8W
Milan, Mich. 29 42 5N 83 41W
Milan, Minn. 30 45 7N 95 55W
Milan, Mo. 32 40 12N 93 7W
Milan, N.H. 36 44 36N 71 12W
Milan, N. Mex. 38 35 9N 107 54W
Milan, Ohio 42 41 18N 82 37W
Milan, Tenn. 48 35 55N 88 46W
Milan, Wash. 53 47 58N 117 20W
Milano, Italy 94 45 28N 9 10 E
Milano, U.S.A. 51 30 43N 96 52W
Milâs 106 37 20N 27′50 E
Milazzo 94 38 13N 15 13 E
Milbank 47 45 13N 96 38W
Milbridge 26 44 32N 67 53W
Milburn, Nebr. 34 41 43N 99 44W
Milburn, Okla. 43 34 14N 96 33W
Milden 63 51 29N 107 32W
Mildred 24 38 1N 95 10W
Mildura 127 34 13 S 142 9 E
Miles, Australia 127 26 40 S 150 9 E
Miles, Tex. 50 31 36N 100 11W
Miles, Wash. 53 47 55N 118 18W
Miles City 33 46 25N 105 51W
Milesburg 45 40 57N 77 47W
Milestone 63 49 59N 104 31W
Milford, Calif. 14 40 10N 120 22W
Milford, Conn. 28 41 14N 73 3W
Milford, Del. 27 38 55N 75 26W
Milford, Ga. 18 31 23N 84 33W
Milford, Ill. 21 40 38N 87 42W
Milford, Ind. 22 41 25N 85 51W
Milford, Iowa 23 43 20N 95 9W
Milford, Kans. 24 39 10N 96 55W
Milford, Ky. 49 38 35N 84 9W
Milford, Maine 26 44 57N 68 39W
Milford, Mass. 28 42 8N 71 31W
Milford, Mich. 29 42 35N 83 36W
Milford, Mo. 32 37 35N 94 9W
Milford, N.H. 36 42 50N 71 39W
Milford, N.J. 37 40 34N 75 6W
Milford, N.Y. 39 42 35N 74 57W
Milford, Nebr. 34 40 47N 97 3W
Milford, Pa. 45 41 19N 74 48W
Milford, Utah 52 38 24N 113 1W
Milford Center 42 40 11N 83 26W
Milford Haven 83 51 43N 5 2W
Milford Haven, B. 83 51 40N 5 10W
Milford Lake 24 39 5N 96 54W
Milford Sd. 128 44 41 S 167 47 E
Milḩ, Baḩr al 106 32 40N 43 35 E
Milḩ, Ras al 121 31 54N 25 6 E
Miliana 120 27 20N 2 32 E
Mililani Town 19 21 28N 158 1W
Milk → 33 48 4N 106 19W
Milk River 62 49 10N 112 5W
Mill → 29 43 2N 82 35W
Mill City, Nev. 35 40 41N 118 4W
Mill City, Oreg. 44 44 45N 122 29W
Mill Creek 54 38 44N 79 58W
Mill Hall 45 41 6N 77 29W
Mill I. 5 66 0 S 101 30 E
Mill Shoals 21 38 15N 88 21W
Milladore 55 44 36N 89 51W
Millard 32 40 7N 92 33W
Millard County ◇ 52 39 0N 113 0W
Millboro, S. Dak. 47 43 4N 99 58W
Millboro, Va. 54 37 59N 79 36W
Millbrook 39 41 47N 73 42W
Millbury 28 42 12N 71 46W
Millcreek 52 40 42N 111 50W
Mille Lacs, L. des 60 48 45N 90 35W
Mille Lacs County ◇ 30 45 50N 93 45W
Mille Lacs L. 30 46 15N 93 39W
Milledgeville, Ga. 18 33 5N 83 14W
Milledgeville, Ill. 21 41 58N 89 46W
Milledgeville, Ohio 42 39 36N 83 35W
Milledgeville, Tenn. 48 35 22N 88 22W
Millen 18 32 48N 81 57W
Miller, Kans. 24 38 38N 95 59W
Miller, Miss. 31 34 55N 89 46W
Miller, Mo. 32 37 13N 93 50W
Miller, Nebr. 34 40 56N 99 23W
Miller, S. Dak. 47 44 31N 98 59W
Miller County ◇, Ark. 13 33 10N 93 58W
Miller County ◇, Ga. 18 31 10N 84 45W
Miller County ◇, Mo. 32 38 15N 92 25W
Millers → 28 42 35N 72 30W
Millers Creek Res. 51 33 30N 99 20W
Millers Falls 28 42 35N 72 30W
Millers Ferry 10 32 6N 87 22W
Millersburg, Ind. 22 41 32N 85 42W
Millersburg, Iowa 23 41 34N 92 10W
Millersburg, Mich. 29 45 20N 84 4W
Millersburg, Ohio 42 40 33N 81 55W
Millersburg, Pa. 45 40 32N 76 58W
Millersport 42 39 54N 82 32W
Millersville, Md. 27 39 4N 76 39W
Millersville, Pa. 45 40 0N 76 22W
Millerton, Iowa 23 40 51N 93 18W
Millerton, N.Y. 39 41 57N 73 31W
Millerton L. 15 37 1N 119 41W
Millett 51 28 35N 99 12W
Millheim 45 40 54N 77 29W
Millicent 127 37 34 S 140 21 E
Milligan, Fla. 17 30 45N 86 38W
Milligan, Nebr. 34 40 30N 97 23W
Millington, Md. 27 39 16N 75 50W
Millington, Mich. 29 43 17N 83 32W
Millinocket 26 45 39N 68 43W
Millinocket L. 26 45 46N 68 48W
Millis 28 42 10N 71 22W
Millport 10 33 34N 88 5W
Millry 10 31 38N 88 19W
Mills, N. Mex. 38 36 5N 104 15W
Mills, Nebr. 34 42 57N 99 27W
Mills, Wyo. 56 42 50N 106 22W
Mills County ◇, Iowa 23 41 0N 95 35W
Mills County ◇, Tex. 51 31 27N 98 34W
Mills L. 62 61 30N 118 20W
Millsboro 27 38 36N 75 18W
Millstadt 21 38 28N 90 6W
Millstone 54 38 48N 81 6W

Milltown Moju

Milltown, Ind. 22 38 21N 86 17W
Milltown, S. Dak. 47 43 25N 97 48W
Milltown, Wis. 55 45 32N 92 30W
Milltown Malbay 85 52 51N 9 25W
Millville, Del. 27 38 35N 75 8W
Millville, Iowa 23 42 42N 91 5W
Millville, Ky. 49 38 8N 84 49W
Millville, Mass. 28 42 2N 71 35W
Millville, N.J. 37 39 24N 75 2W
Millville, Ohio 42 39 23N 84 39W
Millville, Pa. 45 41 7N 76 32W
Millwood 18 31 16N 82 40W
Millwood L. 13 33 42N 93 58W
Milmay 37 39 26N 74 52W
Milne Inlet 59 72 30N 80 0W
Milner 16 40 29N 107 1W
Milnesand 38 33 39N 103 20W
Milnor 41 46 16N 97 27W
Milo, Canada 62 50 34N 112 53W
Milo, Iowa 23 41 17N 93 27W
Milo, Maine 26 45 15N 68 59W
Milo, Mo. 32 37 45N 94 18W
Milo, Oreg. 44 42 56N 123 3W
Milolii 19 19 11N 155 55W
Mílos 95 36 44N 24 25 E
Milpitas 14 37 26N 121 55W
Milroy, Ind. 22 39 30N 85 28W
Milroy, Minn. 30 44 25N 95 33W
Milroy, Pa. 45 40 43N 77 35W
Milton, N.Z. 128 46 7 S 169 59 E
Milton, U.K. 84 57 18N 4 32W
Milton, Del. 27 38 47N 75 19W
Milton, Fla. 17 30 38N 87 3W
Milton, Ill. 21 39 34N 90 39W
Milton, Iowa 23 40 41N 92 10W
Milton, Kans. 24 37 26N 97 46W
Milton, Ky. 49 38 43N 85 22W
Milton, Mass. 28 42 15N 71 5W
Milton, N. Dak. 41 48 38N 98 3W
Milton, N.H. 36 43 25N 70 59W
Milton, Pa. 45 41 1N 76 51W
Milton, Vt. 36 44 38N 73 7W
Milton, W. Va. 54 38 26N 82 8W
Milton, Wis. 55 42 47N 88 56W
Milton-Freewater 44 45 56N 118 23W
Milton Keynes 83 52 3N 0 42W
Milton Reservoir 16 40 14N 104 38W
Miltona 30 46 3N 95 18W
Miltonvale 24 39 21N 97 27W
Miltou 121 10 14N 17 26 E
Milwaukee 55 43 2N 87 55W
Milwaukee County ◇ 55 43 0N 88 0W
Milwaukie 44 45 27N 122 38W
Mimbres 38 32 51N 107 59W
Mimbres Mts. 38 32 50N 107 45W
Mimoso 75 15 10 S 48 5W
Mims 17 28 40N 80 51W
Min Jiang →, Fujian, China 115 26 0N 119 35 E
Min Jiang →, Sichuan, China 113 28 45N 104 40 E
Min Xian 115 34 25N 104 0 E
Mina 35 38 24N 118 7W
Mina Pirquitas 76 22 40 S 66 30W
Mīnā Su'ud 106 28 45N 48 28 E
Mīnā'al Aḩmadī 106 29 5N 48 10 E
Mīnāb 107 27 10N 57 1 E
Minago → 63 54 33N 98 59W
Minaki 63 49 59N 94 40W
Minam 44 45 38N 117 43W
Minamata 117 32 10N 130 30 E
Minas 77 34 20 S 55 10W
Minas, Sierra de las 66 15 9N 89 31W
Minas Basin 61 45 20N 64 12W
Minas de Rio Tinto 91 37 42N 6 35W
Minas Gerais □ 75 18 50 S 46 0W
Minas Novas 75 17 15 S 42 36W
Minatare 34 41 49N 103 30W
Minatitlán 65 17 58N 94 35W
Minbu 109 20 10N 94 52 E
Minburn 23 41 45N 94 2W
Minco 43 35 19N 97 57W
Mindanao 111 8 0N 125 0 E
Mindanao Trench 111 8 0N 128 0 E
Minden, Germany 88 52 18N 8 45 E
Minden, Iowa 23 41 28N 95 32W
Minden, La. 25 32 37N 93 17W
Minden, Nebr. 34 40 30N 98 57W
Minden, Nev. 35 38 57N 119 46W
Minden City 29 43 40N 82 47W
Mindenmines 32 37 28N 94 35W
Mindiptana 111 5 55 S 140 22 E
Mindoro 111 13 0N 121 0 E
Mindoro Strait 111 12 30N 120 30 E
Mindouli 122 4 12 S 14 28 E
Mine 117 34 12N 131 7 E
Minehead 83 51 12N 3 29W
Mineiros 73 17 34 S 52 34W
Mineola, N.Y. 39 40 45N 73 39W
Mineola, Tex. 51 32 40N 95 29W
Miner County ◇ 47 44 1N 97 36W
Mineral, Calif. 14 40 21N 121 36W
Mineral, Va. 54 38 1N 77 55W
Mineral, Wash. 53 46 43N 122 11W
Mineral Bluff 18 34 55N 84 17W
Mineral County ◇, Colo. 16 37 40N 106 50W
Mineral County ◇, Mont. 33 47 4N 115 0W
Mineral County ◇, Nev. 35 38 30N 118 25W
Mineral County ◇, W. Va. 54 39 21N 79 0W
Mineral Mts. 52 38 30N 112 45W
Mineral Point, Mo. 32 37 57N 90 44W
Mineral Point, Wis. 55 42 52N 90 11W
Mineral Springs 13 33 53N 93 55W
Mineral Wells 51 32 48N 98 7W
Minersville, Pa. 45 40 41N 76 16W
Minersville, Utah 52 38 13N 112 56W
Minerva, N.Y. 39 43 47N 73 59W
Minerva, Ohio 42 40 44N 81 6W
Mingan 61 50 20N 64 0W
Mingechaurskoye Vdkhr. 99 40 56N 47 20 E
Minggang 115 32 24N 114 3 E
Mingin 109 22 50N 94 30 E
Mingo County ◇ 54 37 43N 82 11W
Mingo Junction 42 40 19N 80 37W
Mingxi 115 26 18N 117 12 E
Minho □ 91 41 25N 8 20W
Minho → 91 41 58N 8 40W
Minidoka 20 42 45N 113 29W
Minidoka County ◇ 20 42 50N 113 38W
Minier 21 40 26N 89 19W
Minigwal L. 126 29 31 S 123 14 E
Minipi, L. 61 52 25N 60 45W
Mink L. 62 61 54N 117 40W
Minna 120 9 37N 6 30 E
Minneapolis, Kans. 24 39 8N 97 42W
Minneapolis, Minn. 30 44 59N 93 16W
Minnedosa 63 50 14N 99 50W
Minnehaha County ◇ 47 43 40N 96 49W
Minneiska 30 44 12N 91 52W
Minneola 24 37 26N 100 1W
Minneota 30 44 34N 95 59W
Minnesota □ 30 46 0N 94 15W
Minnesota → 30 44 54N 93 9W
Minnesota City 30 44 6N 91 46W
Minnesota Lake 30 43 51N 93 50W
Minnetonka 30 44 56N 93 27W
Minnewaukan 41 48 4N 99 15W
Minnitaki L. 60 49 57N 92 10W
Mino 117 35 32N 136 55 E
Miño → 91 41 52N 8 40W
Minong 55 46 6N 91 49W
Minonk 21 40 54N 89 2W
Minooka 21 41 27N 88 16W
Minor Hill 48 35 4N 87 9W
Minorca = Menorca 91 40 0N 4 0 E
Minot 41 48 14N 101 18W
Minqing 115 26 15N 118 50 E
Minsk 98 53 52N 27 30 E
Mińsk Mazowiecki 89 52 10N 21 33 E
Minster 42 40 24N 84 23W
Mint Hill 40 35 13N 80 41W
Mintaka Pass 108 37 0N 74 58 E
Minto, Alaska 11 64 53N 149 11W
Minto, N. Dak. 41 48 17N 97 22W
Minton 63 49 10N 104 35W
Minturn 16 39 35N 106 26W
Minusinsk 101 53 50N 91 20 E
Minutang 109 28 15N 96 30 E
Minvoul 122 2 9N 12 8 E
Mio 29 44 39N 84 8W
Mir 121 14 5N 11 59 E
Mira → 70 1 36N 79 1W
Mira por vos Cay 67 22 9N 74 30W
Miracema do Norte 74 9 33 S 48 24W
Mirador 74 6 22 S 44 22W
Miraflores, Colombia 70 1 25N 72 13W
Miraflores, Mexico 64 23 21N 109 45W
Miraflores Locks 57 9 0N 79 36W
Miraj 108 16 50N 74 45 E
Miram Shah 108 33 0N 70 2 E
Miramar, Argentina 76 38 15 S 57 50W
Miramar, U.S.A. 17 25 59N 80 15W
Miramichi B. 61 47 15N 65 0W
Miranda 73 20 10 S 56 15W
Miranda □ 70 10 15N 66 25W
Miranda → 73 19 25 S 57 20W
Miranda de Ebro 91 42 41N 2 57W
Mirando City 50 27 26N 99 0W
Mirandópolis 77 21 9 S 51 6W
Mirassol 77 20 46 S 49 28W
Mirbāţ 105 17 0N 54 45 E
Miri 110 4 18N 114 0 E
Mirim, Lagoa 77 32 45 S 52 50W
Mirimire 70 11 10N 68 43W
Miriti 73 6 15 S 59 0W
Mirnyy, Antarct. 5 66 33 S 93 1 E
Mirnyy, U.S.S.R. 101 62 33N 113 53 E
Mirond L. 63 55 6N 102 47W
Mirpur Khas 108 25 30N 69 0 E
Mirror 62 52 30N 113 7W
Mîrşani 95 44 1N 23 59 E
Miryang 114 35 31N 128 44 E
Mirzapur 109 25 10N 82 34 E
Mirzapur-cum-Vindhyachal = Mirzapur 109 25 10N 82 34 E
Misantla 65 19 56N 96 50W
Misawa 116 40 41N 141 24 E
Miscou I. 61 47 57N 64 31W
Misenheimer 40 35 29N 80 17W
Mish'āb, Ra'as al 106 28 15N 48 43 E
Mishagua → 72 11 12 S 72 58W
Mishan 114 45 37N 131 48 E
Mishawaka 22 41 40N 86 11W
Mishima 117 35 10N 138 52 E
Mishmar Ayyalon 104 31 52N 34 57 E
Mishmar Ha' Emeq 104 32 37N 35 7 E
Mishmar Ha Negev 104 31 22N 34 48 E
Mishmar Ha Yarden 104 33 0N 35 36 E
Misión, La 64 32 5N 116 50W
Misión Fagnano 78 54 32 S 67 17W
Misiones □, Argentina 77 27 0 S 55 0W
Misiones □, Paraguay 76 27 0 S 56 0W
Miskīn 107 23 44N 56 52 E
Miskitos, Cayos 66 14 26N 82 50W
Miskolc 89 48 7N 20 50 E
Misool 111 1 52 S 130 10 E
Misquah Hills 30 47 50N 90 30W
Misquamicut 28 41 20N 71 49W
Misrātah 121 32 24N 15 3 E
Misriç 106 37 55N 41 40 E
Missanabie 60 48 20N 84 6W
Missão Velha 74 7 15 S 39 10W
Missaukee County ◇ 29 44 20N 85 10W
Missinaibi → 60 50 43N 81 29W
Missinaibi L. 60 48 23N 83 40W
Mission, S. Dak. 47 43 18N 100 39W
Mission, Tex. 50 26 13N 98 20W
Mission City 62 49 10N 122 15W
Mission Hill 47 42 55N 97 17W
Mission Indian Reservations 15 33 20N 116 50W
Mission Viejo 15 33 36N 117 40W
Missiquoi B. 36 45 5N 73 10W
Missisa L. 60 52 20N 85 7W
Missisquoi → 36 45 0N 73 8W
Mississagi → 60 46 15N 83 9W
Mississinewa L. 22 40 42N 85 52W
Mississippi □ 31 32 0N 90 0W
Mississippi → 25 29 9N 89 15W
Mississippi County ◇, Ark. 13 35 45N 90 5W
Mississippi County ◇, Mo. 32 36 50N 89 15W
Mississippi River Delta 25 29 10N 89 15W
Mississippi Sd. 31 30 20N 89 0W
Missoula 33 46 52N 114 1W
Missoula County ◇ 33 47 4N 114 0W
Missouri □ 32 38 0N 92 0W
Missouri → 32 38 49N 90 7W
Missouri Buttes 56 44 37N 104 47W
Missouri City 32 39 14N 94 18W
Missouri Valley 23 41 34N 95 53W
Mistake B. 63 62 8N 93 0W
Mistassini → 61 48 42N 72 20W
Mistassini L. 60 51 0N 73 30W
Mistastin L. 61 55 57N 63 20W
Mistatim 63 52 52N 103 22W
Mistretta 94 37 56N 14 20 E
Misty L. 63 58 53N 101 40W
Mitchell, Australia 127 26 29 S 147 58 E
Mitchell, Ga. 18 33 13N 82 42W
Mitchell, Ind. 22 38 44N 86 28W
Mitchell, Iowa 23 43 19N 92 53W
Mitchell, Nebr. 34 41 57N 103 49W
Mitchell, Oreg. 44 44 34N 120 9W
Mitchell, S. Dak. 47 43 43N 98 2W
Mitchell → 127 15 12 S 141 35 E
Mitchell, Mt. 40 35 46N 82 16W
Mitchell County ◇, Ga. 18 31 15N 84 10W
Mitchell County ◇, Iowa 23 43 20N 92 45W
Mitchell County ◇, Kans. 24 39 30N 98 10W
Mitchell County ◇, N.C. 40 36 5N 82 10W
Mitchell County ◇, Tex. 50 32 24N 100 52W
Mitchell L. 10 32 48N 86 27W
Mitchellsburg 49 37 36N 84 57W
Mitchellville 23 41 40N 93 22W
Mitchelstown 85 52 16N 8 18W
Mitiaro, I. 128 19 49 S 157 43W
Mitla 65 16 55N 96 24W
Mito 117 36 20N 140 30 E
Mitsinjo 123 16 1 S 45 52 E
Mitsiwa 121 15 35N 39 25 E
Mitsukaidō 117 36 1N 139 59 E
Mitú 70 1 8N 70 3W
Mituas 70 3 52N 68 49W
Mitumba, Chaîne des 122 6 0 S 29 0 E
Mitwaba 122 8 2 S 27 17 E
Mitzic 122 0 45N 11 40 E
Mixteco → 65 18 11N 98 30W
Miyagi □ 116 38 15N 140 45 E
Miyake-Jima 117 34 0N 139 30 E
Miyako 116 39 40N 141 59 E
Miyako-Jima 117 24 45N 125 20 E
Miyako-Rettō 117 24 24N 125 0 E
Miyakonojō 117 31 40N 131 5 E
Miyanoura-Dake 117 30 20N 130 31 E
Miyazaki 117 31 56N 131 30 E
Miyazaki □ 117 32 30N 131 30 E
Miyazu 117 35 35N 135 10 E
Miyoshi 117 34 48N 132 51 E
Miyun 114 40 28N 116 50 E
Mizal 106 23 59N 45 11 E
Mizamis = Ozamis 111 8 15N 123 50 E
Mizdah 121 31 30N 13 0 E
Mize 31 31 52N 89 33W
Mizen Hd., Cork, Ireland 85 51 27N 9 50W
Mizen Hd., Wicklow, Ireland 85 52 52N 6 4W
Mizhi 114 37 47N 110 12 E
Mizil 95 44 59N 26 29 E
Mizoram □ 109 23 30N 92 40 E
Mizpah, Minn. 30 47 55N 94 12W
Mizpah, Mont. 33 46 14N 105 16W
Mizpe Ramon 104 30 34N 34 49 E
Mizuho 5 70 30 S 41 0 E
Mizusawa 116 39 8N 141 8 E
Mjölby 97 58 20N 15 10 E
Mjøsa 97 60 48N 11 0 E
Mkushi 123 14 25 S 29 15 E
Mladá Boleslav 88 50 27N 14 53 E
Mława 89 53 9N 20 25 E
Mo i Rana 96 66 15N 14 7 E
Moa 111 8 0 S 128 0 E
Moab 52 38 35N 109 33W
Moabi 122 2 24 S 10 59 E
Moaco → 72 7 41 S 68 18W
Moala 128 18 36 S 179 53 E
Moapa 35 36 40N 114 37W
Moba 122 7 0 S 29 48 E
Mobaye 122 4 25N 21 5 E
Mobayi 122 4 15N 21 8 E
Mobeetie 50 35 31N 100 26W
Moberly 32 39 25N 92 26W
Moberly → 62 56 12N 120 55W
Mobile, Ala. 10 30 41N 88 3W
Mobile, Ariz. 12 33 3N 112 16W
Mobile B. 10 30 30N 88 0W
Mobile County ◇ 10 30 41N 88 3W
Mobridge 47 45 32N 100 26W
Mobutu Sese Seko, L. 122 1 30N 31 0 E
Moca 57 18 24N 67 10W
Mocajuba 74 2 35 S 49 30W
Moçambique 123 15 3 S 40 42 E
Moçâmedes = Namibe 123 15 7 S 12 11 E
Mocapra → 70 7 56N 66 46W
Moccasin 12 36 55N 112 46W
Moccasin Gap 54 36 38N 82 33W
Mocha, I. 78 38 22 S 73 56W
Mochudi 123 24 27 S 26 7 E
Mocimboa da Praia 122 11 25 S 40 20 E
Mocksville 40 35 54N 80 34W
Moclips 53 47 14N 124 13W
Mocoa 70 1 7N 76 35W
Mococa 77 21 28 S 47 0W
Mocorito 64 25 30N 107 53W
Moctezuma 64 29 50N 109 0W
Moctezuma → 65 21 59N 98 34W
Mocuba 123 16 54 S 36 57 E
Modane 90 45 12N 6 40 E
Model 16 37 22N 104 15W
Módena, Italy 94 44 39N 10 55 E
Modena, U.S.A. 52 37 48N 113 56W
Modesto 14 37 39N 121 0W
Módica 94 36 52N 14 45 E
Modoc, Ga. 18 32 37N 82 19W
Modoc, S.C. 46 33 44N 82 13W
Modoc County ◇ 14 41 40N 120 50W
Modoc Point 44 42 27N 121 52W
Moe 127 38 12 S 146 19 E
Moei → 112 17 25N 98 10 E
Moengo 71 5 45N 54 20W
Moenkopi 12 36 7N 111 13W
Moffat, U.K. 84 55 20N 3 27W
Moffat, U.S.A. 16 37 58N 105 56W
Moffat County ◇ 16 40 45N 108 10W
Mogadishu = Muqdisho 105 2 2N 45 25 E
Mogador = Essaouira 120 31 32N 9 42W
Mogami → 116 38 45N 140 0 E
Mogaung 109 25 20N 97 0 E
Mogi das Cruzes 77 23 31 S 46 11W
Mogi-Guaçu → 77 20 53 S 48 10W
Mogi-Mirim 77 22 29 S 47 0W
Mogilev 98 53 55N 30 18 E
Mogilev-Podolskiy 99 48 20N 27 40 E
Mogincual 123 15 35 S 40 25 E
Mogocha 101 53 40N 119 50 E
Mogoi 111 1 55 S 133 10 E
Mogok 109 23 0N 96 40 E
Mogollon Mts. 38 33 25N 108 40W
Mogollon Rim 12 34 10N 110 50W
Mohács 89 45 58N 18 41 E
Mohall 41 48 46N 101 31W
Moḩammadābād 107 37 52N 59 5 E
Mohave, L. 12 35 12N 114 34W
Mohave County ◇ 12 35 0N 114 0W
Mohave Mts. 12 34 35N 114 10W
Mohawk, Mich. 29 47 18N 88 21W
Mohawk, N.Y. 39 43 0N 75 0W
Mohawk → 39 42 47N 73 41W
Mohawk Mts. 12 32 30N 113 35W
Mohe 114 53 28N 122 17 E
Mohican → 42 40 22N 82 9W
Mohican, C. 11 60 12N 167 25W
Mohicanville Reservoir 42 40 45N 82 0W
Mohon Pk. 12 34 57N 113 9W
Mohoro 122 8 6 S 39 8 E
Moidart, L. 84 56 47N 5 40W
Moineşti 95 46 28N 26 31 E
Mointy 100 47 10N 73 18 E
Moisie 61 50 12N 66 1W
Moisie → 61 50 14N 66 5W
Moïssala 121 8 21N 17 46 E
Mojave 15 35 3N 118 10W
Mojave → 15 35 6N 116 4W
Mojave Desert 15 35 0N 117 20W
Mojo 76 21 48 S 65 33W
Mojokerto 111 7 29 S 112 25 E
Mojos, Llanos de 73 15 0 S 65 0W
Moju → 74 1 40 S 48 25W

Mokai **Moose Jaw Cr.**

Mokai **128** 38 32 S 175 56 E
Mokane **32** 38 41N 91 53W
Mokapu Peninsula **19** 21 25N 157 45W
Mokelumne → **14** 38 13N 121 28W
Mokelumne Hill **14** 38 18N 120 43W
Mokokchung **109** 26 15N 94 30 E
Mokolea Rock **19** 21 27N 157 44W
Moku Manu **19** 21 29N 157 43W
Mokuaeae I. **19** 22 14N 159 25W
Mokuauia I. **19** 21 40N 157 56W
Mokulua Is. **19** 21 24N 157 42W
Mol **87** 51 11N 5 5 E
Molalla **44** 45 9N 122 35W
Molchanovo **100** 57 40N 83 50 E
Mold **82** 53 10N 3 10W
Moldavia = Moldova **95** 46 30N 27 0 E
Moldavian S.S.R. □ **99** 47 0N 28 0 E
Molde **96** 62 45N 7 9 E
Moldova **95** 46 30N 27 0 E
Moldoveanu **95** 45 36N 24 45 E
Molena **18** 33 1N 84 30W
Molepolole **123** 24 28 S 25 28 E
Molfetta **94** 41 12N 16 35 E
Molii Pond **19** 21 31N 157 51W
Molina **16** 39 11N 108 4W
Moline, Ill. **21** 41 30N 90 31W
Moline, Kans. **24** 37 22N 96 18W
Molino **17** 30 43N 87 20W
Molinos **76** 25 28 S 66 15W
Moliro **122** 8 12 S 30 30 E
Molise □ **94** 41 45N 14 30 E
Mollendo **72** 17 0 S 72 0W
Mölndal **97** 57 40N 12 3 E
Molokai **19** 21 8N 157 0W
Molokini I. **19** 20 38N 156 30W
Molopo → **123** 28 30 S 20 13 E
Molotov = Perm **98** 58 0N 57 10 E
Moloundou **122** 2 8N 15 15 E
Molson L. **63** 54 22N 96 40W
Molu **111** 6 45 S 131 40 E
Molucca Sea **111** 4 0 S 124 0 E
Moluccas = Maluku **111** 1 0 S 127 0 E
Moma **123** 16 47 S 39 4 E
Mombaça **74** 5 43 S 39 45W
Mombasa **122** 4 2 S 39 43 E
Mombetsu **116** 44 21N 143 22 E
Momchilgrad **95** 41 33N 25 23 E
Momence **21** 41 10N 87 40W
Mompós **70** 9 14N 74 26W
Møn **97** 54 57N 12 15 E
Mon → **109** 20 25N 94 30 E
Mona **52** 39 49N 111 51W
Mona, Canal de la **67** 18 30N 67 45W
Mona, I. **67** 18 5N 67 54W
Mona, Isla **57** 18 5N 67 54W
Mona, Pta. **66** 9 37N 82 36W
Monach Is. **84** 57 32N 7 40W
Monaco ■ **90** 43 46N 7 23 E
Monadhliath Mts. **84** 57 10N 4 4W
Monadnock, Mt. **36** 42 52N 72 7W
Monagas □ **71** 9 20N 63 0W
Monaghan **85** 54 15N 6 58W
Monaghan □ **85** 54 10N 7 0W
Monahans **50** 31 36N 102 54W
Monango **41** 46 10N 98 36W
Monarch **46** 34 42N 81 34W
Monarch Mt. **62** 51 55N 125 57W
Monarch Pass **16** 38 30N 106 20W
Monastir = Bitola **95** 41 5N 21 10 E
Monastir **121** 35 50N 10 49 E
Moncayo, Sierra del **91** 41 48N 1 50W
Mönchengladbach **88** 51 12N 6 23 E
Monchique **91** 37 19N 8 38W
Monchique, Sa. de **91** 37 18N 8 39W
Moncks Corner **46** 33 12N 80 1W
Monclova **64** 26 50N 101 30W
Moncton **61** 46 7N 64 51W
Mondamin **23** 41 42N 96 1W
Mondego → **91** 40 9N 8 52W
Mondeodo **111** 3 34 S 122 9 E
Mondoví, Italy **94** 44 23N 7 49 E
Mondovi, U.S.A. **55** 44 34N 91 40W
Monee **21** 41 25N 87 44W
Monero **38** 36 55N 106 52W
Monessen **45** 40 9N 79 54W
Moneta **23** 43 13N 95 24W
Monett **32** 36 55N 93 55W
Monette **13** 35 53N 90 21W
Monforte **91** 39 6N 7 25W
Mong Cai **112** 21 27N 107 54 E
Mong Hsu **109** 21 54N 98 30 E
Mong Kung **109** 21 35N 97 35 E
Mong Lang **112** 21 29N 97 52 E
Mong Nai **109** 20 32N 97 46 E
Mong Pawk **109** 22 4N 99 16 E
Mong Ton **109** 20 17N 98 45 E
Mong Wa **109** 21 26N 100 27 E
Mong Yai **109** 22 21N 98 3 E
Mongalla **121** 5 8N 31 42 E
Mongers, L. **126** 29 25 S 117 5 E
Monghyr = Munger **109** 25 23N 86 30 E
Mongo **121** 12 14N 18 43 E
Mongolia ■ **113** 47 0N 103 0 E
Mongororo **121** 12 3N 22 26 E
Mongu **123** 15 16 S 23 12 E
Monhegan I. **26** 43 46N 69 19W
Moniac **18** 30 31N 82 14W
Monico **55** 45 35N 89 9W
Monida **33** 44 34N 112 19W
Moniteau County ◇ **32** 38 35N 92 35W
Monitor **53** 47 29N 120 25W
Monitor Range **35** 38 40N 118 45W
Monkey River **65** 16 22N 88 29W
Monkoto **122** 1 38 S 20 35 E
Monkstown **51** 33 48N 95 56W
Monkton **27** 39 35N 76 37W
Monmouth, U.K. **83** 51 48N 2 43W
Monmouth, Ill. **21** 40 55N 90 39W
Monmouth, Oreg. **44** 44 51N 123 14W
Monmouth County ◇ **37** 40 15N 74 15W
Monmouth Junction **37** 40 23N 74 33W
Mono County ◇ **14** 38 0N 119 0W
Mono L. **14** 38 1N 119 1W
Monocary → **27** 39 13N 77 27W
Monolith **15** 35 7N 118 22W
Monomoy I. **28** 41 36N 69 59W
Monomoy Point **28** 41 33N 70 2W
Monon **22** 40 52N 86 53W
Monona, Iowa **23** 43 3N 91 23W
Monona, Wis. **55** 43 4N 89 20W
Monona County ◇ **23** 42 0N 96 0W
Monongah **54** 39 28N 80 13W
Monongahela **45** 40 12N 79 56W
Monongahela → **45** 40 27N 80 1W
Monongahela National Forest **54** 38 30N 79 57W
Monongalia County ◇ **54** 39 39N 80 1W
Monópoli **94** 40 57N 17 18 E
Monowi **34** 42 50N 98 20W
Monqoumba **122** 3 33N 18 40 E
Monroe, Ark. **13** 34 44N 91 6W
Monroe, Ga. **18** 33 47N 83 43W
Monroe, Ind. **22** 40 45N 84 56W
Monroe, Iowa **23** 41 31N 93 6W
Monroe, La. **25** 32 30N 92 7W
Monroe, Mich. **29** 41 55N 83 24W
Monroe, N.C. **40** 34 59N 80 33W
Monroe, N.Y. **39** 41 20N 74 11W
Monroe, Nebr. **34** 41 28N 97 36W
Monroe, Ohio **42** 39 27N 84 22W
Monroe, Okla. **43** 34 59N 94 30W
Monroe, Oreg. **44** 44 19N 123 18W
Monroe, S. Dak. **47** 43 29N 97 13W
Monroe, Utah **52** 38 38N 112 7W
Monroe, Va. **54** 37 30N 79 8W
Monroe, Wash. **53** 47 51N 121 58W
Monroe, Wis. **55** 42 36N 89 38W
Monroe, L. **17** 28 50N 81 19W
Monroe City **32** 39 39N 91 44W
Monroe County ◇, Ala. **10** 31 31N 87 20W
Monroe County ◇, Ark. **13** 34 42N 91 19W
Monroe County ◇, Fla. **17** 25 30N 81 0W
Monroe County ◇, Ga. **18** 33 0N 83 55W
Monroe County ◇, Ill. **21** 38 15N 90 10W
Monroe County ◇, Ind. **22** 39 10N 86 30W
Monroe County ◇, Iowa **23** 41 0N 92 50W
Monroe County ◇, Ky. **49** 36 45N 85 45W
Monroe County ◇, Mich. **29** 41 50N 83 35W
Monroe County ◇, Miss. **31** 33 49N 88 33W
Monroe County ◇, Mo. **32** 39 30N 92 0W
Monroe County ◇, N.Y. **39** 43 10N 77 40W
Monroe County ◇, Ohio **42** 39 46N 81 7W
Monroe County ◇, Pa. **45** 41 0N 75 15W
Monroe County ◇, Tenn. **49** 35 31N 84 22W
Monroe County ◇, W. Va. **54** 37 36N 80 33W
Monroe County ◇, Wis. **55** 43 50N 90 40W
Monroe L. **22** 39 1N 86 31W
Monroeton **45** 41 43N 76 29W
Monroeville, Ala. **10** 31 31N 87 20W
Monroeville, Ind. **22** 40 59N 84 52W
Monroeville, Ohio **42** 41 15N 82 42W
Monroeville, Pa. **45** 40 26N 79 45W
Monrovia **120** 6 18N 10 47W
Mons **87** 50 27N 3 58 E
Monse **111** 4 0 S 123 10 E
Monsefú **72** 6 52 S 79 52W
Monson **26** 45 17N 69 30W
Mont Alto **45** 39 51N 77 34W
Mont Belvieu **51** 29 51N 94 53W
Mont-de-Marsan **90** 43 54N 0 31W
Mont Ida **24** 38 13N 95 22W
Mont-Joli **61** 48 37N 68 10W
Mont Laurier **60** 46 35N 75 30W
Mont-St-Michel, Le **90** 48 40N 1 30W
Mont Tremblant Prov. Park **60** 46 30N 74 30W
Mont Vernon **36** 42 50N 71 42W
Montagu I. **5** 58 25 S 26 20W
Montague, Canada **61** 46 10N 62 39W
Montague, Calif. **14** 41 44N 122 32W
Montague, Mass. **28** 42 32N 72 32W
Montague, Mich. **29** 43 25N 86 22W
Montague, Tex. **51** 33 42N 97 48W
Montague, I. **64** 31 40N 114 56W
Montague County ◇ **51** 33 47N 97 44W
Montague I. **11** 60 0N 147 30W
Montague Sd. **126** 14 28 S 125 20 E
Montalba **51** 31 53N 95 44W
Montalbán **91** 40 50N 0 45W
Montaña **72** 6 0 S 73 0W
Montana □ **33** 47 0N 110 0W
Montañita **70** 1 22N 75 28W
Montargis **90** 48 0N 2 43 E
Montauban **90** 44 0N 1 21 E
Montauk **39** 41 3N 71 57W
Montbéliard **90** 47 31N 6 48 E
Montcalm County ◇ **29** 43 15N 85 10W
Montclair **37** 40 49N 74 13W
Monte Albán **65** 17 2N 96 45W
Monte Alegre **71** 2 0 S 54 0W
Monte Alegre de Goiás **75** 13 14 S 47 10W
Monte Alegre de Minas **75** 18 52 S 48 52W
Monte Azul **75** 15 9 S 42 53W
Monte Bello Is. **126** 20 30 S 115 45 E
Monte-Carlo **90** 43 46N 7 23 E
Monte Carmelo **75** 18 43 S 47 29W
Monte Caseros **76** 30 10 S 57 50W
Monte Comán **76** 34 40 S 67 53W
Monte Cristi **67** 19 52N 71 39W
Monte Dinero **78** 52 18 S 68 33W
Monte Lindo → **76** 23 56 S 57 12W
Monte Quemado **76** 25 53 S 62 41W
Monte Sant' Ángelo **94** 41 42N 15 59 E
Monte Santu, C. di **94** 40 5N 9 42 E
Monte Vista **16** 37 35N 106 9W
Monteagle **49** 35 15N 85 50W
Monteagudo, Argentina **77** 27 14 S 54 8W
Monteagudo, Bolivia **73** 19 49 S 63 59W
Montebello **60** 45 40N 74 55W
Montecito **15** 34 26N 119 40W
Montecristi **70** 1 0 S 80 40W
Montego Bay **66** 18 30N 78 0W
Montegut **25** 29 28N 90 33W
Monteiro **74** 7 48 S 37 2W
Montelíbano **70** 8 5N 75 29W
Montélimar **90** 44 33N 4 45 E
Montello, Nev. **35** 41 16N 114 12W
Montello, Wis. **55** 43 48N 89 20W
Montemorelos **65** 25 11N 99 42W
Montenegro = Crna Gora □ **95** 42 40N 19 20 E
Montenegro **77** 29 39 S 51 29W
Montepuez **123** 13 8 S 38 59 E
Monterey, Calif. **14** 36 37N 121 55W
Monterey, Ky. **49** 38 25N 84 52W
Monterey, Mass. **28** 42 11N 73 13W
Monterey, Tenn. **49** 36 9N 85 16W
Monterey, Va. **54** 38 25N 79 35W
Monterey B. **14** 36 45N 122 0W
Monterey County ◇ **15** 36 15N 121 20W
Montería **70** 8 46N 75 53W
Montero **73** 17 20 S 63 15W
Monteros **76** 27 11 S 65 30W
Monterrey **64** 25 40N 100 30W
Montes Altos **74** 5 50 S 47 4W
Montes Claros **75** 16 30 S 43 50W
Montesano **53** 46 59N 123 36W
Montevallo **10** 33 6N 86 52W
Montevideo, Uruguay **77** 34 50 S 56 11W
Montevideo, U.S.A. **30** 44 57N 95 43W
Monteview **20** 43 56N 112 32W
Montezuma, Ga. **18** 32 18N 84 2W
Montezuma, Ind. **22** 39 48N 87 22W
Montezuma, Iowa **23** 41 35N 92 32W
Montezuma, Kans. **24** 37 36N 100 27W
Montezuma County ◇ **16** 37 20N 108 30W
Montezuma Cr. → **52** 37 17N 109 20W
Montfort **55** 42 58N 90 26W
Montgomery = Sahiwal **108** 30 45N 73 8 E
Montgomery, U.K. **83** 52 34N 3 9W
Montgomery, Ala. **10** 32 23N 86 19W
Montgomery, Ga. **18** 31 57N 81 7W
Montgomery, La. **25** 31 40N 92 53W
Montgomery, Minn. **30** 44 26N 93 35W
Montgomery, Pa. **45** 41 10N 76 53W
Montgomery, Tex. **51** 30 23N 95 42W
Montgomery, W. Va. **54** 38 11N 81 19W
Montgomery Center **36** 44 53N 73 40W
Montgomery City **32** 38 59N 91 30W
Montgomery County ◇, Ala. **10** 32 15N 86 18W
Montgomery County ◇, Ark. **13** 34 34N 93 38W
Montgomery County ◇, Ga. **18** 32 15N 82 35W
Montgomery County ◇, Ill. **21** 39 10N 89 30W
Montgomery County ◇, Ind. **22** 40 5N 86 55W
Montgomery County ◇, Iowa **23** 41 0N 95 10W
Montgomery County ◇, Kans. **24** 37 15N 95 45W
Montgomery County ◇, Ky. **49** 38 0N 83 55W
Montgomery County ◇, Md. **27** 39 15N 77 15W
Montgomery County ◇, Miss. **31** 33 29N 89 44W
Montgomery County ◇, Mo. **32** 38 55N 91 30W
Montgomery County ◇, N.C. **40** 35 20N 79 50W
Montgomery County ◇, N.Y. **39** 42 50N 74 30W
Montgomery County ◇, Ohio **42** 39 45N 84 12W
Montgomery County ◇, Pa. **45** 40 10N 75 10W
Montgomery County ◇, Tenn. **48** 36 32N 87 21W
Montgomery County ◇, Tex. **51** 30 19N 95 27W
Montgomery County ◇, Va. **54** 37 8N 80 25W
Montgomery Village **27** 39 12N 77 13W
Monticello, Ark. **13** 33 38N 91 47W
Monticello, Fla. **17** 30 33N 83 52W
Monticello, Ga. **18** 33 18N 83 40W
Monticello, Ill. **21** 40 1N 88 34W
Monticello, Ind. **22** 40 45N 86 46W
Monticello, Iowa **23** 42 15N 91 12W
Monticello, Ky. **49** 36 50N 84 51W
Monticello, Maine **26** 46 19N 67 51W
Monticello, Minn. **30** 45 18N 93 48W
Monticello, Miss. **31** 31 33N 90 7W
Monticello, Mo. **32** 40 7N 91 43W
Monticello, N. Mex. **38** 33 24N 107 27W
Monticello, N.Y. **39** 41 39N 74 42W
Monticello, Utah **52** 37 52N 109 21W
Monticello, Wis. **55** 42 45N 89 36W
Montijo **91** 38 52N 6 39W
Montilla **91** 37 36N 4 40W
Montluçon **90** 46 22N 2 36 E
Montmagny **61** 46 58N 70 34W
Montmartre **63** 50 14N 103 27W
Montmorency **61** 46 53N 71 11W
Montmorency County ◇ **29** 45 0N 84 10W
Monto **127** 24 52 S 151 6 E
Montoro **91** 38 1N 4 27W
Montour, Idaho **20** 43 55N 116 20W
Montour, Iowa **23** 41 59N 92 43W
Montour County ◇ **45** 41 0N 76 40W
Montour Falls **39** 42 21N 76 51W
Montoursville **45** 41 15N 76 55W
Montoya **38** 35 6N 104 4W
Montpelier, Idaho **20** 42 19N 111 18W
Montpelier, Ind. **22** 40 33N 85 17W
Montpelier, La. **25** 30 41N 90 39W
Montpelier, Miss. **31** 33 43N 88 57W
Montpelier, N. Dak. **41** 46 42N 98 35W
Montpelier, Ohio **42** 41 35N 84 37W
Montpelier, Vt. **36** 44 16N 72 35W
Montpellier **90** 43 37N 3 52 E
Montréal **60** 45 31N 73 34W
Montreal L. **63** 54 20N 105 45W
Montreal Lake **63** 54 3N 105 46W
Montreuil **90** 50 27N 1 45 E
Montreux **88** 46 26N 6 55 E
Montrose, U.K. **84** 56 43N 2 28W
Montrose, Ark. **13** 33 18N 91 30W
Montrose, Colo. **16** 38 29N 107 53W
Montrose, Ill. **21** 39 10N 88 23W
Montrose, Iowa **23** 40 31N 91 25W
Montrose, Mich. **29** 43 11N 83 54W
Montrose, Miss. **31** 32 8N 89 14W
Montrose, Mo. **32** 38 16N 93 59W
Montrose, Pa. **45** 41 50N 75 53W
Montrose, S. Dak. **47** 43 42N 97 11W
Montrose, W. Va. **54** 39 4N 79 49W
Montrose County ◇ **16** 38 30N 108 15W
Montross **54** 38 6N 76 50W
Monts, Pte. des **61** 49 20N 67 12W
Montserrat **67** 16 40N 62 10W
Montvale **54** 37 23N 79 44W
Montville **28** 41 27N 72 8W
Monument, Kans. **24** 39 6N 101 1W
Monument, Oreg. **44** 44 49N 119 25W
Monument Draw → **50** 32 29N 102 20W
Monument Pass **12** 36 58N 110 5W
Monument Pk. **20** 42 7N 114 14W
Monument Valley **12** 37 0N 110 0W
Monveda **122** 2 52N 21 30 E
Monywa **109** 22 7N 95 11 E
Monze **123** 16 17 S 27 29 E
Monze, C. **108** 24 47N 66 37 E
Monzón **91** 41 52N 0 10 E
Moody, Mo. **32** 36 32N 91 59W
Moody, Tex. **51** 31 18N 97 21W
Moody County ◇ **47** 44 3N 96 36W
Mooleyville **48** 38 1N 86 28W
Moon L. **14** 41 10N 121 10W
Moonbeam **60** 49 20N 82 10W
Moonie → **127** 29 19 S 148 43 E
Moorcroft **56** 44 16N 104 57W
Moore, Idaho **20** 43 44N 113 22W
Moore, Mont. **33** 46 59N 109 42W
Moore, Okla. **43** 35 20N 97 29W
Moore, Tex. **51** 29 3N 99 1W
Moore, Utah **52** 38 58N 111 10W
Moore, L. **126** 29 50 S 117 35 E
Moore County ◇, N.C. **40** 35 20N 79 20W
Moore County ◇, Tenn. **48** 35 17N 86 22W
Moore County ◇, Tex. **50** 35 55N 101 59W
Moore Haven **17** 26 50N 81 6W
Moore Reservoir **36** 44 20N 71 53W
Moorefield, Nebr. **34** 40 41N 100 24W
Moorefield, W. Va. **54** 39 4N 78 58W
Moorefield → **54** 39 5N 78 59W
Mooreland **43** 36 26N 99 12W
Moorestown **37** 39 58N 74 57W
Mooresville, Ind. **22** 39 37N 86 22W
Mooresville, N.C. **40** 35 35N 80 48W
Mooreton **41** 46 16N 96 53W
Moorfoot Hills **84** 55 44N 3 8W
Moorhead, Iowa **23** 41 56N 95 51W
Moorhead, Minn. **30** 46 53N 96 45W
Moorhead, Miss. **31** 33 27N 90 30W
Mooringsport **25** 32 41N 93 58W
Moorland **23** 42 26N 94 18W
Moose →, Canada **60** 51 20N 80 25W
Moose →, N.Y. **39** 43 38N 75 24W
Moose →, Vt. **36** 44 24N 72 1W
Moose Factory **60** 51 16N 80 32W
Moose I. **63** 51 42N 97 10W
Moose Jaw **63** 50 24N 105 30W
Moose Jaw Cr. → **63** 50 34N 105 18W

Moose Lake Mountain

Moose Lake, Canada 63 53 43N 100 20W
Moose Lake, U.S.A. 30 46 27N 92 46W
Moose Mountain Cr. → 63 49 13N 102 12W
Moose Mountain Prov. Park 63 49 48N 102 25W
Moose Pass 11 60 29N 149 22W
Moose River, Canada 60 50 48N 81 17W
Moose River, U.S.A. 26 45 39N 70 16W
Moosehead L. 26 45 38N 69 40W
Mooselookmeguntic L. 26 44 55N 70 49W
Moosilauke, Mt. 36 44 3N 71 40W
Moosomin 63 50 9N 101 40W
Moosonee 60 51 17N 80 39W
Moosup 28 41 43N 71 53W
Mopeia 123 17 30S 35 40E
Mopti 120 14 30N 4 0W
Moquegua 72 17 15S 70 46W
Moquegua □ 72 16 50S 70 55W
Mora, Puerto Rico 57 18 28N 67 2W
Mora, Sweden 97 61 2N 14 38E
Mora, Ga. 18 31 25N 82 57W
Mora, Minn. 30 45 53N 93 18W
Mora, N. Mex. 38 35 58N 105 20W
Mora County ◇ 38 36 0N 104 0W
Morada Nova 74 5 7S 38 23W
Morada Nova de Minas 75 18 37S 45 22W
Moradabad 108 28 50N 78 50E
Morafenobe 123 17 50S 44 53E
Morales, Colombia 70 2 45N 76 38W
Morales, U.S.A. 51 29 8N 96 46W
Moramanga 123 18 56S 48 12E
Moran, Kans. 24 37 55N 95 10W
Moran, Mich. 29 46 0N 84 50W
Moran, Tex. 51 32 33N 99 10W
Morant Cays 66 17 22N 76 0W
Morant Pt. 66 17 55N 76 12W
Morar L. 84 56 57N 5 40W
Moratuwa 108 6 45N 79 55E
Morava → 88 48 10N 16 59E
Moravia, Iowa 23 40 53N 92 49W
Moravia, N.Y. 39 42 43N 76 25W
Moravian Hts. = Ceskomoravská Vrchovina 88 49 30N 15 40E
Morawhanna 71 8 30N 59 40W
Moray Firth 84 57 50N 3 30W
Morbihan □ 90 47 55N 2 50W
Morden 63 49 15N 98 10W
Mordovian A.S.S.R.□ 98 54 20N 44 30E
Møre og Romsdal fylke □ 96 62 30N 8 0E
Moreau → 47 45 18N 100 43W
Morecambe 82 54 5N 2 52W
Morecambe B. 82 54 7N 3 0W
Moree 127 29 28S 149 54E
Morehead 49 38 11N 83 26W
Morehead City 40 34 43N 76 43W
Morehouse 32 36 51N 89 41W
Morehouse Parish ◇ 25 32 47N 91 48W
Moreland, Ga. 18 33 17N 84 46W
Moreland, Ky. 49 37 30N 84 49W
Morelia 64 19 40N 101 11W
Morella 91 40 35N 0 5W
Morelos 64 26 42N 107 40W
Morelos □ 65 18 40N 99 10W
Morena, Sierra 91 38 20N 4 0W
Morenci, Ariz. 12 33 5N 109 22W
Morenci, Mich. 29 41 43N 84 13W
Moreni 95 44 59N 25 36E
Morero 73 11 9S 66 15W
Moreru → 73 10 10S 59 15W
Moresby I. 62 52 30N 131 40W
Moreton B. 127 27 10S 153 10E
Moreton I. 127 27 10S 153 25E
Morgan, Ga. 18 31 32N 84 36W
Morgan, Ky. 49 38 36N 84 24W
Morgan, Minn. 30 44 25N 94 56W
Morgan, Utah 52 41 2N 111 41W
Morgan, Vt. 36 44 53N 73 2W
Morgan, Mt. 15 37 31N 118 47W
Morgan City, Ala. 10 34 28N 86 34W
Morgan City, La. 25 29 42N 91 12W
Morgan County ◇, Ala. 10 34 27N 86 56W
Morgan County ◇, Colo. 16 40 15N 103 50W
Morgan County ◇, Ga. 18 33 40N 83 25W
Morgan County ◇, Ill. 21 39 45N 90 10W
Morgan County ◇, Ind. 22 39 30N 86 25W
Morgan County ◇, Ky. 49 37 55N 83 15W
Morgan County ◇, Mo. 32 38 25N 92 50W
Morgan County ◇, Ohio 42 39 39N 81 51W
Morgan County ◇, Tenn. 49 36 6N 84 36W
Morgan County ◇, Utah 52 41 10N 111 45W
Morgan County ◇, W. Va. 54 39 35N 78 16W
Morgan Hill 14 37 8N 121 39W
Morgan L. 38 36 52N 108 41W
Morgan Mill 51 32 23N 98 10W
Morganfield 48 37 41N 87 55W
Morganton 40 35 45N 81 41W
Morgantown, Ind. 22 39 22N 86 16W
Morgantown, Ky. 48 37 14N 86 41W
Morgantown, Md. 27 38 21N 76 58W
Morgantown, Ohio 42 39 8N 83 12W
Morgantown, W. Va. 54 39 38N 79 57W
Morganville, Ga. 18 34 56N 85 27W
Morganville, Kans. 24 39 28N 97 12W
Morganza 25 30 44N 91 36W
Moriah Mt. 35 39 17N 114 12W
Moriarty 38 34 59N 106 3W
Morice L. 62 53 50N 127 40W
Morichal 70 2 10N 70 34W
Morichal Largo → 71 9 27N 62 25W
Morinville 62 53 49N 113 41W
Morioka 116 39 45N 141 8E
Moris 64 28 8N 108 32W
Morlaix 90 48 36N 3 52W
Morland 24 39 21N 100 5W
Morley, Mich. 29 43 29N 85 27W
Morley, Mo. 32 37 3N 89 37W
Mormon L. 12 34 57N 111 29W
Mormon Lake 12 34 55N 111 28W
Mormon Mts. 35 37 0N 114 0W
Morning Sun 23 41 5N 91 15W
Morningside 27 38 50N 76 54W
Mornington, I. 78 49 50S 75 30W
Mornington I. 127 16 30S 139 30E
Moro, Ark. 13 34 48N 90 59W
Moro, Oreg. 44 45 29N 120 44W
Moro → 13 33 17N 92 21W
Moro G. 111 6 30N 123 0E
Morocco 22 40 57N 87 27W
Morocco ■ 120 32 0N 5 50W
Morococha 72 11 40S 76 5W
Morogoro 122 6 50S 37 40E
Morokweng 123 26 12S 23 45E
Moroleón 64 20 8N 101 32W
Morombe 123 21 45S 43 22E
Moron, Argentina 76 34 39S 58 37W
Morón, Cuba 66 22 8N 78 39W
Mörön → 113 47 14N 110 37E
Morón de la Frontera 91 37 6N 5 28W
Morona → 70 4 40S 77 10W
Morona-Santiago □ 70 2 30S 78 0W
Morondava 123 20 17S 44 17E
Moroni 52 39 32N 111 35W
Morotai 111 2 10N 128 30E
Moroto 122 2 28N 34 42E
Morovis 57 18 20N 66 25W
Morozov 95 42 30N 25 10E
Morpeth 82 55 11N 1 41W
Morphou 106 35 12N 32 59E
Morral 42 40 41N 83 13W
Morrill, Kans. 24 39 56N 95 42W
Morrill, Nebr. 34 41 58N 103 56W
Morrill County ◇ 34 41 45N 103 0W
Morrilton 13 35 9N 92 44W
Morrinhos, Ceara, Brazil 74 3 14S 40 7W
Morrinhos, Minas Gerais, Brazil 75 17 45S 49 10W
Morrinsville 128 37 40S 175 32E
Morris, Canada 63 49 25N 97 22W
Morris, Conn. 28 41 43N 73 15W
Morris, Ga. 18 31 48N 84 57W
Morris, Ill. 21 41 22N 88 26W
Morris, Minn. 30 45 35N 95 55W
Morris, N.Y. 39 42 33N 75 15W
Morris, Okla. 43 35 36N 95 51W
Morris County ◇, Kans. 24 38 30N 96 40W
Morris County ◇, N.J. 37 40 45N 74 30W
Morris County ◇, Tex. 51 33 2N 94 44W
Morrisburg 60 44 55N 75 7W
Morrison, Ill. 21 41 49N 89 58W
Morrison, Okla. 43 36 18N 97 1W
Morrison, Tenn. 49 35 36N 85 55W
Morrison County ◇ 30 46 0N 94 10W
Morrisonville 21 39 25N 89 27W
Morristown, Ariz. 12 33 51N 112 37W
Morristown, Ind. 22 39 40N 85 42W
Morristown, Minn. 30 44 14N 93 27W
Morristown, N.J. 37 40 48N 74 29W
Morristown, N.Y. 39 44 35N 75 39W
Morristown, S. Dak. 47 45 56N 101 43W
Morristown, Tenn. 49 36 13N 83 18W
Morrisville, Mo. 32 37 29N 93 25W
Morrisville, N.C. 40 35 49N 78 50W
Morrisville, N.Y. 39 42 53N 75 35W
Morrisville, Vt. 36 44 34N 72 36W
Morro, Pta. 76 27 6S 71 0W
Morro Bay 15 35 22N 120 51W
Morro do Chapéu 75 11 33S 41 9W
Morros 74 2 52S 44 3W
Morrosquillo, Golfo de 66 9 35N 75 40W
Morrow, La. 25 30 50N 92 5W
Morrow, Ohio 42 39 21N 84 8W
Morrow County ◇, Ohio 42 40 33N 82 50W
Morrow County ◇, Oreg. 44 45 25N 119 40W
Morrowville 24 39 51N 97 10W
Morrumbene 123 23 31S 35 16E
Morse 50 36 4N 101 29W
Morse Bluff 34 41 26N 96 46W
Morse Res. 22 40 7N 86 3W
Morshansk 98 53 28N 41 50E
Morteros 76 30 50S 62 0W
Mortes, L. Aux 41 48 20N 99 7W
Mortes, R. das → 75 11 45S 50 44W
Morton, Ill. 21 40 37N 89 28W
Morton, Minn. 30 44 33N 94 59W
Morton, Miss. 31 32 21N 89 39W
Morton, Tex. 50 33 44N 102 46W
Morton, Wash. 53 46 34N 122 17W
Morton County ◇, Kans. 24 37 15N 101 45W
Morton County ◇, N. Dak. 41 46 45N 101 30W
Mortons Gap 48 37 14N 87 28W
Morvan, Mts. du 90 47 5N 4 0E
Morven, Ga. 18 30 57N 83 30W
Morven, N.C. 40 34 52N 80 0W
Morvern 84 56 38N 5 44W
Morwell 127 38 10S 146 22E
Morzhovets, Ostrov 98 66 44N 42 35E
Mosby 33 47 0N 107 52W
Mosca 16 37 39N 105 52W
Moscos Is. 112 14 0N 97 30E
Moscow = Moskva 98 55 45N 37 35E
Moscow, Idaho 20 46 44N 117 0W
Moscow, Kans. 24 37 20N 101 12W
Moscow, Ky. 48 36 37N 89 2W
Moscow, Ohio 42 38 52N 84 14W
Moscow, Pa. 45 41 20N 75 31W
Moscow, Tenn. 48 35 4N 89 24W
Moscow Mills 32 38 57N 90 55W
Mosel → 90 50 22N 7 36E
Moselle = Mosel → 90 50 22N 7 36E
Moselle 31 31 30N 89 17W
Moselle □ 90 48 59N 6 33E
Moses Lake 53 47 8N 119 17W
Mosgiel 128 45 53S 170 21E
Mosheim 49 36 11N 82 57W
Mosher 47 43 28N 100 18W
Moshi 122 3 22S 37 18E
Mosier 44 45 41N 121 24W
Mosinee 55 44 47N 89 43W
Mosjøen 96 65 51N 13 12E
Moskenesøya 96 67 58N 13 0E
Moskenstraumen 96 67 47N 12 45E
Moskva 98 55 45N 37 35E
Moskva → 98 55 5N 38 51E
Mosquera 70 2 35N 78 24W
Mosquero 38 35 47N 103 58W
Mosquitia 66 15 20N 84 10W
Mosquito Creek L. 42 41 18N 80 46W
Mosquitos, Golfo de los 66 9 15N 81 10W
Moss, Norway 97 59 27N 10 40E
Moss, U.S.A. 49 36 36N 85 37W
Moss Bluff 25 30 18N 93 11W
Moss Point 31 30 25N 88 30W
Mossaka 122 1 15S 16 45E
Mossâmedes 75 16 7S 50 11W
Mossbank 63 49 56N 105 56W
Mossburn 128 45 41S 168 15E
Mosselbaai 123 34 11S 22 8E
Mossendjo 122 2 55S 12 42E
Mossman 127 16 21S 145 15E
Mossoró 74 5 10S 37 15W
Mossuril 123 14 58S 40 42E
Mossy → 63 54 5N 102 58W
Mossy Head 17 30 45N 86 19W
Mossyrock 53 46 32N 122 29W
Most 88 50 31N 13 38E
Mosta 94 35 54N 14 24E
Mostaganem 120 35 54N 0 5E
Mostar 95 43 22N 17 50E
Mostardas 77 31 2S 50 51W
Mosul = Al Mawşil 106 36 15N 43 5E
Motagua → 66 15 44N 88 14W
Motala 97 58 32N 15 1E
Motherwell 84 55 48N 4 0W
Motihari 109 26 30N 84 55E
Motley 30 46 20N 94 40W
Motley County ◇ 50 34 1N 100 50W
Motocurunya 71 4 24N 64 5W
Motozintla de Mendoza 65 15 21N 92 14W
Motru → 95 44 44N 22 59E
Mott 41 46 23N 102 20W
Motters 27 39 40N 77 20W
Motueka 128 41 7S 173 1E
Motul 65 21 0N 89 20W
Mouanda 122 1 28S 13 7E
Mouchalagane → 61 50 56N 68 41W
Moúdhros 95 39 50N 25 18E
Moudjeria 120 17 50N 12 28W
Mouila 122 1 50S 11 0E
Moule 67 16 20N 61 22W
Moulins 90 46 35N 3 19E
Moulmein 109 16 30N 97 40E
Moulton, Ala. 10 34 29N 87 18W
Moulton, Iowa 23 40 41N 92 41W
Moulton, Tex. 51 29 35N 97 9W
Moultonboro 36 43 45N 71 10W
Moultrie 18 31 11N 83 47W
Moultrie, L. 46 33 20N 80 5W
Moultrie County ◇ 21 39 40N 88 35W
Mound 25 32 21N 91 1W
Mound Bayou 31 33 53N 90 44W
Mound City, Ill. 21 37 5N 89 10W
Mound City, Kans. 24 38 8N 94 49W
Mound City, Mo. 32 40 7N 95 14W
Mound City, S. Dak. 47 45 44N 100 4W
Mound Valley 24 37 12N 95 24W
Moundou 121 8 40N 16 10E
Moundridge 24 38 12N 97 31W
Mounds, Ill. 21 37 7N 89 12W
Mounds, Okla. 43 35 53N 96 4W
Moundsville 54 39 55N 80 44W
Moundville, Ala. 10 33 1N 87 37W
Moundville, Mo. 32 37 46N 94 27W
Mount Airy, Md. 27 39 22N 77 10W
Mount Airy, N.C. 40 36 31N 80 37W
Mount Angel 44 45 4N 122 48W
Mount Auburn 23 42 15N 92 6W
Mount Ayr, Ind. 22 40 57N 87 18W
Mount Ayr, Iowa 23 40 43N 94 14W
Mount Baker National Forest 53 48 10N 121 15W
Mount Barker 126 34 38S 117 40E
Mount Blanchard 42 40 54N 83 34W
Mount Calm 51 31 46N 96 53W
Mount Carmel, Ill. 21 38 25N 87 46W
Mount Carmel, Utah 52 37 15N 112 40W
Mount Carroll 21 42 6N 89 59W
Mount Clemens 29 42 35N 82 53W
Mount Darwin 123 16 47S 31 38E
Mount Desert I. 26 44 21N 68 20W
Mount Dora, Fla. 17 28 48N 81 38W
Mount Dora, N. Mex. 38 36 31N 103 29W
Mount Eaton 42 40 42N 81 42W
Mount Eden 49 38 3N 85 9W
Mount Edgecumbe 11 57 3N 135 21W
Mount Enid 126 21 42S 116 26E
Mount Enterprise 51 31 55N 94 41W
Mount Erie 21 38 31N 88 14W
Mount Etna 22 40 45N 85 34W
Mount Forest 60 43 59N 80 43W
Mount Gambier 127 37 50S 140 46E
Mount Gay 54 37 51N 82 0W
Mount Gilead, N.C. 40 35 13N 80 0W
Mount Gilead, Ohio 42 40 33N 82 50W
Mount Holly, N.C. 40 35 18N 81 1W
Mount Holly, N.J. 37 39 59N 74 47W
Mount Holly Springs 45 40 7N 77 12W
Mount Hood National Forest 44 45 15N 122 0W
Mount Hope, Kans. 24 37 52N 97 40W
Mount Hope, W. Va. 54 37 54N 81 10W
Mount Horeb 55 43 1N 89 44W
Mount Ida 13 34 34N 93 38W
Mount Isa 127 20 42S 139 26E
Mount Jackson 54 38 45N 78 39W
Mount Jewett 45 41 44N 78 39W
Mount Joy 45 40 7N 76 30W
Mount Juliet 48 36 12N 86 31W
Mount Kisco 39 41 12N 73 44W
Mount Laguna 15 32 52N 116 25W
Mount Lebanon 45 40 23N 80 3W
Mount Liberty 42 40 21N 82 38W
Mount Lofty Ra. 127 34 35S 139 5E
Mount McKinley National Park 11 63 30N 150 0W
Mount Magnet 126 28 2S 117 47E
Mount Maunganui 128 37 40S 176 14E
Mount Montgomery 35 37 58N 118 20W
Mount Morgan 127 23 40S 150 25E
Mount Moriah 32 40 20N 93 48W
Mount Morris, Ill. 21 42 3N 89 26W
Mount Morris, Mich. 29 43 7N 83 42W
Mount Morris, N.Y. 39 42 44N 77 52W
Mount Nicholas 126 22 54S 120 27E
Mount Olive, Ill. 21 39 4N 89 44W
Mount Olive, Miss. 31 31 46N 89 39W
Mount Olive, N.C. 40 35 12N 78 4W
Mount Olivet 49 38 32N 84 2W
Mount Orab 42 39 2N 83 55W
Mount Pearl 61 47 31N 52 47W
Mount Pleasant, Del. 27 39 32N 75 43W
Mount Pleasant, Iowa 23 40 58N 91 33W
Mount Pleasant, Mich. 29 43 36N 84 46W
Mount Pleasant, Pa. 45 40 9N 79 33W
Mount Pleasant, S.C. 46 32 47N 79 52W
Mount Pleasant, Tenn. 48 35 32N 87 12W
Mount Pleasant, Tex. 51 33 9N 94 58W
Mount Pleasant, Utah 52 39 33N 111 27W
Mount Pocono 45 41 7N 75 22W
Mount Prospect 21 42 4N 87 56W
Mount Pulaski 21 40 1N 89 17W
Mount Rainier National Park 53 46 55N 121 50W
Mount Revelstoke Nat. Park 62 51 5N 118 30W
Mount Robson 62 52 56N 119 15W
Mount Robson Prov. Park 62 53 0N 119 0W
Mount Savage 27 39 42N 78 53W
Mount Shasta 14 41 19N 122 19W
Mount Solon 54 38 21N 79 5W
Mount Sterling, Ill. 21 39 59N 90 45W
Mount Sterling, Ky. 49 38 4N 83 56W
Mount Sterling, Ohio 42 39 43N 83 16W
Mount Storm 54 39 17N 79 15W
Mount Storm L. 54 39 13N 79 16W
Mount Summit 22 40 0N 85 23W
Mount Sunapee 36 43 19N 72 6W
Mount Trumbull 12 36 25N 113 19W
Mount Union, Iowa 23 41 3N 91 23W
Mount Union, Pa. 45 40 23N 77 53W
Mount Vernon, Ala. 10 31 5N 88 1W
Mount Vernon, Ark. 13 35 14N 92 8W
Mount Vernon, Ga. 18 32 11N 82 36W
Mount Vernon, Ill. 21 38 19N 88 55W
Mount Vernon, Ind. 22 37 56N 87 54W
Mount Vernon, Iowa 23 41 55N 91 23W
Mount Vernon, Ky. 49 37 21N 84 21W
Mount Vernon, Md. 27 38 47N 77 6W
Mount Vernon, Mo. 32 37 6N 93 49W
Mount Vernon, N.Y. 39 40 55N 73 50W
Mount Vernon, Ohio 42 40 23N 82 29W
Mount Vernon, Oreg. 44 44 25N 119 7W
Mount Vernon, S. Dak. 47 43 43N 98 16W
Mount Vernon, Tenn. 49 35 25N 84 29W
Mount Vernon, Tex. 51 33 11N 95 13W
Mount Vernon, Wash. 53 48 25N 122 20W
Mount Whaleback 126 23 18S 119 44E
Mount Wolf 45 40 4N 76 43W
Mount Zion 21 39 46N 88 53W
Mountain, N. Dak. 41 48 41N 97 52W

Mountain Nacaome

Mountain, Wis. 55 45 11N 88 28W
Mountain Brook 10 33 30N 86 45W
Mountain City, Ga. 18 34 55N 83 23W
Mountain City, Nev. 35 41 50N 115 58W
Mountain City, Tenn. 49 36 29N 81 48W
Mountain Creek 10 32 43N 86 29W
Mountain Grove 32 37 8N 92 16W
Mountain Home, Ark. 13 36 20N 92 23W
Mountain Home, Idaho 20 43 8N 115 41W
Mountain Home, N.C. 40 35 23N 82 30W
Mountain Home, Tex. 51 30 10N 99 22W
Mountain Iron 30 47 32N 92 37W
Mountain Lake 30 43 57N 94 56W
Mountain Lake Park 27 39 24N 79 23W
Mountain Meadows Reservoir 14 40 17N 120 49W
Mountain Park 43 34 42N 98 57W
Mountain Park 62 52 50N 117 15W
Mountain Pine 13 34 34N 93 10W
Mountain View, Ark. 13 35 52N 92 7W
Mountain View, Calif. 14 37 23N 122 5W
Mountain View, Hawaii 19 19 33N 155 7W
Mountain View, Mo. 32 37 0N 91 42W
Mountain View, Okla. 43 35 6N 98 45W
Mountain Village 11 62 5N 163 43W
Mountainair 38 34 31N 106 15W
Mountainaire 12 35 9N 111 40W
Mountainburg 13 35 38N 94 10W
Mountainview 56 41 16N 110 20W
Mountlake Terrace 53 47 47N 122 19W
Mountmellick 85 53 7N 7 20W
Mountrail County ◇ 41 48 10N 102 30W
Moura 71 1 32 S 61 38W
Mourdi Depression 121 18 10N 23 0 E
Mourdiah 120 14 35N 7 25W
Mourne → 85 54 45N 7 39W
Mourne Mts. 85 54 10N 6 0W
Mouscron 87 50 45N 3 12 E
Mousie 49 37 25N 82 53W
Moussoro 121 13 41N 16 35 E
Moutong 111 0 28N 121 13 E
Movas 64 28 10N 109 25W
Moville, Ireland 85 55 11N 7 3W
Moville, U.S.A. 23 42 29N 96 4W
Moweaqua 21 39 38N 89 1W
Mower County ◇ 30 43 40N 92 45W
Mowrystown 42 39 2N 83 45W
Moxee City 53 46 33N 120 23W
Moxotó → 74 9 19 S 38 14W
Moy → 85 54 5N 8 50W
Moyahua 64 21 16N 103 10W
Moyale, Ethiopia 105 3 34N 39 4 E
Moyale, Kenya 122 3 30N 39 0 E
Moyamba 120 8 4N 12 30W
Moyen Atlas 120 32 0N 5 0W
Moyers 43 34 19N 95 39W
Moyie Springs 20 48 44N 116 11W
Moyle □ 85 55 10N 6 15W
Moylie → 20 48 43N 116 11W
Moyo 110 8 10 S 117 40 E
Moyobamba 72 6 0 S 77 0W
Moyyero → 101 68 44N 103 42 E
Mozambique = Moçambique 123 15 3 S 40 42 E
Mozambique ■ 123 19 0 S 35 0 E
Mozambique Chan. 123 20 0 S 39 0 E
Mozdok 99 43 45N 44 48 E
Mozyr 98 52 0N 29 15 E
Mpanda 122 6 23 S 31 1 E
Mpika 123 11 51 S 31 25 E
Mpwapwa 122 6 23 S 36 30 E
Msaken 121 35 49N 10 33 E
Msoro 123 13 35 S 31 50 E
Mt. Everest = Qomolangma Feng 113 28 0N 86 45 E
Mtwara 122 10 20 S 40 20 E
Mu Us Shamo 114 39 0N 109 0 E
Muaná 74 1 25 S 49 15W
Muang Chiang Rai 112 19 52N 99 50 E
Muang Lamphun 112 18 40N 99 2 E
Muang Phichit 112 16 29N 100 21 E
Muar = Bandar Maharani 112 2 3N 102 34 E
Muar → 112 2 15N 102 48 E
Muarabungo 110 1 28 S 102 52 E
Muaraenim 110 3 40 S 103 50 E
Muarajuloi 110 0 12 S 114 3 E
Muarakaman 110 0 2 S 116 45 E
Muaratebo 110 1 30 S 102 26 E
Muaratembesi 110 1 42 S 103 8 E
Muaratewe 110 0 58 S 114 52 E
Mubende 122 0 33N 31 22 E
Mubi 121 10 18N 13 16 E
Mucajaí → 71 2 25N 60 52W
Mucajaí, Serra do 71 2 23N 61 10W
Muck 84 56 50N 6 15W
Muckalee Cr. → 18 31 38N 84 9W
Muco → 70 4 15N 70 21W
Muconda 122 10 31 S 21 15 E
Mucuim → 73 6 33 S 64 18W
Mucura 71 2 31 S 62 43W
Mucuri 75 18 0 S 39 36W
Mucurici 75 18 6 S 40 31W
Mud → 48 37 13N 86 54W
Mud Butte 47 45 0N 102 54W
Mud Cr. →, Okla. 43 33 55N 97 28W
Mud Cr. →, S. Dak. 47 45 11N 98 24W
Mud L. 35 37 52N 117 4W
Mud Lake Reservoir 47 45 47N 98 15W
Mudanjiang 114 44 38N 129 30 E
Muddy →, Ill. 21 37 33N 89 32W
Muddy →, Nev. 35 36 31N 114 24W
Muddy Boggy Cr. → 43 34 3N 95 47W
Muddy Cr. →, Utah 52 38 24N 110 42W
Muddy Cr. →, Wyo. 56 41 35N 109 58W
Muddy Creek Reservoir 16 37 45N 103 15W
Muddy Gap 56 42 21N 107 28W
Mudgee 127 32 32 S 149 31 E
Mudjatik → 63 56 1N 107 36W
Muenster 51 33 39N 97 23W
Muerto, Mar 65 16 10N 94 10W
Mufulira 123 12 32 S 28 15 E
Mugi 117 33 40N 134 25 E
Muğla 106 37 15N 28 22 E
Mŭglizh 95 42 37N 25 32 E
Mugu 109 29 45N 82 30 E
Muhammad Qol 121 20 53N 37 9 E
Muharraqa = Sa'ad 104 31 28N 34 33 E
Muhlenberg County ◇ 48 37 10N 87 10W
Mühlig Hofmann fjella 5 72 30 S 5 0 E
Mui Bai Bung 112 8 35N 104 42 E
Mui Ron 112 18 7N 106 27 E
Muikamachi 117 37 15N 138 50 E
Muine Bheag 85 52 42N 6 57W
Muir 29 43 0N 84 56W
Muir Woods National Monument 14 37 55N 122 35W
Mukah 110 2 55N 112 5 E
Mukden = Shenyang 114 41 48N 123 27 E
Mukhtuya = Lensk 101 60 48N 114 55 E
Mukilteo 53 47 57N 122 18W
Mukomuko 110 2 30 S 101 10 E
Muktsar 108 30 30N 74 30 E
Mukur 108 32 50N 67 42 E
Mukutawa → 63 53 10N 97 24W
Mukwonago 55 42 52N 88 20W
Mulberry, Ark. 13 35 30N 94 3W
Mulberry, Fla. 17 27 54N 81 59W
Mulberry Fork → 10 33 30N 87 11W
Mulberry Grove 21 38 56N 89 16W
Mulchatna → 11 59 40N 157 7W
Mulchén 76 37 45 S 72 20W
Mulde → 88 51 10N 12 48 E
Muldoon 51 29 49N 97 4W
Muldraugh 49 37 56N 85 59W
Muldrow 43 35 24N 94 36W
Mule Creek, N. Mex. 38 33 7N 108 57W
Mule Creek, Wyo. 56 43 19N 104 8W
Mulegé 64 26 53N 112 1W
Muleshoe 50 34 13N 102 43W
Mulgrave 61 45 38N 61 31W
Mulhacén 91 37 4N 3 20W
Mulhall 43 36 4N 97 25W
Mülheim 88 51 26N 6 53 E
Mulhouse 90 47 40N 7 20 E
Muling He → 114 45 53N 133 30 E
Mull 84 56 27N 6 0W
Mullaittvu 108 9 15N 80 49 E
Mullan 20 47 28N 115 48W
Mullen 34 42 3N 101 1W
Mullens 54 37 35N 81 23W
Muller, Pegunungan 110 0 30N 113 30 E
Mullet Pen. 85 54 10N 10 2W
Mullett L. 29 45 31N 84 31W
Mullett Lake 29 45 34N 84 32W
Mullewa 126 28 29 S 115 30 E
Mullica → 37 39 33N 74 25W
Mullin 51 31 33N 98 40W
Mullingar 85 53 31N 7 20W
Mullins 46 34 12N 79 15W
Mullinville 24 37 35N 99 29W
Multan 108 30 15N 71 36 E
Multnomah County ◇ 44 45 30N 122 10W
Mulvane 24 37 29N 97 15W
Mumbwa 123 15 0 S 27 0 E
Mun → 112 15 17N 103 0 E
Muna 111 5 0 S 122 30 E
München 88 48 8N 11 33 E
Munchen-Gladbach = Mönchengladbach 88 51 12N 6 23 E
Muncho Lake 62 59 0N 125 50W
Muncie 22 40 12N 85 23W
Muncy 45 41 12N 76 47W
Mundala 111 4 30 S 141 0 E
Mundare 62 53 35N 112 20W
Munday 51 33 27N 99 38W
Mundelein 21 42 16N 88 0W
Münden, Germany 88 51 25N 9 42 E
Munden, U.S.A. 24 39 55N 97 32W
Mundo Novo 75 11 50 S 40 29W
Munducurus 71 4 47 S 58 16W
Munford 48 35 27N 89 49W
Munfordville 49 37 16N 85 54W
Mungbere 122 2 36N 28 28 E
Munger 109 25 23N 86 30 E
Mungindi 127 28 58 S 149 1 E
Munhango 123 12 10 S 18 38 E
Munhango → 123 11 30 S 19 30 E
Munich = München 88 48 8N 11 33 E
Munich 41 48 40N 98 50W
Munising 29 46 25N 86 40W
Munjor 24 38 49N 99 16W
Munku-Sardyk 101 51 45N 100 20 E
Munnsville 39 42 59N 75 35W
Muñoz Gamero, Pen. 78 52 30 S 73 5 E
Munroe L. 63 59 13N 98 35W
Munson 17 30 52N 86 52W
Münster 88 51 58N 7 37 E
Munster □ 85 52 20N 8 40W
Munsungan L. 26 46 22N 69 0W
Muntele Mare 95 46 30N 23 12 E
Muntok 110 2 5 S 105 10 E
Munyak 100 43 30N 59 15 E
Muon Pak Beng 112 19 51N 101 4 E
Muonio 96 67 57N 23 40 E
Mupa 123 16 5 S 15 50 E
Muping 114 37 22N 121 36 E
Muqdisho 105 2 2N 45 25 E
Mûr → 88 47 7N 13 55 E
Murakami 116 38 14N 139 29 E
Murallón, Cuerro 78 49 48 S 73 30W
Murang'a 122 0 45 S 37 9 E
Murashi 98 59 30N 49 0 E
Murayama 116 38 30N 140 25 E
Murchison → 126 27 45 S 114 0 E
Murchison, Mt. 5 73 0 S 168 0 E
Murchison Falls = Kabarega Falls 122 2 15N 31 30 E
Murchison Ra. 126 20 0 S 134 10 E
Murcia 91 38 20N 1 10W
Murcia □ 91 37 50N 1 30W
Murdo 47 43 53N 100 43W
Murdock, Kans. 24 37 37N 97 56W
Murdock, Minn. 30 45 13N 95 24W
Murdock, Nebr. 34 40 55N 96 17W
Mureş □ 95 46 45N 24 40 E
Mureş → 89 46 15N 20 13 E
Mureşul = Mureş → 89 46 15N 20 13 E
Murfatlar 95 44 10N 28 26 E
Murfreesboro, Ark. 13 34 4N 93 41W
Murfreesboro, N.C. 40 36 27N 77 6W
Murfreesboro, Tenn. 48 35 51N 86 24W
Murgab 100 38 10N 74 2 E
Murgeni 95 46 12N 28 1 E
Murgon 127 26 15 S 151 54 E
Muriaé 75 21 8 S 42 23W
Murici 74 9 19 S 35 56W
Müritz See 88 53 25N 12 40 E
Murmansk 98 68 57N 33 10 E
Murom 98 55 35N 42 3 E
Muroran 116 42 25N 141 0 E
Muroto 117 33 18N 134 9 E
Muroto-Misaki 117 33 15N 134 10 E
Murphy, Idaho 20 43 13N 116 33W
Murphy, N.C. 40 35 5N 84 2W
Murphy, Oreg. 44 42 21N 123 20W
Murphys Corner 53 47 53N 122 12W
Murphysboro 21 37 46N 89 20W
Murray, Iowa 23 41 3N 93 57W
Murray, Ky. 48 36 37N 88 19W
Murray, Utah 52 40 40N 111 53W
Murray →, Australia 127 35 20 S 139 22 E
Murray →, Canada 62 56 11N 120 45W
Murray, L., Okla. 43 34 2N 97 3W
Murray, L., S.C. 46 34 3N 81 13W
Murray Bridge 127 35 6 S 139 14 E
Murray City 42 39 31N 82 10W
Murray County ◇, Ga. 18 34 50N 84 45W
Murray County ◇, Minn. 30 44 0N 95 45W
Murray County ◇, Okla. 43 34 30N 97 0W
Murray Harbour 61 46 0N 62 28W
Murray Seascarp 125 30 0N 135 0W
Murraysburg 123 31 58 S 23 47 E
Murrayville 21 39 35N 90 15W
Murree 108 33 56N 73 28 E
Murrells Inlet 46 33 33N 79 2W
Murrumbidgee → 127 34 43 S 143 12 E
Mursala 110 1 41N 98 28 E
Murtaugh 20 42 30N 114 10W
Murtle L. 62 52 8N 119 38W
Muru → 72 8 9 S 70 45W
Murvaul L. 51 32 2N 94 25W
Murwara 109 23 46N 80 28 E
Murwillumbah 127 28 18 S 153 27 E
Muryo 111 6 36 S 110 53 E
Mürzzuschlag 88 47 36N 15 41 E
Muş 106 38 45N 41 30 E
Mûsa, G. 106 28 33N 33 59 E
Musa Khel 108 30 59N 69 52 E
Mūsá Qal'eh 107 32 20N 64 50 E
Musaffargarh 108 30 10N 71 10 E
Musala 95 42 13N 23 37 E
Musan 114 42 12N 129 12 E
Musay'īd 107 25 0N 51 33 E
Muscat = Masqat 107 23 37N 58 36 E
Muscat & Oman = Oman ■ 105 23 0N 58 0 E
Muscatine 23 41 25N 91 3W
Muscatine County ◇ 23 41 30N 91 0W
Muscle Shoals 10 34 45N 87 40W
Muscoda 55 43 11N 90 27W
Muscogee County ◇ 18 32 30N 84 58W
Musconetcong → 37 40 36N 75 11W
Muscotah 24 39 33N 95 31W
Musella 18 32 48N 84 2W
Musgrave Ras. 126 26 0 S 132 0 E
Mushie 122 2 56 S 16 55 E
Musi → 110 2 20 S 104 56 E
Muskeg → 62 60 20N 123 20W
Muskeg B. 30 48 55N 95 10W
Muskeget Channel 28 41 25N 70 25W
Muskego 55 42 55N 88 8W
Muskegon 29 43 14N 86 16W
Muskegon → 29 43 14N 86 21W
Muskegon County ◇ 29 43 15N 86 15W
Muskegon Heights 29 43 12N 86 16W
Muskingum → 42 40 3N 81 59W
Muskingum County ◇ 42 39 56N 82 1W
Muskogee 43 35 45N 95 22W
Muskogee County ◇ 43 35 40N 95 25W
Muskwa → 62 58 47N 122 48W
Musmar 121 18 13N 35 40 E
Musoma 122 1 30 S 33 48 E
Musquaro, L. 61 50 38N 61 5W
Musquodoboit Harbour 61 44 50N 63 9W
Musselburgh 84 55 57N 3 3W
Mussell Cr. → 32 39 26N 92 57W
Musselshell → 33 47 21N 107 57W
Musselshell County ◇ 33 46 35N 108 30W
Mussoorie 108 30 27N 78 6 E
Mustang, Nepal 109 29 10N 83 55 E
Mustang, U.S.A. 43 35 24N 97 42W
Mustang Draw → 50 31 58N 102 40W
Mustang I. 51 27 52N 97 3W
Musters, L. 78 45 20 S 69 25W
Mustinka → 30 45 45N 96 38W
Muswellbrook 127 32 16 S 150 56 E
Mût, Egypt 121 25 28N 28 58 E
Mut, Turkey 106 36 40N 33 28 E
Mutaray 101 60 56N 101 0 E
Mutare 123 18 58 S 32 38 E
Muting 111 7 23 S 140 20 E
Mutsu 116 41 5N 140 55 E
Mutsu-Wan 116 41 5N 140 55 E
Muttaburra 127 22 38 S 144 29 E
Mutual, Ohio 42 40 5N 83 38W
Mutual, Okla. 43 36 14N 99 9W
Mutunópolis 75 13 40 S 49 15W
Muxima 122 9 33 S 13 58 E
Muy Muy 66 12 39N 85 36W
Muya 101 56 27N 115 50 E
Muzaffarabad 108 34 25N 73 30 E
Muzaffarnagar 108 29 26N 77 40 E
Muzaffarpur 109 26 7N 85 23 E
Muzhi 100 65 25N 64 40 E
Muzon, C. 11 54 40N 132 42W
Muztag 113 36 20N 87 28 E
Mvuma 123 19 16 S 30 30 E
Mwanza, Tanzania 122 2 30 S 32 58 E
Mwanza, Zaïre 122 7 55 S 26 43 E
Mwaya 122 9 32 S 33 55 E
Mweelrea 85 53 37N 9 48W
Mweka 122 4 50 S 21 34 E
Mwenezi 123 21 15 S 30 48 E
Mwenga 122 3 1 S 28 28 E
Mweru, L. 122 9 0 S 28 40 E
Mwinilunga 123 11 43 S 24 25 E
My Tho 112 10 29N 106 23 E
Myakka → 17 26 56N 82 11W
Myanaung 109 18 18N 95 22 E
Myaungmya 109 16 30N 94 40 E
Mycenae = Mikínai 95 37 43N 22 46 E
Myeik Kyunzu 112 11 30N 97 30 E
Myerstown 45 40 22N 76 19W
Myingyan 109 21 30N 95 20 E
Myitkyina 109 25 24N 97 26 E
Mylo 41 48 38N 99 37W
Mymensingh 109 24 45N 90 24 E
Mynydd Du 83 51 45N 3 45W
Mýrdalsjökull 96 63 40N 19 6W
Myrtle, Miss. 31 34 34N 89 7W
Myrtle, Mo. 32 36 31N 91 16W
Myrtle, W. Va. 54 37 46N 82 12W
Myrtle Beach 46 33 42N 78 53W
Myrtle Creek 44 43 1N 123 17W
Myrtle Point 44 43 4N 124 8W
Myrtlewood 10 32 16N 87 57W
Mysore 108 12 17N 76 41 E
Mysore □ = Karnataka □ 108 13 15N 77 0 E
Mystic, Conn. 28 41 21N 71 58W
Mystic, Iowa 23 40 47N 92 57W
Mystic Island 37 39 34N 74 22W
Myton 52 40 12N 110 4W
Mývatn 96 65 36N 17 0W
Mzimvubu → 123 31 38 S 29 33 E

N

Naab → 88 49 1N 12 2 E
Naalehu 19 19 4N 155 35W
Na'an 104 31 53N 34 52 E
Naantali 97 60 29N 22 2 E
Naas 85 53 12N 6 40W
Nabadwip = Navadwip 109 23 34N 88 20 E
Nabari 117 34 37N 136 5 E
Nabesna 11 62 22N 143 0W
Nabeul 121 36 30N 10 44 E
Nabire 111 3 15 S 135 26 E
Nabisipi → 61 50 14N 62 13W
Nablus = Nābulus 104 32 14N 35 15 E
Nābulus 104 32 14N 35 15 E
Nacala-Velha 123 14 32 S 40 34 E
Nacaome 66 13 31N 87 30W

Naches Nebo, Mt.

Naches 53 46 44N 120 42W
Naches → 53 46 38N 120 31W
Nachingwea 122 10 23 S 38 49 E
Nacimiento Reservoir 15 35 46N 120 53W
Naco, Mexico 64 31 20N 109 56W
Naco, U.S.A. 12 31 20N 109 57W
Nacogdoches 51 31 36N 94 39W
Nacogdoches County ◇ 51 31 35N 94 40W
Nácori Chico 64 29 39N 109 1W
Nacozari 64 30 24N 109 39W
Nadiad 108 22 41N 72 56 E
Nadūshan 107 32 2N 53 35 E
Nadvoitsy 98 63 52N 34 14 E
Nadym 100 65 35N 72 42 E
Nadym → 100 66 12N 72 0 E
Nafada 120 11 8N 11 20 E
Naftshahr 106 34 0N 45 30 E
Nafūd ad Dahy 106 22 0N 45 0 E
Naga 111 13 38N 123 15 E
Naga Hills 109 26 0N 94 30 E
Nagagami → 60 49 40N 84 40W
Nagahama 117 35 23N 136 16 E
Nagai 116 38 6N 140 2 E
Nagai I. 11 55 5N 160 0W
Nagaland □ 109 26 0N 94 30 E
Nagano 117 36 40N 138 10 E
Nagano □ 117 36 15N 138 0 E
Nagaoka 117 37 27N 138 51 E
Nagappattinam 108 10 46N 79 51 E
Nagar Parkar 108 24 30N 70 35 E
Nagasaki 117 32 47N 129 50 E
Nagasaki □ 117 32 50N 129 40 E
Nagato 117 34 19N 131 5 E
Nagaur 108 27 15N 73 45 E
Nageezi 38 36 16N 107 45W
Nagercoil 108 8 12N 77 26 E
Nagīneh 107 34 20N 57 15 E
Nagornyy 101 55 58N 124 57 E
Nagoya 117 35 10N 136 50 E
Nagpur 108 21 8N 79 10 E
Nags Head 40 35 57N 75 38W
Nagua 67 19 23N 69 50W
Naguabo 57 18 13N 65 44W
Nagykanizsa 88 46 28N 17 0 E
Nagykörös 89 47 5N 19 48 E
Naha 117 26 13N 127 42 E
Nahalal 104 32 41N 35 12 E
Nahanni Butte 62 61 2N 123 31W
Nahanni Nat. Park 62 61 15N 125 0W
Nahant 28 42 26N 70 55W
Nahariyya 104 33 1N 35 5 E
Nahāvand 106 34 10N 48 22 E
Nahf 104 32 56N 35 18 E
Nahlin 62 58 55N 131 38W
Nahma 29 45 50N 86 40W
Nahuel Huapi, L. 78 41 0 S 71 32W
Nahunta 18 31 12N 81 59W
Naicá 64 27 53N 105 31W
Naicam 63 52 30N 104 30W
Nā'ifah 105 19 59N 50 46 E
Nain, Canada 61 56 34N 61 40W
Nā'īn, Iran 107 32 54N 53 0 E
Nainpur 108 22 30N 80 10 E
Naipu 95 44 12N 25 47 E
Naira 111 4 28 S 130 0 E
Nairn 84 57 35N 3 54W
Nairobi 122 1 17 S 36 48 E
Naivasha 122 0 40 S 36 30 E
Najafābād 107 32 40N 51 15 E
Najd 106 26 30N 42 0 E
Najibabad 108 29 40N 78 20 E
Najin 114 42 12N 130 15 E
Nakadōri-Shima 117 32 57N 129 4 E
Nakalele Pt. 19 21 2N 156 35W
Nakaminato 117 36 21N 140 36 E
Nakamura 117 33 0N 133 0 E
Nakano 117 36 45N 138 22 E
Nakano-Shima 117 29 51N 129 52 E
Nakashibetsu 116 43 33N 144 59 E
Nakfa 121 16 40N 38 32 E
Nakhichevan A.S.S.R. □ 99 39 14N 45 30 E
Nakhodka 101 42 53N 132 54 E
Nakhon Phanom 112 17 23N 104 43 E
Nakhon Ratchasima 112 14 59N 102 12 E
Nakhon Sawan 112 15 35N 100 10 E
Nakhon Si Thammarat 112 8 29N 100 0 E
Nakina, B.C., Canada 62 59 12N 132 52W
Nakina, Ont., Canada 60 50 10N 86 40W
Naknek 11 58 44N 157 1W
Nakskov 97 54 50N 11 8 E
Naktong → 114 35 7N 128 57 E
Nakuru 122 0 15 S 36 4 E
Nakusp 62 50 20N 117 45W
Nal → 108 25 20N 65 30 E
Nalchik 99 43 30N 43 33 E
Nalgonda 108 17 6N 79 15 E
Nallamalai Hills 108 15 30N 78 50 E
Nallen 54 38 7N 80 53W
Nalón → 91 43 32N 6 4W
Nālūt 121 31 54N 11 0 E
Nam Co 113 30 30N 90 45 E
Nam Dinh 112 20 25N 106 5 E
Nam-Phan 112 10 30N 106 0 E
Nam Phong 112 16 42N 102 52 E
Nam Tha 112 20 58N 101 30 E
Namacurra 123 17 30 S 36 50 E
Namak, Daryācheh-ye 107 34 30N 52 0 E
Namak, Kavir-e 107 34 30N 57 30 E
Namakan L. 30 48 27N 92 36W
Namaland 123 24 30 S 17 0 E
Namangan 100 41 0N 71 40 E
Namapa 123 13 43 S 39 50 E
Namber 111 1 2 S 134 49 E
Nambour 127 26 32 S 152 58 E
Nameh 110 2 34N 116 21 E
Namekagon → 55 46 5N 92 6W
Namew L. 63 54 14N 101 56W
Namib Desert = Namib-Woestyn 123 22 30 S 15 0 E
Namib-Woestyn 123 22 30 S 15 0 E
Namibe 123 15 7 S 12 11 E
Namibe □ 123 16 35 S 12 30 E
Namibia ■ 123 22 0 S 18 9 E
Namlea 111 3 18 S 127 5 E
Nampa 20 43 34N 116 34W
Nampō-Shotō 117 30 0N 140 0 E
Nampula 123 15 6N 39 15 E
Namrole 111 3 46 S 126 46 E
Namse Shankou 109 30 0N 82 25 E
Namsen → 96 64 27N 11 42 E
Namsos 96 64 29N 11 30 E
Namtay 101 62 43N 129 37 E
Namtu 109 23 5N 97 28 E
Namu 62 51 52N 127 50W
Namucha Shank'ou 109 30 0N 82 28 E
Namur 87 50 27N 4 52 E
Namur □ 87 50 17N 5 0 E
Namutoni 123 18 49 S 16 55 E
Namwala 123 15 44 S 26 30 E
Nan 112 18 52N 100 42 E
Nana 95 44°17N 26 34 E
Nanaimo 62 49 10N 124 0W
Nanakuli 19 21 24N 158 9W
Nanam 114 41 44N 129 40 E
Nanan 115 24 59N 118 21 E
Nanango 127 26 40 S 152 0 E
Nan'ao, China 115 23 28N 117 5 E
Nanao, Japan 117 37 0N 137 0 E
Nanbu 115 31 18N 106 3 E
Nance County ◇ 34 41 25N 98 0W
Nanchang 115 28 42N 115 55 E
Nancheng 115 27 33N 116 35 E
Nanching = Nanjing 115 32 2N 118 47 E
Nanchong 115 30 43N 106 2 E
Nanchuan 115 29 9N 107 6 E
Nancy, France 90 48 42N 6 12 E
Nancy, U.S.A. 49 37 4N 84 45W
Nanda Devi 108 30 23N 79 59 E
Nandan, China 115 24 58N 107 29 E
Nandan, Japan 117 34 10N 134 42 E
Nanded 108 19 10N 77 20 E
Nandi 128 17 42 S 177 20 E
Nandurbar 108 21 20N 74 15 E
Nandyal 108 15 30N 78 30 E
Nanga-Eboko 122 4 41N 12 22 E
Nanga Parbat 108 35 10N 74 35 E
Nangahtayae 110 1 32 S 110 34 E
Nangapinoh 110 0 20 S 111 44 E
Nangarhár □ 107 34 20N 70 0 E
Nanjemoy 27 38 27N 77 13W
Nanjiang 115 32 28N 106 51 E
Nanjing 115 32 2N 118 47 E
Nankang 115 25 40N 114 45 E
Nankoku 117 33 39N 133 44 E
Nanning 115 22 48N 108 20 E
Nanpi 114 38 2N 116 45 E
Nanping 115 26 38N 118 10 E
Nansei-Shotō 117 26 0N 128 0 E
Nansemond County ◇ 54 36 45N 76 40W
Nansen Sd. 4 81 0N 91 0W
Nantahala L. 40 35 10N 83 40W
Nantahala National Forest 40 35 15N 83 30W
Nantes 90 47 12N 1 33W
Nanticoke, Md. 27 38 16N 75 54W
Nanticoke, Pa. 45 41 12N 76 0W
Nanticoke → 27 38 16N 75 56W
Nanton 62 50 21N 113 46W
Nantong 115 32 1N 120 52 E
Nantucket 28 41 17N 70 6W
Nantucket County ◇ 28 41 15N 70 5W
Nantucket Harbor 28 41 17N 70 6W
Nantucket I. 28 41 16N 70 5W
Nantucket Sd. 28 41 30N 70 15W
Nanty Glo 45 40 28N 78 50W
Nanuque 75 17 50 S 40 21W
Nanxiong 115 25 6N 114 15 E
Nanyang 115 33 11N 112 30 E
Nanyuan 114 39 44N 116 22 E
Nanyuki 122 0 2N 37 4 E
Nanzhang 115 31 45N 111 50 E
Náo, C. de la 91 38 44N 0 14 E
Naococane L. 61 52 50N 70 45W
Naoetsu 117 37 12N 138 10 E
Naoli He → 114 47 18N 134 9 E
Naomi Peak 52 41 55N 111 41W
Napa 14 38 18N 122 17W
Napa County ◇ 14 38 30N 122 20W
Napaimiut 11 61 33N 158 42W
Napakiak 11 60 42N 161 57W
Napanee 60 44 15N 77 0W
Napaskiak 11 60 43N 161 55W
Napavine 53 46 35N 122 54W
Naper 34 42 58N 99 6W
Naperville 21 41 46N 88 9W
Napier 128 39 30 S 176 56 E
Naples = Nápoli 94 40 50N 14 17 E
Naples, Fla. 17 26 8N 81 48W
Naples, Idaho 20 48 34N 116 24W
Naples, N.Y. 39 42 37N 77 24W
Naples, Tex. 51 33 12N 94 41W
Napo □ 70 0 30 S 77 0W
Napo → 70 3 20 S 72 40W
Napoleanville 25 29 56N 91 2W
Napoleon, Ind. 22 39 12N 85 20W
Napoleon, N. Dak. 41 46 30N 99 46W
Napoleon, Ohio 42 41 23N 84 8W
Nápoli 94 40 50N 14 17 E
Naponee 34 40 5N 99 9W
Nappanee 22 41 27N 86 0W
Nara, Japan 117 34 40N 135 49 E
Nara, Mali 120 15 10N 7 20W
Nara □ 117 34 30N 136 0 E
Nara Visa 38 35 37N 103 6W
Naracoorte 127 36 58 S 140 45 E
Naranja 17 25 31N 80 26W
Naranjito 57 18 18N 66 15W
Narasapur 109 16 26N 81 40 E
Narathiwat 112 6 30N 101 48 E
Narayanganj 109 23 40N 90 33 E
Narayanpet 108 16 45N 77 30 E
Narbonne 90 43 11N 3 0 E
Nardin 43 36 47N 97 27W
Nardò 95 40 10N 18 0 E
Narin 108 36 5N 69 0 E
Narindra, Helodranon' i 123 14 55 S 47 30 E
Narino □ 70 1 30N 78 0W
Narita 117 35 47N 140 19 E
Narka 24 39 58N 97 25W
Narmada → 108 21 38N 72 36 E
Narodnaya, G. 98 65 5N 60 0 E
Narrabri 127 30 19 S 149 46 E
Narragansett Bay 28 41 0N 71 0W
Narragansett Pier 28 41 26N 71 27W
Narrandera 127 34 42 S 146 31 E
Narraway → 62 55 44N 119 55W
Narrogin 126 32 58 S 117 14 E
Narromine 127 32 12 S 148 12 E
Narrows 54 37 20N 80 49W
Narsimhapur 108 22 54N 79 14 E
Naruto 117 34 11N 134 37 E
Narva 98 59 23N 28 12 E
Narvik 96 68 28N 17 26 E
Naryan-Mar 98 68 0N 53 0 E
Narym 100 59 0N 81 30 E
Narymskoye 100 49 10N 84 15 E
Naryn 100 41 26N 75 58 E
Nasa 96 66 29N 15 23 E
Nasarawa 120 8 32N 7 41 E
Naseby 128 45 1 S 170 10 E
Naselle 53 46 22N 123 49W
Naser, Buheirat en 121 23 0N 32 30 E
Nash 43 36 40N 98 3W
Nash County ◇ 40 36 0N 78 0W
Nashawena I. 28 41 26N 70 53W
Nashoba 43 34 29N 95 13W
Nashua, Iowa 23 42 57N 92 32W
Nashua, Minn. 30 46 2N 96 19W
Nashua, Mont. 33 48 8N 106 22W
Nashua, N.H. 36 42 45N 71 28W
Nashville, Ark. 13 33 57N 93 51W
Nashville, Ga. 18 31 12N 83 15W
Nashville, Ill. 21 38 21N 89 23W
Nashville, Ind. 22 39 12N 86 15W
Nashville, Kans. 24 37 27N 98 25W
Nashville, Mich. 29 42 36N 85 5W
Nashville, Mo. 32 37 23N 94 30W
Nashville, N.C. 40 35 58N 77 58W
Nashville, Ohio 42 40 36N 82 7W
Nashville, Tenn. 48 36 10N 86 47W
Nashwauk 30 47 23N 93 10W
Nasik 108 19 58N 73 50 E
Nasirabad 108 26 15N 74 45 E
Naskaupi → 61 53 47N 60 51W
Nass → 62 55 0N 129 40W
Nassau, Bahamas 66 25 0N 77 20W
Nassau, Minn. 30 45 4N 96 26W
Nassau, N.Y. 39 42 31N 73 37W
Nassau, Bahía 78 55 20 S 68 0W
Nassau County ◇, Fla. 17 30 40N 81 45W
Nassau County ◇, N.Y. 39 40 45N 73 40W
Nassawadox 54 37 28N 75 52W
Nasser, L. = Naser, Buheirat en 121 23 0N 32 30 E
Nässjö 97 57 39N 14 42 E
Nastopoka Is. 60 57 0N 77 0W
Nat Kyizin 112 14 57N 97 59 E
Nata, Botswana 123 20 12 S 26 12 E
Nata, Tanzania 123 2 0 S 34 25 E
Natagaima 70 3 37N 75 6W
Natal, Brazil 74 5 47 S 35 13W
Natal, Canada 62 49 43N 114 51W
Natal, Indonesia 110 0 35N 99 7 E
Natal □ 123 28 30 S 30 30 E
Natalbany → 25 30 20N 90 30W
Natalia 51 29 11N 98 52W
Naṭanz 107 33 30N 51 55 E
Natashquan 61 50 14N 61 46W
Natashquan → 61 50 7N 61 50W
Natchez, La. 25 31 41N 93 3W
Natchez, Miss. 31 31 34N 91 24W
Natchitoches 25 31 46N 93 5W
Natchitoches Parish ◇ 25 31 41N 93 3W
Nathdwara 108 24 55N 73 50 E
Nathrop 16 38 45N 106 5W
Natick 28 42 17N 71 21W
Nation → 62 55 30N 123 32W
National 23 42 57N 91 17W
National City 15 32 41N 117 6W
Natitingou 120 10 20N 1 26 E
Natividad, I. 64 27 50N 115 10W
Natoma 24 39 11N 99 2W
Natron, L. 122 2 20 S 36 0 E
Natrona County ◇ 56 43 0N 107 0W
Natrona Heights 45 40 37N 79 44W
Natuna Besar, Kepulauan 110 4 0N 108 15 E
Natuna Selatan, Kepulauan 110 2 45N 109 0 E
Natural Bridge, Ala. 10 34 6N 87 36W
Natural Bridge, Va. 54 37 38N 79 33W
Natural Bridge Station 54 37 37N 79 30W
Naturaliste, C. 126 33 32 S 115 0 E
Naturaliste Channel 126 25 20 S 113 0 E
Naturita 16 38 14N 108 34W
Natwick 56 41 58N 105 4W
Naubinway 29 46 6N 85 27W
Naugatuck 28 41 30N 73 3W
Naumburg 88 51 10N 11 48 E
Nauru ■ 124 1 0 S 166 0 E
Nauru Is. 124 0 32 S 166 55 E
Naushahra = Nowshera 108 34 0N 72 0 E
Nauta 70 4 31 S 73 35W
Nautanwa 109 27 20N 83 25 E
Nautla 65 20 20N 96 50W
Nauvoo 21 40 33N 91 23W
Nava 64 28 25N 100 46W
Navadwip 109 23 34N 88 20 E
Navajo 12 35 7N 109 32W
Navajo County ◇ 12 36 0N 110 20W
Navajo Cr. → 12 36 59N 111 24W
Navajo Indian Reservation 12 35 20N 110 0W
Navajo Mt. 52 37 2N 110 52W
Navajo Reservoir 38 36 48N 107 36W
Navalcarnero 91 40 17N 4 5W
Navan = An Uaimh 85 53 39N 6 40W
Navarino, I. 78 55 0 S 67 40W
Navarra □ 91 42 40N 1 40W
Navarre 17 30 24N 86 52W
Navarro → 14 39 11N 123 45W
Navarro County ◇ 51 32 6N 96 28W
Navarro Mills L. 51 31 57N 96 42W
Navasota 51 30 23N 96 5W
Navasota → 51 30 21N 96 10W
Navassa, U.S.A. 40 34 18N 78 0W
Navassa, W. Indies 67 18 30N 75 0W
Naver → 84 58 34N 4 15W
Navgatuck → 28 41 18N 73 7W
Navidad 76 33 57 S 71 50W
Navidad → 51 28 50N 96 35W
Navoi 100 40 9N 65 22 E
Navojoa 64 27 0N 109 30W
Navolato 64 24 47N 107 42W
Navolok 98 62 33N 39 57 E
Návpaktos 95 38 23N 21 50 E
Návplion 95 37 33N 22 50 E
Navsari 108 20 57N 72 59 E
Nawabshah 108 26 15N 68 25 E
Nawakot 109 27 55N 85 10 E
Nawalgarh 108 27 50N 75 15 E
Nawāsīf, Harrat 106 21 20N 42 10 E
Náxos 95 37 8N 25 25 E
Nāy Band 107 27 20N 52 40 E
Naya → 70 3 13N 77 22W
Nayakhan 101 61 56N 159 0 E
Nayarit □ 64 22 0N 105 0W
Naylor 32 36 34N 90 36W
Nayoro 116 44 21N 142 28 E
Nazaré, Bahia, Brazil 75 13 2 S 39 0W
Nazaré, Goiás, Brazil 74 6 23 S 47 40W
Nazaré, Pará, Brazil 73 6 25 S 52 29W
Nazareth = Naẓerat 104 32 42N 35 17 E
Nazareth, Pa. 45 40 44N 75 19W
Nazareth, Tex. 50 34 33N 102 6W
Nazas 64 25 10N 104 6W
Nazas → 64 25 35N 103 25W
Naze, The 83 51 53N 1 19 E
Naẓerat 104 32 42N 35 17 E
Nazir Hat 109 22 35N 91 49 E
Nazko 62 53 1N 123 37W
Nazko → 62 53 7N 123 34W
Ncheu 123 14 50 S 34 47 E
Ndalatando 122 9 12 S 14 48 E
Ndélé 121 8 25N 20 36 E
Ndendé 122 2 22 S 11 23 E
Ndjamena 121 12 10N 14 59 E
Ndjolé 122 0 10 S 10 45 E
Ndola 123 13 0 S 28 34 E
Neagh, Lough 85 54 35N 6 25W
Neah Bay 53 48 22N 124 37W
Neal 24 37 50N 96 5W
Near Is. 11 52 30N 174 0 E
Neath 83 51 39N 3 49W
Nebit Dag 100 39 30N 54 22 E
Nebo, Ill. 21 39 27N 90 47W
Nebo, La. 25 31 35N 92 9W
Nebo, Mt. 52 39 49N 111 46W

Nebraska **Newark-on-Trent**

Nebraska □ 34 41 30N 99 30W
Nebraska City 34 40 41N 95 52W
Nebraska National Forest 34 42 45N 103 10W
Nébrodi, Monti 94 37 55N 14 50 E
Necedah 55 44 2N 90 4W
Nechako → 62 53 30N 122 44W
Neche 41 48 59N 97 33W
Neches → 51 29 58N 93 51W
Neckar → 88 49 31N 8 26 E
Necker I. 19 23 35N 164 42W
Necochea 76 38 30 S 58 50W
Nederland, Colo. 16 39 58N 105 31W
Nederland, Tex. 51 29 59N 94 0W
Neebish I. 29 46 16N 84 9W
Needham 28 42 17N 71 14W
Needle Range 52 38 25N 113 55W
Needles 15 34 51N 114 37W
Needles, The 83 50 39N 1 35W
Needmore, Ga. 18 30 41N 82 43W
Needmore, Tex. 50 34 2N 102 45W
Needville 51 29 24N 95 50W
Neely 31 31 10N 88 45W
Neely Henry L. 10 33 55N 86 2W
Neelyville 32 36 34N 90 30W
Ñeembucú □ 76 27 0 S 58 0W
Neemuch = Nimach 108 24 30N 74 56 E
Neenah 55 44 11N 88 28W
Neepawa 63 50 15N 99 30W
Neeses 46 33 33N 81 7W
Neft-chala = imeni 26 Bakinskikh Komissarov 99 39 19N 49 12 E
Nefta 120 33 53N 7 50 E
Neftyannyye Kamni 99 40 20N 50 55 E
Negapatam = Nagappattinam 108 10 46N 79 51 E
Negaunee 29 46 30N 87 36W
Negba 104 31 40N 34 41 E
Negele 105 5 20N 39 36 E
Negeri Sembilan □ 112 2 50N 102 10 E
Negev = Hanegev 104 30 50N 35 0 E
Negoiu 95 45 35N 24 32 E
Negoiu, Vf. 89 43 35N 24 31 E
Negombo 108 7 12N 79 50 E
Negotin 95 44 16N 22 37 E
Negra, La 76 23 46 S 70 18W
Negra, Pta. 72 6 6 S 81 10W
Negra Pt. 111 18 40N 120 50 E
Negreet 25 31 28N 93 35W
Negro →, Argentina 78 41 2 S 62 47W
Negro →, Bolivia 73 14 11 S 63 7W
Negro →, Brazil 71 3 0 S 60 0W
Negro →, Uruguay 77 33 24 S 58 22W
Negros 111 10 0N 123 0 E
Negru Vodă 95 43 47N 28 21 E
Nehalem → 44 45 40N 123 56W
Nehawka 34 40 50N 95 59W
Nehbandān 107 31 35N 60 5 E
Nehoiaşu 95 45 24N 26 20 E
Nei Monggol Zizhiqu □ 114 42 0N 112 0 E
Neidpath 63 50 12N 107 20W
Neijiang 115 29 35N 104 55 E
Neillsville 55 44 34N 90 36W
Neilton 53 47 25N 123 53W
Neisse → 88 52 4N 14 46 E
Neiva 70 2 56N 75 18W
Neixiang 115 33 10N 111 52 E
Nejanilini L. 63 59 33N 97 48W
Nekemte 121 9 4N 36 30 E
Nekoma, Kans. 24 38 28N 99 27W
Nekoma, N. Dak. 41 48 35N 98 22W
Nekoosa 55 44 19N 89 54W
Neksø 97 55 4N 15 8 E
Nelhart 33 46 56N 110 44W
Neligh 34 42 8N 98 2W
Nelkan 101 57 40N 136 4 E
Nellore 108 14 27N 79 59 E
Nelma 101 47 39N 139 0 E
Nelson, Canada 62 49 30N 117 20W
Nelson, N.Z. 128 41 18 S 173 16 E
Nelson, U.K. 82 53 50N 2 14W
Nelson, Ariz. 12 35 31N 113 19W
Nelson, Mo. 32 38 59N 93 3W
Nelson, N.H. 36 42 58N 72 8W
Nelson, Nebr. 34 40 12N 98 4W
Nelson, Wis. 55 44 25N 92 0W
Nelson □ 128 42 11 S 172 15 E
Nelson → 63 54 33N 98 2W
Nelson, Estrecho 78 51 30 S 75 0W
Nelson County ◇, Ky. 49 37 50N 85 30W
Nelson County ◇, N. Dak. 41 48 0N 98 5W
Nelson County ◇, Va. 54 37 50N 78 52W
Nelson Forks 62 59 30N 124 0W
Nelson House 63 55 47N 98 51W
Nelson L. 63 55 48N 100 7W
Nelson Reservoir 33 48 32N 107 31W
Nelspruit 123 25 29 S 30 59 E
Néma 120 16 40N 7 15W
Nemah 53 46 31N 123 53W
Nemaha, Iowa 23 42 31N 95 6W
Nemaha, Nebr. 34 40 20N 95 41W
Nemaha County ◇, Kans. 24 39 45N 96 0W
Nemaha County ◇, Nebr. 34 40 20N 95 45W
Neman → 98 55 25N 21 10 E
Nemeiben L. 63 55 20N 105 20W
Nemira 95 46 17N 26 19 E
Nemunas = Neman → 98 55 25N 21 10 E
Nemuro 116 43 20N 145 35 E
Nemuro-Kaikyō 116 43 30N 145 30 E
Nemuy 101 55 40N 136 9 E
Nen Jiang → 114 45 28N 124 30 E
Nenagh 85 52 52N 8 11W
Nenana 11 64 34N 149 5W
Nene → 82 52 38N 0 13 E
Nenjiang 114 49 10N 125 10 E
Nenusa, Kepulauan 111 4 45N 127 1 E
Nenzel 34 42 56N 101 6W
Neodesha 24 37 25N 95 41W
Neoga 21 39 19N 88 27W
Neola, Iowa 23 41 27N 95 37W
Neola, Utah 52 40 26N 110 2W
Neopit 55 44 59N 88 50W
Neópolis 74 10 18 S 36 35W
Neosho 32 36 52N 94 22W
Neosho → 43 36 48N 95 18W
Neosho County ◇ 24 37 30N 95 15W
Neosho Falls 24 37 59N 95 33W
Neosho Rapids 24 38 22N 95 59W
Nepal ■ 109 28 0N 84 30 E
Nepalganj 109 28 5N 81 40 E
Nephi 52 39 43N 111 50W
Nephin 85 54 1N 9 21W
Neptune 37 40 13N 74 2W
Nerchinsk 101 52 0N 116 39 E
Nerchinskiy Zavod 101 51 20N 119 40 E
Nereju 95 45 43N 26 43 E
Néret L. 61 54 45N 70 44W
Neretva → 95 43 1N 17 27 E
Nerstrand 30 44 20N 93 4W
Nerva 91 37 42N 6 30W
Nes 96 65 53N 17 24W
Nes Ziyyona 104 31 56N 34 48W
Nesbit 31 34 53N 90 1W
Nesebŭr 95 42 41N 27 46 E
Neshkoro 55 43 58N 89 13W
Neshoba 31 32 37N 89 8W
Neshoba County ◇ 31 32 46N 89 7W
Neskaupstaður 96 65 9N 13 42W
Nesmith 46 33 39N 79 31W
Nespelem 53 48 10N 118 59W
Ness, Loch 84 57 15N 4 30W
Ness City 24 38 27N 99 54W
Ness County ◇ 24 38 30N 100 0W
Nesttun 97 60 19N 5 21 E
Netanya 104 32 20N 34 51 E
Netarts 44 45 26N 123 57W
Netawaka 24 39 36N 95 43W
Netcong 37 40 54N 74 42W
Nète → 87 51 7N 4 14 E
Nether Stowey 83 51 0N 3 10W
Netherbury 83 50 46N 2 45W
Netherdale 127 21 10 S 148 33 E
Netherlands ■ 87 52 0N 5 30 E
Netherlands Antilles ■ 70 12 15N 69 0W
Netherlands Guiana = Surinam ■ 71 4 0N 56 0W
Nett L. 30 48 7N 93 7W
Nett Lake Indian Reservation 30 48 5N 93 5W
Nettilling L. 59 66 30N 71 0W
Nettleton 31 34 5N 88 37W
Netzahualcoyotl, Presa 65 17 10N 93 30W
Neubrandenburg 88 53 33N 13 17 E
Neuchâtel 88 47 0N 6 55 E
Neuchâtel, Lac de 88 46 53N 6 50 E
Neufchâteau 87 49 50N 5 25 E
Neumünster 88 54 4N 9 58 E
Neunkirchen 88 49 23N 7 12 E
Neuquén 78 38 55 S 68 0 E
Neuquén □ 76 38 0 S 69 50W
Neuquén → 78 38 59 S 68 0W
Neuruppin 88 52 56N 12 48 E
Neuse → 40 35 6N 76 29W
Neusiedler See 88 47 50N 16 47 E
Neustrelitz 88 53 22N 13 4 E
Neuville 51 31 41N 94 9W
Neva → 98 59 50N 30 30 E
Nevada, Iowa 23 42 1N 93 27W
Nevada, Mo. 32 37 51N 94 22W
Nevada □ 35 39 0N 117 0W
Nevada, Sierra 91 37 3N 3 15W
Nevada City 14 39 16N 121 1W
Nevada County ◇, Ark. 13 33 36N 93 17W
Nevada County ◇, Calif. 14 39 15N 121 0W
Nevada de Sta. Marta, Sa. 72 10 55N 73 50W
Nevado, Cerro 78 35 30 S 68 32W
Nevanka 101 56 31N 98 55 E
Nevers 90 47 0N 3 9 E
Neversink → 39 41 21N 74 42W
Neversink Res. 39 41 48N 74 42W
Neville 63 49 58N 107 39W
Nevis, U.S.A. 30 46 58N 94 51W
Nevis, W. Indies 67 17 0N 62 30W
Nevrokop = Gotse Delchev 95 41 43N 23 46 E
Nevşehir 106 38 33N 34 40 E
Nevyansk 98 57 30N 60 13 E
New →, Guyana 71 3 20N 57 37W
New →, Fla. 17 29 50N 84 40W
New →, W. Va. 54 38 10N 81 12W
New Albany, Ind. 22 38 18N 85 49W
New Albany, Kans. 24 37 34N 95 56W
New Albany, Miss. 31 34 29N 89 0W
New Albany, Pa. 45 41 36N 76 27W
New Alluwe 43 36 37N 95 29W
New Almelo 24 39 36N 100 7W
New Amsterdam 71 6 15N 57 36W
New Athens, Ill. 21 38 19N 89 53W
New Athens, Ohio 42 40 11N 81 0W
New Auburn, Minn. 30 44 40N 94 14W
New Auburn, Wis. 55 45 12N 91 33W
New Augusta 31 31 12N 89 2W
New Baden 21 38 32N 89 42W
New Baltimore, Mich. 29 42 41N 82 44W
New Baltimore, Pa. 45 39 59N 78 46W
New Bavaria 42 41 12N 84 10W
New Bedford 28 41 38N 70 56W
New Berlin, Ill. 21 39 44N 89 55W
New Berlin, N.Y. 39 42 37N 75 20W
New Berlin, Wis. 55 42 59N 88 6W
New Bern 40 35 7N 77 3W
New Bethlehem 45 41 0N 79 20W
New Bloomfield, Mo. 32 38 43N 92 5W
New Bloomfield, Pa. 45 40 25N 77 11W
New Boston, Ill. 21 41 10N 91 0W
New Boston, Mass. 28 42 6N 73 5W
New Boston, N.H. 36 42 59N 71 41W
New Boston, Ohio 42 38 45N 82 56W
New Boston, Tex. 51 33 28N 94 25W
New Braunfels 51 29 42N 98 8W
New Bremen 42 40 26N 84 23W
New Brighton 128 43 29 S 172 43 E
New Britain, Papua N. G. 124 5 50 S 150 20 E
New Britain, U.S.A. 28 41 40N 72 47W
New Brockton 10 31 23N 85 56W
New Brunswick 37 40 30N 74 27W
New Brunswick □ 61 46 50N 66 30W
New Buffalo 29 41 47N 86 45W
New Caledonia = Nouvelle Calédonie 124 21 0 S 165 0 E
New Cambria 24 38 53N 97 30W
New Canaan 28 41 9N 73 30W
New Canton 54 37 42N 78 18W
New Carlisle 42 39 56N 84 2W
New Carrollton 27 38 58N 76 53W
New Castile = Castilla La Nueva 91 39 45N 3 20W
New Castle, Colo. 16 39 34N 107 32W
New Castle, Del. 27 39 40N 75 34W
New Castle, Ind. 22 39 55N 85 22W
New Castle, Ky. 49 38 26N 85 10W
New Castle, Pa. 45 41 0N 80 21W
New Castle, Va. 54 37 30N 80 7W
New Castle County ◇ 27 39 30N 75 40W
New City 39 41 9N 73 59W
New Concord, Ky. 48 36 33N 88 9W
New Concord, Ohio 42 39 59N 81 54W
New Cumberland 54 40 30N 80 36W
New Deal 50 33 44N 101 50W
New Delhi 108 28 37N 77 13 E
New Denver 62 50 0N 117 25W
New Don Pedro Reservoir 14 37 43N 120 24W
New Edinburg 13 33 46N 92 14W
New Effington 47 45 51N 96 55W
New Egypt 37 40 4N 74 32W
New Ellenton 46 33 28N 81 41W
New England 41 46 32N 102 52W
New England Ra. 127 30 20 S 151 45 E
New Era 29 43 34N 86 21W
New Fairfield 28 41 27N 73 14W
New Florence, Mo. 32 38 55N 91 27W
New Florence, Pa. 45 40 23N 79 5W
New Forest 83 50 53N 1 40W
New Fork Lakes 56 43 6N 109 57W
New Franklin 32 39 1N 92 44W
New Freedom 45 39 44N 76 42W
New Glarus 55 42 49N 89 38W
New Glasgow 61 45 35N 62 36W
New Guinea 124 4 0 S 136 0 E
New Hampshire □ 36 44 0N 71 30W
New Hampton, Iowa 23 43 3N 92 19W
New Hampton, Mo. 32 40 16N 94 12W
New Hampton, N.H. 36 43 36N 71 39W
New Hanover County ◇ 40 34 15N 77 50W
New Harmony, Ind. 22 38 8N 87 56W
New Harmony, Utah 52 37 29N 113 19W
New Hartford, Conn. 28 41 53N 72 59W
New Hartford, Iowa 23 42 34N 92 37W
New Hartford, N.Y. 39 43 4N 75 18W
New Haven, Conn. 28 41 18N 72 55W
New Haven, Ill. 21 37 55N 88 8W
New Haven, Ind. 22 41 4N 85 1W
New Haven, Ky. 49 37 40N 85 36W
New Haven, Mich. 29 42 44N 82 48W
New Haven, Mo. 32 38 37N 91 13W
New Haven, N.Y. 39 43 29N 76 19W
New Haven, W. Va. 54 38 59N 81 58W
New Haven County ◇ 28 41 25N 72 50W
New Hazelton 62 55 20N 127 30W
New Hebrides = Vanuatu ■, Pac. Oc. 124 15 0 S 168 0 E
New Hebrides = Vanuatu ■, Pac. Oc. 124 15 0 S 168 0 E
New Hebron 31 31 44N 89 59W
New Hogan L. 14 38 9N 120 49W
New Holstein 55 43 57N 88 5W
New Hope, Ala. 10 34 32N 86 24W
New Hope, Pa. 45 40 22N 74 57W
New Iberia 25 30 1N 91 49W
New Ipswich 36 42 46N 71 51W
New Ireland 124 3 20 S 151 50 E
New Jersey □ 37 40 0N 74 30W
New Johnsonville 48 36 1N 87 58W
New Kensington 45 40 34N 79 46W
New Kent 54 37 31N 76 59W
New Kent County ◇ 54 37 31N 76 59W
New L. 40 35 39N 76 20W
New Leipzig 41 46 22N 101 57W
New Lexington 42 39 43N 82 13W
New Lisbon 55 43 53N 90 10W
New Liskeard 60 47 31N 79 41W
New London, Conn. 28 41 22N 72 6W
New London, Iowa 23 40 55N 91 24W
New London, Md. 27 39 25N 77 16W
New London, Minn. 30 45 18N 94 56W
New London, Mo. 32 39 35N 91 24W
New London, N.H. 36 43 25N 71 59W
New London, Ohio 42 41 5N 82 24W
New London, Wis. 55 44 23N 88 45W
New London County ◇ 28 41 30N 72 15W
New Madison 42 39 58N 84 43W
New Madrid 32 36 36N 89 32W
New Madrid County ◇ 32 36 40N 89 35W
New Market, Ala. 10 34 55N 86 26W
New Market, Ind. 22 39 57N 86 55W
New Market, Iowa 23 40 44N 94 54W
New Market, Md. 27 39 23N 77 16W
New Market, Tenn. 49 36 6N 83 33W
New Market, Va. 54 38 39N 78 40W
New Martinsville 54 39 39N 80 52W
New Matamoras 42 39 31N 81 4W
New Meadows 20 44 58N 116 18W
New Melle 32 38 43N 90 53W
New Melones L. 14 37 57N 120 31W
New Mexico □ 38 34 30N 106 0W
New Miami 42 39 26N 84 32W
New Milford, Conn. 28 41 35N 73 25W
New Milford, Pa. 45 41 52N 75 44W
New Munich 30 45 38N 94 45W
New Norfolk 127 42 46 S 147 2 E
New Orleans 25 29 58N 90 4W
New Oxford 45 39 52N 77 4W
New Paltz 39 41 45N 74 5W
New Paris 42 39 51N 84 48W
New Philadelphia, Ohio 42 40 30N 81 27W
New Philadelphia, Pa. 45 40 43N 76 7W
New Pine Creek 44 42 0N 120 18W
New Plymouth, N.Z. 128 39 4 S 174 5 E
New Plymouth, U.S.A. 20 43 58N 116 49W
New Port Richey 17 28 16N 82 43W
New Prague 30 44 32N 93 35W
New Preston 28 41 40N 73 21W
New Princeton 44 43 15N 118 35W
New Providence, Bahamas 66 25 25N 78 35W
New Providence, U.S.A. 22 38 28N 85 57W
New Radnor 83 52 15N 3 10W
New Raymer 16 40 36N 103 51W
New Richland 30 43 54N 93 30W
New Richmond, Ohio 42 38 57N 84 17W
New Richmond, Wis. 55 45 7N 92 32W
New Riegel 42 41 3N 83 19W
New Roads 25 30 42N 91 26W
New Rochelle 39 40 55N 73 47W
New Rockford 41 47 41N 99 8W
New Ross 85 52 24N 6 58W
New Salem, Mass. 28 42 30N 72 20W
New Salem, N. Dak. 41 46 51N 101 25W
New Sharon 23 41 28N 92 39W
New Siberian Is. = Novosibirskiye Ostrava 101 75 0N 142 0 E
New Smyrna Beach 17 29 1N 80 56W
New South Wales □ 127 33 0 S 146 0 E
New Straitsville 42 39 35N 82 14W
New Stuyahok 11 59 29N 157 20W
New Tazewell 49 36 27N 83 36W
New Town 41 47 59N 102 30W
New Tulsa 43 36 9N 95 48W
New Ulm 30 44 19N 94 28W
New Underwood 47 44 6N 102 50W
New Vienna, Iowa 23 42 33N 91 7W
New Vienna, Ohio 42 39 19N 83 42W
New Vineyard 26 44 48N 70 7W
New Virginia 23 41 11N 93 44W
New Washington 42 40 58N 82 51W
New Waterford 61 46 13N 60 4W
New Waverly 51 30 32N 95 29W
New Westminster 62 49 13N 122 55W
New Whiteland 22 39 33N 86 5W
New Windsor 27 39 33N 77 9W
New Woodville 43 33 56N 96 36W
New York 39 40 43N 74 0W
New York □ 39 43 0N 75 0W
New York County ◇ 39 40 45N 73 59W
New York Mills 30 46 31N 95 22W
New Zealand ■ 128 40 0 S 176 0 E
New Zion 46 33 51N 80 2W
Newala 122 10 58 S 39 18 E
Newark, Ark. 13 35 42N 91 27W
Newark, Calif. 14 37 32N 122 2W
Newark, Del. 27 39 41N 75 46W
Newark, Md. 27 38 15N 75 17W
Newark, N.J. 37 40 44N 74 10W
Newark, N.Y. 39 43 3N 77 6W
Newark, Ohio 42 40 4N 82 24W
Newark, Tex. 51 33 0N 97 29W
Newark L. 35 39 42N 115 44W
Newark-on-Trent 82 53 6N 0 48W

Newark Valley Nong Khai

Newark Valley 39 42 14N 76 11W
Newaygo 29 43 25N 85 48W
Newaygo County ◇ 29 43 30N 85 50W
Newberg 44 45 18N 122 58W
Newbern, Ala. 10 32 36N 87 32W
Newbern, Tenn. 48 36 7N 89 16W
Newberry, Fla. 17 29 39N 82 37W
Newberry, Ind. 22 38 55N 87 1W
Newberry, Mich. 29 46 21N 85 30W
Newberry, S.C. 46 34 17N 81 37W
Newberry County ◇ 46 34 20N 81 40W
Newberry Springs 15 34 50N 116 41W
Newbrook 62 54 24N 112 57W
Newburg, Md. 27 38 22N 76 37W
Newburg, Mo. 32 37 55N 91 54W
Newburg, N. Dak. 41 48 43N 100 55W
Newburg, Pa. 45 40 8N 77 33W
Newburg, W. Va. 54 39 23N 79 51W
Newburgh, Ind. 22 37 57N 87 24W
Newburgh, N.Y. 39 41 30N 74 1W
Newbury, U.K. 83 51 24N 1 19W
Newbury, U.S.A. 36 43 19N 72 3W
Newburyport 28 42 49N 70 53W
Newcastle, Australia 127 33 0 S 151 46 E
Newcastle, Canada 61 47 1N 65 38W
Newcastle, S. Africa 123 27 45 S 29 58 E
Newcastle, U.K. 85 54 13N 5 54W
Newcastle, Calif. 14 38 53N 121 8W
Newcastle, Maine 26 44 2N 69 32W
Newcastle, Nebr. 34 42 39N 96 53W
Newcastle, Okla. 43 35 15N 97 36W
Newcastle, Tex. 51 33 12N 98 44W
Newcastle, Utah 52 37 40N 113 33W
Newcastle, Wyo. 56 43 50N 104 11W
Newcastle Emlyn 83 52 2N 4 29W
Newcastle Ra. 127 15 45 S 130 15 E
Newcastle-under-Lyme 82 53 2N 2 15W
Newcastle-upon-Tyne 82 54 59N 1 37W
Newcastle Waters 126 17 30 S 133 28 E
Newcomb, Md. 27 38 45N 76 12W
Newcomb, N. Mex. 38 36 17N 108 42W
Newcomb, N.Y. 39 43 58N 74 10W
Newcomerstown 42 40 16N 81 36W
Newdegate 126 33 6 S 119 0 E
Newe Etan 104 32 30N 35 32 E
Newe Sha'anan 104 32 47N 34 59 E
Newe Zohar 104 31 9N 35 21 E
Newell, Ark. 13 33 10N 92 45W
Newell, Iowa 23 42 36N 95 0W
Newell, S. Dak. 47 44 43N 103 25W
Newellton 25 32 4N 91 14W
Newenham, C. 11 58 39N 162 11W
Newfane 39 43 17N 78 43W
Newfield 37 39 33N 75 1W
Newfolden 30 48 21N 96 20W
Newfound L. 36 43 40N 71 47W
Newfoundland, Canada 61 48 30N 56 0W
Newfoundland, U.S.A. 49 38 8N 83 6W
Newfoundland □ 61 53 0N 58 0W
Newfoundland Mts. 52 41 10N 113 20W
Newhalem 53 48 40N 121 15W
Newhalen 11 59 43N 154 54W
Newhall, Calif. 15 34 23N 118 32W
Newhall, Iowa 23 41 59N 91 59W
Newham 83 51 31N 0 2 E
Newhaven 83 50 47N 0 4 E
Newington, Conn. 28 41 43N 72 45W
Newington, Ga. 18 32 35N 81 30W
Newkirk, N. Mex. 38 35 4N 104 16W
Newkirk, Okla. 43 36 53N 97 3W
Newland 40 36 5N 81 56W
Newllano 25 31 7N 93 16W
Newman, Calif. 14 37 19N 121 1W
Newman, Ill. 21 39 48N 87 59W
Newman Grove 34 41 45N 97 47W
Newmans L. 17 29 40N 82 12W
Newmarket, Ireland 85 52 13N 9 0W
Newmarket, U.K. 83 52 15N 0 23 E
Newmarket, U.S.A. 36 43 5N 70 56W
Newnan 18 33 23N 84 48W
Newport, Gwent, U.K. 83 51 35N 3 0W
Newport, I. of W., U.K. 83 50 42N 1 18W
Newport, Salop, U.K. 83 52 47N 2 22W
Newport, Ark. 13 35 37N 91 16W
Newport, Del. 27 39 43N 75 37W
Newport, Ind. 22 39 53N 87 25W
Newport, Ky. 49 39 5N 84 30W
Newport, Maine 26 44 50N 69 17W
Newport, N.C. 40 34 48N 76 52W
Newport, N.H. 36 43 22N 72 10W
Newport, N.J. 37 39 18N 75 11W
Newport, N.Y. 39 43 11N 75 1W
Newport, Nebr. 34 42 36N 99 20W
Newport, Oreg. 44 44 39N 124 3W
Newport, Pa. 45 40 29N 77 8W
Newport, R.I. 28 41 29N 71 19W
Newport, Tenn. 49 35 58N 83 11W
Newport, Vt. 36 44 56N 72 13W
Newport, Wash. 53 48 11N 117 3W
Newport Beach 15 33 37N 117 56W
Newport County ◇ 28 41 30N 71 20W
Newport News 54 36 59N 76 25W
Newquay 83 50 24N 5 6W
Newry 85 54 10N 6 20W
Newry & Mourne □ 85 54 10N 6 15W
Newsoms 54 36 38N 77 8W
Newtok 11 60 56N 164 38W
Newton, Ga. 18 31 19N 84 20W
Newton, Ill. 21 38 59N 88 10W
Newton, Iowa 23 41 42N 93 3W
Newton, Kans. 24 38 3N 97 21W
Newton, Mass. 28 42 21N 71 12W
Newton, Miss. 31 32 19N 89 10W
Newton, N.C. 40 35 40N 81 13W
Newton, N.J. 37 41 3N 74 45W
Newton, Tex. 51 30 51N 93 46W
Newton, Utah 52 41 52N 112 0W
Newton Abbot 83 50 32N 3 37W
Newton County ◇, Ark. 13 35 50N 93 13W
Newton County ◇, Ga. 18 33 30N 83 50W
Newton County ◇, Ind. 22 41 0N 87 25W
Newton County ◇, Miss. 31 32 26N 89 7W
Newton County ◇, Mo. 32 36 55N 94 20W
Newton County ◇, Tex. 51 30 32N 93 49W
Newton Falls, N.Y. 39 44 13N 74 59W
Newton Falls, Ohio 42 41 11N 80 59W
Newton Grove 40 35 14N 78 21W
Newton L. 21 38 55N 88 15W
Newton Stewart 84 54 57N 4 30W
Newtonia 32 36 53N 94 11W
Newtonmore 84 57 4N 4 7W
Newtonsville 42 39 11N 84 5W
Newtonville 10 33 33N 87 48W
Newtown, U.K. 83 52 31N 3 19W
Newtown, Conn. 28 41 25N 73 19W
Newtown, Md. 27 39 18N 76 9W
Newtown, Mo. 32 40 22N 93 20W
Newtown, Pa. 45 40 14N 74 57W
Newtownabbey 85 54 40N 5 55W
Newtownabbey □ 85 54 45N 6 0W
Newtownards 85 54 37N 5 40W
Newville 45 40 10N 77 24W
Ney 42 41 23N 84 32W
Neya 98 58 21N 43 49 E
Neyrīz 107 29 15N 54 19 E
Neyshābūr 107 36 10N 58 50 E
Nez Perce County ◇ 20 46 10N 116 55W
Nez Perce Indian Reservation 20 46 15N 116 30W
Nezhin 99 51 5N 31 55 E
Nezperce 20 46 14N 116 14W
Nezperce National Forest 20 45 50N 115 20W
Ngabang 110 0 23N 109 55 E
Ngabordamlu, Tanjung 111 6 56 S 134 11 E
Ngami Depression 123 20 30 S 22 46 E
Nganglong Kangri 109 33 0N 81 0 E
Nganjuk 111 7 32 S 111 55 E
Ngaoundéré 122 7 15N 13 35 E
Ngapara 128 44 57 S 170 46 E
Ngawi 111 7 24 S 111 26 E
Ngha Lo 112 21 33N 104 28 E
Ngoring Hu 113 34 55N 97 5 E
Ngudu 122 2 58 S 33 25 E
Nguigmi 121 14 20N 13 20 E
Nguru 120 12 56N 10 29 E
Nha Trang 112 12 16N 109 10 E
Nhambiquara 73 12 50 S 59 49W
Nhamundá 71 2 14 S 56 43W
Nhamundá → 71 2 12 S 56 41W
Nhecolândia 73 19 17 S 56 58W
Niafounké 120 16 0N 4 5W
Niagara 41 48 0N 97 54W
Niagara → 39 43 16N 79 4W
Niagara County ◇ 39 43 15N 78 45W
Niagara Falls, Canada 60 43 7N 79 5W
Niagara Falls, U.S.A. 39 43 5N 79 4W
Niah 110 3 58N 113 46 E
Niamey 120 13 27N 2 6 E
Niangara 122 3 42N 27 50 E
Niangua 32 37 23N 92 50W
Niangua → 32 38 58N 92 48W
Niantic 28 41 20N 72 11W
Nianzishan 114 47 31N 122 53 E
Niarada 33 47 49N 114 36W
Nias 110 1 0N 97 30 E
Nibong Tebal 112 5 10N 100 29 E
Nicaragua ■ 66 11 40N 85 30W
Nicaragua, Lago de 66 12 0N 85 30W
Nicastro 94 39 0N 16 18 E
Nicatous L. 26 45 5N 68 9W
Nice, France 90 43 42N 7 14 E
Nice, U.S.A. 14 39 7N 122 51W
Niceville 17 30 31N 86 30W
Nichinan 117 31 38N 131 23 E
Nicholás, Canal 66 23 30N 80 5W
Nicholas County ◇, Ky. 49 38 20N 84 0W
Nicholas County ◇, W. Va. 54 38 17N 80 51W
Nicholasville 49 37 53N 84 34W
Nicholls 18 31 31N 82 38W
Nichols, Iowa 23 41 29N 91 19W
Nichols, N.Y. 39 42 1N 76 22W
Nichols, S.C. 46 34 14N 79 9W
Nichols, Wis. 55 44 40N 88 28W
Nicholson, Ga. 18 34 7N 83 26W
Nicholson, Miss. 31 30 29N 89 43W
Nickel Creek 50 31 55N 104 45W
Nickerie □ 71 4 0N 57 0W
Nickerie → 71 5 58N 57 0W
Nickerson, Kans. 24 38 8N 98 5W
Nickerson, Nebr. 34 41 32N 96 28W
Nicobar Is. 102 9 0N 93 0 E
Nicoclí 70 8 26N 76 48W
Nicodemus 24 39 24N 99 37W
Nicola 62 50 12N 120 40W
Nicolet 60 46 17N 72 35W
Nicolet National Forest 55 45 35N 88 45W
Nicollet 30 44 17N 94 11W
Nicollet County ◇ 30 44 20N 94 15W
Nicolls Town 66 25 8N 78 0W
Nicoma Park 43 35 30N 97 19W
Nicosia 106 35 10N 33 25 E
Nicoya 66 10 9N 85 27W
Nicoya, G. de 66 10 0N 85 0W
Nicoya, Pen. de 66 9 45N 85 40W
Nidd → 82 54 1N 1 32W
Nielsville 30 47 32N 96 49W
Nienburg 88 52 38N 9 15 E
Nieuw Amsterdam 71 5 53N 55 5W
Nieuw Nickerie 71 6 0N 56 59W
Nieuwpoort 87 51 8N 2 45 E
Nièvre □ 90 47 10N 3 40 E
Niğde 106 38 0N 34 40 E
Niger ■ 120 13 30N 10 0 E
Niger → 120 5 33N 6 33 E
Nigeria ■ 120 8 30N 8 0 E
Nightcaps 128 45 57 S 168 2 E
Nighthawk 53 48 58N 119 38W
Nightmute 11 60 29N 164 44W
Nihoa 19 23 6N 161 58W
Nii-Jima 117 34 20N 139 15 E
Niigata 116 37 58N 139 0 E
Niigata □ 117 37 15N 138 45 E
Niihama 117 33 55N 133 16 E
Niihau 19 21 54N 160 9W
Niimi 117 34 59N 133 28 E
Niitsu 116 37 48N 139 7 E
Nijkerk 87 52 13N 5 30 E
Nijmegen 87 51 50N 5 52 E
Nijverdal 87 52 22N 6 28 E
Nikel 96 69 24N 30 12 E
Nikep 27 39 32N 79 1W
Nikiniki 111 9 49 S 124 30 E
Nikki 120 9 58N 3 12 E
Nikkō 117 36 45N 139 35 E
Nikolai 11 62 58N 154 10W
Nikolayev 99 46 58N 32 0 E
Nikolayevsk 99 50 0N 45 35 E
Nikolayevsk-na-Amur 101 53 8N 140 44 E
Nikolski 11 52 56N 168 52W
Nikolskoye 101 55 12N 166 0 E
Nikopol, Bulgaria 95 43 43N 24 54 E
Nikopol, U.S.S.R. 99 47 35N 34 25 E
Nīkshahr 107 26 15N 60 10 E
Nîl, Nahr en → 121 30 10N 31 6 E
Nîl el Abyad → 121 15 38N 32 31 E
Nîl el Azraq → 121 15 38N 32 31 E
Niland 15 33 14N 115 31W
Nile = Nîl, Nahr en → 121 30 10N 31 6 E
Niles, Kans. 24 38 58N 97 28W
Niles, Mich. 29 41 50N 86 15W
Niles, Ohio 42 41 11N 80 46W
Nill 19 21 19N 157 44W
Nilo Peçanha 75 13 37 S 39 6W
Nimach 108 24 30N 74 56 E
Nîmes 90 43 50N 4 23 E
Nimneryskiy 101 57 50N 125 10 E
Nimrod 30 46 38N 94 53W
Nimrod L. 13 34 57N 93 10W
Nīmrūz □ 107 30 0N 62 0 E
Nimule 122 3 32N 32 3 E
Ninaview 16 37 39N 103 15W
Nīnawá 106 36 25N 43 10 E
Ninety Mile Beach, The 127 38 15 S 147 24 E
Ninety Six 46 34 11N 82 1W
Nineveh = Nīnawá 106 36 25N 43 10 E
Ning'an 114 44 22N 129 20 E
Ningbo 115 29 51N 121 28 E
Ningde 115 26 38N 119 23 E
Ningdu 115 26 25N 115 59 E
Ningjin 114 37 35N 114 57 E
Ningming 115 22 8N 107 4 E
Ningpo = Ningbo 115 29 51N 121 28 E
Ningqiang 115 32 47N 106 15 E
Ningshan 115 33 21N 108 21 E
Ningsia Hui A.R. = Ningxia Huizu Zizhiqu □ 114 38 0N 106 0 E
Ningwu 114 39 0N 112 18 E
Ningxia Huizu Zizhiqu □ 114 38 0N 106 0 E
Ningxiang 115 28 15N 112 30 E
Ningyuan 115 25 37N 111 57 E
Ninh Binh 112 20 15N 105 55 E
Ninini Pt. 19 21 58N 159 20W
Ninnekah 43 34 57N 97 56W
Ninnescah → 24 37 20N 97 10W
Ninove 87 50 51N 4 2 E
Nioaque 77 21 5 S 55 50W
Niobrara 34 42 45N 98 2W
Niobrara → 34 42 46N 98 3W
Niobrara County ◇ 56 43 0N 104 25W
Nioro du Sahel 120 15 15N 9 30W
Niort 90 46 19N 0 29W
Ni ta 49 35 31N 84 33W
Nipawin 63 53 20N 104 0W
Nipawin Prov. Park 63 54 0N 104 37W
Nipigon 60 49 0N 88 17W
Nipigon, L. 60 49 50N 88 30W
Nipin → 63 55 46N 108 35W
Nipishish L. 61 54 12N 60 45W
Nipissing L. 60 46 20N 80 0W
Nipomo 15 35 3N 120 29W
Nipton 15 35 28N 115 16W
Niquelândia 75 14 33 S 48 23W
Nirasaki 117 35 42N 138 27 E
Nirmal 108 19 3N 78 20 E
Nirmali 109 26 20N 86 35 E
Niš 95 43 19N 21 58 E
Nişāb 105 14 25N 46 29 E
Nishinomiya 117 34 45N 135 20 E
Nishin'omote 117 30 43N 130 59 E
Nishiwaki 117 34 59N 134 58 E
Niskibi → 60 56 29N 88 9W
Nisland 47 44 40N 103 33W
Nisswa 30 46 31N 94 17W
Nisutlin → 62 60 14N 132 34W
Niţā' 106 27 15N 48 35 E
Nitchequon 61 53 10N 70 58W
Niterói 75 22 52 S 43 0W
Nith → 84 55 20N 3 5W
Nitra 89 48 19N 18 4 E
Nitra → 89 47 46N 18 10 E
Nitro 54 38 25N 81 51W
Nitta Yuma 31 33 2N 90 51W
Niuafo'ou 128 15 30 S 175 58W
Niue I. 125 19 2 S 169 54W
Niut 110 0 55N 110 6 E
Nivelles 87 50 35N 4 20 E
Nivernais 90 47 0N 3 40 E
Niwot 16 40 6N 105 10W
Nixa 32 37 3N 93 18W
Nixon, Tenn. 48 35 7N 88 16W
Nixon, Tex. 51 29 16N 97 46W
Nizamabad 108 18 45N 78 7 E
Nizamghat 109 28 20N 95 45 E
Nizhne Kolymsk 101 68 34N 160 55 E
Nizhne-Vartovskoye 100 60 56N 76 38 E
Nizhneangarsk 101 55 47N 109 30 E
Nizhneudinsk 101 54 54N 99 3 E
Nizhneyansk 101 71 26N 136 4 E
Nizhniy Novgorod = Gorkiy 98 56 20N 44 0 E
Nizhniy Tagil 98 57 55N 59 57 E
Nizhnyaya Tunguska → 101 64 20N 93 0 E
Nizip 106 37 5N 37 50 E
Nizké Tatry 89 48 55N 20 0 E
Njombe 122 9 20 S 34 50 E
Nkambe 120 6 35N 10 40 E
Nkawkaw 120 6 36N 0 49W
Nkhata Bay 122 11 33 S 34 16 E
Nkhota Kota 123 12 56 S 34 15 E
Nkongsamba 122 4 55N 9 55 E
Nmai → 109 25 30N 97 25 E
Noakhali = Maijdi 109 22 48N 91 10 E
Noank 28 41 19N 72 1W
Noatak 11 67 34N 162 58W
Nobeoka 117 32 36N 131 41 E
Noble, Ill. 21 38 42N 88 14W
Noble, La. 25 31 41N 93 41W
Noble, Okla. 43 35 8N 97 24W
Noble County ◇, Ind. 22 41 25N 85 25W
Noble County ◇, Ohio 42 39 45N 81 31W
Noble County ◇, Okla. 43 36 20N 97 10W
Nobles County ◇ 30 43 45N 95 45W
Noblesville 22 40 3N 86 1W
Nocatee 17 27 10N 81 53W
Nocera Inferiore 94 40 45N 14 37 E
Nochixtlán 65 17 28N 97 14W
Nocona 51 33 47N 97 44W
Nocrich 95 45 55N 24 26 E
Noda 117 35 56N 139 52 E
Nodaway 23 40 56N 94 54W
Nodaway → 32 39 54N 94 58W
Nodaway County ◇ 32 40 20N 94 50W
Noel 32 36 33N 94 29W
Nogales, Mexico 64 31 20N 110 56W
Nogales, U.S.A. 12 31 20N 110 56W
Nōgata 117 33 48N 130 44 E
Noginsk 101 64 30N 90 50 E
Nogoa → 127 23 40 S 147 55 E
Nogoyá 76 32 24 S 59 48W
Nohili Pt. 19 22 4N 159 47W
Noi → 112 14 50N 100 15 E
Noirmoutier, Î. de 90 46 58N 2 10W
Nojima-Zaki 117 34 54N 139 53 E
Nok Kundi 107 28 50N 62 45 E
Nokhtuysk 101 60 0N 117 45 E
Nokomis, Canada 63 51 35N 105 0W
Nokomis, Fla. 17 27 7N 82 27W
Nokomis, Ill. 21 39 18N 89 18W
Nokomis L. 63 57 0N 103 0W
Nola 122 3 35N 16 4 E
Nolan County ◇ 50 32 28N 100 25W
Nolensville 48 35 57N 86 40W
Nolin River L. 48 37 17N 86 15W
Noma 17 30 59N 85 37W
Noman L. 63 62 15N 108 55W
Nomans Land 28 41 15N 70 49W
Nombre de Dios 66 9 34N 79 28W
Nome, Alaska 11 64 30N 165 25W
Nome, Tex. 51 30 2N 94 25W
Nome ◇ 11 64 30N 165 0W
Nomo-Zaki 117 32 35N 129 44 E
Nonacho L. 63 61 42N 109 40W
Nondalton 11 59 58N 154 51W
Nong Khae 112 14 29N 100 53 E
Nong Khai 112 17 50N 102 46 E

Nong'an	114 44 25N 125 5 E	North Bend, Canada	62 49 50N 121 27W
Nonoava	64 27 28N 106 44W	North Bend, Nebr.	34 41 28N 96 47W
Noonan	41 48 54N 103 1W	North Bend, Oreg.	44 43 24N 124 14W
Noord Brabant □	87 51 40N 5 0 E	North Bennington	36 42 56N 73 15W
Noord Holland □	87 52 30N 4 45 E	North Bergen	37 40 48N 74 1W
Noordbeveland	87 51 35N 3 50 E	North Berwick, U.K.	84 56 4N 2 44W
Noordoostpolder	87 52 45N 5 45 E	North Berwick, U.S.A.	26 43 18N 70 44W
Noordwijk aan Zee	87 52 14N 4 26 E	North Bonneville	53 45 39N 121 57W
Noorvik	11 66 50N 161 3W	North Branch, Mich.	29 43 14N 83 12W
Noorvik Indian Reservation	11 66 50N 161 5W	North Branch, Minn.	30 45 31N 92 59W
Nootka	62 49 38N 126 38W	North Branch Elkhorn →	34 41 59N 97 27W
Nootka I.	62 49 32N 126 42W	North Branch Potomac →	27 39 32N 78 35W
Nopah Range	15 36 10N 116 10W	North Branch	
Nóqui	122 5 55 S 13 30 E	Shenandoah →	54 38 59N 78 22W
Nora	34 40 10N 97 58W	North Branford	28 41 20N 72 46W
Nora Springs	23 43 9N 93 1W	North Brookfield	28 42 16N 72 5W
Noranda	60 48 20N 79 0W	North Brunswick	37 40 28N 74 28W
Norborne	32 39 18N 93 40W	North Buena Vista	23 42 41N 90 58W
Norcatur	24 39 50N 100 11W	North Butte	56 43 54N 105 57W
Norco	15 33 56N 117 33W	North Canadian →	43 35 16N 95 31W
Norcross, Ga.	18 33 56N 84 13W	North Canton	42 40 53N 81 24W
Norcross, Minn.	30 45 52N 96 12W	North C., Canada	61 47 2N 60 20W
Nord □	90 50 15N 3 30 E	North C., N.Z.	128 34 23 S 173 4 E
Nord-Ostsee Kanal	88 54 15N 9 40 E	North Cape May	37 38 59N 74 57W
Nord-Trøndelag fylke □	96 64 20N 12 0 E	North Caribou L.	60 52 50N 90 40W
Nordaustlandet	4 79 14N 23 0 E	North Carolina □	40 35 30N 80 0W
Nordegg	62 52 29N 116 5W	North Cascades National	
Norden	34 42 52N 100 5W	Park	53 48 45N 121 10W
Nordhausen	88 51 29N 10 47 E	North Channel, Br. Is.	84 55 0N 5 30W
Nordheim	51 28 55N 97 37W	North Channel, Canada	60 46 0N 83 0W
Nordkapp, Norway	96 71 10N 25 44 E	North Channel, U.S.A.	29 46 5N 83 30W
Nordkapp, Svalbard	4 80 31N 20 0 E	North Charleston, N.H.	36 43 18N 72 24W
Nordland fylke □	96 65 40N 13 0 E	North Charleston, S.C.	46 32 53N 79 58W
Nordman	20 48 38N 116 57W	North Chelmsford	28 42 38N 71 23W
Nordrhein-Westfalen □	88 51 45N 7 30 E	North Chicago	21 42 19N 87 51W
Nordvik	101 74 2N 111 32 E	North Chichester	36 43 15N 71 22W
Nore	85 52 40N 7 0W	North College Hill	42 39 13N 84 33W
Norembega	60 48 59N 80 43W	North Collins	39 42 36N 78 56W
Norfolk, Conn.	28 41 59N 73 12W	North Concho →	50 31 27N 100 25W
Norfolk, N.Y.	39 44 50N 71 1W	North Conway	36 44 3N 71 8W
Norfolk, Nebr.	34 42 2N 97 25W	North Dakota □	41 47 30N 100 15W
Norfolk, Va.	54 36 51N 76 17W	North Dartmouth	28 41 36N 70 59W
Norfolk □	82 52 39N 1 0 E	North Down □	85 54 40N 5 45W
Norfolk Broads	82 52 30N 1 15 E	North Downs	83 51 17N 0 30 E
Norfolk County ◇	28 42 10N 71 20W	North Druid Hills	18 33 49N 84 19W
Norfolk I.	124 28 58 S 168 3 E	North East, Md.	27 39 36N 75 57W
Norfork	13 36 13N 92 17W	North East, Pa.	45 42 13N 79 50W
Norfork L.	13 36 15N 92 14W	North East Cape Fear →	40 34 11N 77 57W
Norge	43 34 59N 98 0W	North East Frontier Agency	
Norias	50 26 47N 97 47W	= Arunachal Pradesh □	109 28 0N 95 0 E
Norilsk	101 69 20N 88 6 E	North East Providence Chan.	66 26 0N 76 0W
Norlina	40 36 27N 78 12W	North Eastham	28 41 52N 69 59W
Normal, Ala.	10 34 47N 86 34W	North Easton	28 42 4N 71 6W
Normal, Ill.	21 40 31N 88 59W	North English	23 41 31N 92 5W
Norman, Ark.	13 34 27N 93 41W	North Enid	43 36 26N 97 52W
Norman, N.C.	40 35 10N 79 43W	North Esk →	84 56 44N 2 25W
Norman, Nebr.	34 40 29N 98 48W	North European Plain	80 55 0N 20 0 E
Norman, Okla.	43 35 13N 97 26W	North Fabius →	32 39 54N 91 30W
Norman →	127 17 28 S 140 49 E	North Fairfield	42 41 6N 82 37W
Norman, L.	40 35 26N 80 57W	North Fond du Lac	55 43 48N 88 29W
Norman County ◇	30 47 20N 96 30W	North Foreland	83 51 22N 1 28 E
Norman Park	18 31 16N 83 41W	North Fork	20 45 25N 113 59W
Norman Wells	58 65 17N 126 51W	North Fork American →	14 38 57N 120 59W
Normanby →	127 14 23 S 144 10 E	North Fork Cuivre →	32 39 2N 90 59W
Normandie	90 48 45N 0 10 E	North Fork Edisto →	46 33 16N 80 54W
Normandin	60 48 49N 72 31W	North Fork Feather →	14 38 33N 121 30W
Normandy = Normandie	90 48 45N 0 10 E	North Fork Grand →	47 45 47N 102 16W
Normandy	50 28 55N 100 36W	North Fork Humboldt →	35 40 56N 115 32W
Normangee	51 31 2N 96 7W	North Fork John Day →	44 44 45N 119 38W
Normanton	127 17 40 S 141 10 E	North Fork Moreau →	47 45 9N 102 50W
Norphlet	13 33 19N 92 40W	North Fork Red →	43 34 24N 99 14W
Norquay	63 51 53N 102 5W	North Fork Shoshone →	56 44 29N 109 18W
Norquinco	78 41 51 S 70 55W	North Fork Smoky Hill →	24 38 54N 101 18W
Norrbotten □	96 66 30N 22 30 E	North Fork Solomon →	24 39 28N 99 15W
Norrby	96 64 55N 18 15 E	North Fork South Platte →	16 39 25N 105 0W
Nørresundby	97 57 5N 9 52 E	North Fort Myers	17 26 41N 81 53W
Norris, Mont.	33 45 34N 111 41W	North Fox I.	29 45 29N 85 47W
Norris, S. Dak.	47 43 28N 101 12W	North Freedom	55 43 28N 89 52W
Norris, Tenn.	49 36 12N 84 4W	North Grafton	28 42 14N 71 42W
Norris City	21 37 59N 88 20W	North Grosvenor Dale	28 41 59N 71 54W
Norris L.	49 36 14N 84 6W	North Hampton	36 42 57N 70 48W
Norristown, Ga.	18 32 30N 82 30W	North Haven, Conn.	28 41 23N 72 52W
Norristown, Pa.	45 40 7N 75 21W	North Haven, Maine	26 44 8N 68 53W
Norrköping	97 58 37N 16 11 E	North Henik L.	63 61 45N 97 40W
Norrland □	96 66 50N 18 0 E	North Hero	36 44 49N 73 18W
Norrtälje	97 59 46N 18 42 E	North Highlands	14 38 40N 121 23W
Norsk	101 52 30N 130 0 E	North I., N.Z.	128 38 0 S 175 0 E
Norte, Pta.	78 42 5 S 63 46W	North I., U.S.A.	46 33 17N 79 11W
Norte de Santander □	70 8 0N 73 0W	North Judson	22 41 13N 86 46W
Nortelândia	73 14 25 S 56 48W	North Kingsville	42 41 54N 80 42W
North	46 33 37N 81 6W	North Knife →	63 58 53N 94 45W
North →	28 42 37N 72 44W	North Korea ■	114 40 0N 127 0 E
North Adams, Mass.	28 42 42N 73 7W	North Lakhimpur	109 27 14N 94 7 E
North Adams, Mich.	29 41 58N 84 32W	North Las Vegas	35 36 12N 115 7W
North America	6 40 0N 100 0W	North Lewisburg	42 40 13N 83 33W
North Amherst	28 42 25N 72 32W	North Liberty, Ind.	22 41 32N 86 26W
North Andaman I.	112 13 15N 92 40 E	North Liberty, Iowa	23 41 46N 91 35W
North Andover	28 42 42N 71 8W	North Little Rock	13 34 45N 92 16W
North Anna →	54 37 48N 77 25W	North Loon Mt.	20 45 7N 115 52W
North Atlanta	18 33 52N 84 21W	North Loup	34 41 30N 98 46W
North Attleboro	28 41 59N 71 20W	North Loup →	34 41 17N 98 24W
North Augusta	46 33 30N 81 59W	North Manchester	22 41 0N 85 46W
North Battleford	63 52 50N 108 17W	North Manitou I.	29 45 7N 86 1W
North Bay	60 46 20N 79 30W	North Mankato	30 44 10N 94 0W
North Beach	27 38 43N 76 32W	North Miami	17 25 54N 80 11W
North Belcher Is.	60 56 50N 79 50W	North Miami Beach	17 25 56N 80 10W

North Middletown	49 38 9N 84 7W	Northfield, Mass.	28 42 42N 72 27W
North Minch	84 58 5N 5 55W	Northfield, Minn.	30 44 27N 93 9W
North Muskegon	29 43 15N 86 17W	Northfield, N.H.	36 43 26N 71 36W
North Myrtle Beach	46 33 48N 78 42W	Northfield, N.J.	37 39 22N 74 33W
North Nahanni →	62 62 15N 123 20W	Northfield, Vt.	36 44 9N 72 40W
North Naples	17 26 12N 81 48W	Northford	28 41 24N 72 48W
North New River Canal →	17 26 30N 80 30W	Northglenn	16 39 53N 104 58W
North Oaks	15 34 25N 118 31W	Northland □	128 35 30 S 173 30 E
North Ogden	52 41 19N 111 58W	Northome	30 47 52N 94 17W
North Olmsted	42 41 25N 81 56W	Northport, Ala.	10 33 14N 87 35W
North Ossetian A.S.S.R. □	99 43 30N 44 30 E	Northport, Mich.	29 45 8N 85 37W
North Palisade	15 37 6N 118 31W	Northport, N.Y.	39 40 54N 73 21W
North Pease →	50 34 15N 100 7W	Northport, Nebr.	34 41 41N 103 5W
North Perry	42 41 47N 81 9W	Northport, Wash.	53 48 55N 117 48W
North Plains, N. Mex.	38 34 45N 108 10W	Northrop	30 43 44N 94 26W
North Plains, Oreg.	44 45 37N 123 0W	Northumberland	45 40 54N 76 48W
North Platte	34 41 8N 100 46W	Northumberland □	82 55 12N 2 0W
North Platte →	34 41 7N 100 42W	Northumberland, C.	127 38 5 S 140 40 E
North Pt.	61 47 5N 64 0W	Northumberland County ◇,	
North Pole, Arctic	4 90 0N 0 0 E	Pa.	45 40 55N 76 50W
North Pole, U.S.A.	11 64 45N 147 21W	Northumberland County ◇,	
North Portal	63 49 0N 102 33W	Va.	54 37 55N 76 29W
North Powder	44 45 2N 117 55W	Northumberland Str.	61 46 20N 64 0W
North Prairie	55 42 56N 88 24W	Northview	32 37 17N 93 0W
North Providence	28 41 50N 71 25W	Northville, N.Y.	39 43 13N 74 11W
North Pt., Mich.	29 45 2N 83 16W	Northville, S. Dak.	47 45 9N 98 35W
North Pt., Mich.	29 45 22N 83 30W	Northway	11 62 58N 141 56W
North Richland Hills	51 32 50N 97 14W	Northwest Territories □	58 65 0N 100 0W
North Rim	12 36 12N 112 3W	Northwich	82 53 16N 2 30W
North Ronaldsay	84 59 20N 2 30W	Northwood, Iowa	23 43 27N 93 13W
North Salem	22 39 52N 86 39W	Northwood, N. Dak.	41 47 44N 97 34W
North Salt Lake	52 40 50N 111 55W	Northwood, N.H.	36 43 12N 71 9W
North Santiam →	44 44 41N 123 0W	Northwye	32 37 59N 91 46W
North Saskatchewan →	63 53 15N 105 5W	Norton, Kans.	24 39 50N 99 53W
North Schell Peak	35 39 25N 114 36W	Norton, Mass.	28 41 58N 71 11W
North Sea	86 56 0N 4 0 E	Norton, Va.	54 36 56N 82 38W
North Sentinel I.	112 11 35N 92 15 E	Norton, Vt.	36 45 0N 71 48W
North Sioux City	47 42 32N 96 29W	Norton B.	11 64 45N 161 15W
North Slope ◇	11 69 0N 154 0W	Norton County ◇	24 39 45N 99 50W
North Sporades = Voríai		Norton Reservoir	28 41 59N 99 56W
Sporádhes	95 39 15N 23 30 E	Norton Sd.	11 63 50N 164 0W
North Springfield, Pa.	45 41 59N 80 26W	Nortonville, Kans.	24 39 25N 95 20W
North Springfield, Vt.	36 43 20N 72 32W	Nortonville, Ky.	48 37 12N 87 27W
North Stonington	28 41 0N 72 0W	Norwalk, Calif.	15 33 54N 118 5W
North Stradbroke I.	127 27 35 S 153 28 E	Norwalk, Conn.	28 41 7N 73 22W
North Stratford	36 44 45N 71 38W	Norwalk, Iowa	23 41 29N 93 41W
North Sulphur →	51 33 23N 95 18W	Norwalk, Ohio	42 41 15N 82 37W
North Sutton	36 43 22N 71 56W	Norway, Iowa	23 41 54N 91 55W
North Sydney	61 46 12N 60 15W	Norway, Kans.	24 39 42N 97 47W
North Syracuse	39 43 8N 76 7W	Norway, Maine	26 44 13N 70 32W
North Terre Haute	22 39 31N 87 22W	Norway, Mich.	29 45 47N 87 55W
North Thompson →	62 50 40N 120 20W	Norway, S.C.	46 33 27N 81 7W
North Toe →	40 36 0N 82 16W	Norway ■	97 63 0N 11 0 E
North Tonawanda	39 43 2N 78 53W	Norway House	63 53 59N 97 50W
North Troy	36 45 0N 72 24W	Norwegian Dependency □	5 66 0 S 15 0 E
North Truro	28 42 2N 70 5W	Norwegian Sea	97 66 0N 1 0 E
North Twin I.	60 53 20N 80 0W	Norwich, U.K.	82 52 38N 1 17 E
North Tyne →	82 54 59N 2 7W	Norwich, Conn.	28 41 31N 72 5W
North Uist	84 57 40N 7 15W	Norwich, Kans.	24 37 27N 97 51W
North Umpqua →	44 43 16N 123 27W	Norwich, N.Y.	39 42 32N 75 32W
North Vancouver	62 49 25N 123 3W	Norwich, Vt.	36 43 42N 72 18W
North Vernon	22 39 0N 85 38W	Norwood, Colo.	16 38 8N 108 20W
North Wabiskaw L.	62 56 0N 113 55W	Norwood, La.	25 30 58N 91 6W
North Wales	45 40 13N 75 17W	Norwood, Mass.	28 42 12N 71 12W
North Walsham	82 52 49N 1 22 E	Norwood, Minn.	30 44 46N 93 55W
North Washington	23 43 7N 92 25W	Norwood, Mo.	32 37 7N 92 24W
North West Basin	126 25 45 S 115 0 E	Norwood, N.C.	40 35 14N 80 7W
North West C.	126 21 45 S 114 9 E	Norwood, N.Y.	39 44 45N 75 0W
North West Christmas I.		Norwood, Ohio	42 39 10N 84 27W
Ridge	125 6 30N 165 0W	Norwoodville	23 41 39N 93 33W
North West Frontier □	108 34 0N 71 0 E	Nos Kaliakra	95 43 21N 28 30 E
North West Highlands	84 57 35N 5 2W	Noshiro	116 40 12N 140 0 E
North West Providence		Nosok	100 70 10N 82 20 E
Channel	66 26 0N 78 0W	Noşratābād	107 29 55N 60 0 E
North West River	61 53 30N 60 10W	Noss Hd.	84 58 29N 3 4W
North West Territories □	58 67 0N 110 0W	Nossa Senhora da Glória	74 10 14 S 37 25W
North Wichita →	51 33 43N 99 29W	Nossa Senhora das Dores	74 10 29 S 37 13W
North Wildwood	37 39 0N 74 48W	Nossa Senhora do	
North Wilkesboro	40 36 10N 81 9W	Livramento	73 15 48 S 56 22W
North Windham	26 43 50N 70 26W	Nossob →	123 26 55 S 20 37 E
North York Moors	82 54 25N 0 50W	Nosy Bé	123 13 25 S 48 15 E
North Yorkshire □	82 54 15N 1 25W	Nosy Boraha	123 16 50 S 49 55 E
Northallerton	82 54 20N 1 26W	Nosy Mitsio	123 12 54 S 48 36 E
Northam, Australia	126 31 35 S 116 42 E	Nosy Varika	123 20 35 S 48 32 E
Northampton, U.K.	83 52 14N 0 54W	Notasulga	10 32 34N 85 41W
Northampton, Mass.	28 42 19N 72 38W	Notch Peak	52 39 9N 113 25W
Northampton, Pa.	45 40 41N 75 30W	Notigi Dam	63 56 40N 99 10W
Northampton □	83 52 16N 0 55W	Notikewin →	62 57 2N 117 38W
Northampton County ◇,		Noto	94 36 52N 15 4 E
N.C.	40 36 20N 77 30W	Notre-Dame	61 46 18N 64 46W
Northampton County ◇, Pa.	45 40 50N 75 20W	Notre Dame B.	61 49 45N 55 30W
Northampton County ◇, Va.	54 37 15N 75 55W	Notre Dame de Koartac =	
Northborough	28 42 19N 71 39W	Koartac	59 60 55N 69 40W
Northbridge	28 42 9N 71 39W	Notre Dame d'Ivugivic =	
Northeast C.	11 63 18N 168 42W	Ivugivik	59 62 24N 77 55W
Northern Cheyenne Indian		Notrees	50 31 55N 102 45W
Reservation	33 45 30N 106 40W	Nottaway →	60 51 22N 78 55W
Northern Circars	109 17 30N 82 30 E	Nottely L.	18 34 58N 84 5W
Northern Group	128 10 0 S 160 0W	Nottingham, U.K.	82 52 57N 1 10W
Northern Indian L.	63 57 20N 97 20W	Nottingham, U.S.A.	36 43 7N 71 6W
Northern Light, L.	60 48 15N 90 39W	Nottingham □	82 53 10N 1 0W
Northern Marianas	124 17 0N 145 0 E	Nottoway →	54 36 33N 76 55W
Northern Territory □	126 16 0 S 133 0 E	Nottoway County ◇	54 37 8N 78 5W
Northfield, Maine	26 44 52N 67 34W	Nottoway Court House	54 37 8N 78 5W
		Notus	20 43 43N 116 48W
		Nouâdhibou	120 20 54N 17 0W

Nouâdhibou, Ras Ogden

Nouâdhibou, Ras 120 20 50N 17 0W
Nouakchott 120 18 9N 15 58W
Noumea 124 22 17 S 166 30 E
Noupoort 123 31 10 S 24 57 E
Nouveau Comptoir 60 53 0N 78 49W
Nouvelle Calédonie 124 21 0 S 165 0 E
Nova Cruz 74 6 28 S 35 25W
Nova Era 75 19 45 S 43 3W
Nova Esperança 77 23 8 S 52 24W
Nova Friburgo 75 22 16 S 42 30W
Nova Gaia 122 10 10 S 17 35 E
Nova Granada 75 20 30 S 49 20W
Nova Iguaçu 75 22 45 S 43 28W
Nova Iorque 74 7 0 S 44 5W
Nova Lima 75 19 59 S 43 51W
Nova Lisboa = Huambo 123 12 42 S 15 54 E
Nova Mambone 123 21 0 S 35 3 E
Nova Ponte 75 19 8 S 47 41W
Nova Scotia □ 61 45 10N 63 0W
Nova Sofala 123 20 7 S 34 42 E
Nova Venécia 75 18 45 S 40 24W
Nova Vida 73 10 11 S 62 47W
Nova Zagora 95 42 32N 25 59 E
Novaci 95 45 10N 23 42 E
Noval Iorque 74 6 48 S 44 0W
Novara 94 45 27N 8 36 E
Novato 14 38 6N 122 35W
Novaya Ladoga 98 60 7N 32 16 E
Novaya Lyalya 100 59 10N 60 35 E
Novaya Sibir, O. 101 75 10N 150 0 E
Novaya Zemlya 100 75 0N 56 0 E
Nové Zámky 89 48 2N 18 8 E
Novgorod 98 58 30N 31 25 E
Novgorod-Severskiy 98 52 2N 33 10 E
Novi Krichim 95 42 8N 24 31 E
Novi Pazar 95 43 25N 27 15 E
Novi Sad 95 45 18N 19 52 E
Novinger 32 40 14N 92 43W
Novo Acôrdo 74 10 10 S 46 48W
Novo Aripuanã 71 5 8 S 60 22W
Nôvo Cruzeiro 75 17 29 S 41 53W
Nôvo Hamburgo 77 29 37 S 51 7W
Novo Horizonte 75 21 25 S 49 10W
Novoaltaysk 100 53 30N 84 0 E
Novocherkassk 99 47 27N 40 5 E
Novokachalinsk 116 45 5N 132 0 E
Novokazalinsk 100 45 48N 62 6 E
Novokuybyshevsk 98 53 7N 49 58 E
Novokuznetsk 100 53 45N 87 10 E
Novomoskovsk 98 54 5N 38 15 E
Novorossiysk 99 44 43N 37 46 E
Novorybnoye 101 72 50N 105 50 E
Novoshakhtinsk 99 47 46N 39 58 E
Novosibirsk 100 55 0N 83 5 E
Novosibirskiye Ostrava 101 75 0N 142 0 E
Novotroitsk 98 51 10N 58 15 E
Novouzensk 99 50 32N 48 17 E
Novska 94 45 19N 17 0 E
Novvy Port 100 67 40N 72 30 E
Now Shahr 107 36 40N 51 30 E
Nowata 43 36 42N 95 38W
Nowata County ◇ 43 36 50N 95 40W
Nowater Cr. → 56 43 57N 108 0W
Nowgong 109 26 20N 92 50 E
Nowood Cr. → 56 44 17N 107 58W
Nowra 127 34 53 S 150 35 E
Nowshera 108 34 0N 72 0 E
Nowy Sącz 89 49 40N 20 41 E
Nowy Tomyśl 88 52 19N 16 10 E
Noxapater 31 33 1N 89 1W
Noxon Reservoir 33 47 57N 115 44W
Noxubee → 10 32 50N 88 10W
Noxubee County ◇ 31 33 7N 88 34W
Noyes 30 49 0N 97 12W
Nsanje 123 16 55 S 35 12 E
Nsawam 120 5 50N 0 24W
Nsukka 120 6 51N 7 29 E
Nubieber 14 41 6N 121 11W
Nûbîya, Es Sahrâ En 121 21 30N 33 30 E
Nuble □ 76 37 0 S 72 0W
Nuboai 111 2 10 S 136 30 E
Nuckolls County ◇ 34 40 15N 98 0W
Nucla 16 38 16N 108 33W
Nueces → 51 27 51N 97 30W
Nueces County ◇ 51 27 47N 97 40W
Nueima → 104 31 54N 35 25 E
Nueltin L. 63 60 30N 99 30W
Nueva, I. 78 55 13 S 66 30W
Nueva Antioquia 70 6 5N 69 26W
Nueva Casas Grandes 64 30 25N 107 55W
Nueva Esparta □ 71 11 0N 64 0W
Nueva Gerona 66 21 53N 82 49W
Nueva Imperial 78 38 45 S 72 58W
Nueva Palmira 76 33 52 S 58 20W
Nueva Rosita 64 28 0N 101 11W
Nueva San Salvador 66 13 40N 89 18W
Nuéve de Julio 76 35 30 S 61 0W
Nuevitas 66 21 30N 77 20W
Nuevo, Golfo 78 43 0 S 64 30W
Nuevo Guerrero 65 26 34N 99 15W
Nuevo Laredo 65 27 30N 99 30W
Nuevo León □ 64 25 0N 100 0W
Nuevo Mundo, Cerro 72 21 55 S 66 53W
Nuevo Rocafuerte 70 0 55 S 75 27W
Nugget Pt. 128 46 27 S 169 50 E
Nuhaka 128 39 3 S 177 45 E
Nukheila 121 19 1N 26 21 E
Nuku'alofa 128 21 10 S 174 0W
Nukus 100 42 20N 59 7 E
Nulato 11 64 43N 158 6W
Nulhegan → 36 44 45N 71 38W
Nullarbor Plain 126 30 45 S 129 0 E
Numa 23 40 41N 92 59W
Numan 121 9 29N 12 3 E
Numata 117 36 45N 139 4 E
Numazu 117 35 7N 138 51 E
Numfoor 111 1 0 S 134 50 E
Nunaksaluk I. 61 55 49N 60 20W
Nunda, N.Y. 39 42 35N 77 56W
Nunda, S. Dak. 47 44 10N 97 1W
Nuneaton 83 52 32N 1 29W
Nunivak I. 11 60 10N 166 30W
Nunkun 108 33 57N 76 2 E
Nunn 16 40 42N 104 47W
Nunnelly 48 35 52N 87 28W
Nunspeet 87 52 21N 5 45 E
Nuomin He → 114 46 45N 126 55 E
Nuorgam 94 70 5N 27 51 E
Nuquí 70 5 42N 77 17W
Nuremburg = Nürnberg 88 49 26N 11 5 E
Nuri 64 28 2N 109 22W
Nürnberg 88 49 26N 11 5 E
Nursery 51 28 56N 97 6W
Nusa Barung 111 8 22 S 113 20 E
Nusa Kambangan 111 7 47 S 109 0 E
Nusa Tenggara Barat □ 110 8 50 S 117 30 E
Nusa Tenggara Timur □ 111 9 30 S 122 0 E
Nusaybin 99 37 3N 41 10 E
Nushki 108 29 35N 66 0 E
Nutak 59 57 28N 61 59W
Nutley 37 40 49N 74 9W
Nutrioso 12 33 57N 109 13W
Nuwakot 109 28 10N 83 55 E
Nuweveldberge 123 32 10 S 21 45 E
Nuyts, Pt. 126 35 4 S 116 38 E
Nuyts Arch. 126 32 35 S 133 20 E
Nyack 39 41 5N 73 55W
Nyahanga 122 2 20 S 33 37 E
Nyahururu 122 0 2N 36 27 E
Nyainqentanglha Shan 113 30 0N 90 0 E
Nyâlâ 121 12 2N 24 58 E
Nyandoma 98 61 40N 40 12 E
Nyarling → 62 60 41N 113 23W
Nyasa, L. = Malawi, L. 123 12 30 S 34 30 E
Nyazepetrovsk 98 56 3N 59 36 E
Nybro 97 56 44N 15 55 E
Nyda 100 66 40N 72 58 E
Nye County ◇ 35 37 0N 116 40W
Nyeri 122 0 23 S 36 56 E
Nyíregyháza 89 47 58N 21 47 E
Nykarleby 96 63 22N 22 31 E
Nykøbing 97 54 56N 11 52 E
Nyköping 97 58 45N 17 0 E
Nylstroom 123 24 42 S 28 22 E
Nynäshamn 97 58 54N 17 57 E
Nysa 89 50 30N 17 22 E
Nysa → 88 52 4N 14 46 E
Nyssa 44 43 53N 117 0W
Nyurba 101 63 17N 118 28 E
Nzega 122 4 10 S 33 12 E
N'Zérékoré 120 7 49N 8 48W
Nzeto 122 7 10 S 12 52 E

O

Ō-Shima, Nagasaki, Japan 117 34 29N 129 33 E
Ō-Shima, Shizuoka, Japan 117 34 44N 139 24 E
O. C. Fisher L. 50 31 29N 100 29W
Oacoma 47 43 48N 99 24W
Oahe, L. 47 44 27N 100 24W
Oahe Dam 47 44 27N 100 24W
Oahu 19 21 28N 157 58W
Oak 34 40 14N 97 54W
Oak Bluffs 28 41 27N 70 34W
Oak City, N.C. 40 35 58N 77 18W
Oak City, Utah 52 39 22N 112 20W
Oak Cr. → 47 45 35N 100 30W
Oak Creek, Colo. 16 40 16N 106 57W
Oak Creek, Wis. 55 42 52N 87 55W
Oak Grove, Ky. 48 36 40N 87 26W
Oak Grove, La. 25 32 52N 91 23W
Oak Grove, Mo. 32 39 0N 94 8W
Oak Harbor, Ohio 42 41 30N 83 9W
Oak Harbor, Wash. 53 48 18N 122 39W
Oak Hill, Fla. 17 28 52N 80 51W
Oak Hill, Kans. 24 39 15N 97 21W
Oak Hill, Ohio 42 38 54N 82 35W
Oak Hill, Tenn. 48 36 5N 86 47W
Oak Hill, W. Va. 54 37 59N 81 9W
Oak Knolls 15 34 51N 120 27W
Oak Lawn 21 41 43N 87 44W
Oak Orchard 27 38 36N 75 12W
Oak Park, Ga. 18 32 22N 82 19W
Oak Park, Ill. 21 41 53N 87 47W
Oak Park, Mich. 29 42 28N 83 11W
Oak Ridge, La. 25 32 38N 91 47W
Oak Ridge, Mo. 32 37 30N 89 44W
Oak Ridge, Tenn. 49 36 1N 84 16W
Oak Vale 31 31 26N 89 58W
Oak Valley 24 37 20N 96 1W
Oak View 15 34 24N 119 18W
Oakan-Dake 116 43 27N 144 10 E
Oakboro 40 35 13N 80 20W
Oakdale, Calif. 14 37 46N 120 51W
Oakdale, Ill. 21 38 16N 89 30W
Oakdale, La. 25 30 49N 92 40W
Oakdale, Nebr. 34 42 4N 97 58W
Oakengates 82 52 42N 2 29W
Oakes 41 46 8N 98 6W
Oakesdale 53 47 8N 117 15W
Oakfield, Ga. 18 31 47N 83 58W
Oakfield, N.Y. 39 43 4N 78 16W
Oakfield, Wis. 55 43 41N 88 33W
Oakford 21 40 6N 89 58W
Oakgrove 13 36 27N 93 26W
Oakham 82 52 40N 0 43W
Oakhill 10 31 55N 87 5W
Oakhurst, Calif. 14 37 19N 119 40W
Oakhurst, N.J. 37 40 16N 74 1W
Oakland, Ark. 13 36 28N 92 35W
Oakland, Calif. 14 37 49N 122 16W
Oakland, Ill. 21 39 39N 88 2W
Oakland, Iowa 23 41 19N 95 23W
Oakland, Ky. 48 37 2N 86 15W
Oakland, Maine 26 44 33N 69 43W
Oakland, Md. 27 39 25N 79 24W
Oakland, Miss. 31 34 3N 89 55W
Oakland, N.J. 37 41 2N 74 14W
Oakland, Nebr. 34 41 50N 96 28W
Oakland, Okla. 43 34 7N 96 49W
Oakland, Oreg. 44 43 25N 123 18W
Oakland, Pa. 45 41 57N 75 37W
Oakland, Tenn. 48 35 14N 89 31W
Oakland City 22 38 20N 87 21W
Oakland County ◇ 29 42 35N 83 20W
Oakland Park 17 26 10N 80 8W
Oaklawn 24 37 36N 97 18W
Oakley, Idaho 20 42 15N 113 53W
Oakley, Kans. 24 39 8N 100 51W
Oakley, Mich. 29 43 9N 84 10W
Oakley, Utah 52 40 43N 111 18W
Oakman 10 33 43N 87 23W
Oakridge 44 43 45N 122 28W
Oakton 48 36 40N 89 4W
Oaktown 22 38 52N 87 27W
Oakville, Conn. 28 41 36N 73 5W
Oakville, Iowa 23 41 6N 91 3W
Oakville, Wash. 53 46 51N 123 14W
Oakwood, Ohio 42 39 43N 84 11W
Oakwood, Ohio 42 41 6N 84 23W
Oakwood, Okla. 43 35 56N 98 42W
Oakwood, Tex. 51 31 35N 95 51W
Oamaru 128 45 5 S 170 59 E
Oark 13 35 41N 93 35W
Oasis 35 41 2N 114 29W
Oates Coast 5 69 0 S 160 0 E
Oaxaca 65 17 2N 96 40W
Oaxaca □ 65 17 0N 97 0W
Ob → 100 66 45N 69 30 E
Oba 60 49 4N 84 7W
Obama 117 35 30N 135 45 E
Oban 84 56 25N 5 30W
Obbia 105 5 25N 48 30 E
Obed 62 53 30N 117 10W
Obera 77 27 21 S 55 2W
Oberhausen 88 51 28N 6 50 E
Oberlin, Kans. 24 39 49N 100 32W
Oberlin, La. 25 30 37N 92 46W
Oberlin, Ohio 42 41 18N 82 13W
Oberon 41 47 55N 99 13W
Obert 34 42 41N 97 2W
Obi, Kepulauan 111 1 23 S 127 45 E
Óbidos 71 1 50 S 55 30W
Obihiro 116 42 56N 143 12 E
Obilatu 111 1 25 S 127 20 E
Obion 48 36 16N 89 12W
Obion → 48 35 55N 89 39W
Obion County ◇ 48 36 20N 89 10W
Oblong 21 39 0N 87 55W
Obluchye 101 49 1N 131 4 E
Obo 122 5 20N 26 32 E
O'Brien, Fla. 17 30 2N 82 57W
O'Brien, Oreg. 44 42 4N 123 42W
O'Brien, Tex. 51 33 23N 99 51W
O'Brien County ◇ 23 43 5N 95 35W
Observatory Inlet 62 55 10N 129 54W
Obskaya Guba 100 69 0N 73 0 E
Obuasi 120 6 17N 1 40W
Obzor 95 42 50N 27 52 E
Ocala 17 29 11N 82 8W
Ocamo → 71 2 48N 65 14W
Ocampo 64 28 9N 108 24W
Ocaña, Colombia 70 8 15N 73 20W
Ocaña, Spain 91 39 55N 3 30W
Occidental 38 36 11N 105 3W
Occidental, Cordillera, Colombia 70 5 0N 76 0W
Occidental, Cordillera, Peru 72 14 0 S 74 0W
Ocean, I. = Banaba 124 0 45 S 169 50 E
Ocean Bluff 28 42 6N 70 39W
Ocean City, Md. 27 38 20N 75 5W
Ocean City, N.J. 37 39 17N 74 35W
Ocean City, Wash. 53 47 4N 124 10W
Ocean County ◇ 37 39 50N 74 15W
Ocean L. 56 43 12N 108 36W
Ocean Park 53 46 30N 124 3W
Ocean Springs 31 30 25N 88 50W
Oceana 54 37 42N 81 38W
Oceana County ◇ 29 43 40N 86 20W
Oceano 15 35 6N 120 37W
Oceanport 37 40 19N 74 3W
Oceanside, Calif. 15 33 12N 117 23W
Oceanside, N.Y. 39 40 38N 73 38W
Oceanville 37 39 28N 74 28W
Ochelata 43 36 36N 95 59W
Ocheyedan 23 43 25N 95 32W
Ocheyedan Mound 23 43 24N 95 31W
Ochil Hills 84 56 14N 3 40W
Ochiltree County ◇ 50 36 10N 100 55W
Ochlocknee 18 30 58N 84 3W
Ochlockonee → 17 29 59N 84 26W
Ochoco Mts. 44 44 30N 120 35W
Ochoco National Forest 44 44 20N 120 15W
Ochopee 17 25 54N 81 18W
Ochre River 63 51 4N 99 47W
Ocilla 18 31 36N 83 15W
Ocmulgee → 18 31 58N 82 33W
Ocna Mureş 95 46 23N 23 55 E
Ocna Sibiului 95 45 52N 24 2 E
Ocnele Mari 95 45 8N 24 18 E
Ocoee, Fla. 17 28 34N 81 33W
Ocoee, Tenn. 49 35 7N 84 43W
Ocoña 72 16 26 S 73 8W
Ocoña → 72 16 28 S 73 8W
Oconee 21 39 17N 89 7W
Oconee → 18 31 58N 82 33W
Oconee, L. 18 33 28N 83 15W
Oconee County ◇, Ga. 18 33 50N 83 25W
Oconee County ◇, S.C. 46 34 45N 83 0W
Oconee National Forest 18 33 15N 83 45W
Oconomowoc 55 43 7N 88 30W
Oconto, Nebr. 34 41 9N 99 46W
Oconto, Wis. 55 44 53N 87 52W
Oconto → 55 44 53N 87 50W
Oconto County ◇ 55 45 0N 88 15W
Oconto Falls 55 44 52N 88 9W
Ocosingo 65 17 10N 92 15W
Ocotal 66 13 41N 86 31W
Ocotlán 64 20 21N 102 42W
Ocracoke 40 35 7N 75 58W
Ocracoke I. 40 35 10N 75 50W
Octavia 34 41 21N 97 4W
Ocumare del Tuy 70 10 7N 66 46W
Ocuri 73 18 45 S 65 50W
Ōda 117 35 11N 132 30 E
Ódáðahraun 96 65 5N 17 0W
Odate 116 40 16N 140 34 E
Odawara 117 35 20N 139 6 E
Odda 97 60 3N 6 35 E
Oddur 105 4 11N 43 52 E
Odebolt 23 42 19N 95 15W
Odei → 63 56 6N 96 54W
Odell, Ill. 21 41 0N 88 31W
Odell, Nebr. 34 40 3N 96 48W
Odell, Oreg. 44 45 38N 121 32W
Odell, Tex. 51 34 21N 99 25W
Odem 51 27 57N 97 35W
Ödemiş 106 38 15N 28 0 E
Oden 13 34 37N 93 47W
Odense 97 55 22N 10 23 E
Odenton 27 39 5N 76 42W
Oder → 88 53 33N 14 38 E
Odessa, Del. 27 39 27N 75 40W
Odessa, Minn. 30 45 16N 96 20W
Odessa, Mo. 32 39 0N 93 57W
Odessa, Tex. 50 31 52N 102 23W
Odessa, Wash. 53 47 20N 118 41W
Odessa, U.S.S.R. 99 46 30N 30 45 E
Odienné 120 9 30N 7 34W
Odobeşti 95 45 43N 27 4 E
Odon 22 38 51N 86 59W
O'Donnell 50 32 58N 101 50W
Odorheiul Secuiesc 89 46 21N 25 21 E
Odra → 88 53 33N 14 38 E
Odum 18 31 40N 82 2W
Odžak 95 45 3N 18 18 E
Odzi 123 19 0 S 32 20 E
Oeiras 74 7 0 S 42 8W
Oelrichs 47 43 11N 103 14W
Oelwein 23 42 41N 91 55W
O'Fallon 32 38 49N 90 42W
Ofanto → 94 41 22N 16 13 E
Offa 120 8 13N 4 42 E
Offaly □ 85 53 15N 7 30W
Offenbach 88 50 6N 8 46 E
Offerle 24 37 54N 99 33W
Ofotfjorden 96 68 27N 16 40 E
Ōfunato 116 39 4N 141 43 E
Oga 116 39 55N 139 50 E
Oga-Hantō 116 39 58N 139 47 E
Ogahalla 60 50 6N 85 51W
Ōgaki 117 35 21N 136 37 E
Ogallah 24 38 59N 99 44W
Ogallala 34 41 8N 101 43W
Ogbomosho 120 8 1N 4 11 E
Ogden, Ark. 13 33 35N 94 3W
Ogden, Iowa 23 42 2N 94 2W
Ogden, Kans. 24 39 7N 96 43W
Ogden, Utah 52 41 13N 111 58W

Ogdensburg Oracle

Ogdensburg, N.J. 37 41 5N 74 36W
Ogdensburg, N.Y. 39 44 42N 75 30W
Ogeechee → 18 31 50N 81 3W
Ogema 30 47 6N 95 56W
Ogemaw 13 33 28N 93 2W
Ogemaw County ◇ 29 44 15N 84 10W
Ogilvie 30 45 50N 93 26W
Oglala 47 43 17N 102 44W
Oglala National Grassland 34 42 55N 103 45W
Ogle County ◇ 21 42 0N 89 20W
Oglesby, Ill. 21 41 18N 89 4W
Oglesby, Tex. 51 31 25N 97 30W
Oglethorpe 18 32 18N 84 4W
Oglethorpe County ◇ 18 33 50N 83 0W
Oglio → 94 45 2N 10 39 E
Ogoki → 60 51 38N 85 57W
Ogoki L. 60 50 50N 87 10W
Ogoki Res. 60 50 45N 88 15W
Ogooué → 122 1 0S 10 0E
Ogosta → 95 43 48N 23 55 E
Ogowe = Ogooué → 122 1 0S 10 0E
Ohai 128 44 55 S 168 0 E
Ohakune 128 39 24 S 175 24 E
Ohanet, Oued → 120 28 44N 8 46 E
Ohata 116 41 24N 141 10 E
Ohatchee 10 33 47N 86 0W
Ohau, L. 128 44 15 S 169 53 E
Ohey 87 50 26N 5 8 E
Ohio, Colo. 16 38 34N 106 37W
Ohio, Ill. 21 41 34N 89 28W
Ohio □ 42 40 15N 82 45W
Ohio → 48 36 59N 89 8W
Ohio City 42 40 46N 84 37W
Ohio County ◇, Ind. 22 38 55N 85 0W
Ohio County ◇, Ky. 48 37 30N 86 50W
Ohio County ◇, W. Va. 54 40 6N 80 34W
Ohioville 45 40 41N 80 30W
Ohre → 88 50 30N 14 10 E
Ohridsko, Jezero 95 41 8N 20 52 E
Oiapoque → 71 4 8N 51 40W
Oil Center 38 32 30N 103 16W
Oil City, La. 25 32 45N 93 58W
Oil City, Pa. 45 41 26N 79 42W
Oil Trough 13 35 38N 91 28W
Oildale 15 35 25N 119 1W
Oilmont 33 48 44N 111 51W
Oilton 43 36 5N 96 35W
Oise □ 90 49 28N 2 30 E
Ōita 117 33 14N 131 36 E
Ōita □ 117 33 15N 131 30 E
Oiticica 74 5 3 S 41 5W
Ojai 15 34 27N 119 15W
Ojinaga 64 29 34N 104 25W
Ojiya 117 37 18N 138 48 E
Ojo Feliz 38 36 4N 105 7W
Ojo Sarco 38 36 7N 105 47W
Ojos del Salado, Cerro 76 27 0 S 68 40W
Okaba 111 8 6 S 139 42 E
Okabena 30 43 44N 95 19W
Okahandja 123 22 0 S 16 59 E
Okahukura 124 38 48 S 175 14 E
Okaloosa County ◇ 17 30 30N 86 40W
Okanagan L. 62 50 0N 119 30W
Okanagan Ra. 53 48 40N 119 45W
Okandja 122 0 35 S 13 45 E
Okanogan 53 48 22N 119 35W
Okanogan → 53 48 6N 119 44W
Okanogan County ◇ 53 48 30N 120 0W
Okanogan National Forest 53 48 30N 120 10W
Okarche 43 35 44N 97 58W
Okarito 128 43 15 S 170 9 E
Okaton 47 43 53N 100 53W
Okaukuejo 123 19 10 S 16 0 E
Okavango Swamps 123 18 45 S 22 45 E
Okay 43 35 51N 95 19W
Okaya 117 36 0N 138 10 E
Okayama 117 34 40N 133 54 E
Okayama □ 117 35 0N 133 50 E
Okazaki 117 34 57N 137 10 E
O'Kean 13 36 10N 90 49W
Okeechobee 17 27 15N 80 50W
Okeechobee, L. 17 27 0N 80 50W
Okeechobee County ◇ 17 27 30N 81 0W
Okeene 43 36 7N 98 19W
Okefenokee Swamp 18 30 40N 82 20W
Okehampton 83 50 44N 4 1W
Okemah 43 35 26N 96 19W
Okemos 29 42 43N 84 26W
Okene 120 7 32N 6 11 E
Oketo 24 39 58N 96 36W
Okfuskee County ◇ 43 35 25N 96 15W
Okha 101 53 40N 143 0 E
Okhotsk 101 59 20N 143 10 E
Okhotsk, Sea of 101 55 0N 145 0 E
Okhotskiy Perevoz 101 61 52N 135 35 E
Okhotsko Kolymskoye 101 63 0N 157 0 E
Oki-Shotō 117 36 5N 133 15 E
Okiep 123 29 39 S 17 53 E
Okinawa □ 117 26 40N 128 0 E
Okinawa-Guntō 117 26 40N 128 0 E
Okinawa-Jima 117 26 32N 128 0 E
Okino-erabu-Shima 117 27 21N 128 33 E
Oklahoma □ 43 36 0N 97 0W
Oklahoma City 43 35 30N 97 30W
Oklahoma County ◇ 43 35 35N 97 20W
Oklaunion 51 34 8N 99 9W
Oklawaha → 17 29 28N 81 41W
Oklawaha, L. 17 29 30N 81 45W
Oklee 30 47 50N 95 51W
Okmulgee 43 35 37N 95 58W
Okmulgee County ◇ 43 35 40N 96 0W
Okoboji 23 43 23N 95 8W
Okolona, Ark. 13 34 0N 93 20W
Okolona, Ky. 49 38 8N 85 41W
Okolona, Miss. 31 34 0N 88 45W
Okrika 120 4 40N 7 10 E
Oktabrsk 100 49 28N 57 25 E
Oktaha 43 35 35N 95 29W
Oktibbeha County ◇ 31 33 28N 88 49W
Oktyabrskiy 98 54 28N 53 28 E
Oktyabrskoy Revolyutsii, Os. 101 79 30N 97 0 E
Oktyabrskoye 100 62 28N 66 3 E
Okuru 128 43 55 S 168 55 E
Okushiri-Tō 116 42 15N 139 30 E
Ola, Ark. 13 35 2N 93 13W
Ola, Idaho 20 44 11N 116 18W
Ólafsfjörður 96 66 4N 18 39W
Ólafsvík 96 64 53N 23 43W
Olamon 26 45 7N 68 37W
Olancha 15 36 17N 118 1W
Olanchito 66 15 30N 86 30W
Öland 97 56 45N 16 38 E
Olanta 46 33 56N 79 56W
Olar 46 33 11N 81 11W
Olascoaga 76 35 15 S 60 39W
Olathe, Colo. 16 38 36N 107 59W
Olathe, Kans. 24 38 53N 94 49W
Olavarría 76 36 55 S 60 20W
Olberg 12 33 6N 111 41W
Ólbia 94 40 55N 9 30 E
Old Bahama Chan. =
Bahama, Canal Viejo de 66 22 10N 77 30W
Old Bridge 37 40 25N 74 22W
Old Castile = Castilla La
Vieja 91 41 55N 4 0W
Old Castle 85 53 46N 7 10W
Old Crow 58 67 30N 140 5 E
Old Faithful 56 44 28N 110 50W
Old Forge, N.Y. 39 43 43N 74 58W
Old Forge, Pa. 45 41 22N 75 45W
Old Fort 40 35 38N 82 11W
Old Fort → 63 58 36N 110 24W
Old Harbor 11 57 12N 153 18W
Old Hickory L. 48 36 18N 86 40W
Old Logan Cr. → 34 41 37N 96 30W
Old Lyme 28 41 19N 72 20W
Old Mines 32 38 1N 90 45W
Old Monroe 32 38 56N 90 45W
Old Ocean 51 29 5N 95 45W
Old Orchard Beach 26 43 31N 70 23W
Old Saybrook 28 41 18N 72 23W
Old Speck Mt. 26 44 34N 70 57W
Old Town, Fla. 17 29 36N 82 59W
Old Town, Maine 26 44 56N 68 39W
Old Washington 42 40 2N 81 27W
Old Wives L. 63 50 5N 106 0W
Old Woman Mts. 15 34 20N 115 0W
Oldbury 83 51 38N 2 30W
Oldenburg, Germany 88 53 10N 8 10 E
Oldenburg, U.S.A. 22 39 21N 85 12W
Oldenzaal 87 52 19N 6 53 E
Oldham, U.K. 82 53 33N 2 8W
Oldham, U.S.A. 47 44 14N 97 19W
Oldham County ◇, Ky. 49 38 25N 85 30W
Oldham County ◇, Tex. 50 35 30N 102 30W
Oldman → 62 49 57N 111 42W
Olds 62 51 50N 114 10W
Oldsmar 17 28 2N 82 40W
Oldtown 27 39 33N 78 37W
Olean, Mo. 32 38 25N 92 32W
Olean, N.Y. 39 42 5N 78 26W
Olekma → 101 60 22N 120 42 E
Olekminsk 101 60 25N 120 30 E
Olenegorsk 98 68 9N 33 18 E
Olenek 101 68 28N 112 18 E
Olenek → 101 73 0N 120 10 E
Olentangy → 42 39 58N 83 2W
Oléron, Île d' 90 45 55N 1 15W
Oleśnica 89 51 13N 17 22 E
Olex 44 45 30N 120 11W
Olga 101 43 50N 135 14 E
Olga, L. 60 49 47N 77 15W
Olga, Mt. 126 25 20 S 130 50 E
Olgastretet 4 78 35N 25 0 E
Olifants → 123 24 5 S 31 20 E
Ólimbos, Óros 95 40 6N 22 23 E
Olímpia 77 20 44 S 48 54W
Olimpo □ 76 20 30 S 58 45W
Olinda 74 8 1 S 34 51W
Olindiná 74 11 22 S 38 21W
Oliva 76 32 0 S 63 38W
Olive Branch 31 34 58N 89 50W
Olive Hill 49 38 18N 83 13W
Olivehurst 14 39 6N 121 34W
Oliveira 75 20 39 S 44 50W
Oliveira dos Brejinhos 75 12 19 S 42 54W
Olivenza 91 38 41N 7 9W
Oliver, Canada 62 49 13N 119 37W
Oliver, Ga. 18 32 31N 81 32W
Oliver, Wis. 55 46 40N 92 12W
Oliver County ◇ 41 47 2N 101 25W
Oliver L. 63 56 56N 103 22W
Oliver Springs 49 36 3N 84 20W
Olivet, Kans. 24 38 29N 95 45W
Olivet, Md. 27 38 20N 76 26W
Olivet, Mich. 29 42 27N 84 56W
Olivet, S. Dak. 47 43 14N 97 40W
Olivia, Minn. 30 44 47N 94 59W
Olivia, N.C. 40 35 22N 79 7W
Olla 25 31 54N 92 14W
Ollagüe 76 21 15 S 68 10W
Ollie 23 41 12N 92 6W
Olmos 72 5 59 S 79 46W
Olmstead, Ill. 21 37 11N 89 5W
Olmstead, Ky. 48 36 45N 87 1W
Olmsted County ◇ 30 44 0N 92 30W
Olney, Ill. 21 38 44N 88 5W
Olney, Md. 27 39 9N 77 4W
Olney, Mont. 33 48 33N 114 35W
Olney, Tex. 51 33 22N 98 45W
Olney Springs 16 38 10N 103 57W
Olomane → 61 50 14N 60 37W
Olomouc 88 49 38N 17 12 E
Olonets 98 61 10N 33 0 E
Olongapo 111 14 50N 120 18 E
Olovyannaya 101 50 58N 115 35 E
Olowalu 19 20 49N 156 38W
Oloy → 101 66 29N 159 29 E
Olpe 24 38 16N 96 10W
Olsburg 24 39 26N 96 37W
Olsztyn 89 53 48N 20 29 E
Olt □ 95 44 20N 24 30 E
Olt → 89 43 50N 24 40 E
Olteniţa 89 44 7N 26 42 E
Olton 50 34 11N 102 8W
Oltu 106 40 35N 41 58 E
Olustee, Fla. 17 30 12N 82 26W
Olustee, Okla. 43 34 33N 99 25W
Olympia, Greece 95 37 39N 21 39 E
Olympia, U.S.A. 53 47 3N 122 53W
Olympic Mts. 53 47 55N 123 45W
Olympic National Forest 53 47 25N 123 35W
Olympus, Mt. = Ólimbos,
Óros 95 40 6N 22 23 E
Olympus, Mt. 53 47 48N 123 43W
Om → 100 54 59N 73 22 E
Ōma, Japan 116 41 45N 141 5 E
Oma, U.S.A. 31 31 44N 90 9W
Ōmachi 117 36 30N 137 50 E
Omae-Zaki 117 34 36N 138 14 E
Ōmagari 116 39 27N 140 29 E
Omagh 85 54 36N 7 20W
Omagh □ 85 54 35N 7 15W
Omaha, Ark. 13 36 27N 93 11W
Omaha, Nebr. 34 41 17N 96 1W
Omaha, Tex. 51 33 11N 94 45W
Omaha Indian Reservation 34 42 10N 96 30W
Omak 53 48 25N 119 31W
Omak L. 53 48 17N 119 24W
Oman ■ 105 23 0N 58 0 E
Oman, G. of 107 24 30N 58 30 E
Omaruru 123 21 26 S 16 0 E
Omate 72 16 45 S 71 0W
Ombai, Selat 111 8 30 S 124 50 E
Omboué 122 1 35 S 9 15 E
Ombrone → 94 42 39N 11 0 E
Omdurmân 121 15 40N 32 28 E
Omega 18 31 21N 83 36W
Omemee 41 48 42N 100 22W
Omer 29 44 3N 83 51W
Ometepe, Isla de 66 11 32N 85 35W
Ometepec 65 16 39N 98 23W
Omez 104 32 22N 35 0 E
Ominato 116 41 17N 141 10 E
Omineca → 62 56 3N 124 16W
Ōmiya 117 35 54N 139 38 E
Ommaney, C. 11 56 10N 134 40W
Ommen 87 52 31N 6 26 E
Omo → 121 6 25N 36 10 E
Omolon → 101 68 42N 158 36 E
Omono-Gawa → 116 39 46N 140 3 E
Ompompanoosuc → 36 43 45N 72 14W
Omro 55 44 2N 88 45W
Omsk 100 55 0N 73 12 E
Omsukchan 101 62 32N 155 48 E
Ōmu 116 44 34N 142 58 E
Omul, Vf. 89 45 27N 25 29 E
Ōmura 117 32 56N 130 0 E
Omuramba → 123 19 10 S 19 20 E
Omurtag 95 43 8N 26 26 E
Ōmuta 117 33 0N 130 26 E
Ona 17 27 29N 81 55W
Onaga 24 39 29N 96 10W
Onaka 47 45 12N 99 28W
Onalaska 55 43 53N 91 14W
Onamia 30 46 4N 93 40W
Onancock 54 37 43N 75 45W
Onang 111 3 2 S 118 49 E
Onaping L. 60 47 3N 81 30W
Onarga 21 40 43N 88 1W
Onarhã 107 35 30N 71 0 E
Onavas 64 28 28N 109 30W
Onawa 23 42 2N 96 6W
Onaway, Idaho 20 46 56N 116 53W
Onaway, Mich. 29 45 21N 84 14W
Oncesti 95 43 56N 25 52 E
Oncócua 123 16 30 S 13 25 E
Onda 91 39 55N 0 17W
Ondangua 123 17 57 S 16 4 E
Ondas → 75 12 8 S 45 0W
Ondo 120 7 4N 4 47 E
Öndörhaan 113 47 19N 110 39 E
Öndverðarnes 96 64 52N 24 0W
Onega 98 64 0N 38 10 E
Onega → 98 63 58N 37 55 E
Onega, G. of = Onezhskaya
Guba 98 64 30N 37 0 E
Onega, L. = Onezhskoye
Ozero 98 62 0N 35 30 E
Onehunga 128 36 55 S 174 48 E
Oneida, Ill. 21 41 4N 90 13W
Oneida, Iowa 23 42 33N 91 21W
Oneida, Kans. 24 39 52N 95 56W
Oneida, N.Y. 39 43 6N 75 39W
Oneida, Tenn. 49 36 30N 84 31W
Oneida County ◇, Idaho 20 42 10N 112 30W
Oneida County ◇, N.Y. 39 43 20N 75 30W
Oneida County ◇, Wis. 55 45 40N 89 35W
Oneida Indian Reservation 55 44 25N 88 10W
Oneida L. 39 43 12N 75 54W
O'Neill 34 42 27N 98 39W
Onekama 29 44 22N 86 12W
Onekotan, Ostrov 101 49 25N 154 45 E
Oneonta, Ala. 10 33 57N 86 28W
Oneonta, N.Y. 39 42 27N 75 4W
Onezhskaya Guba 98 64 30N 37 0 E
Onezhskoye Ozero 98 62 0N 35 30 E
Ongarue 128 38 42 S 175 19 E
Ongniud Qi 114 43 0N 118 38 E
Ongole 108 15 33N 80 2 E
Onguren 101 53 38N 107 36 E
Onida 47 44 42N 100 4W
Onilahy → 123 23 34 S 43 45 E
Onitsha 120 6 6N 6 42 E
Onley 54 37 41N 75 43W
Ono 14 40 29N 122 37W
Onoda 117 34 2N 131 25 E
Onondaga County ◇ 39 43 0N 76 15W
Onondaga Indian
Reservation 39 42 55N 76 10W
Onset 28 41 45N 70 39W
Onslow, Australia 126 21 40 S 115 12 E
Onslow, U.S.A. 23 42 6N 91 1W
Onslow B. 40 34 20N 77 15W
Onslow County ◇ 40 34 50N 77 30W
Onstwedde 87 53 2N 7 4 E
Ontake-San 117 35 53N 137 29 E
Ontario, Calif. 15 34 4N 117 39W
Ontario, Oreg. 44 44 2N 116 58W
Ontario, Wis. 55 43 45N 90 35W
Ontario □ 60 52 0N 88 10W
Ontario, L.,
U.S.A. 39 43 20N 78 0W
Ontario County ◇ 39 42 50N 77 20W
Ontonagon 29 46 52N 89 19W
Ontonagon County ◇ 29 46 40N 89 25W
Oodnadatta 126 27 33 S 135 30 E
Ookala 19 20 1N 155 17W
Ooldea 126 30 27 S 131 50 E
Oolitic 22 38 54N 86 31W
Oologah 43 36 27N 95 43W
Oologah L. 43 36 26N 95 41W
Ooltewah 49 35 4N 85 4W
Oona River 62 53 57N 130 16W
Oost-Vlaanderen □ 87 51 5N 3 50 E
Oostburg 55 43 37N 87 48W
Oostende 87 51 15N 2 50 E
Oosterhout 87 51 39N 4 47 E
Oosterschelde 87 51 33N 4 0 E
Ootacamund 108 11 30N 76 44 E
Ootsa L. 62 53 50N 126 2W
Opaka 95 43 28N 26 10 E
Opala, U.S.S.R. 101 51 58N 156 30 E
Opala, Zaïre 122 0 40 S 24 20 E
Opan 95 42 13N 25 41 E
Opanake 108 6 35N 80 40 E
Opasatika 60 49 30N 82 50W
Opasquia 63 53 16N 93 34W
Opava 89 49 57N 17 58 E
Opelika 10 32 39N 85 23W
Opelousas 25 30 32N 92 5W
Opémisca, L. 60 49 56N 74 52W
Opheim 33 48 51N 106 24W
Ophir, Alaska 11 63 10N 156 31W
Ophir, Oreg. 44 42 34N 124 23W
Ophthalmia Ra. 126 23 15 S 119 30 E
Opihikao 19 19 26N 154 53W
Opinaca → 60 52 15N 78 2W
Opinaca L. 60 52 39N 76 20W
Opiskotish, L. 61 53 10N 67 50W
Opole 89 50 42N 17 58 E
Oporto = Porto 91 41 8N 8 40W
Opotiki 128 38 1 S 177 19 E
Opp 10 31 17N 86 16W
Oppland fylke □ 97 61 15N 9 40 E
Opportunity, Mont. 33 46 6N 112 50W
Opportunity, Wash. 53 47 39N 117 15W
Optima 43 36 46N 101 21W
Opua 128 35 19 S 174 9 E
Opunake 128 39 26 S 173 52 E
Oquawka 21 40 56N 90 57W
Or Yehuda 104 32 2N 34 50 E
Ora 104 30 55N 35 1 E
Oracle 12 32 37N 110 46W

Oradea Oulu

Oradea **89** 47 2N 21 58 E
Örœfajökull **96** 64 2N 16 39W
Orai **108** 25 58N 79 30 E
Oraibi **12** 35 53N 110 37W
Oran, Algeria **120** 35 45N 0 39W
Oran, Argentina **76** 23 10 S 64 20W
Oran, U.S.A. **32** 37 5N 89 39W
Orange, Australia **127** 33 15 S 149 7 E
Orange, France **90** 44 8N 4 47 E
Orange, Calif. **15** 33 47N 117 51W
Orange, Conn. **28** 41 17N 73 2W
Orange, Mass. **28** 42 35N 72 19W
Orange, Tex. **51** 30 6N 93 44W
Orange, Va. **54** 38 15N 78 7W
Orange, C. **71** 4 20N 51 30W
Orange City, Fla. **17** 28 57N 81 18W
Orange City, Iowa **23** 43 0N 96 4W
Orange County ◇, Calif. **15** 33 30N 117 45W
Orange County ◇, Fla. **17** 28 30N 81 15W
Orange County ◇, Ind. **22** 38 30N 86 30W
Orange County ◇, N.C. **40** 36 0N 79 10W
Orange County ◇, N.Y. **39** 41 20N 74 15W
Orange County ◇, Tex. **51** 30 12N 93 52W
Orange County ◇, Va. **54** 38 15N 78 7W
Orange County ◇, Vt. **36** 44 0N 72 20W
Orange Cove **15** 36 38N 119 19W
Orange Free State = Oranje Vrystaat □ **123** 28 30 S 27 0 E
Orange Grove **51** 27 58N 97 56W
Orange Lake **17** 29 25N 82 13W
Orange Park **17** 30 10N 81 42W
Orange Walk **65** 18 6N 88 33W
Orangeburg **46** 33 30N 80 52W
Orangeburg County ◇ **46** 33 20N 80 30W
Orangevale **14** 38 41N 121 13W
Orangeville, Canada **60** 43 55N 80 5W
Orangeville, Ill. **21** 42 28N 89 39W
Orangeville, Pa. **45** 41 5N 76 25W
Orangeville, Utah **52** 39 14N 111 3W
Oranienburg **88** 52 45N 13 15 E
Oranje → **123** 28 41 S 16 28 E
Oranje Vrystaat □ **123** 28 30 S 27 0 E
Oranjemund **123** 28 38 S 16 29 E
Or'Aquiva **104** 32 30N 34 54 E
Oras **111** 12 9N 125 28 E
Orăştie **95** 45 50N 23 10 E
Oraşul Stalin = Braşov **89** 45 38N 25 35 E
Oraya, La **72** 11 32 S 75 54W
Orbetello **94** 42 26N 11 11 E
Orbisonia **45** 40 15N 77 54W
Orbost **127** 37 40 S 148 29 E
Orcadas **5** 60 44 S 44 37W
Orcas **53** 48 36N 122 57W
Orcas I. **53** 48 42N 122 56W
Orchard, Colo. **16** 40 20N 104 7W
Orchard, Idaho **20** 43 19N 116 2W
Orchard, Iowa **23** 43 14N 92 47W
Orchard, Nebr. **34** 42 20N 98 15W
Orchard City **16** 38 50N 107 58W
Orchard Homes **33** 46 55N 114 4W
Orchard Park **39** 42 46N 78 45W
Orchard Valley **56** 41 6N 104 49W
Orchards **53** 45 40N 122 34W
Orchila, Isla **70** 11 48N 66 10W
Orcopampa **72** 15 20 S 72 23W
Ord **34** 41 36N 98 56W
Ord → **126** 15 33 S 138 15 E
Ord, Mt., Australia **126** 17 20 S 125 34 E
Ord, Mt., U.S.A. **50** 30 18N 103 30W
Orderville **52** 37 17N 112 38W
Ordos = Mu Us Shamo **114** 39 0N 109 0 E
Ordu **106** 40 55N 37 53 E
Ordway **16** 38 13N 103 46W
Ordzhonikidze **99** 43 0N 44 35 E
Ore City **51** 32 48N 94 43W
Ore Mts. = Erzgebirge **88** 50 25N 13 0 E
Orealla **71** 5 15N 57 23W
Oreana, Idaho **20** 43 3N 116 24W
Oreana, Ill. **21** 39 56N 88 52W
Oreana, Nev. **35** 40 20N 118 19W
Örebro **97** 59 20N 15 18 E
Örebro län □ **97** 59 27N 15 0 E
Oregon, Ill. **21** 42 1N 89 20W
Oregon, Mo. **32** 39 59N 95 9W
Oregon, Ohio **42** 41 38N 83 25W
Oregon, Wis. **55** 42 56N 89 23W
Oregon □ **44** 44 0N 121 0W
Oregon Butte **53** 46 7N 117 41W
Oregon Caves National Monument **44** 42 6N 123 24W
Oregon City **44** 45 21N 122 36W
Oregon County ◇ **32** 36 40N 91 25W
Oregon Dunes Nat. Rec. Area **44** 42 3N 123 26W
Orekhovo-Zuyevo **98** 55 50N 38 55 E
Orel **98** 52 57N 36 3 E
Orem **52** 40 19N 111 42W
Orenburg **98** 51 45N 55 6 E
Orense **91** 42 19N 7 55W
Orepuki **128** 46 19 S 167 46 E
Orford Ness **83** 52 6N 1 31 E
Organ **38** 32 26N 106 36W
Organ Pipe Cactus National Monument **12** 32 0N 113 10W
Orgūn **107** 32 55N 69 12 E
Orhon Gol → **113** 49 30N 106 0 E
Orick **14** 41 17N 124 4W
Orient, Iowa **23** 41 12N 94 25W
Orient, Maine **26** 45 49N 67 50W
Orient, S. Dak. **47** 44 54N 99 5W
Orient, Wash. **53** 48 52N 118 12W
Oriental **40** 35 2N 76 42W
Oriental, Cordillera, Bolivia **73** 17 0 S 66 0W
Oriental, Cordillera, Colombia **70** 6 0N 73 0W
Oriente **76** 38 44 S 60 37W
Orihuela **91** 38 7N 0 55W
Orin **56** 42 39N 105 12W
Orinda **14** 37 53N 122 11W
Orinduik **71** 4 40N 60 3W
Orinoco → **71** 9 15N 61 30W
Orion, Ala. **10** 31 58N 86 0W
Orion, Ill. **21** 41 21N 90 23W
Orion, Okla. **43** 36 13N 98 47W
Oriska **41** 46 56N 97 47W
Oriskany **39** 43 10N 75 20W
Orissa □ **109** 20 0N 84 0 E
Oristano **94** 39 54N 8 35 E
Oristano, Golfo di **94** 39 50N 8 22 E
Orituco → **70** 8 45N 67 27W
Orizaba **65** 18 50N 97 10W
Orizare **95** 42 44N 27 39 E
Orizona **75** 17 3 S 48 18W
Orkanger **96** 63 18N 9 52 E
Orkla → **96** 63 18N 9 51 E
Orkney □ **84** 59 0N 3 0W
Orkney Is. **84** 59 0N 3 0W
Orla **50** 31 50N 103 55W
Orland **14** 39 45N 122 12W
Orlando, Fla. **17** 28 33N 81 23W
Orlando, Okla. **43** 36 9N 97 23W
Orléanais **90** 48 0N 2 0 E
Orléans, France **90** 47 54N 1 52 E
Orleans, Calif. **14** 41 18N 123 32W
Orleans, Ind. **22** 38 40N 86 27W
Orleans, Mass. **28** 41 47N 69 59W
Orleans, Nebr. **34** 40 8N 99 27W
Orleans, Vt. **36** 44 49N 72 12W
Orléans, Î. d' **61** 46 54N 70 58W
Orleans County ◇, N.Y. **39** 43 15N 78 10W
Orleans County ◇, Vt. **36** 44 45N 72 15W
Orleans Parish ◇ **25** 29 58N 90 4W
Orlik **101** 52 30N 99 55 E
Orlinda **48** 36 36N 86 43W
Ormara **107** 25 16N 64 33 E
Ormoc **111** 11 0N 124 37 E
Ormond **128** 38 33 S 177 56 E
Ormond Beach **17** 29 17N 81 3W
Ormond-by-the-Sea **17** 29 21N 81 4W
Ormsby **30** 43 51N 94 42W
Orne □ **90** 48 40N 0 5 E
Örnsköldsvik **96** 63 17N 18 40 E
Oro → **64** 25 35N 105 2W
Oro Grande **15** 34 36N 117 20W
Orocovis **57** 18 14N 66 23W
Orocué **70** 4 48N 71 20W
Orofino **20** 46 29N 116 15W
Orogrande **38** 32 24N 106 5W
Oromocto **61** 45 54N 66 29W
Orono **26** 44 53N 68 40W
Oronoco **30** 44 10N 92 32W
Oroqen Zizhiqi **114** 50 34N 123 43 E
Oroquieta **111** 8 32N 123 44 E
Orós **74** 6 15 S 38 55W
Orosei **94** 40 20N 9 40 E
Orotukan **101** 62 16N 151 42 E
Orovada **35** 41 34N 117 47W
Oroville, Calif. **14** 39 31N 121 33W
Oroville, Wash. **53** 48 56N 119 26W
Oroville, L. **14** 39 33N 121 29W
Oroville Dam **14** 39 33N 121 29W
Orpha **56** 42 51N 105 30W
Orr, Minn. **30** 48 3N 92 50W
Orr, Okla. **43** 34 2N 97 32W
Orrick **32** 39 13N 94 7W
Orrin **41** 48 6N 100 10W
Orrville **42** 40 50N 81 46W
Orsha **98** 54 30N 30 25 E
Orsk **98** 51 12N 58 34 E
Orşova **89** 44 41N 22 25 E
Ortegal, C. **91** 43 43N 7 52W
Orteguaza → **70** 0 43N 75 16W
Orthez **90** 43 29N 0 48W
Ortigueira **91** 43 40N 7 50W
Orting **53** 47 6N 122 12W
Ortles **94** 46 31N 10 33 E
Ortley **47** 45 20N 97 12W
Ortón → **72** 10 50 S 67 0W
Ortona **94** 42 21N 14 24 E
Ortonville **30** 45 19N 96 27W
Orūmīyeh **106** 37 40N 45 0 E
Orūmīyeh, Daryācheh-ye **106** 37 50N 45 30 E
Oruro **72** 18 0 S 67 9W
Oruro □ **72** 18 40 S 67 30W
Oruzgān □ **107** 33 30N 66 0 E
Orvieto **94** 42 43N 12 8 E
Orwell **42** 41 32N 80 52W
Orwell → **83** 52 2N 1 12 E
Oryakhovo **95** 43 40N 23 57 E
Osa **98** 57 17N 55 26 E
Osa, Pen. de **66** 8 0N 84 0W
Osage, Ark. **13** 36 11N 93 24W
Osage, Iowa **23** 43 17N 92 49W
Osage, Okla. **43** 36 19N 96 24W
Osage, W. Va. **54** 39 39N 80 1W
Osage, Wyo. **56** 43 59N 104 25W
Osage → **32** 38 36N 92 57W
Osage Beach **32** 38 9N 92 37W
Osage City, Kans. **24** 38 38N 95 50W
Osage City, Mo. **32** 38 33N 92 2W
Osage County ◇, Kans. **24** 38 40N 95 40W
Osage County ◇, Mo. **32** 38 30N 91 45W
Osage County ◇, Okla. **43** 36 40N 96 30W
Ōsaka **117** 34 40N 135 30 E
Osakis **30** 45 52N 95 9W
Osakis, L. **30** 45 54N 95 7W
Osawatomie **24** 38 31N 94 57W
Osborne **24** 39 26N 98 42W
Osborne County ◇ **24** 39 30N 98 45W
Osburn **20** 47 30N 116 0W
Osceola, Ark. **13** 35 42N 89 58W
Osceola, Iowa **23** 41 2N 93 46W
Osceola, Mo. **32** 38 3N 93 42W
Osceola, Nebr. **34** 41 11N 97 33W
Osceola, Wis. **55** 45 19N 92 42W
Osceola County ◇, Fla. **17** 28 0N 81 0W
Osceola County ◇, Iowa **23** 43 20N 95 35W
Osceola County ◇, Mich. **29** 44 0N 85 20W
Osceola Mills **45** 40 51N 78 16W
Osceola National Forest **17** 30 20N 82 30W
Oscoda **29** 44 26N 83 20W
Oscoda County ◇ **29** 44 40N 84 10W
Oscura **38** 33 29N 106 3W
Ösel = Saaremaa **98** 58 30N 22 30 E
Osgood, Ind. **22** 39 8N 85 18W
Osgood, Ohio **42** 40 20N 84 30W
Osgood Mts. **35** 41 10N 117 20W
Osh **100** 40 37N 72 49 E
Oshawa **60** 43 50N 78 50W
Oshkosh, Nebr. **34** 41 24N 102 21W
Oshkosh, Wis. **55** 44 1N 88 33W
Oshogbo **120** 7 48N 4 37 E
Oshwe **122** 3 25 S 19 28 E
Osica de Jos **95** 44 14N 24 20 E
Osierfield **18** 31 40N 83 7W
Osijek **95** 45 34N 18 41 E
Osipenko = Berdyansk **99** 46 45N 36 50 E
Oskaloosa, Iowa **23** 41 18N 92 39W
Oskaloosa, Kans. **24** 39 13N 95 19W
Oskarshamn **97** 57 15N 16 27 E
Oskélanéo **60** 48 5N 75 15W
Oslo, Norway **97** 59 55N 10 45 E
Oslo, U.S.A. **30** 48 12N 97 8W
Oslob **111** 9 31N 123 26 E
Oslofjorden **97** 59 20N 10 35 E
Osmanabad **108** 18 5N 76 10 E
Osmaniye **106** 37 5N 36 10 E
Osmond **34** 42 22N 97 36W
Osnabrock **41** 48 40N 98 9W
Osnabrück **88** 52 16N 8 2 E
Osorio **77** 29 53 S 50 17W
Osorno **78** 40 25 S 73 0W
Osorno □ **78** 40 34 S 73 9W
Osorno, Vol. **78** 41 0 S 72 30W
Osoyoos **62** 49 0N 119 30W
Ospika → **62** 56 20N 124 0W
Osprey **17** 27 12N 82 29W
Osprey Reef **127** 13 52 S 146 36 E
Oss **87** 51 46N 5 32 E
Ossa, Mt. **127** 41 52 S 146 3 E
Óssa, Oros **95** 39 47N 22 42 E
Ossabaw I. **18** 31 50N 81 5W
Ossabaw Sd. **18** 31 50N 81 6W
Osseo, Mich. **29** 41 53N 84 33W
Osseo, Wis. **55** 44 35N 91 13W
Ossian, Ind. **22** 40 53N 85 10W
Ossian, Iowa **23** 43 9N 91 46W
Ossineke **29** 44 55N 83 26W
Ossining **39** 41 10N 73 55W
Ossipee **36** 43 41N 71 7W
Ossipee L. **36** 43 42N 71 10W
Ossokmanuan L. **61** 53 25N 65 0W
Ossora **101** 59 20N 163 13 E
Ostend = Oostende **87** 51 15N 2 50 E
Österdalälven → **97** 61 30N 13 45 E
Östergötlands län □ **97** 58 35N 15 45 E
Östersund **96** 63 10N 14 38 E
Osterville **28** 41 38N 70 22W
Østfold fylke □ **97** 59 25N 11 25 E
Ostfriesische Inseln **88** 53 45N 7 15 E
Ostia **94** 41 40N 12 20 E
Ostrander **30** 43 37N 92 26W
Ostrava **89** 49 51N 18 18 E
Ostróda **89** 53 42N 19 58 E
Ostrołeka **89** 53 4N 21 32 E
Ostrov, Bulgaria **95** 43 40N 24 9 E
Ostrov, Romania **95** 44 6N 27 24 E
Ostrów Mazowiecka **89** 52 50N 21 51 E
Ostrów Wielkopolski **89** 51 36N 17 44 E
Ostrowiec-Świętokrzyski **89** 50 55N 21 22 E
O'Sullivan Dam **53** 46 59N 119 16W
Osum → **95** 43 40N 24 50 E
Ōsumi-Kaikyō **117** 30 55N 131 0 E
Ōsumi-Shotō **117** 30 30N 130 0 E
Osuna **91** 37 14N 5 8W
Oswegatchie → **39** 44 42N 75 30W
Oswego, Ill. **21** 41 41N 88 21W
Oswego, Kans. **24** 37 10N 95 6W
Oswego, N.Y. **39** 43 27N 76 31W
Oswego → **39** 43 27N 76 30W
Oswego County ◇ **39** 43 25N 76 10W
Oswestry **82** 52 52N 3 3W
Osyka **31** 31 0N 90 28W
Otago □ **128** 44 44 S 169 10 E
Otago Harb. **128** 45 47 S 170 42 E
Ōtake **117** 34 12N 132 13 E
Otaki **128** 40 45 S 175 10 E
Otaru **116** 43 10N 141 0 E
Otaru-Wan = Ishikari-Wan **116** 43 25N 141 1 E
Otavalo **70** 0 13N 78 20W
Otavi **123** 19 40 S 17 24 E
Otero County ◇, Colo. **16** 38 0N 103 45W
Otero County ◇, N. Mex. **38** 32 30N 105 45W
Othello **53** 46 50N 119 10W
Otho **23** 42 25N 94 9W
Otira Gorge **128** 42 53 S 171 33 E
Otis, Colo. **16** 40 9N 102 58W
Otis, Kans. **24** 38 32N 99 3W
Otis, Mass. **28** 42 12N 73 6W
Otisville **29** 43 10N 83 31W
Otjiwarongo **123** 20 30 S 16 33 E
Oto **23** 42 17N 95 54W
Otoe **34** 40 43N 96 7W
Otoe County ◇ **34** 40 40N 96 0W
Otoineppu **116** 44 44N 142 16 E
Otorohanga **128** 38 12 S 175 14 E
Otoskwin → **60** 52 13N 88 6W
Otosquen **63** 53 17N 102 1W
Otranto **95** 40 9N 18 28 E
Otranto, C. d' **95** 40 7N 18 30 E
Otranto, Str. of **95** 40 15N 18 40 E
Otsego **29** 42 27N 85 42W
Otsego County ◇, Mich. **29** 45 0N 84 40W
Otsego County ◇, N.Y. **39** 42 40N 75 0W
Otsego L. **39** 42 45N 74 52W
Ōtsu **117** 35 0N 135 50 E
Ōtsuki **117** 35 36N 138 57 E
Ottawa = Outaouais → **60** 45 27N 74 8W
Ottawa, Canada **60** 45 27N 75 42W
Ottawa, Ill. **21** 41 21N 88 51W
Ottawa, Kans. **24** 38 37N 95 16W
Ottawa, Ohio **42** 41 1N 84 3W
Ottawa County ◇, Kans. **24** 39 15N 97 45W
Ottawa County ◇, Mich. **29** 42 50N 86 0W
Ottawa County ◇, Ohio **42** 41 30N 83 9W
Ottawa County ◇, Okla. **43** 36 50N 94 50W
Ottawa Is. **59** 59 35N 80 10W
Ottawa National Forest **29** 46 25N 89 15W
Otter **33** 45 12N 106 12W
Otter Cr. →, Utah **52** 38 10N 112 2W
Otter Cr. →, Vt. **36** 44 13N 73 17W
Otter Creek **17** 29 19N 82 46W
Otter Creek Reservoir **52** 38 10N 112 1W
Otter L. **63** 55 35N 104 39W
Otter Lake, Ill. **21** 39 28N 89 56W
Otter Lake, Mich. **29** 43 13N 83 28W
Otter Rapids, Ont., Canada **60** 50 11N 81 39W
Otter Rapids, Sask., Canada **63** 55 38N 104 44W
Otter Tail → **30** 46 16N 96 36W
Otter Tail County ◇ **30** 46 20N 95 45W
Otter Tail L. **30** 46 24N 95 40W
Otterbein **22** 40 29N 87 6W
Ottertail **30** 46 26N 95 33W
Otterville **32** 38 42N 93 0W
Ottosen **23** 42 54N 94 23W
Ottumwa **23** 41 1N 92 25W
Oturkpo **120** 7 16N 8 8 E
Otway **42** 38 52N 83 11W
Otway, Bahía **78** 53 30 S 74 0W
Otway, C. **127** 38 52 S 143 30 E
Otwock **89** 52 5N 21 20 E
Ötztaler Alpen **88** 46 45N 11 0 E
Ou → **112** 20 4N 102 13 E
Ou-Sammyaku **116** 39 20N 140 35 E
Ouachita **13** 33 51N 92 50W
Ouachita → **25** 31 38N 91 49W
Ouachita, L. **13** 34 34N 93 12W
Ouachita County ◇ **13** 33 35N 92 50W
Ouachita Mts. **43** 34 40N 94 25W
Ouachita National Forest **43** 34 50N 94 50W
Ouachita Parish ◇ **25** 32 30N 92 7W
Ouadâne **120** 20 50N 11 40W
Ouadda **121** 8 15N 22 20 E
Ouagadougou **120** 12 25N 1 30W
Ouahran = Oran **120** 35 45N 0 39W
Ouallene **120** 24 41N 1 11 E
Ouanda Djallé **121** 8 55N 22 53 E
Ouango **122** 4 19N 22 30 E
Ouargla **120** 31 59N 5 16 E
Ouarzazate **120** 30 55N 6 50W
Oubangi → **122** 1 0N 17 50 E
Ouddorp **87** 51 50N 3 57 E
Oude Rijn → **87** 52 12N 4 24 E
Oudenaarde **87** 50 50N 3 37 E
Oudtshoorn **123** 33 35 S 22 14 E
Ouessant, Île d' **90** 48 28N 5 6W
Ouesso **122** 1 37N 16 5 E
Ouest, Pte. **61** 49 52N 64 40W
Ouezzane **120** 34 51N 5 35W
Ouidah **120** 6 25N 2 0 E
Oujda **120** 34 41N 1 55W
Oujeft **120** 20 2N 13 0W
Ouled Djellal **120** 34 28N 5 2 E
Oulu **96** 65 1N 25 29 E

Oulu Pampas

Oulu □ 96 65 10N 27 20 E
Oulujärvi 96 64 25N 27 15 E
Oulujoki → 96 65 1N 25 30 E
Oum Chalouba 121 15 48N 20 46 E
Ounianga-Kébir 121 19 4N 20 29 E
Ounianga Sérir 121 18 54N 19 51 E
Our → 87 49 55N 6 5 E
Ouray, Colo. 16 38 1N 107 40W
Ouray, Utah 52 40 6N 109 41W
Ouray County ◇ 16 38 10N 107 45W
Ourém 74 1 33 S 47 6W
Ouricuri 74 7 53 S 40 5W
Ourinhos 77 23 0 S 49 54W
Ouro Fino 77 22 16 S 46 25W
Ouro Prêto 75 20 20 S 43 30W
Ourthe → 87 50 29N 5 35 E
Ouse →, E. Sussex, U.K. 83 50 43N 0 3 E
Ouse →, N. Yorks., U.K. 82 54 3N 0 7 E
Outagamie County ◇ 55 44 20N 88 30W
Outaouais → 60 45 27N 74 8W
Outardes → 61 49 24N 69 30W
Outer Hebrides 84 57 30N 7 40W
Outer I., Canada 61 51 10N 58 35W
Outer I., U.S.A. 55 47 2N 90 26W
Outer Santa Barbara Passage 15 33 15N 118 40W
Outjo 123 20 5 S 16 7 E
Outlook, Canada 63 51 30N 107 0W
Outlook, U.S.A. 33 48 53N 104 47W
Ouyen 127 35 1 S 142 22 E
Ouzinkie 11 57 56N 152 30W
Ovalau 128 17 40 S 178 48 E
Ovalle 76 30 33 S 71 18W
Ovando 33 47 1N 113 8W
Ovar 91 40 51N 8 40W
Ovejas 70 9 32N 75 14W
Over Flakkee 87 51 45N 4 5 E
Overbrook 24 38 47N 95 33W
Overijssel □ 87 52 25N 6 35 E
Overland 32 38 41N 90 22W
Overland Park 24 38 58N 94 40W
Overlea 27 39 22N 76 32W
Overly 41 48 41N 100 9W
Overpelt 87 51 12N 5 20 E
Overton, Nebr. 34 40 44N 99 32W
Overton, Nev. 35 36 33N 114 27W
Overton, Tex. 51 32 16N 94 59W
Overton County ◇ 49 36 23N 85 19W
Övertorneå 96 66 23N 23 38 E
Ovett 31 31 29N 89 2W
Ovid, Colo. 16 40 58N 102 23W
Ovid, Mich. 29 43 1N 84 22W
Ovid, N.Y. 39 42 41N 76 49W
Oviedo, Spain 91 43 25N 5 50W
Oviedo, U.S.A. 17 28 40N 81 13W
Owaka 128 46 27 S 169 40 E
Owambo 123 17 20 S 16 30 E
Owanka 47 44 1N 102 35W
Owasa 23 42 26N 93 12W
Owasco L. 39 42 50N 76 31W
Owase 117 34 7N 136 12 E
Owasso 43 36 16N 95 51W
Owatonna 30 44 5N 93 14W
Owbeh 107 34 28N 63 10 E
Owego 39 42 6N 76 16W
Owen 55 44 57N 90 33W
Owen County ◇, Ind. 22 39 20N 86 50W
Owen County ◇, Ky. 49 38 30N 84 50W
Owen Sound 60 44 35N 80 55W
Owendo 122 0 17N 9 30 E
Owens → 15 36 32N 117 59W
Owens L. 15 36 26N 117 57W
Owensboro 48 37 46N 87 7W
Owensville, Ark. 13 34 37N 92 49W
Owensville, Ind. 22 38 16N 87 41W
Owensville, Mo. 32 38 21N 91 30W
Owensville, Ohio 42 39 7N 84 8W
Owenton 49 38 32N 84 50W
Owings Mills 27 39 25N 76 47W
Owingsville 49 38 9N 83 46W
Owl → 63 57 51N 92 44W
Owl Creek Mts. 56 43 40N 108 55W
Owls Head 26 44 5N 69 4W
Owo 120 7 10N 5 39 E
Owosso 29 43 0N 84 10W
Owsley County ◇ 49 37 25N 83 40W
Owyhee 35 41 57N 116 6W
Owyhee → 44 43 49N 117 2W
Owyhee, L. 44 43 38N 117 14W
Owyhee County ◇ 20 42 45N 116 0W
Owyhee Mts. 20 42 45N 116 20W
Ox Mts. 85 54 6N 9 0W
Oxapampa 72 10 33 S 75 26W
Oxbow 26 46 25N 68 29W
Oxelösund 97 58 43N 17 15 E
Oxford, N.Z. 128 43 18 S 172 11 E
Oxford, U.K. 83 51 45N 1 15W
Oxford, Ala. 10 33 36N 85 51W
Oxford, Ark. 13 36 13N 91 56W
Oxford, Colo. 16 37 10N 107 43W
Oxford, Ind. 22 40 31N 87 15W
Oxford, Iowa 23 41 43N 91 47W
Oxford, Kans. 24 37 17N 97 10W
Oxford, La. 25 31 56N 93 38W
Oxford, Maine 26 44 8N 70 30W
Oxford, Mass. 28 42 7N 71 52W
Oxford, Md. 27 38 41N 76 11W
Oxford, Mich. 29 42 49N 83 16W
Oxford, Miss. 31 34 22N 89 31W
Oxford, N.C. 40 36 19N 78 35W
Oxford, N.Y. 39 42 27N 75 36W
Oxford, Nebr. 34 40 15N 99 38W
Oxford, Ohio 42 39 31N 84 45W
Oxford, Pa. 45 39 47N 75 59W
Oxford □ 83 51 45N 1 15W
Oxford County ◇ 26 44 30N 70 30W
Oxford Junction 23 41 59N 90 57W
Oxford L. 63 54 51N 95 37W
Oxford Pk. 20 42 16N 112 6W
Oxnard 15 34 12N 119 11W
Oxon Hill 27 38 48N 76 59W
Oya 110 2 55N 111 55 E
Oyama 117 36 18N 139 48 E
Oyapock → 71 4 8N 51 40W
Oyem 122 1 34N 11 31 E
Oyen 63 51 22N 110 28W
Oykel → 84 57 55N 4 26W
Oymyakon 101 63 25N 142 44 E
Oyo 120 7 46N 3 56 E
Oyón 72 10 37 S 76 47W
Oyster Bay 39 40 52N 73 32W
Ōyūbari 116 43 1N 142 5 E
Ozamis 111 8 15N 123 50 E
Ozan 13 33 51N 93 43W
Ozark, Ala. 10 31 28N 85 39W
Ozark, Ark. 13 35 29N 93 50W
Ozark, Mo. 32 37 1N 93 12W
Ozark County ◇ 32 36 40N 92 25W
Ozark National Forest 13 35 40N 93 20W
Ozark Plateau 32 37 0N 93 0W
Ozark Reservoir 13 35 30N 94 10W
Ozarks, L. of the 32 38 12N 92 38W
Ozarks Nat. Scenic Riverways 32 37 25N 91 12W
Ozaukee County ◇ 55 43 20N 88 0W
Ozette L. 53 48 6N 124 38W
Ozona 50 30 43N 101 12W
Ozone 49 35 53N 84 49W
Ozuluama 65 21 40N 97 50W
Ozun 95 45 47N 25 50 E

P

Pa-an 109 16 51N 97 40 E
Pa Sak → 112 15 30N 101 0 E
Paarl 123 33 45 S 18 56 E
Paatsi → 96 68 55N 29 0 E
Paauilo 19 20 2N 155 22W
Pab Hills 108 26 30N 66 45 E
Pablo 33 47 36N 114 7W
Pabna 109 24 1N 89 18 E
Pacaás Novos, Serra dos 73 10 45 S 64 15W
Pacaipampa 72 5 35 S 79 39W
Pacaja → 74 1 56 S 50 50W
Pacajus 74 4 10 S 38 31W
Pacaraima, Sierra 71 4 0N 62 30W
Pacarán 72 12 50 S 76 3W
Pacaraos 72 11 12 S 76 42W
Pacasmayo 72 7 20 S 79 35W
Pace 17 30 36N 87 10W
Pachacamac 72 12 14 S 77 53W
Pachitea → 72 8 46 S 74 33W
Pachiza 72 7 16 S 76 46W
Pacho 70 5 8N 74 10W
Pachpadra 108 25 58N 72 10 E
Pachuca 65 20 10N 98 40W
Pachuta 31 32 2N 88 53W
Pacific, Canada 62 54 48N 128 28W
Pacific, U.S.A. 32 38 29N 90 45W
Pacific-Antarctic Basin 125 46 0 S 95 0W
Pacific-Antarctic Ridge 125 43 0 S 115 0W
Pacific Beach 53 47 13N 124 12W
Pacific City 44 45 12N 123 57W
Pacific County ◇ 53 46 30N 123 55W
Pacific Grove 14 36 38N 121 56W
Pacific Ocean 124 10 0N 140 0W
Pacific Palisades 19 21 25N 157 58W
Pacifica 14 37 36N 122 30W
Pacitan 111 8 12 S 111 7 E
Packwood, Iowa 23 41 8N 92 5W
Packwood, Wash. 53 46 36N 121 40W
Pacofi 62 53 0N 132 30W
Pacolet 46 34 54N 81 46W
Pacolet Mills 46 34 55N 81 45W
Pacuí → 75 16 46 S 45 1W
Padaido, Kepulauan 111 1 5 S 138 0 E
Padang 110 1 0 S 100 20 E
Padangpanjang 110 0 40 S 100 20 E
Padangsidempuan 110 1 30N 99 15 E
Padauari → 71 0 15 S 64 5W
Padcaya 73 21 52 S 64 48W
Paddockwood 63 53 30N 105 30W
Paden 43 35 30N 96 34W
Paderborn 88 51 42N 8 44 E
Padilla 73 19 19 S 64 20W
Padina 95 44 50N 27 8 E
Padloping Island 59 67 0N 62 50W
Pádova 94 45 24N 11 52 E
Padre I. 50 27 10N 97 25W
Padre Island National Seashore 50 27 0N 97 25W
Padroni 16 40 47N 103 10W
Padstow 82 50 33N 4 57W
Padua = Pádova 94 45 24N 11 52 E
Paducah, Ky. 48 37 5N 88 37W
Paducah, Tex. 50 34 1N 100 18W
Paeroa 128 37 23 S 175 41 E
Pag 94 44 30N 14 50 E
Pagadian 111 7 55N 123 30 E
Pagai Selatan 110 3 0 S 100 15W
Pagai Utara 110 2 35 S 100 0 E
Pagalu 119 1 25 S 5 36 E
Pagastikós Kólpos 95 39 15N 23 0 E
Pagatan 110 3 33 S 115 59 E
Page, Ariz. 12 36 57N 111 27W
Page, N. Dak. 41 47 10N 97 34W
Page, Nebr. 34 42 26N 98 25W
Page City 24 39 5N 101 9W
Page County ◇, Iowa 23 40 45N 95 10W
Page County ◇, Va. 54 38 40N 78 28W
Pageland 46 34 46N 80 24W
Pago Pago 128 14 16 S 170 43W
Pagosa Springs 16 37 16N 107 1W
Paguate 38 35 8N 107 23W
Pagwa River 60 50 2N 85 14W
Pahala 19 19 12N 155 29W
Pahang □ 112 3 40N 102 20 E
Pahang → 112 3 30N 103 9 E
Pahaska 56 44 30N 109 58W
Pahiatua 128 40 27 S 175 50 E
Pahoa 19 19 30N 154 57W
Pahokee 17 26 50N 80 40W
Pahrump 35 36 12N 115 59W
Pahute Mesa 35 37 20N 116 45W
Paia 19 20 54N 156 22W
Paige 51 30 13N 97 7W
Paignton 83 50 26N 3 33W
Paiján 72 7 42 S 79 20W
Päijänne, L. 97 61 30N 25 30 E
Pailin 112 12 46N 102 36 E
Pailolo Channel 19 21 0N 156 40W
Painan 110 1 21 S 100 34 E
Paincourtville 25 29 59N 91 3W
Painesdale 29 47 3N 88 40W
Painesville 42 41 43N 81 15W
Paint → 42 45 58N 88 15W
Paint Hills = Nouveau Comptoir 60 53 0N 78 49W
Paint I. 63 55 28N 97 57W
Paint Rock, Ala. 10 34 40N 86 20W
Paint Rock, Tex. 51 31 31N 99 55W
Paint Rock → 10 34 28N 86 28W
Painted Desert 12 36 0N 111 0W
Painted Post 39 42 10N 77 6W
Paintsville 49 37 49N 82 48W
Pais Vasco 91 43 0N 2 30W
Paisley, U.K. 84 55 51N 4 27W
Paisley, U.S.A. 44 42 42N 120 32W
Paita 72 5 11 S 81 9W
Pajarito 38 34 59N 106 42W
Pak Lay 112 18 15N 101 27 E
Pakanbaru 110 0 30N 101 15 E
Pakaraima Mts. 71 6 0N 60 0W
Pakistan ■ 107 30 0N 70 0 E
Pakokku 109 21 20N 95 0 E
Pakse 112 15 5N 105 52 E
Paktīā □ 107 33 0N 69 15 E
Pala, Chad 121 9 25N 15 5 E
Pala, U.S.A. 15 33 22N 117 5W
Palacios 51 28 42N 96 13W
Palagruža 94 42 24N 16 15 E
Palam 108 19 0N 77 0 E
Palamós 91 41 50N 3 10 E
Palampur 108 32 10N 76 30 E
Palana 101 59 10N 159 59 E
Palanan 111 17 8N 122 29 E
Palanan Pt. 111 17 17N 122 30 E
Palangkaraya 110 2 16 S 113 56 E
Palani Hills 108 10 14N 77 33 E
Palanpur 108 24 10N 72 25 E
Palaoa Pt. 19 20 44N 156 58W
Palapye 123 22 30 S 27 7 E
Palatine 21 42 7N 88 3W
Palatka, U.S.A. 17 29 39N 81 38W
Palatka, U.S.S.R. 101 60 6N 150 54 E
Palauk 112 13 10N 98 40 E
Palawan 110 9 30N 118 30 E
Palayankottai 108 8 45N 77 45 E
Palca 72 19 7 S 69 9W
Palco 24 39 15N 99 34W
Paleleh 111 1 10N 121 50 E
Palembang 110 3 0 S 104 50 E
Palen Dry L. 15 33 46N 115 13W
Palena → 78 43 50 S 73 50W
Palena, L. 78 43 55 S 71 40W
Palencia 91 42 1N 4 34W
Palermo, Colombia 70 2 54N 75 26W
Palermo, Italy 94 38 8N 13 20 E
Palermo, Calif. 14 39 26N 121 33W
Palermo, N. Dak. 41 48 21N 102 14W
Palestine, Asia 104 32 0N 35 0 E
Palestine, Ark. 13 34 58N 90 54W
Palestine, Ill. 21 39 0N 87 37W
Palestine, Ohio 42 40 3N 84 45W
Palestine, Tex. 51 31 46N 95 38W
Palestine, L. 51 32 6N 95 27W
Paletwa 109 21 10N 92 50 E
Palghat 108 10 46N 76 42 E
Pali 108 25 50N 73 20 E
Palikea Pk. 19 21 26N 158 6W
Palisade, Colo. 16 39 7N 108 21W
Palisade, Nebr. 34 40 21N 101 7W
Palisades, Idaho 20 43 21N 111 13W
Palisades, Wash. 53 47 25N 119 54W
Palisades Reservoir 20 43 20N 111 12W
Palitana 108 21 32N 71 49 E
Palito Blanco 50 27 35N 98 11W
Palizada 65 18 18N 92 8W
Palk Bay 108 9 30N 79 15 E
Palk Strait 108 10 0N 79 45 E
Palm Bay 17 28 2N 80 35W
Palm Beach 17 26 43N 80 2W
Palm Beach County ◇ 17 26 45N 80 20W
Palm Desert 15 33 43N 116 22W
Palm Is. 127 18 40 S 146 35 E
Palm Springs 15 33 50N 116 33W
Palma, Canary Is. 120 28 40N 17 50W
Palma, Mozam. 122 10 46 S 40 29 E
Palma → 75 12 33 S 47 52W
Palma, B. de 91 39 30N 2 39 E
Palma, La, Canary Is. 120 28 40N 17 50W
Palma, La, Panama 66 8 15N 78 0W
Palma, La, Spain 91 37 21N 6 38W
Palma de Mallorca 91 39 35N 2 39 E
Palma Soriano 66 20 15N 76 0W
Palmaḥim 104 31 56N 34 44 E
Palmares 74 8 41 S 35 28W
Palmarito 70 7 37N 70 10W
Palmas 77 26 29 S 52 0W
Palmas, C. 120 4 27N 7 46W
Pálmas, G. di 94 39 0N 8 30 E
Palmas de Monte Alto 75 14 16 S 43 10W
Palmdale, Calif. 15 34 35N 118 7W
Palmdale, Fla. 17 26 57N 81 19W
Palmeira 75 25 25 S 50 0W
Palmeira dos Índios 74 9 25 S 36 37W
Palmeirais 74 6 0 S 43 0W
Palmeiras → 75 12 22 S 47 8W
Palmeirinhas, Pta. das 122 9 2 S 12 57 E
Palmelo 75 17 20 S 48 27W
Palmer, Alaska 11 61 36N 149 7W
Palmer, Iowa 23 42 38N 94 36W
Palmer, Kans. 24 39 38N 97 8W
Palmer, Mass. 28 42 9N 72 20W
Palmer, Nebr. 34 41 13N 98 15W
Palmer, Tenn. 49 35 21N 85 34W
Palmer → 126 24 46 S 133 25 E
Palmer Arch 5 64 15 S 65 0W
Palmer Lake 16 39 7N 104 55W
Palmer Land 5 73 0 S 60 0W
Palmers Crossing 31 31 16N 89 15W
Palmerston, C. 127 21 32 S 149 29 E
Palmerston North 128 40 21 S 175 39 E
Palmerton 45 40 48N 75 37W
Palmetto, Fla. 17 27 31N 82 34W
Palmetto, Ga. 18 33 31N 84 40W
Palmetto, La. 25 30 43N 91 55W
Palmi 94 38 21N 15 51 E
Palmira, Argentina 76 32 59 S 68 34W
Palmira, Colombia 70 3 32N 76 16W
Palmyra = Tudmur 106 34 36N 38 15 E
Palmyra, Ill. 21 39 26N 90 0W
Palmyra, Ind. 22 38 24N 86 7W
Palmyra, Mo. 32 39 48N 91 32W
Palmyra, N.J. 37 40 1N 75 1W
Palmyra, Nebr. 34 40 42N 96 23W
Palmyra, Pa. 45 40 18N 76 36W
Palmyra, Va. 54 37 52N 78 16W
Palmyra Is. 125 5 52N 162 5W
Palo 23 42 4N 91 48W
Palo Alto 14 37 27N 122 10W
Palo Alto County ◇ 23 43 5N 94 40W
Palo Duro Cr. → 50 35 0N 101 55W
Palo Pinto 51 32 46N 98 18W
Palo Pinto County ◇ 51 32 45N 98 20W
Palo Verde, Ariz. 12 33 21N 112 41W
Palo Verde, Calif. 15 33 26N 114 44W
Paloma, La 76 30 35 S 71 0W
Palopo 111 3 0 S 120 16 E
Palos, Cabo de 91 37 38N 0 40W
Palouse 53 46 55N 117 4W
Palouse → 53 46 35N 118 13W
Palpa 72 14 30 S 75 15W
Palu, Indonesia 111 1 0 S 119 52 E
Palu, Turkey 106 38 45N 40 0 E
Paluan 111 13 26N 120 29 E
Pama 120 11 19N 0 44 E
Pamanukan 111 6 16 S 107 49 E
Pamekasan 111 7 10 S 113 28 E
Pamirs 100 37 40N 73 0 E
Pamlico → 40 35 20N 76 28W
Pamlico County ◇ 40 35 10N 76 45W
Pamlico Sd. 40 35 20N 76 0W
Pampa 50 35 32N 100 58W
Pampa, La □ 76 36 50 S 66 0W
Pampa de Agma 78 43 45 S 69 40W
Pampa de las Salinas 76 32 1 S 66 58W
Pampa Grande 73 18 5 S 64 6W
Pampa Hermosa 72 7 7 S 75 4W
Pampanua 111 4 16 S 120 8 E
Pampas, Argentina 76 35 0 S 63 0W

Pampas Patrocínio

Pampas, Peru 72 12 20 S 74 50W
Pampas → 72 13 24 S 73 12W
Pamplico 46 34 0N 79 34W
Pamplin City 54 37 16N 78 41W
Pamplona, Colombia 70 7 23N 72 39W
Pamplona, Spain 91 42 48N 1 38W
Pamunkey → 54 37 32N 76 48W
Pana 21 39 23N 89 5W
Panaca 35 37 47N 114 23W
Panacea 17 30 2N 84 23W
Panagyurishte 95 42 30N 24 15 E
Panaitan 111 6 35 S 105 10 E
Panaji 108 15 25N 73 50 E
Panama, Panama 57 8 48N 79 55W
Panamá, Panama 66 9 0N 79 25W
Panama, Nebr. 34 40 36N 96 31W
Panama, Okla. 43 35 10N 94 40W
Panama ■ 66 8 48N 79 55W
Panama, Bay of 57 8 50N 79 20W
Panama Canal, Panama 57 9 20N 79 55W
Panama City 17 30 10N 85 40W
Panama City Beach 17 30 11N 85 48W
Panamint Range 15 36 20N 117 20W
Panamint Valley 15 36 15N 117 20W
Panão 72 9 55 S 75 55W
Panarukan 111 7 40 S 113 52 E
Panay 111 11 10N 122 30 E
Panay, G. 111 11 0N 122 30 E
Pancake Range 35 38 30N 115 50W
Pančevo 95 44 52N 20 41 E
Panciu 95 45 54N 27 8 E
Pancorbo, Paso 91 42 32N 3 5W
Pandan 111 11 45N 122 10 E
Pandegelang 111 6 25 S 106 0 E
Pandharpur 108 17 41N 75 20 E
Pando 77 34 44 S 56 0W
Pando □ 72 11 20 S 67 40W
Pandora 42 40 57N 83 58W
Panfilov 100 44 10N 80 0 E
Pang-Long 109 23 11N 98 45 E
Pang-Yang 109 22 7N 98 48 E
Pangani 122 5 25 S 38 58 E
Pangburn 13 35 26N 91 50W
Pangfou = Bengbu 115 32 58N 117 20 E
Pangil 122 3 10 S 26 35 E
Pangkah, Tanjung 111 6 51 S 112 33 E
Pangkajene 111 4 46 S 119 34 E
Pangkalanberandan 110 4 1N 98 20 E
Pangkalanbuun 110 2 41 S 111 37 E
Pangkalansusu 110 4 2N 98 13 E
Pangkalpinang 110 2 0 S 106 0 E
Pangkoh 110 3 5 S 114 8 E
Pangnirtung 59 66 8N 65 54W
Pangong Tso 108 34 0N 78 20 E
Pangrango 111 6 46 S 107 1 E
Panguipulli 78 39 38 S 72 20W
Panguitch 52 37 50N 112 26W
Pangutaran Group 111 6 18N 120 34 E
Panhandle 50 35 21N 101 23W
Paniau 19 21 56N 160 5W
Panjgur 107 27 0N 64 5 E
Panjim = Panaji 108 15 25N 73 50 E
Panjinad Barrage 107 29 22N 71 15 E
Panna 108 24 40N 80 15 E
Panola 10 32 57N 88 16W
Panola County ◇, Miss. 31 34 19N 89 57W
Panola County ◇, Tex. 51 32 9N 94 20W
Panora 23 41 42N 94 22W
Panorama 77 21 21 S 51 51W
Panshan 114 41 3N 122 2 E
Panshi 114 42 58N 126 5 E
Pantar 111 8 28 S 124 10 E
Pantelleria 94 36 52N 12 0 E
Pánuco 65 22 0N 98 15W
Panyam 120 9 27N 9 8 E
Panyu 115 22 51N 113 20 E
Pao →, Anzoátegui, Venezuela 71 8 6N 64 17W
Pao →, Apure, Venezuela 70 8 33N 68 1W
Paola 24 38 35N 94 53W
Paoli, Colo. 16 40 37N 102 28W
Paoli, Ind. 22 38 33N 86 28W
Paoli, Okla. 43 34 50N 97 15W
Paonia 16 38 52N 107 36W
Paoshan 109 25 7N 99 9 E
Paoting = Baoding 114 38 50N 115 28 E
Paot'ou = Baotou 114 40 32N 110 2 E
Paoua 122 7 9N 16 20 E
Papá, Hungary 89 47 22N 17 30 E
Papa, U.S.A. 19 19 13N 155 52W
Papaaloa 19 19 59N 155 13W
Papagayo → 65 16 36N 99 43W
Papagayo, Golfo de 66 10 30N 85 50W
Papago Indian Reservation 12 32 15N 112 0W
Papaikou 19 19 47N 155 6W
Papakura 128 37 4 S 174 59 E
Papantla 65 20 30N 97 30W
Papar 110 5 45N 116 0 E
Paparoa 128 36 6 S 174 16 E
Papawai Pt. 19 20 47N 156 32W
Papien Chiang = Da → 112 21 15N 105 20 E
Papigochic → 64 29 9N 109 40W
Papillion 34 41 9N 96 3W
Papineau 21 40 58N 87 43W
Paposo 76 25 0 S 70 30W
Papua New Guinea ■ 124 8 0 S 145 0 E
Papudo 76 32 29 S 71 27W
Papun 109 18 0N 97 30 E
Pará = Belém 74 1 20 S 48 30W
Pará □, Brazil 73 3 20 S 52 0W
Pará □, Surinam 71 40 0 S 53 0W
Paraburdoo 126 23 14 S 117 32 E
Paracas, Pen. 72 13 53 S 76 20W
Paracatu 75 17 10 S 46 50W
Paracatu → 75 16 30 S 45 4W
Parachinar 108 33 55N 70 5 E
Paracuru 74 3 24 S 39 4W
Parada, Punta 72 15 22 S 75 11W
Paradip 109 20 15N 86 35 E
Paradise, Calif. 14 39 46N 121 37W
Paradise, Kans. 24 39 7N 98 55W
Paradise, Mich. 29 46 38N 85 2W
Paradise, Mont. 33 47 23N 114 48W
Paradise, Nev. 35 36 9N 115 10W
Paradise, Utah 52 41 34N 111 50W
Paradise → 61 53 27N 57 19W
Paradise Hill 43 35 40N 95 5W
Paradise Valley, Ariz. 12 33 32N 111 57W
Paradise Valley, Nev. 35 41 30N 117 32W
Paradise Valley, Wyo. 56 42 49N 106 23W
Parado 111 8 42 S 118 30 E
Paragon 22 39 24N 86 34W
Paragonah 52 37 53N 112 46W
Paragould 13 36 3N 90 29W
Paraguá →, Bolivia 73 13 34 S 61 53W
Paragua →, Venezuela 71 6 55N 62 55W
Paragua, La 71 6 50N 63 20W
Paraguaçu → 75 12 45 S 38 54W
Paraguaçu Paulista 77 22 22 S 50 35W
Paraguaipoa 70 11 21N 71 57W
Paraguaná, Pen. de 70 12 0N 70 0W
Paraguarí 76 25 36 S 57 0W
Paraguarí □ 76 26 0 S 57 10W
Paraguay ■ 76 23 0 S 57 0W
Paraguay → 76 27 18 S 58 38W
Paraíba = João Pessoa 74 7 10 S 34 52W
Paraíba □ 74 7 0 S 36 0W
Paraíba do Sul → 75 21 37 S 41 3W
Parainen 97 60 18N 22 18 E
Paraiso, Mexico 65 18 24N 93 14W
Paraiso, Panama 57 9 3N 79 38W
Parakou 120 9 25N 2 40 E
Paramaribo 71 5 50N 55 10W
Parambu 74 6 13 S 40 43W
Paramillo, Nudo del 70 7 4N 75 55W
Paramirim 75 13 26 S 42 15W
Paramirim → 75 11 34 S 43 18W
Paramus 37 40 55N 74 4W
Paramushir, Ostrov 101 50 24N 156 0 E
Paran → 104 30 20N 35 10 E
Paraná, Argentina 76 31 45 S 60 30W
Paranã, Brazil 75 12 30 S 47 48W
Paraná □ 77 24 30 S 51 0W
Paraná → 76 33 43 S 59 15W
Paranaguá 77 25 30 S 48 30W
Paranaíba → 75 20 6 S 51 4W
Paranapanema → 77 22 40 S 53 9W
Paranapiacaba, Serra do 77 24 31 S 48 35W
Paranavaí 77 23 4 S 52 56W
Parang, Jolo, Phil. 111 5 55N 120 54 E
Parang, Mindanao, Phil. 111 7 23N 124 16 E
Parangaba 74 3 45 S 38 33W
Paratinga 75 12 40 S 43 10W
Paraúna 75 16 55 S 50 26W
Parbhani 108 19 8N 76 52 E
Parchim 88 53 25N 11 50 E
Parchment 29 42 20N 85 34W
Pardee Reservoir 14 38 16N 120 51W
Pardeeville 55 43 32N 89 18W
Pardes Hanna 104 32 28N 34 57 E
Pardo →, Bahia, Brazil 75 15 40 S 39 0W
Pardo →, Mato Grosso, Brazil 75 21 46 S 52 9W
Pardo →, Minas Gerais, Brazil 75 15 48 S 44 48W
Pardo →, São Paulo, Brazil 75 20 10 S 48 38W
Pardubice 88 50 3N 15 45 E
Pare 111 7 43 S 112 12 E
Parecis, Serra dos 73 13 0 S 60 0W
Parelhas 74 6 41 S 36 39W
Paren 101 62 30N 163 15 E
Parent 60 47 55N 74 35W
Parent, Lac 60 48 31N 77 1W
Parepare 111 4 0 S 119 40 E
Parfuri 123 22 28 S 31 17 E
Parguba 98 62 20N 34 27 E
Parguera 57 17 59N 67 3W
Paria → 12 36 52N 111 36W
Paria, Golfo de 70 10 20N 62 0W
Paria, Pen. de 71 10 50N 62 30W
Paria Plateau 12 36 50N 111 50W
Pariaguán 71 8 51N 64 34W
Pariaman 110 0 47 S 100 11 E
Paricatuba 71 4 26 S 61 53W
Paricutín, Cerro 64 19 28N 102 15W
Parigi, Java, Indonesia 111 7 42 S 108 29 E
Parigi, Sulawesi, Indonesia 111 0 50 S 120 5 E
Parika 71 6 50N 58 20W
Parima, Serra 71 2 30N 64 0W
Parinari 72 4 35 S 74 25W
Parincea 95 46 27N 27 9 E
Parîng 95 45 20N 23 37 E
Parîngul-Mare 89 45 20N 23 37 E
Parintins 71 2 40 S 56 50W
Pariparit Kyun 109 14 55 S 93 45 E
Paris, Canada 60 43 12N 80 25W
Paris, France 90 48 50N 2 20 E
Paris, Ark. 13 35 18N 93 44W
Paris, Idaho 20 42 14N 111 24W
Paris, Ill. 21 39 36N 87 42W
Paris, Ky. 49 38 13N 84 15W
Paris, Maine 26 44 16N 70 30W
Paris, Mo. 32 39 29N 92 0W
Paris, Tenn. 48 36 18N 88 19W
Paris, Tex. 51 33 40N 95 33W
Paris, Ville de □ 90 48 50N 2 20 E
Parish 39 43 25N 76 8W
Parishville 39 44 38N 74 49W
Pariti 111 10 15 S 123 45 E
Park 24 39 7N 100 22W
Park → 41 48 28N 97 9W
Park City, Kans. 24 37 48N 97 20W
Park City, Ky. 48 37 6N 86 3W
Park City, Mont. 33 45 38N 108 55W
Park City, Utah 52 40 39N 111 30W
Park County ◇, Colo. 16 39 0N 105 45W
Park County ◇, Mont. 33 45 30N 110 30W
Park County ◇, Wyo. 56 44 30N 109 30W
Park Falls 55 45 56N 90 27W
Park Forest 21 41 29N 87 40W
Park Range 16 40 0N 106 30W
Park Rapids 30 46 55N 95 4W
Park Ridge, Ill. 21 42 2N 87 51W
Park Ridge, N.J. 37 41 2N 74 2W
Park River 41 48 24N 97 45W
Park Valley 52 41 49N 113 20W
Parkdale, Ark. 13 33 7N 91 33W
Parkdale, Colo. 16 38 29N 105 23W
Parkdale, Oreg. 44 45 31N 121 36W
Parke County ◇ 22 39 45N 87 10W
Parker, Ariz. 12 34 9N 114 17W
Parker, Colo. 16 39 31N 104 46W
Parker, Kans. 24 38 18N 95 0W
Parker, S. Dak. 47 43 24N 97 8W
Parker, Wash. 53 46 30N 120 28W
Parker City 22 40 11N 85 12W
Parker County ◇ 51 32 46N 97 48W
Parker Dam 12 34 18N 114 8W
Parkers Prairie 30 46 9N 95 20W
Parkersburg, Ill. 21 38 36N 88 3W
Parkersburg, Iowa 23 42 35N 92 47W
Parkersburg, W. Va. 54 39 16N 81 34W
Parkerview 63 51 21N 103 18W
Parkerville 24 38 46N 96 40W
Parkes, A.C.T., Australia 127 35 18 S 149 8 E
Parkes, N.S.W., Australia 127 33 9 S 148 11 E
Parkesburg 45 39 58N 75 55W
Parkin 13 35 16N 90 34W
Parkland 53 47 9N 122 26W
Parkrose 44 45 34N 122 33W
Parks, Ark. 13 34 48N 93 58W
Parks, Nebr. 34 40 3N 101 44W
Parkside 63 53 10N 106 33W
Parksley 54 37 47N 75 39W
Parkston 47 43 24N 97 59W
Parksville, Canada 62 49 20N 124 21W
Parksville, U.S.A. 46 33 47N 82 13W
Parkton 27 39 38N 76 40W
Parkville 27 39 23N 76 33W
Parle, L. qui 30 45 1N 95 52W
Parlier 15 36 37N 119 32W
Parma, Italy 94 44 50N 10 20 E
Parma, Idaho 20 43 47N 116 57W
Parma, Mich. 29 42 16N 84 36W
Parma, Mo. 32 36 37N 89 48W
Parma, Ohio 42 41 23N 81 43W
Parmelee 47 43 19N 101 2W
Parmer County ◇ 50 34 38N 102 45W
Parnaguá 74 10 10 S 44 38W
Parnaíba, Piauí, Brazil 74 2 54 S 41 47W
Parnaíba, São Paulo, Brazil 73 19 34 S 51 14W
Parnaíba → 74 3 0 S 41 50W
Parnamirim 74 8 5 S 39 34W
Parnarama 74 5 31 S 43 6W
Parnassós 95 38 35N 22 30 E
Parnell, Iowa 23 41 35N 92 0W
Parnell, Mo. 32 40 26N 94 37W
Pärnu 98 58 28N 24 33 E
Paroo → 127 31 28 S 143 32 E
Paroo Chan. 127 30 50 S 143 35 E
Páros 95 37 5N 25 12 E
Parowan 52 37 51N 112 50W
Parral 76 36 10 S 71 52W
Parramore I. 54 37 32N 75 39W
Parras 64 25 30N 102 20W
Parrett → 83 51 7N 2 58W
Parris I. 46 32 20N 80 41W
Parrish, Ala. 10 33 44N 87 17W
Parrish, Fla. 17 27 35N 82 26W
Parrott 18 31 54N 84 31W
Parrsboro 61 45 30N 64 25W
Parry Is. 4 77 0N 110 0W
Parry Sound 60 45 20N 80 0W
Parshall, Colo. 16 40 3N 106 11W
Parshall, N. Dak. 41 47 57N 102 8W
Parsippany 37 40 52N 74 26W
Parsnip → 62 55 10N 123 2W
Parsons, Kans. 24 37 20N 95 16W
Parsons, Tenn. 48 35 39N 88 8W
Parsons, W. Va. 54 39 6N 79 41W
Parsonsburg 27 38 22N 75 28W
Partridge 24 37 58N 98 5W
Paru →, Brazil 71 1 33 S 52 38W
Parú →, Venezuela 70 4 20N 66 27W
Paru de Oeste → 71 1 30N 56 0W
Parucito → 70 5 18N 65 59W
Paruro 72 13 45 S 71 50W
Parvān □ 107 35 0N 69 0 E
Parvatipuram 109 18 50N 83 25 E
Pas-de-Calais □ 90 50 30N 2 30 E
Pasadena, Calif. 15 34 9N 118 9W
Pasadena, Tex. 51 29 43N 95 13W
Pasaje 70 3 23 S 79 50W
Pasaje → 76 25 39 S 63 56W
Pascagoula 31 30 21N 88 33W
Pascagoula → 31 30 23N 88 37W
Pasco 53 46 14N 119 6W
Pasco □ 72 10 40 S 75 0W
Pasco, Cerro de 72 10 45 S 76 10W
Pasco County ◇ 17 28 20N 82 30W
Pascoag 28 41 57N 71 42W
Pasfield L. 63 58 24N 105 20W
Pashmakli = Smolyan 95 41 36N 24 38 E
Pasir Mas 112 6 2N 102 8 E
Pasir Putih 112 5 50N 102 24 E
Pasirian 111 8 13 S 113 8 E
Paskenta 14 39 53N 122 33W
Pasley, C. 126 33 52 S 123 35 E
Pasni 107 25 15N 63 27 E
Paso de Indios 78 43 55 S 69 0W
Paso de los Libres 76 29 44 S 57 10W
Paso de los Toros 76 32 45 S 56 30W
Paso Flores 78 40 35 S 70 38W
Paso Robles 15 35 38N 120 41W
Pasorapa 73 18 16 S 64 37W
Paspébiac 61 48 3N 65 17W
Pasquotank County ◇ 40 36 15N 76 10W
Pass Christian 31 30 19N 89 15W
Passaconaway 36 43 59N 71 22W
Passadumkeag 26 45 11N 68 37W
Passage West 85 51 52N 8 20W
Passaic, Mo. 32 38 19N 94 21W
Passaic, N.J. 37 40 51N 74 7W
Passaic County ◇ 37 41 0N 74 20W
Passau 88 48 34N 13 27 E
Passero, C. 94 36 42N 15 8 E
Passo Fundo 77 28 10 S 52 20W
Passos 75 20 45 S 46 37W
Passumpsic → 36 44 18N 72 3W
Pastaza □ 70 2 0 S 77 0W
Pastaza → 70 4 50 S 76 52W
Pasto 70 1 13N 77 17W
Pastol B. 11 63 7N 163 15W
Pastora Peak 12 36 47N 109 10W
Pastos Bons 74 6 36 S 44 5W
Pastura 38 34 47N 104 57W
Pasuruan 111 7 40 S 112 44 E
Pat Mayse L. 51 33 51N 95 33W
Patagonia, Argentina 78 45 0 S 69 0W
Patagonia, U.S.A. 12 31 33N 110 45W
Patan, India 108 23 54N 72 14 E
Patan, Nepal 109 27 40N 85 20 E
Patani 111 0 20N 128 50 E
Patapsco 27 39 32N 76 54W
Patapsco → 27 39 11N 76 28W
Patch Grove 55 42 56N 90 58W
Patchogue 39 40 46N 73 1W
Patea 128 39 45 S 174 30 E
Pategi 120 8 50N 5 45 E
Paternò 94 37 34N 14 53 E
Pateros 53 48 3N 119 54W
Paterson, N.J. 37 40 55N 74 11W
Paterson, Wash. 53 45 56N 119 36W
Patesville 48 37 47N 86 43W
Pathankot 108 32 18N 75 45 E
Pathfinder Reservoir 56 42 28N 106 51W
Pathfork 49 36 45N 83 28W
Pati 111 6 45 S 111 3 E
Patía 70 2 4N 77 4W
Patía → 70 2 13N 78 40W
Patiala 108 30 23N 76 26 E
Patillas 57 18 1N 66 1W
Patillas, Puerto 57 17 57N 66 0W
Pativilca 72 10 42 S 77 48W
Patkai Bum 109 27 0N 95 30 E
Patman, L. 51 33 19N 94 10W
Pátmos 95 37 21N 26 36 E
Patna 109 25 35N 85 12 E
Patoka 21 38 45N 89 6W
Patoka L. 22 38 20N 86 40W
Paton 23 42 10N 94 16W
Patos 74 6 55 S 37 16W
Patos, Lag. dos 77 31 20 S 51 0 E
Patos de Minas 75 18 35 S 46 32W
Patquía 76 25 30N 102 11W
Pátrai 95 38 14N 21 47 E
Pátraikós, Kólpos 95 38 17N 21 30 E
Patricia 50 32 33N 102 1W
Patricio Lynch, I. 78 48 35 S 75 30W
Patrick 46 34 34N 80 3W
Patrick County ◇ 54 36 55N 80 10W
Patrocínio 75 18 57 S 47 0W

Patsaliga **Perley**

Patsaliga → 10 31 22N 86 31W
Pattani 112 6 48N 101 15 E
Patten 26 46 0N 68 38W
Patterson, Calif. 14 37 28N 121 8W
Patterson, Ga. 18 31 23N 82 8W
Patterson, Idaho 20 44 32N 113 43W
Patterson, La. 25 29 42N 91 18W
Patterson, Mo. 32 37 11N 90 33W
Patterson, Pt. 29 45 58N 85 39W
Patti 94 38 8N 14 57 E
Pattison 31 31 53N 90 53W
Patton 45 40 38N 78 39W
Pattonsburg 32 40 3N 94 8W
Patu 74 6 6 S 37 38W
Patuakhali 109 22 20N 90 25 E
Patuca → 66 15 50N 84 18W
Patuca, Punta 66 15 49N 84 14W
Patuxent → 27 38 18N 76 25W
Pátzcuaro 64 19 30N 101 40W
Pau 90 43 19N 0 25W
Pau d' Arco 74 7 30 S 49 22W
Pau dos Ferros 74 6 7 S 38 10W
Paucartambo 72 13 19 S 71 35W
Pauillac 90 45 11N 0 46W
Pauini 72 7 40 S 66 58W
Pauini → 71 1 42 S 62 50W
Pauk 109 21 27N 94 30 E
Paul 20 42 36N 113 47W
Paul I. 61 56 30N 61 20W
Paul Isnard 71 4 47N 54 1W
Paul Spur 12 31 22N 109 44W
Paulden 12 34 53N 112 28W
Paulding, Miss. 31 32 2N 89 2W
Paulding, Ohio 42 41 8N 84 35W
Paulding County ◇, Ga. 18 34 0N 84 50W
Paulding County ◇, Ohio 42 41 8N 84 35W
Paulina 44 44 8N 119 58W
Paulina Marsh 44 43 15N 121 0W
Paulina Pk. 44 43 41N 121 15W
Paulins Kill → 37 40 55N 75 5W
Paulis = Isiro 122 2 53N 27 40 E
Paulista 74 7 57 S 34 53W
Paulistana 74 8 9 S 41 9W
Paullina 23 42 59N 95 41W
Paulo Afonso 74 9 21 S 38 15W
Paulo de Faria 75 20 2 S 49 24W
Pauls Valley 43 34 44N 97 13W
Paulsboro 37 39 50N 75 15W
Pausa 72 15 16 S 73 22W
Pauto → 70 5 9N 70 55W
Pauwela 19 20 56N 156 19W
Pavant Range 52 39 10N 112 5W
Pavia 94 45 10N 9 10 E
Pavillion 56 43 15N 108 42W
Pavlikeni 95 43 14N 25 20 E
Pavlodar 100 52 33N 77 0 E
Pavlograd 99 48 30N 35 52 E
Pavlovo, Gorkiy, U.S.S.R. 98 55 58N 43 5 E
Pavlovo, Yakut A.S.S.R., U.S.S.R. 101 63 5N 115 25 E
Pavlovsk 99 50 26N 40 5 E
Pavo 18 30 58N 83 45W
Paw Creek 40 35 17N 80 56W
Paw Paw, Mich. 29 42 13N 85 53W
Paw Paw, W. Va. 54 39 32N 78 28W
Paw Paw Lake 29 42 13N 86 16W
Pawcatuck 28 41 22N 71 52W
Pawhuska 43 36 40N 96 20W
Pawlet 36 43 20N 73 12W
Pawling 39 41 34N 73 36W
Pawnee, Ill. 21 39 36N 89 35W
Pawnee, Okla. 43 36 20N 96 48W
Pawnee → 24 38 10N 99 6W
Pawnee City 34 40 7N 96 9W
Pawnee County ◇, Kans. 24 38 10N 99 15W
Pawnee County ◇, Nebr. 34 40 10N 96 20W
Pawnee County ◇, Okla. 43 36 20N 96 50W
Pawnee Cr. → 16 40 34N 103 14W
Pawnee National Grassland 16 40 40N 104 20W
Pawnee Rock 24 38 16N 99 1W
Pawpaw 21 41 41N 88 59W
Pawtucket 28 41 53N 71 23W
Paxico 24 39 4N 96 10W
Paxson 11 63 2N 145 30W
Paxton, Ill. 21 40 27N 88 6W
Paxton, Mass. 28 42 19N 71 56W
Paxton, Nebr. 34 41 7N 101 21W
Paya Bakri 112 2 3N 102 44 E
Payakumbuh 110 0 20 S 100 35 E
Payette 20 44 5N 116 56W
Payette → 20 44 5N 116 57W
Payette County ◇ 20 44 0N 116 55W
Payette L. 20 44 55N 116 7W
Payette National Forest 20 45 10N 115 30W
Payne 42 41 5N 84 44W
Payne Bay = Bellin 59 60 0N 70 0W
Payne County ◇ 43 36 5N 97 0W
Payne L. 59 59 30N 74 30W
Paynesville 30 45 23N 94 43W
Paysandú 76 32 19 S 58 8W
Payson, Ariz. 12 34 14N 111 20W
Payson, Ill. 21 39 49N 91 15W
Payson, Utah 52 40 3N 111 44W
Paytes 54 38 13N 77 49W
Paz → 66 13 44N 90 10W
Paz, Bahía de la 64 24 15N 110 25W
Paz, La, Entre Ríos, Argentina 76 30 50 S 59 45W
Paz, La, San Luis, Argentina 76 33 30 S 67 20W
Paz, La, Bolivia 72 16 20 S 68 10W
Paz, La, Hond. 66 14 20N 87 47W
Paz, La, Mexico 64 24 10N 110 20W
Paz, La □ 72 15 30 S 68 0W
Paz Centro, La 66 12 20N 86 41W
Pazar 106 41 10N 40 50 E
Pazardzhik 95 42 12N 24 20 E
Pazña 72 18 36 S 66 55W
Pe Ell 53 46 34N 123 18W
Pea → 17 31 1N 85 51W
Pea Ridge 13 36 27N 94 7W
Peabody, Kans. 24 38 10N 97 7W
Peabody, Mass. 28 42 31N 70 56W
Peace →, Canada 62 59 0N 111 25W
Peace →, U.S.A. 17 26 56N 82 6W
Peace Dale 28 41 27N 71 30W
Peace Point 62 59 7N 112 27W
Peace River 62 56 15N 117 18W
Peach County ◇ 18 32 30N 83 50W
Peach Creek 54 37 53N 81 59W
Peach Orchard 13 36 17N 90 40W
Peach Springs 12 35 32N 113 25W
Peachtree City 18 33 25N 84 35W
Peak, The 82 53 24N 1 53W
Peak Range 127 22 50 S 148 20 E
Peale, Mt. 52 38 26N 109 14W
Pearblossom 15 34 30N 117 55W
Pearce 12 31 54N 109 49W
Pearisburg 54 37 20N 80 44W
Pearl, Ill. 21 39 28N 90 38W
Pearl, Miss. 31 32 18N 90 12W
Pearl → 31 30 11N 89 32W
Pearl and Hermes Reef 19 27 55N 175 45W
Pearl City, Hawaii 19 21 24N 157 59W
Pearl City, Ill. 21 42 16N 89 50W
Pearl Harbor 19 21 21N 157 57W
Pearl River, La. 25 30 23N 89 45W
Pearl River, N.Y. 39 41 4N 74 2W
Pearl River County ◇ 31 30 40N 89 38W
Pearland 51 29 34N 95 17W
Pearsall 51 28 54N 99 6W
Pearse I. 62 54 52N 130 14W
Pearson 18 31 18N 82 51W
Peary Land 4 82 40N 33 0W
Pease 30 45 42N 93 39W
Pease → 51 34 12N 99 2W
Pebane 123 17 10 S 38 8 E
Pebas 70 3 10 S 71 46W
Pebble, I. 78 51 20 S 59 40W
Pebble Beach 14 36 34N 121 57W
Peč 95 42 40N 20 17 E
Peçanha 75 18 33 S 42 34W
Pecatonica 21 42 19N 89 22W
Pecatonica → 21 42 26N 89 12W
Pechea 95 45 36N 27 49 E
Pechenga 98 69 30N 31 25 E
Pechora → 98 68 13N 54 15 E
Pechorskaya Guba 98 68 40N 54 0 E
Peck 29 43 16N 82 49W
Peckerwood L. 13 34 40N 91 30W
Pecos, N. Mex. 38 35 35N 105 41W
Pecos, Tex. 50 31 26N 103 30W
Pecos → 50 29 42N 101 22W
Pecos County ◇ 50 30 53N 102 53W
Pecos Plains 38 33 15N 104 10W
Pécs 89 46 5N 18 15 E
Peculiar 32 38 43N 94 28W
Pédernales 67 18 2N 71 44W
Pedernales → 51 30 26N 98 4W
Pedra Azul 75 16 2 S 41 17W
Pedra Grande, Recifes de 75 17 45 S 38 58W
Pedras Negras 73 12 51 S 62 54W
Pedreiras 74 4 32 S 44 40W
Pedrera, La 70 1 18 S 69 43W
Pedro Afonso 74 9 0 S 48 10W
Pedro Antonio Santos 65 18 54N 88 15W
Pedro Bay 11 59 47N 154 7W
Pedro Cays 66 17 5N 77 48W
Pedro Chico 70 1 4N 70 25W
Pedro de Valdivia 76 22 55 S 69 38W
Pedro Juan Caballero 77 22 30 S 55 40W
Pedro Miguel 57 9 2N 79 37W
Pedro Miguel Locks 57 9 1N 79 36W
Peduyim 104 31 20N 34 37 E
Pee Dee → 46 33 22N 79 16W
Peebles, U.K. 84 55 40N 3 12W
Peebles, U.S.A. 42 38 57N 83 24W
Peekskill 39 41 17N 73 55W
Peel 82 54 14N 4 40W
Peel → 58 67 0N 135 0W
Peerless 33 48 47N 105 50W
Peers 62 53 40N 116 0W
Peetz 16 40 58N 103 7W
Peever 47 45 33N 96 57W
Pegasus Bay 128 43 20 S 173 10 E
Pegram 48 36 6N 87 3W
Pegu 109 17 20N 96 29 E
Pegu Yoma 109 19 0N 96 0 E
Pehuajó 76 35 45 S 62 0W
Peine 76 23 45 S 68 8W
Peixe 75 12 0 S 48 40W
Peixe → 75 21 31 S 51 58W
Peixoto de Azeredo → 73 10 6 S 55 31W
Pekalongan 111 6 53 S 109 40 E
Pekan 112 3 30N 103 25 E
Pekin, Ill. 21 40 35N 89 40W
Pekin, Ind. 22 38 30N 86 0W
Pekin, N. Dak. 41 47 48N 98 20W
Peking = Beijing 114 39 55N 116 20 E
Pelabuhan Kelang 110 3 0N 101 23 E
Pelabuhan Ratu, Teluk 111 7 5 S 106 30 E
Pelabuhanratu 111 7 0 S 106 32 E
Pelahatchie 31 32 19N 89 48W
Pelaihari 110 3 55 S 114 45 E
Peleaga 89 45 22N 22 55 E
Pelechuco 72 14 48 S 69 4W
Pelée, Mt. 67 14 48N 61 0W
Pelee, Pt. 60 41 54N 82 31W
Pelee I. 60 41 47N 82 40W
Pelejo 72 6 10 S 75 49W
Peleng 111 1 20 S 123 30 E
Pelham, Ga. 18 31 8N 84 9W
Pelham, Mass. 28 42 24N 72 24W
Pelham, N.C. 40 36 31N 79 28W
Pelican, Alaska 11 57 58N 136 14W
Pelican, La. 25 31 53N 93 35W
Pelican L., Canada 63 52 28N 100 20W
Pelican L., U.S.A. 30 48 4N 92 55W
Pelican Narrows 63 55 10N 102 56W
Pelican Portage 62 55 51N 112 35W
Pelican Rapids, Canada 63 52 45N 100 42W
Pelican Rapids, U.S.A. 30 46 34N 96 5W
Pelion 46 33 46N 81 15W
Pelkosenniemi 96 67 6N 27 28 E
Pell City 10 33 35N 86 17W
Pella 23 41 25N 92 55W
Pellston 29 45 33N 84 47W
Pellville 48 37 45N 86 49W
Pelly → 58 62 47N 137 19W
Pelly Bay 59 68 38N 89 50W
Pelly L. 58 66 0N 102 0W
Peloncillo Mts. 12 32 20N 109 0W
Peloponnes = Pelopónnisos □ 95 37 10N 22 0 E
Pelopónnisos □ 95 37 10N 22 0 E
Peloro, C. 94 38 15N 15 40 E
Pelorus Sound 128 40 59 S 173 59 E
Pelotas 77 31 42 S 52 23W
Pelòvo 95 43 26N 24 17 E
Pelvoux, Massif de 90 44 52N 6 20 E
Pemadumcook L. 26 45 42N 68 57W
Pemalang 111 6 53 S 109 23 E
Pematang 110 0 12 S 102 4 E
Pematangsiantar 110 2 57N 99 5 E
Pemba 123 5 0 S 39 45 E
Pemberton, Australia 126 34 30 S 116 0 E
Pemberton, Canada 62 50 25N 122 50W
Pemberton, Minn. 30 44 1N 93 47W
Pemberton, N.J. 37 39 58N 74 41W
Pemberville 42 41 25N 83 28W
Pembina 41 48 58N 97 15W
Pembina →, Canada 63 49 0N 98 12W
Pembina →, U.S.A. 41 48 58N 97 14W
Pembina County ◇ 41 48 48N 97 37W
Pembine 55 45 38N 87 59W
Pembroke, Canada 60 45 50N 77 7W
Pembroke, U.K. 83 51 41N 4 57W
Pembroke, Ga. 18 32 8N 81 37W
Pembroke, Ky. 48 36 47N 87 21W
Pembroke, Mass. 28 42 5N 70 48W
Pembroke, N.C. 40 34 41N 79 12W
Pembroke Pines 17 26 0N 80 14W
Pemigewasset → 36 43 26N 71 40W
Pemiscot County ◇ 32 36 10N 89 50W
Pen Argyl 45 40 52N 75 16W
Pen-y-Ghent 82 54 10N 2 15W
Peña de Francia, Sierra de 91 40 32N 6 10W
Peñalara, Pico 91 40 51N 3 57W
Penalosa 24 37 43N 98 19W
Penalva 74 3 18 S 45 10W
Penang = Pinang 112 5 25N 100 15 E
Penápolis 77 21 30 S 50 0W
Peñarroya-Pueblonuevo 91 38 19N 5 16W
Peñas, C. de 91 43 42N 5 52W
Penas, G. de 78 47 0 S 75 0W
Peñas, Pta. 71 11 17N 62 0W
Penasco 38 36 10N 105 41W
Pench'i = Benxi 114 41 20N 123 48 E
Pend Oreille → 53 49 4N 117 37W
Pend Oreille County ◇ 53 48 30N 117 10W
Pend Oreille L. 20 48 10N 116 21W
Pendembu 120 9 7N 12 14W
Pendências 74 5 15 S 36 43W
Pender 34 42 7N 96 43W
Pender County ◇ 40 34 30N 78 0W
Pendergrass 18 34 10N 83 41W
Pendleton, Ind. 22 40 0N 85 45W
Pendleton, Oreg. 44 45 40N 118 47W
Pendleton, S.C. 46 34 39N 82 47W
Pendleton County ◇, Ky. 49 38 40N 84 20W
Pendleton County ◇, W. Va. 54 38 47N 79 17W
Pendroy 33 48 4N 112 18W
Penedo 74 10 15 S 36 36W
Penelope 51 31 52N 96 56W
Penetanguishene 60 44 50N 79 55W
Penfield 45 41 13N 78 35W
Pengalengan 111 7 9 S 107 30 E
Penglai 114 37 48N 120 42 E
Pengshui 115 29 17N 108 12 E
Peniche 91 39 19N 9 22W
Penicuik 84 55 50N 3 14W
Penida 110 8 45 S 115 30 E
Peninsular Malaysia □ 112 4 0N 102 0 E
Penitente, Serra dos 74 8 45 S 46 20W
Penmarch, Pte. de 90 47 48N 4 22W
Penn Hills 45 40 28N 79 52W
Penn Yan 39 42 40N 77 3W
Pennant 63 50 32N 108 14W
Pennell, Mt. 52 37 58N 110 47W
Penner → 108 14 35N 80 10 E
Pennines 82 54 50N 2 20W
Pennington, Ala. 10 32 13N 88 3W
Pennington, N.J. 37 40 19N 74 48W
Pennington County ◇, Minn. 30 48 5N 96 0W
Pennington County ◇, S. Dak. 47 44 0N 103 0W
Pennington Gap 54 36 46N 83 2W
Pennock 30 45 9N 95 10W
Penns Grove 37 39 44N 75 28W
Pennsauken 37 39 58N 75 3W
Pennsboro 54 39 17N 80 58W
Pennsburg 45 40 23N 75 29W
Pennsville 37 39 39N 75 31W
Pennsylvannia □ 45 40 45N 77 30W
Pennville 22 40 30N 85 9W
Penny 62 53 51N 121 20W
Penobscot → 26 44 30N 68 48W
Penobscot B. 26 44 35N 68 50W
Penobscot County ◇ 26 45 0N 69 0W
Penola 127 37 25 S 140 21 E
Penong 126 31 59 S 133 5 E
Penonomé 66 8 31N 80 21W
Penrhyn Is. 125 9 0 S 158 30W
Penrith, Australia 127 33 43 S 150 38 E
Penrith, U.K. 82 54 40N 2 45W
Pensacola, Fla. 17 30 25N 87 13W
Pensacola, Okla. 43 36 28N 95 7W
Pensacola Mts. 5 84 0 S 40 0W
Pense 63 50 25N 104 59W
Pentecoste 74 3 48 S 39 17W
Penticton 62 49 30N 119 38W
Pentland 127 20 32 S 145 25 E
Pentland Firth 84 58 43N 3 10W
Pentland Hills 84 55 48N 3 25W
Pentwater 29 43 47N 86 26W
Penuelas 57 18 4N 66 43W
Penwell 50 31 45N 102 36W
Penylan L. 63 61 50N 106 20W
Penza 98 53 15N 45 5 E
Penzance 83 50 7N 5 32W
Penzhino 101 63 30N 167 55 E
Penzhinskaya Guba 101 61 30N 163 0 E
Peoria, Ariz. 12 33 35N 112 14W
Peoria, Ill. 21 40 42N 89 36W
Peoria, Okla. 43 36 54N 94 41W
Peoria County ◇ 21 40 45N 89 45W
Peoria Heights 21 40 45N 89 35W
Peotone 21 41 20N 87 48W
Pep 38 33 50N 103 20W
Pepacton Reservoir 39 42 5N 74 58W
Pepeekeo 19 19 51N 155 6W
Pepin 55 44 27N 92 9W
Pepin County ◇ 55 44 30N 92 10W
Pepperell 28 42 40N 71 35W
Pequest → 37 40 50N 75 5W
Pequop Mts. 35 40 45N 114 40W
Pequot Lakes 30 46 36N 94 19W
Perabumilih 110 3 27 S 104 15 E
Perak → 112 5 10N 101 4 E
Peralta 38 34 50N 106 41W
Percé 61 48 31N 64 13W
Perche 90 48 31N 1 1 E
Perche Cr. → 32 38 49N 92 24W
Percy 31 33 7N 90 53W
Perdido 10 31 0N 87 38W
Perdido →, Argentina 78 42 55 S 67 0W
Perdido →, U.S.A. 10 30 27N 87 23W
Perdido, Mte. 90 42 40N 0 5 E
Perdido B. 10 30 20N 87 30W
Pereira 70 4 49N 75 43W
Pereira Barreto 75 20 38 S 51 7W
Perekop 99 46 10N 33 42 E
Perené → 72 11 9 S 74 14W
Pereyaslav Khmelnitskiy 99 50 3N 31 28 E
Pérez, I. 65 22 24N 89 42W
Pergamino 76 33 52 S 60 30W
Perham 30 46 36N 95 34W
Perhentian, Kepulauan 112 5 54N 102 42 E
Péribonca → 61 48 45N 72 5W
Péribonca, L. 61 50 1N 71 10W
Perico 76 24 20 S 65 5W
Pericos 64 25 3N 107 42W
Peridot 12 33 18N 110 28W
Périgord 90 45 0N 0 40 E
Périgueux 90 45 10N 0 42 E
Perijá, Sierra de 70 9 30N 73 3W
Perito Moreno 78 46 36 S 70 56W
Peritoró 74 4 20 S 44 18W
Perkasie 45 40 22N 75 18W
Perkins 43 35 58N 97 2W
Perkins County ◇, Nebr. 34 40 45N 101 45W
Perkins County ◇, S. Dak. 47 45 30N 102 30W
Perkinston 31 30 47N 89 8W
Perlas, Arch. de las 66 8 41N 79 7W
Perlas, Punta de 66 12 30N 83 30W
Perley 30 47 11N 96 48W

Perlis Pine Apple

Perlis □ 112 6 30N 100 15 E
Perm 98 58 0N 57 10 E
Perma 33 47 22N 114 35W
Pernambuco = Recife 74 8 0 S 35 0W
Pernambuco □ 74 8 0 S 37 0W
Pernell 43 34 34N 97 31W
Perouse Str., La 116 45 40N 142 0 E
Perow 62 54 35N 126 10W
Perpignan 90 42 42N 2 53 E
Perquimans County ◇ 40 36 10N 76 30W
Perrin 51 33 2N 98 4W
Perrine 17 25 36N 80 21W
Perris 15 33 47N 117 14W
Perro, L. del 38 34 41N 105 58W
Perry, Ark. 13 35 3N 92 48W
Perry, Fla. 17 30 7N 83 35W
Perry, Ga. 18 32 28N 83 44W
Perry, Ill. 21 39 47N 90 45W
Perry, Iowa 23 41 51N 94 6W
Perry, Kans. 24 39 5N 95 24W
Perry, Maine 26 44 58N 67 5W
Perry, Mich. 29 42 50N 84 13W
Perry, Mo. 32 39 26N 91 40W
Perry, N.Y. 39 42 43N 78 0W
Perry, Okla. 43 36 17N 97 14W
Perry, S.C. 46 33 38N 81 19W
Perry, Utah 52 41 28N 112 2W
Perry County ◇, Ala. 10 32 38N 87 19W
Perry County ◇, Ark. 13 35 0N 92 48W
Perry County ◇, Ill. 21 38 5N 89 20W
Perry County ◇, Ind. 22 38 5N 86 40W
Perry County ◇, Ky. 49 37 15N 83 15W
Perry County ◇, Miss. 31 31 12N 89 2W
Perry County ◇, Mo. 32 37 45N 89 50W
Perry County ◇, Ohio 42 39 43N 82 13W
Perry County ◇, Pa. 45 40 35N 77 5W
Perry County ◇, Tenn. 48 35 39N 87 50W
Perry Hall 27 39 25N 76 28W
Perry Lake 24 39 7N 95 26W
Perrydale 44 45 3N 123 16W
Perrysburg 42 41 34N 83 38W
Perrysville 42 40 40N 82 19W
Perryton 50 36 24N 100 48W
Perryville, Alaska 11 55 55N 159 9W
Perryville, Ark. 13 35 0N 92 48W
Perryville, Ky. 49 37 39N 84 57W
Perryville, Md. 27 39 34N 76 4W
Perryville, Mo. 32 37 43N 89 52W
Persepolis 107 29 55N 52 50 E
Perseverancia 73 14 44 S 62 48W
Pershing County ◇ 35 40 20N 118 10W
Persia = Iran ■ 107 33 0N 53 0 E
Persia 23 41 35N 95 33W
Persian Gulf = The Gulf 107 27 0N 50 0 E
Person County ◇ 40 36 15N 79 0W
Perth, Australia 126 31 57 S 115 52 E
Perth, Canada 60 44 55N 76 15W
Perth, U.K. 84 56 24N 3 27W
Perth, Kans. 24 37 11N 97 31W
Perth, N. Dak. 41 48 43N 99 28W
Perth Amboy 37 40 31N 74 16W
Peru, Ill. 21 41 20N 89 8W
Peru, Ind. 22 40 45N 86 4W
Peru, Kans. 24 37 5N 96 6W
Peru, N.Y. 39 44 35N 73 32W
Peru, Nebr. 34 40 29N 95 44W
Peru, Vt. 36 43 14N 72 54W
Peru ■ 70 8 0 S 75 0W
Peru-Chile Trench 125 20 0 S 72 0W
Perúgia 94 43 6N 12 24 E
Pervomaysk 99 48 10N 30 46 E
Pervouralsk 98 56 55N 60 0 E
Pésaro 94 43 55N 12 53 E
Pesca, La 65 23 46N 97 47W
Pescara 94 42 28N 14 13 E
Peshawar 108 34 2N 71 37 E
Peshtera 95 42 2N 24 18 E
Peshtigo → 55 44 58N 87 40W
Pesotum 21 39 55N 88 16W
Pesqueira 74 8 20 S 36 42W
Pesqueria → 64 25 54N 99 11W
Petah Tiqwa 104 32 6N 34 53 E
Petal 31 31 21N 89 16W
Petaling Jaya 112 3 4N 101 42 E
Petaluma 14 38 14N 122 39W
Petange 87 49 33N 5 55 E
Petatlán 64 17 31N 101 16W
Petauke 123 14 14 S 31 20 E
Petawawa 60 45 54N 77 17W
Petén Itzá, Lago 66 16 58N 89 50W
Petenwell L. 55 44 4N 90 1W
Peter 1st, I. 5 69 0 S 91 0W
Peter Pond L. 63 55 55N 108 44W
Peterbell 60 48 36N 83 21W
Peterborough, Australia 127 32 58 S 138 51 E
Peterborough, U.K. 83 52 35N 0 14W
Peterborough, U.S.A. 36 42 53N 71 57W
Peterhead 84 57 30N 1 49W
Peter's Mine 71 6 14N 59 20W
Petersburg, Alaska 11 56 48N 132 58W
Petersburg, Ill. 21 40 1N 89 51W
Petersburg, Ind. 22 38 30N 87 17W
Petersburg, Mich. 29 41 54N 83 43W
Petersburg, N. Dak. 41 48 0N 98 0W
Petersburg, N.J. 37 39 15N 74 43W
Petersburg, Nebr. 34 41 51N 98 5W
Petersburg, Ohio 42 40 55N 80 32W
Petersburg, Pa. 45 40 34N 78 3W
Petersburg, Tenn. 48 35 19N 86 38W
Petersburg, Tex. 50 33 52N 101 36W
Petersburg, Va. 54 37 14N 77 24W
Petersburg, W. Va. 54 39 1N 79 5W
Petersham 28 42 29N 72 11W
Peterson, Iowa 23 42 55N 95 21W
Peterson, Minn. 30 43 47N 91 50W
Peterstown 54 37 24N 80 48W
Petersville 49 38 27N 83 30W
Petit Bois I. 31 30 12N 88 26W
Petit-Cap 61 48 3N 64 30W
Petit Goâve 67 18 27N 72 51W
Petit Manan Pt. 26 44 24N 67 54W
Petitcodiac 61 45 57N 65 11W
Petite Baleine → 60 56 0N 76 45W
Petite Saguenay 61 48 15N 70 4W
Petitsikapau, L. 61 54 37N 66 25W
Petlad 108 22 30N 72 45 E
Peto 65 20 10N 88 53W
Petone 128 41 13 S 174 53 E
Petoskey 29 45 22N 84 57W
Petra 104 30 20N 35 22 E
Petra, Ostrova 4 76 15N 118 30 E
Petra Velikogo, Zaliv 116 42 40N 132 0 E
Petrey 10 31 51N 86 13W
Petrich 95 41 24N 23 13 E
Petrified Forest National Park 12 35 0N 109 30W
Petrila 95 45 29N 23 29 E
Petrolândia 74 9 5 S 38 20W
Petroleum 54 39 11N 81 16W
Petroleum County ◇ 33 47 7N 108 25W
Petrolia, Canada 60 42 54N 82 9W
Petrolia, Kans. 24 37 45N 95 29W
Petrolia, Tex. 51 34 1N 98 14W
Petrolina 74 9 24 S 40 30W
Petropavlovsk 100 54 53N 69 13 E
Petropavlovsk-Kamchatskiy 101 53 3N 158 43 E
Petrópolis 75 22 33 S 43 9W
Petros 49 36 6N 84 27W
Petroşeni 89 45 28N 23 20 E
Petrovaradin 95 45 16N 19 55 E
Petrovsk 98 52 22N 45 19 E
Petrovsk-Zabaykalskiy 101 51 20N 108 55 E
Petrozavodsk 98 61 41N 34 20 E
Pettibone 41 47 7N 99 31W
Pettis County ◇ 32 38 40N 93 15W
Pettus 51 28 37N 97 48W
Peumo 76 34 21 S 71 12W
Peureulak 110 4 48N 97 45 E
Pevek 101 69 41N 171 19 E
Pfeifer 24 38 43N 99 10W
Pforzheim 88 48 53N 8 43 E
Phagwara 108 31 10N 75 40 E
Phala 123 23 45 S 26 50 E
Phalodi 108 27 12N 72 24 E
Phan Rang 112 11 34N 109 0 E
Phan Thiet 112 11 1N 108 9 E
Phangan, Ko 112 9 45N 100 0 E
Phangnga 112 8 28N 98 30 E
Phanh Bho Ho Chi Minh 112 10 58N 106 40 E
Pharr 50 26 12N 98 11W
Phatthalung 112 7 39N 100 6 E
Pheba 31 33 35N 88 57W
Phelps, Ky. 49 37 32N 82 9W
Phelps, N.Y. 39 42 58N 77 3W
Phelps, Wis. 55 46 4N 89 5W
Phelps County ◇, Mo. 32 37 55N 91 45W
Phelps County ◇, Nebr. 34 40 30N 99 30W
Phelps L., Canada 63 59 15N 103 15W
Phelps L., U.S.A. 40 35 46N 76 27W
Phenix 54 37 5N 78 45W
Phenix City 10 32 28N 85 0W
Phetchabun 112 16 25N 101 8 E
Phetchabun, Thiu Khao 112 16 0N 101 20 E
Phetchaburi 112 13 1N 99 55 E
Phichai 112 17 22N 100 10 E
Phil Campbell 10 34 21N 87 42W
Philadelphia, Miss. 31 32 46N 89 7W
Philadelphia, N.Y. 39 44 9N 75 43W
Philadelphia, Pa. 45 39 57N 75 10W
Philadelphia, Tenn. 49 35 41N 84 24W
Philadelphia County ◇ 45 39 57N 75 10W
Philip 47 44 2N 101 40W
Philip Smith Mts. 11 68 0N 148 0W
Philippeville 87 50 12N 4 33 E
Philippi 54 39 9N 80 3W
Philippines ■ 111 12 0N 123 0 E
Philippopolis = Plovdiv 95 42 8N 24 44 E
Philipsburg, Mont. 33 46 20N 113 18W
Philipsburg, Pa. 45 40 54N 78 13W
Phillip, I. 127 38 30 S 145 12 E
Phillips, Maine 26 44 49N 70 21W
Phillips, Nebr. 34 40 54N 98 13W
Phillips, Okla. 43 34 30N 96 12W
Phillips, Tex. 50 35 42N 101 22W
Phillips, Wis. 55 45 42N 90 24W
Phillips County ◇, Ark. 13 34 19N 90 51W
Phillips County ◇, Colo. 16 40 40N 102 20W
Phillips County ◇, Kans. 24 39 45N 99 15W
Phillips County ◇, Mont. 33 48 12N 108 0W
Phillipsburg, Ga. 18 31 25N 83 30W
Phillipsburg, Kans. 24 39 45N 99 19W
Phillipsburg, Mo. 32 37 33N 92 47W
Phillipsburg, N.J. 37 40 42N 75 12W
Phillipsburg, Ohio 42 39 54N 84 24W
Philmont 39 42 15N 73 39W
Philo, Calif. 14 39 4N 123 26W
Philo, Ill. 21 40 1N 88 9W
Philomath, Ga. 18 33 44N 82 59W
Philomath, Oreg. 44 44 32N 123 22W
Philpott L. 54 36 47N 80 2W
Phippsburg 16 40 14N 106 57W
Phitsanulok 112 16 50N 100 12 E
Phnom Dangrek 112 14 20N 104 0 E
Phnom Penh 112 11 33N 104 55 E
Phnom Thbeng 112 13 50N 104 56 E
Phoenix, Ariz. 12 33 27N 112 4W
Phoenix, La. 25 29 39N 89 56W
Phoenix, N.Y. 39 43 14N 76 18W
Phoenix, Oreg. 44 42 16N 122 49W
Phoenix Is. 124 3 30 S 172 0W
Phoenixville 45 40 8N 75 31W
Phong Saly 112 21 42N 102 9 E
Phra Chedi Sam Ong 112 15 16N 98 23 E
Phra Nakhon Si Ayutthaya 112 14 25N 100 30 E
Phrae 112 18 7N 100 9 E
Phrao 112 19 23N 99 15 E
Phu Doan 112 21 40N 105 10 E
Phu Loi 112 20 14N 103 14 E
Phu Ly 112 20 35N 105 50 E
Phuket 112 7 52N 98 22 E
Piacá 74 7 42 S 47 18W
Piacenza 94 45 2N 9 42 E
Piaçubaçu 74 10 24 S 36 25W
Pialba 127 25 20 S 152 45 E
Piapot 63 49 59N 109 8W
Piatã 75 13 9 S 41 48W
Piatra 95 43 51N 25 9 E
Piatra Neamţ 89 46 56N 26 21 E
Piatra Olt 95 44 22N 24 16 E
Piatt County ◇ 21 40 0N 88 35W
Piauí □ 74 7 0 S 43 0W
Piaui → 74 6 38 S 42 42W
Piave → 94 45 32N 12 44 E
Piazza Ármerina 94 37 21N 14 20 E
Pibor Post 121 6 47N 33 3 E
Pica 72 20 35 S 69 25W
Picacho, Ariz. 12 32 43N 111 30W
Picacho, N. Mex. 38 33 21N 105 9W
Picardie 90 50 0N 2 15 E
Picardy = Picardie 90 50 0N 2 15 E
Picayune 31 30 32N 89 41W
Piceance Cr. → 16 40 5N 108 14W
Picher 43 36 59N 94 50W
Pichilemu 76 34 22 S 72 0W
Pichincha, □ 70 0 10 S 78 40W
Pickaway County ◇ 42 39 43N 82 59W
Pickens, Ark. 13 33 51N 91 29W
Pickens, Miss. 31 32 53N 89 58W
Pickens, Okla. 43 34 23N 95 2W
Pickens, S.C. 46 34 53N 82 42W
Pickens, W. Va. 54 38 39N 80 13W
Pickens County ◇, Ala. 10 33 16N 88 6W
Pickens County ◇, Ga. 18 34 30N 84 25W
Pickens County ◇, S.C. 46 34 50N 82 45W
Pickerel L. 60 48 40N 91 25W
Pickering 32 40 27N 94 49W
Pickett County ◇ 49 36 34N 85 8W
Pickford 29 46 10N 84 22W
Pickle Lake 60 51 30N 90 12W
Pickrell 34 40 23N 96 44W
Pickstown 47 43 4N 98 32W
Pickwick L. 10 35 4N 88 15W
Pico Truncado 78 46 40 S 68 0W
Picos 74 7 5 S 41 28W
Picota 72 6 54 S 76 24W
Picton, Canada 60 44 1N 77 9W
Picton, N.Z. 128 41 18 S 174 3 E
Picton, I. 78 55 2 S 66 57W
Picton 61 45 41N 62 42W
Picture Butte 62 49 55N 112 45W
Pictured Rocks Nat. Lakeshore 29 46 30N 86 30W
Picuí 74 6 31 S 36 21W
Picún Leufú 78 39 30 S 69 5W
Pidurutalagala 108 7 10N 80 50 E
Pie Town 38 34 18N 108 9W
Piedad, La 64 20 20N 102 1W
Piedecuesta 70 6 59N 73 3W
Piedmont = Piemonte □ 94 45 0N 7 30 E
Piedmont, Ala. 10 33 55N 85 37W
Piedmont, Kans. 24 37 37N 96 22W
Piedmont, Mo. 32 37 9N 90 42W
Piedmont, Okla. 43 35 39N 97 44W
Piedmont, S.C. 46 34 42N 82 28W
Piedmont, S. Dak. 47 44 14N 103 24W
Piedmont L. 42 40 11N 81 13W
Piedra del Anguila 78 40 2 S 70 4W
Piedra Lais 70 3 10N 65 50W
Piedras, R. de las → 72 12 30 S 69 15W
Piedras Negras 64 28 35N 100 35W
Piemonte □ 94 45 0N 7 30 E
Pierce, Colo. 16 40 38N 104 45W
Pierce, Idaho 20 46 30N 115 48W
Pierce, Nebr. 34 42 12N 97 32W
Pierce City 32 36 57N 94 0W
Pierce County ◇, Ga. 18 31 20N 82 10W
Pierce County ◇, N. Dak. 41 48 0N 100 0W
Pierce County ◇, Nebr. 34 42 20N 97 40W
Pierce County ◇, Wash. 53 47 0N 122 0W
Pierce County ◇, Wis. 55 44 45N 92 25W
Pierceton 22 41 12N 85 42W
Pierceville 24 37 53N 100 40W
Piercy 14 39 59N 123 48W
Pierpont 47 45 30N 97 50W
Pierre 47 44 22N 100 21W
Pierron 21 38 47N 89 36W
Pierson, Fla. 17 29 14N 81 28W
Pierson, Iowa 23 42 33N 95 52W
Pierz 30 45 59N 94 6W
Piet Retief 123 27 1 S 30 50 E
Pietarsaari = Jakobstad 96 63 40N 22 43 E
Pietermaritzburg 123 29 35 S 30 25 E
Pietersburg 123 23 54 S 29 25 E
Pietrosul 89 47 35N 24 43 E
Pigeon, La. 25 30 4N 91 17W
Pigeon, Mich. 29 43 50N 83 16W
Pigeon →, Ind. 22 41 47N 85 49W
Pigeon →, Tenn. 49 36 2N 83 17W
Pigeon Cove 28 42 41N 70 38W
Pigeon Cr. → 10 31 20N 86 42W
Pigeon Falls 55 44 26N 91 13W
Pigeon Forge 49 35 48N 83 33W
Pigg → 54 37 0N 79 29W
Piggott 13 36 23N 90 11W
Pigüe 76 37 36 S 62 25W
Pike 54 39 17N 81 5W
Pike County ◇, Ala. 10 31 48N 85 58W
Pike County ◇, Ark. 13 34 14N 93 45W
Pike County ◇, Ga. 18 33 5N 84 20W
Pike County ◇, Ill. 21 39 35N 90 50W
Pike County ◇, Ind. 22 38 25N 87 10W
Pike County ◇, Ky. 49 37 30N 82 25W
Pike County ◇, Miss. 31 31 15N 90 27W
Pike County ◇, Mo. 32 39 20N 91 10W
Pike County ◇, Ohio 42 39 4N 83 1W
Pike County ◇, Pa. 45 41 20N 75 0W
Pike National Forest 16 39 15N 105 20W
Pike Road 10 32 17N 86 6W
Pikes Peak 16 38 50N 105 3W
Pikesville 27 39 23N 76 43W
Piketberg 123 32 55 S 18 40 E
Piketon 42 39 4N 83 1W
Pikeville, Ky. 49 37 29N 82 31W
Pikeville, N.C. 40 35 30N 77 59W
Pikeville, Tenn. 49 35 36N 85 11W
Pikwitonei 63 55 35N 97 9W
Pilão Arcado 74 10 9 S 42 26W
Pilar, Brazil 74 9 36 S 35 56W
Pilar, Paraguay 76 26 50 S 58 20W
Pilas 111 6 39N 121 37 E
Pilaya → 73 20 55 S 64 4W
Pilbara 126 21 15 S 118 16 E
Pilcomayo → 76 25 21 S 57 42W
Pilger 34 42 0N 97 3W
Pilibhit 108 28 40N 79 50 E
Pilica → 89 51 25N 20 45 E
Pillager 30 46 20N 94 28W
Pillaro 70 1 10 S 78 32W
Pillsbury 41 47 13N 97 48W
Pillsbury, L. 14 39 25N 122 57W
Pillsbury Sd. 57 18 20N 64 50W
Pílos 95 36 55N 21 42 E
Pilot Grove 32 38 53N 92 55W
Pilot Knob, Ark. 13 35 42N 93 57W
Pilot Knob, Ky. 48 36 50N 86 41W
Pilot Knob, Mo. 32 37 40N 90 40W
Pilot Mound 63 49 15N 98 54W
Pilot Mountain 40 36 23N 80 28W
Pilot Pk. 56 44 58N 109 53W
Pilot Point, Alaska 11 57 34N 157 35W
Pilot Point, Tex. 51 33 24N 96 58W
Pilot Rock 44 45 29N 118 50W
Pilot Station 11 61 56N 162 53W
Pilsen = Plzen 88 49 45N 13 22 E
Pima 12 32 54N 109 50W
Pima County ◇ 12 32 0N 112 0W
Pimba 127 31 18 S 136 46 E
Pimenta Bueno 73 11 35 S 61 10W
Pimentel 72 6 45 S 79 55W
Pinal County ◇ 12 33 0N 111 15W
Pinang 112 5 25N 100 15 E
Pinar del Río 66 22 26N 83 40W
Pinaroo 127 35 17 S 140 53 E
Pinas, Mt. 15 34 50N 119 9W
Pincher Creek 62 49 30N 113 57W
Pinchi L. 62 54 38N 124 30W
Pinckard 10 31 19N 85 33W
Pinckneyville, Ill. 21 38 5N 89 23W
Pinckneyville, Miss. 31 31 1N 91 29W
Pinconning 29 43 51N 83 58W
Pinczów 89 50 30N 20 35 E
Pindall 13 36 4N 92 53W
Pindaré → 74 3 17 S 44 47W
Pindaré Mirim 74 3 37 S 45 21W
Pindiga 120 9 58N 10 53 E
Pindobal 74 3 16 S 48 25W
Pindos Óros 95 40 0N 21 0 E
Pindus Mts. = Pindos Óros 95 40 0N 21 0 E
Pine, Ariz. 12 34 23N 111 27W
Pine, Oreg. 44 44 52N 117 5W
Pine →, Canada 63 58 50N 105 38W
Pine →, U.S.A. 29 43 35N 84 8W
Pine, C. 61 46 37N 53 32W
Pine Apple 10 31 52N 87 0W

Pine Barrens Pocatalico

Pine Barrens 37 39 30N 74 30W
Pine Bluff 13 34 13N 92 1W
Pine Bluffs 56 41 11N 104 4W
Pine Castle 17 28 28N 81 22W
Pine City, Minn. 30 45 50N 92 59W
Pine City, Wash. 53 47 12N 117 31W
Pine County ◊ 30 46 5N 92 50W
Pine Cr. →, Nev. 35 40 36N 116 12W
Pine Cr. →, Pa. 45 41 10N 77 16W
Pine Creek 126 13 50 S 132 10 E
Pine Creek L. 43 34 7N 95 5W
Pine Falls 63 50 34N 96 11W
Pine Flat L. 15 36 50N 119 20W
Pine Forest Range 35 41 45N 118 50W
Pine Grove, La. 25 30 43N 90 45W
Pine Grove, Pa. 45 40 33N 76 23W
Pine Grove, W. Va. 54 39 34N 80 41W
Pine Hill 37 39 47N 74 59W
Pine Is. 17 26 36N 82 7W
Pine Island 30 44 12N 92 39W
Pine Knot 49 36 39N 84 26W
Pine Level 10 32 4N 86 4W
Pine Log 18 34 21N 84 44W
Pine Mountain 18 32 52N 84 51W
Pine Mt., Ga. 18 34 56N 83 12W
Pine Mt., Ky. 49 37 0N 83 45W
Pine Mt., Wyo. 56 41 2N 109 1W
Pine Pass 62 55 25N 122 42W
Pine Point 62 60 50N 114 28W
Pine Prairie 25 30 47N 92 25W
Pine Ridge, S. Dak. 47 42 30N 102 40W
Pine Ridge, S. Dak. 47 43 2N 102 33W
Pine Ridge Indian Reservation 47 43 30N 102 0W
Pine River, Canada 63 51 45N 100 30W
Pine River, U.S.A. 30 46 43N 94 24W
Pine Springs 50 31 54N 104 49W
Pine Valley 52 38 20N 113 45W
Pinebluff 40 35 6N 79 28W
Pinedale, Calif. 15 36 50N 119 48W
Pinedale, Wyo. 56 42 52N 109 52W
Pinega → 98 64 8N 46 54 E
Pinehurst, Ga. 18 32 12N 83 46W
Pinehurst, N.C. 40 35 12N 79 28W
Pineland 51 31 15N 93 58W
Pinellas County ◊ 17 28 0N 82 45W
Pinellas Park 17 27 50N 82 43W
Pinerolo 94 44 47N 7 21 E
Pines, Lake O The 51 32 45N 94 30W
Pinetop 12 34 8N 109 56W
Pinetops 40 35 46N 77 38W
Pinetown, S. Africa 123 29 48 S 30 54 E
Pinetown, U.S.A. 40 35 37N 76 52W
Pinetta 17 30 36N 83 21W
Pineview 18 32 7N 83 30W
Pineville, Iowa 23 36 36N 94 23W
Pineville, Ky. 49 36 46N 83 42W
Pineville, La. 25 31 19N 92 26W
Pineville, N.C. 40 35 5N 80 53W
Pineville, S.C. 46 33 26N 80 1W
Pineville, W. Va. 54 37 35N 81 32W
Pinewood 46 33 44N 80 27W
Piney → 32 37 54N 92 4W
Piney Buttes 33 47 35N 106 45W
Piney Grove 27 39 42N 78 24W
Piney Point 27 38 9N 76 31W
Piney Woods 31 32 2N 90 0W
Ping → 112 15 42N 100 9 E
Pingding 114 37 47N 113 38 E
Pingdingshan 115 33 43N 113 27 E
Pingdong 115 22 39N 120 30 E
Pingdu 114 36 42N 119 59 E
Pingguo 115 23 19N 107 36 E
Pinghe 115 24 17N 117 21 E
Pingjiang 115 28 45N 113 36 E
Pingle 115 24 40N 110 40 E
Pingliang 114 35 35N 106 31 E
Pingluo 114 38 52N 106 30 E
Pingnan 115 23 33N 110 22 E
Pingree 41 47 10N 98 55W
Pingtan Dao 115 25 29N 119 47 E
Pingwu 115 32 25N 104 30 E
Pingxiang, Guangxi Zhuangzu, China 115 22 6N 106 46 E
Pingxiang, Jiangxi, China 115 27 43N 113 48 E
Pingyao 114 37 12N 112 10 E
Pinhal 77 22 10 S 46 46W
Pinheiro 74 2 31 S 45 5W
Pinhel 91 40 50N 7 1W
Pinhuá → 73 6 21 S 65 0W
Pini 110 0 10N 98 40 E
Piniós → 95 39 55N 22 10 E
Pinjarra 126 32 37 S 115 52 E
Pink 43 35 18N 97 6W
Pink → 63 56 50N 103 50W
Pink Cliffs 52 37 25N 112 20W
Pink Hill 40 35 3N 77 45W
Pinnacle 40 36 20N 80 26W
Pinnacle Buttes 56 43 44N 109 57W
Pinnacle Peak 56 43 23N 110 32W
Pinnacles National Monument 15 36 25N 121 12W
Pino Hachado, Paso 78 38 39 S 70 54W
Pinola 31 31 53N 89 58W
Pinole 14 38 0N 122 17W
Pinon 12 36 6N 110 14W
Pinos 64 22 20N 101 40W
Pinotepa Nacional 65 16 19N 98 3W
Pinrang 111 3 46 S 119 41 E
Pinsk 98 52 10N 26 1 E
Pinson, Ala. 10 33 41N 86 41W
Pinson, Tenn. 48 35 29N 88 43W
Pinta, Sierra 12 32 15N 113 30W
Pintados 72 20 35 S 69 40W
Pintlalla Cr. → 10 32 21N 86 30W
Pinyang 115 27 42N 120 31 E
Pinyug 98 60 5N 48 0 E
Pio XII 74 3 53 S 45 17W
Pioche 35 37 56N 114 27W
Piombino 94 42 54N 10 30 E
Pioneer, Iowa 23 42 39N 94 23W
Pioneer, La. 25 32 44N 91 26W
Pioneer, Ohio 42 41 41N 84 33W
Pioneer, Tenn. 49 36 25N 84 19W
Pioner, Os. 101 79 50N 92 0 E
Piorini → 71 3 23 S 63 30W
Piorini, L. 71 3 15 S 62 35W
Piotrków Trybunalski 89 51 23N 19 43 E
Pīp 107 26 45N 60 10 E
Pipe Creek 51 29 43N 98 56W
Pipe Spring National Monument 12 36 50N 112 55W
Pipestone 30 44 0N 96 19W
Pipestone → 60 52 53N 89 23W
Pipestone County ◊ 30 44 0N 96 15W
Pipestone Cr. → 63 49 42N 100 45W
Pipmuacan, Rés. 61 49 45N 70 30W
Piqua, Kans. 24 37 56N 95 32W
Piqua, Ohio 42 40 9N 84 15W
Piquet Carneiro 74 5 48 S 39 25W
Piquiri → 77 24 3 S 54 14W
Piracanjuba 75 17 18 S 49 1W
Piracicaba 77 22 45 S 47 40W
Piracuruca 74 3 50 S 41 50W
Piræus = Piraiévs 95 37 57N 23 42 E
Piraiévs 95 37 57N 23 42 E
Pirajuí 77 21 59 S 49 29W
Pirané 76 25 42 S 59 6W
Piranhas 74 9 27 S 37 46W
Pirapemas 74 3 43 S 44 14W
Pirapora 75 17 20 S 44 56W
Pirata, Monte 57 18 6N 65 33W
Piray → 73 16 32 S 63 45W
Pirdop 95 42 40N 24 10 E
Pires do Rio 75 17 18 S 48 17W
Pírgos 95 37 40N 21 27 E
Pirgovo 95 43 44N 25 43 E
Piribebuy 76 25 26 S 57 2W
Pirin Planina 95 41 40N 23 30 E
Pirineos 91 42 40N 1 0 E
Piripiri 74 4 15 S 41 46W
Piritu 70 9 23N 69 12W
Pirot 95 43 9N 22 39 E
Piru 111 3 4 S 128 12 E
Pisa 94 43 43N 10 23 E
Pisac 72 13 25 S 71 50W
Pisagua 72 19 40 S 70 15W
Piscataquis → 26 45 15N 68 58W
Piscataquis County ◊ 26 46 0N 69 0W
Piscataway, Md. 27 38 42N 76 58W
Piscataway, N.J. 37 40 34N 74 27W
Pisco 72 13 50 S 76 12W
Piscu 95 45 30N 27 43 E
Písek, Czech. 88 49 19N 14 10 E
Pisek, U.S.A. 41 48 19N 97 43W
Pisgah, Iowa 23 41 50N 95 55W
Pisgah, Md. 27 38 32N 77 8W
Pisgah Forest 40 35 15N 82 44W
Pisgah National Forest 40 35 50N 82 0W
Pishan 113 37 30N 78 33 E
Pising 111 5 8 S 121 53 E
Pisinimo 12 32 2N 112 19W
Pismo Beach 15 35 9N 120 38W
Pistóia 94 43 57N 10 53 E
Pistol B. 63 62 25N 92 37W
Pistol River 44 42 17N 124 24W
Pisuerga → 91 41 33N 4 52W
Pit → 14 40 47N 122 6W
Pitalito 70 1 51N 76 2W
Pitanga 75 24 46 S 51 44W
Pitangui 75 19 40 S 44 54 E
Pitcairn I. 125 25 5 S 130 5W
Pite älv → 96 65 20N 21 25 E
Piteå 96 65 20N 21 25 E
Piteşti 89 44 52N 24 54 E
Pithapuram 109 17 10N 82 15 E
Pitiquito 64 30 42N 112 2W
Pitkin, Colo. 16 38 37N 106 31W
Pitkin, La. 25 30 56N 92 56W
Pitkin County ◊ 16 39 10N 106 50W
Pitlochry 84 56 43N 3 43W
Pitman 37 39 44N 75 8W
Pitrufquén 78 38 59 S 72 39W
Pitt County ◊ 40 35 30N 77 20W
Pitt I. 62 53 30N 129 50W
Pittsboro, Ind. 22 39 52N 86 28W
Pittsboro, Miss. 31 33 56N 89 20W
Pittsboro, N.C. 40 35 43N 79 11W
Pittsburg, Calif. 14 38 2N 121 53W
Pittsburg, Ill. 21 37 47N 88 51W
Pittsburg, Kans. 24 37 25N 94 42W
Pittsburg, N.H. 36 45 3N 71 24W
Pittsburg, Okla. 43 34 43N 95 52W
Pittsburg, Tex. 51 33 0N 94 59W
Pittsburg County ◊ 43 34 50N 95 50W
Pittsburgh 45 40 26N 80 1W
Pittsfield, Ill. 21 39 36N 90 49W
Pittsfield, Maine 26 44 47N 69 23W
Pittsfield, Mass. 28 42 27N 73 15W
Pittsfield, N.H. 36 43 18N 71 20W
Pittsfield, Vt. 36 43 46N 72 48W
Pittsford 36 43 42N 73 3W
Pittsgrove 37 39 37N 75 14W
Pittston 45 41 19N 75 47W
Pittstown 37 40 36N 74 56W
Pittsview 10 32 11N 85 10W
Pittsville, Md. 27 38 24N 75 52W
Pittsville, Mo. 32 38 50N 93 0W
Pittsville, Wis. 55 44 27N 90 8W
Pittsylvania County ◊ 54 36 55N 79 15W
Piuí 75 20 28 S 45 58W
Pium 74 10 27 S 49 11W
Piura 72 5 15 S 80 38W
Piura □ 72 5 10 S 80 0W
Piute County ◊ 52 38 20N 112 10W
Pivijay 70 10 28N 74 37W
Pixley 15 35 58N 119 18W
Pizarro 70 4 58N 77 22W
Pizzo 94 38 44N 16 10 E
Placedo 51 28 41N 96 50W
Placentia 61 47 20N 54 0W
Placentia B. 61 47 0N 54 40W
Placer County ◊ 14 39 10N 120 30W
Placerville, Calif. 14 38 44N 120 48W
Placerville, Colo. 16 38 1N 108 3W
Placerville, Idaho 20 43 57N 115 57W
Placetas 66 22 15N 79 44W
Placid, L. 17 27 15N 81 22W
Placitas 38 35 18N 106 25W
Plain City 52 41 18N 112 6W
Plain Dealing 25 32 54N 93 42W
Plainfield, Conn. 28 41 41N 71 56W
Plainfield, Ind. 22 39 42N 86 24W
Plainfield, Iowa 23 42 51N 92 32W
Plainfield, Mass. 28 42 0N 72 0W
Plainfield, N.H. 36 43 32N 72 21W
Plainfield, N.J. 37 40 37N 74 25W
Plainfield, Vt. 36 44 17N 72 26W
Plainfield, Wis. 55 44 13N 89 30W
Plainfield Heights 29 43 1N 85 37W
Plains, Ga. 18 32 2N 84 24W
Plains, Kans. 24 37 16N 100 35W
Plains, Mont. 33 47 28N 114 53W
Plains, Pa. 45 41 15N 75 37W
Plains, Tex. 50 33 11N 102 50W
Plainview, Ark. 13 35 2N 93 18W
Plainview, Minn. 30 44 10N 92 10W
Plainview, N.Y. 39 40 46N 73 29W
Plainview, Nebr. 34 42 21N 97 47W
Plainview, Tex. 50 34 11N 101 43W
Plainville, Conn. 28 41 41N 72 51W
Plainville, Ga. 18 34 24N 85 2W
Plainville, Ind. 22 38 48N 87 9W
Plainville, Kans. 24 39 14N 99 18W
Plainwell 29 42 27N 85 38W
Plaistow 36 42 50N 71 6W
Pláka 95 40 0N 25 24 E
Plakhino 100 67 45N 86 5 E
Plana Cays 67 22 38N 73 30W
Planada 14 37 16N 120 19W
Planeta Rica 70 8 25N 75 36W
Plankinton 47 43 43N 98 29W
Plano, Ill. 21 41 40N 88 32W
Plano, Tex. 51 33 1N 96 42W
Plant City 17 28 1N 82 7W
Plantation 17 26 8N 80 15W
Plantersville, Ala. 10 32 40N 86 56W
Plantersville, Miss. 31 34 12N 88 40W
Plantersville, S.C. 46 33 33N 79 13W
Plantsite 12 33 2N 109 21W
Plaquemine 25 30 17N 91 14W
Plaquemines Parish ◊ 25 29 29N 89 42W
Plasencia 91 40 3N 6 8W
Plaster Rock 61 46 53N 67 22W
Plastun 116 44 45N 136 19 E
Plata, La, Argentina 76 35 0 S 57 55W
Plata, La, Colombia 70 2 23N 75 53W
Plata, La, L. 78 44 55 S 71 50W
Plata, Rio de la 57 18 29N 66 15W
Plata, Río de la → 76 34 45 S 57 30W
Platani → 94 37 23N 13 16 E
Platí, Ákra- 95 40 27N 24 0 E
Platina 14 40 22N 122 53W
Platinum 11 59 1N 161 49W
Plato 70 9 47N 74 47W
Platte 47 43 23N 98 51W
Platte →, Mo. 32 39 16N 94 50W
Platte →, Nebr. 34 41 4N 95 53W
Platte Center 34 41 32N 97 29W
Platte City 32 39 22N 94 47W
Platte County ◊, Mo. 32 39 20N 94 45W
Platte County ◊, Nebr. 34 41 30N 97 30W
Platte County ◊, Wyo. 56 42 0N 105 0W
Platteville, Colo. 16 40 13N 104 49W
Platteville, Wis. 55 42 44N 90 29W
Plattsburg 32 39 34N 94 27W
Plattsburgh 39 44 42N 73 28W
Plattsmouth 34 41 1N 95 53W
Plauen 88 50 29N 12 9 E
Playa Azul 64 17 59N 102 24W
Playa de Guayanés 57 18 4N 65 49W
Playa de Humacao 57 18 10N 65 45W
Playas L. 38 31 51N 108 35W
Playgreen L. 63 54 0N 98 15W
Plaza, N. Dak. 41 48 1N 101 58W
Plaza, Wash. 53 47 19N 117 23W
Pleasant, L. 12 33 51N 112 16W
Pleasant B. 28 41 40N 69 57W
Pleasant Bay 61 46 51N 60 48W
Pleasant Dale 34 40 48N 96 56W
Pleasant Garden 40 35 58N 79 46W
Pleasant Grove 52 40 22N 111 44W
Pleasant Hill, Calif. 14 37 57N 122 4W
Pleasant Hill, Ill. 21 39 27N 90 52W
Pleasant Hill, La. 25 31 49N 93 31W
Pleasant Hill, Mo. 32 38 47N 94 16W
Pleasant Hill, N. Mex. 38 34 31N 103 4W
Pleasant Hill, Ohio 42 40 3N 84 21W
Pleasant Hill, Tenn. 49 35 59N 85 12W
Pleasant Lake 30 45 30N 94 17W
Pleasant Plains, Ark. 13 35 33N 91 38W
Pleasant Plains, Ill. 21 39 52N 89 55W
Pleasant Site 10 34 33N 88 4W
Pleasant View, Colo. 16 37 35N 108 46W
Pleasant View, Wash. 53 46 29N 118 20W
Pleasanton, Iowa 23 40 35N 93 45W
Pleasanton, Kans. 24 38 11N 94 43W
Pleasanton, N. Mex. 38 33 17N 108 53W
Pleasanton, Nebr. 34 40 58N 99 5W
Pleasanton, Tex. 51 28 58N 98 29W
Pleasants County ◊ 54 39 22N 81 12W
Pleasantville, Iowa 23 41 23N 93 18W
Pleasantville, N.J. 37 39 24N 74 32W
Pleasantville, Ohio 42 39 49N 82 32W
Pleasure Ridge Park 49 38 9N 85 50W
Pleasureville 49 38 21N 85 7W
Pleiku 112 13 57N 108 0 E
Pleniţa 95 44 14N 23 10 E
Plenty, Bay of 128 37 45 S 177 0 E
Plentywood 33 48 47N 104 34W
Plesetsk 98 62 40N 40 10 E
Plessisville 61 46 14N 71 47W
Pletipi L. 61 51 44N 70 6W
Pleven 95 43 26N 24 37 E
Plevlja 95 43 21N 19 21 E
Plevna, Kans. 24 37 59N 98 19W
Plevna, Mont. 33 46 25N 104 31W
Ploieşti 89 44 57N 26 5 E
Plonge, Lac La 63 55 8N 107 20W
Plovdiv 95 42 8N 24 44 E
Plover, Iowa 23 42 53N 94 38W
Plover, Wis. 55 44 27N 89 32W
Plover → 55 44 29N 89 35W
Plum 45 40 29N 79 47W
Plum City 55 44 38N 92 11W
Plum I., Mass. 28 42 45N 70 48W
Plum I., N.Y. 39 41 11N 72 12W
Plum Point 27 38 0N 76 0W
Plum Springs 48 37 0N 86 20W
Plumas County ◊ 14 40 0N 121 0W
Plumas National Forest 14 39 50N 120 40W
Plumerville 13 35 10N 92 38W
Plummer, Idaho 20 47 20N 116 53W
Plummer, Minn. 30 47 55N 96 3W
Plumtree 123 20 27 S 27 55 E
Plush 44 42 25N 119 54W
Plymouth, U.K. 83 50 23N 4 9W
Plymouth, Calif. 14 38 29N 120 51W
Plymouth, Ill. 21 40 18N 90 58W
Plymouth, Ind. 22 41 21N 86 19W
Plymouth, Iowa 23 43 15N 93 7W
Plymouth, Kans. 24 38 25N 96 20W
Plymouth, Mass. 28 41 57N 70 40W
Plymouth, Minn. 30 45 2N 93 27W
Plymouth, N.C. 40 35 52N 76 43W
Plymouth, N.H. 36 43 46N 71 41W
Plymouth, Nebr. 34 40 18N 97 0W
Plymouth, Pa. 45 41 14N 75 57W
Plymouth, Utah 52 41 53N 112 9W
Plymouth, Vt. 36 43 34N 72 45W
Plymouth, W. Va. 54 38 31N 81 51W
Plymouth, Wis. 55 43 45N 87 59W
Plymouth Bay 28 41 57N 70 37W
Plymouth County ◊, Iowa 23 42 45N 96 10W
Plymouth County ◊, Mass. 28 41 45N 70 45W
Plymouth Sd. 83 50 20N 4 10W
Plynlimon = Pumlumon Fawr 83 52 29N 3 47W
Plzen 88 49 45N 13 22 E
Po → 94 44 57N 12 4 E
Po Hai = Bo Hai 114 39 0N 120 0 E
Pobeda 101 65 12N 146 12 E
Pobedino 101 49 51N 142 49 E
Pobedy Pik 100 40 45N 79 58 E
Poca 54 38 28N 81 49W
Pocahontas, Ark. 13 36 16N 90 58W
Pocahontas, Ill. 21 38 50N 89 33W
Pocahontas, Iowa 23 42 44N 94 40W
Pocahontas County ◊, Iowa 23 42 45N 94 40W
Pocahontas County ◊, W. Va. 54 38 10N 80 2W
Pocasset, Mass. 28 41 41N 70 37W
Pocasset, Okla. 43 35 12N 97 58W
Pocatalico 54 38 29N 81 40W

Pocatalico Porter L.

Pocatalico → 54 38 29N 81 49W
Pocatello 20 42 52N 112 27W
Pochontas 62 53 10N 117 51W
Pochutla 65 15 50N 96 31W
Poci 71 5 57N 61 29W
Pocinhos 74 7 4S 36 3W
Pocito Casas 64 28 32N 111 6W
Poções 75 14 31S 40 21W
Pocomoke → 27 37 58N 75 39W
Pocomoke City 27 38 5N 75 34W
Pocomoke Sd. 54 37 50N 75 50W
Pocomoke Sound 27 37 56N 75 45W
Poconé 73 16 15S 56 37W
Pocono Mts. 45 41 7N 75 22W
Poços de Caldas 75 21 50S 46 33W
Podgorica = Titograd 95 42 30N 19 19E
Podkamennaya
Tunguska → 101 61 50N 90 13E
Podolsk 98 55 25N 37 30E
Podor 120 16 40N 15 2W
Podporozhy 98 60 55N 34 2E
Podu Turcului 95 46 11N 27 25E
Pofadder 123 29 10S 19 22E
Pogamasing 60 46 55N 81 50W
Pogoanele 95 44 55N 27 0E
Pogranitšnyi 116 44 25N 131 24E
Poh 111 0 46S 122 51E
Pohang 114 36 1N 129 23E
Pohue B. 19 19 0N 155 48W
Poiana Mare 95 43 57N 23 5E
Poinsett, C. 5 65 42S 113 18E
Poinsett, L. 47 44 34N 97 5W
Poinsett County ◇ 13 35 34N 90 43W
Point Arena 14 38 55N 123 41W
Point au Fer I. 25 29 18N 91 15W
Point Baker 11 56 21N 133 37W
Point Comfort 51 28 41N 96 33W
Point Edward 60 43 0N 82 30W
Point Hope 11 68 21N 166 47W
Point Lay 11 69 46N 163 3W
Point Lookout 27 38 5N 76 18W
Point of Rocks 56 41 41N 108 47W
Point Pedro 108 9 50N 80 15E
Point Pleasant, N.J. 37 40 5N 74 3W
Point Pleasant, W. Va. 54 38 51N 82 8W
Point Reyes National
Seashore 14 38 10N 122 55W
Point Stephens 127 32 38S 152 12E
Pointblank 51 30 45N 95 13W
Pointe a la Hache 25 29 35N 89 48W
Pointe-à-Pitre 67 16 10N 61 30W
Pointe Coupee Parish ◇ 25 30 36N 91 37W
Pointe Noire 122 4 48S 11 53E
Poitiers 90 46 35N 0 20E
Pojoaque Valley 38 35 54N 106 1W
Pokai B. 19 21 27N 158 12W
Pokaran 108 27 0N 71 50E
Pokegama L. 30 47 12N 93 35W
Poko 122 5 41N 31 55E
Pokrovsk 101 61 29N 126 12E
Polacca 12 35 50N 110 23W
Polacca Wash → 12 35 22N 110 50W
Polan 107 25 30N 61 10E
Poland, N.Y. 39 43 14N 75 4W
Poland, Ohio 42 41 1N 80 37W
Poland ■ 89 52 0N 20 0E
Polar Sub-Glacial Basin 5 85 0S 110 0E
Polcura 76 37 17S 71 43W
Polden Hills 83 51 7N 2 50W
Pole Mt. 56 41 14N 105 23W
Polesye 98 52 0N 28 10E
Polevskoy 98 56 26N 60 11E
Polewali, Sulawesi, Indonesia 111 4 8S 119 43E
Polewali, Sulawesi, Indonesia 111 3 21S 119 23E
Poli 122 8 34N 13 15E
Polillo Is. 111 14 56N 122 0E
Políyiros 95 40 23N 23 25E
Polk, Nebr. 34 41 5N 97 46W
Polk, Ohio 42 40 57N 82 13W
Polk, Pa. 45 41 22N 79 56W
Polk City 23 41 46N 93 43W
Polk County ◇, Ark. 13 34 35N 94 15W
Polk County ◇, Fla. 17 28 0N 81 45W
Polk County ◇, Ga. 18 34 0N 85 10W
Polk County ◇, Iowa 23 41 40N 93 35W
Polk County ◇, Minn. 30 47 40N 96 30W
Polk County ◇, Mo. 32 37 35N 93 25W
Polk County ◇, N.C. 40 35 15N 82 10W
Polk County ◇, Nebr. 34 41 15N 97 40W
Polk County ◇, Oreg. 44 44 55N 123 20W
Polk County ◇, Tenn. 49 35 10N 84 39W
Polk County ◇, Tex. 51 30 43N 94 56W
Polk County ◇, Wis. 55 45 30N 92 30W
Polkton 40 35 1N 80 12W
Polkville, Miss. 31 32 11N 89 42W
Polkville, N.C. 40 35 25N 81 39W
Pollachi 108 10 35N 77 0E
Pollock, Idaho 20 45 19N 116 21W
Pollock, La. 25 31 32N 92 25W
Pollock, Mo. 32 40 21N 93 5W
Pollock, S. Dak. 47 45 55N 100 17W
Pollock Pines 14 38 46N 120 34W
Pollocksville 40 35 0N 77 14W
Polnovat 100 63 50N 65 54E
Polo, Ill. 21 41 59N 89 35W
Polo, Mo. 32 39 33N 94 3W

Polotsk 98 55 30N 28 50E
Polski Trŭmbesh 95 43 20N 25 38E
Polsko Kosovo 95 43 23N 25 38E
Polson 33 47 41N 114 9W
Poltava 99 49 35N 34 35E
Polunochnoye 98 60 52N 60 25E
Polvadera 38 34 12N 106 55W
Polyanovgrad 95 42 39N 26 59E
Polyarny 98 69 8N 33 20E
Polynesia 125 10 0S 162 0W
Pomaria 46 34 16N 81 25W
Pomaro 64 18 20N 103 18W
Pombal, Brazil 74 6 45S 37 50W
Pombal, Portugal 91 39 55N 8 40W
Pomeroy, Iowa 23 42 33N 94 41W
Pomeroy, Ohio 42 39 2N 82 2W
Pomeroy, Wash. 53 46 28N 117 36W
Pomfret, Conn. 28 41 54N 71 58W
Pomfret, Md. 27 38 0N 77 0W
Pomme de Terre →, Minn. 30 45 10N 96 5W
Pomme de Terre →, Mo. 32 38 11N 93 25W
Pomme de Terre L. 32 37 54N 93 19W
Pomona, Calif. 15 34 4N 117 45W
Pomona, Kans. 24 38 36N 95 27W
Pomona, Md. 27 39 10N 76 7W
Pomona, Mo. 32 36 52N 91 55W
Pomona, N.J. 37 39 29N 74 35W
Pomona Lake 24 38 39N 95 34W
Pomona Park 17 29 30N 81 36W
Pomorie 95 42 32N 27 41E
Pompano Beach 17 26 14N 80 8W
Pompeys Pillar 33 45 59N 107 57W
Pompton Lakes 37 41 0N 74 17W
Ponape 124 6 55N 158 10E
Ponask, L. 60 54 0N 92 41W
Ponass L. 63 52 16N 103 58W
Ponca 34 42 34N 96 43W
Ponca City 43 36 42N 97 5W
Ponca Cr. → 34 42 48N 98 5W
Ponce 57 18 1N 66 37W
Ponce ◇ 57 18 10N 66 30W
Ponce de Leon 17 30 44N 85 56W
Ponce de Leon B. 17 25 15N 81 10W
Poncha Springs 16 38 31N 106 5W
Ponchatoula 25 30 26N 90 26W
Poncheville, L. 60 50 10N 76 55W
Pond Creek 43 36 40N 97 48W
Pond Inlet 59 72 40N 77 0W
Pondera County ◇ 33 48 12N 112 30W
Ponderosa 38 35 40N 106 40W
Pondicherry 108 11 59N 79 50E
Pondosa 14 41 12N 121 41W
Ponds, I. of 61 53 27N 55 52W
Poneto 22 40 39N 85 13W
Ponferrada 91 42 32N 6 35W
Ponnani 108 10 45N 75 59E
Ponnyadaung 109 22 0N 94 10E
Ponoi 98 67 0N 41 0E
Ponoi → 98 66 59N 41 17E
Ponoka 62 52 42N 113 40W
Ponorogo 111 7 52S 111 29E
Ponta de Pedras 74 1 23S 48 52W
Ponta Grossa 77 25 7S 50 10W
Ponta Pora 77 22 20S 55 35W
Pontal → 74 9 8S 40 12W
Pontalina 75 17 31S 49 27W
Pontarlier 90 46 54N 6 20E
Pontchartrain L. 25 30 5N 90 5W
Ponte Alta, Serra do 75 19 42S 47 40W
Ponte Alta do Norte 74 10 45S 47 34W
Ponte Branca 73 16 27S 52 40W
Ponte Macassar 111 9 30S 123 58E
Ponte Nova 75 20 25S 42 54W
Ponte Vedra Beach 17 30 15N 81 23W
Pontedera 94 43 40N 10 37E
Pontefract 82 53 42N 1 19W
Ponteix 63 49 46N 107 29W
Pontevedra 91 42 26N 8 40W
Pontiac, Ill. 21 40 53N 88 38W
Pontiac, Mich. 29 42 38N 83 18W
Pontian Kecil 112 1 29N 103 23E
Pontianak 110 0 3S 109 15E
Pontine Is. = Ponziane, Isole 94 40 55N 13 0E
Ponton → 62 58 27N 116 11W
Pontotoc 31 34 15N 89 0W
Pontotoc County ◇, Miss. 31 34 15N 89 0W
Pontotoc County ◇, Okla. 43 34 45N 96 45W
Pontypool 83 51 42N 3 1W
Pontypridd 83 51 36N 3 21W
Ponziane, Isole 94 40 55N 13 0E
Poole, U.K. 83 50 42N 1 58W
Poole, Ky. 48 37 38N 87 39W
Poole, Nebr. 34 40 59N 98 58W
Pooler 18 32 7N 81 15W
Pooles I. 27 39 17N 76 16W
Poolesville 27 39 9N 77 25W
Pooley I. 62 52 45N 128 15W
Poona = Pune 108 18 29N 73 57E
Poopó 72 18 23S 66 59W
Poopó, Lago de 72 18 30S 67 35W
Popayán 70 2 27N 76 36W
Pope 31 34 13N 89 57W
Pope County ◇, Ark. 13 35 28N 92 59W
Pope County ◇, Ill. 21 37 25N 88 35W
Pope County ◇, Minn. 30 45 40N 95 25W
Pope Cr. → 21 41 8N 90 58W

Popejoy 23 42 36N 93 26W
Poperinge 87 50 51N 2 42E
Popes Creek 27 38 24N 76 58W
Popigay 101 72 1N 110 39E
Popina 95 44 7N 26 57E
Poplar, Mont. 33 48 7N 105 12W
Poplar, N.C. 40 36 4N 82 21W
Poplar, Wis. 55 46 35N 91 48W
Poplar →, Man., Canada 63 53 0N 97 19W
Poplar →, N.W.T., Canada 62 61 22N 121 52W
Poplar →, U.S.A. 33 48 5N 105 11W
Poplar Bluff 32 36 46N 90 24W
Poplar Branch 40 36 17N 75 53W
Poplar Grove 21 42 22N 88 49W
Poplar I. 27 38 46N 76 23W
Poplar Mt. 49 36 43N 85 3W
Poplar Plains 49 38 21N 83 41W
Poplarville 31 30 51N 89 32W
Popo Aggie → 56 43 1N 108 21W
Popocatepetl 65 19 10N 98 40W
Popokabaka 122 5 41S 16 40E
Popovo 95 43 21N 26 18E
Poquetanuck 28 41 29N 72 3W
Poquonock Bridge 28 41 19N 72 11W
Poquoson 54 37 8N 76 24W
Porangaba 72 8 48S 70 36W
Porangatu 75 13 26S 49 10W
Porbandar 108 21 44N 69 43E
Porce → 70 7 28N 74 53W
Porcher I. 62 53 50N 130 30W
Porco 73 19 50S 65 59W
Porcos → 75 12 42S 45 7W
Porcupine →, Canada 63 59 11N 104 46W
Porcupine →, U.S.A. 11 66 34N 145 19W
Porcupine Mts. 29 46 40N 89 40W
Pordim 95 43 23N 24 51E
Porecatu 75 22 43S 51 24W
Pori 97 61 29N 21 48E
Porjus 96 66 57N 19 50E
Porkkala 97 59 59N 24 26E
Porlamar 71 10 57N 63 51W
Poronaysk 101 49 13N 143 0E
Poroshiri-Dake 116 42 41N 142 52E
Porpoise B. 5 66 0S 127 0E
Porreta Pass 94 44 0N 11 10E
Porsangen 96 70 40N 25 40E
Port Alberni 62 49 40N 124 50W
Port Alexander 11 56 15N 134 38W
Port Alfred, Canada 61 48 18N 70 53W
Port Alfred, S. Africa 123 33 36S 26 55E
Port Alice 62 50 20N 127 25W
Port Allegany 45 41 48N 78 17W
Port Allen 25 30 27N 91 12W
Port Angeles 53 48 7N 123 27W
Port Antonio 66 18 10N 76 30W
Port Aransas 51 27 50N 97 4W
Port Arthur = Lüshun 114 38 45N 121 15E
Port Arthur, Australia 127 43 7S 147 50E
Port Arthur, U.S.A. 51 29 54N 93 56W
Port au Port B. 61 48 40N 58 50W
Port-au-Prince 67 18 40N 72 20W
Port Augusta 127 32 30S 137 50E
Port Augusta West 127 32 29S 137 29E
Port Austin 29 44 3N 83 1W
Port Barre 25 30 34N 91 57W
Port Bergé Vaovao 123 15 33S 47 40E
Port Blair 112 11 40N 92 30E
Port Blandford 61 48 20N 54 10W
Port Bradshaw 127 12 30S 137 20E
Port Burwell 60 42 40N 80 48W
Port-Cartier 61 50 2N 66 50W
Port Chalmers 128 45 49S 170 30E
Port Charlotte 17 26 59N 82 6W
Port Chester 39 41 0N 73 40W
Port Clements 62 53 40N 132 10W
Port Clinton 42 41 31N 82 56W
Port Clyde 26 43 56N 69 16W
Port Colborne 60 42 50N 79 10W
Port Coquitlam 62 49 15N 122 45W
Port Darwin, Australia 126 12 24S 130 45E
Port Darwin, Falk. Is. 78 51 50S 59 0W
Port Davey 127 43 16S 145 55E
Port-de-Paix 67 19 50N 72 50W
Port Dickson 112 2 30N 101 49E
Port Edward 62 54 12N 130 10W
Port Edwards 55 44 21N 89 52W
Port Elgin 60 44 25N 81 25W
Port Elizabeth, S. Africa 123 33 58S 25 40E
Port Elizabeth, U.S.A. 37 39 19N 74 59W
Port Ellen 84 55 38N 6 10W
Port-en-Bessin 90 49 21N 0 45W
Port Erin 82 54 5N 4 45W
Port Etienne = Nouâdhibou 120 20 54N 17 0W
Port Ewen 39 41 54N 73 59W
Port Fairy 127 38 22S 142 12E
Port Gamble 53 47 51N 122 35W
Port-Gentil 122 0 40S 8 50E
Port Gibson 31 31 58N 90 59W
Port Glasgow 84 55 57N 4 40W
Port Harcourt 120 4 40N 7 10E
Port Hardy 62 50 41N 127 30W
Port Harrison = Inoucdjouac 59 58 25N 78 15W
Port Hawkesbury 61 45 36N 61 22W
Port Hedland 126 20 25S 118 35E
Port Heiden 11 56 55N 158 41W
Port Henry 39 44 3N 73 28W

Port Hood 61 46 0N 61 32W
Port Hope, Canada 60 43 56N 78 20W
Port Hope, U.S.A. 29 43 57N 82 43W
Port Hueneme 15 34 7N 119 12W
Port Huron 29 42 58N 82 26W
Port Isabel 50 26 5N 97 12W
Port Jackson 127 33 50S 151 18E
Port Jefferson, N.Y. 39 40 57N 73 3W
Port Jefferson, Ohio 42 40 20N 84 6W
Port Jervis 39 41 22N 74 41W
Port-la-Nouvelle 90 43 1N 3 3E
Port Laoise 85 53 2N 7 20W
Port Lavaca 51 28 37N 96 38W
Port Lincoln 126 34 42S 135 52E
Port Lions 11 57 52N 152 53W
Port Loko 120 8 48N 12 46W
Port Ludlow 53 47 56N 122 41W
Port Lyautey = Kenitra 120 34 15N 6 40W
Port Macquarie 127 31 25S 152 25E
Port Mansfield 50 26 34N 97 26W
Port Maria 66 18 25N 77 5W
Port Matilda 45 40 48N 78 3W
Port Mayaca 17 26 59N 80 36W
Port Mellon 62 49 32N 123 31W
Port-Menier 61 49 51N 64 15W
Port Moller 11 55 59N 160 34W
Port Morant 66 17 54N 76 19W
Port Moresby 124 9 24S 147 8E
Port Mourant 71 6 15N 57 20W
Port Mouton 61 43 58N 64 50W
Port Musgrave 127 11 55S 141 50E
Port Neches 51 30 0N 93 59W
Port Nelson 63 57 3N 92 36W
Port Nolloth 123 29 17S 16 52E
Port Norris 37 39 15N 75 2W
Port Nouveau-Québec 59 58 30N 65 59W
Port of Spain 67 10 40N 61 31W
Port Orange 17 29 9N 80 59W
Port Orchard 53 47 32N 122 38W
Port Orford 44 42 45N 124 30W
Port Pegasus 128 47 12S 167 41E
Port Penn 27 39 31N 75 35W
Port Perry 60 44 6N 78 56W
Port Phillip B. 127 38 10S 144 50E
Port Pirie 127 33 10S 138 1E
Port Radium = Echo Bay 58 66 5N 117 55W
Port Renfrew 62 48 30N 124 20W
Port Republic, Md. 27 38 30N 76 33W
Port Republic, N.J. 37 39 31N 74 29W
Port Rowan 60 42 40N 80 30W
Port Royal, Ky. 49 38 33N 85 5W
Port Royal, Va. 54 38 10N 77 12W
Port Royal Sd. 46 32 15N 80 40W
Port Safaga = Bûr Safâga 121 26 43N 33 57E
Port Said = Bûr Sa'îd 121 31 16N 32 18E
Port St. Joe 17 29 49N 85 18W
Port-St-Louis-du-Rhône 90 43 23N 4 49E
Port Salerno 17 27 9N 80 12W
Port Sanilac 29 43 26N 82 33W
Port Saunders 61 50 40N 57 18W
Port Shepstone 123 30 44S 30 28E
Port Simpson 62 54 30N 130 20W
Port Stanley 60 42 40N 81 10W
Port Sudan = Bûr Sûdân 121 19 32N 37 9E
Port Sulphur 25 29 29N 89 42W
Port Susan 53 48 5N 122 15W
Port Talbot 83 51 35N 3 48W
Port Tobacco 27 38 27N 77 2W
Port Townsend 53 48 7N 122 45W
Port-Vendres 90 42 32N 3 8E
Port Vincent 25 30 20N 90 51W
Port Vladimir 98 69 25N 33 6E
Port Washington, N.Y. 39 40 50N 73 41W
Port Washington, Ohio 42 40 20N 81 31W
Port Washington, Wis. 55 43 23N 87 53W
Port Weld 112 4 50N 100 38E
Port Wentworth 18 32 9N 81 10W
Port Wing 55 46 47N 91 23W
Portachuelo 73 17 10S 63 20W
Portadale 18 30 34N 83 54W
Portadown 85 54 27N 6 26W
Portage, Ind. 22 41 34N 87 11W
Portage, Maine 26 46 46N 68 29W
Portage, Mich. 29 42 12N 85 35W
Portage, Pa. 45 40 23N 78 41W
Portage, Utah 52 41 59N 112 14W
Portage, Wis. 55 43 33N 89 28W
Portage → 42 41 31N 83 5W
Portage County ◇, Ohio 42 41 9N 81 15W
Portage County ◇, Wis. 55 44 25N 89 30W
Portage La Prairie 63 49 58N 98 18W
Portageville 32 36 26N 89 42W
Portal, Ariz. 12 31 55N 109 9W
Portal, Ga. 18 32 33N 81 56W
Portal, N. Dak. 41 48 59N 102 33W
Portalegre 91 39 19N 7 25W
Portalegre □ 91 39 20N 7 40W
Portales 38 34 11N 103 20W
Portarlington 85 53 10N 7 10W
Porteirinha 75 15 44S 43 2W
Portel 74 1 57S 50 49W
Porter, Minn. 30 44 38N 96 10W
Porter, Okla. 43 35 52N 95 31W
Porter, Wash. 53 46 56N 123 18W
Porter County ◇ 22 41 25N 87 5W
Porter L., N.W.T., Canada 63 61 41N 108 5W

Porter L. Priština

Porter L., Sask., Canada **63** 56 20N 107 20W
Porterville, Calif. **15** 36 4N 119 1W
Porterville, Miss. **31** 32 41N 88 28W
Porthcawl **83** 51 28N 3 42W
Porthill **20** 48 59N 116 30W
Portile de Fier **89** 44 42N 22 30 E
Portimão **91** 37 8N 8 32W
Portis **24** 39 34N 98 41W
Portland, Australia **127** 38 20 S 141 35 E
Portland, Ark. **13** 33 14N 91 31W
Portland, Conn. **28** 41 34N 72 38W
Portland, Fla. **17** 30 31N 86 12W
Portland, Ind. **22** 40 26N 84 59W
Portland, Maine **26** 43 39N 70 16W
Portland, Mich. **29** 42 52N 84 54W
Portland, Mo. **32** 38 43N 91 43W
Portland, N. Dak. **41** 47 30N 97 22W
Portland, Oreg. **44** 45 32N 122 37W
Portland, Tenn. **48** 36 35N 86 31W
Portland, Tex. **51** 27 53N 97 20W
Portland, Bill of **83** 50 31N 2 27W
Portland, C. **127** 40 46 S 148 0 E
Portland, I. of **83** 50 32N 2 25W
Portland Prom. **59** 58 40N 78 33W
Portneuf **61** 46 43N 71 55W
Portneuf → **20** 42 58N 112 35W
Portneuf Range **20** 42 50N 112 0W
Pôrto, Brazil **74** 3 54 S 42 42W
Porto, Portugal **91** 41 8N 8 40W
Pôrto Acre **72** 9 34 S 67 31W
Pôrto Alegre, Pará, Brazil **71** 4 22 S 52 44W
Pôrto Alegre, Rio Grande do Sul, Brazil **77** 30 5 S 51 10W
Porto Amboim = Gunza **122** 10 50 S 13 50 E
Pôrto Cajueiro **73** 11 3 S 55 53W
Pôrto da Fôlha **74** 9 55 S 37 17W
Pôrto de Móz **74** 1 41 S 52 13W
Pôrto de Pedras **74** 9 10 S 35 17W
Pôrto des Meinacos **73** 12 33 S 53 7W
Porto Empédocle **94** 37 18N 13 30 E
Pôrto Esperança **73** 19 37 S 57 29W
Pôrto Esperidão **73** 15 51 S 58 28W
Pôrto Franco **74** 6 20 S 47 24W
Pôrto Grande **71** 0 42N 51 24W
Pôrto Jofre **73** 17 20 S 56 48W
Porto Mendes **77** 24 30 S 54 15W
Pôrto Murtinho **73** 21 45 S 57 55W
Pôrto Nacional **74** 10 40 S 48 30W
Porto Novo **120** 6 23N 2 42 E
Pôrto Santana **71** 0 3 S 51 11W
Porto Santo **120** 33 45N 16 25W
Pôrto São José **77** 22 43 S 53 10W
Pôrto Seguro **75** 16 26 S 39 5W
Porto Tórres **94** 40 50N 8 23 E
Pôrto União **77** 26 10 S 51 10W
Pôrto Válter **72** 8 15 S 72 40W
Porto-Vecchio **90** 41 35N 9 16 E
Pôrto Velho **73** 8 46 S 63 54W
Portobelo **66** 9 35N 79 42W
Portoferráio **94** 42 50N 10 20 E
Portola **14** 39 49N 120 28W
Portoscuso **94** 39 12N 8 22 E
Portovíejo **70** 1 7 S 80 28W
Portpatrick **84** 54 50N 5 7W
Portree **84** 57 25N 6 11W
Portrush **85** 55 13N 6 40W
Portsmouth, Domin. **67** 15 34N 61 27W
Portsmouth, U.K. **83** 50 48N 1 6W
Portsmouth, N.H. **36** 43 5N 70 45W
Portsmouth, Ohio **42** 38 44N 82 57W
Portsmouth, R.I. **28** 41 36N 71 15W
Portsmouth, Va. **54** 36 50N 76 18W
Portsoy **84** 57 41N 2 41W
Porttipahta **96** 68 5N 26 40 E
Portugal ■ **91** 40 0N 7 0W
Portuguesa □ **70** 9 10N 69 15W
Portuguese-Guinea = Guinea-Bissau ■ **120** 12 0N 15 0W
Portuguese Timor □ = Timor **111** 9 0 S 125 0 E
Portumna **85** 53 5N 8 12W
Portville **39** 42 3N 78 20W
Porum **43** 35 22N 95 16W
Porvenir, Bolivia **72** 11 10 S 68 50W
Porvenir, Chile **78** 53 10 S 70 16W
Porvoo **97** 60 24N 25 40 E
Posadas **77** 27 30 S 55 50W
Posen **29** 45 16N 83 42W
Posey County ◇ **22** 38 0N 87 50W
Poseyville **22** 38 10N 87 47W
Poshan = Boshan **114** 36 28N 117 49 E
Poso **111** 1 20 S 120 55 E
Posoegroenoe **71** 4 23N 55 43W
Posse **75** 14 4 S 46 18W
Possel **122** 5 5N 19 10 E
Possession I. **5** 72 4 S 172 0 E
Possum Kingdom L. **51** 32 52N 98 26W
Post, Oreg. **44** 44 10N 120 29W
Post, Tex. **50** 33 12N 101 23W
Post Falls **20** 47 43N 116 57W
Poste Maurice Cortier **120** 22 14N 1 2 E
Postojna **89** 45 46N 14 12 E
Poston **46** 33 53N 79 26W
Postville **23** 43 5N 91 34W
Potagannissing B. **29** 46 5N 83 50W
Potatch → **20** 46 26N 116 47W
Potawatomi Indian Reservation **24** 39 20N 95 52W
Potchefstroom **123** 26 41 S 27 7 E
Potcoava **95** 44 30N 24 39 E
Poté **75** 17 49 S 41 49W
Poteau **43** 35 3N 94 37W
Poteau → **43** 35 23N 94 26W
Poteet **51** 29 2N 98 35W
Potelu, Lacul **95** 43 44N 24 20 E
Potenza **94** 40 40N 15 50 E
Poteriteri, L. **128** 46 5 S 167 10 E
Potgietersrus **123** 24 10 S 28 55 E
Poth **51** 29 4N 98 5W
Potholes Reservoir **53** 46 59N 119 16W
Poti **99** 42 10N 41 38 E
Potiraguá **75** 15 36 S 39 53W
Potiskum **120** 11 39N 11 2 E
Potlatch **20** 46 55N 116 54W
Potlogi **95** 44 34N 25 34 E
Potomac, Ill. **21** 40 18N 87 48W
Potomac, Md. **27** 39 1N 77 13W
Potomac → **27** 38 0N 76 23W
Potomac Heights **27** 38 36N 77 8W
Potosí, Bolivia **73** 19 38 S 65 50W
Potosi, U.S.A. **32** 37 56N 90 47W
Potosí □ **72** 20 31 S 67 0W
Pototan **111** 10 54N 122 38 E
Potrerillos **76** 26 30 S 69 30W
Potsdam, Germany **88** 52 23N 13 4 E
Potsdam, U.S.A. **39** 44 40N 74 59W
Pottawatomie County ◇, Kans. **24** 39 20N 96 15W
Pottawatomie County ◇, Okla. **43** 35 10N 97 0W
Pottawattamie County ◇ **23** 41 20N 95 30W
Potter, Kans. **24** 39 26N 95 9W
Potter, Nebr. **34** 41 13N 103 19W
Potter County ◇, Pa. **45** 41 50N 78 0W
Potter County ◇, S. Dak. **47** 45 0N 100 0W
Potter County ◇, Tex. **50** 35 22N 101 50W
Potterville, Ga. **18** 32 31N 84 7W
Potterville, Mich. **29** 42 38N 84 45W
Potts Camp **31** 34 39N 89 18W
Pottsboro **51** 33 46N 96 40W
Pottstown **45** 40 15N 75 39W
Pottsville **45** 40 41N 76 12W
Pottuvil **108** 6 55N 81 50 E
Potwin **24** 37 56N 97 1W
Pouce Coupé **62** 55 40N 120 10W
Poughkeepsie **39** 41 42N 73 56W
Poulan **18** 31 31N 83 47W
Poulaphouca Res. **85** 53 8N 6 30W
Poulsbo **53** 47 44N 122 39W
Poultney **36** 43 31N 73 14W
Pound **54** 37 8N 82 36W
Pouso Alegre, Mato Grosso, Brazil **73** 11 46 S 57 16W
Pouso Alegre, Minas Gerais, Brazil **77** 22 14 S 45 57W
Povenets **98** 62 50N 34 50 E
Poverty Bay **128** 38 43 S 178 2 E
Póvoa de Varzim **91** 41 25N 8 46W
Powassan **60** 46 5N 79 25W
Poway **15** 32 58N 117 2W
Powder →, Mont. **33** 46 45N 105 26W
Powder →, Oreg. **44** 44 45N 117 3W
Powder River **56** 43 2N 106 59W
Powder River County ◇ **33** 45 20N 105 40W
Powder Springs **18** 33 52N 84 41W
Powderhorn **16** 38 17N 107 7W
Powell **56** 44 45N 108 46W
Powell → **49** 36 29N 83 52W
Powell Butte **44** 44 15N 121 1W
Powell County ◇, Ky. **49** 37 50N 83 50W
Powell County ◇, Mont. **33** 47 0N 113 0W
Powell Creek **126** 18 6 S 133 46 E
Powell L. **52** 36 57N 111 29W
Powell River **62** 49 50N 124 35W
Powellville **27** 38 20N 75 22W
Powelton **18** 33 26N 82 52W
Power County ◇ **20** 42 50N 112 50W
Powers, Mich. **29** 45 41N 87 32W
Powers, Oreg. **44** 42 53N 124 4W
Powers Lake **41** 48 34N 102 39W
Powersville **32** 40 33N 93 15W
Poweshiek County ◇ **23** 41 40N 92 30W
Powhatan, Ark. **13** 36 5N 91 7W
Powhatan, Va. **54** 37 32N 77 55W
Powhatan County ◇ **54** 37 32N 77 55W
Powhatan Point **42** 39 52N 80 49W
Powhattan **24** 39 46N 95 38W
Pownal **36** 42 46N 73 14W
Powys □ **83** 52 20N 3 20W
Poxoreu **73** 15 50 S 54 23W
Poyang Hu **115** 29 5N 116 20 E
Poyarkovo **101** 49 36N 128 41 E
Poygan L. **55** 44 19N 88 50W
Poynette **55** 43 24N 89 24W
Poza Rica **65** 20 33N 97 27W
Požarevac **95** 44 35N 21 18 E
Poznań **88** 52 25N 16 55 E
Pozo Almonte **72** 20 10 S 69 50W
Pozo Colorado **76** 23 30 S 58 45W
Pozo del Dátil **64** 30 0N 112 15W
Pozoblanco **91** 38 23N 4 51W
Pozuzo **72** 10 5 S 75 35W
Prachin Buri **112** 14 0N 101 25 E
Prachuap Khiri Khan **112** 11 49N 99 48 E
Pradera **70** 3 25N 76 15W
Prado **75** 17 20 S 39 13W
Prague = Praha **88** 50 5N 14 22 E
Prague, Nebr. **34** 41 19N 96 49W
Prague, Okla. **43** 35 29N 96 41W
Praha **88** 50 5N 14 22 E
Prahova □ **95** 45 10N 26 0 E
Prahova → **95** 44 50N 25 50 E
Praid **89** 46 32N 25 10 E
Prainha, Amazonas, Brazil **73** 7 10 S 60 30W
Prainha, Pará, Brazil **71** 1 45 S 53 30W
Prairie **31** 33 48N 88 40W
Prairie City, Iowa **23** 41 36N 93 14W
Prairie City, Oreg. **44** 44 28N 118 43W
Prairie City, S. Dak. **47** 45 32N 102 48W
Prairie County ◇, Ark. **13** 34 47N 91 35W
Prairie County ◇, Mont. **33** 46 57N 105 30W
Prairie Dog Cr. → **24** 40 0N 99 18W
Prairie Dog Town Ford Red → **50** 34 27N 99 21W
Prairie du Chien **55** 43 3N 91 9W
Prairie du Rocher **21** 38 5N 90 6W
Prairie du Sac **55** 43 17N 89 43W
Prairie Farm **55** 45 14N 91 59W
Prairie Grove **13** 35 59N 94 19W
Prairie Hill **32** 39 31N 92 44W
Prairie Home **32** 38 49N 92 35W
Prairie View, Kans. **24** 39 50N 99 34W
Prairie View, Tex. **51** 30 6N 95 59W
Prairie Village **24** 38 58N 94 38W
Prapat **110** 2 41N 98 58 E
Prata **75** 19 25 S 48 54W
Prato **94** 43 53N 11 5 E
Pratt **24** 37 39N 98 44W
Pratt County ◇ **24** 37 35N 98 45W
Prattville **10** 32 28N 86 29W
Pravia **91** 43 30N 6 12W
Praya **110** 8 39 S 116 17 E
Preble **39** 42 44N 76 9W
Preble County ◇ **42** 39 45N 84 38W
Precordillera **76** 30 0 S 69 1W
Preeceville **63** 51 57N 102 40W
Pregonero **70** 8 1N 71 46W
Prelate **63** 50 51N 109 24W
Premier **62** 56 4N 129 56W
Premier Downs **126** 30 30 S 126 30 E
Premont **50** 27 22N 98 7W
Prentice **55** 45 33N 90 17W
Prentiss **31** 31 36N 89 52W
Prentiss County ◇ **31** 34 39N 88 34W
Prenzlau **88** 53 19N 13 51 E
Preobrazheniye **116** 42 54N 133 54 E
Prepansko Jezero **95** 40 55N 21 0 E
Preparis North Channel **112** 15 12N 93 40 E
Preparis South Channel **112** 14 36N 93 40 E
Přerov **89** 49 28N 17 27 E
Prescott, Canada **60** 44 45N 75 30W
Prescott, Ariz. **12** 34 33N 112 28W
Prescott, Ark. **13** 33 48N 93 23W
Prescott, Iowa **23** 41 1N 94 37W
Prescott, Kans. **24** 38 4N 94 42W
Prescott, Mich. **29** 44 11N 83 56W
Prescott, Wash. **53** 46 18N 118 19W
Prescott National Forest **12** 34 30N 112 30W
Preservation Inlet **128** 46 8 S 166 35 E
Presho **47** 43 54N 100 3W
Presidencia de la Plaza **76** 27 0 S 29 50W
Presidencia Roque Saenz Peña **76** 26 45 S 60 30W
Presidente Epitácio **75** 21 56 S 52 6W
Presidente Hayes □ **76** 24 0 S 59 0W
Presidente Hermes **73** 11 17 S 61 55W
Presidente Prudente **75** 22 5 S 51 25W
Presidential Lakes **37** 39 54N 74 35W
Presidio, Mexico **64** 29 29N 104 23W
Presidio, U.S.A. **50** 29 34N 104 22W
Presidio County ◇ **50** 30 0N 104 0W
Preslav **95** 43 10N 26 52 E
Preslavska Planina **95** 43 10N 26 45 E
Prespa **95** 41 44N 24 55 E
Prespa, L. = Prepansko Jezero **95** 40 55N 21 0 E
Presque Isle, Maine **26** 46 41N 68 1W
Presque Isle, Mich. **29** 45 18N 83 29W
Presque Isle County ◇ **29** 45 15N 84 0W
Prestbury **83** 51 54N 2 2W
Presteigne **83** 52 17N 3 0W
Presto **73** 18 55 S 64 56W
Preston, U.K. **82** 53 46N 2 42W
Preston, Ga. **18** 32 4N 84 32W
Preston, Idaho **20** 42 6N 111 53W
Preston, Iowa **23** 42 3N 90 24W
Preston, Kans. **24** 37 46N 98 33W
Preston, Md. **27** 38 43N 75 55W
Preston, Minn. **30** 43 40N 92 5W
Preston, Nev. **35** 38 55N 115 4W
Preston, Okla. **43** 35 43N 95 59W
Preston, C. **126** 20 51 S 116 12 E
Preston City **28** 41 33N 72 57W
Preston County ◇ **54** 39 31N 79 48W
Prestonpans **84** 55 58N 3 0W
Prestonsburg **49** 37 40N 82 47W
Prestwick **84** 55 30N 4 38W
Prêto →, Amazonas, Brazil **71** 0 8 S 64 6W
Prêto →, Bahia, Brazil **74** 11 21 S 43 52W
Prêto do Igapó-Açu → **71** 4 26 S 59 48W
Pretoria **123** 25 44 S 28 12 E
Pretty Prairie **24** 37 47N 98 1W
Prettyboy Reservoir **27** 39 37N 76 43W
Préveza **95** 38 57N 20 47 E
Prewitt **38** 35 22N 108 3W
Prewitt Reservoir **16** 40 26N 103 22W
Prey-Veng **112** 11 35N 105 29 E
Pribilof Is., Bering S. **4** 56 0N 170 0W
Pribilof Is., U.S.A. **11** 57 0N 170 0W
Pribram **88** 49 41N 14 2 E
Price, Md. **27** 39 6N 75 58W
Price, Tex. **51** 32 8N 94 57W
Price, Utah **52** 39 36N 110 49W
Price → **52** 39 10N 110 6W
Price County ◇ **55** 45 45N 90 20W
Price I. **62** 52 23N 128 41W
Prichard, Ala. **10** 30 44N 88 5W
Prichard, W. Va. **54** 38 15N 82 36W
Prichett **16** 37 22N 102 52W
Priddy **51** 31 41N 98 31W
Pride **48** 37 34N 87 53W
Prieska **123** 29 40 S 22 42 E
Priest → **20** 48 12N 116 54W
Priest L. **20** 48 35N 116 52W
Priest Rapids Dam **53** 46 39N 119 54W
Priestly **62** 54 8N 125 20W
Prieta Loma **14** 37 7N 121 50W
Prikaspiyskaya Nizmennost **99** 47 0N 48 0 E
Prikumsk **99** 44 50N 44 10 E
Prilep **95** 41 21N 21 37 E
Priluki **99** 50 30N 32 24 E
Primeira Cruz **74** 2 30 S 43 26W
Primghar **23** 43 5N 95 38W
Primorsko **95** 42 15N 27 44 E
Primrose **34** 41 38N 98 14W
Primrose L. **63** 54 55N 109 45W
Prince Albert **63** 53 15N 105 50W
Prince Albert Mts. **5** 76 0 S 161 30 E
Prince Albert Nat. Park **63** 54 0N 106 25W
Prince Albert Pen. **58** 72 30N 116 0W
Prince Albert Sd. **58** 70 25N 115 0W
Prince Alfred C. **4** 74 20N 124 40W
Prince Charles I. **59** 67 47N 76 12W
Prince Charles Mts. **5** 72 0 S 67 0 E
Prince Edward County ◇ **54** 37 18N 78 25W
Prince Edward I. □ **61** 46 20N 63 20W
Prince Edward Is. **3** 45 15 S 39 0 E
Prince Frederick **27** 38 33N 76 35W
Prince George, Canada **62** 53 55N 122 50W
Prince George, U.S.A. **54** 37 13N 77 17W
Prince George County ◇ **54** 37 13N 77 17W
Prince Georges County ◇ **27** 38 45N 76 50W
Prince of Wales, C. **11** 65 36N 168 5W
Prince of Wales I., Canada **58** 73 0N 99 0W
Prince of Wales I., U.S.A. **11** 55 47N 132 50W
Prince of Wales Is. **127** 10 40 S 142 10 E
Prince of Wales-Outer Ketchikan ◇ **11** 55 0N 131 30W
Prince Patrick I. **4** 77 0N 120 0W
Prince Regent Inlet **4** 73 0N 90 0W
Prince Rupert **62** 54 20N 130 20W
Prince William County ◇ **54** 38 45N 77 29W
Prince William Sd. **11** 60 40N 147 0W
Princesa Isabel **74** 7 44 S 38 0W
Princess Anne **27** 38 12N 75 42W
Princess Charlotte B. **127** 14 25 S 144 0 E
Princess Royal I. **62** 53 0N 128 40W
Princeton, Canada **62** 49 27N 120 30W
Princeton, Ark. **13** 33 59N 92 38W
Princeton, Calif. **14** 39 24N 122 1W
Princeton, Ill. **21** 41 23N 89 28W
Princeton, Ind. **22** 38 21N 87 34W
Princeton, Iowa **23** 41 40N 90 20W
Princeton, Kans. **24** 38 29N 95 16W
Princeton, Ky. **48** 37 7N 87 53W
Princeton, Maine **26** 45 13N 67 34W
Princeton, Mass. **28** 42 0N 71 0W
Princeton, Mich. **29** 46 17N 87 29W
Princeton, Minn. **30** 45 34N 93 35W
Princeton, Mo. **32** 40 24N 93 35W
Princeton, N.C. **40** 35 28N 78 10W
Princeton, N.J. **37** 40 21N 74 39W
Princeton, S.C. **46** 34 30N 82 17W
Princeton, W. Va. **54** 37 22N 81 6W
Princeton, Wis. **55** 43 51N 89 8W
Princeville **21** 40 56N 89 46W
Principe, I. de **119** 1 37N 7 27 E
Principe Chan. **62** 53 28N 130 0W
Principe da Beira **73** 12 20 S 64 30W
Prineville **44** 44 18N 120 51W
Prineville Reservoir **44** 44 7N 120 47W
Pringle, S. Dak. **47** 43 37N 103 36W
Pringle, Tex. **50** 35 57N 101 27W
Prins Harald Kyst **5** 70 0 S 35 1 E
Prinsburg **30** 44 56N 95 11W
Prinsesse Astrid Kyst **5** 70 45 S 12 30 E
Prinsesse Ragnhild Kyst **5** 70 15 S 27 30 E
Prinzapolca **66** 13 20N 83 35W
Prior Lake **30** 44 43N 93 25W
Priozersk **98** 61 2N 30 7 E
Pripet = Pripyat → **98** 51 20N 30 9 E
Pripet Marshes = Polesye **98** 52 0N 28 10 E
Pripyat → **98** 51 20N 30 9 E
Priština **95** 42 40N 21 13 E

Privas Qondū

Privas 90 44 45N 4 37 E
Privolzhskaya Vozvyshennost 99 51 0N 46 0 E
Prizren 95 42 13N 20 45 E
Probolinggo 111 7 46 S 113 13 E
Proctor, Colo. 16 40 48N 102 57W
Proctor, Minn. 30 46 45N 92 14W
Proctor, Vt. 36 43 40N 73 2W
Proctor, W. Va. 54 39 43N 80 49W
Proctor L. 51 31 58N 98 29W
Proctorsville 36 43 23N 72 40W
Proctorville 42 38 26N 82 23W
Proddatur 108 14 45N 78 30 E
Prof. Van Blommestein Meer 71 4 45N 55 5W
Progreso 65 21 20N 89 40W
Prokopyevsk 100 54 0N 86 45 E
Prome = Pyè 109 18 49N 95 13 E
Promise City 23 40 45N 93 9W
Promontory Mts. 52 41 30N 112 30W
Prophet ⟶ 62 58 48N 122 40W
Prophetstown 21 41 40N 89 56W
Propriá 74 10 13 S 36 51W
Proserpine 127 20 21 S 148 36 E
Prospect, Conn. 28 41 30N 72 59W
Prospect, Ohio 42 40 27N 83 11W
Prospect, Oreg. 44 42 45N 122 29W
Prospect, Pa. 45 40 54N 80 3W
Prosperity 46 34 12N 81 32W
Prosser, Nebr. 34 40 41N 98 34W
Prosser, Wash. 53 46 12N 119 46W
Prostějov 88 49 30N 17 9 E
Protection 24 37 12N 99 29W
Protem 32 36 32N 92 51W
Protivin 23 43 13N 92 6W
Provadiya 95 43 12N 27 30 E
Provence 90 43 40N 5 46 E
Providence, Ky. 48 37 24N 87 46W
Providence, R.I. 28 41 49N 71 24W
Providence, Utah 52 41 43N 111 49W
Providence Bay 60 45 41N 82 15W
Providence County ◇ 28 41 50N 71 40W
Providence Mts. 15 35 10N 115 15W
Providencia 70 0 28 S 76 28W
Providencia, I. de 66 13 25N 81 26W
Provideniya 101 64 23N 173 18W
Provincetown 28 42 3N 70 11W
Provins 90 48 33N 3 15 E
Provo, S. Dak. 47 43 12N 103 50W
Provo, Utah 52 40 14N 111 39W
Provost 63 52 25N 110 20W
Prowers County ◇ 16 38 0N 102 30W
Prudence I. 28 41 37N 71 19W
Prudentópolis 75 25 12 S 50 57W
Prudhoe Bay 11 70 18N 148 22W
Prud'homme 63 52 20N 105 54W
Prue 43 36 15N 96 15W
Pruszków 89 52 9N 20 49 E
Prut ⟶ 89 46 3N 28 10 E
Prydz B. 5 69 0S 74 0 E
Pryor 43 36 19N 95 19W
Przemyśl 89 49 50N 22 45 E
Przeworsk 89 50 6N 22 32 E
Przhevalsk 100 42 30N 78 20 E
Pskov 98 57 50N 28 25 E
Puaena Pt. 19 21 36N 158 6W
Puán 76 37 30 S 62 45W
Pucacuro ⟶ 70 3 20 S 74 58W
Pucallpa 72 8 25 S 74 30W
Pucará, Bolivia 73 18 43 S 64 11W
Pucará, Peru 72 15 5 S 70 24W
Pucarani 72 16 23 S 68 30W
Pucheng 115 27 59N 118 31 E
Pucheni 95 45 12N 25 17 E
Puckaway L. 55 43 45N 89 10W
Puckett 31 32 5N 89 47W
Pudozh 98 61 48N 36 32 E
Pudukkottai 108 10 28N 78 47 E
Puebla 65 19 0N 98 10W
Puebla □ 65 18 30N 98 0W
Pueblo 16 38 16N 104 37W
Pueblo Colorado Wash ⟶ 12 35 5N 110 22W
Pueblo County ◇ 16 38 15N 104 30W
Pueblo Hundido 76 26 20 S 70 5W
Pueblo Mt. 44 42 6N 118 39W
Pueblo Nuevo, Puerto Rico 57 18 28N 66 51W
Pueblo Nuevo, Venezuela 70 8 26N 71 26W
Puelches 76 38 5 S 65 51W
Puelén 76 37 32 S 67 38W
Puente Alto 76 33 32 S 70 35W
Puente-Genil 91 37 22N 4 47W
Pueo Pt. 19 21 54N 160 4W
Puerca, Pta. 57 18 13N 65 36W
Puerco ⟶, Ariz. 12 34 54N 110 2W
Puerco ⟶, N. Mex. 12 34 22N 107 50W
Puerto Acosta 72 15 32 S 69 15W
Puerto Aisén 78 45 27 S 73 0W
Puerto Ángel 65 15 40N 96 29W
Puerto Arista 65 15 56N 93 48W
Puerto Armuelles 66 8 20N 82 51W
Puerto Ayacucho 70 5 40N 67 35W
Puerto Barrios 66 15 40N 88 32W
Puerto Bermejo 76 26 55 S 58 34W
Puerto Bermúdez 72 10 20 S 75 0W
Puerto Bolívar 70 3 19 S 79 55W
Puerto Cabello 70 10 28N 68 1W
Puerto Cabezas 66 14 0N 83 30W
Puerto Cabo Gracias á Dios 66 15 0N 83 10W
Puerto Carreño 70 6 12N 67 22W
Puerto Castilla 66 16 0N 86 0W
Puerto Chicama 72 7 45 S 79 20W
Puerto Coig 78 50 54 S 69 15W
Puerto Cortes, C. Rica 66 8 55N 84 0W
Puerto Cortés, Hond. 66 15 51N 88 0W
Puerto Cumarebo 70 11 29N 69 30W
Puerto de Santa María 91 36 36N 6 13W
Puerto del Rosario 120 28 30N 13 52W
Puerto Deseado 78 47 55 S 66 0W
Puerto Guaraní 73 21 18 S 57 55W
Puerto Heath 72 12 34 S 68 39W
Puerto Huitoto 70 0 18N 74 3W
Puerto Inca 72 9 22 S 74 54W
Puerto Juárez 65 21 11N 86 49W
Puerto La Cruz 71 10 13N 64 38W
Puerto Leguízamo 70 0 12 S 74 46W
Puerto Libertad 64 29 55N 112 41W
Puerto Limón 70 3 23N 73 30W
Puerto Lobos 78 42 0 S 65 3W
Puerto López 70 4 5N 72 58W
Puerto Madryn 78 42 48 S 65 4W
Puerto Maldonado 72 12 30 S 69 10W
Puerto Manotí 66 21 22N 76 50W
Puerto Mercedes 70 1 11N 72 53W
Puerto Miraña 70 1 20 S 70 19W
Puerto Montt 78 41 28 S 73 0W
Puerto Morelos 65 20 49N 86 52W
Puerto Nariño 70 4 56N 67 48W
Puerto Natales 78 51 45 S 72 15W
Puerto Nuevo 70 5 53N 69 56W
Puerto Nuevo, Pta. 57 18 30N 66 24W
Puerto Nutrias 70 8 5N 69 18W
Puerto Ordaz 71 8 16N 62 44W
Puerto Padre 66 21 13N 76 35W
Puerto Páez 70 6 13N 67 28W
Puerto Peñasco 64 31 20N 113 33W
Puerto Pinasco 76 22 36 S 57 50W
Puerto Pirámides 78 42 35 S 64 20W
Puerto Plata 67 19 48N 70 45W
Puerto Portillo 72 9 45 S 72 42W
Puerto Princesa 111 9 46N 118 45 E
Puerto Quellón 78 43 7 S 73 37W
Puerto Quepos 66 9 29N 84 6W
Puerto Rico 72 11 5 S 67 38W
Puerto Rico ■ 57 18 15N 66 30W
Puerto Saavedra 78 38 47 S 73 24W
Puerto Sastre 76 22 2 S 57 55W
Puerto Siles 73 12 48 S 65 5W
Puerto Suárez 73 18 58 S 57 52W
Puerto Tejada 70 3 14N 76 24W
Puerto Umbría 70 0 52N 76 33W
Puerto Vallarta 64 20 36N 105 15W
Puerto Varas 78 41 19 S 72 59W
Puerto Villazón 73 13 32 S 61 57W
Puerto Wilches 70 7 21N 73 54W
Puertollano 91 38 43N 4 7W
Puesto Cunambo 70 2 10 S 76 0W
Pueyrredón, L. 78 47 20 S 72 0W
Pugachev 98 52 0N 48 49 E
Puget Sound 53 47 50N 122 30W
Púglia □ 94 41 0N 16 30 E
Puica 72 15 0 S 72 33W
Puieşti 95 46 25N 27 33 E
Puigcerdá 91 42 24N 1 50 E
Pujilí 70 0 57 S 78 41W
Pukaki L. 128 44 4 S 170 1 E
Pukalani 19 20 51N 156 20W
Pukapuka 125 10 53 S 165 49W
Pukatawagan 63 55 45N 101 20W
Pukekohe 128 37 12 S 174 55 E
Pukoo 19 21 4N 156 48W
Pukou 115 32 7N 118 38 E
Pula 94 39 0N 9 0 E
Pulacayo 72 20 25 S 66 41W
Pulaski, Ill. 21 37 12N 89 12W
Pulaski, Iowa 23 40 45N 92 12W
Pulaski, N.Y. 39 43 34N 76 8W
Pulaski, Tenn. 48 35 12N 87 2W
Pulaski, Va. 54 37 3N 80 47W
Pulaski, Wis. 55 44 41N 88 14W
Pulaski County ◇, Ark. 13 34 45N 92 20W
Pulaski County ◇, Ga. 18 32 15N 83 30W
Pulaski County ◇, Ill. 21 37 15N 89 5W
Pulaski County ◇, Ind. 22 41 0N 86 40W
Pulaski County ◇, Ky. 49 37 5N 84 35W
Pulaski County ◇, Mo. 32 37 50N 92 10W
Pulaski County ◇, Va. 54 37 0N 80 45W
Pulicat, L. 108 13 40N 80 15 E
Pullman 53 46 44N 117 10W
Pulog, Mt. 111 16 40N 120 50 E
Puloraja 110 4 55N 95 24 E
Pumlumon Fawr 83 52 29N 3 47W
Pumpville 50 29 53N 101 45W
Puna 73 19 45 S 65 28W
Puná, I. 70 2 55 S 80 5W
Punakha 109 27 42N 89 52 E
Punaluu 19 21 35N 157 53W
Punata 73 17 32 S 65 50W
Punch 108 33 48N 74 4 E
Pune 108 18 29N 73 57 E
Pungo L. 40 35 42N 76 33W
Puning 115 23 20N 116 12 E
Punjab □, India 108 31 0N 76 0 E
Punjab □, Pakistan 108 30 0N 72 0 E
Puno 72 15 55 S 70 3W
Punta, Cerro de 57 18 10N 66 37W
Punta Alta 78 38 53 S 62 4W
Punta Arenas 78 53 10 S 71 0W
Punta Cardón 70 11 38N 70 14W
Punta Coles 72 17 43 S 71 23W
Punta de Agua ⟶ 50 35 32N 102 27W
Punta de Bombón 72 17 10 S 71 48W
Punta de Díaz 76 28 0 S 70 45W
Punta de Piedras 70 10 54N 64 6W
Punta Delgado 78 42 43 S 63 38W
Punta Gorda, Belize 65 16 10N 88 45W
Punta Gorda, U.S.A. 17 26 56N 82 3W
Punta Prieta 64 28 58N 114 17W
Punta Rassa 17 26 26N 81 59W
Puntarenas 66 10 0N 84 50W
Punto Fijo 70 11 50N 70 13W
Punxsatawney 45 40 57N 78 59W
Puolo Pt. 19 21 54N 159 36W
Puqi 115 29 40N 113 50 E
Puquio 72 14 45 S 74 10W
Pur ⟶ 100 67 31N 77 55 E
Purace, Vol. 70 2 21N 76 23W
Purbeck, Isle of 83 50 40N 2 5W
Purcell 43 35 1N 97 22W
Purcell Mts. 33 48 30N 115 0W
Purcellville 54 39 8N 77 43W
Purdin 32 39 57N 93 10W
Purdon 51 31 57N 96 37W
Purdy, Mo. 32 36 49N 93 55W
Purdy, Okla. 43 34 43N 97 35W
Purdy, Va. 54 36 49N 77 36W
Purgatoire ⟶ 16 38 4N 103 11W
Puri 109 19 50N 85 58 E
Purificación 70 3 51N 74 55W
Purísima, La 64 26 10N 112 4W
Purmerend 87 52 30N 4 58 E
Purnia 109 25 45N 87 31 E
Pursat 112 12 34N 103 50 E
Purukcau 110 0 35 S 114 35 E
Puruliya 109 23 17N 86 24 E
Purus ⟶ 71 3 42 S 61 28W
Purvis 31 31 9N 89 25W
Pŭrvomay 95 42 8N 25 17 E
Purwakarta 111 6 35 S 107 29 E
Purwodadi, Jawa, Indonesia 111 7 7 S 110 55 E
Purwodadi, Jawa, Indonesia 111 7 51 S 110 0 E
Purwokerto 111 7 25 S 109 14 E
Purworejo 111 7 43 S 110 2 E
Puryear 48 36 27N 88 20W
Pusan 114 35 5N 129 0 E
Pushaw L. 26 44 56N 68 48W
Pushchino 101 54 10N 158 0 E
Pushkino 99 51 16N 47 0 E
Pushmataha County ◇ 43 34 25N 95 20W
Put-in Bay 42 41 39N 82 49W
Putahow L. 63 59 54N 100 40W
Putao 109 27 28N 97 30 E
Putaruru 128 38 2 S 175 50 E
Puţeni 95 45 49N 27 42 E
Puthein Myit ⟶ 109 15 56N 94 18 E
Putian 115 25 23N 119 0 E
Putignano 94 40 50N 17 5 E
Putina 72 14 55 S 69 55W
Puting, Tanjung 110 3 31 S 111 46 E
Putna ⟶ 95 45 42N 27 26 E
Putnam, Conn. 28 41 55N 71 55W
Putnam, Okla. 43 35 51N 98 58W
Putnam, Tex. 51 32 22N 99 12W
Putnam County ◇, Fla. 17 29 35N 81 45W
Putnam County ◇, Ga. 18 33 20N 83 15W
Putnam County ◇, Ill. 21 41 10N 89 15W
Putnam County ◇, Ind. 22 39 40N 86 50W
Putnam County ◇, Mo. 32 40 30N 93 0W
Putnam County ◇, N.Y. 39 41 25N 73 45W
Putnam County ◇, Ohio 42 40 59N 84 12W
Putnam County ◇, Tenn. 49 36 10N 85 30W
Putnam County ◇, W. Va. 54 38 32N 81 54W
Putney, Ga. 18 31 29N 84 8W
Putney, S. Dak. 47 45 34N 98 11W
Putney, Vt. 36 42 58N 72 31W
Putorana, Gory 101 69 0N 95 0 E
Putre 72 18 12 S 69 35W
Puttalam 108 8 1N 79 55 E
Putten 87 52 16N 5 36 E
Puttgarden 88 54 28N 11 15 E
Putumayo ⟶ 70 3 7 S 67 58W
Putussibau 110 0 50N 112 56 E
Puu Kaaumakua 19 21 30N 157 54W
Puu Keahiakahoe 19 21 23N 157 49W
Puu o Keokeo 19 19 13N 155 44W
Puuanahulu 19 19 49N 155 51W
Puukolii 19 20 56N 156 41W
Puunene 19 20 53N 156 23W
Puuwai 19 21 54N 160 12W
Puxico 32 36 57N 90 10W
Puy, Le 90 45 3N 3 52 E
Puy-de-Dôme 90 45 46N 2 57 E
Puy-de-Dôme □ 90 45 47N 3 0 E
Puyallup 53 47 12N 122 18W
Puyang 114 35 40N 115 1 E
Puyehue 78 40 40 S 72 37W
Puyo 70 1 28 S 77 59W
Pweto 122 8 25 S 28 51 E
Pwllheli 82 52 54N 4 26W
Pya-ozero 98 66 5N 30 58 E
Pyapon 109 16 20N 95 40 E
Pyasina ⟶ 101 73 30N 87 0
Pyatigorsk 99 44 2N 43 6
Pyè 109 18 49N 95 13
Pyinmana 109 19 45N 96 12
Pymatuning Reservoir 42 41 30N 80 28
Pyŏngyang 114 39 0N 125 30
Pyote 50 31 32N 103 8
Pyramid L. 35 40 1N 119 35
Pyramid Lake Indian Reservation 35 40 20N 119 35
Pyramid Pk. 56 43 27N 110 28
Pyrenees = Pyrénées 90 42 45N 0 18
Pyrénées 90 42 45N 0 18
Pyrénées-Atlantiques □ 90 43 15N 1 0
Pyrénées-Orientales □ 90 42 35N 2 26
Pyu 109 18 30N 96 28

Q

Qabalān 104 32 8N 35 17
Qabātiyah 104 32 25N 35 16
Qādib 105 12 35N 54 2
Qā'emshahr 107 36 30N 52 55
Qahremānshahr 106 34 23N 47 0
Qaidam Pendi 113 37 0N 95 0
Qa'iya 106 24 33N 43 15
Qalāt 107 32 15N 66 58
Qal'at al Akhḍar 106 28 0N 37 10
Qal'at al Mu'azzam 106 27 45N 37 31
Qal'eh Shaharak 108 34 10N 64 20
Qal'eh-ye Now 107 35 0N 63 5
Qalqīlya 104 32 12N 34 58
Qam 104 32 36N 35 43
Qamar, Ghubbat al 105 16 20N 52 30
Qamruddin Karez 108 31 45N 68 20
Qāna 104 33 12N 35 17
Qandahār 108 31 32N 65 30
Qandahār □ 108 31 0N 65 0
Qâra 121 29 38N 26 30
Qarachuk 106 37 0N 42 2
Qārah 106 29 55N 40 3
Qarqan 113 38 5N 85 20
Qarqan He ⟶ 113 39 30N 88 30
Qasim, Si. Arabia 106 26 0N 43 0
Qāsim, Syria 104 32 59N 36 2
Qaṣr-e Qand 107 26 15N 60 45
Qasr Farâfra 121 27 0N 28 1
Qatar ■ 107 25 30N 51 15
Qattâra, Munkhafed el 121 29 30N 27 30
Qattâra Depression = Qattâra, Munkhafed el 121 29 30N 27 30
Qāyen 107 33 40N 59 10
Qazvin 106 36 15N 50 0
Qena 121 26 10N 32 43
Qeshm 107 26 55N 56 10
Qezi'ot 104 30 52N 34 26
Qian Xian 115 34 31N 108 15
Qianshan 115 30 37N 116 35
Qianxi 115 27 3N 106 3
Qianyang 115 27 18N 110 10
Qijiang 115 28 57N 106 35
Qila Safed 107 29 0N 61 30
Qila Saifullāh 108 30 45N 68 17
Qilian Shan 113 38 30N 96 0
Qin Ling = Qinling Shandi 115 33 50N 108 10
Qin'an 115 34 48N 105 40
Qingdao 114 36 5N 120 20
Qinghai □ 113 36 0N 98 0
Qinghai Hu 113 36 40N 100 10
Qingjiang, Jiangsu, China 115 33 30N 119 2
Qingjiang, Jiangxi, China 115 28 4N 115 29
Qingliu 115 26 11N 116 48
Qingshuihe 114 39 55N 111 35
Qingyang 114 36 2N 107 55
Qingyuan 115 23 40N 112 59
Qinhuangdao 114 39 56N 119 30
Qinling Shandi 115 33 50N 108 10
Qinyang 115 35 7N 112 57
Qinyuan 114 36 29N 112 20
Qinzhou 115 21 58N 108 38
Qiongshan 115 19 51N 110 26
Qiongzhou Haixia 115 20 10N 110 15
Qiqihar 114 47 26N 124 0
Qiryat 'Anavim 104 31 49N 35 7
Qiryat Ata 104 32 47N 35 6
Qiryat Bialik 104 32 50N 35 5
Qiryat Gat 104 31 32N 34 46
Qiryat Ḥayyim 104 32 49N 35 4
Qiryat Mal'akhi 104 31 44N 34 44
Qiryat Shemona 104 33 13N 35 3
Qiryat Yam 104 32 51N 35 4
Qishan 115 22 52N 120 25
Qishon ⟶ 104 32 49N 35 2
Qitai 113 44 2N 89 35
Qiyahe 114 53 0N 120 35
Qiyang 115 26 35N 111 50
Qizān 105 17 0N 42 20
Qom 107 34 40N 51 0
Qomolangma Feng 113 28 0N 86 45
Qomsheh 107 32 0N 51 55
Qondūz 107 36 50N 68 50
Qondūz □ 107 36 50N 68 50

Qu Jiang Rarden

Qu Jiang → 115 30 1N 106 24 E
Qu Xian, Sichuan, China 115 30 48N 106 58 E
Qu Xian, Zhejiang, China 115 28 57N 118 54 E
Quabbin Reservoir 28 42 20N 72 20W
Quail 50 34 55N 100 30W
Quakertown 45 40 26N 75 21W
Quan Long 112 9 7N 105 8 E
Quanah 51 34 18N 99 44W
Quang Ngai 112 15 13N 108 58 E
Quang Yen 112 20 56N 106 52 E
Quantico 27 38 23N 75 44W
Quantock Hills 83 51 8N 3 10W
Quanzhou, Fujian, China 115 24 55N 118 34 E
Quanzhou, Guangxi Zhuangzu, China 115 25 57N 111 5 E
Quapaw 43 36 58N 94 50W
Quaraí 76 30 15 S 56 20W
Quarryville 45 39 54N 76 10W
Quartz Hill 15 34 39N 118 13W
Quartzsite 12 33 40N 114 13W
Quatsino 62 50 30N 127 40W
Quatsino Sd. 62 50 25N 127 58W
Quay 38 34 56N 103 45W
Quay County ◇ 38 35 0N 103 30W
Qubab = Mishmar Ayyalon 104 31 52N 34 57 E
Qūchān 107 37 10N 58 27 E
Queanbeyan 127 35 17 S 149 14 E
Québec 61 46 52N 71 13W
Québec □ 61 50 0N 70 0W
Quebradillas 57 18 29N 66 56W
Quechee 36 43 40N 72 25W
Queen Alexandra Ra. 5 85 0 S 170 0 E
Queen Anne 27 38 55N 75 57W
Queen Annes County ◇ 27 39 10N 76 0W
Queen Charlotte 62 53 15N 132 2W
Queen Charlotte Bay 78 51 50 S 60 40W
Queen Charlotte Is. 62 53 20N 132 10W
Queen Charlotte Sd. 128 41 10 S 174 15 E
Queen Charlotte Str. 62 51 0N 128 0W
Queen City, Mo. 32 40 25N 92 34W
Queen City, Tex. 51 33 9N 94 9W
Queen Creek 12 33 15N 111 35W
Queen Elizabeth Is. 6 76 0N 95 0W
Queen Mary Coast 5 70 0 S 95 0 E
Queen Maud G. 58 68 15N 102 30W
Queen Maud Ra. 5 86 0 S 160 0W
Queens Chan. 126 15 0 S 129 30 E
Queens County ◇ 39 40 40N 73 50W
Queenscliff 127 38 16 S 144 39 E
Queensland 18 31 46N 83 14W
Queensland □ 127 22 0 S 142 0 E
Queenstown, Australia 127 42 4 S 145 35 E
Queenstown, N.Z. 128 45 1 S 168 40 E
Queenstown, S. Africa 123 31 52 S 26 52 E
Queenstown, U.S.A. 27 38 59N 76 9W
Queets → 53 47 33N 124 21W
Queguay Grande → 76 32 9 S 58 9W
Queimadas 74 11 0 S 39 38W
Quela 122 9 10 S 16 56 E
Quelimane 123 17 53 S 36 58 E
Quelpart = Cheju Do 115 33 29N 126 34 E
Quemado 38 34 20N 108 30W
Quemú-Quemú 76 36 3 S 63 36W
Quenemo 24 38 35N 95 30W
Quequén 76 38 30 S 58 30W
Querco 72 13 50 S 74 52W
Querétaro 64 20 40N 100 23W
Querétaro □ 64 20 30N 100 0W
Queshan 115 32 55N 114 2 E
Quesnel 62 53 0N 122 30W
Quesnel → 62 52 58N 122 29W
Quesnel L. 62 52 30N 121 20W
Questa 38 36 42N 105 36W
Quetena 72 22 10 S 67 25W
Quetico Prov. Park 60 48 30N 91 45W
Quetrequile 78 41 33 S 69 22W
Quetta 107 30 15N 66 55 E
Quevedo 70 1 2 S 79 29W
Quezaltenango 66 14 50N 91 30W
Quezon City 111 14 38N 121 0 E
Qui Nhon 112 13 40N 109 13 E
Quiaca, La 76 22 5 S 65 35W
Quibaxe 122 8 24 S 14 27 E
Quibdo 70 5 42N 76 40W
Quiberon 90 47 29N 3 9W
Quíbor 70 9 56N 69 37W
Quick 62 54 36N 126 54W
Quidnet 28 41 18N 69 58W
Quiet L. 62 61 5N 133 5W
Quiindy 76 25 58 S 57 14W
Quila 64 24 23N 107 13W
Quilán, C. 78 43 15 S 74 30W
Quilcene 53 47 49N 122 53W
Quilengues 123 14 12 S 14 12 E
Quilimarí 76 32 5 S 71 30W
Quilino 76 30 14 S 64 29W
Quillabamba 72 12 50 S 72 50W
Quillacollo 72 17 26 S 66 17W
Quillagua 76 21 40 S 69 40W
Quillaicillo 76 31 17 S 71 40W
Quillota 76 32 54 S 71 16W
Quilmes 76 34 43 S 58 15W
Quilon 108 8 50N 76 38 E
Quilpie 127 26 35 S 144 11 E
Quilpué 76 33 5 S 71 33W
Quimby 23 42 38N 95 38W
Quime 72 17 2 S 67 15W
Quimilí 76 27 40 S 62 30W
Quimper 90 48 0N 4 9W
Quimperlé 90 47 53N 3 33W
Quinault 53 47 28N 123 51W
Quinault → 53 47 21N 124 18W
Quinault Indian Reservation 53 47 30N 124 5W
Quincemil 72 13 15 S 70 40W
Quincy, Calif. 14 39 56N 120 57W
Quincy, Fla. 17 30 35N 84 34W
Quincy, Ill. 21 39 56N 91 23W
Quincy, Mass. 28 42 15N 71 0W
Quincy, Mich. 29 41 57N 84 53W
Quincy, Ohio 42 10 18N 83 58W
Quinebaug 28 42 1N 71 57W
Quinebaug → 28 41 33N 72 3W
Quines 76 32 13 S 65 48W
Quinga 123 15 49 S 40 15 E
Quinhagak 11 59 45N 161 54W
Quinlan, Okla. 43 36 27N 99 3W
Quinlan, Tex. 51 32 55N 96 8W
Quinn → 35 40 53N 119 3W
Quintana Roo □ 65 19 0N 88 0W
Quintanar de la Orden 91 39 36N 3 5W
Quintanar de la Sierra 91 41 57N 2 55W
Quinter 24 39 4N 100 14W
Quintero 76 32 45 S 71 30W
Quinton 43 35 7N 95 22W
Quinwood 54 38 4N 80 42W
Quipungo 123 14 37 S 14 40 E
Quirihue 76 36 15 S 72 35W
Quiriquire 70 9 59N 63 13W
Quiruvilca 72 8 1 S 78 19W
Quissanga 123 12 24 S 40 28 E
Quitaque 50 34 22N 101 4W
Quitilipi 76 26 50 S 60 13W
Quitman, Ark. 13 35 23N 92 13W
Quitman, Ga. 18 30 47N 83 34W
Quitman, La. 25 32 21N 92 43W
Quitman, Miss. 31 32 2N 88 44W
Quitman, Tex. 51 32 48N 95 27W
Quitman County ◇, Ga. 18 31 50N 85 0W
Quitman County ◇, Miss. 31 34 12N 90 17W
Quitman Mts. 50 31 0N 105 16W
Quito 70 0 15 S 78 35W
Quixadá 74 4 55 S 39 0W
Quixeramobim 74 5 12 S 39 17W
Qulin 32 36 36N 90 15W
Qumrān 104 31 43N 35 27 E
Quneitra 104 33 7N 35 48 E
Quonochontaug 28 41 21N 71 43W
Quorn 127 32 25 S 138 0 E
Qûs 121 25 55N 32 50 E
Quseir 121 26 7N 34 16 E
Qusrah 104 32 5N 35 20 E

R

Raahe 96 64 40N 24 28 E
Ra'anana 104 32 12N 34 52 E
Raasay 84 57 25N 6 4W
Raasay, Sd. of 84 57 30N 6 8W
Raba 111 8 36 S 118 55 E
Rabat, Malta 94 35 53N 14 25 E
Rabat, Morocco 120 34 2N 6 48W
Rabaul 124 4 24 S 152 18 E
Rabbit → 62 59 41N 127 12W
Rabbit Cr. → 47 45 13N 102 10W
Rabbit Lake 63 53 8N 107 46W
Rabbitskin → 62 61 47N 120 42W
Rābigh 106 22 50N 39 5 E
Rabun County ◇ 18 34 50N 83 30W
Raccoon →, Iowa 23 41 35N 93 37W
Raccoon →, Ohio 42 40 2N 82 24W
Race, C. 61 46 40N 53 5W
Race Point 28 42 4N 70 14W
Raceland, Ky. 49 38 32N 82 44W
Raceland, La. 25 29 44N 90 36W
Rach Gia 112 10 5N 105 5 E
Racine 30 43 48N 92 31W
Rădăuţi 89 47 50N 25 59 E
Radcliff 49 37 51N 85 57W
Radcliffe 23 42 20N 93 25W
Radford 54 37 8N 80 34W
Radhwa, Jabal 106 24 34N 38 18 E
Radisson, Canada 63 52 30N 107 20W
Radisson, U.S.A. 55 45 45N 91 40W
Radium 24 38 12N 98 56W
Radium Hill 127 32 30 S 140 42 E
Radium Hot Springs 62 50 35N 116 2W
Radium Springs 38 32 30N 106 55W
Radnevo 95 42 17N 25 58 E
Radnor 42 40 23N 83 9W
Radnor Forest 83 52 17N 3 10W
Radom 89 51 23N 21 12 E
Radomir 95 42 37N 23 4 E
Radomsko 89 51 5N 19 28 E
Radstock 83 51 17N 2 25W
Radstock, C. 126 33 12 S 134 20 E
Radville 63 49 30N 104 15W
Rae 62 62 50N 116 3W
Rae Bareli 109 26 18N 81 20 E
Rae Isthmus 59 66 40N 87 30W
Raeren 87 50 41N 6 7 E
Raeside, L. 126 29 20 S 122 0 E
Raetihi 128 39 25 S 175 17 E
Rafaela 76 31 10 S 61 30W
Rafai 122 4 59N 23 58 E
Rafḥā 106 29 35N 43 35 E
Rafsanjān 107 30 30N 56 5 E
Raft → 20 42 37N 113 15W
Raft River Mts. 52 41 55N 113 25W
Ragama 108 7 0N 79 50 E
Ragan 34 40 19N 99 15W
Raglan 128 37 55 S 174 55 E
Ragland 10 33 45N 86 9W
Ragley 25 30 30N 93 15W
Rago 24 37 26N 98 4W
Ragusa 94 36 56N 14 42 E
Raha 111 4 55 S 123 0 E
Rahad al Bardī 121 11 20N 23 40 E
Rahaeng = Tak 112 16 52N 99 8 E
Rahway 37 40 37N 74 17W
Raichur 108 16 10N 77 20 E
Raiford 17 30 4N 82 14W
Raigarh 109 21 56N 83 25 E
Raiis 106 23 33N 38 43 E
Raijua 111 10 37 S 121 36 E
Railroad Valley 35 38 25N 115 40W
Rainbow City 10 33 57N 86 0W
Rainbow Lake 62 58 30N 119 23W
Rainbow Plateau 12 36 55N 111 0W
Rainelle 54 37 58N 80 47W
Rainier 53 46 53N 122 41W
Rainier, Mt. 53 46 52N 121 46W
Rains County ◇ 51 32 52N 95 46W
Rainsburg 45 39 54N 78 30W
Rainsville 10 34 30N 85 50W
Rainy → 30 48 50N 94 42W
Rainy L. 63 48 42N 93 10W
Rainy River 63 48 43N 94 29W
Raipur 109 21 17N 81 45 E
Raj Nandgaon 109 21 0N 81 0 E
Raja, Ujung 110 3 40N 96 25 E
Raja Ampat, Kepulauan 111 0 30 S 130 0 E
Rajahmundry 109 17 1N 81 48 E
Rajang → 110 2 30N 112 0 E
Rajapalaiyam 108 9 25N 77 35 E
Rajasthan □ 108 26 45N 73 30 E
Rajasthan Canal 108 28 0N 72 0 E
Rajgarh 108 24 2N 76 45 E
Rajkot 108 22 15N 70 56 E
Rajojooseppi 96 68 25N 28 30 E
Rajpipla 108 21 50N 73 30 E
Rajshahi 109 24 22N 88 39 E
Rajshahi □ 109 25 0N 89 0 E
Rakaia 128 43 45 S 172 1 E
Rakaia → 128 43 36 S 172 15 E
Rakan, Ra's 107 26 10N 51 20 E
Rakaposhi 108 36 10N 74 25 E
Rakata, Pulau 110 6 10 S 105 20 E
Rake 23 43 35N 93 50W
Rakitnoye 116 45 36N 134 17 E
Rakitovo 95 41 59N 24 5 E
Rakovski 95 42 21N 24 57 E
Raleigh, Fla. 17 29 25N 82 32W
Raleigh, N.C. 40 35 47N 78 39W
Raleigh, N. Dak. 41 46 20N 101 20W
Raleigh B. 40 34 50N 76 15W
Raleigh County ◇ 54 37 45N 81 10W
Ralls 50 33 41N 101 24W
Ralls County ◇ 32 39 30N 91 30W
Ralston, Nebr. 34 41 12N 96 3W
Ralston, Okla. 43 36 30N 96 44W
Ralston, Pa. 45 41 30N 76 57W
Ralston, Wyo. 56 44 43N 108 52W
Ram → 62 62 1N 123 41W
Rām Allāh 104 31 55N 35 10 E
Rama, Israel 104 32 56N 35 21 E
Rama, Nic. 66 12 9N 84 15W
Ramah 16 39 7N 104 10W
Ramalho, Serra do 75 13 45 S 44 0W
Ramanathapuram 108 9 25N 78 55 E
Ramat Gan 104 32 4N 34 48 E
Ramat HaSharon 104 32 7N 34 50 E
Rambipuji 111 8 12 S 113 37 E
Ramea 61 47 31N 57 23W
Ramechhap 109 27 25N 86 10 E
Ramelau 111 8 55 S 126 22 E
Ramer, Ala. 10 32 3N 86 13W
Ramer, Tenn. 48 35 4N 88 37W
Ramey 45 40 48N 78 24W
Ramgarh, Bihar, India 109 23 40N 85 35 E
Ramgarh, Raj., India 108 27 30N 70 36 E
Rāmhormoz 106 31 15N 49 35 E
Ramla 104 31 55N 34 52 E
Rammūn 104 31 55N 35 17 E
Ramnad = Ramanathapuram 108 9 25N 78 55 E
Ramon, Har 104 30 30N 34 38 E
Ramona, Calif. 15 33 2N 116 52W
Ramona, Kans. 24 38 36N 97 4W
Ramona, Okla. 43 36 32N 95 55W
Ramona, S. Dak. 47 44 7N 97 13W
Ramore 60 48 30N 80 25W
Ramos → 64 25 35N 105 3W
Rampart 11 65 30N 150 10W
Rampur 108 28 50N 79 5 E
Rampur Hat 109 24 10N 87 50 E
Ramree Kyun 109 19 0N 94 0 E
Ramsay, Mich. 29 46 28N 90 0W
Ramsay, Mont. 33 46 1N 112 42W
Ramseur 40 35 44N 79 39W
Ramsey, Canada 60 47 25N 82 20W
Ramsey, U.K. 82 54 20N 4 21W
Ramsey, Ill. 21 39 8N 89 7W
Ramsey, N.J. 37 41 4N 74 9W
Ramsey County ◇, Minn. 30 45 0N 93 5W
Ramsey County ◇, N. Dak. 41 48 15N 98 50W
Ramsgate 83 51 20N 1 25 E
Ramtek 108 21 20N 79 15 E
Ranaghat 109 23 15N 88 35 E
Ranau 110 6 2N 116 40 E
Rancagua 76 34 10 S 70 50W
Rancharia 75 22 15 S 50 55W
Rancheria → 62 60 13N 129 7W
Ranches of Taos 38 36 22N 105 37W
Ranchester 56 44 54N 107 10W
Ranchi 109 23 19N 85 27 E
Rancho Cordova 14 38 36N 121 18W
Ranco, L. 78 40 15 S 72 25W
Rancu 95 44 32N 24 15 E
Rand, Colo. 16 40 27N 106 11W
Rand, W. Va. 54 38 17N 81 34W
Randalia 23 42 52N 91 53W
Randall, Iowa 23 42 14N 93 35W
Randall, Kans. 24 39 38N 98 3W
Randall, Minn. 30 46 5N 94 30W
Randall County ◇ 50 34 59N 101 55W
Randallstown 27 39 22N 76 48W
Randers 97 56 29N 10 1 E
Randle 53 46 32N 121 57W
Randleman 40 35 49N 79 48W
Randlett 43 34 11N 98 28W
Randolph, Iowa 23 40 52N 95 34W
Randolph, Kans. 24 39 26N 96 46W
Randolph, Maine 26 44 14N 69 46W
Randolph, Mass. 28 42 10N 71 2W
Randolph, Miss. 31 34 11N 89 10W
Randolph, N.Y. 39 42 10N 78 59W
Randolph, Nebr. 34 42 23N 97 22W
Randolph, Utah 52 41 40N 111 11W
Randolph, Vt. 36 43 55N 72 40W
Randolph Center 36 43 55N 72 37W
Randolph County ◇, Ala. 10 33 20N 85 25W
Randolph County ◇, Ark. 13 36 20N 91 0W
Randolph County ◇, Ga. 18 31 45N 84 45W
Randolph County ◇, Ill. 21 38 0N 89 50W
Randolph County ◇, Ind. 22 40 10N 85 0W
Randolph County ◇, Mo. 32 39 25N 92 30W
Randolph County ◇, N.C. 40 35 40N 79 50W
Randolph County ◇, W. Va. 54 38 45N 80 0W
Råne älv → 96 65 50N 22 20 E
Rangaunu B. 128 34 51 S 173 15 E
Rangeley 26 44 58N 70 39W
Rangeley L. 26 44 55N 70 43W
Rangely 16 40 5N 108 48W
Ranger 51 32 28N 98 41W
Rangia 109 26 28N 91 38 E
Rangiora 128 43 19 S 172 36 E
Rangitaiki → 128 37 54 S 176 49 E
Rangitata → 128 43 45 S 171 15 E
Rangkasbitung 111 6 22 S 106 16 E
Rangon → 109 16 28N 96 40 E
Rangoon 109 16 45N 96 20 E
Rangpur 109 25 42N 89 22 E
Ranibennur 108 14 35N 75 30 E
Ranier 30 48 36N 93 20W
Raniganj 109 23 40N 87 5 E
Raniwara 108 24 50N 72 10 E
Rankin, Ill. 21 40 28N 87 54W
Rankin, Tex. 50 31 13N 101 56W
Rankin County ◇ 31 32 15N 90 0W
Rankin Inlet 58 62 30N 93 0W
Rannoch, L. 84 56 41N 4 20W
Rannoch Moor 84 56 38N 4 48W
Ranohira 123 22 29 S 45 24 E
Ranong 112 9 56N 98 40 E
Ransiki 111 1 30 S 134 10 E
Ransom, Ill. 21 41 9N 88 39W
Ransom, Kans. 24 38 38N 99 58W
Ransom County ◇ 41 46 30N 97 40W
Rantau 110 2 56 S 115 9 E
Rantauprapat 110 2 15N 99 50 E
Rantekombola 111 3 15 S 119 57 E
Rantīs 104 32 4N 35 3 E
Rantoul, Ill. 21 40 19N 88 9W
Rantoul, Kans. 24 38 33N 95 7W
Raohe 114 46 47N 134 0 E
Rapa Iti 125 27 35 S 144 20W
Rapang 111 3 45 S 119 55 E
Rāpch 107 25 40N 59 15 E
Rapelje 33 45 58N 109 14W
Rapid →, Canada 62 59 15N 129 5W
Rapid →, U.S.A. 30 48 42N 94 26W
Rapid City 47 44 5N 103 14W
Rapid Cr. → 47 43 54N 102 37W
Rapid River 29 45 55N 86 58W
Rapidan → 54 38 22N 77 37W
Rapides des Joachims 60 46 13N 77 43W
Rapides Parish ◇ 25 31 15N 92 30W
Rappahannock → 54 37 34N 76 18W
Rappahannock County ◇ 54 38 40N 78 10W
Raquette → 39 45 0N 74 42W
Rarden 42 38 55N 83 12W

Raritan Reynolds

Raritan 37 40 34N 74 38W
Raritan → 37 40 29N 74 17W
Raritan Bay 37 40 27N 74 15W
Rarotonga 125 21 30S 160 0W
Ra's al Khaymah 107 25 50N 56 5E
Ra's al-Unuf 121 30 25N 18 15E
Ras Bânâs 121 23 57N 35 59E
Ras Dashen 122 13 8N 38 26E
Ra's Tannūrah 106 26 40N 50 10E
Râs Timirist 120 19 21N 16 30W
Rasa, Punta 78 40 50S 62 15W
Rashad 121 11 55N 31 0E
Rashîd 121 31 21N 30 22E
Rasht 106 37 20N 49 40E
Rason, L. 126 28 45S 124 25E
Raşova 95 44 15N 27 55E
Rasovo 95 43 42N 23 17E
Rastu 95 43 53N 23 16E
Rat Buri 112 13 30N 99 54E
Rat Islands 11 52 0N 178 0W
Rat River 62 61 7N 112 36W
Ratangarh 108 28 5N 74 35E
Ratcliff 51 31 24N 95 8W
Rath Luirc 85 52 21N 8 40W
Rathbun 23 40 50N 92 50W
Rathbun L. 23 40 54N 93 5W
Rathdrum 85 52 57N 6 13W
Rathenow 88 52 38N 12 23E
Rathkeale 85 52 32N 8 57W
Rathlin I. 85 55 18N 6 14W
Rathlin O'Birne I. 85 54 40N 8 50W
Ratlam 108 23 20N 75 0E
Ratliff City 43 34 25N 97 30W
Ratnagiri 108 16 57N 73 18E
Raton 38 36 54N 104 24W
Rattan 43 34 12N 95 25W
Rattlesnake Cr. → 44 42 44N 117 47W
Rattlesnake Hills 56 42 45N 107 10W
Rattray Hd. 84 57 38N 1 50W
Ratz, Mt. 62 57 23N 132 12W
Raub 112 3 47N 101 52E
Rauch 76 36 45S 59 5W
Raufarhöfn 96 66 27N 15 57W
Raukumara Ra. 128 38 5S 177 55E
Raul Soares 75 20 5S 42 22W
Rauma 97 61 10N 21 30E
Rausu-Dake 116 44 4N 145 7E
Ravalli 33 47 17N 114 11W
Ravalli County ◇ 33 46 0N 114 0W
Rāvar 107 31 20N 56 51E
Ravena 39 42 28N 73 49W
Ravendale 14 40 48N 120 22W
Ravenel 46 32 46N 80 15W
Ravenna, Italy 94 44 28N 12 15E
Ravenna, Nebr. 34 41 1N 98 55W
Ravenna, Ohio 42 41 9N 81 15W
Ravenna, Tex. 51 33 40N 96 15W
Ravensburg 88 47 48N 9 38E
Ravenshoe 127 17 37S 145 29E
Ravensthorpe 126 33 35S 120 2E
Ravenswood 54 38 57N 81 46W
Ravenwood 32 40 22N 94 41W
Ravi → 108 30 35N 71 49E
Ravinia 47 43 8N 98 26W
Rawalpindi 108 33 38N 73 8E
Rawāndūz 106 36 40N 44 30E
Rawang 112 3 20N 101 35E
Rawdon 60 46 3N 73 40W
Rawene 128 35 25S 173 32E
Rawlinna 126 30 58S 125 28E
Rawlins 56 41 47N 107 14W
Rawlins County ◇ 24 39 45N 101 0W
Rawlinson Range 126 24 40S 128 30E
Rawson 78 43 15S 65 0W
Rawsonville 36 43 10N 72 50W
Ray, Minn. 30 48 25N 93 13W
Ray, N. Dak. 41 48 21N 103 10W
Ray, C. 61 47 33N 59 15W
Ray City 18 31 5N 83 11W
Ray County ◇ 32 39 20N 94 0W
Ray Mts. 11 66 0N 152 0W
Rayadurg 108 14 40N 76 50E
Rayagada 109 19 15N 83 20E
Raychikhinsk 101 49 46N 129 25E
Rayle 18 33 48N 82 54W
Raymond, Canada 62 49 30N 112 35W
Raymond, Calif. 14 37 13N 119 54W
Raymond, Ga. 18 33 20N 84 43W
Raymond, Ill. 21 39 19N 89 34W
Raymond, Kans. 24 38 17N 98 25W
Raymond, Minn. 30 45 2N 95 14W
Raymond, Miss. 31 32 16N 90 25W
Raymond, N.H. 36 43 2N 71 11W
Raymond, Nebr. 34 40 57N 96 47W
Raymond, S. Dak. 47 44 55N 97 56W
Raymond, Wash. 53 46 41N 123 44W
Raymondville, Mo. 32 37 20N 91 50W
Raymondville, Tex. 50 26 29N 97 47W
Raymore 63 51 25N 104 31W
Rayne 25 30 14N 92 16W
Rayón 64 29 43N 110 35W
Rayong 112 12 40N 101 20E
Raystown Branch → 45 40 27N 77 59W
Raystown L. 45 40 25N 78 5W
Raytown 32 39 1N 94 28W
Rayville, La. 25 32 29N 91 46W
Rayville, Mo. 32 39 21N 94 4W
Raz, Pte. du 90 48 2N 4 47W
Razdelna 95 43 13N 27 41E
Razdolnoye 116 43 30N 131 52E
Razelm, Lacul 95 44 50N 29 0E
Razgrad 95 43 33N 26 34E
Razlog 95 41 53N 23 28E
Ré, Île de 90 46 12N 1 30W
Reader 13 33 46N 93 6W
Reading, U.K. 83 51 27N 0 57W
Reading, Kans. 24 38 31N 95 58W
Reading, Mass. 28 42 32N 71 6W
Reading, Mich. 29 41 50N 84 45W
Reading, Ohio 42 39 13N 84 26W
Reading, Pa. 45 40 20N 75 56W
Readland 13 33 4N 91 13W
Readlyn 23 42 42N 92 14W
Readsboro 36 42 46N 72 57W
Readstown 55 43 27N 90 45W
Reagan 48 35 31N 88 20W
Reagan County ◇ 50 31 25N 101 34W
Real, Cordillera 72 17 0S 67 10W
Real County ◇ 51 29 55N 99 55W
Realicó 76 35 0S 64 15W
Realitos 50 27 27N 98 32W
Ream 112 10 34N 103 39E
Reardan 53 47 40N 117 53W
Reasnor 23 41 35N 93 1W
Reata 64 26 8N 101 5W
Rebi 111 6 23S 134 7E
Rebiana 121 24 12N 22 10E
Rebun-Tō 116 45 23N 141 2E
Recherche, Arch. of the 126 34 15S 122 50E
Recife 74 8 0S 35 0W
Reconquista 76 29 10S 59 45W
Recreio 73 8 0S 58 25W
Recreo 76 29 25S 65 10W
Rector 13 36 16N 90 17W
Recuay 72 9 43S 77 28W
Red →, Canada 63 50 24N 96 48W
Red →, Ky. 49 37 51N 84 5W
Red →, La. 25 31 1N 91 45W
Red →, N. Dak. 41 49 0N 97 15W
Red →, Tenn. 48 36 32N 87 22W
Red Bank, N.J. 37 40 21N 74 5W
Red Bank, Tenn. 49 35 7N 85 17W
Red Bay 61 51 44N 56 25W
Red Bluff 14 40 11N 122 15W
Red Bluff L. 38 31 54N 103 55W
Red Boiling Springs 49 36 32N 85 51W
Red Bud 21 38 13N 89 59W
Red Cedar → 55 44 42N 91 53W
Red Cliff Ind. Reservation 55 46 50N 90 47W
Red Cloud 34 40 5N 98 32W
Red Cr. → 31 30 41N 88 40W
Red Deer 62 52 20N 113 50W
Red Deer →, Alta., Canada 63 50 58N 110 0W
Red Deer →, Man., Canada 63 52 53N 101 1W
Red Deer L. 63 52 55N 101 20W
Red Devil 11 61 46N 157 19W
Red Feather Lakes 16 40 48N 105 35W
Red Head 17 30 29N 85 51W
Red Hills 24 37 40N 98 50W
Red Hook 39 41 55N 73 53W
Red Indian L. 61 48 35N 57 0W
Red L., Ariz. 12 35 40N 114 4W
Red L., S. Dak. 47 43 44N 99 13W
Red Lake 63 51 3N 93 49W
Red Lake → 30 47 55N 97 1W
Red Lake County ◇ 30 47 50N 96 0W
Red Lake Falls 30 47 53N 96 16W
Red Lake Indian Reservation 30 48 0N 95 20W
Red Level 10 31 24N 86 36W
Red Lion, N.J. 37 39 53N 74 45W
Red Lion, Pa. 45 39 54N 76 36W
Red Lodge 33 45 11N 109 15W
Red Mountain 15 35 37N 117 38W
Red Oak, Iowa 23 41 1N 95 14W
Red Oak, N.C. 40 36 2N 77 54W
Red Oak, Okla. 43 34 57N 95 5W
Red River County ◇ 51 33 37N 95 3W
Red River Parish ◇ 25 32 1N 93 21W
Red River Valley 41 48 0N 96 50W
Red Rock, Canada 60 48 55N 88 15W
Red Rock, Ariz. 12 36 36N 109 3W
Red Rock, Mont. 33 44 55N 112 50W
Red Rock, Okla. 43 36 28N 97 11W
Red Rock, L. 23 41 22N 92 59W
Red Rock Cr. → 43 36 30N 96 59W
Red Sea 105 25 0N 36 0E
Red Springs, N.C. 40 34 49N 79 11W
Red Springs, Tex. 51 33 37N 99 25W
Red Sucker L. 63 54 9N 93 40W
Red Tower Pass = Turnu Rosu Pasul 89 45 33N 24 17E
Red Willow County ◇ 34 40 15N 100 30W
Red Willow Cr. → 34 40 13N 100 29W
Red Wing 30 44 34N 92 31W
Redbay 17 30 35N 85 57W
Redbird 43 35 54N 95 36W
Redbridge 83 51 35N 0 7E
Redcar 82 54 37N 1 4W
Redcliff, Canada 63 50 10N 110 50W
Redcliff, U.S.A. 16 39 31N 106 22W
Reddell 25 30 40N 92 25W
Reddick, Fla. 17 29 22N 82 12W
Reddick, Ill. 21 41 6N 88 15W
Redding, Calif. 14 40 35N 122 24W
Redding, Iowa 23 40 36N 94 23W
Redding Ridge 28 41 19N 73 21W
Redditch 83 52 18N 1 57W
Redenção 74 4 13S 38 43W
Redfield, Ark. 13 34 27N 92 11W
Redfield, Iowa 23 41 35N 94 12W
Redfield, Kans. 24 37 50N 94 53W
Redfield, S. Dak. 47 44 53N 98 31W
Redford 50 29 27N 104 11W
Redkey 22 40 21N 85 9W
Redknife → 62 61 14N 119 22W
Redlake 30 47 53N 95 1W
Redlands 15 34 4N 117 11W
Redmesa 16 37 6N 108 11W
Redmon 21 39 39N 87 52W
Redmond, Oreg. 44 44 17N 121 11W
Redmond, Utah 52 39 0N 111 52W
Redmond, Wash. 53 47 41N 122 7W
Redonda 67 16 58N 62 19W
Redondela 91 42 15N 8 38W
Redondo 91 38 39N 7 37W
Redondo Beach 15 33 50N 118 23W
Redoubt Volcano 11 60 29N 152 45W
Redrock 38 32 41N 108 44W
Redrock Pt. 62 62 11N 115 2W
Redruth 83 50 14N 5 14W
Redstone 16 39 11N 107 14W
Redstone Cr. → 47 44 4N 98 5W
Redvale 16 38 10N 108 25W
Redvers 63 49 35N 101 40W
Redwater 62 53 55N 113 6W
Redwater → 33 48 3N 105 13W
Redwood 31 32 29N 90 48W
Redwood → 30 44 34N 95 5W
Redwood City 14 37 30N 122 15W
Redwood County ◇ 30 44 20N 95 15W
Redwood Cr. → 14 41 18N 124 5W
Redwood Falls 30 44 32N 95 7W
Redwood National Park 14 41 40N 124 5W
Ree, L. 85 53 35N 8 0W
Ree Heights 47 44 31N 99 12W
Reece 24 37 48N 96 27W
Reed, Ky. 48 37 51N 87 21W
Reed, Okla. 43 34 54N 99 42W
Reed, L. 63 54 38N 100 30W
Reed City 29 43 53N 85 31W
Reeder 41 46 7N 102 57W
Reedley 15 36 36N 119 27W
Reeds 32 37 7N 94 10W
Reeds Pk. 38 33 9N 107 51W
Reeds Spring 32 36 45N 93 23W
Reedsburg 55 43 32N 90 0W
Reedsport 44 43 42N 124 6W
Reedsville, Va. 54 37 51N 76 17W
Reedsville, W. Va. 54 39 31N 79 48W
Reedy 54 38 54N 81 26W
Reedy → 46 28 4N 81 21W
Reefton 128 42 6S 171 51E
Reelfoot L. 48 36 25N 89 22W
Reese 29 43 27N 83 42W
Reese → 35 40 48N 117 4W
Reeves 25 30 31N 93 3W
Reeves County ◇ 50 31 13N 103 45W
Reform 10 33 23N 88 1W
Refugio 51 28 18N 97 17W
Refugio County ◇ 51 28 14N 97 20W
Regan 41 47 10N 100 32W
Regavim 104 32 32N 35 2E
Regeneração 74 6 15S 42 41W
Regensburg 88 49 1N 12 7E
Regent 41 46 25N 102 33W
Réggio di Calábria 94 38 7N 15 38E
Réggio nell' Emilia 94 44 42N 10 38E
Regina, Canada 63 50 27N 104 35W
Régina, Fr. Gui. 71 4 19N 52 8W
Register 18 32 22N 81 53W
Registro 77 24 29S 47 49W
Rehoboth, Namibia 123 23 15S 17 4E
Rehoboth, U.S.A. 38 35 32N 108 39W
Rehoboth Bay 27 38 40N 75 6W
Rehoboth Beach 27 38 43N 131 15W
Rehovot 104 31 54N 34 48E
Rei-Bouba 121 8 40N 14 15E
Reichenbach 88 50 36N 12 19E
Reidsville, Ga. 18 32 6N 82 7W
Reidsville, N.C. 40 36 21N 79 40W
Reigate 83 51 14N 0 11W
Reims 90 49 15N 4 0E
Reina 104 32 43N 35 18E
Reina Adelaida, Arch. 78 52 20S 74 0W
Reinbeck 23 42 19N 92 36W
Reindeer → 63 55 36N 103 11W
Reindeer I. 63 52 30N 98 0W
Reindeer L. 63 57 15N 102 15W
Reinga, C. 128 34 25S 172 43E
Reisterstown 27 39 28N 76 50W
Rekinniki 101 60 51N 163 40E
Reliance, Canada 63 63 0N 109 20W
Reliance, Del. 27 38 38N 75 43W
Reliance, S. Dak. 47 43 53N 99 36W
Reliance, Wyo. 56 41 40N 109 12W
Remanso 74 9 41S 42 4W
Rembang 111 6 42S 111 21E
Rembert 46 34 6N 80 32W
Rembrandt 23 42 50N 95 10W
Remedios, Colombia 70 7 2N 74 41W
Remedios, Panama 66 8 15N 81 50W
Remer 30 47 4N 93 55W
Remeshk 107 26 55N 58 50E
Remetea 95 46 45N 25 29E
Remich 87 49 32N 6 22E
Remington, Ind. 22 40 46N 87 9W
Remington, Va. 54 38 32N 77 49W
Rémire 71 4 53N 52 17W
Remscheid 88 51 11N 7 12E
Remsen, Iowa 23 42 49N 95 58W
Remsen, N.Y. 39 43 20N 75 11W
Renascença 70 3 50S 66 21W
Rend Lake 21 38 2N 88 58W
Rendsburg 88 54 18N 9 41E
Rene 101 66 2N 179 25W
Renfrew, Canada 60 45 30N 76 40W
Renfrew, U.K. 84 55 52N 4 24W
Renfroe 18 32 14N 84 43W
Rengat 110 0 30S 102 45E
Rengo 76 34 24S 70 50W
Renhuai 115 27 48N 106 24E
Renick 54 38 1N 80 22W
Renk 121 11 50N 32 50E
Renkum 87 51 58N 5 43E
Renmark 127 34 11S 140 43E
Rennell Sd. 62 53 23N 132 35W
Renner Springs T.O. 126 18 20S 133 47E
Rennes 90 48 7N 1 41W
Reno, Minn. 30 43 36N 91 17W
Reno, Nev. 35 39 31N 119 48W
Reno → 94 44 37N 12 17E
Reno County ◇ 24 38 0N 98 0W
Renovo 45 41 20N 77 45W
Rensselaer, Ind. 22 40 57N 87 9W
Rensselaer, N.Y. 39 42 38N 73 45W
Rensselaer County ◇ 39 42 40N 73 30W
Rentiesville 43 35 35N 95 30W
Renton 53 47 29N 122 12W
Rentz 18 32 25N 82 59W
Renville 30 44 48N 95 13W
Renville County ◇, Minn. 30 44 45N 95 0W
Renville County ◇, N. Dak. 41 48 37N 101 35W
Renwick 23 42 50N 93 59W
Repton 10 31 25N 87 14W
Republic, Kans. 24 39 55N 97 49W
Republic, Mich. 29 46 25N 87 59W
Republic, Mo. 32 37 7N 93 29W
Republic, Ohio 42 41 8N 83 1W
Republic, Wash. 53 48 39N 118 44W
Republic County ◇ 24 39 45N 97 40W
Republican → 24 39 4N 96 48W
Republican City 34 40 6N 99 13W
Republiek 71 5 30N 55 13W
Repulse B., Antarct. 5 64 30S 99 30E
Repulse B., Australia 127 20 31S 148 45E
Repulse Bay 59 66 30N 86 30W
Requena, Peru 72 5 5S 73 52W
Requena, Spain 91 39 30N 1 4W
Reserve, Canada 63 52 28N 102 39W
Reserve, Kans. 24 39 59N 95 34W
Reserve, La. 25 30 3N 90 33W
Reserve, N. Mex. 38 33 43N 108 45W
Resht = Rasht 106 37 20N 49 40E
Resistencia 76 27 30S 59 0W
Reşiţa 89 45 18N 21 53E
Resolution I., Canada 59 61 30N 65 0W
Resolution I., N.Z. 128 45 40S 166 40E
Resplandes 74 6 17S 45 13W
Resplendor 75 19 20S 41 15W
Reston 63 49 33N 101 6W
Retalhuleu 66 14 33N 91 46W
Réthímnon 95 35 18N 24 30E
Réunion 3 22 0S 56 0E
Reutlingen 88 48 28N 9 13E
Reval = Tallinn 98 59 22N 24 48E
Revda 98 56 48N 59 57E
Revelstoke 62 51 0N 118 10W
Reventazón 72 6 10S 80 58W
Revere, Mass. 28 42 25N 71 1W
Revere, Mo. 32 40 35N 91 41W
Revilla Gigedo, Is. 125 18 40N 112 0W
Revillo 47 45 1N 96 34W
Rewa 109 24 33N 81 25E
Rewa → 71 3 19N 58 42W
Rewari 108 28 15N 76 40E
Rewey 55 42 51N 90 24W
Rexburg 20 43 49N 111 47W
Rexford, Kans. 24 39 28N 100 45W
Rexford, Mont. 33 48 53N 115 13W
Rey Malabo 122 3 45N 8 50E
Reydon 43 35 39N 99 55W
Reyes 72 14 19S 67 23W
Reyes, Pt. 14 38 0N 123 0W
Reykjahlið 96 65 40N 16 55W
Reykjanes 96 63 48N 22 40W
Reykjavík 96 64 10N 21 57E
Reynolds, Canada 63 49 40N 95 55W
Reynolds, Ga. 18 32 33N 84 6W
Reynolds, Ill. 21 41 20N 90 40W
Reynolds, Ind. 22 40 45N 86 52W
Reynolds, N. Dak. 41 47 40N 97 7W
Reynolds, Nebr. 34 40 4N 97 20W

Reynolds County Robbinsville

Reynolds County **32** 37 20N 91 0W
Reynolds Ra. **126** 22 30 S 133 0 E
Reynoldsville **18** 30 51N 84 47W
Reynosa **65** 26 5N 98 18W
Reynosa Draz **50** 26 15N 98 30W
Rezovo **95** 42 0N 28 0 E
Rhame **41** 46 14N 103 39W
Rhayader **83** 52 19N 3 30W
Rhea County ◇ **49** 35 30N 85 0W
Rheden **87** 52 0N 6 3 E
Rhein **63** 51 25N 102 15W
Rhein → **87** 51 52N 6 20 E
Rheine **88** 52 17N 7 25 E
Rheinland-Pfalz □ **88** 50 0N 7 0 E
Rhin = Rhein → **87** 51 52N 6 20 E
Rhine = Rhein → **87** 51 52N 6 20 E
Rhine **18** 31 59N 83 12W
Rhinelander **55** 45 38N 89 25W
Rhode Island **28** 41 30N 71 15W
Rhode Island □ **28** 41 40N 71 30W
Rhode Island Sd. **28** 41 20N 71 10W
Rhodes = Ródhos **95** 36 15N 28 10 E
Rhodesia = Zimbabwe ■ **123** 20 0 S 30 0 E
Rhodhiss L. **40** 35 47N 81 26W
Rhodope Mts. = Rhodopi Planina **95** 41 40N 24 20 E
Rhodopi Planina **95** 41 40N 24 20 E
Rhome **51** 33 3N 97 28W
Rhön **88** 50 24N 9 58 E
Rhondda **83** 51 39N 3 30W
Rhône □ **90** 45 54N 4 35 E
Rhône → **90** 43 28N 4 42 E
Rhum **84** 57 0N 6 20W
Rhumney **83** 51 32N 3 7W
Rhyl **82** 53 19N 3 29W
Riachão **74** 7 20 S 46 37W
Riacho de Santana **75** 13 37 S 42 57W
Rialma **75** 15 18 S 49 34W
Riasi **108** 33 10N 74 50 E
Riau □ **110** 0 0 102 35 E
Riau, Kepulauan **110** 0 30N 104 20 E
Rib Lake **55** 45 19N 90 12W
Ribadeo **91** 43 35N 7 5W
Ribamar **74** 2 33 S 44 3W
Ribas do Rio Pardo **73** 20 27 S 53 46W
Ribat **123** 29 50N 60 55 E
Ribatejo □ **91** 39 15N 8 30W
Ribble → **82** 54 13N 2 20W
Ribe **97** 55 19N 8 44 E
Ribeira do Pombal **74** 10 50 S 38 32W
Ribeirão Prêto **75** 21 10 S 47 50W
Ribeiro Gonçalves **74** 7 32 S 45 14W
Ribera **38** 35 23N 105 27W
Riberalta **73** 11 0 S 66 0W
Ricardo **50** 27 25N 97 51W
Riccarton **128** 43 32 S 172 37 E
Rice, Calif. **15** 34 5N 114 51W
Rice, Minn. **30** 45 45N 94 13W
Rice, Tex. **51** 32 14N 96 30W
Rice County ◇, Kans. **24** 38 25N 98 10W
Rice County ◇, Minn. **30** 44 20N 93 15W
Rice Lake **55** 45 30N 91 44W
Riceboro **18** 31 44N 81 26W
Riceville, Iowa **23** 43 22N 92 33W
Riceville, Ky. **49** 37 44N 82 55W
Riceville, Tenn. **49** 35 23N 84 42W
Rich County ◇ **52** 41 30N 111 10W
Rich Fountain **32** 38 24N 91 53W
Rich Hill **32** 38 6N 94 22W
Rich Square **40** 36 16N 77 17W
Richards, Mo. **32** 37 54N 94 33W
Richards, Tex. **51** 30 32N 95 51W
Richards L. **63** 59 10N 107 10W
Richardson **51** 32 57N 96 44W
Richardson → **63** 58 25N 111 14W
Richardson County ◇ **34** 40 15N 95 45W
Richardson Lakes **26** 44 46N 70 58W
Richardton **41** 46 53N 102 19W
Richey **33** 47 39N 105 4W
Richfield, Idaho **20** 43 3N 114 9W
Richfield, Kans. **24** 37 16N 101 47W
Richfield, Minn. **30** 44 53N 93 17W
Richfield, Pa. **45** 40 41N 77 7W
Richfield, Utah **52** 38 46N 112 5W
Richfield Springs **39** 42 51N 74 59W
Richford **36** 45 0N 72 40W
Richgrove **15** 35 48N 119 7W
Richibucto **61** 46 42N 64 54W
Richland, Ga. **18** 32 5N 84 40W
Richland, Mich. **29** 42 22N 85 27W
Richland, Mo. **32** 37 51N 92 26W
Richland, Nebr. **34** 41 26N 97 13W
Richland, Oreg. **44** 44 46N 117 10W
Richland, S. Dak. **47** 42 46N 96 39W
Richland, Tex. **51** 31 57N 96 26W
Richland, Wash. **53** 46 17N 119 18W
Richland Center **55** 43 21N 90 23W
Richland County ◇, Ill. **21** 38 45N 88 5W
Richland County ◇, Mont. **33** 47 48N 104 40W
Richland County ◇, N. Dak. **41** 46 15N 97 0W
Richland County ◇, Ohio **42** 40 45N 82 31W
Richland County ◇, S.C. **46** 34 10N 81 0W
Richland County ◇, Wis. **55** 43 20N 90 30W
Richland Parish ◇ **25** 32 22N 91 52W
Richland Springs **51** 31 16N 98 57W
Richlands, N.C. **40** 34 54N 77 34W
Richlands, Va. **54** 37 6N 81 48W
Richmond, Australia **127** 20 43 S 143 8 E
Richmond, N.Z. **128** 41 20 S 173 12 E
Richmond, S. Africa **123** 29 51 S 30 18 E
Richmond, N. Yorks., U.K. **82** 54 24N 1 43W
Richmond, Surrey, U.K. **83** 51 28N 0 18W
Richmond, Calif. **14** 37 56N 122 21W
Richmond, Ill. **21** 42 29N 88 18W
Richmond, Ind. **22** 39 50N 84 53W
Richmond, Kans. **24** 38 24N 95 15W
Richmond, Ky. **49** 37 45N 84 18W
Richmond, Maine **26** 44 5N 69 48W
Richmond, Mich. **29** 42 49N 82 45W
Richmond, Mo. **32** 39 17N 93 58W
Richmond, N.H. **36** 42 45N 72 18W
Richmond, Tex. **51** 29 35N 95 46W
Richmond, Utah **52** 41 56N 111 48W
Richmond, Va. **54** 37 33N 77 27W
Richmond, Vt. **36** 44 24N 72 59W
Richmond County ◇, Ga. **18** 33 15N 82 5W
Richmond County ◇, N.C. **40** 35 0N 79 45W
Richmond County ◇, N.Y. **39** 40 40N 74 15W
Richmond County ◇, Va. **54** 37 58N 76 46W
Richmond Heights **17** 25 38N 80 23W
Richmond Highlands **53** 47 46N 122 21W
Richmond Hill **18** 31 56N 81 18W
Richmond Ra. **128** 41 32 S 173 22 E
Richmondville **39** 42 38N 74 34W
Richton **31** 31 16N 88 56W
Richville, Minn. **30** 46 31N 95 38W
Richville, N.Y. **39** 44 25N 75 22W
Richwood, Ohio **42** 40 26N 83 18W
Richwood, W. Va. **54** 38 14N 80 32W
Richwoods **32** 38 10N 90 50W
Ricketts **23** 42 8N 95 35W
Rico **16** 37 42N 108 2W
Riddle, Idaho **20** 42 11N 116 7W
Riddle, Oreg. **44** 42 57N 123 22W
Ridge **27** 38 8N 76 24W
Ridge Farm **21** 39 54N 87 39W
Ridge Spring **46** 33 51N 81 40W
Ridgecrest **15** 35 38N 117 40W
Ridgedale **63** 53 0N 104 10W
Ridgefield, Conn. **28** 41 17N 73 30W
Ridgefield, Wash. **53** 45 49N 122 45W
Ridgeland, Miss. **31** 32 26N 90 8W
Ridgeland, S.C. **46** 32 29N 80 59W
Ridgeland, Wis. **55** 45 12N 91 54W
Ridgely **48** 36 16N 89 29W
Ridgetop **48** 36 24N 86 46W
Ridgetown **60** 42 26N 81 52W
Ridgeville, Ind. **22** 40 18N 85 2W
Ridgeville, S.C. **46** 33 6N 80 19W
Ridgeway, Iowa **23** 43 18N 91 59W
Ridgeway, Mo. **32** 40 23N 93 57W
Ridgeway, Ohio **42** 40 31N 83 35W
Ridgeway, S.C. **46** 34 18N 80 58W
Ridgeway, Va. **54** 36 35N 79 52W
Ridgeway, Wis. **55** 43 1N 90 1W
Ridgewood **37** 40 59N 74 7W
Ridgway, Colo. **16** 38 9N 107 46W
Ridgway, Ill. **21** 37 48N 88 16W
Ridgway, Pa. **45** 41 25N 78 44W
Riding Mt. Nat. Park **63** 50 50N 100 0W
Ried **88** 48 14N 13 30 E
Rienzi **31** 34 46N 88 32W
Riesco, I. **78** 52 55 S 72 40W
Riesel **51** 31 29N 96 55W
Rieth **44** 45 40N 118 54W
Rieti **94** 42 23N 12 50 E
Riffe L. **53** 46 32N 122 26W
Rifle **16** 39 32N 107 47W
Rifstangi **96** 66 32N 16 12W
Rig Rig **121** 14 13N 14 25 E
Riga **98** 56 53N 24 8 E
Riga, G. of = Rīgas Jūras Līcis **98** 57 40N 23 45 E
Rīgas Jūras Līcis **98** 57 40N 23 45 E
Rigby **20** 43 40N 111 55W
Rīgestān □ **107** 30 15N 65 0 E
Riggins **20** 45 25N 116 19W
Rigolet **61** 54 10N 58 23W
Riihimäki **97** 60 45N 24 48 E
Riiser-Larsen-halvøya **5** 68 0 S 35 0 E
Rijeka **94** 45 20N 14 21 E
Rijn → **87** 52 12N 4 21 E
Rijssen **87** 52 19N 6 30 E
Rijswijk **87** 52 4N 4 22 E
Rikuzentakada **116** 39 0N 141 40 E
Rila **95** 42 7N 23 7 E
Riley, Ind. **22** 39 23N 87 18W
Riley, Kans. **24** 39 18N 96 50W
Riley, Oreg. **44** 43 32N 119 28W
Riley County ◇ **24** 39 20N 96 40W
Rillito **12** 32 25N 111 9W
Rimah, Wadi ar → **106** 26 5N 41 30 E
Rimbey **62** 52 35N 114 15W
Rimersburg **45** 41 3N 79 30W
Rímini, Italy **94** 44 3N 12 33 E
Rimini, U.S.A. **46** 33 40N 80 30W
Rîmna → **95** 45 36N 27 3 E
Rîmnicu Sărat **89** 45 26N 27 3 E
Rîmnicu Vîlcea **89** 45 9N 24 21 E
Rimouski **61** 48 27N 68 30W
Rinard **23** 42 20N 94 29W
Rinca **111** 8 45 S 119 35 E
Rincon, Puerto Rico **57** 18 20N 67 15W
Rincon, U.S.A. **18** 32 18N 81 14W
Rincon, Bahia de **57** 17 55N 66 20W
Rincón de Romos **64** 22 14N 102 18W
Rinconada **76** 22 26 S 66 10W
Rineanna **85** 52 42N 85 7W
Rineyville **49** 37 45N 85 58W
Ringgold, Ga. **18** 34 55N 85 7W
Ringgold, La. **25** 32 20N 93 17W
Ringgold, Nebr. **34** 41 31N 100 47W
Ringgold County ◇ **23** 40 45N 94 15W
Ringkøbing **97** 56 5N 8 15 E
Ringling, Mont. **33** 46 16N 110 49W
Ringling, Okla. **43** 34 11N 97 36W
Ringoes **37** 40 26N 74 52W
Ringsted **23** 43 18N 94 31W
Ringvassøy **96** 69 56N 19 15 E
Ringwood, N.J. **37** 41 7N 74 15W
Ringwood, Okla. **43** 36 23N 98 15W
Rinía **95** 37 23N 25 13 E
Rinjani **110** 8 24 S 116 28 E
Rio, Ill. **21** 41 7N 90 24W
Rio, Wis. **55** 43 27N 89 14W
Rio Arriba County ◇ **38** 36 30N 106 45W
Rio Blanco **16** 39 44N 107 57W
Rio Blanco County ◇ **16** 40 0N 108 15W
Rio Branco, Brazil **72** 9 58 S 67 49W
Río Branco, Uruguay **77** 32 40 S 53 40W
Rio Brilhante **77** 21 48 S 54 33W
Río Bueno **78** 40 19 S 72 58W
Río Chico **70** 10 19N 65 59W
Rio Claro, Brazil **77** 22 19 S 47 35W
Rio Claro, Trin. & Tob. **67** 10 20N 61 25W
Río Colorado **78** 39 0 S 64 0W
Río Cuarto **76** 33 10 S 64 25W
Rio de Contas **75** 13 36 S 41 48W
Rio de Janeiro **75** 23 0 S 43 12W
Rio de Janeiro □ **75** 22 50 S 43 0W
Rio Dell **14** 40 30N 124 6W
Rio do Prado **75** 16 35 S 40 34W
Rio do Sul **77** 27 13 S 49 37W
Río Gallegos **78** 51 35 S 69 15W
Río Grande, Argentina **78** 53 50 S 67 45W
Río Grande, Bolivia **72** 20 51 S 67 17W
Rio Grande, Brazil **77** 32 0 S 52 20W
Río Grande, Mexico **64** 23 50N 103 2W
Río Grande, Nic. **66** 12 54N 83 33W
Río Grande, Puerto Rico **57** 18 23N 65 50W
Rio Grande, N.J. **37** 39 1N 74 53W
Rio Grande, Ohio **42** 38 56N 82 21W
Rio Grande City **50** 26 23N 98 49W
Rio Grande County ◇ **16** 37 40N 106 20W
Rio Grande do Norte □ **74** 5 40 S 36 0W
Rio Grande do Sul □ **77** 30 0 S 53 0W
Rio Grande National Forest **16** 37 30N 106 30W
Río Hato **66** 8 22N 80 10W
Rio Hondo **50** 26 14N 97 35W
Rio Lagartos **65** 21 36N 88 10W
Rio Largo **74** 9 28 S 35 50W
Río Mayo **78** 45 40 S 70 15W
Río Mulatos **72** 19 40 S 66 50W
Río Muni = Mbini □ **122** 1 30N 10 0 E
Rio Negro, Brazil **77** 26 0 S 50 0W
Río Negro, Chile **78** 40 47 S 73 14W
Río Negro, Pantanal do **73** 19 0 S 56 0W
Rio Pardo **77** 30 0 S 52 30W
Río Pico **78** 44 0 S 70 22W
Rio Piedras **57** 18 24N 66 3W
Rio Real **75** 11 28 S 37 56W
Río Segundo **76** 31 40 S 63 59W
Río Tercero **76** 32 15 S 64 8W
Río Tinto **74** 6 48 S 35 5W
Rio Verde, Brazil **75** 17 50 S 51 0W
Río Verde, Mexico **65** 21 56N 99 59W
Rio Verde de Mato Grosso **73** 18 56 S 54 52W
Rio Vista **14** 38 10N 121 42W
Ríobamba **70** 1 50 S 78 45W
Ríohacha **70** 11 33N 72 55W
Rioja **72** 6 11 S 77 5W
Rioja, La **76** 29 20 S 67 0W
Rioja, La □, Argentina **76** 29 30 S 67 0W
Rioja, La □, Spain **91** 42 20N 2 20W
Rion **46** 34 18N 81 8W
Rionegro **70** 6 9N 75 22W
Riosucio, Caldas, Colombia **70** 5 30N 75 40W
Riosucio, Choco, Colombia **70** 7 27N 77 7W
Riou L. **63** 59 7N 106 25W
Riozinho → **70** 2 55 S 67 7W
Ripley, Ill. **21** 40 1N 90 38W
Ripley, Miss. **31** 34 44N 88 57W
Ripley, N.Y. **39** 42 16N 79 43W
Ripley, Ohio **42** 38 45N 83 51W
Ripley, Okla. **43** 36 1N 96 54W
Ripley, Tenn. **48** 35 45N 89 32W
Ripley, W. Va. **54** 38 49N 81 43W
Ripley County ◇, Ind. **22** 39 5N 85 15W
Ripley County ◇, Mo. **32** 36 40N 90 50W
Ripon, U.K. **82** 54 8N 1 31W
Ripon, Calif. **14** 37 44N 121 7W
Ripon, Wis. **55** 43 51N 88 50W
Rippey **23** 41 56N 94 12W
Ririe **20** 43 38N 111 47W
Ririe L. **20** 43 30N 111 43W
Risaralda □ **70** 5 0N 76 10W
Risco **32** 36 33N 89 49W
Rishiri-Tō **116** 45 11N 141 15 E
Rishon le Ẕiyyon **104** 31 58N 34 48 E
Rishpon **104** 32 12N 34 49 E
Rising City **34** 41 12N 97 18W
Rising Fawn **18** 34 46N 85 32W
Rising Star **51** 32 6N 98 58W
Rising Sun, Ind. **22** 38 57N 84 51W
Rising Sun, Md. **27** 39 42N 76 4W
Rîsnov **95** 45 35N 25 27 E
Rison **13** 33 58N 92 11W
Risør **97** 58 43N 9 13 E
Rita Blanca Cr. → **50** 35 40N 102 29W
Rita Blanca National Grassland **50** 36 20N 102 30W
Ritchie County ◇ **54** 39 13N 81 3W
Ritchies Archipelago **112** 12 5N 94 0 E
Ritter, Mt. **14** 37 41N 119 12W
Rittman **42** 40 58N 81 47W
Ritzville **53** 47 8N 118 23W
Riva **27** 38 57N 76 35W
Rivadavia, Buenos Aires, Argentina **76** 35 29 S 62 59W
Rivadavia, Mendoza, Argentina **76** 33 13 S 68 30W
Rivadavia, Salta, Argentina **76** 24 5 S 62 54W
Rivadavia, Chile **76** 29 57 S 70 35W
Rivas **66** 11 30N 85 50W
River Falls **55** 44 52N 92 38W
Rivera **77** 31 0 S 55 50W
Riverbank **14** 37 44N 120 56W
Riverdale, Calif. **15** 36 26N 119 52W
Riverdale, Ga. **18** 33 34N 84 25W
Riverdale, N. Dak. **41** 47 30N 101 22W
Riverdale, Nebr. **34** 40 47N 99 10W
Riverdsale **123** 34 7 S 21 15 E
Riverhead **39** 40 55N 72 40W
Riverhurst **63** 50 55N 106 50W
Riverina **127** 35 30 S 145 20 E
Rivers **63** 50 2N 100 14W
Rivers, L. of the **63** 49 49N 105 44W
Rivers Inlet **62** 51 40N 127 20W
Riverside, Calif. **15** 33 59N 117 22W
Riverside, Iowa **23** 41 29N 91 35W
Riverside, Md. **27** 38 22N 77 11W
Riverside, N.J. **37** 40 2N 74 58W
Riverside, Oreg. **44** 43 32N 118 10W
Riverside, Tex. **51** 30 51N 95 24W
Riverside, Wash. **53** 48 30N 119 30W
Riverside, Wyo. **56** 41 13N 106 47W
Riverside County ◇ **15** 33 45N 116 0W
Riverside Reservoir **16** 40 20N 104 15W
Riverton, Canada **63** 51 1N 97 0W
Riverton, N.Z. **128** 46 21 S 168 0 E
Riverton, Ill. **21** 39 51N 89 33W
Riverton, Iowa **23** 40 41N 95 34W
Riverton, Kans. **24** 37 5N 94 42W
Riverton, La. **25** 32 10N 92 6W
Riverton, Nebr. **34** 40 5N 98 46W
Riverton, Oreg. **44** 43 10N 124 16W
Riverton, Utah **52** 40 31N 111 56W
Riverton, W. Va. **54** 38 45N 79 26W
Riverton, Wyo. **56** 43 2N 108 23W
Riverton Heights **53** 47 28N 122 17W
Riverview **17** 27 52N 82 20W
Rivesville **54** 39 32N 80 7W
Riviera, Ariz. **12** 35 8N 114 32W
Riviera, Tex. **50** 27 18N 97 49W
Riviera Beach, Fla. **17** 26 47N 80 3W
Riviera Beach, Md. **27** 39 10N 76 31W
Rivière-à-Pierre **61** 46 59N 72 11W
Rivière-au-Renard **61** 48 59N 64 23W
Rivière-du-Loup **61** 47 50N 69 30W
Rivière-Pentecôte **61** 49 57N 67 1W
Rivière-Pilot **67** 14 26N 60 53W
Riyadh = Ar Riyāḍ **106** 24 41N 46 42 E
Rize **106** 41 0N 40 30 E
Rizhao **115** 35 25N 119 30 E
Rizzuto, C. **94** 38 54N 17 5 E
Rjukan **97** 59 54N 8 33 E
Roach L. **35** 35 41N 115 22W
Roachdale **22** 39 51N 86 48W
Roag, L. **84** 58 10N 6 55W
Roan Cliffs **52** 39 20N 109 40W
Roan Cr. → **16** 39 20N 108 13W
Roan Mountain **49** 36 12N 82 4W
Roan Plateau **52** 39 20N 109 20W
Roanaoke I. **40** 35 53N 75 39W
Roane County ◇, Tenn. **49** 35 52N 84 31W
Roane County ◇, W. Va. **54** 38 48N 81 21W
Roanne **90** 46 3N 4 4 E
Roanoke, Ala. **10** 33 9N 85 22W
Roanoke, Ill. **21** 40 48N 89 12W
Roanoke, Ind. **22** 40 58N 85 22W
Roanoke, Tex. **51** 33 0N 97 10W
Roanoke, Va. **54** 37 16N 79 56W
Roanoke → **40** 35 57N 76 42W
Roanoke County ◇ **54** 37 16N 79 56W
Roanoke Rapids **40** 36 28N 77 40W
Roanoke Rapids L. **40** 36 29N 77 40W
Roaring Spring **45** 40 20N 78 24W
Roaring Springs **50** 33 54N 100 52W
Roatán **66** 16 18N 86 35W
Robards **48** 37 41N 87 33W
Robbins, N.C. **40** 35 26N 79 35W
Robbins, Tenn. **49** 36 21N 84 35W
Robbinsville **40** 35 19N 83 48W

Robe Ross Ice Shelf

Robe → 85 53 38N 9 10W
Robersonville 40 35 50N 77 15W
Robert Lee 50 31 54N 100 29W
Robert S. Kerr Reservoir 43 35 21N 94 47W
Roberta 18 32 43N 84 1W
Roberts, Idaho 20 43 43N 112 8W
Roberts, Ill. 21 40 37N 88 11W
Roberts, Mont. 33 45 22N 109 10W
Roberts County ◇, S. Dak. 47 45 33N 96 57W
Roberts County ◇, Tex. 50 35 55N 100 55W
Robertsdale 10 30 33N 87 43W
Robertson 123 33 46 S 19 50 E
Robertson County ◇, Ky. 49 38 30N 84 5W
Robertson County ◇, Tenn. 48 36 31N 86 53W
Robertson County ◇, Tex. 51 31 2N 96 29W
Robertson I. 5 65 15 S 59 30W
Robertsport 120 6 45N 11 26W
Robertsville 37 40 21N 74 17W
Roberval 61 48 32N 72 15W
Robeson Ch. 4 82 0N 61 30W
Robeson County ◇ 40 34 30N 79 10W
Robesonia 45 40 21N 76 8W
Robinson, Ill. 21 39 0N 87 44W
Robinson, Kans. 24 39 49N 95 25W
Robinson, N. Dak. 41 47 9N 99 47W
Robinson, Tex. 51 31 28N 97 7W
Robinson, L. 46 34 30N 80 12W
Robinson Crusoe I. 125 33 38 S 78 52W
Robinson Mt. 33 48 58N 115 25W
Robinson Ranges 126 25 40 S 119 0 E
Robla, La 91 42 50N 5 41W
Roblin 63 51 14N 101 21W
Roboré 73 18 10 S 59 45W
Robson, Mt. 62 53 10N 119 10W
Robstown 51 27 47N 97 40W
Roby, Mo. 32 37 31N 92 8W
Roby, Tex. 50 32 45N 100 23W
Roca 34 40 39N 96 40W
Roca, C. da 91 38 40N 9 31W
Roca Partida, I. 64 19 1N 112 2W
Rocas, I. 74 4 0 S 34 1W
Rocha 77 34 30 S 54 25W
Rochdale, U.K. 82 53 36N 2 10W
Rochdale, U.S.A. 28 42 12N 71 54W
Roche, La 90 46 4N 6 19 E
Rochedo 73 19 57 S 54 52W
Rochefort, Belgium 87 50 9N 5 12 E
Rochefort, France 90 45 56N 0 57W
Rochelle, Ga. 18 31 57N 83 27W
Rochelle, Ill. 21 41 56N 89 4W
Rochelle, Tex. 51 31 14N 99 13W
Rochelle, La 90 46 10N 1 9W
Rocheport 32 38 59N 92 34W
Rocher River 62 61 23N 112 44W
Rochester, Canada 62 54 22N 113 27W
Rochester, U.K. 83 51 22N 0 30 E
Rochester, Ill. 21 39 45N 89 32W
Rochester, Ind. 22 41 4N 86 13W
Rochester, Ky. 48 37 13N 86 53W
Rochester, Mass. 28 41 44N 70 49W
Rochester, Mich. 29 42 41N 83 8W
Rochester, Minn. 30 44 1N 92 28W
Rochester, N.H. 36 43 18N 70 59W
Rochester, N.Y. 39 43 10N 77 37W
Rochester, Ohio 42 41 8N 82 18W
Rochester, Tex. 51 33 19N 99 51W
Rochester, Vt. 36 43 51N 72 48W
Rochester, Wash. 53 46 49N 123 6W
Rociu 95 44 43N 25 2 E
Rock 29 46 4N 87 10W
Rock →, Canada 62 60 7N 127 7W
Rock →, U.S.A. 21 41 29N 90 37W
Rock Cave 54 38 50N 80 21W
Rock County ◇, Minn. 30 43 45N 96 15W
Rock County ◇, Nebr. 34 42 30N 99 30W
Rock County ◇, Wis. 55 42 45N 89 10W
Rock Cr. →, Ill. 21 41 42N 90 3W
Rock Cr. →, Nev. 35 40 39N 116 55W
Rock Cr. →, Oreg. 44 45 34N 120 25W
Rock Cr. →, S. Dak. 47 43 44N 97 58W
Rock Cr. →, Utah 52 40 17N 110 30W
Rock Cr. →, Mont. 33 46 43N 113 40W
Rock Cr. →, Mont. 33 48 27N 107 6W
Rock Creek 42 41 40N 80 52W
Rock Creek Butte 44 44 49N 118 7W
Rock Falls, Ill. 21 41 47N 89 41W
Rock Falls, Iowa 23 43 13N 93 5W
Rock Hall 27 39 8N 76 14W
Rock Hill 46 34 56N 81 1W
Rock Island, Ill. 21 41 30N 90 34W
Rock Island, Wash. 53 47 22N 120 8W
Rock Island County ◇ 21 41 25N 90 30W
Rock Island Dam 53 47 23N 120 4W
Rock Point 27 38 16N 76 50W
Rock Rapids 23 43 26N 96 10W
Rock River 56 41 44N 105 58W
Rock Sound 66 24 54N 76 12W
Rock Spring 18 34 50N 85 14W
Rock Springs, Mont. 33 46 49N 106 15W
Rock Springs, Wyo. 56 41 35N 109 14W
Rock Valley 23 43 12N 96 18W
Rockall 80 57 37N 13 42W
Rockaway 44 45 37N 123 57W
Rockbridge 21 39 16N 90 12W
Rockbridge County ◇ 54 37 55N 79 20W
Rockcastle → 49 36 58N 84 21W
Rockcastle County ◇ 49 37 20N 84 20W
Rockdale 51 30 39N 97 0W
Rockdale County ◇ 18 33 40N 84 0W
Rockefeller Plat. 5 80 0 S 140 0W
Rockford, Ala. 10 32 53N 86 13W
Rockford, Ill. 21 42 16N 89 6W
Rockford, Iowa 23 43 3N 92 57W
Rockford, Mich. 29 43 7N 85 34W
Rockford, Minn. 30 45 5N 93 44W
Rockford, Ohio 42 40 41N 84 39W
Rockford, Wash. 53 47 27N 117 8W
Rockglen 63 49 11N 105 57W
Rockham 47 44 55N 98 49W
Rockhampton 127 23 22 S 150 32 E
Rockingham 40 34 57N 79 46W
Rockingham County ◇, N.C. 40 36 20N 79 50W
Rockingham County ◇, N.H. 36 43 0N 71 10W
Rockingham County ◇, Va. 54 38 27N 78 52W
Rockingham Forest 83 52 28N 0 42W
Rocklake 41 48 47N 99 15W
Rockland, Idaho 20 42 34N 112 53W
Rockland, Maine 26 44 6N 69 7W
Rockland, Mass. 28 42 8N 70 55W
Rockland, Mich. 29 46 44N 89 11W
Rockland, Wis. 55 43 54N 90 55W
Rockland County ◇ 39 41 10N 74 5W
Rockledge 17 28 20N 80 43W
Rocklin 14 38 48N 121 14W
Rockmart 18 34 0N 85 3W
Rockport, Calif. 14 39 44N 123 49W
Rockport, Ind. 22 37 53N 87 3W
Rockport, Mass. 28 42 39N 70 37W
Rockport, Mo. 32 40 25N 95 31W
Rockport, Tex. 51 28 2N 97 3W
Rockport, Wash. 53 48 29N 121 36W
Rocksprings 50 30 1N 100 13W
Rockton 21 42 27N 89 4W
Rockville, Conn. 28 41 52N 72 28W
Rockville, Ind. 22 39 46N 87 14W
Rockville, Md. 27 39 5N 77 9W
Rockville, Mo. 32 38 4N 94 5W
Rockville, Nebr. 34 41 7N 98 50W
Rockwall 51 32 56N 96 28W
Rockwall County ◇ 51 32 56N 96 28W
Rockwell, Iowa 23 42 59N 93 11W
Rockwell, N.C. 40 35 33N 80 25W
Rockwell City 23 42 24N 94 38W
Rockwood, Maine 26 45 41N 69 45W
Rockwood, Pa. 45 39 55N 79 9W
Rockwood, Tenn. 49 35 52N 84 41W
Rocky 43 35 9N 99 3W
Rocky → 40 35 9N 80 4W
Rocky Boy 33 48 16N 109 47W
Rocky Boys Indian Reservation 33 48 25N 109 30W
Rocky Comfort Cr. → 18 32 59N 82 25W
Rocky Ford, Colo. 16 38 3N 103 43W
Rocky Ford, Ga. 18 32 40N 81 50W
Rocky Fork 49 36 2N 82 33W
Rocky Hill 28 41 40N 72 39W
Rocky Lane 62 58 31N 116 22W
Rocky Mount, N.C. 40 35 57N 77 48W
Rocky Mount, Va. 54 37 12N 79 57W
Rocky Mountain House 62 52 22N 114 55W
Rocky Mountain National Park 16 40 25N 105 45W
Rocky Mts., N. Amer. 62 55 0N 121 0W
Rocky Mts., U.S.A. 16 39 0N 106 0W
Rocky Pt. 126 33 30 S 123 57 E
Rocky Point 40 34 26N 77 53W
Rocky Ridge 27 39 38N 77 20W
Rocky Top 44 44 47N 122 17W
Rockyford 62 51 14N 113 10W
Rod 107 28 10N 63 5 E
Roda, La 91 39 13N 2 15W
Rødbyhavn 97 54 39N 11 22 E
Roddickton 61 50 51N 56 8W
Rodeo 38 31 50N 109 2W
Roderick I. 62 52 38N 128 22W
Rodez 90 44 21N 2 33 E
Ródhos 95 36 15N 28 10 E
Rodman 23 43 2N 94 32W
Rodney 23 42 12N 95 57W
Rodney, C. 128 36 17 S 174 50 E
Rodoni, C. 95 41 32N 19 30 E
Rodriguez 3 19 45 S 63 20 E
Roe → 85 55 10N 6 59W
Roebling 37 40 7N 74 47W
Roebourne 126 20 44 S 117 9 E
Roebuck B. 126 18 5 S 122 20 E
Roeland Park 24 39 2N 94 39W
Roermond 87 51 12N 6 0 E
Roes Welcome Sd. 59 65 0N 87 0W
Roeselare 87 50 57N 3 7 E
Roff 43 34 38N 96 50W
Rogagua, L. 72 13 43 S 66 50W
Rogaland fylke □ 97 59 12N 6 20 E
Roger Mills County ◇ 43 35 45N 99 45W
Rogers, Ark. 13 36 20N 94 7W
Rogers, La. 25 31 32N 92 14W
Rogers, N. Dak. 41 47 4N 98 12W
Rogers, Nebr. 34 41 28N 96 55W
Rogers, Tex. 51 30 56N 97 14W
Rogers, Mt. 54 36 40N 81 33W
Rogers City 29 45 25N 83 49W
Rogers County ◇ 43 36 20N 95 40W
Rogers L. 15 34 55N 117 50W
Rogerson 20 42 13N 114 36W
Rogersville, Ala. 10 34 50N 87 18W
Rogersville, Mo. 32 37 7N 93 3W
Rogersville, Tenn. 49 36 24N 83 1W
Roggan 60 54 25N 79 32W
Roggen 16 40 10N 104 22W
Rogoaguado, L. 73 13 0 S 65 30W
Rogue → 44 42 26N 124 26W
Rogue River 44 42 26N 123 10W
Rogue River Nat. Forest 44 42 54N 122 22W
Rohnerville 14 40 34N 124 8W
Rohri 108 27 45N 68 51 E
Rohtak 108 28 55N 76 43 E
Roi Et 112 16 4N 103 40 E
Rojas 76 34 10 S 60 45W
Rojo, Cabo 57 17 56N 67 12W
Rojo, C. 65 21 33N 97 20W
Rokan → 110 2 0N 100 50 E
Roland, Iowa 23 42 10N 93 30W
Roland, Okla. 43 35 25N 94 31W
Rolândia 77 23 18 S 51 23W
Rolette 41 48 40N 99 51W
Rolette County ◇ 41 48 55N 99 55W
Rolfe 23 42 49N 94 31W
Roll 12 32 45N 113 59W
Rolla, Kans. 24 37 7N 101 38W
Rolla, Mo. 32 37 57N 91 46W
Rolla, N. Dak. 41 48 52N 99 37W
Rolling Fork 31 32 55N 90 53W
Rolling Fork → 49 37 55N 85 50W
Roma, Australia 127 26 32 S 148 49 E
Roma, Italy 94 41 54N 12 30 E
Roma, Sweden 97 57 32N 18 26 E
Roma-Los Saenz 50 26 24N 99 5W
Romain C. 46 33 0N 79 22W
Roman, Bulgaria 95 43 8N 23 54 E
Roman, Romania 89 46 57N 26 55 E
Roman, U.S.S.R. 101 66 4N 112 14 E
Romana, La 67 18 27N 68 57W
Romang 111 7 30 S 127 20 E
Romania ■ 89 46 0N 25 0 E
Romano, Cayo 66 22 0N 77 30W
Romano C. 17 25 51N 81 41W
Romanzof C. 11 61 49N 166 6W
Romblon 111 12 33N 122 17 E
Rome = Roma 94 41 54N 12 30 E
Rome, Ga. 18 34 15N 85 10W
Rome, Ill. 21 40 53N 89 30W
Rome, N.Y. 39 43 13N 75 27W
Rome, Pa. 45 41 51N 76 21W
Rome City 22 41 30N 85 23W
Romeo, Colo. 16 37 10N 105 59W
Romeo, Mich. 29 42 48N 83 1W
Romeoville 21 41 39N 88 3W
Romero 50 35 44N 102 56W
Romîni 95 44 59N 24 11 E
Romney 54 39 21N 78 45W
Romney Marsh 83 51 0N 1 0 E
Romorantin-Lanthenay 90 47 21N 1 45 E
Romsdalen 96 62 25N 8 0 E
Rona 84 57 33N 6 0W
Ronan 33 47 32N 114 6W
Roncador, Cayos 66 13 32N 80 4W
Roncador, Serra do 75 12 30 S 52 30W
Ronceverte 54 37 45N 80 28W
Ronda 91 36 46N 5 12W
Rondane 97 61 57N 9 50 E
Rondón 70 6 17N 71 6W
Rondônia 73 10 52 S 61 57W
Rondônia □ 73 11 0 S 63 0W
Rondonópolis 73 16 28 S 54 38W
Rondout Res. 39 41 50N 74 29W
Rong, Koh 112 10 45N 103 15 E
Rong Xian 115 29 23N 104 22 E
Rong'an 115 25 14N 109 22 E
Ronge, L. la 63 55 6N 105 17W
Ronge, La 63 55 5N 105 20W
Rongshui 115 25 5N 109 12 E
Ronkonkoma 39 40 48N 73 7W
Ronne Ice Shelf 5 78 0 S 60 0W
Ronse 87 50 45N 3 35 E
Ronuro → 73 11 56 S 53 33W
Roodepoort-Maraisburg 123 26 8 S 27 52 E
Roodhouse 21 39 29N 90 24W
Roof Butte 12 36 28N 109 5W
Rooks County ◇ 24 39 20N 99 15W
Roopville 18 33 27N 85 8W
Roorkee 108 29 52N 77 59 E
Roosendaal 87 51 32N 4 29 E
Roosevelt, Ariz. 12 33 41N 111 9W
Roosevelt, Minn. 30 48 48N 95 6W
Roosevelt, Okla. 43 34 51N 99 1W
Roosevelt, Utah 52 40 18N 109 59W
Roosevelt → 73 7 35 S 60 20W
Roosevelt, Mt. 62 58 26N 125 20W
Roosevelt County ◇, Mont. 33 48 20N 105 20W
Roosevelt County ◇, N. Mex. 38 34 0N 103 30W
Roosevelt I. 5 79 30 S 162 0W
Roosevelt National Forest 16 40 45N 105 40W
Roper 40 35 53N 76 37W
Roper → 126 14 43 S 135 27 E
Ropesville 50 33 26N 102 9W
Roque Pérez 76 35 25 S 59 24W
Roraima □ 71 2 0N 61 30W
Roraima, Mt. 71 5 10N 60 40W
Rorketon 63 51 24N 99 35W
Røros 96 62 35N 11 23 E
Rosa 122 9 33 S 31 15 E
Rosa, Monte 88 45 57N 7 53 E
Rosalia 53 47 14N 117 22W
Rosamond L. 15 34 50N 118 4W
Rosario, Argentina 76 33 0 S 60 40W
Rosário, Brazil 74 3 0 S 44 15W
Rosario, Baja Calif. N., Mexico 64 30 0N 115 50W
Rosario, Durango, Mexico 64 26 30N 105 35W
Rosario, Sinaloa, Mexico 64 23 0N 105 52W
Rosario, Paraguay 76 24 30 S 57 35W
Rosario, Villa del 70 10 19N 72 19W
Rosario de la Frontera 76 25 50 S 65 0W
Rosario de Lerma 76 24 59 S 65 35W
Rosario del Tala 76 32 20 S 59 10W
Rosário do Sul 77 30 15 S 54 55W
Rosário Oeste 73 14 50 S 56 25W
Rosarito 64 28 38N 114 4W
Rosas 91 42 19N 3 10 E
Rosas, G. de 91 42 10N 3 15 E
Rosburg 53 46 20N 123 38W
Roscoe, Ill. 21 42 25N 89 1W
Roscoe, S. Dak. 47 45 27N 99 20W
Roscoe, Tex. 50 32 27N 100 32W
Roscommon, Ireland 85 53 38N 8 11W
Roscommon, U.S.A. 29 44 30N 84 35W
Roscommon □ 85 53 40N 8 15W
Roscommon County ◇ 29 44 15N 84 40W
Roscrea 85 52 58N 7 50W
Rose 34 42 9N 99 28W
Rose, Mt. 35 39 21N 119 55W
Rose Blanche 61 47 38N 58 45W
Rose Bud 13 35 20N 92 5W
Rose City 29 44 25N 84 7W
Rose Creek 30 43 36N 92 50W
Rose Harbour 62 52 15N 131 10W
Rose Hill, Ill. 21 39 6N 88 9W
Rose Hill, Iowa 23 41 19N 92 28W
Rose Hill, Kans. 24 37 34N 97 7W
Rose Hill, N.C. 40 34 50N 78 2W
Rose Pk. 12 33 25N 109 21W
Rose Pt. 62 54 11N 131 39W
Rose Valley 63 52 19N 103 49W
Roseau, Domin. 67 15 20N 61 24W
Roseau, U.S.A. 30 48 51N 95 46W
Roseau → 30 49 0N 96 30W
Roseau County ◇ 30 48 45N 95 50W
Roseboro 40 34 58N 78 31W
Rosebud, Mo. 32 38 23N 91 25W
Rosebud, Mont. 33 46 16N 106 27W
Rosebud, S. Dak. 47 43 14N 100 51W
Rosebud, Tex. 51 31 4N 96 59W
Rosebud County ◇ 33 46 30N 106 45W
Rosebud Indian Reservation 47 43 10N 101 0W
Roseburg 44 43 13N 123 20W
Rosebush 29 43 42N 84 46W
Rosedale, Md. 27 39 19N 76 31W
Rosedale, Miss. 31 33 51N 91 2W
Rosedale, Okla. 43 34 55N 97 11W
Rosedale, W. Va. 54 38 44N 80 57W
Roseglen 41 47 45N 101 50W
Roseland, La. 25 30 46N 90 31W
Roseland, Nebr. 34 40 28N 98 34W
Rosemary 62 50 46N 112 5W
Rosemont 27 39 20N 77 37W
Rosemount 30 44 45N 93 8W
Rosenberg 51 29 34N 95 49W
Rosendale 30 45 2N 94 43W
Rosenhayn 37 39 29N 75 8W
Rosenheim 88 47 51N 12 9 E
Rosepine 25 30 55N 93 17W
Rosetown 63 51 35N 107 59W
Rosetta = Rashîd 121 31 21N 30 22 E
Rosette 52 41 49N 113 25W
Roseville, Calif. 14 38 45N 121 17W
Roseville, Ill. 21 40 44N 90 40W
Roseville, Mich. 29 42 30N 82 56W
Roseville, Minn. 30 45 1N 93 10W
Roseville, Ohio 42 39 49N 82 5W
Roseville, Pa. 45 41 52N 76 58W
Rosh Haniqra, Kefar 104 33 5N 35 5 E
Rosh Pinna 104 32 58N 35 32 E
Rosharon 51 29 21N 95 28W
Rosholt, S. Dak. 47 45 52N 96 44W
Rosholt, Wis. 55 44 38N 89 18W
Rosiclare 21 37 26N 88 21W
Rosier 18 32 59N 82 15W
Rosignol 71 6 15N 57 30W
Roşiori de Vede 95 44 9N 25 0 E
Rositsa 95 43 57N 27 57 E
Rositsa → 95 43 10N 25 30 E
Roskilde 97 55 38N 12 3 E
Roslavl 98 53 57N 32 55 E
Roslyn, S. Dak. 47 45 30N 97 29W
Roslyn, Wash. 53 47 13N 120 59W
Rosman 40 35 9N 82 49W
Ross, N.Z. 128 42 53 S 170 49 E
Ross, U.S.A. 41 48 19N 102 33W
Ross County ◇ 42 39 20N 82 59W
Ross Dependency □ 5 70 0 S 170 5W
Ross I. 5 77 30 S 168 0 E
Ross Ice Shelf 5 80 0 S 180 0 E

Ross L. Sage Cr.

Ross L. 53 48 44N 121 4W
Ross Lake National Recreation Area 53 48 43N 121 4W
Ross on Wye 83 51 55N 2 34W
Ross R. Barnett Reservoir 31 32 24N 90 4W
Ross Sea 5 74 0 S 178 0 E
Rossan Pt. 85 54 42N 8 47W
Rossburg 42 40 17N 84 38W
Rossburn 63 50 40N 100 49W
Rossford 42 41 36N 83 34W
Rossie 23 43 1N 95 11W
Rossignol, L., N.S., Canada 61 44 12N 65 10W
Rossignol, L., Qué., Canada 60 52 43N 73 40W
Rossiter 45 40 54N 78 56W
Rossland 62 49 6N 117 50W
Rosslare 85 52 17N 6 23W
Rosso 120 16 40N 15 45W
Rossosh 99 50 15N 39 28 E
Rossport 60 48 50N 87 30W
Rosston, Ark. 13 33 36N 93 17W
Rosston, Okla. 43 36 49N 99 56W
Røssvatnet 96 65 45N 14 5 E
Rossville, Ill. 21 40 23N 87 40W
Rossville, Ind. 22 40 25N 86 36W
Rossville, Kans. 24 39 8N 95 57W
Rosthern 63 52 40N 106 20W
Rostock 88 54 4N 12 9 E
Rostov, Don, U.S.S.R. 99 47 15N 39 45 E
Rostov, Moskva, U.S.S.R. 98 57 14N 39 25 E
Roswell, Ga. 18 34 2N 84 22W
Roswell, N. Mex. 38 33 24N 104 32W
Rosyth 84 56 2N 3 26W
Rotan 50 32 51N 100 28W
Rothaargebirge 88 51 0N 8 20 E
Rother → 83 50 59N 0 40 E
Rotherham 82 53 26N 1 21W
Rothes 84 57 31N 3 12W
Rothesay, Canada 61 45 23N 66 0W
Rothesay, U.K. 84 55 50N 5 3W
Rothsay 30 46 28N 96 17W
Rothschild 55 44 53N 89 37W
Roti 111 10 50 S 123 0 E
Roto 127 33 0 S 145 30 E
Rotoroa, L. 128 41 55 S 172 39 E
Rotorua 128 38 9 S 176 16 E
Rotorua, L. 128 38 5 S 176 18 E
Rotterdam, Neth. 87 51 55N 4 30 E
Rotterdam, U.S.A. 39 42 48N 74 1W
Rottumeroog 87 53 33N 6 34 E
Rottweil 88 48 9N 8 38 E
Rotuma 124 12 25 S 177 5 E
Roubaix 90 50 40N 3 10 E
Rouen 90 49 27N 1 4 E
Rougemont 40 36 13N 78 56W
Rough River L. 48 37 37N 86 30W
Rouleau 63 50 10N 104 56W
Roulette 45 41 47N 78 9W
Round Hill 54 39 8N 77 46W
Round Lake 30 43 32N 95 28W
Round Mt. 127 30 26 S 152 16 E
Round Mountain, Nev. 35 38 43N 117 4W
Round Mountain, Tex. 51 30 26N 98 21W
Round Oak 18 33 7N 83 37W
Round Rock, Ariz. 12 36 31N 109 28W
Round Rock, Tex. 51 30 31N 97 41W
Round Top 51 30 4N 96 42W
Round Valley Indian Reservation 14 39 50N 123 20W
Roundup 33 46 27N 108 33W
Roura 71 4 44N 52 20W
Rousay 84 59 10N 3 2W
Rouses Point 39 44 59N 73 22W
Rouseville 45 41 28N 79 42W
Roussillon 90 42 30N 2 35 E
Routt County ◇ 16 40 30N 107 0W
Routt National Forest 16 40 45N 107 0W
Rouyn 60 48 20N 79 0W
Rovaniemi 96 66 29N 25 41 E
Rover 48 35 40N 86 36W
Rovereto 94 45 53N 11 3 E
Rovigo 94 45 4N 11 48 E
Rovinj 94 45 5N 13 40 E
Rovira 70 4 15N 75 20W
Rovno 99 50 40N 26 10 E
Rovuma → 122 10 29 S 40 28 E
Rowan 23 42 45N 93 33W
Rowan County ◇, Ky. 49 38 10N 83 25W
Rowan County ◇, N.C. 40 35 40N 80 30W
Rowe 38 35 30N 105 41W
Rowena 51 31 39N 100 3W
Rowesville 46 33 22N 80 50W
Rowland 40 34 32N 79 18W
Rowlesburg 54 39 21N 79 40W
Rowlett 51 32 54N 96 34W
Rowley 23 42 22N 91 51W
Rowley Shoals 126 17 30 S 119 0 E
Roxana 27 38 30N 75 10W
Roxas 111 11 36N 122 49 E
Roxboro 40 36 24N 78 59W
Roxburgh 128 45 33 S 169 19 E
Roxbury, Conn. 28 41 45N 73 11W
Roxbury, Kans. 24 38 33N 97 26W
Roxbury, N.Y. 39 42 17N 74 34W
Roxbury, Vt. 36 44 8N 72 44W
Roxie 31 31 30N 91 4W
Roxton 51 33 33N 95 44W
Roy, Fla. 17 29 37N 81 29W
Roy, Mont. 33 47 20N 108 58W
Roy, N. Mex. 38 35 57N 104 12W
Roy, Utah 52 41 10N 112 2W
Roy, Wash. 53 47 0N 122 33W
Royal 23 43 4N 95 17W
Royal Center 22 40 52N 86 30W
Royal City 53 46 54N 119 38W
Royal Oak, Md. 27 38 44N 76 11W
Royal Oak, Mich. 29 42 30N 83 9W
Royalston 28 42 40N 72 12W
Royalton 30 45 50N 94 18W
Royalty 50 31 22N 102 52W
Royan 90 45 37N 1 2W
Royersford 45 40 11N 75 33W
Royse City 51 32 59N 96 20W
Royston 18 34 17N 83 7W
Rozel 24 38 12N 99 24W
Rtishchevo 98 55 16N 43 50 E
Ruahine Ra. 128 39 55 S 176 2 E
Ruapehu 128 39 17 S 175 35 E
Ruapuke I. 128 46 46 S 168 31 E
Rub' al Khali 105 18 0N 48 0 E
Rubh a' Mhail 84 55 55N 6 10W
Rubha Hunish 84 57 42N 6 20W
Rubiataba 75 15 8 S 49 48W
Rubicone → 94 44 8N 12 28 E
Rubinéia 75 20 13 S 51 2W
Rubio 70 7 43N 72 22W
Rubtsovsk 100 51 30N 81 10 E
Ruby, Alaska 11 64 45N 155 30W
Ruby, S.C. 46 34 44N 80 11W
Ruby Dome 35 40 37N 115 28W
Ruby L. 35 40 10N 115 28W
Ruby Mts. 35 40 30N 115 20W
Ruby Valley 35 40 30N 115 21W
Rudnichnyy 98 59 38N 52 26 E
Rudnik 95 42 36N 27 30 E
Rudnogorsk 101 57 15N 103 42 E
Rudnyy 100 52 57N 63 7 E
Rudolf, Ostrov 100 81 45N 58 30 E
Rudolph 55 44 30N 89 48W
Rudozem 95 41 29N 24 51 E
Rudy 13 35 31N 94 16W
Rudyard, Mich. 29 46 14N 84 36W
Rudyard, Mont. 33 48 34N 110 33W
Rufa'a 121 14 44N 33 22 E
Rufflin 46 33 0N 80 49W
Rufiji → 122 7 50 S 39 15 E
Rufino 76 34 20 S 62 50W
Rufisque 120 14 40N 17 15W
Rufus 44 45 42N 120 44W
Rugao 115 32 23N 120 31 E
Rugby, U.K. 83 52 23N 1 16W
Rugby, U.S.A. 41 48 22N 100 0W
Rügen 88 54 22N 13 25 E
Ruhama 104 31 31N 34 43 E
Ruhr → 88 51 25N 6 44 E
Rui Barbosa 75 12 18 S 40 27W
Rui'an 115 27 47N 120 40 E
Ruidosa 50 29 59N 104 41W
Ruidoso 38 33 20N 105 41W
Ruidoso Downs 38 33 20N 105 32W
Rukwa L. 122 8 0 S 32 20 E
Rule 51 33 11N 99 54W
Ruleville 31 33 44N 90 33W
Rulo 34 40 3N 95 26W
Rum → 30 45 11N 93 23W
Rum Cay 66 23 40N 74 58W
Rum Jungle 126 13 0 S 130 59 E
Rumāḩ 106 25 29N 47 10 E
Rumania = Romania ■ 89 46 0N 25 0 E
Rumbêk 121 6 54N 29 37 E
Rumbley 27 38 6N 75 51W
Rumford 26 44 33N 70 33W
Rumney 36 43 47N 71 48W
Rumoi 116 43 56N 141 39W
Rump Mt. 26 45 12N 71 4W
Rumsey 62 51 51N 112 48W
Rumson 37 40 23N 74 0W
Runan 115 33 0N 114 30 E
Runanga 128 42 25 S 171 15 E
Runcorn 82 53 20N 2 44W
Runge 51 28 53N 97 43W
Rungwa 122 6 55 S 33 32 E
Runnells 23 41 31N 93 21W
Runnels County ◇ 51 31 51N 99 57W
Running Water → 50 34 0N 101 30W
Ruoqiang 113 38 55N 88 10 E
Rupa 109 27 15N 92 21 E
Rupat 110 1 45N 101 40 E
Rupea 95 46 2N 25 13 E
Rupert, Idaho 20 42 37N 113 41W
Rupert, Vt. 36 43 16N 73 13W
Rupert, W. Va. 54 37 58N 80 41W
Rupert → 60 51 29N 78 45W
Rupert House = Fort Rupert 60 51 30N 78 40W
Rupununi → 71 4 3N 58 35W
Rural Hall 40 36 15N 80 18W
Rural Retreat 54 36 54N 81 17W
Rurrenabaque 72 14 30 S 67 32W
Rusape 123 18 35 S 32 8 E
Ruschuk = Ruse 95 43 48N 25 59 E
Ruse 95 43 48N 25 59 E
Ruşeţu 95 44 57N 27 14 E
Rush 49 38 20N 82 46W
Rush Center 24 38 28N 99 19W
Rush City 30 45 41N 92 58W
Rush County ◇, Ind. 22 39 35N 85 30W
Rush County ◇, Kans. 24 38 30N 99 15W
Rush Cr. → 16 38 22N 102 32W
Rush Springs 43 34 47N 97 58W
Rushden 83 52 17N 0 37W
Rushford 30 43 49N 91 46W
Rushmore, Mt. 47 43 53N 103 28W
Rushville, Ill. 21 40 7N 90 34W
Rushville, Ind. 22 39 37N 85 27W
Rushville, Mo. 32 39 35N 95 1W
Rushville, Nebr. 34 42 43N 102 28W
Rusk 51 31 48N 95 9W
Rusk County ◇, Tex. 51 32 9N 94 48W
Rusk County ◇, Wis. 55 45 25N 91 10W
Ruskin, Fla. 17 27 43N 82 26W
Ruskin, Nebr. 34 40 9N 97 52W
Ruso 41 47 50N 100 56W
Russas 74 4 55 S 37 50W
Russell, Canada 63 50 50N 101 20W
Russell, N.Z. 128 35 16 S 174 10 E
Russell, Fla. 17 30 3N 81 45W
Russell, Kans. 24 38 54N 98 52W
Russell County ◇, Ala. 10 32 18N 85 10W
Russell County ◇, Kans. 24 39 0N 98 45W
Russell County ◇, Ky. 49 37 0N 85 0W
Russell County ◇, Va. 54 36 0N 82 0W
Russell Cr. → 49 37 14N 85 30W
Russell L., Man., Canada 63 56 15N 101 30W
Russell L., N.W.T., Canada 62 63 5N 115 44W
Russell Springs, Kans. 24 38 55N 101 11W
Russell Springs, Ky. 49 37 3N 85 5W
Russellkonda 109 19 57N 84 42 E
Russellville, Ala. 10 34 30N 87 44W
Russellville, Ark. 13 35 17N 93 8W
Russellville, Ky. 48 36 51N 86 53W
Russellville, Mo. 32 38 31N 92 26W
Russellville, Ohio 42 38 52N 83 47W
Russellville, Tenn. 49 36 15N 83 12W
Russian → 14 38 27N 123 8W
Russian Mission 11 61 47N 161 19W
Russian S.F.S.R. □ 101 62 0N 105 0 E
Russiaville 22 40 25N 86 16W
Russkaya Polyana 100 53 47N 73 53 E
Russkoye Ustie 4 71 0N 149 0 E
Rustburg 54 37 17N 79 6W
Rustenburg 123 25 41 S 27 14 E
Ruston 25 32 32N 92 38W
Ruteng 111 8 35 S 120 30 E
Ruth, Miss. 31 31 23N 90 19W
Ruth, Nev. 35 39 17N 114 59W
Rutherford 48 36 8N 88 59W
Rutherford County ◇, N.C. 40 35 20N 81 50W
Rutherford County ◇, Tenn. 48 35 51N 86 24W
Rutherfordton 40 35 22N 81 58W
Rutherglen 84 55 50N 4 11W
Ruthsburg 27 39 0N 75 58W
Ruthton 30 44 11N 96 6W
Ruthven 23 43 8N 94 54W
Rutland, Ill. 21 40 59N 89 3W
Rutland, Iowa 23 42 46N 94 18W
Rutland, Mass. 28 42 23N 71 57W
Rutland, N. Dak. 41 46 3N 97 30W
Rutland, Ohio 42 39 3N 82 8W
Rutland, S. Dak. 47 44 5N 96 58W
Rutland, Vt. 36 43 37N 72 58W
Rutland County ◇ 36 43 35N 73 0W
Rutland I. 112 11 25N 92 40 E
Rutledge, Ga. 18 33 38N 83 37W
Rutledge, Minn. 30 46 16N 92 52W
Rutledge, Tenn. 49 36 17N 83 31W
Rutledge → 63 61 4N 112 0W
Rutledge L. 63 61 33N 110 47W
Rutshuru 122 1 13 S 29 25 E
Ruurlo 87 52 5N 6 24 E
Ruwenzori 122 0 30N 29 55 E
Růžhevo Konare 95 42 23N 24 46 E
Ružomberok 89 49 3N 19 17 E
Rwanda ■ 122 2 0 S 30 0 E
Ryakhovo 95 44 0N 26 18 E
Ryan, Iowa 23 42 21N 91 29W
Ryan, Okla. 43 34 1N 97 57W
Ryan, L. 84 55 0N 5 2W
Ryazan 98 54 40N 39 40 E
Ryazhsk 98 53 45N 40 3 E
Rybache 100 46 40N 81 20 E
Rybachiy Poluostrov 98 69 43N 32 0 E
Rybinsk = Andropov 98 58 5N 38 50 E
Rybinskoye Vdkhr. 98 58 30N 38 25 E
Ryde 83 50 44N 1 9W
Ryder 41 47 55N 101 40W
Ryderwood 53 46 23N 123 3W
Rye, U.K. 83 50 57N 0 46 E
Rye, Ark. 13 33 45N 91 59W
Rye, Colo. 16 37 55N 104 56W
Rye, N.H. 36 43 2N 70 50W
Rye → 82 54 12N 0 53W
Rye Beach 36 42 59N 70 46W
Rye Patch Reservoir 35 40 28N 118 19W
Ryegate 33 46 18N 109 15W
Ryōthu 116 38 5N 138 26 E
Rypin 89 53 3N 19 25 E
Ryūgasaki 117 35 54N 140 11 E
Ryūkyū Is. = Nansei-Shotō 117 26 0N 128 0 E
Rzeszów 89 50 5N 21 58 E
Rzhev 98 56 20N 34 20 E

S

Sa Dec 112 10 20N 105 46 E
Sa'ad 104 31 28N 34 33 E
Sa'ādatābād 107 30 10N 53 5 E
Saale → 88 51 57N 11 56 E
Saar → 88 49 41N 6 32 E
Saarbrücken 88 49 15N 6 58 E
Saaremaa 98 58 30N 22 30 E
Saariselkä 96 68 16N 28 15 E
Saba 67 17 42N 63 26W
Sabadell 91 41 28N 2 7 E
Sabagalet 110 1 36 S 98 40 E
Sabah □ 110 6 0N 117 0 E
Sábana de la Mar 67 19 7N 69 24W
Sabana Grande 57 18 5N 66 58W
Sábanalarga 70 10 38N 74 55W
Sabang 110 5 50N 95 15 E
Sabará 75 19 55 S 43 46W
Sabarania 111 2 5 S 138 18 E
Sabasţiyah 104 32 17N 35 12 E
Sabáudia 94 41 17N 13 2 E
Sabaya 72 19 1 S 68 23W
Sabetha 24 39 54N 95 48W
Sabhah 121 27 9N 14 29 E
Sabin 30 46 47N 96 39W
Sabina 42 39 29N 83 38W
Sabinal, Mexico 64 30 58N 107 25W
Sabinal, U.S.A. 51 29 19N 99 28W
Sabinas 64 27 50N 101 10W
Sabinas → 64 27 37N 100 42W
Sabinas Hidalgo 64 26 33N 100 10W
Sabine → 25 29 59N 93 47W
Sabine County ◇ 51 31 20N 93 51W
Sabine L. 25 29 53N 93 51W
Sabine National Forest 51 31 38N 94 0W
Sabine Parish ◇ 25 31 38N 93 39W
Sabine Pass 51 29 44N 93 54W
Sabinópolis 75 18 40 S 43 6W
Sabinoso 38 35 42N 104 24W
Sablayan 111 12 50N 120 50 E
Sable, C., U.S.A. 17 25 9N 81 8W
Sable, C., Canada 61 43 29N 65 38W
Sable I. 61 44 0N 60 0W
Sables-d'Olonne, Les 90 46 30N 1 45W
Saboeiro 74 6 32 S 39 54W
Sabolev 101 54 20N 155 30 E
Sabrina Coast 5 68 0 S 120 0 E
Sabula, Iowa 23 42 4N 90 10W
Sabula, Mo. 32 37 27N 90 42W
Sabzevār 107 36 15N 57 40 E
Sabzvārān 107 28 45N 57 50 E
Sac → 32 38 1N 93 43W
Sac City 23 42 25N 95 0W
Sac County ◇ 23 42 25N 95 5W
Sacajawea, L. 53 46 20N 118 45W
Sacajawea Peak 44 45 15N 117 17W
Sacandaga Reservoir 39 43 6N 74 16W
Sacaton 12 33 5N 111 44W
Sachigo → 60 55 6N 88 58W
Sachigo, L. 60 53 50N 92 12W
Sackets Harbor 39 43 57N 76 7W
Saco, Maine 26 43 30N 70 27W
Saco, Mont. 33 48 28N 107 21W
Saco → 26 43 28N 70 23W
Sacramento, Brazil 75 19 53 S 47 27W
Sacramento, Calif. 14 38 35N 121 29W
Sacramento, Ky. 48 37 25N 87 16W
Sacramento, N. Mex. 38 32 48N 105 34W
Sacramento → 14 38 3N 121 56W
Sacramento County ◇ 14 38 20N 121 20W
Sacramento Mts. 38 32 30N 105 30W
Sacramento South 14 38 32N 121 26W
Sacramento Valley 14 39 30N 122 0W
Sacramento Wash → 12 34 43N 114 28W
Sádaba 91 42 19N 1 12W
Sadani 122 5 58 S 38 35 E
Sadao 112 6 38N 100 26 E
Sadd el Aali 121 23 54N 32 54 E
Saddle Mt., Oreg. 44 45 58N 123 41W
Saddle Mt., Wyo. 56 44 43N 109 59W
Saddle Mts. 53 46 55N 120 0W
Saddle Peak 53 48 58N 120 9W
Sadieville 49 38 23N 84 32W
Sado 116 38 0N 138 25 E
Sadon 109 25 28N 98 0 E
Sadorus 21 39 58N 88 21W
Saegerstown 45 41 43N 80 9W
Säffle 97 59 8N 12 55 E
Safford 12 32 50N 109 43W
Saffron Walden 83 52 2N 0 15 E
Safi 120 32 18N 9 20W
Safīd Kūh 107 34 45N 63 0 E
Sag Harbor 39 41 0N 72 18W
Saga, Indonesia 111 2 40 S 132 55 E
Saga, Japan 117 33 15N 130 16 E
Saga □ 117 33 15N 130 20 E
Sagadahoc County ◇ 26 44 0N 70 0W
Sagae 116 38 22N 140 17 E
Sagaing □ 109 23 55N 95 56 E
Sagala 120 14 9N 6 38W
Sagamore 28 41 45N 70 33W
Sagavanirktok → 11 70 19N 147 53W
Sage 56 41 49N 110 58W
Sage Cr. → 33 47 16N 109 43W

Sagerton **Salālah**

Sagerton **51** 33 5N 99 58W
Sageville **23** 42 36N 90 43W
Sagil **113** 50 15N 91 15 E
Saginaw **29** 43 26N 83 56W
Saginaw → **29** 43 39N 83 51W
Saginaw B. **29** 43 50N 83 40W
Saginaw County ◇ **29** 43 20N 84 0W
Sagīr, Zab al **106** 35 10N 43 20 E
Saglouc **59** 62 14N 75 38W
Sagra, La **91** 37 57N 2 35W
Sagres **91** 37 0N 8 58W
Sagua la Grande **66** 22 50N 80 10W
Saguache **16** 38 5N 106 8W
Saguache County ◇ **16** 38 10N 106 15W
Saguaro Nat. Monument **12** 32 12N 110 38W
Saguenay → **61** 48 22N 71 0W
Sagunto **91** 39 42N 0 18W
Sahagún, Colombia **70** 8 57N 75 27W
Sahagún, Spain **91** 42 18N 5 2W
Saham **104** 32 42N 35 46 E
Saḥam al Jawlān **104** 32 45N 35 55 E
Sahand, Kūh-e **106** 37 44N 46 27 E
Sahara **120** 23 0N 5 0 E
Saharan Atlas **118** 34 9N 3 29 E
Saharanpur **108** 29 58N 77 33 E
Saharien, Atlas **120** 33 30N 1 0 E
Sahiwal **108** 30 45N 73 8 E
Sahtaneh → **62** 59 2N 122 28W
Sahuaripa **64** 29 0N 109 13W
Sahuarita **12** 31 57N 110 58W
Sahuayo **64** 20 4N 102 43W
Sai-Cinza **73** 6 17 S 57 42W
Sa'id Bundas **121** 8 24N 24 48 E
Saïda **120** 34 50N 0 11 E
Saīdābād **107** 29 30N 55 45 E
Sa'idiyeh **106** 36 20N 48 55 E
Saidu **108** 34 43N 72 24 E
Saigon = Phanh Bho Ho Chi Minh, Vietnam **112** 10 58N 106 40 E
Saigon = Phanh Bho Ho Chi Minh, Vietnam **112** 10 58N 106 40 E
Saigon = Phanh Bho Ho Chi Minh, Vietnam **112** 10 58N 106 40 E
Saih-al-Malih **107** 23 37N 58 31 E
Saijō **117** 33 55N 133 11 E
Saikhoa Ghat **109** 27 50N 95 40 E
Saiki **117** 32 58N 131 51 E
Sailolof **111** 1 7 S 130 46 E
Sailor Springs **21** 38 46N 88 22W
St. Abb's Head **84** 55 55N 2 10W
St. Alban's, Canada **61** 47 51N 55 50W
St. Albans, U.K. **83** 51 44N 0 19W
St. Albans, Vt. **36** 44 49N 73 5W
St. Albans, W. Va. **54** 38 23N 81 50W
St. Alban's Head **83** 50 34N 2 3W
St. Albert **62** 53 37N 113 32W
St. Andrew Sd. **18** 31 0N 81 25W
St. Andrew's, Canada **61** 47 45N 59 15W
St. Andrews, U.K. **84** 56 20N 2 48W
St. Ann B. **61** 46 22N 60 25W
St. Anne **21** 41 1N 87 43W
St. Ann's Bay **66** 18 26N 77 15W
St. Ansgar **23** 43 23N 92 55W
St. Anthony, Canada **61** 51 22N 55 35W
St. Anthony, U.S.A. **20** 43 58N 111 41W
St. Arnaud Ra. **128** 42 1 S 172 53 E
St. Arthur **61** 47 33N 67 46W
St. Asaph **82** 53 15N 3 27W
St-Augustin-Saguenay **61** 51 13N 58 38W
St. Augustine **17** 29 54N 81 19W
St. Augustine Beach **17** 29 51N 81 16W
St. Austell **83** 50 20N 4 48W
St.-Barthélemy, I. **67** 17 50N 62 50W
St. Bee's Hd. **82** 54 30N 3 38 E
St. Benedict **24** 39 53N 96 6W
St. Bernard Parish ◇ **25** 29 55N 89 10W
St. Boniface **63** 49 53N 97 5W
St. Bride's **61** 46 56N 54 10W
St. Bride's B. **83** 51 48N 5 15W
St-Brieuc **90** 48 30N 2 46W
St. Catharines **60** 43 10N 79 15W
St. Catherines I. **18** 31 40N 81 10W
St. Catherine's Pt. **83** 50 34N 1 18W
St. Charles, Ark. **13** 34 23N 91 8W
St. Charles, Idaho **20** 42 7N 111 23W
St. Charles, Ill. **21** 41 54N 88 19W
St. Charles, Iowa **23** 41 17N 93 49W
St. Charles, Mich. **29** 43 18N 84 9W
St. Charles, Minn. **30** 43 58N 92 4W
St. Charles, Mo. **32** 38 47N 90 29W
St. Charles, S. Dak. **47** 43 5N 99 6W
St. Charles, Va. **54** 36 48N 83 4W
St. Charles County ◇ **32** 38 45N 90 40W
St. Charles Parish ◇ **25** 29 59N 90 25W
St. Christopher-Nevis ■ **67** 17 20N 62 40W
St. Clair, Ga. **18** 33 9N 82 13W
St. Clair, Mich. **29** 42 50N 82 30W
St. Clair, Minn. **30** 44 5N 93 51W
St. Clair, Mo. **32** 38 21N 90 59W
St. Clair, Pa. **45** 40 43N 76 12W
St. Clair → **29** 42 19N 82 31W
St. Clair, L., Canada **60** 42 30N 82 45W
St. Clair, L., U.S.A. **29** 42 27N 82 39W
St. Clair County ◇, Ala. **10** 33 35N 86 17W
St. Clair County ◇, Ill. **21** 38 30N 89 55W
St. Clair County ◇, Mich. **29** 43 0N 82 30W
St. Clair County ◇, Mo. **32** 38 0N 93 45W
St. Clair Shores **29** 42 30N 82 53W
St. Clairsville **42** 40 5N 80 54W
St. Claude **63** 49 40N 98 20W
St. Cloud, Fla. **17** 28 15N 81 17W
St. Cloud, Minn. **30** 45 34N 94 10W
St-Coeur de Marie **61** 48 39N 71 43W
St. Croix →, Maine **26** 45 4N 67 5W
St. Croix →, Wis. **55** 44 45N 92 48W
St. Croix County ◇ **55** 45 0N 92 20W
St. Croix Falls **55** 45 24N 92 38W
St. Croix Flowage **55** 46 15N 91 56W
St. Croix L. **30** 44 57N 92 45W
St. David, Ariz. **12** 31 54N 110 13W
St. David, Ill. **21** 40 30N 90 3W
St. David's, Canada **61** 48 12N 58 52W
St. David's, U.K. **83** 51 54N 5 16W
St. David's Head **83** 51 55N 5 16W
St-Denis **90** 48 56N 2 22 E
St. Donatus **23** 42 22N 90 33W
St. Edward **34** 41 34N 97 52W
St. Elias, Mt. **11** 60 18N 140 56W
St. Elias Mts., Canada **62** 60 33N 139 28W
St. Elias Mts., U.S.A. **11** 60 0N 138 0W
St.-Elie **71** 4 49N 53 17W
St. Elizabeth **32** 38 15N 92 16W
St. Elmo **21** 39 2N 88 51W
St-Étienne **90** 45 27N 4 22 E
St. Eustatius **67** 17 20N 63 0W
St-Félicien **60** 48 40N 72 25W
St-Flour **90** 45 2N 3 6 E
St. Frances **47** 43 9N 100 54W
St. Francis, Kans. **24** 39 47N 101 48W
St. Francis, Maine **26** 47 10N 68 54W
St. Francis, Minn. **30** 45 23N 93 22W
St. Francis, Wis. **55** 42 58N 87 52W
St. Francis → **13** 34 38N 90 36W
St. Francis, C. **123** 34 14 S 24 49 E
St. Francis County ◇ **13** 35 1N 90 47W
St. Francisville, Ill. **21** 38 36N 87 39W
St. Francisville, La. **25** 30 47N 91 23W
St. Francois County ◇ **32** 37 50N 90 30W
St. Francois Mts. **32** 37 30N 90 35W
St. Froid, L. **26** 46 57N 68 37W
St. Gabriel **25** 30 16N 91 6W
St-Gabriel-de-Brandon **60** 46 17N 73 24W
St. Gallen **88** 47 25N 9 20 E
St. Genevieve County ◇ **32** 37 50N 90 10W
St. George, Australia **127** 28 1 S 148 30 E
St. George, Canada **61** 45 11N 66 50W
St. George, Ga. **18** 30 31N 82 2W
St. George, Kans. **24** 39 12N 96 25W
St. George, S.C. **46** 33 11N 80 35W
St. George, Utah **52** 37 6N 113 35W
St. George, C. **61** 48 30N 59 16W
St. George, Pt. **14** 41 47N 124 15W
St. George I., Alaska **11** 56 35N 169 35W
St. George I., Fla. **17** 29 35N 84 55W
St. George Island **27** 38 7N 76 29W
St-Georges **87** 50 37N 5 20 E
St. George's, Newf., Canada **61** 48 26N 58 31W
St. Georges, Qué., Canada **60** 46 42N 72 35W
St-Georges **61** 46 8N 70 40W
St. Georges, Fr. Gui. **71** 4 0N 52 0W
St. George's, Grenada **67** 12 5N 61 43W
St. George's B. **61** 48 24N 58 53W
St. George's Channel **86** 52 0N 6 0W
St. Helena, Atl. Oc. **2** 15 55 S 5 44W
St. Helena, Calif. **14** 38 30N 122 28W
St. Helena, Nebr. **34** 42 49N 97 15W
St. Helena Parish ◇ **25** 30 50N 90 40W
St. Helena Sd. **46** 32 15N 80 25W
St. Helenabaai **123** 32 40 S 18 10 E
St. Helens, U.K. **82** 53 28N 2 44W
St. Helens, U.S.A. **44** 45 52N 122 48W
St. Helens, Mt. **53** 46 12N 122 12W
St. Helier **83** 49 11N 2 6W
St. Henry **42** 40 25N 84 38W
St. Hilaire **30** 48 1N 96 14W
St-Hubert **87** 50 2N 5 23 E
St-Hyacinthe **60** 45 40N 72 58W
St. Ignace **29** 45 52N 84 44W
St. Ignace I. **60** 48 45N 88 0W
St. Ignatius **33** 47 19N 114 6W
St. Ives, Cambs., U.K. **83** 52 20N 0 5W
St. Ives, Cornwall, U.K. **83** 50 13N 5 29W
St. James, Mich. **29** 45 45N 85 31W
St. James, Minn. **30** 43 59N 94 38W
St. James, Mo. **32** 38 0N 91 37W
St. James, N.Y. **39** 40 53N 73 9W
St. James City **17** 26 29N 82 5W
St. James Parish ◇ **25** 30 1N 90 50W
St. Jean **60** 45 20N 73 20W
St-Jean → **61** 50 17N 64 20W
St-Jean, L. **61** 48 40N 72 0W
St. Jean Baptiste **63** 49 15N 97 20W
St-Jean-Port-Joli **61** 47 15N 70 13W
St-Jérôme, Qué., Canada **60** 45 47N 74 0W
St-Jérôme, Qué., Canada **61** 48 26N 71 53W
St. Jo **51** 33 42N 97 31W
St. Joe, Ark. **13** 36 2N 92 48W
St. Joe, Idaho **20** 47 19N 116 21W
St. Joe National Forest **20** 47 5N 115 30W
St. John, Canada **61** 45 20N 66 8W
St. John, Kans. **24** 38 0N 98 46W
St. John, N. Dak. **41** 48 57N 99 43W
St. John, Wash. **53** 47 6N 117 35W
St. John →, Canada **61** 45 15N 66 4W
St. John →, U.S.A. **26** 45 12N 66 5W
St. John, C. **61** 50 0N 55 32W
St. John I. **57** 18 20N 64 42W
St. John The Baptist Parish ◇ **25** 30 3N 90 33W
St. John's, Antigua **67** 17 6N 61 51W
St. John's, Canada **61** 47 35N 52 40W
St. Johns, Ariz. **12** 34 30N 109 22W
St. Johns, Mich. **29** 43 0N 84 33W
St. Johns → **17** 30 24N 81 24W
St. Johns County ◇ **17** 29 45N 81 25W
St. Johnsbury **36** 44 25N 72 1W
St. Joseph, Ill. **21** 40 7N 88 2W
St. Joseph, La. **25** 31 55N 91 14W
St. Joseph, Mich. **29** 42 6N 86 29W
St. Joseph, Mo. **32** 39 46N 94 50W
St. Joseph, Tenn. **48** 35 2N 87 30W
St. Joseph →, Ind. **22** 41 5N 85 8W
St. Joseph →, Mich. **29** 42 7N 86 29W
St. Joseph, I. **60** 46 12N 83 58W
St. Joseph, L. **60** 51 10N 90 35W
St. Joseph County ◇ **22** 41 35N 86 15W
St. Joseph Pt. **17** 29 52N 85 24W
St-Jovite **60** 46 8N 74 38W
St. Kilda **128** 45 53 S 170 31 E
St. Kitts = St. Christopher **67** 17 20N 62 40W
St. Kitts-Nevis ■ **67** 17 20N 62 40W
St. Landry Parish ◇ **25** 30 40N 92 0W
St. Laurent **63** 50 25N 97 58W
St-Laurent **71** 5 29N 54 3W
St. Lawrence, Canada **61** 46 54N 55 23W
St. Lawrence, U.S.A. **47** 44 31N 98 56W
St. Lawrence → **61** 49 30N 66 0W
St. Lawrence, Gulf of **61** 48 25N 62 0W
St. Lawrence County ◇ **39** 44 30N 75 0W
St. Lawrence I. **11** 63 30N 170 30W
St. Leo **30** 44 43N 96 3W
St. Leonard, Canada **61** 47 12N 67 58W
St. Leonard, U.S.A. **27** 38 28N 76 30W
St. Lewis → **61** 52 26N 56 11W
St. Libory **34** 41 5N 98 21W
St-Lô **90** 49 7N 1 5W
St-Louis **120** 16 8N 16 27W
St. Louis, Mich. **29** 43 25N 84 36W
St. Louis, Mo. **32** 38 37N 90 12W
St. Louis, Okla. **43** 35 5N 96 53W
St. Louis → **30** 46 44N 92 9W
St. Louis County ◇, Minn. **30** 47 40N 92 20W
St. Louis County ◇, Mo. **32** 38 40N 90 25W
St. Louis Park **30** 44 57N 93 21W
St. Louisville **42** 40 10N 82 25W
St. Lucia ■ **67** 14 0N 60 50W
St. Lucia, Lake **123** 28 5 S 32 30 E
St. Lucia Channel **67** 14 15N 61 0W
St. Lucie **17** 27 29N 80 20W
St. Lucie Canal **17** 27 10N 80 18W
St. Lucie County ◇ **17** 27 25N 80 30W
St. Lunaire-Griquet **61** 51 31N 55 28W
St. Maarten **67** 18 0N 63 5W
St-Malo **90** 48 39N 2 1W
St-Marc **67** 19 10N 72'41W
St. Marie **21** 38 56N 88 1W
St. Maries **20** 47 19N 116 35W
St. Maries → **20** 47 19N 116 33W
St. Marks **17** 30 9N 84 12W
St. Marks → **17** 30 8N 84 12W
St-Martin, I. **67** 18 0N 63 0W
St. Martin I. **29** 45 30N 86 46W
St. Martin L. **63** 51 40N 98 30W
St. Martin Parish ◇ **25** 30 7N 91 50W
St. Martins **61** 45 22N 65 34W
St. Martinville **25** 30 7N 91 50W
St. Mary B. **61** 46 50N 53 50W
St. Mary Parish ◇ **25** 29 48N 91 30W
St. Mary Pk. **127** 31 32 S 138 34 E
St. Marys, Australia **127** 41 35 S 148 11 E
St. Mary's, U.K. **83** 49 55N 6 17W
St. Mary's, Alaska **11** 62 4N 163 10W
St. Marys, Ga. **18** 30 44N 81 33W
St. Marys, Iowa **23** 41 19N 93 44W
St. Marys, Kans. **24** 39 12N 96 4W
St. Marys, Mo. **32** 37 53N 89 57W
St. Marys, Ohio **42** 40 33N 84 24W
St. Marys, Pa. **45** 41 26N 78 34W
St. Marys, W. Va. **54** 39 23N 81 12W
St. Marys →, Ga. **18** 30 43N 81 27W
St. Marys →, Ind. **22** 41 5N 85 8W
St. Marys →, Mich. **29** 46 0N 83 55W
St. Mary's, C. **61** 46 50N 54 12W
St. Marys Bay **61** 44 25N 66 10W
St. Marys City **27** 38 11N 76 26W
St. Marys County ◇ **27** 38 15N 76 40W
St-Mathieu, Pte. de **90** 48 20N 4 45W
St. Matthew I. **11** 60 24N 172 42W
St. Matthews, Ky. **49** 38 15N 85 39W
St. Matthews, S.C. **46** 33 40N 80 46W
St. Matthews, I. = Zadetkyi Kyun **110** 10 0N 98 25 E
St-Maurice → **60** 46 21N 72 31W
St. Meinrad **22** 38 10N 86 49W
St. Michael **11** 63 29N 162 2W
St. Michaels **27** 38 47N 76 14W
St. Michael's Mt. **83** 50 7N 5 30W
St-Nazaire **90** 47 17N 2 12W
St. Nazianz **55** 44 0N 87 55W
St. Neots **83** 52 14N 0 16W
St. Olaf **23** 42 56N 91 23W
St-Omer **90** 50 45N 2 15 E
St. Onge **47** 44 33N 103 43W
St-Pacome **61** 47 24N 69 58W
St-Pamphile **61** 46 58N 69 48W
St. Paris **42** 40 8N 83 58W
St. Pascal **61** 47 32N 69 48W
St. Patrick Peak **33** 46 59N 114 51W
St. Paul, Canada **62** 54 0N 111 17W
St. Paul, Ind. Oc. **3** 30 40 S 77 34 E
St. Paul, Alaska **11** 57 7N 170 17W
St. Paul, Ark. **13** 35 50N 93 46W
St. Paul, Ind. **22** 39 26N 85 38W
St. Paul, Iowa **23** 40 46N 91 31W
St. Paul, Kans. **24** 37 31N 95 10W
St. Paul, Minn. **30** 44 57N 93 6W
St. Paul, Nebr. **34** 41 13N 98 27W
St. Paul, Va. **54** 36 54N 82 19W
St. Paul, I. **61** 47 12N 60 9W
St. Paul I. **11** 57 10N 170 15W
St. Pauls **40** 34 48N 78 58W
St. Peter, Ill. **21** 38 52N 88 51W
St. Peter, Minn. **30** 44 20N 93 57W
St. Peter Port **83** 49 27N 2 31W
St. Peters, N.S., Canada **61** 45 40N 60 53W
St. Peters, P.E.I., Canada **61** 46 25N 62 35W
St. Petersburg **17** 27 46N 82 39W
St. Petersburg Beach **17** 27 45N 82 45W
St. Phillip **33** 46 50N 104 9W
St Pierre **61** 46 46N 56 12W
St-Pierre, L. **60** 46 12N 72 52W
St-Pierre et Miquelon □ **61** 46 55N 56 10W
St-Quentin **90** 49 50N 3 16 E
St. Regis **33** 47 18N 115 6W
St. Regis Falls **39** 44 41N 74 33W
St. Sebastien, Tanjon' i **123** 12 26 S 48 44 E
St-Siméon **61** 47 51N 69 54W
St. Simons I. **18** 31 12N 81 15W
St. Stephen, Canada **61** 45 16N 67 17W
St. Stephen, U.S.A. **46** 33 24N 79 55W
St. Tammany Parish ◇ **25** 30 29N 90 2W
St. Thomas, Canada **60** 42 45N 81 10W
St. Thomas, Mo. **32** 38 23N 92 13W
St. Thomas, N. Dak. **41** 48 37N 97 27W
St. Thomas I. **57** 18 20N 64 55W
St-Tite **60** 46 45N 72 34W
St-Tropez **90** 43 17N 6 38 E
St. Troud = Sint Truiden **87** 50 48N 5 10 E
St-Valéry **90** 50 10N 1 38 E
St. Vincent, U.S.A. **30** 48 58N 97 14W
St. Vincent, W. Indies **67** 13 10N 61 10W
St. Vincent, G. **127** 35 0 S 138 0 E
St. Vincent and the Grenadines ■ **67** 13 0N 61 10W
St. Vincent I. **17** 29 42N 85 3W
St. Vincent Passage **67** 13 30N 61 0W
St-Vith **87** 50 17N 6 9 E
St. Vrain **38** 34 25N 103 29W
Ste-Agathe-des-Monts **60** 46 3N 74 17W
Ste Anne de Beaupré **61** 47 2N 70 58W
Ste-Anne-des-Monts **61** 49 8N 66 30W
Ste-Marguerite → **61** 50 9N 66 36W
Ste Marie **67** 14 48N 61 1W
Ste-Marie de la Madeleine **61** 46 26N 71 0W
Ste-Rose **67** 16 20N 61 45W
Ste.-Rose du Lac **63** 51 4N 99 30W
Saintes **90** 45 45N 0 37W
Saintes, Île des **67** 15 50N 61 35W
Saintonge **90** 45 40N 0 50W
Sairang **109** 23 50N 92 45 E
Sairecábur, Cerro **76** 22 43 S 67 54W
Saitama □ **117** 36 25N 139 30 E
Sajama **72** 18 7 S 69 0W
Sakai **117** 34 30N 135 30 E
Sakaide **117** 34 15N 133 50 E
Sakaiminato **117** 35 38N 133 11 E
Sakākah **106** 30 0N 40 8 E
Sakakawea, L. **41** 47 30N 101 25W
Sakami, L. **60** 53 15N 77 0W
Sakania **123** 12 43 S 28 30 E
Sakarya → **99** 41 7N 30 39 E
Sakashima-Guntō **117** 24 46N 124 0 E
Sakata **116** 38 55N 139 50 E
Sakhalin, Ostrov **101** 51 0N 143 0 E
Sakhalinskiy Zaliv **101** 54 0N 141 0 E
Sakhnīn **104** 32 52N 35 12 E
Sakon Nakhon **112** 17 10N 104 9 E
Sakuma **117** 35 3N 137 49 E
Sakurai **117** 34 30N 135 51 E
Sala **97** 59 58N 16 35 E
Sala-y-Gómez **125** 26 28 S 105 28W
Salaberry-de-Valleyfield **60** 45 15N 74 8W
Salada, La **64** 24 30N 111 30W
Saladas **76** 28 15 S 58 40W
Saladillo **76** 35 40 S 59 55W
Salado **13** 35 42N 91 36W
Salado →, Buenos Aires, Argentina **76** 35 44 S 57 22W
Salado →, La Pampa, Argentina **78** 37 30 S 67 0W
Salado →, Río Negro, Argentina **78** 41 34 S 65 3W
Salado →, Santa Fe, Argentina **76** 31 40 S 60 41W
Salado →, Mexico **64** 26 52N 99 19W
Salado, Rio **38** 34 16N 106 52W
Salaga **120** 8 31N 0 31W
Salālah **105** 16 56N 53 59 E

Salamanca San José do Anauá

Salamanca, Chile 76 31 46 S 70 59W
Salamanca, Spain 91 40 58N 5 39W
Salamanca, U.S.A. 39 42 10N 78 43W
Salamina 70 5 25N 75 29W
Salamis 95 37 56N 23 30 E
Salamonia 22 40 23N 84 52W
Salamonie L. 22 40 46N 85 37W
Salar de Atacama 76 23 30 S 68 25W
Salar de Uyuni 72 20 30 S 67 45W
Salatiga 111 7 19 S 110 30 E
Salavat 98 53 21N 55 55 E
Salaverry 72 8 15 S 79 0W
Salawati 111 1 7 S 130 52 E
Salayar 111 6 7 S 120 30 E
Salcia 95 43 56N 24 55 E
Salcombe 83 50 14N 3 47W
Saldaña 91 42 32N 4 48W
Saldanha 123 33 0 S 17 58 E
Sale, Australia 127 38 6 S 147 6 E
Salé, Morocco 120 34 3N 6 48W
Sale, U.K. 82 53 26N 2 19W
Sale City 18 31 16N 84 1W
Sale Creek 49 35 23N 85 7W
Salekhard 100 66 30N 66 35 E
Salem, India 108 11 40N 78 11 E
Salem, Ala. 10 32 36N 85 14W
Salem, Ark. 13 36 22N 91 50W
Salem, Conn. 28 41 0N 72 0W
Salem, Fla. 17 29 53N 83 25W
Salem, Ill. 21 38 38N 88 57W
Salem, Ind. 22 38 36N 86 6W
Salem, Iowa 23 40 51N 91 38W
Salem, Ky. 48 37 16N 88 15W
Salem, Mass. 28 42 31N 70 53W
Salem, Md. 27 38 32N 75 55W
Salem, Mo. 32 37 39N 91 32W
Salem, N.J. 37 39 34N 75 28W
Salem, N.Y. 39 43 10N 73 20W
Salem, Nebr. 34 40 5N 95 43W
Salem, Ohio 42 40 54N 80 52W
Salem, Oreg. 44 44 56N 123 2W
Salem, S. Dak. 47 43 44N 97 23W
Salem, Utah 52 40 3N 111 40W
Salem, Va. 54 37 18N 80 3W
Salem, W. Va. 54 39 17N 80 34W
Salem County ◇ 37 39 40N 75 20W
Salem Plateau 32 37 30N 91 30W
Salemburg 40 35 1N 78 30W
Salen 97 64 41N 11 27 E
Salerno 94 40 40N 14 44 E
Salfit 104 32 5N 35 11 E
Salford 82 53 30N 2 17W
Salgueiro 74 8 4 S 39 6W
Salida 16 38 32N 106 0W
Salima 123 13 47 S 34 28 E
Salina, Italy 94 38 35N 14 50 E
Salina, Ariz. 12 36 1N 109 52W
Salina, Kans. 24 38 50N 97 37W
Salina, Okla. 43 36 18N 95 9W
Salina, Utah 52 38 58N 111 51W
Salina Cruz 65 16 10N 95 10W
Salinas, Brazil 75 16 10 S 42 10W
Salinas, Chile 76 23 31 S 69 29W
Salinas, Ecuador 70 2 10 S 80 58W
Salinas, Puerto Rico 57 17 59N 66 18W
Salinas, U.S.A. 14 36 40N 121 39W
Salinas →, Mexico 65 16 28N 90 31W
Salinas →, U.S.A. 14 36 45N 121 48W
Salinas, B. de 66 11 4N 85 45W
Salinas, Pampa de las 76 31 58 S 66 42W
Salinas, Punta 57 18 29N 66 11W
Salinas, Sierra de 15 36 20N 121 20W
Salinas Ambargasta 76 29 0 S 65 0W
Salinas de Hidalgo 64 22 30N 101 40W
Salinas Grandes 76 30 0 S 65 0W
Salinas Nat. Monument 38 34 6N 106 4W
Salinas Pk. 38 33 22N 106 35W
Salinas Valley 15 36 15N 121 15W
Saline, La. 25 32 10N 92 59W
Saline, Mich. 29 42 10N 83 47W
Saline →, Ill. 21 37 35N 88 8W
Saline →, Kans. 24 38 52N 97 30W
Saline →, Ark. 13 33 10N 92 8W
Saline →, Ark. 13 33 44N 93 58W
Saline County ◇, Ark. 13 34 34N 92 35W
Saline County ◇, Ill. 21 37 45N 88 30W
Saline County ◇, Kans. 24 38 45N 97 40W
Saline County ◇, Mo. 32 39 10N 93 10W
Saline County ◇, Nebr. 34 40 30N 97 10W
Saline L. 25 31 52N 92 54W
Saline Valley 15 36 50N 117 50W
Salineno 50 26 31N 99 7W
Salinópolis 74 0 40 S 47 20W
Salisbury = Harare 123 17 43 S 31 2 E
Salisbury, U.K. 83 51 4N 1 48W
Salisbury, Conn. 28 41 59N 73 25W
Salisbury, Mass. 28 42 51N 70 49W
Salisbury, Md. 27 38 22N 75 36W
Salisbury, Mo. 32 39 25N 92 48W
Salisbury, N.C. 40 35 40N 80 29W
Salisbury, N.H. 36 43 22N 71 42W
Salisbury, Pa. 45 39 45N 79 5W
Salisbury, Vt. 36 43 53N 73 6W
Salisbury Heights 36 43 24N 71 44W
Salisbury Plain 83 51 13N 1 50W
Salish Mts. 33 45 30N 115 0W
Sălişte 95 45 45N 23 56 E
Salitpa 10 31 37N 88 1W
Salitre → 74 9 29 S 40 39W
Salix 23 42 19N 96 17W
Salkehatchie → 46 32 37N 80 53W
Salkum 53 46 32N 122 38W
Salladasburg 45 41 17N 77 14W
Salley 46 33 34N 81 18W
Sallisaw 43 35 28N 94 47W
Salmās 106 38 12N 44 45 E
Salmo 62 49 10N 117 20W
Salmon 20 45 11N 113 54W
Salmon →, Canada 62 54 3N 122 40W
Salmon →, U.S.A. 20 45 51N 116 47W
Salmon Arm 62 50 40N 119 15W
Salmon Falls → 36 43 12N 70 50W
Salmon Falls Cr. → 20 42 43N 114 51W
Salmon Mt. 36 45 14N 71 8W
Salmon Mts. 14 41 0N 123 0W
Salmon National Forest 20 45 10N 114 20W
Salmon Res. 61 48 5N 56 0W
Salmon River Mts. 20 44 50N 115 30W
Salmon River Reservoir 39 43 32N 75 55W
Salmon South Fork → 20 45 23N 115 31W
Salo 97 60 22N 23 10 E
Salome 12 33 47N 113 37W
Salonica = Thessaloníki 95 40 38N 22 58 E
Salonta 89 46 49N 21 42 E
Salop = Shropshire □ 83 52 36N 2 45W
Salsacate 76 31 20 S 65 5W
Salsk 99 46 28N 41 30 E
Salso → 94 37 6N 13 55 E
Salt →, Canada 62 60 0N 112 25W
Salt →, Ariz. 12 33 23N 112 19W
Salt →, Ky. 49 38 0N 85 57W
Salt →, Mo. 32 39 28N 91 4W
Salt Basin 50 31 42N 105 2W
Salt Cr. → 21 40 8N 89 50W
Salt Draw → 50 31 19N 103 28W
Salt Flat 50 31 45N 105 5W
Salt Fork 43 36 38N 97 35W
Salt Fork Arkansas → 43 36 36N 97 3W
Salt Fork Brazos → 50 33 16N 100 0W
Salt Fork L. 42 40 3N 81 30W
Salt Fork Red → 43 34 27N 99 21W
Salt L., Hawaii 19 21 21N 157 55W
Salt L., N. Mex. 38 32 18N 104 0W
Salt Lake City 52 40 45N 111 53W
Salt Lake County ◇ 52 40 40N 112 0W
Salt Lick 49 38 7N 83 37W
Salt Marsh L. 52 39 29N 113 55W
Salt River Indian Reservation 12 33 35N 111 50W
Salt Springs 17 29 21N 81 44W
Salta 76 24 57 S 65 25W
Salta □ 76 24 48 S 65 30W
Saltcoats 84 55 38N 4 47W
Saltee Is. 85 52 7N 6 37W
Salters 46 33 36N 79 51W
Saltfjorden 96 67 15N 14 10 E
Salthólmavík 96 65 24N 21 57W
Saltillo, Mexico 64 25 30N 100 57W
Saltillo, Miss. 31 34 23N 88 41W
Saltillo, Pa. 45 40 13N 78 1W
Saltillo, Tenn. 48 35 23N 88 13W
Salto, Argentina 76 34 20 S 60 15W
Salto, Uruguay 76 31 27 S 57 50W
Salto da Divisa 75 16 0 S 39 57W
Salton Sea 15 33 15N 115 45W
Saltpond 120 5 15N 1 3W
Saltspring 62 48 54N 123 37W
Saltville 54 36 53N 81 46W
Saluda, N.C. 40 35 14N 82 21W
Saluda, S.C. 46 34 0N 81 46W
Saluda, Va. 54 37 36N 76 36W
Saluda → 46 34 1N 81 4W
Saluda County ◇ 46 34 0N 81 45W
Salûm 121 31 31N 25 7 E
Salûm, Khâlig el 121 31 30N 25 9 E
Salur 109 18 27N 83 18 E
Salus 13 35 44N 93 24W
Salut, Îs. du 71 5 15N 52 35W
Saluzzo 94 44 39N 7 29 E
Salvación, B. 78 50 50 S 75 10W
Salvador, Brazil 75 13 0 S 38 30W
Salvador, Canada 63 52 10N 109 32W
Salvador, L. 25 29 43N 90 15W
Salvaterra 74 0 46 S 48 31W
Salwa 107 24 45N 50 55 E
Salween → 109 16 31N 97 37 E
Salyany 99 39 10N 48 50 E
Salyersville 49 37 45N 83 4W
Salzburg 88 47 48N 13 2 E
Salzburg □ 88 47 15N 13 0 E
Salzgitter 88 52 13N 10 22 E
Sam Houston National Forest 51 30 32N 95 29W
Sam Neua 112 20 29N 104 0 E
Sam Ngao 112 17 18N 99 0 E
Sam Rayburn Reservoir 51 31 4N 94 5W
Sama 100 60 12N 60 22 E
Sama de Langreo 91 43 18N 5 40W
Samagaltai 101 50 36N 95 3 E
Samaipata 73 18 9 S 63 52W
Samales Group 111 6 0N 122 0 E
Samana Cay 67 23 3N 73 45W
Samangán □ 107 36 15N 68 3 E
Samani 116 42 7N 142 56 E
Samar 111 12 0N 125 0 E
Samaria = Shōmrōn 104 32 15N 35 13 E
Samaria 20 42 7N 112 20W
Samarinda 110 0 30 S 117 9 E
Samarkand 100 39 40N 66 55 E
Sāmarrā' 106 34 16N 43 55 E
Samaúma 73 7 50 S 60 2W
Sambaíba 74 7 8 S 45 21W
Sambalpur 109 21 28N 84 4 E
Sambar, Tanjung 110 2 59 S 110 19 E
Sambas 110 1 20N 109 20 E
Sambava 123 14 16 S 50 10 E
Sambhal 108 28 35N 78 37 E
Sambhar 108 26 52N 75 6 E
Sambiase 94 38 58N 16 16 E
Sambor 112 12 46N 106 0 E
Sambre → 87 50 27N 4 52 E
Samburg 48 36 23N 89 21W
Samchŏk 114 37 30N 129 10 E
Same 122 4 2 S 37 38 E
Samo Alto 76 30 22 S 71 0W
Samokov 95 42 18N 23 35 E
Samoorombón, Bahía 76 36 5 S 57 20W
Sámos 95 37 45N 26 50 E
Samoset 17 27 28N 82 33W
Samothráki 95 40 28N 25 28 E
Sampacho 76 33 20 S 64 50W
Sampang 111 7 11 S 113 13 E
Sampit 110 2 34 S 113 0 E
Sampit, Teluk 110 3 5 S 113 3 E
Sampson County ◇ 40 35 0N 78 30W
Samra 106 25 35N 41 0 E
Samson 10 31 7N 86 3W
Samsun 106 41 15N 36 22 E
Samuel R. McKelvie Nat. Forest 34 42 40N 101 0W
Samui, Ko 112 9 30N 100 0 E
Samut Prakan 112 13 32N 100 40 E
Samut Sakhon 112 13 31N 100 13 E
Samut Songkhram → 112 13 24N 100 1 E
San 120 13 15N 4 57W
San → 89 50 45N 21 51 E
San Agustín 70 1 53N 76 16W
San Agustin, Plains of 38 33 45N 108 15W
San Agustín de Valle Fértil 76 30 35 S 67 30W
San Ambrosio 125 26 28 S 79 53W
San Andreas 14 38 12N 120 41W
San Andrés, I. de 66 12 42N 81 46W
San Andres Mts. 38 33 0N 106 30W
San Andrés Tuxtla 65 18 30N 95 20W
San Angelo 50 31 28N 100 26W
San Anselmo 14 37 59N 122 34W
San Antonio, Belize 65 16 15N 89 2W
San Antonio, Chile 76 33 40 S 71 40W
San Antonio, Colo. 16 37 1N 106 1W
San Antonio, N. Mex. 38 33 55N 106 52W
San Antonio, Tex. 51 29 25N 98 30W
San Antonio, Venezuela 70 3 30N 66 44W
San Antonio → 51 28 30N 96 54W
San Antonio, C., Argentina 76 36 15 S 56 40W
San Antonio, C., Cuba 66 21 50N 84 57W
San Antonio B. 51 28 20N 96 45W
San Antonio de los Baños 66 22 54N 82 31W
San Antonio de los Cobres 76 24 10 S 66 17W
San Antonio do Zaire 122 6 8 S 12 11 E
San Antonio Mt. 50 32 0N 105 30W
San Antonio Oeste 78 40 40 S 65 0W
San Antonio Reservoir 15 35 48N 120 53W
San Ardo 15 36 1N 120 54W
San Augustin, C. 111 6 20N 126 13 E
San Augustine, Calif. 15 34 28N 120 22W
San Augustine, Tex. 51 31 32N 94 7W
San Augustine County ◇ 51 31 30N 94 8W
San Benedetto 94 45 2N 10 57 E
San Benedicto, I. 64 19 18N 110 49W
San Benito 50 26 8N 97 38W
San Benito → 14 36 53N 121 34W
San Benito County ◇ 15 36 30N 121 0W
San Bernard → 51 28 52N 95 27W
San Bernardino 15 34 7N 117 19W
San Bernardino County ◇ 15 34 45N 116 0W
San Bernardino Mts. 15 34 10N 116 45W
San Bernardino Str. 111 13 0N 125 0 E
San Bernardo 76 33 40 S 70 50W
San Bernardo, I. de 70 9 45N 75 50W
San Blas 64 26 4N 108 46W
San Blas, Arch. de 66 9 50N 78 31W
San Blas, C. 17 29 40N 85 21W
San Borja 72 14 50 S 66 52W
San Bruno 14 37 38N 122 25W
San Buenaventura, Bolivia 72 14 28 S 67 35W
San Buenaventura, Mexico 64 27 5N 101 32W
San Carlos, Argentina 76 33 50 S 69 0W
San Carlos, Bolivia 73 17 24 S 63 45W
San Carlos, Chile 76 36 10 S 72 0W
San Carlos, Mexico 64 29 0N 100 54W
San Carlos, Nic. 66 11 12N 84 50W
San Carlos, Phil. 111 10 29N 123 25 E
San Carlos, Uruguay 77 34 46 S 54 58W
San Carlos, U.S.A. 12 33 21N 110 27W
San Carlos, Amazonas, Venezuela 70 1 55N 67 4W
San Carlos, Cojedes, Venezuela 70 9 40N 68 36W
San Carlos de Bariloche 78 41 10 S 71 25W
San Carlos del Zulia 70 9 1N 71 55W
San Carlos Indian Reservation 12 33 25N 110 0W
San Carlos L. 12 33 11N 110 32W
San Clemente, Chile 76 35 30 S 71 29W
San Clemente, U.S.A. 15 33 26N 117 37W
San Clemente I. 15 32 53N 118 29W
San Cristóbal, Argentina 76 30 20 S 61 10W
San Cristóbal, Colombia 70 2 18 S 73 2W
San Cristóbal, Dom. Rep. 67 18 25N 70 6W
San Cristobal, U.S.A. 38 36 36N 105 39W
San Cristóbal, Venezuela 70 16 50N 92 40W
San Cristóbal de las Casas 65 16 50N 92 33W
San Diego, Calif. 15 32 43N 117 9W
San Diego, Tex. 51 27 46N 98 14W
San Diego, C. 78 54 40 S 65 10W
San Diego County ◇ 15 33 0N 117 15W
San Diego de la Unión 64 21 28N 100 52W
San Elizario 50 31 35N 106 16W
San Estanislao 76 24 39 S 56 26W
San Felipe, Chile 76 32 43 S 70 42W
San Felipe, Colombia 70 1 55N 67 6W
San Felipe, Mexico 64 31 0N 114 52W
San Felipe, Venezuela 70 10 20N 68 44W
San Felipe Pueblo 38 35 26N 106 27W
San Felíu de Guíxols 91 41 45N 3 1 E
San Félix 125 26 23 S 80 0W
San Fernando, Chile 76 34 30 S 71 0W
San Fernando, Mexico 64 30 0N 115 10W
San Fernando, Luzon, Phil. 111 15 5N 120 37 E
San Fernando, Luzon, Phil. 111 16 40N 120 23 E
San Fernando, Spain 91 36 28N 6 17W
San Fernando, Trin. & Tob. 67 10 20N 61 30W
San Fernando, U.S.A. 15 34 17N 118 26W
San Fernando → 64 24 55N 98 10W
San Fernando de Apure 70 7 54N 67 15W
San Fernando de Atabapo 70 4 3N 67 42W
San Fidel 38 35 5N 107 36W
San Francisco, Argentina 76 31 30 S 62 5W
San Francisco, Bolivia 73 15 16 S 65 31W
San Francisco, U.S.A. 14 37 47N 122 25W
San Francisco → 12 32 59N 109 22W
San Francisco, Paso de 76 27 0 S 68 0W
San Francisco B. 14 37 40N 122 20W
San Francisco County ◇ 14 37 47N 122 25W
San Francisco Cr. → 50 29 53N 102 19W
San Francisco de Macorís 67 19 19N 70 15W
San Francisco del Monte de Oro 76 32 36 S 66 8W
San Francisco del Oro 64 26 52N 105 50W
San Francisco Mts. 38 33 45N 108 50W
San Francisco Solano, Pta. 70 6 18N 77 29W
San Gabriel 70 0 36N 77 49W
San Gabriel → 51 30 46N 97 1W
San Gabriel Mts. 15 34 20N 118 0W
San German 57 18 5N 67 3W
San Gil 70 6 33N 73 8W
San Gottardo, Paso del 88 46 33N 8 33 E
San Gregorio 77 32 37 S 55 40W
San Ignacio, Belize 65 17 10N 89 0W
San Ignacio, Bolivia 73 16 20 S 60 55W
San Ignacio, Mexico 64 27 27N 113 0W
San Ignacio, Paraguay 76 26 52 S 57 3W
San Ignacio, Laguna 64 26 50N 113 11W
San Ildefonso, C. 111 16 0N 122 1 E
San Isabel National Forest 16 38 0N 105 2W
San Isidro, Argentina 76 34 29 S 58 31W
San Isidro, U.S.A. 50 26 43N 98 27W
San Jacinto, Colombia 70 9 50N 75 8W
San Jacinto, Calif. 15 33 47N 116 57W
San Jacinto, Nev. 35 41 53N 114 47W
San Jacinto County ◇ 51 30 36N 95 8W
San Jacinto Mts. 15 33 45N 116 40W
San Javier, Misiones, Argentina 77 27 55 S 55 5W
San Javier, Santa Fe, Argentina 76 30 40 S 59 55W
San Javier, Beni, Bolivia 73 14 34 S 64 42W
San Javier, Santa Cruz, Bolivia 73 16 18 S 62 30W
San Javier, Chile 76 35 40 S 71 45W
San Jerónimo, Sa. de 70 8 0N 75 50W
San Joaquín, Bolivia 73 13 4 S 64 49W
San Joaquin, U.S.A. 15 36 36N 120 11W
San Joaquín, Venezuela 70 10 16N 67 47W
San Joaquín →, Bolivia 73 13 8 S 63 41W
San Joaquin →, U.S.A. 14 38 4N 121 51W
San Joaquin County ◇ 14 37 50N 121 15W
San Joaquin Valley 14 37 20N 121 0W
San Jon 38 35 6N 103 20W
San Jorge 76 31 54 S 61 50W
San Jorge, Bahía de 64 31 20N 113 20W
San Jorge, Golfo 78 46 0 S 66 0W
San Jorge, G. de 91 40 50N 0 55W
San José, Bolivia 73 17 53 S 60 50W
San José, C. Rica 66 10 0N 84 2W
San José, Guat. 66 14 0N 90 50W
San José, Mexico 64 25 0N 110 50W
San Jose, Luzon, Phil. 111 15 45N 120 55 E
San Jose, Mindoro, Phil. 111 12 27N 121 4 E
San Jose, Calif. 14 37 20N 121 53W
San Jose, Ill. 21 40 18N 89 36W
San José Carpizo 65 19 26N 90 32W
San José de Feliciano 76 30 26 S 58 46W
San José de Jáchal 76 30 15 S 68 46W
San José de Mayo 76 34 27 S 56 40W
San José de Ocune 70 4 15N 70 20W
San José de Uchapiamonas 72 14 13 S 68 5W
San José del Cabo 64 23 0N 109 40W
San José del Guaviare 70 2 35N 72 38W
San José do Anauá 71 0 58N 61 22W

San Jose I. — Santa Isabel

San Jose I. **51** 27 59N 96 59W
San Juan, Argentina **76** 31 30 S 68 30W
San Juan, Colombia **70** 8 46N 76 32W
San Juan, Mexico **64** 21 20N 102 50W
San Juan, Ica, Peru **72** 15 22 S 75 7W
San Juan, Puno, Peru **72** 14 2 S 69 19W
San Juan, Phil. **111** 8 25N 126 20 E
San Juan, Puerto Rico **57** 18 28N 66 7W
San Juan ◇ **57** 18 20N 66 10W
San Juan □, Argentina **76** 31 9 S 69 0W
San Juan □, Dom. Rep. **67** 18 45N 71 25W
San Juan →, Argentina **76** 32 20 S 67 25W
San Juan →, Bolivia **73** 21 2 S 65 19W
San Juan →, Colombia **70** 4 3N 77 27W
San Juan →, Nic. **66** 10 56N 83 42W
San Juan →, U.S.A. **52** 37 16N 110 26W
San Juan →, Venezuela **71** 10 14N 62 38W
San Juan, C. **122** 1 5N 9 20 E
San Juan Basin **38** 36 20N 108 10W
San Juan Bautista, Paraguay **76** 26 37 S 57 6W
San Juan Bautista, U.S.A. **14** 36 51N 121 32W
San Juan Capistrano **15** 33 30N 117 40W
San Juan County ◇, Colo. **16** 37 50N 107 40W
San Juan County ◇, N. Mex. **38** 36 30N 108 30W
San Juan County ◇, Utah **52** 38 0N 109 30W
San Juan County ◇, Wash. **53** 48 32N 123 5W
San Juan Cr. → **15** 35 40N 120 22W
San Juan de Guadalupe **64** 24 38N 102 44W
San Juan de los Morros **70** 9 55N 67 21W
San Juan del César **70** 10 46N 73 1W
San Juan del Norte **66** 10 58N 83 40W
San Juan del Norte, B. de **66** 11 0N 83 40W
San Juan del Río **65** 20 25N 100 0W
San Juan del Sur **66** 11 20N 85 51W
San Juan I. **53** 48 32N 123 5W
San Juan Indian Reservation **38** 36 0N 106 10W
San Juan Mts. **16** 37 30N 107 0W
San Juan National Forest **16** 37 30N 108 0W
San Juan Pueblo **38** 36 3N 106 4W
San Julián **78** 49 15 S 67 45W
San Justo **76** 30 47 S 60 30W
San Lázaro, C. **64** 24 50N 112 18W
San Lázaro, Sa. de **64** 23 25N 110 0W
San Leandro **14** 37 44N 122 9W
San Lorenzo, Argentina **76** 32 45 S 60 45W
San Lorenzo, Beni, Bolivia **73** 15 22 S 65 48W
San Lorenzo, Tarija, Bolivia **73** 21 26 S 64 47W
San Lorenzo, Ecuador **70** 1 15N 78 50W
San Lorenzo, Paraguay **76** 25 20 S 57 32W
San Lorenzo, Puerto Rico **57** 18 11N 65 58W
San Lorenzo, Venezuela **70** 9 47N 71 4W
San Lorenzo → **64** 24 15N 107 24W
San Lorenzo, I., Mexico **64** 28 35N 112 50W
San Lorenzo, I., Peru **72** 12 7 S 77 15W
San Lorenzo, Mt. **78** 47 40 S 72 20W
San Lucas, Bolivia **73** 20 5 S 65 7W
San Lucas, Baja Calif. S., Mexico **64** 22 53N 109 54W
San Lucas, Baja Calif. S., Mexico **64** 27 10N 112 14W
San Lucas, U.S.A. **15** 36 8N 121 1W
San Lucas, C. de **64** 22 50N 110 0W
San Luis, Argentina **76** 33 20 S 66 20W
San Luis, Cuba **66** 22 17N 83 46W
San Luis, Guat. **66** 16 14N 89 27W
San Luis, Ariz. **12** 32 29N 114 47W
San Luis, Colo. **16** 37 12N 105 25W
San Luis □ **76** 34 0 S 66 0W
San Luis, I. **64** 29 58N 114 26W
San Luis, L. de **73** 13 45 S 64 0W
San Luis, Sierra de **76** 32 30 S 66 10W
San Luis Cr. → **16** 37 42N 105 44W
San Luís de la Loma **64** 17 18N 100 55W
San Luis de la Paz **64** 21 19N 100 32W
San Luis Obispo **15** 35 17N 120 40W
San Luis Obispo County ◇ **15** 35 30N 120 30W
San Luis Peak **16** 37 59N 106 56W
San Luis Potosí **64** 22 9N 100 59W
San Luis Potosí □ **64** 22 10N 101 0W
San Luis Reservoir **14** 37 4N 121 5W
San Luis Rey → **15** 33 12N 117 24W
San Luis Río Colorado **64** 32 29N 114 58W
San Luis Valley **16** 37 45N 105 50W
San Manuel **12** 32 36N 110 38W
San Marcos, Colombia **70** 8 39N 75 8W
San Marcos, Guat. **66** 14 59N 91 52W
San Marcos, Mexico **64** 27 13N 112 6W
San Marcos, Calif. **15** 33 9N 117 10W
San Marcos, Tex. **51** 29 53N 97 56W
San Marino **94** 43 56N 12 25 E
San Marino ■ **94** 43 56N 12 25 E
San Martin, Antarct. **5** 68 11 S 67 0W
San Martín, Argentina **76** 33 5 S 68 28W
San Martín, Colombia **70** 3 42N 73 42W
San Martin, U.S.A. **14** 37 5N 121 37W
San Martin → **73** 13 8 S 63 43W
San Martin, C. **15** 35 53N 121 28W
San Martín, L. **78** 48 50 S 72 50W
San Martin de los Andes **78** 40 10 S 71 20W
San Mateo, Calif. **14** 37 34N 122 19W
San Mateo, N. Mex. **38** 35 20N 107 39W
San Mateo County ◇ **14** 37 30N 122 25W
San Mateo Mts. **38** 33 45N 107 25W
San Matías **73** 16 25 S 58 20W
San Matías, Golfo **78** 41 30 S 64 0W
San Miguel, El Salv. **66** 13 30N 88 12W
San Miguel, Panama **66** 8 27N 78 55W
San Miguel, Calif. **15** 35 45N 120 42W
San Miguel, N. Mex. **38** 32 9N 106 44W
San Miguel, Venezuela **70** 9 40N 65 11W
San Miguel →, Bolivia **73** 13 52 S 63 56W
San Miguel →, S. Amer. **70** 0 25N 76 30W
San Miguel →, U.S.A. **16** 38 23N 108 48W
San Miguel County ◇, Colo. **16** 38 0N 108 30W
San Miguel County ◇, N. Mex. **38** 35 30N 105 0W
San Miguel de Huachi **72** 15 40 S 67 15W
San Miguel de Tucumán **76** 26 50 S 65 20W
San Miguel del Monte **76** 35 23 S 58 50W
San Miguel I. **15** 34 2N 120 23W
San Narciso **111** 15 2N 120 3 E
San Nicolás de los Arroyas **76** 33 25 S 60 10W
San Nicolas I. **15** 33 15N 119 30W
San Onofre **70** 9 44N 75 32W
San Pablo, Bolivia **76** 21 43 S 66 38W
San Pablo, Calif. **14** 37 58N 122 21W
San Pablo, Colo. **16** 37 9N 105 24W
San Pablo B. **14** 38 5N 122 20W
San Patricio **38** 33 25N 105 20W
San Patricio County ◇ **51** 28 2N 97 31W
San Pedro, Buenos Aires, Argentina **77** 26 30 S 54 10W
San Pedro, Jujuy, Argentina **76** 24 12 S 64 55W
San Pedro, Colombia **70** 4 56N 71 53W
San-Pédro, Ivory C. **120** 4 50N 6 33W
San Pedro, Mexico **64** 23 55N 110 17W
San Pedro, Peru **72** 14 49 S 74 5W
San Pedro, U.S.A. **51** 27 48N 97 41W
San Pedro □ **76** 24 0 S 57 0W
San Pedro →, Chihuahua, Mexico **64** 28 20N 106 10W
San Pedro →, Michoacan, Mexico **64** 19 23N 103 51W
San Pedro →, Nayarit, Mexico **64** 21 45N 105 30W
San Pedro →, U.S.A. **12** 32 59N 110 47W
San Pedro, Pta. **76** 25 30 S 70 38W
San Pedro Channel **15** 33 30N 118 25W
San Pedro de Arimena **70** 4 37N 71 42W
San Pedro de Atacama **76** 22 55 S 68 15W
San Pedro de Jujuy **76** 24 12 S 64 55W
San Pedro de las Colonias **64** 25 50N 102 59W
San Pedro de Lloc **72** 7 15 S 79 28W
San Pedro de Macorís **67** 18 30N 69 18W
San Pedro del Norte **66** 13 4N 84 33W
San Pedro del Paraná **76** 26 43 S 56 13W
San Pedro Mártir, Sierra **64** 31 0N 115 30W
San Pedro Mixtepec **65** 16 2N 97 7W
San Pedro Ocampo = Melchor Ocampo **64** 24 52N 101 40W
San Pedro Sula **66** 15 30N 88 0W
San Perlita **50** 26 30N 97 39W
San Pitch → **52** 39 3N 111 51W
San Quintín **64** 30 29N 115 57W
San Rafael, Argentina **76** 34 40 S 68 21W
San Rafael, Calif. **14** 37 58N 122 32W
San Rafael, N. Mex. **38** 35 7N 107 53W
San Rafael, Venezuela **70** 10 58N 71 46W
San Rafael → **52** 38 47N 110 7W
San Rafael Mts. **15** 34 40N 119 50W
San Rafael Swell **52** 38 45N 110 45W
San Ramón, Bolivia **73** 13 17 S 64 43W
San Ramón, Peru **72** 11 8 S 75 20W
San Ramón de la Nueva Orán **76** 23 10 S 64 20W
San Remo **94** 43 48N 7 47 E
San Román, C. **70** 12 12N 70 0W
San Roque **76** 28 25 S 58 45W
San Rosendo **76** 37 16 S 72 43W
San Saba **51** 31 12N 98 43W
San Saba → **51** 31 15N 98 36W
San Saba County ◇ **51** 31 13N 98 47W
San Salvador, Bahamas **67** 24 0N 74 40W
San Salvador, El Salv. **66** 13 40N 89 10W
San Salvador de Jujuy **76** 24 10 S 64 48W
San Salvador I. **67** 24 0N 74 32W
San Sebastián, Argentina **78** 53 10 S 68 30W
San Sebastian, Puerto Rico **57** 18 20N 66 59W
San Sebastián, Spain **91** 43 17N 1 58W
San Sebastián, Venezuela **70** 9 57N 67 11W
San Simeon **15** 35 39N 121 11W
San Simon **12** 32 16N 109 14W
San Simon → **12** 32 50N 109 39W
San Telmo **64** 30 58N 116 6W
San Tiburcio **64** 24 8N 101 32W
San Valentin, Mte. **78** 46 30 S 73 30W
San Vicente de la Barquera **91** 43 23N 4 29W
San Vicente del Caguán **70** 2 7N 74 46W
San Xavier Indian Reservation **12** 32 10N 111 0W
San Yanaro **70** 2 47N 69 42W
San Ygnacio **50** 27 3N 99 26W
San Ysidro **38** 35 34N 106 46W
Saña, Peru **72** 6 54 S 79 36W
Sana', Yemen **105** 15 27N 44 12 E
Sana → **94** 45 3N 16 23 E
Sanaga → **122** 3 35N 9 38 E
Sanak I. **11** 54 25N 162 40W
Sanaloa, Presa **64** 24 50N 107 20W
Sanana **111** 2 5 S 125 59 E
Sanandaj **106** 35 18N 47 1 E
Sanandita **76** 21 40 S 63 45W
Sanborn, Minn. **30** 44 13N 95 8W
Sanborn, N. Dak. **41** 46 57N 98 14W
Sanborn County ◇ **47** 44 0N 98 0W
Sanbornville **36** 43 33N 71 2W
Sancha He → **115** 26 48N 106 7 E
Sánchez **67** 19 15N 69 36W
Sanco, Pt. **111** 8 15N 126 24 E
Sancti-Spíritus **66** 21 52N 79 33W
Sand Cr. →, Ind. **22** 39 3N 85 51W
Sand Cr. →, Wyo. **56** 43 20N 105 2W
Sand Fork **54** 38 55N 80 45W
Sand Hill → **30** 47 36N 96 52W
Sand Hills **34** 42 10N 101 30W
Sand I., Hawaii **19** 21 19N 157 53W
Sand I., Wis. **55** 46 59N 90 58W
Sand Lake **29** 43 18N 85 31W
Sand Point **11** 55 20N 160 30W
Sand Pt. **29** 43 55N 83 24W
Sand Res. **43** 36 45N 96 10W
Sand Springs **43** 36 9N 96 7W
Sand Tank Mts. **12** 32 45N 112 30W
Sanda **117** 34 53N 135 14 E
Sandakan **110** 5 53N 118 4 E
Sandan **112** 12 46N 106 0 E
Sandanski **95** 41 35N 23 16 E
Sanday **84** 59 15N 2 30W
Sandborn **22** 38 54N 87 11W
Sanders **12** 35 13N 109 20W
Sanders County ◇ **33** 47 40N 115 30W
Sanderson, Fla. **17** 30 15N 82 16W
Sanderson, Tex. **50** 30 9N 102 24W
Sandersville, Ga. **18** 32 59N 82 48W
Sandersville, Miss. **31** 31 47N 89 2W
Sandfly L. **63** 55 43N 106 6W
Sandía, Peru **72** 14 10 S 69 30W
Sandia, U.S.A. **51** 28 1N 97 53W
Sandıklı **106** 38 30N 30 20 E
Sandnes **97** 58 50N 5 45 E
Sandness **84** 60 18N 1 38W
Sandoa **122** 9 41 S 23 0 E
Sandomierz **89** 50 40N 21 43 E
Sandona **70** 1 17N 77 28W
Sandoval **21** 38 37N 89 7W
Sandoval County ◇ **38** 35 45N 106 45W
Sandover → **127** 21 43 S 136 32 E
Sandoway **109** 18 20N 94 30 E
Sandpoint **20** 48 17N 116 33W
Sandringham **82** 52 50N 0 30 E
Sandspit **62** 53 14N 131 49W
Sandston **54** 37 31N 77 19W
Sandstone, Australia **126** 27 59 S 119 16 E
Sandstone, U.S.A. **30** 46 8N 92 52W
Sandtown **27** 39 4N 75 44W
Sandusky, Mich. **29** 43 25N 82 50W
Sandusky, Ohio **42** 41 27N 82 42W
Sandusky → **42** 41 27N 83 0W
Sandusky County ◇ **42** 41 21N 83 7W
Sandviken **97** 60 38N 16 46 E
Sandwich, Ill. **21** 41 39N 88 37W
Sandwich, Mass. **28** 41 46N 70 30W
Sandwich B. **61** 53 40N 57 15W
Sandwip Chan. **109** 22 35N 91 35 E
Sandy, Oreg. **44** 45 24N 122 16W
Sandy, Pa. **45** 41 6N 78 46W
Sandy, Utah **52** 40 35N 111 50W
Sandy C., Queens., Australia **127** 24 42 S 153 15 E
Sandy C., Tas., Australia **127** 41 25 S 144 45 E
Sandy Cay **67** 23 13N 75 18W
Sandy Cr. → **56** 41 51N 109 47W
Sandy Hook, Ky. **49** 38 5N 83 8W
Sandy Hook, Miss. **31** 31 2N 89 49W
Sandy Hook, N.J. **37** 40 26N 74 0W
Sandy L. **60** 53 2N 93 0W
Sandy Lake **60** 53 0N 93 15W
Sandy Narrows **63** 55 5N 103 4W
Sandy Ridge **40** 36 30N 80 6W
Sandy Springs **18** 33 56N 84 23W
Sandyville **54** 38 54N 81 40W
Sanford, Colo. **16** 37 16N 105 54W
Sanford, Fla. **17** 28 48N 81 16W
Sanford, Maine **26** 43 27N 70 47W
Sanford, Miss. **31** 31 29N 89 26W
Sanford, N.C. **40** 35 29N 79 10W
Sanford, Tex. **50** 35 42N 101 32W
Sanford → **126** 27 22 S 115 53 E
Sanford, Mt. **11** 62 13N 144 8W
Sanga → **122** 1 5 S 17 0 E
Sanga-Tolon **101** 61 50N 149 40 E
Sangamner **108** 19 37N 74 15 E
Sangamon → **21** 40 7N 90 20W
Sangamon County ◇ **21** 39 45N 89 40W
Sangar **101** 64 2N 127 31 E
Sangasangadalam **110** 0 36 S 117 13 E
Sangay **70** 2 0 S 78 20W
Sangeang **111** 8 12 S 119 6 E
Sanger, Calif. **15** 36 42N 119 33W
Sanger, Tex. **51** 33 22N 97 10W
Sanggan He → **114** 38 12N 117 15 E
Sanggau **110** 0 5N 110 30 E
Sangihe, Kepulauan **111** 3 0N 126 0 E
Sangihe, P. **111** 3 45N 125 30 E
Sangkapura **110** 5 52 S 112 40 E
Sangli **108** 16 55N 74 33 E
Sangmélina **122** 2 57N 12 1 E
Sangonera → **91** 37 59N 1 4W
Sangre de Cristo **38** 36 40N 105 15W
Sangre de Cristo Mts. **16** 37 30N 105 20W
Sangudo **62** 53 50N 114 54W
Sangue → **73** 11 1 S 58 39W
Sangzhi **115** 29 25N 110 12 E
Sanibel I. **17** 26 26N 82 6W
Sanilac County ◇ **29** 43 25N 82 50W
Sanjiang **115** 25 48N 109 37 E
Sanjo **116** 37 37N 138 57 E
Sankt Gotthard P. = San Gottardo, Paso del **88** 46 33N 8 33 E
Sankt Moritz **88** 46 30N 9 50 E
Sankuru → **122** 4 17 S 20 25 E
Sanlúcar de Barrameda **91** 36 46N 6 21W
Sanmenxia **115** 34 47N 111 12 E
Sannicandro Gargánico **94** 41 50N 15 34 E
Sanok **89** 49 35N 22 10 E
Sanpete County ◇ **52** 39 30N 111 40W
Sanpoil → **53** 47 57N 118 41W
Sanquhar **84** 55 21N 3 56W
Sanshui **115** 23 10N 112 56 E
Sant Joseph County ◇ **29** 41 50N 85 30W
Santa, Peru **72** 8 59 S 78 40W
Santa, U.S.A. **20** 47 9N 116 27W
Santa Ana, Beni, Bolivia **73** 13 50 S 65 40W
Santa Ana, Santa Cruz, Bolivia **73** 18 43 S 58 44W
Santa Ana, Santa Cruz, Bolivia **73** 16 37 S 60 43W
Santa Ana, Ecuador **70** 1 16 S 80 20W
Santa Ana, El Salv. **66** 14 0N 89 31W
Santa Ana, Mexico **64** 30 31N 111 8W
Santa Ana, U.S.A. **15** 33 46N 117 52W
Santa Ana → **70** 9 30N 71 57W
Santa Ana Indian Reservation **38** 35 26N 106 37W
Santa Ana Mts. **15** 33 40N 117 30W
Santa Ana Pueblo **38** 35 26N 106 37W
Santa Anna **51** 31 45N 99 20W
Santa Bárbara, Colombia **70** 5 53N 75 35W
Santa Barbara, Hond. **66** 14 53N 88 14W
Santa Bárbara, Mexico **64** 26 48N 105 50W
Santa Barbara, U.S.A. **15** 34 25N 119 42W
Santa Bárbara, Venezuela **70** 7 47N 71 10W
Santa Barbara Channel **15** 34 15N 120 0W
Santa Barbara County ◇ **15** 34 40N 120 0W
Santa Barbara I. **15** 33 29N 119 2W
Santa Catalina, Colombia **70** 10 36N 75 17W
Santa Catalina, Mexico **64** 25 40N 110 50W
Santa Catalina, Gulf of **15** 33 10N 117 50W
Santa Catalina I. **15** 33 23N 118 25W
Santa Catarina □ **77** 27 25 S 48 30W
Santa Catarina, I. de **77** 27 30 S 48 40W
Santa Cecília **77** 26 56 S 50 18W
Santa Clara, Cuba **66** 22 20N 80 0W
Santa Clara, Calif. **14** 37 21N 121 57W
Santa Clara, N.Y. **39** 44 38N 74 27W
Santa Clara, Oreg. **44** 44 6N 123 8W
Santa Clara, Utah **52** 37 8N 113 39W
Santa Clara → **15** 34 14N 119 16W
Santa Clara County ◇ **14** 37 15N 121 40W
Santa Clara de Olimar **77** 32 50 S 54 54W
Santa Clara Valley **15** 36 50N 121 30W
Santa Clotilde **70** 2 33 S 73 45W
Santa Cruz, Argentina **78** 50 0 S 68 32W
Santa Cruz, Bolivia **73** 17 43 S 63 10W
Santa Cruz, Brazil **74** 6 13 S 36 1W
Santa Cruz, Chile **76** 34 38 S 71 27W
Santa Cruz, C. Rica **66** 10 15N 85 35W
Santa Cruz, Peru **72** 5 40 S 75 56W
Santa Cruz, Phil. **111** 14 20N 121 24 E
Santa Cruz, U.S.A. **15** 36 58N 122 1W
Santa Cruz, Venezuela **71** 8 3N 64 27W
Santa Cruz □, Argentina **78** 49 0 S 70 0W
Santa Cruz □, Bolivia **73** 17 43 S 63 10W
Santa Cruz →, Argentina **78** 50 10 S 68 20W
Santa Cruz →, U.S.A. **12** 33 20N 112 16W
Santa Cruz, Is. **124** 10 30 S 166 0 E
Santa Cruz Cabrália **75** 16 17 S 39 2W
Santa Cruz County ◇, Ariz. **12** 31 30N 110 45W
Santa Cruz County ◇, Calif. **14** 37 0N 122 0W
Sta. Cruz de Tenerife **120** 28 28N 16 15W
Santa Cruz del Norte **66** 23 9N 81 55W
Santa Cruz del Sur **66** 20 44N 78 0W
Santa Cruz do Rio Pardo **77** 22 54 S 49 37W
Santa Cruz do Sul **77** 29 42 S 52 25W
Santa Cruz I. **15** 34 1N 119 43W
Santa Cruz Mts. **14** 37 15N 122 0W
Santa Cruz Wash → **12** 33 23N 112 12W
Santa Domingo, Cay **66** 21 25N 75 15W
Santa Elena, Argentina **76** 30 58 S 59 47W
Santa Elena, Ecuador **70** 2 16 S 80 52W
Santa Elena, U.S.A. **50** 26 46N 98 29W
Santa Elena, C. **66** 10 54N 85 56W
Santa Fe, Argentina **76** 31 35 S 60 41W
Santa Fe, U.S.A. **38** 35 41N 105 57W
Santa Fé □ **76** 31 50 S 60 55W
Santa Fe → **17** 29 53N 82 53W
Santa Fe, L. **17** 29 45N 82 5W
Santa Fe Baldy **38** 35 50N 105 46W
Santa Fe County ◇ **38** 35 30N 106 0W
Santa Fe Nat. Forest **38** 36 3N 106 42W
Santa Filomena **74** 9 6 S 45 50W
Santa Genoveva **64** 23 18N 109 52W
Santa Helena **74** 2 14 S 45 18W
Santa Helena de Goiás **75** 17 53 S 50 35W
Santa Inês **75** 13 17 S 39 48W
Santa Inés, I. **78** 54 0 S 73 0W
Santa Isabel = Rey Malabo **122** 3 45N 8 50 E
Santa Isabel, Argentina **76** 36 10 S 66 54W
Santa Isabel, Brazil **75** 11 45 S 51 30W

Santa Isabel **Savona**

Santa Isabel, Puerto Rico ... **57** 17 58N 66 24W
Santa Isabel do Araguaia.... **74** 6 7 S 48 19W
Santa Isabel do Morro ...... **75** 11 34 S 50 40W
Santa Lucía, Corrientes, Argentina .... **76** 28 58 S 59 5W
Santa Lucía, San Juan, Argentina .... **76** 31 30 S 68 30W
Santa Lucia, Uruguay....... **76** 34 27 S 56 24W
Santa Lucia Range **15** 36 0N 121 20W
Santa Margarita, Argentina.. **76** 38 28 S 61 35W
Santa Margarita, Mexico **64** 24 30N 111 50W
Santa Margarita L. **15** 35 20N 120 30W
Santa María, Argentina ..... **76** 26 40 S 66 0W
Santa Maria, Brazil .... **77** 29 40 S 53 48W
Santa Maria, U.S.A. **15** 34 57N 120 26W
Santa María →, Mexico...... **64** 31 0N 107 14W
Santa Maria →, U.S.A..... **12** 34 19N 114 31W
Santa María, Bahía de **64** 25 10N 108 40W
Santa Maria da Vitória...... **75** 13 24 S 44 12W
Santa María de Ipire........ **71** 8 49N 65 19W
Santa María del Oro........ **64** 25 58N 105 20W
Santa Maria di Leuca, C. ... **95** 39 48N 18 20 E
Santa Maria do Suaçuí...... **75** 18 12 S 42 25W
Santa Maria dos Marmelos .. **73** 6 7 S 61 51W
Santa Marta **70** 11 15N 74 13W
Santa Marta, Sierra Nevada de **70** 10 55N 73 50W
Santa Marta Grande, C. .... **77** 28 43 S 48 50W
Santa Maura = Levkás ..... **95** 38 40N 20 43 E
Santa Monica **15** 34 1N 118 29W
Santa Paula............... **15** 34 21N 119 4W
Santa Quitéria .... **74** 4 20 S 40 10W
Santa Rita, Mont. **33** 48 42N 112 19W
Santa Rita, N. Mex. **38** 32 48N 108 4W
Santa Rita, Guarico, Venezuela **70** 8 8N 66 16W
Santa Rita, Zulia, Venezuela **70** 10 32N 71 32W
Santa Rita do Araquaia ..... **73** 17 20 S 53 12W
Santa Rosa, La Pampa, Argentina .... **76** 36 40 S 64 17W
Santa Rosa, San Luis, Argentina .... **76** 32 21 S 65 10W
Santa Rosa, Bolivia .... **72** 10 36 S 67 20W
Santa Rosa, Brazil .... **77** 27 52 S 54 29W
Santa Rosa, Colombia **70** 3 32N 69 48W
Santa Rosa, Ecuador .... **70** 3 27 S 79 58W
Santa Rosa, Peru.......... **72** 14 30 S 70 50W
Santa Rosa, Calif. **14** 38 26N 122 43W
Santa Rosa, N. Mex. **38** 34 57N 104 41W
Santa Rosa, Tex. **50** 26 16N 97 50W
Santa Rosa, Venezuela **70** 1 29N 66 55W
Santa Rosa Beach **17** 30 22N 86 14W
Santa Rosa County ◇ **17** 30 45N 87 0W
Santa Rosa de Cabal **70** 4 52N 75 38W
Santa Rosa de Copán....... **66** 14 47N 88 46W
Santa Rosa de Osos **70** 6 39N 75 28W
Santa Rosa de Río Primero.. **76** 31 8 S 63 20W
Santa Rosa de Viterbo...... **70** 5 53N 72 59W
Santa Rosa del Palmar ...... **73** 16 54 S 62 24W
Santa Rosa I., Calif. **15** 33 58N 120 6W
Santa Rosa I., Fla. **17** 30 20N 86 50W
Santa Rosa Mts. **15** 33 20N 116 15W
Santa Rosa Range......... **35** 41 45N 117 40W
Santa Rosa Wash →........ **12** 33 0N 112 0W
Santa Rosalía **64** 27 20N 112 20W
Santa Sylvina .... **76** 27 50 S 61 10W
Santa Tecla = Nueva San Salvador **66** 13 40N 89 18W
Santa Teresa, Argentina .... **76** 33 25 S 60 47W
Santa Teresa, Brazil .... **75** 19 55 S 40 36W
Santa Teresa, Mexico **65** 25 17N 97 51W
Santa Teresa, Venezuela **71** 4 43N 61 4W
Santa Vitória .... **75** 18 50 S 50 8W
Santa Vitória do Palmar .... **77** 33 32 S 53 25W
Santa Ynez →............ **15** 35 41N 120 36W
Santa Ynez Mts. **15** 34 30N 120 0W
Santai.................... **115** 31 5N 104 58 E
Santaluz.................. **74** 11 15 S 39 22W
Santana .... **75** 13 2 S 44 5W
Santana, Coxilha de .... **77** 30 50 S 55 35W
Santana do Ipanema .... **74** 9 22 S 37 14W
Santana do Livramento ..... **77** 30 55 S 55 30W
Santander, Colombia **70** 3 1N 76 28W
Santander, Spain **91** 43 27N 3 51W
Santander Jiménez **65** 24 11N 98 29W
Santaquin **52** 39 59N 111 47W
Santarém, Brazil .... **71** 2 25 S 54 42W
Santarém, Portugal **91** 39 12N 8 42W
Santaren Channel **66** 24 0N 79 30W
Sante Genevieve **32** 37 59N 90 3W
Santee, Calif. **15** 32 50N 116 58W
Santee, Nebr. **34** 42 51N 97 50W
Santee →................. **46** 33 7N 79 17W
Santee Indian Reservation... **34** 42 50N 97 50W
Santiago, Bolivia .... **73** 18 19 S 59 34W
Santiago, Brazil .... **77** 29 11 S 54 52W
Santiago, Chile .... **76** 33 24 S 70 40W
Santiago, Panama **66** 8 0N 81 0W
Santiago, Peru .... **72** 14 11 S 75 43W
Santiago □ .... **76** 33 30 S 70 50W
Santiago →.............. **70** 4 27 S 77 38W
Santiago, C. .... **78** 50 46 S 75 27W
Santiago, Serranía de ...... **73** 18 25 S 59 25W
Santiago de Chuco .... **72** 8 9 S 78 11W
Santiago de Compostela..... **91** 42 52N 8 37W
Santiago de Cuba **66** 20 0N 75 49W
Santiago de los Cabelleros... **67** 19 30N 70 40W
Santiago del Estero......... **76** 27 50 S 64 15W
Santiago del Estero □ ...... **76** 27 40 S 63 15W
Santiago Ixcuintla **64** 21 50N 105 11W
Santiago Mts. **50** 29 55N 103 22W
Santiago Papasquiaro **64** 25 0N 105 20W
Santiago Peak **50** 29 47N 103 25W
Santiaguillo, L. de **64** 24 50N 104 50W
Santiam Pass **44** 44 25N 121 55W
Santo →................. **72** 8 56 S 78 37W
Santo Amaro .... **75** 12 30 S 38 43W
Santo Anastácio........... **77** 21 58 S 51 39W
Santo André .... **77** 23 39 S 46 29W
Santo Ângelo .... **77** 28 15 S 54 15W
Santo Antonio .... **73** 15 50 S 56 0W
Santo Antônio de Jesus ..... **75** 12 58 S 39 16W
Santo Antônio do Içá ...... **70** 3 5 S 67 57W
Santo Antônio do Leverger.. **73** 15 52 S 56 5W
Santo Corazón .... **73** 18 0 S 58 45W
Santo Domingo, Dom. Rep.. **67** 18 30N 64 54W
Santo Domingo, Baja Calif. N., Mexico **64** 30 43N 116 2W
Santo Domingo, Baja Calif. S., Mexico **64** 25 32N 112 2W
Santo Domingo, Nic. **66** 12 14N 84 59W
Santo Domingo de los Colorados .... **70** 0 15 S 79 9W
Santo Domingo Indian Reservation **38** 35 30N 106 30W
Santo Domingo Pueblo **38** 35 31N 106 22W
Santo Tomás, Mexico **64** 31 33N 116 24W
Santo Tomás, Peru .... **72** 14 26 S 72 8W
Santo Tomé .... **77** 28 40 S 56 5W
Santo Tomé de Guayana **71** 8 22N 62 40W
Santoña **91** 43 29N 3 27W
Santos .... **77** 24 0 S 46 20W
Santos Dumont .... **77** 22 55 S 43 10W
Sānūr .... **104** 32 22N 35 15 E
Sanyuan.................. **115** 34 35N 108 58 E
Sanza Pombo .... **122** 7 18 S 15 56 E
São Anastácio .... **77** 22 0 S 51 40W
São Benedito .... **74** 4 3 S 40 53W
São Bento .... **74** 2 42 S 44 50W
São Bento do Norte .... **74** 5 4 S 36 2W
São Borja .... **77** 28 39 S 56 0W
São Caitano .... **74** 8 21 S 36 6W
São Carlos .... **77** 22 0 S 47 50W
São Cristóvão .... **74** 11 1 S 37 15W
São Domingos .... **75** 13 25 S 46 19W
São Domingos do Maranhão. **74** 5 42 S 44 22W
São Félix .... **75** 11 36 S 50 39W
São Francisco .... **75** 16 0 S 44 50W
São Francisco →.......... **74** 10 30 S 36 24W
São Francisco do Maranhão . **74** 6 15 S 42 52W
São Francisco do Sul .... **77** 26 15 S 48 36W
São Gabriel .... **77** 30 20 S 54 20W
São Gabriel da Palha .... **75** 18 47 S 40 39W
São Gonçalo .... **77** 22 48 S 43 5W
São Gotardo .... **75** 19 19 S 46 3W
São João da Boa Vista ..... **77** 22 0 S 46 52W
São João da Ponte .... **75** 15 56 S 44 1W
São João del Rei .... **75** 21 8 S 44 15W
São João do Araguaia ...... **74** 5 23 S 48 46W
São João do Paraíso .... **75** 15 19 S 42 1W
São João do Piauí .... **74** 8 21 S 42 15W
São João dos Patos .... **74** 6 30 S 43 42W
São Joaquim da Barra ...... **75** 20 35 S 47 53W
São José, B. de .... **74** 2 38 S 44 4W
São José da Laje .... **74** 9 1 S 36 3W
São José de Mipibu .... **74** 6 5 S 35 15W
São José do Peixe .... **74** 7 24 S 42 34W
São José do Rio Prêto ...... **77** 20 50 S 49 20W
São José dos Campos ...... **77** 23 7 S 45 52W
São Leopoldo............. **77** 29 50 S 51 10W
São Lourenço .... **75** 22 7 S 45 3W
São Lourenço →.......... **73** 17 53 S 57 27W
São Lourenço, Pantanal do .. **73** 17 30 S 56 20W
São Luís .... **74** 2 39 S 44 15W
São Luís do Curu .... **74** 3 40 S 39 14W
São Luís Gonzaga .... **77** 28 25 S 55 0W
São Marcos →............ **75** 18 15 S 47 37W
São Marcos, B. de .... **74** 2 0 S 44 0W
São Mateus .... **75** 18 44 S 39 50W
São Mateus →............ **75** 18 35 S 39 44W
São Miguel do Araguaia .... **75** 13 19 S 50 13W
São Miguel dos Campos..... **74** 9 47 S 36 5W
São Nicolau →............ **74** 5 45 S 42 2W
São Paulo .... **77** 23 32 S 46 37W
São Paulo □ .... **77** 22 0 S 49 0W
São Paulo, I. **2** 0 50N 31 40W
São Paulo de Olivença ..... **70** 3 27 S 68 48W
São Rafael .... **74** 5 47 S 36 55W
São Raimundo das Mangabeiras .... **74** 7 1 S 45 29W
São Raimundo Nonato ...... **74** 9 1 S 42 42W
São Romão .... **75** 16 22 S 45 4W
São Roque, C. de .... **74** 5 30 S 35 16W
São Sebastião, I. de .... **77** 23 50 S 45 18W
São Sebastião do Paraíso ... **77** 20 54 S 46 59W
São Simão............... **75** 18 56 S 50 30W
São Tomé, Atl. Oc. .... **119** 0 10N 6 39 E
São Tomé, Brazil .... **74** 5 58 S 36 4W
São Tomé, C. de .... **75** 22 0 S 40 59W
São Tomé & Principe ■ .... **119** 0 12N 6 39 E
São Vicente .... **77** 23 57 S 46 23W
São Vicente, Cabo de....... **91** 37 0N 9 0W
Saona, I. **67** 18 10N 68 40W
Saône →................. **90** 45 44N 4 50 E
Saône-et-Loire □ .... **90** 46 25N 4 50 E
Saonek................... **111** 0 22 S 130 55 E
Sapão →................. **74** 11 1 S 45 32W
Saparua .... **111** 3 33 S 128 40 E
Sapé .... **74** 7 6 S 35 13W
Sapele .... **120** 5 50N 5 40 E
Sapelo I. **18** 31 25N 81 12W
Sapelo Island **18** 31 23N 81 17W
Sapelo Sound **18** 31 30N 81 10W
Saposoa .... **72** 6 55 S 76 45W
Sappa Cr. →............. **34** 40 7N 99 39W
Sappho **53** 48 4N 124 16W
Sappington **33** 45 48N 111 46W
Sapporo................. **116** 43 0N 141 21 E
Sapudi .... **111** 7 2 S 114 17 E
Sapulpa **43** 35 59N 96 5W
Saqqez .... **106** 36 15N 46 20 E
Sar-e Pol .... **107** 36 10N 66 0 E
Sar Planina .... **95** 42 10N 21 0 E
Sara, L. **21** 39 8N 88 36W
Sarāb .... **106** 38 0N 47 30 E
Sarada →................ **109** 27 21N 81 23 E
Saragosa **50** 31 2N 103 39W
Saragossa = Zaragoza **91** 41 39N 0 53W
Saraguro .... **70** 3 35 S 79 16W
Sarah **31** 34 34N 90 13W
Sarajevo .... **95** 43 52N 18 26 E
Saraland **10** 30 50N 88 4W
Saralu .... **95** 44 43N 28 10 E
Saramacca □ **71** 5 0N 56 0W
Saramacca →............ **71** 5 50N 55 55W
Saran, G. .... **110** 0 30 S 111 25 E
Saranac, Mich. **29** 42 56N 85 13W
Saranac, N.Y. **39** 44 39N 73 45W
Saranac →............... **39** 44 42N 73 27W
Saranac L. **39** 44 20N 74 10W
Saranac Lake **39** 44 20N 74 8W
Sarandí del Yi .... **77** 33 18 S 55 38W
Sarandí Grande .... **76** 33 44 S 56 20W
Sarangani B. .... **111** 6 0N 125 13 E
Sarangani Is. .... **111** 5 25N 125 25 E
Sarangarh .... **109** 21 30N 83 5 E
Saransk .... **98** 54 10N 45 10 E
Sarapul .... **98** 56 28N 53 48 E
Sarasota................. **17** 27 20N 82 32W
Sarasota County ◇ **17** 27 15N 82 20W
Saratoga, Calif. **14** 37 16N 122 2W
Saratoga, Ind. **22** 40 14N 84 55W
Saratoga, N.C. **40** 35 39N 77 47W
Saratoga, Tex. **51** 30 17N 94 31W
Saratoga, Wyo. **56** 41 27N 106 49W
Saratoga County ◇........ **39** 43 10N 73 50W
Saratoga L. **39** 43 1N 73 45W
Saratoga Springs **39** 43 5N 73 47W
Saratov .... **98** 51 30N 46 2 E
Saravane .... **112** 15 43N 106 25 E
Sarawak □ .... **110** 2 0N 113 0 E
Sarbāz .... **107** 26 38N 61 19 E
Sarbīsheh .... **107** 32 30N 59 40 E
Sarcoxie **32** 37 3N 94 7W
Sardalas .... **120** 25 50N 10 34 E
Sardarshahr .... **108** 28 30N 74 29 E
Sardegna .... **94** 39 57N 9 0 E
Sardinata **70** 8 5N 72 48W
Sardinia = Sardegna .... **94** 39 57N 9 0 E
Sardinia **42** 39 0N 83 49W
Sardis, Ala. **10** 32 17N 86 59W
Sardis, Ga. **18** 32 58N 81 46W
Sardis, Miss. **31** 34 26N 89 55W
Sardis L. **31** 34 25N 89 48W
Sardis Res. **43** 34 40N 95 25W
Sarepta **25** 32 54N 93 27W
Sargeant **30** 43 48N 92 48W
Sargent, Ga. **18** 33 26N 84 52W
Sargent, Nebr. **34** 41 39N 99 22W
Sargent County ◇ **41** 46 3N 97 45W
Sargents................. **16** 38 25N 106 24W
Sargodha .... **108** 32 10N 72 40 E
Sarh .... **121** 9 5N 18 23 E
Sārī .... **107** 36 30N 53 4 E
Sarida →................ **104** 32 4N 34 45 E
Sarikamiş .... **106** 40 22N 42 35 E
Sarikei .... **110** 2 8N 111 30 E
Sarina .... **127** 21 22 S 149 13 E
Sarita **50** 27 13N 97 47W
Sariyer .... **95** 41 10N 29 3 E
Sark **83** 49 25N 2 20W
Sarlat-la-Canéda .... **90** 44 54N 1 13 E
Sarmi .... **111** 1 49 S 138 44 E
Sarmiento .... **78** 45 35 S 69 5W
Sarnia **60** 42 58N 82 23W
Sarny .... **98** 51 17N 26 40 E
Sarolangun .... **110** 2 19 S 102 42 E
Saronikós Kólpos .... **95** 37 45N 23 45 E
Saros Körfezi .... **95** 40 30N 26 15 E
Sarpsborg .... **97** 59 16N 11 12 E
Sarpy County ◇ **34** 41 10N 96 10W
Sarre = Saar →........... **88** 49 41N 6 32 E
Sarre, La **60** 48 45N 79 15W
Sarro **120** 13 40N 5 15W
Sartell **30** 45 37N 94 12W
Sartène .... **94** 41 38N 8 58 E
Sarthe □ .... **90** 47 58N 0 10 E
Sarthe →................. **90** 47 33N 0 31W
Sartynya .... **100** 63 22N 63 11 E
Sarvestān .... **107** 29 20N 53 10 E
Sary-Tash .... **100** 39 44N 73 15 E
Saryshagan .... **100** 46 12N 73 38 E
Sasa .... **104** 33 2N 35 23 E
Sasabe **12** 31 29N 111 33W
Sasabeneh .... **105** 7 59N 44 43 E
Sasakwa................. **43** 34 57N 96 31W
Sasaram................. **109** 24 57N 84 5 E
Sasebo .... **117** 33 10N 129 43 E
Saser Mt. .... **108** 34 50N 77 50 E
Saskatchewan □ **63** 54 40N 106 0W
Saskatchewan →.......... **63** 53 37N 100 40W
Saskatoon **63** 52 10N 106 38W
Saskylakh .... **101** 71 55N 114 1 E
Sasovo .... **98** 54 25N 41 55 E
Sassafras **27** 39 22N 75 20W
Sassandra **120** 5 0N 6 8W
Sassandra →............. **120** 4 58N 6 5W
Sássari .... **94** 40 44N 8 33 E
Sasser **18** 31 43N 84 21W
Sassnitz .... **88** 54 29N 13 39 E
Sasyk, Ozero .... **95** 45 45N 30 0 E
Sata-Misaki.............. **117** 30 59N 130 40 E
Satadougou **120** 12 25N 11 25W
Satanta **24** 37 26N 100 59W
Satara .... **82** 17 44N 73 58 E
Satartia **31** 32 40N 90 33W
Satellite Beach **17** 28 10N 80 36W
Satilla →................ **18** 30 59N 81 29W
Satipo .... **72** 11 15 S 74 25W
Satka .... **98** 55 3N 59 1 E
Satmala Hills .... **108** 20 15N 74 40 E
Satna .... **109** 24 35N 80 50 E
Satolah **18** 34 59N 83 11W
Sátoraljaújhely .... **89** 48 25N 21 41 E
Satpura Ra. .... **108** 21 25N 76 10 E
Satsuma **10** 30 51N 88 4W
Satsuna-Shotō .... **117** 30 0N 130 0 E
Satu Mare .... **89** 47 46N 22 55 E
Satui .... **110** 3 50 S 115 27 E
Satun .... **112** 6 43N 100 2 E
Saturnina →............. **73** 12 15 S 58 10W
Sauce .... **76** 30 5 S 58 46W
Sauceda **64** 25 55N 101 18W
Sauceda Mts. **12** 32 35N 112 35W
Saucier **31** 30 39N 89 8W
Saucillo **64** 28 1N 105 17W
Sauda .... **97** 59 40N 6 20 E
Saúde .... **74** 10 56 S 40 24W
Sauðarkrókur **96** 65 45N 19 40W
Saudi Arabia ■ .... **105** 26 0N 44 0 E
Saugatuck **29** 42 40N 86 12W
Saugatuck →............. **28** 41 7N 73 22W
Saugerties **39** 42 5N 73 57W
Saugus, Calif. **15** 34 25N 118 32W
Saugus, Mass. **28** 42 28N 71 1W
Sauk Centre **30** 45 44N 94 57W
Sauk City **55** 43 17N 89 43W
Sauk County ◇ **55** 43 25N 89 50W
Sauk Rapids **30** 45 35N 94 10W
Saukville **55** 43 23N 87 56W
Saül **71** 3 37N 53 12W
Saulsbury **48** 35 3N 89 5W
Sault Ste. Marie, Canada.... **60** 46 30N 84 20W
Sault Ste. Marie, U.S.A..... **29** 46 30N 84 21W
Saumlaki .... **111** 7 55 S 131 20 E
Saumur **90** 47 15N 0 5W
Saunders C. .... **128** 45 53 S 170 45 E
Saunders County ◇ **34** 41 15N 96 40W
Saunders I. .... **5** 57 48 S 26 28W
Saunemin **21** 40 54N 88 24W
Sauquoit **39** 43 0N 75 16W
Saurbœr, Borgarfjarðarsýsla, Iceland **96** 64 24N 21 35W
Saurbœr, Eyjafjarðarsýsla, Iceland **96** 65 27N 18 13W
Sauri .... **120** 11 42N 6 44 E
Saurimo................. **122** 9 40 S 20 12 E
Sautatá **70** 7 50N 77 4W
Savá **66** 15 32N 86 15W
Sava →.................. **95** 44 50N 20 26 E
Savage, Md. **27** 39 8N 76 50W
Savage, Mont. **33** 47 27N 104 21W
Savage I. = Niue I. .... **125** 19 2 S 169 54W
Savai'i .... **128** 13 28 S 172 24W
Savalou .... **120** 7 57N 1 58 E
Savana I. **57** 18 21N 65 5W
Savanna, Ill. **21** 42 5N 90 8W
Savanna, Okla. **43** 34 50N 95 51W
Savanna la Mar **66** 18 10N 78 10W
Savannah, Ga. **18** 32 5N 81 6W
Savannah, Mo. **32** 39 56N 94 50W
Savannah, Ohio **42** 40 58N 82 22W
Savannah, Tenn. **48** 35 14N 88 15W
Savannah →.............. **46** 32 2N 80 53W
Savannah Beach **18** 32 1N 80 51W
Savannakhet .... **112** 16 30N 104 49 E
Savant L. **60** 50 16N 90 44W
Savant Lake **60** 50 14N 90 40W
Savanur .... **108** 14 59N 75 21 E
Savé .... **120** 8 2N 2 29 E
Save →.................. **123** 21 16 S 34 0 E
Sāveh .... **106** 35 2N 50 20 E
Savelugu **120** 9 38N 0 54W
Savoie □ .... **90** 45 26N 6 35 E
Savona .... **94** 44 19N 8 29 E

Savonburg Senador Pompeu

Savonburg 24 37 45N 95 9W
Savonlinna 98 61 52N 28 53 E
Savoonga 11 63 42N 170 29W
Savoy 21 40 3N 88 15W
Saw Pit 16 37 56N 108 6W
Sawahlunto 110 0 40 S 100 52 E
Sawai 111 3 0 S 129 5 E
Sawai Madhopur 108 26 0N 76 25 E
Sawara 117 35 55N 140 30 E
Sawatch Range 16 39 0N 106 30W
Sawel, Mt. 85 54 48N 7 5W
Sawknah 121 29 4N 15 47 E
Sawmills 123 19 30 S 28 2 E
Sawtooth Mts. 30 47 30N 91 0W
Sawtooth Nat. Rec. Area 20 44 0N 114 50W
Sawtooth National Forest 52 41 50N 113 20W
Sawtooth Range 20 44 3N 114 58W
Sawu 111 10 35 S 121 50 E
Sawu Sea 111 9 30 S 121 50 E
Sawyer, Kans. 24 37 30N 98 41W
Sawyer, Mich. 29 41 53N 86 35W
Sawyer, N. Dak. 41 48 5N 101 3W
Sawyer, Okla. 43 34 1N 95 23W
Sawyer County ◇ 55 45 50N 91 0W
Sawyers Bar 14 41 18N 123 7W
Saxapahaw 40 35 57N 79 19W
Saxonburg 45 40 45N 79 49W
Saxton, Ky. 49 36 38N 84 7W
Saxton, Pa. 45 40 13N 78 15W
Say 120 13 8N 2 22 E
Sayabec 61 48 35N 67 41W
Sayán 72 11 8 S 77 12W
Sayan, Vostochnyy 101 54 0N 96 0 E
Sayan, Zapadnyy 101 52 30N 94 0 E
Saybrook 21 40 26N 88 32W
Saydā 106 33 35N 35 25 E
Sayghān 107 35 10N 67 55 E
Sayḥut 105 15 12N 51 10 E
Saylorville L. 23 41 48N 93 46W
Saynshand 113 44 55N 110 11 E
Sayre, Okla. 43 35 18N 99 38W
Sayre, Pa. 45 41 59N 76 32W
Sayreville 37 40 28N 74 22W
Sayula 64 19 50N 103 40W
Sayville 39 40 44N 73 5W
Sazan 95 40 30N 19 20 E
Săzava → 88 49 53N 14 24 E
Sazin 108 35 35N 73 30 E
Sazlika → 95 41 59N 25 50 E
Sca Fell 86 54 27N 3 14W
Scafell Pikes 82 54 26N 3 14W
Scaggsville 27 39 9N 76 54W
Scales Mound 21 42 29N 90 15W
Scalpay 84 57 51N 6 40W
Scammon 24 37 17N 94 49W
Scammon Bay 11 61 51N 165 35W
Scandia, Canada 62 50 20N 112 0W
Scandia, U.S.A. 24 39 48N 97 47W
Scandinavia, Europe 80 64 0N 12 0 E
Scandinavia, U.S.A. 55 44 27N 89 9W
Scanlon 30 46 42N 92 26W
Scapa Flow 84 58 52N 3 6W
Scappoose 44 45 45N 122 53W
Scarborough, Trin. & Tob. 67 11 11N 60 42W
Scarborough, U.K. 82 54 17N 0 24W
Scarsdale 39 40 59N 73 49W
Scarville 23 43 28N 93 37W
Scenic 47 43 47N 102 33W
Schaffhausen 88 47 42N 8 39 E
Schagen 87 52 49N 4 48 E
Schaller 23 42 30N 95 18W
Schefferville 61 54 48N 66 50W
Schelde → 87 51 15N 4 16 E
Schell City 32 38 1N 94 7W
Schell Creek Range 35 39 25N 114 40W
Schellsburg 45 40 3N 78 39W
Schenectady 39 42 49N 73 57W
Schenectady County ◇ 39 42 50N 74 0W
Scheveningen 87 52 6N 4 16 E
Schiedam 87 51 55N 4 25 E
Schiermonnikoog 87 53 30N 6 15 E
Schio 94 45 42N 11 21 E
Schlater 31 33 39N 90 21W
Schleicher County ◇ 50 30 52N 100 36W
Schleswig, Germany 88 54 32N 9 34 E
Schleswig, U.S.A. 23 42 10N 95 26W
Schleswig-Holstein □ 88 54 10N 9 40 E
Schley County ◇ 18 32 15N 84 15W
Schoenchen 24 38 43N 99 20W
Schofield 55 44 54N 89 36W
Schoharie 39 42 40N 74 19W
Schoharie → 39 42 57N 74 18W
Schoharie County ◇ 39 42 35N 74 30W
Schoharie Res. 39 42 22N 74 26W
Schoodic L. 26 45 23N 68 56W
Schoolcraft 29 42 7N 85 38W
Schoolcraft County ◇ 29 46 10N 86 15W
Schouwen 87 51 43N 3 45 E
Schreiber 60 48 45N 87 20W
Schroon L. 39 43 47N 73 47W
Schroon Lake 39 43 50N 73 46W
Schulenburg 51 29 41N 96 54W
Schuler 63 50 20N 110 6W
Schumacher 60 48 30N 81 16W
Schurz 35 38 57N 118 49W
Schuylkill Haven 45 40 38N 76 10W
Schuyler, Nebr. 34 41 27N 97 4W
Schuyler, Va. 54 37 47N 78 42W
Schuyler County ◇, Ill. 21 40 10N 90 40W
Schuyler County ◇, Mo. 32 40 25N 92 30W
Schuyler County ◇, N.Y. 39 42 20N 76 50W
Schuylkill → 45 39 53N 75 12W
Schuylkill County ◇ 45 40 48N 76 50W
Schwäbische Alb 88 48 30N 9 30 E
Schwarzwald 88 48 0N 8 0 E
Schwatka Mts. 11 67 20N 156 30W
Schweinfurt 88 50 3N 10 12 E
Schwerin 88 53 37N 11 22 E
Schwyz 88 47 2N 8 39 E
Sciacca 94 37 30N 13 3 E
Scie, La 61 49 57N 55 36W
Science Hill 49 37 11N 84 38W
Scilla 94 38 18N 15 44 E
Scilly, Isles of 83 49 55N 6 15W
Scio, Ohio 42 40 24N 81 5W
Scio, Oreg. 44 44 42N 122 51W
Scioto → 42 38 44N 83 1W
Scioto County ◇ 42 38 53N 82 59W
Scipio, Okla. 43 35 3N 95 58W
Scipio, Utah 52 39 15N 112 6W
Scituate 28 42 12N 70 44W
Scituate Reservoir 28 41 45N 71 35W
Scobey 33 48 47N 105 25W
Scofield 52 39 44N 111 10W
Scofield Reservoir 52 39 49N 111 8W
Scone 84 56 25N 3 26W
Scooba 31 32 50N 88 29W
Scoresbysund 4 70 20N 23 0W
Scotch Plains 37 40 39N 74 24W
Scotia, Calif. 14 40 29N 124 6W
Scotia, N.Y. 39 42 50N 73 58W
Scotia, Nebr. 34 41 28N 98 42W
Scotia, S.C. 46 32 41N 81 15W
Scotia Sea 5 56 5 S 56 0W
Scotland, Ark. 13 35 32N 92 37W
Scotland, Conn. 28 41 42N 72 7W
Scotland, Md. 27 38 5N 76 22W
Scotland, S. Dak. 47 43 9N 97 43W
Scotland □ 83 57 0N 4 0W
Scotland County ◇, Mo. 32 40 25N 92 10W
Scotland County ◇, N.C. 40 34 50N 79 30W
Scotland Neck 40 36 8N 77 25W
Scotlandville 25 30 31N 91 11W
Scott, Antarct. 5 77 0 S 165 0 E
Scott, Ark. 13 34 42N 92 6W
Scott, Miss. 31 33 36N 91 5W
Scott, Ohio 42 40 59N 84 35W
Scott → 14 41 48N 123 2W
Scott, Mt. 44 42 56N 122 1W
Scott Bar Mts. 14 41 50N 123 0W
Scott City, Kans. 24 38 29N 100 54W
Scott City, Mo. 32 37 12N 89 30W
Scott County ◇, Ark. 13 34 54N 94 5W
Scott County ◇, Ill. 21 39 40N 90 30W
Scott County ◇, Ind. 22 38 40N 85 45W
Scott County ◇, Iowa 23 41 35N 90 35W
Scott County ◇, Kans. 24 38 30N 101 0W
Scott County ◇, Ky. 49 38 15N 84 35W
Scott County ◇, Minn. 30 44 40N 93 30W
Scott County ◇, Miss. 31 32 22N 89 29W
Scott County ◇, Mo. 32 37 0N 89 35W
Scott County ◇, Tenn. 49 36 25N 84 29W
Scott County ◇, Va. 54 36 55N 82 45W
Scott Glacier 5 66 15 S 100 5 E
Scott I. 5 67 0 S 179 0 E
Scott Inlet 59 71 0N 71 0W
Scott Is. 62 50 48N 128 40W
Scott L. 63 59 55N 106 18W
Scott Mts. 14 41 15N 122 45W
Scott Peak 20 44 21N 112 49W
Scott Reef 126 14 0 S 121 50 E
Scottdale 45 40 6N 79 35W
Scotts Bluff County ◇ 34 41 50N 103 45W
Scotts Bluff National Monument 34 41 50N 103 40W
Scotts Hill 48 35 31N 88 15W
Scottsbluff 34 41 52N 103 40W
Scottsboro 10 34 40N 86 2W
Scottsburg, Ind. 22 38 41N 85 47W
Scottsburg, Oreg. 44 43 39N 123 49W
Scottsburg, Va. 54 36 45N 78 48W
Scottsdale, Australia 127 41 9 S 147 31 E
Scottsdale, U.S.A. 12 33 29N 111 56W
Scottsville, Kans. 24 39 32N 97 57W
Scottsville, Ky. 49 36 45N 86 11W
Scottville 29 43 58N 86 17W
Scranton, Iowa 23 42 1N 94 33W
Scranton, Kans. 24 38 47N 95 44W
Scranton, N. Dak. 41 46 9N 103 9W
Scranton, Pa. 45 41 25N 75 40W
Screven 18 31 29N 82 1W
Screven County ◇ 18 32 45N 81 40W
Scribner 34 41 40N 96 40W
Scunthorpe 82 53 35N 0 38W
Scurry 51 32 31N 96 23W
Scurry County ◇ 50 32 44N 100 55W
Scusciuban 105 10 18N 50 12 E
Scutari = Üsküdar 106 41 0N 29 5 E
Sea Breeze 37 39 18N 75 20W
Sea Bright 37 40 22N 73 59W
Sea Isle City 37 39 9N 74 42W
Seaboard 40 36 29N 77 26W
Seabra 75 12 25 S 41 46W
Seabrook, N.H. 36 42 53N 70 52W
Seabrook, Tex. 51 29 34N 95 2W
Seadrift 51 28 25N 96 43W
Seaford, Del. 27 38 39N 75 37W
Seaford, Va. 54 37 12N 76 26W
Seaforth, Canada 60 43 35N 81 25W
Seaforth, U.S.A. 30 44 29N 95 20W
Seagoville 51 32 38N 96 32W
Seagraves 50 32 57N 102 34W
Seagrove 40 35 33N 79 46W
Seal → 63 58 50N 97 30W
Seal Cove 61 49 57N 56 22W
Seal I. 26 43 53N 68 45W
Seal L. 61 54 20N 61 30W
Seale 10 32 18N 85 10W
Sealevel 40 34 52N 76 23W
Sealy 51 29 47N 96 9W
Seaman 42 38 57N 83 34W
Searchlight 35 35 28N 114 55W
Searcy 13 35 15N 91 44W
Searcy County ◇ 13 35 55N 92 38W
Searles L. 15 35 44N 117 21W
Searsboro 23 41 35N 92 42W
Searsburg 36 42 52N 72 58W
Searsport 26 44 28N 68 56W
Seaside, Calif. 14 36 37N 121 50W
Seaside, Oreg. 44 46 0N 123 56W
Seaside Heights 37 39 55N 74 6W
Seaside Park 37 39 55N 74 5W
Seat Pleasant 27 38 54N 76 55W
Seattle 53 47 36N 122 20W
Seaview Ra. 127 18 40 S 145 45 E
Seaville 37 39 12N 74 42W
Sebago L. 26 43 52N 70 34W
Sebastian 17 27 49N 80 28W
Sebastian, C. 44 42 20N 124 26W
Sebastian County ◇ 13 35 10N 94 10W
Sebastián Vizcaíno, Bahía 64 28 0N 114 30W
Sebastopol = Sevastopol 99 44 35N 33 30 E
Sebastopol, Calif. 14 38 24N 122 49W
Sebastopol, Miss. 31 32 34N 89 20W
Sebec L. 26 45 16N 69 15W
Sebeka 30 46 38N 95 5W
Sebeş 95 45 58N 23 34 E
Sebeşului, Munţii 95 45 36N 23 40 E
Sebewaing 29 43 44N 83 27W
Şebinkarahisar 106 40 22N 38 28 E
Seboeis 26 45 22N 68 43W
Seboeis L. 26 45 28N 68 53W
Seboomook L. 26 45 56N 69 51W
Seboyeta 38 35 12N 107 23W
Sebree 48 37 36N 87 32W
Sebrell 54 36 47N 77 8W
Sebring 17 27 30N 81 27W
Sebta = Ceuta 120 35 52N 5 18W
Sebuku 110 3 30 S 116 25 E
Sebuku, Teluk 110 4 0N 118 10 E
Secession L. 46 34 18N 82 39W
Sechelt 62 49 25N 123 42W
Sechura 72 5 39 S 80 50W
Sechura, Desierto de 72 6 0 S 80 30W
Second L. 36 45 9N 71 10W
Secor 21 40 45N 89 8W
Secretary 27 38 37N 75 57W
Secretary I. 128 45 15 S 166 56 E
Section 10 34 35N 85 59W
Secunderabad 108 17 28N 78 30 E
Sécure → 73 15 10 S 64 52W
Security 16 38 45N 104 45W
Sedalia, Colo. 16 39 26N 104 58W
Sedalia, Mo. 32 38 42N 93 14W
Sedan, France 90 49 43N 4 57 E
Sedan, Kans. 24 37 8N 96 11W
Sedan, Minn. 30 45 35N 95 15W
Sedan, N. Mex. 38 36 9N 103 8W
Seddon 128 41 40 S 174 7 E
Seddonville 128 41 33 S 172 1 E
Sede Ya'aqov 104 32 43N 35 7 E
Sedgefield 40 36 1N 79 54W
Sedgewick 62 52 48N 111 41W
Sedgewick, Mt. 38 35 11N 108 6W
Sedgwick, Colo. 16 40 56N 102 32W
Sedgwick, Kans. 24 37 55N 97 26W
Sedgwick, Maine 26 44 18N 68 37W
Sedgwick County ◇, Colo. 16 40 50N 102 15W
Sedgwick County ◇, Kans. 24 37 30N 97 20W
Sedhiou 120 12 44N 15 30W
Sedienie 95 42 16N 24 33 E
Sedley 63 50 10N 104 0W
Sedom 104 31 5N 35 20 E
Sedona 12 34 52N 111 46W
Sedova, Pik 100 73 29N 54 58 E
Sedro-Woolley 53 48 30N 122 14W
Seeheim 123 26 50 S 17 45 E
Seekonk 28 41 49N 71 20W
Seeley Lake 33 47 11N 113 29W
Se'elim, Nahal 104 31 21N 35 24 E
Seelyville 22 39 30N 87 16W
Seg-ozero 98 63 0N 33 10 E
Segamat 112 2 30N 102 50 E
Segarcea 95 44 6N 23 43 E
Seget 111 1 24 S 130 58 E
Segezha 98 63 44N 34 19 E
Ségou 120 13 30N 6 16W
Segovia = Coco → 66 15 0N 83 8W
Segovia, Colombia 70 7 7N 74 42W
Segovia, Spain 91 40 57N 4 10W
Segre → 91 41 40N 0 43 E
Seguam I. 11 52 19N 172 30W
Seguam Pass 11 52 0N 172 30W
Séguéla 120 7 55N 6 40W
Seguin 51 29 34N 97 58W
Segundo → 76 30 53 S 62 44W
Segura → 91 38 6N 0 54W
Sehithwa 123 20 30 S 22 30 E
Sehore 108 23 10N 77 5 E
Seibert 16 39 18N 102 53W
Şeica Mare 95 46 1N 24 7 E
Seiland 96 70 25N 23 15 E
Seiling 43 36 9N 98 56W
Seinäjoki → 96 62 40N 22 45 E
Seine → 90 49 26N 0 26 E
Seine-et-Marne □ 90 48 45N 3 0 E
Seine-Maritime □ 90 49 40N 1 0 E
Seine-Saint-Denis □ 90 48 58N 2 24 E
Seistan 107 30 50N 61 0 E
Seistan, Daryâcheh-ye 107 31 0N 61 0 E
Sekayu 110 2 51 S 103 51 E
Sekondi-Takoradi 120 4 58N 1 45W
Selah 53 46 39N 120 32W
Selama 112 5 12N 100 42 E
Selangor □ 112 3 20N 101 30 E
Selaru 111 8 9 S 131 0 E
Selawik 11 66 36N 160 0W
Selawik L. 11 66 30N 160 45W
Selby, U.K. 82 53 47N 1 5W
Selby, U.S.A. 47 45 31N 100 2W
Selbyville 27 38 28N 75 14W
Selden, Kans. 24 39 33N 100 34W
Selden, N.Y. 39 40 52N 73 2W
Seldovia 11 59 26N 151 43W
Sele → 94 40 27N 14 58 E
Selemdzha → 101 51 42N 128 53 E
Selenge → 113 49 25N 103 59 E
Seletan, Tg. 110 4 10 S 114 40 E
Selfridge 41 46 2N 100 56W
Sélibabi 120 15 10N 12 15W
Seligman, Ariz. 12 35 20N 112 53W
Seligman, Mo. 32 36 31N 93 56W
Selîma, El Wâhât el 121 21 22N 29 19 E
Selinsgrove 45 40 48N 76 52W
Selkirk, Canada 63 50 10N 96 55W
Selkirk, U.K. 84 55 33N 2 50W
Selkirk, U.S.A. 24 38 29N 101 32W
Selkirk I. 63 53 20N 99 6W
Selkirk Mts., Canada 62 51 15N 117 40W
Selkirk Mts., U.S.A. 20 48 30N 116 40W
Selleck 53 47 23N 121 52W
Sellers 46 34 17N 79 28W
Sellersburg 22 38 24N 85 45W
Sells 12 31 55N 111 53W
Selma, Ala. 10 32 25N 87 1W
Selma, Ark. 13 33 42N 91 34W
Selma, Calif. 15 36 34N 119 37W
Selma, N.C. 40 35 32N 78 17W
Selma, Oreg. 44 42 17N 123 37W
Selman 43 36 48N 99 30W
Selmer 48 35 10N 88 36W
Selpele 111 0 1 S 130 5 E
Selsey Bill 83 50 44N 0 47W
Selu 111 7 32 S 130 55 E
Selva 76 29 50 S 62 0W
Selvas 72 6 30 S 67 0W
Selway → 20 46 9N 115 36W
Selwyn 127 21 32 S 140 30 E
Selwyn L. 63 60 0N 104 30W
Selwyn Ra. 127 21 10 S 140 0 E
Selz 41 47 52N 99 54W
Seman → 95 40 45N 19 50 E
Semarang 111 7 0 S 110 26 E
Semau 111 10 13 S 123 22 E
Semeru 111 8 4 S 112 55 E
Semichi Is. 11 52 42N 174 0 E
Seminary 31 31 34N 89 30W
Seminoe Reservoir 56 42 9N 106 55W
Seminole, Fla. 17 27 50N 82 47W
Seminole, Okla. 43 35 14N 96 41W
Seminole, Tex. 50 32 43N 102 39W
Seminole, L. 18 30 43N 84 52W
Seminole County ◇, Fla. 17 28 40N 81 15W
Seminole County ◇, Ga. 18 31 0N 84 55W
Seminole County ◇, Okla. 43 35 10N 96 40W
Semiozernoye 100 52 22N 64 8 E
Semipalatinsk 100 50 30N 80 10 E
Semirara Is. 111 12 0N 121 20 E
Semisopochnoi I. 11 51 55N 179 36 E
Semitau 110 0 29N 111 57 E
Semiyarskoye 100 50 55N 78 23 E
Semmering Pass 88 47 41N 15 45 E
Semmes 10 30 47N 88 16W
Semnān 107 35 55N 53 25 E
Semnān □ 107 36 0N 54 0 E
Semois → 87 49 53N 4 44 E
Semporna 111 4 30N 118 33 E
Semuda 110 2 51 S 112 58 E
Sen → 112 13 45N 105 12 E
Sena 72 11 32 S 67 11W
Sena → 72 11 31 S 67 11W
Sena Madureira 72 9 5 S 68 45W
Senachwine L. 21 41 10N 89 20W
Senador Pompeu 74 5 40 S 39 20W

Senai Shenandoah

Senai **112** 1 38N 103 38 E
Senaja **110** 6 45N 117 3 E
Senanga **123** 16 2 S 23 14 E
Senath **32** 36 8N 90 10W
Senatobia **31** 34 37N 89 58W
Sendai, Kagoshima, Japan **117** 31 50N 130 20 E
Sendai, Miyagi, Japan **116** 38 15N 140 53 E
Sendai-Wan **116** 38 15N 141 0 E
Seneca, Ill. **21** 41 19N 88 37W
Seneca, Kans. **24** 39 50N 96 4W
Seneca, Md. **27** 39 5N 77 20W
Seneca, Mo. **32** 36 51N 94 37W
Seneca, Nebr. **34** 42 3N 100 50W
Seneca, Oreg. **44** 44 8N 118 58W
Seneca, S.C. **46** 34 41N 82 57W
Seneca, S. Dak. **47** 45 4N 99 31W
Seneca County ◇, N.Y. **39** 42 45N 76 45W
Seneca County ◇, Ohio **42** 41 7N 83 11W
Seneca Falls **39** 42 55N 76 48W
Seneca L. **39** 42 40N 76 54W
Senecaville L. **42** 39 55N 81 25W
Senegal ■ **120** 14 30N 14 30W
Senegal → **120** 15 48N 16 32W
Senegambia **118** 12 45N 12 0W
Senge Khambab = Indus → **108** 24 20N 67 47 E
Sengkang **111** 4 8 S 120 1 E
Senguerr → **78** 45 35 S 68 50W
Senhor-do-Bonfim **74** 10 30 S 40 10W
Senigállia **94** 43 42N 13 12 E
Senj **94** 45 0N 14 58 E
Senja **96** 69 25N 17 30 E
Senlis **90** 49 13N 2 35 E
Senmonorom **112** 12 27N 107 12 E
Sennâr **121** 13 30N 33 35 E
Senneterre **60** 48 25N 77 15W
Senoia **18** 33 18N 84 33W
Sens **90** 48 11N 3 15 E
Senta **95** 45 55N 20 3 E
Sentinel, Ariz. **12** 32 52N 113 13W
Sentinel, Okla. **43** 35 9N 99 11W
Sentinel Butte **41** 46 55N 103 51W
Sento Sé **74** 9 40 S 41 18W
Sentola **111** 7 55 S 110 13 E
Seo de Urgel **91** 42 22N 1 23 E
Seoul = Sŏul **114** 37 31N 126 58 E
Separation Point **61** 53 37N 57 25W
Sepīdān **107** 30 20N 52 5 E
Sepone **112** 16 45N 106 13 E
Sept-Îles **61** 50 13N 66 22W
Septemvri **95** 42 13N 24 6 E
Sepulga → **10** 31 11N 86 46W
Sequatchie County ◇ **49** 35 23N 85 23W
Sequim **53** 48 5N 123 6W
Sequoia National Forest **15** 36 0N 118 20W
Sequoia National Park **15** 36 30N 118 30W
Sequoyah County ◇ **43** 35 30N 94 45W
Serafina **38** 35 24N 105 19W
Seraing **87** 50 35N 5 32 E
Seram **111** 3 10 S 129 0 E
Seram Laut, Kepulauan **111** 4 5 S 131 25 E
Seram Sea **111** 2 30 S 128 30 E
Serang **111** 6 8 S 106 10 E
Serasan **110** 2 29N 109 4 E
Serbia = Srbija □ **95** 43 30N 21 0 E
Sercaia **95** 45 49N 25 9 E
Serdobsk **98** 52 28N 44 10 E
Seremban **112** 2 43N 101 53 E
Serena, La **76** 29 55 S 71 10W
Serenje **123** 13 14 S 30 15 E
Sereth = Siret → **89** 47 58N 26 5 E
Sergeant Bluff **23** 42 24N 96 22W
Sergino **100** 62 30N 65 38 E
Sergipe □ **74** 10 30 S 37 30W
Seria **110** 4 37N 114 23 E
Serian **110** 1 10N 110 31 E
Seribu, Kepulauan **110** 5 36 S 106 33 E
Sermata **111** 8 15 S 128 50 E
Serny Zavod **100** 39 59N 58 50 E
Serov **100** 59 29N 60 35 E
Serowe **123** 22 25 S 26 43 E
Serpukhov **98** 54 55N 37 28 E
Serra do Navio **71** 0 59N 52 3W
Serra Talhada **74** 7 59 S 38 18W
Sérrai **95** 41 5N 23 31 E
Serrezuela **76** 30 40 S 65 20W
Serrinha **75** 11 39 S 39 0W
Serrita **74** 7 56 S 39 19W
Sertânia **74** 8 5 S 37 20W
Sertanópolis **77** 23 4 S 51 2W
Serua **111** 6 18 S 130 1 E
Serui **111** 1 53 S 136 10 E
Serule **123** 21 57 S 27 20 E
Sesepe **111** 1 30 S 127 59 E
Sesfontein **123** 19 7 S 13 39 E
Sesheke **123** 17 29 S 24 13 E
Sesser **21** 38 5N 89 1W
Sestao **91** 43 18N 3 0W
Setana **116** 42 26N 139 51 E
Sète **90** 43 25N 3 42 E
Sete Lagôas **75** 19 27 S 44 16W
Seth Ward **50** 34 13N 101 42W
Sétif **120** 36 9N 5 26 E
Seto **117** 35 14N 137 6 E
Setonaikai **117** 34 20N 133 30 E
Settat **120** 33 0N 7 40W
Setté-Cama **122** 2 32 S 9 45 E
Setting L. **63** 55 0N 98 38W
Settle **82** 54 5N 2 18W
Setúbal **91** 38 30N 8 58W
Setúbal, B. de **91** 38 40N 8 56W
Seul, Lac-Rés. **60** 50 25N 92 30W
Seul Choix Pt. **29** 45 55N 85 55W
Seulimeum **110** 5 27N 95 15 E
Sevan, Ozero **99** 40 30N 45 20 E
Sevastopol **99** 44 35N 33 30 E
Seven Devils Mts. **20** 44 45N 116 40W
Seven Sisters **62** 54 56N 128 10W
Seven Springs **40** 35 14N 77 51W
Seven Troughs Range **35** 40 30N 118 40W
Seven Valleys **45** 39 51N 76 46W
Severn **40** 36 31N 77 11W
Severn →, Canada **60** 56 2N 87 36W
Severn →, U.K. **83** 51 35N 2 38W
Severn L. **60** 53 54N 90 48W
Severna Park **27** 39 4N 76 33W
Severnaya Zemlya **101** 79 0N 100 0 E
Severnyye Uvaly **98** 58 0N 48 0 E
Severo-Kurilsk **101** 50 40N 156 8 E
Severo-Yeniseyskiy **101** 60 22N 93 1 E
Severodinsk **98** 64 27N 39 58 E
Severomorsk **98** 69 5N 33 27 E
Severouralsk **98** 60 9N 59 57 E
Severy **24** 37 37N 96 14W
Sevier → **52** 39 4N 113 6W
Sevier Bridge Reservoir **52** 39 22N 112 2W
Sevier County ◇, Ark. **13** 33 58N 94 10W
Sevier County ◇, Tenn. **49** 35 48N 83 33W
Sevier County ◇, Utah **52** 38 45N 111 50W
Sevier Desert **52** 39 40N 112 45W
Sevier L. **52** 38 54N 113 9W
Sevier Plateau **52** 38 20N 112 10W
Sevierville **49** 35 52N 83 34W
Sevilla, Colombia **70** 4 16N 75 57W
Sevilla, Spain **91** 37 23N 6 0W
Seville = Sevilla **91** 37 23N 6 0W
Seville, Fla. **17** 29 19N 81 30W
Seville, Ga. **18** 31 58N 83 36W
Sevlievo **95** 43 2N 25 3 E
Sewanee **49** 35 12N 85 55W
Seward, Alaska **11** 60 7N 149 27W
Seward, Ill. **21** 42 14N 89 22W
Seward, Kans. **24** 38 11N 98 48W
Seward, Nebr. **34** 40 55N 97 6W
Seward, Pa. **45** 40 25N 79 1W
Seward County ◇, Kans. **24** 37 15N 100 45W
Seward County ◇, Nebr. **34** 40 50N 97 10W
Seward Peninsula **11** 65 30N 166 0W
Sewell **76** 34 10 S 70 23W
Sewer **111** 5 53 S 134 40 E
Sewickley **45** 40 32N 80 12W
Sexsmith **62** 55 21N 118 47W
Seychelles ■ **3** 5 0S 56 0 E
Seyðisfjörður **96** 65 16N 14 0W
Seyhan → **99** 36 38N 35 8 E
Seymchan **101** 62 54N 152 30 E
Seymour, Conn. **28** 41 24N 73 4W
Seymour, Ind. **22** 38 58N 85 53W
Seymour, Iowa **23** 40 45N 93 7W
Seymour, Mo. **32** 37 9N 92 46W
Seymour, Tex. **51** 33 35N 99 16W
Seymour, Wis. **55** 44 31N 88 20W
Seymourville **25** 30 16N 91 14W
Sfax **121** 34 49N 10 48 E
Sfintu Gheorghe **89** 45 52N 25 48 E
Sha Xian **115** 26 23N 117 45 E
Shaanxi □ **115** 35 0N 109 0 E
Shaba □ **122** 8 0 S 25 0 E
Shabla **95** 43 31N 28 32 E
Shabunda **122** 2 40 S 27 16 E
Shache **113** 38 20N 77 10 E
Shackelford County ◇ **51** 32 45N 99 18W
Shackleton Ice Shelf **5** 66 0 S 100 0 E
Shackleton Inlet **5** 83 0 S 160 0 E
Shadehill Reservoir **47** 45 45N 102 12W
Shadow Mt. Nat. Rec. Area **16** 40 7N 105 48W
Shadrinsk **100** 56 5N 63 32 E
Shady Cove **44** 42 37N 122 49W
Shady Dale **18** 33 24N 83 36W
Shady Grove, Fla. **17** 30 17N 83 38W
Shady Grove, Ky. **48** 37 20N 87 53W
Shady Point **43** 35 8N 94 40W
Shady Side **27** 38 50N 76 31W
Shady Spring **54** 37 42N 81 6W
Shafer, L. **22** 40 46N 86 46W
Shafter, Calif. **15** 35 30N 119 16W
Shafter, Tex. **50** 29 49N 104 18W
Shaftesbury **83** 51 0N 2 12W
Shaftsbury **36** 43 1N 73 11W
Shageluk **11** 62 41N 159 34W
Shāhābād **107** 37 40N 56 50 E
Shahdād **107** 30 30N 57 40 E
Shahdadkot **108** 27 50N 67 55 E
Shahgarh **108** 27 15N 69 50 E
Shaḫḫāt **121** 32 48N 21 54 E
Shahr Kord **107** 32 15N 50 55 E
Shahrig **108** 30 15N 67 40 E
Shahsād, Namakzār-e **107** 30 20N 58 20 E
Shaikhabad **108** 34 2N 68 45 E
Shajapur **108** 23 27N 76 21 E
Shaker Heights **42** 41 29N 81 32W
Shakhty **99** 47 40N 40 16 E
Shakhunya **98** 57 40N 46 46 E
Shaki **120** 8 41N 3 21 E
Shakopee **30** 44 48N 93 32W
Shaktoolik **11** 64 20N 161 9W
Shala, L. **121** 7 30N 38 30 E
Shalimar **17** 30 27N 86 36W
Shallotte **40** 33 58N 78 23W
Shallow Water **24** 38 23N 100 55W
Shallowater **50** 33 36N 102 0W
Sham, J. ash **107** 23 10N 57 5 E
Shamâl Dârfûr □ **121** 15 0N 25 0 E
Shamâl Kordofân □ **121** 15 0N 30 0 E
Shamattawa **63** 55 51N 92 5W
Shamattawa → **60** 55 1N 85 23W
Shambaugh **23** 40 42N 95 3W
Shamīl **107** 27 30N 56 55 E
Shammar, Jabal **106** 27 40N 41 0 E
Shamo = Gobi **114** 44 0N 111 0 E
Shamo, L. **121** 5 45N 37 30 E
Shamokin **45** 40 47N 76 34W
Shamrock, Okla. **43** 35 56N 96 35W
Shamrock, Tex. **50** 35 13N 100 15W
Shamva **123** 17 20 S 31 32 E
Shan □ **109** 21 30N 98 30 E
Shanchengzhen **114** 42 20N 125 20 E
Shandon **15** 35 39N 120 23W
Shandong □ **114** 36 0N 118 0 E
Shang Xian **115** 33 50N 109 58 E
Shangani → **123** 18 41 S 27 10 E
Shangbancheng **114** 40 50N 118 1 E
Shangcheng **115** 31 47N 115 26 E
Shangchuan Dao **115** 21 40N 112 50 E
Shangdu **114** 41 30N 113 30 E
Shanggao **115** 28 17N 114 55 E
Shanghai **115** 31 15N 121 26 E
Shangqiu **115** 34 26N 115 36 E
Shangrao **115** 28 25N 117 59 E
Shangshui **115** 33 42N 114 35 E
Shangsi **115** 22 8N 107 58 E
Shangyou **115** 25 48N 114 32 E
Shangzhi **114** 45 22N 127 56 E
Shaniko **44** 45 0N 120 45W
Shannon, Greenland **4** 75 10N 18 30W
Shannon, N.Z. **128** 40 33 S 175 25 E
Shannon, Ga. **18** 34 20N 85 4W
Shannon, Ill. **21** 42 9N 89 44W
Shannon, Miss. **31** 34 7N 88 43W
Shannon → **85** 52 35N 9 30W
Shannon, L. **53** 48 33N 121 45W
Shannon County ◇, Mo. **32** 37 10N 91 20W
Shannon County ◇, S. Dak. **47** 43 15N 102 35W
Shannontown **46** 33 53N 80 21W
Shansi = Shanxi □ **114** 37 0N 112 0 E
Shantar, Ostrov Bolshoy **101** 55 9N 137 40 E
Shantou **115** 23 18N 116 40 E
Shantung = Shandong □ **114** 36 0N 118 0 E
Shanxi □ **114** 37 0N 112 0 E
Shanyang **115** 33 31N 109 55 E
Shaoguan **115** 24 48N 113 35 E
Shaowu **115** 27 22N 117 28 E
Shaoxing **115** 30 0N 120 35 E
Shaoyang **115** 27 14N 111 25 E
Shapinsay **84** 59 2N 2 50W
Shaqrā', S. Yemen **105** 13 22N 45 44 E
Shaqra', Si. Arabia **106** 25 15N 45 16 E
Shari **116** 43 55N 144 40 E
Sharjah = Ash Shāriqah **107** 25 23N 55 26 E
Shark B. **126** 25 55 S 113 32 E
Sharkey County ◇ **31** 32 55N 90 53W
Sharon, Conn. **28** 41 53N 73 29W
Sharon, Kans. **24** 37 15N 98 25W
Sharon, Mass. **28** 42 7N 71 11W
Sharon, N. Dak. **41** 47 36N 97 54W
Sharon, Okla. **43** 36 17N 99 20W
Sharon, Pa. **45** 41 14N 80 31W
Sharon, Tenn. **48** 36 14N 88 50W
Sharon, Vt. **36** 43 47N 72 25W
Sharon, Wis. **55** 42 30N 88 44W
Sharon, Plain of = Hasharon **104** 32 12N 34 49 E
Sharon Springs **24** 38 54N 101 45W
Sharonville **42** 39 16N 84 25W
Sharp County ◇ **13** 36 4N 91 37W
Sharpe, L. **47** 44 1N 99 23W
Sharpe L. **63** 54 5N 93 40W
Sharpes **17** 28 26N 80 46W
Sharpsburg, Iowa **23** 40 48N 94 38W
Sharpsburg, Md. **27** 39 28N 77 45W
Sharpsburg, N.C. **40** 35 53N 77 50W
Sharpsville, Ind. **22** 40 23N 86 5W
Sharpsville, Pa. **45** 41 15N 80 29W
Sharptown, Md. **27** 38 0N 75 0W
Sharptown, N.J. **37** 39 40N 75 22W
Sharq el Istiwa'iya □ **121** 5 0N 33 0 E
Sharya **98** 58 22N 45 20 E
Shashi, Botswana **123** 21 15 S 27 27 E
Shashi, China **115** 30 25N 112 14 E
Shasta **14** 40 36N 122 29W
Shasta, Mt. **14** 41 25N 122 12W
Shasta County ◇ **14** 40 40N 122 0W
Shasta Dam **14** 40 43N 122 25W
Shasta L. **14** 40 43N 122 25W
Shasta National Forest **14** 41 10N 122 20W
Shattuck **43** 36 16N 99 53W
Shaunavon **63** 49 35N 108 25W
Shaver L. **15** 37 9N 119 18W
Shaw **31** 33 36N 90 47W
Shaw → **126** 20 21 S 119 17 E
Shawan **113** 44 34N 85 50 E
Shawangunk Mts. **39** 41 35N 74 30W
Shawano **55** 44 47N 88 36W
Shawano County ◇ **55** 44 45N 88 40W
Shawboro **40** 36 24N 76 6W
Shawhan **49** 38 18N 84 16W
Shawinigan **60** 46 35N 72 50W
Shawnee, Ga. **18** 32 29N 81 25W
Shawnee, Kans. **24** 39 1N 94 43W
Shawnee, Ohio **42** 39 36N 82 13W
Shawnee, Okla. **43** 35 20N 96 55W
Shawnee County ◇ **24** 39 0N 95 45W
Shawnee National Forest **21** 37 40N 88 20W
Shawneetown **21** 37 42N 88 8W
Shcherbakov = Rybinsk **98** 58 5N 38 50 E
Shchuchiosk **100** 52 56N 70 12 E
She Xian **115** 29 50N 118 25 E
Shea **71** 2 48N 59 4W
Shebele, Wabi → **105** 2 0N 44 0 E
Sheboygan **55** 43 46N 87 45W
Sheboygan County ◇ **55** 43 45N 87 50W
Sheboygan Falls **55** 43 44N 87 49W
Shechem **104** 32 13N 35 21 E
Shedd **44** 44 28N 123 7W
Shediac **61** 46 14N 64 32W
Sheelin, Lough **85** 53 48N 7 20W
Sheenjek → **11** 66 45N 144 33W
Sheep Haven **85** 55 12N 7 55W
Sheep Hole Mts. **15** 34 10N 117 40W
Sheep Mt. **56** 43 31N 110 28W
Sheep Range **35** 36 35N 115 15W
Sheerness **83** 51 26N 0 47 E
Sheet Harbour **61** 44 56N 62 31W
Shefar'am **104** 32 48N 35 10 E
Sheffield, U.K. **82** 53 23N 1 28W
Sheffield, Ala. **10** 34 46N 87 41W
Sheffield, Ill. **21** 41 21N 89 44W
Sheffield, Iowa **23** 42 54N 93 13W
Sheffield, Mass. **28** 42 5N 73 21W
Sheffield, Tex. **50** 30 41N 101 49W
Sheho **63** 51 35N 103 13W
Shehuen → **78** 49 35 S 69 34W
Shekhupura **108** 31 42N 73 58 E
Shelbiana **49** 37 26N 82 30W
Shelbina **32** 39 47N 92 2W
Shelburn **22** 39 11N 87 24W
Shelburne, N.S., Canada **61** 43 47N 65 20W
Shelburne, Ont., Canada **60** 44 4N 80 15W
Shelburne, U.S.A. **36** 44 23N 73 14W
Shelburne B. **127** 11 50 S 142 50 E
Shelburne Falls **28** 42 36N 72 45W
Shelby, Iowa **23** 41 31N 95 27W
Shelby, Mich. **29** 43 37N 86 22W
Shelby, Miss. **31** 33 57N 90 46W
Shelby, Mont. **33** 48 30N 111 51W
Shelby, N.C. **40** 35 17N 81 32W
Shelby, Nebr. **34** 41 12N 97 26W
Shelby, Ohio **42** 40 53N 82 40W
Shelby County ◇, Ala. **10** 33 15N 86 49W
Shelby County ◇, Ill. **21** 39 25N 88 45W
Shelby County ◇, Ind. **22** 39 30N 85 50W
Shelby County ◇, Iowa **23** 41 40N 95 20W
Shelby County ◇, Ky. **49** 38 10N 85 10W
Shelby County ◇, Mo. **32** 39 50N 92 0W
Shelby County ◇, Ohio **42** 40 17N 84 9W
Shelby County ◇, Tenn. **48** 35 5N 89 55W
Shelby County ◇, Tex. **51** 31 48N 94 11W
Shelbyville, Ill. **21** 39 24N 88 48W
Shelbyville, Ind. **22** 39 31N 85 47W
Shelbyville, Ky. **49** 38 13N 85 14W
Shelbyville, Mo. **32** 39 48N 92 2W
Shelbyville, Tenn. **48** 35 29N 86 28W
Shelbyville, Tex. **51** 31 46N 94 5W
Shelbyville, L. **21** 39 26N 88 46W
Sheldahl **23** 41 52N 93 42W
Sheldon, Iowa **23** 43 11N 95 51W
Sheldon, Mo. **32** 37 40N 94 18W
Sheldon, N. Dak. **41** 46 35N 97 30W
Sheldon, S.C. **46** 32 36N 80 48W
Sheldon, Wis. **55** 45 19N 90 58W
Sheldon Point **11** 62 32N 164 52W
Sheldrake **61** 50 20N 64 51W
Shelikhova, Zaliv **101** 59 30N 157 0 E
Shelikof Strait **11** 57 30N 155 0W
Shell Lake, Canada **63** 53 19N 107 2W
Shell Lake, U.S.A. **55** 45 45N 91 55W
Shell Rock **23** 42 43N 92 35W
Shellbrook **63** 53 13N 106 24W
Shelley **20** 43 23N 112 7W
Shellharbour **127** 34 31 S 150 51 E
Shelling Rocks **85** 51 45N 10 35W
Shellman **18** 31 46N 84 37W
Shellman Bluff **18** 31 35N 81 19W
Shellrock → **23** 42 35N 92 25W
Shellsburg **23** 42 6N 91 52W
Shelltown **27** 37 58N 75 40W
Shelly **30** 47 28N 96 49W
Shelton, Conn. **28** 41 19N 73 5W
Shelton, Nebr. **34** 40 47N 98 44W
Shelton, S.C. **46** 34 30N 81 25W
Shelton, Wash. **53** 47 13N 123 6W
Shemakha **99** 40 38N 48 37 E
Shenandoah, Iowa **23** 40 46N 95 22W
Shenandoah, Pa. **45** 40 49N 76 12W
Shenandoah, Va. **54** 38 29N 78 37W
Shenandoah → **54** 39 19N 77 44W

Shenandoah County **Silver Creek**

Shenandoah County ◇ **54** 38 53N 78 30W
Shenandoah Mt. **54** 38 40N 77 15W
Shenandoah National Park **54** 38 35N 78 22W
Shenchi **114** 39 8N 112 10 E
Shendam **120** 8 49N 9 30 E
Shendī **121** 16 46N 33 22 E
Sheng Xian **115** 29 35N 120 50 E
Shenmu **114** 38 50N 110 29 E
Shenqiucheng **115** 33 24N 115 2 E
Shensi = Shaanxi □ **115** 35 0N 109 0 E
Shenyang **114** 41 48N 123 27 E
Sheopur Kalan **108** 25 40N 76 40 E
Shephelah = Hashefela **104** 31 30N 34 43 E
Shepherd, Mich. **29** 43 32N 84 41W
Shepherd, Mont. **33** 45 57N 108 21W
Shepherd, Tex. **51** 30 31N 95 1W
Shepherdsville **49** 37 59N 85 43W
Shepparton **127** 36 23 S 145 26 E
Sheqi **115** 33 12N 112 57 E
Sher Khan Qala **108** 29 55N 66 20 E
Sherada **121** 7 18N 36 30 E
Sherborne **83** 50 56N 2 31W
Sherbro I. **120** 7 30N 12 40W
Sherbrooke **61** 45 28N 71 57W
Sherburn **30** 43 39N 94 43W
Sherburne, N.Y. **39** 42 41N 75 30W
Sherburne, Vt. **36** 43 10N 72 47W
Sherburne County ◇ **30** 45 20N 93 45W
Sheridan, Ark. **13** 34 19N 92 24W
Sheridan, Ill. **21** 41 32N 88 41W
Sheridan, Ind. **22** 40 8N 86 13W
Sheridan, Ky. **48** 37 21N 88 12W
Sheridan, Mo. **32** 40 31N 94 37W
Sheridan, Mont. **33** 45 27N 112 12W
Sheridan, Oreg. **44** 45 6N 123 24W
Sheridan, Wyo. **56** 44 48N 106 58W
Sheridan County ◇, Kans. **24** 39 20N 100 30W
Sheridan County ◇, Mont. **33** 48 48N 104 30W
Sheridan County ◇, N. Dak. **41** 47 45N 100 20W
Sheridan County ◇, Nebr. **34** 42 30N 102 20W
Sheridan County ◇, Wyo. **56** 44 50N 106 45W
Sheridan Lake **16** 38 28N 102 18W
Sherman, Conn. **28** 41 35N 73 30W
Sherman, Ill. **21** 39 54N 89 36W
Sherman, Miss. **31** 34 22N 88 50W
Sherman, N. Mex. **38** 32 45N 107 51W
Sherman, N.Y. **39** 42 10N 79 36W
Sherman, Tex. **51** 33 38N 96 36W
Sherman County ◇, Kans. **24** 39 20N 101 45W
Sherman County ◇, Nebr. **34** 41 15N 99 0W
Sherman County ◇, Oreg. **44** 45 30N 120 40W
Sherman County ◇, Tex. **50** 36 10N 101 58W
Sherman Reservoir **34** 41 18N 98 53W
Sherman Station **26** 45 54N 68 26W
Sherrard **21** 41 19N 90 31W
Sherridon **63** 55 8N 101 5W
Sherrill **13** 34 23N 91 57W
Sherwood, Ark. **13** 34 48N 92 16W
Sherwood, Md. **27** 38 46N 76 19W
Sherwood, N. Dak. **41** 48 57N 101 38W
Sherwood, Ohio **42** 41 17N 84 33W
Sherwood, Tenn. **49** 35 5N 85 56W
Sherwood Forest **82** 53 5N 1 5W
Shesheke **123** 17 14 S 24 22 E
Sheslay **62** 58 17N 131 52W
Sheslay → **62** 58 48N 132 5W
Shetek, L. **30** 44 7N 95 42W
Shethanei L. **63** 58 48N 97 50W
Shetland □ **84** 60 30N 1 30W
Shetland Is. **84** 60 30N 1 30W
Shetucket **28** 41 0N 72 0W
Shevlin **30** 47 32N 95 15W
Shewa Gimira **121** 7 4N 35 51 E
Sheyenne **41** 47 50N 99 7W
Sheyenne → **41** 47 2N 96 50W
Shiawassee County ◇ **29** 42 55N 84 10W
Shibām **105** 16 0N 48 36 E
Shibata **116** 37 57N 139 20 E
Shibecha **116** 43 17N 144 36 E
Shibetsu **116** 44 10N 142 23 E
Shibogama L. **60** 53 35N 88 15W
Shibushi **117** 31 25N 131 8 E
Shickley **34** 40 25N 97 43W
Shickshinny **45** 41 9N 76 9W
Shidao **114** 36 50N 122 25 E
Shidler **43** 36 47N 96 40W
Shidler Res. **43** 36 50N 96 40W
Shido **117** 34 19N 134 10 E
Shiel, L. **84** 56 48N 5 32W
Shields **24** 38 37N 100 27W
Shiga □ **117** 35 20N 136 0 E
Shigaib **121** 15 5N 23 35 E
Shiguaigou **114** 40 52N 110 15 E
Shihchiachuangi =
Shijiazhuang **114** 38 2N 114 28 E
Shijiazhuang **114** 38 2N 114 28 E
Shikarpur **108** 27 57N 68 39 E
Shikoku □ **117** 33 30N 133 30 E
Shikoku-Sanchi **117** 33 30N 133 30 E
Shilabo **105** 6 22N 44 32 E
Shiliguri **109** 26 45N 88 25 E
Shilka **101** 52 0N 115 55 E
Shilka → **101** 53 20N 121 26 E
Shillelagh **85** 52 46N 6 32W
Shillington **45** 40 18N 75 58W
Shillong **109** 25 35N 91 53 E
Shilo **104** 32 4N 35 18 E
Shiloh, Ga. **18** 32 49N 84 42W
Shiloh, N.C. **40** 36 17N 76 5W
Shiloh, N.J. **37** 39 28N 75 18W
Shiloh, Ohio **42** 40 58N 82 36W
Shilong **115** 23 5N 113 52 E
Shimabara **117** 32 48N 130 20 E
Shimada **117** 34 49N 138 10 E
Shimane □ **117** 35 0N 132 30 E
Shimanovsk **101** 52 15N 127 30 E
Shimizu **117** 35 0N 138 30 E
Shimodate **117** 36 20N 139 55 E
Shimoga **108** 13 57N 75 32 E
Shimonoseki **117** 33 58N 131 0 E
Shin, L. **84** 58 7N 4 30W
Shin Pond **26** 46 6N 68 33W
Shin-Tone → **117** 35 44N 140 51 E
Shinano → **117** 36 50N 138 30 E
Shīndand **107** 33 12N 62 8 E
Shiner **51** 29 26N 97 10W
Shinglehouse **45** 41 58N 78 12W
Shingler **18** 31 35N 83 47W
Shingleton **29** 46 21N 86 28W
Shingletown **14** 40 30N 121 53W
Shingū **117** 33 40N 135 55 E
Shinjō **116** 38 46N 140 18 E
Shinnston **54** 39 24N 80 18W
Shinyanga **122** 3 45 S 33 27 E
Shiogama **116** 38 19N 141 1 E
Shiojiri **117** 36 6N 137 58 E
Ship Bottom **37** 39 39N 74 11W
Ship I. **31** 30 13N 88 55W
Ship Rock **38** 36 41N 108 50W
Shipehenski Prokhod **95** 42 45N 25 15 E
Shipka **95** 42 46N 25 33 E
Shipki La **108** 31 45N 78 40 E
Shipman, Ill. **21** 39 7N 90 3W
Shipman, Va. **54** 37 43N 78 51W
Shippegan **61** 47 45N 64 45W
Shippensburg **45** 40 3N 77 31W
Shippenville **45** 41 15N 79 28W
Shiprock **38** 36 47N 108 41W
Shipshewana **22** 41 41N 85 35W
Shiqian **115** 27 32N 108 13 E
Shiqma, N. → **104** 31 37N 34 30 E
Shiquan **115** 33 5N 108 15 E
Shīr Kūh **107** 31 39N 54 3 E
Shirakawa, Fukushima,
Japan **117** 37 7N 140 13 E
Shirakawa, Gifu, Japan **117** 36 17N 136 56 E
Shirane-San, Gumma, Japan **117** 36 48N 139 22 E
Shirane-San, Yamanashi,
Japan **117** 35 42N 138 9 E
Shiraoi **116** 42 33N 141 21 E
Shīrāz **107** 29 42N 52 30 E
Shire → **123** 17 42 S 35 19 E
Shiretoko-Misaki **116** 44 21N 145 20 E
Shirigami-Misaki **116** 41 24N 140 12 E
Shiriya-Zaki **116** 41 25N 141 30 E
Shirley, Ark. **13** 35 39N 92 19W
Shirley, Ind. **22** 39 53N 85 35W
Shirley, Mass. **28** 42 33N 71 39W
Shirley Mills **26** 45 22N 69 37W
Shiroishi **116** 38 0N 140 37 E
Shīrvān **107** 37 30N 57 50 E
Shirwa L. = Chilwa, L. **123** 15 15 S 35 40 E
Shishaldin Volcano **11** 54 45N 163 58W
Shishmanova **95** 42 58N 23 12 E
Shishmaref **11** 66 15N 166 4W
Shisur **105** 17 30N 54 0 E
Shitai **115** 30 12N 117 25 E
Shively **49** 38 12N 85 49W
Shivers **31** 31 48N 89 59W
Shivpuri **108** 25 26N 77 42 E
Shivta **104** 30 53N 34 40 E
Shivwits Plateau **12** 36 15N 113 30W
Shiwei **114** 51 19N 119 55 E
Shixing **115** 24 46N 114 5 E
Shizuishan **114** 39 15N 106 50 E
Shizuoka **117** 35 0N 138 24 E
Shizuoka □ **117** 35 15N 138 40 E
Shkoder = Shkodra **95** 42 6N 19 20 E
Shkodra **95** 42 6N 19 20 E
Shkumbini → **95** 41 5N 19 50 E
Shmidt, O. **101** 81 0N 91 0 E
Shō-Gawa → **117** 36 47N 137 4 E
Shoal Cr. →, Ill. **21** 38 28N 89 35W
Shoal Cr. →, Mo. **32** 39 44N 93 32W
Shoal Lake **63** 50 30N 100 35W
Shoals **22** 38 40N 86 47W
Shōdo-Shima **117** 34 30N 134 15 E
Shoeburyness **83** 51 31N 0 49 E
Shoemakersville **45** 40 30N 75 58W
Sholapur = Solapur **108** 17 43N 75 56 E
Shologontsy **101** 66 13N 114 0 E
Shomera **104** 33 4N 35 17 E
Shōmrōn **104** 32 15N 35 13 E
Shonto **12** 36 36N 110 39W
Shopville **49** 37 9N 84 29W
Shoreacres **51** 29 36N 95 1W
Shoreham **36** 43 54N 73 19W
Shorewood **55** 43 5N 87 54W
Shorter **10** 32 24N 85 57W
Shorterville **10** 31 34N 85 6W
Shortsville **39** 42 57N 77 14W
Shoshone, Calif. **15** 35 58N 116 16W
Shoshone, Idaho **20** 42 56N 114 25W
Shoshone → **56** 44 52N 108 11W
Shoshone Basin **56** 43 5N 108 5W
Shoshone County ◇ **20** 47 30N 116 0W
Shoshone L. **56** 44 22N 110 43W
Shoshone Mts. **35** 39 20N 117 25W
Shoshone National Forest **56** 44 20N 109 45W
Shoshone Range **35** 40 20N 116 50W
Shoshong **123** 22 56 S 26 31 E
Shoshoni **56** 43 14N 108 7W
Shoup **20** 45 23N 114 17W
Shouyang **114** 37 54N 113 8 E
Show Low **12** 34 15N 110 2W
Showell **27** 38 24N 75 13W
Shreve **42** 40 41N 82 1W
Shreveport **25** 32 31N 93 45W
Shrewsbury, U.K. **82** 52 42N 2 45W
Shrewsbury, U.S.A. **28** 42 18N 71 43W
Shrirampur **109** 22 44N 88 21 E
Shropshire □ **83** 52 36N 2 45W
Shuangcheng **114** 45 20N 126 15 E
Shuangliao **114** 43 29N 123 30 E
Shuangyashan **114** 46 28N 131 5 E
Shubert **34** 40 14N 95 41W
Shubuta **31** 31 52N 88 42W
Shucheng **115** 31 28N 116 57 E
Shu'eib, Wadi → **104** 31 54N 35 38 E
Shuksan, Mt. **53** 48 50N 121 36W
Shulan **114** 44 28N 127 0 E
Shule **113** 39 25N 76 3 E
Shullsburg **55** 42 35N 90 13W
Shumagin Is. **11** 55 7N 159 45W
Shumikha **100** 55 10N 63 15 E
Shunchang **115** 26 54N 117 48 E
Shunde **115** 22 42N 113 14 E
Shungnak **11** 66 52N 157 9W
Shuo Xian **114** 39 20N 112 33 E
Shuqualak **31** 32 59N 88 34W
Shūr → **107** 28 30N 55 0 E
Shurugwi **123** 19 40 S 30 0 E
Shūsf **107** 31 50N 60 5 E
Shūshtar **106** 32 0N 48 50 E
Shuswap L. **62** 50 55N 119 3W
Shutesbury **28** 42 25N 72 25W
Shuwaykah **104** 32 20N 35 1 E
Shuyak I. **11** 58 31N 152 30W
Shwebo **109** 22 30N 95 45 E
Shwegu **109** 24 15N 96 26 E
Shweli → **109** 23 45N 96 45 E
Shyok **108** 34 15N 78 12 E
Shyok → **108** 35 13N 75 53 E
Si Kiang = Xi Jiang → **115** 22 5N 113 20 E
Si Racha **112** 13 10N 100 48 E
Siah **106** 22 0N 47 0 E
Siahan Range **107** 27 30N 64 40 E
Siaksrindrapura **110** 0 51N 102 0 E
Sialkot **108** 32 32N 74 30 E
Siam = Thailand ■ **110** 16 0N 102 0 E
Sian = Xi'an **115** 34 15N 109 0 E
Siantan, P. **110** 3 10N 106 15 E
Siàpo → **70** 2 7N 66 28W
Siāreh **107** 28 5N 60 14 E
Siargao **111** 9 52N 126 3 E
Siasconset **28** 41 16N 69 58W
Siasi **111** 5 34N 120 50 E
Siau **111** 2 50N 125 25 E
Siauliai **98** 55 56N 23 15 E
Şibay **98** 52 42N 58 39 E
Šibenik **94** 43 48N 15 54 E
Siberia **102** 60 0N 100 0 E
Siberut **110** 1 30 S 99 0 E
Sibi **108** 29 30N 67 54 E
Sibil **111** 4 59 S 140 35 E
Sibiti **122** 3 38 S 13 19 E
Sibiu **89** 45 45N 24 9 E
Sibiu □ **95** 45 50N 24 15 E
Sibley, Ill. **21** 40 35N 88 23W
Sibley, Iowa **23** 43 24N 95 45W
Sibley, La. **25** 32 33N 93 18W
Sibley, Miss. **31** 31 23N 91 24W
Sibley County ◇ **30** 44 35N 94 15W
Sibolga **110** 1 42N 98 45 E
Sibsagar **109** 27 0N 94 36 E
Sibu **110** 2 18N 111 49 E
Sibuco **111** 7 20N 122 10 E
Sibuguey B. **111** 7 50N 122 45 E
Sibutu **111** 4 45N 119 30 E
Sibutu Passage **111** 4 50N 120 0 E
Sibuyan **111** 12 25N 122 40 E
Sibuyan Sea **111** 12 30N 122 20 E
Sicamous **62** 50 49N 119 0W
Sichuan □ **115** 31 0N 104 0 E
Sicilia **94** 37 30N 14 30 E
Sicilia □ **94** 37 30N 14 30 E
Sicily = Sicilia **94** 37 30N 14 30 E
Sicily Island **25** 31 51N 91 40W
Sicuani **72** 14 21 S 71 10W
Siddipet **108** 18 0N 78 51 E
Sidell **21** 39 55N 87 49W
Sidéradougou **120** 10 42N 4 12W
Sîdi Barrâni **121** 31 38N 25 58 E
Sidlaw Hills **84** 56 32N 3 10W
Sidley, Mt. **5** 77 2 S 126 2W
Sidmouth **83** 50 40N 3 13W
Sidnaw **29** 46 30N 88 43W
Sidney, Canada **62** 48 39N 123 24W
Sidney, Ark. **13** 36 0N 91 40W
Sidney, Ill. **21** 40 1N 88 4W
Sidney, Iowa **23** 40 45N 95 39W
Sidney, Mont. **33** 47 43N 104 9W
Sidney, N.Y. **39** 42 19N 75 24W
Sidney, Nebr. **34** 41 8N 102 59W
Sidney, Ohio **42** 40 17N 84 9W
Sidney Lanier L. **18** 34 10N 84 4W
Sidoarjo **111** 7 30 S 112 46 E
Sidon = Saydā **106** 33 35N 35 25 E
Sidon **31** 33 25N 90 12W
Sidra, G. of = Surt, Khalīj **121** 31 40N 18 30 E
Siedlce **89** 52 10N 22 20 E
Siegen **88** 50 52N 8 2 E
Siem Reap **112** 13 20N 103 52 E
Siena **94** 43 20N 11 20 E
Sierpe, Bocas de la **70** 10 0N 61 30W
Sierra Blanca **50** 31 11N 105 22W
Sierra Blanca Peak **38** 33 23N 105 49W
Sierra City **14** 39 34N 120 38W
Sierra Colorada **78** 40 35 S 67 50W
Sierra County ◇, Calif. **14** 39 40N 121 30W
Sierra County ◇, N. Mex. **38** 33 0N 107 0W
Sierra Gorda **76** 22 50 S 69 15W
Sierra Grande **78** 41 36 S 65 22W
Sierra Leone ■ **120** 9 0N 12 0W
Sierra Madre **56** 41 15N 107 5W
Sierra Mojada **64** 27 19N 103 42W
Sierra National Forest **15** 37 15N 119 10W
Sierra Nevada **15** 37 30N 119 0W
Sierra Vista **12** 31 33N 110 18W
Sierraville **14** 39 36N 120 22W
Sífnos **95** 37 0N 24 45 E
Sifton **63** 51 21N 100 8W
Sifton Pass **62** 57 52N 126 15W
Sighetul Marmatiei **89** 47 57N 23 52 E
Sighişoara **89** 46 12N 24 50 E
Sigli **110** 5 25N 96 0 E
Siglufjörður **96** 66 12N 18 55W
Signal Mountain **49** 35 7N 85 21W
Signal Pk. **12** 33 20N 114 2W
Signy I. **5** 60 45 S 45 56W
Sigourney **23** 41 20N 92 12W
Sigsbee **18** 31 16N 83 52W
Sigsig **70** 3 0 S 78 50W
Sigtuna **97** 59 36N 17 44 E
Sigüenza **91** 41 3N 2 40W
Siguiri **120** 11 31N 9 10W
Sigurd **52** 38 50N 111 58W
Sihanoukville = Kompong
Som **110** 10 38N 103 30 E
Sihaus **72** 8 40 S 77 40W
Sihui **115** 23 20N 112 40 E
Si'īr **104** 31 35N 35 9 E
Siirt **106** 37 57N 41 55 E
Sikar **108** 27 33N 75 10 E
Sikasso **120** 11 18N 5 35W
Sikes **25** 32 5N 92 29W
Sikeston **32** 36 53N 89 35W
Sikhote Alin, Khrebet **101** 46 0N 136 0 E
Síkinos **95** 36 40N 25 8 E
Sikkani Chief → **62** 57 47N 122 15W
Sikkim □ **109** 27 50N 88 30 E
Sikotu-Ko **116** 42 45N 141 25 E
Sil → **91** 42 27N 7 43W
Sil Nakya **12** 32 13N 111 49W
Silacayoapan **65** 17 30N 98 9W
Silas **10** 31 46N 88 20W
Sīlat az Ẓahr **104** 32 19N 35 11 E
Silchar **109** 24 49N 92 48 E
Silcox **63** 57 12N 94 10W
Siler City **40** 35 44N 79 28W
Silesia = Slask **88** 51 0N 16 30 E
Siletz **44** 44 43N 123 55W
Silgarhi Doti **109** 29 15N 81 0 E
Silghat **109** 26 35N 93 0 E
Silifke **106** 36 22N 33 58 E
Siling Co **113** 31 50N 89 20 E
Silistra **95** 44 6N 27 19 E
Siljan **97** 60 55N 14 45 E
Silkeborg **97** 56 10N 9 32 E
Sillajhuay, Cordillera **72** 19 46 S 68 40W
Sillustani **72** 15 50 S 70 7W
Silo **43** 34 3N 96 29W
Siloam **18** 33 32N 83 5W
Siloam Springs **13** 36 11N 94 32W
Silogui **110** 1 10 S 9 0 E
Silsbee **51** 30 21N 94 11W
Silt **16** 39 33N 107 40W
Siltcoos L. **44** 43 53N 124 6W
Silva Porto = Kuito **123** 12 22 S 16 55 E
Silver **50** 32 4N 100 40W
Silver Bay **30** 47 18N 91 16W
Silver Bell **12** 32 23N 111 30W
Silver Bow County ◇ **33** 45 48N 112 45W
Silver Bow Park **33** 46 1N 112 28W
Silver City, Iowa **23** 41 7N 95 39W
Silver City, Mich. **29** 46 50N 89 35W
Silver City, Miss. **31** 33 6N 90 30W
Silver City, N.C. **40** 35 2N 79 12W
Silver City, N. Mex. **38** 32 46N 108 17W
Silver Cliff **16** 38 8N 105 27W
Silver Cr. →, Ariz. **12** 34 44N 110 2W
Silver Cr. →, Oreg. **44** 43 16N 119 13W
Silver Creek, N.Y. **39** 42 33N 79 10W
Silver Creek, Nebr. **34** 41 19N 97 40W

Silver L. Sneads Ferry

Silver L., Calif. 15 35 21N 116 7W
Silver L., Wash. 53 46 17N 122 47W
Silver L., Oreg. 44 43 22N 119 25W
Silver L., Oreg. 44 43 6N 120 53W
Silver Lake, Kans. 24 39 6N 95 52W
Silver Lake, Minn. 30 44 54N 94 12W
Silver Lake, Oreg. 44 43 8N 121 3W
Silver Lake, Wis. 55 44 4N 89 14W
Silver Run 27 39 42N 77 3W
Silver Spring 27 38 59N 77 2W
Silver Springs, Fla. 17 29 13N 82 3W
Silver Springs, Nev. 35 39 25N 119 14W
Silverdale 24 37 3N 96 54W
Silverstreet 46 34 13N 81 43W
Silverton, Colo. 16 37 49N 107 40W
Silverton, N.J. 37 40 1N 74 10W
Silverton, Oreg. 44 45 1N 122 47W
Silverton, Tex. 50 34 28N 101 19W
Silverton, Wash. 53 48 5N 121 35W
Silvia 70 2 37N 76 21W
Silvies → 44 43 34N 119 2W
Silwād 104 31 59N 35 15 E
Simanggang 110 1 15N 111 32 E
Simão Dias 74 10 44 S 37 49W
Simard, L. 60 47 40N 78 40W
Sîmărtin 95 46 19N 25 58 E
Simcoe 60 42 50N 80 20W
Simcoe, L. 60 44 25N 79 20W
Simenga 101 62 42N 108 25 E
Simeulue 110 2 45N 95 45 E
Simferopol 99 44 55N 34 3 E
Simi Valley 15 34 16N 118 47W
Simikot 109 30 0N 81 50 E
Simití 70 7 58N 73 57W
Simla, India 108 31 2N 77 9 E
Simla, U.S.A. 16 39 9N 104 5W
Simmesport 25 30 59N 91 49W
Simmie 63 49 56N 108 6W
Simms 33 47 30N 111 56W
Simnasho 44 44 58N 121 21W
Simões 74 7 36 S 40 49W
Simojärvi 96 66 5N 27 3 E
Simojoki → 96 65 35N 25 1 E
Simojovel 65 17 12N 92 38W
Simonette → 62 55 9N 118 15W
Simonton Lake 22 41 44N 85 59W
Simpang, Indonesia 110 1 16 S 104 5 E
Simpang, Malaysia 112 4 50N 100 40 E
Simplício Mendes 74 7 51 S 41 54W
Simplon Pass 88 46 15N 8 0 E
Simpson, Kans. 24 39 23N 97 56W
Simpson, La. 25 31 16N 93 1W
Simpson County ◇, Ky. 48 36 45N 86 35W
Simpson County ◇, Miss. 31 31 53N 89 58W
Simpson Des. 127 25 0 S 137 0 E
Simpson Park Range 35 39 50N 116 35W
Simpsonville, Ky. 49 38 13N 85 22W
Simpsonville, S.C. 46 34 44N 82 15W
Sims 21 38 22N 88 32W
Simsbury 28 41 53N 72 48W
Simunjan 110 1 25N 110 45 E
Simushir, Ostrov 101 46 50N 152 30 E
Sinabang 110 2 30N 96 24 E
Sinadogo 105 5 50N 47 0 E
Sinai = Es Sînâ' 121 29 0N 34 0 E
Sinai 47 44 15N 97 3W
Sinai, Mt. = Mûsa, G. 106 28 33N 33 59 E
Sinaia 95 45 21N 25 38 E
Sinaloa 64 25 50N 108 20W
Sinaloa □ 64 25 0N 107 30W
Sinan 115 27 56N 108 13 E
Sînāwan 120 31 0N 10 37 E
Sincé 70 9 15N 75 9W
Sincelejo 70 9 18N 75 24W
Sinclair 56 41 47N 107 7W
Sinclair, L. 18 33 8N 83 12W
Sinclair Mills 62 54 5N 121 40W
Sinclairville 39 42 16N 79 16W
Sincorá, Serra do 75 13 30 S 41 0W
Sind □ 108 26 0N 69 0 E
Sind Sagar Doab 108 32 0N 71 30 E
Sindangan 111 8 10N 123 5 E
Sindangbarang 111 7 27 S 107 1 E
Sines 91 37 56N 8 51W
Singa 121 13 10N 33 57 E
Singapore ■ 112 1 17N 103 51 E
Singapore, Straits of 112 1 15N 104 0 E
Singaraja 110 8 6 S 115 10 E
Singer 25 30 39N 93 25W
Singida 122 4 49 S 34 48 E
Singitikós Kólpos 95 40 6N 24 0 E
Singkaling Hkamti 109 26 0N 95 39 E
Singkawang 110 1 0N 108 57 E
Singkep 110 0 30 S 104 20 E
Singleton 127 32 33 S 151 0 E
Singleton, Mt. 126 29 27 S 117 15 E
Singora = Songkhla 112 7 13N 100 37 E
Sinjai 111 5 7 S 120 20 E
Sinjār 106 36 19N 41 52 E
Sinjil 104 32 3N 35 15 E
Sinkat 121 18 55N 36 49 E
Sinkiang Uighur = Xinjiang Uygur Zizhiqu □ 113 42 0N 86 0 E
Sinking Spring 42 39 4N 83 23W
Sinnemahoning 45 41 19N 78 6W
Sinni → 94 40 9N 16 42 E
Sinnuris 121 29 26N 30 31 E
Sinoe, L. 95 44 35N 28 50 E
Sinop 106 42 1N 35 11 E
Sinskoye 101 61 8N 126 48 E
Sint Eustatius, I. 67 17 30N 62 59W
Sint Maarten, I. 67 18 4N 63 4W
Sint Niklaas 87 51 10N 4 9 E
Sint Truiden 87 50 48N 5 10 E
Sintang 110 0 5N 111 35 E
Sinton 51 28 2N 97 31W
Sintra 91 38 47N 9 25W
Sinŭiju 114 40 5N 124 24 E
Siocon 111 7 40N 122 10 E
Sioma 123 16 25 S 23 28 E
Sion 88 46 14N 7 20 E
Sioux Center 23 43 5N 96 11W
Sioux City 23 42 30N 96 24W
Sioux County ◇, Iowa 23 43 5N 96 10W
Sioux County ◇, N. Dak. 41 46 0N 101 0W
Sioux County ◇, Nebr. 34 42 30N 103 45W
Sioux Falls 47 43 33N 96 44W
Sioux Lookout 60 50 10N 91 50W
Sioux Rapids 23 42 53N 95 9W
Siping 114 43 8N 124 21 E
Sipiwesk L. 63 55 5N 97 35W
Siple 5 75 0 S 74 0 E
Sipora 110 2 18 S 99 40 E
Sipsey → 10 33 0N 88 10W
Siquia → 66 12 10N 84 20W
Siquijor 111 9 12N 123 35 E
Siquirres 66 10 6N 83 30W
Siquisique 70 10 34N 69 42W
Sir Edward Pellew Group 127 15 40 S 137 10 E
Siracusa 94 37 4N 15 17 E
Sirajganj 109 24 25N 89 47 E
Siren 55 45 47N 92 24W
Siret → 89 47 58N 26 5 E
Sirmans 17 30 21N 83 39W
Sirohi 108 24 52N 72 53 E
Sironj 108 24 5N 77 39 E
Síros 95 37 28N 24 57 E
Sirsa 108 29 33N 75 4 E
Sisak 94 45 30N 16 21 E
Sisaket 112 15 8N 104 23 E
Sishui 115 34 48N 113 15 E
Sisipuk L. 63 55 45N 101 50W
Siskiyou County ◇ 14 41 40N 122 40W
Siskiyou Mts. 14 42 0N 122 40W
Siskiyou National Forest 44 42 20N 124 0W
Sisophon 112 13 38N 102 59 E
Sisquoc → 15 34 54N 120 18W
Sisseton 47 45 40N 97 3W
Sisseton Indian Reservation 41 46 0N 126 30W
Sissonville 54 38 32N 81 38W
Sīstān va Balūchestān □ 107 27 0N 62 0 E
Sister Bay 55 45 11N 87 7W
Sisters 44 44 18N 121 33W
Sisterville 54 39 34N 80 59W
Sitapur 109 27 38N 80 45 E
Sitges 91 41 17N 1 47 E
Sítio da Abadia 75 14 48 S 46 16W
Sitka, Alaska 11 57 3N 135 20W
Sitka, Kans. 24 37 11N 99 39W
Sitka ◇ 11 57 0N 135 0W
Sitkinak I. 11 56 33N 154 10W
Sittang → 109 17 10N 96 58 E
Sittang Myit → 109 17 20N 96 45 E
Sittard 87 51 0N 5 52 E
Sittwe 109 20 18N 92 45 E
Situbondo 111 7 45 S 114 0 E
Siuna 66 13 37N 84 45W
Siuri 109 23 50N 87 34 E
Siuslaw → 44 44 1N 124 8W
Siuslaw National Forest 44 44 15N 123 50W
Sivand 107 30 5N 52 55 E
Sivas 106 39 43N 36 58 E
Siverek 106 37 50N 39 19 E
Sivomaskinskiy 98 66 40N 62 35 E
Sivrihisar 106 39 30N 31 35 E
Sîwa 121 29 11N 25 31 E
Siwalik Range 109 28 0N 83 0 E
Siwan 109 26 13N 84 21 E
Sizewell 83 52 13N 1 38 E
Sjælland 97 55 30N 11 30 E
Sjíptjenski P. 95 42 46N 25 33 E
Sjumen = Kolarovgrad 95 43 18N 26 55 E
Skagafjörður 96 65 54N 19 35W
Skagastølstindane 97 61 28N 7 52 E
Skagen 97 68 37N 14 27 E
Skagerrak 97 57 30N 9 0 E
Skagit → 53 48 23N 122 22W
Skagit County ◇ 53 48 30N 121 30W
Skagway 11 59 28N 135 19W
Skagway-Yakutat-Angoon ◇ 11 59 0N 139 0W
Skaidi 96 70 26N 24 30 E
Skalni Dol = Kamenyak 95 43 24N 26 57 E
Skamania County ◇ 53 46 0N 122 0W
Skaneateles 39 42 57N 76 26W
Skara 97 58 25N 13 30 E
Skaraborgs län □ 97 58 20N 13 30 E
Skardu 108 35 20N 75 44 E
Skedee 43 36 23N 96 42W
Skeena → 62 54 9N 130 5W
Skeena Mts. 62 56 40N 128 30W
Skegness 82 53 9N 0 20 E
Skeldon 71 5 55N 57 20W
Skellefte älv → 96 64 45N 21 10 E
Skellefteå 96 64 45N 20 58 E
Skelleftehamn 96 64 47N 20 59 E
Skellytown 50 35 34N 101 11W
Skerries, The 82 53 27N 4 40W
Skhwaner, Pegunungan 110 1 0 S 112 30 E
Skiatook 43 36 20N 96 0W
Skiatook Res. 43 36 20N 96 10W
Skibbereen 85 51 33N 9 16W
Skiddaw 82 54 39N 3 9W
Skidmore, Mo. 32 40 17N 95 5W
Skidmore, Tex. 51 28 15N 97 41W
Skien 97 59 12N 9 35 E
Skierniewice 89 51 58N 20 10 E
Skikda 120 36 50N 6 58 E
Skillet → 21 38 5N 88 5W
Skipton 82 53 57N 2 1W
Skíros 95 38 55N 24 34 E
Skive 97 56 33N 9 2 E
Skjálfandafljót → 96 65 59N 17 25W
Skjálfandi 96 66 5N 17 30W
Skoghall 97 59 20N 13 30 E
Skokie 21 42 3N 87 45W
Skopje 95 42 1N 21 32 E
Skövde 97 58 15N 13 59 E
Skovorodino 101 54 0N 125 0 E
Skowhegan 26 44 46N 69 43W
Skownan 63 51 58N 99 35W
Skudeneshavn 97 59 10N 5 10 E
Skull 85 51 32N 9 40W
Skull Valley 12 34 30N 112 41W
Skull Valley Indian Reservation 52 40 24N 112 45W
Skuna → 31 33 54N 89 41W
Skunk → 23 40 42N 91 7W
Skwierzyna 88 52 33N 15 30 E
Skye 84 57 15N 6 10W
Skykomish 53 47 42N 121 22W
Skyland 40 35 29N 82 32W
Skyros = Skíros 95 38 55N 24 34 E
Slagle 25 31 12N 93 8W
Slamet 110 7 16 S 109 8 E
Slaney → 85 52 52N 6 45W
Slănic 95 45 14N 25 58 E
Slask 88 51 0N 16 30 E
Slate Is. 60 48 40N 87 0W
Slate Spring 31 33 44N 89 22W
Slater, Iowa 23 41 53N 93 41W
Slater, Mo. 32 39 13N 93 4W
Slatina 89 44 28N 24 22 E
Slaton 50 33 26N 101 39W
Slaughter 25 30 43N 91 9W
Slaughter Beach 27 38 52N 75 18W
Slaughters 48 37 29N 87 30W
Slaughterville 43 35 5N 97 20W
Slave → 62 61 18N 113 39W
Slave Coast 118 6 0N 2 30 E
Slave Lake 62 55 17N 114 43W
Slave Pt. 62 61 11N 115 56W
Slavgorod 100 53 1N 78 37 E
Slavkov 88 49 10N 16 52 E
Slavyanka 116 42 53N 131 21 E
Slavyansk 99 48 55N 37 36 E
Slayden 31 34 57N 89 27W
Slayton 30 43 59N 95 45W
Sleaford 82 53 0N 0 22W
Sleat, Sd. of 84 57 5N 5 47W
Sledge 31 34 26N 90 13W
Sleeper 32 37 46N 92 36W
Sleeper Is. 59 58 30N 81 0W
Sleeping Bear Dunes Nat. Lakeshore 29 44 50N 86 5W
Sleeping Bear Pt. 29 44 55N 86 3W
Sleepy Eye 30 44 18N 94 43W
Sleetmute 11 61 42N 157 10W
Sleman 111 7 40 S 110 20 E
Slemon L. 62 63 13N 116 4W
Slemp 49 37 5N 83 6W
Slick 43 35 47N 96 16W
Slick Rock 16 38 3N 108 54W
Slide Mt. 39 42 0N 74 25W
Slidell 25 30 17N 89 47W
Sliedrecht 87 51 50N 4 45 E
Slieve Aughty 85 53 4N 8 30W
Slieve Bloom 85 53 4N 7 40W
Slieve Donard 85 54 10N 5 57W
Slieve Gullion 85 54 8N 6 26W
Slieve Mish 85 52 12N 9 50W
Slievenamon 85 52 25N 7 37W
Sligo, Ireland 85 54 17N 8 28W
Sligo, U.S.A. 45 41 6N 79 29W
Sligo □ 85 54 10N 8 35W
Sligo B. 85 54 20N 8 40W
Slim Buttes 47 45 20N 103 15W
Slite 97 57 42N 18 48 E
Sliven 95 42 42N 26 19 E
Sloan 23 42 14N 96 14W
Sloat 14 39 52N 120 44W
Slobodskoy 98 58 40N 50 6 E
Slobozia, Argeş, Romania 95 44 30N 25 14 E
Slobozia, Ialomiţa, Romania 95 44 34N 27 23 E
Slocan 62 49 48N 117 28W
Slochteren 87 53 12N 6 48 E
Slocomb 10 31 7N 85 36W
Slocum 28 41 32N 71 31W
Slope County ◇ 41 46 20N 103 30W
Slough 83 51 30N 0 35W
Slovakia = Slovensko □ 89 48 30N 19 0 E
Slovakian Ore Mts. = Slovenské Rudohorie 89 48 45N 20 0 E
Slovenia = Slovenija □ 94 45 58N 14 30 E
Slovenija □ 94 45 58N 14 30 E
Slovenské Rudohorie 89 48 45N 20 0 E
Slovensko □ 89 48 30N 19 0 E
Sluis 87 51 18N 3 23 E
Slunchev Bryag 95 42 40N 27 41 E
Slyne Hd. 85 53 25N 10 10W
Slyudyanka 101 51 40N 103 40 E
Smakover 13 33 22N 92 44W
Small, C. 26 43 42N 69 51W
Smalltree L. 63 61 0N 105 0W
Smallwood Reservoir 61 54 20N 63 10W
Smara 120 32 9N 8 16W
Smarr 18 32 59N 83 53W
Smarts Mt. 36 43 48N 72 3W
Smartville 14 39 13N 121 18W
Smeaton 63 53 30N 104 49W
Smederevo 95 44 40N 20 57 E
Smethport 45 41 49N 78 27W
Smidovich 101 48 36N 133 49 E
Smiley, Canada 63 51 38N 109 29W
Smiley, U.S.A. 51 29 16N 97 38W
Smilyan 95 41 29N 24 46 E
Smith, Canada 62 55 10N 114 0W
Smith, U.S.A. 35 38 48N 119 20W
Smith →, Canada 62 59 34N 126 30W
Smith →, Mont. 33 47 25N 111 29W
Smith →, N.C. 40 36 27N 79 43W
Smith Arm 58 66 15N 123 0W
Smith B. 11 70 30N 154 20W
Smith Center 24 39 47N 98 47W
Smith County ◇, Kans. 24 39 45N 98 45W
Smith County ◇, Miss. 31 32 1N 89 23W
Smith County ◇, Tenn. 48 36 5N 86 0W
Smith County ◇, Tex. 51 32 21N 95 18W
Smith I., Md. 27 38 0N 76 0W
Smith I., N.C. 40 33 53N 77 59W
Smith I., Va. 54 37 9N 75 53W
Smith Mountain L. 54 37 2N 79 30W
Smith Pk. 20 48 51N 116 40W
Smith River 14 41 56N 124 9W
Smith Sund 4 78 30N 74 0W
Smithburg, N.J. 37 40 13N 74 21W
Smithburg, W. Va. 54 39 17N 80 44W
Smithers 62 54 45N 127 10W
Smithfield, N.C. 40 35 31N 78 21W
Smithfield, Nebr. 34 40 34N 99 45W
Smithfield, Utah 52 41 50N 111 50W
Smithfield, Va. 54 36 59N 76 38W
Smithland, Iowa 23 42 14N 95 56W
Smithland, Ky. 48 37 9N 88 24W
Smiths 10 32 32N 85 6W
Smiths Falls 60 44 55N 76 0W
Smiths Ferry 20 44 18N 116 5W
Smiths Grove 48 37 3N 86 12W
Smithsburg 27 39 39N 77 35W
Smithton 32 38 41N 93 5W
Smithtown 39 40 51N 73 12W
Smithville, Ga. 18 31 54N 84 15W
Smithville, Md. 27 38 46N 75 45W
Smithville, Miss. 31 34 4N 88 23W
Smithville, Mo. 32 39 23N 94 35W
Smithville, Okla. 43 34 28N 94 39W
Smithville, Tenn. 49 35 58N 85 49W
Smithville, Tex. 51 30 1N 97 10W
Smithville, W. Va. 54 39 4N 81 6W
Smoaks 46 33 5N 80 49W
Smoke Bend 25 30 7N 91 1W
Smoke Creek Desert 35 40 30N 119 40W
Smoky → 62 56 10N 117 21W
Smoky Dome 20 43 30N 114 56W
Smoky Falls 60 50 4N 82 10W
Smoky Hill → 24 39 4N 96 48W
Smoky Hills 24 39 15N 99 30W
Smoky Lake 62 54 10N 112 30W
Smøla 96 63 23N 8 3 E
Smolan 24 38 44N 97 41W
Smolensk 98 54 45N 32 0 E
Smolikas, Óros 95 40 9N 20 58 E
Smolyan 95 41 36N 24 38 E
Smoot 56 42 37N 110 55W
Smooth Rock Falls 60 49 17N 81 37W
Smoothstone L. 63 54 40N 106 50W
Smulţi 95 45 57N 27 44 E
Smyadovo 95 43 2N 27 1 E
Smyrna = İzmir 99 38 25N 27 8 E
Smyrna, Del. 27 39 18N 75 36W
Smyrna, Ga. 18 33 53N 84 31W
Smyrna, Tenn. 48 35 59N 86 31W
Smyrna Mills 26 46 8N 68 10W
Smyth County ◇ 54 36 55N 81 25W
Snaefell 82 54 18N 4 26W
Snaefellsjökull 96 64 45N 23 46W
Snake →, Nebr. 34 42 47N 100 47W
Snake →, Wash. 53 46 12N 119 2W
Snake →, Minn. 30 48 26N 97 8W
Snake →, Minn. 30 45 49N 92 46W
Snake L. 63 55 32N 106 35W
Snake Range 35 39 0N 114 20W
Snake River Plain 20 42 50N 114 0W
Snake Valley 52 39 30N 113 55W
Sneads Ferry 40 34 33N 77 24W

Sneedville South Webster

Sneedville 49 36 32N 83 13W
Sneek 87 53 2N 5 40 E
Snelling, Calif. 14 37 31N 120 26W
Snelling, S.C. 46 33 15N 81 27W
Snizort, L. 84 57 33N 6 28W
Snøhetta 96 62 19N 9 16 E
Snohomish 53 47 55N 122 6W
Snohomish County ◇ 53 48 0N 121 30W
Snoqualmie 53 47 31N 121 49W
Snoqualmie National Forest 53 47 35N 121 20W
Snoqualmie Pass 53 47 25N 121 25W
Snover 29 43 28N 82 58W
Snow Hill, Ala. 10 32 0N 87 0W
Snow Hill, Md. 27 38 11N 75 24W
Snow Hill, N.C. 40 35 27N 77 40W
Snow Lake 63 54 52N 100 3W
Snow Mt., Calif. 14 39 23N 122 45W
Snow Mt., Maine 26 45 18N 70 48W
Snow Shoe 45 41 2N 77 57W
Snow Water L. 35 40 48N 114 59W
Snowball 13 35 55N 92 49W
Snowbird L. 63 60 45N 103 0W
Snowdon 82 53 4N 4 8W
Snowdoun 10 32 15N 86 18W
Snowdrift 63 62 24N 110 44W
Snowdrift → 63 62 24N 110 44W
Snowflake 12 34 30N 110 5W
Snowmass 16 39 20N 106 59W
Snowmass Mt. 16 39 8N 107 5W
Snowshoe Pk. 33 48 13N 115 41W
Snowville 52 41 58N 112 43W
Snowy → 127 37 46 S 148 30 E
Snowy Mt. 39 43 42N 74 23W
Snowyside Pk. 20 43 57N 114 58W
Snug Corner 67 22 33N 73 52W
Snyder, Colo. 16 40 20N 103 36W
Snyder, Nebr. 34 41 43N 96 47W
Snyder, Okla. 43 34 40N 98 57W
Snyder, Tex. 50 32 44N 100 55W
Snyder County ◇ 45 40 50N 77 0W
Soacha 70 4 35N 74 13W
Soalala 123 16 6 S 45 20 E
Soap Lake 53 47 23N 119 29W
Sobat, Nahr → 121 9 22N 31 33 E
Sobral 74 3 50 S 40 20W
Soc Trang 112 9 37N 105 50 E
Sochi 99 43 35N 39 40 E
Social Circle 18 33 39N 83 43W
Société, Is. de la 125 17 0 S 151 0W
Society Hill, Ala. 10 32 26N 85 27W
Society Hill, S.C. 46 34 31N 79 51W
Society Is. = Société, Is. de la 125 17 0 S 151 0W
Socompa, Portezuelo de 76 24 27 S 68 18W
Socorro, Colombia 70 6 29N 73 16W
Socorro, U.S.A. 38 34 4N 106 54W
Socorro, I. 64 18 45N 110 58W
Socorro County ◇ 38 34 0N 107 0W
Socotra 105 12 30N 54 0 E
Soda L. 15 35 10N 116 4W
Soda Plains 108 35 30N 79 0 E
Soda Springs, Calif. 14 39 20N 120 23W
Soda Springs, Idaho 20 42 39N 111 36W
Soddy-Daisy 49 35 17N 85 10W
Söderhamn 97 61 18N 17 10 E
Söderköping 97 58 31N 16 20 E
Södermanlands län □ 97 59 10N 16 30 E
Södertälje 97 59 12N 17 39 E
Sodiri 121 14 27N 29 0 E
Sodo 121 7 0N 37 41 E
Sodus 39 43 14N 77 4W
Sodus Point 39 43 16N 76 59W
Soest 87 52 9N 5 19 E
Sofia = Sofiya 95 42 45N 23 20 E
Sofia → 123 15 27 S 47 23 E
Sofiiski 101 52 15N 133 59 E
Sofiya 95 42 45N 23 20 E
Sōfu-Gan 117 29 49N 140 21 E
Sogamoso 70 5 43N 72 56W
Sogn og Fjordane fylke □ 97 61 40N 6 0 E
Sogndalsfjøra 97 61 14N 7 5 E
Sognefjorden 97 61 10N 5 50 E
Sohâg 121 26 33N 31 43 E
Soignies 87 50 35N 4 5 E
Soissons 90 49 25N 3 19 E
Sōja 117 34 40N 133 45 E
Söke 106 37 48N 27 28 E
Sokodé 120 9 0N 1 11 E
Sokol 98 59 30N 40 5 E
Sokółka 89 53 25N 23 30 E
Sokolo 120 14 53N 6 8W
Sokoto 120 13 2N 5 16 E
Sol Iletsk 98 51 10N 55 0 E
Solano 111 16 31N 121 15 E
Solano County ◇ 14 38 20N 121 50W
Solapur 108 17 43N 75 56 E
Soldier, Iowa 23 41 59N 95 46W
Soldier, Kans. 24 39 32N 95 58W
Soldier Summit 52 39 56N 111 5W
Soldiers Grove 55 43 24N 90 47W
Soldotna 11 60 29N 151 3W
Soledad, Colombia 70 10 55N 74 46W
Soledad, U.S.A. 14 36 26N 121 20W
Soledad, Venezuela 71 8 10N 63 34W
Solen 41 46 23N 100 48W
Solent, The 83 50 45N 1 25W
Solfonn 97 60 2N 6 57 E
Soligalich 98 59 5N 42 10 E
Solikamsk 100 59 38N 56 50 E
Solimões → = Amazonas → 71 0 5 S 50 0W
Sollefteå 96 63 12N 17 20 E
Sóller 91 39 46N 2 43 E
Sologne 90 47 40N 2 0 E
Solok 110 0 45 S 100 40 E
Sololá 66 14 49N 91 10 E
Solomon, Ariz. 12 32 49N 109 38W
Solomon, Kans. 24 38 55N 97 22W
Solomon → 24 38 55N 97 22W
Solomon Is. ■ 124 6 0 S 155 0 E
Solomons 27 38 19N 76 27W
Solomon's Pools = Birak Sulaymān 104 31 42N 35 7 E
Solon, China 114 46 32N 121 10 E
Solon, Iowa 23 41 48N 91 30W
Solon, Maine 26 44 57N 69 52W
Solon Springs 55 46 22N 91 49W
Solonópole 74 5 44 S 39 1W
Solor 111 8 27 S 123 0 E
Solothurn 88 47 13N 7 32 E
Solṭānābād 107 36 29N 58 5 E
Solunska Glava 95 41 44N 21 31 E
Solvang 14 34 36N 120 8W
Solvay 39 43 3N 76 13W
Solvychegodsk 98 61 21N 46 56 E
Solway 33 47 35N 84 11W
Solway Firth 82 54 45N 3 38W
Solwezi 123 12 11 S 26 21 E
Sōma 116 37 40N 140 50 E
Somali Rep. ■ 105 7 0N 47 0 E
Sombor 95 45 46N 19 9 E
Sombrerete 64 23 40N 103 40W
Sombrero 67 18 37N 63 30W
Somers, Conn. 28 41 59N 72 27W
Somers, Iowa 23 42 23N 94 26W
Somers, Mont. 33 48 5N 114 13W
Somers Point 37 39 20N 74 36W
Somerset, Canada 63 49 25N 98 39W
Somerset, Colo. 16 38 56N 107 28W
Somerset, Ky. 49 37 5N 84 36W
Somerset, Mass. 28 41 47N 71 8W
Somerset, Ohio 42 39 48N 82 18W
Somerset, Pa. 45 40 1N 79 5W
Somerset, Tex. 51 29 14N 98 40W
Somerset □ 83 51 9N 3 0W
Somerset County ◇, Maine 26 45 30N 70 0W
Somerset County ◇, Md. 27 38 10N 75 50W
Somerset County ◇, N.J. 37 40 35N 74 35W
Somerset County ◇, Pa. 45 40 0N 79 0W
Somerset East 123 32 42 S 25 35 E
Somerset I. 58 73 30N 93 0W
Somerset Res. 36 43 0N 72 57W
Somersworth 36 43 16N 70 52W
Somerton 12 32 36N 114 43W
Somervell County ◇ 51 32 14N 97 45W
Somerville, Mass. 28 42 23N 71 6W
Somerville, N.J. 37 40 35N 74 38W
Somerville, Ohio 42 39 34N 84 38W
Somerville, Tenn. 48 35 15N 89 21W
Somerville, Tex. 51 30 21N 96 32W
Somerville L. 51 30 19N 96 31W
Someş → 89 47 15N 23 45 E
Somes Bar 14 41 23N 123 29W
Somme □ 90 50 0N 2 20 E
Somoto 66 13 28N 86 37W
Somovit 95 43 40N 24 45 E
Somport, Puerto de 91 42 48N 0 31W
Somuncurá, Meseta de 78 41 30 S 67 0W
Son La 112 21 20N 103 50 E
Soná 66 8 0N 81 20W
Sønderborg 97 54 55N 9 49 E
Sondheimer 25 32 33N 91 11W
Sonepur 109 20 55N 83 50 E
Song Cau 112 13 27N 109 18 E
Song Xian 115 34 12N 112 8 E
Songea 122 10 40 S 35 40 E
Songhua Hu 114 43 35N 126 50 E
Songhua Jiang → 114 47 45N 132 30 E
Songjiang 115 31 1N 121 12 E
Songkhla 112 7 13N 100 37 E
Songling 114 48 2N 121 9 E
Songpan 113 32 40N 103 30 E
Songtao 115 28 11N 109 10 E
Songzi 115 30 12N 111 45 E
Sonipat 108 29 0N 77 5 E
Sonmiani 108 25 25N 66 40 E
Sono →, Goiás, Brazil 74 9 58 S 48 11W
Sono →, Minas Gerais, Brazil 75 17 2 S 45 32W
Sonoma 14 38 18N 122 28W
Sonoma County ◇ 14 38 30N 123 0W
Sonoma Peak 35 40 52N 117 36W
Sonora, Calif. 14 37 59N 120 23W
Sonora, Ky. 49 37 32N 85 54W
Sonora, Tex. 50 30 34N 100 39W
Sonora □ 64 29 0N 111 0W
Sonora → 64 28 50N 111 33W
Sonora Desert 12 33 40N 114 15W
Sonoyta 64 31 51N 112 50W
Sonsomate 66 13 43N 89 44W
Sontag 31 31 39N 90 12W
Sopachuy 73 19 29 S 64 31W
Sopchoppy 17 30 4N 84 29W
Soper 43 34 2N 95 42W
Soperton 18 32 23N 82 35W
Sophia 40 35 50N 79 52W
Sopi 111 2 34N 128 28 E
Sopot 89 54 27N 18 31 E
Sop's Arm 61 49 46N 56 56W
Sør-Rondane 5 72 0 S 25 0 E
Sør-Trøndelag fylke □ 96 63 0N 10 0 E
Sorata 72 15 50 S 68 40W
Sorel 60 46 0N 73 10W
Sorento 21 39 1N 89 35W
Soreq, N. → 104 31 57N 34 43 E
Sorgono 94 40 0N 9 0 E
Soria 91 41 43N 2 32W
Soriano 76 33 24 S 58 19W
Sorkh, Kuh-e 107 35 40N 58 30 E
Sorocaba 77 23 31 S 47 27W
Sorochinsk 98 52 26N 53 10 E
Sorong 111 0 55 S 131 15 E
Soroti 122 1 43N 33 35 E
Sørøya 96 70 40N 22 30 E
Sørøysundet 96 70 25N 23 0 E
Sorrento, Italy 94 40 38N 14 23 E
Sorrento, U.S.A. 25 30 11N 90 51W
Sorsele 96 65 31N 17 30 E
Sorsogon 111 13 0N 124 0 E
Sortavala 98 61 42N 30 41 E
Soscumica, L. 60 50 15N 77 27W
Sosnogorsk 98 63 37N 53 51 E
Sosnovka 101 54 9N 109 35 E
Sosnowiec 89 50 20N 19 10 E
Soso 31 31 45N 89 17W
Sosva 98 59 10N 61 50 E
Soto la Marina → 65 23 40N 97 40W
Sotuta 65 20 29N 89 43W
Souanké 122 2 10N 14 3 E
Souderton 45 40 19N 75 19W
Soúdhas, Kólpos 95 35 25N 24 10 E
Souhegan → 36 42 51N 71 29W
Sŏul 114 37 31N 126 58 E
Sound, The 97 56 7N 12 30 E
Sour Lake 51 30 9N 94 25W
Sources, Mt. aux 123 28 45 S 28 50 E
Soure 74 0 35 S 48 30W
Souris, Man., Canada 63 49 40N 100 20W
Souris, P.E.I., Canada 61 46 21N 62 15W
Souris, U.S.A. 41 48 55N 100 40W
Souris →, Canada 63 49 40N 99 34W
Souris →, U.S.A. 41 49 0N 100 57W
Sousa 74 6 45 S 38 10W
Sousel 74 2 38 S 52 29W
Sousse 121 35 50N 10 38 E
South → 40 34 20N 78 3W
South Africa, Rep. of, ■ 123 32 0 S 17 0 E
South Amboy 37 40 29N 74 18W
South America 68 10 0 S 60 0W
South Anna → 54 37 48N 77 25W
South Ashburnam 28 42 37N 71 57W
South Aulatsivik I. 61 56 45N 61 30W
South Australia □ 126 32 0 S 139 0 E
South Baldy 38 33 59N 107 11W
South Bay 17 26 40N 80 43W
South Beloit 21 42 29N 89 2W
South Bend, Ind. 22 41 41N 86 15W
South Bend, Wash. 53 46 40N 123 48W
South Bloomfield 42 39 43N 82 59W
South Boardman 29 44 38N 85 17W
South Boston 54 36 42N 78 54W
South Branch 61 47 55N 59 2W
South Branch Potomac → 54 39 32N 78 35W
South Brook 61 49 26N 56 5W
South Burlington 36 44 28N 73 13W
South Carolina □ 46 34 0N 81 0W
South Carver 28 41 51N 70 54W
South Chaplin 28 41 46N 72 9W
South Charleston, Ohio 42 39 50N 83 38W
South Charleston, W. Va. 54 38 22N 81 44W
South Charlestown 36 43 12N 72 26W
South China 26 44 24N 69 34W
South China Sea 112 10 0N 113 0 E
South Coffeyville 43 36 59N 95 37W
South Congaree 46 33 53N 81 9W
South Dakota □ 47 44 15N 100 0W
South Dartmouth 28 41 36N 70 57W
South Daytona 17 29 10N 81 0W
South Deerfield, Mass. 28 42 29N 72 37W
South Deerfield, N.H. 36 43 6N 71 18W
South Downs 83 50 53N 0 10W
South East C. 127 43 40 S 146 50 E
South-East Fairbanks ◇ 11 64 0N 144 0W
South-East Indian Rise 124 43 0 S 80 0 E
South Easton 28 42 3N 71 5W
South Egremont 28 42 10N 73 25W
South Elgin 21 42 0N 88 18W
South English 23 41 27N 92 5W
South Esk → 84 56 44N 3 3W
South Fabius → 32 39 54N 91 30W
South Foreland 83 51 7N 1 23 E
South Fork, Colo. 16 37 40N 106 37W
South Fork, Pa. 45 40 22N 78 48W
South Fork American → 14 38 57N 120 59W
South Fork Edisto → 46 33 16N 80 54W
South Fork Grand → 47 45 43N 102 17W
South Fork Indian Reservation 35 40 45N 115 40W
South Fork John Day → 44 44 28N 119 31W
South Fork Moreau 47 45 9N 102 50W
South Fork Owyhee → 20 42 16N 116 53W
South Fork Powder → 56 43 40N 106 30W
South Fork Republican → 34 40 3N 101 31W
South Fork Salmon → 20 45 23N 115 31W
South Fork Sappa Cr. → 24 39 47N 100 35W
South Fork Selway → 20 46 10N 115 58W
South Fork Shenandoah → 54 38 57N 78 12W
South Fork Shoshone → 56 44 27N 109 14W
South Fork Solomon → 24 39 28N 98 26W
South Fork Spring → 13 36 19N 91 30W
South Fox I. 29 45 25N 85 51W
South Fulton 48 36 30N 88 52W
South Georgia 5 54 30 S 37 0W
South Glamorgan □ 83 51 30N 3 20W
South Grand → 32 38 17N 93 25W
South Greensburg 45 40 17N 79 33W
South Hadley 28 42 16N 72 35W
South Hadley Falls 28 42 14N 72 36W
South Hamilton 28 42 37N 70 53W
South Haven, Kans. 24 37 3N 97 24W
South Haven, Mich. 29 42 24N 86 16W
South Henik, L. 63 61 30N 97 30W
South Hero 36 44 39N 73 19W
South Hill 54 36 44N 78 8W
South Holston L. 49 36 31N 82 5W
South Honshu Ridge 124 23 0N 143 0 E
South Horr 122 2 12N 36 56 E
South Houston 51 29 40N 95 14W
South Hutchinson 24 38 2N 97 56W
South I., N.Z. 128 44 0 S 170 0 E
South I., U.S.A. 46 33 10N 79 14W
South Invercargill 128 46 26 S 168 23 E
South Jacksonville 21 39 44N 90 12W
South Jordan 52 40 34N 111 55W
South Junction 44 44 51N 121 5W
South Knife → 63 58 55N 94 37W
South Korea ■ 114 36 0N 128 0 E
South Lake Tahoe 14 38 57N 119 59W
South Lancaster 28 42 27N 71 41W
South Lebanon 42 39 22N 84 13W
South Loup → 34 41 4N 98 39W
South Lyon 29 42 28N 83 39W
South Magnetic Pole 5 65 36 S 139 24 E
South Manitou I. 29 45 2N 86 8W
South Marsh I. 27 38 6N 76 2W
South Merrimac 36 42 49N 71 34W
South Miami 17 25 42N 80 18W
South Middleboro 28 41 45N 70 50W
South Mills 40 36 27N 76 20W
South Milwaukee 55 42 55N 87 52W
South Molton 83 51 1N 3 50W
South Mountain 27 39 30N 77 40W
South Mt. 20 42 44N 116 54W
South Nahanni → 62 61 3N 123 21W
South Negril Pt. 66 18 14N 78 30W
South Newport 18 31 38N 81 24W
South Newtane 36 42 55N 72 42W
South Ogden 52 41 12N 112 0W
South Orkney Is. 5 63 0 S 45 0W
South Otselic 39 42 39N 75 47W
South Paris 26 44 14N 70 31W
South Passage 126 26 7 S 113 9 E
South Pekin 21 40 30N 89 39W
South Pittsburg 49 35 1N 85 42W
South Platte → 34 41 7N 100 42W
South Pole 5 90 0 S 0 0 E
South Pomfret 36 43 40N 72 33W
South Ponte Vedra Beach 17 30 3N 81 20W
South Porcupine 60 48 30N 81 12W
South Portland 26 43 38N 70 15W
South Range 29 47 4N 88 38W
South River, Canada 60 45 52N 79 23W
South River, U.S.A. 37 40 27N 74 23W
South Ronaldsay 84 58 46N 2 58W
South Royalton 36 43 49N 72 32W
South St. Paul 30 44 53N 93 2W
South San Francisco 14 37 39N 122 24W
South Sandwich Is. 2 57 0 S 27 0W
South Saskatchewan → 63 53 15N 105 5W
South Seal → 63 58 48N 98 8W
South Seaville 37 39 11N 74 46W
South Sentinel I. 112 11 1N 92 16 E
South Shetland Is. 5 62 0 S 59 0W
South Shields 82 54 59N 1 26W
South Shore, Ky. 49 38 43N 82 59W
South Shore, S. Dak. 47 45 7N 96 56W
South Sioux City 34 42 28N 96 24W
South Skunk → 23 41 15N 92 2W
South Stoddard 36 43 4N 72 7W
South Strafford 36 43 49N 72 23W
South Sulphur → 51 33 23N 95 18W
South Superior 56 41 46N 108 58W
South Taranaki Bight 128 39 40 S 174 5 E
South Thompson → 62 50 40N 120 20W
South Torrington 56 42 3N 104 11W
South Tucson 12 32 12N 110 58W
South Twin I. 60 53 7N 79 52W
South Tyne → 82 54 46N 2 25W
South Uist 84 57 20N 7 15W
South Umpqua → 44 43 16N 123 27W
South Venice 17 27 3N 82 25W
South Wayne 55 42 34N 89 53W
South Weare 36 43 5N 71 45W
South Webster 42 38 49N 82 44W

South Wellfleet **Statham**

South Wellfleet **28** 41 55N 69 58W
South West Africa =
Namibia ■ **123** 22 0S 18 9E
South West City **32** 36 31N 94 37W
South Whitley **22** 41 5N 85 38W
South Williamson **49** 37 40N 82 17W
South Williamsport **45** 41 13N 77 0W
South Windsor **28** 41 49N 72 37W
South Woodstock **36** 43 35N 72 32W
South Yarmouth **28** 41 40N 70 10W
South Yemen ■ **105** 15 0N 48 0E
South Yorkshire □ **82** 53 30N 1 20W
South Zanesville **42** 39 54N 82 2W
Southampton, Canada **60** 44 30N 81 25W
Southampton, U.K. **83** 50 54N 1 23W
Southampton, Mass. **28** 42 14N 72 44W
Southampton, N.Y. **39** 40 53N 72 23W
Southampton County ◇ **54** 36 43N 77 4W
Southampton I. **59** 64 30N 84 0W
Southard **43** 36 4N 98 29W
Southbeach **44** 44 37N 124 3W
Southbridge, N.Z. **128** 43 48S 172 16E
Southbridge, U.S.A. **28** 42 5N 72 2W
Southbury **28** 41 29N 73 13W
Southeast C. **11** 62 56N 169 39W
Southeast Pacific Basin **125** 16 30S 92 0W
Southend **63** 56 19N 103 22W
Southend-on-Sea **83** 51 32N 0 42E
Southern Alps **128** 43 41S 170 11E
Southern Cross **126** 31 12S 119 15E
Southern Indian L. **63** 57 10N 98 30W
Southern Ocean **5** 62 0S 60 0E
Southern Pines **40** 35 11N 79 24W
Southern Uplands **84** 55 30N 3 3W
Southern Ute Indian
Reservation **16** 37 10N 107 30W
Southfield **29** 42 29N 83 17W
Southington **28** 41 36N 72 53W
Southland **50** 33 22N 101 33W
Southport, Australia **127** 27 58S 153 25E
Southport, U.K. **82** 53 38N 3 1W
Southport, N.C. **40** 33 55N 78 1W
Southport, N.Y. **39** 42 3N 76 49W
Southwest Harbor **26** 44 17N 68 20W
Southwest Pt. **57** 17 40N 64 55W
Southwestern Pacific Basin **124** 42 0S 170 0W
Southwick **28** 42 3N 72 46W
Southwold **83** 52 19N 1 41E
Southwood Acres **28** 41 59N 72 32W
Soutpansberge **123** 23 0S 29 30E
Sovata **95** 46 35N 25 3E
Sovetsk, Lithuania, U.S.S.R. **98** 55 6N 21 50E
Sovetsk, R.S.F.S.R.,
U.S.S.R. **98** 57 38N 48 53E
Sovetskaya Gavan **101** 48 50N 140 0E
Sōya-Kaikyō = Perouse Str.,
La **116** 45 40N 142 0E
Sōya-Misaki **116** 45 30N 142 0E
Soyo **122** 6 13S 12 20E
Soyopa **64** 28 41N 109 37W
Sozh → **98** 51 57N 30 48E
Sozopol **95** 42 23N 27 42E
Spa **87** 50 29N 5 53E
Spain ■ **91** 40 0N 5 0W
Spalding, U.K. **82** 52 47N 0 9W
Spalding, Idaho **20** 46 27N 116 49W
Spalding, Nebr. **34** 41 42N 98 22W
Spalding County ◇ **18** 33 15N 84 15W
Spanaway **53** 47 6N 122 26W
Spandau **88** 52 35N 13 7E
Spangle **53** 47 26N 117 23W
Spaniard's Bay **61** 47 38N 53 20W
Spanish **60** 46 12N 82 20W
Spanish Fork **52** 40 7N 111 39W
Spanish Fort **10** 30 40N 87 53W
Spanish Town **66** 18 0N 76 57W
Sparkman **13** 33 55N 92 51W
Sparks, Ga. **18** 31 11N 83 26W
Sparks, Nebr. **34** 42 56N 100 15W
Sparks, Nev. **35** 39 32N 119 45W
Sparks, Okla. **43** 35 37N 96 50W
Sparland **21** 41 2N 89 26W
Sparlingville **29** 42 58N 82 32W
Sparr **17** 29 20N 82 7W
Sparta = Spárti **95** 37 5N 22 25E
Sparta, Ga. **18** 33 17N 82 58W
Sparta, Ill. **21** 38 8N 89 42W
Sparta, Ky. **49** 38 41N 84 54W
Sparta, Mich. **29** 43 10N 85 42W
Sparta, Mo. **32** 37 0N 93 5W
Sparta, N.C. **40** 36 30N 81 7W
Sparta, Tenn. **49** 35 56N 85 28W
Sparta, Wis. **55** 43 56N 90 49W
Spartanburg **46** 34 56N 81 57W
Spartanburg County ◇ **46** 34 50N 82 0W
Spartansburg **45** 41 49N 79 41W
Spárti **95** 37 5N 22 25E
Spartivento, C., Calabria,
Italy **94** 37 56N 16 4E
Spartivento, C., Sard., Italy **94** 38 52N 8 50E
Spassk-Dalniy **101** 44 40N 132 48E
Spátha, Akra **95** 35 42N 23 43E
Spatsizi → **62** 57 42N 128 7W
Spavinaw **43** 36 23N 95 3W
Speaks **51** 29 15N 96 42W
Spearfish **47** 44 30N 103 52W
Spearman **50** 36 12N 101 12W
Spearsville **25** 32 56N 92 36W
Spearville **24** 37 51N 99 45W
Speed **24** 39 41N 99 25W
Speedway **22** 39 47N 86 15W
Speers **63** 52 43N 107 34W
Speightstown **67** 13 15N 59 39W
Spenard **11** 61 11N 149 55W
Spence Bay **58** 69 32N 93 32W
Spencer, Idaho **20** 44 22N 112 11W
Spencer, Ind. **22** 39 17N 86 46W
Spencer, Iowa **23** 43 9N 95 9W
Spencer, Mass. **28** 42 15N 71 59W
Spencer, N.C. **40** 35 41N 80 26W
Spencer, N.Y. **39** 42 13N 76 30W
Spencer, Nebr. **34** 42 53N 98 42W
Spencer, Ohio **42** 41 6N 82 8W
Spencer, S. Dak. **47** 43 44N 97 36W
Spencer, Tenn. **49** 35 45N 85 28W
Spencer, W. Va. **54** 38 48N 81 21W
Spencer, Wis. **55** 44 46N 90 18W
Spencer, C. **127** 35 20S 136 53E
Spencer County ◇, Ind. **22** 38 0N 87 0W
Spencer County ◇, Ky. **49** 38 0N 85 20W
Spencer G. **127** 34 0S 137 20E
Spencerville, Ohio **42** 40 43N 84 21W
Spencerville, Okla. **43** 34 8N 95 21W
Spences Bridge **62** 50 25N 121 20W
Spenser Mts. **128** 42 15S 172 45E
Sperrin Mts. **85** 54 50N 7 0W
Sperry **43** 36 18N 95 59W
Sperryville **54** 38 39N 78 14W
Spessart **88** 50 10N 9 20E
Spey → **84** 57 26N 3 25W
Speyer **88** 49 19N 8 26E
Spézia, La **94** 44 8N 9 50E
Spiceland **22** 39 50N 85 26W
Spickard **32** 40 14N 93 36W
Spinazzola **94** 40 58N 16 5E
Spindale **40** 35 22N 81 56W
Spineni **95** 44 43N 24 37E
Spink **47** 42 51N 96 45W
Spink County ◇ **47** 45 0N 98 18W
Spirit L. **23** 43 29N 95 6W
Spirit Lake, Idaho **20** 47 58N 116 52W
Spirit Lake, Iowa **23** 43 26N 95 6W
Spirit River **62** 55 45N 118 50W
Spiritwood, Canada **63** 53 24N 107 33W
Spiritwood, U.S.A. **41** 46 56N 98 30W
Spiro **43** 35 15N 94 37W
Spithead **83** 50 43N 1 5W
Spitzbergen = Svalbard **4** 78 0N 17 0E
Splendora **51** 30 14N 95 10W
Split **94** 43 31N 16 26E
Split L. **63** 56 8N 96 15W
Splügenpass **88** 46 30N 9 20E
Spofford **50** 29 10N 100 25W
Spokane **53** 47 40N 117 24W
Spokane → **53** 47 54N 118 20W
Spokane County ◇ **53** 47 35N 117 25W
Spokane Indian Reservation **53** 47 57N 118 0W
Spoleto **94** 42 46N 12 47E
Spoon → **21** 40 19N 90 4W
Spooner **55** 45 50N 91 53W
Sporyy Navolok, Mys **100** 75 50N 68 40E
Spotswood **37** 40 23N 74 23W
Spotsylvania **54** 38 12N 77 36W
Spotsylvania County ◇ **54** 38 12N 77 36W
Spotted Horse **56** 44 43N 105 50W
Spragge **60** 46 15N 82 40W
Sprague, Nebr. **34** 40 38N 96 45W
Sprague, Wash. **53** 47 18N 117 59W
Sprague → **44** 42 34N 121 51W
Sprague River **44** 42 27N 121 30W
Spratly, I. **110** 8 20N 112 0E
Spray **44** 44 50N 119 48W
Spree → **88** 52 32N 13 13E
Spremberg **88** 51 33N 14 21E
Spring **51** 30 5N 95 25W
Spring →, Mo. **32** 37 5N 94 45W
Spring →, S. Dak. **47** 45 45N 100 18W
Spring Butte **56** 41 51N 108 53W
Spring City, Tenn. **49** 35 42N 84 52W
Spring City, Utah **52** 39 29N 111 30W
Spring Cr. →, Ga. **18** 30 54N 84 45W
Spring Cr. →, N. Dak. **41** 47 15N 101 48W
Spring Cr. →, Nebr. **34** 40 20N 101 6W
Spring Cr. →, Nev. **35** 39 55N 117 50W
Spring Glen **52** 39 40N 110 51W
Spring Green **55** 43 11N 90 4W
Spring Grove **30** 43 34N 91 38W
Spring Hill, Ala. **10** 31 42N 85 58W
Spring Hill, Ark. **13** 33 35N 93 39W
Spring Hill, Iowa **23** 41 25N 93 39W
Spring Hill, Minn. **30** 45 32N 94 50W
Spring Hill, Tenn. **48** 35 45N 86 56W
Spring Hope **40** 35 57N 78 6W
Spring Lake, N.C. **40** 35 10N 78 58W
Spring Lake, N.J. **37** 40 9N 74 2W
Spring Mts. **35** 36 0N 115 45W
Spring Valley, Calif. **15** 32 45N 117 0W
Spring Valley, Ill. **21** 41 20N 89 12W
Spring Valley, Minn. **30** 43 41N 92 23W
Spring Valley, Nev. **35** 39 10N 114 25W
Spring Valley, Wis. **55** 44 51N 92 14W
Springbok **123** 29 42S 17 54E
Springbrook **23** 42 10N 90 29W
Springdale, Canada **61** 49 30N 56 6W
Springdale, Ark. **13** 36 11N 94 8W
Springdale, Ohio **42** 39 17N 84 29W
Springdale, Utah **52** 37 10N 113 0W
Springdale, Wash. **53** 48 4N 117 45W
Springer, N. Mex. **38** 36 22N 104 36W
Springer, Okla. **43** 34 19N 97 8W
Springerton **21** 38 11N 88 21W
Springerville **12** 34 8N 109 17W
Springfield, N.Z. **128** 43 19S 171 56E
Springfield, Colo. **16** 37 24N 102 37W
Springfield, Fla. **17** 30 10N 85 37W
Springfield, Ga. **18** 32 22N 81 18W
Springfield, Idaho **20** 43 5N 112 41W
Springfield, Ill. **21** 39 48N 89 39W
Springfield, Ky. **49** 37 41N 85 13W
Springfield, La. **25** 30 26N 90 33W
Springfield, Maine **26** 45 24N 68 8W
Springfield, Mass. **28** 42 6N 72 35W
Springfield, Minn. **30** 44 14N 94 59W
Springfield, Mo. **32** 37 13N 93 17W
Springfield, Nebr. **34** 41 5N 96 8W
Springfield, Ohio **42** 39 55N 83 49W
Springfield, Oreg. **44** 44 3N 123 1W
Springfield, S.C. **46** 33 30N 81 17W
Springfield, S. Dak. **47** 42 49N 97 54W
Springfield, Tenn. **48** 36 31N 86 53W
Springfield, Va. **54** 38 47N 77 11W
Springfield, Vt. **36** 43 18N 72 29W
Springfield, L. **21** 39 46N 89 36W
Springfield Plateau **32** 37 30N 92 45W
Springfontein **123** 30 15S 25 40E
Springhill, Canada **61** 45 40N 64 4W
Springhill, U.S.A. **25** 33 0N 93 28W
Springhouse **62** 51 56N 122 7W
Springlake **50** 34 14N 102 18W
Springport **29** 42 22N 84 42W
Springs **123** 26 13S 28 25E
Springsure **127** 24 8S 148 6E
Springtown **51** 32 58N 97 41W
Springvale, Ga. **18** 31 50N 84 53W
Springvale, Maine **26** 43 28N 70 48W
Springview **34** 42 50N 99 45W
Springville, Ala. **10** 33 46N 86 29W
Springville, Calif. **15** 36 8N 118 49W
Springville, Iowa **23** 42 3N 91 27W
Springville, N.Y. **39** 42 31N 78 40W
Springville, Utah **52** 40 10N 111 37W
Springwater **63** 51 58N 108 23W
Spruce Knob **54** 38 42N 79 32W
Spruce Knob-Seneca Rocks
Nat. Rec. Area **54** 38 50N 79 30W
Spruce Pine **40** 35 55N 82 4W
Spur **50** 33 28N 100 52W
Spurn Hd. **82** 53 34N 0 8E
Spuzzum **62** 49 37N 121 23W
Squa Pan L. **26** 46 31N 68 13W
Squam L. **36** 43 45N 71 32W
Squamish **62** 49 45N 123 10W
Square Islands **61** 52 47N 55 47W
Square L. **26** 47 3N 68 20W
Squaw Lake **30** 47 38N 94 8W
Squibnocket Point **28** 41 18N 70 47W
Squillace **94** 38 50N 16 26E
Squire **54** 37 14N 81 37W
Squires **32** 36 51N 92 37W
Sragen **111** 7 28S 110 59E
Srbija □ **95** 43 30N 21 0E
Sre Umbell **112** 11 8N 103 46E
Sredinnyy Khrebet **101** 57 0N 160 0E
Sredna Gora **95** 42 40N 24 20E
Sredne Tambovskoye **101** 50 55N 137 45E
Srednekolymsk **101** 67 27N 153 40E
Srednevilyuysk **101** 63 50N 123 5E
Sredni Rodopi **95** 41 40N 24 45E
Sremska Mitrovica **95** 44 59N 19 35E
Sretensk **101** 52 10N 117 40E
Sri Lanka ■ **108** 7 30N 80 50E
Srikakulam **109** 18 14N 83 58E
Srinagar **108** 34 5N 74 50E
Srnetica **94** 44 25N 16 35E
Staatsburg **39** 41 51N 73 56W
Stacy **30** 45 24N 92 59W
Stacyville **23** 43 26N 92 47W
Staðarhólskirkja **96** 65 23N 21 58W
Stadlandet **96** 62 10N 5 10E
Stadskanaal **87** 53 4N 6 55E
Stafafell **96** 64 25N 14 52W
Staffa **84** 56 26N 6 21W
Stafford, U.K. **82** 52 49N 2 9W
Stafford, Kans. **24** 37 58N 98 36W
Stafford, Tex. **51** 29 37N 95 34W
Stafford, Va. **54** 38 25N 77 25W
Stafford □ **82** 52 53N 2 10W
Stafford, L. **17** 29 20N 82 29W
Stafford County ◇, Kans. **24** 38 0N 98 45W
Stafford County ◇, Va. **54** 38 25N 77 25W
Stafford Springs **28** 41 57N 72 18W
Staines **83** 51 26N 0 30W
Stakhanov **99** 48 35N 38 40E
Stalingrad = Volgograd **99** 48 40N 44 25E
Staliniri = Tskhinvali **99** 42 14N 44 1E
Stalino = Donetsk **99** 48 0N 37 45E
Stalinogorsk =
Novomoskovsk **98** 54 5N 38 15E
Stalybridge **82** 53 29N 2 4W
Stambaugh **29** 46 5N 88 38W
Stamford, U.K. **83** 52 39N 0 29W
Stamford, Conn. **28** 41 3N 73 32W
Stamford, N.Y. **39** 42 25N 74 38W
Stamford, Nebr. **34** 40 8N 99 36W
Stamford, Tex. **51** 32 57N 99 48W
Stamford, Vt. **36** 42 45N 73 4W
Stamford, L. **51** 33 4N 99 34W
Stamping Ground **49** 38 16N 84 41W
Stamps **13** 33 22N 93 30W
Stanardsville **54** 38 18N 78 26W
Stanberry **32** 40 13N 94 35W
Stančevo = Kalipetrovo **95** 44 5N 27 14E
Standerton **123** 26 55S 29 7E
Standing Rock **38** 35 48N 108 22W
Standing Rock Indian
Reservation **47** 45 45N 101 10W
Standish, Calif. **14** 40 22N 120 25W
Standish, Mich. **29** 43 59N 83 57W
Standrod **52** 41 59N 113 25W
Stanfield, Ariz. **12** 32 53N 111 58W
Stanfield, Oreg. **44** 45 47N 119 13W
Stanford, Ky. **49** 37 32N 84 40W
Stanford, Mont. **33** 47 9N 110 13W
Stanhope **23** 42 17N 93 48W
Stanislaus → **14** 37 40N 121 14W
Stanislaus County ◇ **14** 37 30N 121 0W
Stanislaus National Forest **14** 38 10N 120 0W
Stanislav = Ivano-Frankovsk **99** 48 40N 24 40E
Stanke Dimitrov **95** 42 17N 23 9E
Stanley, N.B., Canada **61** 46 20N 66 44W
Stanley, Sask., Canada **63** 55 24N 104 22W
Stanley, Falk. Is. **78** 51 40S 59 51W
Stanley, Idaho **20** 44 13N 114 56W
Stanley, Kans. **24** 38 51N 94 40W
Stanley, Ky. **48** 37 50N 87 15W
Stanley, La. **25** 31 58N 93 54W
Stanley, N.C. **40** 35 21N 81 6W
Stanley, N. Dak. **41** 48 19N 102 23W
Stanley, N. Mex. **38** 35 9N 105 59W
Stanley, Va. **54** 38 35N 78 30W
Stanley, Wis. **55** 44 58N 90 56W
Stanley County ◇ **47** 44 30N 101 0W
Stanleyville **40** 36 12N 80 17W
Stanly County ◇ **40** 35 20N 80 10W
Stanovoy Khrebet **101** 55 0N 130 0E
Stanthorpe **127** 28 36S 151 59E
Stanton, Iowa **23** 40 59N 95 6W
Stanton, Ky. **49** 37 54N 83 52W
Stanton, Mich. **29** 43 18N 85 5W
Stanton, Mo. **32** 38 17N 91 6W
Stanton, N. Dak. **41** 47 19N 101 23W
Stanton, Nebr. **34** 41 57N 97 14W
Stanton, Tenn. **48** 35 28N 89 24W
Stanton, Tex. **50** 32 8N 101 48W
Stanton County ◇, Kans. **24** 37 30N 101 45W
Stanton County ◇, Nebr. **34** 41 50N 97 10W
Stanwood **53** 48 15N 122 23W
Staplehurst **34** 40 58N 97 10W
Staples **30** 46 21N 94 48W
Stapleton **34** 41 29N 100 31W
Star **40** 35 24N 79 47W
Star City, Canada **63** 52 50N 104 20W
Star City, Ark. **13** 33 56N 91 51W
Star City, Ind. **22** 40 58N 86 33W
Star Lake **39** 44 10N 75 2W
Stara Planina **95** 43 15N 23 0E
Stara Zagora **95** 42 26N 25 39E
Staraya Russa **98** 57 58N 31 23E
Starbuck, Minn. **30** 45 37N 95 32W
Starbuck, Wash. **53** 46 31N 118 7W
Starbuck I. **125** 5 37S 155 55W
Stargard **88** 53 29N 13 19E
Staritsa **98** 56 33N 35 0E
Stark **24** 37 42N 95 9W
Stark County ◇, Ill. **21** 41 5N 89 45W
Stark County ◇, N. Dak. **41** 46 55N 102 30W
Stark County ◇, Ohio **42** 40 48N 81 22W
Starke **17** 29 57N 82 7W
Starke County ◇ **22** 41 15N 86 40W
Starks **25** 30 19N 93 40W
Starkville, Colo. **16** 37 8N 104 30W
Starkville, Miss. **31** 33 28N 88 49W
Starkweather **41** 48 27N 98 53W
Starogard **89** 53 59N 18 30E
Starr **46** 34 23N 82 41W
Starr County ◇ **50** 26 30N 98 50W
Starrucca **45** 41 54N 75 28W
Stars Mill **18** 33 19N 84 31W
Start Pt. **83** 50 13N 3 38W
Starvation Reservoir **52** 40 15N 110 30W
Stary Sącz **91** 49 33N 20 35E
Staryy Kheydzhan **101** 60 0N 144 50E
State Center **23** 42 1N 93 10W
State College, Miss. **31** 33 27N 88 47W
State College, Pa. **45** 40 48N 77 52W
State Line **31** 31 26N 88 28W
State Road **40** 36 19N 80 52W
Staten, I. = Estados, I. de
Los **78** 54 40S 64 30W
Staten I. **39** 40 35N 74 9W
Statenville **18** 30 42N 83 2W
Statesboro **18** 32 27N 81 47W
Statesville **40** 35 47N 80 53W
Statham **18** 33 58N 83 35W

Staunton Sublette County

Staunton, Ill. 21 39 1N 89 47W
Staunton, Va. 54 38 9N 79 4W
Stavanger 97 58 57N 5 40 E
Staveley 128 43 40 S 171 32 E
Stavelot 87 50 23N 5 55 E
Staveren 87 52 53N 5 22 E
Stavern 97 59 0N 10 1 E
Stavropol 99 45 5N 42 0 E
Stawell 127 37 5 S 142 47 E
Stayton 44 44 48N 122 48W
Staytonville 27 38 50N 75 32W
Stead 38 36 6N 103 12W
Steamboat Canyon 12 35 45N 109 51W
Steamboat Rock 23 42 25N 93 4W
Steamboat Springs 16 40 29N 106 50W
Stearns County ◇ 30 45 35N 94 30W
Stebbins 11 63 31N 162 17W
Stedman 40 35 0N 78 41W
Steel, Mt. 56 41 50N 107 0W
Steele, Ala. 10 33 56N 86 12W
Steele, Mo. 32 36 5N 89 50W
Steele, N. Dak. 41 46 51N 99 55W
Steele City 34 40 2N 97 2W
Steele County ◇, Minn. 30 44 0N 93 10W
Steele County ◇, N. Dak. 41 47 31N 97 50W
Steeleville 21 38 0N 89 40W
Steelton 45 40 14N 76 50W
Steelville 32 37 58N 91 22W
Steen 30 43 31N 96 16W
Steen River 62 59 40N 117 12W
Steenkool = Bintuni 111 2 7 S 133 32 E
Steens Mt. 44 42 35N 118 40W
Steenwijk 87 52 47N 6 7 E
Steep Pt. 126 26 8 S 113 8 E
Steep Rock 63 51 30N 98 48W
Stefanie L. = Chew Bahir 121 4 40N 36 50 E
Stefansson Bay 5 67 20 S 59 8 E
Stehekin 53 48 19N 120 39W
Steiermark □ 88 47 26N 15 0 E
Steinauer 34 40 12N 96 14W
Steinbach 63 49 32N 96 40W
Steinfort 87 49 39N 5 55 E
Steinhatchee 17 29 40N 83 23W
Steinkjer 96 63 59N 11 31 E
Steinkopf 123 29 15 S 17 48 E
Stella, Ky. 48 36 38N 88 24W
Stella, Mo. 32 36 46N 94 12W
Stella, Nebr. 34 40 14N 95 46W
Stella, Tenn. 48 35 2N 87 5W
Stellarton 61 45 32N 62 30W
Stellenbosch 123 33 58 S 18 50 E
Stelvio, Paso dello 94 46 32N 10 27 E
Stem 40 36 12N 78 43W
Stendal 88 52 36N 11 50 E
Stensele 96 65 3N 17 8 E
Stepanakert 99 39 40N 46 25 E
Stephen 30 48 27N 96 53W
Stephens 13 33 25N 93 4W
Stephens City 54 39 5N 78 13W
Stephens County ◇, Ga. 18 34 35N 83 15W
Stephens County ◇, Okla. 43 34 30N 97 50W
Stephens County ◇, Tex. 51 32 45N 98 54W
Stephens I. 62 54 10N 130 45W
Stephens Knob 49 36 37N 84 20W
Stephenson 29 45 25N 87 36W
Stephenson County ◇ 21 42 20N 89 40W
Stephenville, Canada 61 48 31N 58 35W
Stephenville, U.S.A. 51 32 13N 98 12W
Stepnoi = Elista 99 46 16N 44 14 E
Stepnyak 100 52 50N 70 50 E
Steppe 102 50 0N 50 0 E
Steptoe 53 47 0N 117 21W
Steptoe Valley 35 39 50N 114 45W
Sterling, Alaska 11 60 32N 150 46W
Sterling, Colo. 16 40 37N 103 13W
Sterling, Ga. 18 31 16N 81 34W
Sterling, Idaho 20 43 2N 112 44W
Sterling, Ill. 21 41 48N 89 42W
Sterling, Kans. 24 38 13N 98 12W
Sterling, Mass. 28 42 26N 71 46W
Sterling, Mich. 29 44 2N 84 2W
Sterling, N. Dak. 41 46 49N 100 17W
Sterling, Nebr. 34 40 28N 96 23W
Sterling, Okla. 43 34 45N 98 10W
Sterling, Utah 52 39 12N 111 42W
Sterling, Va. 54 39 1N 77 26W
Sterling City 50 31 51N 101 0W
Sterling County ◇ 50 32 0N 101 0W
Sterling Reservoir 16 40 47N 103 16W
Sterlington 25 32 42N 92 5W
Sterlitamak 98 53 40N 56 0 E
Stetsonville 55 45 4N 90 19W
Stettin = Szczecin 88 53 27N 14 27 E
Stettler 62 52 19N 112 40W
Steuben County ◇, Ind. 22 41 40N 85 0W
Steuben County ◇, N.Y. 39 42 15N 77 20W
Steubens 55 43 11N 90 52W
Steubenville, Ky. 49 36 53N 84 48W
Steubenville, Ohio 42 40 22N 80 37W
Stevens County ◇, Kans. 24 37 15N 101 20W
Stevens County ◇, Minn. 30 45 40N 96 0W
Stevens County ◇, Wash. 53 48 30N 118 0W
Stevens Point 55 44 31N 89 34W
Stevens Pottery 18 32 57N 83 17W
Stevens Village 11 66 1N 149 6W
Stevenson, Ala. 10 34 52N 85 50W
Stevenson, Wash. 53 45 42N 121 53W
Stevenson L. 63 53 55N 96 0W
Stevensville, Md. 27 38 59N 76 19W
Stevensville, Mont. 33 46 30N 114 5W
Steward 21 41 51N 89 1W
Stewardson 21 39 16N 88 38W
Stewart, B.C., Canada 62 55 56N 129 57W
Stewart, N.W.T., Canada 58 63 19N 139 26W
Stewart, Ga. 18 33 25N 83 52W
Stewart, Minn. 30 44 43N 94 29W
Stewart, Miss. 31 33 27N 89 26W
Stewart, I. 78 54 50 S 71 15W
Stewart County ◇, Ga. 18 32 5N 84 50W
Stewart County ◇, Tenn. 48 36 20N 87 55W
Stewart I. 128 46 58 S 167 54 E
Stewarts Point 14 38 39N 123 24W
Stewartstown, N.H. 36 45 0N 71 31W
Stewartstown, Pa. 45 39 45N 76 36W
Stewartsville 32 39 45N 94 30W
Stewartville 30 43 51N 92 29W
Stewiacke 61 45 9N 63 22W
Steyr 88 48 3N 14 25 E
Stickney 47 43 35N 98 26W
Stidham 43 35 22N 95 42W
Stigler 43 35 15N 95 8W
Stikine → 62 56 40N 132 30W
Stiles 50 31 25N 101 34W
Stilesville 22 39 38N 86 38W
Still Pond 27 39 20N 76 3W
Stillhouse Hollow L. 51 31 2N 97 32W
Stillmore 18 32 27N 82 13W
Stillwater, N.Z. 128 42 27 S 171 20 E
Stillwater, Minn. 30 45 3N 92 49W
Stillwater, Nev. 35 39 31N 118 33W
Stillwater, Okla. 43 36 7N 97 4W
Stillwater County ◇ 33 45 48N 109 15W
Stillwater Range 35 39 50N 118 5W
Stillwater Reservoir 39 43 54N 75 3W
Stillwell 18 32 23N 81 15W
Stilwell, Kans. 24 38 46N 94 39W
Stilwell, Okla. 43 35 49N 94 38W
Stinnett 50 35 50N 101 27W
Stinson Lake 36 43 51N 71 48W
Stip 95 41 42N 22 10 E
Stirling, Canada 62 49 30N 112 30W
Stirling, U.K. 84 56 7N 3 57W
Stirling City 14 39 54N 121 32W
Stirling Ra. 126 34 23 S 118 0 E
Stirrat 54 37 44N 82 0W
Stites 20 46 6N 115 59W
Stock Island 17 24 32N 81 34W
Stockbridge, Ga. 18 33 33N 84 14W
Stockbridge, Mass. 28 42 17N 73 19W
Stockbridge, Mich. 29 42 27N 84 11W
Stockbridge Indian Reservation 55 44 50N 88 50W
Stockdale 51 29 14N 97 58W
Stockerau 88 48 24N 16 12 E
Stockett 33 47 21N 111 10W
Stockham 34 40 43N 97 56W
Stockholm, Sweden 97 59 20N 18 3 E
Stockholm, Maine 26 47 3N 68 8W
Stockholm, S. Dak. 47 45 6N 96 48W
Stockholm, Wis. 55 44 29N 92 16W
Stockland 21 40 37N 87 36W
Stockly 27 38 40N 75 20W
Stockport, U.K. 82 53 25N 2 11W
Stockport, Iowa 23 40 51N 91 50W
Stockport, Ohio 42 39 33N 81 48W
Stockton, Ala. 10 31 0N 87 52W
Stockton, Calif. 14 37 58N 121 17W
Stockton, Ill. 21 42 21N 90 1W
Stockton, Kans. 24 39 26N 99 16W
Stockton, Md. 27 38 3N 75 25W
Stockton, Minn. 30 44 2N 91 46W
Stockton, Mo. 32 37 42N 93 48W
Stockton, N.J. 37 40 24N 74 58W
Stockton, Utah 52 40 27N 112 22W
Stockton I. 55 46 57N 90 35W
Stockton L. 32 37 42N 93 46W
Stockton-on-Tees 82 54 34N 1 20W
Stockton Plateau 50 30 30N 102 30W
Stockville 34 40 32N 100 23W
Stoddard 55 43 40N 91 13W
Stoddard County ◇ 32 36 50N 90 0W
Stoke-on-Trent 82 53 1N 2 11W
Stokes Bay 60 45 0N 81 28W
Stokes County ◇ 40 36 20N 80 10W
Stokkseyri 96 63 50N 21 2W
Stokksnes 96 64 14N 14 58W
Stolac 95 43 8N 17 59 E
Stolbovaya 101 64 50N 153 50 E
Stolbovoy, Ostrov 101 56 44N 163 14 E
Stolnici 95 44 31N 24 48 E
Stone 20 42 1N 112 42W
Stone County ◇, Ark. 13 35 52N 92 7W
Stone County ◇, Miss. 31 30 47N 89 8W
Stone County ◇, Mo. 32 36 45N 93 25W
Stone Harbor 37 39 3N 74 45W
Stone Mountain 18 33 49N 84 10W
Stone Mt. 36 44 34N 71 40W
Stoneboro 45 41 20N 80 7W
Stonega 54 36 57N 82 48W
Stoneham 16 40 36N 103 40W
Stonehaven 84 56 58N 2 11W
Stoner 16 37 35N 108 19W
Stoneville 40 36 28N 79 54W
Stonewall, Canada 63 50 10N 97 19W
Stonewall, Ark. 13 36 14N 90 32W
Stonewall, Colo. 16 37 9N 105 1W
Stonewall, La. 25 32 17N 93 50W
Stonewall, Miss. 31 32 8N 88 47W
Stonewall, Okla. 43 34 39N 96 32W
Stonewall County ◇ 50 33 8N 100 14W
Stonington, Colo. 16 37 18N 102 11W
Stonington, Ill. 21 39 44N 89 12W
Stonington, Maine 26 44 9N 68 40W
Stony Creek 54 36 57N 77 24W
Stony Gorge Reservoir 14 39 35N 122 32W
Stony I. 39 43 54N 76 20W
Stony L. 63 58 51N 98 40W
Stony Point, Mich. 29 41 57N 83 16W
Stony Point, N.C. 40 35 52N 81 3W
Stony Pt. 39 43 50N 76 18W
Stony Rapids 63 59 16N 105 50W
Stony Ridge 42 41 31N 83 30W
Stony River 11 61 47N 156 35W
Stony Tunguska = Tunguska, Nizhnyaya → 101 65 48N 88 4 E
Stonyford 14 39 23N 122 33W
Stora Lulevatten 96 67 10N 19 30 E
Stora Sjöfallet 96 67 29N 18 40 E
Storavan 96 65 45N 18 10 E
Store Bælt 97 55 20N 11 0 E
Støren 96 63 3N 10 18 E
Storey County ◇ 35 39 30N 119 35W
Storm B. 127 43 10 S 147 30 E
Storm L. 23 42 38N 95 13W
Storm Lake 23 42 39N 95 13W
Stormberg 123 31 16 S 26 17 E
Stormy Mt. 53 47 54N 120 21W
Stornoway 84 58 12N 6 23W
Storrs 28 41 49N 72 15W
Storsjön 96 62 50N 13 8 E
Storuman 96 65 5N 17 10 E
Storuman,sjö 96 65 13N 16 50 E
Story 56 44 35N 106 53W
Story City 23 42 11N 93 36W
Story County ◇ 23 42 0N 93 25W
Stotesbury 32 37 59N 94 34W
Stoughton, Canada 63 49 40N 103 0W
Stoughton, Mass. 28 42 8N 71 6W
Stoughton, Wis. 55 42 55N 89 13W
Stour →, Dorset, U.K. 83 50 48N 2 7W
Stour →, Hereford & Worcs., U.K. 83 52 25N 2 13W
Stour →, Kent, U.K. 83 51 15N 1 20 E
Stour →, Suffolk, U.K. 83 51 55N 1 5 E
Stourbridge 83 52 28N 2 8W
Stout 23 42 32N 92 43W
Stout, L. 63 52 0N 94 40W
Stoutland 32 37 49N 92 31W
Stoutsville, Mo. 32 39 33N 91 51W
Stoutsville, Ohio 42 39 36N 82 50W
Stovall, Ga. 18 32 58N 84 51W
Stovall, N.C. 40 36 27N 78 35W
Stover 32 38 27N 92 59W
Stowe 36 44 28N 72 41W
Stowell 51 29 47N 94 23W
Stowmarket 83 52 11N 1 0 E
Strabane 85 54 50N 7 28W
Strabane □ 85 54 45N 7 25W
Strafford, Mo. 32 37 16N 93 7W
Strafford, N.H. 36 43 19N 71 12W
Strafford County ◇ 36 43 15N 71 0W
Strahan 127 42 9 S 145 20 E
Straldzha 95 42 35N 26 40 E
Stralsund 88 54 17N 13 5 E
Strand 123 34 9 S 18 48 E
Strandburg 47 45 3N 96 46W
Strandquist 30 48 29N 96 27W
Strang 34 40 25N 97 35W
Strangford, L. 85 54 30N 5 37W
Stranraer 84 54 54N 5 0W
Strasbourg, Canada 63 51 4N 104 55W
Strasbourg, France 90 48 35N 7 42 E
Strasburg, Colo. 16 39 44N 104 20W
Strasburg, Mo. 32 38 46N 94 10W
Strasburg, N. Dak. 41 46 8N 100 10W
Strasburg, Ohio 42 40 36N 81 32W
Strasburg, Pa. 45 39 59N 76 11W
Strasburg, Va. 54 38 59N 78 22W
Stratford, Canada 60 43 23N 81 0W
Stratford, N.Z. 128 39 20 S 174 19 E
Stratford, Calif. 15 36 11N 119 49W
Stratford, Conn. 28 41 12N 73 8W
Stratford, Iowa 23 42 16N 93 56W
Stratford, N.H. 36 44 42N 71 36W
Stratford, Okla. 43 34 48N 96 58W
Stratford, S. Dak. 47 45 19N 98 18W
Stratford, Tex. 50 36 20N 102 4W
Stratford, Wis. 55 44 48N 90 4W
Stratford-on-Avon 83 52 12N 1 42W
Strath Spey 84 57 15N 3 40W
Stratham 36 43 3N 70 55W
Strathclyde □ 84 56 0N 4 50W
Strathcona 30 48 33N 96 10W
Strathcona Prov. Park 62 49 38N 125 40W
Strathmere 37 39 12N 74 40W
Strathmore, Canada 62 51 5N 113 18W
Strathmore, U.K. 84 56 40N 3 4W
Strathmore, U.S.A. 15 36 9N 119 4W
Strathnaver 62 53 20N 122 33W
Strathpeffer 84 57 35N 4 32W
Strathroy 60 42 58N 81 38W
Strathy Pt. 84 58 35N 4 0W
Stratton, U.K. 82 51 41N 1 45W
Stratton, Colo. 16 39 19N 102 36W
Stratton, Maine 26 45 8N 70 26W
Stratton, Nebr. 34 40 9N 101 14W
Stratton, Vt. 36 43 4N 72 55W
Stratton Meadows 16 38 45N 104 48W
Straumnes 96 66 26N 23 8W
Strawberry 13 35 58N 91 19W
Strawberry →, Ark. 13 35 53N 91 13W
Strawberry →, Utah 52 40 10N 110 24W
Strawberry Mt. 44 44 19N 118 43W
Strawberry Point 23 42 41N 91 32W
Strawberry Reservoir 52 40 8N 111 9W
Strawn, Ill. 21 40 39N 88 24W
Strawn, Tex. 51 32 33N 98 30W
Streaky Bay 126 32 48 S 134 13 E
Streator 21 41 8N 88 50W
Streeter 41 46 39N 99 21W
Streetman 51 31 53N 96 19W
Streetsboro 42 41 14N 81 21W
Strehaia 95 44 37N 23 10 E
Strelcha 95 42 25N 24 19 E
Strelka 101 58 5N 93 3 E
Strezhevoy 100 60 42N 77 34 E
Stringer 31 31 52N 89 16W
Stroeder 78 40 12 S 62 37W
Strómboli 94 38 48N 15 12 E
Stromeferry 84 57 20N 5 33W
Stromness 84 58 58N 3 18W
Ströms vattudal 96 64 15N 14 55 E
Stromsburg 34 41 7N 97 36W
Strömstad 97 58 55N 11 15 E
Strömsund 96 63 51N 15 33 E
Strong 13 33 7N 92 21W
Strong → 31 31 51N 90 8W
Strong City, Kans. 24 38 24N 96 32W
Strong City, Okla. 43 35 40N 99 36W
Stronghurst 21 40 45N 90 55W
Strongville 42 41 19N 81 50W
Stronsay 84 59 8N 2 38W
Stroud, U.K. 83 51 44N 2 12W
Stroud, U.S.A. 43 35 45N 96 40W
Stroudsburg 45 40 59N 75 12W
Struer 97 56 30N 8 35 E
Strum 55 44 33N 91 24W
Strumica 95 41 28N 22 41 E
Struthers, Canada 60 48 41N 85 51W
Struthers, U.S.A. 42 41 4N 80 39W
Stryama 95 42 16N 24 54 E
Stryker, Mont. 33 48 41N 114 46W
Stryker, Ohio 42 41 30N 84 25W
Strzelecki Cr. → 127 29 37 S 139 59 E
Stuart, Fla. 17 27 12N 80 15W
Stuart, Iowa 23 41 30N 94 19W
Stuart, Nebr. 34 42 36N 99 8W
Stuart, Okla. 43 34 54N 96 6W
Stuart, Va. 54 36 38N 80 16W
Stuart → 62 54 0N 123 35W
Stuart, Mt. 53 47 29N 120 54W
Stuart I. 11 63 35N 162 30W
Stuart L. 62 54 30N 124 30W
Stuart Range 126 29 10 S 134 56 E
Studen Kladenets, Yazovir 95 41 37N 25 30 E
Studley 24 39 21N 100 10W
Stull, L. 63 54 24N 92 34W
Stump L. 41 47 54N 98 24W
Stumpy Point 40 35 42N 75 44W
Stung Treng 112 13 31N 105 58 E
Stupart → 63 56 0N 93 25W
Sturgeon 32 39 14N 92 17W
Sturgeon →, Mich. 29 45 24N 84 38W
Sturgeon →, Mich. 29 47 2N 88 30W
Sturgeon B., Canada 63 52 0N 97 50W
Sturgeon B., U.S.A. 29 45 45N 85 0W
Sturgeon Bay 55 44 50N 87 23W
Sturgeon Falls 60 46 25N 79 57W
Sturgeon L., Alta., Canada 62 55 6N 117 32W
Sturgeon L., Ont., Canada 60 50 0N 90 45W
Sturgeon Lake 30 46 23N 92 49W
Sturgis, Ky. 48 37 33N 87 59W
Sturgis, Mich. 29 41 48N 85 25W
Sturgis, S. Dak. 47 44 25N 103 31W
Sturt Cr. → 126 20 8 S 127 24 E
Sturtevant 55 42 42N 87 54W
Stutsman County ◇ 41 47 0N 99 0W
Stutterheim 123 32 33 S 27 28 E
Stuttgart, Germany 88 48 46N 9 10 E
Stuttgart, U.S.A. 13 34 30N 91 33W
Stykkishólmur 96 65 2N 22 40W
Styria = Steiermark □ 88 47 26N 15 0 E
Styx → 10 30 31N 87 27W
Su Xian 115 33 41N 116 59 E
Suakin 121 19 8N 37 20 E
Suapure → 70 6 48N 67 1W
Suaqui 64 29 12N 109 41W
Suatá → 71 7 52N 65 22W
Subang 111 6 34 S 107 45 E
Subansiri → 109 26 48N 93 50 E
Subi 110 2 58N 108 50 E
Sublette, Ill. 21 41 39N 89 14W
Sublette, Kans. 24 37 29N 100 51W
Sublette County ◇ 56 43 0N 110 0W

Subotica Svishtov

Subotica **95** 46 6N 19 49 E
Sucarnoochee → **10** 32 25N 88 2W
Success, Canada **63** 50 28N 108 6W
Success, U.S.A. **13** 36 27N 90 43W
Success, L. **15** 36 4N 118 55W
Success, Mt. **36** 44 27N 71 5W
Succor Cr. → **20** 43 37N 116 57W
Suceava **89** 47 38N 26 16 E
Suchan **116** 43 8N 133 9 E
Suchil **64** 23 38N 103 55W
Suchitoto **66** 13 56N 89 0W
Suchou = Suzhou **115** 31 19N 120 38 E
Süchow = Xuzhou **115** 34 18N 117 10 E
Sucio → **70** 7 27N 77 7W
Suck → **85** 53 17N 8 18W
Sucre, Bolivia **73** 19 0 S 65 15W
Sucre, Colombia **70** 8 49N 74 44W
Sucre □, Colombia **70** 8 50N 75 40W
Sucre □, Venezuela **71** 10 25N 63 30W
Sucuaro **70** 4 34N 68 50W
Sucuriju **74** 1 39N 49 57W
Sucuriú → **73** 20 47 S 51 38W
Sud, Pte. **61** 49 3N 62 14W
Sud-Ouest, Pte. du **61** 49 23N 63 36W
Sudair **106** 26 0N 45 0 E
Sudan ■ **121** 15 0N 30 0 E
Sudbury, Canada **60** 46 30N 81 0W
Sudbury, U.K. **83** 52 2N 0 44 E
Sudbury, U.S.A. **28** 42 23N 71 25W
Sûdd **121** 8 20N 30 0 E
Suddie **71** 7 8N 58 29W
Sudetan Mts. = Sudety **88** 50 20N 16 45 E
Sudety **88** 50 20N 16 45 E
Sudirman, Pegunungan **111** 4 30 S 137 0 E
Sudiţi **95** 44 35N 27 38 E
Sudlersville **27** 39 11N 75 52W
Sueca **91** 39 12N 0 21W
Suez = El Suweis **121** 29 58N 32 31 E
Sūf **104** 32 19N 35 49 E
Suffield, Canada **63** 50 12N 111 10W
Suffield, U.S.A. **28** 41 59N 72 39W
Suffolk **54** 36 44N 76 35W
Suffolk □ **83** 52 16N 1 0 E
Suffolk County ◇, Mass. **28** 42 21N 71 5W
Suffolk County ◇, N.Y. **39** 40 50N 73 0W
Sufuk **107** 23 50N 51 50 E
Sugag **95** 45 47N 23 37 E
Sugar →, Ill. **21** 42 26N 89 12W
Sugar →, N.H. **36** 43 24N 72 24W
Sugar City, Colo. **16** 38 14N 103 40W
Sugar City, Idaho **20** 43 52N 111 45W
Sugar Cr. →, Ill. **21** 40 50N 87 45W
Sugar Cr. →, Iroquois, Ind. **22** 39 51N 87 21W
Sugar Cr. →, Mason, Ill. **21** 40 9N 89 38W
Sugar Creek **45** 41 47N 76 27W
Sugar Grove, N.C. **40** 36 15N 81 47W
Sugar Grove, Ohio **42** 39 38N 82 33W
Sugar Hill **18** 34 6N 84 2W
Sugar I. **29** 46 25N 84 12W
Sugar Land **51** 29 37N 95 38W
Sugar Notch **45** 41 12N 75 56W
Sugarloaf Mt. **43** 35 2N 94 28W
Sugartown **25** 30 50N 93 1W
Sugarville **52** 39 28N 112 39W
Sugden **43** 34 5N 97 59W
Sugluk = Saglouc **59** 62 14N 75 38W
Suhaia, L. **95** 43 45N 25 15 E
Suhār **107** 24 20N 56 40 E
Suhbaatar **113** 50 17N 106 10 E
Sui Xian, Henan, China **115** 34 25N 115 2 E
Sui Xian, Henan, China **115** 31 42N 113 24 E
Suiá Missu → **73** 11 13 S 53 15W
Suichang **115** 28 29N 119 15 E
Suichuan **115** 26 20N 114 32 E
Suide **114** 37 30N 110 12 E
Suifenhe **114** 44 25N 131 10 E
Suihua **114** 46 32N 126 55 E
Suining, Hunan, China **115** 26 35N 110 10 E
Suining, Sichuan, China **115** 30 26N 105 35 E
Suiping **115** 33 10N 113 59 E
Suir → **85** 52 15N 7 10W
Suisun B. **14** 38 5N 122 0W
Suisun City **14** 38 15N 122 2W
Suitland **27** 38 51N 76 56W
Suixi **115** 21 19N 110 18 E
Suizhong **114** 40 21N 120 20 E
Sukabumi **111** 6 56 S 106 50 E
Sukadana, Kalimantan, Indonesia **110** 1 10 S 110 0 E
Sukadana, Sumatera, Indonesia **110** 5 5 S 105 33 E
Sukagawa **117** 37 17N 140 23 E
Sukaraja **110** 2 28 S 110 25 E
Sukarnapura = Jayapura **111** 2 28 S 140 38 E
Sukhindol **95** 43 11N 25 10 E
Sukhona → **98** 60 30N 45 0 E
Sukhumi **99** 43 0N 41 0 E
Sukkur **108** 27 42N 68 54 E
Sukkur Barrage **108** 27 50N 68 45 E
Sukumo **117** 32 56N 132 44 E
Sukunka → **62** 55 45N 121 15W
Sul, Canal do **74** 0 10 S 48 30W
Sula, Kepulauan **111** 1 45 S 125 0 E
Sulaco → **66** 15 2N 87 44W
Sulaiman Range **108** 30 30N 69 50 E
Sulam Tsor **104** 33 4N 35 6 E
Sulawesi □ **111** 2 0 S 120 0 E
Sulima **120** 6 58N 11 32W
Sulina **89** 45 10N 29 40 E
Sulitälma **96** 67 17N 17 28 E
Sulitjelma **96** 67 9N 16 3 E
Sullana **72** 4 52 S 80 39W
Sulligent **10** 33 54N 88 8W
Sullivan, Ill. **21** 39 36N 88 37W
Sullivan, Ind. **22** 39 6N 87 24W
Sullivan, Ky. **48** 37 30N 87 57W
Sullivan, Mo. **32** 38 13N 91 10W
Sullivan Bay **62** 50 55N 126 50W
Sullivan County ◇, Ind. **22** 39 5N 87 25W
Sullivan County ◇, Mo. **32** 40 10N 93 5W
Sullivan County ◇, N.H. **36** 43 20N 72 15W
Sullivan County ◇, N.Y. **39** 41 45N 74 45W
Sullivan County ◇, Pa. **45** 41 30N 76 35W
Sullivan County ◇, Tenn. **49** 36 32N 82 19W
Sullivan I. = Lambi Kyun **112** 10 50N 98 20 E
Sully County ◇ **47** 44 45N 100 0W
Sulphur, La. **25** 30 14N 93 23W
Sulphur, Okla. **43** 34 31N 96 58W
Sulphur →, Ark. **13** 33 7N 93 52W
Sulphur →, S. Dak. **47** 44 45N 102 0W
Sulphur →, Tex. **51** 33 7N 93 52W
Sulphur Draw → **50** 33 12N 102 17W
Sulphur Pt. **62** 60 56N 114 48W
Sulphur Rock **13** 35 45N 91 30W
Sulphur Springs, Ark. **13** 36 29N 94 28W
Sulphur Springs, Ind. **22** 40 0N 85 27W
Sulphur Springs, Tex. **51** 33 8N 95 36W
Sulphur Springs Draw → **50** 32 12N 101 36W
Sultan, Canada **60** 47 36N 82 47W
Sultan, U.S.A. **53** 47 52N 121 49W
Sultanpur **109** 26 18N 82 4 E
Sultsa **98** 63 27N 46 2 E
Sulu Arch. **111** 6 0N 121 0 E
Sulu Sea **111** 8 0N 120 0 E
Suluq **121** 31 44N 20 14 E
Sulzberger Ice Shelf **5** 78 0 S 150 0 E
Sumac **18** 34 53N 84 48W
Sumalata **111** 1 0N 122 31 E
Sumampa **76** 29 25 S 63 29W
Sumas **53** 48 59N 122 15W
Sumatera □ **110** 0 40N 100 20 E
Sumatra = Sumatera □ **110** 0 40N 100 20 E
Sumatra, Fla. **17** 30 1N 84 59W
Sumatra, Mont. **33** 46 37N 107 33W
Sumba **111** 9 45 S 119 35 E
Sumba, Selat **111** 9 0 S 118 40 E
Sumbawa **110** 8 26 S 117 30 E
Sumbawa Besar **110** 8 30 S 117 26 E
Sumbe **122** 11 10 S 13 48 E
Sumburgh Hd. **84** 59 52N 1 17W
Sumé **74** 7 39 S 36 55W
Sumedang **111** 6 52 S 107 55 E
Sumenep **111** 7 1 S 113 52 E
Summer I. **29** 45 34N 86 39W
Summer L. **44** 42 50N 120 45W
Summer Lake **44** 42 58N 120 47W
Summerdale **10** 30 28N 87 55W
Summerfield, Kans. **24** 39 59N 96 21W
Summerfield, Ohio **42** 39 48N 81 20W
Summerfield, Tex. **50** 34 44N 102 31W
Summerland **62** 49 32N 119 41W
Summerland Key **17** 24 40N 81 27W
Summers County ◇ **54** 37 40N 80 54W
Summerside **61** 46 24N 63 47W
Summersville, Mo. **32** 37 11N 91 40W
Summersville, W. Va. **54** 38 17N 80 51W
Summersville L. **54** 38 13N 80 53W
Summerton **46** 33 36N 80 20W
Summertown, Ga. **18** 32 45N 82 16W
Summertown, Tenn. **48** 35 26N 87 18W
Summerville, Ga. **18** 34 29N 85 21W
Summerville, S.C. **46** 33 1N 80 11W
Summit, Alaska **11** 63 20N 149 7W
Summit, Ill. **21** 41 48N 87 48W
Summit, Ky. **48** 37 34N 86 5W
Summit, Miss. **31** 31 17N 90 28W
Summit, N.J. **37** 40 43N 74 22W
Summit, Okla. **43** 35 40N 95 26W
Summit, Oreg. **44** 44 38N 123 35W
Summit, S. Dak. **47** 45 18N 97 2W
Summit, Utah **52** 37 48N 112 56W
Summit County ◇, Colo. **16** 39 30N 106 0W
Summit County ◇, Ohio **42** 41 8N 81 29W
Summit County ◇, Utah **52** 40 55N 111 0W
Summit L. **35** 41 31N 119 4W
Summit Lake **62** 54 20N 122 40W
Summit Lake Indian Reservation **35** 41 33N 119 2W
Summit Peak **16** 37 21N 106 42W
Sumner, Iowa **23** 42 51N 92 6W
Sumner, Miss. **31** 33 58N 90 22W
Sumner, Mo. **32** 39 39N 93 15W
Sumner, Nebr. **34** 40 57N 99 31W
Sumner, L. **38** 34 40N 104 25W
Sumner County ◇, Kans. **24** 37 15N 97 20W
Sumner County ◇, Tenn. **48** 36 24N 86 27W
Sumoto **117** 34 21N 134 54 E
Šumperk **88** 49 59N 17 0 E
Sumpter **44** 44 45N 118 12W
Sumrall **31** 31 25N 89 33W
Sumter **46** 33 55N 80 21W
Sumter County ◇, Ala. **10** 32 35N 88 11W
Sumter County ◇, Fla. **17** 28 45N 82 10W
Sumter County ◇, Ga. **18** 32 0N 84 10W
Sumter County ◇, S.C. **46** 33 50N 80 30W
Sumter National Forest **46** 34 50N 83 0W
Sumy **99** 50 57N 34 50 E
Sun **25** 30 39N 89 54W
Sun → **33** 47 29N 111 19W
Sun City, Ariz. **12** 33 36N 112 17W
Sun City, Calif. **15** 33 42N 117 11W
Sun City, Kans. **24** 37 23N 98 55W
Sun Prairie **55** 43 11N 89 13W
Sun River **33** 47 32N 111 43W
Sun Valley **20** 43 42N 114 21W
Sunagawa **116** 43 29N 141 55 E
Sunapee **36** 43 23N 72 7W
Sunapee L. **36** 43 23N 72 5W
Sunart, L. **84** 56 42N 5 43W
Sunbright **49** 36 15N 84 40W
Sunburg **30** 45 21N 95 14W
Sunburst **33** 48 53N 111 55W
Sunbury, N.C. **40** 36 27N 76 37W
Sunbury, Pa. **45** 40 52N 76 48W
Sunchales **76** 30 58 S 61 35W
Suncho Corral **76** 27 55 S 63 27W
Sunchon **115** 34 52N 127 31 E
Suncook **36** 43 8N 71 27W
Suncook → **36** 43 8N 71 28W
Sunda, Selat **110** 6 20 S 105 30 E
Sunda Is. **124** 5 0 S 105 0 E
Sundance **56** 44 24N 104 23W
Sundarbans, The **109** 22 0N 89 0 E
Sundargarh **109** 22 4N 84 5 E
Sunderland, U.K. **82** 54 54N 1 22W
Sunderland, U.S.A. **27** 38 40N 76 36W
Sundre **62** 51 49N 114 38W
Sundridge **60** 45 45N 79 25W
Sundsvall **96** 62 23N 17 17 E
Sunflower **31** 33 33N 90 32W
Sunflower → **31** 32 40N 90 40W
Sunflower, Mt. **24** 39 6N 102 2W
Sunflower County ◇ **31** 33 44N 90 33W
Sungaigerung **110** 2 59 S 104 52 E
Sungailiat **110** 1 51 S 106 8 E
Sungaipakning **110** 1 19N 102 0 E
Sungaipenuh **110** 2 1 S 101 20 E
Sungaitiram **110** 0 45 S 117 8 E
Sungei Patani **112** 5 38N 100 29 E
Sungei Siput **112** 4 51N 101 6 E
Sungguminasa **111** 5 17 S 119 30 E
Sunghua Chiang = Songhua Jiang → **114** 47 45N 132 30 E
Sungtao Hu **115** 19 20N 109 35 E
Sungurlu **106** 40 12N 34 21 E
Sunland Park **38** 31 50N 106 40W
Sunman **22** 39 14N 85 6W
Sunnyside, Utah **52** 39 34N 110 23W
Sunnyside, Wash. **53** 46 20N 120 0W
Sunnyvale **14** 37 23N 122 2W
Sunol **34** 41 9N 102 46W
Sunray, Okla. **43** 34 25N 97 58W
Sunray, Tex. **50** 36 1N 101 49W
Sunrise **56** 42 20N 104 42W
Sunrise Manor **35** 36 12N 115 3W
Sunset, La. **25** 30 25N 92 4W
Sunset, Utah **52** 41 10N 112 2W
Sunset Beach **19** 21 40N 158 3W
Sunset Crater National Monument **12** 35 20N 111 20W
Suntar **101** 62 15N 117 30 E
Suntrana **11** 63 52N 148 51W
Suoyarvi **98** 62 12N 32 23 E
Supai **12** 36 15N 112 41W
Supamo → **71** 6 48N 61 50W
Supaul **109** 26 10N 86 40 E
Supe **72** 11 0 S 77 30W
Superior, Ariz. **12** 33 18N 111 6W
Superior, Iowa **23** 43 26N 94 57W
Superior, Mont. **33** 47 12N 114 53W
Superior, Nebr. **34** 40 1N 98 4W
Superior, Wis. **55** 46 44N 92 6W
Superior, L. **55** 47 0N 90 0W
Superior National Forest **30** 47 40N 92 45W
Suphan Buri **112** 14 14N 100 10 E
Suphan Dağı **106** 38 54N 42 48 E
Suphur Springs Range **35** 40 15N 116 0W
Supriori, Kepulauan **111** 1 0 S 136 0 E
Suqian **115** 33 54N 118 8 E
Suqualena **31** 32 27N 88 50W
Sūr, Lebanon **104** 33 19N 35 16 E
Sūr, Oman **107** 22 34N 59 32 E
Sur, Pt. **14** 36 18N 121 54W
Sura → **98** 56 6N 46 0 E
Surabaja = Surabaya **111** 7 17 S 112 45 E
Surabaya **111** 7 17 S 112 45 E
Suraia **95** 45 40N 27 25 E
Surakarta **111** 7 35 S 110 48 E
Surat **108** 21 12N 72 55 E
Surat Thani **112** 9 6N 99 20 E
Suratgarh **108** 29 18N 73 55 E
Surduc Pasul **95** 45 21N 23 23 E
Sûre → **87** 49 44N 6 31 E
Surf City, N.C. **40** 34 26N 77 33W
Surf City, N.J. **37** 39 40N 74 10W
Surfside **17** 25 53N 80 8W
Surfside Beach **46** 33 37N 78 57W
Surgut **100** 61 14N 73 20 E
Surianu **95** 45 33N 23 31 E
Suriapet **108** 17 10N 79 40 E
Şūrīf **104** 31 40N 35 4 E
Surigao **111** 9 47N 125 29 E
Surin **112** 14 50N 103 34 E
Surinam ■ **71** 4 0N 56 0W
Suriname □ **71** 5 30N 55 0W
Suriname → **71** 5 50N 55 15W
Suring **55** 44 59N 88 22W
Surprise, Ariz. **12** 33 38N 112 19W
Surprise, Nebr. **34** 41 6N 97 19W
Surprise L. **62** 59 40N 133 15W
Surrency **18** 31 44N 82 12W
Surrey **41** 48 14N 101 6W
Surrey □ **83** 51 16N 0 30W
Surry, N.H. **36** 43 3N 72 18W
Surry, Va. **54** 37 8N 76 50W
Surry County ◇, N.C. **40** 36 20N 80 45W
Surry County ◇, Va. **54** 37 8N 76 50W
Surt **121** 31 11N 16 39 E
Surt, Khalīj **121** 31 40N 18 30 E
Surtsey **96** 63 20N 20 30W
Surubim **74** 7 50 S 35 45W
Suruga-Wan **117** 34 45N 138 30 E
Surumu → **71** 3 22N 60 19W
Susa **94** 45 8N 7 3 E
Susaki **117** 33 22N 133 17 E
Sūsangerd **106** 31 35N 48 6 E
Susanino **101** 52 50N 140 14 E
Susank **24** 38 38N 98 46W
Susanville **14** 40 25N 120 39W
Susquehanna → **45** 39 33N 76 5W
Susquehanna County ◇ **45** 41 55N 75 50W
Susquehanna Depot **45** 41 57N 75 36W
Susques **76** 23 35 S 66 25W
Sussex, Canada **61** 45 45N 65 37W
Sussex, N.J. **37** 41 13N 74 37W
Sussex, Va. **54** 36 55N 77 17W
Sussex, Wis. **55** 43 8N 88 13W
Sussex, Wyo. **56** 43 42N 106 18W
Sussex, E. □ **83** 51 0N 0 20 E
Sussex, W. □ **83** 51 0N 0 30W
Sussex County ◇, Del. **27** 38 45N 75 20W
Sussex County ◇, N.J. **37** 41 15N 74 45W
Sussex County ◇, Va. **54** 36 55N 77 17W
Sustut → **62** 56 20N 127 30W
Susuman **101** 62 47N 148 10 E
Susunu **111** 3 20 S 133 25 E
Sutcliffe **35** 39 57N 119 36W
Şuteşti **95** 45 13N 27 27 E
Sutherland, S. Africa **123** 32 33 S 20 40 E
Sutherland, Iowa **23** 42 58N 95 29W
Sutherland, Nebr. **34** 41 10N 101 8W
Sutherland Falls **128** 44 48 S 167 46 E
Sutherland Pt. **127** 28 15 S 153 35 E
Sutherland Reservoir **34** 41 6N 101 10W
Sutherlin **44** 43 23N 123 19W
Sutlej → **108** 29 23N 71 3 E
Sutter **14** 39 10N 121 45W
Sutter County ◇ **14** 39 0N 121 45W
Sutter Creek **14** 38 24N 120 48W
Suttle **10** 32 32N 87 11W
Sutton, N. Dak. **41** 47 24N 98 27W
Sutton, Nebr. **34** 40 36N 97 52W
Sutton, Vt. **36** 44 39N 72 3W
Sutton, W. Va. **54** 38 40N 80 43W
Sutton → **60** 55 15N 83 45W
Sutton County ◇ **50** 30 34N 100 39W
Sutton-in-Ashfield **82** 53 7N 1 20W
Sutton L. **54** 38 40N 80 41W
Suttsu **116** 42 48N 140 14 E
Sutwik I. **11** 56 34N 157 12W
Suva **124** 18 6 S 178 30 E
Suva Planina **95** 43 10N 22 5 E
Suvorov Is. = Suwarrow Is. **125** 15 0 S 163 0W
Suvorovo **95** 43 20N 27 35 E
Suwałki **89** 54 8N 22 59 E
Suwanee **18** 34 3N 84 4W
Suwannee **17** 29 20N 83 9W
Suwannee → **17** 29 17N 83 10W
Suwannee County ◇ **17** 30 15N 83 0W
Suwannee Sd. **17** 29 20N 83 15W
Suwanose-Jima **117** 29 38N 129 43 E
Suwarrow Is. **125** 15 0 S 163 0W
Suweis, Khalîg el **121** 28 40N 33 0 E
Suwŏn **114** 37 17N 127 1 E
Suzdal **98** 56 29N 40 26 E
Suzhou **115** 31 19N 120 38 E
Suzu **117** 37 25N 137 17 E
Suzu-Misaki **117** 37 31N 137 21 E
Suzuka **117** 34 55N 136 36 E
Svalbard **4** 78 0N 17 0 E
Svalbarð **96** 66 12N 15 43W
Svanvik **96** 69 25N 30 3 E
Svappavaara **96** 67 40N 21 3 E
Svartisen **96** 66 40N 13 50 E
Svay Rieng **112** 11 9N 105 45 E
Svealand □ **97** 59 55N 15 0 E
Sveg **97** 62 2N 14 21 E
Svendborg **97** 55 4N 10 35 E
Sverdlovsk **98** 56 50N 60 30 E
Sverdrup Is. **4** 79 0N 97 0W
Svetlaya **116** 46 33N 138 18 E
Svilengrad **95** 41 49N 26 12 E
Svir → **98** 60 30N 32 48 E
Svishtov **95** 43 36N 25 23 E

T

Tâmchekket Tekonsha

Tâmchekket 120 17 25N 10 40W
Tame 70 6 28N 71 44W
Tamega → 91 41 5N 8 21W
Tamenglong 109 25 0N 93 35 E
Tamgak, Mts. 120 19 12N 8 35 E
Tamiahua, Laguna de 65 21 30N 97 30W
Tamiami Canal 17 25 50N 81 0W
Tamil Nadu □ 108 11 0N 77 0 E
Tammerfors = Tampere 97 61 30N 23 50 E
Tammisaari 97 60 0N 23 26 E
Tamms 21 37 14N 89 16W
Ţammūn 104 32 18N 35 23 E
Tamo Abu, Pegunungan 110 3 10N 115 0 E
Tamora 34 40 54N 97 14W
Tampa, Fla. 17 27 57N 82 27W
Tampa, Kans. 24 38 33N 97 9W
Tampa B. 17 27 50N 82 30W
Tampere 97 61 30N 23 50 E
Tampico, Mexico 65 22 20N 97 50W
Tampico, U.S.A. 21 41 38N 89 47W
Tampin 112 2 28N 102 13 E
Tamrida = Qādib 105 12 35N 54 2 E
Tamsagbulag 113 47 14N 117 21 E
Tamu 109 24 13N 94 12 E
Tamworth, Australia 127 31 7 S 150 58 E
Tamworth, U.K. 83 52 38N 1 41W
Tamworth, U.S.A. 36 43 50N 71 18W
Tana 96 70 26N 28 14 E
Tana →, Kenya 122 2 32 S 40 31 E
Tana →, Norway 96 70 30N 28 23 E
Tana, L. 121 13 5N 37 30 E
Tanabe 117 33 44N 135 22 E
Tanabi 75 20 37 S 49 37W
Tanacross 11 63 23N 143 21W
Tanafjorden 96 70 45N 28 25 E
Tanaga I. 11 51 48N 177 53W
Tanaga Volcano 11 51 53N 178 8W
Tanahbala 110 0 30 S 98 30 E
Tanahgrogot 110 1 55 S 116 15 E
Tanahjampea 111 7 10 S 120 35 E
Tanahmasa 110 0 12 S 98 39 E
Tanahmerah 111 6 5 S 140 16 E
Tanakura 117 37 10N 140 20 E
Tanama → 57 18 25N 66 42W
Tanami Des. 126 18 50 S 132 0 E
Tanana 11 65 10N 152 4W
Tanana → 11 65 10N 151 58W
Tananarive = Antananarivo 123 18 55 S 47 31 E
Tânaro → 94 45 1N 8 47 E
Tanchŏn 114 40 27N 128 54 E
Tandag 111 9 4N 126 9 E
Tăndărei 95 44 39N 27 40 E
Tandil 76 37 15 S 59 6W
Tandil, Sa. del 76 37 30 S 59 0W
Tando Adam 108 25 45N 68 40 E
Tane-ga-Shima 117 30 30N 131 0 E
Taneatua 128 38 4 S 177 1 E
Tanen Tong Dan 109 16 30N 98 30 E
Taney County ◇ 32 36 40N 93 0W
Taneytown 27 39 40N 77 11W
Taneyville 32 36 44N 93 2W
Tanezrouft 120 23 9N 0 11 E
Tanga 122 5 5 S 39 2 E
Tanganyika, L. 122 6 40 S 30 0 E
Tangent 44 44 33N 123 7W
Tanger 120 35 50N 5 49W
Tangerang 111 6 12 S 106 39 E
Tanggu 114 39 2N 117 40 E
Tanggula Shan 113 32 40N 92 10 E
Tanghe 115 32 47N 112 50 E
Tangier = Tanger 120 35 50N 5 49W
Tangier I. 54 37 55N 75 59W
Tangier Sd. 27 38 0N 75 57W
Tangipahoa, La. 25 30 52N 90 30W
Tangipahoa, La. 25 30 53N 90 31W
Tangipahoa Parish ◇ 25 30 30N 90 28W
Tangkak 112 2 18N 102 34 E
Tangshan 114 39 38N 118 10 E
Tanimbar, Kepulauan 111 7 30 S 131 30 E
Tanjay 111 9 30N 123 5 E
Tanjore = Thanjavur 108 10 48N 79 12 E
Tanjung 110 2 10 S 115 25 E
Tanjungbalai 110 2 55N 99 44 E
Tanjungbatu 110 2 23N 118 3 E
Tanjungkarang 110 5 20 S 105 10 E
Tanjungpandan 110 2 43 S 107 38 E
Tanjungpinang 110 1 5N 104 30 E
Tanjungpriok 111 6 8 S 106 55 E
Tanjungredeb 110 2 9N 117 29 E
Tanjungselor 110 2 55N 117 25 E
Tankersley 50 31 21N 100 39W
Tanner 54 38 59N 80 57W
Tannu-Ola 101 51 0N 94 0 E
Tanout 120 14 50N 8 55 E
Tanquinho 75 11 58 S 39 6W
Tanta 121 30 45N 30 57 E
Tantoyuca 65 21 21N 98 10W
Tantung = Dandong 114 40 10N 124 20 E
Tantūra = Dor 104 32 37N 34 55 E
Tanzania ■ 122 6 40 S 34 0 E
Tanzilla → 62 58 8N 130 43W
Tao'an 114 45 22N 122 40 E
Taopi 30 43 34N 92 38W
Taos 38 36 24N 105 35W
Taos County ◇ 38 36 30N 105 40W
Taos Indian Reservation 38 36 35N 105 25W
Taos Pueblo 38 36 24N 105 33W
Taoudenni 120 22 40N 3 55W
Taourirt 120 34 25N 2 53W
Taoyuan, China 115 28 55N 111 16 E
Taoyuan, Taiwan 115 25 0N 121 13 E
Tapa Shan = Daba Shan 115 32 0N 109 0 E
Tapachula 65 14 54N 92 17W
Tapah 112 4 12N 101 15 E
Tapajós → 71 2 24 S 54 41W
Tapaktuan 110 3 15N 97 10 E
Tapanahoni → 71 4 20N 54 25W
Tapanui 128 45 56 S 169 18 E
Tapauá 73 5 40 S 64 20W
Tapauá → 73 5 40 S 64 21W
Tapeta 120 6 29N 8 52W
Tapi → 108 21 8N 72 41 E
Tapiraí 75 19 52 S 46 1W
Tapirapé → 74 10 41 S 50 38W
Tapirapecó, Serra 71 1 10N 65 0W
Tapirapuã 73 14 51 S 57 45W
Tapoeripa 71 5 22N 56 34W
Tappahannock 54 37 56N 76 52W
Tappan L. 42 40 22N 81 14W
Tappen 41 46 52N 99 38W
Tapuaenuku, Mt. 128 42 0 S 173 39 E
Tapul Group 111 5 35N 120 50 E
Tapurucuará 71 0 24 S 65 2W
Taquara 77 29 36 S 50 46W
Taquari → 73 19 15 S 57 17W
Taquaritinga 75 21 24 S 48 30W
Tar → 40 35 33N 77 6W
Tar Island 62 57 3N 111 40W
Tara 100 56 55N 74 24 E
Tara →, U.S.S.R. 100 56 42N 74 36 E
Tara →, Yugoslavia 95 43 21N 18 51 E
Tarabagatay, Khrebet 100 48 0N 83 0 E
Tarabuco 73 19 10 S 64 57W
Tarābulus, Lebanon 106 34 31N 35 50 E
Tarābulus, Libya 121 32 49N 13 7 E
Tarakan 110 3 20N 117 35 E
Tarama-Jima 117 24 39N 124 42 E
Taranaki □ 128 39 5 S 174 51 E
Taranga Hill 108 24 0N 72 40 E
Táranto 94 40 30N 17 11 E
Táranto, G. di 94 40 0N 17 15 E
Tarapacá 70 2 56 S 69 46W
Tarapacá □ 76 20 45 S 69 30W
Tarapoto 72 6 30 S 76 20W
Taraquá 70 0 6N 68 28W
Tararua Range 128 40 45 S 175 25 E
Tarat 120 25 55N 9 3 E
Tarata 72 17 27 S 70 2W
Tarauacá 72 8 6 S 70 48W
Tarauacá → 72 6 42 S 69 48W
Tarawera 128 39 2 S 176 36 E
Tarawera L. 128 38 13 S 176 27 E
Tarbat Ness 84 57 52N 3 48W
Tarbela Dam 108 34 8N 72 52 E
Tarbert, Strathclyde, U.K. 84 55 55N 5 25W
Tarbert, W. Isles, U.K. 84 57 54N 6 49W
Tarbes 90 43 15N 0 3 E
Tarboro, Ga. 18 31 1N 81 48W
Tarboro, N.C. 40 35 54N 77 32W
Tarcoola 126 30 44 S 134 36 E
Taree 127 31 50 S 152 30 E
Tarentaise 90 45 30N 6 35 E
Tarfaya 120 27 55N 12 55W
Targhee National Forest 20 44 15N 111 20W
Táriba 70 7 49N 72 13W
Tarifa 91 36 1N 5 36W
Tarija 76 21 30 S 64 40W
Tarija □ 76 21 30 S 63 30W
Tariku → 111 2 55 S 138 26 E
Tarim He → 113 39 30N 88 30 E
Tarim Pendi 113 40 0N 84 0 E
Taritatu → 111 2 54 S 138 27 E
Tarkhankut, Mys 99 45 25N 32 30 E
Tarkio, Mo. 32 40 27N 95 23W
Tarkio, Mont. 33 47 1N 114 44W
Tarkio → 32 40 27N 95 23W
Tarko Sale 100 64 55N 77 50 E
Tarkwa 120 5 20N 2 0W
Tarlac 111 15 29N 120 35 E
Tarlton 42 39 33N 82 47W
Tarma 72 11 25 S 75 45W
Tarn □ 90 43 49N 2 8 E
Tarn → 90 44 5N 1 6 E
Tarn-et-Garonne □ 90 44 8N 1 20 E
Tarnov 34 41 37N 97 30W
Tarnów 89 50 3N 21 0 E
Tarnowskie Góry 89 50 27N 18 54 E
Taroom 127 25 36 S 149 48 E
Taroudannt 120 30 30N 8 52W
Tarpon Springs 17 28 9N 82 45W
Tarqūmiyah 104 31 35N 35 1 E
Tarragona 91 41 5N 1 17 E
Tarrant City 10 33 34N 86 47W
Tarrant County ◇ 51 32 44N 97 7W
Tarrasa 91 41 34N 2 1 E
Tarryall 16 39 7N 105 29W
Tarryall Cr. → 16 39 5N 105 19W
Tarrytown, Ga. 18 32 19N 82 34W
Tarrytown, N.Y. 39 41 4N 73 52W
Tarshiha = Me'ona 104 33 1N 35 15 E
Tarso Emissi 121 21 27N 18 36 E
Tarsus 106 36 58N 34 55 E
Tartagal 76 22 30 S 63 50W
Tartu 98 58 20N 26 44 E
Tarţūs 106 34 55N 35 55 E
Tarumirim 75 19 16 S 41 59W
Tarumizu 117 31 29N 130 42 E
Tarutao, Ko 112 6 33N 99 40 E
Tarutung 110 2 0N 98 54 E
Tarzan 50 32 18N 101 58W
Tasāwah 121 26 0N 13 30 E
Taschereau 60 48 40N 78 40W
Taseko → 62 52 4N 123 9W
Tash-Kumyr 100 41 40N 72 10 E
Tashauz 100 41 49N 59 58 E
Tashi Chho Dzong = Thimphu 109 27 31N 89 45 E
Tashkent 100 41 20N 69 10 E
Tashtagol 100 52 47N 87 53 E
Tasikmalaya 111 7 18 S 108 12 E
Tåsjön 96 64 15N 16 0 E
Taskan 101 62 59N 150 20 E
Tasman B. 128 40 59 S 173 25 E
Tasman Mts. 128 41 3 S 172 25 E
Tasman Pen. 127 43 10 S 148 0 E
Tasman Sea 124 36 0 S 160 0 E
Tasmania □ 127 42 0 S 146 30 E
Tasu Sd. 62 52 47N 132 2W
Tatar A.S.S.R. □ 98 55 30N 51 30 E
Tatarsk 100 55 14N 76 0 E
Tate 18 34 25N 84 23W
Tate County ◇ 31 34 37N 89 58W
Tateyama 117 35 0N 139 50 E
Tathlina L. 62 60 33N 117 39W
Tatinnai L. 63 60 55N 97 40W
Tatitlek 11 60 52N 146 41W
Tatnam, C. 63 57 16N 91 0W
Tatra = Tatry 89 49 20N 20 0 E
Tatry 89 49 20N 20 0 E
Tatsuno 117 34 52N 134 33 E
Tatta 108 24 42N 67 55 E
Tattnall County ◇ 18 32 0N 82 0W
Tatuī 77 23 25 S 47 53W
Tatum, N. Mex. 38 33 16N 103 19W
Tatum, Tex. 51 32 19N 94 31W
Tatum Cr. → 18 30 43N 82 32W
Tat'ung = Datong 114 40 6N 113 18 E
Tatvan 106 38 31N 42 15 E
Tauá 74 6 1 S 40 26W
Taubaté 77 23 0 S 45 36W
Tauern 88 47 15N 12 40 E
Taum Sauk Mt. 32 37 34N 90 44W
Taumarunui 128 38 53 S 175 15 E
Taumaturgo 72 8 54 S 72 51W
Taungdwingyi 109 20 1N 95 40 E
Taunggyi 109 20 50N 97 0 E
Taungup 109 18 51N 94 14 E
Taungup Pass 109 18 40N 94 45 E
Taungup Taunggya 109 18 20N 93 40 E
Taunton, U.K. 83 51 1N 3 7W
Taunton, Mass. 28 41 54N 71 6W
Taunton, Minn. 30 44 36N 96 4W
Taunton Lakes 37 39 51N 74 52W
Taunus 88 50 15N 8 20 E
Taupo 128 38 41 S 176 7 E
Taupo, L. 128 38 46 S 175 55 E
Tauranga 128 37 42 S 176 11 E
Tauranga Harb. 128 37 30 S 176 5 E
Taurianova 94 38 22N 16 1 E
Taurus Mts. = Toros Daglari 106 37 0N 35 0 E
Tavares 17 28 48N 81 44W
Tavda 100 58 7N 65 8 E
Tavda → 100 59 20N 63 28 E
Tavernier 17 25 1N 80 31W
Taveta 122 3 23 S 37 37 E
Taveuni 128 16 51 S 179 58W
Taviche 65 16 38N 96 32W
Tavira 91 37 8N 7 40W
Tavistock 83 50 33N 4 9W
Tavoy 112 14 2N 98 12 E
Taw → 83 17 37 S 177 55 E
Tawakoni, L. 51 32 49N 95 55W
Tawas City 29 44 16N 83 31W
Tawau 110 4 20N 117 55 E
Tawitawi 111 5 10N 120 0 E
Tay → 84 56 37N 3 38W
Tay, Firth of 84 56 25N 3 8W
Tay, L. 84 56 30N 4 10W
Tay Ninh 112 11 20N 106 5 E
Tayabamba 72 8 15 S 77 16W
Taylakovy 100 59 13N 74 0 E
Taylor, Canada 62 56 13N 120 40W
Taylor, Ariz. 12 34 28N 110 5W
Taylor, Ark. 13 33 6N 93 28W
Taylor, Fla. 17 30 26N 82 18W
Taylor, Mich. 29 42 14N 83 16W
Taylor, Miss. 31 34 16N 89 35W
Taylor, N. Dak. 41 46 54N 102 26W
Taylor, Nebr. 34 41 46N 99 23W
Taylor, Tex. 51 30 34N 97 25W
Taylor, Wis. 55 44 19N 91 7W
Taylor → 16 38 32N 106 55W
Taylor, Mt. 38 35 14N 107 37W
Taylor County ◇, Fla. 17 30 0N 83 30W
Taylor County ◇, Ga. 18 32 33N 84 15W
Taylor County ◇, Iowa 23 40 45N 94 40W
Taylor County ◇, Ky. 49 37 20N 85 20W
Taylor County ◇, Tex. 51 32 21N 99 53W
Taylor County ◇, W. Va. 54 39 21N 80 2W
Taylor County ◇, Wis. 55 45 10N 90 30W
Taylor Mill 49 38 55N 84 32W
Taylor Park Reservoir 16 38 49N 106 36W
Taylor Ridge 18 34 35N 85 12W
Taylors Bridge 27 39 23N 75 36W
Taylors Island 27 38 28N 76 18W
Taylorsville, Ind. 22 39 18N 85 57W
Taylorsville, Ky. 49 38 2N 85 21W
Taylorsville, Md. 27 39 27N 77 8W
Taylorsville, Miss. 31 31 50N 89 26W
Taylorsville, N.C. 40 35 55N 81 11W
Taylorville 21 39 33N 89 18W
Taymā 106 27 35N 38 45 E
Taymyr, Poluostrov 101 75 0N 100 0 E
Tayport 84 56 27N 2 52W
Ţayr Zibnā 104 33 14N 35 23 E
Tayshet 101 55 58N 98 1 E
Tayside □ 84 56 25N 3 30W
Taytay 111 10 45N 119 30 E
Taz → 100 67 32N 78 40 E
Taza 120 34 16N 4 6W
Tazawa-Ko 116 39 43N 140 40 E
Tazewell, Tenn. 49 36 27N 83 34W
Tazewell, Va. 54 37 7N 81 31W
Tazewell County ◇, Ill. 21 40 30N 89 30W
Tazewell County ◇, Va. 54 37 7N 81 31W
Tazin → 63 60 26N 110 45W
Tazin L. 63 59 44N 108 42W
Tazlina 11 62 4N 146 27W
Tazovskiy 100 67 30N 78 44 E
Tbilisi 99 41 43N 44 50 E
Tchad = Chad ■ 121 12 30N 17 15 E
Tchad, L. 121 13 30N 14 30 E
Tch'eng-tou = Chengdu 113 30 38N 104 2 E
Tchentlo L. 62 55 15N 125 0W
Tchibanga 122 2 45 S 11 0 E
Tch'ong-k'ing = Chongqing 115 29 35N 106 25 E
Tchula 31 33 11N 90 13W
Te Anau, L. 128 45 15 S 167 45 E
Te Aroha 128 37 32 S 175 44 E
Te Awamutu 128 38 1 S 175 20 E
Te Kuiti 128 38 20 S 175 11 E
Te Puke 128 37 46 S 176 22 E
Te Waewae B. 128 46 13 S 167 33 E
Tea 47 43 27N 96 50W
Tea → 70 0 30 S 65 9W
Teague 51 31 38N 96 17W
Teaneck 37 40 53N 74 1W
Teapa 65 18 35N 92 56W
Teasdale 52 38 17N 111 29W
Tebakang 110 1 6N 110 30 E
Tébessa 120 35 22N 8 8 E
Tebicuary → 76 26 36 S 58 16W
Tebingtinggi, Bengkulu, Indonesia 110 3 38 S 103 9 E
Tebingtinggi, Sumatera Utara, Indonesia 110 3 20N 99 9 E
Tecate 64 32 34N 116 38W
Techirghiol 95 44 4N 28 32 E
Tecka 78 7 35N 1 43W
Tecomán 64 18 55N 103 53W
Tecopa 15 35 51N 116 13W
Tecoripa 64 28 37N 109 57W
Tecuala 64 22 23N 105 27W
Tecuci 89 45 51N 27 27 E
Tecumseh, Mich. 29 42 0N 83 57W
Tecumseh, Nebr. 34 40 22N 96 11W
Tecumseh, Okla. 43 35 15N 96 56W
Tecumseh, Mt. 36 43 57N 71 34W
Tedzhen 100 37 23N 60 31 E
Teec Nos Pas 12 36 55N 109 6W
Tees → 82 54 36N 1 25W
Teesside 82 54 37N 1 13W
Tefé 71 3 25 S 64 50W
Tefé → 71 3 35 S 64 47W
Tegal 111 6 52 S 109 8 E
Tegelen 87 51 20N 6 9 E
Tegid, L. 82 52 53N 3 38W
Tegina 120 10 5N 6 11 E
Tegucigalpa 66 14 5N 87 14W
Tehachapi 15 35 8N 118 27W
Tehachapi Mts. 15 35 0N 118 30W
Tehachapi Pass 15 35 6N 118 18W
Tehama 14 40 2N 122 7W
Tehama County ◇ 14 40 5N 122 15W
Tehrān 107 35 44N 51 30 E
Tehuacán 65 18 30N 97 30W
Tehuantepec 65 16 21N 95 13W
Tehuantepec, Golfo de 65 15 50N 95 0W
Tehuantepec, Istmo de 65 17 0N 94 30W
Teifi → 83 52 4N 4 14W
Teign → 83 50 41N 3 42W
Teignmouth 83 50 33N 3 30W
Teiuş 95 46 12N 23 40 E
Teixeira 74 7 13 S 37 15W
Tejo → 91 38 40N 9 24W
Tejon Pass 15 34 49N 118 53W
Tekamah 34 41 47N 96 13W
Tekapo, L. 128 43 53 S 170 33 E
Tekax 65 20 11N 89 18W
Tekeli 100 44 50N 79 0 E
Tekirdağ 106 40 58N 27 30 E
Tekkali 109 18 37N 84 15 E
Tekoa 53 47 14N 117 4W
Tekonsha 29 42 5N 84 59W

Tel Adashim Throckmorton

Tel Adashim 104 32 30N 35 17 E
Tel Aviv-Yafo 104 32 4N 34 48 E
Tel Lakhish 104 31 34N 34 51 E
Tel Megiddo 104 32 35N 35 11 E
Tel Mond 104 32 15N 34 56 E
Tela 66 15 40N 87 28W
Telanaipura = Jambi 110 1 38 S 103 30 E
Telavi 99 42 0N 45 30 E
Telegraph Cr. 62 58 0N 131 10W
Telemark fylke □ 97 59 25N 8 30 E
Telén 76 36 15 S 65 31W
Teleorman □ 95 44 0N 25 0 E
Teleorman → 95 44 15N 25 20 E
Teles Pires → 73 7 21 S 58 3W
Telescope Pk. 15 36 10N 117 5W
Telfair County ◇ 18 31 55N 83 0W
Telford 82 52 42N 2 31W
Telida 11 63 23N 153 16W
Télimélé 120 10 54N 13 2W
Telkwa 62 54 41N 127 5W
Tell City 22 37 57N 86 46W
Teller 11 65 16N 166 22W
Teller County ◇ 16 38 50N 105 10W
Tellicherry 108 11 45N 75 30 E
Tellico Plains 49 35 22N 84 18W
Telluride 16 37 56N 107 49W
Telocaset 44 45 6N 117 49W
Telogia 17 30 21N 84 49W
Teloloapán 65 18 21N 99 51W
Telom → 112 4 20N 101 46 E
Telpos Iz 98 63 35N 57 30 E
Telsen 78 42 30 S 66 50W
Teluk Intan 110 4 3N 101 0 E
Telukbetung 110 5 29 S 105 17 E
Telukbutun 110 4 13N 108 12 E
Telukdalem 110 0 33N 97 50 E
Tema 120 5 41N 0 0 E
Temanggung 111 7 18 S 110 10 E
Temapache 65 21 4N 97 38W
Temax 65 21 10N 88 50W
Tembeling → 112 4 20N 102 23 E
Temblador 71 8 59N 62 44W
Temblor Range 15 35 20N 119 50W
Teme → 83 52 23N 2 15W
Temecula 15 33 30N 117 9W
Temerloh 112 3 27N 102 25 E
Temir 100 49 21N 57 3 E
Temirtau, Kazakh S.S.R., U.S.S.R. 100 50 5N 72 56 E
Temirtau, R.S.F.S.R., U.S.S.R. 100 53 10N 87 30 E
Témiscaming 60 46 44N 79 5W
Temosachic 64 28 58N 107 50W
Tempe 12 33 25N 111 56W
Temperance 29 41 47N 83 34W
Tempino 110 1 42 S 103 30 E
Tempiute 35 37 39N 115 38W
Temple, N.H. 36 42 48N 71 50W
Temple, Okla. 43 34 16N 98 14W
Temple, Tex. 51 31 6N 97 21W
Temple B. 127 12 15 S 143 3 E
Temple Hill 49 36 53N 85 51W
Temple Terrace 17 28 2N 82 23W
Templemore 85 52 48N 7 50W
Templeton, Calif. 15 35 33N 120 42W
Templeton, Mass. 28 42 33N 72 4W
Tempoal 65 21 31N 98 23W
Temuco 78 38 45 S 72 40W
Temuka 128 44 14 S 171 17 E
Ten Thousand Is. 17 25 55N 81 45W
Tena 70 0 59 S 77 49W
Tenabo 65 20 2N 90 12W
Tenaha 51 31 57N 94 15W
Tenakee Springs 11 57 47N 135 13W
Tenali 108 16 15N 80 35 E
Tenancingo 65 19 0N 99 33W
Tenango 65 19 7N 99 33W
Tenasserim 112 12 6N 99 3 E
Tenasserim □ 112 14 0N 98 30 E
Tenby 83 51 40N 4 42W
Tendaho 105 11 48N 40 54 E
Tendoy 20 44 57N 113 38W
Tenente Marques → 73 11 10 S 59 56W
Tenerife 120 28 15N 16 35W
Teng → 112 20 30N 98 10 E
Teng Xian, Guangxi Zhuangzu, China 115 23 21N 110 56 E
Teng Xian, Shandong, China 115 35 5N 117 10 E
Tengah □ 111 2 0 S 122 0 E
Tengah Kepulauan 110 7 5 S 118 15 E
Tengchong 113 25 0N 98 28 E
Tengchowfu = Penglai 114 37 48N 120 42 E
Tenggara □ 111 3 0 S 122 0 E
Tenggarong 110 0 24 S 116 58 E
Tengiz, Ozero 100 50 30N 69 0 E
Tenino 53 46 51N 122 51W
Tenkasi 108 8 55N 77 20 E
Tenke 122 10 32 S 26 7 E
Tenkiller Ferry L. 43 35 35N 95 2W
Tenkodogo 120 11 54N 0 19W
Tennant 23 41 35N 95 26W
Tennant Creek 126 19 30 S 134 15 E
Tennessee 21 40 18N 90 52W
Tennessee □ 48 35 50N 85 30W
Tennessee → 48 37 4N 88 34W
Tennessee Pass 16 39 22N 106 19W
Tennessee Ridge 48 36 19N 87 47W
Tennille 18 32 56N 82 48W
Tennyson, Ind. 22 38 5N 87 7W
Tennyson, Wis. 55 42 41N 90 41W
Tenom 110 5 4N 115 57 E
Tenosique 65 17 30N 91 24W
Tenryū-Gawa → 117 35 39N 137 48 E
Tensas → 25 31 38N 91 49W
Tensas Parish ◇ 25 32 0N 91 10W
Tensed 20 47 10N 116 55W
Tensleep 56 44 2N 107 27W
Tenstrike 30 47 39N 94 41W
Tent L. 63 62 25N 107 54W
Tenterfield 127 29 0 S 152 0 E
Teófilo Otoni 75 17 50 S 41 30W
Teotihuacán 65 19 44N 98 50W
Tepa 111 7 52 S 129 31 E
Tepalcatepec → 64 18 35N 101 59W
Tepehuanes 64 25 21N 105 44W
Tepequem, Serra 71 3 45N 61 45W
Tepetongo 64 22 28N 103 9W
Tepic 64 21 30N 104 54W
Teplice 88 50 40N 13 48 E
Tepoca, C. 64 30 20N 112 25W
Tequila 64 20 54N 103 47W
Ter → 91 42 0N 3 12 E
Ter Apel 87 52 53N 7 5 E
Téra 120 14 0N 0 45 E
Teraina, I. 125 4 43N 160 25W
Téramo 94 42 40N 13 40 E
Tercero → 76 32 58 S 61 47W
Terek → 99 44 0N 47 30 E
Terengganu □ 112 4 55N 103 0 E
Terenos 73 20 26 S 54 50W
Teresina 74 5 9 S 42 45W
Teresinha 71 0 58N 52 2W
Terhazza 120 23 38N 5 22W
Terlingua 50 29 19N 103 36W
Terlingua Cr. → 50 29 10N 103 36W
Terlton 43 36 8N 96 29W
Termez 100 37 15N 67 15 E
Términos, Laguna de 65 18 35N 91 30W
Térmoli 94 42 0N 15 0 E
Ternate 111 0 45N 127 25 E
Terneuzen 87 51 20N 3 50 E
Terney 101 45 3N 136 37 E
Terni 94 42 34N 12 38 E
Terra Alta 54 39 27N 79 33W
Terra Bella 15 35 58N 119 3W
Terra Nova B. 5 74 50 S 164 40 E
Terrace 62 54 30N 128 35W
Terrace Bay 60 48 47N 87 5W
Terracina 94 41 17N 13 12 E
Terral 43 33 54N 97 57W
Terralba 94 39 42N 8 38 E
Terranova = Ólbia 94 40 55N 9 30 E
Terre Haute 22 39 28N 87 25W
Terrebonne 44 44 21N 121 11W
Terrebonne B. 25 29 5N 90 35W
Terrebonne Parish ◇ 25 29 20N 91 0W
Terrell 51 32 44N 96 17W
Terrell County ◇, Ga. 18 31 50N 84 25W
Terrell County ◇, Tex. 50 30 0N 102 0W
Terrenceville 61 47 40N 54 44W
Terreton 20 43 51N 112 26W
Terril 23 43 18N 94 58W
Terry, La. 25 32 56N 91 21W
Terry, Miss. 31 32 6N 90 18W
Terry, Mont. 33 46 47N 105 19W
Terry County ◇ 50 33 11N 102 17W
Terry Pk. 47 44 19N 103 50W
Terryville 28 41 41N 73 3W
Terschelling 87 53 25N 5 20 E
Teruel 91 40 22N 1 8W
Tervel 95 43 45N 27 28 E
Tervola 96 66 6N 24 49 E
Tešanj 95 44 38N 17 59 E
Tescott 24 39 1N 97 53W
Teshekpuk L. 11 70 35N 153 26W
Teshio 116 44 53N 141 44 E
Teshio-Gawa → 116 44 53N 141 45 E
Tesiyn Gol → 113 50 40N 93 20 E
Teslin 62 60 10N 132 43W
Teslin → 62 61 34N 134 35W
Teslin L. 62 60 15N 132 57W
Tesouro 73 16 4 S 53 34W
Tessalit 120 20 12N 1 0 E
Tessaoua 120 13 47N 7 56 E
Test → 83 51 7N 1 30W
Tetachuck L. 62 53 18N 125 55W
Tetas, Pta. 76 23 31 S 70 38W
Tete 123 16 13 S 33 33 E
Teteven 95 42 58N 24 17 E
Tethul → 62 60 35N 112 12W
Tetlin 11 63 8N 142 31W
Tetlin Indian Reservation 11 63 0N 142 30W
Teton 20 43 53N 111 40W
Teton →, Idaho 20 43 54N 111 51W
Teton →, Mont. 33 47 56N 110 31W
Teton County ◇, Idaho 20 43 55N 111 5W
Teton County ◇, Mont. 33 47 52N 112 20W
Teton County ◇, Wyo. 56 44 0N 110 30W
Teton Pass 56 43 30N 110 57W
Teton Range 56 43 45N 111 0W
Tetonia 20 43 49N 111 10W
Tétouan 120 35 35N 5 21W
Tetovo 95 42 1N 21 2 E
Tetuán = Tétouan 120 35 35N 5 21W
Tetyukhe Pristan 116 44 22N 135 48 E
Teuco → 76 25 35 S 60 11W
Teulon 63 50 23N 97 16W
Teun 111 6 59 S 129 8 E
Teutoburger Wald 88 52 5N 8 20 E
Teutopolis 21 39 8N 88 29W
Tevere → 94 41 44N 12 14 E
Teverya 104 32 47N 35 32 E
Teviot → 84 55 21N 2 51W
Tewkesbury 83 51 59N 2 8W
Tewksbury 28 42 37N 71 14W
Texada I. 62 49 40N 124 25W
Texana, L. 51 29 0N 96 35W
Texarkana, Ark. 13 33 26N 94 2W
Texarkana, Tex. 51 33 26N 94 3W
Texas □ 50 31 0N 101 0W
Texas City 51 29 24N 94 54W
Texas County ◇, Mo. 32 37 20N 92 0W
Texas County ◇, Okla. 43 36 45N 101 30W
Texel 87 53 5N 4 50 E
Texhoma 43 36 30N 101 47W
Texico 38 34 24N 103 3W
Texline 50 36 23N 103 2W
Texola 43 35 12N 99 59W
Texoma, L. 51 33 50N 96 34W
Texon 50 31 13N 101 42W
Teyvareh 107 33 30N 64 24 E
Teziutlán 65 19 50N 97 22W
Tezpur 109 26 40N 92 45 E
Tezzeron L. 62 54 43N 124 30W
Tha-anne → 63 60 31N 94 37W
Tha Nun 112 8 12N 98 17 E
Thabana Ntlenyana 123 29 30 S 29 16 E
Thabazimbi 123 24 40 S 27 21 E
Thackerville 43 33 48N 97 9W
Thai Hoa 112 19 20N 105 20 E
Thai Nguyen 112 21 35N 105 55 E
Thailand ■ 110 16 0N 102 0 E
Thailand, G. of 112 11 30N 101 0 E
Thakhek 112 17 25N 104 45 E
Thal 108 33 28N 70 33 E
Thala La 109 28 25N 97 23 E
Thalia 51 33 59N 99 32W
Thalmann 18 31 18N 81 41W
Thame → 83 51 35N 1 8W
Thames 128 37 7 S 175 34 E
Thames →, Canada 60 42 20N 82 25W
Thames →, U.K. 83 51 30N 0 35 E
Thames →, U.S.A. 28 41 18N 72 5W
Thane 108 19 12N 72 59 E
Thanet, I. of 83 51 21N 1 20 E
Thang Binh 112 15 50N 108 20 E
Thanh Hoa 112 19 48N 105 46 E
Thanjavur 108 10 48N 79 12 E
Thanlwin Myit → 109 20 0N 98 0 E
Thar Desert 108 28 0N 72 0 E
Tharad 108 24 30N 71 44 E
Thargomindah 127 27 58 S 143 46 E
Tharrawaddy 109 17 38N 95 48 E
Thásos 95 40 40N 24 40 E
Thatcher, Ariz. 12 32 51N 109 46W
Thatcher, Colo. 16 37 33N 104 7W
Thaton 109 16 55N 97 22 E
Thaungdut 109 24 30N 94 40 E
Thawville 21 40 41N 88 7W
Thaxton 31 34 18N 89 11W
Thayer, Kans. 24 37 29N 95 28W
Thayer, Mo. 32 36 31N 91 33W
Thayer, Nebr. 34 40 58N 97 30W
Thayer County ◇ 34 40 15N 97 40W
Thayetmyo 109 19 20N 95 10 E
Thayne 56 42 55N 111 0W
Thazi 109 21 0N 96 5 E
The Bight 67 24 19N 75 24W
The Dalles 44 45 36N 121 10W
The English Company's Is. 127 11 50 S 136 32 E
The Granites 126 20 35 S 130 21 E
The Grenadines, Is. 67 12 40N 61 20W
The Grove 51 31 16N 97 32W
The Hamilton → 126 26 40 S 135 19 E
The Macumba → 127 27 52 S 137 12 E
The Pas 63 53 45N 101 15W
The Plains 54 38 52N 77 47W
The Village 43 35 35N 97 33W
Theba 12 32 55N 112 53W
Thebes = Thívai 95 38 19N 23 19 E
Thebes 21 37 13N 89 28W
Thedford 34 41 59N 100 35W
Thekulthili L. 63 61 3N 110 0W
Thelon → 63 62 35N 104 3W
Theodore, Australia 127 24 55 S 150 3 E
Theodore, U.S.A. 10 30 33N 88 10W
Theodore Roosevelt L. 12 33 40N 111 10W
Theodore Roosevelt National Memorial Park 41 47 0N 103 25W
Theodosia 32 36 35N 92 39W
Theresa 39 44 13N 75 48W
Theressa 17 29 50N 82 4W
Theriot 25 29 28N 90 45W
Thermaïkos Kólpos 95 40 15N 22 45 E
Thermal 15 33 39N 116 9W
Thermalito 14 39 31N 121 36W
Thermopolis 56 43 39N 108 13W
Thermopylae P. 95 38 48N 22 35 E
Thessalía □ 95 39 30N 22 0 E
Thessalon 60 46 20N 83 30W
Thessaloníki 95 40 38N 22 58 E
Thessaly = Thessalía □ 95 39 30N 22 0 E
Theta 48 35 47N 87 3W
Thetford 83 52 25N 0 44 E
Thetford Mines 61 46 8N 71 18W
Thibodaux 25 29 48N 90 49W
Thicket Portage 63 55 19N 97 42W
Thief L. 30 48 30N 95 54W
Thief River Falls 30 48 7N 96 10W
Thiel Mts. 5 85 15 S 91 0W
Thielsen, Mt. 44 43 9N 122 4W
Thiérache 90 49 51N 3 45 E
Thies 120 14 50N 16 51W
Thika 122 1 1 S 37 5 E
Thikombia 128 15 44 S 179 55W
Thimphu 109 27 31N 89 45 E
þingvallavatn 96 64 11N 21 9W
Thionville 90 49 20N 6 10 E
Thíra 95 36 23N 25 27 E
Thirsk 82 54 15N 1 20W
Thisted 97 56 58N 8 40 E
Thistle I. 126 35 0 S 136 8 E
Thívai 95 38 19N 23 19 E
þjórsá → 96 63 47N 20 48W
Thlewiaza →, Man., Canada 63 59 43N 100 5W
Thlewiaza →, N.W.T., Canada 63 60 29N 94 40W
Thoa → 63 60 31N 109 47W
Thomas, Md. 27 38 36N 76 18W
Thomas, Okla. 43 35 45N 98 45W
Thomas, W. Va. 54 39 9N 79 30W
Thomas A. Edison, L. 15 37 25N 119 0W
Thomas County ◇, Ga. 18 30 50N 83 55W
Thomas County ◇, Kans. 24 39 20N 101 0W
Thomas County ◇, Nebr. 34 41 50N 100 30W
Thomas Hill Reservoir 32 39 34N 92 39W
Thomasboro 21 40 15N 88 11W
Thomaston, Ala. 10 32 16N 87 38W
Thomaston, Conn. 28 41 41N 73 4W
Thomaston, Ga. 18 32 53N 84 20W
Thomaston, Maine 26 44 5N 69 11W
Thomaston Res. 28 41 42N 73 5W
Thomastown 31 32 52N 89 40W
Thomasville, Ala. 10 31 55N 87 44W
Thomasville, Ga. 18 30 50N 83 59W
Thomasville, N.C. 40 35 53N 80 5W
Thompson, Canada 63 55 45N 97 52W
Thompson, Iowa 23 43 22N 93 46W
Thompson, N. Dak. 41 47 47N 97 6W
Thompson, Pa. 45 41 52N 75 31W
Thompson, Utah 52 38 58N 109 43W
Thompson →, Canada 62 50 15N 121 24W
Thompson →, U.S.A. 32 39 46N 93 37W
Thompson Falls 33 47 36N 115 21W
Thompson Landing 63 62 56N 110 40W
Thompson Pk. 14 41 0N 123 0W
Thompsons Cr. → 31 31 10N 88 55W
Thompsonville, Ill. 21 37 55N 88 46W
Thompsonville, Mich. 29 44 31N 85 56W
Thomson, Ga. 18 33 28N 82 30W
Thomson, Ill. 21 41 58N 90 6W
Thomson → 127 25 11 S 142 53 E
Thomson's Falls = Nyahururu 122 0 2N 36 27 E
Thon Buri 112 13 43N 100 29 E
Thoreau 38 35 24N 108 13W
þórisvatn 96 64 20N 18 55W
þorlákshöfn 96 63 51N 21 22W
Thornaby on Tees 82 54 36N 1 19W
Thornapple →, Mich. 29 42 56N 85 28W
Thornapple →, Wis. 55 45 28N 91 16W
Thornburg 23 41 27N 92 20W
Thorndale 51 30 37N 97 12W
Thornton, Colo. 16 39 52N 104 58W
Thornton, Idaho 20 43 45N 111 51W
Thornton, Iowa 23 42 57N 93 23W
Thornton, Miss. 31 33 5N 90 19W
Thornton, Tex. 51 31 25N 96 34W
Thornton, Wash. 53 47 7N 117 23W
Thorntown 22 40 8N 86 36W
Thornville 42 39 54N 82 25W
Thorny Mt. 32 37 6N 91 10W
Thorp, Wash. 53 47 4N 120 40W
Thorp, Wis. 55 44 58N 90 48W
Thorsby 10 32 55N 86 43W
þórshöfn 96 66 12N 15 20W
Thousand Oaks 15 34 10N 118 50W
Thousand Springs Cr. → 35 41 17N 113 51W
Thrace = Thráki □ 95 41 9N 25 30 E
Thráki □ 95 41 9N 25 30 E
Thrall 51 30 35N 97 18W
Thrashers 31 34 43N 88 32W
Three Forks 33 45 54N 111 33W
Three Hills 62 51 43N 113 15W
Three Lakes 55 45 48N 89 10W
Three Oaks 29 41 48N 86 36W
Three Points, C. 120 4 42N 2 6W
Three Rivers, Calif. 15 36 26N 118 54W
Three Rivers, Mich. 29 41 57N 85 38W
Three Rivers, N. Mex. 38 33 19N 106 5W
Three Rivers, Tex. 51 28 28N 98 11W
Three Sisters 44 44 4N 121 51W
Throckmorton 51 33 11N 99 11W

Throckmorton County Tombigee National Forest

Throckmorton County ◇ **51** 33 10N 99 10W
Throssell Ra. **126** 22 3S 121 43 E
Thubun Lakes **63** 61 30N 112 0W
Thuin **87** 50 20N 4 17 E
Thule, Antarct. **5** 59 27S 27 19W
Thule, Greenland **4** 77 40N 69 0W
Thun **88** 46 45N 7 38 E
Thunder B. **29** 45 0N 83 20W
Thunder Basin National Grassland **56** 43 45N 105 5W
Thunder Bay **60** 48 20N 89 15W
Thunder Butte **47** 45 19N 101 53W
Thunder Hawk **47** 45 56N 101 58W
Thunderbird, L. **43** 35 14N 97 18W
Thunderbolt **18** 32 3N 81 4W
Thung Song **112** 8 10N 99 40 E
Thunkar **109** 27 55N 91 0 E
Thüringer Wald **88** 50 35N 11 0 E
Thurles **85** 52 40N 7 53W
Thurman **23** 40 49N 95 45W
Thurmont **27** 39 37N 77 25W
Thursday I. **127** 10 30S 142 3 E
Thurso, Canada **60** 45 36N 75 15W
Thurso, U.K. **84** 58 34N 3 31W
Thurston, Nebr. **34** 42 11N 96 42W
Thurston, Ohio **42** 39 50N 82 33W
Thurston County ◇, Nebr. **34** 42 15N 96 40W
Thurston County ◇, Wash. **53** 46 58N 122 59W
Thurston I. **5** 72 0S 100 0W
Thutade L. **62** 57 0N 126 55W
Thysville = Mbanza Ngungu **122** 5 12S 14 53 E
Tiahuanacu **72** 16 33S 68 42W
Tian Shan **113** 43 0N 84 0 E
Tiandu **115** 18 18N 109 36 E
Tian'e **115** 25 1N 107 9 E
Tianguá **74** 3 44S 40 59W
Tianhe **115** 24 48N 108 40 E
Tianjin **114** 39 8N 117 10 E
Tianshui **115** 34 32N 105 40 E
Tianyang **115** 23 42N 106 53 E
Tianzhen **114** 40 24N 114 5 E
Tiaret **120** 35 20N 1 21 E
Tiassalé **120** 5 58N 4 57W
Tibagi **77** 24 30S 50 24W
Tibagi → **77** 22 47S 51 1W
Tibati **121** 6 22N 12 30 E
Tibble **10** 31 22N 88 15W
Tiber = Tevere → **94** 41 44N 12 14 E
Tiber Reservoir **33** 48 19N 111 6W
Tiberias, L. = Kinneret, Yam **104** 32 45N 35 35 E
Tiberias, L. = Yam Kinneret **104** 32 45N 35 35 E
Tibesti **121** 21 0N 17 30 E
Tibet = Xizang □ **113** 32 0N 88 0 E
Tibnīn **104** 33 12N 35 24 E
Tibooburra **127** 29 26S 142 1 E
Tibugá, Golfo de **70** 5 45N 77 20W
Tiburón **64** 29 0N 112 30W
Tice **17** 26 40N 81 49W
Tīchīt **120** 18 21N 9 29W
Tichnor **13** 34 8N 91 16W
Ticino □ **88** 46 20N 8 45 E
Ticino → **94** 45 9N 9 14 E
Ticonderoga **39** 43 51N 73 26W
Ticul **65** 20 20N 89 31W
Tiddim **109** 23 28N 93 45 E
Tidewater **54** 37 51N 76 42W
Tidioute **45** 41 41N 79 24W
Tidjikja **120** 18 29N 11 35W
Tidore **111** 0 40N 127 25 E
Tie Plant **31** 33 44N 89 47W
Tiel, Neth. **87** 51 53N 5 26 E
Tiel, Senegal **120** 14 55N 15 5W
Tieling **114** 42 20N 123 55 E
Tielt **87** 51 0N 3 20 E
Tien Shan **107** 42 0N 80 0 E
Tienen **87** 50 48N 4 57 E
Tientsin = Tianjin **114** 39 8N 117 10 E
Tierra Amarilla, Chile **76** 27 28S 70 18W
Tierra Amarilla, U.S.A. **38** 36 42N 106 33W
Tierra Blanca Cr. → **50** 34 58N 101 55W
Tierra Colorada **65** 17 10N 99 35W
Tierra de Campos **91** 42 10N 4 50W
Tierra del Fuego □ **78** 54 0S 67 45W
Tierra del Fuego, I. Gr. de **78** 54 0S 69 0W
Tierralta **70** 8 11N 76 4W
Tiétar → **91** 39 50N 6 1W
Tietê → **77** 20 40S 51 35W
Tieton **53** 46 42N 120 45W
Tiffany **16** 37 2N 107 32W
Tiffany Mt. **53** 48 40N 119 56W
Tiffin, Iowa **23** 41 42N 91 40W
Tiffin, Ohio **42** 41 7N 83 11W
Tiflis = Tbilisi **99** 41 43N 44 50 E
Tifrah **104** 31 19N 34 42 E
Tift County ◇ **18** 31 30N 83 30W
Tifton **18** 31 27N 83 31W
Tifu **111** 3 39S 126 24 E
Tigalda I. **11** 54 6N 165 5W
Tigard **44** 45 26N 122 46W
Tiger **53** 48 42N 117 24W
Tigil **101** 57 49N 158 40 E
Tignall **18** 33 52N 82 44W
Tignish **61** 46 58N 64 2W
Tigre →, Peru **72** 4 30S 74 10W
Tigre →, Venezuela **71** 9 20N 62 30W
Tigris = Dijlah, Nahr → **106** 31 0N 47 25 E
Tigveni **95** 45 10N 24 31 E
Tigyaing **109** 23 45N 96 10 E
Tîh, Gebel el **121** 29 32N 33 26 E
Tihāmah **106** 22 0N 39 0 E
Tijeras **38** 35 5N 106 23W
Tijuana **64** 32 30N 117 10W
Tikal **66** 17 13N 89 24W
Tikamgarh **108** 24 44N 78 50 E
Tikhoretsk **99** 45 56N 40 5 E
Tikrīt **106** 34 35N 43 37 E
Tiksi **101** 71 40N 128 45 E
Tilamuta **111** 0 32N 122 23 E
Tilburg **87** 51 31N 5 6 E
Tilbury, Canada **60** 42 17N 82 23W
Tilbury, U.K. **83** 51 27N 0 24 E
Tilcara **76** 23 36S 65 23W
Tilden, Ill. **21** 38 13N 89 41W
Tilden, Nebr. **34** 42 3N 97 50W
Tilden, Tex. **51** 28 28N 98 33W
Tilghman **27** 38 43N 76 20W
Tilichiki **101** 60 27N 166 5 E
Tiline **48** 37 11N 88 15W
Till → **82** 55 35N 2 3W
Tillabéri **120** 14 28N 1 28 E
Tillamook **44** 45 27N 123 51W
Tillamook B. **44** 45 30N 123 53W
Tillamook County ◇ **44** 45 20N 123 45W
Tillamook Head **44** 45 57N 124 0W
Tillar **13** 33 43N 91 27W
Tiller **44** 42 56N 122 57W
Tillery, L. **40** 35 12N 80 4W
Tillman **46** 32 28N 81 6W
Tillman County ◇ **43** 34 25N 99 0W
Tillmans Corner **10** 30 46N 88 8W
Tillsonburg **60** 42 53N 80 44W
Tílos **95** 36 27N 27 27 E
Tilsit = Sovetsk **98** 55 6N 21 50 E
Tilt → **84** 56 50N 3 50W
Tilton, Ga. **18** 34 40N 84 56W
Tilton, Ill. **21** 40 6N 87 38W
Tilton, N.H. **36** 43 27N 71 36W
Timagami L. **60** 47 0N 80 10W
Timanskiy Kryazh **98** 65 58N 50 5 E
Timaru **128** 44 23S 171 14 E
Timbalier B. **25** 29 3N 90 20W
Timbalier I. **25** 29 3N 90 28W
Timbaúba **74** 7 31S 35 19W
Timbedgha **120** 16 17N 8 16W
Timber **44** 45 43N 123 18W
Timber Lake **47** 45 26N 101 5W
Timberlake **40** 36 17N 78 57W
Timbío **70** 2 20N 76 40W
Timbiqui **70** 2 46N 77 42W
Timbo **13** 35 52N 92 19W
Timbuktu = Tombouctou **120** 16 50N 3 0W
Timimoun **120** 29 14N 0 16 E
Timişoara **89** 45 43N 21 15 E
Timken **24** 38 29N 99 11W
Timmins **60** 48 28N 81 25W
Timmonsville **46** 34 8N 79 57W
Timnath **16** 40 32N 104 59W
Timok → **95** 44 10N 22 40 E
Timon **74** 5 8S 42 52W
Timor **111** 9 0S 125 0 E
Timor □ **111** 9 0S 125 0 E
Timor Sea **127** 10 0S 127 0 E
Timpas **16** 37 49N 103 46W
Timpson **51** 31 54N 94 24W
Tims Ford L. **48** 35 15N 86 10W
Tin Mt. **15** 36 50N 117 10W
Tina **32** 39 32N 93 27W
Tinaca Pt. **111** 5 30N 125 25 E
Tinaco **70** 9 42N 68 26W
Tinaquillo **70** 9 55N 68 18W
Tindall **32** 40 10N 93 36W
Tindouf **120** 27 42N 8 10W
Tinemaha Reservoir **15** 37 3N 118 13W
Tingley **23** 40 51N 94 12W
Tingo Maria **72** 9 10S 75 54W
Tinharé, I. de **75** 13 30S 38 58W
Tinjoub **120** 29 45N 5 40W
Tinmouth **36** 43 26N 73 4W
Tinnevelly = Tirunelveli **108** 8 45N 77 45 E
Tinnoset **97** 59 55N 9 3 E
Tinogasta **76** 28 5S 67 32W
Tínos **95** 37 33N 25 8 E
Tinsley **31** 32 44N 90 28W
Tinsman **13** 33 38N 92 21W
Tinta **72** 14 3S 71 20W
Tintah **30** 46 1N 96 19W
Tintina **76** 27 2S 62 45W
Tioga, N. Dak. **41** 48 24N 102 56W
Tioga, Pa. **45** 41 55N 77 8W
Tioga, Tex. **51** 33 28N 96 55W
Tioga, W. Va. **54** 38 25N 80 40W
Tioga County ◇, N.Y. **39** 42 10N 76 20W
Tioga County ◇, Pa. **45** 41 50N 77 10W
Tioga Pass **14** 37 54N 119 15W
Tioman, Pulau **112** 2 50N 104 10 E
Tionesta **45** 41 30N 79 28W
Tipongpani **109** 27 20N 95 55 E
Tipp City **42** 39 58N 84 11W
Tippah County ◇ **31** 34 44N 88 57W
Tippecanoe County ◇ **22** 40 25N 86 55W
Tipperary **85** 52 28N 8 10W
Tipperary □ **85** 52 37N 7 55W
Tipton, U.K. **83** 52 32N 2 4W
Tipton, Calif. **15** 36 4N 119 19W
Tipton, Ind. **22** 40 17N 86 2W
Tipton, Iowa **23** 41 46N 91 8W
Tipton, Kans. **24** 39 21N 98 28W
Tipton, Mo. **32** 38 39N 92 47W
Tipton, Okla. **43** 34 30N 99 8W
Tipton County ◇, Ind. **22** 40 20N 86 5W
Tipton County ◇, Tenn. **48** 35 29N 89 43W
Tipton Mt. **12** 35 32N 114 12W
Tiptonville **48** 36 23N 89 29W
Tiquié → **70** 0 5N 68 25W
Tiracambu, Serra do **74** 3 15S 46 30W
Tīrān **107** 32 45N 51 8 E
Tirana **95** 41 18N 19 49 E
Tiraspol **99** 46 55N 29 35 E
Tirat Karmel **104** 32 46N 34 58 E
Tirat Yehuda **104** 32 1N 34 56 E
Tirat Ẓevi **104** 32 26N 35 31 E
Tire **106** 38 5N 27 50 E
Tirebolu **106** 40 58N 38 45 E
Tiree **84** 56 31N 6 55W
Tîrgovişte **89** 44 55N 25 27 E
Tîrgu-Jiu **89** 45 5N 23 19 E
Tîrgu Mureş **89** 46 31N 24 38 E
Tîrgu Ocna **95** 46 16N 26 39 E
Tîrgu Secuiesc **95** 46 0N 26 10 E
Tirich Mir **107** 36 15N 71 55 E
Tiririca, Serra da **75** 17 6S 47 6W
Tîrnava Mare → **95** 46 15N 24 30 E
Tîrnava Mică → **95** 46 17N 24 30 E
Tîrnăveni **95** 46 19N 24 13 E
Tirodi **108** 21 40N 79 44 E
Tirol □ **88** 47 3N 10 43 E
Tiros **75** 19 0S 45 58W
Tirso → **94** 39 52N 8 33 E
Tiruchchirappalli **108** 10 45N 78 45 E
Tirunelveli **108** 8 45N 77 45 E
Tirupati **108** 13 39N 79 25 E
Tiruvannamalai **108** 12 15N 79 5 E
Tisa → **89** 45 15N 20 17 E
Tisdale **63** 52 50N 104 0W
Tishomingo, Miss. **31** 34 38N 88 14W
Tishomingo, Okla. **43** 34 14N 96 41W
Tishomingo County ◇ **31** 34 49N 88 12W
Tiskilwa **21** 41 18N 89 30W
Tit-Ary **101** 71 55N 127 2 E
Titicaca, L. **72** 15 30S 69 30W
Titograd **95** 42 30N 19 19 E
Titonka **23** 43 14N 94 3W
Titov Veles **95** 41 46N 21 47 E
Titovo Užice **95** 43 55N 19 50 E
Tittabawassee → **29** 43 23N 83 59W
Titule **122** 3 15N 25 31 E
Titumate **70** 8 19N 77 5W
Titus County ◇ **51** 33 9N 94 58W
Titusville, Fla. **17** 28 37N 80 49W
Titusville, Pa. **45** 41 38N 79 41W
Tivaouane **120** 14 56N 16 45W
Tiverton, U.K. **83** 50 54N 3 30W
Tiverton, U.S.A. **28** 41 38N 71 12W
Tívoli, Italy **94** 41 58N 12 45 E
Tivoli, U.S.A. **51** 28 27N 96 53W
Tīwī **107** 22 45N 59 12 E
Tizi-Ouzou **120** 36 42N 4 3 E
Tizimín **65** 21 0N 88 1W
Tiznados → **70** 8 16N 67 47W
Tiznit **120** 29 48N 9 45W
Tjeggelvas **96** 66 37N 17 45 E
Tjirebon = Cirebon **111** 6 45S 108 32 E
Tlacolula **65** 16 57N 96 23W
Tlacotalpan **65** 18 37N 95 40W
Tlahualilo **64** 26 20N 103 30W
Tlaquepaque **64** 20 39N 103 19W
Tlaxcala **65** 19 20N 98 14W
Tlaxcala □ **65** 19 30N 98 20W
Tlaxiaco **65** 17 18N 97 40W
Tlell **62** 53 34N 131 56W
Tlemcen **120** 34 52N 1 21W
Tmassah **121** 26 19N 15 51 E
Toa Alta **57** 18 23N 66 15W
Toa Baja **57** 18 27N 66 15W
Toad → **62** 59 25N 124 57W
Toamasina **123** 18 10S 49 25 E
Toana Range **35** 40 50N 114 20W
Toano **54** 37 23N 76 48W
Toast **40** 36 30N 80 38W
Toay **76** 36 43S 64 38W
Toba **117** 34 30N 136 51 E
Toba Kakar **108** 31 30N 69 0 E
Tobago **67** 11 10N 60 30W
Tobelo **111** 1 45N 127 56 E
Tobermory, Canada **60** 45 12N 81 40W
Tobermory, U.K. **84** 56 37N 6 4W
Tobias **34** 40 25N 97 20W
Tobin L. **63** 53 35N 103 30W
Tobin Range **35** 40 20N 117 30W
Toboali **110** 3 0S 106 25 E
Tobol **100** 52 40N 62 39 E
Toboli **111** 0 38S 120 5 E
Tobolsk **100** 58 15N 68 10 E
Tobruk = Tubruq **121** 32 7N 23 55 E
Tobyhanna **45** 41 11N 75 25W
Tocache Nuevo **72** 8 9S 76 26W
Tocantínia **74** 9 33S 48 22W
Tocantinópolis **74** 6 20S 47 25W
Tocantins → **74** 1 45S 49 10W
Toccoa **18** 34 35N 83 19W
Toccopola **31** 34 15N 89 14W
Tochigi **117** 36 25N 139 45 E
Tochigi □ **117** 36 45N 139 45 E
Tocopilla **76** 22 5S 70 10W
Tocuyo → **70** 11 3N 68 23W
Tocuyo de la Costa **70** 11 2N 68 23W
Todd County ◇, Ky. **48** 36 50N 87 10W
Todd County ◇, Minn. **30** 46 10N 94 50W
Todd County ◇, S. Dak. **47** 43 5N 101 0W
Toddville **27** 38 18N 76 4W
Todeli **111** 1 38S 124 34 E
Todenyang **122** 4 35N 35 56 E
Todos os Santos, Baía de **75** 12 48S 38 38W
Todos Santos **64** 23 27N 110 13W
Tofield **62** 53 25N 112 40W
Tofino **62** 49 11N 125 55W
Tofte **30** 47 35N 90 50W
Tofua **128** 19 45S 175 5W
Tōgane **117** 35 33N 140 22 E
Togba **120** 17 26N 10 12W
Togiak **11** 59 4N 160 24W
Togian, Kepulauan **111** 0 20S 121 50 E
Togliatti **98** 53 32N 49 24 E
Togo ■ **120** 6 15N 1 35 E
Togowatee Pass **56** 43 45N 110 4W
Togtoh **114** 40 15N 111 10 E
Tohatchi **38** 35 52N 108 47W
Tōhoku □ **116** 39 50N 141 45 E
Tohopekaliga L. **17** 28 12N 81 24W
Toinya **121** 6 17N 29 46 E
Toiyabe National Forest **35** 38 40N 117 0W
Toiyabe Range **35** 39 30N 117 0W
Tojo, Indonesia **111** 1 20S 121 15 E
Tōjō, Japan **117** 34 53N 133 16 E
Tok **11** 63 20N 142 59W
Toka **71** 3 58N 59 17W
Tokachi-Dake **116** 43 17N 142 5 E
Tokachi-Gawa → **116** 42 44N 143 42 E
Tokaj **89** 48 8N 21 27 E
Tokala **111** 1 30S 121 40 E
Tōkamachi **117** 37 8N 138 43 E
Tokanui **128** 46 34S 168 56 E
Tokar **121** 18 27N 37 56 E
Tokara-Rettō **117** 29 37N 129 43 E
Tokarahi **128** 44 56S 170 39 E
Tokashiki-Shima **117** 26 11N 127 21 E
Tokat **106** 40 22N 36 35 E
Tokeland **53** 46 42N 123 59W
Tokelau Is. **124** 9 0S 171 45W
Tokmak **100** 42 49N 75 15 E
Tokong **112** 5 27N 100 23 E
Tokoro-Gawa → **116** 44 7N 144 5 E
Toksook Bay **11** 60 32N 165 0W
Tokuno-Shima **117** 27 56N 128 55 E
Tokushima **117** 34 4N 134 34 E
Tokushima □ **117** 34 15N 134 0 E
Tokuyama **117** 34 3N 131 50 E
Tōkyō **117** 35 45N 139 45 E
Tolbert **51** 34 13N 99 24W
Tolbukhin **95** 43 37N 27 49 E
Tolchester Beach **27** 39 13N 76 14W
Toledo, Spain **91** 39 50N 4 2W
Toledo, Ill. **21** 39 16N 88 15W
Toledo, Iowa **23** 42 0N 92 35W
Toledo, Ohio **42** 41 39N 83 33W
Toledo, Oreg. **44** 44 37N 123 56W
Toledo, Wash. **53** 46 26N 122 51W
Toledo, Montes de **91** 39 33N 4 20W
Toledo Bend Reservoir **25** 31 11N 93 34W
Tolga **120** 34 40N 5 22 E
Toliara **123** 23 21S 43 40 E
Tolima □ **70** 3 45N 75 15W
Tolima, Vol. **70** 4 40N 75 19W
Tolitoli **111** 1 5N 120 50 E
Tolland **28** 41 52N 72 22W
Tolland County ◇ **28** 41 45N 72 20W
Tolleson **12** 33 27N 112 16W
Tolley **41** 48 44N 101 50W
Tolna **41** 47 50N 98 26W
Tolo **122** 2 55S 18 34 E
Tolo, Teluk **111** 2 20S 122 10 E
Tolono **21** 39 59N 88 16W
Tolosa **91** 43 8N 2 5W
Toltén **78** 39 13S 74 14W
Tolu **48** 37 26N 88 15W
Toluca **65** 19 20N 99 40W
Tom **43** 33 44N 94 35W
Tom Green County ◇ **50** 31 28N 100 26W
Tom Price **126** 22 40S 117 48 E
Tom Steed Res. **43** 34 46N 98 50W
Tomah **55** 43 59N 90 30W
Tomahawk **55** 45 28N 89 44W
Tomakomai **116** 42 38N 141 36 E
Tomales Pt. **14** 38 14N 122 59W
Tomar **91** 39 36N 8 25W
Tomás Barrón **72** 17 35S 67 31W
Tomaszów Mazowiecki **89** 51 30N 19 57 E
Tomatlán **64** 19 56N 105 15W
Tombador, Serra do **73** 12 0S 58 0W
Tomball **51** 30 6N 95 37W
Tombé **121** 5 53N 31 40 E
Tombigbee → **10** 31 8N 87 57W
Tombigee National Forest **31** 33 10N 89 0W

Tombouctou Trinity

Tombouctou 120 16 50N 3 0W
Tombstone 12 31 43N 110 4W
Tombua 123 15 55S 11 55E
Tomé, Chile 76 36 36S 72 57W
Tome, U.S.A. 38 34 44N 106 44W
Tomé-Açu 74 2 25S 48 9W
Tomelloso 91 39 10N 3 2W
Tomichi → 16 38 31N 106 58W
Tomini 111 0 30N 120 30E
Tomini, Teluk 111 0 10S 122 0E
Tommot 101 59 4N 126 20E
Tomnavoulin 84 57 19N 3 18W
Tomo 70 2 38N 67 32W
Tomo → 70 5 20N 67 48W
Tomorrit 95 40 40N 20 30E
Tompkins County ◇ 39 42 30N 76 30W
Tompkinsville, Ky. 49 36 42N 85 41W
Tompkinsville, Md. 27 38 18N 76 54W
Toms → 37 39 57N 74 7W
Toms Brook 54 38 57N 78 26W
Toms River 37 39 58N 74 12W
Tomsk 100 56 30N 85 5E
Tonalá 65 16 8N 93 41W
Tonalea 12 36 19N 110 56W
Tonantins 70 2 45S 67 45W
Tonasket 53 48 42N 119 26W
Tonate 71 5 0N 52 28W
Tonawanda 39 43 1N 78 53W
Tonawanda Indian Reservation 39 43 5N 78 25W
Tonbridge 83 51 12N 0 18E
Tondano 111 1 35N 124 54E
Tonekābon 107 36 45N 51 12E
Tong Xian 114 39 55N 116 35E
Tonga ■ 128 19 50S 174 30W
Tonga Trench 124 18 0S 175 0W
Tonganoxie 24 39 7N 95 5W
Tongareva 125 9 0S 158 0W
Tongass National Forest 11 56 30N 134 0W
Tongatapu 128 21 10S 174 0W
Tongcheng 115 31 4N 116 56E
Tongchuan 115 35 6N 109 3E
Tongdao 115 26 10N 109 42E
Tongeren 87 50 47N 5 28E
Tongguan 115 34 40N 110 25E
Tonghua 114 41 42N 125 58E
Tongjiang, Heilongjiang, China 114 47 40N 132 27E
Tongjiang, Sichuan, China 115 31 58N 107 11E
Tongking, G. of 112 20 0N 108 0E
Tongliao 114 43 38N 122 18E
Tongling 115 30 55N 117 48E
Tonglu 115 29 45N 119 37E
Tongnan 115 30 9N 105 50E
Tongoy 76 30 16S 71 31W
Tongren 115 27 43N 109 11E
Tongres = Tongeren 87 50 47N 5 28E
Tongsa Dzong 109 27 31N 90 31E
Tongue 84 58 29N 4 25W
Tongue → 33 46 25N 105 52W
Tongue River Reservoir 33 45 8N 106 46W
Tongyu 114 44 45N 123 4E
Tongzi 115 28 9N 106 49E
Tonica 21 41 13N 89 4W
Tonk 108 26 6N 75 54E
Tonkawa 43 36 41N 97 18W
Tonkin = Bac Phan 112 22 0N 105 0E
Tonlé Sap 112 13 0N 104 0E
Tono 116 39 19N 141 32E
Tonopah, Ariz. 12 33 30N 112 56W
Tonopah, Nev. 35 38 4N 117 14W
Tonosí 66 7 20N 80 20W
Tønsberg 97 59 19N 10 25E
Tonsina 11 61 39N 145 11W
Tontitown 13 36 11N 94 14W
Tonto National Forest 12 34 0N 111 20W
Tooele 52 40 32N 112 18W
Tooele County ◇ 52 40 25N 113 0W
Toole County ◇ 33 48 48N 111 50W
Toombs County ◇ 18 32 10N 82 15W
Toomsboro 18 32 50N 83 5W
Toone 48 35 21N 88 57W
Toora-Khem 101 52 28N 96 17E
Toowoomba 127 27 32S 151 56E
Top 108 34 15N 68 35E
Top-ozero 98 65 35N 32 0E
Topalu 95 44 31N 28 3E
Topawa 12 31 48N 111 51W
Topaz L. 35 38 41N 119 33W
Topeka, Ind. 22 41 32N 85 32W
Topeka, Kans. 24 39 3N 95 40W
Topki 100 55 20N 85 35E
Topley 62 54 49N 126 18W
Topocalma, Pta. 76 34 10S 72 2W
Topolnitsa → 95 42 11N 24 18E
Topolobampo 64 25 40N 109 4W
Topolovgrad 95 42 5N 26 20E
Toponas 16 40 4N 106 48W
Toppenish 53 46 23N 120 19W
Topsail Beach 40 34 23N 77 37W
Topsfield, Maine 26 45 25N 67 44W
Topsfield, Mass. 28 42 38N 70 57W
Topton, N.C. 40 35 15N 83 42W
Topton, Pa. 45 40 30N 75 42W
Toquepala 72 17 24S 70 25W
Toquerville 52 37 15N 113 17W
Toquima Range 35 38 55N 116 50W
Tor Bay 126 35 5S 117 50E
Toraka Vestale 123 16 20S 43 58E
Torata 72 17 23S 70 1W
Torbat-e Heydārīyeh 107 35 15N 59 12E
Torbat-e Jām 107 35 16N 60 35E
Torbay, Canada 61 47 40N 52 42W
Torbay, U.K. 83 50 26N 3 31W
Torch L. 29 44 58N 85 18W
Tordesillas 91 41 30N 5 0W
Torey 101 50 33N 104 50E
Torfajökull 96 63 54N 19 0W
Torgau 88 51 32N 13 0E
Torhout 87 51 5N 3 7E
Tori-Shima 117 30 29N 140 19E
Torin 64 27 33N 110 15W
Torino 94 45 4N 7 40E
Torit 121 4 27N 32 31E
Tormentine 61 46 6N 63 46W
Tormes → 91 41 18N 6 29W
Tornado Mt. 62 49 55N 114 40W
Torne älv → 96 65 50N 24 12E
Torneå = Tornio 96 65 50N 24 12E
Torneträsk 96 68 24N 19 15E
Tornillo 50 31 27N 106 5W
Tornio 96 65 50N 24 12E
Tornionjoki → 96 65 50N 24 12E
Tornquist 76 38 8S 62 15W
Toro 25 31 17N 93 33W
Toro, Cerro del 76 29 10S 69 50W
Toroníos Kólpos 95 40 5N 23 30E
Toronto, Canada 60 43 39N 79 20W
Toronto, Iowa 23 41 54N 90 52W
Toronto, Kans. 24 37 48N 95 57W
Toronto, Ohio 42 40 28N 80 36W
Toronto, S. Dak. 47 44 34N 96 39W
Toronto, L. 64 27 40N 105 30W
Toronto Lake 24 37 46N 95 57W
Toropets 98 56 30N 31 40E
Tororo 122 0 45N 34 12E
Toros Daglari 106 37 0N 35 0E
Torotoro 73 18 7S 65 46W
Torquay, Canada 63 49 9N 103 30W
Torquay, U.K. 83 50 27N 3 31W
Torrance 15 33 50N 118 19W
Torrance County ◇ 38 34 40N 106 0W
Torre Annunziata 94 40 45N 14 26E
Tôrre de Moncorvo 91 41 12N 7 8W
Torrelavega 91 43 20N 4 5W
Torremolinos 91 36 38N 4 30W
Torrens, L. 127 31 0S 137 50E
Torréon 64 25 33N 103 25W
Torres 64 28 46N 110 47W
Torres Strait 127 9 50S 142 20E
Torres Vedras 91 39 5N 9 15W
Torrevieja 91 37 59N 0 42W
Torrey 52 38 18N 111 25W
Torridge → 83 50 51N 4 10W
Torridon, L. 84 57 35N 5 50W
Torrington, Conn. 28 41 48N 73 7W
Torrington, Wyo. 56 42 4N 104 11W
Tortilla Flat 12 33 32N 111 23W
Tortosa 91 40 49N 0 31E
Tortosa, C. 91 40 41N 0 52E
Tortue, Î. de la 67 20 5N 72 57W
Tortuga, La 71 11 0N 65 22W
Tortuguero, L. 57 18 28N 66 26W
Ţorūd 107 35 25N 55 5E
Toruń 89 53 0N 18 39E
Tory I. 85 55 17N 8 12W
Tosa 117 33 24N 133 23E
Tosa-Shimizu 117 32 52N 132 58E
Tosa-Wan 117 33 15N 133 30E
Toscana 94 43 30N 11 5E
Tostado 76 29 15S 61 50W
Toston 33 46 11N 111 26W
Tosu 117 33 22N 130 31E
Tosya 106 41 1N 34 2E
Toteng 123 20 22S 22 58E
Totma 98 60 0N 42 40E
Totnes 83 50 26N 3 41W
Totness 71 5 53N 56 19W
Totonicapán 66 14 58N 91 12W
Totora 73 17 42S 65 9W
Totten Glacier 5 66 45S 116 10E
Tottori 117 35 30N 134 15E
Tottori □ 117 35 30N 134 12E
Touba 120 8 22N 7 40W
Toubkal, Djebel 120 31 0N 8 0W
Tougan 120 13 11N 2 58W
Touggourt 120 33 6N 6 4E
Toughy 34 41 8N 96 50W
Tougué 120 11 25N 11 50W
Toul 90 48 40N 5 53E
Toulepleu 120 6 32N 8 24W
Toulon, France 90 43 10N 5 55E
Toulon, U.S.A. 21 41 6N 89 52W
Toulouse 90 43 37N 1 27E
Toummo 121 22 45N 14 8E
Toungoo 109 19 0N 96 30E
Touraine 90 47 20N 0 30E
Tourane = Da Nang 112 16 4N 108 13E
Tourcoing 90 50 42N 3 10E
Tournai 87 50 35N 3 25E
Tournon 90 45 4N 4 50E
Touros 74 5 12S 35 28W
Tours 90 47 22N 0 40E
Tovar 70 8 20N 71 46W
Towada 116 40 37N 141 13E
Towada-Ko 116 40 28N 140 55E
Towanda, Kans. 24 37 44N 97 0W
Towanda, Pa. 45 41 46N 76 27W
Towang 109 27 37N 91 50E
Towaoc 16 37 12N 108 44W
Tower 30 47 48N 92 17W
Tower City, N. Dak. 41 46 56N 97 40W
Tower City, Pa. 45 40 35N 76 33W
Tower Hill 21 39 23N 88 58W
Towner, Colo. 16 38 28N 102 5W
Towner, N. Dak. 41 48 21N 100 25W
Towner County ◇ 41 48 45N 99 10W
Towns 18 32 0N 82 45W
Towns County ◇ 18 34 55N 83 45W
Townsend, Del. 27 39 24N 75 41W
Townsend, Ga. 18 31 33N 81 31W
Townsend, Mass. 28 42 40N 71 42W
Townsend, Mont. 33 46 19N 111 31W
Townshend 36 43 3N 72 41W
Townshend, C. 127 22 18S 150 30E
Townshend I. 127 22 10S 150 31E
Townsville, Australia 127 19 15S 146 45E
Townsville, U.S.A. 40 36 30N 78 25W
Townville 45 41 41N 79 53W
Towson 27 39 24N 76 36W
Towyn 83 52 36N 4 5W
Toxey 10 31 55N 88 19W
Toya-Ko 116 42 35N 140 51E
Toyah 50 31 19N 103 48W
Toyah Cr. → 50 31 18N 103 27W
Toyah L. 50 31 15N 103 20W
Toyahvale 50 30 57N 103 47W
Toyama 117 36 40N 137 15E
Toyama □ 117 36 45N 137 30E
Toyama-Wan 117 37 0N 137 30E
Toyohashi 117 34 45N 137 25E
Toyokawa 117 34 48N 137 27E
Toyonaka 117 34 50N 135 28E
Toyooka 117 35 35N 134 48E
Toyota 117 35 3N 137 7E
Tozeur 120 33 56N 8 8E
Trabzon 106 41 0N 39 45E
Tracadie 61 47 30N 64 55W
Tracy, Calif. 14 37 44N 121 26W
Tracy, Minn. 30 44 14N 95 37W
Tracy City 49 35 16N 85 44W
Tradewater → 48 37 31N 88 3W
Tradovoye 116 43 17N 132 5E
Traer 23 42 12N 92 28W
Trafalgar 22 39 25N 86 9W
Trafalgar, C. 91 36 10N 6 2W
Traian 95 45 2N 28 15E
Traiguén 78 38 15S 72 41W
Trail, Canada 62 49 5N 117 40W
Trail, U.S.A. 30 47 47N 95 42W
Traill County ◇ 41 47 30N 97 20W
Trainor L. 62 60 24N 120 17W
Traíra → 70 1 4S 69 26W
Tralee 85 52 16N 9 42W
Tralee B. 85 52 17N 9 55W
Trammel 54 37 1N 82 18W
Tramore 85 52 10N 7 10W
Tramway 40 35 27N 79 13W
Tran Ninh, Cao Nguyen 112 19 30N 103 10E
Tranås 97 58 3N 14 59E
Trancas 76 26 11S 65 20W
Trang 112 7 33N 99 38E
Trangan 111 6 40S 134 20E
Trani 94 41 17N 16 24E
Tranqueras 77 31 13S 55 45W
Tranquillity 15 36 39N 120 15W
Transantarctic Mts. 5 85 0S 170 0W
Transcona 63 49 55N 97 0W
Transilvania 89 46 19N 25 0E
Transkei 123 32 15S 28 15E
Transvaal □ 123 25 0S 29 0E
Transylvania = Transilvania 89 46 19N 25 0E
Transylvania 25 32 41N 91 11W
Transylvania County ◇ 40 35 10N 82 50W
Transylvanian Alps 95 45 30N 25 0E
Trápani 94 38 1N 12 30E
Trappe 27 38 40N 76 4W
Trapper Pk. 33 45 54N 114 18W
Traralgon 127 38 12S 146 34E
Tras os Montes e Alto Douro □ 91 41 25N 7 20W
Trăscău, Munţii 95 46 14N 23 14E
Trasimeno, L. 94 43 10N 12 5E
Trask Mt. 44 45 22N 123 27W
Traskwood 13 34 27N 92 39W
Trat 112 12 14N 102 33E
Travelers Rest 46 34 58N 82 27W
Travers, Mt. 128 42 1S 172 45E
Traversay Is. 5 57 0S 28 0W
Traverse, L. 47 45 46N 96 38W
Traverse City 29 44 46N 85 38W
Traverse County ◇ 30 45 45N 96 25W
Traverse Pt. 29 47 9N 88 14W
Travis, L. 51 30 24N 97 55W
Travis County ◇ 51 30 17N 97 45W
Travnik 95 44 17N 17 39E
Treasure County ◇ 33 46 15N 107 20W
Treasure Island 17 27 46N 82 46W
Trébbia → 94 45 4N 9 41E
Trebinje 95 42 44N 18 22E
Třeboň 88 48 59N 14 48E
Tredegar 83 51 47N 3 16W
Treece 24 37 0N 94 51W
Tregaron 83 52 14N 3 56W
Trego 33 48 42N 114 52W
Trego County ◇ 24 38 55N 99 50W
Tréguier 90 48 47N 3 16W
Treherne 63 49 38N 98 42W
Treinta y Tres 77 33 16S 54 17W
Trelew 78 43 10S 65 20W
Trelleborg 97 55 20N 13 10E
Tremont, Ill. 21 40 28N 89 29W
Tremont, Miss. 31 34 14N 88 16W
Tremonton 52 41 43N 112 10W
Tremp 91 42 10N 0 52E
Trempealeau 55 44 0N 91 26W
Trempealeau County ◇ 55 44 15N 91 20W
Trenche → 60 47 46N 72 53W
Trenggalek 111 8 5S 111 38E
Trenque Lauquen 76 36 5S 62 45W
Trent 47 43 54N 96 39W
Trent →, U.K. 82 53 33N 0 44W
Trent →, U.S.A. 40 35 5N 77 2W
Trentino-Alto Adige □ 94 46 30N 11 0E
Trento 94 46 5N 11 8E
Trenton, Canada 60 44 10N 77 34W
Trenton, Fla. 17 29 37N 82 49W
Trenton, Ga. 18 34 52N 85 31W
Trenton, Ill. 21 38 36N 89 41W
Trenton, Ky. 48 36 43N 87 16W
Trenton, Maine 26 44 27N 68 22W
Trenton, Mich. 29 42 8N 83 11W
Trenton, Mo. 32 40 5N 93 37W
Trenton, N.C. 40 35 4N 77 21W
Trenton, N. Dak. 41 48 4N 103 51W
Trenton, N.J. 37 40 14N 74 46W
Trenton, Nebr. 34 40 11N 101 1W
Trenton, Ohio 42 39 29N 84 28W
Trenton, S.C. 46 33 45N 81 51W
Trenton, Tenn. 48 35 59N 88 56W
Trepassey 61 46 43N 53 25W
Tréport, Le 90 50 3N 1 20E
Tres Arroyos 76 38 26S 60 20W
Três Corações 75 21 44S 45 15W
Três Lagoas 75 20 50S 51 43W
Tres Lagos → 78 49 35S 71 25W
Tres Marías 64 21 25N 106 28W
Três Marias, Reprêsa 75 18 12S 45 15W
Tres Montes, C. 78 46 50S 75 30W
Tres Palacios B. 51 28 30N 96 25W
Tres Piedras 38 36 39N 105 58W
Tres Pinos 14 36 48N 121 19W
Três Pontas 75 21 23S 45 29W
Tres Puentes 76 27 50S 70 15W
Tres Puntas, C. 78 47 0S 66 0W
Três Rios 75 22 6S 43 15W
Tres Valles 65 18 15N 96 8W
Treungen 97 59 1N 8 31E
Treutlen County ◇ 18 32 25N 82 30W
Treviso 94 45 40N 12 15E
Trevorton 45 40 47N 76 41W
Treynor 23 41 14N 95 36W
Trezevant 48 36 1N 88 37W
Triangle 54 38 33N 77 20W
Tribbey 43 35 7N 97 4W
Tribly 17 28 28N 82 12W
Tribulation, C. 127 16 5S 145 29E
Tribune 24 38 28N 101 45W
Trichinopoly = Tiruchchirappalli 108 10 45N 78 45E
Trichur 108 10 30N 76 18E
Trident 33 45 57N 111 28W
Trident Peak 35 41 54N 118 25W
Trier 88 49 45N 6 37E
Trieste 94 45 39N 13 45E
Trigg County ◇ 48 36 50N 87 55W
Triglav 94 46 21N 13 50E
Trigo Mountains 12 33 15N 114 40W
Tríkkala 95 39 34N 21 47E
Trikora, Puncak 111 4 15S 138 45E
Trim 85 53 34N 6 48W
Trimble, Mo. 32 39 28N 94 34W
Trimble, Tenn. 48 36 12N 89 11W
Trimble County 49 38 35N 85 20W
Trimont 30 43 46N 94 43W
Trinchera 16 37 2N 104 3W
Trincomalee 108 8 38N 81 15E
Trindade 75 16 40S 49 30W
Trindade, I. 2 20 20S 29 50W
Trinidad, Bolivia 73 14 46S 64 50W
Trinidad, Colombia 70 5 25N 71 40W
Trinidad, Cuba 66 21 48N 80 0W
Trinidad, Uruguay 76 33 30S 56 50W
Trinidad, Calif. 14 41 4N 124 9W
Trinidad, Colo. 16 37 10N 104 31W
Trinidad, Tex. 51 32 9N 96 6W
Trinidad, W. Indies 67 10 30N 61 15W
Trinidad → 65 17 49N 95 9W
Trinidad, G. 78 49 55S 75 25W
Trinidad, I. 78 39 10S 62 0W
Trinidad & Tobago ■ 67 10 30N 61 20W
Trinidad Head 14 41 3N 124 9W
Trinity, Canada 61 48 59N 53 55W
Trinity, U.S.A. 51 30 57N 95 22W

Trinity Tuscumbia

Trinity →, Calif. 14 41 11N 123 42W
Trinity →, Tex. 51 29 45N 94 43W
Trinity B., Australia 127 16 30 S 146 0 E
Trinity B., Canada 61 48 20N 53 10W
Trinity B., U.S.A. 51 29 42N 94 55W
Trinity Center 14 41 0N 122 41W
Trinity County ◇, Calif. 14 40 40N 123 0W
Trinity County ◇, Tex. 51 31 4N 95 8W
Trinity Is. 11 56 33N 154 25W
Trinity Mt. 20 43 36N 115 26W
Trinity Mts. 14 40 50N 122 40W
Trinity National Forest 14 40 40N 123 15W
Trinity Range 35 40 15N 118 45W
Trinkitat 121 18 45N 37 51 E
Trinway 42 40 9N 82 1W
Trion 18 34 33N 85 19W
Triplett 32 39 30N 93 12W
Tripoli = Tarābulus, Lebanon 106 34 31N 35 50 E
Tripoli = Tarābulus, Libya 121 32 49N 13 7 E
Tripoli 23 42 49N 92 16W
Trípolis 95 37 31N 22 25 E
Tripp 47 43 13N 97 58W
Tripp County ◇ 47 43 20N 100 0W
Tripura □ 109 24 0N 92 0 E
Tristan da Cunha 2 37 6 S 12 20W
Triumph 25 29 20N 89 30W
Trivandrum 108 8 41N 77 0 E
Trnava 89 48 23N 17 35 E
Trochu 62 51 50N 113 13W
Trodely I. 60 52 15N 79 26W
Troglav 94 43 56N 16 36 E
Troilus, L. 60 50 50N 74 35W
Trois-Pistoles 61 48 5N 69 10W
Trois-Rivières 60 46 25N 72 34W
Troitsk 100 54 10N 61 35 E
Troitsko Pechorsk 98 62 40N 56 10 E
Trölladyngja 96 64 54N 17 16W
Trollhättan 97 58 17N 12 20 E
Trombetas → 71 1 55 S 55 35W
Troms fylke □ 96 68 56N 19 0 E
Tromsø 96 69 40N 18 56 E
Trona 15 35 46N 117 23W
Tronador 78 41 10 S 71 50W
Trondheim 96 63 36N 10 25 E
Trondheimsfjorden 96 63 35N 10 30 E
Troon 84 55 33N 4 40W
Tropic 52 37 37N 112 5W
Trossachs, The 84 56 14N 4 24W
Trostan 85 55 4N 6 10W
Trotternish 84 57 32N 6 15W
Troup 51 32 9N 95 7W
Troup County ◇ 18 33 0N 85 0W
Trousdale 24 37 49N 99 5W
Trousdale County ◇ 48 36 24N 86 10W
Trout → 62 61 19N 119 51W
Trout Cr. →, Oreg. 44 42 23N 118 3W
Trout Cr. →, Oreg. 44 44 48N 121 3W
Trout Creek, Mich. 29 46 29N 89 1W
Trout Creek, Mont. 33 47 50N 115 36W
Trout Creek, Utah 52 39 42N 113 50W
Trout Dale 54 36 42N 81 26W
Trout L., N.W.T., Canada 62 60 40N 121 40W
Trout L., Ont., Canada 63 51 20N 93 15W
Trout Lake, Mich. 29 46 12N 85 1W
Trout Lake, Wash. 53 46 0N 121 32W
Trout Pk. 56 44 36N 109 32W
Trout River 61 49 29N 58 8W
Troutmans 40 35 42N 80 53W
Troutville 54 37 25N 79 53W
Trouville 90 49 21N 0 5 E
Trowbridge 83 51 18N 2 12W
Troy, Turkey 106 39 57N 26 12 E
Troy, Ala. 10 31 48N 85 58W
Troy, Idaho 20 46 44N 116 46W
Troy, Ind. 22 37 59N 86 55W
Troy, Kans. 24 39 47N 95 5W
Troy, Mich. 29 42 37N 83 9W
Troy, Miss. 31 34 7N 88 53W
Troy, Mo. 32 38 59N 90 59W
Troy, Mont. 33 48 28N 115 53W
Troy, N.C. 40 35 22N 79 53W
Troy, N.H. 36 42 49N 72 11W
Troy, N.Y. 39 42 44N 73 41W
Troy, Ohio 42 40 2N 84 12W
Troy, Oreg. 44 45 57N 117 27W
Troy, Pa. 45 41 47N 76 47W
Troy, S.C. 46 33 59N 82 17W
Troy, S. Dak. 47 45 2N 96 52W
Troy, Tenn. 48 36 20N 89 10W
Troy, Tex. 51 31 12N 97 18W
Troy, Vt. 36 44 52N 72 25W
Troy Peak 35 38 19N 115 30W
Troyan 95 42 57N 24 43 E
Troyes 90 48 19N 4 3 E
Truchas 38 36 3N 105 49W
Truchas Peak 38 35 58N 105 39W
Trucial States = United Arab Emirates ■ 107 23 50N 54 0 E
Truckee 14 39 20N 120 11W
Truckee → 35 39 51N 119 24W
Truesdale 23 42 44N 95 11W
Trufant 29 43 19N 85 21W
Trujillo, Colombia 70 4 10N 76 19W
Trujillo, Hond. 66 16 0N 86 0W
Trujillo, Peru 72 8 6 S 79 0W
Trujillo, Spain 91 39 28N 5 55W
Trujillo, U.S.A. 38 35 32N 104 42W
Trujillo, Venezuela 70 9 22N 70 38W
Trujillo □ 70 9 25N 70 30W
Trujillo Alto 57 18 21N 66 1W
Truk 124 7 25N 151 46 E
Truman 30 43 50N 94 26W
Trumann 13 35 41N 90 31W
Trumansburg 39 42 33N 76 40W
Trumbull, Conn. 28 41 15N 73 12W
Trumbull, Nebr. 34 40 41N 98 16W
Trumbull County ◇ 42 41 14N 80 49W
Trung-Phan 110 16 0N 108 0 E
Truro, Canada 61 45 21N 63 14W
Truro, U.K. 83 50 17N 5 2W
Truro, U.S.A. 28 42 0N 70 3W
Truscott 51 33 45N 99 49W
Trussville 10 33 37N 86 35W
Truth or Consequences 38 33 8N 107 15W
Trutnov 88 50 37N 15 54 E
Truxton 12 35 29N 113 34W
Tryavna 95 42 54N 25 25 E
Tryon, N.C. 40 35 13N 82 14W
Tryon, Nebr. 34 41 33N 100 57W
Tryon, Okla. 43 35 52N 96 58W
Tsala Apopka L. 17 28 53N 82 19W
Tsaratanana 123 16 47 S 47 39 E
Tsarevo = Michurin 95 42 9N 27 51 E
Tsau 123 20 8 S 22 22 E
Tschida L. 41 46 36N 101 49W
Tselinograd 100 51 10N 71 30 E
Tsetserleg 113 47 36N 101 32 E
Tshabong 123 26 2 S 22 29 E
Tshane 123 24 5 S 21 54 E
Tshela 122 4 57 S 13 4 E
Tshikapa 122 6 28 S 20 48 E
Tshofa 122 5 13 S 25 16 E
Tshwane 123 22 24 S 22 1 E
Tsihombe 123 25 10 S 45 41 E
Tsimlyanskoye Vdkhr. 99 48 0N 43 0 E
Tsinan = Jinan 114 36 38N 117 1 E
Tsinghai = Qinghai □ 113 36 0N 98 0 E
Tsingtao = Qingdao 114 36 5N 120 20 E
Tsivory 123 24 4 S 46 5 E
Tskhinvali 99 42 14N 44 1 E
Tsna → 98 54 55N 41 58 E
Tsu 117 34 45N 136 25 E
Tsu L. 62 60 40N 111 52W
Tsuchiura 117 36 5N 140 15 E
Tsugaru-Kaikyō 116 41 35N 141 0 E
Tsumeb 123 19 9 S 17 44 E
Tsumis 123 23 39 S 17 29 E
Tsuruga 117 35 45N 136 2 E
Tsurugi-San 117 33 51N 134 6 E
Tsuruoka 116 38 44N 139 50 E
Tsushima, Gifu, Japan 117 35 10N 136 43 E
Tsushima, Nagasaki, Japan 117 34 20N 129 20 E
Tual 111 5 38 S 132 44 E
Tuam 85 53 30N 8 50W
Tuamotu Arch. 125 17 0 S 144 0W
Tuamotu Ridge 125 20 0 S 138 0W
Tuao 111 17 55N 122 22 E
Tuapse 99 44 5N 39 10 E
Tuatapere 128 46 8 S 167 41 E
Tuba City 12 36 8N 111 14W
Tubac 12 31 37N 111 3W
Tuban 111 6 54 S 112 3 E
Tubarão 77 28 30 S 49 0W
Tūbās 104 32 20N 35 22 E
Tubau 110 3 10N 113 40 E
Tübingen 88 48 31N 9 4 E
Tubruq 121 32 7N 23 55 E
Tubuaeran I. 125 3 51N 159 22W
Tubuai Is. 125 25 0 S 150 0W
Tucacas 70 10 48N 68 19W
Tucano 74 10 58 S 38 48W
Tuchodi → 62 58 17N 123 42W
Tuckahoe 37 39 17N 74 45W
Tuckahoe → 27 38 0N 75 0W
Tucker, Ark. 13 34 26N 91 57W
Tucker, Ga. 18 33 51N 84 13W
Tucker County ◇ 54 39 9N 79 30W
Tuckerman 13 35 44N 91 12W
Tuckernuck Island 28 41 18N 70 15W
Tuckerton 37 39 36N 74 20W
Tucson 12 32 13N 110 58W
Tucumán □ 76 26 48 S 66 2W
Tucumcari 38 35 10N 103 44W
Tucunaré 73 5 18 S 55 51W
Tucupido 70 9 17N 65 47W
Tucupita 71 9 2N 62 3W
Tucuruí 74 3 42 S 49 44W
Tudela 91 42 4N 1 39W
Tudmur 106 34 36N 38 15 E
Tudor, Lac 61 55 50N 65 25W
Tueré → 74 2 48 S 50 59W
Tuftonboro 36 43 42N 71 13W
Tug Fork → 54 38 7N 82 36W
Tugidak I. 11 56 30N 154 40W
Tuguegarao 111 17 35N 121 42 E
Tugur 101 53 44N 136 45 E
Tukangbesi, Kepulauan 111 6 0 S 124 0 E
Tukarak I. 60 56 15N 78 45W
Tūkrah 121 32 30N 20 37 E
Tuktoyaktuk 58 69 27N 133 2W
Tukuyu 122 9 17 S 33 35 E
Tukzar 108 35 55N 66 25 E
Tula, Hidalgo, Mexico 65 20 0N 99 20W
Tula, Tamaulipas, Mexico 65 23 0N 99 40W
Tula, U.S.A. 31 34 14N 89 22W
Tula, U.S.S.R. 98 54 13N 37 38 E
Tulak 107 33 55N 63 40 E
Tulalip Indian Reservation 53 48 4N 122 13W
Tulancingo 65 20 5N 99 22W
Tulare, Calif. 15 36 13N 119 21W
Tulare, S. Dak. 47 44 44N 98 31W
Tulare County ◇ 15 36 10N 118 50W
Tulare Lake Bed 15 36 0N 119 48W
Tularosa 38 33 5N 106 1W
Tularosa Mts. 38 33 45N 108 40W
Tularosa Valley 38 32 45N 106 0W
Tulbagh 123 33 16 S 19 6 E
Tulcán 70 0 48N 77 43W
Tulcea 89 45 13N 28 46 E
Tulcea □ 95 45 0N 29 0 E
Tule → 15 36 3N 119 50W
Tule Cr. → 50 34 40N 101 14W
Tule L. 14 41 53N 121 30W
Tule River Indian Reservation 15 36 0N 118 50W
Tule Valley 52 39 25N 113 30W
Tulelake 14 41 57N 121 29W
Tulemalu L. 63 62 58N 99 25W
Tuli, Indonesia 111 1 24 S 122 26 E
Tuli, Zimbabwe 123 21 58 S 29 13 E
Tulia 50 34 32N 101 46W
Ţülkarm 104 32 19N 35 2 E
Tullahassee 43 35 50N 95 26W
Tullahoma 48 35 22N 86 13W
Tullamore 85 53 17N 7 30W
Tulle 90 45 16N 1 46 E
Tulloch Reservoir 14 37 53N 120 36W
Tullos 25 31 49N 92 19W
Tullow 85 52 48N 6 45W
Tully 39 42 48N 76 7W
Ţulmaythah 121 32 40N 20 55 E
Tulnici 95 45 51N 26 38 E
Tulovo 95 42 33N 25 32 E
Tulsa 43 36 10N 95 55W
Tulsa County ◇ 43 36 0N 95 55W
Tulsequah 62 58 39N 133 35W
Tulua 70 4 6N 76 11W
Tuluksak 11 61 6N 160 58W
Tulun 101 54 32N 100 35 E
Tulungagung 110 8 5 S 111 54 E
Tum 111 3 36 S 130 21 E
Tuma → 66 13 6N 84 35W
Tumaco 70 1 50N 78 45W
Tumaco, Ensenada 70 1 55N 78 45W
Tumatumari 71 5 20N 58 55W
Tumba, L. 122 0 50 S 18 0 E
Tumbaya 76 23 50 S 65 26W
Túmbes 72 3 37 S 80 27W
Tumbes □ 72 3 50 S 80 30W
Tumen 114 43 0N 129 50 E
Tumen Jiang → 114 42 20N 130 35 E
Tumeremo 71 7 18N 61 30W
Tumiritinga 75 18 58 S 41 38W
Tumkur 108 13 18N 77 6 E
Tummel, L. 84 56 43N 3 55W
Tump 107 26 7N 62 16 E
Tumpat 112 6 11N 102 10 E
Tumu 120 10 56N 1 56W
Tumucumaque, Serra 71 2 0N 55 0W
Tumupasa 72 14 9 S 67 55W
Tumut 127 35 16 S 148 13 E
Tumwater 53 47 1N 122 54W
Tunas de Zaza 66 21 39N 79 34W
Tunbridge Wells 83 51 7N 0 16 E
Tunduru 122 11 8 S 37 25 E
Tundzha → 95 41 40N 26 35 E
Tunga Pass 109 29 0N 94 14 E
Tungabhadra → 108 15 57N 78 15 E
Tungaru 121 10 9N 30 52 E
Tungla 66 13 24N 84 21W
Tungnafellsjökull 96 64 45N 17 55W
Tungsten 62 61 57N 128 16W
Tungurahua □ 70 1 15 S 78 35W
Tunguska, Nizhnyaya → 101 65 48N 88 4 E
Tunguska, Podkamennaya → 101 61 36N 90 18 E
Tunia 70 2 41N 76 31W
Tunica, La. 25 30 56N 91 33W
Tunica, Miss. 31 34 41N 90 23W
Tunica County ◇ 31 34 41N 90 23W
Tunis 120 36 50N 10 11 E
Tunis Mills 27 38 49N 76 10W
Tunisia ■ 120 33 30N 9 10 E
Tunja 70 5 33N 73 25W
Tunkhannock 45 41 32N 75 57W
Tunliu 114 36 13N 112 52 E
Tunnell Hill 21 37 32N 88 50W
Tunnelton 54 39 24N 79 45W
Tunnsjøen 96 64 45N 13 25 E
Tuntutuliak 11 60 22N 162 38W
Tununak 11 60 37N 165 15W
Tunungayualok I. 61 56 0N 61 0W
Tunuyán 76 33 35 S 69 0W
Tunuyán → 76 33 33 S 67 30W
Tunxi 115 29 42N 118 25 E
Tuolumne 14 37 58N 120 15W
Tuolumne County ◇ 14 38 0N 120 0W
Tuoy-Khaya 101 62 32N 111 25 E
Tupã 77 21 57 S 50 28W
Tupaciguara 75 18 35 S 48 42W
Tupelo, Miss. 31 34 16N 88 43W
Tupelo, Okla. 43 34 36N 96 26W
Tupik 101 54 26N 119 57 E
Tupinambaranas 71 3 0 S 58 0W
Tupiratiria 74 8 58 S 48 12W
Tupiratins 74 8 23 S 48 8W
Tupiza 76 21 30 S 65 40W
Tupper 62 55 32N 120 1W
Tupper L. 39 44 12N 74 35W
Tupper Lake 39 44 14N 74 28W
Tupungato, Cerro 76 33 15 S 69 50W
Tuquan 114 45 18N 121 38 E
Tuque, La 60 47 30N 72 50W
Túquerres 70 1 5N 77 37W
Tura 101 64 20N 100 17 E
Turabah 106 28 20N 43 15 E
Turagua, Serranía 71 7 20N 64 35W
Tūrān, Iran 107 35 39N 56 42 E
Turan, U.S.S.R. 101 51 55N 95 0 E
Turayf 106 31 41N 38 39 E
Turbeville 46 33 54N 80 1W
Turda 95 46 34N 23 47 E
Turek 89 52 3N 18 30 E
Turen 70 9 17N 69 6W
Turfan = Turpan 113 43 58N 89 10 E
Turfan Depression = Turpan Hami 113 42 40N 89 25 E
Turfan Depression 113 42 45N 89 0 E
Tŭrgovishte 95 43 17N 26 38 E
Turgutlu 106 38 30N 27 48 E
Turhal 106 40 24N 36 5 E
Turia → 91 39 27N 0 19W
Turiaçu 74 1 40 S 45 19W
Turiaçu → 74 1 36 S 45 19W
Turin = Torino 94 45 4N 7 40 E
Turin, Canada 62 49 47N 112 24W
Turin, U.S.A. 23 42 1N 95 58W
Turkana, L. 122 3 30N 36 5 E
Turkestan 100 43 17N 68 16 E
Turkey, Ky. 49 37 29N 83 31W
Turkey, Tex. 50 34 24N 100 54W
Turkey ■ 106 39 0N 36 0 E
Turkey → 23 42 43N 91 2W
Turkey Cr. → 43 35 58N 97 56W
Turkey Creek 25 30 53N 92 25W
Turkey Mt. 50 29 22N 100 12W
Turkey Ridge 47 43 25N 97 25W
Turkmen S.S.R. □ 100 39 0N 59 0 E
Turks Is. 67 21 20N 71 20W
Turks Island Passage 67 21 30N 71 30W
Turku 97 60 30N 22 19 E
Turlock 14 37 30N 120 51W
Turlock L. 14 37 37N 120 35W
Turnagain → 62 59 12N 127 35W
Turnagain, C. 128 40 28 S 176 38 E
Turneffe Is. 65 17 20N 87 50W
Turner, Mich. 29 44 9N 83 47W
Turner, Mont. 33 48 51N 108 24W
Turner, Oreg. 44 44 51N 122 57W
Turner, Wash. 53 46 25N 117 51W
Turner County ◇, Ga. 18 31 45N 83 45W
Turner County ◇, S. Dak. 47 43 17N 97 5W
Turner Valley 62 50 40N 114 17W
Turners Falls 28 42 36N 72 33W
Turnhout 87 51 19N 4 57 E
Turnor L. 63 56 35N 108 35W
Tŭrnovo 95 43 5N 25 41 E
Turnu Măgurele 89 43 46N 24 56 E
Turnu Rosu Pasul 89 45 33N 24 17 E
Turnu-Severin 89 44 39N 22 41 E
Turon 24 37 48N 98 26W
Turpan 113 43 58N 89 10 E
Turpan Hami 113 42 40N 89 25 E
Turpin 43 36 52N 100 52W
Turrell 13 35 23N 90 15W
Turriff 84 57 32N 2 28W
Turtle → 47 44 55N 98 29W
Turtle-Flambeau Flowage 55 46 4N 90 14W
Turtle L. 63 53 36N 108 38W
Turtle Lake, N. Dak. 41 47 31N 100 53W
Turtle Lake, Wis. 55 45 24N 92 8W
Turtle Mountain Indian Reservation 41 48 58N 99 58W
Turtle Mountains 41 48 58N 100 0W
Turtle River 30 47 35N 94 46W
Turtleford 63 53 23N 108 57W
Turukhansk 101 65 21N 88 5 E
Turun ja Porin lääni □ 97 60 27N 22 15 E
Tuscaloosa 10 33 12N 87 34W
Tuscaloosa County ◇ 10 33 11N 87 27W
Tuscany = Toscana 94 43 30N 11 5 E
Tuscarawas 42 40 24N 81 25W
Tuscarawas County ◇ 42 40 22N 81 26W
Tuscarora 35 41 19N 116 14W
Tuscarora Indian Reservation 39 43 10N 78 55W
Tuscarora Mt. 45 40 55N 77 55W
Tuscarora Mts. 35 41 0N 116 20W
Tuscola, Ill. 21 39 48N 88 17W
Tuscola, Tex. 51 32 12N 99 48W
Tuscola County ◇ 29 43 25N 83 20W
Tusculum 49 36 10N 82 46W
Tuscumbia, Ala. 10 34 44N 87 42W
Tuscumbia, Mo. 32 38 14N 92 28W

Tushar Mts. Uralsk

Tushar Mts. 52 38 20N 112 30W
Tushka 43 34 19N 96 10W
Tuskahoma 43 34 37N 95 17W
Tuskar Rock 85 52 12N 6 10W
Tuskegee 10 32 25N 85 42W
Tustin 29 44 6N 85 28W
Tutóia 74 2 45 S 42 20W
Tutong 110 4 47N 114 40 E
Tutova → 95 46 20N 27 30 E
Tutrakan 95 44 2N 26 40 E
Tutshi L. 62 59 56N 134 30W
Tuttle, N. Dak. 41 47 9N 100 0W
Tuttle, Okla. 43 35 17N 97 49W
Tuttle Creek Lake 24 39 15N 96 36W
Tuttlingen 88 47 59N 8 50 E
Tutuala 111 8 25 S 127 15 E
Tutuila 128 14 19 S 170 50W
Tututepec 65 16 9N 97 38W
Tutwiler 31 34 1N 90 26W
Tuva A.S.S.R. □ 101 51 30N 95 0 E
Tuvalu ■ 124 8 0 S 178 0 E
Tuweep 12 36 25N 113 4W
Tuxpan 65 20 58N 97 23W
Tuxtla Gutiérrez 65 16 50N 93 10W
Tuy 91 42 3N 8 39W
Tuy Hoa 112 13 5N 109 10 E
Tuya L. 62 59 7N 130 35W
Tuyen Hoa 112 17 50N 106 10 E
Tuz Gölü 106 38 45N 33 30 E
Ţūz Khurmātū 106 34 56N 44 38 E
Tuzla 95 44 34N 18 41 E
Tvŭrditsa 95 42 42N 25 53 E
Twain Harte 14 38 2N 120 14W
Tweed → 84 55 42N 2 10W
Tweedsmuir Prov. Park 62 53 0N 126 20W
Twentynine Palms 15 34 8N 116 3W
Twiggs County ◇ 18 32 40N 83 30W
Twillingate 61 49 42N 54 45W
Twin Bridges 33 45 33N 112 20W
Twin Brooks 47 45 12N 96 47W
Twin Buttes Reservoir 50 31 22N 100 32W
Twin City 18 32 35N 82 10W
Twin Falls 20 42 34N 114 28W
Twin Falls County ◇ 20 42 30N 114 45W
Twin Hills 11 59 23N 159 58W
Twin Lakes, Colo. 16 39 5N 106 23W
Twin Lakes, Ga. 18 30 43N 83 13W
Twin Lakes, Minn. 30 43 34N 93 25W
Twin Mountain 36 44 16N 71 32W
Twin Mts. 50 30 25N 103 50W
Twin Oaks 43 36 10N 94 51W
Twin Peaks 20 44 35N 114 29W
Twin Rivers 37 40 15N 74 32W
Twin Valley 30 47 16N 96 16W
Twisp 53 48 22N 120 7W
Twitchell Reservoir 15 34 59N 120 19W
Twitty 50 35 19N 100 14W
Two Butte → 16 38 2N 102 9W
Two Buttes 16 37 34N 102 24W
Two Buttes Reservoir 16 37 38N 102 32W
Two Harbors 30 47 2N 91 40W
Two Hills 62 53 43N 111 52W
Two Medicine → 33 48 29N 112 14W
Two Rivers 55 44 9N 87 34W
Twofold B. 127 37 8 S 149 59 E
Ty Ty 18 31 28N 83 39W
Tyaskin 27 38 18N 75 52W
Tye 51 32 27N 99 52W
Tygart L. 54 39 19N 80 2W
Tyger → 46 34 28N 81 26W
Tygh Valley 44 45 15N 121 10W
Tyhee 20 42 57N 112 28W
Tyler, Tex. 51 32 21N 95 18W
Tyler, Wash. 53 47 26N 117 47W
Tyler County ◇, Tex. 51 30 47N 94 25W
Tyler County ◇, W. Va. 54 39 30N 80 54W
Tylertown 31 31 7N 90 9W
Tymochtee → 42 40 57N 83 16W
Tynan 51 28 10N 97 45W
Tynda 101 55 10N 124 43 E
Tyndall 47 43 0N 97 50W
Tyne → 82 54 58N 1 28W
Tyne & Wear □ 82 54 55N 1 35W
Tynemouth 82 55 1N 1 27W
Tyner 40 36 13N 76 37W
Tyonek 11 61 4N 151 8W
Tyonek Indian Reservation 11 61 5N 151 10W
Tyre = Sūr 104 33 19N 35 16 E
Tyrifjorden 97 60 2N 10 8 E
Tyro, Ark. 13 33 50N 91 43W
Tyro, Kans. 24 37 2N 95 49W
Tyro, Miss. 31 34 35N 89 42W
Tyrol = Tirol □ 88 47 3N 10 43 E
Tyrone, N. Mex. 38 32 40N 108 22W
Tyrone, Okla. 43 36 57N 101 4W
Tyrone, Pa. 45 40 40N 78 14W
Tyrrell Arm 63 62 27N 97 30W
Tyrrell County ◇ 40 35 50N 76 10W
Tyrrell L. 63 63 7N 105 27W
Tyrrhenian Sea 94 40 0N 12 30 E
Tysfjorden 96 68 7N 16 25 E
Tyson 36 43 27N 72 44W
Tyulgan 98 52 22N 56 12 E
Tyumen 100 57 11N 65 29 E
Tywi → 83 51 48N 4 20W
Tzaneen 123 23 47 S 30 9 E
Tzukong = Zigong 115 29 15N 104 48 E

U

Uachadi, Sierra 71 4 54N 65 18W
Uainambi 70 1 43N 69 51W
Uarsciek 105 2 28N 45 55 E
Uato-Udo 111 9 7 S 125 36 E
Uatumã → 71 2 26 S 57 37W
Uauá 74 9 50 S 39 28W
Uaupés 70 0 8 S 67 5W
Uaxactún 66 17 25N 89 29W
Ubá 77 21 8 S 43 0W
Ubaitaba 75 14 18 S 39 20W
Ubangi = Oubangi → 122 1 0N 17 50 E
Ubaté 70 5 19N 73 49W
Ubauro 108 28 15N 69 45 E
Ube 117 33 56N 131 15 E
Ubeda 91 38 3N 3 23W
Uberaba 75 19 50 S 47 55W
Uberaba, L. 73 17 30 S 57 50W
Uberlândia 75 19 0 S 48 20W
Ubly 29 43 43N 82 56W
Ubon Ratchathani 112 15 15N 104 50 E
Ubundu 122 0 22 S 25 30 E
Ucayali → 72 4 30 S 73 30W
Uchi Lake 63 51 5N 92 35W
Uchiura-Wan 116 42 25N 140 40 E
Uchiza 72 8 25 S 76 20W
Uchur → 101 58 48N 130 35 E
Ucluelet 62 48 57N 125 32W
Ucon 20 43 36N 111 58W
Uda → 101 54 42N 135 14 E
Udaipur 108 24 36N 73 44 E
Udaipur Garhi 109 27 0N 86 35 E
Udall 24 37 23N 97 7W
Uddevalla 97 58 21N 11 55 E
Uddjaur 96 65 25N 21 15 E
Udell 23 40 47N 92 45W
Udgir 108 18 25N 77 5 E
Udhampur 108 33 0N 75 5 E
Udi 120 6 23N 7 21 E
Údine 94 46 5N 13 10 E
Udmurt A.S.S.R. □ 98 57 30N 52 30 E
Udon Thani 112 17 29N 102 46 E
Udupi 108 13 25N 74 42 E
Udvoy Balkan 95 42 50N 26 50 E
Ueda 117 36 24N 138 16 E
Uedineniya, Os. 4 78 0N 85 0 E
Uehling 34 41 44N 96 30W
Uelen 101 66 10N 170 0W
Uelzen 88 53 0N 10 33 E
Uere → 122 3 45N 24 45 E
Ufa 98 54 45N 55 55 E
Ufa → 98 54 40N 56 0 E
Ugad → 123 20 55 S 14 30 E
Ugalla → 122 5 8 S 30 42 E
Uganda ■ 122 2 0N 32 0 E
Uglegorsk 101 49 5N 142 2 E
Ugolyak 101 64 33N 120 30 E
Ugŭrchin 95 43 6N 24 26 E
Uhrichsville 42 40 24N 81 21W
Uíge 122 7 30 S 14 40 E
Uiju 114 40 15N 124 35 E
Uinta → 52 40 14N 109 51W
Uinta County ◇ 56 41 15N 110 30W
Uinta Mts. 52 40 45N 110 30W
Uinta National Forest 52 40 10N 111 20W
Uintah and Ouray Indian Reservation 52 40 15N 110 20W
Uintah County ◇ 52 40 20N 109 30W
Uitenhage 123 33 40 S 25 28 E
Uithuizen 87 53 24N 6 41 E
Uji-guntō 117 31 15N 129 25 E
Ujjain 108 23 9N 75 43 E
Újpest 89 47 32N 19 6 E
Ujung Pandang 111 5 10 S 119 20 E
Uka 101 57 50N 162 0 E
Uke-Shima 117 28 2N 129 14 E
Ukerewe I. 122 2 0 S 33 0 E
Ukhrul 109 25 10N 94 25 E
Ukhta 98 63 55N 54 0 E
Ukiah, Calif. 14 39 9N 123 13W
Ukiah, Oreg. 44 45 8N 118 56W
Ukrainian S.S.R. □ 99 49 0N 32 0 E
Ulaanbaatar 113 47 55N 106 53 E
Ulaangom 113 50 0N 92 10 E
Ulak I. 11 51 22N 178 57W
Ulan Bator = Ulaanbaatar 113 47 55N 106 53 E
Ulan Ude 101 51 45N 107 40 E
Ulcinj 95 41 58N 19 10 E
Ulen 30 47 5N 96 16W
Ulhasnagar 108 19 15N 73 10 E
Ullapool 84 57 54N 5 10W
Ullin 21 37 17N 89 11W
Ullswater 82 54 35N 2 52W
Ullung-do 114 37 30N 130 30 E
Ulm 88 48 23N 10 0 E
Ulmeni 95 45 4N 26 40 E
Ulonguè 123 14 37 S 34 19 E
Ulricehamn 97 57 46N 13 26 E
Ulster □ 85 54 35N 6 30W
Ulster County ◇ 39 41 50N 74 15W
Ulstrem 95 42 1N 26 27 E
Ulungur He → 113 47 1N 87 24 E
Ulupalakua 19 20 39N 156 24W
Ulutau 100 48 39N 67 1 E
Ulverston 82 54 13N 3 7W
Ulverstone 127 41 11 S 146 11 E
Ulya 101 59 10N 142 0 E
Ulyanovsk 98 54 20N 48 25 E
Ulyasutay 113 47 56N 97 28 E
Ulysses, Kans. 24 37 35N 101 22W
Ulysses, Nebr. 34 41 4N 97 12W
Ulysses, Pa. 45 41 54N 77 46W
Umala 72 17 25 S 68 5W
Uman 99 48 40N 30 12 E
Umaria 109 23 35N 80 50 E
Umarkot 108 25 15N 69 40 E
Umatilla 44 45 55N 119 21W
Umatilla → 44 45 55N 119 20W
Umatilla, L. 53 45 53N 119 40W
Umatilla County ◇ 44 45 40N 118 45W
Umatilla Indian Reservation 44 45 41N 118 31W
Umatilla National Forest 44 45 0N 118 50W
Umba 98 66 50N 34 20 E
Umbagog L. 36 44 46N 71 3W
Umbarger 50 34 57N 102 7W
Umbrella Mts. 128 45 35 S 169 5 E
Umbria □ 94 42 53N 12 30 E
Ume älv → 96 63 45N 20 20 E
Umeå 96 63 45N 20 20 E
Umera 111 0 12 S 129 37 E
Umiat 11 69 22N 152 8W
Umm al Qaywayn 107 25 30N 55 35 E
Umm az Zamul 107 22 42N 55 18 E
Umm Bel 121 13 35N 28 0 E
Umm el Fahm 104 32 31N 35 9 E
Umm Lajj 106 25 0N 37 23 E
Umm Qays 104 32 40N 35 41 E
Umm Ruwaba 121 12 50N 31 20 E
Umnak I. 11 53 15N 168 20W
Umniati → 123 16 49 S 28 45 E
Umpang 112 16 3N 98 54 E
Umpire 13 34 17N 94 3W
Umpqua 44 43 22N 123 28W
Umpqua → 44 43 40N 124 12W
Umpqua National Forest 44 43 10N 122 40W
Umtata 123 31 36 S 28 49 E
Unac → 94 44 30N 16 9 E
Unadilla, Ga. 18 32 16N 83 44W
Unadilla, N.Y. 39 42 20N 75 19W
Unadilla, Nebr. 34 40 41N 96 16W
Unadilla → 39 42 20N 75 25W
Unalakleet 11 63 52N 160 47W
Unalaska 11 53 53N 166 32W
Unalaska I. 11 53 35N 166 50W
Uncía 72 18 25 S 66 40W
Uncompahgre → 16 38 45N 108 6W
Uncompahgre National Forest 16 38 30N 108 30W
Uncompahgre Peak 16 38 4N 107 28W
Uncompahgre Plateau 16 38 20N 108 15W
Underhill Flats 36 44 33N 72 56W
Underwood 41 47 27N 101 9W
Uneiuxi → 70 0 37 S 65 34W
Unga I. 11 55 15N 160 40W
Ungava B. 59 59 30N 67 30W
Ungava Pen. 59 60 0N 74 0W
Unggi 114 42 16N 130 28 E
União da Vitória 77 26 13 S 51 5W
União dos Palmares 74 9 10 S 36 2W
Unicoi 49 36 12N 82 21W
Unicoi County ◇ 49 36 9N 82 25W
Unimak I. 11 54 45N 164 0W
Unimak Pass 11 54 15N 164 30W
Unini → 71 1 41 S 61 31W
Union, Iowa 23 42 15N 93 4W
Union, La. 25 30 5N 90 54W
Union, Maine 26 44 13N 69 17W
Union, Miss. 31 32 34N 89 7W
Union, Mo. 32 38 27N 91 0W
Union, N.J. 37 40 42N 74 17W
Union, Nebr. 34 40 49N 95 55W
Union, Oreg. 44 45 13N 117 52W
Union, S.C. 46 34 43N 81 37W
Union, W. Va. 54 37 36N 80 33W
Union, Wash. 53 47 22N 123 6W
Unión, La, Chile 78 40 10 S 73 0W
Unión, La, Colombia 70 1 35N 77 5W
Unión, La, El Salv. 66 13 20N 87 50W
Unión, La, Mexico 64 17 58N 101 49W
Unión, La, Peru 72 9 43 S 76 45W
Union Bridge 27 39 34N 77 11W
Union Center, S. Dak. 47 44 34N 102 40W
Union Center, Wis. 55 43 41N 90 16W
Union City, Calif. 14 37 36N 122 1W
Union City, Ga. 18 33 35N 84 33W
Union City, Ind. 22 40 12N 84 49W
Union City, Mich. 29 42 4N 85 8W
Union City, N.J. 37 40 45N 74 2W
Union City, Ohio 42 40 12N 84 48W
Union City, Okla. 43 35 23N 97 57W
Union City, Pa. 45 41 54N 79 51W
Union City, Tenn. 48 36 26N 89 3W
Union County ◇, Ark. 13 33 12N 92 40W
Union County ◇, Fla. 17 30 0N 82 25W
Union County ◇, Ga. 18 34 50N 84 0W
Union County ◇, Ill. 21 37 30N 89 15W
Union County ◇, Ind. 22 39 35N 84 55W
Union County ◇, Iowa 23 41 0N 94 15W
Union County ◇, Ky. 48 37 40N 87 55W
Union County ◇, Miss. 31 34 29N 89 0W
Union County ◇, N.C. 40 35 0N 80 40W
Union County ◇, N.J. 37 40 40N 74 20W
Union County ◇, N. Mex. 38 36 30N 103 30W
Union County ◇, Ohio 42 40 14N 83 22W
Union County ◇, Oreg. 44 45 15N 118 0W
Union County ◇, Pa. 45 41 0N 77 0W
Union County ◇, S.C. 46 34 45N 81 45W
Union County ◇, S. Dak. 47 42 51N 96 45W
Union County ◇, Tenn. 49 36 15N 83 48W
Union Creek 44 42 55N 122 27W
Union Gap 53 46 33N 120 28W
Union Grove 55 42 41N 88 3W
Union of Soviet Socialist Republics ■ 101 60 0N 100 0 E
Union Parish ◇ 25 32 47N 92 24W
Union Park 17 28 34N 81 17W
Union Point 18 33 37N 83 4W
Union Springs, Ala. 10 32 9N 85 43W
Union Springs, N.Y. 39 42 51N 76 42W
Union Star 32 39 59N 94 36W
Union Valley Reservoir 14 38 52N 120 26W
Uniondale, Ind. 22 40 50N 85 15W
Uniondale, N.Y. 39 40 43N 73 36W
Uniondale, Pa. 45 41 43N 75 30W
Uniontown, Ala. 10 32 27N 87 31W
Uniontown, Kans. 24 37 51N 94 59W
Uniontown, Ky. 48 37 47N 87 56W
Uniontown, Md. 27 39 36N 77 7W
Uniontown, Pa. 45 39 54N 79 44W
Uniontown, Wash. 53 46 32N 117 5W
Unionville, Ga. 18 31 26N 83 30W
Unionville, Iowa 23 40 49N 92 42W
Unionville, Md. 27 39 28N 77 12W
Unionville, Mich. 29 43 39N 83 28W
Unionville, Mo. 32 40 29N 93 1W
Unionville, N.Y. 39 41 18N 74 34W
Unionville, Nev. 35 40 27N 118 8W
Unionville, Pa. 45 40 55N 77 53W
Unionville, Va. 54 38 16N 77 58W
Uniopolis 42 40 36N 84 5W
Unirea 95 44 15N 27 35 E
United 45 40 13N 79 30W
United Arab Emirates ■ 107 23 50N 54 0 E
United Kingdom ■ 86 55 0N 3 0W
United States Trust Terr. of the Pacific Is. 124 10 0N 160 0 E
Unity, Canada 63 52 30N 109 5W
Unity, Maine 26 44 37N 69 20W
Unity, Md. 27 39 13N 77 5W
Unity, Oreg. 44 44 26N 118 12W
Unity, Wis. 55 44 51N 90 19W
Universal City 51 29 33N 98 17W
University City 32 38 40N 90 20W
University Park 38 32 17N 106 45W
Unnao 109 26 35N 80 30 E
Unst 84 60 50N 0 55W
Unuk → 62 56 5N 131 3W
Ünye 106 41 5N 37 15 E
Uozu 117 36 48N 137 24 E
Upata 71 8 1N 62 24W
Upatoie → 18 32 22N 84 58W
Upemba, L. 122 8 30 S 26 20 E
Upernavik 4 72 49N 56 20W
Upham 41 48 35N 100 44W
Upington 123 28 25 S 21 15 E
Upland, Calif. 15 34 6N 117 39W
Upland, Ind. 22 40 28N 85 30W
Upland, Nebr. 34 40 19N 98 54W
Upolu 128 13 58 S 172 0W
Upolu Pt. 19 20 16N 155 52W
Upper Arlington 42 40 0N 83 4W
Upper Arrow L. 62 50 30N 117 50W
Upper Crossroads 27 39 33N 76 29W
Upper Darby 45 39 58N 75 16W
Upper Foster L. 63 56 47N 105 20W
Upper Hutt 128 41 8 S 175 5 E
Upper Iowa → 23 43 29N 91 14W
Upper Klamath L. 44 42 25N 121 55W
Upper L. 14 41 45N 120 9W
Upper L. Erne 85 54 14N 7 22W
Upper Lake 14 39 10N 122 54W
Upper Marlboro 27 38 49N 76 45W
Upper Musquodoboit 61 45 10N 62 58W
Upper Preoria L. 21 40 52N 89 24W
Upper Red L. 30 48 8N 94 45W
Upper Sandusky 42 40 50N 83 17W
Upper Taimyr → 101 74 15N 99 48 E
Upper Tract 54 38 47N 79 17W
*Upper Volta ■ 120 12 0N 1 0W
Uppsala 97 59 53N 17 38 E
Uppsala län □ 97 60 0N 17 30 E
Upshur County ◇, Tex. 51 32 44N 94 57W
Upshur County ◇, W. Va. 54 39 0N 80 8W
Upson 55 46 22N 90 24W
Upson County ◇ 18 32 50N 84 20W
Upton, Ky. 49 37 28N 85 54W
Upton, Maine 26 44 42N 71 1W
Upton, Mass. 28 42 11N 71 37W
Upton, Wyo. 56 44 6N 104 38W
Upton County ◇ 50 31 15N 102 0W
Ur 106 30 55N 46 25 E
Urabá, Golfo de 70 8 25N 76 53W
Uracara 72 2 20 S 57 50W
Urad Qianqi 114 40 40N 108 30 E
Urakawa 116 42 9N 142 47 E
Ural → 100 47 0N 51 48 E
Ural Mts. = Uralskie Gory 98 60 0N 59 0 E
Uralsk 98 51 20N 51 20 E

*Renamed Burkina Faso

Uralskie Gory **Vascongadas**

Uralskie Gory **98** 60 0N 59 0 E
Urandangi **127** 21 32 S 138 14 E
Urania **25** 31 52N 92 18W
Uranium City **63** 59 34N 108 37W
Uraricaá → **71** 3 20N 61 56W
Uraricuera → **71** 3 2N 60 30W
Uravan **16** 38 22N 108 44W
Urawa **117** 35 50N 139 40 E
Uray **100** 60 5N 65 15 E
Urbana, Ark. **13** 33 10N 92 27W
Urbana, Ill. **21** 40 7N 88 12W
Urbana, Iowa **23** 42 13N 91 52W
Urbana, Mo. **32** 37 51N 93 10W
Urbana, Ohio **42** 40 7N 83 45W
Urbana, La **70** 7 8N 66 56W
Urbandale **23** 41 38N 93 43W
Urbank **30** 46 8N 95 31W
Urbano Santos **74** 3 12 S 43 23W
Urbino **94** 43 43N 12 38 E
Urbión, Picos de **91** 42 1N 2 52W
Urcos **72** 13 40 S 71 38W
Urda **99** 48 52N 47 23 E
Urdinarrain **76** 32 37 S 58 52W
Urdzhar **100** 47 5N 81 38 E
Ure → **82** 54 20N 1 25W
Urengoy **100** 65 58N 28 25 E
Ures **64** 29 30N 110 30W
Urfa **106** 37 12N 38 50 E
Urfahr **88** 48 19N 14 17 E
Urgench **100** 41 40N 60 41 E
Uribante → **70** 7 25N 71 50W
Uribe **70** 3 13N 74 24W
Uribia **70** 11 43N 72 16W
Urich **32** 38 28N 94 2W
Urim **104** 31 18N 34 32 E
Uriondo **76** 21 41 S 64 41W
Urique **64** 27 13N 107 55W
Urique → **64** 26 29N 107 58W
Urk **87** 52 39N 5 36 E
Urla **106** 38 20N 26 47 E
Urlati **95** 44 59N 26 15 E
Urmia = Orūmīyeh **106** 37 40N 45 0 E
Urmia, L. = Orūmīyeh, Daryācheh-ye **106** 37 50N 45 30 E
Uroyan, Montanas de **57** 18 12N 67 0W
Urrao **70** 6 20N 76 11W
Ursa **21** 40 4N 91 22W
Ursine **35** 37 59N 114 13W
Uruaçu **75** 14 30 S 49 10W
Uruana **75** 15 30 S 49 41W
Uruapan **64** 19 30N 102 0W
Uruará → **71** 2 6 S 53 38W
Urubamba **72** 13 20 S 72 10W
Urubamba → **72** 10 43 S 73 48W
Urubaxi → **71** 0 31 S 64 50W
Urubu → **71** 2 55 S 58 25W
Uruçara **71** 2 32 S 57 45W
Uruçuí **74** 7 20 S 44 28W
Uruçuí, Serra do **74** 9 0 S 44 45W
Uruçuí Prêto → **74** 7 20 S 44 38W
Urucuia → **75** 16 8 S 45 5W
Urucurituba **71** 2 41 S 57 40W
Uruguai → **77** 26 0 S 53 30W
Uruguaiana **76** 29 50 S 57 0W
Uruguay ■ **76** 32 30 S 56 30W
Uruguay → **76** 34 12 S 58 18W
Ürümqi **113** 43 45N 87 45 E
Urup, Os. **101** 46 0N 151 0 E
Urutaí **75** 17 28 S 48 12W
Uryung-Khaya **101** 72 48N 113 23 E
Urziceni **95** 44 40N 26 42 E
Usa → **98** 65 57N 56 55 E
Uşak **106** 38 43N 29 28 E
Usakos **123** 22 0 S 15 31 E
Usborne, Mt. **78** 51 42 S 58 50W
Usedom **88** 53 50N 13 55 E
Useko **122** 5 8 S 32 24 E
Ush-Tobe **100** 45 16N 78 0 E
Ushakova, O. **4** 82 0N 80 0 E
Ushant = Ouessant, Île d' **90** 48 28N 5 6W
Usher **17** 29 24N 82 49W
Ushibuka **117** 32 11N 130 1 E
Ushuaia **78** 54 50 S 68 23W
Ushumun **101** 52 47N 126 32 E
Usk **53** 48 19N 117 17W
Usk → **83** 51 37N 2 56W
Üsküdar **106** 41 0N 29 5 E
Usman **98** 52 5N 39 48 E
Usolye Sibirskoye **101** 52 48N 103 40 E
Uspallata, P. de **76** 32 37 S 69 22W
Uspenskiy **100** 48 41N 72 43 E
Ussuri → **116** 48 27N 135 0 E
Ussuriysk **101** 43 48N 131 59 E
Ussurka **116** 45 12N 133 31 E
Ust-Aldan = Batamay **101** 63 30N 129 15 E
Ust Amginskoye = Khandyga **101** 62 42N 135 35 E
Ust-Bolsheretsk **101** 52 50N 156 15 E
Ust chaun **101** 68 47N 170 30 E
Ust'-Ilga **101** 55 5N 104 55 E
Ust Ilimpeya = Yukti **101** 63 26N 105 42 E
Ust-Ilimsk **101** 58 3N 102 39 E
Ust Ishim **100** 57 45N 71 10 E
Ust-Kamchatsk **101** 56 10N 162 28 E
Ust-Kamenogorsk **100** 50 0N 82 36 E
Ust-Karenga **101** 54 25N 116 30 E
Ust Khayryuzova **101** 57 15N 156 45 E
Ust-Kut **101** 56 50N 105 42 E
Ust Kuyga **101** 70 1N 135 43 E
Ust Maya **101** 60 30N 134 28 E
Ust-Mil **101** 59 40N 133 11 E
Ust-Nera **101** 64 35N 143 15 E
Ust-Nyukzha **101** 56 34N 121 37 E
Ust Olenek **101** 73 0N 119 48 E
Ust-Omchug **101** 61 9N 149 38 E
Ust Port **100** 69 40N 84 26 E
Ust Tsilma **98** 65 25N 52 0 E
Ust-Tungir **101** 55 25N 120 36 E
Ust Urt = Ustyurt, Plato **100** 44 0N 55 0 E
Ust Usa **98** 66 0N 56 30 E
Ust Vorkuta **100** 67 24N 64 0 E
Ústí nad Labem **88** 50 41N 14 3 E
Ustica **94** 38 42N 13 10 E
Ustinov **98** 56 51N 53 14 E
Ustye **101** 57 46N 94 37 E
Ustyurt, Plato **100** 44 0N 55 0 E
Usu **113** 44 27N 84 40 E
Usuki **117** 33 8N 131 49 E
Usulután **66** 13 25N 88 28W
Usumacinta → **65** 17 0N 91 0W
Usumbura = Bujumbura **122** 3 16 S 29 18 E
Uta **111** 4 33 S 136 0 E
Utah □ **52** 39 20N 111 30W
Utah County ◇ **52** 40 10N 111 50W
Utah L. **52** 40 12N 111 48W
Ute **23** 42 3N 95 42W
Ute Creek → **38** 35 21N 103 50W
Ute Mountain Indian Reservation **38** 36 55N 108 20W
Ute Park **38** 36 34N 105 6W
Ute Reservoir **38** 35 21N 103 27W
Utete **122** 8 0 S 38 45 E
Uthai Thani **112** 15 22N 100 3 E
Utiariti **73** 13 0 S 58 10W
Utica, Kans. **24** 38 39N 100 10W
Utica, Mich. **29** 42 38N 83 2W
Utica, Miss. **31** 32 7N 90 37W
Utica, N.Y. **39** 43 6N 75 14W
Utica, Ohio **42** 40 14N 82 27W
Utica, S. Dak. **47** 42 59N 97 30W
Utik L. **63** 55 15N 96 0W
Utikuma L. **62** 55 50N 115 30W
Utinga **75** 12 6 S 41 5W
Utleyville **16** 37 17N 103 4W
Utopia **51** 29 37N 99 32W
Utrecht, Neth. **87** 52 5N 5 8 E
Utrecht, S. Africa **123** 27 38 S 30 20 E
Utrecht □ **87** 52 6N 5 7 E
Utrera **91** 37 12N 5 48W
Utsjoki **96** 69 51N 26 59 E
Utsunomiya **117** 36 30N 139 50 E
Uttar Pradesh □ **108** 27 0N 80 0 E
Uttaradit **112** 17 36N 100 5 E
Uttoxeter **82** 52 53N 1 50W
Utuado **57** 18 16N 66 42W
Uudenmaan lääni □ **97** 60 25N 25 0 E
Uusikaarlepyy **96** 63 32N 22 31 E
Uusikaupunki **97** 60 47N 21 25 E
Uva **98** 56 59N 52 13 E
Uvá → **70** 3 41N 70 3W
Uvalda **18** 32 2N 82 31W
Uvalde **51** 29 13N 99 47W
Uvalde County ◇ **51** 29 30N 99 43W
Uvat **100** 59 5N 68 50 E
Uvinza **122** 5 5 S 30 24 E
Uvira **122** 3 22 S 29 3 E
Uvs Nuur **113** 50 20N 92 30 E
Uwajima **117** 33 10N 132 35 E
Uwharrie → **40** 35 23N 80 3W
Uwharrie National Forest **40** 35 20N 80 0W
Uxbridge **28** 42 5N 71 38W
Uxin Qi **114** 38 50N 109 5 E
Uxmal **65** 20 22N 89 46W
Uyak **11** 57 38N 154 0W
Uyandi **101** 69 19N 141 0 E
Uyuni **72** 20 28 S 66 47W
Uzbek S.S.R. □ **100** 41 30N 65 0 E
Uzen **99** 43 27N 53 10 E
Uzerche **90** 45 25N 1 34 E
Uzunköprü **95** 41 16N 26 43 E

V

Vaal → **123** 29 4 S 23 38 E
Vaasa **96** 63 6N 21 38 E
Vaasan lääni □ **96** 63 2N 22 50 E
Vác **89** 47 49N 19 10 E
Vacaria **77** 28 31 S 50 52W
Vacaville **14** 38 21N 121 59W
Vach → **100** 60 45N 76 45 E
Vache, Î.-à- **67** 18 2N 73 35W
Vacherie **25** 30 0N 90 48W
Vacia Talega, Pta. **57** 18 26N 65 53W
Vader **53** 46 24N 122 58W
Vadodara **108** 22 20N 73 10 E
Vadsø **96** 70 3N 29 50 E
Vœrøy **96** 67 40N 12 40 E
Váh → **89** 47 55N 18 0 E
Vahsel B. **5** 75 0 S 35 0W
Vaiden **31** 33 20N 89 45W
Vaigach **100** 70 10N 59 0 E
Vail, Ariz. **12** 32 3N 110 43W
Vail, Colo. **16** 39 40N 106 20W
Vail, Iowa **23** 42 4N 95 12W
Vakarel **95** 42 35N 23 40 E
Val-de-Marne □ **90** 48 45N 2 28 E
Val-d'Oise □ **90** 49 5N 2 10 E
Val d'Or **60** 48 7N 77 47W
Val Marie **63** 49 15N 107 45W
Val Verde County ◇ **50** 30 0N 101 0W
Valahia **89** 44 35N 25 0 E
Valatie **39** 42 25N 73 41W
Valcheta **78** 40 40 S 66 8W
Valdayskaya Vozvyshennost **98** 57 0N 33 30 E
Valdepeñas **91** 38 43N 3 25W
Valders **55** 44 4N 87 53W
Valdés, Pen. **78** 42 30 S 63 45W
Valdese **40** 35 44N 81 34W
Valdez, Ecuador **70** 1 15N 79 0W
Valdez, Alaska **11** 61 7N 146 16W
Valdez, N. Mex. **38** 36 32N 105 35W
Valdez-Cordova ◇ **11** 61 0N 144 0W
Valdivia, Chile **78** 39 50 S 73 14W
Valdivia, Colombia **70** 7 11N 75 27W
Valdivia □ **78** 40 0 S 73 0W
Valdosta **18** 30 50N 83 17W
Vale, Oreg. **44** 43 59N 117 15W
Vale, S. Dak. **47** 44 37N 103 24W
Valença **75** 13 20 S 39 5W
Valença do Piauí **74** 6 20 S 41 45W
Valence **90** 44 57N 4 54 E
Valencia, Spain **91** 39 27N 0 23W
Valencia, Venezuela **70** 10 11N 68 0W
Valencia □ **91** 39 20N 0 40W
Valencia, Albufera de **91** 39 20N 0 27W
Valencia, G. de **91** 39 30N 0 20 E
Valencia County ◇ **38** 34 45N 107 0W
Valencia de Alcántara **91** 39 25N 7 14W
Valenciennes **90** 50 20N 3 34 E
Văleni **95** 44 15N 24 45 E
Valentia Harb. **85** 51 56N 10 17W
Valentia I. **85** 51 54N 10 22W
Valentim, Sa. do **74** 6 0 S 43 30W
Valentin **116** 43 8N 134 17 E
Valentine, Ariz. **12** 35 23N 113 40W
Valentine, Nebr. **34** 42 52N 100 33W
Valentine, Tex. **50** 30 35N 104 30W
Valera **70** 9 19N 70 37W
Valeria **23** 41 44N 93 20W
Valhalla **40** 36 8N 76 40W
Valier, Ill. **21** 38 1N 89 3W
Valier, Mont. **33** 48 18N 112 16W
Valjevo **95** 44 18N 19 53 E
Valkeakoski **97** 61 16N 24 2 E
Valkenswaard **87** 51 21N 5 29 E
Valladolid, Mexico **65** 20 40N 88 11W
Valladolid, Spain **91** 41 38N 4 43W
Valle d'Aosta □ **94** 45 45N 7 22 E
Valle de la Pascua **70** 9 13N 66 0W
Valle de Santiago **64** 20 25N 101 15W
Valle de Zaragoza **64** 27 28N 105 49W
Valle del Cauca □ **70** 3 45N 76 30W
Valle Fértil, Sierra del **76** 30 20 S 68 0W
Valle Hermoso **65** 25 35N 97 40W
Valle Nacional **65** 17 47N 96 19W
Vallecas **91** 40 23N 3 41W
Vallecito **16** 37 23N 107 35W
Vallecito Reservoir **16** 37 23N 107 34W
Valledupar **70** 10 29N 73 15W
Vallejo **14** 38 7N 122 14W
Vallenar **76** 28 30 S 70 50W
Valles Mines **32** 38 2N 90 30W
Valletta **94** 35 54N 14 30 E
Valley, Nebr. **34** 41 19N 96 21W
Valley, Wash. **53** 48 11N 117 44W
Valley Center, Calif. **15** 33 13N 117 2W
Valley Center, Kans. **24** 37 50N 97 22W
Valley City **41** 46 55N 98 0W
Valley County ◇, Idaho **20** 44 45N 115 30W
Valley County ◇, Mont. **33** 48 35N 106 30W
Valley County ◇, Nebr. **34** 41 30N 99 0W
Valley Falls, Kans. **24** 39 21N 95 28W
Valley Falls, N.Y. **39** 42 54N 73 34W
Valley Falls, Oreg. **44** 42 29N 120 17W
Valley Falls, R.I. **28** 41 54N 71 24W
Valley Grove **54** 40 6N 80 34W
Valley Head, Ala. **10** 34 34N 85 37W
Valley Head, W. Va. **54** 38 33N 80 2W
Valley Lee **27** 38 12N 76 31W
Valley Mills **51** 31 40N 97 28W
Valley Park **32** 38 33N 90 29W
Valley Springs, Calif. **14** 38 12N 120 50W
Valley Springs, S. Dak. **47** 43 35N 96 28W
Valley Station **49** 38 6N 85 52W
Valley Stream **39** 40 40N 73 42W
Valley View, Pa. **45** 40 39N 76 33W
Valley View, Tex. **51** 33 29N 97 10W
Valleyview **62** 55 5N 117 17W
Valliant **43** 34 0N 95 6W
Vallimanca, Arroyo **76** 35 40 S 59 10W
Valls **91** 41 18N 1 15 E
Valmeyer **21** 38 18N 90 19W
Valmora **38** 35 49N 104 55W
Valmy **35** 40 48N 117 8W
Valognes **90** 49 30N 1 28W
Valparaíso, Chile **76** 33 2 S 71 40W
Valparaíso, Mexico **64** 22 50N 103 32W
Valparaiso, Fla. **17** 30 29N 86 30W
Valparaiso, Ind. **22** 41 28N 87 4W
Valparaiso, Nebr. **34** 41 5N 96 50W
Valparaíso □ **76** 33 2 S 71 40W
Vals, Tanjung **111** 8 26 S 137 25 E
Valsad **108** 20 40N 72 58 E
Valsbaai **123** 34 15 S 18 40 E
Valsetz **44** 44 50N 123 39W
Valverde del Camino **91** 37 35N 6 47W
Van, Turkey **106** 38 30N 43 20 E
Van, U.S.A. **51** 32 31N 95 38W
Van Alstyne **51** 33 25N 96 35W
Van Bruyssel **61** 47 56N 72 9W
Van Buren, Canada **61** 47 10N 67 55W
Van Buren, Ark. **13** 35 26N 94 21W
Van Buren, Ind. **22** 40 37N 85 30W
Van Buren, Ky. **49** 37 59N 85 10W
Van Buren, Maine **26** 47 10N 67 58W
Van Buren, Mo. **32** 37 0N 91 1W
Van Buren, Ohio **42** 41 8N 83 39W
Van Buren County ◇, Ark. **13** 35 36N 92 28W
Van Buren County ◇, Iowa **23** 40 45N 91 55W
Van Buren County ◇, Mich. **29** 42 15N 86 0W
Van Buren County ◇, Tenn. **49** 35 45N 85 28W
Van Buskirk **55** 46 23N 90 9W
Van Diemen, C. **127** 16 30 S 139 46 E
Van Diemen G. **126** 11 45 S 132 0 E
Van Gölü **106** 38 30N 43 0 E
Van Horn **50** 31 3N 104 50W
Van Meter **23** 41 32N 93 57W
Van Rees, Pegunungan **111** 2 35 S 138 15 E
Van Tassell **56** 42 40N 104 5W
Van Wert, Iowa **23** 40 52N 93 48W
Van Wert, Ohio **42** 40 52N 84 35W
Van Wert County ◇ **42** 40 52N 84 35W
Van Zandt County ◇ **51** 32 33N 95 52W
Vanavara **101** 60 22N 102 16 E
Vance **46** 33 26N 80 25W
Vance County ◇ **40** 36 15N 78 20W
Vanceboro **26** 45 34N 67 26W
Vanceburg **49** 38 36N 83 19W
Vancleave **31** 30 32N 88 42W
Vancleve **49** 37 38N 83 25W
Vancorum **16** 38 14N 108 36W
Vancourt **50** 31 21N 100 11W
Vancouver, Canada **62** 49 15N 123 10W
Vancouver, U.S.A. **53** 45 38N 122 40W
Vancouver, Mt. **11** 60 20N 139 41W
Vancouver I. **62** 49 50N 126 0W
Vandalia, Ill. **21** 38 58N 89 6W
Vandalia, Mo. **32** 39 19N 91 29W
Vandalia, Ohio **42** 39 54N 84 12W
Vandemere **40** 35 11N 76 41W
Vanderbilt **29** 45 9N 84 40W
Vanderburgh County ◇ **22** 38 5N 87 35W
Vandergrift **45** 40 36N 79 34W
Vanderhoof **62** 54 0N 124 0W
Vanderlin I. **127** 15 44 S 137 2 E
Vanderpool **51** 29 45N 99 33W
Vanduser **32** 36 59N 89 42W
Vänern **97** 58 47N 13 30 E
Vänersborg **97** 58 26N 12 19 E
Vang Vieng **112** 18 58N 102 32 E
Vanga **122** 4 35 S 39 12 E
Vangaindrano **123** 23 21 S 47 36 E
Vanguard **63** 49 55N 107 20W
Vanier **60** 45 27N 75 40W
Vankarem **101** 67 51N 175 50 E
Vankleek Hill **60** 45 32N 74 40W
Vanna **96** 70 6N 19 50 E
Vännäs **96** 63 58N 19 48 E
Vannes **90** 47 40N 2 47W
Vanoss **43** 34 46N 96 52W
Vanrhynsdorp **123** 31 36 S 18 44 E
Vansbro **97** 60 32N 14 15 E
Vansittart B. **126** 14 3 S 126 17 E
Vanua Levu **128** 16 33 S 179 15 E
Vanua Mbalavu **128** 17 40 S 178 57W
Vanuatu ■ **124** 15 0 S 168 0 E
Var □ **90** 43 27N 6 18 E
Varanasi **109** 25 22N 83 0 E
Varangerfjorden **96** 70 3N 29 25 E
Varaždin **94** 46 20N 16 20 E
Varberg **97** 57 6N 12 20 E
Vardak □ **107** 34 0N 68 0 E
Vardaman **31** 33 53N 89 11W
Vardar → **95** 40 35N 22 50 E
Varese **94** 45 49N 8 50 E
Vargem Bonita **75** 20 20 S 46 22W
Vargem Grande **74** 3 33 S 43 56W
Varginha **77** 21 33 S 45 25W
Varillas **76** 24 0 S 70 10W
Varina **23** 42 40N 94 54W
Värmlands län □ **97** 60 0N 13 20 E
Varna, Bulgaria **95** 43 13N 27 56 E
Varna, U.S.A. **21** 41 2N 89 14W
Varnado **25** 30 54N 89 50W
Värnamo **97** 57 10N 14 3 E
Varnville **46** 32 51N 81 5W
Varzaneh **107** 32 25N 52 40 E
Várzea Alegre **74** 6 47 S 39 17W
Várzea da Palma **75** 17 36 S 44 44W
Várzea Grande **73** 15 39 S 56 8W
Vasa **96** 63 6N 21 38 E
Vasa Barris → **74** 11 10 S 37 10W
Vascongadas **91** 42 50N 2 45W

Vasht Vilyuy

Vasht = Khāsh **108** 28 15N 61 15 E
Vaslui **89** 46 38N 27 42 E
Vaslui □ **95** 46 30N 27 45 E
Vass **40** 35 15N 79 17W
Vassar, Canada **63** 49 10N 95 55W
Vassar, Kans. **24** 38 42N 95 37W
Vassar, Mich. **29** 43 22N 83 35W
Västerås **97** 59 37N 16 38 E
Västerbottens län □ **96** 64 58N 18 0 E
Västernorrlands län □ **96** 63 30N 17 30 E
Västervik **97** 57 43N 16 43 E
Västmanlands län □ **97** 59 45N 16 20 E
Vasto **94** 42 8N 14 40 E
Vatnajökull **96** 64 30N 16 48W
Vatneyri **96** 65 35N 24 0W
Vatoa **128** 19 50 S 178 13W
Vatomandry **123** 19 20 S 48 59 E
Vatra-Dornei **89** 47 22N 25 22 E
Vättern **97** 58 25N 14 30 E
Vaucluse **46** 33 37N 81 49W
Vaucluse □ **90** 44 3N 5 10 E
Vaughan **31** 32 48N 90 3W
Vaughn, Mont. **33** 47 33N 111 33W
Vaughn, N. Mex. **38** 34 36N 105 13W
Vaupe □ **70** 1 0N 71 0W
Vaupés → **70** 0 2N 67 16W
Vauxhall **62** 50 5N 112 9W
Vava'u **128** 18 36 S 174 0W
Växjö **97** 56 52N 14 50 E
Vaygach, Ostrov **100** 70 0N 60 0 E
Vazovgrad **95** 42 39N 24 45 E
Veadeiros **75** 14 7 S 47 31W
Veblen **47** 45 52N 97 17W
Vechte → **87** 52 34N 6 6 E
Vedea → **89** 44 0N 25 20 E
Vedia **76** 34 30 S 61 31W
Veedersburg **22** 40 7N 87 16W
Veendam **87** 53 5N 6 52 E
Veenendaal **87** 52 2N 5 34 E
Vefsna → **96** 65 48N 13 10 E
Vega, Norway **96** 65 40N 11 55 E
Vega, U.S.A. **50** 35 15N 102 26W
Vega, La, Dom. Rep. **67** 19 20N 70 30W
Vega, La, Peru **72** 10 41 S 77 44W
Vega Alta **57** 18 25N 66 20W
Vega Baja **57** 18 27N 66 23W
Vegafjorden **96** 65 37N 12 0 E
Veghel **87** 51 37N 5 32 E
Vegreville **62** 53 30N 112 5W
Veguita **38** 34 31N 106 46W
Vejer de la Frontera **91** 36 15N 5 59W
Vejle **97** 55 43N 9 30 E
Vela, La **70** 11 27N 69 34W
Velas, C. **66** 10 21N 85 52W
Velasco, Sierra de **76** 29 20 S 67 10W
Velay, Mts. du **90** 45 0N 3 40 E
Velebit Planina **94** 44 50N 15 20 E
Veleka → **95** 42 4N 27 58 E
Vélez **70** 6 1N 73 41W
Vélez Málaga **91** 36 48N 4 5W
Vélez Rubio **91** 37 41N 2 5W
Velhas → **75** 17 13 S 44 49W
Velikaya → **98** 57 48N 28 20 E
Velikaya Kema **116** 45 30N 137 12 E
Veliki Ustyug **98** 60 47N 46 20 E
Velikiye Luki **98** 56 25N 30 32 E
Velikonda Range **108** 14 45N 79 10 E
Velingrad **95** 42 4N 23 58 E
Velletri **94** 41 43N 12 43 E
Vellore **108** 12 57N 79 10 E
Velma **43** 34 28N 97 40W
Velsen-Noord **87** 52 27N 4 40 E
Velsk **98** 61 10N 42 5 E
Velva **41** 48 4N 100 56W
Venado **64** 22 56N 101 10W
Venado Tuerto **76** 33 50 S 62 0W
Venango County ◇ **45** 41 20N 79 50W
Vendée □ **90** 46 50N 1 35W
Vendée, Collines de **90** 46 35N 0 45W
Venedocia **42** 40 47N 84 28W
Veneta **44** 44 3N 123 21W
Venetie **11** 67 1N 146 25W
Venetie Indian Reservation **11** 67 20N 146 0W
Véneto □ **94** 45 40N 12 0 E
Venézia **94** 45 27N 12 20 E
Venézia, Golfo di **94** 45 20N 13 0 E
Venezuela ■ **70** 8 0N 65 0W
Venezuela, Golfo de **70** 11 30N 71 0W
Vengurla **108** 15 53N 73 45 E
Venice = Venézia **94** 45 27N 12 20 E
Venice, Fla. **17** 27 6N 82 27W
Venice, La. **25** 29 17N 89 22W
Venkatapuram **109** 18 20N 80 30 E
Venleer **48** 36 14N 87 27W
Venlo **87** 51 22N 6 11 E
Venraij **87** 51 31N 6 0 E
Venta, La **65** 18 8N 94 3W
Ventana, Punta de la **64** 24 4N 109 48W
Ventana, Sa. de la **76** 38 0 S 62 30W
Ventnor **83** 50 35N 1 12W
Ventnor City **37** 39 20N 74 29W
Venton **27** 38 12N 75 18W
Ventspils **98** 57 25N 21 32 E
Ventuarí → **70** 3 58N 67 2W
Ventura **15** 34 17N 119 18W
Ventura, La **64** 24 38N 100 54W
Ventura County ◇ **15** 34 30N 119 0W
Venturosa, La **70** 6 8N 68 48W
Venus **17** 27 4N 81 22W
Vera, Argentina **76** 29 30 S 60 20W
Vera, Spain **91** 37 15N 1 51W
Vera, U.S.A. **43** 36 27N 95 53W
Veracruz **65** 19 10N 96 10W
Veracruz □ **65** 19 0N 96 15W
Veraval **108** 20 53N 70 27 E
Verbena **10** 32 45N 86 31W
Vercelli **94** 45 19N 8 25 E
Verda **25** 31 42N 92 46W
Verdalsøra **96** 63 48N 11 30 E
Verde →, Argentina **78** 41 56 S 65 5W
Verde →, Goiás, Brazil **75** 19 11 S 50 44W
Verde →, Goiás, Brazil **75** 18 1 S 50 14W
Verde →, Mato Grosso, Brazil **73** 11 54 S 55 48W
Verde →, Mato Grosso, Brazil **73** 21 25 S 56 20W
Verde →, Chihuahua, Mexico **64** 26 29N 107 58W
Verde →, Oaxaca, Mexico **65** 15 59N 97 50W
Verde →, Veracruz, Mexico **64** 21 10N 102 50W
Verde →, Paraguay **76** 23 9 S 57 37W
Verde →, U.S.A. **12** 33 33N 111 40W
Verde, Cay **66** 23 0N 75 5W
Verde Grande → **75** 16 13 S 43 49W
Verde Pequeno → **75** 14 48 S 43 31W
Verdel **34** 42 49N 98 12W
Verden, Germany **89** 52 58N 9 18 E
Verden, U.S.A. **43** 35 5N 98 5W
Verdery **46** 34 7N 82 15W
Verdi **35** 39 31N 119 59W
Verdigre **34** 42 36N 98 2W
Verdigre Cr. → **34** 42 42N 98 3W
Verdigris → **43** 35 48N 95 19W
Verdon **34** 40 9N 95 43W
Verdon-sur-Mer, Le **90** 45 33N 1 4W
Verdun **90** 49 12N 5 24 E
Vereeniging **123** 26 38 S 27 57 E
Vérendrye, Parc Prov. de la **60** 47 20N 76 40W
Verga, C. **120** 10 30N 14 10W
Vergas **30** 46 40N 95 48W
Vergennes **36** 44 10N 73 15W
Verkhnevilyuysk **101** 63 27N 120 18 E
Verkhneye Kalinino **101** 59 54N 108 8 E
Verkhniy Baskunchak **99** 48 14N 46 44 E
Verkhoyansk **101** 67 35N 133 25 E
Verkhoyansk Ra. **102** 66 0N 129 0 E
Verkhoyanskiy Khrebet **101** 66 0N 129 0 E
Verlo **63** 50 19N 108 35W
Vermilion, Canada **63** 53 20N 110 50W
Vermilion, Ill. **21** 39 35N 87 35W
Vermilion, Ohio **42** 41 25N 82 22W
Vermilion →, Alta., Canada **63** 53 22N 110 51W
Vermilion →, Qué., Canada **60** 47 38N 72 56W
Vermilion →, U.S.A. **21** 41 19N 89 4W
Vermilion B. **25** 29 42N 92 0W
Vermilion Bay **63** 49 51N 93 34W
Vermilion Chutes **62** 58 22N 114 51W
Vermilion Cliffs **52** 37 10N 112 30W
Vermilion County ◇ **21** 40 10N 87 45W
Vermilion L. **30** 47 53N 92 26W
Vermilion Parish ◇ **25** 29 55N 92 15W
Vermilion Ra. **30** 47 50N 92 0W
Vermillion **47** 42 47N 96 56W
Vermillion → **47** 42 44N 96 53W
Vermillion Bluffs **16** 40 50N 108 20W
Vermillion County ◇ **22** 39 50N 87 30W
Vermont □ **36** 44 0N 73 0W
Verna **17** 27 23N 82 16W
Vernal **52** 40 27N 109 32W
Verndale **30** 46 24N 95 1W
Verner **60** 46 25N 80 8W
Vernon, Canada **62** 50 20N 119 15W
Vernon, Ala. **10** 33 45N 88 7W
Vernon, Colo. **16** 39 57N 102 19W
Vernon, Conn. **28** 41 50N 72 28W
Vernon, Ill. **21** 38 48N 89 5W
Vernon, Ind. **22** 38 59N 85 36W
Vernon, Tex. **51** 34 9N 99 17W
Vernon, Utah **52** 40 6N 112 26W
Vernon Center **30** 43 58N 94 10W
Vernon County ◇, Mo. **32** 37 50N 94 20W
Vernon County ◇, Wis. **55** 43 30N 90 50W
Vernon Parish ◇ **25** 31 9N 93 16W
Vernonia **44** 45 52N 123 11W
Vero Beach **17** 27 38N 80 24W
Véroia **95** 40 34N 22 12 E
Verona, Italy **94** 45 27N 11 0 E
Verona, Miss. **31** 34 12N 88 43W
Verona, N.C. **40** 34 40N 77 28W
Verona, N. Dak. **41** 46 22N 98 4W
Verona, Wis. **55** 42 59N 89 32W
Veropol **101** 65 15N 168 40 E
Verret, L. **25** 29 53N 91 10W
Versailles, France **90** 48 48N 2 8 E
Versailles, Ill. **21** 39 53N 90 39W
Versailles, Ind. **22** 39 4N 85 15W
Versailles, Ky. **49** 38 3N 84 44W
Versailles, Mo. **32** 38 26N 92 51W
Versailles, Ohio **42** 40 13N 84 29W
Versalles **73** 12 44 S 63 18W
Vert, C. **120** 14 45N 17 30W
Verviers **87** 50 37N 5 52 E
Verwood **63** 49 30N 105 40W
Veseliye **95** 42 18N 27 38 E
Veselovskoye Vdkhr. **99** 47 0N 41 0 E
Vesoul **90** 47 40N 6 11 E
Vesper, Kans. **24** 39 2N 98 17W
Vesper, Wis. **55** 44 29N 89 58W
Vest-Agder fylke □ **97** 58 30N 7 15 E
Vesta, C. Rica **66** 9 43N 83 3W
Vesta, Ga. **18** 33 58N 82 56W
Vesta, Nebr. **34** 40 21N 96 20W
Vesterålen **96** 68 45N 15 0 E
Vestfjorden **96** 67 55N 14 0 E
Vestfold fylke □ **97** 59 15N 10 0 E
Vestmannaeyjar **96** 63 27N 20 15W
Vestspitsbergen **4** 78 40N 17 0 E
Vestvågøy **96** 68 18N 13 50 E
Vesuvio **94** 40 50N 14 22 E
Vesuvius, Mt. = Vesuvio **94** 40 50N 14 22 E
Veszprém **89** 47 8N 17 57 E
Vetal **47** 43 13N 101 23W
Vetlanda **97** 57 24N 15 3 E
Vetovo **95** 43 42N 26 16 E
Vetren **95** 42 15N 24 3 E
Veurne **87** 51 5N 2 40 E
Vevay **22** 38 45N 85 4W
Veys **106** 31 30N 49 0 E
Vezhen **95** 42 50N 24 20 E
Viacha **72** 16 39 S 68 18W
Vian **43** 35 30N 94 58W
Viana, Brazil **74** 3 13 S 45 0W
Viana, Portugal **91** 38 20N 8 0W
Viana do Castelo **91** 41 42N 8 50W
Vianópolis **75** 16 40 S 48 35W
Vibank **63** 50 20N 103 56W
Viborg, Denmark **97** 56 27N 9 23 E
Viborg, U.S.A. **47** 43 10N 97 5W
Viburnum **32** 37 43N 91 8W
Vicco **49** 37 13N 83 4W
Vicenza **94** 45 32N 11 31 E
Vich **91** 41 58N 2 19 E
Vichada □ **70** 5 0N 69 30W
Vichada → **70** 4 55N 67 50W
Vichy **90** 46 9N 3 26 E
Vici **43** 36 9N 99 18W
Vick **13** 33 20N 92 6W
Vicksburg, Mich. **29** 42 7N 85 32W
Vicksburg, Miss. **31** 32 21N 90 53W
Viçosa **74** 9 28 S 36 14W
Viçosa do Ceará **74** 3 34 S 41 5W
Victor, India **108** 21 0N 71 30 E
Victor, Colo. **16** 38 43N 105 9W
Victor, Idaho **20** 43 36N 111 7W
Victor, Iowa **23** 41 44N 92 18W
Victor, Mont. **33** 46 25N 114 9W
Victor Harbor **127** 35 30 S 138 37 E
Victoria, Argentina **76** 32 40 S 60 10W
Victoria, Canada **62** 48 30N 123 25W
Victoria, Chile **78** 38 13 S 72 20W
Victoria, Guinea **120** 10 50N 14 32W
Victoria, H.K. **115** 22 16N 114 15 E
Victoria, Malaysia **110** 5 20N 115 14 E
Victoria, Ill. **21** 41 2N 90 6W
Victoria, Kans. **24** 38 52N 99 9W
Victoria, Tex. **51** 28 48N 97 0W
Victoria, Va. **54** 36 59N 78 8W
Victoria □ **127** 37 0 S 144 0 E
Victoria → **126** 15 10 S 129 40 E
Victoria, Grand L. **60** 47 31N 77 30W
Victoria, L. **122** 1 0 S 33 0 E
Victoria, La **70** 10 14N 67 20W
Victoria Beach **63** 50 40N 96 35W
Victoria County ◇ **51** 28 45N 96 55W
Victoria de las Tunas **66** 20 58N 76 59W
Victoria Falls **123** 17 58 S 25 52 E
Victoria Harbour **60** 44 45N 79 45W
Victoria I. **58** 71 0N 111 0W
Victoria Ld. **5** 75 0 S 160 0 E
Victoria Ra. **128** 42 12 S 172 7 E
Victoria Res. **61** 48 20N 57 27W
Victoria River Downs **126** 16 25 S 131 0 E
Victoria Taungdeik **109** 21 15N 93 55 E
Victoria West **123** 31 25 S 23 4 E
Victoriaville **61** 46 4N 71 56W
Victorica **76** 36 20 S 65 30W
Victorville **15** 34 32N 117 18W
Vicuña **76** 30 0 S 70 50W
Vicuña Mackenna **76** 33 53 S 64 25W
Vidal **15** 34 7N 114 31W
Vidalia, Ga. **18** 32 13N 82 25W
Vidalia, La. **25** 31 34N 91 26W
Vidauri **51** 28 26N 97 8W
Vidette **18** 33 2N 82 15W
Vidin **95** 43 59N 22 50 E
Vidisha **108** 23 28N 77 53 E
Vidor **51** 30 7N 94 1W
Vidra **95** 45 56N 26 55 E
Viedma **78** 40 50 S 63 0W
Viedma, L. **78** 49 30 S 72 30W
Vieja, Sierra **50** 30 35N 104 40W
Vien Pou Kha **112** 20 45N 101 5 E
Vienna = Wien **88** 48 12N 16 22 E
Vienna, Ga. **18** 32 6N 83 47W
Vienna, Ill. **21** 37 25N 88 54W
Vienna, Md. **27** 38 29N 75 50W
Vienna, Mo. **32** 38 11N 91 57W
Vienna, S. Dak. **47** 44 42N 97 30W
Vienna, W. Va. **54** 39 20N 81 33W
Vienne **90** 45 31N 4 53 E
Vienne □ **90** 46 30N 0 42 E
Vienne → **90** 47 13N 0 5 E
Vientiane **112** 17 58N 102 36 E
Vientos, Paso de los **67** 20 0N 74 0W
Vieques, Isla de **57** 18 8N 65 25W
Vieques, Pasaje de **57** 18 10N 65 35W
Vieques, Sonda de **57** 18 15N 65 15W
Vierzon **90** 47 13N 2 5 E
Vietnam ■ **112** 19 0N 106 0 E
Vieux Desert, L. **29** 46 8N 89 7W
Vigan **111** 17 35N 120 28 E
Vigia **74** 0 50 S 48 5W
Vigía Chico **65** 19 46N 87 35W
Vigo **91** 42 12N 8 41W
Vigo County ◇ **22** 39 25N 87 25W
Vigo Park **50** 34 39N 101 30W
Vijayawada **109** 16 31N 80 39 E
Viking, Canada **62** 53 7N 111 50W
Viking, U.S.A. **30** 48 13N 96 24W
Vikna **96** 64 55N 10 58 E
Vikulovo **100** 56 50N 70 40 E
Vila da Maganja **123** 17 18 S 37 30 E
Vila de João Belo = Xai-Xai **123** 25 6 S 33 31 E
Vila de Manica **123** 18 58 S 32 59 E
Vila Franca de Xira **91** 38 57N 8 59W
Vila Machado **123** 19 15 S 34 14 E
Vila Real **91** 41 17N 7 48W
Vila Real de Santo António **91** 37 10N 7 28W
Vila Velha, Amapá, Brazil **71** 3 13N 51 13W
Vila Velha, Espirito Santo, Brazil **75** 20 20 S 40 17W
Vilaine → **90** 47 30N 2 27W
Vilanculos **123** 22 1 S 35 17 E
Vilas, Colo. **16** 37 22N 102 27W
Vilas, S. Dak. **47** 44 1N 97 36W
Vilas County ◇ **55** 46 0N 89 30W
Vilcabamba, Cordillera **72** 13 0 S 73 0W
Vilcanchos **72** 13 40 S 74 25W
Vîlcea □ **95** 45 0N 24 10 E
Vilhelmina **96** 64 35N 16 39 E
Vilhena **73** 12 40 S 60 5W
Viliga **101** 61 36N 156 56 E
Villa Abecia **76** 21 0 S 68 18W
Villa Ahumada **64** 30 38N 106 30W
Villa Ana **76** 28 28 S 59 40W
Villa Ángela **76** 27 34 S 60 45W
Villa Bella **73** 10 25 S 65 22W
Villa Bens = Tarfaya **120** 27 55N 12 55W
Villa Cañás **76** 34 0 S 61 35W
Villa Cisneros = Dakhla **120** 23 50N 15 53W
Villa Colón **76** 31 38 S 68 20W
Villa Constitución **76** 33 15 S 60 20W
Villa de Cura **70** 10 2N 67 29W
Villa de María **76** 29 55 S 63 43W
Villa del Rosario **70** 10 19N 72 19W
Villa Dolores **76** 31 58 S 65 15W
Villa Frontera **64** 26 56N 101 27W
Villa Grove, Colo. **16** 38 15N 105 59W
Villa Grove, Ill. **21** 39 52N 88 10W
Villa Guillermina **76** 28 15 S 59 29W
Villa Hayes **76** 25 0 S 57 20W
Villa Iris **76** 38 12 S 63 12W
Villa María **76** 32 20 S 63 10W
Villa Mazán **76** 28 40 S 66 30W
Villa Montes **76** 21 10 S 63 30W
Villa Ocampo, Argentina **76** 28 30 S 59 20W
Villa Ocampo, Mexico **64** 26 29N 105 30W
Villa Ojo de Agua **76** 29 30 S 63 44W
Villa Pérez **57** 18 12N 66 47W
Villa Rica **18** 33 44N 84 55W
Villa San José **76** 32 12 S 58 15W
Villa San Martín **76** 28 15 S 64 9W
Villa Unión **64** 23 12N 106 14W
Villach **88** 46 37N 13 51 E
Villagarcía de Arosa **91** 42 34N 8 46W
Village of Superior **55** 46 40N 92 6W
Villagrán **65** 24 29N 99 29W
Villaguay **76** 32 0 S 59 0W
Villahermosa **65** 18 0N 92 50W
Villalba, Puerto Rico **57** 18 8N 66 30W
Villalba, Spain **91** 43 26N 7 40W
Villanueva, Colombia **70** 10 37N 72 59W
Villanueva, U.S.A. **38** 35 16N 105 22W
Villanueva de la Serena **91** 38 59N 5 50W
Villard **30** 45 43N 95 16W
Villarreal **91** 39 55N 0 3W
Villarrica, Chile **78** 39 15 S 72 15W
Villarrica, Paraguay **76** 25 40 S 56 30W
Villarrobledo **91** 39 18N 2 36W
Villas **37** 39 2N 74 56W
Villavicencio, Argentina **76** 32 28 S 69 0W
Villavicencio, Colombia **70** 4 9N 73 37W
Villaviciosa **91** 43 32N 5 27W
Villazón **76** 22 0 S 65 35W
Ville-Marie **60** 47 20N 79 30W
Ville Platte **25** 30 41N 92 17W
Villegrande **73** 18 30 S 64 10W
Villegreen **16** 37 18N 103 31W
Villena **91** 38 39N 0 52W
Villisca **23** 40 56N 94 59W
Vilna **62** 54 7N 111 55W
Vilnius **98** 54 38N 25 19 E
Vilonia **13** 35 5N 92 13W
Vilskutskogo, Proliv **101** 78 0N 103 0 E
Vilvoorde **87** 50 56N 4 26 E
Vilyuy → **101** 64 24N 126 26 E

Vilyuysk Walker

Vilyuysk 101 63 40N 121 35 E
Vina 10 34 23N 88 4W
Viña del Mar 76 33 0 S 71 30W
Vinalhaven 26 44 3N 68 50W
Vinalhaven I. 26 44 5N 68 51W
Vinaroz 91 40 30N 0 27 E
Vincennes 22 38 41N 87 32W
Vincent, Ala. 10 33 23N 86 25W
Vincent, Iowa 23 42 36N 94 1W
Vincentown 37 39 56N 74 45W
Vinces 70 1 32 S 79 45W
Vinchina 76 28 45 S 68 15W
Vindel älven → 96 63 55N 19 50 E
Vindeln 96 64 12N 19 43 E
Vindhya Ra. 108 22 50N 77 0 E
Vine Grove 49 37 49N 85 59W
Vineland 37 39 29N 75 2W
Vinemont 10 34 15N 86 52W
Vineyard Haven 28 41 27N 70 36W
Vineyard Sd. 28 41 25N 70 45W
Vinh 112 18 45N 105 38 E
Vining 30 46 16N 95 32W
Vinita 43 36 39N 95 9W
Vinkovci 95 45 19N 18 48 E
Vinnitsa 99 49 15N 28 30 E
Vinson 43 34 54N 99 52W
Vinson Massif 5 78 35 S 85 25W
Vinton, Calif. 14 39 48N 120 10W
Vinton, Iowa 23 42 10N 92 1W
Vinton, La. 25 30 11N 93 35W
Vinton, Ohio 42 38 59N 82 21W
Vinton County ◇ 42 39 15N 82 29W
Vinţu de Jos 95 46 0N 23 30 E
Viola, Ark. 13 36 24N 91 59W
Viola, Del. 27 39 5N 75 34W
Viola, Ill. 21 41 12N 90 35W
Viola, Kans. 24 37 29N 97 39W
Viola, Tenn. 49 35 32N 85 52W
Viola, Wis. 55 43 31N 90 40W
Violet 25 29 54N 89 54W
Viqueque 111 8 52 S 126 23 E
Virac 111 13 30N 124 20 E
Virago Sd. 62 54 0N 132 30W
Viramgam 108 23 5N 72 0 E
Viranşehir 106 37 13N 39 45 E
Virden, Canada 63 49 50N 100 56W
Virden, Ill. 21 39 30N 89 46W
Virden, N. Mex. 38 32 41N 109 0W
Vire 90 48 50N 0 53W
Virgem da Lapa 75 16 49 S 42 21W
Vírgenes, C. 78 52 19 S 68 21W
Virgil, Kans. 24 37 59N 96 1W
Virgil, S. Dak. 47 44 17N 98 25W
Virgilina 54 36 33N 78 47W
Virgin 52 37 12N 113 11W
Virgin →, Canada 63 57 2N 108 17W
Virgin →, U.S.A. 35 36 28N 114 21W
Virgin Islands □ 57 18 30N 64 25W
Virginia, Idaho 20 42 30N 112 10W
Virginia, Ill. 21 39 57N 90 13W
Virginia, Minn. 30 47 31N 92 32W
Virginia □ 54 37 30N 78 45W
Virginia Beach 54 36 51N 75 59W
Virginia City, Mont. 33 45 18N 111 56W
Virginia City, Nev. 35 39 19N 119 39W
Virginia Falls 62 61 38N 125 42W
Virginia Mts. 35 39 50N 119 30W
Virginiatown 60 48 9N 79 36W
Viroqua 55 43 34N 90 53W
Virton 87 49 35N 5 32 E
Virú 72 8 25 S 78 45W
Virudunagar 108 9 30N 78 0 E
Vis 94 43 0N 16 10 E
Visalia 15 36 20N 119 18W
Visayan Sea 111 11 30N 123 30 E
Visby 97 57 37N 18 18 E
Viscount Melville Sd. 4 74 10N 108 0W
Visé 87 50 44N 5 41 E
Višegrad 95 43 47N 19 17 E
Viseu, Brazil 74 1 10 S 46 5W
Viseu, Portugal 91 40 40N 7 55W
Vishakhapatnam 109 17 45N 83 20 E
Visikoi I. 5 56 43 S 27 15W
Viso, Mte. 94 44 38N 7 5 E
Vista, Calif. 15 33 12N 117 14W
Vista, Mo. 32 37 58N 93 40W
Vistula = Wisła → 89 54 22N 18 55 E
Vit → 95 43 30N 24 30 E
Vitebsk 98 55 10N 30 15 E
Viterbo 94 42 25N 12 8 E
Viti Levu 128 17 30 S 177 30 E
Vitim 101 59 28N 112 35 E
Vitim → 101 59 26N 112 34 E
Vitória, Brazil 75 20 20 S 40 22W
Vitoria, Spain 91 42 50N 2 41W
Vitória da Conquista 75 14 51 S 40 51W
Vitória de São Antão 74 8 10 S 35 20W
Vitorino Friere 74 4 4 S 45 10W
Vittória 94 36 58N 14 30 E
Vittório Véneto 94 45 59N 12 18 E
Vivero 91 43 39N 7 38W
Vivian, La. 25 32 53N 93 59W
Vivian, S. Dak. 47 43 56N 100 18W
Vizcaíno, Desierto de 64 27 40N 113 50W
Vizcaíno, Sierra 64 27 30N 114 0W
Vizianagaram 109 18 6N 83 30 E
Viziru 95 45 0N 27 43 E
Vlaardingen 87 51 55N 4 21 E
Vladimir 98 56 15N 40 30 E
Vladimirovo 95 43 32N 23 22 E
Vladivostok 101 43 10N 131 53 E
Vlieland 87 53 16N 4 55 E
Vlissingen 87 51 26N 3 34 E
Vlonë = Vlórë 95 40 32N 19 28 E
Vlórë 95 40 32N 19 28 E
Vltava → 88 50 21N 14 30 E
Vogelkop = Doberai, Jazirah 111 1 25 S 133 0 E
Vogelsberg 88 50 37N 9 15 E
Vohibinany 123 18 49 S 49 4 E
Vohimarina 123 13 25 S 50 0 E
Vohimena, Tanjon' i 123 25 36 S 45 8 E
Vohipeno 123 22 22 S 47 51 E
Voi 122 3 25 S 38 32 E
Voineşti 95 45 5N 25 14 E
Voisey B. 61 56 15N 61 50W
Vojmsjön 96 64 55N 16 40 E
Volborg 33 45 51N 105 41W
Volcano 19 19 26N 155 14W
Volcano Is. 124 25 0N 141 0 E
Volchayevka 101 48 40N 134 30 E
Volda 96 62 9N 6 5 E
Volga, Iowa 23 42 48N 91 33W
Volga, S. Dak. 47 44 19N 96 56W
Volga → 99 48 30N 46 0 E
Volga Hts. = Privolzhskaya Vozvyshennost 99 51 0N 46 0 E
Volgograd 99 48 40N 44 25 E
Volgogradskoye Vdkhr. 99 50 0N 45 20 E
Volin 47 42 58N 97 11W
Volkhov → 98 60 8N 32 20 E
Vollenhove 87 52 40N 5 58 E
Volochanka 101 71 0N 94 28 E
Vologda 98 59 10N 40 0 E
Vólos 95 39 24N 22 59 E
Volsk 98 52 5N 47 22 E
Volta → 118 5 46N 0 41 E
Volta, L. 120 7 30N 0 15 E
Volta Redonda 75 22 31 S 44 5W
Volterra 94 43 24N 10 50 E
Volturno → 94 41 1N 13 55 E
Voluntown 28 41 34N 71 52W
Volusia County ◇ 17 29 0N 81 15W
Volzhskiy 99 48 56N 44 46 E
Vona 16 39 18N 102 45W
Vonore 49 35 36N 84 14W
Voorburg 87 52 5N 4 24 E
Voorheesville 39 42 39N 73 56W
Vopnafjörður 96 65 45N 14 40W
Vorarlberg □ 88 47 20N 10 0 E
Voríai Sporádhes 95 39 15N 23 30 E
Vorkuta 98 67 48N 64 20 E
Voronezh 98 51 40N 39 10 E
Voroshilovgrad 99 48 38N 39 15 E
Vorovskoye 101 54 30N 155 50 E
Vosges 90 48 20N 7 10 E
Vosges □ 90 48 12N 6 20 E
Voss 97 60 38N 6 26 E
Vostochnyy Sayan 101 54 0N 96 0 E
Vostok I. 125 10 5 S 152 23W
Votkinsk 98 57 0N 53 55 E
Votkinskoye Vdkhr. 98 57 30N 55 0 E
Vouga → 91 40 41N 8 40W
Voyageurs Nat. Park 30 48 32N 93 0W
Vozhe Oz. 98 60 45N 39 0 E
Voznesenka 101 56 40N 95 3 E
Voznesensk 99 47 35N 31 21 E
Voznesenye 98 61 0N 35 45 E
Vrancea □ 95 45 50N 26 45 E
Vrancei, Munţii 95 46 0N 26 30 E
Vrangelya, Ostrov 101 71 0N 180 0 E
Vranje 95 42 34N 21 54 E
Vratsa 95 43 13N 23 30 E
Vrbas → 95 45 8N 17 29 E
Vrede 123 27 24 S 29 6 E
Vredenburg 123 32 51 S 18 0 E
Vršac 95 45 8N 21 18 E
Vryburg 123 26 55 S 24 45 E
Vryheid 123 27 45 S 30 47 E
Vucha → 95 42 10N 24 26 E
Vught 87 51 38N 5 20 E
Vulcan, Canada 62 50 25N 113 15W
Vulcan, Romania 95 45 23N 23 17 E
Vulcan, U.S.A. 29 45 47N 87 53W
Vulcano 94 38 25N 14 58 E
Vŭlchedruma 95 43 42N 23 27 E
Vulture Mts. 12 33 45N 113 0W
Vung Tau 112 10 21N 107 4 E
Vŭrbitsa 95 42 59N 26 40 E
Vurshets 95 43 15N 23 23 E
Vutcani 95 46 26N 27 59 E
Vya 35 41 35N 119 52W
Vyatka → 98 56 30N 51 0 E
Vyatskiye Polyany 98 56 5N 51 0 E
Vyazemskiy 101 47 32N 134 45 E
Vyazma 98 55 10N 34 15 E
Vyborg 98 60 43N 28 47 E
Vychegda → 98 61 18N 46 36 E
Vychodné Beskydy 89 49 30N 22 0 E
Vyg-ozero 98 63 30N 34 0 E
Vyrnwy, L. 82 52 48N 3 30W
Vyshniy Volochek 98 57 30N 34 30 E
Vyshzha = imeni 26 Bakinskikh Komissarov 99 39 22N 54 10 E
Vytegra 98 61 0N 36 27 E

W

W.A.C. Bennett Dam 62 56 2N 122 6W
Wa 120 10 7N 2 25W
Waal → 87 51 59N 4 30 E
Wabakimi L. 60 50 38N 89 45W
Wabana 61 47 40N 53 0W
Wabasca 62 55 57N 113 56W
Wabash 22 40 48N 85 49W
Wabash → 22 37 48N 88 2W
Wabash County ◇, Ill. 21 38 30N 87 50W
Wabash County ◇, Ind. 22 40 50N 85 45W
Wabasha 30 44 23N 92 2W
Wabasha County ◇ 30 44 15N 92 15W
Wabasso, Fla. 17 27 45N 80 26W
Wabasso, Minn. 30 44 24N 95 15W
Wabaunsee 24 39 9N 96 21W
Wabaunsee County ◇ 24 39 0N 96 15W
Wabeno 55 45 26N 88 39W
Wabigoon L. 63 49 44N 92 44W
Wabowden 63 54 55N 98 38W
Wąbrzeźno 89 53 16N 18 57 E
Wabuk Pt. 60 55 20N 85 5W
Wabush 61 52 55N 66 52W
Wabuska 35 39 9N 119 11W
Waccamaw, L. 40 34 18N 78 31W
Waccasassa B. 17 29 10N 82 50W
Wachapreague 54 37 36N 75 42W
Wachusett Reservoir 28 42 24N 71 41W
Wacissa 17 30 22N 83 59W
Waco, Nebr. 34 40 54N 97 28W
Waco, Tex. 51 31 33N 97 9W
Waco L. 51 31 35N 97 12W
Waconda Lake 24 39 29N 98 19W
Waconichi, L. 60 50 8N 74 0W
Wad Banda 121 13 10N 27 56 E
Wad Hamid 121 16 30N 32 45 E
Wâd Medanî 121 14 28N 33 30 E
Wadayama 117 35 19N 134 52 E
Waddeneilanden 87 53 25N 5 10 E
Waddenzee 87 53 6N 5 10 E
Waddington 39 44 52N 75 12W
Waddington, Mt. 62 51 23N 125 15W
Wade 40 35 10N 78 44W
Wade Hampton ◇ 11 62 0N 164 0W
Wadena, Canada 63 51 57N 103 47W
Wadena, U.S.A. 30 46 26N 95 8W
Wadena County ◇ 30 46 30N 95 0W
Wadesboro 40 34 58N 80 5W
Wadhams 62 51 30N 127 30W
Wadi Halfa 121 21 53N 31 19 E
Wadi Şabāḩ 106 23 50N 48 30 E
Wading River 37 39 38N 74 31W
Wadley, Ala. 10 33 7N 85 34W
Wadley, Ga. 18 32 52N 82 24W
Wadsworth, Nev. 35 39 38N 119 17W
Wadsworth, Ohio 42 41 2N 81 44W
Wadsworth, Tex. 51 28 50N 95 56W
Waelder 51 29 42N 97 18W
Wafrah 106 28 33N 47 56 E
Wagener 46 33 39N 81 22W
Wageningen, Neth. 87 51 58N 5 40 E
Wageningen, Surinam 71 5 50N 56 50W
Wager B. 59 65 26N 88 40W
Wager Bay 59 65 56N 90 49W
Wagga Wagga 127 35 7 S 147 24 E
Waghete 111 4 10 S 135 50 E
Wagin 126 33 17 S 117 25 E
Wagner 47 43 5N 98 18W
Wagon Mound 38 36 1N 104 42W
Wagon Wheel Gap 16 37 46N 106 49W
Wagoner 43 35 58N 95 22W
Wagoner County ◇ 43 36 0N 95 30W
Wagontire 44 43 15N 119 52W
Wagontire Mt. 44 43 21N 119 53W
Wagram 40 34 54N 79 22W
Wah Wah Mts. 52 38 25N 113 40W
Wahai 111 2 48 S 129 35 E
Wahiawa 19 21 30N 158 2W
Wahiawa Reservoir 19 21 30N 158 3W
Wahkiakum County ◇ 53 46 10N 123 30W
Wahkon 30 46 7N 93 31W
Wahoo 34 41 13N 96 37W
Wahpeton 41 46 16N 96 36W
Waialee 19 21 41N 158 1W
Waialua 19 21 34N 158 8W
Waialua B. 19 21 35N 158 5W
Waianae 19 21 27N 158 11W
Waianae Mts. 19 21 30N 158 10W
Waiau → 128 42 47 S 173 22 E
Waiawa → 19 21 23N 157 59W
Waibeem 111 0 30 S 132 59 E
Waigeo 111 0 20 S 130 40 E
Waihi 128 37 23 S 175 52 E
Waihou → 128 37 15 S 175 40 E
Waikabubak 111 9 45 S 119 25 E
Waikaremoana 128 38 42 S 177 12 E
Waikari 128 42 58 S 172 41 E
Waikato → 128 37 23 S 174 43 E
Waikiki 19 21 17N 157 50W
Waikokopu 128 39 3 S 177 52 E
Waikouaiti 128 45 36 S 170 41 E
Wailua, Hawaii 19 22 3N 159 20W
Wailua, Hawaii 19 20 51N 156 8W
Wailuku 19 20 53N 156 30W
Waimanalo 19 21 21N 157 43W
Waimanalo B. 19 21 20N 157 40W
Waimanalo Beach 19 21 21N 157 42W
Waimano → 19 21 25N 157 58W
Waimate 128 44 45 S 171 3 E
Waimea, Hawaii 19 21 39N 158 3W
Waimea, Hawaii 19 21 58N 159 40W
Waimea B. 19 21 40N 158 5W
Wainganga → 108 18 50N 79 55 E
Waingapu 111 9 35 S 120 11 E
Waini → 71 8 20N 59 50W
Wainwright, Canada 63 52 50N 110 50W
Wainwright, Alaska 11 70 38N 160 2W
Wainwright, Okla. 43 35 37N 95 34W
Waiouru 128 39 28 S 175 41 E
Waipahu 19 21 23N 158 1W
Waipara 128 43 3 S 172 46 E
Waipawa 128 39 56 S 176 38 E
Waipio Acres 19 21 28N 158 1W
Waipio Peninsula 19 21 20N 158 0W
Waipiro 128 38 2 S 178 22 E
Waipu 128 35 59 S 174 29 E
Waipukurau 128 40 1 S 176 33 E
Wairakei 128 38 37 S 176 6 E
Wairarapa, L. 128 41 14 S 175 15 E
Wairoa 128 39 3 S 177 25 E
Waita Reservoir 19 21 55N 159 28W
Waitaki → 128 44 56 S 171 7 E
Waitara 128 38 59 S 174 15 E
Waite 26 45 20N 67 42W
Waite Park 30 45 33N 94 14W
Waits → 36 43 59N 72 8W
Waitsburg 53 46 16N 118 9W
Waitsfield 36 44 42N 72 50W
Waiuku 128 37 15 S 174 45 E
Wajima 117 37 30N 137 0 E
Wajir 122 1 42N 40 5 E
Waka 50 36 17N 101 3W
Wakarusa 22 41 32N 86 1W
Wakasa 117 35 20N 134 24 E
Wakasa-Wan 117 35 40N 135 30 E
Wakatipu, L. 128 45 5 S 168 33 E
Wakaw 63 52 39N 105 44W
Wakayama 117 34 15N 135 15 E
Wakayama-ken □ 117 33 50N 135 30 E
Wake County ◇ 40 35 40N 78 45W
Wake Forest 40 35 59N 78 30W
Wake I. 124 19 18N 166 36 E
WaKeeney 24 39 1N 99 53W
Wakefield, N.Z. 128 41 24 S 173 5 E
Wakefield, U.K. 82 53 41N 1 31W
Wakefield, Kans. 24 39 13N 97 1W
Wakefield, Mass. 28 42 30N 71 4W
Wakefield, Mich. 29 46 29N 89 56W
Wakefield, N.H. 36 43 35N 71 4W
Wakefield, Nebr. 34 42 16N 96 52W
Wakefield, R.I. 28 41 26N 71 30W
Wakefield, Va. 54 36 58N 76 59W
Wakema 109 16 30N 95 11 E
Wakita 43 36 53N 97 55W
Wakkanai 116 45 28N 141 35 E
Wakonda 47 43 0N 97 6W
Wakpala 47 45 40N 100 32W
Wakre 111 0 19 S 131 5 E
Wakuach L. 61 55 34N 67 32W
Wakulla 17 30 14N 84 14W
Wakulla Beach 17 30 6N 84 16W
Wakulla County ◇ 17 30 15N 84 20W
Wałbrzych 88 50 45N 16 18 E
Walbury Hill 83 51 22N 1 28W
Walcheren 87 51 30N 3 35 E
Walcott, Iowa 23 41 35N 90 47W
Walcott, N. Dak. 41 46 33N 96 56W
Walcott, Wyo. 56 41 46N 106 51W
Walcott L. 20 42 40N 113 29W
Walden, Colo. 16 40 44N 106 17W
Walden, N.Y. 39 41 34N 74 11W
Walden Reservoir 16 40 43N 106 17W
Walden Ridge 49 35 30N 85 15W
Waldo, Ark. 13 33 21N 93 18W
Waldo, Fla. 17 29 48N 82 10W
Waldo, Maine 26 44 31N 69 5W
Waldo, Ohio 42 40 28N 83 5W
Waldo County ◇ 26 44 25N 69 0W
Waldoboro 26 44 6N 69 23W
Waldorf, Md. 27 38 38N 76 55W
Waldorf, Minn. 30 43 56N 93 42W
Waldport 44 44 26N 124 4W
Waldron, Canada 63 50 53N 102 35W
Waldron, Ark. 13 34 54N 94 5W
Waldron, Ind. 22 39 27N 85 40W
Waldron, Mich. 29 41 44N 84 25W
Waldwick 37 41 1N 74 7W
Wales, Alaska 11 65 37N 168 5W
Wales, N. Dak. 41 48 54N 98 36W
Wales, Utah 52 39 29N 111 38W
Wales □ 86 52 30N 3 30W
Walford 23 41 53N 91 50W
Walgett 127 30 0 S 148 5 E
Walgreen Coast 5 75 15 S 105 0W
Walhalla, N. Dak. 41 48 55N 97 55W
Walhalla, S.C. 46 34 46N 83 4W
Walk, L. 50 29 31N 100 59W
Walker, Iowa 23 42 17N 91 47W
Walker, Mich. 29 42 58N 85 46W
Walker, Minn. 30 47 6N 94 35W
Walker, Mo. 32 37 54N 94 14W

Walker Watertowr

Walker, S. Dak. 47 45 55N 101 5W
Walker ➝ 35 38 54N 118 47W
Walker County ◇, Ala. 10 33 50N 87 17W
Walker County ◇, Ga. 18 34 45N 85 15W
Walker County ◇, Tex. 51 30 43N 95 33W
Walker L., Man., Canada 63 54 42N 95 57W
Walker L., Qué., Canada 61 50 20N 67 11W
Walker L., U.S.A. 35 38 42N 118 43W
Walker River Indian Reservation 35 39 0N 118 50W
Walkers Pt. 26 43 21N 70 28W
Walkersville 27 39 29N 77 21W
Walkerton 22 41 28N 86 29W
Walkertown 40 36 10N 80 10W
Walkerville 29 43 43N 86 8W
Wall, S. Dak. 47 44 0N 102 8W
Wall, Tex. 50 31 22N 100 18W
Wall Lake 23 42 16N 95 5W
Walla Walla 53 46 4N 118 20W
Walla Walla County ◇ 53 46 18N 118 37W
Wallace, Idaho 20 47 28N 115 56W
Wallace, Kans. 24 38 58N 101 36W
Wallace, N.C. 40 34 44N 77 59W
Wallace, Nebr. 34 40 50N 101 10W
Wallace, S. Dak. 47 45 5N 97 29W
Wallace County ◇ 24 38 50N 101 45W
Wallaceburg 60 42 34N 82 23W
Wallachia = Valahia 89 44 35N 25 0E
Walland 49 35 44N 83 49W
Wallaroo 127 33 56S 137 39E
Wallasey 82 53 26N 3 2W
Wallenpaupack, L. 45 41 25N 75 15W
Waller 51 30 4N 95 56W
Waller County ◇ 51 30 0N 96 0W
Wallingford, U.K. 82 51 40N 1 15W
Wallingford, Conn. 28 41 27N 72 50W
Wallingford, Iowa 23 43 19N 94 48W
Wallingford, Vt. 36 43 28N 72 59W
Wallis 51 29 38N 96 4W
Wallis & Futuna 124 13 18S 176 10W
Wallisville L. 51 29 57N 94 54W
Walloon L. 29 45 17N 85 0W
Wallowa 44 45 34N 117 32W
Wallowa ➝ 44 45 43N 117 47W
Wallowa County ◇ 44 45 30N 117 10W
Wallowa Mts. 44 45 20N 117 30W
Wallowa-Whitman National Forest 44 45 15N 117 20W
Walls 31 34 58N 90 9W
Wallsburg 52 40 23N 111 25W
Wallsend 82 54 59N 1 30W
Wallula 53 46 5N 118 54W
Wallula, L. 53 46 2N 118 59W
Walmsley, L. 63 63 25N 108 36W
Walney, Isle of 82 54 5N 3 15W
Walnut, Ill. 21 41 33N 89 36W
Walnut, Iowa 23 41 29N 95 13W
Walnut, Kans. 24 37 36N 95 5W
Walnut, Miss. 31 34 57N 88 54W
Walnut, N.C. 40 35 51N 82 44W
Walnut ➝ 24 37 3N 97 0W
Walnut Canyon National Monument 12 35 15N 111 20W
Walnut Cove 40 36 18N 80 9W
Walnut Creek 14 37 54N 122 4W
Walnut Grove, Ala. 10 34 4N 86 18W
Walnut Grove, Miss. 31 32 36N 89 28W
Walnut Grove, Mo. 32 37 25N 93 33W
Walnut Hill 17 30 53N 87 30W
Walnut Ridge 13 36 4N 90 57W
Walnut Springs 51 32 3N 97 45W
Walpole, Mass. 28 42 9N 71 15W
Walpole, N.H. 36 43 5N 72 26W
Walsall 83 52 36N 1 59W
Walsenburg 16 37 38N 104 47W
Walsh 16 37 23N 102 17W
Walsh County ◇ 41 48 24N 97 45W
Walter F. George Reservoir 10 31 38N 85 4W
Walterboro 46 32 55N 80 40W
Walters 43 34 22N 98 19W
Walterville 44 44 4N 122 48W
Walthall 31 33 37N 89 17W
Walthall County ◇ 31 31 7N 90 9W
Waltham, Maine 26 44 43N 68 20W
Waltham, Mass. 28 42 23N 71 14W
Waltham Sta. 60 45 57N 76 57W
Walthill 34 42 9N 96 30W
Waltman 56 43 4N 107 12W
Walton, Ind. 22 40 40N 86 15W
Walton, Kans. 24 38 7N 97 15W
Walton, Ky. 49 38 52N 84 37W
Walton, N.Y. 39 42 10N 75 8W
Walton County ◇, Fla. 17 30 30N 86 10W
Walton County ◇, Ga. 18 33 45N 83 45W
Waltonville 21 38 13N 89 2W
Walvisbaai 123 23 0S 14 28E
Walworth County ◇, S. Dak. 47 45 30N 100 0W
Walworth County ◇, Wis. 55 42 40N 88 30W
Wamac 21 38 31N 89 8W
Wamba 122 2 10N 27 57E
Wamego 24 39 12N 96 18W
Wamena 111 4 4S 138 57E
Wampsville 39 43 5N 75 42W
Wampum 45 40 54N 80 21W
Wamsasi 111 3 27S 126 7E
Wamsutter 56 41 40N 107 58W
Wana 108 32 20N 69 32E
Wanaka L. 128 44 33S 169 7E
Wanamingo 30 44 18N 92 47W
Wan'an 115 26 26N 114 49E
Wanapiri 111 4 30S 135 59E
Wanapitei L. 60 46 45N 80 40W
Wanaque 37 41 2N 74 18W
Wanaque Reservoir 37 41 2N 74 18W
Wanatah 22 41 26N 86 54W
Wanblee 47 43 34N 101 40W
Wanchese 40 35 51N 75 38W
Wanda 30 44 19N 95 13W
Wanda Shan 114 46 0N 132 0E
Wandaik 71 4 27N 59 35W
Wandoan 127 26 5S 149 55E
Wanette 43 34 58N 97 2W
Wang Saphung 112 17 18N 101 46E
Wangal 111 6 8S 134 9E
Wanganui 128 39 56S 175 3E
Wangaratta 127 36 21S 146 19E
Wangdu 114 38 40N 115 7E
Wangerooge 88 53 47N 7 52E
Wangiwangi 111 5 22S 123 37E
Wangjiang 115 30 10N 116 42E
Wango 27 38 20N 75 25W
Wangqing 114 43 12N 129 42E
Wanless 63 54 11N 101 21W
Wann 43 36 55N 95 48W
Wanning 115 18 48N 110 22E
Wanquan 114 40 50N 114 40E
Wanxian 115 30 42N 108 20E
Wanyuan 115 32 4N 108 3E
Wanzai 115 28 7N 114 30E
Wapakoneta 42 40 34N 84 12W
Wapanucka 43 34 23N 96 26W
Wapato 53 46 27N 120 25W
Wapawekka L. 63 54 55N 104 40W
Wapello 23 41 11N 91 11W
Wapello County ◇ 23 41 0N 92 25W
Wapikopa L. 60 52 56N 87 53W
Wapinitia Pass 44 45 14N 121 42W
Wapiti 56 44 28N 109 26W
Wappapello, L. 32 36 56N 90 17W
Wappingers Falls 39 41 36N 73 55W
Wapsipinicon ➝ 23 41 44N 90 19W
War 54 37 18N 81 41W
Warangal 108 17 58N 79 35E
Warburton ➝ 127 28 4S 137 28E
Ward, N.Z. 128 41 49S 174 11E
Ward, U.S.A. 47 44 9N 96 28W
Ward County ◇, N. Dak. 41 48 5N 101 30W
Ward County ◇, Tex. 50 31 32N 103 8W
Wardell 32 36 21N 89 49W
Warden 53 46 58N 119 2W
Wardensville 54 39 5N 78 36W
Wardha 108 20 45N 78 39E
Wardha ➝ 108 19 57N 79 11E
Wardlow 62 50 56N 111 31W
Wardsville 32 38 29N 92 11W
Ware, Canada 62 57 26N 125 41W
Ware, U.S.A. 28 42 16N 72 14W
Ware ➝ 28 42 11N 72 22W
Ware County ◇ 18 31 10N 82 20W
Ware Shoals 46 34 24N 82 15W
Wareham 28 41 46N 70 43W
Warehouse Point 28 41 56N 72 37W
Waresboro 18 31 15N 82 29W
Warialda 127 29 29S 150 33E
Wariap 111 1 30S 134 5E
Warkopi 111 1 12S 134 9E
Warley 83 52 30N 2 0W
Warm Springs, Ga. 18 32 53N 84 41W
Warm Springs, Oreg. 44 44 46N 121 16W
Warm Springs, Va. 54 38 3N 79 47W
Warm Springs Indian Reservation 44 45 0N 121 25W
Warm Springs Reservoir 44 43 35N 118 13W
Warman 63 52 19N 106 30W
Warmbad, Namibia 123 28 25S 18 42E
Warmbad, S. Africa 123 24 51S 28 19E
Warnemünde 88 54 9N 12 5E
Warner, Canada 62 49 17N 112 12W
Warner, N.H. 36 43 17N 71 49W
Warner, Okla. 43 35 30N 95 18W
Warner, S. Dak. 47 45 20N 98 30W
Warner Mts. 14 41 40N 120 15W
Warner Range 44 42 25N 120 5W
Warner Robins 18 32 37N 83 36W
Warner Valley 44 42 25N 119 50W
Warnes 73 17 30S 63 10W
Warr Acres 43 35 31N 97 37W
Warrego ➝ 127 30 24S 145 21E
Warrego Ra. 127 24 58S 146 0E
Warren, Ark. 13 33 37N 92 4W
Warren, Conn. 28 41 0N 73 0W
Warren, Idaho 20 45 16N 115 41W
Warren, Ill. 21 42 29N 90 0W
Warren, Ind. 22 40 41N 85 26W
Warren, Minn. 30 48 12N 96 46W
Warren, N.H. 36 43 56N 71 54W
Warren, Ohio 42 41 14N 80 49W
Warren, Pa. 45 41 51N 79 9W
Warren, R.I. 28 41 43N 71 17W
Warren, Tex. 51 30 37N 94 24W
Warren, Vt. 36 44 7N 72 50W
Warren County ◇, Ga. 18 33 20N 82 40W
Warren County ◇, Ill. 21 40 50N 90 35W
Warren County ◇, Ind. 22 40 20N 87 25W
Warren County ◇, Iowa 23 41 20N 93 35W
Warren County ◇, Ky. 48 37 0N 86 25W
Warren County ◇, Miss. 31 32 21N 90 53W
Warren County ◇, Mo. 32 38 45N 91 10W
Warren County ◇, N.C. 40 36 15N 78 0W
Warren County ◇, N.J. 37 40 50N 75 0W
Warren County ◇, N.Y. 39 43 35N 73 45W
Warren County ◇, Ohio 42 39 26N 84 13W
Warren County ◇, Pa. 45 41 50N 79 15W
Warren County ◇, Tenn. 49 35 41N 85 46W
Warren County ◇, Va. 54 38 55N 78 12W
Warren Grove 37 39 44N 74 22W
Warren Pks. 56 44 29N 104 28W
Warrenpoint 85 54 7N 6 15W
Warrens 55 44 8N 90 30W
Warrensburg, Ill. 21 39 56N 89 4W
Warrensburg, Mo. 32 38 46N 93 44W
Warrensburg, N.Y. 39 43 29N 73 46W
Warrenton, S. Africa 123 28 9S 24 47E
Warrenton, Ga. 18 33 24N 82 40W
Warrenton, Mo. 32 38 49N 91 9W
Warrenton, N.C. 40 36 24N 78 9W
Warrenton, Oreg. 44 46 10N 123 56W
Warrenton, Va. 54 38 43N 77 48W
Warrenville 46 33 32N 81 48W
Warri 120 5 30N 5 41E
Warrick County ◇ 22 38 5N 87 15W
Warrina 126 28 12S 135 50E
Warrington, U.K. 82 53 25N 2 38W
Warrington, U.S.A. 17 30 23N 87 17W
Warrior 10 33 49N 86 49W
Warrnambool 127 38 25S 142 30E
Warroad 30 48 54N 95 19W
Warsa 111 0 47S 135 55E
Warsaw = Warszawa 89 52 13N 21 0E
Warsaw, Ill. 21 40 22N 91 26W
Warsaw, Ind. 22 41 14N 85 51W
Warsaw, Ky. 49 38 47N 84 54W
Warsaw, Mo. 32 38 15N 93 23W
Warsaw, N.C. 40 35 0N 78 5W
Warsaw, N.Y. 39 42 45N 78 8W
Warsaw, Va. 54 37 58N 76 46W
Warszawa 89 52 13N 21 0E
Warta ➝ 88 52 35N 14 39E
Wartburg 49 36 6N 84 36W
Warthe = Warta ➝ 88 52 35N 14 39E
Warthen 18 33 6N 82 48W
Wartrace 48 35 32N 86 20W
Waru 111 3 30S 130 36E
Warwick, Australia 127 28 10S 152 1E
Warwick, U.K. 83 52 17N 1 36W
Warwick, Ga. 18 31 50N 83 57W
Warwick, Mass. 28 42 0N 72 0W
Warwick, Md. 27 39 25N 75 47W
Warwick, N. Dak. 41 47 51N 98 43W
Warwick, N.Y. 39 41 16N 74 22W
Warwick, R.I. 28 41 42N 71 28W
Warwick □ 83 52 20N 1 30W
Wasa 62 49 45N 115 50W
Wasatch County ◇ 52 40 20N 111 15W
Wasatch National Forest 52 40 50N 110 40W
Wasatch Plateau 52 39 20N 111 30W
Wasatch Range 52 40 0N 111 30W
Wasco, Calif. 15 35 36N 119 20W
Wasco, Oreg. 44 45 36N 120 42W
Wasco County ◇ 44 45 15N 121 15W
Waseca 30 44 5N 93 30W
Waseca County ◇ 30 44 0N 93 40W
Wasekamio L. 63 56 45N 108 45W
Wash, The 82 52 58N 0 20E
Washakie County ◇ 56 44 0N 107 40W
Washburn, Ill. 21 40 55N 89 17W
Washburn, Maine 26 46 47N 68 9W
Washburn, Mo. 32 36 35N 93 58W
Washburn, N. Dak. 41 47 17N 101 2W
Washburn, Tex. 50 35 11N 101 34W
Washburn, Wis. 55 46 40N 90 54W
Washburn County ◇ 55 45 50N 91 50W
Washim 108 20 3N 77 0E
Washington, Ark. 13 33 47N 93 41W
Washington, Conn. 28 41 39N 73 19W
Washington, D.C. 27 38 54N 77 2W
Washington, Ga. 18 33 44N 82 44W
Washington, Ill. 21 40 42N 89 24W
Washington, Ind. 22 38 40N 87 10W
Washington, Iowa 23 41 18N 91 42W
Washington, Kans. 24 39 49N 97 3W
Washington, Ky. 49 38 37N 83 49W
Washington, La. 25 30 37N 92 4W
Washington, Maine 26 44 16N 69 22W
Washington, Mo. 32 38 33N 91 1W
Washington, N.C. 40 35 33N 77 3W
Washington, N.H. 36 43 11N 72 8W
Washington, N.J. 37 40 46N 74 59W
Washington, Nebr. 34 41 24N 96 13W
Washington, Okla. 43 35 4N 97 29W
Washington, Pa. 45 40 10N 80 15W
Washington, Utah 52 37 8N 113 31W
Washington, Va. 54 38 43N 78 10W
Washington □ 53 47 30N 120 30W
Washington, Mt. 36 44 16N 71 18W
Washington County ◇, Ala. 10 31 22N 88 15W
Washington County ◇, Ark. 13 36 4N 94 10W
Washington County ◇, Colo. 16 40 0N 103 10W
Washington County ◇, Fla. 17 30 30N 85 45W
Washington County ◇, Ga. 18 33 0N 82 50W
Washington County ◇, Idaho 20 44 30N 116 50W
Washington County ◇, Ill. 21 38 20N 89 25W
Washington County ◇, Ind. 22 38 35N 86 5W
Washington County ◇, Iowa 23 41 20N 91 40W
Washington County ◇, Kans. 24 39 45N 97 0W
Washington County ◇, Ky. 49 37 45N 85 10W
Washington County ◇, Maine 26 45 0N 67 30W
Washington County ◇, Md. 27 39 40N 78 0W
Washington County ◇, Minn. 30 45 10N 92 55W
Washington County ◇, Miss. 31 33 16N 90 53W
Washington County ◇, Mo. 32 38 0N 90 50W
Washington County ◇, N.C. 40 35 50N 76 30W
Washington County ◇, N.Y. 39 43 20N 73 25W
Washington County ◇, Nebr. 34 41 30N 96 15W
Washington County ◇, Ohio 42 39 25N 81 27W
Washington County ◇, Okla. 43 36 40N 95 55W
Washington County ◇, Oreg. 44 45 30N 123 0W
Washington County ◇, Pa. 45 40 8N 80 8W
Washington County ◇, R.I. 28 41 30N 71 40W
Washington County ◇, Tenn. 49 36 18N 82 29W
Washington County ◇, Tex. 51 30 10N 96 24W
Washington County ◇, Utah 52 37 20N 113 30W
Washington County ◇, Va. 54 36 55N 82 0W
Washington County ◇, Vt. 36 44 15N 72 40W
Washington County ◇, Wis. 55 43 20N 88 15W
Washington Court House 42 39 32N 83 26W
Washington Grove 27 39 8N 77 11W
Washington I. 55 45 23N 86 54W
Washington Island 55 45 24N 86 56W
Washington Parish ◇ 25 30 51N 90 9W
Washington Terrace 52 41 11N 111 59W
Washir 108 32 15N 63 50E
Washita ➝ 43 34 8N 96 36W
Washita County ◇ 43 35 15N 99 0W
Washoe City 35 39 19N 119 49W
Washoe County ◇ 35 41 0N 119 40W
Washoe L. 35 39 16N 119 48W
Washta 23 42 35N 95 43W
Washtenaw County ◇ 29 42 15N 83 50W
Washtucna 53 46 45N 118 19W
Wasian 111 1 47S 133 19E
Wasilla 11 61 35N 149 26W
Wasior 111 2 43S 134 30E
Waskaiowaka, L. 63 56 33N 96 23W
Waskesiu Lake 63 53 55N 106 5W
Waskish 30 48 10N 94 31W
Waskom 51 32 29N 94 4W
Wassaw I. 18 31 53N 80 58W
Wassaw Sd. 18 31 55N 80 55W
Wassenaar 87 52 8N 4 24E
Wassuk Range 35 38 40N 118 50W
Wasta 47 44 4N 102 27W
Waswanipi 60 49 40N 76 29W
Waswanipi, L. 60 49 35N 76 40W
Watangpone 111 4 29S 120 25E
Watauga County ◇ 40 36 15N 81 45W
Watauga L. 49 36 19N 82 7W
Water Valley, Ky. 48 36 34N 88 49W
Water Valley, Miss. 31 34 10N 89 38W
Waterberg 123 20 30S 17 18E
Waterbury, Conn. 28 41 33N 73 3W
Waterbury, Nebr. 34 42 27N 96 44W
Waterbury, Vt. 36 44 20N 72 46W
Waterbury Center 36 44 22N 72 43W
Waterbury L. 63 58 10N 104 22W
Wateree ➝ 46 33 45N 80 37W
Wateree L. 46 34 20N 80 42W
Waterflow 38 36 45N 108 27W
Waterford, Ireland 85 52 16N 7 8W
Waterford, Calif. 14 37 38N 120 46W
Waterford, Conn. 28 41 20N 72 9W
Waterford, Maine 26 44 14N 70 46W
Waterford, Miss. 31 34 39N 89 28W
Waterford, Pa. 45 41 57N 79 59W
Waterford, Wis. 55 42 46N 88 13W
Waterford □ 85 52 10N 7 40W
Waterford Harb. 85 52 10N 6 58W
Watergap 49 37 38N 82 45W
Waterhen L., Man., Canada 63 52 10N 99 40W
Waterhen L., Sask., Canada 63 54 28N 108 25W
Waterloo, Belgium 87 50 43N 4 25E
Waterloo, Canada 60 43 30N 80 32W
Waterloo, S. Leone 120 8 26N 13 8W
Waterloo, Ala. 10 34 55N 88 4W
Waterloo, Ark. 13 33 33N 93 15W
Waterloo, Ill. 21 38 20N 90 9W
Waterloo, Ind. 22 41 26N 85 1W
Waterloo, Iowa 23 42 30N 92 21W
Waterloo, Mont. 33 45 43N 112 12W
Waterloo, N.Y. 39 42 54N 76 52W
Waterloo, Wis. 55 43 11N 88 59W
Waterman 21 41 46N 88 47W
Waterproof 25 31 48N 91 23W
Watersmeet 29 46 16N 89 11W
Waterton-Glacier International Peace Park 33 48 45N 115 0W
Waterton Lakes Nat. Park 62 49 5N 114 15W
Watertown, Conn. 28 41 36N 73 7W
Watertown, Fla. 17 30 11N 82 36W
Watertown, Mass. 28 42 22N 71 11W

Watertown West Frankfort

Watertown, N.Y. **39** 43 59N 75 55W
Watertown, S. Dak. **47** 44 54N 97 7W
Watertown, Tenn. **48** 36 6N 86 8W
Watertown, Wis. **55** 43 12N 88 43W
Waterville, Kans. **24** 39 42N 96 45W
Waterville, Maine **26** 44 33N 69 38W
Waterville, Minn. **30** 44 13N 93 34W
Waterville, N.Y. **39** 42 56N 75 23W
Waterville, Ohio **42** 41 30N 83 43W
Waterville, Vt. **36** 44 42N 72 47W
Waterville, Wash. **53** 47 39N 120 4W
Waterville Valley **36** 43 57N 71 31W
Watervliet **39** 42 44N 73 42W
Wates **111** 7 53 S 110 6 E
Watford **83** 51 38N 0 23W
Watford City **41** 47 48N 103 17W
Wathaman → **63** 57 16N 102 59W
Wathena **24** 39 46N 94 57W
Watkins **30** 45 19N 94 24W
Watkins Glen **39** 42 23N 76 52W
Watkinsville **18** 33 52N 83 25W
Watonga **43** 35 51N 98 25W
Watonwan County ◇ **30** 44 0N 94 40W
Watova **43** 36 37N 95 39W
Watrous, Canada **63** 51 40N 105 25W
Watrous, U.S.A. **38** 35 48N 104 59W
Watsa **122** 3 4N 29 30 E
Watseka **21** 40 47N 87 44W
Watson, Canada **63** 52 10N 104 30W
Watson, Ark. **13** 33 54N 91 15W
Watson, Ill. **21** 39 2N 88 34W
Watson, Minn. **30** 45 1N 95 48W
Watson, Mo. **32** 40 29N 95 40W
Watson Lake **62** 60 6N 128 49W
Watsontown **45** 41 5N 76 52W
Watsonville **14** 36 55N 121 45W
Watts **43** 36 7N 94 34W
Watts Bar L. **49** 35 37N 84 47W
Wattsburg **45** 42 0N 79 49W
Wattsville **46** 34 31N 82 2W
Watuata = Batuata **111** 6 12 S 122 42 E
Watubela, Kepulauan **111** 4 28 S 131 35 E
Watuppa Pond **28** 41 42N 71 6W
Waubay **47** 45 20N 97 18W
Waubay L. **47** 45 25N 97 24W
Waubun **30** 47 11N 95 57W
Wauchula **17** 27 33N 81 49W
Waucoba Mt. **15** 37 1N 118 0W
Waucoma **23** 43 2N 92 1W
Waugh **63** 49 40N 95 11W
Waugoshance Pt. **29** 45 46N 85 1W
Waukee **23** 41 37N 93 53W
Waukeenah **17** 30 25N 83 57W
Waukegan **21** 42 22N 87 50W
Waukesha **55** 43 1N 88 14W
Waukesha County ◇ **55** 43 0N 88 15W
Waukomis **43** 36 17N 97 54W
Waukon **23** 43 16N 91 29W
Waunakee **55** 43 11N 89 27W
Wauneta **34** 40 25N 101 23W
Waupaca **55** 44 21N 89 5W
Waupaca County ◇ **55** 44 25N 89 0W
Waupun **55** 43 38N 88 44W
Waurika **43** 34 10N 98 0W
Waurika Res. **43** 34 10N 98 0W
Wausa **34** 42 30N 97 32W
Wausau, Fla. **17** 30 38N 85 35W
Wausau, Wis. **55** 44 58N 89 38W
Wausaukee **55** 45 23N 87 57W
Wauseon **42** 41 33N 84 8W
Waushara County ◇ **55** 44 10N 89 15W
Wautoma **55** 44 4N 89 18W
Wauwatosa **55** 43 3N 88 0W
Wauzeka **55** 43 5N 90 53W
Wave Hill **126** 17 32 S 131 0 E
Waveland, Ind. **22** 39 53N 87 3W
Waveland, Miss. **31** 30 17N 89 23W
Waveney → **83** 52 24N 1 20 E
Waverley **128** 39 46 S 174 37 E
Waverley Hall **18** 32 41N 84 44W
Waverly, Ala. **10** 32 44N 85 35W
Waverly, Fla. **17** 27 59N 81 37W
Waverly, Ga. **18** 31 6N 81 43W
Waverly, Ill. **21** 39 36N 89 57W
Waverly, Iowa **23** 42 44N 92 29W
Waverly, Kans. **24** 38 23N 95 36W
Waverly, Ky. **48** 37 43N 87 48W
Waverly, Mo. **32** 39 13N 93 31W
Waverly, N.Y. **39** 42 1N 76 32W
Waverly, Nebr. **34** 40 55N 96 32W
Waverly, Tenn. **48** 36 5N 87 48W
Waverly, Va. **54** 37 2N 77 6W
Waverly, Wash. **53** 47 21N 117 14W
Wavre **87** 50 43N 4 38 E
Wâw **121** 7 45N 28 1 E
Waw al Kabir **121** 25 20N 17 20 E
Wawa **60** 47 59N 84 47W
Wawanesa **63** 49 36N 99 40W
Wawasee, L. **22** 41 24N 85 42W
Wawona **14** 37 32N 119 39W
Waxahachie **51** 32 24N 96 51W
Waxhaw **40** 34 56N 80 45W
Way **31** 32 45N 90 2W
Wayabula Rau **111** 2 29N 128 17 E
Wayan **20** 42 58N 111 23W
Waycross **18** 31 13N 82 21W
Wayland, Iowa **23** 41 8N 91 40W
Wayland, Ky. **49** 37 27N 82 48W
Wayland, Mass. **28** 42 22N 71 22W
Wayland, Mich. **29** 42 40N 85 39W
Wayland, N.Y. **39** 42 34N 77 35W
Wayne, Kans. **24** 39 43N 97 33W
Wayne, Mich. **29** 42 17N 83 23W
Wayne, N.J. **37** 40 55N 74 17W
Wayne, Nebr. **34** 42 14N 97 1W
Wayne, Ohio **42** 41 18N 83 29W
Wayne, Okla. **43** 34 55N 97 19W
Wayne, W. Va. **54** 38 13N 82 27W
Wayne County ◇, Ga. **18** 31 30N 82 0W
Wayne County ◇, Ill. **21** 38 25N 88 25W
Wayne County ◇, Ind. **22** 39 50N 85 0W
Wayne County ◇, Iowa **23** 40 45N 93 20W
Wayne County ◇, Ky. **49** 36 45N 84 50W
Wayne County ◇, Mich. **29** 42 15N 83 15W
Wayne County ◇, Miss. **31** 31 40N 88 39W
Wayne County ◇, Mo. **32** 37 5N 90 30W
Wayne County ◇, N.C. **40** 35 20N 78 0W
Wayne County ◇, N.Y. **39** 43 10N 77 0W
Wayne County ◇, Nebr. **34** 42 15N 97 5W
Wayne County ◇, Ohio **42** 40 48N 81 56W
Wayne County ◇, Pa. **45** 41 35N 75 15W
Wayne County ◇, Tenn. **48** 35 10N 87 44W
Wayne County ◇, Utah **52** 38 15N 111 0W
Wayne County ◇, W. Va. **54** 38 13N 82 27W
Wayne National Forest **42** 39 33N 81 4W
Waynesboro, Ga. **18** 33 6N 82 1W
Waynesboro, Miss. **31** 31 40N 88 39W
Waynesboro, Pa. **45** 39 45N 77 35W
Waynesboro, Tenn. **48** 35 19N 87 46W
Waynesboro, Va. **54** 38 4N 78 53W
Waynesburg **45** 39 54N 80 11W
Waynesville, Ill. **21** 40 15N 89 8W
Waynesville, Mo. **32** 37 50N 92 12W
Waynesville, N.C. **40** 35 28N 82 58W
Waynesville, Ohio **42** 39 32N 84 5W
Waynetown **22** 40 5N 87 4W
Waynoka **43** 36 35N 98 53W
Wayside, Ga. **18** 33 4N 83 37W
Wayside, Miss. **31** 33 16N 91 2W
Wayside, Wis. **55** 44 15N 87 57W
Waza **108** 33 22N 69 22 E
Wazirabad **108** 32 30N 74 8 E
We **110** 5 51N 95 18 E
Weakley County ◇ **48** 36 14N 88 50W
Weald, The **83** 51 7N 0 9 E
Wear → **82** 54 55N 1 22W
Weare **36** 43 6N 71 44W
Weatherby **32** 39 55N 94 14W
Weatherford, Okla. **43** 35 32N 98 43W
Weatherford, Tex. **51** 32 46N 97 48W
Weatherly **45** 40 57N 75 50W
Weathersby **31** 31 56N 89 50W
Weaubleau **32** 37 54N 93 32W
Weaverville, Calif. **14** 40 44N 122 56W
Weaverville, N.C. **40** 35 42N 82 34W
Webb, Iowa **23** 42 57N 95 1W
Webb, Miss. **31** 33 57N 90 21W
Webb City, Mo. **32** 37 9N 94 28W
Webb City, Okla. **43** 36 48N 96 42W
Webb County ◇ **51** 27 30N 99 10W
Webber **24** 39 56N 98 2W
Webbville **49** 38 11N 82 52W
Weber → **52** 41 10N 112 10W
Weber County ◇ **52** 41 20N 111 40W
Webster, Fla. **17** 28 37N 82 3W
Webster, Iowa **23** 41 26N 92 10W
Webster, Mass. **28** 42 3N 71 53W
Webster, N. Dak. **41** 48 17N 98 53W
Webster, N.Y. **39** 43 13N 77 26W
Webster, S. Dak. **47** 45 20N 97 31W
Webster, Wis. **55** 45 53N 92 22W
Webster City **23** 42 28N 93 49W
Webster County ◇, Ga. **18** 32 0N 84 35W
Webster County ◇, Iowa **23** 42 25N 94 10W
Webster County ◇, Ky. **48** 37 30N 87 40W
Webster County ◇, Miss. **31** 33 37N 89 17W
Webster County ◇, Mo. **32** 37 15N 92 50W
Webster County ◇, Nebr. **34** 40 15N 98 30W
Webster County ◇, W. Va. **54** 38 29N 80 25W
Webster Parish ◇ **25** 32 40N 93 20W
Webster Reservoir **24** 39 25N 99 26W
Webster Springs **54** 38 29N 80 25W
Weda **111** 0 21N 127 50 E
Weda, Teluk **111** 0 30N 127 50 E
Weddell I. **78** 51 50 S 61 0W
Weddell Sea **5** 72 30 S 40 0W
Wedgefield **46** 33 53N 80 31W
Wedgeport **61** 43 44N 65 59W
Wedowee **10** 33 19N 85 29W
Weed, Calif. **14** 41 25N 122 23W
Weed, N. Mex. **38** 32 48N 105 31W
Weed Heights **35** 38 59N 119 13W
Weedville **45** 41 17N 78 30W
Weekapaug **28** 41 20N 71 45W
Weeks **25** 29 48N 91 49W
Weekstown **37** 39 37N 74 37W
Weeksville **40** 36 13N 76 10W
Weeping Water **34** 40 52N 96 8W
Weert **87** 51 15N 5 43 E
Wei He →, Hebei, China **114** 36 10N 115 45 E
Wei He →, Shaanxi, China **115** 34 38N 110 15 E
Weifang **114** 36 44N 119 7 E
Weihai **114** 37 30N 122 6 E
Weimar, Germany **88** 51 0N 11 20 E
Weimar, Calif. **14** 39 2N 120 59W
Weimar, Tex. **51** 29 42N 96 47W
Weinan **115** 34 31N 109 29 E
Weiner **13** 35 37N 90 54W
Weipa **127** 12 40 S 141 50 E
Weippe **20** 46 23N 115 56W
Weir, Kans. **24** 37 19N 94 46W
Weir, Ky. **48** 37 7N 87 13W
Weir, Miss. **31** 33 16N 89 18W
Weir → **63** 56 54N 93 21W
Weir, L. **17** 29 0N 81 57W
Weir River **63** 56 49N 94 6W
Weirsdale **17** 28 59N 81 55W
Weirton **54** 40 24N 80 35W
Weiser **20** 44 45N 116 58W
Weiser → **20** 44 14N 116 58W
Weishan **115** 34 47N 117 5 E
Weiss L. **10** 34 8N 85 48W
Weissert **34** 41 28N 99 27W
Weiyuan **114** 35 7N 104 10 E
Weizhou Dao **115** 21 0N 109 5 E
Wejherowo **89** 54 35N 18 12 E
Wekusko **63** 54 30N 99 45W
Wekusko L. **63** 54 40N 99 50W
Welby **63** 50 33N 101 29W
Welch, Okla. **43** 36 52N 95 6W
Welch, Tex. **50** 32 56N 102 8W
Welch, W. Va. **54** 37 26N 81 35W
Welcome, Md. **27** 38 28N 77 8W
Welcome, Minn. **30** 43 40N 94 37W
Welcome, N.C. **40** 35 55N 80 15W
Weld **26** 44 42N 70 25W
Weld County ◇ **16** 40 45N 104 15W
Welda **24** 38 10N 95 18W
Weldon, Ill. **21** 40 7N 88 45W
Weldon, Iowa **23** 40 54N 93 44W
Weldon, N.C. **40** 36 25N 77 36W
Weldon Spring **32** 38 43N 90 41W
Weldona **16** 40 21N 103 58W
Weleetka **43** 35 20N 96 8W
Welkom **123** 28 0 S 26 50 E
Welland **60** 43 0N 79 15W
Welland → **82** 52 43N 0 10W
Wellborn **51** 30 32N 96 18W
Wellesley **28** 42 18N 71 18W
Wellesley Is. **127** 16 42 S 139 30 E
Wellfleet, Mass. **28** 41 56N 70 2W
Wellfleet, Nebr. **34** 40 45N 100 44W
Wellin **87** 50 5N 5 6 E
Wellingborough **83** 52 18N 0 41W
Wellington, Australia **127** 32 35 S 148 59 E
Wellington, Canada **60** 43 57N 77 20W
Wellington, N.Z. **128** 41 19 S 174 46 E
Wellington, Salop, U.K. **82** 52 42N 2 31W
Wellington, Somerset, U.K. **83** 50 58N 3 13W
Wellington, Colo. **16** 40 42N 105 0W
Wellington, Ill. **21** 40 32N 87 41W
Wellington, Kans. **24** 37 16N 97 24W
Wellington, Maine **26** 45 2N 69 36W
Wellington, Mo. **32** 39 8N 93 59W
Wellington, Nev. **35** 38 45N 119 23W
Wellington, Ohio **42** 41 10N 82 13W
Wellington, Tex. **50** 34 51N 100 13W
Wellington, Utah **52** 39 32N 110 44W
Wellington □ **128** 40 8 S 175 36 E
Wellington, I. **78** 49 30 S 75 0W
Wellman, Iowa **23** 41 28N 91 50W
Wellman, Tex. **50** 33 3N 102 26W
Wellpinit **53** 47 53N 117 59W
Wells, Norfolk, U.K. **82** 52 57N 0 51 E
Wells, Somerset, U.K. **83** 51 12N 2 39W
Wells, Kans. **24** 39 5N 97 33W
Wells, Maine **26** 43 20N 70 35W
Wells, Minn. **30** 43 45N 93 44W
Wells, N.Y. **39** 43 24N 74 17W
Wells, Nev. **35** 41 7N 114 58W
Wells, Tex. **51** 31 29N 94 56W
Wells, Vt. **36** 43 25N 73 10W
Wells → **36** 44 10N 72 3W
Wells County ◇, Ind. **22** 40 45N 85 15W
Wells County ◇, N. Dak. **41** 47 35N 99 45W
Wells Gray Prov. Park **62** 52 30N 120 15W
Wells L. **126** 26 44 S 123 15 E
Wellsboro **45** 41 45N 77 18W
Wellsburg, Iowa **23** 42 26N 92 56W
Wellsburg, N.Y. **39** 42 1N 76 44W
Wellsburg, W. Va. **54** 40 16N 80 37W
Wellsford **24** 37 37N 99 2W
Wellston, Mich. **29** 44 13N 85 58W
Wellston, Ohio **42** 39 7N 82 32W
Wellston, Okla. **43** 35 42N 97 4W
Wellsville, Kans. **24** 38 43N 95 5W
Wellsville, Mo. **32** 39 4N 91 34W
Wellsville, N.Y. **39** 42 7N 77 57W
Wellsville, Ohio **42** 40 36N 80 39W
Wellsville, Pa. **45** 40 3N 76 56W
Wellsville, Utah **52** 41 38N 111 56W
Wellton **12** 32 40N 114 8W
Wels **88** 48 9N 14 1 E
Welsh **25** 30 14N 92 49W
Welshpool **83** 52 40N 3 9W
Welton **23** 41 55N 90 36W
Welwyn **63** 50 20N 101 30W
Wem **82** 52 52N 2 45W
Wen Xian **115** 32 43N 104 36 E
Wenatchee **53** 47 25N 120 19W
Wenatchee → **53** 47 27N 120 19W
Wenatchee Mts. **53** 47 15N 120 30W
Wenatchee National Forest **53** 47 55N 120 55W
Wenchang **115** 19 38N 110 42 E
Wenchi **120** 7 46N 2 8W
Wenchow = Wenzhou **115** 28 0N 120 38 E
Wendell, Idaho **20** 42 47N 114 42W
Wendell, Minn. **30** 46 2N 96 6W
Wendell, N.C. **40** 35 47N 78 22W
Wendell, N.H. **36** 43 22N 72 9W
Wenden **12** 33 49N 113 33W
Wendeng **114** 37 15N 122 5 E
Wendesi **111** 2 30 S 134 17 E
Wendover **52** 40 44N 114 2W
Wengcheng **115** 24 22N 113 50 E
Wenlock → **127** 12 2 S 141 55 E
Wenona, Ill. **21** 41 3N 89 3W
Wenona, Md. **27** 38 8N 75 57W
Wensu **113** 41 15N 80 10 E
Wentworth, Australia **127** 34 2 S 141 54 E
Wentworth, Mo. **32** 36 59N 94 4W
Wentworth, N.C. **40** 36 24N 79 46W
Wentworth, N.H. **36** 43 52N 71 55W
Wentzville **32** 38 49N 90 51W
Wenut **111** 3 11 S 133 19 E
Wenxi **115** 35 20N 111 10 E
Wenzhou **115** 28 0N 120 38 E
Weott **14** 40 20N 123 55W
Wepener **123** 29 42 S 27 3 E
Werda **123** 25 24 S 23 15 E
Werder **105** 6 58N 45 1 E
Weri **111** 3 10 S 132 38 E
Werley **55** 43 1N 90 46W
Wersar **111** 1 30 S 131 55 E
Weser → **88** 53 33N 8 30 E
Wesiri **111** 7 30 S 126 30 E
Weskan **24** 38 52N 101 57W
Weslaco **50** 26 10N 97 58W
Wesley, Ga. **18** 32 29N 82 20W
Wesley, Iowa **23** 43 5N 93 59W
Wesley, Maine **26** 44 57N 67 40W
Wesleyville, Canada **61** 49 8N 53 36W
Wesleyville, U.S.A. **45** 42 9N 80 0W
Wessel Is. **127** 11 10 S 136 45 E
Wessington **47** 44 27N 98 42W
Wessington Springs **47** 44 5N 98 34W
Wesson, Ark. **13** 33 7N 92 46W
Wesson, Miss. **31** 31 42N 90 24W
West **51** 31 48N 97 6W
West → **36** 42 52N 72 33W
West Acton **28** 42 29N 71 29W
West Alexandria **42** 39 45N 84 32W
West Allis **55** 43 1N 88 0W
West Arlington **36** 43 8N 73 12W
West Arm Grand Traverse B. **29** 44 50N 85 40W
West B., Fla. **17** 30 10N 85 45W
West B., La. **25** 29 3N 89 22W
West B., Tex. **51** 29 14N 95 0W
West Babylon **39** 40 42N 73 21W
West Baton Rouge Parish ◇ **25** 30 27N 91 12W
West Bend, Iowa **23** 42 57N 94 27W
West Bend, Wis. **55** 43 25N 88 11W
West Bengal □ **109** 23 0N 88 0 E
West Blocton **10** 33 7N 87 7W
West Boylston **28** 42 22N 71 47W
West Branch, Iowa **23** 41 40N 91 20W
West Branch, Mich. **29** 44 17N 84 14W
West Branch Susquehanna → **45** 40 53N 76 48W
West Bridgewater **28** 42 1N 71 0W
West Bromwich **83** 52 32N 2 1W
West Brookfield **28** 42 14N 72 9W
West Burke **36** 44 39N 71 59W
West Burlington **23** 40 49N 91 9W
West Campton **36** 43 40N 71 41W
West Canaan **36** 43 40N 72 2W
West Cape May **37** 38 56N 74 56W
West Carroll Parish ◇ **25** 32 50N 92 52W
West Carthage **39** 43 59N 75 37W
West Chester, Iowa **23** 41 20N 91 49W
West Chester, Pa. **45** 39 58N 75 36W
West Columbia, S.C. **46** 34 0N 81 4W
West Columbia, Tex. **51** 29 9N 95 39W
West Concord **30** 44 9N 92 54W
West Cote Blanche B. **25** 29 45N 91 55W
West Covina **15** 34 4N 117 54W
West Creek **37** 39 38N 74 18W
West Cummington **28** 42 29N 72 57W
West Des Moines **23** 41 35N 93 43W
West Dover **36** 42 56N 72 51W
West Dummerston **36** 42 55N 72 38W
West Elk Mts. **16** 38 35N 107 15W
West Elkton **42** 39 35N 84 33W
West End, Bahamas **66** 26 41N 78 58W
West End, U.S.A. **40** 35 15N 79 34W
West Fairlee **36** 43 54N 72 16W
West Falkland **78** 51 40 S 60 0W
West Fargo **41** 46 52N 96 54W
West Feliciana Parish ◇ **25** 30 50N 91 23W
West Fork Cuivre → **32** 39 2N 90 59W
West Fork Poplar → **33** 48 31N 105 22W
West Fork Trinity → **51** 32 48N 96 54W
West Forks **26** 45 20N 69 58W
West Frankfort **21** 37 54N 88 55W

West Germany **Whitesboro**

West Germany ■ **88** 52 0N 9 0 E
West Glacier **33** 48 30N 113 59W
West Glamorgan □ **83** 51 40N 3 55W
West Grand L. **26** 45 14N 67 51W
West Green **18** 31 37N 82 44W
West Hamlin **54** 38 17N 82 12W
West Hartford **28** 41 45N 72 44W
West Haven **28** 41 17N 72 57W
West Helena **13** 34 33N 90 38W
West Ice Shelf **5** 67 0 S 85 0 E
West Indies **67** 15 0N 70 0W
West Jefferson, N.C. **40** 36 24N 81 30W
West Jefferson, Ohio **42** 39 57N 83 17W
West Kingston **28** 41 29N 71 34W
West Lafayette **22** 40 27N 86 55W
West Lebanon **22** 40 16N 87 23W
West Leipsic **42** 41 7N 84 0W
West Liberty, Iowa **23** 41 34N 91 16W
West Liberty, Ky. **49** 37 55N 83 16W
West Liberty, Ohio **42** 40 15N 83 45W
West Looe **83** 50 21N 4 29W
West Louisville **48** 37 42N 87 17W
West Mansfield **42** 40 24N 83 33W
West Mayfield **45** 40 47N 80 20W
West Memphis **13** 35 9N 90 11W
West Midlands □ **83** 52 30N 1 55W
West Mifflin **45** 40 22N 79 52W
West Milan **36** 44 37N 71 18W
West Milford **54** 39 12N 80 24W
West Millgrove **42** 41 15N 83 30W
West Milton **42** 39 58N 84 20W
West Mineral **24** 37 17N 94 55W
West Monroe **25** 32 31N 92 9W
West Moors **82** 50 49N 1 50W
West Newbury **28** 42 48N 70 0W
West Nicholson **123** 21 2 S 29 20 E
West Nishnabotna → **23** 40 39N 95 38W
West Nueces → **51** 29 16N 99 56W
West Okoboji L. **23** 43 23N 95 9W
West Orange **51** 30 5N 93 46W
West Ossipee **36** 43 48N 71 12W
West Palm Beach **17** 26 43N 80 3W
West Palm Beach Canal **17** 26 40N 80 15W
West Panama City Beach **17** 30 13N 85 53W
West Pawlet **36** 43 21N 73 15W
West Pensacola **17** 30 25N 87 16W
West Plains **32** 36 44N 91 51W
West Plymouth **36** 43 45N 71 45W
West Point, Calif. **14** 38 24N 120 32W
West Point, Ga. **18** 32 53N 85 11W
West Point, Ill. **21** 40 15N 91 11W
West Point, Iowa **23** 40 43N 91 27W
West Point, Ky. **49** 37 59N 85 57W
West Point, Miss. **31** 33 36N 88 39W
West Point, N.Y. **39** 41 24N 73 58W
West Point, Nebr. **34** 41 51N 96 43W
West Point, Va. **54** 37 32N 76 48W
West Point L. **10** 33 0N 85 5W
West Richland **53** 46 18N 119 20W
West Rindge **36** 42 47N 72 3W
West River **27** 38 52N 76 31W
West Road → **62** 53 18N 122 53W
West Rutland **36** 43 36N 73 3W
West Sacramento **14** 38 35N 121 32W
West Salem, Ill. **21** 38 31N 88 1W
West Salem, Ohio **42** 40 58N 82 7W
West Salem, Wis. **55** 43 54N 91 5W
West Schelde → = Westerschelde → **87** 51 25N 3 25 E
West Seneca **39** 42 51N 78 48W
West Siberian Plain **102** 62 0N 75 0 E
West Siloam Springs **43** 36 12N 94 39W
West Springfield **28** 42 6N 72 38W
West Stewartstown **36** 44 59N 71 32W
West Sussex □ **83** 50 55N 0 30W
West Tavaputs Plateau **52** 39 50N 110 20W
West Terre Haute **22** 39 28N 87 27W
West-Terschelling **87** 53 22N 5 13 E
West Thompson Res. **28** 41 57N 71 54W
West Thorton **36** 43 55N 71 42W
West Thumb **56** 44 25N 110 34W
West Tisbury **28** 41 23N 70 41W
West Topsham **36** 44 7N 72 19W
West Union, Iowa **23** 42 57N 91 49W
West Union, Minn. **30** 45 48N 95 5W
West Union, Ohio **42** 38 48N 83 33W
West Union, W. Va. **54** 39 18N 80 47W
West Unity **42** 41 35N 84 26W
West University Place **51** 29 42N 95 26W
West Valley **52** 40 42N 111 58W
West Virginia □ **54** 38 45N 80 30W
West-Vlaanderen □ **87** 51 0N 3 0 E
West Warwick **28** 41 43N 71 32W
West Winfield **39** 42 53N 75 12W
West Yarmouth **28** 41 39N 70 15W
West Yellowstone **33** 44 40N 111 6W
West York **45** 39 57N 76 46W
West Yorkshire □ **82** 53 45N 1 40W
Westbay **17** 30 18N 85 52W
Westboro **32** 40 32N 95 19W
Westborough **28** 42 16N 71 37W
Westbrook, Conn. **28** 41 17N 72 27W
Westbrook, Maine **26** 43 41N 70 22W
Westbrook, Minn. **30** 44 3N 95 26W
Westbrook, Tex. **50** 32 21N 101 1W
Westby, Mont. **33** 48 52N 104 3W
Westby, Wis. **55** 43 39N 90 51W
Westchester County ◇ **39** 41 40N 73 45W
Westcliffe **16** 38 9N 105 28W
Westend **15** 35 42N 117 24W
Westerly **28** 41 22N 71 50W
Western **34** 40 24N 97 12W
Western □ **123** 15 15 S 24 30 E
Western Australia □ **128** 25 0 S 118 0 E
Western Ghats **108** 14 0N 75 0 E
Western Grove **13** 36 6N 92 57W
Western Isles □ **84** 57 30N 7 10W
Western Sahara ■ **120** 25 0N 13 0W
Western Samoa ■ **128** 14 0 S 172 0W
Westernport **27** 39 29N 79 3W
Westerschelde → **87** 51 25N 3 25 E
Westerville, Nebr. **34** 41 24N 99 23W
Westerville, Ohio **42** 40 8N 82 56W
Westerwald **88** 50 39N 8 0 E
Westfall **44** 43 59N 117 48W
Westfield, Ill. **21** 39 27N 88 0W
Westfield, Ind. **22** 40 2N 86 8W
Westfield, Iowa **23** 42 45N 96 36W
Westfield, Maine **26** 46 34N 67 55W
Westfield, Mass. **28** 42 7N 72 45W
Westfield, N.J. **37** 40 39N 74 21W
Westfield, N.Y. **39** 42 20N 79 35W
Westfield, Pa. **45** 41 55N 77 32W
Westfield, Wis. **55** 43 53N 89 30W
Westfield → **28** 42 5N 72 35W
Westfir **44** 43 46N 122 31W
Westford **28** 42 35N 71 26W
Westgate **23** 42 46N 92 0W
Westhoff **51** 29 12N 97 28W
Westhope **41** 48 55N 101 1W
Westland □ **128** 43 33 S 169 59 E
Westland Bight **128** 42 55 S 170 5 E
Westlock **62** 54 9N 113 55W
Westmeath □ **85** 53 30N 7 30W
Westminster, Calif. **15** 33 46N 118 1W
Westminster, Colo. **16** 39 50N 105 2W
Westminster, Mass. **28** 42 33N 71 55W
Westminster, Md. **27** 39 34N 76 59W
Westminster, S.C. **46** 34 40N 83 6W
Westminster, Vt. **36** 43 5N 72 27W
Westmont **45** 40 19N 78 58W
Westmore **36** 44 0N 72 0W
Westmoreland, Kans. **24** 39 24N 96 25W
Westmoreland, N.H. **36** 42 57N 72 25W
Westmoreland, Tenn. **48** 36 34N 86 15W
Westmoreland County ◇, Pa. **45** 40 20N 79 25W
Westmoreland County ◇, Va. **54** 38 6N 76 50W
Westmorland **15** 33 2N 115 37W
Weston, Malaysia **110** 5 10N 115 35 E
Weston, Colo. **16** 37 8N 104 48W
Weston, Mo. **32** 39 25N 94 54W
Weston, Nebr. **34** 41 12N 96 45W
Weston, Oreg. **44** 45 49N 118 26W
Weston, Vt. **36** 43 18N 72 38W
Weston, W. Va. **54** 39 2N 80 28W
Weston, Wis. **55** 44 49N 92 4W
Weston County ◇ **56** 43 55N 104 35W
Weston I. **60** 52 33N 79 36W
Weston-super-Mare **83** 51 20N 2 59W
Westover, Md. **27** 38 7N 75 42W
Westover, Pa. **45** 40 45N 78 40W
Westover, S. Dak. **47** 43 45N 100 40W
Westover, Tenn. **48** 35 37N 88 53W
Westphalia, Mich. **29** 42 56N 84 48W
Westphalia, Mo. **32** 38 26N 92 0W
Westpoint **48** 35 8N 87 32W
Westport, Ireland **85** 53 44N 9 31W
Westport, N.Z. **128** 41 46 S 171 37 E
Westport, Calif. **14** 39 38N 123 47W
Westport, Conn. **28** 41 9N 73 22W
Westport, Ind. **22** 39 11N 85 34W
Westport, Minn. **30** 45 43N 95 10W
Westport, N.H. **36** 42 49N 72 20W
Westport, N.Y. **39** 44 11N 73 26W
Westport, Okla. **43** 36 8N 96 20W
Westport, Oreg. **44** 46 8N 123 23W
Westport, Wash. **53** 46 53N 124 6W
Westray, Canada **63** 53 36N 101 24W
Westray, U.K. **84** 59 18N 3 0W
Westree **60** 47 26N 81 34W
Westview **62** 49 50N 124 31W
Westville, Fla. **17** 30 46N 85 51W
Westville, Ill. **21** 40 2N 87 38W
Westville, Okla. **43** 35 58N 94 40W
Westville, S.C. **46** 34 27N 80 36W
Westwego **25** 29 54N 90 8W
Westwood, Calif. **14** 40 18N 121 0W
Westwood, Ky. **49** 38 30N 82 50W
Westwood, Mass. **28** 42 13N 71 14W
Westwood, Md. **27** 38 40N 76 45W
Westwood, N.J. **37** 40 58N 74 2W
Westwood Lakes **17** 25 44N 80 23W
Wet Mts. **16** 38 0N 105 10W
Wetar **111** 7 30 S 126 30 E
Wetaskiwin **62** 52 55N 113 24W
Wethersfield **28** 41 42N 72 40W
Wetmore, Colo. **16** 38 14N 105 5W
Wetmore, Kans. **24** 39 38N 95 49W
Wetteren **87** 51 0N 3 53 E
Wetumka **43** 35 14N 96 15W
Wetumpka **10** 32 32N 86 13W
Wetzel County ◇ **54** 39 34N 80 41W
Wetzlar **88** 50 33N 8 30 E
Wewahitchka **17** 30 7N 85 12W
Wewoka **43** 35 9N 96 30W
Wexford **85** 52 20N 6 28W
Wexford □ **85** 52 20N 6 25W
Wexford County ◇ **29** 44 20N 85 40W
Wexford Harb. **85** 52 20N 6 25W
Weyauwega **55** 44 19N 88 56W
Weyburn **63** 49 40N 103 50W
Weyburn L. **62** 63 0N 117 59W
Weyerhaeuser **55** 45 26N 91 25W
Weymouth, Canada **61** 44 30N 66 1W
Weymouth, U.K. **83** 50 36N 2 28W
Weymouth, U.S.A. **28** 42 13N 70 58W
Weymouth, C. **127** 12 37 S 143 27 E
Whakatane **128** 37 57 S 177 1 E
Whalan **30** 43 44N 91 55W
Whale → **61** 58 15N 67 40W
Whale Cove **58** 62 11N 92 36W
Whales, B. of **5** 78 0 S 165 0W
Whaleysville **27** 38 24N 75 18W
Whalsay **84** 60 22N 1 0W
Whangamomona **128** 39 8 S 174 44 E
Whangarei **128** 35 43 S 174 21 E
Whangarei Harbour **128** 35 45 S 174 28 E
Wharfe → **82** 53 55N 1 30W
Wharfedale **82** 54 7N 2 4W
Wharton, N.J. **37** 40 54N 74 35W
Wharton, Ohio **42** 40 52N 83 28W
Wharton, Tex. **51** 29 19N 96 6W
Wharton County ◇ **51** 29 12N 96 16W
Wharton State Forest **37** 39 45N 74 40W
What Cheer **23** 41 24N 92 21W
Whatcom, L. **53** 48 44N 122 20W
Whatcom County ◇ **53** 48 56N 122 0W
Whatley **10** 31 39N 87 42W
Wheat Ridge **16** 39 46N 105 5W
Wheatcroft **48** 37 30N 87 52W
Wheatland, Calif. **14** 39 1N 121 25W
Wheatland, Ind. **22** 38 40N 87 19W
Wheatland, Iowa **23** 41 50N 90 51W
Wheatland, Mo. **32** 37 57N 93 24W
Wheatland, Wyo. **56** 42 3N 104 58W
Wheatland County ◇ **33** 46 30N 109 50W
Wheatland Reservoir No.2 **56** 41 50N 105 38W
Wheatley **13** 34 55N 91 7W
Wheaton, Ill. **21** 41 52N 88 6W
Wheaton, Kans. **24** 39 30N 96 19W
Wheaton, Md. **27** 39 3N 77 3W
Wheaton, Minn. **30** 45 48N 96 30W
Wheeler, Ill. **21** 39 3N 88 19W
Wheeler, Kans. **24** 39 46N 101 43W
Wheeler, Miss. **31** 34 35N 88 37W
Wheeler, Oreg. **44** 45 41N 123 53W
Wheeler, Tex. **50** 35 27N 100 16W
Wheeler, Wis. **55** 45 3N 91 55W
Wheeler → **63** 57 25N 105 30W
Wheeler County ◇, Ga. **18** 32 5N 82 45W
Wheeler County ◇, Nebr. **34** 41 50N 98 30W
Wheeler County ◇, Oreg. **44** 44 45N 120 0W
Wheeler County ◇, Tex. **50** 35 30N 100 15W
Wheeler L. **10** 34 48N 87 23W
Wheeler Peak, N. Mex. **38** 36 33N 105 25W
Wheeler Peak, Nev. **35** 38 59N 114 19W
Wheeler Ridge **15** 35 0N 118 57W
Wheelersburg **42** 38 44N 82 51W
Wheeling, Ill. **21** 42 8N 87 55W
Wheeling, W. Va. **54** 40 4N 80 43W
Wheelock **41** 48 18N 103 15W
Wheelwright **49** 37 20N 82 43W
Whelen Springs **13** 33 50N 93 7W
Whernside **82** 54 14N 2 24W
Whidbey I. **53** 48 12N 122 17W
Whidbey Is. **126** 34 30 S 135 3 E
Whiskey Gap **62** 49 0N 113 3W
Whiskey Jack L. **63** 58 23N 101 55W
Whiskey Pk. **56** 42 18N 107 35W
Whiskeytown-Shasta-Trinity Nat. Rec. Area **14** 40 45N 122 15W
Whispering Pines **40** 35 17N 79 26W
Whitakers **40** 36 6N 77 43W
Whitby **82** 54 29N 0 37W
White, Ga. **18** 34 17N 84 45W
White, S. Dak. **47** 44 26N 96 39W
White →, Ariz. **12** 33 44N 110 13W
White →, Ark. **13** 33 57N 91 5W
White →, Ind. **22** 38 25N 87 45W
White →, Nev. **35** 37 19N 115 8W
White →, S. Dak. **47** 43 42N 99 27W
White →, Tex. **50** 33 14N 100 56W
White →, Utah **52** 40 4N 109 41W
White →, Vt. **36** 43 37N 72 20W
White Apple **31** 31 27N 91 4W
White B. **61** 50 0N 56 35W
White Bear Lake **30** 45 5N 93 1W
White Bear Res. **61** 48 10N 57 5W
White Bird **20** 45 46N 116 18W
White Bluff **48** 36 6N 87 13W
White Butte, N. Dak. **41** 46 23N 103 18W
White Butte, S. Dak. **47** 45 56N 102 22W
White Canyon **52** 37 49N 110 26W
White Castle **25** 30 10N 91 9W
White City, Fla. **17** 29 53N 85 13W
White City, Kans. **24** 38 48N 96 44W
White City, Ky. **49** 37 35N 85 40W
White City, Oreg. **44** 42 26N 122 51W
White Cloud, Kans. **24** 39 59N 95 18W
White Cloud, Mich. **29** 43 33N 85 46W
White County ◇, Ark. **13** 35 15N 91 44W
White County ◇, Ga. **18** 34 40N 83 45W
White County ◇, Ill. **21** 38 5N 88 10W
White County ◇, Ind. **22** 40 45N 86 50W
White County ◇, Tenn. **49** 35 56N 85 28W
White Deer **50** 35 26N 101 10W
White Earth **41** 48 23N 102 46W
White Earth → **41** 48 9N 102 42W
White Earth Indian Reservation **30** 47 20N 95 45W
White Hall, Ala. **10** 32 20N 86 43W
White Hall, Ill. **21** 39 26N 90 24W
White Haven **45** 41 4N 75 47W
White Horse **37** 40 11N 74 42W
White I. **128** 37 30 S 177 13 E
White L. **25** 29 44N 92 30W
White Lake, N.C. **40** 34 39N 78 30W
White Lake, S. Dak. **47** 43 44N 98 43W
White Lake, Wis. **55** 45 10N 88 46W
White Mountain **11** 64 41N 163 24W
White Mountain National Forest **36** 44 10N 71 25W
White Mountain Peak **15** 37 38N 118 15W
White Mts., Alaska **11** 65 30N 146 30W
White Mts., Calif. **15** 37 30N 118 15W
White Mts., N.H. **36** 44 10N 71 20W
White Nile = Nîl el Abyad → **121** 15 38N 32 31 E
White Oak, Ga. **18** 31 2N 81 43W
White Oak, S.C. **46** 34 28N 81 7W
White Oak, Tex. **51** 32 32N 94 52W
White Oak Cr. → **51** 33 14N 94 42W
White Otter L. **60** 49 5N 91 55W
White Owl **47** 44 36N 102 26W
White Pass, Canada **62** 59 40N 135 3W
White Pass, U.S.A. **53** 46 38N 121 24W
White Pigeon **29** 41 48N 85 39W
White Pine, Mich. **29** 46 45N 89 35W
White Pine, Mont. **33** 47 45N 115 29W
White Pine, Tenn. **49** 36 7N 83 17W
White Pine County ◇ **35** 39 30N 115 0W
White Pine Range **35** 39 10N 115 20W
White Plains, Ga. **18** 33 28N 83 1W
White Plains, Md. **27** 38 36N 76 55W
White Plains, N.Y. **39** 41 2N 73 46W
White River, Canada **60** 48 35N 85 20W
White River, U.S.A. **47** 43 34N 100 45W
White River Junction **36** 43 39N 72 19W
White River National Forest **16** 39 20N 106 45W
White River Reservoir **50** 33 27N 101 5W
White Rock **49** 36 48N 83 26W
White Rock Cr. → **24** 39 55N 97 50W
White Russia = Byelorussian S.S.R. □ **98** 53 30N 27 0 E
White Salmon **53** 45 44N 121 29W
White Sands National Monument **38** 32 46N 106 20W
White Sea = Beloye More **98** 66 30N 38 0 E
White Springs **17** 30 20N 82 45W
White Stone **54** 37 39N 76 23W
White Sulphur Springs, Mont. **33** 46 33N 110 54W
White Sulphur Springs, W. Va. **54** 37 48N 80 18W
White Swan **53** 46 23N 120 44W
Whiteburg **27** 38 12N 75 32W
Whiteclay **34** 42 57N 102 33W
Whitecliffs **128** 43 26 S 171 55 E
Whitecourt **62** 54 10N 115 45W
Whiteface **50** 33 36N 102 37W
Whiteface → **30** 46 58N 92 48W
Whiteface Reservoir **30** 47 17N 92 11W
Whitefield, Maine **26** 44 10N 69 38W
Whitefield, N.H. **36** 44 23N 71 37W
Whitefish **33** 48 25N 114 20W
Whitefish → **29** 45 55N 86 57W
Whitefish B. **29** 46 40N 84 55W
Whitefish Bay **55** 43 23N 87 54W
Whitefish L. **63** 62 41N 106 48W
Whitefish Point **29** 46 45N 84 59W
Whitefish Pt. **29** 46 46N 84 57W
Whiteford **27** 39 42N 76 21W
Whitegull, L. **61** 55 27N 64 17W
Whitehall, Ark. **13** 35 29N 90 44W
Whitehall, Mich. **29** 43 24N 86 21W
Whitehall, Mont. **33** 45 52N 112 6W
Whitehall, N.Y. **39** 43 33N 73 24W
Whitehall, Wis. **55** 44 22N 91 19W
Whitehaven **82** 54 33N 3 35W
Whitehorse **62** 60 43N 135 3W
Whitehorse, Vale of **83** 51 37N 1 30W
Whitehouse **42** 41 31N 83 48W
Whiteland **22** 39 33N 86 5W
Whitelaw **55** 44 9N 87 49W
Whiteleysburg **27** 38 57N 75 45W
Whitemouth **63** 49 57N 95 58W
Whiteriver **12** 33 50N 109 58W
Whites City **38** 32 11N 104 22W
Whitesail, L. **62** 53 35N 127 45W
Whitesboro, N.Y. **39** 43 7N 75 18W
Whitesboro, Okla. **43** 34 41N 94 53W
Whitesboro, Tex. **51** 33 39N 96 54W

Whitesburg Winona

Whitesburg 49 37 7N 82 49W
Whiteshell Prov. Park 63 50 0N 95 40W
Whiteside, Canal 78 53 55 S 70 15W
Whiteside County ◇ 21 41 45N 89 55W
Whitestown 22 40 0N 86 21W
Whitesville, Ky. 48 37 41N 86 52W
Whitesville, W. Va. 54 37 59N 81 32W
Whitetail 33 48 54N 105 10W
Whiteville, La. 25 30 47N 92 9W
Whiteville, N.C. 40 34 20N 78 42W
Whiteville, Tenn. 48 35 20N 89 9W
Whitewater, Colo. 16 38 59N 108 27W
Whitewater, Kans. 24 37 58N 97 9W
Whitewater, Mo. 32 37 14N 89 48W
Whitewater, Mont. 33 48 46N 107 38W
Whitewater, Wis. 55 42 50N 88 44W
Whitewater B. 17 25 15N 81 0W
Whitewater Baldy 38 33 20N 108 39W
Whitewater L. 60 50 50N 89 10W
Whitewood, Canada 63 50 20N 102 20W
Whitewood, U.S.A. 47 44 28N 103 39W
Whitewright 51 33 31N 96 24W
Whitfield County ◇ 18 34 50N 84 55W
Whithorn 84 54 44N 4 25W
Whitianga 128 36 47 S 175 41 E
Whiting, Iowa 23 42 8N 96 9W
Whiting, Kans. 24 39 35N 95 37W
Whiting, Maine 26 44 48N 67 11W
Whiting, N.J. 37 39 57N 74 23W
Whiting, Vt. 36 43 50N 73 12W
Whitinsville 28 42 7N 71 40W
Whitlash 33 48 55N 111 15W
Whitley City 49 36 44N 84 28W
Whitley County ◇, Ind. 22 41 10N 85 30W
Whitley County ◇, Ky. 49 36 45N 84 10W
Whitman, Mass. 28 42 5N 70 56W
Whitman, Nebr. 34 42 3N 101 31W
Whitman County ◇ 53 47 0N 117 30W
Whitmire 46 34 30N 81 37W
Whitmore Village 19 21 31N 158 1W
Whitnel 40 35 53N 81 32W
Whitney, Canada 60 45 31N 78 14W
Whitney, Nebr. 34 42 47N 103 15W
Whitney, Tex. 51 31 57N 97 19W
Whitney, L. 51 31 52N 97 22W
Whitney, Mt. 15 36 35N 118 18W
Whitney Point 39 42 20N 75 58W
Whitsett 51 28 38N 98 16W
Whitstable 83 51 21N 1 2 E
Whitsunday I. 127 20 15 S 149 4 E
Whittemore, Iowa 23 43 4N 94 26W
Whittemore, Mich. 29 44 14N 83 48W
Whitten 23 42 16N 93 0W
Whittier, Alaska 11 60 47N 148 41W
Whittier, Calif. 15 33 58N 118 3W
Whitwell 49 35 12N 85 31W
Wholdaia L. 63 60 43N 104 20W
Whyalla 127 33 2 S 137 30 E
Wiarton 60 44 40N 81 10W
Wibaux 33 46 59N 104 11W
Wibaux County ◇ 33 46 50N 104 20W
Wichabai 71 2 57N 59 35W
Wichita 24 37 42N 97 20W
Wichita → 51 34 4N 98 10W
Wichita County ◇, Kans. 24 38 30N 101 20W
Wichita County ◇, Tex. 51 33 57N 98 40W
Wichita Falls 51 33 54N 98 30W
Wichita Mt. 43 34 52N 99 17W
Wichita Mts. 43 34 50N 98 45W
Wick 84 58 26N 3 5W
Wickenburg 12 33 58N 112 44W
Wickes 13 34 18N 94 20W
Wickiup Reservoir 44 43 41N 121 41W
Wickliffe, Ky. 48 36 58N 89 5W
Wickliffe, Ohio 42 41 36N 81 28W
Wicklow 85 53 0N 6 2W
Wicklow □ 85 52 59N 6 25W
Wicklow Hd. 85 52 59N 6 3W
Wicklow Mts. 85 53 0N 6 30W
Wicomico → 27 38 13N 75 55W
Wicomico County ◇ 27 38 25N 75 45W
Widnes 82 53 22N 2 44W
Wieliczka 89 50 0N 20 5 E
Wieluń 89 51 15N 18 34 E
Wien 88 48 12N 16 22 E
Wiener Neustadt 88 47 49N 16 16 E
Wierden 87 52 22N 6 35 E
Wiesbaden 88 50 7N 8 17 E
Wigan 82 53 33N 2 38W
Wiggins, Colo. 16 40 14N 104 4W
Wiggins, Miss. 31 32 42N 89 38W
Wiggins, Miss. 31 30 51N 89 8W
Wight, I. of 83 50 40N 1 20W
Wigtown 84 54 52N 4 27W
Wigtown B. 84 54 46N 4 15W
Wilbarger County ◇ 51 34 9N 99 17W
Wilber 34 40 29N 96 58W
Wilberforce, C. 127 11 54 S 136 35 E
Wilbur, Oreg. 44 43 19N 123 21W
Wilbur, Wash. 53 47 46N 118 42W
Wilburton 43 34 55N 95 19W
Wilcannia 127 31 30 S 143 26 E
Wilcox, Nebr. 34 40 22N 99 10W
Wilcox, Pa. 45 41 35N 78 41W
Wilcox County ◇, Ala. 10 31 59N 87 17W
Wilcox County ◇, Ga. 18 32 0N 83 25W
Wild Horse 16 38 50N 103 0W
Wild Horse Reservoir 35 41 41N 115 51W
Wild Rice →, Minn. 30 47 20N 96 50W
Wild Rice →, N. Dak. 41 46 45N 96 47W
Wild Rose 55 44 11N 89 15W
Wildcat → 22 40 28N 86 52W
Wilder, Idaho 20 43 41N 116 55W
Wilder, Minn. 30 43 50N 95 12W
Wildersville 48 35 47N 88 22W
Wilderville 44 42 23N 123 28W
Wildhorse → 43 34 32N 97 10W
Wildorado 50 35 13N 102 12W
Wildrose 41 48 38N 103 11W
Wildwood, Fla. 17 28 52N 82 2W
Wildwood, N.J. 37 38 59N 74 50W
Wildwood Crest 37 38 58N 74 50W
Wiley 16 38 10N 102 20W
Wiley City 53 46 33N 120 41W
Wilhelm II Coast 5 68 0 S 90 0 E
Wilhelmina, Geb. 71 3 50N 56 30W
Wilhelmshaven 88 53 30N 8 9 E
Wilkes-Barre 45 41 15N 75 53W
Wilkes County ◇, Ga. 18 33 50N 82 45W
Wilkes County ◇, N.C. 40 36 10N 81 10W
Wilkes Land 5 69 0 S 120 0 E
Wilkes Sub-Glacial Basin 5 75 0 S 130 0 E
Wilkesboro 40 36 9N 81 10W
Wilkesboro Res. 40 36 10N 81 20W
Wilkesville 42 39 5N 82 20W
Wilkie 63 52 27N 108 42W
Wilkin County ◇ 30 46 20N 96 25W
Wilkinsburg 45 40 26N 79 53W
Wilkinson 31 31 13N 91 14W
Wilkinson County ◇, Ga. 18 32 45N 83 10W
Wilkinson County ◇, Miss. 31 31 6N 91 18W
Will County ◇ 21 41 25N 88 0W
Willacoochee 18 31 20N 83 3W
Willacy County ◇ 50 26 29N 97 47W
Willamette → 44 45 39N 122 46W
Willamette National Forest 44 44 20N 122 10W
Willamina 44 45 5N 123 29W
Willapa B. 53 46 40N 124 0W
Willard, Colo. 16 40 33N 103 29W
Willard, Mo. 32 37 18N 93 26W
Willard, N. Mex. 38 34 36N 106 2W
Willard, Ohio 42 41 3N 82 44W
Willard, Utah 52 41 25N 112 2W
Willards 27 38 24N 75 21W
Willcox 12 32 15N 109 50W
Willcox Playa 12 32 8N 109 51W
Willemstad 67 12 5N 69 0W
Willette 49 36 27N 85 52W
Willey 23 41 59N 94 49W
William → 63 59 8N 109 19W
William B. Bankhead National Forest 10 34 10N 87 15W
Williams, Ariz. 12 35 15N 112 11W
Williams, Calif. 14 39 9N 122 9W
Williams, Minn. 30 48 45N 94 54W
Williams → 36 43 12N 72 27W
Williams County ◇, N. Dak. 41 48 20N 103 30W
Williams County ◇, Ohio 42 41 35N 84 37W
Williams Fork → 16 40 28N 107 40W
Williams Fork Reservoir 16 40 0N 106 8W
Williams Lake 62 52 10N 122 10W
Williamsburg, Iowa 23 41 40N 92 1W
Williamsburg, Kans. 24 38 29N 95 28W
Williamsburg, Ky. 49 36 44N 84 10W
Williamsburg, Mass. 28 42 23N 72 44W
Williamsburg, Md. 27 38 40N 75 50W
Williamsburg, Ohio 42 39 3N 84 4W
Williamsburg, Pa. 45 40 28N 78 12W
Williamsburg, Va. 54 37 16N 76 43W
Williamsburg County ◇ 46 33 40N 79 40W
Williamsfield 21 40 55N 90 1W
Williamson, Ga. 18 33 11N 84 22W
Williamson, Iowa 23 41 5N 93 15W
Williamson, N.Y. 39 43 14N 77 11W
Williamson, W. Va. 54 37 41N 82 17W
Williamson → 44 42 28N 121 57W
Williamson County ◇, Ill. 21 37 40N 88 55W
Williamson County ◇, Tenn. 48 35 55N 86 52W
Williamson County ◇, Tex. 51 30 38N 97 41W
Williamsport, Ind. 22 40 17N 87 17W
Williamsport, Md. 27 39 37N 77 50W
Williamsport, Ohio 42 39 35N 83 7W
Williamsport, Pa. 45 41 15N 77 0W
Williamston, Mich. 29 42 41N 84 17W
Williamston, N.C. 40 35 51N 77 4W
Williamston, S.C. 46 34 37N 82 29W
Williamstown, Ky. 49 38 38N 84 34W
Williamstown, Mass. 28 42 43N 73 12W
Williamstown, N.J. 37 39 40N 74 59W
Williamstown, N.Y. 39 43 26N 75 53W
Williamstown, W. Va. 54 39 24N 81 27W
Williamsville, Del. 27 38 27N 75 8W
Williamsville, Ill. 21 39 57N 89 33W
Williamsville, Mo. 32 36 58N 90 33W
Williford 13 36 15N 91 21W
Willimantic 28 41 43N 72 13W
Willimantic → 28 41 43N 72 12W
Willingboro 37 40 3N 74 54W
Willis, Kans. 24 39 43N 95 31W
Willis, Tex. 51 30 25N 95 29W
Williston, Fla. 17 29 23N 82 27W
Williston, Md. 27 38 48N 75 52W
Williston, N. Dak. 41 48 9N 103 37W
Williston, S.C. 46 33 24N 81 25W
Williston Basin 33 48 0N 104 30W
Williston L. 62 56 0N 124 0W
Willisville 21 37 59N 89 35W
Willits 14 39 25N 123 21W
Willmar 30 45 7N 95 3W
Willoughby 42 41 39N 81 24W
Willow, Alaska 11 61 45N 150 3W
Willow, Ark. 13 34 8N 92 45W
Willow, Okla. 43 35 3N 99 31W
Willow Bunch 63 49 20N 105 35W
Willow City 41 48 36N 100 18W
Willow Cr. →, Utah 52 40 2N 109 45W
Willow Cr. →, Oreg. 44 45 48N 120 1W
Willow Cr. →, Oreg. 44 44 0N 117 13W
Willow Creek, Calif. 14 40 56N 123 38W
Willow Creek, Mont. 33 45 49N 111 39W
Willow Creek Reservoir 35 41 14N 116 32W
Willow Grove, Del. 27 40 8N 75 6W
Willow Grove, Pa. 45 40 9N 75 7W
Willow L., Canada 62 62 10N 119 8W
Willow L., U.S.A. 56 43 0N 109 52W
Willow Lake 47 44 38N 97 38W
Willow Ranch 14 41 54N 120 21W
Willow Reservoir 55 45 43N 89 51W
Willow River, Canada 62 54 6N 122 28W
Willow River, U.S.A. 30 46 19N 92 51W
Willow Springs 32 37 0N 91 58W
Willowbrook 24 38 8N 97 57W
Willowdale 44 44 48N 120 57W
Willowick 42 41 38N 81 28W
Willowlake → 62 62 42N 123 8W
Willowmore 123 33 15 S 23 30 E
Willows 14 39 31N 122 12W
Wills Point 51 32 43N 96 1W
Willshire 42 40 45N 84 48W
Wilma 17 30 9N 84 58W
Wilmar 13 33 38N 91 56W
Wilmer 51 32 35N 96 41W
Wilmette 21 42 5N 87 42W
Wilmington, Del. 27 39 45N 75 33W
Wilmington, Ill. 21 41 18N 88 9W
Wilmington, Mass. 28 42 33N 71 10W
Wilmington, N.C. 40 34 14N 77 55W
Wilmington, Ohio 42 39 27N 83 50W
Wilmington, Vt. 36 42 52N 72 52W
Wilmont 30 43 46N 95 50W
Wilmore, Kans. 24 37 20N 99 13W
Wilmore, Ky. 49 37 52N 84 40W
Wilmot, Ark. 13 33 4N 91 34W
Wilmot, Kans. 24 37 22N 96 53W
Wilmot, S. Dak. 47 45 25N 96 52W
Wilsey 24 38 38N 96 41W
Wilson, Ark. 13 35 34N 90 3W
Wilson, Kans. 24 38 50N 98 29W
Wilson, La. 25 30 55N 91 7W
Wilson, N.C. 40 35 44N 77 55W
Wilson, N.Y. 39 43 19N 78 50W
Wilson, Okla. 43 34 10N 97 26W
Wilson, Tex. 50 33 19N 101 44W
Wilson, Mt. 16 37 50N 107 59W
Wilson County ◇, Kans. 24 37 30N 95 45W
Wilson County ◇, N.C. 40 35 45N 78 0W
Wilson County ◇, Tenn. 48 36 12N 86 18W
Wilson County ◇, Tex. 51 29 8N 98 10W
Wilson Creek 53 47 25N 119 7W
Wilson L. 10 34 48N 87 38W
Wilson Lake 24 38 58N 98 30W
Wilsons Mills 26 44 57N 71 2W
Wilsons Promontory 127 38 55 S 146 25 E
Wilsonville, Nebr. 34 40 7N 100 7W
Wilsonville, Oreg. 44 45 18N 122 46W
Wilton, U.K. 83 51 5N 1 52W
Wilton, Ark. 13 33 45N 94 9W
Wilton, Conn. 28 41 12N 73 26W
Wilton, Maine 26 44 36N 70 14W
Wilton, Minn. 30 47 30N 95 0W
Wilton, N. Dak. 41 47 10N 100 47W
Wilton, N.H. 36 42 51N 71 44W
Wilton, Wis. 55 43 49N 90 32W
Wiltshire □ 83 51 20N 2 0W
Wiltz 87 49 57N 5 55 E
Wiluna 126 26 36 S 120 14 E
Wimauma 17 27 43N 82 18W
Wimbledon 41 47 10N 98 28W
Wimmera 127 36 30 S 142 0 E
Winamac 22 41 3N 86 36W
Winchendon 28 42 41N 72 3W
Winchester, U.K. 83 51 4N 1 19W
Winchester, Ark. 13 33 47N 91 29W
Winchester, Idaho 20 46 14N 116 38W
Winchester, Ill. 21 39 38N 90 27W
Winchester, Ind. 22 40 10N 84 59W
Winchester, Ky. 49 38 0N 84 11W
Winchester, N.H. 36 42 46N 72 23W
Winchester, Tenn. 48 35 11N 86 7W
Winchester, Va. 54 39 11N 78 10W
Winchester Bay 44 43 41N 124 10W
Wind → 56 43 12N 108 12W
Wind Cave National Park 47 43 32N 103 17W
Wind Mt. 38 32 2N 105 31W
Wind Point 55 42 47N 87 46W
Wind River Indian Reservation 56 43 20N 109 0W
Wind River Pk. 56 42 42N 109 7W
Wind River Range 56 43 0N 109 30W
Windber 45 40 14N 78 50W
Windcrest 51 29 31N 98 19W
Winder 18 34 0N 83 45W
Windermere, L. 82 54 20N 2 57W
Windfall, Canada 62 54 12N 116 13W
Windfall, U.S.A. 22 40 22N 85 57W
Windflower L. 62 62 52N 118 30W
Windham 26 43 49N 70 26W
Windham County ◇, Conn. 28 41 45N 72 0W
Windham County ◇, Vt. 36 43 0N 72 45W
Windhoek 123 22 35 S 17 4 E
Windom, Kans. 24 38 23N 97 55W
Windom, Minn. 30 43 52N 95 7W
Windom Pk. 16 37 35N 107 35W
Windorah 127 25 24 S 142 36 E
Window Rock 12 35 41N 109 3W
Windrush → 83 51 48N 1 35W
Windsor, N.S., Canada 61 44 59N 64 5W
Windsor, Newf., Canada 61 48 57N 55 40W
Windsor, Ont., Canada 60 42 18N 83 0W
Windsor, U.K. 83 51 28N 0 36W
Windsor, Colo. 16 40 29N 104 54W
Windsor, Conn. 28 41 50N 72 39W
Windsor, Ill. 21 39 26N 88 36W
Windsor, Mo. 32 38 32N 93 31W
Windsor, N.C. 40 36 0N 76 57W
Windsor, S.C. 46 33 29N 81 31W
Windsor, Va. 54 36 49N 76 45W
Windsor, Vt. 36 43 29N 72 24W
Windsor County ◇ 36 43 35N 72 35W
Windsor Forest 18 31 59N 81 5W
Windsor Hts. 23 41 36N 93 42W
Windsor Locks 28 41 56N 72 38W
Windthorst 51 33 34N 98 26W
Windward Is., Atl. Oc. 67 13 0N 63 0W
Windward Is., Pac. Oc. 125 18 0 S 149 0W
Windward Passage = Vientos, Paso de los 67 20 0N 74 0W
Windy L. 63 60 20N 100 2W
Windy Pk. 53 48 56N 119 58W
Winefred L. 63 55 30N 110 30W
Winema National Forest 44 43 10N 121 50W
Winfall 40 36 13N 76 28W
Winfield, Ala. 10 33 56N 87 49W
Winfield, Iowa 23 41 7N 91 26W
Winfield, Kans. 24 37 15N 96 59W
Winfield, Md. 27 39 26N 77 4W
Winfield, Mo. 32 39 0N 90 44W
Winfield, S. Dak. 47 44 0N 96 59W
Winfield, W. Va. 54 38 32N 81 54W
Winfred 47 44 0N 97 19W
Wing 41 47 9N 100 17W
Wingate 40 34 59N 80 26W
Winger 30 47 32N 95 59W
Wingham 60 43 55N 81 20W
Wingo 48 36 39N 88 44W
Winifred 33 47 34N 109 23W
Winigan 32 40 3N 92 54W
Winisk 60 55 20N 85 15W
Winisk → 60 55 17N 85 5W
Winisk L. 60 52 55N 87 22W
Wink 50 31 45N 103 9W
Winkelman 12 32 59N 110 46W
Winkler 63 49 10N 97 56W
Winkler County ◇ 50 31 52N 103 6W
Winlock 53 46 30N 122 56W
Winn Parish ◇ 25 31 56N 92 38W
Winnabow 40 34 9N 78 6W
Winneba 120 5 25N 0 36W
Winnebago, Ill. 21 42 16N 89 15W
Winnebago, Minn. 30 43 46N 94 10W
Winnebago, Nebr. 34 42 14N 96 28W
Winnebago, L. 55 44 0N 88 26W
Winnebago County ◇, Ill. 21 42 20N 89 10W
Winnebago County ◇, Iowa 23 43 20N 93 40W
Winnebago County ◇, Wis. 55 44 0N 88 45W
Winnebago Indian Reservation 34 42 15N 96 40W
Winneconne 55 44 7N 88 43W
Winnemucca 35 40 58N 117 44W
Winnemucca L. 35 40 7N 119 21W
Winner 47 43 22N 99 52W
Winneshiek County ◇ 23 43 15N 91 50W
Winnetoon 34 42 31N 97 58W
Winnett 33 47 0N 108 21W
Winnfield 25 31 56N 92 38W
Winnibigoshish, L. 30 47 27N 94 13W
Winnie 51 29 49N 94 23W
Winnipeg 63 49 54N 97 9W
Winnipeg → 63 50 38N 96 19W
Winnipeg, L. 63 52 0N 97 0W
Winnipeg Beach 63 50 30N 96 58W
Winnipegosis 63 51 39N 99 55W
Winnipegosis L. 63 52 30N 100 0W
Winnipesaukee 36 43 40N 71 20W
Winnipesaukee, L. 36 43 38N 71 21W
Winnisquam L. 36 43 33N 71 31W
Winnsboro, La. 25 32 10N 91 43W
Winnsboro, S.C. 46 34 23N 81 5W
Winnsboro, Tex. 51 32 58N 95 17W
Winokapau, L. 61 53 15N 62 50W
Winona, Kans. 24 39 4N 101 15W
Winona, Minn. 30 44 3N 91 39W
Winona, Miss. 31 33 29N 89 44W
Winona, Mo. 32 37 1N 91 20W

Xiachengzi York, Kap

Xiachengzi **114** 44 40N 130 18 E
Xiachuan Dao **115** 21 40N 112 40 E
Xiaguan **113** 25 32N 100 16 E
Xiajiang **115** 27 30N 115 10 E
Xiamen **114** 24 25N 118 4 E
Xi'an **115** 34 15N 109 0 E
Xianfeng **115** 29 40N 109 8 E
Xiang Jiang → **115** 28 55N 112 50 E
Xiangfan **115** 32 2N 112 8 E
Xiangning **114** 35 58N 110 50 E
Xiangtan **115** 27 51N 112 54 E
Xiangxiang **115** 27 43N 112 28 E
Xiangyang **115** 32 1N 112 8 E
Xiangyin **115** 28 38N 112 54 E
Xiangzhou **115** 23 58N 109 40 E
Xianju **115** 28 51N 120 44 E
Xianyang **115** 34 20N 108 40 E
Xiao Hinggan Ling **114** 49 0N 127 0 E
Xiaogan **115** 30 52N 113 55 E
Xiapu **115** 26 54N 119 59 E
Xichang **113** 27 51N 102 19 E
Xichuan **115** 33 0N 111 30 E
Xieng Khouang **112** 19 17N 103 25 E
Xifeng **115** 27 7N 106 42 E
Xigazê **113** 29 5N 88 45 E
Xihe **115** 34 2N 105 20 E
Xiliao He → **114** 43 32N 123 35 E
Xilin **115** 24 30N 105 6 E
Xin Xian **114** 38 22N 112 46 E
Xinavane **123** 25 2 S 32 47 E
Xinbin **114** 41 40N 125 2 E
Xincheng **115** 24 5N 108 39 E
Xinfeng **115** 25 27N 114 58 E
Xing'an, Guangxi Zhuangzu, China **115** 25 38N 110 40 E
Xingan, Jiangxi, China **115** 27 46N 115 20 E
Xingcheng **114** 40 40N 120 45 E
Xingguo **115** 26 21N 115 21 E
Xinghua **115** 32 58N 119 48 E
Xinghua Wan **115** 25 15N 119 20 E
Xingning **115** 24 3N 115 42 E
Xingren **113** 25 24N 105 11 E
Xingshan **115** 31 15N 110 45 E
Xingtai **114** 37 3N 114 32 E
Xingu → **71** 1 30 S 51 53W
Xingyang **115** 34 45N 112 52 E
Xinhua **115** 27 42N 111 13 E
Xining **113** 36 34N 101 40 E
Xinjiang **114** 35 34N 111 11 E
Xinjiang Uygur Zizhiqu □ **113** 42 0N 86 0 E
Xinjin **114** 39 25N 121 58 E
Xinle **114** 38 25N 114 40 E
Xinmin **114** 41 59N 122 50 E
Xinning **115** 26 28N 110 50 E
Xinxiang **115** 35 18N 113 50 E
Xinyang **115** 32 6N 114 3 E
Xinzheng **115** 34 20N 113 45 E
Xinzhou **115** 19 43N 109 17 E
Xinzhu **115** 24 49N 120 57 E
Xiongyuecheng **114** 40 12N 122 5 E
Xiping **115** 33 22N 114 0 E
Xique-Xique **74** 10 50 S 42 40W
Xiruá → **72** 6 3 S 67 50W
Xiuyan **114** 40 18N 123 11 E
Xixabangma Feng **109** 28 20N 85 40 E
Xixiang **115** 33 0N 107 44 E
Xizang □ **113** 32 0N 88 0 E
Xuancheng **115** 30 56N 118 43 E
Xuan'en **115** 30 0N 109 30 E
Xuanhan **115** 31 18N 107 38 E
Xuanhua **114** 40 40N 115 2 E
Xuchang **115** 34 2N 113 48 E
Xuguit Qi **114** 49 17N 120 44 E
Xunke **114** 49 35N 128 27 E
Xupu **115** 27 53N 110 32 E
Xuwen **115** 20 20N 110 10 E
Xuyong **115** 28 10N 105 22 E
Xuzhou **115** 34 18N 117 10 E

Y

Ya 'Bad **104** 32 27N 35 10 E
Yaak **33** 48 50N 115 43W
Ya'an **113** 29 58N 103 5 E
Yabelo **121** 4 50N 38 8 E
Yablanitsa **95** 43 2N 24 5 E
Yablonovy Khrebet **101** 53 0N 114 0 E
Yablonovyy Ra. **102** 53 0N 114 0 E
Yabucoa **57** 18 3N 65 53W
Yabucoa, Puerto **57** 18 8N 65 48W
Yachats **44** 44 19N 124 6W
Yacheng **115** 18 22N 109 6 E
Yacolt **53** 45 51N 122 24W
Yacuiba **76** 22 0 S 63 43W
Yacuma → **73** 13 38 S 65 23W
Yadgir **108** 16 45N 77 5 E
Yadkin → **40** 35 29N 80 9W
Yadkin County ◇ **40** 36 10N 80 40W
Yadkinville **40** 36 8N 80 39W
Yagodnoye **101** 62 33N 149 40 E
Yagoua **122** 10 20N 15 13 E
Yaguas → **70** 2 45 S 70 10W
Yagur **104** 32 45N 35 4 E
Yahk **62** 49 6N 116 10W
Yahuma **122** 1 0N 23 10 E
Yaita **117** 36 48N 139 56 E
Yakima **53** 46 36N 120 31W
Yakima → **53** 46 15N 119 14W
Yakima County ◇ **53** 46 30N 120 30W
Yakima Indian Reservation **53** 46 10N 120 30W
Yakoruda **95** 42 1N 23 39 E
Yakovlevka **116** 44 26N 133 28 E
Yaku-Shima **117** 30 20N 130 30 E
Yakut A.S.S.R. □ **101** 62 0N 130 0 E
Yakutat **11** 59 33N 139 44W
Yakutat B. **11** 59 45N 140 45W
Yakutsk **101** 62 5N 129 50 E
Yala **112** 6 33N 101 18 E
Yale, Ill. **21** 39 7N 88 2W
Yale, Iowa **23** 41 47N 94 21W
Yale, Mich. **29** 43 8N 82 48W
Yale, Okla. **43** 36 7N 96 42W
Yale, S. Dak. **47** 44 26N 97 59W
Yale, Va. **54** 36 51N 77 17W
Yale L. **53** 45 58N 122 20W
Yalgoo **126** 28 16 S 116 39 E
Yalinga **122** 6 33N 23 10 E
Yalkubul, Punta **65** 21 32N 88 37W
Yalobusha → **31** 33 33N 90 10W
Yalobusha County ◇ **31** 33 59N 89 41W
Yalong Jiang → **113** 26 40N 101 55 E
Yalpukh, Oz. **95** 45 30N 28 41 E
Yalta **99** 44 30N 34 10 E
Yalu Chiang → **114** 41 30N 126 30 E
Yalu He → **114** 46 56N 123 30 E
Yalu Jiang → **114** 40 0N 124 22 E
Yalutorovsk **100** 56 41N 66 12 E
Yam Ha Melaḥ = Dead Sea **106** 31 30N 35 30 E
Yam Kinneret **104** 32 45N 35 35 E
Yamada **117** 33 33N 130 49 E
Yamagata **116** 38 15N 140 15 E
Yamagata □ **116** 38 30N 140 0 E
Yamaguchi **117** 34 10N 131 32 E
Yamaguchi □ **117** 34 20N 131 40 E
Yamal, Poluostrov **100** 71 0N 70 0 E
Yamanashi □ **117** 35 40N 138 40 E
Yamantau **98** 54 20N 57 40 E
Yamantau, Gora **98** 54 15N 58 6 E
Yâmbiô **121** 4 35N 28 16 E
Yambol **95** 42 30N 26 36 E
Yamdena **111** 7 45 S 131 20 E
Yame **117** 33 13N 130 35 E
Yamethin **109** 20 29N 96 18 E
Yamhill County ◇ **44** 45 15N 123 10W
Yamma-Yamma, L. **127** 26 16 S 141 20 E
Yampa **16** 40 9N 106 55W
Yampa → **16** 40 32N 108 59W
Yampi Sd. **126** 16 8 S 123 38 E
Yamrukchal **95** 42 44N 24 52 E
Yamsay Mt. **44** 42 56N 121 22W
Yamuna → **109** 25 30N 81 53 E
Yamzho Yumco **113** 28 48N 90 35 E
Yana → **101** 71 30N 136 0 E
Yanagawa **117** 33 10N 130 24 E
Yanai **117** 33 58N 132 7 E
Yan'an **114** 36 35N 109 26 E
Yanaul **98** 56 25N 55 0 E
Yanbu 'al Baḥr **106** 24 0N 38 5 E
Yancey **51** 29 8N 99 9W
Yancey County ◇ **40** 35 50N 82 20W
Yanceyville **40** 36 24N 79 20W
Yanchang **114** 36 43N 110 1 E
Yancheng, Henan, China **115** 33 35N 114 0 E
Yancheng, Jiangsu, China **115** 33 23N 120 8 E
Yanchi **114** 37 48N 107 20 E
Yanchuan **114** 36 51N 110 10 E
Yandoon **109** 17 0N 95 40 E
Yangambi **122** 0 47N 24 20 E
Yangch'ü = Taiyuan **114** 37 52N 112 33 E
Yangchun **115** 22 11N 111 48 E
Yanggao **114** 40 21N 113 55 E
Yangi-Yer **100** 40 17N 68 48 E
Yangjiang **115** 21 50N 110 59 E
Yangquan **114** 37 58N 113 31 E
Yangshan **115** 24 30N 112 40 E
Yangshuo **115** 24 48N 110 29 E
Yangtze Kiang = Chang Jiang → **115** 31 48N 121 10 E
Yangxin **115** 29 50N 115 12 E
Yangzhou **115** 32 21N 119 26 E
Yanhee Res. **112** 17 30N 98 45 E
Yanji **114** 42 59N 129 30 E
Yankton **47** 42 53N 97 23W
Yankton County ◇ **47** 43 0N 97 30W
Yanqi **113** 42 5N 86 35 E
Yanqing **114** 40 30N 115 58 E
Yanshan **115** 28 15N 117 41 E
Yantai **114** 37 34N 121 22 E
Yanting **115** 31 11N 105 24 E
Yantra → **95** 43 40N 25 37 E
Yanush **43** 34 43N 95 19W
Yanzhou **114** 35 35N 116 49 E
Yao **121** 12 56N 17 33 E
Yaoundé **122** 3 50N 11 35 E
Yap **124** 9 31N 138 6 E
Yapen **111** 1 50 S 136 0 E
Yapen, Selat **111** 1 20 S 136 10 E
Yaqui → **64** 27 37N 110 39W
Yaquina Head **44** 44 41N 124 5W
Yar-Sale **100** 66 50N 70 50 E
Yaracuy □ **70** 10 20N 68 45W
Yaracuy → **70** 10 33N 68 15W
Yaraka **127** 24 53 S 144 3 E
Yarangüme **106** 37 35N 29 8 E
Yaransk **98** 57 22N 47 49 E
Yarbo **10** 31 32N 88 17W
Yardville **37** 40 11N 74 40W
Yare → **83** 52 36N 1 28 E
Yarensk **98** 61 10N 49 8 E
Yarí → **70** 0 20 S 72 20W
Yaritagua **70** 10 5N 69 8W
Yarkand = Shache **113** 38 20N 77 10 E
Yarkhun → **108** 36 17N 72 30 E
Yarmouth, Canada **61** 43 50N 66 7W
Yarmouth, U.S.A. **26** 43 48N 70 11W
Yarmūk → **104** 32 42N 35 40 E
Yarnell **12** 34 13N 112 45W
Yaroslavl **98** 57 35N 39 55 E
Yartsevo **101** 60 20N 90 0 E
Yarumal **70** 6 58N 75 24W
Yasawa Group **128** 17 0 S 177 23 E
Yasinski, L. **60** 53 16N 77 35W
Yasothon **112** 15 50N 104 10 E
Yass **127** 34 49 S 148 54 E
Yas'ur **104** 32 54N 35 10 E
Yata → **73** 10 29 S 65 26W
Yates Center **24** 37 53N 95 44W
Yates City **21** 40 47N 90 1W
Yates County ◇ **39** 42 40N 77 10W
Yatesboro **45** 40 48N 79 20W
Yatesville **18** 32 55N 84 9W
Yathkyed L. **63** 62 40N 98 0W
Yatsushiro **117** 32 30N 130 40 E
Yaṭṭah **104** 31 27N 35 6 E
Yauca **72** 15 39 S 74 35W
Yauco **57** 18 2N 66 51W
Yauco, Rio → **57** 17 59N 66 49W
Yauya **72** 8 59 S 77 17W
Yauyos **72** 12 19 S 75 50W
Yavapai County ◇ **12** 34 30N 112 30W
Yavari → **72** 4 21 S 70 2W
Yavatmal **108** 20 20N 78 15 E
Yavne **104** 31 52N 34 45 E
Yawatahama **117** 33 27N 132 24 E
Yayama-Rettō **117** 24 30N 123 40 E
Yazd **107** 31 55N 54 27 E
Yazd □ **107** 32 0N 55 0 E
Yazdān **107** 33 30N 60 50 E
Yazoo → **31** 32 22N 90 54W
Yazoo City **31** 32 51N 90 25W
Yazoo County ◇ **31** 32 50N 90 25W
Yding Skovhøj **97** 55 59N 9 46 E
Ye Xian **114** 37 8N 119 57 E
Yeager **43** 35 9N 96 21W
Yebyu **109** 14 15N 98 13 E
Yecla **91** 38 35N 1 5W
Yécora **64** 28 20N 108 58W
Yegros **76** 26 20 S 56 25W
Yeguas, Punta **57** 18 1N 65 50W
Yehuda, Midbar **104** 31 35N 35 15 E
Yei **121** 4 9N 30 40 E
Yelabuga **98** 55 45N 52 4 E
Yelanskoye **101** 61 25N 128 0 E
Yelcho, L. **78** 43 18 S 72 18W
Yelets **98** 52 40N 38 30 E
Yell **84** 60 35N 1 5W
Yell County ◇ **13** 35 3N 93 24W
Yell Sd. **84** 60 33N 1 15W
Yellow →, Fla. **17** 30 30N 87 0W
Yellow →, Ind. **22** 41 16N 86 50W
Yellow →, Wis. **55** 46 1N 92 22W
Yellow →, Wis. **55** 44 58N 91 18W
Yellow Jacket **16** 37 32N 108 43W
Yellow Medicine County ◇ **30** 44 40N 95 45W
Yellow Pine **20** 44 58N 115 30W
Yellow Sea **114** 35 0N 123 0 E
Yellow Springs **42** 39 48N 83 53W
Yellowhead P. **62** 52 53N 118 25W
Yellowknife **62** 62 27N 114 29W
Yellowknife → **58** 62 31N 114 19W
Yellowstone → **33** 47 59N 103 59W
Yellowstone County ◇ **33** 46 10N 108 0W
Yellowstone L. **56** 44 27N 110 22W
Yellowstone National Park **56** 44 40N 110 30W
Yellville **13** 36 14N 92 41W
Yelm **53** 46 57N 122 36W
Yemassee **46** 32 41N 80 51W
Yemen ■ **105** 15 0N 44 0 E
Yenangyaung **109** 20 30N 95 0 E
Yenisey → **100** 71 50N 82 40 E
Yeniseysk **101** 58 27N 92 13 E
Yeniseyskiy Zaliv **100** 72 20N 81 0 E
Yenyuka **101** 57 57N 121 15 E
Yeo, L. **126** 28 0 S 124 30 E
Yeola **108** 20 0N 74 30 E
Yeoman **22** 40 40N 86 44W
Yeovil **83** 50 57N 2 38W
Yeppoon **127** 23 5 S 150 47 E
Yerbent **100** 39 30N 58 50 E
Yerbogachen **101** 61 16N 108 0 E
Yerevan **99** 40 10N 44 31 E
Yerington **35** 38 59N 119 10W
Yermak **100** 52 2N 76 55 E
Yermakovo **101** 52 25N 126 20 E
Yermo **15** 34 54N 116 50W
Yerofey Pavlovich **101** 54 0N 122 0 E
Yershov **99** 51 22N 48 16 E
Yerunaja, Cerro **72** 10 16 S 76 55W
Yerushalayim **104** 31 47N 35 10 E
Yes Tor **83** 50 41N 3 59W
Yeso **38** 34 26N 104 37W
Yessey **101** 68 29N 102 10 E
Yetter **23** 42 19N 94 51W
Yeu, I. d' **90** 46 42N 2 20W
Yevpatoriya **99** 45 15N 33 20 E
Yeysk **99** 46 40N 38 12 E
Yezd = Yazd **107** 31 55N 54 27 E
Yhati **76** 25 45 S 56 35W
Yhú **77** 25 0 S 56 0W
Yi → **76** 33 7 S 57 8W
Yi Xian **114** 41 30N 121 22 E
Yiannitsa **95** 40 46N 22 24 E
Yibin **113** 28 45N 104 32 E
Yichang **115** 30 40N 111 20 E
Yicheng **114** 35 42N 111 40 E
Yichuan **114** 36 2N 110 10 E
Yichun, Heilongjiang, China **114** 47 44N 128 52 E
Yichun, Jiangxi, China **115** 27 48N 114 22 E
Yidu **114** 36 43N 118 28 E
Yihuang **115** 27 30N 116 12 E
Yijun **114** 35 28N 109 8 E
Yilan, China **114** 46 19N 129 34 E
Yilan, Taiwan **115** 24 51N 121 44 E
Yilehuli Shan **114** 51 20N 124 20 E
Yimianpo **114** 45 7N 128 2 E
Yinchuan **114** 38 30N 106 15 E
Ying He → **115** 32 30N 116 30 E
Ying Xian **114** 39 32N 113 10 E
Yingcheng **115** 30 56N 113 35 E
Yingde **115** 24 10N 113 25 E
Yingkou **114** 40 37N 122 18 E
Yingshan **115** 30 41N 115 32 E
Yingshang **115** 32 38N 116 12 E
Yingtan **113** 28 12N 117 0 E
Yining **113** 43 58N 81 10 E
Yinjiang **115** 28 1N 108 21 E
Yinmabin **109** 22 10N 94 55 E
Yinnietharra **126** 24 39 S 116 12 E
Yipinglang **113** 25 10N 101 52 E
Yirshi **114** 47 18N 119 49 E
Yishan **115** 24 28N 108 38 E
Yíthion **95** 36 46N 22 34 E
Yitong **114** 43 13N 125 20 E
Yituliho **114** 50 38N 121 34 E
Yixing **115** 31 21N 119 48 E
Yiyang, Henan, China **115** 34 27N 112 10 E
Yiyang, Hunan, China **115** 28 35N 112 18 E
Yizhang **115** 25 27N 112 57 E
Yizre'el **104** 32 34N 35 19 E
Ylitornio **96** 66 19N 23 39 E
Ylivieska **96** 64 4N 24 28 E
Ynykchanskiy **101** 60 15N 137 35 E
Yoakum **51** 29 17N 97 9W
Yoakum County ◇ **50** 33 11N 102 50W
Yocona → **31** 34 11N 90 10W
Yoder **56** 41 55N 104 18W
Yog Pt. **111** 14 6N 124 12 E
Yogyakarta **111** 7 49 S 110 22 E
Yoho Nat. Park **62** 51 25N 116 30W
Yojoa, L. de **66** 14 53N 88 0W
Yokadouma **122** 3 26N 15 6 E
Yokkaichi **117** 35 0N 136 38 E
Yoko **121** 5 32N 12 20 E
Yokohama **117** 35 27N 139 28 E
Yokosuka **117** 35 20N 139 40 E
Yokote **116** 39 20N 140 30 E
Yola **121** 9 10N 12 29 E
Yolaina, Cordillera de **66** 11 30N 84 0W
Yolo County ◇ **14** 38 45N 121 50W
Yonago **117** 35 25N 133 19 E
Yonaguni-Jima **117** 24 27N 123 0 E
Yoncalla **44** 43 36N 123 17W
Yonezawa **116** 37 57N 140 4 E
Yong Peng **112** 2 0N 103 3 E
Yong'an **115** 25 59N 117 25 E
Yongchun **115** 25 16N 118 20 E
Yongding **115** 24 43N 116 45 E
Yongfeng **115** 27 20N 115 22 E
Yongfu **115** 24 59N 109 59 E
Yonghe **114** 36 46N 110 38 E
Yongji **115** 34 52N 110 28 E
Yongshun **115** 29 2N 109 51 E
Yongxin **115** 26 58N 114 15 E
Yongxing **115** 26 9N 113 8 E
Yongxiu **115** 29 2N 115 42 E
Yonibana **120** 8 30N 12 19W
Yonkers **39** 40 56N 73 54W
Yonne □ **90** 47 50N 3 40 E
Yonne → **90** 48 23N 2 58 E
Yoqne'am **104** 32 40N 35 6 E
York, Australia **126** 31 52 S 116 47 E
York, U.K. **82** 53 58N 1 7W
York, Ala. **10** 32 29N 88 18W
York, N. Dak. **41** 48 19N 99 34W
York, Nebr. **34** 40 52N 97 36W
York, Pa. **45** 39 58N 76 44W
York, S.C. **46** 35 0N 81 12W
York → **54** 37 15N 76 23W
York, C. **127** 10 42 S 142 31 E
York, Kap **4** 75 55N 66 25W

York County Zyryanovsk

York County ◇, Maine **26** 43 25N 70 50W
York County ◇, Nebr. **34** 40 45N 97 40W
York County ◇, Pa. **45** 39 58N 76 44W
York County ◇, S.C. **46** 34 55N 81 10W
York County ◇, Va. **54** 37 14N 76 30W
York Sd. **126** 14 50 S 125 5 E
York Springs **45** 40 0N 77 7W
Yorke Pen. **127** 34 50 S 137 40 E
Yorkshire Wolds **82** 54 0N 0 30W
Yorkton **63** 51 11N 102 28W
Yorktown, Ark. **13** 34 1N 91 49W
Yorktown, Ind. **22** 40 10N 85 30W
Yorktown, Tex. **51** 28 59N 97 30W
Yorktown, Va. **54** 37 14N 76 30W
Yorkville, Ga. **18** 33 55N 84 58W
Yorkville, Ill. **21** 41 38N 88 27W
Yoro **66** 15 9N 87 7W
Yoron-Jima **117** 27 2N 128 26 E
Yos Sudarso, Pulau **111** 8 0 S 138 30 E
Yosemite **49** 37 21N 84 50W
Yosemite National Park **14** 37 45N 119 40W
Yosemite Village **14** 37 45N 119 35W
Yoshkar Ola **98** 56 38N 47 55 E
Yost **52** 41 58N 113 33W
Yŏsu **115** 34 47N 127 45 E
Yotala **73** 19 10 S 65 17W
Yotvata **104** 29 55N 35 2 E
You Jiang ⟶ **115** 23 22N 110 3 E
Youbou **62** 48 53N 124 13W
Youghal **85** 51 58N 7 51W
Youghal B. **85** 51 55N 7 50W
Youghiogheny ⟶ **45** 40 22N 79 52W
Youghiogheny Reservoir **27** 39 48N 79 22W
Young, Australia **127** 34 19 S 148 18 E
Young, Canada **63** 51 47N 105 45W
Young, Uruguay **76** 32 44 S 57 36W
Young County ◇ **51** 33 12N 98 44W
Young Harris **18** 34 56N 83 51W
Youngstown, Canada **63** 51 35N 111 10W
Youngstown, Fla. **17** 30 22N 85 26W
Youngstown, N.Y. **39** 43 15N 79 3W
Youngstown, Ohio **42** 41 6N 80 39W
Youngsville, La. **25** 30 3N 92 0W
Youngsville, N.C. **40** 36 1N 78 29W
Youngsville, N. Mex. **38** 36 11N 106 34W
Youngsville, Pa. **45** 41 51N 79 19W
Yountville **14** 38 24N 122 22W
Youyang **115** 28 47N 108 42 E
Youyu **114** 40 10N 112 20 E
Yozgat **106** 39 51N 34 47 E
Ypané ⟶ **76** 23 29 S 57 19W
Ypres = Ieper **87** 50 51N 2 53 E
Ypsilanti, Mich. **29** 42 14N 83 37W
Ypsilanti, N. Dak. **41** 46 47N 98 34W
Yreka **14** 41 44N 122 38W
Ystad **97** 55 26N 13 50 E
Ythan ⟶ **84** 57 26N 2 12W
Ytyk-Kel **101** 62 30N 133 45 E
Yu Shan **115** 23 30N 120 58 E
Yu Xian, Hebei, China **114** 39 50N 114 35 E
Yu Xian, Henan, China **115** 34 10N 113 28 E
Yuan Jiang ⟶ **115** 28 55N 111 50 E
Yuanling **115** 28 29N 110 22 E
Yuanyang **113** 23 10N 102 43 E
Yuba **55** 43 33N 90 26W
Yuba City **14** 39 8N 121 37W
Yuba County ◇ **14** 39 15N 121 30W
Yūbari **116** 43 4N 141 59 E
Yūbetsu **116** 43 13N 144 5 E
Yucatán □ **65** 21 30N 86 30W
Yucatán, Canal de **66** 22 0N 86 30W
Yucca **12** 34 52N 114 9W
Yucca House National
Monument **16** 37 16N 108 38W
Yucca L. **35** 36 57N 116 2W
Yucca Valley **15** 34 8N 116 27W
Yucheng **114** 36 55N 116 32 E
Yuci **114** 37 42N 112 46 E
Yudino **100** 55 10N 67 55 E
Yudu **115** 25 59N 115 30 E
Yueqing **115** 28 9N 120 59 E
Yueyang **115** 29 21N 113 5 E
Yugan **115** 28 43N 116 37 E
Yugoslavia ■ **95** 44 0N 20 0 E
Yuhuan **115** 28 9N 121 12 E
Yujiang **115** 28 10N 116 43 E
Yukon **43** 35 31N 97 45W
Yukon ⟶ **11** 62 32N 163 54W
Yukon-Koyukuk ◇ **11** 65 0N 154 0W
Yukon Territory □ **58** 63 0N 135 0W
Yukti **101** 63 26N 105 42 E
Yukuhashi **117** 33 44N 130 59 E
Yule ⟶ **126** 20 41 S 118 17 E
Yulee **17** 30 38N 81 36W
Yülin, China **115** 18 10N 109 31 E
Yulin, Guangxi Zhuangzu,
China **115** 22 40N 110 8 E
Yulin, Shaanxi, China **114** 38 20N 109 30 E
Yuma, Ariz. **12** 32 43N 114 37W
Yuma, Colo. **16** 40 8N 102 43W
Yuma, B. de **67** 18 20N 68 35W
Yuma County ◇, Ariz. **12** 33 30N 114 0W
Yuma County ◇, Colo. **16** 40 0N 102 20W
Yuma Desert **12** 32 25N 110 30W
Yumbo **70** 1 20 S 26 15 E
Yumen **113** 39 50N 97 30 E
Yun Xian **115** 32 50N 110 46 E
Yunaska I. **11** 52 38N 170 40W
Yungas **73** 17 0 S 66 0W
Yungay, Chile **76** 37 10 S 72 5W
Yungay, Peru **72** 9 2 S 77 45W
Yunhe **115** 28 8N 119 33 E
Yunlin **115** 23 42N 120 30 E
Yunnan □ **113** 25 0N 102 0 E
Yunxiao **115** 23 59N 117 18 E
Yupukarri **71** 3 45N 59 20W
Yur **101** 59 52N 137 41 E
Yurgao **100** 55 42N 84 51 E
Yuribei **100** 71 8N 76 58 E
Yurimaguas **72** 5 55 S 76 7W
Yuscarán **66** 13 58N 86 45W
Yushu, Jilin, China **114** 44 43N 126 38 E
Yushu, Qinghai, China **113** 33 5N 96 55 E
Yutan **34** 41 15N 96 24W
Yuyao **115** 30 3N 121 10 E
Yuzawa **116** 39 10N 140 30 E
Yuzhno-Sakhalinsk **101** 46 58N 142 45 E
Yvelines □ **90** 48 40N 1 45 E
Yvetot **90** 49 37N 0 44 E

Z

Zaandam **87** 52 26N 4 49 E
Zabaykalskiy **101** 49 40N 117 25 E
Zabid **105** 14 0N 43 10 E
Zābol **107** 31 0N 61 32 E
Zābol □ **107** 32 0N 67 0 E
Zābolī **107** 27 10N 61 35 E
Zabrze **89** 50 18N 18 50 E
Zacapa **66** 14 59N 89 31W
Zacapu **64** 19 50N 101 43W
Zacatecas **64** 22 49N 102 34W
Zacatecas □ **64** 23 30N 103 0W
Zacatecoluca **66** 13 29N 88 51W
Zachary **25** 30 39N 91 9W
Zacoalco **64** 20 14N 103 33W
Zacualtipán **65** 20 39N 98 36W
Zadar **94** 44 8N 15 14 E
Zadetkyi Kyun **110** 10 0N 98 25 E
Zafra **91** 38 26N 6 30W
Zafriya **104** 31 59N 34 51 E
Żagań **88** 51 39N 15 22 E
Zagazig **121** 30 40N 31 30 E
Zagreb **94** 45 50N 16 0 E
Zāgros, Kuhhā-ye **107** 33 45N 47 0 E
Zāhedān **107** 29 30N 60 50 E
Zahl **41** 48 34N 103 42W
Zahlah **106** 33 52N 35 50 E
Zaïre ■ **122** 3 0 S 23 0 E
Zaïre ⟶ **122** 6 4 S 12 24 E
Zaječar **95** 43 53N 22 18 E
Zakamensk **101** 50 23N 103 17 E
Zakavkazye **99** 42 0N 44 0 E
Zākhū **106** 37 10N 42 50 E
Zákinthos **95** 37 47N 20 57 E
Zaleski **42** 39 17N 82 24W
Zalingei **121** 12 51N 23 29 E
Zalma **32** 37 9N 90 5W
Zama **31** 32 59N 89 23W
Zambeze ⟶ **123** 18 55 S 36 4 E
Zambezi = Zambeze ⟶ **123** 18 55 S 36 4 E
Zambezi **123** 13 30 S 23 15 E
Zambia ■ **123** 15 0 S 28 0 E
Zamboanga **111** 6 59N 122 3 E
Zambrano **70** 9 45N 74 49W
Zamora, Ecuador **70** 4 4 S 78 58W
Zamora, Mexico **64** 20 0N 102 21W
Zamora, Spain **91** 41 30N 5 45W
Zamora-Chinchipe □ **70** 4 15 S 78 50W
Zamość **89** 50 43N 23 15 E
Zamuro, Sierra del **71** 4 0N 62 30W
Zanaga **122** 2 48 S 13 48 E
Zandvoort **87** 52 22N 4 32 E
Zanesville **42** 39 56N 82 1W
Zanjan **106** 36 40N 48 35 E
Zanjān □ **106** 37 20N 49 30 E
Zante = Zákinthos **95** 37 47N 20 57 E
Zanthus **126** 31 2 S 123 34 E
Zanzibar **122** 6 12 S 39 12 E
Zaouiet El-Kala = Bordj
Omar Driss **120** 28 10N 6 40 E
Zaouiet Reggane **120** 26 32N 0 3 E
Zap **41** 47 17N 101 55W
Zapadnaya Dvina ⟶ **98** 57 4N 24 3 E
Západné Beskydy **89** 49 30N 19 0 E
Zapadni Rodopi **95** 41 50N 24 0 E
Zapadnyy Sayan **101** 52 30N 94 0 E
Zapala **78** 39 0 S 70 5W
Zapaleri, Cerro **76** 22 49 S 67 11W
Zapata **50** 26 55N 99 16W
Zapata County ◇ **50** 27 0N 99 0W
Zapiga **72** 19 40 S 79 0W
Zapolyarnyy **98** 69 26N 30 51 E
Zaporozhye **99** 47 50N 35 10 E
Zara **106** 39 58N 37 43 E
Zaragoza, Colombia **70** 7 30N 74 52W
Zaragoza, Coahuila, Mexico **64** 28 30N 101 0W
Zaragoza, Nuevo León,
Mexico **65** 24 0N 99 46W
Zaragoza, Spain **91** 41 39N 0 53W
Zaragoza □ **91** 41 35N 1 0W
Zarand **107** 30 46N 56 34 E
Zaranj **107** 30 55N 61 55 E
Zarate **76** 34 7 S 59 0W
Zaraza **71** 9 21N 65 19W
Zaria **120** 11 0N 7 40 E
Zarqā' ⟶ **104** 32 10N 35 37 E
Zaruma **70** 3 40 S 79 38W
Zary **88** 51 37N 15 10 E
Zarzal **70** 4 24N 76 4W
Zarzis **121** 33 31N 11 2 E
Zashiversk **101** 67 25N 142 40 E
Zaskar Mountains **108** 33 15N 77 30 E
Zavala County ◇ **51** 28 57N 99 51W
Zavalla **51** 31 10N 94 26W
Zavāreh **107** 33 29N 52 28 E
Zavitinsk **101** 50 10N 129 20 E
Zavodoski **5** 56 0 S 27 45W
Zawiercie **89** 50 30N 19 24 E
Zāwiyat al Bayḑā **121** 32 30N 21 40 E
Zāyandeh ⟶ **107** 32 35N 52 0 E
Zayarsk **101** 56 12N 102 55 E
Zaysan **100** 47 28N 84 52 E
Zaysan, Oz. **100** 48 0N 83 0 E
Zaytā **104** 32 23N 35 2 E
Zduńska Wola **89** 51 37N 18 59 E
Zearing **23** 42 10N 93 18W
Zeballos **62** 49 59N 126 50W
Zebulon, Ga. **18** 33 6N 84 21W
Zebulon, Ky. **49** 37 32N 82 28W
Zebulon, N.C. **40** 35 49N 78 19W
Zeebrugge **87** 51 19N 3 12 E
Zeehan **127** 41 52 S 145 25 E
Zeeland, Mich. **29** 42 49N 86 1W
Zeeland, N. Dak. **41** 45 58N 99 50W
Zeeland □ **87** 51 30N 3 50 E
Ze'elim **104** 31 13N 34 32 E
Zeerust **123** 25 31 S 26 4 E
Zefat **104** 32 58N 35 29 E
Zeigler **21** 37 54N 89 3W
Zeila **105** 11 21N 43 30 E
Zeist **87** 52 5N 5 15 E
Zeitz **88** 51 3N 12 9 E
Zelienople **45** 40 48N 80 8W
Zell **47** 44 54N 98 44W
Zelzate **87** 51 13N 3 47 E
Zémio **122** 5 2N 25 5 E
Zemlya Frantsa Iosifa **4** 81 0N 55 0 E
Zemun **95** 44 51N 20 25 E
Zenda **24** 37 27N 98 17W
Zephyr Cove **35** 39 0N 119 57W
Zephyrhills **17** 28 14N 82 11W
Zerbst **88** 51 59N 12 8 E
Zeya **101** 53 48N 127 14 E
Zeya ⟶ **101** 53 13N 127 35 E
Zhailma **100** 51 37N 61 33 E
Zhangguangcai Ling **114** 45 0N 129 0 E
Zhanghua **115** 24 6N 120 29 E
Zhangjiakou **114** 40 48N 114 55 E
Zhangping **115** 25 17N 117 23 E
Zhangpu **115** 24 8N 117 35 E
Zhangwu **114** 42 43N 123 52 E
Zhangye **113** 38 50N 100 23 E
Zhangzhou **115** 24 30N 117 35 E
Zhanhua **114** 37 40N 118 8 E
Zhanjiang **115** 21 15N 110 20 E
Zhanyi **113** 25 38N 103 48 E
Zhanyu **114** 44 30N 122 30 E
Zhao Xian **114** 37 43N 114 45 E
Zhao'an **115** 23 41N 117 10 E
Zhaoping **115** 24 11N 110 48 E
Zhaoqing **115** 23 0N 112 20 E
Zhaotong **113** 27 20N 103 44 E
Zhaoyuan **114** 37 20N 120 23 E
Zhdanov **99** 47 5N 37 31 E
Zhecheng **115** 34 7N 115 20 E
Zhejiang □ **115** 29 0N 120 0 E
Zheleznodorozhny **98** 62 35N 50 55 E
Zheleznogorsk-Ilimskiy **101** 56 34N 104 8 E
Zhen'an **115** 33 27N 109 9 E
Zhenfeng **115** 25 22N 105 40 E
Zheng'an **115** 28 32N 107 27 E
Zhengding **114** 38 8N 114 32 E
Zhenghe **115** 27 20N 118 50 E
Zhengyang **115** 32 37N 114 22 E
Zhengyangguan **115** 32 30N 116 29 E
Zhengzhou **115** 34 45N 113 34 E
Zhenjiang **115** 32 11N 119 26 E
Zhenlai **114** 45 50N 123 5 E
Zhenning **115** 26 4N 105 45 E
Zhenyuan, Gansu, China **114** 35 35N 107 30 E
Zhenyuan, Guizhou, China **115** 27 4N 108 21 E
Zhigansk **101** 66 48N 123 27 E
Zhijiang **115** 27 27N 109 42 E
Zhitomir **99** 50 20N 28 40 E
Zhlobin **98** 52 55N 30 0 E
Zhokhova, Ostrov **101** 76 4N 152 40 E
Zhong Xian **115** 30 21N 108 1 E
Zhongdian **113** 27 48N 99 42 E
Zhongshan **115** 22 26N 113 20 E
Zhongwei **114** 37 30N 105 12 E
Zhongxiang **115** 31 12N 112 34 E
Zhoushan Dao **115** 30 5N 122 10 E
Zhouzhi **115** 34 10N 108 12 E
Zhuanghe **114** 39 40N 123 0 E
Zhucheng **114** 36 0N 119 27 E
Zhugqu **115** 33 40N 104 30 E
Zhuji **115** 29 40N 120 10 E
Zhumadian **115** 32 59N 114 2 E
Zhuo Xian **114** 39 28N 115 58 E
Zhupanovo **101** 53 40N 159 52 E
Zhushan **115** 32 15N 110 13 E
Zhuxi **115** 32 25N 109 40 E
Zhuzhou **115** 27 49N 113 12 E
Zia Indian Reservation **38** 35 30N 106 50W
Zibo **114** 36 47N 118 3 E
Zidarovo **95** 42 20N 27 24 E
Ziebach County ◇ **47** 45 0N 101 50W
Zielona Góra **88** 51 57N 15 31 E
Zierikzee **87** 51 40N 3 55 E
Zigey **121** 14 43N 15 50 E
Zigong **115** 29 15N 104 48 E
Zigui **115** 31 0N 110 40 E
Ziguinchor **120** 12 35N 16 20W
Zihuatanejo **64** 17 38N 101 33W
Zikhron Ya'Aqov **104** 32 34N 34 56 E
Zile **106** 40 15N 35 52 E
Žilina **89** 49 12N 18 42 E
Zillah, Libya **121** 28 30N 17 33 E
Zillah, U.S.A. **53** 46 24N 120 16W
Zima **101** 54 0N 102 5 E
Zimapán **65** 20 54N 99 20W
Zimbabwe ■ **123** 20 0 S 30 0 E
Zimmerman **30** 45 37N 93 34W
Zimnicea **95** 43 40N 25 22 E
Zinder **120** 13 48N 9 0 E
Zion **21** 42 27N 87 50W
Zion National Park **52** 37 15N 113 5W
Zion Reservoir **12** 34 37N 109 29W
Zionsville **22** 39 57N 86 16W
Zipaquirá **70** 5 0N 74 0W
Zippori **104** 32 45N 35 16 E
Zirkel, Mt. **16** 40 50N 106 40W
Zirko **107** 25 0N 53 40 E
Zitácuaro **64** 19 28N 100 21W
Ziway, L. **121** 8 0N 38 50 E
Zixi **115** 27 45N 117 4 E
Ziyang **115** 32 32N 108 31 E
Zizhong **115** 29 48N 104 47 E
Zlataritsa **95** 43 2N 25 55 E
Zlatitsa **95** 42 41N 24 7 E
Zlatna **95** 46 8N 23 11 E
Zlatograd **95** 41 22N 25 7 E
Zlatoust **98** 55 10N 59 40 E
Zlin = Gottwaldov **89** 49 14N 17 40 E
Zlītan **121** 32 32N 14 35 E
Zmeinogorsk **100** 51 10N 82 13 E
Znojmo **88** 48 50N 16 2 E
Zolfo Springs **17** 27 30N 81 48W
Zomba **123** 15 22 S 35 19 E
Zongo **122** 4 20N 18 35 E
Zonguldak **106** 41 28N 31 50 E
Zorleni **95** 46 14N 27 44 E
Zornitsa **95** 42 23N 26 58 E
Zorra I. **57** 9 18N 79 52W
Zorritos **72** 3 43 S 80 40W
Zou Xiang **115** 35 30N 116 58 E
Zouar **121** 20 30N 16 32 E
Zouérate **120** 22 44N 12 21W
Zoutkamp **87** 53 20N 6 18 E
Zrenjanin **95** 45 22N 20 23 E
Zudáñez **73** 19 6 S 64 44W
Zuetina **121** 30 58N 20 7 E
Zufar **105** 17 40N 54 0 E
Zug **88** 47 10N 8 31 E
Zuid-Holland □ **87** 52 0N 4 35 E
Zuidhorn **87** 53 15N 6 23 E
Zula **121** 15 17N 39 40 E
Zulia □ **70** 10 0N 72 10W
Zumbo **123** 15 35 S 30 26 E
Zumbro Falls **30** 44 17N 92 26W
Zumbrota **30** 44 17N 92 40W
Zumpango **65** 19 48N 99 6W
Zungeru **120** 9 48N 6 8 E
Zunhua **114** 40 18N 117 58 E
Zuni **38** 35 4N 108 51W
Zuni ⟶ **12** 34 39N 109 40W
Zuni Indian Reservation **38** 35 0N 108 50W
Zuni Mts. **38** 35 10N 108 30W
Zunyi **115** 27 42N 106 53 E
Zürich, Switz. **88** 47 22N 8 32 E
Zurich, U.S.A. **24** 39 14N 99 26W
Zutphen **87** 52 9N 6 12 E
Zuwārah **121** 32 58N 12 1 E
Zverinogolovskoye **100** 54 23N 64 40 E
Zvezdets **95** 42 6N 27 26 E
Zvishavane **123** 20 17 S 30 2 E
Zvolen **89** 48 33N 19 10 E
Zwettl **88** 48 35N 15 9 E
Zwickau **88** 50 43N 12 30 E
Zwingle **23** 42 18N 90 41W
Zwolle, Neth. **87** 52 31N 6 6 E
Zwolle, U.S.A. **25** 31 38N 93 39W
Zymoetz ⟶ **62** 54 33N 128 31W
Żyrardów **89** 52 3N 20 28 E
Zyryanka **101** 65 45N 150 51 E
Zyryanovsk **100** 49 43N 84 20 E